For Reference

Not to be taken from this room

ENCYCLOPEDIA OF
AMERICAN
JOURNALISM

ENCYCLOPEDIA OF AMERICAN JOURNALISM

For Reference

Not to be taken from this room

STEPHEN L. VAUGHN

EDITOR

Routledge
Taylor & Francis Group
New York   London

Routledge
Taylor & Francis Group
270 Madison Avenue
New York, NY 10016

Routledge
Taylor & Francis Group
2 Park Square
Milton Park, Abingdon
Oxon OX14 4RN

Printed in the United States of America on acid-free paper
10 9 8 7 6 5 4 3 2 1

International Standard Book Number-13: 978-0-415-96950-5 (Hardcover)

Library of Congress Cataloging-in-Publication Data

Vaughn, Stephen L.
    Encyclopedia of American journalism / Stephen L. Vaughn.
        p. cm.
    Includes bibliographical references and index.
    ISBN-10: 0-415-96950-6 (alk. paper)
    ISBN-13: 978-0-415-96950-5
    1. Journalism--United States--Encyclopedias. I. Title.

PN4855.V38 2008
070.03--dc22
                                                                                          2007018022

Visit the Taylor & Francis Web site at
http://www.taylorandfrancis.com

and the Routledge Web site at
http://www.routledge.com

Contents

Associate Editors

Bruce J. Evensen
DePaul University

James Landers
Colorado State University

Contributors

David Abrahamson
Northwestern University

Sue Westcott Alessandri
Syracuse Unversity

Craig Allen
Arizona State University

Paul Ashdown
University of Tennessee

James L. Aucoin
University of South Alabama

Guy T. Baehr
Rutgers University

Gerald J. Baldasty
University of Washington

James L. Baughman
University of Wisconsin

Maureen Beasley
University of Maryland

Jon Bekken
Albright College

Jose Luis Benavides
California State University, Northridge

Sandra Combs Birdiett
Michigan State University

Ulf Jonas Bjork
IUPUI

Frederick Blevens
University of Oklahoma

Manahem Blondheim
Hebrew University of Jerusalem

Gregory Borchard
University of Nevada at Las Vegas

Paul Boyer
University of Wisconsin–Madison

Patricia Bradley
Temple University

Carolyn Bronstein
DePaul University

Donald R. Browne
University of Minnesota

Judith Buddenbaum
Colorado State University

Kissette Bundy
Hampton University

Todd Steven Burroughs
University of Maryland

Elizabeth V. Burt
University of Hartford

Ginger Carter
Georgia College & State University

Ed Caudill
University of Tennessee

Lloyd Chiasson
Nicholls State University

Carmen E. Clark
University of Wisconsin–Madison

Contributors

Jeremy Cohen
Pennsylvania State University

Mike Conklin
DePaul University

Tom Connery
University of St. Thomas

Mark Conrad
Fordham University

Russell J. Cook
Bethany College

David A. Copeland
Elon University

Joseph P. Cosco
Old Dominion University

John M. Coward
University of Tulsa

R. Bruce Craig
National Coalition for History

Dale Cressman
Brigham Young University

Douglass K. Daniel
Associated Press

Roei Davidson
University of Michigan

Wayne Dawkins
Hampton University

Everett Dennis
Fordham University

Anju Desai
University of Wisconsin–Madison

Hazel Dicken-Garcia
University of Minnesota

Donna Dickerson
University of Texas at Tyler

Michael Dillon
Duquesne University

Greg Downey
University of Wisconsin–Madison

Robert Drechsel
University of Wisconsin–Madison

Wally Eberhard
University of Georgia

Matthew Ehrlich
University of Illinois at Champaign-Urbana

Kathleen Endres
University of Akron

Emily Erickson
Louisiana State University

Bruce J. Evensen
DePaul University

Frank E. Fee, Jr.
University of North Carolina

Robert Ferrell
Indiana University

Eric Fettmann
New York Post

Robert Fortner
Calvin College

Ralph Frasca
Marymount University

Richard Fried
University of Illinois at Chicago

Barbara Friedman
University of North Carolina at Chapel Hill

Michael R. Frontani
Elon University

Michael Gauger
Independent Scholar

Robert J. Goldstein
Oakland University

Douglas Gomery
University of Maryland

Agnes Hooper Gottlieb
Seton Hall University

Tracy Gottlieb
Seton Hall University

Calvin L. Hall
Appalachian State University

Kirk Hallahan
Colorado State University

Donna Halper
Emerson College

Kathleen Hansen
University of Minnesota

Christopher Harper
Temple University

John Allen Hendricks
Southeastern Oklahoma State University

Carol Sue Humphrey
Oklahoma Baptist University

William Huntzicker
St. Cloud State University

Frankie Hutton
Montclair State University

Gordon Jackson
University of Wisconsin–Madison

Robert Jensen
University of Texas

Owen Johnson
Indiana University

Richard Junger
Western Michigan University

Richard Katula
University of Illinois at Champaign-Urbana

Richard B. Kielbowicz
University of Washington

Paulette Kilmer
University of Toledo

Richard Kirkendall
University of Washington

Kris Kodrich
Colorado State University

Carol Koehler
University of Missouri–Kansas City

Bill Kovarik
Radford University

Brooke Kroeger
New York University

Michele Kroll
University of Wisconsin–Madison

Sanford Lakoff
University of California, San Diego

James Landers
Colorado State University

Julie Lane
University of Wisconsin–Madison

Amy Mattson Lauters
Wichita State University

Edmund Lawler
DePaul University

Linda Lawson
University of Washington

Kevin C. Lee
Western Carolina University

Thomas Leonard
University of California at Berkeley

William J. Leonhirth
Independent Scholar

Ralph Levering
Davidson University

Robert Lichter
Center for Media and Public Affairs

Louis Liebovich
University of Illinois

Christopher Long
University of Wisconsin–Madison

Therese L. Lueck
University of Akron

Linda Lumsden
Western Kentucky University

Jeffrey M. McCall
DePauw University

Contributors

Jane S. McConnell
Minnesota State University

James McGrath Morris
West Springfield High School

Gwyn Mellinger
Baker University

Fritz Messere
State University of New York at Oswego

Robert Miraldi
State University of New York at New Paltz

Jack Mitchell
University of Wisconsin–Madison

James Moses
Arkansas Technology University

Lawrence Mullen
University of Nevada at Las Vegas

Michael D. Murray
University of Missouri at St. Louis

Seungahn Nah
University of Kentucky

David Nord
Indiana University

Sarah Burke Odland
University of Iowa

Kathleen K. Olson
Lehigh University

Michael Oriard
Oregon State University

Paul Parsons
Elon University

John Pavlik
Rutgers University

Lee Anne Peck
University of Northern Colorado

Rob Pierce
State University of New York at Cortland

Wes Pippert
University of Missouri

Stephen Ponder
University of Oregon

Robert Pondillo
Middle Tennessee State University

Peter W. Quigley
Independent Scholar

Robert A. Rabe
University of Wisconsin–Madison

Nick Ravo
Lynn University

Bill Reader
Ohio University

Barbara Straus Reed
Rutgers University

Sam Riley
Virginia Polytechnical Institute and
   State University

Don Ritchie
U.S. Senate Office

Nancy Roberts
State University of New York at Albany

Laura Ruel
University of North Carolina at Chapel Hill

Debra A. Schwartz
Columbia College, Chicago

Hemant Shah
University of Wisconsin–Madison

Jason Shepard
University of Wisconsin–Madison

Peter Simonson
University of Pittsburgh

Christopher Simpson
American University

Hugh Slotten
University of Otago

Jeffery Smith
University of Wisconsin–Milwaukee

Meg Spratt
University of Washington

Nigel Starck
University of South Australia

James Startt
Valparaiso University

Linda Steiner
Rutgers University

Guido Stempel
Ohio University

Edmund J. Sullivan
Columbia University

David Sumner
Ball State University

Randall Sumpter
Texas A&M University

Wendy Swanberg
University of Wisconsin–Madison

Michael Sweeney
Utah State University

Saman Talib
Rutgers University

Jaimie Tallman
University of Nebraska

Dwight L. Teeter
University of Tennessee

Athan Theoharis
Marquette University

Shayla Thiel
DePaul University

Andie Tucher
Columbia University

Kathleen Turner
Davidson College

Lou Ureneck
Boston University

Stephen Vaughn
University of Wisconsin–Madison

Kimberly Voss
Southern Illinois University

Peter Wallace
Independent Scholar

Patrick Washburn
Ohio University

Charles A. Weeks
St. Paul's School, Concord, NH

Gabriel Weimann
University of Haifa

Andrew B. Wertheimer
University of Hawaii at Manoa

Betty Houchin Winfield
University of Missouri

Allan Winkler
University of Miami at Ohio

Ben Yagoda
University of Delaware

Bernice Yeung
berniceyeung.com

Ronald Zboray
University of Pittsburgh

Alphabetical List of Entries

Thematic List of Entries

Associations and Organizations
American Society of Newspaper Editors
    (ASNE)
Committee on Public Information
Federal Communications Commission
    (FCC)
Gannett Center for Media Studies
National Association of Black Journalists
Office of War Information
Society of Professional Journalists
U.S. Information Agency
Vanderbilt Television News Archives
Women's National Press Club
Women's Press Organizations

Historical Overview and Practice
Advertising
Agricultural Journalism
Alternative Press
Archives and Newspapers
Archiving and Preservation
Asian American Journalists and Press
Baseball Journalism
Black Press
Blogs
Boxing Journalism
Business and Financial Reporting
Cameras in the Courtroom
Chinese American Press
Classical Music Criticism
Clear and Present Danger
Columnists
Communist Press
Copyright and Photography
Copyright, The Legal Issues of
Entertainment Press
Ethics
Ethnic/Immigrant Press
Fairness Doctrine

Feminist Journalism
Football Journalism
Frontier Press
German-Language Press in America,
    1732-1945
Hutchins Commission Report
Interpretative Reporting
Inverted Pyramid
Investigative Journalism
Japanese-American Press
Jewish Press in America
Labor Press
Latino Press
Legislative Branch Reporting: The Congress
Libel
Licensing
Literary Journalism
Local News
Magazines, Men's
Magazines, News
Maps and the News
Motion Pictures
Muckraking
Native American Journalism
Newspaper Readers
Obituaries
Objectivity in Reporting
Office of Censorship
Op-Ed Page
Photojournalism
Polk Awards, George
Popular Music Criticism
Pornography
Propaganda
Public Relations
Radio and the News
Reading Notices
Reform Journalism
Religion and the Press

Introduction

The *Encyclopedia of American Journalism* explores in depth those journalists and their organizations who have observed and recorded the events of American history. In 1930, John H. Finley of the *New York Times* said that journalists were "the historians of the present tense" and he called journalism "the religion of democracy" (*NYT*, Dec. 19, 1930, p. 24). Although Finley made these observations well before the advent of television, computers, the Internet, and many of the other modern media that we now take for granted, his assessment of the importance of journalists and journalism still remains relevant in our own time. A free society requires good journalists, and their job is demanding, and always has been, if for no other reason than that their work covers the entire scope of human endeavor. To achieve their goals, having a sense of history is no less critical than having the ability to communicate clearly and effectively.

Yet there are many components in modern media and modern living that distort, or even ignore, history, and these forces inevitably affect journalism. If it is true, as has been said, that journalists write the "first draft of history," then it is also true that they are often accused of lacking knowledge of the past. The *Encyclopedia of American Journalism* provides an antidote to such criticism by offering readers an account of journalism's past that is relevant to the twenty-first century. As it makes clear, journalism has a rich history, one whose origins trace back to the American colonies. It is the full scope of that history that helps us to understand better the extraordinary changes that have transformed journalism in recent decades.

The 405 articles in this *Encyclopedia*, which vary in length from 500 to 5,000 words, touch on a wide range of subjects, many of which have been too often neglected or given short shrift in other reference works. Although presented in alphabetical order, the entries cover seven major themes.

ASSOCIATIONS AND ORGANIZATIONS

These articles detail groups that support or regulate journalists' work from "American Society of Newspaper Editors (ASNE)" to "Women's Press Organizations." Some are governmental, such as the "Office of War Information" and some are voluntary special interest groups, such as the "National Association of Black Journalists."

HISTORICAL OVERVIEW AND PRACTICE

These articles cover the whole scope of American history; however, special attention has been given to developments since 1945 and the end of World War II. Where earlier reference works in the field tend to trail off after the mid-twentieth century, this *Encyclopedia* covers the major events and trends since that period, ranging from "Archiving and Preservation," "Baseball Journalism," "Citizen Reporters," "Ethics," "Hutchins Commission Report," "Travel Journalism," to "Youth Television News."

Introduction

There are several essays on the ethnic and immigrant media. Throughout much of its history, the United States has had a vibrant ethnic and immigrant press. Literally hundreds of foreign-language newspapers have been published at one time or another, a dimension of American journalism that has been given too little attention in earlier reference works. Users of this *Encyclopedia of American Journalism* will find essays on the Chinese-American, German-Language, Japanese-American, Jewish, Native-American, and Latino presses, and more.

Significant attention is also devoted to the Black press, beginning with its first newspaper, *Freedom's Journal*, published in 1827. Readers will find essays on such prominent people and topics as Frederick Douglass and the *North Star*, Robert Abbott and the *Chicago Defender*, and the *Pittsburgh Courier*'s "Double V" campaign during World War II.

Other essays discuss issues arising from the powerful and lucrative image industries —advertising, public relations, and entertainment—that intersect with journalism in many ways. To that mix, we must also add government propaganda, which since the First World War, has grown increasingly sophisticated and pervasive. Advertising and public relations have had a major impact on news media throughout the twentieth century, if not before. During the latter half of the century, the union of marketing, publicity, and the news grew stronger as the teaching of advertising and public relations (aka, strategic communication) became deeply embedded in the curricula of many journalism schools. Modern entertainment has likewise blended with news reporting and has heightened the emphasis on celebrities and pseudo-events. In addition, during the past century, propaganda that has resulted from modern warfare and the rise of a national security state has placed great pressures on journalists and has presented obstacles to reporting. In the modern media environment, the lines separating advertising, public relations, entertainment, propaganda, and journalism have blurred, making it more difficult to distinguish between the significant and the trivial, between hard news and that which is fabricated. This *Encyclopedia* has several articles that provide perspective on the problems these issues pose for good journalism practice.

Still other articles examine aspects of the "new journalism" of the 1960s and 1970s. Other essays look at such topics as ethics, Investigative Journalism, the news media and the Vietnam War, as well as the temperance, pacifist, underground, and alternative presses.

INDIVIDUALS

These entries examine the careers of such well-known radio commentators as Walter Winchell and H. V. Kaltenborn, and such notable television anchors as Walter Cronkite, Chet Huntley and David Brinkley, Peter Jennings, Dan Rather, and Tom Brokaw. This volume also covers the too-often-neglected contributions of African American women journalists, such as Lucy Wilmot Smith and Victoria Mathews. It is not only African American women who have been denied the space they deserve in older and more traditional journalism reference works, but all women journalists in general and so essays deal with, for example, Mary Katherine Goddard and Anne Royall. Considerable attention is given to journalists who have been involved in reform such as Jacob Riis and Lincoln Steffens. A number of articles deal with the efforts of muckrakers and other reformers such as Mark Sullivan and Samuel Hopkins Adams to expose corruption during the early twentieth century.

Readers will find numerous examples of stories about courageous reporters in these pages. Edward R. Murrow, who rose to prominence while covering the London air raids during World War II and then achieved distinction for his opposition to the demagoguery of Senator Joseph McCarthy during the 1950s, appears here as do the stories of reporters who covered the wars in Korea, Vietnam, and the Middle East.

Herein also are histories of major media entrepreneurs who have shaped modern journalism. The stories of such moguls as Joseph Pulitzer and William Randolph Hearst are well known and their lives and work are freshly chronicled here. But this volume also covers other and more recent personalities and developments, including E. W. Scripps; the Newhouses, father and son; Walter Annenberg; Ted Turner; and Rupert Murdock.

JOURNALISM IN AMERICAN HISTORY

Politics and journalism compose one of the main currents running through this volume. Clearly, there is a close connection between image-making and political power. Several articles (in the chronological format of "Presidency and the Press:...") focus on how modern presidents have dealt with the media, starting with the William McKinley administration at the time of the Spanish-American War in 1898 and continuing through the administration of George W. Bush in the early twenty-first century. A number of other essays deal with reporting from the American Revolution to two entries on aspects of terrorism and the news.

LAWS, ACTS, AND LEGISLATION

The articles in this *Encyclopedia of American Journalism* make it abundantly clear that freedom of the press and having access to information have been hard-won rights. Several articles in this work deal with important legislation in American history that has tried to restrict the freedom of the press and with U. S. Supreme Court cases that have involved censorship and freedom of expression, such as the Alien and Sedition Acts of 1798 and *New York Times v. U.S.*, 1971.

PRINT, BROADCAST, NEWSGROUPS, AND CORPORATIONS

Many articles in this volume discuss the impact of radio, television, the Internet and other computer-related media on the news, including coverage of magazines, local newspapers, media conglomerates, and ABC, CBS, and NBC News as well as the emergence of National Public Radio, C-Span, Cable News Network (CNN), and Fox News.

TECHNOLOGIES

The *Encyclopedia of American Journalism* gives major attention to new communication technologies and their influence on the practice of journalism. Readers of this volume will find essays by scholars on specific topics such as "Digital Photography and Journalism," "Satellite Technology," "Videotape," and "Digital Information Technologies." But the discussion of new technologies and their influence can also be found in many other articles on such topics as the "Progressive Era and the Press," "Photojournalism," "Copyright," "Youth Television News," and "Terrorism and Mass Media," to name but a few. New technologies have changed, and continue to change, the practice of journalism, and they present profound challenges to the profession. In all, more than forty articles in this volume reference the impact of technology on journalism. For example, "Blogs"—listed thematically under Historical Overview and Practice—is clearly a journalistic practice made possible by technology.

Readers will find a commitment to three principles that form the foundation for this *Encyclopedia*. They are a belief in the importance of reason and the honest pursue of the truth, a conviction that freedom of information and freedom of the news media are essential to our way of life, and a confidence in the vital role that history plays in helping us understand our own time and prepare for the future. As many of these essays make clear, our belief in the rationality of human beings and our faith that the "truth" can be found have been tested severely during the past century. And yet without faith that people are rational and that the fair-minded pursuit of truth is noble, we lose the rationale underlying the mission of journalism: to inform the citizenry and the government that rests on the decisions of those citizens.

There is much in history, and perhaps in human nature, to suggest that freedom of information and freedom of the press are fragile. That these rights have taken root and thrived in the United States owes much to the courageous work of journalists. That much is made clear in the pages that follow.

History offers us a way of thinking that is unlike that found in most other disciplines. It asks us to orient issues and problems in a stream of time. Without understanding the historical context of contemporary affairs, it is unlikely that we will gain the perspectives we need to deal intelligently with the great issues of our own age. It is to that difficult but important task that this volume is dedicated.

HOW TO USE THIS *ENCYCLOPEDIA*

Although the entries herein are arranged alphabetically, there is both an **Alphabetical List of Entries** and a **Thematic List of Entries**. The thematic list suggests the major theme of each entry but cannot fully encompass the richness of the multiple strands found in individual entries. Following each entry is a **Further Reading** section to lead readers to other relevant literature. Many of the people, themes, and organizations discussed are frequently covered in several of essays and so a thorough, analytical **Index** is provided.

ACKNOWLEDGMENTS

Several people at Routledge played an important part in making the *Encyclopedia of American Journalism* possible and I wish to thank them for their help. Acquisitions editor Mark Georgiev first suggested this project in 2003 and then worked closely with us to define the project's scope and its table of contents. Mark was a constant source of encouragement and first-rate advice. He was assisted early in the project by associate development editor Kristen Holt, and then by assistant development editor, Christopher Flores. Kate Aker, director of development, then guided the project through its most difficult passages. It was her energy and commitment to the *Encyclopedia* that brought it to fruition.

To the many writers who contributed to this project I offer my heartfelt thanks. Although I have taught journalism history for more than a quarter century, I learned many new things in reading your essays. You have helped to make this a highly readable and valuable reference work.

Finally, I would like to express my appreciation to my two associate editors, James Landers and Bruce Evensen. The *Encyclopedia* benefited greatly from Jim Landers's levelheaded judgment and superb knowledge of twentieth-century journalism. I owe a special debt of thanks to Bruce Evensen. From the beginning, he devoted an extraordinary amount of time and energy to this project well beyond what might have been expected of him. Rarely have I meant anyone with a greater knowledge of American journalism history or who writes about this area with greater speed and lucidity. His contribution to this *Encyclopedia* has been immense.

STEPHEN VAUGHN

ABBOTT, ROBERT S.

The story of Robert Sengstacke Abbot's (Nov. 24, 1870–Feb. 29, 1940) life and eventual success in newspaper publishing epitomizes the challenges educated and enterprising African Americans faced during the Jim Crow and Progressive eras. It also embodies African American urban journalism rising by its bootstraps into a million-dollar enterprise in the twentieth century.

Abbott's life and entrepreneurship grew from unusual roots in the most predictable of slave cultures, enhanced by strict German values and a reasonably strong education and training for printing and law careers. His shoestring startup Chicago newspaper, the *Chicago Defender* (established in 1905) served a neglected black population. It progressed into a resounding voice against discrimination, advocating "race" opportunity (he shunned the terms *Negro*, *black*, and *Afro-American*) and the needs of Chicagoans of color. Its million-dollar success and added publications supported both a community and an extended-family dynasty that continued to produce the *Chicago Defender* for more than sixty years after Abbott's death.

If there ever was a slave aristocracy, Robert Abbott's roots (from his father's side) came from it. His father managed all servants in a Georgia plantation house and his exemplary dedication and status with the owners was both his antebellum mainstay and his post-emancipation undoing. Although he treasured his freedom, Thomas Abbott never could find the status and structure he enjoyed in servitude. Robert's mother, a dark-skinned hairdresser from the close-knit and independent Geechee culture of the Georgia islanders gave Robert the family roots and cultural heritage visible at times in his adult personality.

Robert's father died when Robert was four months old. His light-skinned German mulatto stepfather, John Sengstacke, who became a Congregationalist minister, mentored him with Calvinist rigor from early childhood. Yet, the social meaning of light and dark skin—along with cultural differences from Sengstacke's German upbringing—stigmatized the family, despite their high standards and education. Abbott experienced the constant discomfort wrought by his dark skin and the comfort of living in an all-black community outside of Savannah and visiting relatives on St. Simons Island in his childhood, where a proud history of resistance to slavery endured.

Abbott's first experience working on a newspaper was with the four-page paper his father began, produced, distributed, and read from the pulpit to parishioners. After studying unsuccessfully in a light-skin dominated school, Abbott eventually attended Hampton Institute and spent eight years there, learning the printing trade, completing his college degree, and touring with a singing group that solicited donations for the college.

Color was a constant source of frustration to Abbott. Even his move to Chicago was tied to rejection in love by his light-skinned girlfriend's family, who regarded Robert as below their daughter's station for marriage, despite a life-long acquaintance with him. He had already worked as a printer's devil, had labored on his stepfather's newspaper, and was a trained printer, but his efforts to find gainful work in skilled printing crafts were frustrated by his skin color. He earned a diploma in law at Kent College in Chicago, only to find that his dark skin posed too big a risk of courtroom defeat to prospective partners or clients.

Abbott began *The Chicago Defender* doing everything but the printing himself, including selling the two-cent weekly from door-to-door and person-to-person on the street. By 1929, its circulation had grown to 250,000 and the *Defender* had its own building, press, and several departments. It had risen through typical urban strategies, such as sensationalizing crime and other scandals, but it had also gained enormously from Abbott's ability to hire good people, including J. Hockley Smiley in 1910, who managed operations.

Abbott lashed out at Jim Crow and discrimination in the South and North. He believed the North, and Chicago in particular, offered far more jobs and economic opportunity for southern blacks than the South and subsequently produced special promotional issues of *The Defender*, which he distributed in enormous numbers throughout the South. Thus, Abbott not only influenced history in the South by using mass media to spur migration to Chicago, but he provided a newspaper to inform, lead, entertain, assure and maintain a community for the newcomers after they arrived. He loudly objected to the ghettoizing of blacks on Chicago's South Side, decried the racial incidents and lynching of the early twentieth century, and promoted race achievement through awards and by publishing the work of talented writers and poets, including Langston Hughes and others.

Further Reading

Doreski, C. K. "From News to History: Robert Abbott and Carl Sandburg Read the 1919 Chicago Riot." *African American Review* 26, no. 4 (Winter, 1992).

———. *Writing America Black: Race Rhetoric and the Public Sphere.* New York: Cambridge University Press, 1998.

Herbst, Susan. "Public Expression Outside the Mainstream" *Annals of the American Academy of Political and Social Science* 546, *The Media and Politics* (July, 1996), 120–131.

Ottley, Roi. *The Lonely Warrior: The Life and Times of Robert S. Abbott.* Chicago: Henry Regnery Company, 1955.

CARMEN E. CLARK

AMERICAN BROADCASTING COMPANY (ABC) NEWS

ABC News helped to bring broadcast journalism fully into the television age. It was one of the "big three" networks prior to the growth of cable and satellite TV. Yet when ABC began, CBS and NBC already were broadcast news institutions. ABC's achievements were not so much in the reporting of news events, which CBS and NBC also covered. ABC surpassed its rivals with concepts that loosened TV news from newspaper influences. Journalism became a television experience for viewers.

ABC's signatures were the daily broadcasts of "The World News Tonight" and "Nightline." Both programs were major innovations. ABC was also the first major broadcast organization to recognize the importance of local TV news. Local stations owned by ABC challenged more traditional CBS-NBC newscasting designs.

ABC had to fight to become a major network. Its maverick approach traced to its star-crossed inception. In 1926, NBC had fortified the strongest national radio network. To limit newcomer CBS, NBC formed a third network called the Blue Network. CBS and others protested NBC's ownership of two systems. The FCC concurred and, in 1943, forced NBC to sell the Blue Network. It went to Edward Nobel, the founder of Lifesavers candies. NBC stripped the Blue Network of its assets and kept its few popular entertainers. What was left of the Blue Network became ABC.

The rudiments of ABC News were news commentary programs on radio. Popular during the 1930s, news commentaries faded during World War II. CBS and NBC introduced regular newscasts. ABC became a haven for famed commentators whose programs had been dropped by CBS and NBC. The best known of these personalities was Walter Winchell. Others were Drew Pearson and Gabriel Heatter. The most venerable was Paul Harvey, whose ABC commentaries began in 1950 and continued for well over a half century.

ABC television began in 1948. For the next twenty years, the expense of TV broadcasting kept ABC close to collapse. In 1953, Nobel sold ABC to Leonard Goldenson. In 1955, assistance came from the Disney corporation, and ABC managed to stay afloat through the black-and-white era of television. Financial problems reached crisis proportions again when television began its conversion to color. In 1965, Goldenson attempted to sell ABC to International Telegraph and Telephone (ITT), a large conglomerate that during the 1960s owned many businesses. Fearful of mounting debt,

ITT backed out. Three years later, ABC barely survived a hostile takeover attempt by the reclusive billionaire Howard Hughes.

Lacking resources, ABC News was a marginal operation. In 1954, it provided the only live coverage of the Army-McCarthy hearings, but largely because it had no daytime programming during the period when the hearings occurred.

When CBS and NBC initiated nightly news programs in 1948, it became a problem for ABC. ABC did not follow until 1954. While CBS and NBC had noted journalists, ABC became a revolving door for newscasters. The first seven were John Daly, Murphy Martin, John Lawrence, William Sheehan, Alex Drier, Ron Cochran, and Bill Shadel. In 1961, Goldenson hired President Dwight Eisenhower's acclaimed press secretary James Hagerty to be the first official president of ABC News, but Hagerty struggled. A low point came in 1968 when ABC could not afford full coverage of that year's political conventions.

Fortunes changed later in 1968 when Al Primo became news director of the ABC-owned New York station WABC. Primo believed that TV news was too serious, dominated by elder stentorian newscasters who sat in studios and read worded accounts. CBS's Walter Cronkite, the period's most popular newscaster, best personified this "Olympian" approach.

Primo took advantage of new technology such as videotape and mobile cameras. He showcased a large team of on-camera anchors and roving reporters who communicated news while posing as the viewers' friends. This concept, known as "Eyewitness News," moved WABC from last to first place in audience ratings. The idea then was introduced at ABC's other owned stations that included WLS in Chicago, KABC in Los Angeles, WXYZ in Detroit, and KGO in San Francisco. These stations, too, became Number 1 in the ratings.

"Eyewitness News" was a turning point both for ABC and for television news. The five ABC stations became one of the largest profit centers in the history of broadcasting. During the 1970s, these five stations generated more than $1 billion in profits. By 1975, almost every other ABC, CBS, and NBC local affiliate abandoned the "Olympian" style in favor of ABC's freer and more energetic design. "Eyewitness News" facilitated the first regular "live shots" and other applications of "electronic newsgathering" technology. The concept later served as a model for reporting on CNN and ABC's cable sports channel ESPN.

Professional uncertainty testified to the ferment ABC had stirred. Fearful that "Eyewitness News" would move from local to network news, Cronkite joined with many CBS and NBC News veterans in denouncing conversational language, reporter involvement, and friendly newscasting as "show business" techniques. Critics further felt that video undermined the flow of information that came from newscasters' written scripts. Among those who defended ABC was media theorist Marshall McLuhan, who felt that "Eyewitness News" at last had proven television's potential for "shared" news communication. McLuhan asserted, no doubt prematurely, that written scripts and printed news were obsolete.

Despite thriving from its initiatives in local TV news, ABC still was mired in the last-place ratings of its national newscast, the "ABC Evening News." The ABC news division resisted attempts to change the broadcast's "Olympian" format. Former CBS reporter Harry Reasoner was ABC's main anchor between 1970 and 1977. Competing against CBS and Cronkite, Reasoner's ratings were small.

In 1976, low ratings precipitated an ill-fated display of ABC ingenuity. ABC hired NBC "Today Show" host Barbara Walters as Reasoner's co-anchor. Although this gave ABC the distinction of introducing the first female network main anchor, Walters was removed after one year. Walters and Reasoner disliked each other and viewers, who sensed that fact, were uncomfortable.

Success finally came with ABC's most-noted unconventional move. In 1977, ABC named Roone Arledge, the mastermind of ABC Sports, as president of the network news division. Again, critics denounced ABC's debasement of news traditions. The hiring of Arledge marked the first time in journalism that a person with no news background was placed in charge of a major news organization. Nevertheless, borrowing some "Eyewitness News" techniques but mostly those from "The Wide World of Sports," Arledge transformed network news.

Arledge ended the "ABC Evening News." In 1978 he launched a new nightly newscast called "The World News Tonight." Anchored by Frank Reynolds until Reynold's death in 1983, and then by Peter Jennings until 2005, "The World News Tonight" featured co-anchors from different locations around the world. They included Max Robinson, the first African American network newscaster. Seen for the first time in network news were regular "live" reports, extensive visualization, animations, digital graphics, and thematic music.

ABC's next breakthrough came in 1980. Arledge persuaded ABC affiliates to permit an extra half-hour of network news late at night for coverage of the Iran Hostage Crisis. Anchored by Ted Koppel, these reports were permanently established as the broadcast "Nightline." By this time, a third broadcast begun in 1976, "Good Morning America," became a major showcase for ABC's expanded news reporting.

After Cronkite's retirement in 1981, ABC became the leader in broadcast news. In addition to its expansion in television, ABC was the only national broadcast entity to build up operations in radio news. Most leading local news radio stations became an ABC News affiliate.

Acclaimed journalism and public affairs figures who in the 1980s joined Arledge were David Brinkley, pioneer of NBC's "Huntley-Brinkley Report"; Pierre Salinger, former press secretary to President John Kennedy; and Carl Bernstein, whose 1972 exposés in the *Washington Post* exposed the Watergate scandal. Others who identified ABC News were correspondents Sam Donaldson, Brit Hume, John

McWethy, Cokie Roberts, and Bettina Gregory; and analyst George Will.

ABC News had ascended when cable and satellite delivery first appeared. In 1982, ABC was alone among the three original broadcast networks in launching a twenty-four-hour all-news channel on cable TV. This venture, called the Satellite News Channel, had been preceded by Ted Turner's Cable News Network. Because cable systems already provided CNN, SNC collapsed. Although from SNC emerged ABC's twenty-four-hour all-sports channel ESPN, ABC's "The World News Tonight" and other news programs were overshadowed by CNN.

In 1985, Goldenson sold ABC to Capital Cities, a local station group that in the 1970s grew from obscurity from profits gained by applying ABC's revisions in local TV news. To meet plummeting ABC ratings and revenues caused by cable competition, Capital Cities cut budgets for ABC News. Several of ABC's thirty foreign and domestic bureaus were closed. However, the downsizing of ABC News was less severe than at CBS and NBC, where hundreds of journalists lost their jobs.

More reductions came in 1997. Capital Cities was absorbed by Disney, the corporation that had saved ABC forty-two years earlier. Disney shored news operations in New York and Washington but eliminated remaining bureaus.

Despite decline, ABC remained prominent in broadcast news. Appointed as anchor in 1983, Peter Jennings headed "The World News Tonight" until his death in 2005. Jennings's tenure was one of the longest of any broadcast journalist. ABC's most celebrated news figure was Arledge. Arledge's death in 2002 generated worldwide news. Arledge was eulogized for epitomizing ABC's tradition of fighting the establishment and coming out ahead.

Further Reading

Craig Allen, *News Is People: The Rise of Local TV News and the Fall of News from New York*. Ames: Iowa State Press, 2001.

Ken Auletta, *Three Blind Mice: How the TV Networks Lost Their Way*. New York: Random House, 1991.

James B. Duffy, *The Wind in the Trees*. New York: Endimiyon, 1997.

Marc Gunther, *The House that Roone Built: The Inside Story of ABC News*. Boston: Little, Brown, 1994.

Leonard H. Goldenson, *Beating the Odds: The Untold Story Behind the Rise of ABC*. New York: Scribner, 1991.

Sterling Quinlan, *Inside ABC: American Broadcasting Company's Rise to Power*. New York : Hastings House, 1979.

CRAIG ALLEN

ABOLITIONIST PRESS

Beginning around 1830, some American anti-slavery activists known as *abolitionists* or *immediatists* undertook to emancipate all slaves and to grant them full rights and U.S. citizenship. Many abolitionists were Christian evangelists to whom ending slavery was a moral imperative and publishing was a means toward that end. Early abolitionists used newspapers as grass-roots organizing tools in Ohio, Pennsylvania, and New England, forming groups and societies around the papers. They aimed to make the North a haven for liberty and equality and to build a power base for overturning slavery throughout the land. Their extensive media included newspapers, tracts, prayer books, broadsides (single-sheet imprints), pamphlets, textbooks, primers, sheet music, novels, magazines, hymnals, symbols, symbolic objects, and children's publications.

Whether all slaves in the nation would be freed and whether free blacks would assimilate as equals were hotly contested issues in the North when abolitionism arose. Northern states passed laws restricting the rights of free blacks and the Constitution protected slaveholders' property rights. Anti-slavery moderates favored gradualism and resisted abolitionist challenges to desegregate their churches or support Negro and women's rights. Some southern and conservative churches backed the *colonization* movement begun in 1817 to send free Negroes to Africa as an alternative to universal emancipation and assimilation.

Controversy played out in the abolitionist press for more than forty years leading to the Emancipation Proclamation (1863) and Thirteenth Amendment (1865). A scattering of studies list the main abolitionist newspapers, document violence against them and address related First Amendment issues, but they do not include the breadth of immediatist publications or the diversity of media during this critical era.

New studies of the abolitionist press might include expanded bibliographies of anti-slavery newspapers, magazines, tracts, and serials—including those edited and published by blacks that were clearly abolitionist in purpose and vision; studies connecting newspapers and publishers within the social history of the era; attention to regional and community newspapers promoting abolitionist activities; interconnections between the abolitionist press and religious, political, and social activity; and communication strategies of abolitionist, anti-slavery, and pro-slavery forces.

Newspaper Chronology

Anti-slavery newspaper commentary and articles, books, organizational reports, pamphlets, open letters, and sermons increased throughout the 1700s into the 1800s, but no anti-slavery focused American newspaper is known to have published before 1817.

Quakers began the earliest anti-slavery newspapers. Charles Osborn, an Ohio Quaker, established *The Philanthropist*, in 1817. Elihu Embree's *Manumission Intelligencer* (1819) became *The Emancipator* in 1820. In 1821, another Quaker, Benjamin Lundy bought *The Emancipator* and renamed it *The Genius of Universal Emancipation*. A newspaper was central to Lundy's strategy as he migrated from Vermont to Ohio to Tennessee to New England, speaking against slavery and starting anti-slavery societies. He settled on making New England a hotbed of anti-slavery

influence and a haven for free blacks. Walking throughout the region, he reportedly carried the *Genius*'s page beds with him—publishing wherever a friendly printer lent his shop—until setting up a Baltimore office in 1830.

Universal emancipation was controversial in the North. As southern states passed laws banishing freed slaves, they moved north but were not very welcome. An 1821, an amendment to the New York state constitution did away with the property qualification for white voters but increased the property qualification for blacks from $100 to $250, thus drastically cutting New York City's black electorate when black settlement was rising and feeding a cultural Renaissance. Free blacks met increasing barriers as the state's 1827 emancipation date arrived.

That year, two black New Yorkers, Samuel Cornish and John Russwurm, started *Freedom's Journal*. It championed freedom and the rights of free blacks, called for immediate emancipation, denouncing lynching and the colonization movement as anti-black and pro-slavery. It met violent opposition but claimed a thousand subscribers and dozens of subscription agents in the United States, England, Canada, and Haiti.

Cornish left the paper briefly and Russwurm abandoned the abolitionist mission. Cornish returned but could not revive the paper's audience. He replaced *Freedom's Journal* with *The Rights of All* (1829-30). One agent, David Walker, wrote four important articles in *The Rights of All* known as "Walker's Appeal," supporting slave rebellion as self defense and championing black liberation. The pamphlet version of "Walker's Appeal" was banned throughout the South. Cornish, a Presbyterian minister and an abolitionist leader, later published *The Colored American* in New York, in the late 1830s.

The rise of abolitionism and the abolitionist press is usually credited to William Lloyd Garrison, a fiery white editor, leader and orator who briefly co-edited the *Genius of Universal Emancipation* with Lundy in 1830. In 1831 Garrison began *The Liberator* as an organ for the New England Anti-slavery Society (1831–) and the American Anti-Slavery Society (1832–). Uncompromising in its stand for immediate abolition throughout the nation and full equality for blacks, it circulated longer than any anti-slavery newspaper—thirty-five years—throughout New England, the nation, and the world.

Anti-slavery, abolitionist, and abolitionist-sympathetic daily newspapers proliferated in every Northern state between 1830 and the Civil War. Most notable was Horace Greeley's adamantly anti-slavery *New York Tribune*, whose national circulation was greater than any other in the era.

Lewis and Arthur Tappan, silk traders who became abolitionists around 1830 were key benefactors of the abolitionist press. They originally sponsored *The Liberator*; Lewis later funded the *Emancipator*, the most widely circulated anti-slavery newspaper of the era. He got involved with the *Amistad* case (a case involving blacks who had been kidnapped and sold into slavery in Africa and who rebelled as their ship traveled near Cuba) and wrote daily reports on its developments to the *Emancipator*. Tappan also began a journal, *Human Rights*, and a children's magazine, *The Slave's Friend*.

Violence against the abolitionist press was widespread in the 1830s. A mob attacked Lewis Tappan's New York home in 1834 and burned his furniture in the street. When Elijah Lovejoy, a New England Congregationalist minister, went to St. Louis and began publishing the abolitionist *St. Louis Observer* (1834–36), mobs destroyed his press three times. He moved to nearby Alton, Illinois in 1837, began the *Alton Observer*, and was killed by a mob that threw his fourth press into the Mississippi. That year free blacks lost the vote in Pennsylvania and Michigan and the *Antislavery Herald* began in Boston.

New papers in the 1840s reflected splits in anti-slavery societies over female activism, electoral involvement, and church segregation. The Liberty Party in 1842 founded *The Abolitionist* while Cornish, the Tappan brothers, and James Birney published for the American and Foreign Anti-Slavery Society. An African American, Martin Delaney, began the Pittsburgh *Mystery* in 1843. The *Antislavery Bugle* began in 1845.

In December 1847, Frederick Douglass, a former slave, after years of public speaking and organizing, began *The North Star*. Unlike the *Liberator*, it defended slave rebellions and acknowledged the African American experience. The *North Star* merged with the *Emancipator* in 1851, and continued as *Frederick Douglass' Paper* until he began *Douglass' Monthly*, an abolitionist magazine, in 1860. Douglass had a tremendous following. Newspaper debates arose between Douglass and Garrison over slave rebellions, electoral activity, and the Constitution.

By the late 1840s, *The Liberator* went to the fringe, sponsoring Constitution burnings and declaring a moral imperative for whites to harbor escaping slaves. *Uncle Tom's Cabin* was first serialized in an anti-slavery newspaper, *The National Era*, in 1851, illustrating layers of media in abolitionist publishing. In the United States, there are no known female abolitionist newspapers, although Canada's *Provincial Freeman*, begun in 1853, was edited and published by Mary Ann Shadd Carey, a black woman born in Delaware.

Anti-Slavery Imprints as Organizing Tools

Imprints allowed organizers to present their cases and enabled audiences to review and consider them. Abolitionists societies formed around newspapers, appointing members as subscription agents. Literature including newspapers, magazines, tracts, and other serials flowed at anti-slavery fairs, speaking tours and public meetings, in Sunday Schools, and countless other activities.

Abolitionists aggressively wrote letters to newspapers and launched a national petition campaign to outlaw slavery in the District of Columbia in the 1830s. Sympathetic newspapers published petition text and mailing instructions for filled petitions, enabling readers to copy the words and circulate petitions independently. In response to floods of petitions, an 1835 gag rule banned the traditional reading of petitions in Congress for nearly a decade.

Abolitionists sent thousands of newspapers broadsides, letters, pamphlets, tracts, and petitions to post offices in the South for general distribution. Southern postmasters refused to distribute them and states passed laws banning postal distribution of abolitionist materials including newspapers when federal courts did not uphold the postmasters' actions. Georgetown, D.C., outlawed any Negro leaving a post office in possession of seditious materials, and in 1835 the Charleston post office was ransacked, anti-slavery newspapers and other literature sent by abolitionists removed and burned. Northern female activists organized to visit friends and relatives in the South to personally deliver publications about the evils of slavery.

The abolitionist press is an important part of the history of the events leading to the Civil War and in the eventual end of slavery? Certainly, among America's many reform movements this was one of the most successful, and that success came at a terrible price.

Further Reading

Jacobs, Donald M., Heath Paley, Susan Parker, and Dana Silverman. *Antebellum Black Newspapers: Indices to New York Freedom's Journal* (1827–1829), *The Rights of All* (1829), *The Weekly Advocate* (1837), *and The Colored American* (1837-1841) Westport, CT: Greenwood Press, 1976.

McFeely, William S. *Frederick Douglass*. NewYork: W. W. Norton, 1991.

Nye, Russel B. *Fettered Freedom: A Discussion of Civil Liberties and the Slavery Controversy in the United States, 1830–1860*. East Lansing: Michigan State College Press, 1949.

Rogers, William B. *"We Are all Together Now": Frederick Douglass, William Lloyd Garrison, & the Prophetic Tradition*. New York: Garland Publishing, 1995.

Williams, Robert C. *Horace Greeley: Champion of American Freedom*. New York: New York University Press, 2006.

CARMEN E. CLARK

ABRAMS V. UNITED STATES

More than two thousand Americans were arrested and convicted during the World War I era under provisions of the 1917 Espionage Act and its 1918 Sedition Act amendments. The courts were unwilling to accept the argument that the First Amendment protected speech that challenged the United States' participation in, or prosecution of the war with Germany. The dissent by Supreme Court Justices Oliver Wendell Holmes and Louis Brandeis in the *Abrams* case marked a significant step in the expansion of freedom of speech.

Justice Holmes created the *clear and present danger test* in March 1919 in *Schenck v. United States* in which he wrote that challenging the government during war time was analogous to shouting fire in a theater and causing a panic. Under such circumstances, Holmes wrote, speech could not be protected. But by the next October, Holmes was ready in *Abrams v. United States* to clarify the meaning of the *clear and present danger test* in what has become one of the most powerful rationales for freedom of expression voiced by the Supreme Court. Based upon the principle that a public *marketplace of ideas* is a keystone of democratic government, Holmes wrote that only the "present danger of immediate evil or an intent to bring it about" can justify limits on the expression of opinion. Holmes did not believe Jacob Abrams and his four co-defendants had crossed that dangerous threshold.

The defendants were Russian-born Jews who immigrated to the United States to escape the Czar's anti-Semitic pogroms. Claiming loyalty to the United States, they believed that when an American military force arrived in northern Russian in 1918, it was to crush the Russian revolutionaries who had overthrown the Czar. The actual motive for intervention has never been clear. The revolutionaries had signed a peace treaty in 1917 with Germany when that country was at war with the United States.

Abrams and the others wrote and printed two leaflets. They distributed them from the windows of buildings in New York City. One circular said that President Woodrow Wilson's "cowardly silence" about sending the U.S. military into Russia was the work of a "plutocratic gang" in Washington, D.C., and called for support of workers in Russian. The second leaflet was written in Yiddish and called on readers to engage in a general strike.

The defendants received prison sentences ranging from three to twenty years. By a vote of 7–2, the Supreme Court upheld the convictions under Sedition Act prohibitions against conspiracy to "incite, provoke or encourage resistance to the United States," or to "unlawfully and willfully, by utterance, writing, printing and publication, to urge, incite and advocate curtailment of production of things and products, to wit, ordnance and ammunition, necessary and essential to the prosecution of the war."

Justices Holmes and Brandeis dissented. Holmes wrote that "when men have realized that time has upset many fighting faiths, they may come to believe … that the ultimate good desired is better reached by free trade in ideas—that the best test of truth is the power of the thought to get itself accepted in the competition of the market, and that truth is the only ground upon which their wishes safely can be carried out. That at any rate is the theory of our Constitution."

Holmes wrote that the Constitution required the nation to be "eternally vigilant against attempts to check the expression of opinions that we loathe and believe to be fraught with death, unless they so imminently threaten immediate interference with the lawful and pressing purposes of the law that an immediate check is required to save the country." Although Holmes and Brandeis were in the minority at the time, the marketplace theory has become well accepted constitutional doctrine. "Only the emergency that makes it immediately dangerous to leave the correction of evil counsels to time," Holmes concluded, "warrants making any exception to the sweeping command, 'Congress shall make no law abridging the freedom of speech.'"

Further Reading

Abrams v. United States 250 U.S. 616 (1919).
Polenburg, Richard. *Fighting Faiths: The Abrams Case, the Supreme Court, and Free Speech*. Ithaca, NY: Cornell University Press, 1988.
Schenck v. United States 249 U.S. 47 (1919).
Stone, Geoffrey R. *Perilous Times: Free Speech in Wartime*. New York: W.W. Norton & Co., 2004.
White, Edward G. *Justice Oliver Wendell Holmes: Law and the Inner Self.* New York: Oxford University Press, 1993.

JEREMY COHEN

ADAMS, SAMUEL HOPKINS

Samuel Hopkins Adams (1871–1958) came by his crusading zeal naturally. He was the son of Myron Adams, a Presbyterian minister from Dunkirk, New York, and Hester Rose Hopkins Adams, the daughter of Auburn Theological Seminary Professor Samuel W. Hopkins. His grandparents were distant relatives of the Boston Adamses. He grew up along Erie Canal and in later years wrote about New York State history.

At sixteen, he was the Hamilton College correspondent for the *New York Tribune*, briefly taking up residence in New York City's tenderloin district to report on the area's immigrant population. He later graduated to the *New York Sun*, Charles A. Dana's school of "new journalism" that included Richard Harding Davis, Jacob Riis, Arthur Brisbane, David Graham Phillips, and Will Irwin. There, Adams learned how to recognize the important detail that placed readers at the center of the story and "how to get at facts," (Kennedy, p. 27), qualities he put to use as a muckraking magazine reporter.

In 1900, Adams, now married and the father of an infant daughter, became managing editor of McClure's syndicate. Later he became its advertising manager, and in 1903, a staff writer at *McClure's Magazine*. Joined by Lincoln Steffens, Ray Stannard Baker, and Ida Tarbell, Adams developed a national reputation for exposing the hidden facts behind public and corporate abuse. Adams investigated miscarriages of justice in Kentucky and lawlessness in Appalachian West Virginia. He was lured to *Collier's Weekly* in 1904 to write about coal strikes, beef trusts, and political corruption in the West. Back at *McClure's* in 1905, he investigated the use of disinfection in the prevention of tuberculosis, then the nation's third leading killer.

Adams would be best remembered for his muckraking series on the patent medicine industry. *Collier's* began the six-part exposé "The Great American Fraud" on October 7, 1905. "Gullible America will spend some seventy-five millions of dollars in the purchase of patent medicines," he wrote. "In consideration of this sum it will swallow huge quantities of alcohol, an appalling amount of opiates and narcotics, a wide assortment of varied drugs ranging from powerful and dangerous heart depressants to insidious liver stimulants, and, far in excess of all other ingredients, undiluted fraud." (p. 14) His five-month investigation demonstrated the health threats caused by patent medicines, the press's complicity in publishing false advertising, and the government's failure to protect the health of Americans. In a follow-up series on quacks and quackery Adams identified more than 250 nostrums, many of which were more dangerous than the diseases they purported to cure. Adams's work established him as the nation's leading writer on health and medicine, forced many in the press to police their advertising, and helped convince Congress to pass the Pure Food and Drug Act in 1906.

Adams muckraked the trusts as chief editorial writer for *Ridgway's* magazine in 1906. In 1907, he began a long career as a free lance journalist by reporting the sensational Stanford White murder case for the *New York World*. Health articles for *McClure's*, *Collier's*, and *Hampton's* followed. Adams also turned to writing detective stories and romantic novels. *Flaming Youth* in 1923 became one of the most vivid chronicles of the Jazz Age. Seventeen novels and stories became motion pictures, including 1934's Academy Award winner *It Happened One Night*. In his later years, Adams wrote biography and juvenile fiction. His fifty-sixth book, *Tenderloin*, published posthumously in 1959, was an affectionate remembrance of his newspaper days. At his death, Adams seven-decade career that included perhaps ten million words was celebrated for bringing medical science to American readers.

Further Reading

Adams, Samuel Hopkins. *The Great American Fraud: Collier's Expose of the Patent Medicine Fraud, 1905–1906*. New York: P.F. Collier & Son, 1906.
Adams, Samuel Hopkins. *The Health Master*. Boston: Houghton Mifflin, 1914.
Adams, Samuel Hopkins. "The Solving of the Milk Problem." *McClure's*, December 1908.
Kennedy III, Samuel V. *Samuel Hopkins Adams and the Business of Writing*. Syracuse: Syracuse University Press, 1999.
Miraldi, Robert. *Muckraking and Objectivity: Journalism's Colliding Traditions*. New York: Greenwood Press, 1990.
New York Times. November 17, 1958.
"Samuel Hopkins Adams." *Contemporary Authors*, vol. 220. Detroit: Gale Publishing, 2004.
Samuel Hopkins Adams Papers are located at Syracuse University and Hamilton College in Clinton, New York.

BRUCE J. EVENSEN

ADVERTISING

Here we examine two ways to think about the relationship between advertising and journalism, which have profound consequences for democracy. First, we consider the role that advertising plays in relation to news production. We then turn briefly to how political advertising, in the Age of Television became the major source of campaign information for voters campaigns, often replacing news in this regard.

The sources of income for news-sellers have varied over time. The initial producers were supported by political parties and also made a living by selling their publications to partisan supporters. The arrival of the penny press lifted much of the financial pressures from the publishers and allowed them to start offering products without a partisan slant. Ironically, it was advertising that initially allowed publishers freedom from partisan financiers or supporters. Once they were able to defray more of the costs through advertising, publishers started focusing on audiences that would attract more advertisers. In order to attract the most advertisers and to be able to charge higher prices for the advertisements, publishers needed to increase the circulation of their papers. To do this they had to provide information that appealed to as wide an audience as possible. This need to appeal to the largest possible number of people led to an increasingly nonbiased stance in journalism.

However, over the years, particularly since the development of media industry conglomerates, the increasing confounding of journalism and entertainment resources in these companies, has led to a new trend in journalism: segmentation and soft news. Advertising can be seen as influencing a news producer in two ways: first, in the actual news content of the programming, for example soft news, which can be catered to attracting the highest number of viewers. The second way that advertising influences news is in the way that the producers of news content position themselves in the media market. This need to position themselves most favorably has led to increasing segmentation, which is just another word used for focusing on specific demographics within the audience.

In the late nineteenth century, advertising served to liberate journalism from dependence on individual benefactors and political parties; a century later advertising was once again shifting the journalism landscape. During the 1990s, the three major television networks faced increasing competition for audiences by cable television. In the 2000s, the Internet further eroded the audiences available to network news and print publications. This increased competition led to networks focusing both on "marginal" or casual viewers and to viewers from particular segments of society.

The effect of focusing on marginal viewers, viewers who were likely to choose from a variety of shows, was that more and more soft news was offered. Since news required high fixed cost investment, news producers were forced to either focus directly on particular and lucrative audiences or on a wider mix of soft news and hard news. Since most network and cable shows focused on women during the day, and the evening programming was largely targeted towards the eighteen to thirty-five-year-old audience, this explained much of the criticism of news as both too liberal and largely soft news.

Segmentation of the market led to the success of such outlets as Fox News which catered to people with particular news preferences. Once again, segmentation influenced the content and style of journalism offered. This was particularly true on the Internet, radio, and in the publishing industries. A segmented outlet, such as a local newspaper like *Newsday* on Long Island, New York, would focus its newsgathering and production capacities towards satisfying the information demands of its targeted audience—people on

Long Island. Advertisers rewarded news production outfits such as *Newsday* to the extent that it was able to attract and retain its audiences. Segmentation, therefore, could take on many forms, including geographic, economic, gender, ethnic, religious, and political foci.

Another aspect of advertising's impact on journalism was the growing consolidation within the media world. Five conglomerates came to dominate the media and entertainment world: Time Warner, the Walt Disney Company, News Corporation, Viacom, and Bertelsmann. Each of these conglomerates held major interests in all forms of media from publication to the Internet and exerted immense influence on American journalism. Consider, for example, the four major networks: NBC was owned by GE (a major media conglomerate), CBS by Viacom, ABC by Disney, and Fox by News Corporation. One of the most prominent and obvious effects on journalism was the cross-promotion of entertainment products. This development meant that once a product was produced by the parent company, it was promoted through its various holdings including the news outlets. Therefore, it was not uncommon to see "specials" on network and local news programs on current shows or movies produced by the sister company of the network.

Another impact of this kind of widespread ownership was the increasing reach of a single product produced by one company. A good example of this kind of occurrence was Clear Channel Communication which owned 1,240 radio stations in the first years of the twenty-first century. However, these 1,240 stations were run by only two hundred employees in order to maximize the profits earned from the advertising operations of the parent company. This meant that much of the same content was played across the country including the same talk shows which served as a soft news source for a number of Americans. The leading talk show personality on Clear Channel was the highly partisan Rush Limbaugh. Although other talk show personalities were also offered, the choice for radio listeners was nevertheless severely constrained when compared to situations where stations were owned by multiple companies.

In contrast to this state of affairs, there was another strong tradition in journalism, one reflected in the 1947 report of the Commission on Freedom of the Press—familiarly known as the Hutchins Commission, after the University of Chicago president Robert Hutchins who led it. It held that while corporations should be in business solely to make money, the press should be guided by a higher moral principle, that of providing the public with the information needed for a functioning democracy. This tradition reflected the thinking of major publishers, and was marked by ethical standards which drew a sharp line between the business and reporting side of the enterprise. Joseph Pulitzer, the founder of one of the first newspaper chains, developed an ultimately powerful market niche by championing the "common man" in the late nineteenth century. Pulitzer argued in favor of news for the public good. He steadfastly held that news should be "drastically independent of government and public opinion" and thus set a high standard for journalism which continued into the twentieth century.

For example, *St. Louis Post Dispatch* reporters who traveled to North Vietnam during the cold war brought home reports which countered U.S. policy. Their findings were reinforced by reporting from other major news outlets including the *New York Times*, the Associated Press, and, ultimately, by television news.

The tradition of "drastically independent" reporting—bolstered by public mistrust of government stemming from the Vietnam War and Watergate scandal—contributed to recognition of the value of a "firewall" between news and advertising. In the early twenty-first century, this idea was still strongly supported at such major news outlets National Public Radio, Cable News Network, the *Washington Post*, and *New Yorker*. The most coveted award for quality investigative reporting continued to bear Joseph Pulitzer's name. In this tradition, there was a real effort to differentiate between advertising and news decision-making processes.

In the early twenty-first century, there was no doubt that a crisis existed in contemporary newspaper publishing. But, as the Commission on the Role of the Press in a Democracy noted, it was important to point out that not all ownership models were alike. In regard to influential "hard news" newspapers, the biggest problems emerged as chains took their stock "public" in the 1990s, resulting in Wall Street demands for large profit margins. However, at such prestigious newspapers as the *Washington Post*, the *Wall Street Journal*, and the *New York Times*, not all stocks were publicly traded. Indeed "mixed" stock models emerged, with owners, frequently from major families, owning private stock with a controlling vote. Moreover, multiple other online news formats were developing, some of which were creating successful citizen formats with advertising.

It is worth noting a second problem that emerged during the age of television in the United States. Political advertising became the major source of information for voters in election campaigns; and in competitive races, much of it was negative, or directed at attacking the opponent. By 1984, even though television news programs, such as the one anchored by Dan Rather at CBS, clearly dominated the U.S. information environment, negative ads on TV, or polispots, actually overwhelmed news in a general election in terms of total airtime by a ratio of four to one. This advertising predominance continued through the 1990s as research made it clear that advertising had an impact on voter impressions of candidates particularly during presidential primaries. Research studies also made it clear that negative political advertising contained more information about campaign issues than the predominant, more marketable "horserace oriented news."

Positive advertising was often criticized for lacking substance, although it did tap the more positive emotions of "hope" and "trust." Negative advertising targeted opponents in emotional and personal ways, and "stealth negative advertising" often occurred toward the end of a campaign, beneath the press radar. Significantly, it was not unusual that this kind of advertising appealed to racial or ethnic prejudices.

Further Reading

Brader, Ted. *Campaigning for Hearts and Minds: How Emotional Appeals in Political Ads Work.* Chicago: University of Chicago Press, 2006.

Geer, John. *In Defense of Negativity.* Chicago: University of Chicago Press, 2006.

Hamilton, James T. *All the News That's Fit to Sell.* Princeton, NJ: Princeton University Press, 2004.

Just, Marion, et al. *Crosstalk: News, Candidates and the Public in a Presidential Campaign.* Chicago: University of Chicago Press, 1996.

Kern, Montague. *30 Second Politics: Political Advertising in the 80s.* Westport, CT: Praeger-Greenwood, 1989.

West, Darrell, Montague Kern, Dean Alger, and Janice Groggin. "Ad Buys in Presidential Politics: The Strategies of Electoral Persuasion," *Journal of Political Communication* (Spring 1996).

SAMAN TALIB

MONTAGUE KERN

AGEE, JAMES

James Agee's (Nov. 27, 1909–May 16, 1955) reputation as a groundbreaking literary journalist derives from one great book, *Let Us Now Praise Famous Men*, a collaboration with the photographer Walker Evans. Ostensibly a report on tenant farming in Alabama assigned by *Fortune* magazine in 1936, *Let Us Now Praise Famous Men* is actually metajournalism, Agee's personal critique of corporate journalism and his own reportage, which Agee viewed as cynical exploitation of the disadvantaged for profit. Although the Luce publishing empire considered Agee one of its star writers, it rejected *Let Us Now Praise Famous Men* and released it to the authors who published it in 1941 with the Houghton Mifflin Company to little notice. Republished in 1960, the book won acclaim as one of the great journalistic classics of the twentieth century.

Agee was born in Knoxville, Tennessee, in 1909. The death of his father in an automobile accident in 1916 troubled Agee for the rest of his life. *A Death in the Family*, Agee's posthumously published novel about the event, won the Pulitzer Prize in 1958. In 1919, Agee was enrolled by his mother at St. Andrew's, an Episcopal school on the Cumberland Plateau near Sewanee, Tennessee. There he was befriended by Father James Flye, with whom he later carried on a lifelong correspondence, published as *The Letters of James Agee to Father Flye* in 1962. *The Morning Watch*, a novel about his experiences at St. Andrew's, was published in 1951.

Agee's earliest experiments in journalistic writing appeared in the *Monthly*, a literary magazine published by Phillips Exeter Academy in Exeter, New Hampshire, which Agee attended from 1925 to 1928. Admitted to Harvard, he was elected president of the Harvard *Advocate* and edited its parody of *Time* in 1932. He was then hired by *Fortune* and worked for the magazine until 1939. A collection of poems, *Permit Me Voyage*, was published in 1934. His editors at *Fortune* assigned Agee to write lengthy articles on such topics as the Tennessee Valley Authority, Roman society, the American roadside, the cruise line industry, art, and cockfighting.

After leaving *Fortune*, Agee reviewed films for *The Nation* and *Time*, securing a reputation as one of America's greatest film critics. He also wrote notable articles on film topics for *Life* and contributed news articles, book reviews, and essays to *Time*, the most memorable of which was "Victory: The Peace," a meditation on the atomic bomb. Many of these articles have been collected in *Agee on Film: Reviews and Comments* (1958), and *James Agee: Selected Journalism* (1985, 2005), and *Agee: Selected Literary Documents* (1996). *The Collected Poems of James Agee* and *The Collected Short Prose of James Agee* both appeared in 1968.

Agee's last years were highly productive despite the fact that he was in ill health. He died in 1955 of a heart attack while riding in a New York City taxi. He worked on screenplays including *The African Queen* and *The Night of the Hunter*, and wrote *Mr. Lincoln*, a television film that appeared in serial form on the CBS program *Ominbus*. *Agee on Film: Five Film Scripts* by James Agee was published in 1960.

Agee's influence on journalistic practice has been significant due, in part, to his accomplished writing across many different genres. His style influenced later movements such as New Journalism although he remains difficult to categorize. While his journalistic work was once disparaged as a distraction from his poetry and fiction, it has come to be regarded as distinctively excellent. His best journalism has a quality of prescience and prophecy. *Let Us Now Praise Famous Men* challenges journalists to consider the implications of their trade and to view their work in a moral context.

Further Reading

Ashdown, Paul, ed. *James Agee: Selected Journalism.* Knoxville: University of Tennessee, 1985, 2005.

Ashdown, Paul, "James Agee." In *A Sourcebook of American Literary Journalism*, edited by Thomas B. Connery, Westport: Greenwood, 1992.

Ashdown, Paul, "Prophet from Highland Avenue: Agee's Visionary Journalism." In *James Agee: Reconsiderations*, edited by Michael A. Lofaro, Knoxville: University of Tennessee, 1992.

Bergreen, Laurence. *James Agee: A Life.* New York: Dutton, 1984.

Kramer, Victor A., ed. *Agee: Selected Literary Documents*, edited by Troy, NY: Whitson, 1996.

Lofaro, Michael A., and Hugh Davis. *James Agee Rediscovered: The Journals of Let Us Now Praise Famous Men and Other New Manuscripts.* Knoxville: University of Tennessee, 2005.

Lowe, James. *The Creative Process of James Agee.* Baton Rouge: Louisiana State University, 1994.

Madden, David, and Jeffrey J. Folks, eds. *Remembering James Agee*, 2nd ed. Athens: University of Georgia, 1997.

Maharidge, Dale and Michael Williamson. *And Their Children After Them.* New York: Pantheon, 1989.

Moreau, Geneviéve. *The Restless Journey of James Agee.* New York: Morrow, 1977.

Stott, William. *Documentary Expression and Thirties America.* New York: Oxford University Press, 1973.

PAUL ASHDOWN

AGRICULTURAL JOURNALISM

Agricultural journalism can be described as specific content within any publication or entire niche publications about any agricultural specializations or interests. In any form it embodies practices, values and interplay between timely social forces. Agricultural journalistic content may be found in daily and weekly newspapers, magazines, pamphlets, pictures, cartoons, editorials, data such as weather and market reports, government publications, boilerplate, broadcasts, newsletters, almanacs, cookbooks, rural or farm lifestyle publications, handbills, or advertisements connected or related to agriculture. Readers and audiences could be planters, yeoman farmers, gentleman farmers, farm women, farm families, pioneer sod-breakers, herdsmen, livestock breeders, cash croppers, share croppers, dairy producers, truck farmers, fruit and nut growers, hybrid seed producers, modern family farm enterprises, corporate farmers or investors, and commodity brokers—or the general public.

It was often through the press that colonial agriculture became steeped in social convention and anecdotal sharing of experience before scientific methods seeped into farming practices. Nineteenth-century agriculture had far-flung communication, a yeoman ideal, and hungry city dwellers to feed. The Morrill Acts beginning in 1862 created land-grant schools of agriculture that strongly influenced agricultural journalism. The twentieth century brought widespread education and cooperative movements, along with organic farming. New technologies, such as hydroponics, arose on small-scale while chemical farming and biotechnology grew rapidly. Corporate farms and vertical consolidation of the food industry after World War II could not keep farm exports from steadily dropping. Prices also dropped, from overproduction, while students increasingly enrolled in agricultural programs. The computer age accelerated change as it open new forums and exchange. All these developments were reflected in agricultural journalism.

Chronology

Agricultural journalism historians often have started with the first specialized agricultural newspaper in 1819—John Stuart Skinner's weekly, *The American Farmer.* But agriculture was the central economic force in colonial America. Important news in any town and region was often related to it. The early press introduced new methods, data, technology, philosophical and moral attitudes about agriculture and farming. Newspapers reported on markets and exports, freely expressing opinions about agricultural issues. Almanacs allowed farmers to plan on the weather. Other colonial media probably enriched agricultural practices, as well.

At the turn of the nineteenth century, newspapers and their editors were frequently important agents for changes in farming practices. New specialized newspapers, magazines and serials on many topics circulated via new transportation networks under favorable postal rates. Expansion and farming went hand-in-hand while the yeoman citizen-farmer and Renaissance man became cultural ideals. Farming meant survival for some and a mission for others. Overfarming of cash crops had already depleted expanses of soil at a time when demand for food rose with urbanization. Animal husbandry was new to many farmers. Science and informed farming methods offered solutions.

Skinner had a dream when he began publishing *The American Farmer* in Baltimore on April 2, 1819. In the first issue, he wrote, "The great aim and the chief pride of *The American Farmer* will be to collect information from every source, on every branch of husbandry, thus to enable the reader to study the various systems which experience has proved to be the best, under given circumstances." His eight-page quarto continued for about fifteen years. It was sold in 1834 to E. P. Roberts and published as *The Farmer and Gardener* for five years until reverting to Skinner and its original name for another six years. During that time Skinner published two monthlies: *The American Turf Register and Sporting Magazine* and *The American Silk Society and Rural Economist.* He also wrote and published about doctoring livestock—a subject of which little had been written. Agricultural change was underway.

In 1845, Skinner joined Horace Greeley and Thomas McElrath to produce an agricultural supplement to the *New York Tribune,* called *A Monthly Journal of Agriculture.* The *Tribune* was a penny daily, but its weekly edition had enormous circulation in rural areas. Greeley's mission was to educate citizens. He disseminated information and solicited reader participation. The *Monthly Journal* continued that tradition. Greeley's following was great and his famous refrain, "Go West, young man," tied in with an agricultural ideal enhanced by better methods and knowledge. Skinner's final contribution was a voluminous monthly journal of integrated agricultural, legal, and economic development, *The Plough, the Loom, and the Anvil.* It continued from 1848 to Skinner's untimely death in 1851.

Judge Jesse Buel's *The Cultivator,* illustrated a direction in early agricultural journalism apart from Skinner: a value-and-information-driven vision to uplift farming methods in New England. Buel, a self-educated editor-publisher of non-agricultural newspapers, had retired to an eighty-five-acre farm at age forty-two to learn farming. Through that undertaking, he developed *The Cultivator* (1834–1840), "To improve the soil, and the mind," was its masthead motto.

Another long-acknowledged agricultural journalist of the nineteenth century was Luther Tucker, founder of the *Genesee Farmer and Gardener's Journal,* "the first really great long-lived farm paper in America," according to historian William E. Ogilvie. The *Genesee Farmer* merged with Judge Buel's *Cultivator* to form *The Country Gentleman* (1840) when Tucker took it over after Buel's death. Tucker also published *The Horticulturalist* magazine (1846–1853).

William E. Ogilvie's *Pioneer Agricultural Journalists* (1974) profiles Skinner, Tucker, and thirteen other important nineteenth-century editors and publishers through Herbert W. Collingwood, editor of the *Rural New Yorker*.

Twentieth-Century Farm and Specialty Newspapers, Newsletters, and Magazines

Hoard's Dairyman and *Wallace's Farmer* had roots in the late nineteenth century but carried their influence into the twentieth century through their agricultural journalism. Editor-publisher W. D. Hoard in Wisconsin helped establish a regional dairy economy in the 1870s through the *Jefferson County Union*, his regional general-audience newspaper, a decade before he launched the national *Hoard's Dairyman*. *Wallace's Farmer* was to farming what *Hoard's Dairyman* was to dairying—the largest and most respected one-stop source for current information and exchange about agriculture. The aristocratic Wallace family was so influential, partly through generations of publishing *Wallace's Farmer*, that Henry C. Wallace was named Secretary of Agriculture (under Warren Harding) and Henry A. Wallace served as Vice President (under Franklin D. Roosevelt). Henry C. Wallace was influential in Iowa farming in many ways, including working to lower taxes (the Homestead Act) and starting a Master Farmer Awards program in 1926.

Countless branches of farm organizations including cooperatives, the Grange, the Farm Bureau, and farm political groups such as Farmer's Holiday Association, the National Farmer's Union, the Farm Bureau, and the National Farm Organization published internal newspapers, newsletters, or magazines. Youth groups including 4-H and Future Farmers of America arose mid-century and also published.

The New Deal during the Great Depression of the 1930s stimulated agricultural journalism. The Works Projects Administration (WPA) also sponsored the writing of extensive histories of horticulture and other agricultural development in states such as Minnesota.

Radio and Television

Twentieth-century agricultural journalism ushered in farm radio. Regular weather reporting began on University of Wisconsin's 9XM, America's first licensed radio station, on January 3, 1921, three months before the first exclusively farm station, WDZ in Tuscola, Illinois went on the air. WDZ broadcast only a few minutes a day, sending grain prices to regional grain elevators. Market reports began that autumn on the Wisconsin station, renamed WHA, and its first farm talk broadcast aired in July 1922. Agriculture departments and agricultural extension services had been positioning themselves to instruct and lead the nation's farmers over the airways to increasingly technological agriculture. Similar radio stations in Springfield and Worcester, Massachusetts, and in other states such as Iowa, Illinois, Kansas, Michigan, Texas, Tennessee, and Missouri quickly followed.

Radio was revolutionizing farm life through educators' involvement. The annual convention of the Association of Agricultural College Education (AACE) sponsored a discussion of uses of radio and movies in 1922. (Cinema may seem marginal to agricultural journalism historians but it is not beyond its scope.)

As radio expanded from a few minutes or hours of sporadic daily broadcasts to more substantial programming, agricultural broadcasting was front and center. KDKA in Pittsburgh hired the first full-time agricultural reporter in March 1923. By 1924, the USDA estimated 370,000 farm families owned and listened to radios. That same year the USDA called a conference to set standards for agricultural broadcasting and established annual conferences overseen by the Secretary of Agriculture.

In the decade of the Great Depression and Dust Bowl, rural electrification and radio entered farm houses together, bringing education, weather and market reports but also music and other popular entertainment. Farm radio blossomed in the post World War II era and rural stations continued to thrive into the twenty-first century. The first sixty years of farm broadcasting are meticulously documented by John C. Baker's *Farm Broadcasting* (1981). From the Baker work and from the extensive agricultural extension publications throughout the first two-thirds of the twentieth century, a reader might conclude that agricultural extension services directed rural life, through the sheer volume and scope of its contributions to agricultural journalism. However, independent agricultural journalism—in national, state, local, and regional newspapers, radio, and television—thrived at the same time.

Farming was already in decline when television became popular. No extension or agriculture departments were granted dominion over the medium which was far more commercial than educational from the outset. By the mid-1950s, fertilizer and farm chemical companies sponsored television programming, as they also advertised in farm and trade magazines. Yet agricultural programming was primarily local, and outside of rural areas where fertilizer and pesticide commercials fetched hefty returns, farmers were generally not valued as audiences. Market reports had all but disappeared from local television in most regions by the 1980s.

Recent Decades

A courtship of agriculture departments by agrichemical industries promoted pesticides, hybrid seed, pharmaceuticals, and commercial genetics. Through the remainder of the century, these large-scale and high-profit private interests targeted agricultural journalism, funding research and development in agriculture departments as scientific farming.

An organic farming movement and related journalism paralleled the rise of chemical farming at mid-century. J. I. Rodale, owner of Rodale Press in Emmaus, Pennsylvania, began *Organic Farming and Gardening* magazine in 1942. He died in 1971 but the magazine continued through his son, Robert, who died suddenly in the Soviet Union while negotiating a joint-venture to produce a Russian-language magazine, *Novii Fermer*, to promote sustainable agriculture. American involvement in international agricultural journalism history has hardly been pursued. Rodale Press, primarily a health and wellness publisher, still gave prominent voice to alternative farming.

In the early twenty-first century, farmers still relied on mass media for information about everything from weather to technology, methods, markets, animal health, and pestilence. Few editors, though, saw it as their mission to empower farmers or to promote agricultural economies in the way they had during the nineteenth century. Although the Internet introduced new communication and better access to weather maps, products, and data, farming remained underreported. And even though agricultural journalism took a developmental and service path, providing resources for farmers and agricultural entrepreneurs across the nation and the world, coverage of farm issues for general audiences was rare.

Further Reading

Baker, John C. *Farm Broadcasting; The First Sixty Years.* Ames: Iowa State University Press, 1981.

Demaree, Albert Lowther. "The American Agricultural Press; 1819–1860." *American Journal of Sociology* 47, no. 4 (1942): 646–647.

Marti, D. B. "Agricultural Journalism and the Diffusion of Knowledge: The First Half-Century in America." *Agricultural History* 54, no. 1(1980): 28–37.

Ogilvie, William E. *Pioneer Agricultural Journalists.* New York: Beekman, 1974.

Pawlick, Thomas F. *The Invisible Farm: The Worldwide Decline of Farm News and Agricultural Journalism Training.* Chicago: Burnham, Inc., 2001.

Schlebecker, John T. and Andrew W. Hopkins. *A History of Dairy Journalism in the United States, 1810–1950.* Madison, Wisconsin: University of Wisconsin Press, 1957.

CARMEN E. CLARK

ALIEN AND SEDITION ACTS

In the United States, ironically, freedom of expression is taught by discussing governmental efforts to crush speech and press attacking those in power. The Alien and Sedition Acts of 1798 are famous examples of governmental overreaching, sacrificing liberty in the name of security during a period that President John Adams called the "half war with France." These four Acts were adopted in the summer of 1798 with little attention paid to the words of the First Amendment to the Constitution of the United States, adopted less than seven years earlier, on December 15, 1791. The First Amendment's words explicitly guaranteed freedom of speech and press in addition to freedom of religion, a right of assembly and a right to protest against federal government actions. The First Amendment's wording was clear: "Congress shall make no law . . . abridging the freedom of speech, or of the press. . . ."

The Alien and Sedition Acts arose in the context of bitter political tensions with England and France and angry divisions within the United States, a new nation fearing for its very survival. Although France provided crucial support to the Americans during the War for Independence, France was angered by the United States' Jay Treaty of 1794 which was seen as favoring England. French raids on American shipping further heightened tensions. After the infamous "XYZ affair" in which American envoys in France were asked to provide the then-enormous sum of a quarter-million dollars as an American war loan, the price for France's willingness to negotiate with the United States, Americans were infuriated. War fever rose, and in 1797, President Adams called for war preparations.

The more powerful Federalist Party favored England. The Republicans, led by Vice President Thomas Jefferson, stubbornly continued to support France. Outrage at the terror of the French Revolution was political trouble for the Republicans, who were associated by the Federalists with anarchy and mob rule endangering an orderly society.

Jeffersonians, as historian James Morton Smith wrote, "stressed liberty and the pursuit of happiness rather than authority and security, demanding a government responsive to public opinion, without the guidance of an elite ruling class." Name-calling from both sides escalated in the newspapers. Adams was termed a man bent on establishing a monarchy; Jefferson was called the Anti-Christ. Political vituperation in the minority of the newspapers opposing the Adams Federalists—perhaps 20 percent of the press—was scathing. Adams's loyal wife, Abigail, complained bitterly in her correspondence about Republican incendiaries such as Benjamin Franklin Bache of the Philadelphia *Aurora*, who called "'the President old, querulous, Bald, blind, crippled, Toothless Adams.'"

In that atmosphere of war hysteria and political extremism, with Federalists controlling the Congress, the presidency, and the federal courts, and after heated debates, Congress enacted the Sedition Act on July 10 by a vote of 44 to 41. Technically, this was a peacetime enactment, but the Adams Federalists believed the nation should be on a war footing. President Adams signed the Sedition Act into law on July 14. The Alien Act lengthened the period for a resident to become a naturalized citizen from five to fourteen years, and the Alien Enemies Act gave the president or the federal courts the power to imprison or deport non-citizens. Acts dealing with Aliens were aimed, at least in part, at troublesome editors or writers who were not citizens.

Republican newspapers denounced the Sedition Act, with the *Aurora* declaring that Americans "'had better hold their tongues and make tooth picks out of their pens.'"

The Boston *Independent Chronicle* defiantly declared that despite the Sedition Act, citizens of the United States had the right to criticize government and government officials. The Act, however, made it a crime to "conspire . . . with intent to oppose any measure or measures of the government of the United States." Further, any person who "shall write, print, utter or publish . . . any false, scandalous or malicious writing or writings against the government of the United States, or either House of the Congress . . ., or the President, with intent to defame . . .or to stir up sedition within the United States. . . . " could be fined up to $2,000 and imprisoned for up to two years. The office of vice president [opposition leader Jefferson] was not included in the list of people or institutions to be placed above criticism.

Critics of the Sedition Act were prescient. Fourteen indictments were brought under the Act, largely aimed at Republican newspapermen or spokesmen. The first prosecution convicted the tempestuous Vermont Congressman Matthew Lyon. He was jailed for four months and fined $1,000. His crime was that he had written to a Windsor, Vermont, newspaper that President Adams's Executive Branch showed an "unbounded thirst for ridiculous pomp, foolish adulation, and selfish avarice," swallowing up the public welfare "in a continual grasp for power." When Anthony Haswell, editor of the *Vermont Gazette*, defended Lyon, he also was indicted and convicted, paying a $200 fine and spending two months in federal prison. Others convicted included a prominent scientist and educator, the London-born Thomas Cooper; William Duane, who assumed the editorship of the *Aurora* after Benjamin Bache died of yellow fever in 1798; and leading Jeffersonians James T. Callender and Thomas Daly Burk.

Even though the Sedition Act included a provision that truth would be a defense against prosecutions, this proved to be no protection at all. For one thing, the judges in the federal courts were all Federalists. For another, it was anti-Administration opinions that drew the indictments, and proving the truth of an opinion would be highly difficult in a hostile court, with Federalist officials selecting Federalist jurors to serve under a Federalist judge.

Opposition to the Alien and Sedition Acts led to James Madison's authorship of the Virginia Resolutions, arguing that a free, republican government cannot be libeled and that the First Amendment provided absolute protection for criticism of the federal government. The Virginia Resolutions, and the Kentucky Resolutions written by Thomas Jefferson, were early interpretations supporting the First Amendment in opposition to the authoritarianism of the Alien and Sedition Acts.

The unfairness of those Acts, and their punitive enforcement by Federalist against political opponents became an instructive part of American civil liberties history. Thomas Jefferson and his supporters made the acts a major campaign issue in 1800. The Sedition Act expired in 1801 when Jefferson became president; the acts regarding aliens were later repealed or expired and not re-enacted. After being bitterly assailed in the press during his years as president, however, Jefferson—who continued to oppose a federal sedition law—nevertheless advocated some selected state sedition prosecutions. The Federalists never elected another president and eventually disbanded as a political force.

Further Reading

Levy, Leonard W., *Emergence of a Free Press*. New York, Oxford University Press, 1985.

Lofton, John. *The Press As Guardian of the First Amendment*. Columbia, University of South Carolina Press, 1980.
Miller, John C. *Crisis in Freedom*. Boston, Little, Brown & Co., 1951.
Smith, James Morton, *Freedom's Fetters*.Ithaca, NY: Cornell University Press, 1956.

DWIGHT L. TEETER, JR.

ALTERNATIVE PRESS

Although the term *alternative press* is commonly understood to refer to those publications emerging since the early 1960s that have both championed the rights of groups and individuals, and have stood against the excesses of governmental and corporate power, an alternative press has been in service in the United States throughout its history. The immediate precursors to the alternative press of the 1960s were journalists I. F. Stone, Carey McWilliams, and Dorothy Day. Stone, a vociferous opponent of the McCarthyism of the early 1950s, began publication of *I. F. Stone's Weekly* in 1953, a paper that championed the cause of blacks, opposed early intervention in Vietnam, and ran numerous exposés of government and corporate malfeasance. Beginning in 1955, under the editorship of Carey McWilliams, the *Nation* was one of the great liberal magazines, and a strident opponent of U.S. involvement in Southeast Asia. The *Nation* became a center for investigative journalism. Dorothy Day's *Catholic Worker* campaigned for the poor and was a bastion of pacifist politics, opposing U.S. entry into World War II and Vietnam.

In the 1960s, demographics determined the direction of much of the alternative press. In 1964, seventeen-year-olds constituted the largest single group in the U.S. population—the ranks of fifteen-to-twenty-four year olds would increase by nearly 50 percent by the end of the decade. Civil rights and the war in Vietnam were of particular interest to this cohort. The alternative press, at this time most visible in the underground newspapers, with their uninhibited style and content, and their philosophical ties to the counterculture, challenged the Establishment and its mass media. The alternative press was instrumental in defining not only the Establishment, and opposition to it, but as a corollary, the values and aspirations of the counterculture and New Left. The first so-called "underground paper" was Greenwich Village's anti-Establishment *Village Voice*, founded in 1955 by Daniel Wolf (who became editor), Edward Fancher (who was publisher), and the novelist and early practitioner of what became called the "new journalism," Norman Mailer. The *Village Voice* maintained its "underground" status even after achieving a circulation of 150,000 in the 1970s. Art Kunkin started the *Los Angeles Free Press* in 1964, and by 1970 the publication had a circulation of 95,000. One of the most radical of the new papers, the *Free Press* provided a steady diet of anti-Establishment fare, at one point printing the names of undercover narcotics agents, leading to rejection of Kunkin's application for a press pass (he left the publication in 1971, after the U.S. Supreme Court held that he did not automatically qualify for a press pass under the First Amendment).

Other publications included protest journals like New York's *East Village Other* and satirical *Realist,* Chicago's *Seed,* Milwaukee's *Kaleidoscope,* the *San Francisco Oracle,* and the most successful of the campus papers, the *Berkeley Barb,* which published major Bay area exposés, organized student protests, and supported the sexual revolution.

A hallmark of 1960s alternative journalism was the reinvigoration of muckraking and investigative journalism. *Ramparts,* founded in 1962 by Edward Keating as a Roman Catholic journal, was transformed from an intellectual quarterly teetering on extinction into a slick, muckraking monthly in 1964, when Warren Hinkle took editorial control. Its exposés on the war in Vietnam and Central Intelligence Agency funding and control of the National Student Association are representative of the muckraking style of journalism that was coming back into vogue. This tradition was continued with the publication of *Mother Jones,* named for socialist organizer Mary Jones, and founded in 1976 by *Ramparts* editors and writers Adam Hochschild, Paul Jacobs, and Richard Parker. It quickly established itself as a modern muckraking paragon, and its publisher, the Foundation for National Progress has funded numerous efforts in investigative journalism. In 2004, *Mother Jones*'s circulation surpassed 250,000. Another influential muckraking journal was *The Progressive,* founded in 1909, which has published important stories documenting American sweatshops, the fallacy of American upward mobility, and the radiation-related health problems of GIs who had taken part in the cleanup after the dropping of the atomic bomb on Nagasaki.

The most successful of the alternative publications to emerge in the 1960s was *Rolling Stone* magazine, founded in 1967. It focused on rock stars such as the Rolling Stones, Doors, Jimi Hendrix, Bob Dylan and, especially, the Beatles, and promoted the countercultural lifestyle embodied by the "hippies." The underground press of the 1960s was composed of two types of publications, primarily—those advocating political mobilization, and those advocating the countercultural lifestyle. *Rolling Stone* established itself as the premier publication catering to the counterculture, and reflected founder and editor Jann Wenner's largely apolitical stance, a position maintained throughout the 1960s. During the 1970s, it became a mainstream publication with a reputation for trenchant political and cultural analysis and a center for the "new journalism" of Tom Wolfe, Hunter S. Thompson, P. J. O'Rourke, and others.

Much alternative journalism has been ethnically and racially based. During the 1960s, militant community-based papers, among them San Francisco's *The Black Panther,* Jamaica, New York's *The Voice,* and Tampa's *Sentinel-Bulletin,* were popular among younger members of the black community. These publications dominated the discourse on issues including black militancy, political mobilization, and education; more conservative national papers like the *Pittsburgh Courier,* the *Chicago Defender,* and the *Afro-American* of Baltimore saw their readership dwindle. In picking up the cause of civil rights, the black alternative press of the 1960s was building upon a long tradition. In the years leading up to the Civil War, the black press helped to unify the African American community, providing information and education, and exhorting its readers to the Abolitionist cause. New York City's *Freedom's Journal,* first published in 1827 by Samuel Cornish and John Russworm, was the nation's first black newspaper; the first *successful* black paper was Samuel Cornish's *The Colored American* (1837 to 1842), which took as its mission "the moral, social and political elevation of the free colored people; and the peaceful emancipation of the slaves," and chronicled the activities of northern blacks in the local and national abolitionist movement, as well as their efforts in various educational and cultural societies.

Prior to the Civil War, most black editors advocated nonviolence, but enactment of the Fugitive Slave Law (1850). The Dred Scott decision (1859) incensed black editors and leaders and swelled the ranks of the militants among them. Frederick Douglass, whose abolitionist *North Star,* begun in 1847, was the first black publication to draw both a substantial white readership; it also attracted the ire of the Rochester community in which it was published—Douglass's home and papers were destroyed by fire. Douglass founded other abolitionist publications, including *Douglass' Monthly,* which continued in publication until 1863. Other important pre-Civil War newspapers include the weeklies, *Ram's Horn,* which enjoyed a run of seven years and 2,500 subscribers after its founding by Willis Hodges in 1941, and Albany, New York's *The Elevator,* which had the support, financial and otherwise, of Horace Greeley, founder of the *Tribune,* his assistant Henry Raymond (founder of the *New York Times*), and other Abolitionists.

During the Civil War, the black press collapsed in the South, and weathered difficult times in the North. With the end of the Civil War, the black press again flourished, rapidly increasing from the twenty-four journals that remained. By 1890, more than 1,200 new black newspapers and magazines had been created, many in the metropolises of the East and Midwest. Important publications included W.E.B. DuBois's *The Crisis,* the official journal of the National Association for the Advancement of Colored People, which achieved a peak circulation of 100,000 by 1918. Robert S. Abbott's *Chicago Defender,* founded in 1905, pioneered a black press for the masses by presenting a muckraking brand of journalism concentrating on the Ku Klux Klan, crime, lynchings, and race riots. With its distribution in the North and South, the *Defender* helped to spark the great movement of blacks from the rural South to the industrial North. Given the dire conditions still suffered by the nation's blacks, the black press was less than enthusiastic in its support for the declaration of war against Germany in April 1917, and the ongoing criticism of discrimination in the armed forces that was to be found in the *Defender* and *Crisis* was viewed as such a threat as to prompt George Creel's Committee on Public Information to warn of German agitation of the black community; the Justice Department voiced its belief that Russian Bolsheviks were providing funding for propaganda efforts to fuel race antagonisms. Race riots and violence against blacks proliferated in the years following the war; state legislatures in the South enacted discriminatory laws that curbed discussion of equality; lynchings continued. In this deteriorating environment, Marcus Garvey promoted his "Back to Africa" movement in his eight journals, including *Negro World*, with more than 200,000 subscribers worldwide.

Historically, the alternative press has addressed the concerns of other minority communities. During the 1960s, Latino consciousness reached a new peak when Cesar Chavez's lead the United Farm Workers (UFW) union against the California grape. In 1964, the San Joaquin Valley's *El Malcriado* became the official publication of the UFW. In the ensuing years, dozens of newspapers were started to speak to and for Latino communities across the Southwest and beyond. Los Angeles's *La Raza*, started in 1967, called for better educational and employment opportunities, and helped to raise the awareness of urban Latinos in much the same way that *El Malcriado* had for the rural population. The UFW followed its success in California in improving the working conditions of migrant workers with efforts in Texas and in Florida. Other papers started in the 1960s included Denver's *El Gallo*, *La Guardia* in Milwaukee, and San Antonio's *El Rebozo*, published by women. These publications continued a tradition of protest dating back to the previous century, with more than one hundred Spanish-language publications appearing in the last half of the nineteenth century. Among those challenging the Anglo establishment were *El Clamor Público* (1855–1859), which spoke out against mob violence in Los Angeles, and Santa Fé's *El Gato*, which championed the working class's call for higher pay in 1894.

The Native American periodicals that emerged in the late 1960s and 1970s also contributed to a greater ethnic consciousness, though usually printed in English. *Akwesasne Notes*, founded in 1968 as the official publication of the Mohawk Nation, was the largest Indian paper, and loosely associated with the American Indian Movement (AIM). *Wassaja* is another newspaper, published by the American Indian Historical Society, which has promoted self-determination. These publications build on a long history: Georgia's *Cherokee Phoenix* (1828–1832) was the first Native American newspaper; the *Cherokee Advocate*, Sioux-language *Siwinowe Kesibwi*, and *Cherokee Rose Bud*, were other early papers speaking to and for the various Latino communities.

From the first women's movement of the 1840s to the present, feminist newspapers and periodicals have been a constant voice championing equality and an end to discrimination. The feminist press emerged from the Abolitionist movement, which produced some of the earliest examples of feminist journalism. The *Lily*, established as a temperance publication in 1849, picked up the cause of suffrage within a year as women's rights leader Elizabeth Cady Stanton joined editor Amelia Bloomer. From 1853 to 1856, Paulina Wright Davis, organizer of the first suffrage convention in 1850, published *Una*. Other pre-Civil War feminist publications were *The Sibyl* in New York and Rhode Island's *The Pioneer* and *Woman's Advocate*.

Like their Black counterparts, women's rights advocates expected enfranchisement to follow the Civil War. The ratification of the Fourteenth and Fifteenth Amendments, and women's exclusion from their rights and protections, effectively mobilized the women's movement and spurred the creation of numerous new publications. The first, *The Revolution*, with a run from 1868 to 1871, was published by Susan B. Anthony and edited by Elizabeth Cady Stanton. It argued forcefully for the enfranchisement of women, and further advocated equal opportunity and pay for women, unionization, and liberalized divorce laws; it discussed controversial topics such as domestic violence and sexual health. *Woodhull and Claflin's Weekly* (1870) championed voting rights, and provided candid discussion of free love, prostitution, abortion and venereal disease. Margaret Sanger's the *Woman Rebel*, started in 1914, helped to focus and bring attention to the issue of women's reproductive health in the early twentieth century. The enactment of the Fourteenth and Fifteenth Amendments of the Constitution prompted Lucy Stone and others to form the American Woman Suffrage Association, which published the suffragist *Woman's Journal* (1870–1917). The passage of the Nineteenth Amendment in 1920 laid to rest this issue, but women's issues were brought to the forefront once again during the social upheaval of the 1960s and 1970s, and the so-called "second wave" of feminism had its own publications. The newspaper *off our backs* began publication in 1970, and today enjoys a presence in print and on the World Wide Web. Popular from its inception, with a circulation of 250,000 in 1972, the most influential feminist publication of this period was *Ms.*, edited by Gloria Steinem, which produced the most consistent attack on the white patriarchal establishment. In 1989, Steinem relaunched the magazine as a nonprofit organization and ad-free magazine.

Another alternative press genre closely allied with the feminist press has been that of the lesbian community. The lesbian press was an important bridge between the feminist and lesbian communities of the 1970s. Like their counterparts in the feminist press, these newspapers and magazines were the products of collectives of women who shunned the top-down hierarchy of most organizations as a product of patriarchal domination. Publications included New York City's *Majority Report*, Denver's *Big Mama Rag*, *Plexus* in San Francisco, *Sister* and *The Lesbian Tide* in Los Angeles, and *Ain't I a Woman*, a lesbian-feminist paper published in Iowa City, Iowa.

The radical gay press took root in major cities following riots ignited by a police raid on the Stonewall Inn in New York City in June 1969. Publications catering to the new movement included New York's *Come Out!*, Detroit's *Gay Liberator*, and *Fag Rag* in Boston. This first generation of militant publications assumed the anti-Vietnam, anti-Establishment posture of other alternative publications, and celebrated gay love through fiction, poetry, photographs, and reportage on the movement. In the mid-1970s, the gay press adopted slicker packaging, as had other alternative publications from the 1960s, and focused on culture, entertainment, and news. *Gay Sunshine*, revived in 1971, is emblematic of this conversion—as an underground publication of the Berkeley Gay Liberation Front it had failed; in its new incarnation it found success, and provided a model for the monthly magazine *Christopher Street*, which debuted in 1976, and quickly earned a reputation as the gay *New Yorker*. Newspapers, too, moved away from polemics and towards the arts, as exemplified in *The Advocate*. With a circulation of 110,000 in 1977 among a relatively affluent readership, *The Advocate* successfully drew national advertising dollars, and paved the way for other gay publications. Gay and lesbian publications continue to crusade for the rights of homosexuals, and many, like *The San Francisco Sentinel*, have a print and Web presence.

From the beginning, there have been foreign-language publications meeting the needs of immigrant populations. The emergence of the various foreign-language publications mirrored the makeup of the immigrant population. Before the Civil War, most foreign-language publications were in French or German. Numbering three hundred in 1860, the number of foreign-language papers rose steadily as new waves of immigrants entered the country. By the turn of the century, southern Europeans accounted for 50 percent of immigrants, and Italians, Russians, and Austro-Hungarians composed over 75 percent of immigrants in the first decades of the twentieth century. The pre-1870s publications were intended for immigrants from northern Europe, primarily, who tended to move into rural areas; the southern and eastern Europeans that immigrated to the country after 1870 were primarily refugees settling in the urban centers. Meeting the needs of immigrant communities, there were 1,200 foreign-language publications in 1910, and a peak of 1,323 in 1917 serving an increasingly urban population. Dailies, more than a third German-language, reached their peak in 1914, when 160 were published.

The pattern of publication has remained constant: Every wave of immigration has been accompanied by the publication of foreign-language publications. As immigrant groups are assimilated into the dominant English-speaking culture, the need for the foreign-language press dissipates, though many of the community-based papers persevere. Often, these publications find themselves at odds with the Establishment. A case in point is the German-language press of the early twentieth century. Assimilation and a decrease in immigration led to a decrease in the number of publications, with the hostilities in Europe contributing to further decline in the years leading up to America's entrance into World War I. The mainstream press was decidedly pro-British. Many of the German-language publications called for American neutrality. Publications such as the *Der Deutsch Correspondent* espoused loyalty to the United States while stressing social and cultural ties to Germany. Once the United States joined the hostilities, most German-language papers that had championed the German cause instead advocated pacifism. German publications became a major target of government efforts to control the press, and the Espionage Act and Sedition Act, enacted in 1917 and 1918, respectively, empowered the government to imprison and fine anyone deemed to be acting contrary to

the interests of the American war effort, among them German-language and pacifist, non-interventionist Socialist publications. Anti-German hysteria, government intervention, and assimilation, led to a rapid decline in the German-language press during the interwar years.

The end of the nineteenth century saw the emergence of publications aimed at the excesses of capitalism embodied in the empires of robber barons like J. P. Morgan, John D. Rockefeller, and Andrew Carnegie. Carrying forth the most radical program were the papers of the anarchist movement. Seeking an end to capitalism and the modern nation-state, the anarchist periodicals called for armed rebellion. Albert R. Parsons championed the anarchist view in *The Alarm*, published in Chicago in the 1880s. Parsons was hanged in 1887 for his alleged role in a bomb attack on police during the Haymarket riots (1886). Without his efforts, the Anarchist movement lacked a national presence until the publication in 1906 of Emma Goldman's *Mother Earth*, in New York City, which ran until banned from the U.S. mail under provisions of the Espionage Act of 1917. Goldman was arrested and eventually deported. While the anarchist movement failed to capture the imagination of the American public and gain sufficient adherents to become a real force, it has persevered, and today enjoys a substantial presence on the World Wide Web.

Far more successful in making inroads among American labor was the socialist movement. Socialism provided a potent critique of capitalism and its exploitation of the working class. The Socialist Party was an important third party for a time, the popularity of which was evident in the 1920 election in which Socialist presidential candidate Eugene Debs received nearly a million votes, or 6 percent of votes cast, and nearly eighty other Socialist Party candidates were elected mayor in twenty-four states. The weekly *Appeal to Reason* (1895–1922) was the national voice for the Socialist movement, and counted among its journalists Helen Keller, Jack London, and Upton Sinclair, whose muckraking exposé on the Chicago meat packing industry, later published as *The Jungle*, led to federal regulation of the industry. Published in Girard, Kansas, the publication had a paid subscription base of 760,000—the most of any dissident publication in American history. Under the command of founder and editor J. A. Wayland, the *Appeal* condemned the inequalities of capitalism while promoting organized labor. The product of a network of thousands of writers across the country, the *Appeal* was the newspaper of record for the American Socialist movement. Other early socialist papers included the *New York Evening Call* (1908–1923) and the *Milwaukee Leader* (1911–1942), which thrived with the Socialist Party in the decades leading up to U.S. entry into World War I. The Espionage Act of 1917 and its successor, the Sedition Act of 1918, which criminalized the writing or publication of "any disloyal, profane, scurrilous or abusive language about the form of government of the United States or the Constitution, military or naval forces, flag, or the uniform," were used to shut down the pacifist Socialist press. These actions coincided with the so-called "Palmer raids" (1918–1921) that led to the arrest of some 15,000 Socialists, Communists, Industrial Workers of the World unionists, and other leftists. Nevertheless, the popularity of the Socialist Party was on the rise before its pacifism during World War II put it at odds with most Americans and it suffered a sharp decline in membership.

Also arguing the cause of labor was the American Communist Party, which had a number of publications including the *Ohio Socialist,* the *Toiler,* the *Worker,* the *Midweek Worker,* the *Southern Worker,* and the *Daily Worker,* started in 1924 by the American Communist Party. The daily had a peak circulation of 100,000 in the late1930s; by 1958, when the now weekly paper ceased publication, circulation had fallen to 5,600 in the wake of McCarthyism. It resumed publication in 1968 as the *Daily World* (1968–1986), passed through a number of other incarnations, and is published today as the *People's Weekly World* (since 1999). McCarthyism and the cold war effectively ended the political aspirations of leftist parties in the United States, but these voices have persevered in the underground press and recently have benefited from the access possible through World Wide Web.

In the twenty-first century, the alternative press continues to champion the rights of women, labor, and minorities, and to criticize the excesses of capitalism it sees in globalization and global wealth disparity. Animal rights activists and environmentalists make their arguments in their own publications (for instance, the *Animal Rights Journal* and *Earth First!,* respectively), as do a growing number of right-leaning publications such as *Human Events, Campus Report,* and *The Wanderer.* Among the recent developments has been the proliferation of zines advocating the views of their creator(s), commonly an individual or small group. Computers have allowed these independent, self-published, low-budget publications, to become widespread. The digital age has also seen an explosion in alternative publications as the alternative press has established a strong and growing presence on the World Wide Web. Znet (http://www.zmag.org/weluser.htm), and the Independent Media Institute's Alternet project (http://www.alternet.org) are among those sites providing directories of the thousands of zines and alternative publications with a presence on the Web, as well as information on the activities of citizens groups, student organizations, and non-profits. The Web has proven a boon to the alternative press, expanding its reach and coverage, and helping to assure its presence into the future.

Further Reading

Alternative Press Center, http://www.altpress.org.

Armstrong, David. *A Trumpet to Arms: Alternate Media in America.* Boston: South End Press, 1981.

Draper, Robert. *Rolling Stone Magazine: The Uncensored History.* New York: Doubleday, 1990.

Emery, Michael, and Edwin Emery. *The Press in America: An Interpretive History of the Mass Media.* 9th ed. Englewood Cliffs, NJ: Prentice Hall, 1999.

Gitlin, Todd. *The Whole World is Watching: Mass Media in the Making and Unmaking of the New Left.* Berkeley: University of California Press, 1980.

Glessing, Robert J. *The Underground Press in America.* Bloomington: Indiana University Press, 1970.

Independent Media Institute,. Alternet, http://www.alternet.org.

Kessler, Lauren. *The Dissident Press Alternative Journalism in American History.* Beverly Hills: Sage, 1984.

Lewis, Roger, *Outlaws of America: The Underground Press and its Context.* London: Heinrich Hanau Publication, 1972.

Murphy, James E., and Sharon M. Murphy. *Let My People Know: American Indian Journalism.* Norman: University of Oklahoma Press, 1981.

Streitmatter, Rodger. *Voices of Revolution: The Dissident Press in America.* New York: Columbia University Press, 2001.

Washburn, Patrick. *A Question of Sedition: The Federal Government's Investigation of the Black Press During World War II.* New York: Oxford, 1986.

MICHAEL R. FRONTANI

AMERICAN REVOLUTION

The press played an important role during the American Revolution by keeping Americans engaged in the war even when the fighting occurred in distant locales. Some writers used the newspapers to stir up the people's passions against the mother country, but the press served primarily to keep Americans informed about the progress of the fight with Great Britain. From the moment that the colonials received word of Britain's new taxes in 1764 until news of the peace treaty arrived in 1783, newspapers constituted the major source of information about events and developments in the conflict with the mother country. Without the press, many Americans would have known practically nothing about what was happening.

American newspaper printers sought to keep their readers informed about the events of the war, but they also sought to keep people encouraged about how the Revolution was going. Thus, they often put a positive spin on the reports they published. Military victories and successes were extolled and expanded while defeats and setbacks were downplayed and minimized. For example, printers lavished praise on George Washington and the Continental Army for the relatively small victory at Trenton in 1776 while passing off the loss of a 5,000-man army at Charleston in 1780 as a minor setback that would quickly be overcome. Through the use of such reporting techniques, newspaper printers helped to boost morale and keep people engaged in the war even when the actual events took place hundreds of miles away.

But the press also helped shape the ideological basis for the revolt from Great Britain. Many of the ideas that provided the intellectual support for the Revolution first appeared in pamphlets. In the eighteenth century British world, pamphlets served as an important forum for the expression of opinion. The ideas of some of England's more radical political and social thinkers were transmitted to colonial leaders in this manner. These ideas were then summarized and reprinted in the newspapers which reached even more people. The ideas expressed in these publications challenged traditional authority and led to a change in colonials' beliefs and attitudes. The pamphlets and newspapers thus helped set the ideological context for revolution and independence.

Background

The growth of the colonies in the eighteenth century produced many differences with the mother country which helped produce the divisions that led to the Revolution. But the spark that started the vocal arguments came from an argument over taxes. Britain began passing additional taxes for the American colonies in order to pay off the war debt that had resulted from their victory over France in the Seven Years' War (known as the French and Indian War in America). Parliament adopted the Sugar Act in 1764, the Stamp Act in 1765, and the Townshend Duties in 1767. Each time, American leaders expressed their opposition through essays and resolutions that appeared in newspapers throughout the colonies. Most American protests centered around the issue of legislative representation. Colonials cried "no taxation without representation," insisting that they were not represented in the British Parliament because they did not vote for its members. The British responded by stating that every member of Parliament represented every citizen of the Empire.

Both town meetings and colonial assemblies passed resolutions protesting the new taxes, and the newspapers published them all. Accompanying the official resolutions were also a variety of essays stating the American position. Probably the most famous group of essays against the British taxes appeared in the *Pennsylvania Chronicle* in 1767–1768. Written by John Dickinson, the eleven "Letter(s) from a Farmer in Pennsylvania" declared that the British Parliament did not have the authority to levy taxes on Americans.

Along with resolutions and essays, newspapers published reports of public protests against the British taxes. A variety of trade boycotts were organized beginning in 1764. The Stamp Act placed a tax on several types of printed materials. The most vocal members of American society— merchants, lawyers, and printers—faced a loss of income because of the tax and wrote many of the protests against the Stamp Act. They also organized public demonstrations. Several of these produced near riots in the streets as colonials marched in protest during the summer and fall of 1765. These marches sometimes resulted in property destruction. For example, in Boston the crowd destroyed the home of Lieutenant Governor Thomas Hutchinson because of his support for the Stamp Act. Most of these organized protests resulted in the forced resignation of the local stamp distributor in an effort to prevent the act from taking effect. In the days immediately prior to the act taking effect, printers used their newspapers to protest the act. The most visible, and probably the most famous, newspaper protest appeared in the *Pennsylvania Journal* on October 31, 1765. By turning the rules that held the type in place upside down and using a woodcut of a skull, printer William Bradford made the newspaper look like a tombstone. In the masthead, he declared that the newspaper was "EXPIRING: In Hopes of a Resurrection to Life again." When the Stamp Act officially took effect on November 1, 1765, most printers either ceased printing the stamped items or claimed there was no stamped paper available. The British Parliament repealed the Stamp Act in 1766 and sought other sources of revenue.

The city of Boston, Massachusetts, quickly became a center for many of the protests. The first effort at an organized exchange of news and propaganda originated in Boston. The "Journal of Occurrences," although first published in the *New York Journal*, dealt primarily with reported British tyranny and atrocities in the Boston area. It appeared in 1768 and 1769. But one of the local newspapers, the *Boston Gazette*, quickly became the leader in publishing materials attacking British actions. The printers of the *Boston Gazette*, Benjamin Edes and John Gill, opened the pages of their newspaper to protests against the new taxes. Taking particular advantage of this access was Samuel Adams, who became the leader of the Sons of Liberty in Boston. Through the pages of the *Boston Gazette*, Adams and his supporters communicated to the citizens of Massachusetts and the other colonies their ideas about Great Britain and its actions against the colonies. In 1772, Adams led the way in organizing the Committees of Correspondence which provided a means of communication between the colonies that was separate from official channels.

Further events in the 1770s sparked Edes and Gill to continue to use the pages of the *Boston Gazette* to criticize the actions of the British government. On March 5, 1770, British troops fired into a snowball-throwing crowd, killing five men. The *Boston Gazette* outlined their story published on March 12 with black borders and reported in great detail how the British army had attacked innocent Americans. The article concluded that "The Town of Boston affords a recent and melancholy Demonstration of the destructive Consequences of quartering Troops among Citizens in a Time of Peace, under a pretense of supporting the Laws and invading Civil Authority. . . ." The story re-appeared in newspapers throughout the colonies, informing Americans everywhere about the loss of life in Boston. Paul Revere also produced an engraving that portrayed the event as an attack by British soldiers on the American crowd. This image reenforced the printed reports appearing in the newspapers.

The conflict with Great Britain calmed down following the Boston Massacre as people on both sides of the Atlantic reacted in horror. Samuel Adams, in an effort to convince Americans that they could no longer trust the mother country, used the pages of the *Boston Gazette* to keep the discussion alive. Thus, Adams and his associates were ready when word of the Tea Act reached the colonies. Intended to save the floundering East India Company, the Tea Act lowered the tax on tea and allowed for the shipment of tea directly to the colonies (thus reducing costs further by eliminating the British middlemen). Many merchants opposed the legislation because it threatened their smuggling operations. Adams and other colonial leaders perceived the lowering of the tea tax as an underhanded way to get colonials to surrender their stand against Parliamentary-imposed taxes.

Edes and Gill reported on town meetings that protested the Tea Act. Arguments over what to do with the East India Company tea when it arrived resulted in the Boston Tea Party, where Americans "disguised as Indians" dumped 342 chests of tea into the harbor. The *Boston Gazette* covered all of these events and provided stories that appeared again and again throughout the colonies. At the time, printers exchanged copies of their newspapers with each other in order to gain news about events in other colonies. The Committees of Correspondence also produced statements about the conflict with Great Britain, but the exchange system constituted the major means of news diffusion at the time.

The Boston Tea Party made reconciliation in the conflict between Great Britain and the colonies extremely difficult. The British Parliament passed the Coercive Acts to punish the colony of Massachusetts, and particularly the city of Boston. Americans responded by supporting Boston through resolutions and supplies. Newspapers throughout the colonies called on their readers to stand with Boston against British tyranny. One of the results of such calls was the meeting of the First Continental Congress in Philadelphia from September 25 to October 26 in 1774, a final effort to settle the differences between the colonies and the mother country short of war. This effort failed.

War

People in Boston and Massachusetts began to gather arms and to organize in preparation for the confrontation they expected to come. The confrontation finally came on April 19, 1775. British forces headed to Concord to seize colonial arms and ammunition stored there. They met a group of Massachusetts militiamen on the village green in Lexington. Shots were exchanged, and the war portion of the American Revolution had begun. Many newspaper printers in Boston fled the city in order to continue publishing. Benjamin Edes moved the *Boston Gazette* to Watertown. Edes's flight from Boston broke his partnership with John Gill, and they never worked together again. Both continued to publish a newspaper for a number of years, but they did not continue as the leading Patriot printers in Massachusetts. That position fell to Isaiah Thomas, who used his *Massachusetts Spy* to call on Americans to defend their rights against British tyranny. Thomas had established the *Spy* in Boston in 1770. He fled to Worcester following the Battles of Lexington and Concord. From there he printed probably the most famous account of these battles. His story in the May 3, 1775, issue of the *Massachusetts Spy* began with a call to arms: "Americans! Forever bear in mind the BATTLE OF LEXINGTON! — where British troops, unmolested and unprovoked, wantonly and in a most inhuman manner, fired upon and killed a number of our countrymen, then robbed, ransacked, and burned their houses! nor could the tears of defenseless women, some of whom were in the pains of childbirth, the cries of helpless babes, nor the prayers of age, confined to beds of sickness, appease their thirst for blood! — or divert them from their DESIGN OF MURDER AND ROBBERY!"

When news of the fighting at Lexington and Concord reached Philadelphia, men from throughout the colonies were gathering for the meeting of the Second Continental Congress. As the meeting began on May 10, 1775, the delegates realized that the conflict with Great Britain had changed. They organized the Continental Army and appointed George Washington of Virginia as its commander. Appointing a Virginian to command the troops was an attempt by the Continental Congress to pull the colonies closer together. Newspapers throughout the colonies praised the decision for that reason and quickly spread the word that the fight in Massachusetts was everyone's war.

The majority of the newspapers in the colonies supported the Patriot side. Printers like Benjamin Edes, John Gill, and Isaiah Thomas led the way in using newspapers to attack British tyranny. In doing so, they moved away from the previously-held standard of trying to present both sides of any issue they covered. To present both sides could help lead to injustice through the spreading of erroneous ideas. John Holt, printer of the *New York Journal*, declared in the January 5, 1775, issue that "My paper is sacred to the cause of truth and justice, and I have preferred the pieces, that in my opinion, are the most necessary to the support of that cause." Holt and other like-minded newspaper printers had not become full-fledged editors yet, but they had begun to pick and choose what they published in order to support the cause they were working for.

Although most newspaper printers supported the Patriot cause, a few favored the British side of the argument. Prior to the war, these Loyalist printers had difficulty continuing in business because of intimidation by the Patriots. Once the war started, they could only survive in areas controlled by the British army. Probably the two most famous Loyalist printers were James Rivington and Hugh Gaine, both of whom published newspapers in New York City. Both initially tried to follow the tradition of printing both sides, but found they could not continue in business that way. Forced to choose, they chose to support the British and earned the hatred of the Patriots as a result. Rivington, probably the best printer in America in the 1770s, became the "King's Printer" and used the pages of his *Royal Gazette* to attack the Patriots, extol British successes, and downplay British losses. In this, Rivington proved no different from his American opponents who used the pages of their news sheets in a similar manner—to support their cause.

Besides news about the fighting and other events of the Revolution, most newspapers continued to publish letters and essays designed to convince more Americans of the reality of British tyranny. By the end of 1775, some essays even started to call for Americans to break away from the mother country by declaring independence. The most famous of these calls for independence appeared in January 1776. *Common Sense*, written by Thomas Paine, first appeared as a pamphlet, but many newspapers throughout the colonies reprinted all or part of it. Paine placed the blame for the troubles of the colonies at the feet of King George III and called on Americans to kick off their chains and declare independence. Many printers endorsed this call as they sought to spread Paine's ideas by reprinting *Common Sense*. Once the Continental Congress reached agreement and adopted the Declaration of Independence on July 4, 1776, newspaper printers published the text of the Declaration so that all Americans could read to what the delegates had agreed.

Role of the Press

Once independence had been declared, Americans focused on winning the war. Newspaper printers reported as much information about the various battles as they could acquire. As had always been true with American newspapers, the printer closest to the battle tried to print as complete an account as possible. Newspaper printers continued to regularly exchange copies of their productions with each other, and they freely copied from each other in order to communicate as much information as possible. This exchange system enabled most newspaper printers to keep their readers informed about and engaged in the war even when events occurred far away.

Various newspaper essayists encouraged Americans to keep fighting for the cause. Thomas Paine once more put pen to paper through a series of newspaper essays (called the *Crisis* papers) that appeared throughout the country during the Revolution. The most famous of these essays was the first one, originally published in the *Pennsylvania Journal* on December 19, 1776. In this piece, Paine called on Americans to fight for freedom and liberty: "These are the times that try men's souls. The summer soldier and the sunshine patriot will, in this crisis, shrink from the service of their country; but he that stands it now, deserves the love and thanks of man and woman." Paine thus urged Americans to stay true to the cause in order to achieve ultimate victory and freedom.

The Revolutionary War had a tremendous impact on the press. When the war began, thirty-seven newspapers appeared throughout the colonies. Only twenty of them survived until war's end. Printers founded thirty-three new publications during the war, but all of them did not survive either. When the war ended, thirty-five newspapers were being published in the new country. Although a loss of two does not sound large, the numbers of starts and losses show a much larger impact from the war. Readership had increased as people sought out newspapers in an effort to keep up with what was happening elsewhere. Publication totals approached 40,000, but most issues were read by many more people than the individual purchaser. But the fighting also created many problems. The war cut off access to imported supplies of presses, types, paper, and ink from Great Britain. Americans attempted to produce the needed materials, but could not keep up with demand. So, printers often reduced the size of their newspaper or did not publish at all because of the lack of the necessary supplies. A number of printers also had to move their offices in the face of

the approach of the enemy. As previously mentioned, both Benjamin Edes and Isaiah Thomas fled Boston in order to keep publishing after the Battles of Lexington and Concord. John Holt moved his operation from New York City to Kingston and then to Poughkeepsie in order to avoid the British army. James Robertson, a Loyalist printer, moved with the British army from New York to Philadelphia to Charleston because he could only continue to print under the protection of British authorities. All newspaper printers, whether Patriot or Loyalist, experienced production problems of one sort or another during the war.

Historians have debated for years just how much impact the press had on the Revolutionary War. David Ramsay, one of the earliest historians of the Revolution, declared (*The History of the American Revolution*, 1789) that "in establishing American independence, the pen and the press had a merit equal to that of the sword." Most historians since Ramsay have agreed, stating that the newspaper printers had an important role to play in the American Revolution because they kept the people informed and sought to urge them on to victory. Arthur Schlesinger, in *Prelude to Independence* (1957), concluded that the press played an essential role in rallying Americans to the cause of independence. Most historians have emphasized the function of the press in the American Revolution because contemporaries believed the newspapers played an essential role in the outcome of the war. Both Benjamin Franklin and Ambrose Serle, a Loyalist, described the press as an "engine" that should be used to advance the cause. And most Americans concluded that the efforts of Patriot newspaper printers to keep readers informed about the war helped ensure ultimate success by boosting morale and rallying Americans to the cause until victory was achieved. In other words, independence would not have been won without the press.

Further Reading

Bailyn, Bernard. *The Ideological Origins of the American Revolution*. Cambridge, MA: Harvard University Press, 1967.

Bailyn, Bernard, and John B. Hench, eds. *The Press and the American Revolution*. Worcester, MA: American Antiquarian Society, 1980.

Berger, Carl. *Broadsides and Bayonets: The Propaganda War of the American Revolution*. Revised edition. San Rafael, CA: Presidio Press, 1976.

Davidson, Philip. *Propaganda and the American Revolution, 1763–1783*. Chapel Hill: University of North Carolina Press, 1941.

Hart, Jim Allee. *The Developing Views on the News: Editorial Syndrome, 1500–1800*. Carbondale: Southern Illinois University Press, 1970.

Humphrey, Carol Sue. *"This Popular Engine": New England Newspapers During the American Revolution, 1775–1789*. Newark: University of Delaware Press, 1992.

Levy, Leonard W. *Emergence of a Free Press*. New York: Oxford University Press, 1985.

Morgan, Edmund S., and Helen M. *The Stamp Act Crisis: Prologue to Revolution*. Chapel Hill: University of North Carolina Press, 1953.

Schlesinger, Arthur M. *Prelude to Independence: The Newspaper War on Britain, 1764–1776*. New York: Random House, 1957.

Sloan, Wm. David, and Julie Hedgepeth Williams. *The Early American Press, 1690–1783*. Westport, CT: Greenwood Press, 1994.

Smith, Jeffery A. *Printers and Press Freedom: The Ideology of Early American Journalism*. New York: Oxford University Press, 1988.

CAROL SUE HUMPHREY

AMERICAN SOCIETY OF NEWSPAPER EDITORS

The American Society of Newspaper Editors (ASNE) was founded in 1922 by a group of editors headed by Casper S. Yost of the *St. Louis Globe-Democrat*, as a response to public criticism of press ethics and credibility. The ASNE's constitution envisioned an organization that would advance professional ideals and standards, defend newspapers against its detractors, and develop an "esprit de corps" among the elite editors of daily journalism. The ASNE's most prominent and enduring efforts have included advocacy for freedom of information and, since the 1970s, newsroom diversity. The organization also has piloted initiatives to enhance newspaper readership and credibility as well as to champion the cause of international press freedom.

From its earliest years, the centerpiece of the organization has been its annual convention, which provides a forum for discussion not only of matters affecting the newspaper profession but also for political and social issues of the day. The prominence of the ASNE's annual speakers is a testament to the organization's access to power. All U.S. presidents since Warren Harding, who was an ASNE member, have addressed the organization. During World War II and the Korean conflict, the ASNE was routinely granted off-the-record briefings with top military leaders. Perhaps the most notable, and controversial, political figure to take the ASNE podium was Cuban leader Fidel Castro, who spoke at the 1959 convention over the objections of the U.S. State Department. Owing to their news value, portions of the program have garnered national media coverage and, more recently, have been telecast on C-SPAN. ASNE founders were so certain of the annual meeting's historical importance that they began, with the 1924 convention, to transcribe the proceedings and to distribute bound copies to university libraries. As a result, the serialized ASNE proceedings are entrenched in the journalism canon housed in many American research libraries.

Because concerns about journalism ethics compelled the ASNE's founding, early leaders wasted no time in formally aligning themselves with this issue. At its first convention in 1923, the ASNE adopted an ethics code that pushed the organization to the forefront of the newspaper industry's evolving recognition of the press's democratic obligations to its public and of the need for standards of professional conduct. These Canons of Journalism—which emphasized the press' responsibility to protect the public welfare, the obligation to advance press freedom, and the need for independence, sincerity, truthfulness, accuracy, impartiality, fair play, and decency—remained in place until 1975. At that time a new Statement of Principles updated the language and conceptual framework of the founders' vision, codified the value of a watchdog press, and incorporated proscriptions against such ethical failings as the appearance of conflicts of interest.

The role of the ethics code was tested by a scandal that erupted in 1924, when *Denver Post* publisher Fred Bonfils, an ASNE member, became the subject of a congressional inquiry and the cause of great embarrassment to the organization. Bonfils was accused of unethical conduct for editorials and news coverage that supported the awarding of no-bid leases on government oil reserves at the same time that he had a stake in such agreements at Teapot Dome, Wyoming, and Elk River, California. The issue divided ASNE members between those who wished to see the organization exercise ethical enforcement powers and those, like founder Yost, who feared that any policing of members' conduct would violate their free-press rights. When the matter was finally resolved, after about eight years of debate and organizational strife, Yost's side generally prevailed. This was a defining moment for the organization and for the construct of journalism ethics; as a result, the ASNE's code was framed as a set of ideals rather than regulations for editor conduct.

Founded as an exclusive organization for daily newspaper editors in cities with populations of 100,000 or more, the ASNE remained an elite organization even as it relaxed its membership to include editors of daily newspapers of any circulation. Membership in 2006 was about 750, down from the peak of 1,010 in 1988. Throughout its history, the ASNE has honored its founders' wish that a newspaper's influence within the organization be proportional to its size. It had generally limited membership to editors of daily newspapers, but gradually relaxed the requirements to include other leaders of daily newspapers, such as top editorial executives of newspaper chains and wire services. One result of the daily newspaper restriction was the disproportionate exclusion of women and non-whites from ASNE membership. The ASNE first granted membership to an African-American, John Sengstacke of the *Chicago Daily Defender*, in 1965 but did not elect a non-white editor, William Hilliard of the *Portland Oregonian*, to the presidency until 1993. Although the first woman joined in 1928, just a handful of women were active members at any one time until the 1970s, when the organization made a concerted effort to attract women. In 1947 Oveta Culp Hobby of the *Houston Post* became the first woman elected to the ASNE board but was the only woman director until the 1970s. In 1987 Katherine Fanning of the *Christian Science Monitor* became the ASNE's first woman president.

One of the ASNE's most prominent, and controversial, efforts has been a newsroom diversity initiative founded in 1978, which has sought to bring the proportion of non-whites employed in daily newspaper newsrooms into parity with the U.S. non-white population. Each year prior to its convention, the ASNE reports the results of its annual newsroom census. In 2006, the ASNE's newsroom census found that 13.87 percent of employees in daily newsrooms were non-white, compared to a U.S. non-white population of 33 percent. Nearly every year the ASNE's census disclosure draws criticism from diversity advocates, including organizations representing non-white journalists, who fault the ASNE and newspaper industry for failing to remedy historical disadvantages for non-white journalists.

The erosion of the ASNE's membership can be attributed in large part to the decline in the number of daily papers and the ever-growing number of papers owned by chains. At the same time that newspaper economics have forced editors to trim their budgets for attending conventions, corporate owners provide more opportunities for professional development and interaction with editors from other newspapers. Thus far the ASNE leadership has resisted pressure to merge with the Associated Press Managing Editors or to be absorbed by the Newspaper Association of America, which brought seven organizations into one organization in 1992.

Further Reading

American Society of Newspaper Editors. *The ASNE Bulletin*, vols. 71–767, 2 March 1934 to April 1995; *The American Editor*, vols. 768- , May-June 1995 to present.

American Society of Newspaper Editors. *Problems of Journalism: Proceedings of the American Society of Newspaper Editors*, 1924–44 and 1946–80; *Proceedings of the American Society of Newspaper Editors*, 1981–present.

Mellinger, Gwyneth. "Counting Color: Ambivalence and Contradiction in the American Society of Newspaper Editors' Discourse of Diversity." *Journal of Communication Inquiry* 27, no. 2 (2003): 129–51.

Najjar, Orayb. "ASNE Efforts Increase Minorities in Newsrooms." *Newspaper Research Journal* 16, no. 4 (1995): 126–40.

Pitts, Alice Fox. *Read All About It! 50 Years of ASNE*. American Society of Newspaper Editors, 1974.

Pratte, Paul A. *Gods Within the Machine: A History of the American Society of Newspaper Editors, 1923–1993*. Westport, CT: Praeger, 1995.

GWYNETH MELLINGER

ANNENBERG, WALTER

Publishing magnate Walter Annenberg (March 13, 1908–October 21, 2002) owned newspaper, television, radio, and magazine properties, which at various times included the *Philadelphia Inquirer, Philadelphia Daily News, Daily Racing Form, Seventeen* magazine, *TV Guide*, and several radio and television stations.

Annenberg was born in Milwaukee, Wisconsin, and attended the Wharton School of Finance at the University of Pennsylvania from 1927–28. He joined his father's company as a bookkeeping assistant in 1928. He married Veronica Dunkelman in 1938, but they were divorced in 1950. They had a daughter, Wallis, and a son, Roger, who committed suicide in 1962. In 1951, Mr. Annenberg married Leonore Cohn Rosenstiel, to whom he remained married until his death.

In 1920 his father, Moses Annenberg, moved his family from Milwaukee to Great Neck, Long Island, where he established his newspaper distribution business. He later purchased the *Daily Racing Form* and expanded it into seven racing papers across the country. In 1936, he purchased the *Philadelphia Inquirer*.

In 1939, Moses was indicted by a Chicago federal grand jury for income tax evasion. Walter and two other business associates were also indicted. Moses agreed to plead guilty, pay $9.5 million in back taxes, and serve three years in prison. As part of the settlement, charges against Walter and other business associates were dropped. Moses died of a brain tumor thirty-nine days after his release from prison in 1942.

As the sole son in a family of eight, Walter was named heir to the newly named Triangle Corporation, which included the *Inquirer* and several other publications. His years as publisher of the *Philadelphia Inquirer* from 1942 to 1969 were sometimes controversial because of charges that he used the newspaper for personal vendettas against his enemies.

Annenberg created and launched *Seventeen* magazine in 1944 and *TV Guide* in 1953, which were both highly successful. *TV Guide* became America's highest-circulation magazine at its peak, selling almost twenty million copies per week.

Active in Republican politics, Annenberg was appointed by President Richard Nixon as U.S. Ambassador to Great Britain from 1968 to 1974. He was a close friend and substantial contributor to Ronald Reagan's presidential campaigns.

Annenberg sold the *Philadelphia Inquirer* and the *Philadelphia Daily News* to Knight Newspapers in 1969 and the broadcast companies in the early 1970s. In 1988, he sold *Seventeen* and *TV Guide* and remaining portions of Triangle Publications to Rupert Murdoch for $3.2 billion. He said that he planned to devote the rest of his life to education and philanthropy.

He became renowned for his philanthropic activity and gave more than $2 billion in donations to various causes, including $150 million to the Corporation for Public Broadcasting. His gifts established schools of communication at the University of Pennsylvania in 1962 and the University of Southern California in 1971. Annenberg was also one of the country's leading collectors of art, and bequeathed his extensive collection, valued at more than $1 billion, to New York's Metropolitan Museum of Art in 1991. Annenberg died in 2002 at the age of 94.

Further Reading

Cooney, John. *The Annenbergs*. New York: Simon and Schuster, 1982.

Fonzi, Gaeton. *Annenberg: A Biography of Power*. New York: Weybright and Talley, 1970.

Glueck, Grace. "Walter Annenberg, Philanthropist and Publisher, Dies at 94," *New York Times*, Oct. 2, 2002.

Laswell, Mark. *TV Guide: 50 Years of Television*. New York, Crown, 2002.

Ogden, Christopher, *Legacy: A Biography of Moses and Walter Annenberg*. New York: Little, Brown and Company, 1999.

Nourie, Alan, and Barbara Nouri, eds. *American Mass-Market Magazines*. Westport, CT: Greenwood, 1990.

DAVID E. SUMNER

ANTHONY, SUSAN B.

Susan Brownell Anthony (1820–1906) was a leader of the woman suffrage movement who, like many of her contemporary suffragists, started her career as an activist and publicist in the temperance and abolition movements of the 1850s and 1860s. Frustrated by the limitations placed on women's full participation in public life, Anthony recognized woman's rights as paramount to a healthy and just society and devoted her considerable energies to secure women's political, economic, and social equality. She was a co-founder of the National Woman Suffrage Association (NWSA) in 1868 and manager of its publication, the *Revolution,* for the next two years. Through her writings and speeches, and in testimony in support of woman's rights before Congress, state legislatures, and the courts, she helped to overturn social conventions that restricted the rights of women.

Anthony was born in South Adams, Massachusetts, the second of the six children of Daniel and Lucy Read Anthony. Her father, a Quaker, was a storekeeper who also owned and managed small cotton mills. In her early years, the family was relatively prosperous and at sixteen, Susan was sent to a finishing school for a year until her father went bankrupt in the financial panic of 1838. In 1839, she began teaching at a Quaker school for girls in New Rochelle, the first of a number of low-paying teaching positions. Although she had a number of suitors over the years, when later asked if she had ever been in love, Anthony said she had no desire to give up her life of freedom to become a man's housekeeper.

During the 1840s, Anthony became an activist in the temperance movement, which, though largely supported by women, was dominated by male leaders and organizations. She joined one of the few women's temperance organizations, the Daughters of Temperance, and in 1848 formed a new chapter in Albany. When, as a delegate of the Daughters, she was refused the opportunity to speak at the 1851 convention of the Sons of Temperance, Anthony stormed out of the meeting. Shortly after, she organized the Woman's State Temperance Society (WSTS) of New York, with Elizabeth Cady Stanton as president and herself as one of two secretaries. With Stanton and Anthony as organizers, the WSTS got off to a strong start, but when they began to devote too much of the discussion to woman's rights, dissention began in the ranks. At the 1853 WSTS convention, the more conservative members voted to allow men to speak and hold office. The men then denounced Stanton for her advocacy of woman's rights and the membership voted her out of the presidency. Anthony resigned in protest. By then, the two women had become fast friends and remained so for the rest of their lives.

By this time, Anthony had already gained some stature in the woman's rights movement. In 1852, she had been elected secretary of the Women's Rights Convention in Syracuse, New York. In the winter of 1854 she conducted a lecture tour and house-to-house campaign in upstate New York to collect signatures on a petition to the legislature for a married women's property bill, which within four years won partial success. She also became an untiring worker for the abolition movement and often equated slavery with the virtual slavery of women.

The momentum of the woman's rights movement slowed during the Civil War, when Anthony and many Northern feminists supported of the war and assisted fugitive slaves. Anthony and Stanton criticized President Abraham Lincoln when the Emancipation Proclamation freed only Southern blacks but remained silent about the role of women. Later they opposed passage of the Fourteenth Amendment that guaranteed citizenship rights to all *males* regardless of race but effectively denied such rights to women. While campaigning in Kansas for the simultaneous enfranchisement of women and blacks in 1867, Anthony and Stanton met the wealthy eccentric reformer, George Francis Train, who offered to provide financial backing for a reform newspaper. Anthony was to serve as proprietor and manager, while Stanton and Parker Pillsbury, an abolitionist writer, were named editors. The first issue of the *Revolution* appeared January 8, 1868 and for the next two years it was the mouthpiece of the radical wing of the women's movement. publishing polemical articles on such controversial topics as prostitution, birth control, the exploitation of servant girls, and women's divorce rights. At the same time, Anthony, Stanton, and other members of the radical wing founded the National Woman Suffrage Association. In response, the more conservative wing of the movement shortly after established the American Woman Suffrage Association and a second publication, the *Woman's Journal*. A series of personal and financial difficulties ended Train's financial support and, faced by stiff competition from the well-financed *Woman's Journal*, Anthony agreed in May 1870 to relinquish control of the *Revolution*. Under new management, the paper declined rapidly and in 1872 disappeared entirely.

Despite this failure, Anthony remained one of the most visible leaders in the suffrage movement, always pushing the boundaries and confronting the system. In 1872, she went on a six-month lecture tour urging women to register and vote to test a theory that the fourteenth and fifteenth amendments enfranchised all citizens, including women. When she did so in Rochester, she was arrested and convicted. At the same time, she campaigned for a suffrage amendment to the federal Constitution, and convinced legislators to introduce it into every session of Congress from 1877 until 1904 so that it eventually became known as the Anthony Amendment.

The press grudgingly came to admire Anthony's courage, dedication, and ability. Mainstream newspapers joined reform journals in publishing her speeches and letters, and she was frequently interviewed for her views on a range of topics in addition to woman's rights and suffrage. Her most significant publishing venture was the multi-volume *History of Woman Suffrage*, which she started writing with Elizabeth Cady Stanton and Mathilda Gage in 1880. The first three volumes were published between 1881 and 1886; the fourth, which she co-authored with Ida Husted Harper, was published in 1902.

Further Reading

Archer, Jules. "Susan B. Anthony," in *Breaking Barriers: The Feminist Revolution from Susan B. Anthony to Margaret Sanger to Betty Friedan*. New York: Viking Press, 1991.

Baker, Jean. *Sisters: The Lives of American Suffragists*. New York: Hill and Wang, 2005.

Barry, Kathleen. *Susan B. Anthony: A Biography of a Singular Woman*, rev. ed. Bloomington, IN: 1st Books Library, 2000.

Cullen-Dupont, Kathryn. *American Women Activists' Writings" An Anthology, 1637–2002*. New York: Cooper Square Press, 2002.

Flexner, Eleanor. *Century of Struggle: The Woman's Rights Movement in the United States*, rev. ed. Cambridge, MA: Belknap Press, 1975.

Harper, Ida Husted. *Life and Work of Susan B. Anthony,* 3 vols. Indianapolis, IN: Hollenbeck Press, 1898–1908; reprint, North Stratford, NH: Ayer Co., 1998.

Sherr, Lynn. *Failure is Impossible: Susan B. Anthony in her Own Words*. New York: Times Books, 1995.

Stalcup, Brenda. *Susan B. Anthony*. San Diego: Greenhaven Press, 2002.

Stanton, Elizabeth Cady, Susan B. Anthony, and Ann D. Gordon. *The Selected Papers of Elizabeth Cady Stanton and Susan B. Anthony*. Vol 3, *National Protection for National Citizens, 1873 to 1880*. New Brunswick, NJ: Rutgers University Press, 2003.

Ward, Geoffrey C., Martha Saxton, Ann D. Gordon, and Ellen Carol DuBois. *Not for Ourselves Alone: The Story of Elizabeth Cady Stanton and Susan B. Anthony: An Illustrated History*. New York: Alfred A. Knopf, 1999.

ELIZABETH V. BURT

AOL TIME WARNER

AOL Time Warner existed as a corporate entity from January 2001 until October 2003. America Online, the United States' largest Internet service provider, announced in January 2000 that it planned to acquire Time Warner, with its holdings in cable systems, cable networks, movies, books, magazines, and recordings. The $183 billion merger, the largest up to that time, was to be on the basis of AOL's stock value and not on the relative revenue of the two companies. At the time, AOL had annual revenue of $5.5 billion, and Time Warner had annual revenue of $23 billion. On the basis of the final agreement, AOL was to control 55 percent of the enterprise and Time Warner was to control 45 percent of the enterprise. Steve Case, who had become the face of AOL, became chairman of AOL Time Warner, succeeding Gerald Levin. The stock symbol for the merged company changed from TWX to AOL. By October 2003, AOL Time Warner had written off nearly $100 billion in

assets because of the merger and faced investigations of inflated revenue statements for AOL. The corporate entity re-emerged as Time Warner with AOL as a division and in 2004 paid $510 million to settle investigations of the Justice Department and the Securities and Exchange Commission. Case became an affiliated director of Time Warner. Richard D. Parsons became chairman of Time Warner, and the stock symbol again was TWX.

The combination of AOL and Time Warner culminated nearly a century of media concentration and technological advances. The Warner brothers, Henry, Albert, Sam, and Jack, founded Warner Bros. studios in 1923. In 1927, Warner Bros. released one of the earliest talkies, the "The Jazz Singer." By 1958 the Warner enterprises included Warner Bros. Records. The studio went through a series of acquisitions and mergers and by 1972 had become Warner Communications Inc.

Henry Luce and Britton Haddon founded Time Inc. also in 1923. By 1930 it had added *Fortune* magazine, and by 1936 came *Life* magazine. Time-Life Books became a division of Time Inc. in 1961. In 1972, Time Life backed the creation of Home Box Office (HBO). In 1990, Time purchased Warner Communications for $14 billion, creating at the time what was the largest entertainment and media enterprise in the world. Time Warner acquired the Turner Broadcasting System, which included CNN, in 1996.

America Online had its origins in the provision of computer-based messaging, games and other entertainment, and news and information. Initially through computer "bulletin-board" systems and subsequently through the Internet, users of such systems could participate interactively with other users around the country and around the world. America Online emerged from Quantum Computer Services Inc. America Online Inc. appeared in 1991 and began trading on NASDAQ in 1992. America Online became part of the New York Stock Exchange in 1996. Although Steve Case was not the founder of AOL, he became identified as its personification and chief promoter. America Online began as a bulletin board system, but provided a gateway to the Internet in 1995. The development of the World Wide Web in the early 1990s and of graphical browsers had created a new media force and a new economic force.

Time Warner, before its combination with AOL, had made two unsuccessful attempts at creating interactive systems. Prior to the creation of Time Warner, Warner Amex had been the developer of Qube, a two-way cable system experiment in Columbus, Ohio. Qube allowed subscribers to make program choices, participate in polls, and receive other interactive services through a two-way link with the cable system's headquarters. Qube failed to prosper in Columbus and as a national network, and it closed in 1985. Time Warner tried again with its Full Service Network in the early 1990s, but that effort also failed. The combination with AOL provided another effort to stake a claim on the new online technologies.

In many ways, the rise of AOL and fall of AOL Time Warner was indicative of the turn-of-the-century phenomenon known as the "dotcom bubble." The appellation dot.

com came from the domain name of many online companies—.com. These firms attracted massive investments. Eventually, however, the issues of physical assets, effective business models, and dependable revenue streams brought a bursting of the bubble and the loss millions of dollars for investors and for employees who had received stock options in lieu of salaries. The era had its survivors including amazon.com, eBay, and AOL.

The combination of AOL and Time Warner also brought into focus issues of consumer access to online systems, convergence, and corporate malfeasance. Prior to the combination of AOL and Time Warner, AOL was a strong advocate of providing equal access to competitive broadband providers on cable systems. After its combination with the second largest cable system in the United States, AOL ceased its advocacy of such open access. The U.S. Supreme Court in 2005 ruled that cable systems do not have to provide such open access, and the Federal Communications Commission has had under study the limiting of such access to the regulated telecommunications system. The undoing of the combination, however, included investigations into corporate malfeasance at AOL. A *Washington Post* investigative series in 2002 showed that AOL through a variety of devices had inflated its revenue. Time Warner eventually had to write off nearly $100 billion in assets as a result of the combination. Time Warner also paid $300 million to the Securities and Exchange Commission and $210 million to the Justice Department to settle the claims against AOL.

AOL now is one of several Time Warner divisions that also include HBO, Time Warner Cable, New Line Cinema, the Turner Broadcasting System, Time Inc., and Warner Bros. Entertainment. Time Warner, with its AOL division, remains one of the megamedia companies that is battling to gain dominance in the use of existing and emerging communication technologies to provide information and entertainment services. Although AOL remains a success story in the commercial development of the Internet, its "acquisition" of Time Warner may serve more as a cautionary tale for future investors in new technologies.

Further Reading

Bruck, Connie. *Master of the Game: Steve Ross and the Creation of Time Warner.* East Rutherford, NJ: Penguin Books, 1995.

Clurman, Richard. *To the End of Time: The Seduction and Conquest of a Media Empire.* New York: Simon & Schuster: 1992.

Klein, Alec. *Steve Case, Jerry Levin, and the Collapse of AOL Time Warner.* New York: Simon & Schuster, 2003.

Munk, Nina. *Steve Case, Jerry Levin, and the Unmaking of AOL Time Warner.* New York: HarperBusiness, 2004.

Swisher, Kara. *AOL.COM : How Steve Case Beat Bill Gates, Nailed the Netheads, and Made Millions in the War for the Web.* New York: Times Books: 1998.

Swisher, Kara with Lisa Dickey. *There Must Be a Pony in Here Somewhere: The AOL Time Warner Debacle and the Quest for a Digital Future.* New York: Crown Business, 2003.

Wilkinson, Julia. *My Life at AOL.* Bloomington, IN: Authorhouse, 2001.

WILLIAM J. LEONHIRTH

ARCHIVES AND NEWSPAPERS

Historians have long debated the use of news content as a source of historical information. John Bach McMaster's book *History of the People of the United States*, begun in 1883, was based largely on newspaper sources. Historian James Ford Rhodes urged in an *Atlantic Monthly* article in 1909 that newspapers should hold an honorable place in the study of the past. In the 1923 book *The Newspaper and the Historian*, Lucy Maynard Salmon suggested that historians should use newspapers to reconstruct a picture of contemporary life. For journalism historians, the newspaper is a primary source when the subject of study is the product or practice of journalism itself, or when the research question involves the impact of various media accounts. For general historians, the newspaper is a secondary source that supplements, complements or contradicts primary sources such as original manuscripts, letters, official documents, memoirs, first person accounts and other such materials.

Librarians and archivists have a long tradition of including newspapers in their collections. The *Maryland Gazette* index (1727–1746) was the first of its kind in the United States. The *New York Herald* started a news index in book form in 1875 and continued indexing until 1906. Members of the American Library Association urged development of a national newspaper index as early as 1893. The *New York Times* began publishing a quarterly index of subjects found in its pages starting in 1913. In part because of demand from subscribing libraries, the company eventually published the index going all the way back to 1851. Despite enormous collection, organization, indexing, storage and preservation problems, librarians have gone to great lengths to provide newspaper content to their patrons. Collections of bound newspapers have been replaced by microfilm, which is itself being converted to digital systems of storage and retrieval.

Technology of Newspaper Archives

Newsprint used since the 1870s turns to dust in a relatively short period of time. Early microfilm technology did not provide a secure alternative, since the film developed spots or defects over time that made the images illegible. Reliable digital archives have yet to be established. The story of newspaper archives is inextricably linked to the technology used to preserve the newspapers.

Binding back issues of newspapers was the archival technology in place until microfilming became practical in the 1930s. As early as 1898, historian Albert Bushnell Hart urged libraries to accumulate files of newspapers even if it meant that the whole of Manhattan Island had to be used to store the volumes. Finding space for the collected papers eventually became a problem that overwhelmed librarians and archivists. As many as one million bound copies of more than 180 newspapers from twenty-two states covering two centuries of American history were offered to the public in an auction by the Kansas State Historical Society in 1997 because the society's library and archives director said they could not take care of them anymore.

A camera capable of creating full-page images of newspaper pages for display on microfilm was introduced in 1932 by Eastman Kodak, which had worked in collaboration with *New York Herald Tribune* librarian David G. Rogers to develop the system. Microfilm quickly became the medium of choice for storage and preservation of newspaper collections and a number of service firms sprang up to meet the demand for microfilming thousands of newspaper titles, both contemporaneously and retrospectively. However, early microfilm technology proved unacceptable for archival-quality preservation and many libraries that discarded bound volumes of newspapers when the microfilm arrived found themselves years later with illegible images on deteriorating film that could not be restored.

Optical storage technology seemed to provide a solution in the late 1980s as CD-ROMs gained acceptance. However, the incompatible technical standards of early systems and the expensive and unreliable equipment used for scanning newspaper pages once more created stumbling blocks. News organizations and libraries quickly recognized that such technology was not cost-efficient and would require constant vigilance in transferring content to whatever the next new format might be. This "backward compatibility" issue continues to bedevil anyone working on standards for archiving and preserving content digitally.

Critics have decried the conversion of bound newspapers to alternative storage media, but practical considerations have taken precedence. The Library of Congress and the National Endowment for the Humanities have provided funding to all fifty states for projects to identify, catalog and microfilm newspaper collections in libraries, museums, archives, historical societies, newspaper libraries and other sources. Researchers can now use a national database to locate newspaper collections from 500,000 locations around the country through the United States Newspaper Program.

Electronic Newspaper Archives

In addition to the work that libraries and archival institutions do to make newspaper collections accessible, news libraries have played an important role. The news library in a newspaper organization serves both as a library and an archive. News librarians provide the news staff with information resources to add depth and context to the news. They also organize and preserve the work product that the newspaper staff generates every day. The dusty filing cabinets stuffed with yellowed and dog-eared newspaper clippings have been replaced, however, by electronic systems.

Newspaper companies were among the early innovators in developing computer storage and retrieval systems for text. The *New York Times*'s Information Bank service, consisting of a computer index and abstracts of newspaper content, started in 1971 with coverage back to 1969. Full-text storage and retrieval capability was added in 1981. The Toronto *Globe and Mail* introduced the first truly full-text, online electronic newspaper in 1976. Other major vendors such as Nexis/Lexis, DataTimes, Vu/Text, BRS, Dialog and Dow Jones News Retrieval began offering their online services of full-text newspaper content in the early 1980s. By the early 1990s, more than 150 full-text newspaper files in the United States were available through database vendors. That number has increased steadily ever since.

With some important exceptions, the full-text electronic file of a newspaper corresponds to the content that appeared in the newsprint version. However, the only somewhat complete version of any electronic newspaper database is the in-house, internal database that is kept by each newspaper for its own reporters and editors. That version is not accessible to anyone outside the organization and contains material that is not included in any electronic version vended by outside services.

Newspapers have different policies for how much of the printed product is sent to commercial database vendors. Many papers have regional editions or editions throughout the day, but not all of the stories in all of the editions are stored in the database vended to the public. Many newspapers do not send wire-service copy that ran in the newspaper to the database vendors. In the wake of a major legal case (*Tasini v. New York Times*) in 2001, most newspapers do not send free-lance content that appeared in print to the database services. Some papers include only selected syndicated columns from among all that ran in the newspaper, based on internal selection policies that are not discernable to the searcher.

Early electronic database versions of newspapers, internal or external, did not include agate type material such as box scores, funeral notices, stock-market listings, calendars, classified or legal notice advertising or similar materials. Nor did they include any visual materials. Photos, charts, graphs, tables, drawings, or other illustrative materials are noted at the bottom of the story, but there is no way for systems vended to the public to capture those materials. In these cases, the news librarians preparing the electronic files refer a searcher to the microfilm edition of the newspaper to see the visual elements. Obviously, the electronic database also excludes display advertising and commercial inserts, once again requiring the searcher to use the microfilm to get a full record of what the print subscriber received on his or her doorstep. These kinds of materials, though, are included in more recent electronic databases such ProQuest Historical Newspapers for such publications as the *New York Times*, *Chicago Tribune*, and *Los Angeles Times*.

Newspapers have always archived the negatives and photos that ran in their own pages, and have kept a small number of the photos from wire services and from promotional sources. As with the clipping files, photos and negatives were stored in filing cabinets and were retrieved using an in-house cataloging system, if any was in place at all. However, in the 1980s many news organizations began shifting from wet darkrooms to the electronic darkroom, and digital storage of images became possible.

News organizations such as the Associated Press have been innovators in the digital capture and storage of photos. As early as 1990, the AP was working on a system for electronic photo selection and editing that would eliminate entirely the need to print a hard copy of a photo. This posed special problems for news librarians, who had to determine how a photo that was "born digital" and was placed in the newspaper electronically was going to be stored, identified and retrieved. News organizations that had already established electronic database standards for their text content typically created a separate and usually incompatible system for storage and retrieval of images. Most news organizations are struggling to this day to develop digital asset management systems that can seamlessly handle content from both.

Despite these difficulties, many newspapers continue to generate revenue from the sale of content from their text and photo archives. Libraries, businesses, law firms, and many others subscribe to the major newspaper database vendors, which pay a handsome royalty to the newspapers for the privilege of vending their content. Newspapers sell individual stories to the public from their text archives through services accessible through their own Web sites. Photo archives vended by the AP, the *New York Times,* and other news organizations are accessible via the Internet to the general public. Newspapers have recognized the monetary value in their archives and have found ways to capitalize on the market for that content.

Web Archives

Newspapers have not been so successful in capturing the content of their Web sites for archival purposes. One of the first newspaper Web sites was launched by Knight-Ridder in 1994. However, the early engineers and designers who launched the "Mercury Center" site failed to capture any electronic record of the site's initial appearance and architecture, and that history is lost. The earliest page from the "Mercury Center" that can be viewed using the Internet Archive is from December 1, 1998. The early Web site efforts of other newspapers have suffered the same fate. While the Library of Congress and the National Endowment for the Humanities have established programs to capture and store printed newspaper content electronically, there is no such effort focused on capturing newspaper Web site content.

Indeed, there is a debate about whether such content should even be archived at all. Some newspaper professionals argue that their sites are more like a service than a publication. Because the content changes by the minute and because the Web sites include many interactive, and hence fluid, features such as forums, discussions, bulletin boards, and searchable databases, there is no way to "fix" a Web site the way that archivists require for traditional documents. Some newspaper Web masters burn a CD every few months just to capture a snapshot of the site's content, but that is certainly not an archival strategy.

While newspaper Web site content is not archived, the site does serve as a platform from which to sell stories from the text archive of the printed newspaper. As mentioned, most newspaper Web sites generate revenue from the sale to the public of individual stories from the electronic database of stories that appeared in the newspaper. Many also use the news Web site to vend photos from their photo archives. Once again, this is an example of the newspaper Web site as a service rather than a publication.

Unarguably, however, audiences also use the newspaper Web site as a source of news and information. Future scholars will find themselves in a difficult position if they wish to study the content of newspaper Web sites to determine their influence and effect as they do using archives of printed newspapers. No such archives exist, with the exception of the Internet Archive which is focused on the entirety of the Internet, not just news Web sites. And since many newspaper Web sites refuse entry to the "crawler" software that the Internet Archive uses to map sites, they will not be archived there either. Just as with the early history of television and radio, the early history of newspaper Web sites is lost, and will continue to be at risk as long as there is no reliable method for archiving content, or even a consensus that archiving is necessary.

Further Reading

Baker, Nicholson. *Double Fold: Libraries and the Assault on Paper.* New York : Random House, 2001.

Cox, Richard J. *Vandals in the Stacks?: A Response to Nicholson Baker's Assault on Libraries.* Westport, CT: Greenwood Press, 2002.

Martin, Shannon E., and Kathleen A. Hansen. *Newspapers of Record in a Digital Age: From Hot Type to Hot Link.* Westport, CT: Praeger, 1998.

Salmon, Lucy Maynard. *The Newspaper and the Historian.* New York : Oxford University Press, 1923.

Semonche, Barbara P., ed. *News Media Libraries: A Management Handbook.* Westport, CT: Greenwood Press, 1993.

KATHLEEN A. HANSEN

ARCHIVING AND PRESERVATION

News content provides a chronicle of the important events of the day. News content and newsmaking behavior also reflect the official power structures in society. Social historians rely heavily on local news content to understand the day-to-day life of communities and citizens. Consequently, there is significant value in collecting, preserving and making accessible the news content from a wide range of time periods and from a variety of distribution channels.

Media content is notoriously difficult for archivists to manage. Archivists consider five characteristics of information integrity when considering what type of material to collect and how to preserve it. These are content, fixity, reference, provenance, and context. Each of these poses special problems when applied to media content.

Content refers to the format and structure of the item to be archived. For a printed text, content includes the actual words as well as the layout and design of the document. Image content includes both the photo or video itself and things such as the resolution, accuracy of color representation and image quality. Physically preserving content in a manner that allows for future accessibility has always been an issue for news in whatever medium has been used for initial distribution. Maintaining the archaic equipment necessary to display historical content poses another set of difficulties.

Fixity refers to the way content is fixed as a discrete object. If content is subject to change or withdrawal without notice, its value as a cultural record is severely diminished. For instance, a published document is considered a fixed object. The act of producing and broadcasting a radio or television program qualifies those programs as discrete objects. Fixity of content on the World Wide Web is an entirely different matter.

Reference refers to the characteristics of an information object that allow it to be definitively and reliably located over time among other objects. Systems of citation, description and classification provide this means of reference. But these reference systems are incomplete and difficult to manage archivally when applied to media content.

Provenance requires that an information object must include a record of its origin and chain of custody. The formal process of publication, for instance, creates a channel of distribution and establishes a record of provenance. As media content migrates from one distribution platform to another, however, provenance becomes much more difficult to establish.

Context refers to the ways information objects interact with one another. For instance, a news photo exists within a larger context when it is printed on a newspaper page surrounding by text or graphics. The context for that photo changes if it is distributed via a broadcast channel. A Web page consists of links to items outside the content of that specific page and those links constitute the context for understanding that Web page as an information object.

These archival concepts have influenced the decisions about what media content should be preserved and how that material should be accessed. Media organizations have implemented one set of decisions for their internal archives (storage of their own content) and a different set of decisions for the material they make available to the wider community of scholars, librarians and the general public.

Archiving Print Content

Newspaper preservation in the United States, up until the 1930s, involved binding the back issues in book form. Because newspapers switched after 1870 from rag-stock paper to the highly acidic newsprint we recognize today, much of the archived content was already badly deteriorated by the 1920s. In 1932, *New York Herald Tribune* news librarian David G. Rogers teamed up with Eastman Kodak to develop a camera that could film newspaper pages and display them in full-page format, allowing newspaper content to be captured on microfilm. In the intervening decades, many newspapers have been photographed and stored as microfilm. The silver halide microfilm edition of a newspaper is the "edition of record" that is sent to the Library of Congress with a fee for copyright registration. The full-page format captures the content and meets the fixity, provenance, and context requirements for archival integrity.

The Library of Congress and the National Endowment for the Humanities have collaborated since 1982 in an effort to locate, catalog, and preserve newspapers published throughout the United States. Called the United States Newspaper Project, the effort has supported projects in each of the fifty states to inventory and microfilm newspaper collections in public libraries, courthouses, newspaper offices, historical museums, college and university libraries, archives and private collections. Records of the holdings in a state are entered into a national database maintained by the Online Computer Library Center (OCLC) and are accessible throughout the world via OCLC's WorldCat service on the Internet. Microfilm copies of the 200,000 newspaper titles in the system are available to researchers through interlibrary loan from more than 500,000 locations. Eight national newspaper repositories around the country also provide access to portions of the collections. This project has helped meet the reference requirement for archival integrity.

The National Endowment for the Humanities also established the National Digital Newspaper Program in 2004, intended to create a national digital resource of historically significant newspapers from all U.S. states and territories published between 1836 and 1922. When this long-term project is completed, the database will be maintained by the Library of Congress and available via the Internet. Microfilm files of the newspaper pages are converted into digital files to create this database. Also, many institutions responsible for collecting newspapers have scanned some microfilm files into digital format.

In addition to the efforts of library and historical institutions, newspaper organizations themselves have always maintained internal archives of their own content. News libraries were innovators in the capture of newspaper text files into electronic form for the newspaper's internal database and for vending to the public through commercial services. News librarians regularly "enhance" the raw files with information such as keywords and descriptors; with corrections; with notations about the graphics, photos and design elements that might have accompanied the story; and by stripping out the editing and layout instructions from the pagination technicians. This work helps ensure that the electronic version of the printed newspaper accurately reflects at least a portion of what appeared in print.

There is no archival copy of news organizations' Web sites. Researchers cannot use the Web version of a newspaper as a substitute for the newspaper itself since the content differs and is not accessible beyond a few weeks' time. This issue will be discussed in more detail in the section on archiving online content below.

Archiving Radio and Television Content

Much of the early history of radio and television is lost. Live radio programs were captured starting in 1928 using commercial 78 rpm 12-inch discs to record programs for replay by radio stations. This technique was replaced by the "electrical transcription" (ET) process introduced in 1932 using a 33 1/3 rpm 16-inch disc with 15 minutes of play time per side. This ET process became the broadcast standard but because discs were fragile and cumbersome, few ETs are still in existence. The first commercial audio tape recorder was introduced in 1948, used to tape Bing Crosby's radio program for ABC. Again, tapes from this time period have been lost or have deteriorated and the equipment needed to play different formats is obsolete and may exist only in museums.

Few early live television broadcasts were captured. When they were, kinescope or film recording technology was employed. Many of those recordings that did exist were discarded or have deteriorated beyond use. Videotape recording technology was introduced in 1956 but the industry adopted many incompatible formats and technological obsolescence has been a major issue. Most broadcast news operations re-used tapes over and over, thus obliterating any record of earlier work. Videotape is also highly susceptible to degradation, and the costs of storage facilities and qualified staff to maintain multiple formats and equipment were prohibitive.

Recognizing that the history of the broadcast media was being lost, the American Television and Radio Act of 1976 authorized the Library of Congress to establish and maintain an archive to preserve a permanent record of the broadcast programs considered a part of the country's cultural heritage. The content archived by the Library of Congress is available through its Motion Picture, Broadcasting and Recorded Sound Division. Other archives of broadcast news content exist in universities, museums and through the Vanderbilt Television News Archive, established in 1968.

The television networks themselves greatly expanded their internal archiving practices starting in the 1970s when home videotaping technology, copyright issues and the potential for revenue from sales of taped content became apparent. In addition to use by their own news producers, the archives of NBC News, ABC News, CBS News, and CNN News (among others) are publicized via the Internet; members of the public and independent producers can purchase tapes of programs aired.

Both radio and television organizations also archive content that has not been aired. For example, the Broadcast Library for National Public Radio maintains raw tapes of briefings, press conferences, and White House statements made during important news events such as the early months of war or the terrorist attacks of September 11, 2001. The NPR library also includes music, spoken word, and sound effects tapes for use in program production. Most television tape libraries include stock footage, unaired news items, outtakes, and syndicated news items.

Inevitably, broadcast content will be accessible in digital form. National radio networks "stream" their programs over the Internet and archive broadcasts digitally. Several Internet search engine firms have developed a computerized system for transcribing and abstracting television broadcasts and assigning keywords that can be searched electronically. The television broadcasts need to be converted into digital format, but once they are, they can be easily stored and made accessible via the Internet. These companies are working with the television networks to develop a fee-based system that could offer users access to an unlimited, fully searchable digital video library of network content.

Archiving Online Content

Just as with broadcast content, much of the early history of the online environment is lost. From its origins in the 1970s, the "killer application" of the Internet was e-mail between engineers and scientists, a form of communication that does not immediately suggest a need for an archive of content. Before the development of the World Wide Web, bulletin boards and Usenet forums generated stockpiles of postings arranged into "newsgroups" but the content was difficult to search and required impossible-to-remember numerical addresses to access. With the development of the World Wide Web and graphical browser software in the early 1990s, the Internet became accessible to the masses, content increased exponentially, and the archiving issues began to emerge.

Engineer Brewster Kahle created the Internet Archive in 1996 in an attempt to capture a record of the text and images in the documents that appear on the Web. Since then the Archive has expanded to include audio, moving images, and software as well as Web pages in the collection. The Internet Archive is certainly not comprehensive because the crawler software used to capture content cannot gain access to hundreds of thousands of sites that block such crawlers. However, the Archive creates a small window onto a portion the Web at a particular point in time.

Media companies were early experimenters with, and adopters of, digital content storage and delivery systems. News librarians were instrumental in the development of the text database systems that dominated the online industry in the 1970s and 1980s. But as the Web emerged as the digital medium of choice, news organizations were as slow to adapt as were many other large organizations.

Knight-Ridder launched the "Mercury Center" news Web site in 1994, becoming one of the first news organizations to recognize the potential of the Web. Given the newspaper's importance to its technology-savvy Silicon Valley readers, it is no surprise that the innovation started there. However, the early engineers and designers who launched that site failed to capture any electronic record of the site's initial appearance and architecture, and that history is lost. Using the Internet Archive, the earliest page from the "Mercury Center" that can be viewed is from December 1, 1998.

Most newspapers and broadcast/cable operations now have Web sites, but none of them has any way to reliably archive the content that appears on these sites. Indeed, there is a debate about whether an archive is even necessary for such content. Since much of the content of online news sites changes by the minute, and a good deal of the rest of the content is created by users through features such as forums, community discussion sections and interactive, personally tailored use of content, many argue that such sites are more like a service than a publication that must be archived for future use.

Electronic publications are distinguished from printed documents in a number of ways. They are easily manipulable, internally and externally linkable, readily transformable, inherently searchable and infinitely replicable. With these characteristics, archivists and preservationists are suggesting that it may be necessary to rethink the nature of a document. Certainly, the differences between the printed newspaper or televised newscast and that news organization's Web site are significant, especially in the context of a discussion about archiving content.

Despite such considerations, the Library of Congress was authorized by Congress in 2000 to develop and execute a plan for a National Digital Information Infrastructure and Preservation Program. Congress appropriated $99.8 million to establish the program. The Library of Congress, along with other federal and nonfederal entities, was charged with identifying a national network of libraries and other organizations with responsibilities for collecting digital materials and providing access to, and long-term preservation of, those materials. The Library of Congress issued its plan in 2002 which was approved by Congress in December of that year.

In 2005, the Library of Congress and the National Science Foundation awarded research grants of $3 million to ten university teams to begin developing standards and systems for digital information collection and preservation. However, news content from online sites has yet to be identified as a priority for inclusion in any archive project. The archival standards of content, fixity, reference, provenance, and context seem almost impossible to meet when applied to news content on the Web. It is an open question whether online news content will be accessible to future historians, sociologists, communications scholars and the general public. For now, the archival fate of information that is "born digital" remains precarious.

Further Reading

Ellis, Judith, ed. *Keeping Archives*. Melbourne, Australia: Thorpe Bowker, 2004.

Kahle, Brewster. "Preserving the Internet." *Scientific American* (March 1997): 82.

Martin, Shannon E., and Kathleen A. Hansen. *Newspapers of Record in a Digital Age: From Hot Type to Hot Link*. Westport, CT: Praeger, 1998.

Progress made by the National Digital Information Infrastructure and Preservation Program can be followed at http://www.digitalpreservation.gov (2001–).

Semonche, Barbara P., ed. *News Media Libraries: A Management Handbook*. Westport, CT: Greenwood Press, 1993.

KATHLEEN A. HANSEN

ARIZONA REPUBLIC

The *Arizona Republic* was originally a political trumpet that helped bring statehood to America's last frontier territory. A century later, it was the nation's fastest-growing news-

paper. It became the tenth largest newspaper in the United States and in the West was exceeded in circulation only by the *Los Angeles Times* and *San Francisco Chronicle*.

Located in Phoenix, the newspaper began in 1890 as the *Arizona Republican*. The political climate was favorable to the paper's early growth. Eastern business interests controlled Arizona's dominant Democratic Party and those interests attempted to block statehood using the Democrat-aligned *Phoenix Gazette* in the process. Statehood became the main theme of an embryonic Republican Party, and its leaders, Lewis Wolfley and Clark Churchill, founded the *Republican*. The *Republican* cultivated vast local support for Arizona to join the Union. By campaigning for statehood, the *Republican* rapidly grew. It was Arizona's largest newspaper when statehood finally came in 1912. The *Republican* and *Gazette* remained bitter political rivals.

The rivalry ended in 1930 when Phoenix became the first sizable city with a newspaper monopoly. During a "bust" cycle in Arizona's up-and-down economy, the *Republican* and the *Gazette* agreed to merge. The newspapers dropped their political flags. The first edition of the *Arizona Republic* appeared on Veterans Day of that year.

The *Republic's* modern era began in 1946 with its purchase by Eugene C. Pulliam, the owner of the *Indianapolis Star* and *News*. Pulliam was a fixture at the *Arizona Republic* until his death in 1975. Ownership by his successors continued until 2000. During this fifty-four-year period, circulation of the *Republic* increased from 45,000 to nearly 600,000.

The *Republic* and its artist Steve Benson won a Pulitzer Prize for editorial cartooning in 1993. Its best known journalistic achievement followed the 1976 murder of its investigative reporter Don Bolles, who had covered organized crime. Those eventually convicted of Bolles's murder were exposed in an investigative reporting project that involved newspapers from across the United States.

Under Pulliam, the *Republic* advanced many technical innovations. In 1964, Pulliam acquired a short-lived Phoenix daily newspaper that was the first to publish with "offset" technology. With these first offset presses, the *Republic* pioneered the field's conversion from metal to "cold type" printing. In 1986, the *Republic* was the first newspaper to eliminate compositors and adopt electronic page layout. In 1995, it was one of the first newspapers to provide an online edition on the Internet.

Another innovation in 1994 had been the closure of presses at its downtown Phoenix facility in favor of networked publishing plants in Phoenix's far-flung suburbs. The relocation of presses enabled dramatic circulation gains during a decade when the Phoenix area nearly doubled in population.

In 2000, the Gannett corporation purchased the *Republic*. After *USA Today*, the *Arizona Republic* was Gannett's largest newspaper. In Arizona the *Republic* centered the state's largest media complex which also included Azcentral.com, the *Tucson Citizen*, the *Arizona Business Gazette*, *La Voz*, and KPNX and KNAZ television.

Further Reading

Arizona Media. Tempe, AZ: Arizona Educational Media Association and Arizona State University, 1975.

Arizona Newspapers Association, *Arizona Newspapers.* Phoenix, AZ: ANA Press, 1965.

Pulliam, Russell, *Gene Pulliam: Last of the Newspaper Titans.* Ottawa, IL: Jameson, 1984.

Martin Tallberg, *Don Bolles: An Investigation into His Murder.* New York: Popular Library, 1977

Marshall Trimble, *Arizona: A Cavalcade of History.* Tucson, AZ: Rio Nuevo, 2003.

Earl A. Zarbin, *All the Time a Newspaper: The First 100 years of the Arizona Republic.* Phoenix, AZ: Arizona Republic Books, 1990.

CRAIG ALLEN

ARMED FORCES MEDIA

Media produced about and for the members of the armed forces are published by both the U. S. Department of Defense and by private organizations, The Armed Forces Information Service has the job of providing media for military personnel and Department of Defense civilian employees throughout the world. It works directly with the assistant secretary of defense for public affairs who also has responsibility for media relations and community relations. Its primary mission is to provide high quality news, information and entertainment to U.S. forces. It serves all military installations both in the United States and abroad, all naval ships, and all U.S. embassies that have military attachments. It attempts to provide as much information as possible without censorship.

The Armed Forces Radio and Television Service (AFRTS) provides radio and TV programs to almost one million servicemen and women overseas, aboard ships, and to their family members. It distributes programs by satellite and by mail on video and audiotape. Affiliate stations also produce their own programs. The major broadcast networks, syndicates, stations, and program producers have provided generous support to AFRTS radio and television operations.

The Information Operations Directorate plans and coordinates Department of Defense internal media products to communicate policies, programs, and activities of the office of the secretary of defense. This includes electronic, broadcast, photographic, and print materials. It also has an Internet news and feature service.

The Defense Visual Information Directorate oversees Department of Defense visual information and the Joint Combat Camera program. It is responsible for the Defense Visual Information Center which preserves and provides access to U.S. military films, videos, multimedia collections, and still photographs. The directorate also is the Department of Defense's central storage and distribution facility for such things as constructional videotapes and CD-ROMs.

The Policy and Alliances Directorate oversees policy for all Department of Defense newspapers, pamphlets, and periodicals. It is a Department of Defense contact with Congress, the public and government agencies.

Stars & Stripes is the Department of Defense authorized daily newspaper. It was started during the Civil War, resumed during World War I and World War II, and became a continuous publication after World War II. It has a long tradition of editorial independence and historically has not been the voice of the Department of Defense.

A major factor in armed forces media is the Defense Information School which trains both print and broadcast journalists for all branches of the armed services. Founded at Fort Slocum in 1942, it moved to Fort Benjamin Harrison in 1968 and then to Fort George Meade in 1994. It has entry level and advanced programs in public affairs, journalism, photojournalism, broadcasting, electronic imaging, broadcast systems maintenance, video production, and visual information management. The school is a major factor in staffing the post newspapers at forty-six military bases.

Private Publications

Private publications have been designed for a variety of audiences. Some have been geared to active military personnel, others for defense contractors, and still others have been lifestyle publications for military personnel and their families. The major private effort in military media is the Army Times Publishing Company, which is owned by Gannett, the largest media company in the United States, with ninety-one daily newspapers including *USA Today* and twenty-one television stations. The Army Times Publishing Group is organized into three groups:

1. The Military Times Media Group published the *Army Times, Navy Times, Air Force Times,* and *Marine Corps Times.* These four newsweeklies had a combined circulation of 240,000 in the early twenty-first century and were believed to have a pass-along rate of 4.25 persons, which meant they reached more than one million service personnel, or about 72 percent of the 1,385,116 active duty soldiers. More than 80 percent of all officers saw these publications an average of forty-three times a year, 85 percent of all non-commissioned officers an average of forty-two times a year, and 87 percent of all enlisted personnel an average of forty times a year. They also reached 50 percent of the 728,408 military spouses an average of twenty times a year.

2. The Defense News Media Group published *Defense News, Armed Forces Journal, Training & Simulation Journal,* and *C4ISR Journal (Intelligence, Surveillance and Reconnaissance Journal). Defense News* (circulation: 38,671) served an audience of senior military government decisions makers throughout the world. *Armed Forces Journal* (circulation: 42,000) was the leading joint service magazine for U.S. officers and military leaders. *Training & Simulation Journal* (circulation: 18,000) was a bimonthly journal that deals with trends in training and simulation. *C4ISR Journal* (circulation: 16,000), published ten times a year, dealt with advancing

technology in military intelligence, surveillance, and reconnaissance.

3. The *Federal Times* newsweekly was aimed at federal government decision makers. With a circulation of 40,000, it was passed along to the extent that it was seen by perhaps 130,000 government employees, including 5,300 members of the Senior Executive Service, the top level government executives.

Burrelle's Media Directory listed sixty-four publications under the heading "Military and Defense Industry," with thirty-four of those under the heading "Military Lifestyle." It was a diverse group of publications and some of the most widely circulated ones included:

- *American Legion Magazine* (circulation: 2,528,853) was published by the American Legion, the largest veterans' organization.
- *Army Reserve Magazine* (circulation: 400,000), published by U.S. Army Reserve, was aimed at Army reservists.
- *AUSA News* (circulation:120,000), published by the Association of the United States Army, carried reports on national security issues.
- *Family Magazine* (circulation: 600,000), published by Military Family Communications, focused on such family issues as food, travel, and parenting.
- *Jane's Defense Weekly* (circulation 85,000), put out by Jane's Information Group, was recognized as one of the expert sources on defense issues worldwide.
- *The Lone Sailor Range & Bearings* (circulation: 200,000), written for Navy veterans, was published by U.S. Navy Memorial Foundation.
- *Military Lifestyle Couponer* (circulation: 525,000), published by Downey Communications, contained coupons for commissary products.
- *Naval Affairs* (circulation: 180,000), published by the Fleet Reserve Association, provided legislative updates on personnel issues that affected active duty personnel, reservists, and retired military personnel.
- *Sergeants* (circulation: 160,000), put out by the Air Force Sergeants Association, was aimed at active reserve and retired enlisted Air Force personnel and their families.
- *Soldier of Fortune* (circulation: 1,000,000), published by Omega group, popularized military adventure.
- *V.F.W. Auxiliary* (circulation: 690,000) covered veterans' issues; and *V.F.W, Magazine* (circulation: 2,000,000) treated national issues from a veteran's perspective.

Further Reading

AFIS, http://www.defenselink.mil/afis/about.
Armed Forces Journal, http://www.armedforcesjournal.com.
Army Times Publishing Company, http://www.careerbuilder.com/JobSeeker/Companies/CompanySearch.aspx.
Burrelle's Media Directory, 2003.
C4ISR Journal, http:www.isrjournal.com.
Defense News, http://www.defensenews.com.
DMOZ Open Directory Project, http://dmoz.org.
Media Kit 2006. Federal Times, http://www.federaltimes.com/promos/advertising/.
Military Times Media Group, http//www.militarycity.com.
Radio Services, http://myafn.dodmedia.osd.mil/radio/services/.

GUIDO H. STEMPEL III

ARMY–MCCARTHY HEARINGS

The 1954 United States Senate subcommittee hearings (April 27–June 17, 1954) involving a dispute between Wisconsin Republican Senator Joseph R. McCarthy, one of the leading Communist hunters of the decade, and the Army marked an important event for journalism, particularly television journalism. The televised hearings, some argued, paved the way for McCarthy's political defeat.

McCarthy seized headlines around the country starting in February 1950, when he charged that Communists had infiltrated the State Department. Although a Senate committee discounted the allegation, saying that it had no foundation, he raised more claims of subversion in the United States government and military, launching investigations that damaged the reputations of his targets but supplied little evidence to substantiate his claims. His charges, reported in the press, gave Republicans a weapon against Democrats, who had held the presidency since 1933, yet after the 1952 election, which sent GOP candidate and World War II hero Dwight D. Eisenhower to the White House, the political calculations changed. President Eisenhower and administration leaders, arguing that the anti-Communist fight should be left to them, perceived threats in what they viewed as McCarthy's excesses and sought to check them.

Then in March 1954, after behind-the-scenes encouragement from the Eisenhower administration, Army leaders announced that the senator and his aides had sought improperly to secure special treatment for a McCarthy staff member, Private G. David Schine, who had been drafted into military service. Replying to the charge, McCarthy said authorities had attempted to bribe and blackmail him and his associates in a bid to stymie an inquiry of suspected Communist penetration of an Army base. The accusations prompted the Senate Permanent Subcommittee on Investigations, the panel that McCarthy used for his Communism-in-government inquiries, to scrutinize the matter in hearings that promised to give a national television audience its first extended look at the senator. Toward that result, Eisenhower and his aides quietly sought protracted hearings, although some Republicans worried that the hearings would harm their party.

The hearings, often slow and dull, took 187 hours of television time and preempted thirty-five days of regular telecasts, but the proceedings were carried live in their entirety on only the two smallest networks, the American Broadcasting Company (ABC) and Du Mont. The Columbia Broadcasting System (CBS), fearful of losing advertising revenue from its regular daytime programs, never provided live coverage, which figured to be expensive; the National Broadcasting Company (NBC) carried live telecasts of the first two days of the hearings, then withdrew because of low audience interest and losses in ad revenue (commercial sponsorship was not permitted during the first two weeks of hearings). Lacking lucrative regular daytime programming, ABC, whose programs went to only fifty to seventy-nine stations, and Du Mont, whose programs went to just ten, did not sacrifice ad revenue and were able to afford such public affairs broadcasts. The telecasts and their television ratings were considered important for ABC, buttressing its standing and ultimately helping it become competitive with its rivals. As for newspaper coverage of the hearings, it set records for coverage of a congressional committee. The Associated Press wire service carried one million words on the hearings, editors reckoned.

A number of writers said the pictures from the hearings were not flattering to the senator, showing the nation a reckless, blustering bully whose physical appearance was an unattractive as his behavior. Most damaging, commentators said, was the image of the Army's chief counsel, Joseph N. Welch, as he rebuked McCarthy on June 9 for an attack on a junior member of Welch's law firm—who was not involved in the hearings—for his previous membership in an organization tied to Communists. "[S]o reckless and so cruel," McCarthy had wounded the "young lad," leading Welch to ask: "Have you no sense of decency, sir, at long last? Have you left no sense of decency?" In 1999, experts on public speaking ranked Welch's address as one of the top one hundred speeches of the twentieth century.

Passing judgment on the hearings, the subcommittee was split, releasing majority and minority reports that criticized McCarthy and his side for seeking privileges for Schine and faulted Army officials for trying to mollify the senator and sway McCarthy's investigation of a military base. Press assessments, public opinion polls, and political observers held that the hearings were detrimental to most of the participants. The proceedings themselves did not result in any action against McCarthy, but during the hearings, Vermont Republican Senator Ralph Flanders urged his chamber to censure McCarthy, and months later, in December 1954, the Senate voted to condemn him because of conduct not associated with the Army dispute. Condemnation effectively ended his influence in the Senate and sent McCarthy into a downward spiral, politically and personally, that he could not escape. He died on May 2, 1957, from a liver ailment related to alcoholism.

Journalists and, later historians, claimed that a large television audience tuned in to the hearings and was sufficiently angered by McCarthy to turn against the Wisconsinite, precipitating his decline. But viewership was smaller than assumed. Just sixty percent of the nation had access to live coverage of the hearings; the coverage was not available in major markets, including those in the West. Stations and networks that did not offer the telecasts drew a relatively small volume of public complaints, an indication

of low interest in the hearings, and advertiser interest and television ratings for the telecasts were low. Moreover, it was doubtful whether telecasts such as the hearings could galvanize mass opinion significantly. McCarthy's stature among the public, as measured in the Gallup Poll, had been waning *before* the hearings, hinting of the importance of earlier developments, among them a critical broadcast on Edward R. Murrow's *See It Now* news program on CBS in March 1954, a signal of elite willingness to challenge the senator. If the hearings and journalists' coverage of them did leave a key impression, it was likely on elites, especially the senators who would censure McCarthy.

Further Reading

Barnouw, Erik. *The Image Empire: A History of Broadcasting in the United States,* Vol. 3, From 1953. New York: Oxford University Press, 1970.
Bayley, Edwin R. *Joe McCarthy and the Press*. Madison: University of Wisconsin Press, 1981.
Fried, Richard M. *Men Against McCarthy*. New York: Columbia University Press, 1976.
Friendly, Fred W. *Due to Circumstances Beyond Our Control*. New York: Random House, 1967.
Gauger, Michael. "Flickering Images: Live Television Coverage and Viewership of the Army-McCarthy Hearings." *The Historian* 67 (Winter 2005): 678–93.
Oshinsky, David M. *A Conspiracy So Immense: The World of Joe McCarthy*. New York: Free Press, 1983.
Reeves, Thomas C. *The Life and Times of Joe McCarthy: A Biography*. New York: Stein and Day, 1982.
Straight, Michael. *Trial by Television*. Boston: Beacon Press, 1954.

MICHAEL GAUGER

ASIAN AMERICAN JOURNALISTS AND PRESS

The words "Asian American" and "journalism" usually conjures up images of high-profile media personalities such as broadcast journalist Connie Chung, who became the first Asian American and the second woman to land a primetime news anchor job when she joined the *CBS Evening News* in 1993. But the role of Asians in journalism—whether in the form of media catering specifically to the various ethnic Asian communities or in regard to reporters contributing to the mainstream press—can be traced back to the arrival of Chinese gold prospectors in the mid-nineteenth century. And as Asian Americans have become more integrated into American society, and as the demographics of the population have grown and transformed, the work and coverage of the Asian ethnic press and the work of Asian Americans in mainstream journalism have often served as a reflection of the political, social, and historic dynamics of the time.

The first known newspaper catering to an Asian audience living in the United States was a handwritten Chinese language weekly paper based in San Francisco called the *The Golden Hills' News*, which was launched on April 22, 1854.

The publication covered news from China as well as developments in *Gum San*—or Gold Mountain, as San Francisco was called—where many Chinese had come in search of riches during the Gold Rush era. In one of the early issues of the newspaper, the publisher explained the purpose of the venture: "[we,]...believing that civil and political knowledge is of infinite importance to the Chinese, both in their individual, social and relative state, have established *The Golden Hills' News* for that special mission. The influence of chapel and press is intended to relieve the pressure of religious ignorance, settle and explain our laws, assist the Chinese to provide [for] their wants and soften, dignify and improve their general character. ..."

The Golden Hills' News would cease publication in less than a year, but Rev. William Speer, a Presbyterian missionary soon started a new publication called *The Oriental*, the first to feature an English section in order to expose the general public to China and the Chinese in America. Several Chinese American publications run out of *Gum San* would arise during the nineteenth century, though few of them lasted for very long because illiteracy was high and the readership was small, making the publications' life reliant on a publisher's enthusiasm, persistence, and fundraising abilities.

But an increasing number of ethnic-specific publications—most of them language-specific—would develop, with newspapers popping up to serve burgeoning Asian communities establishing themselves in America. At the turn of the twentieth century, for example, a number of publications serving the Japanese American community arose, including what is believed to be the first publication of its kind, the *The Report*, which was published by the Japanese YMCA in Seattle beginning in 1899.

By World War II, Japanese American newspapers flourished, a number of them dedicated to covering the effects of Executive Order 9066, which called for the national internment of Japanese Americans during the war. Some publications were started within the internment camps themselves, while publishers and editors of existing newspapers such as Los Angeles' *Rafu Shimpo,* which had begun publishing in 1903, found themselves arrested by FBI agents in a roundup of high-profile Japanese American community members.

Rafu Shimpo's publisher, H. T. Komai, was arrested on April 3, 1942, and the newspaper was ordered closed. But in the hours before the staff was forced to leave the newspaper and interned at camps across the country, Aki Komai, the publisher's son, and a few staffers hid the thousands of wood and metal Japanese type pieces that had been imported from Japan in the basement of the newspaper building, knowing that it would be impossible to revive the publication in the future without the type. In 1944, Executive Order 9066 was rescinded and Japanese Americans were released from the internment camps. Aki Komai and three former staff members reunited and returned to the newspaper's original building to miraculously find the Japanese type intact. They pooled their money to relaunch the paper, and the revived edition began publishing on January 1, 1946. *Rafu Shimpo* has been publishing continuously since then, covering issues of pressing concern to the Japanese American community, including the movement for internment redress.

The rise of the Asian ethnic press has continued to reflect the changes, growth, and diversity of Asian America and the community's immigration patterns, with an increasing number of publications—such as *Kore-Am Journal, India West*, and the *Philippine News*—catering to Korean, Indian, and Filipino audiences launched in the mid- and late twentieth century. The growth of the Southeast Asian population in the United States in the late twentieth century, which included a great number of refugees of the Vietnam War and other international conflicts, has spawned a new generation of ethnic publications. Yen Ngoc Do, who had covered the Vietnam War from his hometown of Saigon and then immigrated to America in 1975, was among these journalist-pioneers. In 1978, Do pooled $4,000 to start the first and largest Vietnamese-language newspaper in the United States, *Nguoi Viet,* out of his Garden Grove, California, garage. He would go on to start a Vietnamese-language magazine and radio station, as well. Sensing the strength of this growing Southeast Asian community, media conglomerates such as Knight Ridder, have attempted to reach this demographic by creating publications such as *Viet Mercury,* the Vietnamese-language spin-off of the *San Jose Mercury News.*

As the ethnic press developed and thrived, Asian American pioneers simultaneously made inroads into the mainstream press. Mamie Louise Leung Larson is believed to be one of the first journalists of Asian descent to work at a mainstream newspaper when she took a job at the *Los Angeles Record* in 1926 at the age of twenty-one. She reportedly landed the job after one of the staff reporters came to work drunk and a desperate city editor sent Leung Larson to cover his beat at the Hall of Justice. Leung Larson left the *Record* after three years and took jobs through the 1930s and 1940s at publications such as the *San Francisco News*, the *Chicago Daily Times*, and the *Los Angeles Times Sunday Magazine*, covering everything from her nephew's traditional Chinese month-old party, to Charlie Chaplin's divorce, to the tax evasion trial of Al Capone. In 1958, she joined the staff of the Los Angeles-based *Evening Outlook* before retiring from journalism in the early 1970s.

Bill Hosokawa would follow in Leung Larson's footsteps as one of the first Asian Americans to work for a large metropolitan daily. He faced severe challenges getting there, though. As a student at the University of Washington in the early 1930s, he and two other Asian American students were told to forget about a career in journalism. And unlike the rest of their classmates, Hosokawa and the other Asian American students were not given newspaper internships during their junior year of college because, as Hosokawa has recounted, the professors told them "the publishers wouldn't welcome you." After graduating from college in 1937, Hosokawa did, indeed, difficulty finding a publication that would welcome him and he worked as a secretary before taking on some magazine writing work in Asia. A few weeks before Pearl Harbor, Hosokawa returned to Seattle, at which point he and his family were placed in an internment camp in Wyoming. There, he started a weekly newspaper called the *Hart Mountain Sentinel*, stirring up controversy by supporting the Japanese American Citizens League's backing of the U.S. government's internment policy.

After the war, Hosokawa landed a copyediting job at the *Des Moines Register* before getting a job at the *Denver Post* in the mid 1940s. He would become the paper's first war correspondent, assigned to cover the conflict in Korea in 1950. He retired nearly thirty-five years later as the paper's editorial page editor.

Through the years, a number of other mainstream journalists managed to challenge stereotypes and break into newsrooms across the country. A reporter who grew up in Oakland, California's, Chinatown named William Wong, for example, reportedly "broke a color line" by landing a job in the mid-1960s at the *San Francisco Chronicle*, a mainstream daily newspaper in a city with one of the largest Asian American populations. By 1970, he had been hired as a staff reporter for the *Wall Street Journal*, where Wong made an effort to report stories about the Asian American community, including a profile of a Chinese American civil rights group called Chinese for Affirmative Action, and a feature story about how newly arrived Vietnamese refugees were faring in their new home state of California a year after the fall of Saigon.

At about the same time, another young Asian American journalist name Ben Fong-Torres, who was also a pioneer in local radio, began working as a writer and editor of a start-up magazine called *Rolling Stone*, making Fong-Torres one of the first Asian American staffers of a mainstream magazine.

Asian Americans were steadily climbing the ranks within mainstream media, and by 1986, the William Woo, a native of Shanghai, was named editor of the *St. Louis Post-Dispatch*, the first Asian American to assume the top post at a major metropolitan daily newspaper. Woo started at the *Post-Dispatch* as a reporter in 1962, before becoming a foreign correspondent, Washington columnist, editorial writer, and editorial page editor. Woo served as editor for a decade, and after he retired from daily journalism, he taught at Stanford University, University of California at Berkeley, and the University of Hong Kong.

And as Connie Chung was climbing the ranks, other broadcast pioneers included Barbara Tanabe, who began her journalism career in Seattle in 1970 and became one of the first Asian American TV news anchors. A San Francisco journalist named Jan Yanehiro also blazed trails in broadcast by hosting a program called "Evening Magazine." Launched in 1976, Yanehiro, who started her career in radio, helped revolutionize television by introducing the "magazine format" to broadcast.

There have been Asian American pioneers in radio, as well. In 1989, a Filipino reporter named Emil Guillermo became the first Asian American to host National Public Radio's "All Things Considered." In addition, a Vietnam-born journalist named Nguyen Qui Duc began his radio career in 1979, working for outlets such as the BBC and National Public Radio, where he worked as a commentator for "All Things Considered." Nguyen, a published author, has also served as host of "Pacific Time," a first-of-its-kind public radio program covering Asia and Asian Americans, which began broadcasting in November 2000.

By the 1980s, there were about four hundred Asian Americans working in newspapers across the country, and a group of Los Angeles journalists banded together to create the Asian American Journalists Association (AAJA). One of the group's early missions was to increase the ranks of Asian Americans in the profession by encouraging high school and college students to pursue journalism, a goal the organization continues to pursue today by offering scholarships and mentorship programs.

At its first social even, AAJA attracted fifty journalists; now the organization represents thousands of journalists across the country, and continues to nurture Asian Americans in media and management positions, bring attention to the dearth of Asian American men in broadcast, and advocate for more accurate—and less stereotyped—representations of Asian Americans in media. As with many professional journalism organizations, its members continue to debate its proper role within the field—is it a purely professional development organization, or should it also engage in media watchdog activities? The chapters don't always agree.

In one memorable May 1990 incident, *Newsday*'s Pulitzer Prize-winning columnist Jimmy Breslin reportedly shouted racial epithets at a Korean American reporter when she criticized one of his columns as sexist. AAJA's New York Chapter, with author and journalist Helen Zia at the helm, responded by holding a press conference and demanding that *Newsday* fire Breslin. The press conference led to national media coverage of the issue.

The ethnic press and Asian American journalists are also said to bring unique insight or perspective to developing and writing stories related to Asian Americans. For example, the 1982 Vincent Chin murder—a Chinese American was killed by out-of-work auto employees who mistook him for a Japanese American and thus believed that he was somehow responsible for the loss of their jobs—was covered differently by Asian Americans and the Asian ethnic press than by mainstream media. Whereas the mainstream press saw it as an act of random violence, the ethnic press and some Asian American reporters at mainstream outlets reported that the crime had racist undertones by quoting bystanders and witnesses to the crime.

The Asian American press also owes a great deal to the civil rights movement, which was crucial to the development of an "Asian American community." Indeed, the term *Asian American* wasn't coined until the civil rights movement when one activist began popularizing it. Until that point, people of Asian ancestry living in the United States primarily identified as members of an ethnic-specific community. Though this is still certainly the case today, the term *Asian American* has become commonplace. "Asian American," then, is a political construct that arose out of the politically charged 1960s, and this was certainly reflected in early publications dedicated to serving this new community.

The sociopolitical issues of the late 1960s and early 1970s—ranging from the Civil Rights Movement to the anti-Vietnam War effort, to the call for ethnic studies at college campuses—served as the backdrop that led to the creation of the first Asian American publications. Most of these papers and magazines—including *Getting Together* and *New Dawn*—were started by a motley group of students with left-leaning sensibilities who believed that broadcasting their ideas through a publication could help their cause. One of the most notable newspapers of this era was a monthly publication called *Gidra*, founded by a group of University of California at Los Angeles students. The publication modeled itself after the alternative newspapers published by groups such as the Black Panthers and the Young Lords. Run as a true collective, issues of *Gidra* were edited and assembled out of a house in Los Angeles that was also home to a number of the publication's staff. *Gidra*'s eclectic coverage ranged from essays and articles tackling the Vietnam War to cultural coverage, to a controversial how-to piece on fixing toilets that was meant to promote self-reliance among its readers.

Meanwhile, on the East Coast, a group affiliated with New York City Chinatown's Basement Workshop founded *Bridge* magazine, which also sought to offer an Asian American perspective on American politics, current events, and culture. Started in the early 1970s and printing through the mid-1980s, *Bridge* published stories related to Asian American Studies, labor issues, and Asian American representation in the comics, while also serving as a venue for Asian American poets and fiction writers.

At about the same time, a professor at the City College of San Francisco named Gordon Lew decided to start a bilingual newspaper in order to serve the changing population in San Francisco's Chinatown. He called his new enterprise *East West News*.

East West News was a breeding ground for a number of journalists who would go on to do pioneering work in the mainstream press, including *Rolling Stone*'s Ben Fong-Torres and the *Wall Street Journal*'s William Wong. *East West News* aimed to provide balance and bring an independent perspective to issues affecting Chinese Americans. Published weekly, the paper featured news coverage of the antiwar movement, President Richard Nixon's visit to China, as well as a popular and witty column named Manchester Foo, which chronicled the personalities of Chinatown.

Asian American documentary filmmaking was also developing during this time, with Los Angeles media makers forming an organization called Visual Communications in 1970. It was the first organization dedicated to producing Asian American works, and would lead to the development of organizations such as the San Francisco-based National Asian American Telecommunications Association (now called the Asian American Media Center), whose express purpose is to increase Asian American media representation by funding and broadcasting Asian American documentaries and films on public television.

Pan-Asian media efforts were on a steady rise, and in 1979, a newsweekly called *AsianWeek* was founded by a Chinese immigrant named John T. C. Fang, to cover Asian America. Based out of San Francisco, *AsianWeek* continues to be the only English-language weekly publication dedicated to covering Asian American issues. *AsianWeek* is still owned and operated by the Fang family, which would go on to run a neighborhood paper called *The Independent* as well as the *San Francisco Examiner*, which the family purchased amid great controversy from the Hearst Corporation in 2000. Though the Fangs no longer publish the *Examiner*, in its brief and troubled stint as owners and publishers, the Fangs became the first Asian Americans to run a major metropolitan daily newspaper.

In the 1980s, more Asian American publications were started to appeal to this growing demographic, but with an eye toward culture and lifestyle rather than overt politics. In the process, the publications also played a role in defining and articulating what it means to be Asian American. *Yolk* and *A. magazine* were among the best-known Asian American magazines to emerge during this time. *Yolk* had an explicitly entertainment and pop culture bent while *A.*, started in the late 1980s by Asian American media mogul Jeff Yang, became the longest-running, highest profile Asian American publication to date. Glossy and stylish, the magazine was aimed decidedly at a younger Asian American audience—those that had grown up after the term "Asian American" had been developed. *A.* regularly featured fashion spreads, advice columns, horoscopes, as well as news stories.

During the dot-com boom of the 1990s, a number of Web enterprises were developed in hopes of becoming the primary Web portals for Asian American news and culture. Channel A, started in 1996 by a journalist named Steve Chin, was among the most viable, but it folded after financial backing fell through as a result of the Asian financial crisis. Chin later partnered with *A.* magazine to start A Online, but since its inception, the magazine faced financial challenges—Asian American publications have historically been unable to reach profitability—and the cost of maintaining a Web site eventually forced both the Web site and the magazine to fold in 2002.

But glossy magazines continue to thrive since the demise of *A.*, including the Asian indie pop culture zine Giant Robot, women's magazines like *Audrey* and *Jade,* and independent news magazines like *Hyphen*. These publications, which also cater to a younger Asian American audience, represent a shift in Asian American sensibilities among later generations in that they are less explicit about their racial politics. Tackling Asian American issues through prominent personalities and storytelling, rather than addressing racial politics head-on, is also reflected in new English-language TV programs targeted at young Asian Americans such as the now-defunct "Stir," which was developed in 2004 by the International Channel and Jeff Yang, the former publisher of the *A.* magazine.

Mainstream broadcasting companies are also beginning to tap into the Asian American market, which is among the fastest growing in the country. In 2004, MTV announced the launch of MTV Desi, aimed at young Indian Americans. In 2005, MTV China and MTV Korea hit the airwaves, with a target audience of young Chinese American and Korean American viewers.

Further Reading

Chen, Stanford. 1996. *Counting on Each Other: A History of the Asian American Journalists Association from 1981–1996.* San Francisco: Asian American Journalists Association.

Cheng, Mae M. 2003. "Few Asian Males Work for TV News." *USA Today*, January 31, A-15.

Hua, Vanessa. 2006. "William Woo — acclaimed reporter and editor, Stanford professor." *San Francisco Chronicle,* April 13, B-7.

Hubner, John. 2001. "Asian Stereotypes Addressed at Journalists' Event." *San Jose Mercury News*, August 5, 6-B.

Lai, H. M. 1987. "The Chinese American Press," in *The Ethnic Press in the United States: A Historical Analysis and Handbook*, edited by Sally Miller, pp. 27–43. Westport, CT: Greenwood Press.

Kennedy, Randy. 2004. "Asian-American Trendsetting on a Shoestring," *New York Times*, July 5, E-1.

Mansfield-Richardson, Virginia. 2000. *Asian Americans and the Mass Media: A Content Analysis of Twenty United States Newspapers and a Survey of Asian American Journalists.* New York: Garland Publishing.

Matsumoto, Jon. 1998. "Asian Americans Anchor Their Influence." *Los Angeles Times*, September 4, F-2.

Shaw, David. 1990. "Stereotypes Hinder Minorities' Attempts to Reach Managerial Ranks." *Los Angeles Times*, December 13, A-37.

Tachiki, Amy. 1971. *Roots: An Asian American Reader.* Asian American Studies Center: University of California at Los Angeles.

Wong, William. 2001. *Yellow Journalist: Dispatches from Asian America.* Philadelphia: Temple University Press.

Zia, Helen. 2000. *Asian American Dreams: An Emergence of An American People.* New York: Farrar, Straus and Giroux.

Zia, Helen. 2000. "Asian-Americans: From 'Asian invaders' to emergent Americans." *Quill*, May 1, p. 32.

BERNICE YEUNG

ASSOCIATED PRESS

"I backed off about 35 feet. Here the ground sloped down toward the center of a volcanic crater. I quickly piled up some stones and a Jap sandbag to raise me about two feet. I picked up the camera and climbed up on the pile. Out of the corner of my eye, I had seen the men start the flag up. I swung my camera, and shot the scene."

Joe Rosenthal's famous photograph of six soldiers raising the American flag on Iwo Jima after four days of devastating losses would appear on Sunday morning, February 25, 1945, in newspapers across the United States. In one-four hundredth of a second, the Associated Press (1846–) photographer captured the courage and sacrifice of America's war effort and lifted the nation's spirit. The picture was republished in newspapers and magazines over many weeks. The photograph inspired a Marine Corps War Memorial adjacent to Arlington National Cemetery and is seen by some as the greatest news photograph of the twentieth century. The unassuming photographer would win a Pulitzer Prize for his work, one of twenty-nine photographs taken by Associated Press photographers to win the Pulitzer Prize. The news organization's forty-eight Pulitzers attest to its 160 years of preeminence in news gathering.

By the beginning of 2007, Associated Press operated 242 news bureaus worldwide, serving 1,700 newspapers and 5,000 radio and television stations in the United States. In addition, the organization has 8,500 international subscribers in 121 countries, including 330 international broadcasters who receive AP copy in five languages, as well as its video and photographic services, which had grown to an inventory of more than 10 million images. The company's statement of corporate principles claims it was in the business "of bringing truth to the world" by training its 3,700 worldwide employees to "abhor inaccuracies, carelessness, bias, and distortions." In 1914, AP's general manager Melville Stone had said something similar in promising the organization, begun as an effort at cooperative newsgathering by New York publishers, would always "strive for a truthful, unbiased report of the world's happenings." Cutbacks in international coverage by large news organizations "have placed more of the responsibility for global coverage with us," AP's president Tom Curley noted on April 3, 2006. This prompted AP to restructure its international bureaus, creating global editing desks, blogs, and podcasts, increasing its sports coverage and financial information, and creating an AP Online Video network designed "to meet the content challenges of the digital era."

Associated Press was organized in May 1846 when Moses Yale Beach, publisher of the *New York Sun*, and David Hale, publisher of New York's *Journal of Commerce*, persuaded James Gordon Bennett, publisher of the widely circulated *New York Herald*, to join them in a cooperative news gathering venture that quickly focused on reporting war news along the U.S.-Mexican border. Horace Greeley, publisher of the highly respected *New York Tribune*, along with publishers from New York's *Courier and Journal* and the New York *Express* joined the initiative. In 1849, AP's first foreign bureau was established by Daniel Craig in Halifax, Nova Scotia. Craig's team of reporters intercepted ships coming from Europe and telegraphed their news to New York before the ships arrived in port. By 1858, Associated Press transmitted messages received by transoceanic cable.

Associated Press was a major source of information during the Civil War. Its platoons of reporters covered the fighting, filing under the anonymous byline, "from the Associated Press agent." At first, Secretary of War Edwin Stanton attempted to control war reporting by seizing the telegraph office in Washington, D.C.. The determination of AP reporters to file their stories from Baltimore and other sites foiled sustained efforts at military censorship. During military campaigns, President Abraham Lincoln would frequently arrive at a telegraph office near the White House and read Associated Press dispatches of the fighting. Operators remembered his habit of entering and asking, "What news do you have for me?" The president was provided a cot to rest in the telegraph office and eagerly read AP dispatches as they clattered in. On November 19, 1863, AP agent Joseph L. Gilbert took down Lincoln's remarks at the dedication of a military cemetery in Gettysburg, Pennsylvania. Gilbert's reporting became the most reliable account of Lincoln's memorable words that day. An AP agent traveling with the Army of the Potomac was in Appomattox, Virginia, on April 9, 1865, when Confederate General Robert E. Lee surrendered his forces to Union General Ulysses S. Grant. Six days later, AP's Washington correspondent Lawrence Gobright reported the "terrible news" of Lincoln's assassination at Ford's Theater.

The post-Civil War period was a time of rapid growth in the newspaper industry through the twin forces of immigration and industrialization. Associated Press adapted itself to this new environment by securing its first leased wire, a 226-mile circuit between New York, Philadelphia, Baltimore, and Washington, D.C. This permitted the cooperative to move news more rapidly to its expanding roster of clients. On the eve of the American centennial, Associated Press lost its first correspondent to die in the line of duty when stringer Mark Kellogg, filing from the Little Bighorn, wrote, "I go with Custer and will be at the death." As participating newspapers emphasized speed and accuracy in reporting to gain an edge over competing papers, Associated Press experimented with Guglielmo Marconi's wireless telegraph. In 1899 the device was installed on the steamship *Ponce* to radio results of an America's Cup yacht race off Sandy Hook, New Jersey.

AP general manager Melville Stone appreciated the importance of fairness, balance and impartiality in satisfying the social responsibility of the press. He also knew that it was good business. Since AP was sending stories to papers and readers with competing political points of view, AP editors insisted on sourcing, fact-based reporting, and the inverted pyramid in placing the most important part of a story at the head of their copy. This practice promoted objectivity as a core journalistic value. The *Associated Press Stylebook* would sell more than one million copies and be called "the Bible of journalism." During Stone's twenty-eight years of leadership, AP became a highly professional, nonpartisan news service to 1,200 newspapers, filing 70,000 words daily during World War I. Under Stone's successor, Kent Cooper, AP inaugurated news features, wire photos, and teletype to transmit national news at sixty words per minute. AP's annual poll of sports writers to determine the top ten college football teams in the nation was launched in 1935. In 1939, Louis P. Lochner, AP's Berlin bureau chief, won a Pulitzer Prize for his reporting on the rise of Adolf Hitler's Third Reich. In December 1941, as AP was expanding into radio, Lochner was arrested by the Nazis, when the German Foreign Office wired AP the warning "American journalists no longer exist for you." Lochner would later

be released in a prisoner swap. AP's Joe Morton was not so fortunate. He is the only known journalist to have been executed by the Nazis during World War II.

During the cold war, AP's correspondent in Bucharest, Leonard Kirschen, was jailed for ten years by Romanian authorities for alleged spying. AP's Pulitzer Prize winning photographer Frank "Pappy" Noel spent three years in a North Korean prisoner-of-war camp. AP's Prague bureau chief William N. Oatis was jailed for twenty-eight months on espionage charges. Malcolm Browne and Peter Arnett received Pulitzer Prizes for their reporting on the Vietnam War. The war's two most horrific pictures were taken by AP photographers. Eddie Adams photographed a South Vietnamese general executing a Viet Cong prisoner on a Saigon street in 1968. Nick Ut captured the horror of a Vietnamese girl fleeing in terror after a napalm attack in 1973. Both photographs won Pulitzer Prizes and helped mobilize American public opinion against the controversial war effort. In 1985 AP's chief Middle East correspondent Terry Anderson was kidnapped by Islamic militants in Beirut and held for six years and eight months. His return to the United States was itself a major news event. Three AP employees would be killed covering the allied military campaign in Iraq.

Associated Press introduced the first of its filmless digital cameras in 1994. Its global video newsgathering agency, APTV, was launched later that year. Two years later AP opened The Wire, a continuously updated online news service combining texts, photos, audio and video news. Thomas Curley, former publisher of Gannett's *USA Today*, followed Louis D. Boccardi in 2003 as AP chief and has emphasized "adapting to the new digital media marketplace." This has meant "creating more content for the digital era, not less," improving the accessibility of AP reporting through better search engines, while relying on AP's core values of "being first and being accurate."

Further Reading

Alabiso, Vincent. Kelly Smith Tunney, and Chuck Zoeller. *Flash! The Associated Press Covers the World*. New York: Henry N. Abrams, 1998.

Cooper, Kent. *Kent Cooper and the Associated Press: An Autobiography*. New York: Random House, 1959.

Gramling, Oliver. *AP: The Story of News*. New York: Farrar and Rinehart, 1940.

Rosewater, Victor. *History of Cooperative News-gathering in the United States*. New York: D. Appleton, 1930.

Schwarzlose, Richard A. *The American Wire Services: A Study of Their Development as a Social Institution*. New York: Arno Press, 1979, originally 1965.

Shaw, Donald L. "News Bias and the Telegraph: A Study of Historical Change." *Journalism Quarterly* 44 (Spring 1967): 3–12, 31.

Stone, Melville E. "The Associated Press," a five part series in *Century* 69 (April 1905): 888–95; 70 (May 1905): 143–151; (June 1905): 299–310; (July 1905): 379–86; and (Aug.1905): 504–10.

BRUCE J. EVENSEN

ATLANTA JOURNAL-CONSTITUTION

The history of the *Atlanta Journal-Constitution* reflects more than a century of change in the evolution of newspaper journalism. Personal and often politically aligned publications moved through consolidation, competing new media forms, and changes in American life that in turn changed media use.

The starting point of a now-hyphenated newspaper nameplate came during Reconstruction with the purchase of the *Atlanta Daily Opinion* by Carey Wentworth Styles in 1868, along with his partners James H. Anderson and W. A. Hemphill. He immediately renamed it the *Atlanta Constitution*. By 1876, Hemphill became the controlling stockholder and in the same year sold a half-interest in the company to Evan P. Howell, a lawyer and Confederate Army veteran. The Howell name figured prominently in ownership and editorial leadership until the mid-twentieth century.

1876 proved to be a pivotal year for the *Constitution*. Howell was named editor-in-chief and proved to have an eye for picking writers and editors who would make the *Constitution* successful. In that year he hired Henry Woodfin Grady as managing editor and Joel Chandler Harris as associate editor. Both were young but experienced journalists; both had developed reputations for their work in Georgia journalism.

Grady, born in Athens, Georgia, in 1850, began his writing career at the *Rome Courier* and held part ownership with Robert Alston and Alexander St. Clair Adams in the *Atlanta Daily Herald*. That paper carried his milestone editorial on "The New South" in March 1874, advocating industrial development as a cure for the post-Civil War economic woes of the region. Along with his editorial position, Grady purchased a quarter interest in the newspaper from Howell.

While Grady earned a degree from the University of Georgia before launching his journalism career, Harris entered journalism and the literary world as an apprentice printer on a plantation near Eatonton. At the age of sixteen, he was hired by Joseph Addison Turner on Turnwold, home of the only plantation newspaper during the Civil War. His mentor's work immersed him in journalism and both American and British literature. From Turnwold, he moved to printing and editorial positions in Macon and Forsyth before being hired as associate editor of the *Savannah Morning News* in 1870. He also began to publish literary fiction, culminating in the Uncle Remus tales which were first published in the *Constitution* in 1878. Harris had earlier heard these stories told by plantation slaves and his recounting of them, which by the time of his death in 1908 had amounted to ten volumes, led to national recognition and readership that made him as well known as Mark Twain.

In 1886 Evan Howell's son Clark joined the editorial staff after graduating from the University of Georgia and working as a reporter in Philadelphia and New York. His training continued under Grady and Harris. Grady was by then known as a spokesman from the New South, much in demand on the northern speaking circuit. Complications from a cold that developed during a speaking engagement in Boston led to his death in 1889. By then young Howell was ready to assume the role of managing editor. Thus began one of the longest terms of a newspaper under one editorial leader. Howell was essentially in charge of the newspaper until he died in 1936. The Howell family ownership of the newspaper continued until 1950.

Howell was active in the Democratic Party, serving in the Georgia House and Senate for a number of years. His public political life ended in the gubernatorial campaign of 1906, when a bitter primary race pitted him against the owner of the archrival competing newspaper, The *Atlanta Journal*. This newspaper was established as an evening competitor to the morning *Constitution* by lawyer and politician Edward F. Hoge in 1883 and purchased shortly thereafter by Hoke Smith, then an Atlanta lawyer. Both Howell and Smith were ardent segregationists, with Howell viewed as softer on racial issues by Georgia voters. Howell's loss to Smith did not remove him from activity as a Democratic convention delegate and party leader.

The newspapers were editorially aggressive under Howell, conducting campaigns against the convict lease system, supporting the acceptance of refugees from yellow fever epidemics in the Southeast, and opposing a bill that would have outlawed football at the University of Georgia after a player died. The two newspapers were editorially innovative and sought out promising journalists who flourished in Atlanta or moved on to greater recognition elsewhere. Sports writing legend Grantland Rice wrote for the *Journal* in 1902, and Margaret ("Peggy") Mitchell began her writing career on the *Journal* magazine in 1922. The first staff photographs—taken by Francis E. Price of a cross-country auto race–appeared in 1909.

Howell hired a young man named Ralph McGill as sports editor in 1929, thus launching the career of a future Pulitzer Prize winner and national opinion leader. McGill switched to political reporting in the 1930s, won a fellowship for overseas study, and became executive editor in 1938. That year he began writing a regular column, completing an estimated 10,000 before his death in 1969. He was elevated to editor-in-chief in 1941 and publisher in 1960, all the while continuing to churn out news, columns, and editorials. His 1959 Pulitzer Prize was awarded for columns and editorials on tolerance and peaceful integration, with a front-page editorial on October 13, 1958, titled "A Church, A School." It was written in the wake of bombings of a synagogue in Atlanta and elsewhere in the South.

That Pulitzer was one of nine earned by the *Constitution* between 1931 and 2006. The first was prompted by an investigation lead by Howell into municipal graft. Others were awarded for editorial writing, local reporting, investigative reporting, and explanatory journalism. The *Journal* was honored with a Pulitzer in 1948 for stories on municipal fraud in South Georgia.

Former Ohio Governor James M. Cox expanded his growing newspaper empire into the South by buying the

Journal and WSB Radio for $3,156,350 in 1939. In March 1950 he acquired the *Constitution* from Clark Howell Jr. and combined the two newspapers' Sunday editions. The daily editions of the two newspapers remained independent until they were combined in 1982. Although the *Journal* led the *Constitution* at one point, the circulation of the evening *Journal* began to slide along with that of many other evening newspapers across the country. A version of the *Journal*, essentially the *Constitution* with a few pages made over for an evening edition, was published until November 2001 when the nameplates were combined into their present form—the *Atlanta Journal-Constitution*—with the editorial pages and policies dominated by the more liberal stance of the *Constitution*'s editorialists.

The newspaper is one of the largest holdings of the parent company, Atlanta-based Cox Enterprises, whose interests span newspapers and other print products, radio, television, and cable. They have attempted to meet the challenge of changing readership and media forms with an aggressive presence on the Internet and continue to be among the largest newspapers in the country. In 2006, they were the thirteenth largest Sunday paper in the nation with a circulation of 561,405. The daily edition was ranked fifteenth largest with a circulation of 365,011.

Further Reading

Buckley, R. Bruce Jr. *Joel Chandler Harris: A Biography and Critical Study.* Athens: University of Georgia Press, 1987.

Brasch, Walter M. *Brer Rabbit, Uncle Remus, and the 'Cornfield Journalist': The Tale of Joel Chandler Harris.* Macon, GA: Mercer University Press, 2000.

Bryan, Ferald J. *Henry Grady or Tom Watson? The Rhetorical Struggle for the New South, 1880–1890.* Macon, GA: Mercer University Press, 1994.

Cebula, James E. *James M. Cox: Journalist and Politician.* New York: Garland, 1985.

Clowse, Barbara Barksdale. *Ralph McGill: A Biography.* Macon, GA: Mercer University Press, 1998.

Davis, Harold E. *Henry Grady's New South: Atlanta, a Brave Beautiful City.* Tuscaloosa: University of Alabama Press, 1990.

Glover, Charles E. *Journey Through Our Years: The Story of Cox Enterprises, Inc.* Atlanta: Longstreet Press, 1998.

Grantham, Dewey W. *Hoke Smith and the Politics of the New South.* Baton Rouge: Lousiana State University Press, 1958.

Pfennig, Dennis J. "The Captain Retires: Clark Howell Takes the Helm," *Atlanta Historical Journal* 25 (Summer 1980): 5–20.

Teel, Leonard Ray. *Ralph Emerson McGill: Voice of the Southern Conscience.* Knoxville: University of Tennessee Press, 2001.

WALLACE B. EBERHARD

ATLANTIC MONTHLY

If there is such a thing as an elite of informed opinion in the United States, it has been on display for a long time in the pages of the *Atlantic Monthly* (1857–). Time and again, the *Atlantic* has been a place where accomplished journalists, writers, policy analysts, and political leaders have published opinion leading articles, insightful critiques, and breakthrough works of fiction.

This attribute was present from the *Atlantic's* very beginning in 1857 when it was founded in Boston by a group of intellectuals with ties to Harvard College whose intellectual and social credentials gave the publication considerable influence. Their magazine was to be a "journal of literature, politics, science, and the arts." This remarkably prominent group included Oliver Wendell Holmes, a physician and poet, who coined the term, anesthesia. He has also been credited with helping to save the *USS Constitution* with his popular poem "Old Ironsides." Holmes was the father of Oliver Wendell Holmes Jr., who became an influential Chief Justice on the U.S. Supreme Court. It was Holmes senior who came up with the name for the magazine.

Other prominent writers and editors were associated with the magazine. Henry Wadsworth Longfellow, whose works included "The Song of Hiawatha" and "Evangeline," gave his countrymen a mythic literature about the past and earned the love of his contemporaries and successors. Ralph Waldo Emerson, who embodied and articulated the energy, optimism, and hopes of emerging modern liberal thought, appeared in the publication's pages. The first editor, James Russell Lowell, was a poet and essayist who later served as ambassador to Britain and Spain. As editor, he realized the founders' vision by publishing American writers who were both emerging talents and established authors.

The *Atlantic* had a high-minded mission. In the first issue's "Declaration of Purpose," the magazine said that in politics, it would "be the organ of no party or clique, but will honestly endeavor to be the exponent of what its conductors believe to be the American idea. It will deal frankly with persons and with parties, endeavoring always to keep in view that moral element which transcends all persons and parties, and which alone makes the basis of a true and lasting prosperity. It will not rank itself with any sect ... but with that body of men which is in favor of Freedom, National Progress, and Honor, whether public or private."

The magazine's ideals were energized and directed by the passions and character of the Boston literati who founded it. The *Atlantic* supported the abolitionist movement. In the events leading up to the Civil War and during that conflict, the *Atlantic* provided a platform for activists. Julia Ward Howe's "Battle Hymn of the Republic" first appeared there in 1862. Frederick Douglass, the former slave and eloquent advocate of freedom for his race, appeared several times in the *Atlantic* as did other abolitionist advocates. As their contemporaries saw service in the war, the magazine posted stories from the front.

The centrality of abolition and the Civil War to the magazine's early years is revealed in an episode involving Nathaniel Hawthorne, a contemporary of the magazine's founders and the author of *The Scarlet Letter*. When he submitted a story that was not entirely supportive of the wartime cause and its leadership, his piece was subjected to heavy editing. Frustrated, Hawthorne complained to the editors, "The political complexion of the Magazine has been getting too deep a black Republican tinge."

After the war, the problems of citizenship for the former slaves, reconstruction of the south, and the spread of modern capitalism added reality to the idealism of the early years of the magazine. The *Atlantic* attempted to publish articles that reflected the most current ideas and literature. Henry James and Mark Twain were given space as were Theodore Roosevelt and Woodrow Wilson who published essays in the *Atlantic* before they became presidents of the United States. In 1897, the magazine published John Muir's "The American Forest," which contributed to the establishment of Yosemite as the first national park and the U.S. Forest Service. In 1927, the *Atlantic* bought "Fifty Grand," written by Ernest Hemingway.

In subsequent years, the magazine continued to publish material of contemporary importance. Albert Einstein wrote on nuclear technology and the future. George F. Kennan, the architect of the cold war foreign policy of containment, serialized his memoirs and diaries in the *Atlantic*. Late in 1981, David Stockman, President Reagan's director of the Office of Management and Budget, found himself at the epicenter of the Ronald Reagan administration's efforts to alter the federal government's role in the economy. He also found himself in political hot water after the publication of William Greider's *Atlantic* article on "The Education of David Stockman," which revealed that Stockman had doubts about Reagan administration policies.

The *Atlantic* remained a prominent outlet for opinion in the aftermath of the attacks of September 11, 2001, and during the George W. Bush administration's War on Terror. To cover this period and its global implications, both military and political, the magazine had such able staffers as James Fallows and Robert Kaplan and the leadership of Editor Michael Kelly (1957–2003), who died while on assignment in Iraq. William Langewiesche, a former pilot, also earned a place on the masthead with his powerful three-part series, "American Ground," on the recovery of the area around the World Trade Center that appeared in July of 2002. Based on exclusive access to the site, Langewiesche's writings were published as a book about what the author called a "uniquely American improvisation on an enormous scale." In 2002, Langewiesche joined six other *Atlantic Monthly* contributors who were winners of National Magazine Awards. In 2006 the magazine led the industry with 8 of 115 finalists for the prize with wins in General Excellence, Reporting, Public Interest, Feature Writing, Reviews and Criticism, and Fiction. In January, 2006, under the ownership of David Bradley, the magazine which for 148 years had been in Boston, published its first issue from Washington, DC.

Further Reading

Howe, De Wolfe. *The Atlantic Monthly and its Makers.* Boston: The Atlantic MonthlyPress, 1919.

Menand, Louis. *The Metaphysical Club.* New York: Farrar, Straus and Giroux, 2001.

Sedgwick, Ellery. *The Atlantic Monthly, 1857–1909: Yankee Humanism at High Tide and Ebb.* Amherst: University of Massachusetts Press, 1994.

PETER W QUIGLEY

B

BAKER, RAY STANNARD

"I wanted to know what *I* should do to save the world," Ray Stannard Baker (1870–1946) wrote, when remembering what drew him to a career as one of the Progressive Period's greatest muckraking journalists. Baker admitted "my part in developing the so-called literature of exposure." From the first, his hope had been "to train my eyes, brain and hand" to "set forth the facts as I saw them." What emerged was a journalism "extraordinarily aware of the newness in the world" that featured "an awakening sympathy for the world's down-trodden and oppressed" (*American Chronicle*, 31, 33, 40, 66, and 92).

Baker's moralism was a legacy from a long line of public servants. Captain Remember Baker, his great-great-grandfather, had served with a cousin, General Ethan Allen, during the Revolutionary War. His father Joseph Stannard Baker was a Civil War major captured by the Confederates. Major Baker married Alice Potter, and the two raised their family on "the essential truths of Christianity" and a Presbyterian certainty that "in the sweat of thy face thou shalt eat bread" (*American Chronicle*, 2 and 57). Ray Stannard Baker was born in Lansing, Michigan, and raised in St. Croix, Wisconsin. After graduating Michigan Agricultural College, Baker reported on social unrest for Victor Lawson's liberally minded *Chicago News-Record*. Baker's sympathetic coverage of a worker's march on Washington in 1893 and the Pullman strike in Chicago a year later, deepened his social activism. The widely publicized efforts of British reformer William Stead to clean up Chicago's vice, intensified Baker's sense of mission, an attitude encouraged by Jessie Irene Beal, the daughter of his botany professor, whom he married in 1896. The couple would have four children.

In the spring of 1898, Baker joined the staff of *McClure's Magazine*. Initially, he wrote admiringly of Teddy Roosevelt and the Rough Riders and America's imperial mission in the world. Domestic stories were less idealistic. He uncovered labor and business alliances in the in the building trades, the beef trust, the fruit industry, and within municipal governments that gouged consumers. His work on illegal railway rebates later led to passage of the Hepburn Act that strengthened the ability of the Interstate Commerce Commission to oversee rail rates. In October 1902 Baker arrived in Wilkes-Barre, Pennsylvania, to investigate the strong arm tactics used by the United Mine Workers to ter-rorize seventeen thousand anthracite coal miners who had refused to strike. He visited the miners in their homes and at their meetings and told their story in the January 1903 edition of *McClure's*, the issue that made the magazine the preeminent muckraking magazine of America's Progressive period. He told the tale of Abraham Price, a Dorrance Colliery engineer, who had "his eyes put out" because he "believed a man should have a right to work when and where he pleases." Non-striker John Snyder had his home looted and burned. "Assaulters pounded James Winstone to their satisfaction," killing him. Mob rule risked becoming "an American way of life" (*Muckraking: Three Landmark Articles*, 81–102).

In the fall of 1904 Baker began his investigation of racism in America by reporting on the lynching of African Americans in Alabama, Georgia, Illinois, and Ohio. His articles in the January and February 1905 issues of *McClure's* were an indictment of mob violence. Baker continued "following the color line" in a series of articles published throughout 1908 by *American Magazine*, a publication he edited and partly owned. He revealed unrelenting reasons for "the ocean of antagonism between the white and Negro races in this country" (Baker, *Following the Color Line*, xv and 3). "The Negro is inferior and must be made to keep his place," a Southern white explained to Baker. Behind the remark stood a "good old boy" network linking magistrates to mayors and bankers and businessmen who profited from the chain gang. Baker found that a lack of educational and economic opportunities had created a generation of hopelessness (*Following the Color Line*, 46–47 and 88–89). Baker's hope was that in "presenting a picture of conditions as they were," America's "social conscience" would be stirred so that no one would be barred from the nation's spiritual and material progress (Baker Papers. Library of Congress. Notebook C, 36–38 and Notebook J, 116–118).

By the time Baker left *American Magazine* in 1915 his reputation as one of the nation's outstanding reporters and most prolific authors was well established. In addition to more than two hundred magazine articles, he had become a novelist, whose work under the pen name David Grayson, sold more than two million copies. The books saw the full flowering of Baker's Emersonian idealism through fictionalized, first person, pastoral narratives that expressed "the invisible life which in every man is so far more real, so far more important, than his visible activities" (*David Grayson, Great Possessions*, xi). That moralism made him an eager advocate of Woodrow Wilson's "New Freedom," and its efforts on behalf of child laborers and displaced workers. Baker accompanied Wilson to the Paris Peace Conference in 1919, where he directed the American delegation's press bureau. Baker strongly defended Wilson's League of Nations in a three-volume work *Woodrow Wilson and World Settlement* that urged readers "to make sacrifices of immediate interest for future benefits" (viii).

Baker edited Wilson's public papers and for fifteen years worked on Wilson's authorized biography. The eight-volume work was awarded the Pulitzer Prize for biography in 1940. At his passing, editorial writers eulogized "a man at home in his era and anxious to explore it to the end" (*New York Times*, July 13, 1946, 14). That era gave birth to a progressive impulse in which journalists, in Baker's view, attempted to awaken readers to "a great wind of moral force moving through the world" that encouraged "just men everywhere" to exercise "good-will as the true foundation of a civilized society" (*World Settlement*, 522).

Further Reading

Baker, Ray Stannard. *American Chronicle: The Autobiography of Ray Stannard Baker*, New York: Charles Scribner's Sons, 1945.

——. *Following the Color Line*, New York: Harper & Row, 1964, originally 1908.

——. *The New Industrial Unrest: Reasons and Remedies*, New York: Arno Press, 1971, originally 1920.

——. *The Spiritual Unrest*, New York: Frederick A. Stokes, 1909.

——. *Woodrow Wilson and World Settlement*, Gloucester, MA: Peter Smith, 1960, originally 1922.

Bannister, Robert C. *Ray Stannard Baker: The Mind and Thought of a Progressive*, New Haven: Yale University, 1966.

Chalmers, David M., "Ray Stannard Baker's Search for Reform." *Journal of the History of Ideas* 19, June 1958.

Evensen, Bruce J. "The Evangelical Origins of the Muckrakers." *American Journalism* 6 (1989).

——. "The Media and Reform, 1900–1917." In *The Age of Mass Communication*, edited by Wm. David Sloan. Northport: AL: Vision Press, 1998.

——. "Progressivism, Muckraking and Objectivity." In *Fair & Balanced: A History of Journalistic Objectivity*, edited by Steven R. Knowlton and Karen L. Freeman. Northport, AL: Vision Press, 2005.

Fitzpatrick, Ellen F., ed., *Muckraking: Three Landmark Articles*. Boston: Bedford Books, 1994.

Grayson, David. *Great Possessions*. Garden City: Doubleday, Page, 1917.

Papers of Ray Stannard Baker. Collections of Baker's letters and notebooks can be found in the Library of Congress, Washington, D.C.; the Princeton University Library; the Jones Library in Amherst, Massachusetts; and the Perkins School of Theology at Southern Methodist University.

Semonche, John E. *Ray Stannard Baker: A Quest for Democracy in Modern America, 1870–1918*. Chapel Hill: University of North Carolina, 1969.

Weinberg, Arthur, and Lila Weinberg, eds. *The Muckrakers: The Era in Journalism That Moved America to Reform*. New York: G.P. Putnam's Sons, 1961.

BRUCE J. EVENSEN

BARTON, BRUCE

Renowned as an advertising man, writer on religion, and political figure (he advised presidents, served three years in the House of Representatives and ran for the U.S. Senate in 1940), Bruce Barton (1886–1967) is seldom remembered for his many exploits in journalism.

Born in Tennessee, where his father was a circuit-riding minister, he spent much of his youth in Oak Park, Illinois. He edited his high school newspaper and was a cub reporter for the *Oak Park Oak Leaves*. After graduation from Amherst College, he took a job in 1907 as a jack-of-all-trades for a Chicago publisher of three "household" magazines, including the *Home Herald*. This and his next job in publishing evaporated when the companies failed.

He found a more secure niche in 1912 as assistant sales manager for P. F. Collier & Sons. He supervised the sales force but also composed ads, including a paragon for the Harvard Classics that pictured Marie Antoinette en route to the guillotine. From 1908 on, he wrote for various magazines, church and secular. Some articles detailed efforts to carry the Social Gospel to the urban poor. He penned fiction and nonfiction, signed, pseudonymous, and anonymous. His interviews of luminaries like historian-novelist H. G. Wells, President Woodrow Wilson, and British Prime Minister David Lloyd George drew particular notice.

Editing *Every Week* marked Barton's journalistic zenith. In 1915 he took charge of the Crowell Publishing Company's Sunday supplement. When wartime newsprint prices spiked, newspapers canceled it; Barton countered by adding pithy homilies—for which he had a gift—and fiction and marketed *Every Week* at newsstands on the theory that a customer buying a two-cent daily would part with the rest of his nickel for the magazine. His chief innovation was the captioned two-page picture spread—photo essays of a kind popularized in the 1930s by *Life*. (When a man later sued Henry Luce for taking the idea from him, Luce refuted the claim by bringing back issues of *Every Week* to court.)

As the war ground on, Crowell gave up on *Every Week* in 1918. Barton next ran a national fund-raising drive for seven social-service agencies ministering to America's doughboys. In this endeavor he met Alex F. Osborn and Roy S. Durstine, with whom he founded the advertising agency Barton, Durstine & Osgood in 1919.

At BDO (BBDO after a 1928 merger with the George Batten Agency), Barton at first worked without salary—he survived by writing prolifically for outlets like *American Magazine* and *Ladies Home Journal*. At times he produced a column, often filled with upbeat, inspirational sketches. *Redbook* and later *American Magazine* ran such pieces. He had a column with the McClure Syndicate (1926–1932), the *New York Herald-Tribune* (1932–1934), and the *New York American* (1935–1936). He wrote several books on religious topics; the most famous was his 1925 best-selling depiction of Jesus, *The Man Nobody Knows*.

His great journalistic coup was an exclusive 1926 interview for the AP with President Calvin Coolidge, a folksy colloquy (much edited by both men) at the Coolidge's Adirondack summer vacation home. He won unprecedented permission to quote Coolidge directly, outraging reporters on the White House beat. The excuse was that the piece addressed human interest, not policy. Sensing early on the importance of "personality" in politics, Barton had done much to humanize Coolidge in the media; the interview no doubt rewarded such services.

Journalism always intrigued Barton. He once looked into purchasing a Boston paper. In 1946 he bought an interest in the Phoenix papers owned by his friend Eugene Pulliam. He continued writing for magazines, including *Reader's Digest* and the *Saturday Evening Post,* and from 1949 to 1955 authored a column for King Features. He ended it once convinced that his "hope and hustle" emphasis had lost its erstwhile appeal. "Youth" had always been a key theme in his writings; with age, he sensed he could no longer connect with that group. He died in 1967.

Further Reading

Fried, Richard M. *The Man Everybody Knew: Bruce Barton and Modern America.* (Chicago: Ivan R. Dee, 2005.
Ribuffo, Leo. "Jesus Christ as Business Statesman: Bruce Barton and the Selling of Corporate Capitalism." *American Quarterly* 33 (Summer 1981).

RICHARD M. FRIED

BASEBALL JOURNALISM

On a sunny, late summer day in 1857, men in top hats escorted women under parasols to the edge of a clearing in Hoboken, New Jersey, to watch a baseball game between the Eagles and the Gothams. The engraving in the September 12th edition of *Porter's Spirit of the Times* is the oldest known illustration of baseball in an American periodical. Baseball and journalism since that day have enjoyed a long and mutually satisfying relationship. Newspapers and magazines used baseball to stimulate circulation. And baseball used journalism to become "the national pastime" even though baseball's origins precede America's settlement.

Brooklyn's Henry Chadwick, an enthusiastic cricketer, began playing baseball in 1847 and reporting on games for the *Long Island Star.* Over the next decade as fifty clubs began playing baseball in the New York City area, Chadwick became convinced that the speed and the excitement of the game made it the perfect "national sport for Americans." Chadwick reported baseball for the *New York Times,* beginning in 1856, developed a box score for the sports weekly *New York Clipper* that allowed readers to understand what had happened in the game at a glance. Fans following the Knickerbockers and their challengers, the Gothams, Eagles, Empires, Excelsiors, and Atlantics, could measure one player's performance against another's. These benchmarks created a common language across generations that enabled the devoted to talk about a player's "greatness". On December 5, 1856, Sunday's *New York Mercury* noted this rage to play in calling baseball "the national past-time."

Porter's Spirit of the Times reported that Brooklyn was fast becoming "not a city of churches" but "the city of baseball clubs." In March 1858, fourteen clubs from Brooklyn and Manhattan formed the National Association of Base Ball Players. On July 20, 1858, several thousand fans gathered at Fashion Race Course near Flushing, New York, and paid fifty cents to see their favorite all stars compete in what the *New York Times* considered "a noble and invigorating game." In October of the following year *Harper's Weekly* predicted baseball would soon crowd out cricket as the national game.

Sixty clubs joined the baseball association by the summer of 1860. The *New York Illustrated News* on August 4, 1860, celebrated the "national pastime" as a "manly sport." It observed that "diseased people commit murders, arson, rapes and robberies," but baseball was "good for public health and morals" because "the exercise produced robust fellows with sound stomachs and well-developed muscles." Baseball promoted continuity even in the midst of bitter sectional conflict. Clubs across the country continued playing the game, and soldiers with bats in their rucksacks helped spread the sport throughout training camps, war prisons, and behind the front lines. The *New York Clipper* reported in January 1862 that Union generals encouraged troops to play baseball to "alleviate the monotony of camp life." Spalding reported that many Southerners learned the game in prisoner-of-war camps. Will Irwin would later report in *Collier's Weekly* that prisoners from different states would choose up sides. Chadwick spoke for many when he wrote in the *New York Herald* of his hope that baseball's broad appeal might one day encourage national reconciliation.

Professional baseball was born in civic humiliation. The Cincinnati Base Ball Club, formed just after the war, was trounced the following year by the barnstorming Washington Nationals. The *Cincinnati Daily Times* of June 26, 1868 demanded that municipal pride be restored through "just respect for western talent and skill." Harry Wright, a local jeweler, became manager of the Red Stockings, recruited top talent to the team by raiding other teams and publicly paid them to take on top contenders the following year in the East. Chadwick's highly successful baseball weekly *The Ball Players Chronicle,* joined by New York's *National Chronicle,* deplored play for pay, but *Harper's Weekly* observed that paying certain players had long been baseball's poorly kept secret. The rampaging Red Stockings were a commercial spectacle, traveling eleven thousand miles in 1869, winning fifty-six games and tying one. Henry M. Millar, who covered the team for the *Cincinnati Commercial,* became the Reds publicity man, and carefully cultivated the image of a team trained to military perfection. President Grant and much of his cabinet were on hand when the Reds beat the Nationals 24–8. When word was wired to Cincinnati there was celebration in the streets.

The creation on March 17, 1871, of the National Association of Professional Base Ball Players was front page news in New York, Brooklyn, Boston, Chicago, Philadelphia, Cleveland, and Washington, the central cities in the new alliance. *Harper's* and *Frank Leslie's Illustrated Newspaper* gave the league national exposure, but betting and bribery, particularly on New York Mutual games, sunk the league's reputation, the *Chicago Tribune* calling it "a palpable and unbelievable fraud." On February 2, 1876, William Hulbert, a Chicago civic booster, met with seven other businessmen at New York's Grand Central Hotel, and announced the creation of the National League, making very clear to a *New York Times* reporter that the new league has "nothing whatever to do with the old National Association." Competing leagues, the American Association in 1881, the Union Association in 1884, and the Players League in 1890 challenged the National League's salary ceiling and reserve clause that bound players to certain teams. Rivalries were created and sometimes fought in the press. Oliver Perry Caylor, veteran editor of the *Cincinnati Enquirer*, organized the Cincinnati Red Stockings whose principal opponent was the St. Louis Brown Stockings that were the creation of Canadian-born Alfred M. Spink. Spink's passion for promotion would lead him in the winter of 1886 to start *The Sporting News*, long a leading authority on baseball.

The National League's management-owned teams worked closely with the local press to build a star system designed to keep the customers coming. In this they were greatly aided by ball players who became sports writers. The best known of these was Tim Murnane, a light-hitting first baseman/outfielder on Boston and Providence, who became a leading baseball booster in the pages of the *Boston Globe*. Some baseball writers were rewarded for their enthusiasm by important jobs in professional baseball. Ford Frick began his apprenticeship as a baseball writer for the Hearst Press and its newly minted sports section. Frick would later become president of the National League and Baseball Commissioner. Baseball executives and sports writers worked together to give the game a big buildup. The league's biggest star was Michael J. "King" Kelly. The *New York Clipper* wrote that Kelly's "wonderful quickness in desperate situations" endeared him to fans. Kelly had helped pace the White Stockings to five league championships with his league leading hitting and run scoring. He patented the hit and run, baiting umpires, stealing signs, backing up throws, and as catcher, finger signs to pitchers and throwing out opposing runners. Kids fought over his baseball card.

The National League finally met its match in 1903, when the American League joined the senior circuit to re-create the Major Leagues with October's season-ending World Series classic. Ban Johnson, a sports writer and editor on the *Cincinnati Commercial-Gazette*, and Charles Comiskey, eventual owner of the Chicago White Sox, were the driving forces behind the merger. The National League's determination to cap salaries at $2,400, led more than one hundred players to jump to the American League at the start of the 1901 season, including Boston's Cy Young, Philadelphia's Nap Lajoie, and "Wee" Willie Keeler. The American League's family-friendly, star-laden lineups were a hit with fans and were puffed in the press. In 1902, American League teams in Philadelphia, St. Louis, Boston, Chicago, Cleveland, Washington, Detroit, and Baltimore

outdrew National League clubs in Pittsburgh, Brooklyn, Boston, Cincinnati, Chicago, St. Louis, Philadelphia, and New York by more than half a million. The *New York Times* on August 20, 1903, predicted the end of "the baseball war" would lead to the "perpetuation of baseball as the National pastime of America." A gifted group of sports writers—Heywood Broun, Ring Lardner, Grantland Rice, Damon Runyon and Paul Gallico—nationally syndicated their celebration of the sport.

The Chicago Cubs were the first dominant team in the expanded Major Leagues, appearing in four of the first seven World Series, winning two. In eight years the team's net worth soared from $125,000 to $780,000. Baseball was becoming big business. Baseball's "dead ball era" was dominated by pitching, speed, and a few determined, superior players, chief among these were Walter "Big Train" Johnson, Detroit's Ty Cobb, Tris Speaker, an icon in Boston and Cleveland, Christy Mathewson of the New York Giants, and Grover Cleveland Alexander, who played with the Phillies, Cubs, and Cardinals. The Giants John J. McGraw and Connie Mack of the A's and Phillies were the most publicized managers of the period.

The press was initially reluctant to report what it suspected about eight members of the Chicago White Sox who were later indicted for throwing the 1919 World Series. Puffing paid and tearing down sports celebrities did not. Babe Ruth got star treatment as the greatest home run hitter of the 1920s. Ruth helped make the New York Yankees the dominant team of the century. The team began life in the American League as the Highlanders and was first called the "Yankees" in William Randolph Hearst's *New York Journal* on April 14, 1904. The team would win thirty-nine pennants and twenty-six World Series over the next century under managers Miller Huggins, Joe McCarthy, Casey Stengel, Ralph Houk, Billy Martin and Joe Torre. The Columbia Broadcasting System bought the team for $11.2 million, and sold it to a Cleveland shipbuilder, George Steinbrenner, for $10 million in 1973. In the three decades since, Steinbrenner increased the team's payroll to $200 million and its estimated net worth to $730 million. For seven consecutive years the team drew more than three million fans to Yankee Stadium, "the house that Ruth built." In 2005 its attendance topped four million. The team was rich enough to launch its own cable network.

The Yankees were not baseball's only success story. Branch Rickey's decision in 1947 to desegregate major league baseball by bringing Jackie Robinson to the Brooklyn Dodgers, opened the gates to Henry Aaron, Ernie Banks, Roberto Clemente, Willie Mays, Frank Robinson and an extraordinary group of African American athletes. Wonderfully talented Latin players would follow. Baseball became an international spectacle with an infusion of talent from Japan and Korea. Popular excitement was captured and promoted by network television. Ted Turner purchased the Atlanta Braves to launch Turner Broadcasting System in the 1970s. The *Chicago Tribune* bought the Chicago Cubs to market their cable network in the 1980s. In 1998, News Corporation, owned by Rupert Murdoch acquired the Los

Angeles Dodgers for $311 million with plans to start a cable sports station in Southern California. Two years later, $323 million would be paid for the Cleveland Indians. It would take $700 million to purchase the Boston Red Sox in 2002 and feature them on a New England cable sports network.

For generations, sports writers were seen as arbiters of baseball greatness and a fan's connection to a favorite team. The Baseball Writers Association in 1931 began its annual selection of Most Valuable Players in the American and National Leagues. Two years later, Arch Ward, a baseball writer on the *Chicago Tribune*, came up with the idea of an All-Star Game to promote the Chicago World's Fair. The spectacle has been an annual event on the sports calendar ever since. In 1947, baseball writers devised a rookie-of-the-year award. The Cy Young Award, honoring the best pitcher in baseball, was the brainchild of Ford Frick and has been the annual selection of baseball writers. Jerome Holtzman, a long-time Chicago sports writer, came up with the idea of "saves" for relievers.

During the second half of the twentieth century, baseball writers had to compete with baseball broadcasters as the ultimate authority on the game and its conduit to fans. Red Smith, Ric Roberts, Jim Murray, Bob Broeg, Bob Burns, Dick Young, Leonard Koppett, and Thomas Boswell contended with radio and television commentators for their take on the game. Peter Gammons of the *Boston Globe* transitioned to reporting for the sports cable network ESPN. Curt Gowdy, the voice of the Boston Red Sox from 1951 to 1965, had preceded Gammons to network baseball broadcasting on the National Broadcasting Company. In modern free agency, players came and went, but the broadcast voice of teams became a fan's point of contact with the team, an affection and affiliation that is felt across generations, wherever the voices were heard. In New York, Red Barber was the voice of the Dodgers and then the Yankees. Mel Allen broadcast the Yanks for thirty-eight years. Bob Prince in Pittsburgh, Ernie Harwell in Detroit, Harry Caray, first in St. Louis and then in Chicago, Jack Brickhouse, also in Chicago, Jack Buck in St. Louis, Vin Scully in Los Angeles, Chuck Thompson in Baltimore, Marty Brennaman in Cincinnati, Byrum Saam and Harry Kalas in Philadelphia, and Herb Carneal in Minnesota became beloved municipal heroes across generations of baseball fans.

Together, these reporters and broadcasters working with league players and owners produced a game of symbolic significance. As a young man growing up in Brooklyn, Walt Whitman already sensed in 1888 "great things in baseball. It's our game, the American game." It became in modernizing and post-modern America, a game of grace, skill, strategy, and stamina that signaled the start of spring, the hope of summer, and often the discouragement of the first snow. In this way, season after season, it became an intrinsic part of family, community, and eventually, national life.

Further Reading

Alexander, Charles C. *Our Game: An American Baseball History.* New York: Henry Holt, 1991.

Caren, Eric C. *Baseball Extra: The Newspaper History of the Glorious Game from Its Beginning to the Present.* Edison, NJ: Castle Books, 2000.

Rader, Benjamin G. *Baseball: A History of America's Game.* Urbana: University of Illinois Press, 2002.

Smith, Curt. *The Storytellers: From Mel Allen to Bob Costas.* New York: Macmillan, 1995.

Tygiel, Jules. *Past Time: Baseball as History.* New York: Oxford University Press, 2000.

Voigt, David Quentin. *American Baseball: From Gentleman's Sport to the Commissioner System.* Norman: University of Oklahoma Press, 1966.

BRUCE J. EVENSEN

BENNETT, JAMES GORDON

James Gordon Bennett (September 1, 1795–June 1, 1872) is generally considered one of the most influential, innovative, and controversial journalists in the history of the American press. As a pioneer of the popular newspaper, he helped define the idea of "news" as a marketable commodity and "sensationalism" as a marketing goldmine, and his *New York Herald* earned an enormous circulation throughout the country with a canny mix of thorough, timely reporting on daily events and great dollops of skirmish and scandal. Boldly innovative, brazenly self-promotional, insatiably ambitious, shamelessly provocative, Bennett enjoyed making news as much as he did covering it. Though he frequently referred to himself as "the Napoleon of the Press," his many critics preferred labels like "Prince of Darkness." Both were right.

Born in Banffshire, Scotland, into a comfortable Catholic farm family, young James was sent at fifteen to a seminary in Aberdeen, where his studies ranged from church history and the classics to science and French. His discovery of Byron, Scott, Hume, and Rousseau, however, fueled his disenchantment with the family faith. In 1819, apparently on a whim, Bennett joined a friend who was emigrating to North America, and after a string of teaching and proofreading jobs in Canada and New England found his way into newspaper work as a translator for the *Charleston Courier,* an influential mercantile daily.

From there he went on to reporting and editing jobs on a series of Democratic papers in New York and (briefly) Philadelphia, winning wide notice for his fresh and iconoclastic voice during a four-year stint as a political correspondent for the *New York Enquirer* and its successor *Courier and Enquirer.* But Bennett was too ambitious and contrary to accommodate himself to the fractious world of party journalism, and by 1833 he had fallen out with nearly all of the key editors of the local political press.

As Bennett was reaching a turning point in his life, however, so was journalism. Inspired in part by the egalitarian spirit and emerging class-consciousness of the Jacksonian era, in part by the availability of faster and cheaper means of production and transportation, in part by economic ambition, some urban editors had been experimenting with a brand-new kind of mass-market daily. Rather than following the traditional model of the political newspaper heavily funded by the party, subservient to its interests, and intended mainly for the professional classes, the new "penny press," led by the pioneering New York *Sun*, sought a wide popular readership, especially among the working class, and depended entirely on advertising and sales revenue for its profits. Cheap, feisty, and politically independent (though rarely politically neutral), easy to buy from hawkers in the streets, the penny papers emphasized the sort of local and human-interest stories rarely before considered worthy of newsprint, and hired enterprising reporters to scour the courts, the theaters, and the streets to dig them up. Within two years of its founding in 1833 the *Sun* was claiming a circulation of nearly twenty thousand, quadruple that of the city's best-selling elite paper. That same year, after failing to wangle a position with any of the established penny dailies, Bennett scraped up five hundred dollars to challenge them with his own, the *New York Herald,* whose first issue appeared on May 6, 1835.

Bennett's *New York Herald*

Bennett fought for notice and circulation with two main tactics: sensation and attack. Like the other penny editors, he often filled his pages with breezy accounts of scandal and crime, but he may well have taken his interest in gossip one step farther: accusations that he collected blackmail from people with secrets to keep were frequent enough to sound plausible. He also understood the news value of a good public assault, attacking in print everything from the best-selling *Sun* to working-class agitators, the nouveau riche, abolitionists, religion in general and Catholicism in particular, and all the other editors in New York. Counterattacks he welcomed—and chronicled—as evidence of his own importance, and he constantly boasted that his paper was saucier, smarter, freer, and bolder than all others. Indefatigably competitive, Bennett used any means necessary, whether carrier pigeon, pony express, or harbor boat, to get the news faster than his rivals—who were then forced to join him in an ever-escalating race to be first.

A breakthrough for Bennett's *Herald* came in the spring of 1836, when during his endless and extravagant coverage of the murder of the glamorous prostitute Helen Jewett he claimed to have unearthed evidence exonerating Richard Robinson, the respectable young clerk accused of her killing. That interpretation, though probably (and deliberately) wrong, attracted to the penny press a large new middle-class readership, which Bennett coveted and cultivated as more desirable than the generally working-class constituency of the earlier penny papers. In the years before the Civil War, Bennett's evident southern sympathies and expressed distaste for Abraham Lincoln won him a large circulation below the Mason-Dixon line, where few other New York papers were welcomed. As the *Herald*'s popularity grew, Bennett moderated his tone somewhat but never tempered his personality. Like his fellow editor Horace Greeley of the *New York Tribune,* he became as well-known as his paper, both men referred to in the national press by surname only and written up like local monuments in city guidebooks.

Yet their reputations were almost perfectly oppositional, Greeley symbolizing rectitude, reformism, and (at least to his admirers) a generally endearing eccentricity, while Bennett's supporters celebrated his acerbic and aggressive manner as evidence of his fearless independence. His enduring image as a sort of roguish Peck's Bad Boy of journalism rests in part on favorable books by Isaac Pray and Frederic Hudson, both of them former employees.

Bennett's opponents and critics were merciless, but rarely effective. During the Moral War of 1840, a group of elite editors and other prominent New Yorkers accused him, in a barrage of hyperbolic epithets, of immorality, irreverence, intrusiveness, exploitation, and vulgarity, but their attempted boycott caused him little permanent harm. Neither did the occasional caning inflicted on him in the street—at least five during the *Herald*'s first two years of life, which the infuriating Bennett would simply describe, gleefully, in his paper—though he did lose several lawsuits for libel. In 1852 someone sent a homemade letter bomb to his office that was discovered and defused before causing any damage. On April 10, 1861, during the tense standoff at Fort Sumter, Bennett called for the "overthrow" of Abraham Lincoln's "demoralizing, disorganizing and destructive" Republican Party. Furious mobs besieged the *Herald* office and demanded that an American flag be hung from the window.

Yet while his excesses drew criticism, Bennett was also at the forefront of many innovations, both technological and journalistic. Nestled among the accounts of scandal and crime was a regular "money article," an informed comment on Wall Street business that soon drew the loyal patronage of merchants and financiers. He introduced the "cash system," ending a long and financially ruinous tradition of extending endless credit to purchasers and advertisers. He was among the first American editors to make extensive use of foreign correspondents and was quick to see the great journalistic potential of the telegraph. Even the hypercompetitive Bennett, however, could understand the benefits of cooperation, too, and in the mid-1840s he numbered among the founders of the newsgathering collaborative later known as the Associated Press. And once the Civil War had begun, Bennett reversed course and pledged his support for the Union cause, pouring staggering resources into covering the war. The *Herald* was said to have fielded more than one hundred correspondents (ten at Gettysburg alone) and spent more than half a million dollars on its war news, which many considered the most thorough and up-to-date offered by any paper of the time. Among the wide circle of secret sources and informants that contributed to the *Herald*'s uncanny ability to scoop the competition was a confidante of Mrs. Lincoln, and even the famously journalist-averse Secretary of War, Edwin Stanton, was occasionally known to cooperate with the *Herald* for mutual advantage.

In 1840, at the height of the Moral War (and perhaps in an attempt to deflate it), the forty-four-year-old Bennett married Henrietta Crean, an Irish-born music teacher half his age whom he'd met barely three months earlier at his prize reporter's wedding. Four children were born to the couple, two of whom, Jeanette and James Gordon Bennett, Jr., reached adulthood. Bennett's insatiable habit of boasting in his columns about his family—beginning on June 1, 1840, with the first-person announcement of his engagement headlined "Caught at Last ... New Movement in Civilization"—inspired such constant vilification of Mrs. Bennett and the children in the streets as well as the press that they spent much of their time in Europe. Bennett retired in 1866, turning the *Herald* over to his son, and died just six months before his archrival Greeley. On his deathbed he asked for a priest to hear his confession, returning at the end to the Catholic Church.

Further Reading

Carlson, Oliver. *The Man Who Made News: James Gordon Bennett.* New York: Duell, Sloan and Pearce, 1942.

Crouthamel, James L. *Bennett's "New York Herald" and the Rise of the Popular Press.* Syracuse: Syracuse University Press, 1989.

Hudson, Frederic. *Journalism in the United States, from 1690 to 1872.* New York: Harper, 1873; repr. ed., 1969.

[Pray, Isaac C.] *Memoirs of James Gordon Bennett and His Times. By a Journalist.* New York: Stringer & Townsend, 1855; repr. ed., 1970.

ANDIE TUCHER

BERGER, VICTOR

Victor Berger (February 28, 1860–August 7, 1929) was a leading American socialist for more than thirty years, as editor and publisher of English- and German-language newspapers and a four-term Socialist Party congressman.

Born February 28, 1860, in Nieder Rebbach, Austria-Hungary, Berger immigrated to the United States in 1878 with his parents, and moved to Milwaukee, Wisconsin, in 1880, where he taught German in the public schools until he was fired for his radicalism. Berger purchased the German-language daily *Wisconsin Vorwarts* in 1893, retrenched as the weekly *Warheit* in 1897. In 1901, Berger took charge of the weekly *Social Democratic Herald.* In December 1911 he launched his best-known newspaper, the daily *Milwaukee Leader,* which served the city's powerful Socialist Party and labor unions until 1942.

Berger was the paper's majority owner and guiding spirit, even while he was attending to his Congressional duties or, in 1919 and 1920, barred under terms of his bail from active management. The *Leader* competed head-on with Milwaukee's other dailies, boasting sports and women's pages, serialized fiction, and general news, as well as extensive labor coverage and commentary from Berger and other prominent socialists.

Berger helped organize the Social Democratic Party (soon reorganized as the Socialist Party) and recruited its best-known figure, Eugene V. Debs. Berger played a key role in the Socialists' local success through his newspapers and organizational skills. The first Socialist to be elected to Congress, in 1910, Berger prided himself on his constructive approach, advocating reform measures such as old-age pensions. He initially served a single term, losing to a fusion Democrat-Republican candidate in 1912. Berger's opposition to World War I led to electoral victories in 1918 and again in 1919 (the latter with 55 percent of the vote), but Congress refused to seat him.

World War I proved a heavy burden, even though popular revulsion to the slaughter resulted in Berger winning five consecutive elections to Congress. On October 13, 1917, Postmaster General Albert S. Burleson revoked the *Milwaukee Leader's* second-class mailing rights; the next year the post office expanded the ban, refusing all mail service. Much of the *Leader's* advertising was withdrawn, and it was forced to turn to donations to sustain publication. Berger was also convicted of interfering with the war effort, although in 1921 his conviction was overturned by the U.S. Supreme Court (which, however, upheld the post office's actions against the *Leader*).

Ironically, Berger and his newspaper had adopted a cautious attitude toward the war, opposing both the war and demonstrations against it; arguing that conscription was unconstitutional, but encouraging socialists to obey the law; and demanding the preservation of civil liberties. In August 1918, Berger issued new editorial guidelines, instructing the staff that the *Leader* should provide readers the information to draw their own conclusions, while avoiding explicit criticism of the administration. "We will say nothing we don't think," he concluded, "although we think a great deal that we can't say."

Berger returned to Congress in 1923, leaving management of the *Leader* to others. Meanwhile, the Socialist Party had suffered a major split, and Berger's brand of pragmatic, "constructive" politics was increasingly marginalized both within the party and in the larger society.

Berger died August 7, 1929, twenty-two days after he was hit by a street car. He had returned to the editor's desk at the *Leader* five months earlier, after completing his fourth and final term in Congress.

Further Reading

Beck, Elmer A. "Autopsy of a Labor Daily: The Milwaukee Leader." *Journalism Monographs* 16 (August 1970).

Berger, Victor L. *Voice and Pen of Victor L. Berger: Congressional Speeches and Editorials.* Milwaukee, WI: The Milwaukee Leader, 1929.

De Leon, Daniel. *Berger's Hits and Misses at the Called Session of the Sixty-Second Congress.* New York: New York Labor News, 1912. (Reissued 1963 as *A Socialist in Congress: His Duties and Responsibilities.*)

Miller, Sally M. *Victor Berger and the Promise of Constructive Socialism, 1910–1920.* Westport, CT: Greenwood Press, 1973.

Nash, Roderick. "Victor L. Berger: Making Marx Respectable." *Wisconsin Magazine of History* 47 (Summer 1964): 301-8.

Stevens, Michael E., ed. *The Family Letters of Victor and Meta Berger: 1849–1929.* Madison, Wisc.: State Historical Society, 1995.

JON BEKKEN

BIRNEY, JAMES GILLESPIE

"What are the abolitionists doing? Have they levied a military force? Laid up magazines of arms? They talk and they print, to persuade their fellow countrymen to do justice and show mercy to the poor. This is the head and front of their offending—no more" (*The Philanthropist*, April 1, 1836, 1). These words from besieged abolitionist editor James Gillespie Birney (February 4, 1792–November 25, 1857) came in the midst of mob action in Cincinnati, Ohio, that smashed his press and threatened his life if he continued his campaign against slavery.

Birney was born near Danville, Kentucky, son of James Birney, a prosperous plantation owner, and Martha Reed. At six, he was given a slave as a birthday present. Birney's anti-slavery sentiment developed through his studies at Transylvania College in Lexington and the College of New Jersey, later Princeton, from where he graduated in 1810. He studied law in Philadelphia and came under the influence of anti-slavery activist Abraham L. Pennock, a Quaker. Birney acquired slaves in 1816, when he married Agatha McDowell, the niece of Kentucky Governor George McDowell. By 1818, the couple oversaw a cotton plantation of forty-three slaves outside Huntsville, Alabama. Six of the couple's eleven children would survive childhood, two becoming Union generals during the Civil War.

As a state legislator, Birney opposed the sale of slaves in Alabama. By 1823 he had sold his plantation and moved to Huntsville, becoming the city's mayor in 1829. Birney's deepening involvement with the revivalist spirit of the Presbyterian Church made him a proponent of Indian rights, universal education, and the Sunday school movement. As an agent for the American Colonization Society, Birney began in 1832 to write editorials and raise funds promoting the emigration of freed slaves to Liberia in West Africa. By the summer of 1835 Birney had moved his family to Cincinnati, where he planned to start a newspaper arguing the moral necessity of immediate abolition. The local press charged he was a "misguided fanatic" (Birney 1843, 205) and on November 1 the city's mayor, marshal, and county sheriff warned him of violence if he proceeded to publish. Birney moved his press twenty miles up the Ohio River to New Richmond, a stop on the Underground Railroad, where the first issue of *The Philanthropist* appeared on January 1, 1836.

Birney claimed "the indisputable right to speak, write and print" his "utter condemnation of slavery" (*The Philanthropist*, January 1, 1836, 1). At anti-abolitionist meetings, provoked by his publication, Birney pushed what he considered "the Constitutional cause of universal freedom" (*The Philanthropist*, February 19, 1836, 1). By May, *The Philanthropist*, now published in Cincinnati as the official organ of the Ohio Anti-Slavery Society, argued that "just government" required for all men the "unalienable right to life, liberty, and the pursuit of happiness" (*The Philanthropist*, May 13, 1836, 1).

On the evening of July 12, 1836, a mob stormed the paper's office, smashed its press and threatened Birney's life if he resumed publication. *The Philanthropist* reported the incident three days later. Birney used the attack to argue abolishing slavery was now linked to "freedom of the press" and the cause "to preserve our own liberties" (*The Philanthropist*, July 22, 1836, 1). On July 30, the mob struck again. Birney's office was destroyed, his press thrown into the river, and his home ransacked, along with Cincinnati's black residential district. Undaunted, Birney continued publication and was arrested in 1837 for harboring a fugitive slave. The case, argued by Salmon P. Chase, would later overturn Ohio's fugitive slave law.

Birney's stand in Cincinnati made him a hero in the abolitionist cause. He became a leader in the American Anti-Slavery Society, moved with his family to New York, and was a tireless organizer on both sides of the Atlantic for abolitionism. In 1840 and 1844 he was the presidential nominee of the Liberty Party, carrying enough votes in the second election to deny Henry Clay, the Whig Party nominee who favored colonization, the presidency. Although injured in a riding accident in 1845, Birney continued to write and publish on behalf of abolitionism. He continued to publish *The Philanthropist* in Cincinnati until 1847, when it was moved to Washington, D.C., and renamed the *National Era*. Five years later the paper, edited by Gamaliel Bailey, greatly energized the abolitionist community with the publication of Harriet Beecher Stowe's *Uncle Tom's Cabin*, a fitting tribute to a man and newspaper intimately identified with the abolitionist cause.

Further Reading

Birney, James G. *The American Churches: The Bulwarks of American Slavery*. New York: Arno Press, 1969, originally 1843.

——. *Letter on Colonization, Addressed to the Rev. Thornton J. Mills, Corresponding Secretary of the Kentucky Colonization Society*. New York: Office of Anti-Slavery Reporter, 1834.

——. *A Letter on the Political Obligations of Abolitionists*. New York: Arno Press, 1969, originally 1839.

——. *James G. Birney and His Times*, New York: D. Appleton & Co., 1890.

Dumond, Dwight L., ed. *Letters of James Gillespie Birney, 1831–1857*. New York: D. Appleton-Century Co., 1938.

Fladeland, Betty. *James Gillespie Birney: Slaveholder to Abolitionist*. New York: Cornell University Press, 1955.

Franklin, Cathy Rogers. "James Gillespie Birney, the Revival Spirit, and The Philanthropist." *American Journalism* 17, (Spring 2000).

Green, Beriah. *Sketches of the Life and Writings of James Gillespie Birney*. Utica, NY: Jackson & Chaplin, 1844.

Papers of James Gillespie Birney. Archival Manuscript Material. Manuscript Reading Room. Library of Congress. Washington, D.C. Also, William L. Clements Library. University of Michigan. Ann Arbor, Michigan.

BRUCE J. EVENSEN

BLACK PRESS

Since its inception on the American publishing landscape in 1827, the black newspaper has been the provocative, courageous conscience of what has been referred to as the democratic experiment. As democratic idealists, black newspapers have worked diligently throughout their 180-year existence to keep America true to her ideals and precepts as outlined in the Declaration of Independence and the United States Constitution. As agents of uplift and as promoters of the abolition of slavery, early weeklies such as *Freedom's Journal*, *The Rights of All*, and *The Colored American* published in New York City were a proud, socially responsible, and politically astute bunch even as they were never financially successful attracting big advertising dollars. Beginning on March 27, 1827, Samuel Cornish and John Russwurm co-edited the *Freedom's Journal* (1827–1829) from a small Varick Street office in lower New York City. Russwurm, a graduate of Bowdoin College in Maine, eventually immigrated to Liberia, West Africa, as convert to a scheme to rid the nation of blacks. Russwurm became disenchanted with American democracy as false and untenable for people of color. Decidedly pro-American, Cornish was a Presbyterian minister who renamed *Freedom's Journal* to *The Rights of All* and continued to publish the weekly until the autumn of 1829. Subsequently he was connected with a number of newspapers, including *The Weekly Advocate* and *The Colored American*, the latter published by a committee including, black New York clergyman Charles Ray and Philip A. Bell, who was said to be the "most ubiquitous black journalist" of the era. The early papers apparently did a fine balancing act of showcasing the best of what free blacks could eke out for themselves in America and encouraging them to do more with less. At the same time, the early newspapers were a consistent moral voice in opposing slavery. The intended readership of the early papers was obviously white as there were only about three hundred thousand blacks in America during the last half of the decade leading to the Civil War.

In the 1830s and 1840s, a number of short-lived weeklies were published, including William Whipper's *National Reformer* (1838–1839) published in Philadelphia, and David Ruggles *Mirror of Liberty* (1838–1840) published in New York City. A Pittsburgh area physician, Martin Delany, managed to launch a short-lived paper in 1843 known as *The Mystery*, the only black-owned publication west of the Alleghenies during this era. Delany joined the Democratic Party and became an officer-physician during the Civil War; both unusual feats for a black man of his time.

The most illustrious of antebellum editors and publishers was Frederick Douglass (1818?–1895), a fugitive slave from the Eastern Shore of Maryland who became a towering abolitionist and orator. Late in his life, Douglass became the highest-ranking black in the federal government service. To aid in his abolitionist, social activist and women's rights work, Douglass published *The North Star* (1847–1851), *Frederick Douglass' Paper* (1851–1860) and *Douglass' Monthly* (1859–1863), all influential publications. Douglass also published several books about his life as a fugitive slave, including *My Bondage and My Freedom* (1855). Aided in his publishing and editorial work by British abolitionist Julia Griffiths and subsidized by a wealthy New York businessman, Gerrit Smith, Douglass's papers were extremely well edited and peddled by a group of subscription agents who were Douglass's supporters and fellow abolitionists.

Black women worked in conjunction with black male publishers from the inception of the black press in various ways, including as subscription agents and editorial assistants and correspondents. Mary Shadd Cary and Ida B. Wells, both black women, deserve special mention because they published their own papers during the nineteenth century. Cary, a contributor to Douglass's newspapers, was born in Delaware but exiled herself to Canada with a group of fugitive blacks who lived in Ontario. With the aid of her brother, Cary published the *Provincial Freeman* (1853–1857) to serve those blacks who left America to reside in what was then commonly called Canada West. Mary Miles Bibbs published *Voice of the Fugitive* (1851–1852) from the same region.

Ida B. Wells was singular in her work as an editor, researcher, and publisher. Born in Holly Springs, Mississippi, in 1862 to slave parents, Wells used her connection with *The Free Speech and Headlight* (1888–1892), based in Memphis, Tennessee, to launch an anti-lynching crusade. Galvanized because a white mob lynched a friend of hers in 1892, Wells concluded that the reason was because his grocery store had become too successful in competition with a local white grocer. Wells took note that the lynching of the innocent grocer was "an excuse to get rid of Negroes who were acquiring wealth and property and thus to keep the race terrorized." Systematically collecting data on lynchings, Wells showed that the South was ruled by violence and racist intimidation. With the name of her paper shortened to *Free Speech*, Wells continued to travel widely to educate the nation about lynchings and even journeyed twice to Britain. She discovered that the horrific practice increased over 200 percent between 1882 and 1892. Noting that over 240 people were murdered during that decade alone, Wells soon took opportunities to put the lynchings on the international agenda. The increase seemed to follow closely the Federal government withdrawing support from Southern blacks. Wells herself eluded death threats and a bounty on her head. The death threats were the result of daring, outspoken speeches and writings. She lost her newspaper. Wells reported that over twenty-five hundred lynchings, mostly of blacks, took place in America between 1884 and 1900. Timothy Thomas Fortune published *New York Age* in the 1890s as a social activist newspaper. Befriending Ida B. Wells as a fellow publisher, he warned her not to go back to Memphis. Wells worked briefly as a reporter for Fortune's paper. Ida B. Wells lived and continued her anti-lynching work in danger and managed also to work with black women's reform groups that were forerunners of the

National Association of Colored Women (NACW), begun in 1896. She eventually moved to Chicago, but continued to take the lead in documenting lynching atrocities and in educating the nation to the dreadful, racist practice well into the twentieth century. Wells died in 1931.

Some black newspapers established during the late nineteenth century survived into the twentieth century, including the *Philadelphia Tribune*, founded in 1884 by Chris J. Perry; the *Afro-American* of Baltimore, Maryland and Washington, D. C., founded in 1892 by John H. Murphy; the Houston *Informer*, started in 1893; the *Indianapolis Recorder* founded in 1895; the Los Angeles *Watts Star Review* begun in 1904; the *Chicago Defender* launched by Robert S. Abbott in 1905; the *Norfolk Journal and Guide*, founded in Norfolk, Virginia, in 1907 by P. B. Young; the *Amsterdam News* established in 1909; and the *Pittsburgh Courier* started by 1910 by Robert E. Vann and still in operation in 2006, although its doors were shut for several years .

During World War II, the black press came into its own as a powerful voice of complaints about the maltreatment of black soldiers during wartime. Although few people would have denied the reality of racial injustices, the black press' strategy of combining criticism with support for the war infuriated many government officials. The *Pittsburgh Courier*, in its heyday, started the Double V Campaign in 1942 calling for a victory abroad in the war effort and a victory at home to combat segregation and discrimination. As a January 1942 letter to the editor of the *Courier*, which sparked the campaign, put it: "first V for victory over enemies from without, the second V for victory over our enemies from within." Following that letter, the *Courier* devoted a lot of column space to a "Double V" campaign. J. Edgar Hoover, chief of a newly created General Intelligence Division (GID) and others suggested that the black press had links to Communism and to get Congress to put pressure on the paper. The *Courier* and other black newspapers would have been shut down if Hoover had had his way, and the government would have stopped the outspoken demands for equality spearheaded by black newspapers. It was Attorney General Francis Biddle who used his office to protect civil liberties in direct opposition to the practices of the former U. S. Attorney General, A. Mitchell Palmer who was one of the prime instigators of the "Red Scare" in America from 1919 to 1921.

Still a relatively small group of mostly weeklies, black newspapers in the early twenty-first century were galvanized by leadership of the National Newspaper Publishers Association (NNPA). The association linked and oversaw more than 120 black weeklies and bi-weeklies nationwide. Such corporations as General Motors aided NNPA to bring more and better technology to black newspapers and to an international wire service, based in Washington, D. C. As of 2007, the NNPA was an association of such newspapers as the *Amsterdam News* published in New York and the *Afro-American* published in Baltimore. Scattered across America from coast to coast and often lagging in circulation figures and advertising, the black press consistently managed, despite many of tribulations, to accomplish a great deal. Throughout their history, black newspapers emphasized liberty, justice, and democracy without avarice as its main principles. Rarely motivated solely by profit, African-American newspapers continued to reflect democratic ideals. Most of these papers focused on community, organization and church news, although some did turn to sensationalism and crime reporting to stay afloat financially.

Further Reading

Hutton, Frankie. *The Early Black Press in America, 1827–1860.* Westport, CT: Greenwood Press, 1993.

Roberts, Gene and Hank Kilbanoff. *The Race Beat: The Press, the Civil Rights Struggle, and the Awakening of a Nation.* New York: Knopf, 2006.

Washburn, Patrick S. *A Question of Sedition: The Federal Government's Investigation of the Black Press during World War II.* New York: Oxford University Press, 1986.

FRANKIE HUTTON

BLEYER, WILLARD GROSVENOR

Willard Grosvenor Bleyer (1873–1935) was a pioneering figure in journalism education, best known for his national leadership in establishing journalism as a university-level field of inquiry and for creating the School of Journalism at the University of Wisconsin in 1927. He was instrumental in creating the first national organizations to promote research and teaching in journalism and mass communication, and set in motion the first program of graduate study in these fields.

Bleyer was born in 1873 into a prominent Wisconsin newspaper family. His father and uncles worked in all aspects of the newspaper business, and as a young boy, Bleyer was a familiar presence in the editorial, circulation, research, and printing departments of many of the state's major newspaper offices. During his undergraduate years at the University of Wisconsin (1892–1896), Bleyer founded the student newspaper, *The Daily Cardinal*, which is still published today, and the University Press Club, a student organization that lobbied the administration to introduce journalism courses into the university curriculum. Bleyer earned a Bachelor's degree in English in 1896 and received his Master's degree two years later. After a brief stint as a high school English teacher, Bleyer returned to the university and earned his PhD in 1904, at which time he joined the faculty. He married Alice Haskell, a midwestern suffragist, in 1911.

As a young professor, Bleyer joined ongoing national debates about the value of university training for journalists. Opponents of formal journalism instruction, such as E.L. Godkin of the *Nation* and Horace White of the *Chicago Tribune*, insisted that "on-the-job" training in the newsroom was the only way to learn reporting. Their views were the dominant ones of the day, but Bleyer and other progressives, including the publisher Joseph Pulitzer, argued that poorly educated reporters were not capable of fulfilling newspapers' social responsibility to bring the world of knowledge to readers, to heighten connections between citizens and their institutions, and to promote democratic participation. Bleyer argued that "adequate preparation" for journalists, which meant a structured program of university study joining liberal arts with practical journalism instruction, was as important for society as the proper training of physicians and lawyers. He built his case for journalism education on forward-thinking ideas, arguing that journalism had a more direct impact upon the welfare of society and the success of democratic government than any other profession.

In the years between the introduction of the first journalism class at Wisconsin in 1905 and the establishment of the School of Journalism, Bleyer transformed journalism at the university into a substantive area of study that drew widely from the liberal arts. His curricular models were adopted by emerging journalism programs nationwide. During this period, he also took important stands against commercialization of the news and sensational journalism, and argued that working journalists ought to unionize to demand better salaries and working conditions, and to enhance the status of their profession.

Bleyer died in 1935, at the age of sixty-two. Frank Luther Mott, the director of the School of Journalism at the University of Iowa, described his passing as "nothing less than a national loss, for I think that we all looked to Doctor Bleyer as the leader of the forces for education in journalism."

Further Reading

Bronstein, Carolyn and Stephen Vaughn. "Willard G. Bleyer and the Relevance of Journalism Education." *Journalism and Mass Communication Monographs* 166 (1998).

Czitrom, Daniel J. *Media and the American Mind: From Morse to McLuhan.* Chapel Hill: University of North Carolina Press, 1982.

Rogers, Everett M. *A History of Communication Study: A Biographical Approach.* New York: Free Press, 1994.

Rogers, Everett M., and Steven H. Chaffee. "Communication and Journalism from 'Daddy' Bleyer to Wilbur Schramm: A Palimpsest," *Journalism and Mass Communication Monographs* 148 (1994).

Sloan, William David. "In Search of Itself: A History of Journalism Education." In *Makers of the Media Mind: Journalism Educators and Their Ideas*, edited by W. D. Sloan. Hillsdale, NJ: Lawrence Erlbaum, 1990.

CAROLYN BRONSTEIN

BLOGS

A weblog, or "blog," refers to any site on the World Wide Web constructed as a time-stamped series of individual news items arranged such that the most recent "postings" appear at the top of the page. Blogs first appeared in the late 1990s as custom-coded, database-driven, dynamic web sites created and used by technology professionals. By 2000, user-friendly services for blog authoring and hosting (such as Blogger.com, purchased by the Internet search firm Google), had become freely available to the growing population of Internet users. Today blogs represent "social networking" technologies, where authors comment on each other's postings and link to each other's sites, creating dense networks of affiliation around various technological, political, and social topics. By late 2006, one blog search engine, Technorati.com, claimed to track over fifty million unique blogs, and the Pew Internet and American Life Project reported that twelve million Americans—8 percent of all U.S. Internet users—blogged.

The potential for blogs to complement or even change the practice of professional journalism became evident in the aftermath of the September 11, 2001, terrorist attacks. As Internet traffic overwhelmed the online properties of corporate news outlets, weblogs designed for technology news like Slashdot.org were suddenly relaying "real news" from online, broadcast, and print media. In addition, weblogs which allowed public comment and participation became sites for concerned citizens to post eyewitness accounts of the tragedy, offers to assist victims, or questions about the whereabouts of loved ones. These rapid, direct, and "unfiltered" communications were in turn picked up by the mainstream media and became part of the wider human interest story around the event. Blogs have continued to grow as important sources of "on the ground" information and opinion in crisis situations around the globe. After the U.S.-led invasion of Iraq in 2003, both journalists and readers turned to unauthorized "milblogs" authored by soldiers engaged in combat operations, and to blogs written from the point of view of civilians, such as the popular "Baghdad Burning" site, hosted by Google's Blogger service and authored pseudononymously by an Iraqi woman under the name of "Riverbend."

In the years leading up to the 2004 U.S. presidential election, the potential for blogs to assist strategic communication efforts—marketing, public relations, and political speech—became evident as well. The campaign staff of Democratic presidential primary candidate Howard Dean not only set up their own blog, but also used a third-party social networking tool called MeetUp.com—designed to facilitate just-in-time physical meetings for the members of online communities—in order to both gain national media attention and to generate grassroots donations. The strategy helped to propel the candidate from also-ran to front-runner status (though in the end it was not enough to secure Dean his party's nomination). The Dean example of using an in-house blog—linking to and trading content back and forth with a large number of individual blogs authored by potential supporters—was echoed in corporate "viral marketing" campaigns which increasingly attempted to use weblogs to generate "buzz" for a new product or service on the Internet, in order to ensure free and widespread exposure by traditional broadcast and print news media.

Besides providing grist for journalists and an outlet for marketers, by the early 2000s blogs had earned a popular reputation as a new form of watchdog reporting, challenging the mainstream of both journalistic writing and political communication. For example, left-wing bloggers claimed credit for motivating the 2002 resignation of Senate Majority Leader Trent Lott, by focusing mainstream media attention on controversial remarks Lott made at a reception for fellow Senator Strom Thurmond. Similarly, right-wing bloggers claimed to have precipitated the resignation of Dan Rather from the CBS Evening News anchor chair in 2005, by focusing mainstream media attention on the legitimacy of documents that CBS cited in a report on President Bush's National Guard service. In both cases, weblogs engaged in so-called "netroots" journalism actually served an agenda-setting function, acting to rapidly and loudly magnify information and arguments already available in the professional media.

In fact, much of what bloggers discuss comes not from their own original reporting, but from professional print and broadcast media organizations, with blogs citing, copying, excerpting and linking to the online content of established media voices. By 2006, many of the best-known journalists at brand-name news outlets had daily blogs themselves, in addition to regular weekly columns and reporting bylines. These journalists claimed that blogs allowed readers to more transparently witness the process of journalism in action—sometimes even allowing them to provide public feedback on the result. And just as with the corporate media many bloggers criticize, a polarization has developed within the supposedly egalitarian "blogosphere." In 2006, a small minority of the estimated fifty million weblogs in existence commanded a vastly disproportionate share of the visitor traffic. The majority of bloggers in the United States still treated their writings not as a challenge to the shortcomings of the mass media, but as personal diaries or hobbies, intended only for an audience of personal friends and family.

The ultimate form and meaning that blogging will develop is still unknown. Widespread adoption of new social networking technologies such as "wikis" (collaboratively authored web sites), "podcasts" (blogs where the postings are audio or video snippets), and "RSS" feeds (bite-sized blog headlines delivered to personal computers or to other web pages) may rapidly change the landscape of blog production and consumption. But in a time when only 39 percent of U.S. Internet users read blogs—and when over 25 percent of the U.S. population doesn't use the Internet at all—weblogs are as of yet unable to serve reliably and equitably as either an information production or an information consumption tool for all citizens.

Further Reading

Lenhart, Amanda, and Susannah Fox. *Bloggers: A portrait of the internet's new storytellers.* Washington, D.C.: Pew Internet & American Life Project, 2006.

Rainie, Lee, Susannah Fox, and Mary Madden. *One year later: September 11 and the Internet.* Washington, D.C.: Pew Internet & American Life Project, 2002.

Riverbend and Aliyah Mamduh. *Baghdad Burning: Girl Blog from Iraq.* New York: CUNY Feminist Press, 2005.

Trippi, Joe. *The Revolution Will Not Be Televised: Democracy, the Internet, and the Overthrow of Everything.* New York: Regan Books, 2004.

GREG DOWNEY

BLOOMBERG, MICHAEL

Unlike media mogul William Randolph Hearst, Michael Bloomberg successfully ran for mayor of New York City. Bloomberg, founder of financial information giant Bloomberg LP, spent more than $40 million of his own money in 2001 to capture the job that eluded Hearst in 1905 and 1909. A lifelong Democrat, Bloomberg ran as a Republican to avoid a congested primary field on the Democratic side.

Born on February 14, 1942, Bloomberg grew up near Boston, the son of a bookkeeper. After earning his MBA from Harvard in 1966, he took a job on Wall Street where he rose through the ranks to become a partner at investment banker Salomon Brothers. But his career in high finance ended abruptly in 1981 when Salomon Brothers was sold and he was not retained.

During his career on Wall Street, Bloomberg was frustrated by the lack of financial data available to the investment industry. Using $4 million of his $10 million windfall from his Salomon Brothers buyout, the aggressive, hard-charging Bloomberg launched a company in 1981 that offered the financial services industry a proprietary terminal with instant access to historical and real-time financial data.

As he explained in his autobiography *Bloomberg on Bloomberg* (1997), the Bloomberg terminal would be the first of its kind in the investment industry where people could get an almost-instant answer to financial questions. The Bloomberg terminal, an information powerhouse, soon became a hit on Wall Street because of its relative simplicity and strong customer support. The terminals did not require specialized training to operate.

Early customers beyond Wall Street included the Bank of England, all of the Federal Reserve Banks, and even the Vatican. The company sold some 180,000 Bloomberg boxes by 2004, capturing more than 40 percent of the $7 billion market-data industry. Bloomberg LP, noted for its risk taking and entrepreneurial energy, successfully challenged Reuters, the British news and financial information agency that had long dominated the market-data industry.

Bloomberg parlayed its success in the market-data industry into the news industry. In 1991, the *New York Times* agreed to become Bloomberg's first newspaper customer. By 1995, Bloomberg News was published in more U.S. newspapers than any other news service except the Associated Press. "We provide what so many newspapers have in short supply: an army of reporters and editors who do nothing but report and explain money, markets, companies, industries and the economy," Bloomberg wrote in his autobiography.

By 2005, Bloomberg News had grown to ninety-four bureaus around the world staffed by more than sixteen hundred journalists who produce more than four thousand news stories each day. In addition, there is Bloomberg TV, Bloomberg Radio, an Internet site and several financial magazines. Regardless of the medium, one of the hallmarks of Bloomberg is its speed and accuracy.

Although Bloomberg retained ownership of about 70 percent of the organization he founded, once he became mayor of New York he gave up the day-to-day management of the company so that he could concentrate on running America's largest city.

Further Reading

Bloomberg, Michael. *Bloomberg by Bloomberg*. New York: John Wiley & Sons Inc., 1997.
"Missing Mike." *The Economist*, September 4, 2004.
Bloomberg LP website. http://about.bloomberg.com/about/ourco/overview.html (Accessed April 9, 2007).

EDMUND LAWLER

BLY, NELLIE (AKA ELIZABETH COCHRAN)

Nellie Bly (May 5, 1864–January 27, 1922), the most celebrated woman journalist of the 1880s and 1890s, pioneered the field of "detective" or "stunt" reporting. The crusading spirit and social welfare agenda in her scores of undercover exploits led to the development of full-scale investigative reporting in the decades that followed.

Bly was born Elizabeth Cochran in Cochran's Mill, Armstrong County, Pennsylvania, May 5, 1864. She was the daughter of Michael Cochran, a county judge and the town mill owner, who died when she was six. She was the thirteenth of his fifteen children, ten by his first wife and five by Bly's mother, Mary Jane Cochran. As a young adult, Bly added a final "e" to the Cochran name. Financial reverses made Bly the sole support of her mother and sister and soon after the family relocated to Pittsburgh. Once there, Bly's impassioned letter to a columnist landed her a job at the *Pittsburg Dispatch* in 1885. For the *Dispatch*, she also reported from Mexico for five months shortly before her move to New York.

Bly's writing life spanned the Victorian and Progressive eras and World War I and its aftermath, but she is best remembered for the three years she reported for Joseph Pulitzer's Sunday *New York World* and became, in the process, the incarnation of "The New Journalism" of the 1880s and 1890s. Joining the staff only a few years after the *World's* inception, Bly began splashily in the fall of 1887 with a two-part chronicle of the intolerable conditions at New York's already infamous women's insane asylum on Blackwell's (now Roosevelt) Island. In her distinctive first-person narrative style, she investigated under cover, feigning insanity to engineer her commitment to the institution and gained release ten days later through another ruse. Her stories brought instant acclaim and helped push through reforms. Soon after came reputation-building exposés of a corrupt statehouse lobbyist, employment agency abuses, the New York baby-buying trade, the lives of chorus girls, jail house life for women, mesmerists and hucksters. Week after week, Bly assumed dozens of guises to bring these reports to the *World's* readers, spawning in the process dozens of imitators at other newspapers across the country and, at last, a place on newspapers for women who wanted to report hard news. In between, as celebrity interviewer, she interviewed presidential wives and merry murderesses. Her last assignment as a full-time member of the staff extended her national celebrity to Europe and beyond: She raced around the world by boat and train to beat the fictional record of Jules Verne's Phileas Fogg with a time of 72 days, 6 hours, 11 minutes and 14 seconds. Nellie Bly board games, caps, lamps, trading cards, and other items proliferated, but she quit in a salary and recognition dispute. In the hiatus, she turned three of her most memorable exploits into books and also tried unsuccessfully to write serial fiction.

In the following years, Bly returned to journalism sporadically. Her most notable assignments in this period were also for the *World*, including her exclusive jailhouse interview with Emma Goldman in 1893; an unsuccessful personal column; her coverage of city, state, and women's movement political conventions; the Midwest drought; and her distinguished coverage of Chicago's Pullman Strike of 1894. Her compassionate portrait of the lives of Pullman workers and their families was Bly at her journalistic best. In 1895, she accepted a lucrative offer from the *Chicago Times-Herald*, but then quit after little more than a month to marry Robert L. Seaman, a New York industrialist thirty years her senior. In 1896, she went back to the *World* briefly at the invitation of her old friend Arthur Brisbane, and then, in 1899, assumed control of her husband's troubled Brooklyn-based ironworks company. Later, she embarked on the manufacture of steel barrels. She ran her two melded companies as a model of social welfare for its 250 employees, but lacked the necessary business acumen to keep the companies going after her husband's death in 1904.

By 1911, with the firm in deep financial trouble, Bly fled to Europe to avoid prosecution and arrived in Vienna at the outbreak of World War I. She immediately joined the foreign press corps and became the first known woman correspondent to tour the battlefields of the eastern front, writing about it for the *New York Evening Journal* and *International News Service* (INS). Brisbane was by then running the *Journal* for William Randolph Hearst. Bly remained in Vienna for the duration of the war, technically an enemy alien for part of the time, but very well-connected among the Austrian nobility. She never returned to the war front, but during this period sent a series of dispatches back to the *Journal*, urging assistance for Austria's widows and war orphans.

She returned to the United States in 1919, stopping in Paris en route to plead Austria's case to U.S. military officials and to President Woodrow Wilson's staff. Though her name was still known to the military intelligence officers who interviewed her, they received her as relic more than icon, and even considered her a bit "hatty" in her vociferous opposition to Bolshevism and her warnings of Russia's threat to central Europe.

Once back in New York, financially strapped, she returned to newspaper work, thanks to Brisbane once again. At her death, he would describe her in a *Journal* editorial as "the best reporter in America." He gave her an editorial page column that Bly quickly turned into a virtual clearing house for unwed mothers who wanted to place their children in good homes. Her other major themes were the increasing number of foreign workers in U.S. shipyards and capital punishment, both of which she opposed. She also covered important front page sensational stories in this period, including kidnappings, the Jess Willard-Jack Dempsey fight, and an electrocution.

At her death, Bly's role in opening the profession of journalism to women reporters was undisputed, as was her place as an enduring journalistic and feminist legend.

Further Reading

Bly, Nellie. *Six Months in Mexico*. New York: John W. Lovell, 1886.
—— *Ten Days in a Madhouse*. New York: Norman L. Munro, 1887.
—— *The Mystery of Central Park*. New York: G.W. Dillingham, 1889.
—— *Nellie Bly's Book: Around the World in 72 Days*. New York: Pictorial Weekly, 1890.
Kroeger, Brooke, *Nellie Bly: Daredevil, Reporter, Feminist*. New York: Times Books, Random House, 1994. (For all known primary and contemporaneous secondary sources, see Kroeger, 523–614.)

BROOKE KROEGER

BOSTON GLOBE

The four-penny *Boston Globe* was launched on March 4, 1872, by six Boston businessmen, led by Eben Jordan, founder of the Jordan Marsh department store, who pooled $150,000 in promising a "commercial and business journal of the first class" that would be "devoted to intelligent and dignified discussion" of issues of real interest to Bostonians. The *Globe* sold by subscription daily for 75 cents a month and three months could be had for two dollars. By August of the following year, twenty-seven-year-old Civil War veteran Charles H. Taylor became business manager. Taylor was a savvy newspaperman, having printed the *Boston Traveller* and reported for the *New York Tribune*. Taylor was brought in as Jordan's partner when the paper's original investors pulled out of the project.

When Taylor became publisher in 1877, the paper had a circulation of less than eight thousand. Taylor immediately launched an evening edition, cut the paper's price to two cents, and began emphasizing local news. The paper's conscientious coverage of D. L. Moody and Ira Sankey's New England Revival between January and April 1877 helped to stimulate circulation. Taylor sent relays of stenographers to Moody's meetings at a specially built, seven thousand-seat tabernacle on Tremont Street to record the evangelist's every utterance and splash it on the front page. The *Globe* then published a bound edition of his sermons to improve its profit margin. The "godly *Globe*," as critics on Newspaper Row called it, tripled its circulation by the end of Moody's meetings, and Taylor's aim was that they add to it.

Boston's newspaper establishment was initially unimpressed by Taylor's success. The *Herald* advertised itself as "a people's paper" and its daily circulation of 116,500

seemed to show it. The *Daily Advertiser* in its sixty-fourth year and the *Post* in its forty-sixth were initially unconcerned by Boston's new daily. The *Journal* sought Republican readers, the *Transcript* "the culturally alert," and the *Traveller* made a play for the female reader. Soon they came to respect Taylor's uncanny capacity to stimulate circulation by promoting stories that moved middle and working class readers. Taylor was tireless, often working 16-hour days to build the paper up through morning and afternoon editions. He knew how to encourage loyalty and zeal in a hand-picked staff that included the college-educated and intellectually engaged. Even competitors grudgingly admired Taylor's engaging forthrightness. One remarked, "He is a good friend and a good enemy. If he opposes a man, he says it to his face. And if he promises a thing, it is sure to be done, no matter what the cost or trouble."

In forty-four years at the *Globe*'s helm, Taylor insisted that "the paper's news columns be independent and impartial." He sought to make the paper "a proper journal for the family circle." He ordered his editors "to never print a piece of news that might injure an innocent person." Reporters were "never to drag in the family of a man who has gone wrong" because "they are suffering enough as it is." He understood "the importance of reporters" and "local news well written" in stimulating and sustaining circulation. Under Taylor, serials became a staple at the *Globe*. The first, "After Dark in Boston," began appearing on November 17, 1879. Baseball was played up as the "national past-time," and as early as May 2, 1878 sports editor Arthur Fowle placed news of the Boston Red Stockings on the front page. Joseph "King" Kelly was puffed by *Globe* sportswriter Tim Murnane. Kentucky-born James Morgan became the *Globe*'s Sunday editor. Edward Bailey was given charge of the paper's aggressively Democratic editorial page and became a champion of Irish immigrant interests that included higher factory wages, an eight-hour work day, the end of the poll tax, and the right of priests to administer last rites to dying patients in local hospitals. Boston's Irish had a newspaper that spoke for them and fought for them. Cyrus Field Willard became the paper's labor editor and reported on the plight of the unions. The paper's appetite for solving murder mysteries can be seen in its sensational summer-long coverage in 1892 of the axe murders of Lizzie Borden's parents. The stories, under managing editor Benjamin Palmer, helped solidify the *Globe* as Boston's circulation leader. During the paper's first three decades, Boston's population would more than double to 560,000 and the *Globe*'s circulation would soar to 200,000. Its forty-page Sunday edition was five times what it had been when Taylor took over the paper and, as it approached 300,000, the *Globe* enjoyed twice the circulation of its nearest competitor.

Taylor's son William became the *Globe*'s publisher in 1921 after his father's death. William O. Taylor was a conservative, Bible-reading, taciturn man who considered the *Globe* a unique "New England institution" during his thirty-five-year leadership of the paper. Liberal critic Oswald Garrison Villard thought the *Globe* under Taylor was "a genuine friend of labor" but "sadly subservient to its advertisers." Frank Sibley and Charles Merrill became the *Globe*'s best-known reporters of the period. Harvard-educated John Harris became the paper's chief political correspondent in 1932. The Depression hit the *Globe* hard. By 1936, the *Globe* sank to third in circulation of Boston's seven dailies. Third generation Irish readers had tired of the paper's uncritical account of the arts and local politics. Many turned to the edgier *Herald* or William Randolph Hearst's more sensational *American*. The *Globe* used the market research of Robert Ahern, Gallup's New England field man, to win back lost readers by aggressively marketing the *Globe* to Boston's growing suburbs and by building a state of the art home delivery system. Sales in the city focused on winning over the expanding number of commuters. Lucien Thayer vastly improved the paper's photographic department. After Pearl Harbor was attacked, John Barry's daily "war diary" became a must read for many Bostonians. The reporting of Victor Jones with the 9th Army and Carlyle Holt's work with the U.S. air campaign in France and Germany helped restore the *Globe*'s reputation as New England's most trusted daily.

When William Davis Taylor took over as the paper's publisher following his father's death in 1955, it marked a generational shift in the *Globe*'s fortunes. Veteran reporter Louis M. Lyons saw "Davis take the lid off," leading *Globe* editors to take "strong editorial positions on civic affairs and public issues," while opening "sensitive situations" to "the uninhibited exploration of reporters." The *Globe* received its first Pulitzer Prize in 1966 for its investigative reporting on the qualifications of a federal district court judge. A 1972 Pulitzer was awarded for the paper's reporting on municipal corruption in the city of Somerville. Three years later the paper was awarded another Pulitzer Prize for its coverage of the desegregation of Boston's public schools.

The Taylor family control of the *Globe* extended until 1997, a period that saw its sports section feature the writing of Bud Collins on tennis, Will McDonough on football, and Peter Gammons on baseball. Paul Szep twice won Pulitzer Prizes for his acerbic editorial cartoons. Stan Grossfeld won a Pulitzer for his photographs of the War in Lebanon in 1984 and Ethiopian hunger in 1985. The *Globe*'s nationally syndicated columnist Ellen Goodman was awarded a Pulitzer Prize in commentary. William Henry received his for criticism. The paper was purchased by the New York Times Company on October 1, 1993. Subsequently, the paper's investigative reporting on sexual abuse allegations within the Catholic Church and its articles on the ethical issues raised by stem cell research were widely praised. In the early twenty-first century, the paper's daily circulation of more than 400,000 and Sunday circulation of 650,000 re-established the *Boston Globe* as one of New England's leading newspapers and a regional institution of national significance.

Further Reading

"Boston Globe." Vertical File, History and Staff, Boston Public Library.

Grossfeld, Stan. *Eyes of the Globe: 25 Years of Photographs from the Boston Globe*, Chester, CT: Globe Pequot Press, 1985.
Harrigan, Jane T. *Read All About It! A Day in the Life of a Metro Newspaper*, Chester, CT: Globe Pequot Press, 1987.
Lyons, Louis M. *Newspaper Story: One Hundred Years of the Boston Globe*, Cambridge: Belknap Press, 1971.
Morgan, James. *Charles H. Taylor: Builder of the Boston Globe*, Boston: Boston Globe, 1923.
Villard, Oswald Garrison. *The Disappearing Daily*, Boston: A.A. Knopf, 1944.

BRUCE J. EVENSEN

BOSTON NEWS-LETTER

The *Boston News-Letter* was America's first continuously published newspaper. Postmaster John Campbell contracted with printer Bartholomew Green to print the paper, and the first issue appeared on April 24, 1704. The paper, through a series of printers and incarnations with various titles, continued to be published until February 1776. By the time of the Revolutionary War, the newspaper served as a mouthpiece for the occupying British army. When the redcoats left Boston, the paper shut down.

The *News-Letter* grew from Campbell's handwritten newsletters, which he started after becoming Boston postmaster. Campbell sent his letters free through the mails and used the same franking privilege with the *News-Letter*. When Campbell could no longer meet the demand for his newsletter, he hired Green to convert it into a newspaper. According to British law, publishing in colonies required sanction. Consequently, the words "Published by Authority" appeared in the nameplate, signifying governmental approval of content. Endorsement continued until Campbell lost his postmaster position in 1719. William Brooker, the new postmaster, assumed the *News-Letter* was a job perk, but Campbell refused to relinquish it, necessitating creation of the *Boston Gazette*.

The *News-Letter* under Campbell obtained information in much the same way printers would for the entire colonial period. Personal and official letters, official colonial and British legislation and decrees, news from sailors and passengers at the docks, clippings from other newspapers, and reports from unpaid correspondents filled Campbell's two-page paper. The *News-Letter*'s information presentation was historical, not timely. Campbell preferred to present information chronologically, especially with news from Europe. Information in his paper was sometimes a year old. By 1720, Campbell sold around three hundred copies per issue.

In 1721, the *News-Letter* was involved in America's first newspaper war. When Boston's third paper, the *New-England Courant*, attacked Cotton Mather's call for smallpox inoculation, Campbell provided pro-inoculation forces a mouthpiece. Campbell gave the paper to printer Green in 1722, who changed the name to the *Weekly News-Letter* in 1726. When Green died in 1733, John Draper assumed control of the paper. It stayed in his family until its demise. Draper's son, Richard, inherited the *News-Letter* in November 1762. He added *New-England Chronicle* to the title. In

1764, the name changed again to the *Massachusetts Gazette (And Boston News-Letter)*. After November 1, 1765, Stamp Act, Draper dropped *Boston News-Letter* from the title. In 1768, the *Gazette* and the *Boston Post-Boy* combined to use *Massachusetts Gazette* as their name. Draper appended *Boston News-Letter* to his *Gazette*. The *Massachusetts Gazette* was published "by Authority" and appeared as the *Post-Boy* on Mondays and as the *News-Letter* on Thursdays. This arrangement lasted until September 1769.

In 1774, Draper died, and his wife Margaret took control with her husband's partner of one month, John Boyle. When this partnership dissolved, Draper and John Howe became associates. When the Revolution began, all of Boston's papers except the *News-Letter* either moved out of the city or shut down.

Further Reading

Bleyer, Willard Grosvenor. *Main Currents in the History of American Journalism*. Boston: Houghton Mifflin, 1927.

Clark, Charles, E., *The Public Prints: The Newspaper in Anglo-American Culture, 1665–1740*. New York: Oxford University Press, 1994.

Kobre, Sidney. *The Development of the Colonial Newspaper*. 1944; reprint, Goucester, MA: Peter Smith, 1960.

Thomas, Isaiah. *The History of Printing in America*. 1810; reprint, New York: Weathervane Books, 1970.

DAVID A. COPELAND

BOURKE-WHITE, MARGARET

Margaret Bourke-White (June 14, 1904–August 27, 1971) was a pioneering photographer who was instrumental in bringing professional standing to twentieth-century photojournalism. For many Americans, her portraits personify Southern poverty, Midwest drought, South African apartheid, and Nazi concentration camps. As a World War II correspondent, she was the first to provide pictures of Germany's bombings of Moscow; she captured the human side of the Korean War by photographing the reunion of a family split by civil war. She and her work came to represent *Life*, America's premiere picture magazine. With covers of world leaders such as Winston Churchill and Josef Stalin, *Life* brought her work to millions.

Even before Bourke-White signed on with *Life*, she had established herself as a daring, innovative photographer and was working for Time Inc. In the late 1920s when she photographed factories in the Midwest, her detail, composition, and perspective revealed the beauty of the machinery that was driving the nation. She experimented with lighting and paper so that her prints were some of the first to capture the drama of the industrial process. They also captured the attention of *Time* magazine publisher Henry Luce. The precision and passion in her photographs of Cleveland, Ohio's, Otis Steel factory meshed with Luce's vision of modern business. He asked her to be the photographer for a magazine he was proposing for the business elite. Auspiciously named *Fortune*, this publication was launched in 1930 during the Great Depression, yet succeeded. It embodied Luce's optimism in the American spirit, defined business in increasingly inclusive terms, and carried the Bourke-White photograph as its trademark. Six years later, Luce would ask her to be one of the four photographers who would launch America's first picture magazine.

The first cover of *Life* magazine, on November 23, 1936, featured Bourke-White's powerful photograph of Montana's Fort Peck Dam. That issue ran another important piece inside. She had been sent to record the dam's completion, a symbol of New Deal progress. While there, she took the initiative to photograph the after-hours lives of the workers. When *Life* ran the photos of the workers with her captions, a new form of journalistic expression in America was created, the photographic essay. She had pioneered a rudimentary structure for such a form as early as the inaugural issue of *Fortune*, with photos of hog-processing.

Margaret White was born on June 14, 1904. Her parents were Minnie Bourke, an independent woman who rode bicycles and read classics, and Joseph White, an engineer and inventor. She grew up in New York and then New Jersey with an older sister and younger brother in a household that encouraged a strong work ethic and a quest for knowledge. Photography became an artistic outlet and occasional source of income after she took a course at the Clarence H. White School at Columbia University. She later finished her education at Cornell University.

She christened herself with a distinctive hyphenated last name when she divorced her first husband after an early two-year marriage. Bourke-White rarely referenced this failed marriage and soon dropped two years from her age (which may explain the 1906 birth date in some accounts). Her other marriage was in 1939 to author Erskine Caldwell, with whom she had documented the poverty of Southern share-croppers. By the time they divorced after almost four years of marriage, she realized that her work was her passion and that a family could not be expected to adapt to her career.

Her *Life* assignments spanned the globe and often came during times of crisis. The jobs required immediate response, and deadlines were tight for the weekly magazine. She gained access where less persistent photographers failed, which assured editors at *Life* a good story, and probably an exclusive. She experimented with newer media, including photomurals, color photography, and movies, as well as innovations such as small-format cameras. But her demand for precise composition lent itself to a large-format camera, with its sturdy construction and big negatives, and usually brought her back to the black-and-white still photograph. *Life* was the journalistic vehicle that gave her work exposure to the mass audience. She not only branded *Life* with her photographs, she institutionalized her influence in its publishing empire. When she came to work for *Life,* she brought from the Bourke-White Studio a skilled printer, Oscar Graubner, who became the head of the *Life* photo labs, and her secretary, Peggy Sargent, who became *Life*'s film editor.

Throughout her career, Bourke-White faced down the jealousy of male co-workers who would reassure themselves that she was merely a front for some male photographer or discredit her reputation in order to claim professional credit for themselves. With daring, determination, and a camera in her hands, she created a confident and dramatic persona whose exploits were covered across the media. Visible, glamorous, and professional, she provided a role model for women, and she enjoyed this celebrity status on lecture tours later in her career.

She did her last photographic assignments for *Life* in 1957, although she would write the text for a later article that her *Life* colleague Alfred Eisenstaedt photographed. That article documented her Parkinson's disease, complications from which would take her life in the summer of 1971. She had begun to lose mobility on her left side in the early 1950s, but, worried she would no longer get the good assignments, "Maggie the Indestructible" did not admit the disease to her editors until it was well advanced.

Bourke-White became the model of a self-made woman by cultivating an independent and high-profile professional career. Her influence on the field of photojournalism ranges from publishing the first photo essay in a U.S. magazine to bringing her staff into the decision-making process at Time Inc. For two decades, her NBC photomural stood in Rockefeller Center as testament to the grand scale of her vision, her precision, and her willingness to blur boundaries. Bourke-White's myriad legacies point to her unstinting efforts to accomplish what she considered the mission of the photojournalist—to record the truth.

Further Reading

Bourke-White, Margaret. *Portrait of Myself.* New York: Simon and Schuster, Inc., 1963.
——. *Red Republic.* RKO Radio Pictures, 1934.
Goldberg, Vicki. *Margaret Bourke-White: A Biography.* New York: Harper & Row, Publishers, 1986.
Rubin, Susan Goldman. *Margaret Bourke-White: Her Pictures Were Her Life.* New York: Harry N. Abrams, Inc., 1999.
"Youth Wants to Know: Margaret Bourke-White." 30 minutes: NBC-TV, 1956.

THERESE L. LUECK

BOURNE, RANDOLPH SILLIMAN

The difficult life of Randolph Bourne (May 30, 1886–December 22, 1918) began in Bloomfield, New Jersey, four miles northwest of Newark. The town's original name "Wardsesson" meant "Crooked Place." Bourne's face was badly deformed at birth. At four, spinal tuberculosis severely stunted his growth and made him a hunchback. His alcoholic father Charles Rogers Bourne abandoned the family. Sarah Barrett Bourne, Randolph's mother and daughter of a Congregational minister, would raise him along with an aunt.

A high school valedictorian, he studied under John Dewey and Charles Beard at Columbia University, paying his bills through proofreading and piano tuning. His liberal idealism was first published in the pages of the *Columbia Monthly* and the *Atlantic Monthly*. Bourne received his masters degree in sociology in 1913. In that year, his

articles celebrating youth culture's "great rich rush and flood of energy" were published as a book, *Youth and Life* (1913, 2–4). A Gilder Fellowship allowed him to travel and study in Europe for a year on the eve of the continent's lurch into war. *Arbitration and International Politics* (1913) and *Towards an Enduring Peace: A Symposium of Peace Proposals and Programs, 1914–1916* (1916) reflect Bourne's early pleas for the peaceful settlement of international disputes. This enthusiasm led to the publication of a series of articles in the *New Republic*, beginning in July 1915, urging American neutrality. These articles stopped in November 1916, when the magazine's editor, Herbert Croly, began to advocate a more interventionist policy that led to the magazine's eventual support of a Congressional war declaration in April 1917.

The Masses, a socialist journal, edited by Max Eastman, whose contributors included John Reed, Sherwood Anderson, Dorothy Day, Carl Sandburg, and Upton Sinclair, was the only publication open to Bourne's anti-war writings. The magazine, however, was soon forced to suspend publication when the Wilson administration prosecuted it under the Espionage Act for undermining the war effort. Bourne quickly launched his own publication, *The Seven Arts*, to vigorously make the case that U.S. involvement in an unjust war of Europe's imperial powers undermined basic American values. "One has a sense of having come to a sudden, short stop at the end of an intellectual era," Bourne lamented, as Dewey and other liberals embraced the war effort (Hansen 1992, 342). In June 1917 Bourne wrote for "those of us who still retain an irreconcilable animus against war." He felt himself deeply estranged from those intellectuals who daily "flood us with the sewage of the war spirit" by embracing Woodrow Wilson's dubious pledge that the "war will secure the triumph of democracy and internationalize the world" (*The Seven Arts*, "The War and the Intellectuals," June 1917, 1–3). In September 1917 he put it bluntly, "The war—or American promise: one must choose" (*The Seven Arts*, September 1917, "A War Diary," 4–5).

Bourne's dissent frightened the journal's financial backers, and in the fall of 1917, *The Seven Arts* ceased publication. "The magazines I write for die violent deaths," he wrote a friend in November 1917. "All my thoughts appear to be unprintable" (Schlissel, 313). Bourne's role at *The Dial* was restricted to literary reviews, where he was an early and articulate supporter of Theodore Dreiser, Willa Cather, and others. Virulent opposition by his pro-war opponents eventually forced him from this job as well. A few weeks later Bourne died in the influenza epidemic of 1918. He was thirty-two-years-old.

After his death, supporters rescued from Bourne's study an unpublished work, "The State," which would include his most somber assessment of the role of propaganda in leading nations to war. "War is the health of the state," he concludes, and is first fought "in the imaginations of men." As assertive president and a compliant press produce propaganda that "gently and irresistibly slides a country into war," in which "the citizen throws off his indifference to government and identifies himself with its purposes" ("War

Is the Health of the State," unpublished manuscript, Papers of Randolph Silliman Bourne)

For an anti-war writer and activist whose early death merited only a single paragraph in the back pages of the mainstream press, Randolph Silliman Bourne has come to symbolize for later generations the potential power of reason and the press in opposing unjust wars. One admirer, John Dos Passos, wrote that, Bourne was "a little sparrow-like man," a "tiny twisted unscared ghost in a black cape," who attempted to warn his World War I generation and every generation afterwards that "war is the health of the state" but no friend to any man (Dos Passos, 105–106).

Further Reading

Abrahams, Edward. *The Lyrical Left: Randolph Bourne, Alfred Stieglitz, and the Origins of Cultural Radicalism in America*. Charlottesville: University of Virginia, 1986.

Blake, Casey Nelson. *Beloved Community: The Cultural Criticism of Randolph Bourne*. Van Wyck Brooks, Waldo Frank, and Lewis Mumford. Chapel Hill: University of North Carolina, 1990.

Bourne, Randolph Silliman. *Youth and Life*. Boston: Houghton Mifflin, 1913.

Brooks, Van Wyck, ed. *The History of a Literary Radical*. New York: B.W. Huebsch, 1920.

Clayton, Bruce. *Forgotten Prophet: The Life of Randolph Bourne*. Columbia: University of Missouri, 1998, originally 1984.

Dos Passos, John. *1919*. New York: Harcourt, Brace & Co., 1932.

Filler, Louis. *Randolph Bourne*. Washington, D.C.: American Council on Public Affairs, 1943.

Hansen, Olaf, ed. *The Radical Will: Randolph Bourne, Selected Writings, 1911–1918*. Berkeley, University of California Press, 1992, originally 1978.

Lasch, Christopher. *The New Radicalism in America, 1889–1963—The Intellectual as a Social Type*. New York: Knopf, 1965.

Moreau, John A. *Randolph Bourne: Legend and Reality*. Washington, D.C.: Public Affairs Press, 1966.

Oppenheim, James, ed. *Untimely papers*. New York: B.W. Huebsch, 1919.

Papers of Randolph Silliman Bourne. New York: Columbia University, Rare Book and Manuscript Library.

Resek, Carl, ed. *War and the Intellectuals: Collected Essays by Randolph S. Bourne*. Indianapolis: Hackett Publishing, 1999, originally 1964.

Sandeen, Eric J., ed. *The Letters of Randolph Bourne*. Troy, NY: Whitson Publishing, 1981.

Schlissel, Lillian, ed. *The World of Randolph Bourne*. New York: E.P. Dutton, 1965.

Vaughan, Leslie J. *Randolph Bourne and the Politics of Cultural Radicalism*. Lawrence: University Press of Kansas, 1997.

BRUCE J. EVENSEN

BOXING JOURNALISM

An estimated one hundred million Americans were listening to the radio on the night of September 22, 1927, when Jack Dempsey and Gene Tunney fought in Chicago's Soldier Field for the heavyweight championship of the world. In the middle of the seventh round —with Dempsey, the fan favorite behind in points—listeners heard NBC's Graham McNamee suddenly say, "Dempsey comes back with a hard right to Tunney's face. Ohhh. Dempsey comes on with a right. He's got Tunney against the ropes. There's another right landing on the champion's jaw, and Tunney is down! Tunney is down!" Ten listeners were so overcome with excitement in that moment that they dropped dead of heart attacks. Another man choked to death on his toothpick. They didn't live to discover that Tunney survived the "long count" and went on to win one of boxing's most controversial fights. The "golden age" of sports journalism made Americans feel they were part of the story. Journalism and boxing had come a long way since their modest beginnings in America.

In the three-hundred-year history of America's colonial and national press, boxing coverage grew from an occasional and anecdotal element in reporting the day's news to a circulation staple. Surveys confirm the sports section is the primary reason American males buy newspapers and read them online, and boxing has long enjoyed a privileged place in the pantheon of athletic contests because of its symbolic significance in certifying the self-actualizing male who subdues through force every enemy and obstacle. As American males increasingly made their money working behind desks, carefully cultivated boxing celebrities seemed an embodiment of our rough hewn ancestors who let nothing stand in their way, while subduing the wilderness to make it a fit place for habitation.

By the first decade of the eighteenth century colonial newspapers began to report on boxing, racing, and harvest festivals for a population that had grown to one quarter million. Agricultural workers, seamen, and slaves enjoyed cock fighting and blood sports. In the Middle Colonies crude men were reported to have hunted deer by fire, and more than one lost an eye or a nose to bare knuckle brawling and gouging. The assurance that you were as good as the next man in the southern backcountry encouraged a culture of violence where colonial papers reported that "gouging and biting, pulling hair and scratching" were ways that "natural men" settled disputes through direct action that certified their honor.

The First Continental Congress in 1774 discouraged "every species of extravagance and dissipation, especially all horse-racing, and all kinds of gaming and cock fighting." But that did not stop Staten Island slave Bill Richmond from settling scores with British soldiers during the Revolution. Lord Percy took the "Black Terror" to London in 1777, where he won a reputation as a worthy opponent in the boxing press then emerging along the Thames. Britain's boxing craze crossed the Atlantic in the early Republican period, largely through the work of sports writer Pierce Egan, whose vivid descriptions of bare-knuckle bouts in London's *Weekly Dispatch* promoted boxing as "a sweet science" that "adds generosity to the national disposition, humanity to our conduct, and courage to our character." Americans were receptive to this message. The "senseless party-spirit" that had been so despised by Puritan fathers was now threatened by the Republican belief that recreation improved the body, soul, and spirit. The *National Intelligencer*, a mouthpiece for Jeffersonian ideals, advocated exercise in 1797 to cultivate "a national spirit." American newspapers gave increasing coverage to tennis, cricket, shinty, rowing, riding, and boxing. Articles began appearing on self-improvement resulting from "physical and moral education." By 1820 the Harvard curriculum included boxing, fencing, and football. Yale President Timothy Dwight gave interviews on the positive power of prayer, study, and gymnastics.

Egan's sixteen-volume *Boxiana*, published between 1813 and 1824 on both sides of the Atlantic, was well received in America, along with William Hazlitt's writing in *The New Monthly Magazine*, and an illustrated journal *The Fancy* that celebrated the lives of Regency "Tom and Jerrys" who used "the art of fives" to settle disputes and separate men from boys. In 1809, Tom Molineaux, a former Virginia slave who won his freedom by fighting, went to England to challenge British champion Tom Cribb, who had defeated Molineaux's mentor, the forty-one-year-old Richmond. Their famous fight on Copthall Common on a bitterly cold night in December 1810 lasted into the fortieth round when Molineaux, exhausted, could not stand for a forty-first. In the eagerly awaited rematch the next year, Cribb broke Molineaux's jaw in the tenth round and knocked him out in the eleventh. No association oversaw boxing's early development, leading several fighters to simultaneously claim they were champions. When Jacob Hyer, a New York bartender, and Tom Beasley, an English sailor, came to blows in a street fight, they decided to settle matters in the squared ring. On the evening of October 15, 1816, the *Boston Post* sent a reporter to Hingham Harbor to cover the contest. He wrote the "vicious" face-off ended when Beasley broke Hyer's arm. Other papers reported after "an hour of fighting" that Hyer had won. Others called it a draw. Another claimed the combatants had "parted as friends."

The period of Jacksonian Democracy saw the creation of a sporting magazine culture and the standardization of rules in professional boxing. The success of John Stuart Skinner's *American Turf Register and Sporting Magazine*, launched in August 1829, led William Trotter Porter and his brothers to publish *Spirit of the Times*, beginning on December 10, 1831, in New York City. During the middle third of the nineteenth century, no sporting journal was more popular or authoritative. Its early coverage of baseball, cricket, fishing, racing and hunting, grew to include boxing, football, the theater, and tall tales from the backwoods. Penny press papers copied Porter's winning formula as his circulation surged past twenty thousand before peaking at forty thousand in the 1840s. Competition also came from Henry William Herbert's *American Monthly Magazine*, the *New York Clipper*, and the *National Police Gazette*. The widely publicized fight between Jacob Hyer's son, Tom, and Yankee Sullivan for the heavyweight championship in 1849 would be the first fought under London Prize Ring Rules that prohibited head butting, hair pulling, eye gouging and neck throttling. The "fearless feat of arms" on February 7, 1849, at Rock Point, Maryland attracted a $10,000 purse at a time when a worker might make $300 in a year. James Gordon Bennett's *New York Herald* could not remember "so great

an excitement in the public mind" since "the first accounts of the Mexican War." Word that Sullivan could not come out for an eighteenth round of fighting was telegraphed to New York. The *Gazette*, George Wilkes' four-page nickel shocker, hoped to be first on the street with reports from ringside that Sullivan "entirely exhausted" had "staggered backward" when "the fight was done" and had to be "helped from the ring."

Competition to stimulate circulation by being the first to report fight results intensified on the eve of the Civil War. When American bare-knuckle champion John C. Heenan fought British champion Tom Sayers to a thirty-seven-round draw outside London on April 17, 1860, Bennett dispatched a boat to intercept a British frigate before it landed in New York harbor with news of the contest. It helped to create a record circulation of 77,000, largest of any American daily. Bennett sent as many as eight reporters to major bouts and published their round-by-round accounts in extra editions. Horace Greeley, publisher of the *New York Tribune*, spoke for many in the establishment press when he equated boxing news with the latest word from "grog shops and brothels," but he still sent reporters to the big fights. Henry Raymond at the *New York Times* griped that since boxing matches were illegal, authorities should "take immediate measures to put a stop to them and arrest the participators." His animosity, however, did not deter the *Times* from being ringside when there was "great and growing excitement in these matters."

By the spring of 1881 the loud-mouthed, pink-paged *National Police Gazette*, now published by Richard Kyle Fox, had become the Bible of the American barbershop by staging sports spectacles that built the personalities of sports celebrities. When John L. Sullivan, a twenty-two-year-old heavyweight contender, refused to walk across Harry Hill's Dance Hall and Boxing Emporium just off the Bowery to shake Fox's hand, he had made an enemy for life. Fox's circulation-building schemes included steeple climbing, oyster opening, haircutting, one-legged dancing, sculling, and female boxing. Early in 1887 he declared that Jake Kilrain was champion and presented him with a diamond-studded belt. Not to be outdone, Sullivan's supporters bought him an even bigger belt. The competing claims were a bonanza for the boxing press that had now grown to include many of the big city dailies in Gilded Age America. When the governor of Louisiana banned the bout, three thousand spectators boarded special trains on July 7, 1889, to a field in Richburg, Mississippi, where the fight was fought. Sullivan's triumph in the seventy-fifth round made him a national celebrity. Sullivan took the stage and made personal appearances. People stood in long lines to shake the hand of the "Boston strong-man."

The end of the bare-knuckle era coincided with the rise of the modern sports section. Joseph Pulitzer, publisher of the *St. Louis Post-Dispatch* and the *New York World*, created a sports department to stimulate the growing sense of civic excitement. His chief competitor, William Randolph Hearst, publisher of the *San Francisco Examiner* and the *New York Journal*, created a daily section devoted to sports in 1895. Hearst had puffed a San Francisco bank clerk, James J. Corbett, as Sullivan's next opponent. Corbett's press agent, theatrical manager William A. Brady pushed reports of "Gentleman Jim" on a willing public. Marquees of Queensbury rules now made fighting faster, with fewer clinches and more movement. The quicker Corbett knocked out the old Irishman in the twenty-first round of their title fight in New Orleans on September 7, 1892, and began touring on both sides of the Atlantic in the play *Gentleman Jack* as a Princeton student of "impeccable moral character." Corbett and Brady would net $150,000 during the play's run, while exposing Corbett, in the eyes of the *Boston Evening Transcript* as "an agreeable disappointment as an actor."

The twentieth century saw sports as a big business. Sports promoters and sports writers needed one another in promoting civic spectacles that commodified sports celebrities. George "Tex" Rickard's powers of promotion knew no peer. He placed a title fight's $30,000 guarantee in gold pieces on public display in a storefront in Goldfield, Nevada to promote the September 3, 1906, light heavyweight contest Battling Nelson and Joe Gans. The stunt worked. Four rows of ringside reporters got in on the boxing ballyhoo, filing stories on Gans's forty-two round win. Rickard saw a golden gate in his $101,000 guarantee of a bout between heavyweight champion Jack Johnson and retired champ Jim Jeffries. Jack London spoke for many in the white community when he implored Jeffries to "remove that golden smile from Johnson's face." The *Boston Globe* stated the racial divide more succinctly. "Mr. Sambo Remo Rastus Brown," alias Jack Johnson, was shown as a bumbling fool, and certainly was no match for "the Great White Hope." Twelve African Americans were killed in racial violence that erupted across the country when word was received that Johnson had knocked out Jeffries in the fifteenth round of their Reno, Nevada fight on Independence Day in 1910. In many areas, film of the fight was banned.

Johnson's win had humiliated the white community by suggesting black prowess in the ultimate arena in which men were measured. The *Nation* deplored "the disgusting exhibition." The *Chicago Tribune* said whites would no longer watch "such ignoble pursuits." Theodore Roosevelt, one of professional boxing's biggest boosters, wrote in the *Outlook* that commercial boxing no longer taught "courage, hardihood, endurance, and self-control." Most states banned the sport. It would be nine years before another title fight was held in the United States. On July 4, 1919, in Toledo, Ohio, Jack Dempsey, a skinny-legged Western fighter with a high-pitched voice would dispatch Jess Willard, "the Pottawatomie Giant" who had defeated Johnson for the title. On that day "the Manassa Mauler" was born and the "Golden Age" of boxing reporting began.

In a decade known for its celebrities—Lindbergh, Valentino, Ford, Chaplin, Ruth, Grange, Jones, Tilden—circulation managers found no one sold more newspapers than Jack Dempsey. Military training for doughboys during World War I had included lessons in the manly art. By the 1920s, twelve million Americans watched boxing matches

or fought themselves. Dempsey's promoter Jack "Doc" Kearns worked well with sports writers, according to Paul Gallico, in making Dempsey "better known than a member of your own family." Grantland Rice, Ring Lardner, Damon Runyon, Heywood Broun, Westbrook Pegler, and others got in on the action, syndicating their columns nationwide, while going on the radio, to become high paid sports celebrities themselves. Forty percent of all local news coverage in the twenties and afterward was now devoted to covering sports. The number increased to 60 percent in the weeks preceding Dempsey's title defenses. Under Rickard's baton, Dempsey's dispatch of French war hero Georges Carpentier in Jersey City, New Jersey on July 2, 1921, drew boxing's first million dollar gate. Sports writers literally hurled Dempsey back through the ropes after Luis Firpo, "the Wild Bull of the Pampas," had knocked the champion out of the ring on September 14, 1923, in the Polo Grounds. The fighters floored each other twelve times before Dempsey won in the second round in what many called the most exciting four minutes in the history of boxing.

Boxing's popularity stimulated the growth of specialty magazines and network radio and television. Nat Fleischer founded *Ring* magazine in 1922 and in the fifty years that followed the magazine published more than forty million words on boxing, making *Ring* the Bible of boxing. The NBC radio network was established in advance of Dempsey's 1926 title defense against Gene Tunney in Philadelphia and the upstart Columbia Broadcasting System used the Dempsey-Tunney rematch in 1927 to create a network of affiliated stations. Joe Louis in the 1930s and 1940s and Rocky Marciano in the 1950s were brought into American homes on radio, and increasingly, television. At the end of World War II, there were only eight thousand television sets in the United States but within eight years, fortry-four million Americans watched television. Many of them could not get enough boxing. *Gillette's Friday Night Fights* enjoyed strong ratings throughout the 1950s, but it was not alone. *Blue Ribbon Bouts* on Wednesday nights, *Fight of the Week* on Saturday Nights, and *Boxing from St. Nick's* on Monday nights gave middle-weight and welter-weight champion Sugar Ray Robinson a national following. Rocky Marciano retired in 1956 as the only undefeated heavyweight champion. Don Dunphy was the era's "voice of boxing," calling two thousand fights on radio and television, including more than two hundred championships with fifty of those in the heavyweight division.

Howard Cosell, a sportscaster for the American Broadcasting Company, became closely identified with heavyweight champion Muhammed Ali in the 1960s and 1970s, and was one of the few journalists to protest the decision by the World Boxing Association to strip Ali of his title in May 1967 because of his refusal to be inducted into the U.S. Army. Ali became a three-time heavyweight champion, and his fights against Joe Frazier and George Foreman drew enormous audiences in pay-per-view. After Ali's retirement in October 1980, promoters Don King and Bob Arum failed to find a heavyweight with Ali's crowd and press appeal. ESPN, a new twenty-four-hour-a-day cable sports station, launched on September 7, 1979, became one of boxing's leading publicists, as it closely followed the careers and contests of Roberto Duran, Marvin Hagler, Sugar Ray Leonard, Thomas Hearns, and Wilfred Benitez. Heavyweights staged a brief comeback when Mike Tyson dominated the division between 1988 and 1990. ESPN2, which began life on October 1, 1993, heavily promoted the careers of Pernell Whitaker, Julio Cesar Chavez, Oscar de la Hoya, and Felix Trinidad. The wide choice, however, in viewing options, the multiplicity of sports and specialty channels, and the absence of a charismatic heavyweight champion became a drag on twenty-first century ratings. By then, boxing had lost much of the symbolic significance it had enjoyed in an earlier, modernizing America. Its champions no longer seemed to stand as the ultimate representative of what it meant to be a man. It was proving harder to persuade communities their fight for respect was necessarily implied by men and women who fought for a living. Postmodern fans now lived in a media-rich environment, where individuals customized their viewing habits and boxing fought with team sports, podcasts, and video games for the attention of its audience.

Further Reading

Cohane, Tim. *Bypaths of Glory: A Sportswriter Looks Back*. New York: Harper & Row, 1963.

Evensen, Bruce J. *When Dempsey Fought Tunney: Heroes, Hokum, and Storytelling in the Jazz Age*. Knoxville: University of Tennessee, 1996.

Gorn, Elliot J. *The Manly Art: Bare-Knuckle Prize Fighting in America*. Ithaca, NY: Cornell University, 1986.

Isenberg, Michael T. *John L. Sullivan and His America*. Urbana: University of Illinois, 1988.

Rader, Benjamin G. *American Sports: From the Age of Folk Games to the Age of Spectators*. Englewood Cliffs, NJ: Prentice-Hall, 1983.

Sammons, Jeffrey T. *Beyond the Ring: The Role of Boxing in American Society*. Urbana: University of Illinois, 1988.

BRUCE J. EVENSEN

BRADFORD, WILLIAM

William Bradford (May 20, 1663–May 23, 1752) was Pennsylvania's first printer, arriving in the colony in 1685, three years after William Penn established it and laid out plans for Philadelphia. Bradford was born in Leicestershire, England, and learned the printing trade from London printer Andrew Sowle, even though Bradford's father was also a printer. Sowle was probably a member of the Society of Friends and printed most of the dissenter group's tracts. Sowle's relationship with Quaker founder George Fox and Penn no doubt affected his apprentice. Bradford joined the Society and obtained a letter of reference from Fox before immigrating to America. Before leaving England, Bradford married Sowle's daughter, Elizabeth. Bradford used Fox's recommendation letter and a newly acquired press, most likely a gift from his father-in-law, to establish a print shop in Pennsylvania. In 1689, the colony hired Bradford to be its official printer, although he began producing official Pennsylvania papers almost immediately after arriving in America.

Bradford printed assorted pamphlets including *Kalendarium Pennsilvaniense* in 1686, the first almanac printed in America. In his eight years in Philadelphia, however, Bradford continually found himself in trouble with Quaker authorities and was admonished by Pennsylvania authorities in 1686, 1687, and 1689 for printing official documents that had not received approval for publication or for including terminology not acceptable to the Quaker faith. In 1692, Bradford printed a series of pamphlets for George Keith, a Quaker who was considered apostate to the mainline doctrine of the Society. Pennsylvania officials ruled Keith's writings seditious and ordered him arrested along with whoever published the offending material. The sheriff found the typeset pages of Keith's tract in Bradford's shop.

The court convicted Keith but acquitted Bradford after the evidence—his typeset frames—were damaged. He then demanded that the government return his confiscated printing tools. Officials finally released them, and Bradford promptly moved to New York, which had hired him as its official printer secretly weeks earlier. Bradford opened his new print shop around June 1, 1693.

In October 1725, Bradford began publishing the *New-York Gazette*. Bradford was then the colony's official printer and the paper was licensed and "published by authority" of the colonial government. In 1734, Bradford's *Gazette* was drawn into the confrontation between James Alexander, William Smith, and those who opposed the government of Governor William Cosby. Alexander and Smith hired Bradford's former apprentice, John Peter Zenger, to publish an opposition paper. As the official publication of the colony, Cosby used Bradford's paper to attack his opponents. After Zenger's arrest for seditious libel and subsequent acquittal based on Andrew Hamilton's famous "truth" defense (truth was not then normally accepted as a defense in libel cases), Cosby lost control of the colony. With a new government in place, Zenger was named New York's printer and Bradford retired. He died in 1752 after working for nearly seventy years as a printer in America. In addition to his print shop, Bradford, with associates, opened the first paper factory in the colonies in 1690.

Bradford's son, Andrew, printed the first newspaper in Philadelphia in December 1719, and family members continued to operate print shops and publish newspapers in Philadelphia and New York throughout the eighteenth century.

Further Reading

Clark, Charles, E. *The Public Prints: The Newspaper in Anglo-American Culture, 1665–1740*. New York: Oxford University Press, 1994.

DeArmond, Anna Janney. *Andrew Bradford: Colonial Printer*. Newark: University of Delaware Press, 1949.

Hildeburn, Charles R. *A Century of Printing. The Issues of the Press in Pennsylvania, 1685-1784*, 2 vols. Philadelphia, 1885–1886; reprint, New York : Burt Franklin, 1968.

Thomas, Isaiah. *The History of Printing in America*. 1810; reprint. New York: Weathervane Books, 1970.

Wroth, Lawrence C. *The Colonial Printer*, 2nd ed. Portland, ME: Southworth-Anthoensen Press, 1938.

DAVID A. COPELAND

BRADLEE, BENJAMIN C.

Benjamin Crowninshield Bradlee, considered one of the most influential newspapers editors of the twentieth century, achieved distinction as the executive editor of the *Washington Post* from 1968 to 1991, a period when the newspaper rose to world prominence. He led its victorious campaign to publish the Pentagon Papers, which detailed the history of the Vietnam War, as well as its coverage of the Watergate political corruption scandal that led to the resignation of President Richard M. Nixon in 1974. Under his direction the newspaper won eighteen Pulitzer prizes.

Bradlee was born on Aug. 26, 1921, in Boston, Massachusetts, to Frederick Josiah and Josephine deGersdorff Bradlee. His father was a well-connected Boston Brahmin and his mother the daughter of a well-to-do New York lawyer and the grandniece of Frank Crowinshield, founding editor of *Vanity Fair*. The family's affluent life style was greatly diminished during the Depression, though, when Frederick Bradlee lost his job in an investment house. Benjamin Bradlee attended St. Mark's in Southboro, Massachusetts, a boarding school for boys from wealthy families, and graduated from Harvard University on August 8, 1942. That same day he received an ensign's commission in the U.S. Navy Reserve and married Jean Saltonstall, the daughter of another Brahmin family. He immediately went on active duty, serving in the Pacific.

After discharge as a lieutenant in 1945, he worked as a reporter for the *New Hampshire Sunday News* in Manchester. In 1948 he became a reporter for the *Washington Post* where he remained for three years until leaving to become the press attache at the U.S. Embassy in Paris. In 1953 he joined *Newsweek* as its European corespondent. Transferred to the Washington bureau in 1957, he became bureau chief in 1961 after he had been instrumental in arranging the magazine's sale to the *Washington Post*. Divorced from his first wife in 1955 by whom he had one son, Benjamin C. Jr., Bradlee married Antoinette Pinchot in 1956. The couple had two children, Dominic and Marina.

As members of the political and media establishment in Washington, the Bradlees lived in Georgetown near Senator John Kennedy, becoming close friends with him and his wife, Jackie. Bradlee's personal relationship with John Kennedy continued as Kennedy successfully campaigned for the Presidency in 1960 and moved into the White House. The friendship enhanced Bradlee's status as a journalist by providing exclusive stories for *Newsweek*, although Bradlee contended he never violated professional objectivity in covering Kennedy. Bradlee's relationship with Kennedy's successor, Lyndon B. Johnson, was less cordial. After Bradlee wrote a story for *Newsweek* indicating that Johnson was looking for a replacement for FBI director, J. Edgar Hoover,

based on information leaked by a confidential source in the White House, an angry President called a press conference to announce that he was reappointing Hoover. Johnson then reportedly told one of Bradlee's friends: "You can tell Ben Bradlee to go [expletive] himself!"

After President Kennedy's assassination in 1963, Bradlee published a eulogy, *That Special Grace* (1964). As a Kennedy confidant, Bradlee kept notes with Kennedy's knowledge on their frequent social contacts and off-the-record chats for the five years preceding his death. These formed the basis for Bradlee's 1975 book, *Conversations with Kennedy*. It pictured Kennedy as perceptive, gossipy, and devoted to his family.

In 1965 Bradlee returned to the *Post*. He was asked to become managing editor of the paper by Katharine Graham, who became publisher following the suicide of Philip Graham, her husband. Three years later Bradlee was named executive editor. With the full backing of Graham, Bradlee hired fresh talent and encouraged competition between staff members for choice assignments. He also oversaw transformation of the women's pages into a feature-oriented "Style" section aimed at drawing in readers of both sexes. This section featured high-caliber writing and was widely copied by other newspapers.

His highest journalism triumph came when the *Post* won the 1972 Pulitzer Prize for public service as a result of its Watergate coverage. This followed the victory of the *Post*, along with that of the *New York Times*, in the Pentagon Papers case when the U.S. Supreme Court ruled in 1971 that the federal government could not forbid publication of these documents that traced the background of the Vietnam War. Known for his salty language, Bradlee became a legendary figure in American journalism, a reputation enhanced by Jason Robards' portrayal of him in the film *All the President's Men* (1976), and by the book by Bob Woodward and Carl Bernstein that told how the two young *Post* reporters had teamed up to uncover the Watergate scandal. His image suffered somewhat in 1981 when the *Post* was forced to return a Pulitzer Prize given to Janet Cooke, a reporter who had fabricated a story about an eight-year-old heroin addict.

Divorced from his second wife in 1975, he married Sally Quinn, a writer for "Style," in 1978. The couple had one child, Quinn, born in 1982. After retirement in 1991, Bradlee was named vice-president-at-large of the *Washington Post*.

Further Reading

Bernstein, Carl, and Bob Woodward. *All the President's Men*. New York: Simon & Schuster, 1974.

Bradlee, Benjamin C. *Conversations with Kennedy*. New York: Norton, 1975.

——. *A Good Life: Newspapering and Other Adventures*. New York: Simon & Schuster, 1975.

——. *That Special Grace*. Philadelphia: Lippincott, 1964.

Graham, Katharine. *Personal History*. New York: Knopf, 1997.

Halberstam, David. The Powers That Be. New York: Knopf, 1979.

Roberts, Chalmers M. *In the Shadow of Power: The Story of the Washington Post*. Cabin John, MD: Seven Locks Press, 1989.

WashingtonPost.com. "Interview with Special Guest Ben Bradlee." http://discuss.washingtonpost.com/zforum/97/bradlee.htm (accessed April 9, 2007).

White, Theodore H. *Lecture with Benjamin C. Bradlee.* Cambridge: Joan Shorenstein Barone Center, Kennedy School of Government, 1991.

MAUREEN BEASLEY

BRINKLEY, DAVID

"The end when it came was illuminated by red flares because there at the end of the tunnel there was no other light," David Brinkley (July 10, 1920–June 11, 2003) reported on April 29, 1975, at the end of America's long involvement in the Viet Nam War, which had killed 58,000 of its soldiers and wounded 153,000 others. "In the smoky red glare at the American embassy in Saigon helicopters were flying from the rooftop" taking away a final few. Marines had to strike the hands of South Vietnamese desperate that they not be left behind. "The war started with B52 bombers," Brinkley lamented, "and ended with the cracking of knuckles."

At two networks over fifty-three years, David Brinkley may have spoken to more people than anyone in the history of broadcast journalism. His spare, conversational, ironic speaking and writing style impressed a generation of newsmen. Tom Brokaw, his long-time colleague at NBC said, "We were all in awe of him. What Hemingway was to literature, Brinkley was to television news." George Will, Brinkley's co-worked at ABC, preferred a sports analogy, "There was never a more graceful center fielder than Joe Di Maggio. And there was never a more graceful writer in the history of broadcast journalism than David Brinkley."

David McClure Brinkley was the youngest of five children born in Wilmington, North Carolina to an old Southern family. His father William Graham Brinkley was a railroad worker who died when David was eight. David was estranged from his mother Mary MacDonald West Brinkley, a respectable Presbyterian and "the fiercest prohibitionist since Carry Nation," who seemed more interested "in dogs, babies, and flowers than me," Brinkley recalled. Brinkley was a loner who took refuge in reading. His high school English teacher, Mrs. Burrows Smith, suggested he consider a career in journalism. At fifteen, he was an unpaid intern at the *Wilmington Morning Star*. After graduating, he went to work there for eleven dollars a week. His first two-sentence story reported that Wilmington was repainting the median on Third Street.

In 1940, Brinkley enlisted in the army and served as a supply sergeant before being misdiagnosed with a kidney ailment and honorably discharged. In 1942 Brinkley got a job writing for the radio wire at United Press based in Atlanta, where he was told to make his copy "easy and breezy." At twenty-two, Brinkley was made manager of the UP bureau in Nashville, where he worked seventy-hour weeks at $42.50 a week. Brinkley developed his famous radio voice through the tutoring of Virginia Mansell, who did commercials at WLAC. "I still talk as she taught me to talk," he said, leaving his Southern accent behind. A year later, UP reassigned Brinkley to Charlotte. In the fall of 1943, Brinkley thought he had a job at CBS radio in Washington. When he arrived, bureau chief Bill White had not heard of Brinkley and would not see him. Brinkley walked four blocks to NBC where he "was hired in ten minutes and stayed thirty-eight years."

At twenty-three, "although I was entirely unprepared," Brinkley was made NBC's White House correspondent. He gathered twice weekly with other reporters at President Franklin Roosevelt's Oval Office press conferences. Tired of "having my stories read wrongly," Brinkley began to do his own on air work. "NBC paid me $60 to write the scripts and paid announcers $600 to read them." On July 25, 1944, Brinkley reported that "friendly fire" in Normandy had accidentally killed 245 of the 250 men he had served with in Company I of the 120th Infantry. On March 5, 1946, Brinkley traveled to Fulton, Missouri to cover the "Iron Curtain" speech of Winston Churchill, "the century's greatest man," warning of Soviet post-war expansionism. Brinkley began appearing on NBC's fledgling television news operation, where he "could make mistakes with no one watching." Brinkley read scripts over five minutes of silent film. In 1946, Brinkley married Ann Fischer, a United Press reporter. The couple had three sons.

NBC television inaugurated coverage of presidential conventions in 1948 and Brinkley was in Philadelphia to report them to several East Coast cities. In February of 1949 *Camel News Caravan*, NBC's nightly fifteen-minute newscast, hosted by John Cameron Swayze, went on the air with Brinkley as its Washington correspondent. Brinkley tried to report in 1954 "as straight as I could" the aftermath of the Supreme Court's order to integrate the nation's public schools. He received death threats and was called "a traitor to the South." Television's reach now extended to seventeen million homes in sixty-four cities and thirty-eight states. NBC paired Brinkley with Chet Huntley, a somewhat stoical correspondent from Los Angeles, to cover the 1956 presidential conventions in Chicago, hoping they would be competitive with coverage at CBS. Brinkley's carefully scripted "ad libs" were a huge hit. On the third night of the convention, Jack Gould, television critic for *The New York Times* wrote, "A quiet Southerner with a dry wit and a heaven-sent appreciation of brevity, has stolen the television limelight this week. Brinkley quite possibly could be the forerunner of a new school of television commentator. He contributes his observations with assurance and not insistence."

Starting on October 29, 1956, NBC's nightly *Huntley-Brinkley Report* dominated the ratings for much of the show's fourteen-year run. The show's close, "Goodnight, Chet." "Goodnight, David," became a national catchphrase. Brinkley observed that "the secret of television is that you are not speaking to ten million people but one or two people at a time in ten million rooms." As the network nightly news expanded to a half hour in the fall of 1963, Brinkley came to see news "as something worth knowing you don't already know." This approach, according to Ted Koppel, let Brinkley "project authority without trying to."

By 1966, television was America's most trusted source for news. Ten Emmy Awards and three Peabody awards affirmed Brinkley's mastery of the medium. "David's command of the single declarative sentence," Walter Cronkite believed, made it the dominant style for a generation of broadcast journalists. One of Brinkley's most famous commentaries followed the June 6, 1968, assassination of Sen. Robert Kennedy, when he told viewers "when Senator Kennedy went down he was speaking for those young people who want to change certain aspects of American life. Well that cause has not been stilled forever because even without him the changes will be made because they have to be."

After Huntley retired in 1970, Brinkley continued as co-host and commentator on the *NBC Nightly News* for eleven years and hosted *NBC Magazine with David Brinkley*. Divorced, Brinkley remarried in 1972, and adopted Susan Adolph's daughter from her previous marriage. At the height of the Watergate scandal in October 1973, Brinkley famously castigated President Richard M. Nixon for obstructing justice. "Our history shows," Brinkley recalled, "that the American people will put up with a great deal. But they will not put up with anyone who claims to be above the law or immune to the rules that apply to everyone else."

On September 4, 1981, Brinkley left NBC after a thirty-eight-year run at the network and repeated clashes with the news division president William Small. "He began dictating to me what I should put on the air," Brinkley wrote in his best-selling memoirs. At sixty-one, several network officials thought Brinkley was too old and washed up. Within a week, Brinkley had been hired by ABC News President Roone Arledge to host a weekly Sunday news show shaped around his personality. Within a month *This Week with David Brinkley* was on the air. Quickly it shot to the top of the ratings, using video clips, panel discussions, interviews, and Brinkley's witty show-ending homilies to easily surpass NBC's venerable *Meet the Press* and CBS's equally stodgy *Face the Nation*. Brinkley's whimsical writings for *This Week* were collected in *Everyone Is Entitled to My Opinion* (1996). His personal favorite was the March 19, 1989, announcement by the Internal Revenue Service that "in the event of war and nuclear attack on this country, the collection of taxes will continue. It says in the areas of this country hardest hit, delinquent taxpayers will be given a little extra time." Brinkley's stories often captured ordinary people doing extraordinary things.

Brinkley retired from ABC in 1996, having won the Presidential Medal of Freedom, the nation's highest civilian award. On that occasion, Brinkley quoted Shakespeare in saying, "all's well that ends well, and my time here ends extremely well."

Further Reading

Appreciations, ABC, CBS, CNN, Fox, MSNBC, NBC, PBS, June 12, 2003.

Chicago Tribune, June 13, 2003, A1 and A21; *The New York Times*, June 13, 2003, A1, A30 and A32.
Brinkley, David. *Brinkley's Beat: People, Places, and Events That Shaped My Time*. New York: Alfred A. Knopf, 2003.
—— *11 Presidents, 4 Wars, 22 Political Conventions, 1 Moon Landing, 3 Assassinations, 2,000 Weeks of News and Other Stuff on Television, and 18 Years of Growing Up in North Carolina*. New York: Alfred A. Knopf, 1995.
—— *Everyone Is Entitled to My Opinion*. New York: Alfred A. Knopf, 1996.
—— *Washington Goes to War*. New York: Alfred A. Knopf, 1988.
Waite, Clayland H. "David Brinkley: U.S. Broadcast Journalist," Museum of Broadcast Communications, Chicago, Illinois.

BRUCE J. EVENSEN

BRISBANE, ARTHUR

Arthur Brisbane (December 12, 1864–December 25, 1936) was an editor whose close alliance with William Randolph Hearst contributed greatly to the newspaper magnate's success and made Brisbane one of the best-paid editors of his era. Born in Buffalo, New York, on December 12, 1864, Brisbane was raised in a wealthy family and named after his father, a follower of French socialist Charles Fourier and a founder of Brook Farm who purchased space on the front page of the *New York Tribune* for a column. As Brisbane's mother died when he was only three years old, he became unusually close to his father and credited him with his interest in writing.

In 1882, armed with a letter of introduction from his father, Brisbane landed a job as a reporter on Charles Dana's *New York Sun*. He learned the craft quickly but was soon bored by the daily grind of reporting. He quit and went to Europe but returned to journalism when he was offered the more glamorous post of London correspondent for the *Sun*. When Dana launched an evening edition of his paper in 1887, he brought Brisbane back to New York as managing editor. Joseph Pulitzer recruited Brisbane in 1890 and made him managing editor of the *Sunday World* and eventually the *Evening World*. Brisbane's ambitious nature clashed with Pulitzer who sought talented but obedient lieutenants. In particular Brisbane wanted to attach his name to the editorials he wrote, something that Pulitzer would not tolerate.

In 1897, when William Randolph Hearst bought the *Morning Journal* and raided Pulitzer's best staff he offered Brisbane editorial freedom of the kind Pulitzer was unwilling to grant. Close in age, with common ambitions, similar larger-than-life fathers, Hearst and Brisbane were natural partners. Brisbane became Hearst's key lieutenant in the hurly burly competition of the evening papers leading the *Evening Journal* to tremendous financial success. In return, Hearst made Brisbane the highest paid newspaper editor in the land. In time, Brisbane relinquished most of his daily managerial duties and became a columnist. His column "Today" was published in all the Hearst papers and his other column "The Week" was syndicated to twelve hundred newspapers. He usually wrote about national and international affairs but he often devoted his column to softer topics that interested many readers less concerned with the news of the world. Brisbane's opposition to the United States entry into World War I, which matched that of his employer, garnered him considerable criticism and accusations that he was pro-German.

Brisbane was not only a powerful editorialist but was one of the first to have made a fortune as a newspaper writer. He used his money to dabble in publishing by acquiring the *Washington Times* in 1917 and the *Evening Wisconsin* in 1918, selling both to Hearst in 1919. He also invested heavily in New York City real estate, and bought a farm on Long Island, a summer home in the Catskills, and vast acreage in Florida where he also had a winter home in Miami. Brisbane died on December 25, 1936.

Further Reading

Brisbane, Arthur. *Editorials from the Hearst Newspapers.* New York: Albertson Publishing co., 1906.
Carlson, Oliver. *Brisbane, a Candid Biography.* Westport, CT: Greenwood Press, 1970.

JAMES MCGRATH MORRIS

BROKAW, TOM

"I thought, oh, my God, these are the people who raised me. These are the people in my home town. These are my parents' best friends, the people that I care about, and I thought, I've got to write about this." Tom Brokaw's (February 6, 1940–) encounter with veterans on the beaches at Normandy forty years after D-Day led to a series of reports and a best-selling book "that introduced the greatest generation to the generations that followed them." Even after more than forty years at NBC and half of that as the anchor of the network's highly rated nightly news, it is the story "of those who sacrificed during the Great Depression, saved the world from the ravages of fascism, and gave us the world we have today" for which Brokaw would be best remembered.

Thomas John Brokaw, son of Anthony Orville Brokaw, a construction foreman with the U.S. Army Corps of Engineers, and Eugenia Conley Brokaw, a clerk who steered her son toward journalism, was born in Webster, South Dakota, and raised on Army bases "where all the talk and all the activity was organized around the war." He attended high school in Yankton and worked as a radio disc jockey, where he was able to interview Meredith Lynn Auld, Miss South Dakota of 1959. They married on August 17, 1962, after Brokaw finished his undergraduate degree in political science at the University of South Dakota and before he began a $100-a-week job as newscaster and morning news editor at KMTV, the NBC affiliate in Omaha, Nebraska. The couple would have three daughters.

In 1965, Brokaw's good looks, deep baritone, and affability on the air got him the job of news anchor at WSB-TV in Atlanta, where his occasional reporting on civil rights began appearing on the network's *Huntley-Brinkley Report.* The following year he was promoted to reporter

and later news anchor for KNBC-TV in Los Angeles. He reported for the network on the drug counter-culture of San Francisco's Haight-Ashbury District and on June 6, 1968, he reported the assassination of Senator Robert Kennedy in Los Angeles. Brokaw covered the California delegation at the Democratic National Convention in Chicago and the violent clashes between protesters and police outside the convention hall. Brokaw's coverage of the rise of Ronald Reagan to California's governor and growing antiwar protests at the University of California-Berkeley increased his national profile. In April 1971, he became host of *First Tuesday,* NBC's early experiment in mounting a monthly news magazine.

Brokaw became NBC's White House correspondent in the summer of 1973 as a Senate Committee began its nationally televised hearings on the Watergate scandal. On October 20, 1973, Brokaw reported what came to be known as the "Saturday Night Massacre" in which President Richard Nixon fired special prosecutor Archibald Cox rather than comply with his subpoena to turn over taped Oval Office conversations. The nation's attorney general and assistant attorney general resigned in protest. On July 24, 1974, the U.S. Supreme Court ordered Nixon to turn over his Watergate tapes to investigators. Five days later, Brokaw reported that "Nixon's impeachment is a certainty." Eleven days later, Nixon resigned the presidency. Brokaw had won the respect of the White House press corps for his determined reporting on Watergate. "It wasn't adversary journalism," he said. Reporters faced sustained "White House hostility." Brokaw believed the episode demonstrated that "presidents are not above or beyond the people."

NBC executives saw Brokaw's intelligence and on air poise as a plus in their efforts to overtake the *CBS Evening News with Walter Cronkite.* His White House responsibilities were expanded to include weekend anchoring of the *NBC Nightly News* and prime time news specials. On August 30, 1976, Brokaw became the host of the *Today Show,* replacing Barbara Walters who had just defected to ABC News. Brokaw's salary increased to half a million dollars a year and the show annually earned twenty million dollars for the network. Along with co-host Jane Pauley, Brokaw strengthened the show's hard news edge, reporting on the oil crisis, inflation, the future of the Panama Canal, talks to limit strategic arms, and a one-on-one interview with President Jimmy Carter. Brokaw's persistence paid off and the *Today Show* began to pull away from ABC's *Good Morning, America* in the morning ratings war.

In 1982, ABC News President Roone Arledge offered Brokaw the anchor job for the network's nightly newscast. Instead, NBC signed Brokaw to co-anchor the *NBC Nightly News* with Roger Mudd, beginning in April 1982. On Labor Day 1983, Brokaw became the sole anchor of the show, a position he retained for twenty-one years. For two decades, Brokaw at NBC, Dan Rather at CBS, and Peter Jennings at ABC competed for the nightly news audience. When they began their run, more than two-thirds of all Americans watched network news. At the end of their era, fewer than half of all Americans were tuning in as the Internet, cable, and web-based technologies fragmented the viewing audience. At first, Rather and then Jennings had the highest rated shows. During his last seven years on the air, however, Brokaw and NBC were the most watched network, boasting fifteen million viewers.

In 1983, Brokaw reported from Poland on Pope John Paul II's visit to his communist homeland and filed stories from Beirut following attacks on American forces in the Middle East. On January 28, 1986, he reported on the explosion of the space shuttle *Challenger* after takeoff, killing all seven astronauts aboard. Later that year he hosted an award-winning documentary on "AIDs: Fear and Fact" that analyzed what little was known of a dreaded disease that had killed an estimated 140,000 in a decade. Brokaw's 1987 "Conversation with Mikhail Gorbachev" at the Kremlin won a DuPont Award and was the first such interview given to a Western newsman. Brokaw traveled to Lockerbie, Scotland, to cover the crash of Pan Am Flight 103 in December 1988 and on June 13, 1989, rode a bike with a concealed camera and microphone into Beijing's Tiananmen Square to report the aftermath of the government's bloody attack on student protesters. On November 9, 1989, Brokaw was the only network news anchor in Berlin to report the smashing of the Berlin Wall and "the beginning of a new age in Europe." The wall had been erected at the height of the Cold War in 1961 to keep East Berliners from fleeing to the democratic West. Brokaw reported from the Brandenburg Gate, where "crowds have gathered to celebrate their new freedom. This is the day the Cold War ended, not with a bang but with a street party," he said as he held in his hand a piece of the shattered wall.

In February and March 1991, Brokaw reported from forward bases the allied attack to repel Iraq from neighboring Kuwait. In April 1992, he returned to Los Angeles to report the grim aftermath of racial rioting that left thirty-eight dead, fourteen hundred injured, and property damage at $550 million. He reported on April 30 that the destruction was "a sickening reminder of how we've failed to deal with racism in this country." Brokaw was criticized for what some considered NBC's excessive coverage in 1994 of the O.J. Simpson case in which the former football star was charged with a double murder. Brokaw admitted being uncomfortable with tabloid journalism but acknowledged "you can't be above the news." NBC, he said, had "an obligation" to cover a story that had captured the public's imagination. The onslaught of cable news and talk radio in the late 1990s, Brokaw believed, was "changing the news business." He began earnestly reporting the Internet revolution in 1995. That revolution helped make President Bill Clinton's sexual involvement with a White House intern the major story of 1998, leading up to the president's impeachment. "It was the story no one turned off," Brokaw said, and his reporting won a Peabody Award in 1998.

"We don't just have egg on our face, we have omelet all over our suits," Brokaw famously said on Election Night 2000 when the networks prematurely called the presidential election before all the votes were counted in Florida. In the aftermath of terrorist attacks on the United States on September 11, 2001, Brokaw "tried to get our people through something we were utterly unprepared for." After touring the devastated World Trade Center site he reported its "ugly legacy" for "the thousands who died violent deaths there," yet it was a "holy place" of national consecration and rededication in the fight to preserve freedom "from appalling inhumanity."

Brokaw retired from nightly anchoring the NBC News in December 2004 to devote more time to his ranch in Montana, his commitment to environmental causes, and his work on news specials. He returned to Normandy on the sixtieth anniversary of D-Day and continued his reporting on America's "greatest generation" for viewers who "more than ever longed for authentic American heroes." On Brokaw's last nightly news broadcast he observed that "the essence of journalism is to report what's new and what we need to know." He thought he could spend the rest of his lifetime reporting "the lessons we can learn" from men and women whose "common effort" saved their beleaguered generation and "serves as an inspiration to our own."

Further Reading

Brokaw, Tom. *The Greatest Generation.* New York: Random House, 1998.
—— *The Greatest Generation Speaks: Letters and Reflections.* Norwalk, CT: Easton Press, 1999.
—— "Lessons from a Life in Journalism," http://www.msnbc.com, October 8, 2004.
——. *A Long Way from Home: Growing Up in the American Heartland.* New York: Random House, 2002.
Goldberg, Robert, and Gerald Jay Goldberg. *Anchors: Brokaw, Jennings, Rather and the Evening News.* New York: Birch Lane, 1990.
"Weighting Anchor: Tom Brokaw Takes Stock and Looks Ahead." *Columbia Journalism Review,* January/February 2004.

BRUCE J. EVENSEN

BROOKLYN DAILY EAGLE

The *Brooklyn Daily Eagle* (1841–1955) was more than a newspaper. For more than a century, it was a local landmark and cultural institution, steadfastly preserving communal continuity, while self-consciously shaping and promoting the city's civic identity. The *Eagle* was one of Brooklyn's biggest boosters.

As a city, Brooklyn was but seven years old when the *Eagle* was born on October 26, 1841, in political protest after Whig President William Henry Harrison landslide electoral win. Kings County Democrats felt that they needed a newspaper to fight for Brooklyn's 35,500 residents. When the paper's founder, Henry Cruse Murphy, became Brooklyn's mayor in 1842, day-to-day operations were turned over to Richard Adams Locke, who seven years earlier had persuaded readers of the *New York Sun* that he had seen batmen and blue unicorns on the moon. Isaac Van Anden, a small, taciturn printer with a passion for order, purchased the paper for $1,500 and by 1843, he had made it profitable through job printing. Walt Whitman strengthened the paper's political independence when he became editor in February, 1846. Twenty-two months later, Whitman, a tireless crusader against slavery, was sacked after continuing battles with Brooklyn's business community. At the start of the Civil War, Whitman's successor Henry McCloskey, a states' rights Democrat, was forced to resign because of his attacks on Abraham Lincoln. His city editor, Joseph Howard, was arrested at his desk after publishing a fake proclamation from the president. On April 17, 1861, a mob forced the *Eagle* to show its loyalty by displaying the flag.

The *Eagle* liked to claim that Brooklyn "makes business a pleasure," and portrayed the rapidly growing metropolis with its sprawling Navy Yard as a "middle class utopia" of churches and affordable housing, benevolent societies, cricket clubs, lyceums and lodges, all of which made for "moral living" and stood in stark contrast to the "Gomorrah" standing on the other side of the East River (August 1, 1846, September 30, 1846, and May 3, 1847). Van Anden and editor Thomas Kinsella, an Irish immigrant, were big boosters of the Brooklyn Bridge, begun on January 23, 1867, within view of the *Eagle*'s office and completed on May 24, 1883, in the midst of a riotous civic celebration. Henry Chadwick, a sports writer on the *Eagle* and other papers, promoted baseball and Brooklyn's team joined the National League in 1890, winning eleven pennants during the life of the *Eagle*.

The paper's campaign to maintain Brooklyn's independence failed. The city, then America's third largest, became a borough of New York City on January 1, 1898, in what the *Eagle* would call "the great mistake." Brooklyn's integration into Greater New York City encouraged Lower East Side Jews and eventually African-Americans and Puerto Ricans to move to the city. The paper came to reflect the diversity of its readers while it also maintained its allegiance of extended families who made Brooklyn home. Few public events in Brooklyn were so small that they didn't merit a line in the *Eagle*. Its Code of Ethics urged reporters and editors to be "helpful rather than harmful" and to see the *Eagle* as a "public service institution." The paper was twice honored by the George Polk Award for community service. The paper developed an international focus under Hans V. Kaltenborn, which led to three Pulitzer Prizes for editorial cartooning. Edward Bok, for thirty years the editor of *The Ladies' Home Journal*, got his start at the *Eagle*. So did Hollywood screenwriter Nunnally Johnson, CBS diplomatic correspondent Winston Burdett, and President Eisenhower's press secretary Murray Snyder.

By the 1950s increasing competition from Brooklyn bureaus of New York dailies threatened the *Eagle*'s weakening grip on afternoon readers and advertising revenues. It cut costs and coverage, further exposing its vulnerability. A protracted strike for higher wages by the American Newspaper Guild paralyzed the paper. For the first time in their long history the "Bums," the beloved Brooklyn Dodgers, would go on to win the 1955 World Series. But the *Eagle* was not alive to report it. The paper perished on March 16, 1955, one hundred fourteen years after its first issue.

Further Reading

Brasher, Thomas L. *Whitman as Editor of the Brooklyn Daily Eagle*. Detroit: Wayne State University Press, 1970.

Brooklyn Daily Eagle. *How a Modern Newspaper Is Made*. Brooklyn: Brooklyn Eagle Press, 1911.

Brooklyn Eagle. *The Brooklyn Daily Eagle*. Brooklyn: Brooklyn Eagle Press, 1911.

Christie, George V. *The Brooklyn Daily Eagle*. Washington, D.C.: published by the author.

Evensen, Bruce J. "'Saucepan Journalism' in an Age of Indifference: Moody, Beecher, and Brooklyn's Gilded Press." *Journalism History*, Winter 2001–2002.

Howard, Henry W.B., ed. *The Eagle and Brooklyn*. Brooklyn: Brooklyn Daily Eagle, 1893.

http://.www.brooklynpubliclibrary.org/eagle has digitalized issues of the *Brooklyn Daily Eagle* from October 26, 1841 through December 31, 1902.

Robinson, William E. "The History of the Press of Brooklyn and Kings County." In *The Civil, Political, Professional History and Commercial and Industrial Record of the County of Kings and the City of Brooklyn, New York, from 1683 to 1884*, vol. 2, edited by Henry R. Stiles. New York: W.W. Munsell, 1884.

Schroth, Raymond A. *The Eagle and Brooklyn: A Community Newspaper, 1841–1855*. Westport, CT: Greenwood Press, 1974.

Weyrauch, Martin H. *The Pictorial History of Brooklyn Issued by the Brooklyn Daily Eagle on Its Seventy-Fifth Anniversary, October 26, 1916*. Brooklyn: Brooklyn Daily Eagle, 1916.

BRUCE J. EVENSEN

BROUN, HEYWOOD CAMPBELL

"We must bring ourselves to realize that it is necessary to support free speech for the things we hate in order to ensure it for the things in which we believe." When Heywood Broun (December 7, 1888–December 18, 1939) made this assertion in the *New York World* on January 26, 1923, he was one of America's most widely read and highest paid columnists. His determination to live up to that standard led him to champion unpopular causes, to lose his job, and to launch a labor union for journalists.

Heywood Campbell Broun was born in Brooklyn, New York, the son of an immigrant Scots printer Heywood Cox Broun, and his German American wife, Henrietta Brose Braun. He was raised in Manhattan, attended private schools, but failed to graduate Harvard, preferring poker and Boston Red Sox baseball. Brown was a large man—six feet, four inches, weighting 250 pounds—who projected a rumpled, genial aversion to hard work. He was drawn to journalism, he later claimed, because "no matter how short they make the working day, it will still be a good deal longer than the time required to complete my work."

Broun had made a good impression as a summer intern at the *New York Morning Telegram* in 1908. Two years later, he was working there full time, reporting sports, and specializing in baseball. Two years later he was fired when he insisted on "a living wage." Publishers tended "to pat their fathead employee on the head," Broun observed, in lieu of a satisfactory salary. Broun next worked re-write at the *New*

York Tribune and soon was back writing about baseball. He covered the Giants and could count ace pitcher Christy Mathewson as a friend and checker-playing partner. Broun was a gentle usurper of the sports cliché. "Sports do not build character," he famously wrote. "They reveal it." Later, he wrote, "God seems always on the side that has the best football coach."

When the *Tribune*'s drama critic died in 1915, Broun took the job. His sometimes acerbic style won readers but could alienate actors. Broun once wrote that Geoffrey Steyne was the worst actor on the American stage. Steyne sued. In a later production, Steyne was left out of the review, except for its final sentence that said, "Mr. Steyne's performance was not up to its usual standard." Even the greats felt Broun's barbs. Tallulah Bankhead was told after one performance "your show is slipping."

In 1917, Broun married feminist writer Ruth Hale. Their son, Heywood Hale Broun, born in 1918, followed his father into sports writing. Broun critically reported from France on General John J. Pershing and the training of America's Expeditionary Force. Ruth Hale filed stories for the overseas edition of the *Chicago Tribune*. Broun became a member of the Algonquin Round Table in 1919. Together with friends Dorothy Parker, Robert Benchley, Robert E. Sherwood, Alexander Woollcott, George S. Kaufman, and Edna Ferber, Broun regularly took his lunch in the Rose Room of New York City's Algonquin Hotel. Brooks Atkinson of the *New York Times* thought the "vicious circle," as Broun liked to call them, "changed the nature of American comedy and established the tastes of a new period in the arts and theater." Broun was an early and eager supporter of the Marx Brothers, Ernest Hemingway, and F. Scott Fitzgerald.

In 1921, Broun's signed column, "It Seems to Me," began appearing in the *New York World* and was syndicated to a record-setting one million nationwide readers. Broun's column in the summer of 1927 strongly supported an independent review of the death penalties given to anarchists Nicola Sacco and Bartolomeo Venzetti. His column, "Hangman's House," appearing on August 5, attacked the presidents of Harvard and the Massachusetts Institute of Technology for failing to force a commutation of the sentence. Two Italian immigrants, he suggested, could not expect justice from "the tight minds of old men." Broun's column was suspended by *World* publisher Ralph Pulitzer. Broun, writing in the *Nation*, accused the *World* of "timidity" and was fired.

Broun was assured by Roy W. Howard that his socialist sentiments would be left undisturbed by the Scripps-Howard syndicate when his column began appearing in 1928. The Great Depression deepened Broun's commitment to the working class. He was an unsuccessful socialist candidate for Congress in 1930. A year later he wrote and produced a Broadway Revue "Shoot the Works" to give work to unemployed actors and stagehands. On August 7, 1933, a Broun column urged the creation of a journalists union to help "hacks and white collar slaves" who were losing their jobs to the Depression. The American Newspaper Guild was formed in December 1933 with Broun as its president, a position he kept until his death in 1939. An award is annu-

ally given in his name by the guild to a reporter who fights for the rights of the underdog.

Shortly before his death, Broun warned readers of a coming world war. "Appeasers," he wrote, "believe that if you keep on throwing steaks at a tiger, the tiger will become a vegetarian." Adolf Hitler's subsequent invasion of Poland did in fact start World War II. President Franklin Roosevelt remarked that Broun's death had robbed the country "of a hard fighter for the underprivileged, whose staunch champion he always was."

Further Reading

Broun, Heywood. *It Seems to Me*. New York: Harcourt, Brace, 1935.

Broun, Heywood Hale, ed., *The Collected Edition of Heywood Broun*, New York: Harcourt, Brace, 1941.

Broun, Heywood Hale. *Whose Little Boy Are You? A Memoir of the Broun Family*. New York: St. Martin's, 1983.

Leab, Daniel J.. *A League of Individuals: The Organization of the American Newspaper Guild, 1933-1936*, New York: Columbia University Press, 1970.

Lewis, John L., Franklin P. Adams, and Herbert Bayard Swope. *Heywood Broun as He Seemed to Us*. New York: Random House, 1940.

O'Connor, Richard. *Heywood Broun: A Biography*. New York: G.P. Putnam's Sons, 1975.

BRUCE J. EVENSEN

BUSINESS AND FINANCIAL REPORTING

Business and financial reporting embraces several categories of news: news about companies, news about the economy including financial markets, news about government regulation and policy, news about consumer issues and trends, and advice about managing personal finances.

Company news tends to focus on large public companies such as Microsoft, General Motors and Wal-Mart. Investors who hold shares of stock in these companies pay close attention to their financial performance and changes in leadership and strategy. Investors look to business publications, news shows and websites for revealing information about these companies so that they know whether to buy, sell or hold their stock.

Company news often comes from the documents that public companies file with the Securities in Exchange Commission. Federal law requires that companies divulge key financial statements as well as other information of material interest to investors. The requirements arose out of the stock market crash of 1929 as a way to restore confidence in securities markets. Among the most important of these required documents are annual and quarterly reports, proxy and registration statements. In recent years, these documents have become available online through the SEC web site (http://www.sec.gov).

A type of coverage that routinely comes from these filings is the so-called earnings story that reports a company's revenue, profit and expenses for a period, usually a quarter. An earnings story also contains the company's earnings per share of common stock and explanations from company executives about the company's performance during the period.

In recent years, some companies filed inaccurate financial statements in an effort to mislead investors. Congress responded by passing the Public Company Accounting Reform and Investor Protection Act of 2002. The law, sponsored by Sen. Paul Sarbanes (D-Md) and Michael Oxley (R-Ohio) is referred to as the Sarbanes-Oxley Act. The law requires corporate CEO's to personally certify the integrity of their companies' disclosures.

Company news also comes from trials and documents arising from litigation. A shareholder suit against Disney Corp., which ended in August 2005, provided a window into the management practices and style of the company's controversial chairman and chief executive, Michael Eisner. Peripheral litigation can also provide information for journalists. For example, information about the generous retirement benefits offered by General Electric to its former CEO Jack Welch came out in court documents related to his divorce.

Journalists find it more difficult to report on private companies. One important source of information is bond-rating companies. Companies that want to sell bonds to raise capital are required to file extensive financial information with these companies, and that information is available, typically for a fee, to potential investors or the media.

Economic news is mostly concerned with the rate of economic activity as measured by a variety of economic indicators, including the nation's gross domestic product and the rate of unemployment. Other closely watched indicators are housing starts, new factory orders and orders for durable goods. News about the Federal Reserve, which manages the nation's monetary policy, also falls under the rubric of economic news. The chairman of the Federal Reserve is now an important news figure whose speeches and testimony to Congress are closely covered by reporters. The number followed most closely by reporters covering the Fed is the federal funds rate, which is rate banks charge for short-term loans among themselves. It is a bellwether for interest rates through throughout the economy.

News about the stock, bond, commodities and other markets also tends to be handled as economic news. The performance of stock markets is often summarized in the media by the use of indicators such as the Standard & Poor's 500-stock Index or the Dow Jones Industrial Average, which are composite figures representing the prices of many stocks.

News of government regulation focuses largely on the government agencies that watch over key industries such as food, drugs, communication, transportation and securities. These agencies fall within the Executive Branch of the government, and their heads are appointed by the President. Consequently, coverage of these agencies includes important political dimensions. Of course, Congress can pass laws that affect businesses, so business reporters pay close attention to legislation and lobbying as potential sources of news, too.

Consumer news deals with buying trends and the qual-

ity, cost and safety of consumer products. One of the most effective pieces of consumer reporting came in 1965 in a book by Ralph Nader, *Unsafe at any Speed: The Designed-In Dangers of the American Automobile*. It indicted the auto industry for resisting expenditures on such safety features as seat belts.

News about personal finance, which often appears as advice columns in newspapers, gives information about managing and investing money and making big purchases such as a home or a car. In recent years, as the popularity of personal investing for retirement income has grown, these columns frequently discuss mutual funds and other investment options.

While investors make up an important segment of business-news readers and viewers, the principal audience for business news is the general public. Business news has the same goal as other types of journalism: To create an informed citizenry. Its mission is to provide information about how society works so that people can make informed decisions as citizens in a democracy. Like all good journalism, it seeks to hold power accountable and report on malfeasance, corruption, waste, and fraud.

The skepticism that business reporters bring to their work often puts them in conflict with the companies they cover. Company executives usually want to publicize the good news about their companies and downplay the bad news. Good news can raise a company's stock price and benefit executives who own the stock. Of course, journalists eschew the role of publicist and prefer the role of watchdog. As a result, journalists sometimes find it difficult to get anything more out of companies than the law requires them to release. So, along with the ability to read documents and financial statements, source development is especially important for business journalists.

The dangers of suspending journalistic skepticism became apparent in the late 1990s as some in the media, especially on television business-news shows, fanned excessive optimism abut the ascent of the stock market and most particularly stocks in high-tech companies. Some were blind to the bubble that had developed, and they failed to examine the reality of the financial numbers behind the companies who were the decade's high-flyers. The problem was not limited to television: a number of newspapers and magazines treated corporate CEOs as celebrities, including the CEOs at such companies as Enron, which collapsed under the weight of massive debt and corrupt business practices.

Most reputable media companies have codes of ethics that attempt to prevent cheerleading for companies by reporters or commentators. Journalists, according to the prevailing industry ethics, should not report about companies in which they have a financial interest.

Some of the major publications in the United States that report extensively on business are the *Wall Street Journal, New York Times, Washington Post, Los Angeles Times, Business Week, Forbes*, and *Fortune. The Financial Times*, based in London, also is an important source of business news. During the 1990s, Bloomberg News, based in New York, also became a major source of news about business in the economy in the last decade. The company was founded by Michael Bloomberg, who was later elected mayor of New York, as a source of information about the bond market.

Nonfiction books about business topics also have become popular in recent years. They include: *Liar's Poker: Rising Through the Wreckage on Wall Street* (1989), by Michael M. Lewis; *Den of Thieves* (1991) by James B. Stewart, about insider trading on Wall Street; and *A Piece of the Action: How the Middle Class Joined the Money Class* (1994), by Joseph Nocera.

The principal professional organization for business journalists is the Society of American Business Writers and Editors. It is based at the Missouri School of Journalism in Columbia, Missouri.

One of the leading contests to name the best work in the field of business journalism is the Gerald Loeb Awards, which are presented by the UCLA Anderson School of Management. Winners are named in newspaper, magazine, online and television categories. For example, the winner in the large newspaper category in 2005 was Walt Bogdanich of the *New York Times* for his story about the "little recognized problem of clear malfeasance on the part of railroads, using creative in-depth analysis of database records, combined with compelling human stories and court records from around the country, to demonstrate the huge failure of government to regulate a key industry."

Business and economics journalism in the United States is now enjoying a renaissance. It can be traced largely to the wave of deregulation that began in the 1970s and the rise of the global economy. Both developments stimulated interest in business news.

Following the oil shocks and high inflation of the 1970s, the deregulation trend in the United States began in the airline industry and then spread rapidly to other industries, including financial services. Journalism felt the impact of deregulation in two important ways.

First, consumers were interested in new products and services that flowed from deregulation. The new choices ranged from cheaper plane tickets to new kinds of services at banks. For example, consumers, who once may have simply had checking and savings accounts with their local banks, now were confronted with new ways of investing their money as banks became financial-service companies and offered an array of products including brokerage services. Such changes created consumer demand for information about markets. Readers developed interests in mutual funds and stock purchases, and media companies responded with more news about business, the economy, and personal finance.

Second, the growth in financial-services-related advertising in newspapers created more space for business news and generated more revenue to pay for larger business-news staffs. "Business sections," once composed of little more than stocks charts with a routine stock story on the newspaper's back pages, began to turn into stand-alone and well-designed sections with broader and deeper news reports.

Globalization, a more recent trend that arose from advances in technology and the transferability of work

around the world, has stoked interest in business and economics news, too. Americans are far more conscious of the impact on the quality of their daily lives of business decisions and economic trends, even in faraway places. They see the impact in the prices of the products they buy and the losses of jobs to low-wage countries. China's giant economy, for example, has put upward pressure on oil and commodities prices worldwide even as its manufacturers produced low-cost goods for American in low-wage factories.

Interest in business news has created new outlets for journalism. Bloomberg News in New York is now a big worldwide purveyor of business news, and the cable networks offer a plethora of business-news shows. Business news also is widely available on the web at outlets such as marketwatch.com, which is owned by Dow Jones, the company that also owns the *Wall Street Journal*. At local media outlets, the business-news department, if there even was a department, went from being a sleepy corner of many newsrooms, especially in the 1950s, 1960s, and early 1970s, to an important and growing contributor, often producing the day's most exciting front-page stories. And many, if not most, cities have magazines devoted local businesses.

Business journalism has a long and venerable history in the United States. Ida Tarbell, a "muckraker" early in the last century, was doing business journalism when she wrote about the power of the Standard Oil Company in a nineteen-part series for *McClure's* magazine. Upton Sinclair, in his expose of the meat-packing industry, also was producing business journalism. This muckraking journalism, which arose out of the Progressive movement of the early part of the twentieth century, set a high standard for investigative journalism to follow.

Here is an excerpt from Tarbell's work on Standard Oil:

> Very often people who admit the facts, who are willing to see that Mr. Rockefeller has employed force and fraud to secure his ends, justify him by declaring, "It's business." That is, "it's business" has come to be a legitimate excuse for hard dealing, sly tricks, special privileges. It is a common enough thing to hear men arguing that the ordinary laws or morality don't apply in business. Now, if the Standard Oil Company were the only concern in the country guilty of the practices which have given it monopolistic power, this story never would have been written. But it is simply the most conspicuous type of what can be done by these practices.

Other important business stories through the decades have included: *The American Way of Death*, Jessica Mitford's examination of the funeral industry in 1963; "Ask Tighter Law on Meat Inspections," Nick Kotz of the *Des Moines Register*, a report on dirty meat in 1967; and "Blowouts and Roll-Overs," Houston television station KHOU's report on the Ford Motor Co. and Firestone tires in 2000.

Some of the best American journalism during the early twenty-first century was business journalism. The *Los Angeles Times* won a Pulitzer Prize in national reporting for its examination of Wal-Mart, the largest company in the world. In 2002, Gretchen Morgenson of the *New York*

Times won the Pulitzer Prize in beat reporting for her stories about the practices of Wall Street. Business journalists from the *Wall Street Journal* and *Fortune* magazine were instrumental in uncovering the abuses inside Enron Corp., one of many corporate scandals covered by the press in recent years.

Reporters who cover business and the economy at the best newspapers and broadcast outlets typically have developed their expertise through years of experience and through specialized programs of study, offered in the graduate programs at some journalism schools, or in mid-career fellowships such as the Bagehot Fellowship at Columbia University and the Nieman Fellowship at Harvard University.

Further Reading

Lewis, Michael M. *Liar's Poker: Rising Through the Wreckage on Wall Street*. New York: Norton, 1989.

Morris, Kenneth, and Virginia Morris. *The Wall Street Journal Guide to Understanding Money & Investing*. New York: Firedise, 2004.

Nocera, Joseph. *A Piece of the Action: How the Middle Class Joined the Money Class*. New York: Simon & Schuester, 1994.

Roush, Chris. *Show Me the Money: Writing Business and Economic Stories for Mass Communication*. Mahwah, NJ.: Lawrence Erlbaum Associates, 2004.

Serrin, Judith, and William Comp. *Muckrakers: the Journalism that Changed America*.New York: The New Press, 2002

Stewart, James B. *Den of Thieves*. New York: Simon & Schuster, 1991.

Thompson, Terri, ed. *Writing About Business: The New Columbia Knight-Bagehot Guide to Economics and Business Journalism*. New York: Columbia University Press, 2001.

Weinberg, Steve. "Ida Tarbell, Patron Saint," *Columbia Journalism Review*, May/June 2001.

Lou Ureneck

C

CABLE NEWS NETWORK (CNN)

Cable News Network (CNN) was the first twenty-four-hour cable news service in the United States. Richard E. "Ted" Turner III, founder of the Turner Broadcasting System, launched CNN in 1980. Turner challenged the dominance of the news operations of the three broadcast television networks, ABC, CBS, and NBC, with news programming that was available twenty-four hours each day and seven days each week. Despite initial disparagements of CNN as the "Chicken Noodle Network," it became a dominant force in news coverage, particularly international news.

The effects of immediate and saturation coverage of world events have been the focus of studies of the so-called "CNN effect." CNN became a model for its cable-news competitors: MSNBC that launched in 1995, and Fox News that started in 1996 and subsequently surpassed CNN as the ratings leader for the cable-news networks. Although Turner was able to keep CNN financially afloat for nearly two decades, Time Warner acquired the Turner Broadcasting System and CNN in 1996. Turner served as vice chairman of Time Warner until 2001 when America Online acquired Time Warner to create AOL Time Warner. Time Warner removed AOL from its title in 2003, and AOL continued as a division of Time Warner as did the Turner Broadcasting System. Turner served on the Time Warner board as an affiliated director.

Turner earned his reputation as a sportsman with his victory in yachting's America's Cup in 1977 and his ownership of the Atlanta Braves baseball and the Atlanta Hawks basketball teams, and as a hard-charging entrepreneur with development of media properties including super-station WTBS. Turner announced to the National Cable Television Association annual convention in May, 1979, his plans to launch the twenty-four-hour cable news network. He chose a former country club site in Atlanta to house the network, and he staffed the operation generally with young professionals who were willing to work long hours for low wages in a non-union shop. Satellite transmissions would bring reports from around the world to the CNN headquarters, and CNN would beam its news coverage and programming to cable customers throughout the country and the world. CNN first went to satellite and to viewers' homes June 1, 1980. CNN's audience during the first week was 1.7 million to 1.8 million viewers. Even with a variety of technical flaws and human foibles and the need for a lawsuit to gain equal standing with the networks in the White House press pool, the new network slowly increased its credibility and its acceptance in U.S. households as a provider of news from around the country and the world. CNN was the first news agency on the scene for the attempted assassination of Pope John Paul II in 1981. Within a decade, the number of CNN's viewers soared. By the early 1990s, CNN was seen by perhaps eighty million viewers in more than one hundred countries.

Agent of Change

With the successes of its coverage of the Challenger shuttle disaster in 1986, the Tiananman Square democracy demonstrations in China in 1989, and the Persian Gulf War in 1991, CNN has been an agent of change in television news coverage. Prior to the creation of CNN, network news coverage generally was limited to a thirty-minute block of time on weekdays. Newspaper coverage included a morning news cycle or an afternoon news cycle depending on the principal time of distribution. CNN essentially erased deadlines and eliminated the news cycles. Immediacy was the hallmark of CNN coverage as was saturation. The networks could and did devote all available time to a breaking story even to the point of airing unedited, real-time camera feeds of news events. Those who presented the broadcast network news daily, the anchors (e.g., Chet Huntley and David Brinkley, Walter Cronkite, Peter Jennings, Tom Brokaw, Dan Rather), were the stars of the news business and readily identified as opinion leaders on national and international topics. With newscasts around the clock, the status of the CNN anchors generally was less than that of the superstars. CNN did create a number of media stars and attracted them from broadcast networks: Bernard Shaw, Larry King, Christianne Armanpour, Peter Arnett, Lou Dobbs, Judy Woodruff, and Wolf Blitzer. For most of its history, CNN's most visible media superstar was Turner, who *Time* magazine chose as its Man of the Year in 1991.

The impact of CNN's news coverage and the number of its viewers around the world have been the subject of much study. CNN's description of itself as the "World News Leader" came under particular scrutiny in 1991 when CNN correspondents and staff members remained in Iraq as the United States and its allies launched attacks to force Saddam Hussein to withdraw from Kuwait. Coverage began with Shaw, John Holliman, and Arnett providing eyewitness accounts of initial U.S. air raids on Baghdad—with seventeen hours of uninterrupted coverage—and continued through the successful land campaign against the Iraqi forces. Despite the view that its coverage of the Persian Gulf War was the crowning moment for CNN, the network and particularly Arnett received criticism for presenting the Iraqi views on the deaths of civilians and attacks that missed military targets.

CNN's role in providing instantaneous and saturation coverage of events was made possible by satellite technology that transmitted television images directly around the world. The role of satellite technology was central to the development of CNN. Cable television had its origins in the use of master antennas to provide broadcast television programs to communities that had limited television reception because of distance from broadcasting stations or other geographical barriers. The original Community Antenna Television or CATV systems were a boon to broadcasters in increasing their audiences. As technology advanced and use of microwave transmissions expedited the delivery of broadcast programming, broadcasters objected to the introduction of "distant" and competing signals into their market areas. In 1972, the Federal Communications Commission in approved a compromise to allow competing "distant" cable signals in the second fifty largest markets in the country. This action proved moot because satellite technology made possible the direct transmission of original programs to cable head-ends for distribution to consumers.

Along with the provision of first-run movies through HBO and live sports events through ESPN, Turner provided cable viewers with WTBS, an independent television station. Here Turner's ownership of the Atlanta Braves and the Atlanta Hawks proved advantageous because he marketed their games to a new national audience. With the success of such original and live satellite programming, Turner turned to the challenge of providing a cable news outlet.

Turner recognized that satellite technology had revolutionized news reporting. Before the use of satellites to provide direct transmission of news coverage, correspondents had to ship film or videotape from the news site to a processing or editing center and then to the point of domestic transmission. Satellite technology helped to eliminate these steps. CNN extended live news reports from around the world from a few seconds or a few minutes on an evening newscast to the possibility of saturation coverage for hours, if not days.

The CNN Effect

By 2003, more than one billion people had access to CNN around the world. Viewers included heads of state and their constituents and the fact that many of them watched breaking news events raised questions about the so-called "CNN effect." Scholars have described the "CNN effect" variously. One view is that the airing of real-time human suffering created pressure on U.S. leaders to intervene in other parts of the world. The pervasiveness of CNN helped to set the agenda for United States foreign policy and provided a medium for diplomacy itself. Proponents of the "CNN effect" cite events such as the quelling of the Tiananaman

Square protests in Beijing in 1989 and the killing of U.S. servicemen in Mogadishu, Somalia, in 1993 as examples of such agenda setting. Another view of the "CNN effect" argued that the cable news channel played a role in establishing a global public sphere and that leaders of most, if not all, nations had the same sources of information and the same medium for discourse. Still another interpretation contended that CNN was more of a medium for the extension of American power and policy than for agenda setting or a forum for a diversity of national interests and ideologies.

If the Persian Gulf War in 1991 was the high point of CNN's credibility, "The Valley of Death" in 1998 may have been its nadir. Ironically, this investigative report was the premiere of "Newstand: CNN & Time," intended to be a collaboration of the new media partners Time Warner and the Turner Broadcasting System. The investigative report chronicled Operation Tailwind during the war in Southeast Asia in the 1970s. The report contended that the United States used nerve gas against U.S. defectors in Laos. CNN generally had built its reputation on saturation coverage and not on investigative journalism, and questions about the credibility of this report brought CNN extensive criticism. "The Valley of Death" aired on June 7, 1998, and CNN issued a retraction July 2, 1998, after an investigation by media attorney Floyd Abrams and internal counsel David Kohler, who had approved the show. The episode led to the firing of the news producers responsible for the report and departure from CNN of Peter Arnett, who had presented the investigation results on CNN and in an article for *Time*. Arnett subsequently argued that he had not participated in the research for the report, but merely had presented the findings.

By the beginning of the Iraqi War in 2003, leaders of CNN found themselves facing a new media terrain. This was an era of horizontal and vertical integration. The major media areas were movies, recordings, television, magazines, and books. By the end of the 1990s, mega-media companies were competing for dominance in all these arenas. Thrown into this mix during the early 1990s was also the popularization of Internet services through the development of the World Wide Web. Additional broadcasting networks also were competing for viewers. Because cross-ownership was dominant, broadcasting and cable networks no longer were competitors except for ratings for specific shows.

CNN faced direct competition from Fox News and MSNBC. In the cable news rankings, Fox News became the leader with CNN second and MSNBC third. The cable news competition was part of a larger battle of communication titans. CNN was the representative of Time Warner while Fox News was the instrument of Rupert Murdoch and News Corp. Inc., and MSNBC was the agent of Microsoft and NBC Universal, whose corporate owners included General Electric and Vivendi. Although Time Warner's acquisition of CNN in 1996 may have come as a surprise to some, Time Warner had long been an investor in the Turner Broadcasting System. It, and Tele-Communications Inc., then the nation's largest cable television company, had bailed out CNN financially in 1988.

What were the effects of the creation of the Cable News Network? Actually it may be difficult to divorce CNN from the events surrounding it, but CNN became the focal point for many changes. It filled a vacuum in international news coverage. The fact that the number of CNN international bureaus totaled more than the combined efforts of the three broadcast networks only revealed the extent to which the networks had cut back on their coverage of international events. Although the networks engaged in saturation coverage only on rare occasions, CNN and its competitors, Fox News and MSNBC, made saturation coverage a mainstay of cable fare, even if it was only the coverage of the crime of the day or the scandal of the moment.

Further Reading

Ammon, Royce J. *Global Television and the Shaping of World Politics: CNN, Telediplomacy, and Foreign Policy.* Jefferson, NC: McFarland, 2001.

Auletta, Ken. *Media Man: Ted Turner's Improbable Empire.* New York: W.W. Norton & Co. 2004.

Collins, Scott. *Crazy Like a Fox: The Inside Story of How Fox News Beat CNN.* East Rutherford, NJ: Portfolio, 2004.

Denton, Robert E., Jr. ed. *The Media and the Persian Gulf War.* Westport, CT: Praeger, 1993.

Goldberg, Robert and Gerald Jay Goldberg. *Citizen Kane: The Wild Rise of an American Tycoon.* New York: Harcourt, Brace & Co., 1995.

Hack, Richard. *Clash of the Titans: How the Unbridled Ambition of Ted Turner and Rupert Murdoch Has Created Global Empires That Control What We Read and Watch.* Beverly Hills, CA: New Millennium Press, 2003.

Küng-Shankleman, Lucy. *Inside the BBC and CNN: Managing Media Organisations.* London: Routledge, 2000.

Robinson, Piers. *The CNN Effect: The Myth of News, Foreign Policy and Intervention.* London: Routledge, 2002.

Schonfeld, Reese. *Me and Ted Against the World: The Unauthorized Story of the Founding of CNN.* New York: HarperBusiness: 2001.

Vaughan, Roger. *Ted Turner: The Man Behind the Mouth.* Boston: Sail Books, 1978.

Volkmer, Ingrid. *News in the Global Sphere: A Study of CNN and Its Impact on Global Communication.* Luton, University of Luton Press: 1999.

Wittemore, Hank. *CNN: The Inside Story: How a Band of Mavericks Changed the Face of Television News.* New York: Little Brown and Co.: 1990.

WILLIAM J. LEONHIRTH

CAHAN, ABRAHAM

Abraham Cahan (July 7, 1860–Aug. 31, 1951) was one of the founders and for forty-three years the editor of the *Jewish Daily Forward*, the most widely read Yiddish-language newspaper in the world. The *Forward* schooled its half million readers on Socialist solutions to the struggles of New York's underclass. No paper was seen as more significant in representing Jewish working class life to the nation or more central in assimilating the Jewish immigrant in America.

Cahan was born on July 7, 1860 in the shtetl of Podberezya, a Jewish slum in Vilna, Lithuania, when the region was ruled by the Russian Empire. He was the son of Hebrew teachers, Schachne and Sarah Goldarbeiter Cahan, and the grandson of a rabbi. He graduated the Vilna Teachers Institute in 1881 but was forced to flee to Switzerland due to his anti-Czarist activities.

Cahan arrived in New York on June 6, 1881, settling within an immigrant influx on the city's Lower East Side. There, he became a community leader by organizing labor unions and lecturing on socialism while writing articles for the Yiddish and Russian-language as well as the English press. His reporting and editing work at the *Neie Tzeit*, a Yiddish-language socialist weekly, combined story-telling and social theory. His hope in *Workman's Advocate* (May 15, 1889) was to create news stories of "life-likeness" that stimulated a sympathetic reaction to the plight of the poor. Beginning in 1890, his editing of *Arbeiter Zeitung*, the newspaper of the United Hebrew Trades, reflected the influence of Cahan's mentor Frederick Engles.

Cahan's reporting for Charles Dana's *New York Sun* used ironic vignettes of "artistic re-creation" designed to depict "life itself" on the Lower East Side (Sept. 2, 1888). Cahan's realistic portrayal of working class life for the *New York World*, *New York Press* and *New York Star* became the basis of his first book, *Yekl: A Tale of the New York Ghetto* (1896). The *World*'s literary critic William Dean Howells hailed the depiction of "a new New York" and considered Cahan the nation's "new star of realism."

Between 1897 and 1902, Cahan joined Lincoln Steffens and Hutchins Hapgood as a police reporter at the *New York Commercial Advertiser*, where he was encouraged to track social problems to their source. The culturally informed reporting that followed interpreted the turbulent spirit and rich complexity of New York's immigrant community to the paper's cosmopolitan audience. Readers learned of the city's 1,500 pushcart peddlers "hardly earning $5 a week," yet forced to give 50 cents of it in bribes to police to continue operating (June 29, 1898). Readers are also introduced to Rabbi Jacob Joseph, once a revered Talmudic scholar, who becomes "a hopeless invalid" in the New World after being discarded by a community seduced by American secularism (Jan. 24, 1901). "Above the babble of a thousand voices" lives the East Side housewife, Cahan writes. She refuses to succumb to "the fetid odors and heat glare from the street below," and prepares herself "to go hungry again" so she can feed the children (June 29, 1902).

Cahan's *Jewish Daily Forward*, which he first edited on March 16, 1902, became must reading over breakfast tables throughout America's Jewish community. The paper's mission became "unfolding the thousands and thousands of life stories of the tenement homes" that increasingly dominated the industrializing nation's urban landscape (Dec. 21, 1903). This conviction transformed the paper from a seldom-read organ of the Socialist Labor Party into a daily guidebook for Yiddish readers anxious to enter the American experience without abandoning their traditions and common history. In his enormously popular "Bintel Brief," Cahan counseled society's downtrodden for more than forty years: a tubercular afraid of suicide; an abandoned wife fearing the loss of her children; a worker who scabs to buy his wife medicine;

a thirteen-year-old raincoat maker docked two cents for arriving ten minutes late; a barber who thinks of cutting his customers' throats; and the cantor who wondered what would happen to him since he no longer believed in God. When 146 ghetto residents died in the Triangle Factory fire on March 25, 1911, the *Forward*'s special edition spoke in behalf of "a whole people who are in mourning."

The *Forward*'s 20,000 circulation in 1900 would increase to top 130,000 in 1918, and then grow to a quarter million by the middle of the next decade. The fact that the paper was passed along to non-subscribers made its penetration of the immigrant community far greater. One million Jews settled on New York's Lower East Side in the three decades leading to the outbreak of World War I. Fewer than one in twenty-five returned to the Old World. For those who remained, few figures were as significant as Abraham Cahan. His writing and reporting during the first half of the twentieth century captures the cultural shock of the early immigrants followed by a careful chronicling of their struggle and sacrifices that would allow a later generation to flee the limitations of the ghetto altogether. Cahan would live to see the substantial integration of the immigrant Jew into the American mainstream, a journey of transition described and thoughtfully encouraged in the pages of the *Daily Forward*.

Further Reading

Cahan, Abraham. *Bleter Fun Mein Lebe, Leaves from My Life*, New York: Forward Association, 1926.

Chametzky, Jules. *From the Ghetto: The Fiction of Abraham Cahan*, Amherst: University of Massachusetts, 1977.

Evensen, Bruce J. "Abraham Cahan," in Thomas B. Connery, ed., *A Sourcebook of American Literary Journalism*, Westport, CT: Greenwood, 1992.

Marovitz, Sanford E. *Abraham Cahan*, New York: Twayne, 1996.

Rischin, Moses. *Grandma Never Lived in America: The New Journalism of Abraham Cahan*, Bloomington: Indiana University, 1985.

Stein, Leon, Abraham P. Conan, and Lynn Davidson. *The Education of Abraham Cahan*, Philadelphia: Jewish Publication Society of America, 1969.

Zlotnick, Joan. "Abraham Cahan, a Neglected Realist," *American Jewish Archives*, April 1971.

BRUCE J. EVENSEN

CAMERAS IN THE COURTROOM

At the heart of the debate over cameras in the courtroom are two conflicting constitutional rights: public access to the courtroom and the right of a criminal defendant to a fair trial. That conflict was evident during the heavily publicized trial of Bruno Richard Hauptmann for the kidnapping and murder of aviator Charles Lindbergh's baby in 1935, in which the intrusiveness of newsreel cameras and flashbulbs contributed to the circus-like atmosphere of the trial. The American Bar Association subsequently adopted Canon 35 of its judicial rules, calling for a ban on photography and radio broadcasting in the courtroom (later amended to

include television). By the 1960s, almost every state had enacted similar bans.

The U. S. Supreme Court first addressed the issue in a 1965 case from Texas, one of the few states without a camera ban at the time. In *Estes v. Texas*, the Court overturned defendant Estes' swindling conviction based on the presence of television cameras during preliminary hearings and part of his trial. The Court found that the bulky cameras, conspicuous microphones, and bright spotlights were so intrusive that they denied Estes a fair trial. The Court did not ban cameras completely, however, and left open the possibility that improvements in technology might require a reexamination of the issue. Sixteen years later, after additional states had begun to experiment with camera coverage of trials, the Court unanimously ruled in *Chandler v. Florida* (1981) that technology had improved enough that the mere presence of cameras would not be considered a per se violation of a defendant's right to a fair trial. Instead, the defendant has the burden of showing that in his specific case the cameras impaired the jury's ability to render a verdict fairly.

Today all fifty states allow still or video cameras in at least some of their courtrooms (the District of Columbia maintains a complete ban). While most states allow televised coverage of both civil and criminal cases, the extent of coverage allowed will vary according to circumstances. Some states, for example, allow coverage of their appellate courts but not trial courts; some allow coverage of criminal trials only if the defendant agrees; some ban coverage of certain types of proceedings, such as juvenile or sex offense cases; and some give trial judges broad discretion over the extent of coverage in individual cases. Court watchers have observed trial judges grow increasingly reluctant to allow coverage of high-profile cases after Court TV's broadcast of the sensational 1995 O.J. Simpson murder trial.

Photography has been banned from federal courtrooms since 1946, but in the early 1990s the federal system experimented with cameras on a limited basis. In 1996, the U.S. Judicial Conference adopted new rules giving federal appellate courts the right to allow coverage of their proceedings, but only the second and ninth circuit courts of appeal have voted to allow cameras. Cameras are banned for criminal trials in federal court and discouraged for civil cases. The Supreme Court maintains a strict ban on photography of any kind in its courtroom.

Further Reading

Barber, Susanna. *News Cameras in the Courtroom: A Free Press-Fair Trial Debate*. Norwood, NJ: Ablex Publishing, 1987.

Chandler v. Florida, 449 U.S. 560 (1981).

Cohn, Marjorie, and David Dow. *Cameras in the Courtroom: Television and the Pursuit of Justice*. Lanham, MD: Rowman & Littlefield, 2002.

Estes v. Texas, 381 U.S. 532 (1965).

Radio-Television News Directors Association & Foundation, "Cameras in the Court: A State-by-State Guide," http://www.rtndf.org/foi/scc.shtml (accessed April 9, 2007).

KATHLEEN K. OLSON

CAPOTE, TRUMAN

In seeking to elevate the art of storytelling, author Truman Capote (Sept. 30, 1924–Aug. 25, 1984) forged together various techniques, and, at least for the second half of his career, he embarked on a fusion of journalistic, cinematic, conversational, and literary writing styles. The result, according to Capote, was the creation of a new art form, something he called the nonfiction novel.

Born Truman Streckfus Persons in New Orleans on September 30, 1924, the son of Archuylus (Archie) Persons and Lillie May Persons Capote, he died in Los Angeles August 25, 1984, of complications of liver disease. Between these two events Truman Capote managed to construct one of the most intriguing and highly visible literary careers in the twentieth century. In part because of his effete and unusual persona, his proclivity for famous friends, his willingness to promote both himself and his work, Capote seemed at times as much a celebrity as an author.

In 1948, Capote's first novel, the dark and dreamlike *Other Voices, Other Rooms*, established him as bright new talent. In 1949, *A Tree of Night and Other Stories* proved to be consistent with his earlier fiction. During the 1950s Capote traveled across Europe, writing travel essays and portraits. The result was *Local Color*, a collection of travel articles

In 1951 while in Sicily he wrote *The Grass Harp*, and a year later adapted it into a Broadway play. In 1954, he wrote the screenplay for *Beat the Devil* (1954), a movie directed by John Huston that became a cult classic. In 1955, Capote accompanied the touring company of Porgy and Bess as it performed in Soviet Union. The result was an article in *The New Yorker*, "Muses are Heard," which was later published in book form. The same year he published *Muses are Heard*, Capote wrote a nonfiction short story, *A Christmas Memory*, published a decade later as a book.

In 1958, *Esquire* published *Breakfast at Tiffany's*. When published in book form with three short stories, many critics felt that Capote had displayed a level of maturity missing in his earlier fiction.

In late 1959, Capote read about a brutal murder in Kansas. Six years of research resulted in *In Cold Blood*, a blending of journalism and literary style that captured Capote's desire to outline events with the fuller description and dialogue given to novelists. Anxious to prove that "journalism is the most underestimated, the least explored of literary mediums," Capote hoped that *In Cold Blood* contained "the credibility of fact, the immediacy of film, the depth and freedom of prose and the precision of poetry."

From the outset, the book was highly successful—it was on the best-seller list for more than a year—and critically acclaimed. However, in due time a literary uproar ensued. The author called it the "nonfiction novel"; others labeled it a type of "new journalism." Supporters said it was a literary masterpiece that heralded a new genre. Critics said it was nothing new at all.

The question after *In Cold Blood* was what would follow. Quantitatively, the answer is very little. In 1973, *The Dogs Bark* was published, a collection of previously published material. In 1975, *Music for Chameleon's* represented fresh, new work by Capote, offering a calliope of writing techniques including short stories, a novella and a series of conversational portraits, one even with himself.

Following publication of *In Cold Blood*, Capote's health began to deteriorate, and professionally he seems to have gone through an artistic crisis. This crisis, which he described as a form of overwriting he termed "dense," occurred in 1977, and can be tied directly to his health problems with alcohol and drugs. It sharply curtailed work on his eagerly awaited *Answered Prayers*. The four chapters published by *Esquire* in 1975 and 1976 represented the final published work of *Answered Prayers*. (The book, minus the chapter "Mojave," was published by Random House in 1987.)

Further Reading

Epstein, Edward J. *Between Fact and Fiction: The Problem of Journalism*. New York: Vintage Books, 1975.

Clarke, Gerald. *Capote*. New York: Simon and Schuster, 1988.

Grobel, Lawrence. *Conversation with Capote*. New York: New American Library, 1985.

Hollowell, John. *Fact & Fiction, The New Journalism and the Nonficiton Novel*. Chapel Hill: University of North Carolina Press, 1977.

Anderson, Chris, ed. *Literary Nonfiction, Theory, Criticism, Pedagogy*. Carbondale and Edwardsville: Southern Illinois University Press, 1989.

Wolfe, Tom. *The New Journalism*. New York: Harper and Row, 1973.

Weber, Ronald, ed. *The Reporter as Artist: A Look at the New Journalism Controversy*. New York: Hastings House, 1974.

Howard, Philip, Jr., The New Journalism: A Nonfiction Concept of Writing. University of Utah, Master's Thesis, 1971.

Nance, William. *The Worlds of Truman Capote*. New York: Stein and Day, 1970.

Garson, Helen S.,*Truman Capote*. New York. Frederick Unger Publishing, 1980.

LLOYD CHIASSON

CARTER, JR., WILLIAM HODDING

Hodding Carter, Jr. (Feb. 3, 1907–April, 4, 1972) was one of the original civil rights journalists of the American South. Writing first in newspapers and later in magazines and novels, Carter spoke out against racism, economic prejudice, and political corruption at a time when such dissent was unpopular and dangerous. In 1946 he won a Pulitzer Prize for his editorials denouncing prejudice and intolerance. Between 1942 and 1970 he authored at least nineteen books, both fiction and non-fiction.

Carter was born on February 3, 1907 in Hammond, Louisiana, to William Hodding Carter and Irma (Dutart) Carter. He learned to read at age four and entered fourth grade at age seven, graduating valedictorian from his Hammond, LA high school at sixteen. In 1923 he left the South to enter Bowdoin College in Brunswick, Maine.

Carter's college years transformed him. One of only

two Southern students in his class, he had brought many regional prejudices with him, openly shunning the school's lone black student and even defending his own racial prejudice in college news articles. But by the time he graduated 1927 with a Bachelor of Arts degree, Carter had broadened his outlook and shed much of his own intolerance.

After graduate work at Columbia University and a year teaching English at Tulane University in New Orleans, Carter got his first newspaper job in 1929, reporting for the New Orleans *Item* for $12.50 a week. In 1931 he joined United Press as a bureau manager, passing up a Rhodes Scholarship to court Ms. Betty Werlein. They married in 1931, and Hodding joined Associated Press to cover the legislatures in Louisiana and Mississippi. After Carter was fired for "insubordination," the couple decided to start their own newspaper.

They returned to Hammond in 1932 and founded the *Daily Courier*, using their entire fortune of $367 to purchase a broken-down press and meager supplies. Still in his twenties, Carter gained national attention with fearless editorial attacks on Sen. Huey P. Long, former Louisiana governor and then the most powerful politician in the state. Carter's editorials were often personal and vicious, but provocative enough to earn him writing invitations from national publications. In 1936, they moved to Greenville, Mississippi, and founded the *Delta Star*. Two years later they bought out their lone competitor and launched the *Delta Democrat-Times,* whose first issue promised: "We shall publish the truth. We shall be tolerant. We hope to be fearless." Many of his editorials were pieces of conscience, challenging readers to examine their own prejudices. Following a Neiman fellowship at Harvard in 1940, Carter devoted more time to writing books, articles, and novels of the South. He served in the military during World War II and returned to the *Democrat-Times* after his discharge in 1945. The paper was still thriving, and in 1960 Carter transferred editorial control to the eldest of his three sons, Wm. Hodding Carter, III.

An admirer of the Kennedy brothers, Carter was working as a speechwriter for Robert Kennedy when the senator was assassinated in June, 1968. Carter's health quickly declined, and he died of a heart attack in Greenville on April 4, 1972. While conservative by modern standards, in his time Hodding Carter, Jr. was the rarest of white, Southern newsmen—an outspoken editor willing to risk his fortune and reputation to stand against racial intolerance.

Further Reading

Carter, Hodding. *Lower Mississippi*. New York: Farrar and Rinehart, 1942.
———. *Where Main Street Meets the River*. New York: Rinehart, 1953.
———. *The Angry Scar: The Story of Reconstruction*. Garden City, NY: Doubleday and Company, 1959.
———. *First Person Rural*. Garden City, NY: Doubleday and Company, 1963.
———. *Their Words Were Bullets: The Southern Press in War, Reconstruction, and Peace*. Athens: University of Georgia Press, 1969.
———. "Huey Long: American Dictator." In *Pols: Great Writers on American Politicians from Bryan to Reagan*, edited by Jack Beatty. New York: Public Affairs, 2004.
Davies, David R., ed. *The Press and Race: Mississippi Journalists Confront the Movement*. Jackson: University Press of Mississippi, 2001.
Hodding and Betty Werlein Carter Papers, Special Collections, University Libraries, Mississippi State University.
Pace, Etta Eckles. "Hodding Carter: A Bio-Bibliography." MA thesis, Florida State niversity, 1958.
Robinson James E. "Hodding Carter: Southern Liberal, 1907–1972." Ph D diss., Mississippi State University, 1974.
Waldron, Ann. *Hodding Carter: The Reconstruction of a Racist*. Chapel Hill: Algonquin Books of Chapel Hill, 1993.
Wheeler, Thomas C., ed. *A Vanishing America: The Life and Times of the Small Town*. New York: Rinehart and Winston, 1964.

WENDY E. SWANBERG

CBS NEWS

CBS News is a division of CBS Television, which in 2006 was a subsidiary of the CBS Corporation which in turn was a subsidiary of National Amusements, Inc., which was based in Dedham, Massachusetts. Another subsidiary of National Amusements was Viacom, Inc., which had such holdings as MTV Networks Company and Paramount Pictures Corporation.

Bearing in mind that these corporate affiliations are of a comparatively recent historical origin, when one considers the longer history of CBS News, it has encompassed over the years radio, television, and a variety of other business interests. In both radio and television, CBS News played a major role in establishing the professional standards of broadcast journalism and was a primary source of news and information in the latter half of the twentieth century. During the 1980s and 1990s, a focus on the value of CBS stock led to significant cuts in the news division's budget, once considered untouchable. At the same time, the influence of CBS News—and traditional network news in general—began to wane as cable television, talk radio, the Internet, and other alternative sources of news fragmented the audience.

The history of CBS precedes that of CBS News, which has always been dependent upon its parent company for funding and direction. News had only a small part in broadcasting while radio developed as a mass medium in the 1920s. Radio Corporation of America created the National Broadcasting System, two radio networks with twenty-five stations, in 1926. A few months later two entrepreneurs, George Coats and Arthur Judson, organized United Independent Broadcasters. Columbia Phonograph Company invested in UIB, and the company became the Columbia Phonograph Broadcasting System.

The Columbia radio network debuted in September 1927. Its money problems persisted, however, and in 1928 its founders sold a controlling interest to Philadelphia businessman William S. Paley for $500,000. Paley was looking for a venture to develop outside of his family's cigar manufacturing company. He had been impressed by the promise of radio as an advertising and entertainment medium;

sales of his company's cigars had more than doubled after it sponsored a radio program.

Under Paley, Columbia attracted stations to its network with more favorable fees and incentives than NBC offered and by doubling its national programming from ten hours per week to twenty. He also gained advertising by offering discounts for commercials airing on the entire network rather than only regional segments. At the same time, Paley bought a radio station and studio to establish the network in New York. By the end of 1928, the reorganized company, Columbia Broadcasting System, Inc., had forty-nine stations in its network and a solid foundation for growth.

Paley and his executives built the CBS audience by moving away from classical music and other high-brow fare that marked early radio. Following the NBC programming model that proved successful, CBS booked singer Bing Crosby, comedians Jack Benny, Fred Allen, George Burns and Gracie Allen, and others—at times raiding NBC with offers of more money—and developed talent for radio. Often, however, such performers left CBS for NBC and the larger audience its more powerful stations pulled in. In 1936 CBS recorded a net profit of $3.9 million, slightly more than NBC. Still, NBC had the most popular shows on the air.

After World War II, Paley directed CBS to develop its own programs so that the most successful could not easily defect to NBC. Not until 1949 did CBS radio programs overtake NBC in terms of audience. By then television was undergoing its development; despite Paley's lukewarm interest in the new medium, CBS President Frank Stanton and other executives put together the company's television network and entertainment programming much the same way radio had developed twenty years earlier.

News was not important to Paley, at least not in the formative years of CBS. Nor was news-gathering important at NBC. For information, early radio tended to rely on wire service dispatches for brief reports, broadcasts of speeches, and coverage of public ceremonies. Commentators from newspapers were part of the mix, but little original news-gathering was taking place.

When newspapers persuaded the wire services to deny their reports to radio in 1933, CBS organized its own news staff under Paul White, a former United Press reporter who was working in the CBS public relations department. White's efforts, which included hiring reporters in cities around the world and establishing three daily news reports, were undercut when Paley committed CBS to an agreement between radio stations and newspapers to allow limited news broadcasts of wire reports. The agreement lasted barely a year because renegade radio stations ignored it. Only then did Paley back news-gathering by CBS, although the company promoted the idea for its image as a public servant.

Interest in news from Europe grew as the continent appeared to be moving toward war. White turned to the person recently hired at CBS to line up prominent speakers, Edward R. Murrow, and sent him to London to build an international news staff. When Germany invaded Austria in March 1938, CBS aired reports from New York, Paris, Rome, Berlin, and Vienna for the first international news broadcast. The program that followed, *World News Tonight*, became a staple of the era. News was turning profitable; advertisers that had shunned sponsoring a newscast in favor of entertainment programming were now anxious to back news programs tuned in by millions of listeners.

Radio news also was gaining in its ability to influence public opinion. White had established a code of ethics at CBS in late 1937, prodded in part by government interest in seeing that the public airwaves remained neutral in matters of politics and public policy. Knowing that controversy was not good for business, Paley wanted to stave off criticism that his broadcasters or their advertisers were partisans of any stripe. Reporting all sides of an issue and remaining neutral was central to White's code. Eventually, CBS moved away from airing commentators, instead preferring "news analysts" who offered more facts than opinions in their reports. The business-minded Paley hampered news gathering by banning recorded interviews. His concern was that entertainers would begin recording their own programs, thus freeing them to sell their broadcasts to anyone.

With the sounds of sirens and explosions framing his voice, Murrow was CBS's first news star, his reports from London under Nazi bombardment galvanizing American sympathies for the British and against Adolf Hitler's Germany. He became a national hero; in the profession itself, he came to embody the ideals of broadcasting as a calling and a public service. His staff, later known as "Murrow's Boys," included newsmen who would become the core of their generation's news broadcasters: William L. Shirer, Eric Sevareid, Larry LeSueur, Charles Collingwood, Bill Downs, Howard K. Smith, and Richard C. Hottelet. Murrow hired them not for their vocal skills but for their ability to think, report, and write. By the end of World War II, Murrow, White, and others in the news division had brought CBS a respect and trust that no entertainment program could deliver.

The challenge for postwar CBS was to succeed in television in spite of Paley's view that radio was still the medium that mattered. Television had undergone its initial development in the 1920s and 1930s, but the war had stunted its commercial applications. Stanton and like-minded executives forged ahead with building a television network even as Paley set about to make his radio network better than NBC's, an attitude that prompted him to buy his rival's most popular talent—comedians Jack Benny and Red Skelton, for example—at exorbitant prices. Ultimately, they made their greatest postwar contributions to CBS in television.

Stanton, meanwhile, was overseeing the development of television programs the network could own. There was Ed Sullivan's variety show, a series for comedian Jackie Gleason, and a television version of the radio hit *Our Miss Brooks*. Along with *I Love Lucy*, they were among the fifteen top-rated televisions shows in 1956—twelve of which were on CBS. That year television was making far more money than radio, which had begun its downturn. CBS scored another entertainment money-maker when it oversaw the development of the long-playing record.

All that success for CBS had bode well for the news division. News for the new medium began as words read over still photos or, at best, footage shot by newsreel cameramen. In 1948, as prime-time entertainment was bringing together a national television audience, CBS began airing the first weekday evening newscast, a fifteen-minute broadcast with Douglas Edwards as anchor. The young newscaster did not share the older generation's suspicion that television was a fad, and he remained in the anchor seat for fourteen years. Sig Mickelson, then in charge of CBS News, used his experience as a radio newsman and broadcasting executive to train a staff to gather the audio and video elements of news and blend them via television. What Edwards had to offer viewers each night improved as Mickelson hired cameramen to shoot footage exclusively for CBS and trained correspondents to write and broadcast words to accompany those images.

Besides being a time for trial and error in television news and other public service programming, the 1950s offered CBS a test of the new medium's influence and courage. Murrow, although an early skeptic of television, brought his reputation for integrity to the influential documentary series *See It Now*, produced by Fred Friendly. Its debut in November 1951 featured a simultaneous broadcast from the East and West coasts, a technological first. More important were the *See It Now* programs on Senator Joseph McCarthy, aired in 1954, at the height of the McCarthy Communist witch hunt that had dominated American politics for years. The broadcasts—and McCarthy's self-defeating response—helped deflate his influence and turn the public against the senator and his methods. CBS News continued to provide many of the era's most informative and provocative news programs, including the regular hour-long program *CBS Reports*.

The news divisions at CBS and NBC were committed rivals in television. ABC was a distant third, committing few resources to news. With the NBC team of Chet Huntley and David Brinkley commanding greater audiences, CBS in 1962 replaced Edwards with Walter Cronkite, who delivered the news for the next nineteen years. A year later, just a few months before the assassination of President John F. Kennedy would bring television news to age, CBS inaugurated the thirty-minute evening newscast. (NBC followed a week later; ABC did not air a thirty-minute evening news program until 1967.)

Behind Cronkite for much of the 1960s was a news staff as good as Murrow had in the war years, among them White House correspondents Dan Rather and Robert Pierpoint, congressional reporter Roger Mudd, correspondents Harry Reasoner and Charles Kuralt, and commentator Eric Sevareid. The network's coverage of the space program during the race to the moon was a hallmark. However, its award-winning coverage of civil rights, the Vietnam War, and Watergate also brought criticism that CBS News was too liberal in its presentation, and it became a standard target of the growing conservative political movement. Meanwhile, in terms of ratings, CBS overtook NBC in 1968 as the most-watched evening newscast, a position of dominance it retained until Cronkite retired in 1981.

The most influential innovation in the third decade of CBS News was producer Don Hewitt's idea for a magazine for television. Hewitt devised a broadcast that would feature three fifteen-minute segments on a variety of subjects that could not carry an hour-long documentary but needed more than a few minutes on the evening news. *60 Minutes*, which began in 1968 with correspondents Harry Reasoner and Mike Wallace, needed a few years to catch on with viewers. When it did, it became one of the top-rated programs on television and, after thirty-five years on the air with no end in sight, perhaps the medium's most successful ever.

Except for its oft-copied magazine broadcast, CBS News had little to celebrate in the 1980s. Cronkite was replaced by Rather, a highly respected correspondent who brought his customary drive and devotion to the job but not the avuncular qualities of his predecessor. The change allowed Cronkite fans to sample the other networks' evening news—ABC had become a worthy competitor in the 1970s—and the CBS grasp on the evening news audience loosened with time.

That would prove to be true for evening news programs in general. In the mid-1970s the three network evening news broadcasts drew forty-six million viewers, roughly three out of four of the people watching television at that time of day. By 2005, the evening news audience numbered thirty million; only one out of three viewers was watching CBS, NBC, or ABC. In between came technology and competition that changed the dynamic: widespread cable television, satellite-delivered programming, twenty-four-hour news networks, and the Internet and other computer-delivered information systems. For CBS, the really bad news was that it routinely lagged behind NBC and ABC during the twenty-four-year reign of Rather.

The decline at CBS had its roots in corporate moves begun during the twilight of Paley's influence. In 1985, five years before his death at age eighty-nine, Paley faced the prospect of battling hostile takeover bids for CBS by CNN founder Ted Turner and others, even a group of politically conservative investors who wanted more control over its broadcasting. Paley found a friendly ally in Laurence A. Tisch, a wealthy investor who eventually bought a quarter of CBS for $750 million.

However, Tisch's ten-year dominance of CBS—he became chairman shortly after Paley's death—focused more on improving its stock value than building the company. He sold off CBS Records and other assets and, in the quest for slashing spending, turned to the news division, until then off limits to economizing. He dismissed 20 percent of the staff and cut its budget by $30 million, moves that observers would say affect the news division to this day. When Tisch sold CBS to Westinghouse Electric Corporation in 1995 for $5.4 billion, investors celebrated. The network, though, had fallen behind its competitors in terms of audience and advertising revenues.

CBS and its news division began the new century with yet another owner. In 1999 Westinghouse had sold CBS to media giant Viacom. It was a promising move because of the energy Viacom likely would inject into CBS as it repositioned the company in the age of Webcasting, Podcasting, and other more personal forms of communications. However, CBS News stumbled when, during the 2004 presidential campaign, it suffered the embarrassment of retracting a story concerning the military service of President George W. Bush, who was seeking re-election. Rather had been the chief correspondent for the piece, which appeared on the program *60 Minutes II*. When the critical report turned out to be based on phony documents, the news division's reputation suffered anew. Under a cloud, Rather retired in March 2005, earlier than expected, as evening news anchor.

The other networks were retooling as well under the demands of time and changes in the industry. (Longtime anchor Tom Brokaw retired from NBC, and ABC's Peter Jennings died of lung cancer.) A bright point for CBS News and the others lay in the fact that the public's appetite for news and information was only stronger. Their challenge in the 21st century remained developing effective means of communicating with the public and maintaining a foundation of integrity.

Further Reading

Auletta, Ken. "Sign-off: The Long and Complicated Career of Dan Rather. *The New Yorker*. March 7, 2005.

Bliss, Edward Jr. *Now the News: The Story of Broadcast Journalism*. New York: Columbia University Press, 1991.

Gates, Gary Paul. *Air Time: The Inside Story of CBS News*. New York: Harper and Row, 1978.

Smith, Sally Bedell. *In All His Glory: The Life and Times of William S. Paley and the Birth of Broadcasting*. New York: Random House, 1990.

DOUGLASS K. DANIEL

CENSORSHIP

American colonial practices with regard to press censorship were largely molded by developments in English law, which, by the eighteenth century, had created the most liberal press regime in Europe. Thus, prior press censorship (i.e., the requirement that all material be approved by the authorities before publication), which lasted until the middle of the nineteenth century in many European countries (and until 1905 in Russia), lapsed in England in 1694 when the 1643 Ordinance for Printing expired. However, journalists in England and in the American colonies continued to face a wide variety of restrictions, including the requirement that a license be obtained from the authorities before a newspaper began operating, special press taxes and vague, common law restrictions which potentially made criticism of the political authorities subject to prosecution under the doctrine of seditious libel. Thus, the first newspaper ever published in the American colonies, *Publick Occurrences*, was quickly suppressed by Massachusetts authorities in 1690 for failing to obtain the needed license, and its publisher, Benjamin Harris, was jailed. Fourteen years elapsed before another newspaper emerged in the colonies, the 1704 *Boston News-Letter*. The Massachusetts licensing requirement, imposed in 1662, was enforced for 60 years, while Pennsylvania maintained a similar restriction until at least 1722.

Under the extremely vague English common law doctrine of seditious libel, published comments, even by licensed newspapers, which criticized the authorities faced the threat of prosecutions which could result in severe fines and jail sentences. Thus James Franklin was jailed in 1722 for his printed criticisms of colonial authorities in his newspaper, the unlicensed Boston-based *New England Courant*, and was subsequently banned from printing or publishing any "pamphlet or paper of the like nature, except it be first supervised by the secretary of the province." After emerging from prison, Franklin thereafter evaded this licensing requirement by naming his soon-to-be-more-famous brother Benjamin as the official publisher of the *Courant*, which subsequently toned down it political attacks. Benjamin later founded the *Pennsylvania Gazette* in 1729, while James started the *Rhode Island Gazette*, the first newspaper in that colony.

The most famous seditious libel prosecution in the American colonies before the American Revolution involved John Peter Zenger (1697–1746), the German immigrant publisher of the *New York Weekly Journal*, who was tried for his repeated attacks on New York Governor William Cosby. Zenger was jailed under high bail for nine months while awaiting trial. The offending issues of his newspaper were ordered burned before his trial began in August, 1735. Chief Justice James DeLancy correctly informed the jury that, under existing seditious libel doctrine, if Zenger's criticisms were accurate "the law says their being true is an aggravation of the crime" (since such comments could damage the image of the authorities more than false criticism). However, Zenger's eighty-year-old lawyer, Andrew Hamilton, while conceding to the jury that Zenger's writing were libelous under existing law since they clearly criticized the authorities, appealed to the jury with stirring oratory to simply disregard the reigning doctrine which held "the greater the truth, the greater the libel," by acquitting his client on the grounds that he had done no more than "opposing arbitrary power" by "speaking and writing truth." Zenger's subsequent sensational acquittal, in which the jury essentially ignored its legal duty to simply decide whether or not he had published the material in question, rather than to evaluate it, did not immediately change existing seditious libel doctrine. However, his case sparked increased demands for press freedom and helped to shape subsequent developments in both American and English law; thus, in England truth was made a defense in seditious libel prosecutions in 1843, while the 1798 American Sedition Act included a similar provision.

The period leading up to the American Revolution witnessed frequent debates concerning press freedom. Some of them were provoked by the 1765 British Stamp Act, which subjected newspaper and all legal documents to a special tax, sparking and bitter criticism and refusal to pay the tax from large segments of the press and, in a number of cases, mob attacks to prevent the sale of newspaper stamps. Considerable debate was also devoted to the subject of whether press liberty required only freedom from prior restraint or if newspapers would only be free if they could publish without both either advance censorship or the threat of subsequent prosecution for libel. In his *Pennsylvania Gazette*, Benjamin Franklin supported the latter view, arguing that "If all printers were determined not to print anything till they were sure it would offend nobody, there would be very little printed." However, press scholar Leonard Levy argued that most Americans did not accept the argument that the seditious libel doctrine posed an unacceptable threat to liberty, instead accepting the argument of English jurist William Blackstone in his *Commentaries on the Laws of England* (1765–1769) that the absence of prior restraints upon publication constituted freedom of the press. Levy's position is clearly bolstered by the fact, upon the outbreak of the American Revolution, all of the colonies passed legislation which essentially outlawed criticism of the revolutionary cause, restrictions so harsh that historian Claude Van Tyne has written that "the freedom of speech was suppressed, the liberty of the press destroyed."

From the Revolution to World War I, 1775–1917

Those who argue that the Founding Fathers sought to abolish all press prosecutions, either before or after publication, point to the text of the First Amendment to the American Constitution, ratified in1791, which barred Congress from passing any law "abridging the freedom of speech or of the press." However, the intent of this provision is far from clear, as it has been argued that, under Blackstone's doctrine, post-publication sanctions would not restrict press freedom, or, alternatively that it was simply intended to remove Federal jurisdiction from press legislation, while leaving the states free to impose whatever restrictions they wished to, even including prior censorship. Moreover, both during the American Revolution (1775–1783) and the Alien and Sedition Acts crisis (1798–1800), i.e., both shortly before and shortly after the First Amendment was ratified, severe controls on the press were implemented by America's founding generation of leaders.

During the Revolutionary War, local committees of safety composed of leading American nationalists enforced harsh censorship regimes on the press and all of the colonial governments enacted laws which imposed penalties ranging from heavy fines and jail terms to, in some cases, the death penalty and property forfeiture, for those who dared to oppose the revolutionary cause. That the First Amendment was not generally interpreted as establishing a sweeping new libertarian doctrine with regard to press freedoms seems clear from the fact that in 1798, only seven years after its ratification, Congress, which still included some of the constitutional framers, passed drastic restrictions on the press in the notorious Alien and Sedition Acts. These laws were essentially an attempt by the Federalist Party led by President John Adams to crush the rise of the opposition Republican Party led by Vice President Thomas Jefferson. Thus, the Sedition Act outlawed the printing or uttering of "any false, scandalous and malicious statements" which sought to "defame" the government, Congress or President Adams (Jefferson was notably exempted), bring them "into contempt or disrepute" or "excite against them the hatred of the good people of the United States." These provisions provoked renewed debates over the meaning of freedom of the press and led the Kentucky and Virginia legislatures (heavily influenced by Thomas Jefferson and James Madison) to pass resolutions denouncing them as violating the First Amendment. Although only about twenty-five arrests were made under the Sedition Act (which did incorporate the Zenger "truth defense"), the Adams administration used it to prosecute leading Republican newspaper editors, and had Jefferson not defeated Adams in the 1800 presidential election and allowed the Sedition Act to expire, the embryonic nation might well have become a one-party state. Although the Madison administration made no attempt to impose censorship against vociferous Federalist Party criticism of his policies during War of 1812, on several occasions his supporters broke into the offices of opposition newspapers and destroyed their property. Thus, during the so-called "Baltimore Massacre" of July 27, 1812, a crowd of Madison backers invaded the offices of the *Federal Republican,* a leading spokesman for anti-war elements and destroyed its printing press.

Press freedom next became a major issue in connection with the rise of anti-slavery movements during the 1830–1860 period. Several of the southern states enacted legislation which effectively outlawed anti-slavery agitation, and many states banned the circulation of any material which might incite slave rebellions: thus, in 1857, Maryland invoked an 1835 law to imprison a black minister for ten years for possessing a copy of Harriet Beecher Stowe's anti-slavery novel *Uncle Tom's Cabin.* Although President Andrew Jackson was rebuffed when he asked Congress in 1836 to ban abolitionist propaganda from the mails (thus legitimating actions already taken by some postal officials), southern postmasters increasingly seized such material thereafter. By the eve of the Civil War many Republican newspapers, such as the New York *Tribune* and the Springfield *Republican* went undelivered in the South, yet pro-slavery papers such as the New York *Observer* regularly reached their destinations.

No government censorship was imposed during the Mexican-American War (1846–1848), as correspondents and sketch artists were allowed to provide both written and visual depictions of battles from the front lines without any hindrance. However, during the Civil War (1861–1865), both sides imposed a sometimes haphazard and arbitrary censorship on reporters by a variety of techniques that frequently depended upon the attitudes of individual generals and other officials. They included, at various times and places, subjecting telegraph communications to prior censorship, barring reporters from the field, and the closure of offending newspapers and imprisonment of their editors. In 1862, Secretary of War Edwin Stanton ordered the seizure of the offices of a Washington, D.C., newspaper which had alleged violated censorship rules, while, in 1864, two New

York newspapers were closed and their editors briefly jailed for printing a forged, supposed government document and the *Chicago Times* was seized and closed for three days by General Ambrose Burnside after it criticized him, President Abraham Lincoln and other government officials. In the latter case, Burnside acted despite a federal court injunction barring soldiers from carrying out his orders.

Although concerns over allegedly obscene publications attracted considerable attention during the post-Civil War era, especially from the anti-pornographic crusader Anthony Comstock, there were few instances of politically oriented regulation of newspapers between the Civil War and American entry into World War I in 1917. One such exception was during the Spanish-American War (1898–1899), when the government censored reporters' cable correspondence to their newspapers (sometimes rendering the resultant stories unintelligible) and withdrew military press credential from journalists who were caught seeking to evade censorship restrictions. Following the war, General E. S. Otis, commander of American forces occupying the Philippines, censored newspaper reports about Philippine resistance activities.

The Two World Wars, 1917–1945

During World War I, American journalists were subjected to harsh censorship controls at the federal, state, and local levels. Major Douglas MacArthur, who headed the War Department's Bureau of Information, argued in 1916 that the press should be subservient to the needs of the military in wartime. The U. S. government's first large-scale propaganda agency, the Committee on Public Information (1917–1919), headed by George Creel, flooded newspaper offices and other media outlets with pro-war materials and publicized the notion that limitations could be placed on freedom of expression during the war emergency. War correspondents could obtain accreditation from the American Expeditionary Force only after swearing they would disclose no facts which might aid the enemy and posting a $10,000 bond to ensure they would not violate censorship rules. Many America newspapers, especially of leftist persuasions, were banned and/or prosecuted under the draconian Espionage Act of 1917 and the Sedition Act of 1918. Together, these measures sought to eliminate virtually any criticism of the government, including publishing any "disloyal, profane, scurrilous or abusive language about the form" of the American government, the Constitution, the armed forces, the flag, or military uniforms, as well as any language seeking to bring these institutions into "contempt, scorn, contumely or disrepute." Many states enacted similar legislation. As if this were not enough, local citizens often took matters into their own hands by attempting to intimidate people who they believed were not sufficiently patriotic. Virtually the entire socialist and anarchist press (including Emma Goldman's *Mother Earth*) and numerous other radical publications were banned from the mails under these laws: in 1918, Socialist Party leader Morris Hillquit reported that his party had decided to cease printing a handbook because, "The mails are so suppressed I don't believe it is worth the money." The *Freeman's Journal and Catholic Register* was banned from the mail for reprinting Jefferson's statement that Ireland should be free (since this was viewed as critical of America's war-time ally, England) and an issue of *The Public* was treated similarly for arguing that more war-time expenditures should be financed by taxes rather than loans.

Although during and immediately after World War I the American courts, including the Supreme Court, repeatedly upheld a wide variety of repressive measures, by the 1930s the Supreme Court began to gradually increase the protection afforded by the First Amendment to dissident newspapers and others. In the 1931 case of *Near v. Minnesota* (283 U.S. 697) the Court established by a 5–4 vote that the First Amendment constrained the states as well as the Federal government and struck down the 1925 Minnesota "gag" law that banned "malicious, scandalous and defamatory" newspapers in an attempt to suppress sensationalistic so-called "yellow journalism." In its ruling, involving the *Saturday Press* newspaper, which a Minnesota court had ordered closed down "perpetually" under the law after it published claims that Minneapolis officials were collaborating with local gangsters, the Court held that "prior restraint," as opposed to post-publication prosecutions, of printed materials violated the First Amendment, thus endorsing Blackstone's doctrine of 150 years earlier. Writing for the majority, Chief Justice Charles Evans Hughes declared, "The fact that liberty of the press may be abused by miscreant purveyors of scandal does not make any the less necessary the immunity of the press from previous restraint in dealing with official misconduct. Subsequent punishment for such abuses as may exist is the appropriate remedy, consistent with constitutional privilege."

During World War II, prior censorship was effectively imposed on the reporting of military news with little controversy. Journalists overwhelmingly cooperated in enforcing "voluntary" guidelines promulgated by the Office of Censorship (headed by former news executive Byron Price) established under the 1941 War Powers Act, which banned publishing material on subjects such as military plans, presidential trips abroad, intelligence operations and new weapons, including the atomic bomb. Censorship clearance was required not only for written accounts but also for photographs concerning the war, and correspondents were allowed into war theaters only if they agreed to submit to military censorship: as a result, for example, full details of the Pearl Harbor attack were censored for a year and no photographs of dead American soldiers were allowed for twenty months. Under the 1917 Espionage Act, particular issues of more than seventy newspapers and other publications were barred from the mails, and in many cases all future issues were excluded on the grounds that they no longer qualified as regular publications under postal regulations: the most notorious such case involved *Social Justice*, published by the well-known anti-Semitic priest Father Charles Coughlin. In making their decisions, postal officials were guided by political scientist Harold

Lasswell, who developed elaborate criteria supposedly scientifically measure subversion: thus, a publication entitled *X-Ray* was banned from the mails after it was found to be "65% subversive." Although the American Civil Liberties Union proclaimed in 1945 that "wartime censorship raised almost no issues in the United States," thirty years later a Canadian journalist for Reuters wrote that reporters had effectively acted as "the propaganda arm of our government" and that "at the start the censors enforced but by the end we were our own censors." In one major instance, censorship effectively continued after World War II ended: General Douglas MacArthur placed all of southern Japan off-limits to journalists, with the result that no reports about the devastating result of the atomic bombing of Hiroshima emerged for a month, and then only when an Australian journalist evaded the restrictions and filed a report with a London newspaper.

The Cold War and After, 1945–2005

During the Korean War (1950–1953) MacArthur, who commanded United Nations forces until his well-publicized firing by President Truman in 1951, imposed full military censorship on all Korean news in December, 1950, following a brief, confused period in which the press was asked to comply with a vague voluntary code of censorship. By early 1951, correspondents were completely forbidden to make any criticism of the Allied conduct of the war, with penalties ranging from a suspension of credentials to court martials. The London *Daily Dispatch* reported that the censorship became so strict that it could no longer officially report anything other than that UN troops were in Korea, while United Press reporter Robert Miller declared that newspapers had published "certain fact and stories from Korea" which were "pure fabrication" but "we had to write them because they were official releases."

Prior press censorship has been largely unknown in the United States since the Korean War, including during the Vietnam War and various other post-World War II American military operations, such as the two Persian Gulf wars. At least partly for this reason, the government's 1971 attempt to suppress publication of the so-called "Pentagon Papers," attracted enormous attention. The Pentagon Papers affair occurred seven years after the Supreme Court, in the 1964 case of *New York Times Co. v. Sullivan* (376 U.S. 254), had severely limited the legal concept of seditious libel. The Sullivan case originated with a 1960 full-page advertisement by a group of black Alabama clergy criticizing the behavior of the Montgomery, Alabama police. After some of the allegations in the ad proved untrue, Montgomery City Commissioner L. B. Sullivan sued the *New York Times* and the ministers on the grounds that he had been libeled. An Alabama court subsequently ordered the newspaper to pay $500,000 damages, a ruling which was upheld by the Alabama Supreme Court, but overturned by the U.S. Supreme Court on March 9, 1964. The Supreme Court held that the First Amendment's freedom of press protections required that public officials demonstrate malice on the part of news-

papers in order to win a libel action, with malice defined as "publishing of material knowing it to be false, or with a reckless disregard of whether it is true or false." The Court held that the incorrect statements made in the *Times* ad did not fall into this category.

The 1971 Pentagon Papers case, also involving the *New York Times*, centered on new accounts about a secret Department of Defense study of the history of American involvement in Vietnam which had been commissioned by Defense Secretary Robert McNamara before he left his post in 1968. The resulting classified study and accompanying documentation, which included about seven thousand pages of text completed in early 1969, revealed that the government had repeatedly misled Congress and the public about the origins and course of American involvement in Vietnam. After the *Times* began publishing a series of articles about the Pentagon Papers on June 17, 1971, the Richard Nixon administration initiated legal action to block further publication, maintaining that military secrets and other American national security interests were in jeopardy, although nothing in the Papers dealt with developments after 1968. Although Attorney General John Mitchell won a temporary federal district court injunction against further publication by the *Times*, the *Washington Post* obtained a copy of the Papers and took up where the *Times* had left off, and then the *Boston Globe* acted similarly after an injunction against the *Post* was obtained. After two federal appeals courts came to different conclusions concerning the Papers on June 23, the government and the *New York Times* agreed to seek a quick resolution by the Supreme Court.

On June 30, 1971, the Supreme Court ruled 6–3 against the Nixon administration's attempts to ban publication of the Papers (*New York Times v. U.S.*, 403 U.S. 713), but a majority of the justices effectively held open the possibility that under some circumstances prior censorship of the press could be justified. While the Court majority issued an unsigned opinion which declared that "any system of prior restraints of expression comes to this court bearing a heavy presumption against its constitutional validity," each justice issued an individual opinion and no consensus was expressed on the fundamental principles involved. Three justices (Black, Douglas, and Brennan) seemed to suggest that prior restraint could never be justified, but the other three justices joining the majority opinion (Marshall, Stewart, and White) indicated that, while they could not support prior restraint with regard to the papers, they could foresee the possibility that such action could be justified in some future case. The other three justices (Burger, Blackmun, and Harlan) dissented on the grounds that the Court should take more time to examine the materials before making a final judgment concerning a permanent injunction. While making clear that the government bore a heavy burden in order to justify prior restraint on the press, the Court majority seemed to indicate that such action could be justified in some circumstances, but failed to give any guidelines to govern such a decision.

With the major exception of the Pentagon Papers case, there was relatively little direct governmental harassment of the "mainstream" press during the Vietnam War era (approximately 1961–1975), but the so-called "underground press" frequently faced severe, often extra-legal reprisals from both local and federal authorities. The term "underground press" was used to describe an estimated 450 locally based small-scale newspapers, with a total circulation of perhaps five million (including about fifty papers published by or for dissident soldiers) that flourished amidst the "counterculture" of the Vietnam War era. They became the subject of severely disruptive infiltration and harassment from local police, as well as from the FBI, the CIA, military intelligence, the Internal Revenue Service, and other agencies. While many such efforts were secret, California authorities successfully charged the *Los Angeles Free Press* with receiving stolen property after it published the identities of state narcotics agents and arrested dozens of San Diego underground newspaper vendors for such offenses as littering and obstructing sidewalks. In October of 1968, Dallas officials raided the office of *Dallas Notes* to supposedly implement a search warrant authorizing the confiscation of "pornographic materials" and carried off over two tons of materials, leaving behind an office in shambles. Street vendors of the *New Orleans Nola Express* were repeatedly charged with vagrancy and peddling without a license, leading a federal judge to issue an injunction against such police interference after finding that the evidence "overwhelmingly established a policy of the police to arrest persons selling underground newspapers under the guise that they were impeding pedestrian traffic." Montgomery County, Maryland, police arrested one man simply for *possessing* an underground paper. Although underground newspapers often won court cases, most of them operated on a financial shoestring, and many were forced to close due to various forms of governmental disruption and/or the legal expenses which resulted from such efforts, which went largely unreported by the "mainstream" press.

Unlike the two world wars and the Korean War, the government did not impose prior censorship during the Vietnam War or during other instances of military intervention during the Cold War. But reporters' access to critical locations was often restricted, thus accomplishing a form of indirect censorship. In Vietnam, reporters were not restricted until the Cambodian invasion of 1970. Since television was still in its infancy during the Korean War, Vietnam became the first truly televised war, and considerable controversy arose concerning journalistic coverage of the conflict, such as a 1965 CBS broadcast which showed American soldiers burning the huts of villagers and the widely circulated film and photographic depictions of the brutal shooting of a captured enemy soldier by a South Vietnamese police chief in 1968. Some American military and civilian officials increasingly blamed the news coverage and the lack of censorship for American failure to win the war, with the result that tighter restrictions were imposed on news coverage in several subsequent conflicts. Thus, although censorship was not imposed, reporters were excluded completely from Grenada during the first two days of the Reagan's administration's invasion of that island in October, 1983, leaving the press entirely dependent upon government pronouncements. During the George H. W. Bush administration's December, 1989, invasion of Panama, the government allowed only a small "pool" of reporters, chosen by the military, to accompany American troops. Similar systems were implemented during the two Persian Gulf wars (1991, 2003–) of the two Bush presidencies (father and son), which effectively imposed a form of indirect censorship on battleground reports. However, once initial fighting was over, journalists were free to cover the subsequent occupations of Panama and Iraq.

Conclusion

Although the repeated impositions of direct and indirect forms of censorship discussed here make clear that the American press has frequently been subjected to varying types of governmental restraint, nonetheless American journalism, viewed in comparative perspective, has unquestionably been relatively free from overt state control. However, the "mainstream" American press, again viewed in comparative perspective, probably exhibits less diversity of coverage and interpretation than that of most other large democracies. The lack of diverse coverage is due to a combination of financial aspects (large newspapers and other influential media outlets such as the major television networks are owned by wealthy people and corporations who generally do not want to significantly challenge the status quo and whose primary goal is to maximize profits rather than to keep the public well informed), a desire by media owners to be viewed as "responsible" members of society, and fears that perceived anti-government and/or anti-capitalist biases could result in a loss of access to critical government sources and/or overt governmental reprisals of the sort discussed in this essay. Carl Jensen, the director of the news media research Project Censored, founded in 1976, which published annual reports on important stories which have gone unreported by the mainstream press, concluded in 1997 that such lapses resulted most often from media self-censorship rather than governmental restraints. Such self-censorship was best explained by concerns about "the media's bottom line," because "many of the stories that can be cited as undercovered, overlooked or censored are contrary in some way to the financial interests of publishers, owners, stockholders or advertisers," and also by the fact that investigate journalism is far more expensive than the "so-called public stenography school of journalism [in which reporters simply pass on to the public governmental pronouncements] that came to dominate the field in the twentieth century."

Further Reading

Eaton, Clement. *The Freedom of Thought Struggle in the Old South*. New York: Harper & Row, 1964.

Friendly, Fred. *Minnesota Rag: Corruption, Yellow Journalism, and the Case That Saved Freedom of the Press [on Near v. Minnesota]*, Minneapolis: University of Minnesota Press, 2003.

Jensen, Carl. *Censored: The News That Didn't Make the News—and Why.* New York: Four Walls Eight Windows, 1995.

Leamer, Laurence, *The Paper Revolutionaries: The Rise of the Underground Press.* New York: Simon & Schuster, 1972.

Levy, Leonard. *Freedom of Speech and Press in Early American History: Legacy of Suppression.* New York: Harper & Row, 1963.

Levy, Leonard, ed.,Freedom of the Press from Zenger to Jefferson. New York: Bobbs-Merrill, 1966.

Lewis, Anthony. *Make no law: The Sullivan case and the First Amendment.*
New York: Random House, 1991.

MacArthur, John. *Second Front: Censorship and Propaganda in the Gulf War.* New York: Hill & Wang, 1992.

Neely, Mark. *The Fate of Liberty: Abraham Lincoln and Civil Liberties.* New York: Oxford University Press, 1991.

Nelson, Harold, ed. *Freedom of the Press from Hamilton to the Warren Court.* New York: Bobbs-Merrill, 1967.

Nerone, John. *Violence against the Press: Policing the Public Sphere in US History.* New York: Oxford University Press, 1994.

Nye, Russell. *Fettered Freedom: Civil Liberties and the Slavery Controversy, 1830–186,* Urbana: University of Illinois Press, 1972.

Peterson, H. C., and Gilbert Fite. *Opponents of War, 1917–1918,* Seattle: University of Washington Press, 1968.

Putnam, William. *John Peter Zenger and the Fundamental Freedom.* Jefferson, NC: McFarland, 1997.

Roeder, George *The Censored War: American Visual Experience During World War Two.* New Haven, CT: Yale University Press, 1995.

Rudenstine, David. *The Day the Presses Stopped: A History of the Pentagon Papers Case.* Berkeley: University of California Press, 1996.

Sharkey, Jacqueline. *Under Fire: U.S. Military Restrictions on the Media from Grenada to the Persian Gulf.* Washington, D.C.: Center for Public Integrity, 1991.

Smith, James Morton. *Freedom's Fetters: The Alien and Sedition Laws and American Civil Liberties.* Ithaca, NY: Cornell University Press, 1966.

Smith, Jeffrey *Printers and Press Freedom: The Ideology of Early American Journalism.* New York: Oxford University Press, 1988.

Steele, Richard. *Free Speech in the Good War* [World War II]. New York: St. Martin's, 1999.

Sweeney, Michael. *Secrets of Victory: The Office of Censorship and the American Press and Radio in World War II.* Chapel Hill: University of North Carolina Press, 2001.

Vaughn, Stephen. *Holding Fast the Inner Lines: Democracy, Nationalism, and the Committee on Public Information.* Chapel Hill: University of North Carolina Press, 1980.

ROBERT JUSTIN GOLDSTEIN

CENTURY

The best in biography, the best in poetry, the best in fiction, the best in travelogues, the best in woodcut illustrations—the trademark of *Century* magazine, a monthly magazine that flourished, however briefly, during the late nineteenth century. As one of a handful of so-called quality magazines of the era that prospered by providing serious fare, *Century* attracted a sizable readership and numerous advertisers for a dozen years soon after its launch in November 1881. The magazine had replaced *Scribner's*

Monthly subsequent to a business dispute involving the namesake book publisher, which was a partner in the magazine company.

Edited for its first twenty-five years by Richard Watson Gilder, *Century* soared in popularity and to financial success with a three-year series on the Civil War. Begun in late 1884, the series included specially written memoirs by famous Union and Confederate generals, interviews with dozens of former soldiers, and hundreds of woodcut illustrations. At the start of the 1890s, *Century* distributed 220,000 copies a month to subscribers and stores.

The appearance of other quality monthly magazines, including *Cosmopolitan* and *McClure's*, gradually eroded *Century*'s circulation. To compete with the newer magazines, *Century* published occasional lengthy articles on important national and international issues, but Gilder did not want to rely on journalistic articles and preferred the literary emphasis of a serious publication for a genteel readership. *Century*'s monthly circulation decreased to about 150,000 copies by the end of the 1890s.

Literary work by William Dean Howells, Henry James, Jack London, Mark Twain, Edith Wharton, Walt Whitman, and other notables maintained the loyal readership of the magazine for years. Readers enjoyed novels in serial form, novellas, and short stories. The magazine also offered serial articles on historical events. *Century* editors commented on standards and trends in the arts, and a "Topics of the Time" column presented editorial opinion on important political and social issues.

The intensely competitive world of monthly magazines early in the twentieth century resulted in lower subscription and single-copy prices, bidding wars for new work by known authors, and a preference by advertisers for large-circulation periodicals, including several highly popular women's magazines. *Century* lacked the financial resources to meet the challenges, and it entered a period of slow decline. Perhaps contributing to its demise was editorial inflexibility. The magazine adhered to its formula, which meant it failed to broaden its appeal to the important middle-class readership necessary to lure advertisers. *Century* always considered itself a magazine for men and women of culture and wealth. The magazine finally switched its format in 1913 to focus on current events, although the switch was ill-timed because reader preferences then favored features and fiction.

Century, its monthly circulation having dwindled to twenty thousand copies and with few pages of advertising, merged with *Forum* in June 1930. The combined titles lasted a decade until *Forum and Century* merged with another magazine in June 1940, and *Century* disappeared from the masthead.

Further Reading

John, Arthur. *The Best Years of the Century: Richard Watson Gilder, Scribner's Monthly, and the Century Magazine, 1870–1909.* Urbana: University of Illinois Press, 1981.

JAMES LANDERS

CHADWICK, HENRY

Visitors to Cooperstown can read the plaque below the name of a Hall-of-Famer who never professionally played the sport. It celebrates Henry Chadwick (1824–1908) "baseball's preeminent pioneer writer for half a century, inventor of the box score, author of the first rule book, and in 1858 chairman of the rules committee in the first nationwide baseball organization."

In the evolution of baseball from boys' game to national past-time, "no man is more important than Father Chadwick," reports baseball's official history (Thorn, Palmer, Wayman, 517). He was born in Exeter, England, the son of Sir James Chadwick, editor of the *Western Times*. His mother's name is unknown. Chadwick's family came to America and settled in Brooklyn when he was thirteen. Trained as a music teacher, he was an enthusiastic cricketer, and began reporting games for the *Long Island Star* in 1844. Tall and athletic, he married Jane Botts of Richmond, Virginia in 1848, and began reporting on the value of outdoor recreation and physical fitness for the nation's industrial workers.

Baseball had been played as a primitive stick and ball game known as "one-old-cat" or "rounders" going back to colonial times. As early as 1847, Chadwick had played shortstop on the Elysian fields of Hoboken, two years after Alexander Cartwright and his Knickerbocker teammates had codified the sport's first set of rules. In *The Game of Baseball*, Chadwick remembered a day in 1856 when he "chanced to go through the Elysian Fields" and saw two New York club teams playing baseball. It was then that he "took note of the possibilities of the game" and "was struck by the idea that base ball was just the game for a national sport for Americans" (Thorn, Palmer, Wayman, 517).

Chadwick reported baseball for the *New York Times*, beginning in 1856, and in the pages of the sports weekly, the *New York Clipper*, where he perfected the box score, a numerical means by which readers could understand what had happened in the game at a glance. Chadwick's statistics on batters, fielders, and pitchers helped elevate baseball from adolescent play to something systematic and serious, and led Chadwick to the rules committee of the National Association of Base Ball Players, where he wrote baseball's first rules book in 1858. Two years later he published *Beadle's Dime Base Ball Player*, the sport's first annual reference guide.

Chadwick's early accounts of baseball games began appearing in the pages of the *New York Herald* in 1862 and the *New York World* and *New York Sun* soon afterward. He filed Civil War stories out of Richmond for the *New York Tribune* and after the war began a long association with the *Brooklyn Eagle* as chief baseball writer. Chadwick began recording batting averages for the *Clipper* in 1865 and two years later in his weekly *The Ball Player's Chronicle*, he created the "batting champion" by recording hits, home runs and total bases. The following year he created the "total bases average" which became the basis of the modern slugging percentage, which measures a player's extra base power.

Chadwick helped oversee baseball's evolution from amateur to professional status. The National League of Professional Base Ball Clubs, founded in 1876, embraced Chadwick's hard line against betting and made official his pitching categories, as they appeared in *DeWitt's Base Ball Guide*, to include earned run average, hits allowed, hits per game, and opponents' batting averages. Strikeouts would not be recorded until 1889 because Chadwick considered them a sign of poor hitting and not good pitching. From 1881 until his death in 1908, Chadwick annually edited *Spalding's Official Base Ball Guide*, the foremost statistical record the sport had yet seen.

In America's centennial year, Chadwick had presciently predicted that there would come a time when baseball would be widely recognized as America's "national past-time" because of its essential "democratic character" that celebrated individual "courage, nerve, judgment, skill and endurance" (Thorn, 4). He lived to see a day in which the American and National Leagues staged annual World Series spectacles, fall classics watched by tens of thousands, and reported to tens of millions. At his death he was widely recognized as much as any single man, the "Father of Modern Base Ball." (*New York Times*, April 21, 1908, 8)

Further Reading

Chadwick, Henry. *Chadwick's Base Ball Manual*. London: George Routledge & Sons, 1874.

——. *The Game of Base Ball: How to Learn It, How to Play It, and How to Teach It*. New York: George Munro & Co., 1868.

——. *How to Play Base Ball*. New York: A.G. Spalding & Bros., 1889.

——. *Technical Terms of Baseball*. Chicago: A.G. Spalding & Bros., 1897.

DeBekker, L. J. "The Father of the Game." *Harper's Weekly* 51, Issue 2633, June 8, 1907, 838.

Dickson, Paul. *The Joy of Keeping Score: How Scoring the Game Has Influenced and Enhanced the History of Baseball*. New York: Walker & Co., 1996.

"Father of Baseball." *New York Times*, April 21, 1908, 8.

Hardy, Stephen. "Entrepreneurs, Structures and the Sportgeist: Old Tensions in a Modern Industry." In, *Essays on Sport History and Sport Mythology*, edited by Donald G. Kyle, Gary D. Stark, and Allen Guttmann, 45–83. College Station: Texas A & M University Press, 1990.

"In Memory of Henry Chadwick: The Father of Baseball." *Baseball Magazine*, June 1908: 9–12.

Hodermarsky, Mark. *Baseball's Greatest Writers*. Dubuque: Kendall/Hunt Publishers, 2003.

Krout, John Allen. "The Rise of the National Game." In *Annals of American Sport*, 114–148. New Haven: Yale University Press, 1929.

Lamoreaux, David. "Baseball in the Late 19th Century: The Source of Its Appeal." *Journal of Popular Culture* 11, Winter 1977: 597–614.

Papers of Henry Chadwick, including scrapbooks, notes and diaries are part of the Albert G. Spalding Baseball Collection, Manuscript Division, New York Public Library.

Thorn, John. "Our Game," 1-10 and John Thorn, Pete Palmer and Joseph M. Wayman, "The History of Major League Baseball Statistics." In *Total Baseball: The Official Encyclopedia of Major League Baseball*, edited by John Thorn, Pete Palmer, and Michael Gershman, 517–531. Kingston, NY: Total Sports Publishing, 2001.

Tygiel, Jules. "Henry Chadwick and the Invention of Baseball Statistics," *Nine: A Journal of Baseball History and Social Policy Perspectives* 4, Spring 1996: 198–217.

———. *Past Time: Baseball as History*. New York: Oxford University Press, 2000.

Voigt, David Quentin. *American Baseball: From Gentleman's Sport to the Commissioner System*. Norman: University of Oklahoma Press, 1966.

———. "From Chadwick to the Chipmunks." Journal of American Culture 7, Fall 1984: 31–38.

BRUCE J. EVENSEN

CHANCELLOR, JOHN

"It was a moment of absolute pure joy," long-time NBC correspondent, news anchor, and commentator John Chancellor (July 14, 1927–July 12, 1996) said. "It shaped everything that happened in my life." Chancellor was not talking his forty years as a fixture in American homes, but instead, the day in 1950 when he was made a reporter on the *Chicago Sun-Times*. Six months later in a company cost-cutting move, he was out of a job and "drifted into broadcasting." The result, according to Tom Brokaw of NBC News, the man who followed Chancellor as *NBC Nightly News* anchor, was a career that "helped define television news."

John William Chancellor was born and raised in Chicago, Illinois, the only child of hotel executives E.M.J. Chancellor and Mary Barrett Chancellor. His parents wanted him to be a lawyer, but Chancellor's infatuation with journalism began when he was thirteen. Chancellor talked himself inside a police line. "I decided then and there," he later said, "that I wanted to spend my life inside the barricades." He was a teenaged copy boy after school for the *Chicago Daily News*. He took "oddball jobs" as hospital orderly, carpenter's assistant, chemical tester, and riverboat deckhand. Chancellor did public relations work while in the Army between 1945 and 1947, married Constance Herbert after an honorable discharge, enrolled at the University of Illinois-Chicago, but dropped out before graduating. Chancellor supported his wife and daughter Mary as a police reporter and rewrite man at the city desk for the *Chicago Sun-Times*. After his layoff, he got a job as a summer replacement radio news writer at WNBQ, the NBC station in Chicago. "I thought I'd spend a few months in broadcasting and pick up another newspaper job," Chancellor remembers. Instead, he stayed for forty-three years and was among those who helped define broadcast journalism.

Starting in 1950, Chancellor began covering the police beat for WNBQ television. Only ten million American households had television in that year. Chancellor found the work "exhilarating, because there were no rules. We made it up. Nobody knew anything about television, so we invented it." Chancellor shot film, learned how to edit it, and wrote his own reports. His ambitious field reporting pushed television's infant news gathering technology to its limits. Lying face down in a Chicago street, he captured the sound of a gun battle between Chicago police and a murder suspect. Falling debris could be heard when he got close to an industrial fire near a steelworks plant. Chancellor covered a major thunderstorm from inside the storm, filming as he went up in a small plane.

In 1952, as NBC's television news network was taking shape, Chancellor became its Chicago bureau chief. "That first generation of television journalists was put together out of strays and hoboes and tramps and bums," he says. "We came from all over. Much of what people see in news programming today stems from the way we put together news in the very early 1950s." Chancellor was an integral part of the network's live programming of the Republican and Democratic conventions which were held in Chicago's International Amphitheatre in the summer of 1952.

As NBC's senior correspondent, Chancellor in September 1957 was the first network reporter to arrive in Little Rock, Arkansas, to cover the forced desegregation of Central High School. Three years earlier, the U.S. Supreme Court had ruled in *Brown V. Topeka Board of Education* that segregated schools are "inherently unequal." As a result of the ruling, nine African American students were enrolled at Central High but faced a mob of one thousand angry whites on September 4 blocking the school's entrance. Chancellor had hoped "to get a good story" but found himself at the story's center when local police and protesters angrily charged he had sided with the black students. Chancellor and NBC's camera captured when a mob closed in on fifteen-year-old Elizabeth Eckford, shouting death threats at her and Chancellor. Local authorities refused to intervene. President Dwight Eisenhower, watching events unfold while vacationing in Newport, Rhode Island, was dismayed. He returned to the White House on September 24 and gave an Oval Office address on television announcing federal troops were being sent to Little Rock because "the national interest demands the President act" to prevent "anarchy and mob rule." Veteran reporter David Halberstam writes that Chancellor's coverage of the Little Rock crisis "was the first time in American history that the signature figure of a breaking story has been a television reporter and not a print reporter." Chancellor believed "Little Rock was the first national crisis seen on television by the whole country" and "showed how powerful television might be. Television coverage is important particularly when what it is covering is important. Then, it can make history move much faster."

Chancellor remarried in 1958. He and Barbara Upshaw would have two children. In 1958, Chancellor went abroad to cover the Algerian civil war. He reported the Moscow trial of downed U-2 pilot Gary Powers in 1960 and the first manned space flight by Yuri Gagarin. He was a panelist on the Richard Nixon-John Kennedy presidential debates of 1960 and began to see "television emerge as the dominant force, for good or ill, in American politics." He observed, "Before 1960, presidential politics was played out in parades, stadiums, and the back platforms of campaign trains." Now, "it's all moving into our living rooms. The making of the presidency has been the merchandising of the presidency."

In 1961 Chancellor replaced Dave Garroway as host of NBC's "Today Show." He fought to give the show a harder news edge, but eventually ended an unhappy fourteen-month assignment that involved "becoming a television character who gets up early to introduce musical and animal acts." After covering the Common Market in Europe, Chancellor in 1964 was a floor correspondent at the national nominating conventions. At San Francisco's Republican convention, Chancellor was arrested for blocking an aisle. "I've been promised bail by my office," he told viewers as he was led away. As Chet Huntley and David Brinkley cracked up in the NBC booth above the convention floor, Chancellor signed off, "This is John Chancellor reporting, somewhere in custody."

Chancellor became NBC's White House correspondent in early 1965, where he came under the intense scrutiny of President Lyndon Johnson who Chancellor found "obsessed with press relations." Johnson would eavesdrop on Chancellor's White House stand ups "and tried to brief me" before Chancellor went on the air. Although "I didn't want to do it," Chancellor reluctantly gave way to Johnson's insistence and in June 1965, accepted the job of director of the Voice of America. Chancellor found himself in the unenviable position of having to explain America's deepening involvement in Viet Nam to the rest of the world. "It was a very difficult time to try to make the United States plausible," Chancellor said in a 1969 interview, two years after leaving the job.

When Chet Huntley retired in 1970, Chancellor became a co-host of the *NBC Nightly News* with David Brinkley and Frank McGee. In August 1971, Chancellor became the show's sole anchor. For much of the Seventies, he chased *The CBS Evening News with Walter Cronkite* in the narrow ratings race. Characteristic of his approach was his low key announcement on August 8, 1974, of Richard Nixon's resignation because of the Watergate scandal. "I got lots of letters afterward from people who said that was the right thing to do. That's a lesson for those of us in this business. Don't stick yourself in there." Chancellor frequently left the anchor chair to cover events in the Soviet Union, China, and the Middle East. He saw news "as a chronicle of conflict and change" and considered a lack of on-the-record sourcing "the biggest problem we have in broadcast journalism."

After anchoring 2,700 newscasts, Chancellor relinquished the anchor duties to Tom Brokaw in April 1982 and for the next eleven years did regular commentaries on the *Nightly News*. "The wrong way to do commentary is to get mad every night," he said. "That gets boring. Rein in your passion. Explain. Educate." Chancellor was a critic of Israeli policy in Lebanon, the "colossal arrogance" of the Ronald Reagan administration in the Iran-Contra scandal, and the spending sprees of the 1980s and early 1990s. At his passing, Brinkley observed, "he talked to viewers as if he was talking to a good friend across the table." In Chancellor's last commentary, he told his audience "the secret of journalism" is for reporters to remember they are always "guests in people's homes."

Further Reading

Chancellor, John. *Peril and Promise: A Commentary on America.* New York: Harper & Row, 1990.

———. "War Stories." *New York Times*, April 1, 1991, A17.

Chancellor, John, and Walter R. Mears. *The New News Business: A Guide to Writing and Reporting.* New York: Harper Collins, 1995.

Matusow, Barbara. *The Evening Stars: The Making of the Network News Anchor.* Boston: Houghton & Mifflin, 1983.

New York Times, July 13, 1996, A26.

Transcript, John Chancellor Oral History Interview, April 25, 1969, by Dorothy Pierce.

McSweeny, Lyndon Baines Johnson Library and Museum, Austin, Texas.

BRUCE J. EVENSEN

CHICAGO DAILY NEWS

Of all the headlines in the 102-year history of the *Chicago Daily News* (1875–1978), perhaps the most personally painful one for so many Chicagoans was the last one. "So Long, Chicago," the last edition said on March 4, 1978, in what would become a collectors item for third and fourth generation Chicagoans whose parents and grandparents had grown up with the *Daily News*, even as the paper grew up with the city it so self-consciously served. From the scandals of the Grant administration to Watergate, few newspapers took their social responsibility more seriously or had a more intimate relationship with their readers than the *Daily News*. Before the rise of the network nightly news, when newspapers served as guide and advocate for citizens and their communities, the *Chicago Daily News* had established itself a primary spokesman of the nation's second city.

Twenty-seven-year-old Melville E. Stone was a veteran reporter and editor in Chicago's newspaper game, where "from the curbstone to the ashpit" it was "war in the mud and mud to the neck" (*Chicago Daily News*, December 20, 1876, 2). In eight square feet of rented space in a four-story walkup on Fifth Avenue, just west of downtown, he produced the first edition of the one penny, four page *Chicago Daily News* on December 23, 1875, by mischievously endorsing Joseph Medill, publisher of the rival *Tribune*, and "a great and idle man" for president (*Chicago Daily News*, December 23, 1875, 2). By July of 1876 the paper got the financial backing it needed when Stone's former schoolmate, Victor F. Lawson, publisher of the *Skandinaven*, became his partner.

The two men saw the paper as "more than a business enterprise" that targeted no particular class but editorially urged the creation of a public community with improved neighborhoods, schools, streets, and sewers (Lawson Papers, Letter of February 28, 1878). This sense of civic responsibility stimulated circulation. At the end of 1876, the paper's fourteen thousand readers made it Chicago's most popular afternoon paper. By 1885, circulation soared to one hundred thousand and was twice that and second largest in the nation when Stone left the paper in 1888. At Lawson's death in 1925, a half million of Chicago's three million residents were *Daily News* readers and the paper had a value of $13.2 million.

Lawson had been among the first to establish foreign news bureaus and to cultivate column writing. Eugene Field, George Ade, Ben Hecht, Finley Peter Dunne, Carl Sandburg, Edgar Ansel Mowrer and John Gunther, and later, Mike Royko, Sydney J. Harris, and Nicholas von Hoffman confirmed the paper's reputation as "a writer's newspaper." Its award-winning editorial cartoonists included John T. McCutcheon and John Fischetti. The paper courted women readers by serializing short stories, having household hints, and handling stories in a way that "a woman could read aloud in mixed company" (*Chicago Daily News*, December 20, 1876, 2). The paper was awarded thirteen Pulitzer Prizes, three for reporting and three in public service. Frank Knox, who had been a moral crusader as campaign manager for Theodore Roosevelt, and an ardent anti-New Dealer, became publisher of the *Daily News* in 1931, the Republican Party's vice presidential candidate in 1936 and Franklin Roosevelt's war-time navy secretary.

After Knox's death in 1944, the *Daily News* became part of one of the nation's largest newspaper chains when it was purchased by John S. Knight. In 1959, Knight sold the *Daily News* for an unprecedented $24 million to Marshall Field, Jr., publisher of the *Chicago Sun-Times*, and heir to a department store fortune. Field's aggressive competition with the *Chicago Tribune* for morning readers irritated a veteran *Daily News* staff who felt it was being mismanaged and underfunded. The rise of television network news in the fall of 1963, soaring production costs, and the flight of readers to the suburbs, intensified the decline of afternoon newspapers across the United States. Throughout the 1970s, the *Daily News* cut costs, changed management, and modernized its look, but circulation continued dropping. In the end, Field closed the paper, reporting it was "no longer a sound business operation" (*Chicago Daily News*, March 4, 1978, 1), while many of the paper's remaining 327,000 readers remembered Lawson's words that making money had never been the paper's mission or measure.

A reader's relationship to a newspaper was often an intimate thing in the world before television. The paper divided the news of the day in predictable ways. It could be counted on. It faithfully recorded your coming and going and the community of which you were a part, including news of weddings and worship, business and culture, sport and spectacle. In it could be found the romance of daily, communal living. John Chancellor, the anchor of the *NBC Nightly News*, had begun his career in journalism as a copyboy on the *Daily News*. He spoke for many when he said the paper's passing was like "a death in the family" (*Chicago Daily News*, March 4, 1978, 35).

Further Reading

Abbot, Willis J. "Chicago Newspapers and Their Makers." *Review of Reviews* 11, June 1895: 646–665.

Abramoske, Donald J. "The Founding of the *Chicago Daily News*." *Journal of the Illinois State Historical Society* 59, 1966: 341–353.

Akers, Milburn P. "Chicago's Newspaper Concentration." *Nieman Reports* 13, July 1959: 20.

Archive of past issues of the *Chicago Daily News*, Chicago Historical Society, Chicago, Illinois.

Chicago Daily News, "The Last Edition," March 4, 1978.

Dennis, Charles F. *Victor Lawson: His Time and His Work*, New York: Greenwood, 1968, originally 1935.

"Knight of the Press," *Newsweek* XLV, April 25, 1955, 97.

"M.E.S." His Book. New York: Harper & Brothers, 1918.

Nord, David Paul. "The Urbanization of Journalism in Chicago." *Journal of Urban History* 11, August 1985: 411–441.

Papers of Frank Knox, Library of Congress, Washington, D.C.

Papers of Victor F. Lawson and Melville E. Stone, Newberry Library, Chicago, Illinois.

Stone, Melville E. *Fifty Years a Journalist*, New York: Greenwood, 1968, originally 1921.

BRUCE J. EVENSEN

CHICAGO SUN-TIMES

The *Chicago Sun-Times*, a tabloid-sized daily newspaper, debuted in February 1948 as an amalgamation of the former *Daily Illustrated Times*—the first tabloid in Chicago that started in 1929 as an afternoon newspaper—and the *Sun* launched in 1941 as a morning broadsheet. The merger was by no means the first in the highly competitive Chicago news market that dwindled from ten English-language dailies at the end of the nineteenth century to a handful in the twentieth century. Despite the rabid rivalries still displayed by the remaining two major metropolitan dailies, the *Chicago Sun-Times* and *Chicago Tribune*, there are many interconnections between the competitors and dynasties of commerce and industry.

The *Daily Times* was founded by Samuel Emory Thomason, a former *Chicago Tribune* executive who bought the *Chicago Journal*, the oldest newspaper in town dating from 1844, and changed its name and look. With the motto, "Easy to handle, easy to read," the *Times* took a liberal Democratic editorial stance and targeted the working class and mass transit riders with big photographs and bold headlines. Right down to the Speed Graphic camera logo on the front page, he patterned his tabloid after the *New York Daily News* created by Joseph Medill Patterson, a cousin of Thomason's former boss, Col. Robert McCormick. Both Patterson and McCormick were grandsons of famous nineteenth century *Chicago Tribune* editor and publisher, co-founder of the Republican Party and one-time Chicago mayor, Joseph Medill.

The *Sun* was the pro-New Deal brainchild of Marshall Field III whose department store millionaire grandfather, Marshall Field I, loaned money to Medill to buy the *Tribune*. Under McCormick, the *Tribune* became archly conservative, isolationistic and anti-Roosevelt. In 1940, just before the *Sun* dawned, Field III began funding *PM*, a politically liberal New York daily tabloid that lasted until 1948—the same year that the newly-merged *Chicago Sun-Times* debuted after a twenty-one-month labor strike at all Chicago newspapers. Shuttling between his native New York and Chicago, Field III faced newspaper supply shortages during World War II and a legal battle in Chicago to get Associated Press membership to access international news that was finally settled in the *Sun's* favor by the U.S. Supreme Court in 1944. In 1947 Field III bought the *Times* and converted the *Sun* to a tabloid so the papers could share presses and a Sunday edition. The actual merger of the two newspapers seemed inevitable and led the way to further consolidations.

In 1959, Marshall Field IV bought the *Chicago Daily News*, an afternoon broadsheet that had been around since 1876 and claimed to be the first penny press west of the Hudson. The former *Daily News* publisher, Frank Knox, had agreed to publish the first editions of the *Sun* when other commercial printers turned it down. Now the *Daily News* shared printing presses, a library and advertising department with the *Sun-Times*. Though conjoined, the papers remained competitive until the *Daily News* folded in 1978, going the way of many afternoon dailies subsumed by TV evening news programs and traffic delays to suburban distribution.

Some of the *News* staff who had transferred to the *Sun-Times* such as columnist Mike Royko moved to the *Tribune* after part of the final Field Enterprises holdings including the *Sun-Times* were sold by Marshall Field V and his half brother Frederick Woodruff "Ted" Field to Rupert Murdoch's News Corporation in 1984. Murdoch was no stranger to tabloids, having developed them in his native Australia as well as in England and the United States, most notably with the *New York Post*, a tabloid rival to the Tribune Company's *New York Daily News*. The sale also involved the Field Newspaper Syndicate of comic strips including "Andy Capp," "B.C." and "Dennis the Menace" and advice columnist Ann Landers whose work was soon appearing in the rival *Tribune* along with her twin sister's column "Dear Abby." In 1985, Murdoch acquired the former Field-owned UHF station, WFLD-TV as part of his planned Fox Network. Federal law of the time prohibiting ownership of major newspaper and broadcast outlets in the same market made Murdoch sell the *Sun-Times*.

In 1986 the *Sun-Times* was purchased by its publisher Robert Page and other investors who in 1994 sold it and other newly acquired Chicago community and suburban newspapers to Conrad Black's American Publishing Company, part of Hollinger International holding company. Black, who owned tabloids in his native Canada as well as Australia, the United Kingdom, and Israel, subsequently left Hollinger amidst management controversy. Hollinger eventually sold the *Sun-Times* riverfront newspaper building site, scene of journalism-themed motion pictures including *Continental Divide* (1981), *The Paper* (1994) and *Never Been Kissed* (1999), to New York developer Donald Trump

and relocated the newspaper staff to a nearby building in 2004.

In October 2002 both the *Sun-Times* and *Tribune* launched four-color youth-oriented tabloids aimed at creating a news reading habit (Monday through Friday) in urban commuters ages eighteen to thirty-four. The *Sun-Times* created the *Red Streak* in just a few weeks after the *Tribune* announced plans to roll out *RedEye*. In 2005 the *Sun-Times* ceased *Red Streak* when the *Tribune* started distributing *RedEye* for free.

Following in the investigative footsteps of its predecessor the *Times* that uncovered details that led to the release of a convicted killer and inspired the 1948 film, *Call Northside 777*, the *Sun-Times* is known for its community crusades and exposés including setting up a tavern, the Mirage, to capture government bribery via hidden cameras. It has won Pulitzer Prizes for editorial cartooning, photography, and reporting as well as first ever commentary awards for film critic Roger Ebert and former television critic Ron Powers. Syndicated columnist Irv Kupcinet was hired as a sports writer in 1935 at the *Times* where he began a celebrity and gossip column and continued to write "Kup's Column" from the first editions of the *Sun-Times* to his death in 2003.

In 2006, Hollinger International renamed itself Sun Times Media Group reflecting one of its most important publications among more than one hundred other Chicago area holdings.

Further Reading

Cahan, Richard. Michael Williams and Neal Samors. *Real Chicago: Photographs from the Files of the Chicago Sun-Times*. Chicago: Chicago Neighborhoods, Inc., 2004.

Dornfeld, A.A. *Behind the Front Page*. Chicago: Academy Chicago Publishers, 1983.

Field V, Marshall. "1941: Liberal 'Sun' dawns" in *20th Century Chicago: 100 Years, 100 Voices*, edited by Adrienne Drell. Chicago: Sports Publishing, 1999.

Hayner, Don, and Tom McNamee. (Four-part history series published on Sundays in *Chicago Sun-Times* Showcase section in conjunction with the paper's fiftieth anniversary). "Start the Presses," 1 February 1998, 12; "The Next Big Story," February 8, 1998, 1; "News Makers: The Sun-Times did more than just report," 15 February 1998, 12; "Changing Times: Looking toward the millennium with new stories, presses, faces," February 22, 1998, 12.

Madsen, Axel. *The Marshall Fields: The Evolution of an American Business Dynasty*. New York: Wiley, 2002.

Weston, Mary Ann. "The Daily Illustrated Times: Chicago's Tabloid Newspaper," *Journalism History* 16: 3-4 (Autumn-Winter 1989): 76–86.

NORMA FAY GREEN

CHICAGO TRIBUNE

The *Chicago Tribune*, founded in 1847, is the midwestern city's oldest, most influential newspaper as well as one of the ten largest dailies in the United States. It is the founding unit of the U.S. media corporate giant Tribune Company, with holdings that include eleven prominent newspapers, more than twenty-five television and radio stations, online advertising outlets, print and broadcast entertainment services, and the Chicago Cubs baseball team.

Businessmen started the *Tribune* newspaper in Chicago as an offshoot of a literary journal called *The Gem of The Prairie*. It absorbed several publications in the railroad community's pioneer years and in 1858 merged with a rival, the *Democratic Press*. By 1860, the paper was known as the *Tribune* and was number one in daily circulation with sixteen thousand readers in a city of just over one hundred thousand residents.

The *Tribune* enjoyed early success due to forceful, print industry leadership from John L. Scripps, Horace White, Alfred Cowles, Henry Demarest Lloyd, and Joseph Medill. An early advocate for Republican politics and abolitionism, the paper was an important booster of Abraham Lincoln, who was known to hand-carry speeches to its offices. The paper was prominent in getting the party's 1860 national convention held in Chicago, which led to Lincoln's nomination for U.S. president.

The *Tribune* gained an early reputation for investing heavily in new technology, including state-of-the-art, steam-powered presses and copper-faced type. In 1849 it became the first paper in what was then considered the "West" to gather news by telegraph. Circulation more than doubled to 53,000 during the Civil War due to extensive use of wired dispatches, which provided battlefront reports ahead of rival papers for eager readers.

The newspaper constructed its first building, a four-story office, in 1869 in the heart of Chicago's Loop and saw it destroyed in the Great Fire of 1871. Two days later, the paper reappeared with an editorial telling residents: "Cheer up. Chicago will rise again."

Medill, a consummate political and business insider, was elected to a two-year term as the city's mayor after the blaze and led reconstruction efforts. He took total control of the paper in 1874 and would rule almost until he died in 1899.

Editorially, Medill charted a paternalistic course in which he saw commerce and government as interchangeable during some of Chicago's most unsettled economic times. He championed rights of property owners and businessmen. His paper opposed the eight-hour workday, unions, and strikes as a way to settle labor disputes. As a stockholder and director in the 1893 World's Fair in Chicago, he was a tireless booster for the event in the paper.

The *Tribune* prospered financially under Medill. He introduced many reader-friendly features in news columns that helped circulation grow. These included liberal use of foreign correspondents, political cartoons, household hints for women, market tables, farm and garden reports, and a horse-care column. In 1879, its introduction of a weather map was regarded as the first, most effective of its kind in a newspaper.

The *Tribune* was run by Robert W. Patterson Jr., a son-in-law, in the decade after Medill's death. In this period, the publication first referred to itself as the World's Greatest Newspaper and saw great growth in advertising efforts as well as first use of color printing. When Patterson died

in 1910, the paper came close to being purchased by rival *Chicago Daily News* publisher Victor Lawson.

Robert R. McCormick, a Medill grandson, emerged from the family in 1912 as the new *Tribune* publisher. Joseph M. Patterson, another grandson who had helped manage the newspaper after Medill's death with his father, Robert W. Patterson Jr., left Chicago for New York. He later founded the *New York Daily News* that became part of Tribune company holdings.

Under McCormick, an innovative businessman, the *Tribune* saw its circulation grow from 230,000 to 650,000 by 1925. Eventually it would exceed one million daily readers. McCormick invested heavily in Canadian paper mills and built his own plant near Niagara Falls to reduce printing costs.

The *Tribune* embraced new broadcast media almost from the start. It purchased radio station WDAP in 1924 and renamed it WGN (World's Greatest Newspaper). The station broke new ground by broadcasting the Indianapolis 500, Kentucky Derby and World Series. It also aired segments of the 1925 Scopes "monkey trial" by placing microphones in the Tennessee courtroom. In 1948, the *Tribune* established WGN-TV, a future cable super station, and followed with New York's WPIX-TV.

In 1925, the *Tribune* moved from its building at Madison and Dearborn streets in the Loop to its present location, Tribune Tower, at 435 N. Michigan Ave. The winning Gothic design for this new, thirty-six-story building, criticized by some because of its anti-modern look, came from architect John Howell in a $100,000 newspaper-sponsored competition.

In conjunction with the 1933 Century of Progress Exposition held in Chicago, Tribune sports editor Arch Ward organized the first-ever Major League Baseball All-Star game in Chicago. The contest was so popular it remains an annual event. The next year, Ward organized the College All-Star Football Game, a match-up of the reigning professional champion team against a squad of graduated collegiate stars. This game was played annually until 1976.

The *Tribune's* editorial stances and news coverage under McCormick were decidedly isolationist, anti-New Deal, and supportive of U.S. Sen. Joseph McCarthy's virulent anti-Communist witch-hunts. He called his newspaper "The American Paper for Americans." A U.S. flag became a staple pictured in each issue's upper corner of the front page.

The *Tribune's* greatest news scoop during McCormick's leadership was obtaining the text of the Treaty of Versailles in 1919. The paper crusaded against Chicago crime king Al Capone, but got embarrassed in 1930 when one of its own reporters, Jake Lingle, who was killed in a gangland slaying, was discovered to have been receiving payoffs. The newspaper also revealed U.S. war plans on the eve of the Pearl Harbor bombing in 1941. Stanley Johnston's story in the *Tribune* on the Battle of Midway during World War II, which implied that the United States had broken the Japanese code, so angered President Franklin D. Roosevelt that he considered charging Colonel McCormick with treason.

The *Tribune's* biggest gaffe was its premature banner headline on election night in 1948: "Dewey defeats Truman." Though only a limited number of the early editions with the mistaken bulletin reached the public, one did find its way to newly elected U.S. President Harry S Truman, who held it aloft for a national audience to see during a post-election press conference.

After McCormick's death in 1955, the newspaper's editorial page continued to endorse only Republicans for the White House through the 2004 election. New editor Clayton Kirkpatrick, who came up from the paper's newsroom ranks, did usher in objective, non-partisan coverage in the news pages in the late 1960s. He added many young journalists to the staff and created new sections.

Twenty of the *Tribune's* twenty-four Pulitzer Prizes were won after Kirkpatrick became editor. In 1974, the *Tribune* scored a major coup in publishing a forty-four-page, complete transcript of the Watergate tapes from the White House. The newspaper did this in twenty-four hours after the tapes' release, beating the Government Printing Office. Two days later, after studying the transcript more closely, the paper called for Richard M. Nixon's resignation, a step that was considered a huge blow in Nixon's fight to remain U.S. president.

The *Tribune* reorganized its corporate structure in 1968, bought the Chicago Cubs in 1981 and in 1983 became a publicly traded company. These were early moves in a great growth period surrounding the newspaper, turning it into the flagship for Tribune Publishing. Others joining the newspaper in the corporate tent were Tribune Entertainment, Tribune Broadcasting, America Online, WB Television Network, and Tribune Interactive.

The *Tribune* sold the *New York Daily News* in 1991, but the *Tribune* was well on an aggressive path to becoming one of America's largest, multi-media conglomerates. In the 1990s, Tribune Co. bought, or launched, eighteen television stations to go with its already-considerable media holdings.

In 2000, the Tribune Co. made its most significant publishing acquisition by purchasing the Times-Mirror Company, which included the *Los Angeles Times* and seven newspapers in the group. Five years later, this acquisition became problematical due to shrinking readership experienced by U.S. newspapers, decline of advertising revenue, layoffs, and a boardroom battle among major shareholders.

In attempts to diversify its appeal as a print medium, the *Tribune* invested heavily in Spanish-language newspapers. The paper also successfully launched *RedEye*, a daily tabloid aimed for young, urban readers, in 2002 in Chicago.

In 2006, after entertaining offers from interested buyers for the entire Tribune Company, all of which were considered by CEO Dennis FitzSimons to be too low, the year ended with leadership considering strategies to sell holdings piecemeal. Auditors placed the newspaper's circulation at the end of that year at 576,132, making it the eighth largest daily in the United States. In spring 2007, however, it was announced that the *Tribune* and its holdings would be sold.

Further Reading

"About the Tribune—History, Timeline, Pulitzers," http://www.tribune.com (accessed Nov. 9, 2006).

Encyclopedia of the World's Greatest Newspaper. Chicago: Chicago Tribune Co., 1928.

Kinsley, Philip. *The Chicago Tribune: Its First Hundred Years*, vols. 1 and 2. Chicago: Chicago Tribune, 1943 and 1945.

Longstreet, Stephen. *Chicago, 1860–1919.* New York: David McKay Co., 1973.

Tebbel, John W. *An American Dynasty: The Story of the McCormicks, Medills and Pattersons.* New York: Doubleday, 1947.

Wendt, Lloyd. *Chicago Tribune: The Rise of a Great American Newspaper*, Chicago: Rand McNally, 1979.

MIKE CONKLIN

CHILDS, MARQUIS W.

Marquis William Childs (March 17, 1903–June 30, 1990) was a reporter, columnist, and television commentator who specialized in national politics and foreign affairs. His reputation was centered on the syndicated "Washington Calling" column that he wrote from 1944 into the early 1980s. The column dealt with an enormous range of domestic and foreign topics and was at times reprinted in over 150 newspapers. Like many of his generation, Childs was a New Deal liberal and editors frequently printed the "Washington Calling" column to provide a liberal voice on their editorial pages. Childs described himself as an "interpretive reporter," one who explains and contextualizes the news rather than merely passing along information. He strongly believed that a successful political column required original reporting and frequent travel to avoid becoming stale.

Childs was born on March 17, 1903, in Clinton, Iowa, and educated at the University of Wisconsin (BA 1923) and the University of Iowa (MA 1925). He worked briefly for the United Press and joined the St. Louis *Post-Dispatch* in 1926. Two trips to Sweden in the early 1930s formed the basis of *Sweden: The Middle Way*, a book that brought the author wide recognition. Childs became a Washington correspondent in 1934. United Feature Syndicate offered Childs a daily column after the death of Raymond Clapper in early 1944. He returned full time to the *Post-Dispatch* Washington Bureau, while continuing the column three to four days a week, in 1954 and stayed with the paper for the rest of his career.

Childs was a liberal anti-Communist committed to limiting Soviet expansion. Alarmed by the Soviet threat, he urged a vigorous defense and foreign aid program that would allow the United States to negotiate from a position of strength. At the same time, he was haunted by the danger of nuclear weapons and urged the strongest possible international cooperation to prevent the spread and use of such weapons. Childs was also an ardent civil libertarian and wrote at length to defend the constitutional rights of those accused by Sen. Joseph McCarthy and other reactionaries during the 1950s. As he recounted in his later years, he believed that power was dangerous, not just because it was easily misused, but because it often made those who held it believe in their own infallibility.

Childs was a prolific author of magazine articles and books, including several novels, as well as a popular lecturer on political topics. Childs was also successful as a broadcaster. He started doing radio news programs in the 1940s and made frequent television appearances later in his career. He briefly hosted the news show "Washington Spotlight," in the early 1950s and was a panelist on *Meet the Press* 163 times. Despite these many broadcast appearances, Childs always saw himself as a "newspaperman" at heart. Among his many awards was the first Pulitzer Prize for commentary, awarded in 1970.

Childs retired from full time work in 1974, but continued to write a column for many years. He published a memoir, *Witness to Power*, in 1975. Marquis W. Childs died in San Francisco on June 30, 1990.

Further Reading

Childs, Marquis W. *I Write From Washington*. New York: Harper & Brothers, 1942.

——"The Interpretive Reporter in a Troubled World." *Journalism Quarterly* 27 (June 1950): 134–140.

Childs, Marquis W. *Witness to Power*. New York: McGraw Hill, 1975.

Papers of Marquis Childs. University of Iowa Libraries. Iowa City, IA.

ROBERT A. RABE

CHINESE AMERICAN PRESS

"A disorderly Chinaman is rare, and a lazy one does not exist," wrote Mark Twain in *Roughing It*, a memoir about life in Nevada Territory at the time of the American Civil War. The people who persecute the Chinese, Twain said, are not the ladies and gentlemen of society. "Only the scum of the population do it—they and their children; they, and, naturally and consistently, the policemen and politicians, likewise, for these are the dust-licking pimps and slaves of the scum, there as well as elsewhere in America." Unfortunately, many settlers in the far West qualified as those whom Twain labeled as scum, and Twain himself probably never detected the irony of using an epithet that assumed that all Chinese immigrants were men.

Chinese-language newspapers in the United States were mostly started by missionaries and merchants who worked in both the United States and China. They were begun, in part, to provide a sense of community of the immigrants who came to seek gold in California or to work on the transcontinental railroad. Often, they fought discrimination like the kind that Twain witnessed as a frontier journalist in Virginia City. By the end of the century, these newspapers were defending the basic rights of Chinese against laws to exclude them from entering the United States.

Doing research on Chinese-language newspapers provides a significant challenge. The language used in the nineteenth-century newspapers was often a hybrid of classical and Cantonese language with local names for people and places thrown in. This dialect is found neither in Cantonese folk literature or classical literature. Karl Lo and H. M. Lai have undertaken the most comprehensive effort to list existing newspapers and their locations, but they found that only a small portion of the nineteenth-century publications survive, and the history of them is hard to find, often in contradictory and skimpy accounts and in a few available scattered copies of the earliest newspapers.

Many claims have been made for the first Chinese-language newspaper in the United States. Historians disagree about when the first Chinese paper appeared, but all agree it was in San Francisco. In 1851, the Rev. William Speer published his first one-sheet religious tract variously referred to as the *Gold Hill News*, *Golden Hill News*, and *Golden Mountain News*. It lasted less than a year. Speer, corresponding secretary of the Presbyterian Church Board of Education, also started the first regularly published newspaper, *The Oriental*, probably in November 1853.

In May 1856, *The Oriental*, a monthly broadsheet newspaper, contained pages in both English and Chinese; the two outside pages appeared in English and the two inside pages in Chinese. The San Francisco newspaper listed Speer as editor and Lee Kan as associate editor. The paper, "Devoted to Information relating to the Chinese People, the Eastern World, and the Promotion of Christianity," published a report from the Presbytery of California celebrating the Speer's missionary work among the Chinese.

Because of the disparity in wealth and opportunity between China and the United States, the report said, Americans should not begrudge Chinese who wish to work in California. "But we submit that after a tax proportionate to the wants of our state has been levied on the Chinese, that they should be allowed the privilege of working in the mines, and be defended in the rights of property which they have acquired in them, by purchase, or labor. We do not advocate this course on mere grounds of political economy, nor from dictates of commercial expediency, but *because God has been liberal to us,* and a niggard parsimony on our part is not consistent with the liberality with which He has granted His bounties…." Speer later characterized the contributors to *The Oriental* as influential people who gained from the presence of Chinese in California.

The U.S. Census Bureau conducted a comprehensive survey of U.S. newspapers, including what was known about Chinese-language publications. The author, S. N. D. North, describes two contemporary Chinese-language newspapers in San Francisco and the lithography process necessary to publish them. Yee Jenn, who published *The Oriental* (*Wah Kee*) at the time, had learned printing in the United States, and he made all of the seven thousand Chinese characters he used by hand. North reported that *The Oriental*'s office was at 809 Washington St., claimed a circulation of one thousand (much of which went to China), was twenty-one by twenty-eight inches in size, and appeared on Fridays. There were several reasons why people in China might be interested in reading this kind of newspaper from America including to track the activities of extended families and to learn about work opportunities for Chinese who came to the United States. North mentioned a second Chinese paper, *The Chinese-English Newspaper* (*Tong Fan San Bo*), founded in 1876 and claimed a circulation of 750. Both papers were weeklies, contained advertisements, some San Francisco local news and excerpts from the Chinese press. Both sold for 10 cents each or $5 per year. *The Oriental,* after being renamed *Oriental Chinese Newspaper,* disappeared in 1903.

Most printing in Chinese remained complex. The typical compositor had to become familiar with perhaps as many as eleven thousand characters in contrast to the twenty-six letters, ten figures and other signs and symbols of the English language. "A font of type in the Chinese language," the *Scientific American* reported in 1902, "requires eleven thousand spaces, and in the large and spacious racks … each word instead of each letter, as in English, has a place for itself." The compositor had to be calm and focused to get through the daily or weekly task of setting a four-page newspaper. One of the papers displayed considerable enterprise by making a contract with an American paper in Oakland, California, to print a daily edition which was first hand-written and then photoengraved and electrotyped.

After religious groups, business and political organizations were the main sponsors of Chinese-language newspapers. San Francisco's Chinatown covered about a dozen square blocks in the late nineteenth century and the Chinese Consolidated Benevolent Association, commonly known as the Six Companies, dominated its politics and business. This group, controlled by wealthy merchants, often spoke for the Chinese communities throughout the United States and it subsidized the news.

Many newspapers were dominated by shipping and market news. Information on shipping schedules and products often dominated front pages. Sometimes advertisements filled so much space that only a small portion of the paper was left for news and opinion from China and elsewhere. Most news concerned routine items from afar, but some news reflected concern about the anti-Chinese mood sweeping the country. In San Francisco, advertisements pushed a range of products and services from printing to false teeth. One recurring ad promoted gold teeth. Others sold professional sewing and laundry equipment and supplies. A few insurance companies and liquor stores advertised repeatedly.

A business directory, published in a combination of English and Chinese by Wells Fargo & Co. Express in 1882, focused on businesses in San Francisco, but it also listed some businesses in Sacramento, Oakland, Portland, Stockton, San Jose, Virginia City, Marysville, Los Angeles, Denver, and Victoria, B.C. The "Directory of Principal Chinese Business Firms in San Francisco" lists a variety of businesses, including laundries, opium dealers, churches and missions, cigar companies, butchers, tailors, shoe factories, clothing factories, doctors, boot makers, and confectioners. Among them are: The Oriental News Co., 800 Washington St.; Sing Sung & Co., photographer, 743 Washington St.; and Man Kee & Co., Chinese Newspaper, 821 Washington St.—all in San Francisco.

At the turn of the century, news of the Boxer Rebellion—a violent Chinese reaction to foreign interference in China—reached American newspapers as revolutionary groups were forming to overthrow dynastic rule. Future leaders and their advocates studied in the United States and some began newspapers in the United States to support their causes.

Chung Sai Yat Po, Chinese and West Daily Newspaper (copies available at the Huntington Library in San Marino, California), begun in early 1900 and written in some English and some Chinese, was published in San Francisco daily except Sunday. Subscriptions cost $6 a year including postage or $5 if picked up at the printing house. It ran advertisements daily with take-out copies of advertisements available to the printers. The newspaper carried world news with an emphasis on the United States and China. The front page contained both news and commentary, including a cartoon using a quack doctor as a metaphor, saying that the immunization of stopping commercial goods from China did not stop the disease but it increased prices for everything in Chinatown. The February 16, 1900, issue was printed in red ink to celebrate the Chinese New Year. The paper was folded on the right and opened from the left.

Throughout much of the twentieth century, some American newspapers remained freer than those in China or Taiwan to discuss political issues within those countries and Hong Kong. As recently as 2004, the *San Francisco Chronicle* reported a "newspaper war" among six Chinese-language daily newspapers in the Bay Area at a time when mainstream newspapers were experiencing losses in circulation. The six dailies were *Sing Tao Daily, World Journal, China Times, International Daily News, China Press,* and *Ming Pao.* They were joined in 2000 by *Epoch Times,* a free newspaper distributed Monday through Friday. *Sing Tao Daily* began in 1976 as a Bay Area editor of a Hong Kong newspaper. *Ming Pao* also competed against *World Journal* and *Sing Tao Daily* editions in Toronto, Vancouver, and New York. Each ethnic Asian group seemed to prefer certain editions over others. One San Francisco bookstore sold ten different Chinese-language newspapers in 2004, including two editions from Hong Kong and one from Los Angeles. The *New York Times* reported in 2003 a "newspaper war" among four Chinese-language newspapers. By 2006, the Asian American Journalists Association, founded in 1981, claimed a membership of twenty-three hundred members in nineteen chapters at both ethnic and mainstream newspapers across the United States and Asia.

Further Reading

Berger, Joseph. "Newspaper War, Waged a Character at a Time; Chinese-Language Dailies." Battle Fiercely in New York," *New York Times*, November 10, 2003.

Dorman, Michael. "What Really Makes New York Work: The Ethnic Press; Read All About It … In Any Language," *World of New York Magazine, New York Times*, April 8, 1990.

Hua, Vanessa. "Newspaper War in the Bay Area: *Ming Pao* Becomes 6th Chinese-Language Daily," *San Francisco Chronicle*, August 3, 2004, http://www.sfgate.com.

Huntzicker, William E. "Chinese-American Newspapers." In, *Outsiders in 19th-Century Press History: Multicultural Perspective* , edited by Frankie Hutton, and Barbara Straus. Reed. Bowling Green, OH: Bowling Green State University Popular Press, 1995.

Holder, Charles P. "The Chinese Press in America," *Scientific American*, October 11, 1902: 241.

Lai, H.M. "The Chinese-American Press." In *The Ethnic Press in the United States: A Historical Analysis and Handbook*, edited by Sally M. Miller. Westport, CT: Greenwood Press, 1987.

Lo, Karl, and H.M. Lai. *Chinese Newspapers Published in North America, 1854–1975* . Washington, D.C.: Association of Research Libraries, Center for Chinese Research Materials, 1977.

Lum, Casey Man Kong. "Communication and Cultural Insularity: The Chinese Immigrant Experience" *Critical Studies in Mass Communication* 8 (1991): 91–101.

Lydon, Sandy. *Chinese Gold: The Chinese in the Monterey Bay Region* Capitola, CA: Capitola Book Company, 1985.

Stellmann, Louis J. "Yellow Journals: San Francisco's Oriental Newspapers," *Sunset* XIV: 2 (February 1910): 197–201.

Sun, Yumei. "San Francisco's *Chung Sai Yat* Po and the Transformation of Chinese Consciousness, 1900–1920." In *Print Culture in a Diverse America,* edited by James P. Danky, and Wayne A. Wiegand, 85–97 Urbana: University of Illinois Press, 1998.

WILLIAM E. HUNTZICKER

CHRISTIAN BROADCASTING NETWORK (CBN)

The Christian Broadcasting Network (CBN) went on the air October 1, 1961, in a cramped UHF station in Portsmouth, Virginia, through the initiative of Marion Gordon "Pat" Robertson, the thirty-one-year-old son of A. Willis Robertson, a thirty-four-year veteran of the U.S. House and Senate. The young Robertson received a Masters of Divinity degree from New York Theological Seminary in 1959 and was determined to use television as an instrument of mass evangelism. Initially, the station struggled financially. In the fall of 1963 it held its first telethon, asking seven hundred viewers to pledge $10 monthly to meet the ministry's $7,000 in operating expenses. The success of the strategy led to the premier in 1966 of "The 700 Club," a daily broadcast of prayer, interviews, and Christian music, based on the format of NBC's "The Tonight Show." By the end of the decade nearly one hundred affiliated stations were broadcasting the show. CBN became a network when it purchased an Atlanta television station in 1971, a Dallas station in 1973, and a Boston station in 1977. By the 1970s, CBN was the nation's most watched religious broadcast network producing news and public affairs programming through a cable and satellite distribution system designed to serve as an alternative to the nation's three major television networks.

Using satellite communication, CBN expanded worldwide. "The 700 Club" was first broadcast internationally on July 2, 1975, to Europe. Its debut in Asia began on November 7, 1976. The network unveiled a new "700 Club" magazine format on April 29, 1977, focusing on news and public affairs reporting that reached a domestic and international audience over the network's earth satellite station based in Virginia Beach. Satcom and Weststar satellites transmitted the show and other network programming to an estimated audience of more than one million through two hundred affiliated stations. By late 1977, the network aired in cities in Japan, Taiwan, and Puerto Rico, and beginning in 1978, Hong Kong. In April, 1979, the network opened a news bureau in Washington, D.C., responsible for producing live satellite feeds from Capitol Hill and through transmission facilities in the National Press Building. Its first overseas news bureau filed stories and conducted satellite interviews from Jerusalem, beginning in May, 1981. The Jerusalem bureau also produced news and public affairs programming in English and Arabic through Middle East Television, a CBN subsidiary, to six countries in the region.

By 1985, CBN generated $250 million in annual revenues from a state of the art broadcast facility in Virginia Beach, Virginia, that featured four large studios and a staff of more than four hundred. "The 700 Club," hosted by Robertson, could now reach 96 percent of all American households on 228 television stations and an estimated 300 radio stations. News stories focused on the major problems of the period, including the arms race, the environment, the collapsing infrastructure of American cities, the inequalities of the developed and developing worlds, the rise of organized crime, the sexual revolution, racism, drug abuse, attacks on the integrity of the family, abortion, the deterioration of the nation's public schools, its activist courts, and the social and spiritual consequences of unchecked affluence.

The network's news operation experienced growing internal debate over story treatments. News professionals emphasized balance, fairness and essential impartiality. Robertson, preparing a presidential run, favored stories that played to the network's conservative supporters.

Robertson's annual appearances before the National Religious Broadcasters convention in Washington increasingly took on the appearance of campaign rallies. On October 1, 1987, Robertson temporarily left the network to run for the Republican Party's presidential nomination. His second place finish in the Iowa caucus stimulated an upsurge in news stories on the growth of the "Christian right" and its use of mass media to push a conservative political agenda. Religious broadcasting was now big business. Fourteen hundred radio stations, thirty television stations and sixty-six cable systems, reaching thirty-six million viewers a week, specialized in religious broadcasting. They produced annual revenues of half a billion dollars. Robertson's efforts to harness this spiritual enthusiasm for his presidential campaign ultimately failed and by mid-July, 1988, he returned to serve as president of the Christian Broadcasting Network and host of "The 700 Club." There, he decried a "liberal media establishment" whose news organizations claimed objectivity while "masking their basic bias" (off-air recording of "The 700 Club," July 14, 1988).

CBN's reach expanded as the new millennium approached. Network programming penetrated the former Soviet Union on December 23, 1990 with East Bloc countries joining the network in 1992 and 1993. CBN targeted parts of Africa and the Caribbean in the years that followed. RCA's Satcom III satellite began broadcasting the network's programming worldwide twenty-four hours a day and the sale of CBN's Family Entertainment subsidiary on June 11, 1997, to Fox created $136.1 million in additional revenues that the network used in satellite programming throughout the Middle East and Asia. The network's Regent University produced graduates in journalism and mass communication who developed programming for two hundred nations, heard in more than seventy languages, including Russian, Arabic, Spanish, French, and Chinese. A new initiative by the network in 2001 built alliances with producers in local communities in programming to Latin America, Africa, the Muslim world, Europe, Indonesia, Southeast Asia, the Philippines, and China.

Robertson may not have succeeded in building a fourth alternative television network to rival ABC, CBS, and NBC. However, the network's news operation demonstrated there was a public appetite for a conservative alternative to establishment broadcast media, a recognition that paved the way for Fox News and cable's niche news programming in the years that followed.

Further Reading

Abelman, Robert. "News on the '700 Club' after Pat Robertson's Political Fall," *Journalism Quarterly*, Winter 1990.

Gaddy, Gary D. "The Power of the Religious Media: Religious Broadcast Use and the Role of Religious Organizations in Public Affairs," *Review of Religious Research*, Spring 1984.

Gerbner, George, Larry Gross, Stewart Hoover, Michael Morgan, and Nancy Signorielli. *Religion and Television*, Philadelphia: University of Pennsylvania, 1982.

Hadden, Jeffrey, and Charles Swann. *Prime Time Preachers*, Reading, MA: Addison-Wesley, 1981.

Harrell, Jr., David Edwin. *Pat Robertson: A Personal, Religious and Political Portrait*, San Francisco: Harper & Row, 1987.

Robertson, Pat, and Jamie Buckingham. *Shout It from the Housetops*, Plainfield, NJ: Logos International, 1972.

Robertson, Pat and Bob Slosser. *The Secret Kingdom*, Nashville: Thomas Nelson, 1982.

BRUCE J. EVENSEN

CHRISTIAN SCIENCE MONITOR

The purpose of the *Christian Science Monitor*, Mary Baker Eddy suggested in the lead editorial of the paper's first issue on November 25, 1908, was "to injure no man, but to bless all mankind." The conviction came from an episode of personal humiliation administered by the press. The year before Eddy, then eighty-six, had been targeted by Joseph Pulitzer's *New York World* for her unconventional religious beliefs that in Pulitzer's view only appealed to "hysterical women and weak-minded men." Pulitzer encouraged a competency hearing, filed by Eddy's estranged son, to determine her ability to administer a considerable estate. She won, the case was dropped, and one hundred years later the newspaper she started had won seven Pulitzer Prizes for journalistic excellence.

Eddy's claim that she had discovered a divine principle that all physical diseases could be cured by spiritual and not medical means led to her founding of the "Christian Science" Church in 1879 and her derisive criticism in the press. Mark Twain wrote that Eddy preyed upon the vulnerable for profit and was "vain, untruthful, jealous, despotic, arrogant, insolent, and pitiless." Willa Cather, Burton Hendricks, and Georgine Milmine, writing in the muckraking *McClure's Magazine*, were equally merciless. It was Eddy's view that what reaches and affects thought shapes experience. This was why "looking over the newspapers of the day, one naturally reflects that it is dangerous to live, so loaded with diseases seems the very air." The *Christian Science Monitor* was designed to "counteract this public nuisance" that "carries fears to many minds."

The *Monitor*'s first editor, Archibald McLellan, made sure the paper "neither proselytizes nor preaches," but instead "published the real news of the world in a clean, wholesome manner, devoid of the sensational methods employed by so many newspapers." McLellan's city editor was John L. Wright, who quit the *Boston Globe* to work for a newspaper "that will place principle before dividends" and could be "fair, frank, and honest" with its readers regardless of "commercial or political pressures." The *Monitor* did not rely on news services for its content, but developed its own U.S. and world news bureaus that eventually syndicated stories to clients in the United States, Europe, the Middle East, and Asia. Erwin D. Canham, the *Monitor*'s editor throughout World War II and the early Cold War believed the paper's purpose was to help "citizens make informed decisions and take intelligent action for themselves and for society." By the 1980s, *Monitor* editor Katherine W. Fanning maintained the paper's "devotion to public service" remained undiluted as was its aim "to enlighten, elevate, and educate the reader."

From the outset, the *Monitor* minimized reporting on deaths and disasters, largely leaving crime news to other dailies. The paper closely followed efforts to break large trusts, quoting those in the reform community who claimed the U.S. Supreme Court's break up of the Standard Oil Trust in May of 1911 "was designed to curb the rapacious exercise of money power." The story of the sinking of the *Titanic* in April 1912 focused on the stories of survivors and corporate responsibility for the calamity. The assassination of Archduke Franz Ferdinand in Sarajevo that sparked World War I in June 1914 was described by the *Monitor*'s European bureau as "another of those terrible incidents in the history of the house of Hapsburg" and warned "of the effects of this tragedy." When the United States entered the war in April 1917, the paper predicted the coming conflict and its resolution would be "the most important in the history of nations." The war's end in November 1918 provoked "universal rejoicing in every allied capital." Under Frederick Dixon's editorship, the *Monitor* finished this first decade of its life with a circulation of 120,000 on both sides of the Atlantic.

Willis J. Abbot fought for newspaper reform as *Monitor* editor in the 1920s. He had been a key player in the creation of the American Society of Newspaper Editors (ASNE) in 1923 and favored the creation of a "Code of Journalism" to quarantine the profession from the effect of the tabloids. Abbot wanted a code of conduct that would be enforceable on members who abused the public trust. He was convinced that journalism's drive toward professionalism was confounded by the era's "appetite for sensationalism." It had led, he argued, "to the daily chronicling of that which is offensive in life and repugnant to ordinary decency." Throughout the 1920s, Abbot argued that it was "intolerable" and "indefensible" that the nation's leading editors could not punish members for "unethical conduct." Abbot's argument proved particularly persuasive to journalism's young and college-educated editors, who thought the *Monitor*'s success showed a paper did not have to celebrate scandal, sex, sport, celebrity, and spectacle to turn a profit. ASNE's older, less idealistic editors, narrowly outvoted Abbot's initiative, arguing that "ethics are tied to box office receipts," and made ethics requirements on public service non-binding for the nation's newspaper editors.

Erwin D. Canham was drawn to the *Monitor*'s staff because of its unabashed idealism. He served as its Washington correspondent during the New Deal years and early saw signs that "in this great national emergency" that Franklin D. Roosevelt would "make history." Then Canham became a foreign correspondent, where he warned of Adolf Hitler's silencing of political opponents and "the great tragedy of his Jewish persecution." Before Hitler's military might and German occupation of Austria and dismemberment of Czechoslovakia, Canham wrote, Western democracies seemed "unwilling to do anything bolder than make speeches." Canham became the *Monitor*'s managing news editor in 1940, and its editor at the end of the war. He oversaw a staff widely recognized as one of the best in the newspaper industry. This included Joseph C. Harsch, who reported from Berlin; Mallory Browne, Mary Hornaday, and Peter Lyne, based in London; Saville R. Davis, who covered Mussolini; Edmund Stevens and Alexcander Werth, who filed from Moscow; Ronald Stead, who reported the Mediterranean campaign; and Randall Gould, Gordon Walker, and Walter Robb, who reported developments in the Far East. Canham's Washington staff included Richard L. Strout, Roscoe Drummond, William H. Stringer, Neal A. Stanford, Joseph G. Harrison, and Josephine Ripley.

By 1961, the *Monitor* was firmly established as a nationwide newspaper boasting a circulation of 250,000. During the decade, polls of editors, publishers, and journalism professors consistently rated the *Christian Science Monitor* as one of the nation's outstanding papers. In the decades that followed, the paper concentrated on its Washington and foreign reporting, while also focusing on literature, music, and art. Its interpretative analyses identified long-term issues in world affairs, economics, and culture. In 1978, the paper received a special citation from the Pulitzer Prize Committee for "57 years of excellence in journalism." Falling circulation figures in the 1980s, however, led to staff cutbacks and mass resignations in 1989 that included Kay Fanning, the paper's editor, David Anable, managing editor, and David Winder, associate editor. The *Monitor,* under news editor Richard J. Cattani, promised to continue the paper's commitment to "unrelenting but fair-minded journalism." The paper maintained reporters in eleven countries and six regional offices within the United States, providing stories for the *Monitor* and a nationwide network of small weeklies and metropolitan dailies that subscribed to the Monitor News Service.

Special projects of the *Monitor* included Rushworth Kidder's *An Agenda for the 21st Century* (1987), which had interviews with twenty-two prominent Americans on the major issues facing humanity in the twenty-first century; and more broadly, the paper focused on important issues that had been underreported in the mainstream media. The *Monitor* went online in 1996 and launched a radio news network. In the wake of terrorist attacks on the United States on September 11, 2001, the paper received praise for John K. Cooley's reporting from the Middle East. The January 7, 2006, kidnapping of *Monitor* reporter Jill Carroll, in Baghdad, was a major media story until her release eighty-two days later. Richard Bergenheim, a Christian Science practitioner who became the *Monitor*'s editor in 2005, was charged with the responsibility of improving the paper's profitability, while maintaining its long held view that "no human situation is beyond healing or rectification if approached with sufficient understanding of man's God-given potentiality."

Further Reading

Canham, Erwin D. *Commitment to Freedom: The Story of the Christian Science Monitor.* Boston: Houghton Mifflin, 1958.

Christian Science Monitor. *Understanding Our Century: Commemorating the 75th Anniversary of the Christian Science Monitor.* Boston: Christian Science Publishing Society, 1984.

Danziger, Jeff. *Used Cartoons: Political Cartoons from the Christian Science Monitor.* Boston: The Monitor, 1988.

The First 80 Years: The Christian Science Monitor, 1908–1988. Boston: The Christian Science Publishing Co., 1988.

Hunter, Frederic, ed. *A Home Forum Reader: A Timeless Collection of Essays and Poems from the Forum Page of the Christian Science Monitor.* Boston: The Monitor, 1989.

Ralston, Richard E., ed. *Communism: Its Rise and Fall in the 20th Century: From the Pages of the Christian Science Monitor.* Boston: Christian Science Publishing, 1991.

BRUCE J. EVENSEN

CITIZEN REPORTERS

Broadly defined, citizen reporters refer to individuals who produce, disseminate, and exchange a wide variety of news and information, ranging from current topics and common interests to individual issues. Citizen reporters are interchangeable with citizen journalists. As citizen reporters or journalists are distinguished from professional reporters or journalists, there are various terms that indicate citizen reporters, including but not limited to amateur and grassroots reporters or journalists. In addition, as new communication technologies, such as the World Wide Web (or Web) and Weblogs (or blogs), enable citizens to create and deliver news and information, citizen reporters often are referred to as bloggers, wikimedians, or cyberjournalists (or cyberreporters).

The journalistic practices by citizen reporters are defined as citizen journalism, through which ordinary citizens write, report, edit, and send image, text, video, and audio to other audiences. Citizen journalism (also known as participatory journalism) can be distinguished from civic journalism (also known as public or community journalism). Citizen journalism is maintained by citizens who are often marginalized and dissociated with mainstream news media, whereas civic journalism is operated by professional reporters or journalists. Simply put, citizen journalism is "by" citizens, whereas civic journalism is "of" and "for" citizens.

Historical Background and Origins

Before there were newspapers in America there were citizen journalists. Noah Newman reported "the cry of terrified persons" when more than three hundred Native Americans clashed with Plymouth colonists in the Battle of Medfield on February 21, 1676. The first colonial newspaper, *Public Occurrences, Both Forreign and Domestick*, was still fourteen years away when Newman and John Cotton exchanged reports in a newsletter network of "many overtaken by the enemy and kilt" in what came to be known as King Philip's War in the colonies. Of the 549 Puritan publications that appeared between 1638 and 1690, several include reports from citizen reporters. Typical is the October 30, 1683, correspondence from Portsmouth minister Joshua Moodey to Increase Mather in Boston regarding the "monstrous birth" of a stillborn baby to a follower of Anne Hutchinson, who had been banished from Massachusetts Bay because of her antinomian view that salvation did not rest on obedience to church doctrine. The following year Mather's *Essay for the Recording of Illustrious Providences* made much of what happened to those who disobeyed Puritan authority.

Throughout the nineteenth century, frontier editors relied on citizen journalists to report on events beyond the reach of one-man newspaper operations. Characteristic was the June 1895 investigation by Routt County authorities into the apparent suicide of a mining engineer named Wills outside a prospecting camp near Craig, Colorado. A citizen reporter found that Wills had attended a medical college in Louisville before making $75,000 in mining near Helena. The *Craig Courier* of June 22 would report that before opening his mouth to a 44-40 Martin safety gun, Wills had pinned a note to his coat saying, "I cease the struggle for existence. I do myself the mercy to escape the horrors which poverty heaps upon me. Do what you please with what I leave and stick my carcass in a hole any-

where." Citizen reporters frequently captured the poignant impermanence of pioneering culture into the early twentieth century. A citizen journalist offered an eyewitness account in the July 10, 1919, edition of Colorado's *Moffat County Courier* of a Sterling County man who discovered his wife, mother, and two children were drowned when an eight-foot wall of water overturned their car after it stalled in the sands of Pawnee Creek.

During the twentieth century, technology evolved so that not the anonymous but the well-known could be covered by citizen reporters. Abraham Zapruder used a spring-wound Bell and Howell eight-millimeter camera to capture twenty-six seconds of President John F. Kennedy's assassination at Dealey Plaza in Dallas, Texas, on November 22, 1963. Three days later, CBS reporter Dan Rather used the viewing of Zapruder's coverage to speculate that Kennedy had been killed by a lone gunman. On that day, *Life* magazine purchased exclusive rights to the Zapruder film for $150,000. The film would be a critical piece of evidence in the Warren Commission's subsequent investigation of the Kennedy assassination.

In the new millennium, the growth of digital technologies enabled millions to become citizen reporters while permitting millions to see and hear their work. As late as August 16, 2006, 1,613 calls made from individuals trapped in the World Trade Center Towers on September 11, 2001, were released to survivor families and the public. Network television relied heavily on citizen reporters to capture the devastating tsunami that struck the Indian Ocean on December 26, 2004, killing 230,000 people in a swath of death from Indonesia to East Africa. Survivor blogs on the Gulf Coast were among the first reports filed after the August 29–August 30, 2005 passage of Hurricane Katrina across Louisiana, Mississippi, Alabama, and Florida that would kill more than thirteen hundred and displace more than one million others.

The Technology of Citizen Reporting

By the mid-1990s, the Internet and other new communication technologies had created new opportunities for citizens to function as reporters. Blogs, web sites, electronic bulletin boards, and mobile camera phones with wireless access functions gave many citizens the ability to present different perspectives on the news that conventional news media often failed to cover. Citizens could now share news and information about current issues and common interests and also deliver information to other audiences in ways that led to online discussions among individuals.

CompuServe started to provide online services such as electronic mail services and real-time chatting in 1979, but few people received benefits from those services, including people in business, academia, government, and the military. During the late 1980s, when CompuServe and AOL started to offer online services to the general public, ordinary citizens began to have the means to create and deliver their text messages, photographs, and videos to other audiences. Thanks to Hypertext Markup Language (HTML), online users began to generate documents that could be hyperlinked without any space constraint.

Citizen reporters gradually adopted Weblogs as a new reporting tool in the mid-1990s. As Weblogs became popular, citizens could more easily and conveniently produce a wide range of news and information through their blog spheres. Citizen reporters gained popularity through OhMyNews.com, an online based Korean news site. With the motto "every citizen is a reporter," OhMyNews, an alternative newspaper, launched their web site on February 22, 2000, and successfully conducted citizen journalism in collaboration with professional journalists.

Types of Citizen Reporters

Citizen reporters produced and delivered news and information in various forms, such as text, video, and photos, through diverse communication tools, which included mailing lists, online forums, Weblogs, Wiki, mobile phone cameras, and Internet video and radio broadcastings. Up to the mid-1990s, before Weblogs became popular, Usenet, email lists, and electronic Bulletin Board Systems (BBS) were the most widely available communication tools in which citizens could exchange feedback and comments on messages and contents they produced. As citizens started to use Weblog in the late 1990s, bloggers significantly increased the number of citizen reporters.

Some citizen reporters merely posted or added their comments to various news sites written by professional journalists, such as the *New York Times*, *Washington Post*, CNN, and local mainstream news sites. In addition to posting or adding comments on news sites, citizen reporters created and produced news with professional journalists through bloghouses, such as BlufftonToday.com, Lawrence.com, The Denver Post.com, and NJ.com, among others. Finally, citizen reporters participated in news making processes through major news organizations' web sites. For example, MSNBC hired citizen reporters and opened a web site for them when the Katrina disaster occurred in August 2005. Through the web site, citizen reporters posted various news and information about Katrina and its related issues in diverse forms such as text, video, and photographs.

Citizen reporters actively engaged in citizen-based news sites. For example, citizen journalists worked for citizen media, such as MyMissourian.com, WestportNow, iBrattleboro.com, Backfence.com, GetLocalNews.com, and DailyHeights.com. Some citizen news sites published their news and information written by citizen reporters in an offline version, including The Northwest Voice, MyTown, Neighbors, YourHub, and Bluffton Today. Similarly, citizen reporters freely created and edited Web contents through so-called Wiki Journalism. In Wiki Journalism, readers could be both news creators and editors. For example, any citizen could generate or add content to WikiNews, a free online news source, to Backfence.com, a hyperlocal news site, and to Slashdot.org, a technology related news site.

Citizen reporters frequently collaborated with professional journalists to produce news under one umbrella, such as OhMyNews and BlufftonToday. In the case of OhMyNews, in 2006, about fifty professional journalists wrote news articles and columns, whereas about forty-one thousand citizen reporters contributed news articles on a wide range of topics. Citizen reporters also exchanged their news contents with professional journalists in conventional news media. After trained citizen journalists produced news on independent citizen media sites, local mainstream news media produced news articles written by citizen reporters. Also, citizen web sites produced news articles written by professional journalists. Madison Commons, founded in fall, 2005, collaborated with the *Capital Times*, *Wisconsin State Journal*, and the *Isthmus* in Madison, Wisconsin. In January 2006, the Madison Commons Project launched one of the first citizen-based journalism news sites (madison-commons.org) where citizen reporters posted investigative reports about the Madison community. Once a week, such mainstream newspapers as the *Capital Times*, republished news articles written by citizen reporters.

Recent History of Citizen Reporting

During the early twenty-first century, citizen reporters were increasingly going global. They created and disseminated material that because of Web technologies knew no geographic boundaries. As their audiences were worldwide, many of them came to think of themselves as global citizen reporters. For example, Global Voices (GlobalVoices.org) was founded in 2004 with the purpose of building a global network for citizen reporters or bloggers. It was maintained by the Berkman Center for Internet and Society at Harvard University's Law School. In addition, in 2005, OhMyNews hosted OhMyNews International (OMNI) Citizen Reporters' Forum for citizen reporters who were working nationally and internationally. OhMyNews hosted second International Citizen Reporters' Forum in 2006.

Although citizen reporters often claimed they worked as journalists, many had not been trained as journalists. They had little exposure to the traditional norms of objectivity, fairness, balance, and neutrality that have long been a part of a journalist's professional preparation. Citizen reporters can already claim a unique and growing prominence in gathering and disseminating news and, as a consequence, influenced the way journalism was practiced in the twenty-first century and the increasingly democratic, digital marketplace in which news was developed and exchanged.

Further Reading

Friedland, Lewis A. *Public Journalism: Past and Future*. Kettering Foundation Press, 2003.

Gillmore, Dan. *We the media: Grassroots Journalism by the People, for the People*. Cambridge, MA: O'Reilly, 2004.

Glaser, Mark (November 17, 2004). "The New Voices: Hyperlocal Citizen Media Sites Want You (to Write)!" http://ojr.org/ojr/glaser/1098833871.php (accessed April 13, 2007).

Lasica, J. D. (August 7, 2003). "What is Participatory Journalism?" http://www.ojr.org/ojr/workplace/1060217106.php (accessed April 13, 2007).

Lehman, Nicholas. *New Yorker*. Aug. 7, 2006, 44–49.

Outing, Steve (June 15, 2005). "The 11 Layers of Citizen Journalism: A resource guide to help you figure out how to put this industry trend to work for you and your newsroom." Poynteronline, http://www.poynter.org/content/content_view.asp?id=83126 (accessed Aprial 13, 2007).

Related Sites (accessed April 13, 2007):

Backfence.com: http://www.backfence.com/

BlufftonToday: http://www.blufftontoday.com/

DailyHeights.com: http://dailyheights.com/

GetLocalNews.com: http://getlocalnews.com/

Global Voices: http://www.globalvoicesonline.org/

iBrattleboro.com: http://www.ibrattleboro.com/

Lawrence.com: http://www.lawrence.com/

Madison Commons Project: http://www.madisoncommons.org/

MyMissourian.com: http://www.mymissourian.com/

MyTown: http://mytown.dailycamera.com/

Neighbors: http://www.dallasnews.com/neighbors/

NJ.com: http://www.nj.com/

OhMyNews International: http://english.ohmynews.com/index.asp

Slashdot.org: http://slashdot.org/

The Denver Post: http://www.denverpost.com/

The Northwest Voice: http://www.northwestvoice.com/home/

WestportNow: http://www.westportnow.com/

WikiNews: http://en.wikinews.org/wiki/Main_Page

YourHub: http://www.yourhub.com/

Seungahn Nah

CLASSICAL MUSIC CRITICISM

Serious music criticism did not become part of a cultural discourse in the United States until the middle of the nineteenth century. Until then public concerts were only sporadic. With the exception of such groups as Boston's Handel and Haydn Society, founded in 1815, and the New York Philharmonic Society, organized in 1842, music that came to be described as "classical" or "art" was performed by amateur musicians in their homes. Edward Downes has identified a review of the ballad opera "Love in a Village" by Thomas Arne dating from 1767 as the earliest printed review. Oscar Sonneck characterized a lengthy concert review appearing in the *Philadelphia Packet* in May 1786 as "a noteworthy historic document" because of the rarity of such publications.

The growth of New York as a commercial center, increased immigration of Europeans—many of whom were skilled musicians—and the beginnings of the newspaper as a medium of mass communication provided a more favorable environment in that city for regular public performances of music and for critical commentary. A season of Italian grand opera began in 1815. Newspapers costing a penny began to appear in the 1830s. James Gordon Bennett, founder of one such newspaper, the *New York Herald*, began to publish reviews of musical events, for, he argued, newspapers should be "the great organ of social life." Other papers began to include reviews. A composer of some accomplishment and a champion of Beethoven, William Henry Fry (1813–1864), emerged by mid-century as perhaps the most distinguished author of some of these. His prominence as a composer gave his criticism a technical support and credibility that few others could match. Between 1846 and 1852, Fry was a foreign correspondent for the *Philadelphia Public Ledger* and *New York Tribune*, and then from 1852 to 1864, he was arts editor and music critic for the *Tribune*. British-born Henry C. Watson became the first person who probably made a living from music criticism. Musical historian Mark Grant regards him as "the first modern critic." Writing for a number of newspapers, Watson joined others in the ardent promotion of music in American culture. By the end of the century, critic Henry Krehbiel concluded that "'the newspaper now fills the place in the musician's economy which a century ago was filled in Europe by the courts and nobility.'"

Mid-Nineteenth Century to 1920: A Golden Age in the Gilded Age?

Some see the middle of the nineteenth century to World War I, as a kind of golden age for classical music and its criticism in the United States. Others have lamented what they regard as a failure during this time to connect this European derived music to native sources to produce distinctively American art music. Great wealth was amassed and spent to establish musical organizations, especially symphony orchestras, and build concert halls and opera houses. The music of the Viennese school (Haydn, Mozart, and Beethoven) with the additions of Brahms, Wagner, Mendelssohn, and others came to make up a canon of music that Fry and others argued embodied "immutable laws of beauty and truth."

New England transcendentalists Margaret Fuller and Ralph Waldo Emerson used their own magazines in the 1840s and 1850s—among them the *Dial* and *Harbinger*—for essays on music. New cultural magazines that began to appear in the 1850s provided opportunities for expanding discussions of music and made classical music criticism part of a larger discourse on all aspects of culture. *Harper's* and the *Atlantic Monthly* began publishing then, joined by the *Century Illustrated Monthly Magazine* in 1870 and *Scribner's Magazine* in 1887. When William Dean Howells served as the editor of the *Atlantic*, he appointed in 1872 William Foster Apthorp to be its music editor. Apthorp also wrote for Boston newspapers and in that role became that city's first major music critic.

An especially powerful voice of this period came from Boston. Dubbed "the father of American music criticism" by musical scholar Louis Elson, John Sullivan Dwight wrote very much as a missionary on behalf of European art music and came, according to musical historian Joseph Horowitz, to define what Americans meant by classical music. Beginning in 1852, he began to publish his own magazine, *Dwight's Journal of Music*, which employed a number of writers from New York and other parts of the country. It continued until 1881. Through it he and others sustained and amplified Fry's promotion of Beethoven, and he supported the development of musical organizations throughout the United States.

Many critics of distinction succeeded to the earlier group of Apthorp, Dwight, Watson and others. Two might be noted: Henry E. Krehbiel and William J. Henderson. Krehbiel, "the pontiff of musical wisdom" in the words of Grant, worked first as a general-assignment reporter for the *Cincinnati Gazette*, gradually taught himself music, and eventually defined himself as a music critic. He edited for a time the weekly *Musical Review* in New York and then moved to the *New York Tribune*, where he was music critic for more than forty years. Acknowledged by the end of his career as dean of the profession, he did much to aid musicians such as conductor Theodore Thomas and his itinerant orchestra to incorporate Brahms, Wagner, and Dvořák, and perhaps Tchaikovsky into a musical canon. Yet Krehbiel encouraged American composers to use African-American musical material in their music. He thereby found himself at least in partial accord with composer, Arthur Farwell, who in 1905, lamenting "the vise grip which European musical tradition has upon the generation still in power in our musical life," urged American composers to exploit native-American music.

Member of a theatrical family, Henderson identified himself as a preeminent critic of singers and opera, but as a critic for such newspapers as the *New York Times* and the *New York Sun*, he wrote about instrumental music as well. Like Krehbiel, he championed Wagner, and the two thereby became allies of the Wagner protégé and conductor, Anton Seidl, in the promotion of a Wagner cult in New York and elsewhere. Henderson wrote lengthy essays at a time when newspapers provided much more space that they do now for classical music criticism. Horowitz characterizes Henderson's three-thousand word "highly descriptive and shrewdly evaluative" *New York Times* essay on the world premiere of Dvořák's "New World Symphony" in Carnegie Hall in December 1893 as one "of the most astonishing feats of American music journalism." "The attempt to describe a new musical composition may not be quite so futile as an effort to photograph the perfume of a flower," the *Times* review began, "yet it is an experiment of similar nature" (*New York Times*, Dec. 17, 1893, p. 19).

A classical or art music life developed in other cities in the late nineteenth century and the early part of the twentieth. More than in New York, symphony orchestras came to play a larger role in their communities. They developed close relations with local critics. Between 1881 and the end of World War I, Boston, Baltimore, Chicago, Cincinnati, Detroit, Minneapolis, Philadelphia, San Francisco, and St. Louis established resident professional orchestras. Cleveland, Pittsburgh, and Los Angeles added such groups just after the war—enough to make the symphony orchestra a significant symbol of quality urban life in the United States. Establishment of an orchestra in Minneapolis led to the

appointment of that city's first newspaper music critic. In Boston the career of critic Philip Hale was closely tied to the early Boston Symphony for which he wrote program notes of prodigious length. A music enthusiast from a very early age and an accomplished pianist, H. L. Mencken in Baltimore wrote lively criticism for the *Baltimore Sun* and the *American Mercury* as well as program notes for the Baltimore Symphony. In Chicago a good friendship developed between that city's first, and, in the opinion of some, greatest music critic, George P. Upton, and Theodore Thomas, whose career Upton helped change by urging city fathers to create the Chicago Symphony and appoint Thomas its first music director.

Post 1920: Challenges, Change, and Continuity

In the years after World War I, new music required evaluation as did new ways of performing old music. Technology brought radio, television, recordings, the computer, and the iPod—all offering alternative ways to hear music as well as discuss it. What - rightly or wrongly—came to be called popular or pop culture and its music flourished. Discussions of these and other changes expanded and enriched the ongoing conversation about the place of music in the nation's culture.

Radio and television became outlets for musical performances and for commentary and criticism. Both the Metropolitan Opera and the New York Philharmonic began weekly radio broadcasts in the 1930s; and late in the decade the National Broadcasting Company offered Arturo Toscanini an orchestra, the NBC Symphony, to perform weekly concerts for both a live and national radio audience. Conductor Walter Damrosch used the medium for a "Music Appreciation Hour" for children. A composer-critic like Fry, Joseph Deems Taylor, who had written for the *New York American* in the 1920s, built on what Damrosch started and used this new medium to reach a much larger audience and display his very considerable skills as an educator. He provided radio commentary on Metropolitan Opera broadcasts. Conductor and composer Leonard Bernstein used television in much the same way in his Omnibus series in the mid-1950s.

A new Viennese school of composition (Arnold Schoenberg, Anton Webern, and Alban Berg) broke with the tonality of the old and thereby posed challenges to performers, audiences, and critics. These men had American counterparts in Charles Ives, John Cage, Harry Partch, Roger Sessions, and many others. Paul Rosenfeld, who began his critical career in the 1920s, found some of Schoenberg's music difficult to accept, but he wrote with understanding of Ives and other modernist American composers at a time at a time when others either ignored or condemned them. A contemporary of Rosenfeld, Harry Pleasants suggested that the second Viennese school and those who embraced it exemplified a European art tradition whose technical resources had become "exhausted." Like Krehbiel and Farwell he suggested native sources should be exploited more fully. In this context, Olin Downes, principal music critic of the *New York Times* from 1924 to 1955, made an effort to give such music a fair hearing but in the end opted to promote that of the more tonal and accessible Jean Sibelius. Composer Virgil Thomson, who served as music critic for the *New York Herald Tribune* from 1940 to 1954, paid attention to contemporary works, although not always favorably. He applied his very considerable musical talent and verbal skill to analyze all music and its performance in ways that led some to characterize him as a gadfly, "a sacred cow sharpshooter."

Beginning in the 1920s, the popularity of jazz encouraged serious discussion of it and other popular art forms. Gilbert Seldes, who had reviewed classical music for the *Philadelphia Evening Ledger*, became a champion of the popular arts and published in 1923 *The Seven Lively Arts*, a book now regarded as a major text of twentieth-century art criticism. Beginning in the 1970s, John Rockwell sustained this eclecticism. He began as a classical music critic for the *New York Times* in 1972 but almost immediately began writing rock and jazz reviews for that paper as well. He took the position that a "'music critic' had no business excluding entire traditions that most of the world thought of as 'music' just because they didn't conform to his own prejudices...." An accomplished musician and author of critical essays for *Commentary*, *New Criterion*, and the *Times Literary Supplement*, Samuel Lipman dissented from Rockwell's acceptance of the vitality of popular music. Alex Ross of *The New Yorker* has echoed the Rockwell view. The 2005 New York concerts of Catalan viol player Jordi Savall afforded him an opportunity to sustain his view that "music is too personal a medium to support an absolute hierarchy of values." "One musical border after another seemed to melt away," he wrote of those programs, "borders between past and present, composition and improvisation, 'popular' and 'classical.'"

Critics found new ways to discuss these and other matters related to their work. After discussions among critics and conductors during an American Symphony Orchestra League symposium, a North American Music Critics Association was established in 1957. Numbering almost 150 by 2005, it aimed to promote high standards of music criticism in the press and increase general interest in music throughout the Americas. Another opportunity - not limited to just classical music critics but embracing all arts critics – came with the establishment of a National Arts Journalism Program in 1994. Beginning at Northwestern University, it then moved to the Columbia School of Journalism until its demise in 2005. *Symphony* reported, however, in early 2005 the creation of two new programs for arts journalists, one for graduate students at Syracuse University and the other, a National Endowment for the Arts institute for mid-career classical music and opera writers at Columbia University. Finally, the advent of the Internet has provided a resource for broadening and democratizing discussions about music. *Arts Journal.com* provides access to some fifteen arts web logs. It also makes available access to newspaper and periodical articles from the United States, Canada, and the United Kingdom.

Further Reading

Chase, Gilbert. *America's Music: From the Pilgrims to the Present*, rev. 3rd ed., Urbana and Chicago: University of Illinois Press, 1987.

"Criticism." In, *The New Grove Dictionary of Music and Musicians*, 2nd ed., edited by Sadie, Stanley, 687–698. New York: Macmillan, 2001.

Downes, Edward D., and John Rockwell. "Criticism," *The New Grove Dictionary of American Music*, 4 vols., edited by H. Wiley Hitchcock, and Stanley Sadie, 536–546. New York: Macmillan, 1986.

Elson, Louis C. *The History of American Music*, New York: The Macmillan Company, 1925.

Farwell, Arthur "Toward an American Music, *Out West: A Magazine of the Old West and the New*, 10 (January-June 1904): 454–458.

Grant, Mark N. *Maestros of the Pen: A History of Classical Music Criticism in* America. Boston: Northeastern University Press, 1998.

Hart, Philip. *Orpheus in the New World: The Symphony Orchestra as an American Cultural Institution*. New York: W. W. Norton & Company, 1973.

Haskell, Henry, ed. *The Attentive Listener: Three Centuries of Music Criticism*. Princeton, NJ: Princeton University Press, 1996.

Horowitz, Joseph. *Classical Music in America: A History of Its Rise and Fall*. New York and London: W. W. Norton & Company, 2005.

Kammen, Michael. *Gilbert Seldes and the Transformation of Cultural Criticism in the United States*. New York: Oxford University Press, 1996.

Krehbiel, Henry Edward. *Afro-American Folksongs: A Study in Racial and National Music*. New York: G. Schirmer, 1914.

McGill, Lawrence, Willa J. Conrad, Donald Rosenberg, and András Szántó, compilers and editors, "A Survey of Classical Music Critics at General Interest and Specialized New Publications in America: A Collaborative Project of the Music Critics Association of North America and The National Arts Journalism Program at Columbia University," Baltimore and New York, 2005, http://www.mcana.org/images/Critics_Survey_PDF.pdf. (Accessed Aug. 9, 2006).

Randell, Michael, ed. *Harvard Dictionary of Music*, 4th ed. Cambridge: Belknap Press of Harvard University Press, 2003.

Rockwell, John. *All American Music: Composition in the Late Twentieth Century*. New York: Knopf, 1983.

Rosenfeld, Paul. *Discoveries of a Music Critic*. New York: Harcourt, Brace and Co., 1936.

Ross, Alex. "Listen to This," *The New Yorker*, February 16 and 23, 2003, http://www.therestisnoise.com/2004/05/more_to_come_6.html. (Accessed Aug. 9, 2006).

———. "The King of Spain: Jordi Savall at the Metropolitan Museum." *The New Yorker,* May 2, 2005, 108–109.

Sablosky, Irving, *What They Heard: Music in America, 1852–1881. From the Pages of Dwight's Journal of Music*. Baton Rouge and London: Louisiana State University Press, 1986.

Seldes, Gilbert. *The Seven Lively Arts*. New York, London: Harper & Brothers, 1924.

Winzenried, Rebecca, "Pre-emptive Strike," *Symphony*, 56 (Jan.-Feb. 2005), 38–45.

CHARLES A. WEEKS

CLEAR AND PRESENT DANGER

This ringing phrase signifies the most famous test for judging whether the First Amendment to the U.S. Constitution may be temporarily set aside in times of peril to the nation. This famous legal term has become common coinage, borrowed for use in spy novels and as the title for a popular motion picture in 1999. The clear and present danger test is used by judges to balance national security against freedom of expression, thus diluting the First Amendment's command, "Congress shall make no law...abridging the freedom of speech, or of the press. . ." The clear and present danger test, written by U. S. Supreme Court Justice Oliver Wendell Homes, Jr., was part of a unanimous judgment upholding the Espionage Act conviction and fifteen-year sentence of Charles T. Schenck and co-defendants for publishing circulars opposing conscription (of the drafting of men) into the armed services during the World War I era.

Justice Holmes conceded that in normal times, Schenck's words would have been protected under the Constitution. The nature of utterances and actions, however, depends on the circumstances in which they are done. Justice Holmes then wrote one of the most consistently misquoted statements in American legal history: "The most stringent protection of free speech would not protect a man in falsely shouting fire in a theatre and causing a panic" (*Schenck v. United States*, 52). References to this famed statement often omit the word "falsely."

Noting that the United States was at war, Holmes wrote that the question was ". . . whether the words used . . . are of such a nature to create a clear and present danger that they will bring about the substantive evils that Congress has a right to prevent. It is a question of proximity and degree." In two other Espionage Act cases decided by the Court in 1919, *Frohwerk v. United States* and *Debs v. United States*, convictions were again affirmed by Justice Holmes, writing for a unanimous Court. The offenses of Frohwerk and Debs dealt less directly with interference with conscription than with fervent statements in opposition to the war, but they were convicted nonetheless under the clear and present danger language.

The clear and present danger language, however, was not stringent enough to satisfy the majority of the Court. In another World War I decision, *Abrams v. United States* (1919), seven Justices turned to the more repressive concept that words could be punished if they had a "bad tendency" showing a "presumed intent" to cause a harmful result. Jacob Abrams was one of six defendants criticizing the United States' part in the Russian Expeditionary Force at the end of World War I. The prosecution of Abrams and the others was based on the 1918 Sedition Act amending the Espionage Act of 1917 by more broadly criminalizing words that interfered with the United States' prosecution of the war against Germany. Although Abrams and co-defendants published leaflets opposing the United States joining with other nations to send an expeditionary force into Russia, they were not directly concerned with fighting Germany. The leaflets argued that munitions workers go on strike so their bullets could not be used against Russia. For the Court's majority, that was close enough to opposing the war effort against Germany, and the Court upheld the convictions of Abrams and his co-defendants.

In dissent, Holmes—joined by Justice Louis D. Brandeis—wrote that in the *Abrams* case, sentences of twenty years were meted out for publishing two leaflets that the authors had as much right to publish "as the Government has to publish the Constitution now vainly invoked by them." Holmes's language, contending that protesters such as these "poor and puny anonymities" created no clear and present danger, was at its most memorable. Holmes defended the "free trade in ideas," and wrote that "the best test of truth is the power of the thought to get itself accepted in the marketplace of ideas" (*Abrams*, 630).

Holmes and Brandeis also relied on the clear and present danger test in opposing the conviction of Benjamin Gitlow, business manager of a radical socialist newspaper, *The Revolutionary Age*, for violation of the New York criminal anarchy statute (see *Gitlow v. New York*, 1925). Even in upholding the conviction of the unfortunate Gitlow, the Court's majority enunciated the important principle that the First Amendment's power was national, applying not only to actions by Congress, but also to protect speech and press against repressive actions in the states.

The anxious days before World War II led to passage of the Alien Registration Act of 1940, aimed at activities of the Communist Party in the United States. Called the Smith Act, it was the first peacetime sedition law passed by Congress since the Alien and Sedition Acts of 1798. During Cold War tensions with the Soviet Union, the Supreme Court decided *Dennis v. United States* (1951), convictions of communists for attempting to overthrow the government were upheld. The Court borrowed Judge Learned Hand's formula for weighing the "gravity of the 'evil,' as discounted by its improbability," to see whether there is justification for punishing expression. The danger did not have to be imminent because self-preservation of government was the paramount concern (*Dennis*, 510).

In *Yates v. United States* (1957), the Supreme Court overturned Smith Act convictions of fourteen leaders of the Communist Party, By 1969, the U.S. Supreme Court held in a case involving the Ku Klux Klan that states could not punish expression calling for the use of force or violation of law "except where such advocacy is directed to producing imminent lawless action and is likely to incite or produce such action" (*Brandenburg v. Ohio*, 448)

Despite its fame, the clear and present danger test generally turned into an empty slogan for defendants in speech and press cases in wartime. When the Court majority followed the doctrine, the defendants were convicted. When the Court majority shifted to an even less lenient "bad tendency" approach, the defendants were convicted. And in the Communist Party prosecutions, a rewriting of clear and present danger to something akin to "clear and possible danger" still meant that defendants' convictions were upheld, until the Court tried to distinguish between permissible teaching of abstract theory and illegal teaching of doctrine as incitement to action.

The clear and present danger test seemingly worked best apart from wartime or national security concerns. Just before World War II, judges' efforts to mete out punishments for contempt for publishing criticism of their courts was thwarted by the U.S. Supreme Court's use of the clear and present danger formulation. In *Bridges v. California* (1941), the Court dismantled old rules that said that courts could not be criticized while cases were pending before them. Writing for the Court, Justice Hugo L. Black also declared that more than a "reasonable tendency" must be proven to sustain a contempt order. A clear and present danger to the administration of justice must be proven. This use of the clear and present danger test virtually ended contempt-by-publication orders by judges for criticism from outside of the courtroom.

Further Reading

Abrams v. United States, 250 U.S. 616 (1919).

Brandenburg v. Ohio, 395 U.S. 444 (1969).

Bridges v. California, 314 U.S. 252 (1941).

Chafee, Zechariah, Jr. *Free Speech in the United States*. Cambridge, MA: Harvard University Press, 1941.

Debs v. United States, 249 U.S. 211 (1969).

Frohwerk v. United States, 249 U.S. 204 (1919).

Gitlow v. New York, 268 U.S. 652 (1925).

Kalven, Jr. Harry. *A Worthy Tradition: Freedom of Speech in America*, Jamie Kalven, ed. New York, New York University Press, 1988.

Ragan, Fred D. "Justice Oliver Wendell Holmes, Jr., Zechariah Chafee, Jr., and the Clear and Present Danger Test for Free Speech: The First Year, 1919," *Journal of American History*, 58 (June 1971): 24–45.

Schenck v. United States, 249 U.S. 47 (1919).

White, G. Edward. *Justice Oliver Wendell Holmes: Law and the Inner Self*. New York, Oxford University Press, 1993.

DWIGHT L. TEETER, JR.

COBBETT, WILLIAM

William Cobbett (March 9, 1763–June 16, 1835) spent most of his writing career in England, but his talent for searing invective was on display in the United States from 1794 to 1800. He was an extremely prolific polemicist who responded to English corruption, the French Revolution, and American democratic politics by idealizing the traditional values and hierarchical order he associated with his youth in rural England. An egotistical social conservative with racist, sexist, and ultra-patriotic views, Cobbett could be acerbic with his enemies, but he drew attention to political excesses and individual hypocrisy. He was widely read in America and Britain even though he offended many with his scurrility and had contempt for the idea of the sovereignty of the people.

Cobbett was born in Farnham, Surrey, where his father was a small farmer and innkeeper. Although later proud of having a simple country upbringing where God and king were paramount, he left for tedious office work with a London attorney and then joined the army. Stationed in Nova Scotia and New Brunswick, Cobbett taught himself writing, grammar, and other subjects. He used administrative skills to rise in rank to sergeant major in his regiment, but was disgusted with embezzlement by officers. He left the military and prepared evidence to use against four of them in England. Obstructed in court and intimidated by officials, he fled to revolutionary France and then America, but not before writing *The Soldier's Friend* (1792), an anonymous pamphlet detailing abuses and cover-ups in the British military.

Arriving in the United States upset enough to seem sympathetic to republicanism, Cobbett was soon so angry about avaricious Americans, critical British émigrés, and accounts of turmoil in France that he became a journalistic defender of his native country. Starting in 1794, he wrote a steady stream of pamphlets that heaped contempt on Paineites [supporters of Thomas Paine] and Jeffersonians. He opened a store in Philadelphia that sold office supplies, lottery tickets, and his own works. From 1797 to 1799 he published *Porcupine's Gazette*, a daily newspaper that did battle with Benjamin Franklin Bache and other journalists who backed Thomas Jefferson, sympathized with change in France, and attacked Federalists. Contending that America was on the brink of French-inspired moral and political anarchy, Cobbett supported passage of the Sedition Act of 1798 and urged a military alliance with Britain.

As a journalist, Cobbett disdained fears of subscriber reaction and professions of impartiality. He was, however, subjected to threats and legal actions. After losing a financially ruinous libel suit brought by Dr. Benjamin Rush, he returned to England in 1800. Over the next thirty-five years Cobbett founded a number of periodicals and maintained his prodigious journalistic productivity despite occasional problems with the law that included two years in prison for protesting flogging in the military. His writings identified with the common people and appreciated the pre-industrial world of old England. His works included proposals for political reform and the celebrated *Rural Rides* (1830). Elected to Parliament in 1832, he had a heart attack during a debate in 1835 and died several weeks later.

Further Reading

Cobbett, William. *Peter Porcupine in America: Pamphlets of Republicanism and Revolution*, ed. David A. Wilson. Ithaca, NY: Cornell University Press, 1994.

Durey, Michael. *Transatlantic Radicals and the Early American Republic*. Lawrence: University Press of Kansas, 1997.

List, Karen K. "The Role of William Cobbett in Philadelphia's Party Press, 1794–1799," *Journalism Monographs*, no. 82, May 1983.

Nattrass, Leonora. *William Cobbett: The Politics of Style*. Cambridge: Cambridge University Press, 1995.

Smith, Jeffery A. *Franklin and Bache: Envisioning the Enlightened Republic*. New York: Oxford University Press, 1990.

Spater, George. *William Cobbett: The Poor Man's Friend*. Cambridge: Cambridge University Press, 1982.

JEFFREY A. SMITH

COLONIAL PRESS

News that appeared in the early colonial press frequently came from European newspapers and other foreign sources, was several weeks old, and resembled accounts of recent history more than current events. Religion often strongly influenced local news and rumor frequently found its way into the press. Newspapers were allowed to publish by authority of colonial governments and through the first two decades of the eighteenth century it was rare for papers to challenge local leaders.

The press did not exist in the British American colonies from the point of initial settlement. The British first established colonies on the mainland in North America in 1607. From the first days of settlement, many colonists tried to re-create many aspects of the culture they left behind in the mother country. But printing presses were not always included. The Puritans, religious dissidents who settled Massachusetts first, brought printing to the British colonies in North America when they set up a printing press in 1638, and Boston became the first center of printing in the British colonies. The Puritans believed that it was essential for believers to have easy access to the Bible and they needed a printing press in order to make copies of the Bible readily available. The Puritans had established Harvard College in 1636 to train ministers. The printing press was set up at Cambridge to help provide resources for the college and the church. The first book published was the *Bay Psalm Book*, printed in 1640.

Over the course of the seventeenth century, the number of printing presses in the British colonies grew slowly. By the last decades of the century, some printers considered establishing a newspaper. Boston continued to be the center of growth and development in the printing industry in the American colonies. Here, Benjamin Harris became the first printer to actually try a newspaper when he published *Publick Occurrences, Both Foreign and Domestick* on September 25, 1690. Harris published a summary of news from Massachusetts, the other colonies, and Europe. He also published an essay criticizing the colonial government for failing to adequately handle problems with the Native Americans. Harris only produced one issue of *Publick Occurrences*. Local authorities shut down the publication because he failed to get official permission to publish the newspaper. It would be fourteen years before someone tried again.

On April 24, 1704, John Campbell printed the *Boston News-Letter*. Having learned from Harris's experience, Campbell asked for permission to publish and seldom questioned the government because he feared being shut down. Campbell clearly hesitated to criticize the public authorities, but he successfully broke the news drought and made newspapers an accepted part of the printing industry in the British colonies.

Campbell finally faced competition beginning in 1719, when William Brooker, the new postmaster in Boston, began publishing the *Boston Gazette*. Although the *Boston Gazette* became a radical news sheet in later decades, it initially remained fairly predictable and inoffensive in order to continue to gain information from government officials.

In 1721, the friendly and safe relationship between newspaper printers and public officials ended. James Franklin (Benjamin Franklin's older brother) began publishing the *New England Courant*. Franklin had been encouraged to begin the *Courant* by a group of citizens opposed to the leaders of Massachusetts and that opposition showed in the pages of Franklin's newspaper.

Much of the disagreements in Massachusetts also related to religious differences. Supporters of the government tended to be members of the Puritan Congregational Church while those in the opposition tended to be members of the Church of England. Letters and essays in the *Gazette* and the *Courant* reflected disagreements over how to deal with the Native Americans, worries about the French in Canada, and other governmental issues. They even argued over the issue of the validity of smallpox inoculation. Franklin led the attack against the new method of preventing disease, partially in order to attack Increase and Cotton Mather, influential Puritan ministers who supported inoculation.

James Franklin finally went too far in 1722 when he attacked the local authorities for failing to adequately defend against pirate attacks. Franklin was charged with contempt and told he could no longer publish the *Courant*. Franklin just made his apprentice brother Benjamin the official printer and continued publication. The two brothers eventually had a falling-out and Benjamin left Boston for good. James finally ended the *Courant* in 1726. He moved to Newport, Rhode Island, where he later established that colony's first paper, the *Rhode Island Gazette*.

Benjamin Franklin moved to Philadelphia, the other center of printing in the British colonies. William Bradford had established the first press in Philadelphia in 1685, but he moved to New York City in 1693 after a falling-out with Quaker leaders. William Bradford's son, Andrew, published the first paper in Philadelphia on December 22, 1719. Ten years later, Benjamin Franklin took over the management of Samuel Keimer's *Pennsylvania Gazette*, which had first appeared in December 1728. Franklin had opened his own shop in Philadelphia in the spring of 1728 and had planned to publish a paper to rival Bradford's *Mercury*. Keimer, Franklin's first employer when he came to Philadelphia from Boston, learned of Franklin's newspaper plans and rushed to publish the *Gazette* first. But Keimer could not turn the *Gazette* into a successful venture, so he passed it on to Franklin. Franklin quickly succeeded, winning the government printing contract away from Bradford. By age twenty-four, Benjamin Franklin was the sole proprietor of what many regarded as the best newspaper in the colonies.

Franklin's success revolved around a number of ventures. He filled the pages of the *Gazette* with news and materials gleaned from a variety of sources, including other newspapers and letters acquired from readers. He included essays on a variety of topics, both political and otherwise. Although not particularly religious, Franklin may have contributed to the Great Awakening by welcoming George Whitefield into his home, giving his preaching front-page play, and by selling bound editions of Whitefield's sermons. Franklin also ventured into other printing projects, most notably the extremely successful *Poor Richard's Almanack*, which he began publishing in 1732. Benjamin Franklin retired from the active management of the *Pennsylvania Gazette* at age forty-two, but he continued to give advice about the operation of the *Gazette* and helped a number of young printers set up shop and establish newspapers throughout the colonies.

Newspapers appeared in other colonies. William Bradford founded New York's first paper when he issued the *New York Gazette* on November 8, 1733. William Parks founded the *Maryland Gazette* in Annapolis in 1727. Parks later also founded the first paper in Virginia, when he began publishing the *Virginia Gazette* in Williamsburg in 1736.

On June 10, 1731, Benjamin Franklin published an "Apology for Printers" in the *Pennsylvania Gazette*. He declared that "Printers are educated in the Belief, that when Men differ in Opinion, both Sides ought equally to have the Advantage of being heard by the Publick; and that when Truth and Error have fair Play, the former is always an overmatch for the latter: Hence they cheerfully serve all contending Writers that pay them well, without regarding on which side they are of the Question in Dispute." Increasingly, newspaper printers perceived their news sheets as the location for discussion and debate in order to determine the direction for community decisions. But public officials continued to be unsure about how the newspaper press should function and what should be the relationship between newspaper printers and government leaders. This uncertainty helped produce one of the most famous free press trials in history.

The trial of John Peter Zenger grew out of a political conflict in New York. Originally settled by the Dutch as New Amsterdam in the early 1600s, the colony became New York in 1664 when the British conquered the colony. In the 1730s, opponents of Governor William Cosby sought ways to inform the people about Cosby's questionable actions. They provided financial support for the founding of Zenger's *New York Weekly Journal* on November 5, 1733. Throughout the rest of 1733, the *Journal* criticized Governor Cosby and his government for failing to govern properly. By early 1734, Cosby tried to shut down the *Weekly Journal* by seeking grand jury indictments or action by the colonial legislature. Failing in all of these efforts, Cosby had the royal council issue a warrant for Zenger's arrest for encouraging sedition. Zenger was imprisoned for nine months, a fact that produced considerable sympathy for his situation. James Alexander, who had done much of the editing of the *Weekly Journal*, planned to defend Zenger, but Cosby had him disbarred. Zenger's supporters hired Andrew Hamilton of Pennsylvania, one of the most famous lawyers in the colonies.

In defending Zenger, Hamilton helped enunciate principles of great importance for the future. He quickly admitted that Zenger had published the items in question. This admission should have produced a quick guilty verdict because the issue of who printed the seditious material was technically all the jury could deal with. Hamilton, however,

sought to go beyond the point of who published to deal with what was published. He urged the jury to consider the truth of what Zenger had printed. He declared that it was essential for good government that citizens have the freedom to criticize their rulers and to judge the validity of criticisms aimed at ruling authorities. The jury found Zenger "not guilty," which technically meant that Zenger had not printed the material in question. It took years for the implications of this trial to be fully understood and implemented, but Zenger's trial established the first examples for the admissibility of information about the issue of the truth of alleged libels and the role of a jury in determining whether a publication was seditious or defamatory. This verdict was a step toward establishing the press's role as a locale for discussion and debate over the actions of government.

The *New York Weekly Journal* continued to be published while Zenger was in jail, primarily through the efforts of his wife Anna. In that experience, Anna Zenger was not unique. Much of the colonial economy was based on family-run businesses, and husbands and wives often worked side by side in making the family income. As a result, a number of women learned how to run a print shop and took over when their husbands could not work. In the 1730s, James Franklin's wife Ann produced the *Rhode Island Gazette* during his lengthy illness and continued it following his death in 1735. Elizabeth Timothy took over the *South-Carolina Gazette* follow her husband's death in 1738, and she continued the paper for seven years. Mary Katherine Goddard, the sister of William Goddard, joined with her brother and her mother Mary to help run the *Providence Gazette* in 1762. She later helped manage two other papers started by her brother, the *Pennsylvania Chronicle* in Philadelphia and the *Maryland Journal* in Baltimore. Other unheralded women probably participated in the printing business as well as they helped husbands and sons earn the family income.

Throughout the eighteenth century, the colonial press became increasingly important as a source of news and information. In comparison to England and the rest of Europe, Americans became more literate. Literacy increasingly became the mark of a good citizen. By the middle of the eighteenth century, over one-half of the adult men in the colonies could read. But even those who could not read for themselves turned to newspapers for information. Groups gathered in local taverns to hear the newspapers read out loud. The average printing run for a colonial newspaper was between five hundred and one thousand, but each of these issues probably reached two or three people which thus greatly multiplied the impact of each issue. The tavern became an important local institution where people came in contact with newspapers and discussed their contents.

Producing a newspaper in the eighteenth century was a slow process. Thirteen separate processes had to occur in order to print a single page. Type had to be set by hand in the form and then locked into place in the press. Once the form was in position, someone would ink the type using two large deerskin balls and then place a piece of paper on top of the type. Then someone else would pull twice on an iron lever that pressed the paper down onto the inked type. This printed page would be hung up to dry, and the process would be repeated. Two people working ten hours could produce two thousand to twenty-five hundred pages a day. And that count assumes they had all the necessary supplies. Except for ink, almost all the equipment and materials needed to produce a newspaper had to be imported. Christopher Sower, Jr., of Pennsylvania, began to manufacture presses in 1750 and type in 1772, but the best still had to be brought over from Great Britain. And paper, made from rags, continued to be scarce and had to be imported until late in the colonial era.

For most of the eighteenth century colonial newspapers published items of interest primarily from Europe. Most local news apparently passed more by word of mouth than through newspapers. Births, deaths, and trading news appeared most frequently, along with an occasional essay about a local issue. News items from Europe proved popular, followed by materials from the more distant colonies. Advertisements also constituted a major part of each issue, primarily because advertisement revenue helped support the newspaper and because readers wanted to know what wares local merchants had to sell.

The focus of the colonial press began to change with the French and Indian War. Because much of the fighting occurred in the colonies, Americans wanted to know where the enemy was and who was winning. They would have wanted to know this even if all the fighting had occurred in Europe, but the closeness of the fighting made it even more important to know as many details as available. By the end of the war, twenty-three newspapers appeared regularly throughout the colonies. The French and Indian War helped focus the interest of many colonists on the same subject and thus helped set the stage for the Revolutionary War. Through the press—newspapers and pamphlets—the colonists began to think of themselves as Americans, fiercely debated what the character of the republic should be, and stayed informed about events and developments in the fight against the mother country.

Further Reading

Copeland, David A. *Colonial American Newspapers: Character and Content.* Newark: University of Delaware Press, 1997.

Kobre, Sidney. *The Development of the Colonial Newspaper.* Gloucester, MA: Peter Smith, 1960.

Sloan, Wm. David, and Julie Hedgepeth Williams. *The Early American Press, 1690-1783.* Westport, CT: Greenwood Press, 1994.

Smith, Jeffery A. *Printers and Press Freedom: The Ideology of Early American Journalism.* New York: Oxford University Press, 1988.

CAROL SUE HUMPHREY

COLUMNISTS

Columnists are the human face of daily newspapers, and have been an American tradition throughout the twentieth century and well into the twenty-first century. Traditionally, these writers appear in a fixed section of the newspaper such as the opinion pages, or the front of a local news section, or in the entertainment section. Columnists write to a fixed length, usually about eight hundred words. They are published on a consistent cycle, be that weekly, twice or three times a week, or even daily. Columns are signed and reflect personal opinion, and they differ from editorials which are the unsigned institutional opinion of newspapers. Most columnists are general interest writers who may focus on politics, humor, or local issues, and yet they are not limited to write exclusively about their specialty. What is required is that their work be read by a large number of readers.

Columnists began appearing in daily newspapers in the late 1800s and the beginning of the 1900s. George Ade (1866–1944) of Chicago wrote a column called "Stories of the Streets and of the Town" for the *Chicago Record* from 1893–1900. Ade's pieces captured the colorful slang of working-class people. Ringgold "Ring" Lardner (1885–1933) wrote the "In Wake of the News" sports column for the *Chicago Tribune* from 1913 to 1919, then a humor column from 1919 to 1927. William Penn Adair "Will" Rogers (1879–1935) endeared himself to readers with wry cowboy humor. His column was syndicated, meaning it originated at a newspaper or institution then was sold to other newspapers at rates based on circulation. Rogers's column began in 1922 and ended in 1935 after he died in a plane crash. Rogers is associated with the quotation, "Well, all I know is what I read in the papers."

Walter Winchell (1897–1972) shaped the modern gossip column, beginning in the 1920s at the *New York Evening Graphic*, and continuing through the 1960s at *New York's Daily Mirror*. Winchell was the iconic reporter who wore a fedora and barked his column to the beat of teletype clatter. Louella Parsons (1881–1972) emerged as a widely read Hollywood columnist for Hearst Newspapers. By the 1930s, her column reached one in four American households. Parsons was challenged by Hedda Hopper (1885–1966) an actress-turned columnist for the *Los Angeles Times* and other newspapers. Hopper's column at its peak reached thirty-five million readers.

A sibling rivalry developed between twins Esther Pauline Lederer, better known as advice columnist Ann Landers (1918–2002), and Pauline Esther Phillips, known to readers as Abigail Van Buren or Dear Abby. During the last half of the twentieth century, both writers often used humor to answer serious questions about relationships, families, sexuality, substance abuse, and disease.

War provided another serious theme for writers. World War II correspondent Ernie Pyle (1900–1945) is lauded as a patron saint by the National Society of Newspaper Columnists. Pyle's Scripps Howard dispatches emphasized the struggles of foot soldiers instead of the lives of commanders.

Political Columnists

Walter Lippmann (1889–1974) set the standard for the modern political column when he began writing for the *New*

York Herald Tribune in 1931 and continued through 1967. "Today and Tomorrow" appeared in about two hundred newspapers and was read closely by the government leaders and elites. Lippmann's analyses sometimes helped to shape public policy. Dorothy Thompson, also of the *Herald Tribune*, wrote a political column on international affairs from 1936–1958. James Reston (1909–1995) two-time Pulitzer Prize winner and Washington correspondent with the *New York Times*, in 1960 began writing a three times weekly column labeled "Washington," which became must reading for officials and the public. Reston, who admired Lippmann, was a widely respected liberal commentator.

There were also a number of prominent conservative columnists during the latter half of the twentieth century. William F. Buckley Jr. was one of the most influential. Buckley, who came from a privileged background, needled rather than slashed liberal and moderate adversaries with a British-like air of facile intelligence that seemed to give him the high ground in debates. His syndicated column appeared in 350 newspapers during his prime years from 1962 through the 1980s. Buckley also hosted the Public Broadcasting System TV show "Firing Line." That exposure elevated him to iconic status in popular culture. Buckley's successor as leading conservative on op-ed pages was George F. Will, who began syndication through the Washington Post Writers Group in 1973. During the early twentieth-first century, his column appeared in four hundred newspapers twice a week. He also wrote regularly for *Newsweek* magazine. Another significant conservative writer was James Kilpatrick, a Richmond, Virginia, journalist. Kilpatrick wrote "The Writer's Art," a column devoted to language usage. Kilpatrick, the conservative foil in CBS "60 Minutes" Point-Counterpoint segment, was parodied on NBC's "Saturday Night Live."

Another influential conservative was William Safire, who was once active in the Richard Nixon administration, and who during the 1970s was included in the *New York Times's* mix of Op-Ed Page columnists. A speechwriter before he became a columnist, Safire coined the phrase "nattering nabobs of negativism," used by Vice President Spiro Agnew. Safire's humorous column on grammar and usage, "On Language," was long a mainstay of the Sunday *New York Times Magazine*.

Since the 1980s, conservative partisans complained about alleged liberal bias in news coverage, however conservative views dominated American opinion pages. The largest newspapers of two hundred thousand or more circulation often had opinion pages that balanced liberal, conservative and moderate perspectives. However, as the majority of U.S. dailies had a circulation one hundred thousand or less, publishers more so than editors decided who spoke in op-ed spaces. Often, those writers reflected the political climate, which in the late twentieth to early twenty-first centuries was conservative.

There were widely read liberal- and moderate-leaning columnists to be sure. For example, the Washington Post Writers Group syndicate offered David Broder, an observer of Washington politics since the 1950s; Ellen Goodman of the *Boston Globe*, who offered a liberal and feminist viewpoint since the 1970s, and William Raspberry, for four decades from 1966 until 2006 a moderate who was often praised for his political yet non-ideological writing style. A peer of Raspberry was the late Robert C. Maynard (1937–1993), publisher of the *Oakland Tribune* in California. Maynard simulated dinner table-like discussions in his syndicated columns in order to solve social dilemmas.

Metro Columnists

Local section columnists wrote opinionated articles about issues close to home that resonated with their readers. For decades Mike Royko (1932–1997) wrote in the voice of working class, white ethnic Chicagoans for the *Chicago Daily News*, *Sun-Times*, and finally the *Chicago Tribune*. Favorite Royko themes were mayoral politics, social issues, and crime. Jimmy Breslin was a sportswriter before editors coaxed him to become a local columnist with the *New York Herald Tribune* during the 1960s. In 1976, Breslin continued his column at the *New York Daily News*. In 1988, he moved to *Newsday* of Long Island, New York. Breslin took readers to the gritty city neighborhoods he walked, or he had them listen in on the colorful language of politicians, working stiffs, and wise guys the columnist engaged.

Herb Caen (1916–1997) was a San Francisco institution for nearly six decades, from 1938 until his death. Caen is credited with coining the terms "beatnik" and "hippie." Caen's daily column in the *San Francisco Chronicle* consisted of multiple items separated by elipses. Each item was loaded with sarcasm and wit. He wrote authoritatively about people and culture of the San Francisco Bay area. For two decades, Chuck Stone of the *Philadelphia Daily News*, wrote about race, local politics, criminal justice, and social trends. Stone gained national notoriety. From the 1970s and until his retirement from the paper in 1991 when he entered academia, dozens of crime suspects surrendered to Stone, so the columnist could escort them safely to police.

Columnist Tandems and Teams

At the end of World War II, Joseph (1910–1989) and Stewart Alsop (1914–1974) co-wrote "Matter of Fact," a political column originating at the *New York Herald-Tribune* that appeared in about 135 newspapers for 12 years until 1958. What distinguished them was they led the trend of co-written syndicated columns. In 1963, the *New York Herald-Tribune* paired Rowland Evans (1921–2001) with Robert Novak and for three decades they produced Evans & Novak columns. Evans retired and Novak continued writing the column solo after 1993. Jack Germond and Jules Witcover collaborated on a "Politics Today" column distributed by Tribune Media Services. Both writers worked much of their careers at the *Baltimore Sun*. Germond and Witcover were recognizable faces on Sunday morning public affairs television shows.

In 1932, Drew Pearson (1897–1969) began the "Washington Merry-Go-Round" investigative political column that exposed government secrecy, excess and incompetence. After 1942, Pearson wrote the column solo. In 1965, he shared the column byline with assistant Jack Anderson. Upon Pearson's death in 1969, Anderson (1922–2005) became sole proprietor of the column. The "Merry-Go-Round," which Anderson wrote with numerous associates, grew to a high of one thousand newspaper clients in 1997, which makes it one of the most successful columns ever.

Humorists

George Ade, Ring Lardner, and Will Rogers were among early twentieth-century humorists. One of the best-known satirists of the last half of the century was Art Buchwald. His nightclub column "Paris After Dark" began in 1949 in the *New York Herald Tribune*. Then in the early 1950s, Buchwald's column used hyperbole to depict American tourists' perspectives of Europe. Buchwald moved to Washington, D.C., in the 1960s and his political satire column was renamed "Capitol Punishment." At his peak, Buchwald's column appeared in 650 newspapers.

In 1983, Dave Barry began writing a humor column for the *Miami Herald* that was notorious, said one historian, "for its highly developed sense of lunacy." Barry used heaping portions of hyperbole like Buchwald and mocked everyone, including the judges who gave him a Pulitzer Prize for commentary, and linguists such as Kilpatrick and Safire with his "Mr. Language Person" parodies in which Barry "explained" the "marsupial phrase" and "pluperfect consumptive." Barry's column appeared in about five hundred newspapers.

Erma Bombeck (1927–1996) had several nicknames: Socrates of the ironing board, America's housewife at large, and queen of suburbia. Yet what was clear was the success of her domestic humor column, "At Wit's End." From 1965 to 1996 up to 900 newspapers carried the three-times-weekly column. Bombeck's humor was often self-effacing and she rarely poked fun at others. Bombeck once called herself "too old for a paper route, too young for Social Security, and too tired for an affair."

Minority and Women Voices

George Schuyler was a contrarian black conservative voice in the weekly *Pittsburgh Courier* from 1924 to 1966. In 1965 Schuyler began syndication in the North American Newspaper Alliance and wrote until his death in 1977. Carl Rowan (1925–2000) began a syndicated column with the *Chicago Sun-Times* in 1965 that continued until the end of the twentieth century.

In 1992, eighteen African American columnists formed the William Monroe Trotter Group, a society that was a testament to the steady growth of minority columnists who numbered one hundred during the 1980s and 1990s. For example, Leonard Pitts of the *Miami Herald* began his column in 1991 and emerged as one of the fresher voices of the twenty-first century, connecting with minority and mainstream audiences. Pitts' angry column the day after

the terrorist destruction of the World Trade Center towers in September 2001 generated about thirty thousand email responses.

In addition to Dorothy Thompson of the *Herald Tribune* and Ellen Goodman of the *Boston Globe*, noted women opinion page columnists included Mary McGrory (1918–2004) of the *Washington Star* and *Washington Post*; Molly Ivins, an acerbic political writer based in Austin, Texas; Anna Quindlen, whose "Life in the 30s" *New York Times* column was called the voice of the Baby Boom generation, and Maureen Dowd, a reliably sarcastic *New York Times* political columnist.

American newspaper columnists have a wide range of interests: politics, local issues, celebrities and gossip, advice, humor, or general interests—whatever is on their mind on the day they are scheduled to publish about eight hundred words. The common thread that ties these varied writers together has been their skill in connecting with readers.

Further Reading

Goodman, Ellen. *Keeping in Touch*. New York, Summit Books, 1985.

Ivins, Molly. *Molly Ivins Can't Say That, Can She?* New York: Random House, 1991.

Raspberry, William. *Looking Backward at Us*. Jackson: University Press of Mississippi, 1991.

Riley, Sam G. *The American Newspaper Columnist*. Westport, CT: Praeger Publishers, 1998.

Reston, James. *Deadline: A Memoir*. New York: Random House, 1991.

Royko, Mike. *Sez Who? Sez Me*. New York: Warner Books, 1983.

WAYNE DAWKINS

COMMITTEE ON PUBLIC INFORMATION

When President Woodrow Wilson created the first large-scale government propaganda agency, the Committee on Public Information (CPI) (aka Creel Committee), on April 13, 1917 (Executive Order 2594), he turned to his friend, the former muckraking journalist George Creel, to organize and lead the agency. The energetic Creel (one colleague called him "that thunderous steam engine") was temperamental and thin-skinned, and he was a controversial choice to head the CPI but his name soon became synonymous with the government's propaganda efforts. There was no doubt about his enthusiasm for the American cause in World War I, or his loyalty to Wilson. "Democracy is a religion with me," Creel said in May, 1918, "and throughout my whole adult life I have preached America as the hope of the world." He had difficulty, though, separating America and its ideals from Wilson and his policies. As he told the President in late 1917, "I find it hard always to think of you as a person, for you stand for America so absolutely in my mind and heart and are so inseparably connected with the tremendous events of the time."

Creel believed in the power of the press and thought its influence could not be overestimated because, he said, "we know only what it tells us." In more recent times, U. S. presidents have turned first to Madison Avenue to find advertising and public relations specialists to conduct propaganda, but in 1917, Creel turned instinctively to other journalists to build the CPI. In this group, he found a deep reservoir of people who were genuinely committed to spreading democracy. During the Progressive era before the war, many of them had been strongly involved in efforts to reform society. From the outset, Creel sought to control information about the war. One of the first sections he created in the CPI was the Division of News. L. Ames Brown, who had been the White House correspondent for the *New York Sun* and the *Philadelphia Record*, headed this section until he left it to lead the CPI's Division of Syndicated Features, which was created to capture Sunday newspaper readers. Brown's replacement in the Division of News was first J. W. McConaughy, who had been an editorial writer for *Munsey's Magazine* and a correspondent with the *New York Evening Mail*, and then Leigh Reilly, who had been managing editor of the *Chicago Herald*. The news division attempted to flood the country with information. It sent out enough mimeographed material each week to fill twenty thousand news columns. During the war it produced about six thousand news releases. Most newspapers and magazines readily accepted this output.

The CPI established the nation's first government daily newspaper, the *Official Bulletin*. President Wilson thought that the United States needed a national newspaper. Edited by Edward S. Rochester, who had been managing editor of the *Washington Post*, it published official government announcements and acts that directly affected citizens. The *Official Bulletin* usually ran about eight pages (until casualty lists increased its size) and went free to other newspapers, government officials, post offices, and military bases. The paper's circulation peaked in August, 1918, at 118,000; the publication was discontinued on March 31, 1919.

There were many other efforts by the CPI to mobilize the news. A Foreign Language Newspaper Division and a Division of Work with the Foreign Born monitored between 800 and 900 foreign-language newspapers in the United States. Under the Trading-with-the-Enemy Act of 1917, these papers were required to file sworn translations with the postmaster if they carried articles or editorials on the United States or on countries with which America was at war. The CPI also managed to place regular news releases in more than 700 of these papers.

The CPI expanded to involve much more than just journalists. Academicians and other intellectuals were among the most active propagandists during the war. Realizing that not everyone read newspapers or pamphlets, Creel and the CPI attempted to enlist visual media in the war effort. A *Bulletin for Cartoonists* sent material suggesting ideas to more than 750 cartoonists in the U.S. The Division of Films used photography and newsreels to sell the war. In January, 1918, the CPI added a Division of Advertising and a Division of Pictorial Publicity which helped to create some of the most striking visual images of the German enemy used in posters and elsewhere. In a time before regular radio broadcasting, the CPI enlisted 75,000 local speakers who became surrogates for the President and known as the Four Minute Men. Each week the Wilson administration prepared a bulletin for them with sample talks on topics the President wished covered. Newspapers also often carried these speeches.

The CPI tried to influence news not only in the United States but abroad. It established a news service between the Division of News and the American Expeditionary Force in Europe, and despite General John J. Pershing's objections, U. S. correspondents visited war zones. The CPI's Foreign Press Bureau, led by the *Saturday Evening Post*'s European correspondent Ernest Poole, helped the Committee on Public Information maintain a news network that covered events not only in Europe but in many other parts of the world. A wireless and cable service known as COMPUB, also helped the United States send its message abroad.

The CPI attempted to exploit every form of mass communication during the war. By this time there were many new and exciting non-print media that could be used for propaganda including motion pictures, newsreels, and phonograph records. In all, the CPI had more than a dozen subdivisions that specialized in various aspects of propaganda in the United States and offices in more than thirty countries abroad. Creel boasted after the war that even his severest critics "took with his breakfast a daily diet of our material."

Creel maintained that his committee had no formal censorship powers, which while technically true, is also misleading. Creel was a member of the government's Censorship Board that censored messages between the United States and other countries. Creel and the CPI had little interest in news that might be critical of the American war effort and indeed attempted to overwhelm such news with their own information. Moreover, the committee, through its publications, helped to popularize the idea that freedom of expression during the war had severe limitations.

The great slogan of this period was that the war was to "make the world safe for democracy," and many of the people who worked for the CPI did believe in democratic government. In the short-term, the CPI was undoubtedly successful in mobilizing American public opinion behind the war. But whatever enthusiasms journalists may have had during this period, many of them quickly became disillusioned with government propaganda once the war ended. Walter Lippmann concluded that propaganda and censorship had prevented citizens from seeing the real world and that reporters had been "derelict" in their duty to inform the public. When in 1920, he and Charles Merz wrote "A Test of the News," a study of how the *New York Times* had covered the Russian Revolution, they began by quoting from the *Iliad*, which offered an assessment of the news much different from the one Creel had made: "Enlighten me now, O Muses, tenants of Olympian homes. For you are goddesses, inside on everything, know everything. But we mortals hear only the news, and know nothing at all."

During the 1920s, the belief grew that the Creel Committee had oversold the war. During the 1930s, the public was slow to heed warnings about the dangers of Germany's growing military power, in part some believe, because many Americans thought that the threat to freedom during First World War had been overstated. By the time United States entered World War II in 1941, the reputation of Creel and the CPI were in such disrepute that as Elmer Davis and others created a new American propaganda agency, the Office of War Information, they considered the zealous approach taken Creel and his compatriots during World War I to be a model of what should be avoided.

Further Reading

Creel, George. *How We Advertised America*. New York: Arno Press, 1972, originally published 1920.

Lippmann, Walter, and Charles Merz. "A Test of the News." *New Republic*, 23 (suppl. Aug.4, 1920): 1–42.

Mock, James R., and Cedric Larson. *World That Won the War: The Story of the Committee on Public Information*. Princeton, NJ: Princeton University Press, 1939.

Vaughn, Stephen. *Holding Fast the Inner Lines: Democracy, Nationalism, and the Committee on Public Information*. Chapel Hill: University of North Carolina Press, 1980.

STEPHEN VAUGHN

COMMUNIST PRESS

The press has always been key to Communist political activity. Karl Marx began his revolutionary career as a journalist, while V.I. Lenin published several articles exhorting his fellow Bolsheviks to greater efforts to build the Communist press, which he saw as not merely a means of propaganda, but a "collective organizer." But Communists were hardly alone in prioritizing their communication apparatus—dissident movements (and governments as well) of every stripe have sought to harness the power of the press almost from its origins.

The best-known Communist newspaper in the United States was the *Daily Worker*, although in the 1930s the party also published the short-lived *Midwest Daily Record* and the *People's World* (daily from 1938 until 1949, weekly until 1986) as popular front organs, a host of foreign-language dailies and weeklies (many formally independent of the party), literary and theoretical journals, and a host of other specialized periodicals. Magazines such as the *New Masses* (1926–1956; as *Masses and Mainstream* in its final years) published material by some of the leading artistic and literary figures of the left, including Ernestine Caldwell, Jack Conroy, Theodore Dreiser, Mike Gold, Ernest Hemingway, Langston Hughes, Meridel Le Sueur, and Richard Wright during the Popular Front years.

The *Daily Worker* was launched in Chicago in January 1924 with money from the party's foreign-language sections and built on a foundation of weekly newspapers dating to the ferment unleashed within the Socialist Party by the Russian Revolution and the subsequent expulsion of the left-wing tendencies that (for the most part) coalesced to form the Communist (Workers) Party. As factions broke away from the Communist Party over the following decades, each

launched its own newspapers, the most notable of which was the Trotskyist weekly *The Militant*.

The *Daily Worker* was published through 1957, when it was cut back to a weekly. The *Worker* expanded to semiweekly publication in 1961, and resumed daily publication in 1968 as *The Daily World*. In 1986, the paper was consolidated with the west coast *People's World* to form the *People's Daily World*, which was retrenched as the *People's Weekly World* in 1991. At its peak the paper had some thirty-five thousand subscribers, but enjoyed a much greater reach through allied publications and the efforts of readers who were expected to draw on the newspaper's analysis and information in their local organizing.

There are, of course, other Communist parties in the United States, each of which supports its own press. Issued on a weekly basis into the early twenty-first century were the Revolutionary Communist Party's *Revolution* (founded in 1975; also issued in a separate Spanish-language edition), the Socialist Workers Party's *The Militant* (1928–), and the Workers World Party's *Workers World* (1954–). Several now-defunct publications also played significant roles, such as the *National Guardian*, launched in 1948 to support the Progressive Party and continuing as an independent radical weekly that played a significant role in the emergence of the new left, and in catalyzing the new Communist movement of the 1970s, before ceasing publication in 1992. As new Communist groups emerged, each established its own press—often publishing with a frequency far beyond what their numbers could reasonably support—perhaps most spectacularly the semiweekly (from 1973 through 1989) *Bulletin* issued by a Workers' League that never counted more than a couple hundred supporters (the paper has since retrenched to a virtual existence as the world socialist web site).

While the *Daily Worker*, *People's World*, and *New Masses* were certainly the best known of the Communist Party's publications, and the most studied, they may well have been less influential than the myriad shop floor newsletters and foreign-language publications issued by party supporters. Indeed, the party considered its shop floor and neighborhood publications so important that it issued the monthly *Party Organizer* from 1927 until 1938 in large part to offer guidance to the three hundred or so such papers.

The party's foreign-language newspapers always enjoyed a larger circulation than their English-language counterparts, reflecting the party's origins in the Socialists' foreign language federations and the predominantly immigrant character of the American working class. In an immigrant community where it was particularly strong, the party supported three Finnish-language dailies, *Työmies* (1903–1950), *Eteenpäin* (1921–1950), and *Toveri* (1907–1931), as well as the weekly *Toveritar/Naisten Viiri* (1909–1978) aimed at Finnish women, and the combined *Työmies-Eteenpäin* from 1950 until 1998, gradually reducing publication from five times a week to weekly before suspending altogether. But the Communists also published daily newspapers in Croatian, Hungarian, Lithuanian, Russian, Slovakian, Ukrainian, Yiddish, and other languages, many issued by ethnic and mutual aid societies which often enjoyed substantial autonomy. Where daily publication could not be sustained, party supporters issued weekly and monthly papers in nearly every language spoken by workers in the United States. While this commitment to foreign-language publishing is now restricted to a Spanish-language section in the back pages of the party's weekly, the foreign-language federations raised the bulk of the funds to launch the *Daily Worker,* which continues to live off their legacy. In 2006, the *People's Weekly World* was edited from the offices of the Workers Education Society, successor to the Lithuanian association that published the Communist daily *Vilnis* from 1920 to 1989 (as a weekly in its final years). It claimed a total circulation of some twenty-five thousand copies weekly (about two thousand of which are individual subscriptions).

The Communist press was at the height of its influence in the 1930s and 1940s, when the party had established a substantial, if short-lived, base in the labor movement; drawn many artists and intellectuals into its orbit through popular front organizations focused on issues such as racial justice, opposition to the global rise of fascism, and expansion of social welfare programs; and still included many vibrant foreign-language newspapers that in later decades succumbed to government persecution (including the forced dissolution of the party-dominated International Workers Order), the influx of anti-Communist immigrants in the aftermath of World War II, and the assimilation of younger generations.

These newspapers were not mere outlets for official proclamations and news of party activities. Many boasted substantial national and international news (aided by the resources of the independent labor news service Federated Press, by Tass, and by reports sent in by hundreds of grassroots supporters around the country), along with substantial cultural and educational offerings. Most Communist papers included a diversity of voices, even if the party did impose its orthodoxy on major political questions. In 1935, the *Daily Worker* launched a sports section that continued for decades, combining reports of sporting events with critiques of the institutionalized racism that dominated the industry. The paper's eleven-year campaign—through its sports pages, often working in cooperation with African American newspapers—to desegregate major league baseball has drawn substantial scholarly attention in recent years, was but part of a larger effort to integrate the party's commitment to economic and social equality into all aspects of its coverage and of its members' lives. The *Worker* also published comic strips, cultural coverage that focused attention on popular art forms such as jazz and blues, and populist commentary by figures such as Woody Guthrie. By the mid-1930s, its in-depth labor and civil rights coverage drew readers from outside the Communist orbit.

However, in the 1950s McCarthyism and the larger campaign of persecution it has come to represent (coupled with growing awareness of Stalinism's methods) forced the party to the margins of political life, and it became increasingly difficult to sustain its press. Several papers were discontinued or merged, and others cut back their publication schedule. Even its retrenched public presence could only be sustained with external funding. Archival documents establish that the party received substantial financial assistance from the Soviet Union from 1959 to 1989. The end of that funding forced a new round of retrenchment. In 2006, the Communist Party published its weekly newspaper, the monthly *Political Affairs* magazine, and the Young Communist League's quarterly *Dynamic* magazine.

Further Reading

Bekken, Jon. "'No Weapon So Powerful': Working-Class Newspapers in the United States," *Journal of Communication Inquiry 12(2),* 1988.

Howe, Irving, and Lewis Coser. *The American Communist Party: A Critical History.* Boston: Beacon Press, 1957.

Isserman, Maurice. *Which Side Were You On?: The American Communist Party During the Second World War.* Wesleyan University Press, 1987.

Klehr, Harvey. *The Heyday of American Communism: The Depression Decade.* New York: Basic Books, 1984.

Kostiainen, Auvo. *The Forging of Finnish-American Communism, 1917–1924: A Study in Ethnic Radicalism.* Annales Universitatis Turkuensis, University of Turku, Finland, 1978.

Silber, Irwin. *Press Box Red: The Story of Lester Rodney, The Communist Who Helped Break the Color Line in American Sports.* Philadelphia: Temple University Press, 2003.

JON BEKKEN

COMSTOCK LAW

The Comstock Law (1873) was a federal anti-obscenity statute enacted by Congress after heavy lobbying by Anthony Comstock (1844–1915), who became a special agent of the U.S. Post Office to enforce its provisions. A Connecticut native and Brooklyn dry-goods clerk, Comstock in 1872 persuaded the New York Young Men's Christian Association to form a committee to combat the sexually suggestive publications widely available in the city. In 1873, backed by wealthy patrons, it became the New York Society for the Suppression of Vice. The so-called Comstock Law strengthened an 1842 federal ban on importing obscene materials and an 1865 Congressional prohibition against mailing such materials. The new law criminalized the importing, mailing, or advertising of "obscene," "lewd," or lascivious" books, pamphlets, prints, pictures, etc., as well as materials or information relating to abortion or contraception. Ads promoting illegal lotteries were added to the banned list in 1876. An early Comstock-Law victim, D. M. Bennett, was jailed in 1878 for mailing *Cupid's Yokes,* a sex-reform pamphlet. Over the ensuing decades, Comstock seized vast quantities of print material he deemed obscene, ranging from risqué ephemera and racy magazines like the *Illustrated Police Gazette* to classic erotica by the likes of Boccaccio, Rabelais, and John Cleland (author of the 1750 pornographic classic *Fanny Hill*). Boston's New England Watch and Ward Society (1873) pursued similar objectives. The prevailing definition of obscenity was that formulated by Lord Chief Justice Cockburn of England in *Queen* v. *Hicklin* (1868): "[T]he test is this, whether the tendency of the matter charged as obscenity [i.e., specific passages in a longer work] is to deprave and corrupt those whose minds are open to immoral influences and into whose hands a publication of this sort may fall."

From the first, the Comstock Law roused criticism. Thirty Congressmen voted against it. The National Liberal League (1876), supported by the freethinker Robert Ingersoll and the historical writer James Parton, and dedicated to fighting "the Comstock laws, State and National, and ... the wave of intolerance, bigotry, and ignorance which threatens to submerge our cherished liberties," secured fifty thousand signatures on a petition urging Congress to repeal the federal measure.

Overall, however, the Comstock Law and numerous state and local statutes modeled on it initially stirred little protest. The anti-vice societies enjoyed the support of the social elite and won praise from reformers, civic notables, and religious leaders. The *New York Charities Directory* regularly listed the Society for the Suppression of Vice, and the *Encyclopedia of Social Reform* (1898) discussed Comstock favorably. Harvard's Francis G. Peabody, a professor of social ethics, praised the Watch and Ward Society in 1898 for protecting citizens from "the pestiferous evil which at any time may come up into our faces, into our lives, into our children's lives." Many authors, librarians, editors, and journalists endorsed the censorship laws for suppressing material that transgressed the prevailing genteel code.

While Comstock typically targeted obscure, furtively distributed publications, well-known authors occasionally fell under the ban, either through actual prosecution or the fear of prosecution. In 1882, a Boston publisher cancelled a planned edition of Walt Whitman's *Leaves of Grass,* criticized for homoerotic tendencies, when a district attorney threatened prosecution. In 1890, the postmaster-general banned from the mails a newspaper serializing Leo Tolstoy's *Kreutzer Sonata,* a novel involving suspicions of adultery. Several publishers rejected Stephen Crane's *Maggie: A Girl of the Streets* in the early 1890s; only after the success of Crane's *The Red Badge of Courage* (1895) did a publisher (Appleton's) issue an expurgated version of *Maggie.* Theodore Dreiser's *Sister Carrie,* whose protagonist uses sex to advance her career, was initially accepted by Doubleday in 1900, but then effectively suppressed, as the publisher technically fulfilled the contract by printing one thousand copies but simply stored them away. Margaret Sanger fled to England in 1914 after her publications advocating birth control ran afoul of the Comstock Law.

But the cultural climate was changing. In *"Obscene" Literature and Constitutional Law* (1911) and subsequent essays such as "Our Prudish Censorship Unveiled" (*The Forum,* January 1914), the radical New York lawyer Theodore Schroeder vigorously attacked censorship. Obscenity laws violate the First Amendment, Schroeder argued, because they discriminate "according to the subject matter discussed" or "according to differences of literary style in expressing the same thought." The Comstock Law, he said, represented a

futile effort "to control the psycho-sexual condition of postal patrons." In 1913, Comstock's organization failed in its effort to suppress the novel *Hagar Revelly* by Daniel Carson Goodman, a reform-minded physician intent on publicizing the sexual exploitation of working women. Federal judge Learned Hand, who heard the case, commented that Justice Cockburn's definition of obscenity, "however consonant ... with mid-Victorian morals," bore little relation "to the understanding and morality of the present time." Other cases confirmed the liberalizing trend.

Congress reformed the Customs Bureau's censorship practices in 1930 to assure greater First Amendment protection, and in a landmark Customs case of 1933, federal judge John Woolsey cleared James Joyce's novel *Ulysses.* In 1943, with federal censorship practices under increasing scrutiny, a U.S. appeals court overthrew a post-office effort to deny second-class mailing privileges to the men's magazine *Esquire.* The liberalizing trend culminated in 1957 when the U.S. Supreme Court, in the *U.S. v. Roth* and *Alberts v. California,* liberalized the definition of obscenity. Henceforth, the high court ruled, a work must be judged in its entirety, rather than by specific words or passages, and according to "contemporary community standards" rather than on the basis of undefined pejorative terms. Works with "the slightest redeeming social importance," the court held, enjoyed a presumptive right to constitutional protection. Under the *Roth/Alberts* standard, long-banned works such as *Fanny Hill,* D. H. Lawrence's *Lady Chatterley's Lover,* and Henry Miller's *Tropic of Cancer* won First Amendment protection. The Comstock Law continued to cast a long shadow, and the struggle to define the obscene went on, with mixed results. By the mid-twentieth century, however, the once-vast scope of federal, state, and local obscenity laws had, at least for the printed word, been very sharply circumscribed.

Further Reading

Boyer, Paul S. *Purity in Print: Book Censorship in America from the Gilded Age to the Computer Age,* 2nd ed. Madison: University of Wisconsin Press, 2002.

Broun, Heywood, and Leach, Margaret. *Anthony Comstock: Roundsman of the Lord.* New York: A. & C. Boni, 1927.

Comstock, Anthony. *Traps for the Young,* Intro. by J. M. Buckley. Whitefish, MT: Kessinger Publishing, 2005.

Horowitz, Helen Lefkowitz. *Rereading Sex: Battles over Sexual Knowledge and Suppression in Nineteenth-Century America.* New York: Alfred A. Knopf, 2002.

Lewis, Felice Flanery. *Literature, Obscenity and Law.* Carbondale: Southern Illinois University Press, 1976.

Paul, James C.N., and Schwartz, Murray L. *Federal Censorship: Obscenity in the Mail.* New York: The Free Press, 1961.

Tedford, Thomas L. *Freedom of Speech in the United States.* New York: Random House, 1985.

PAUL S. BOYER

CONDÉ NAST PUBLICATIONS

Condé Nast (1873–1942) began his magazine empire when he purchased *Vogue* in 1909. Four years later he purchased

House and Garden, which he helped transform into a leading interior design authority. In 1914, he introduced *Vanity Fair*, a magazine that quickly set publishing standards in arts, politics, sports, and society. In 1939, he launched *Glamour*, the last magazine he would personally develop before his death. By 2005, Condé Nast Publications holdings included about twenty magazines, including *Bon Appetit, Conde Nast Traveler, GQ, Lucky, Mademoiselle, Popular Mechanics, The New Yorker, Redbook, Self, Seventeen*, and *YM*.

Condé Montrose Nast was born March 26, 1873, in New York City but spent most of his early years in St. Louis. He earned a law degree from Washington University after earning his bachelor's degree from Georgetown University. Spurning a law career, he accepted his friend Robert Collier's offer in 1898 to become advertising manager and later business manager at *Collier's Weekly*. During the next nine years, he led the magazine to unprecedented financial success.

In 1909 he bought *Vogue*, a small society magazine founded in 1892, which he repositioned with the editorial mission of helping high-income women dress fashionably. After promoting Edna Chase to editor in 1914, they built *Vogue* into the country's most prestigious fashion magazine.

Nast's enduring contribution to magazine publishing was developing the concept of "class" publications directed at particular groups of readers with common interests. He shunned bulk readership in favor of attracting a select and devoted group of readers of a high social profile. As he pointed out in a 1913 essay, "A 'class' publication is nothing more nor less than a publication that looks for its circulation only to those having in common a certain characteristic marked enough to group them into a class."

Nast proved prophetic in a way he did not realize during his lifetime. Following the advent of television, the decline of general interest magazines and rise of specialized magazines became the most defining characteristic of American magazine publishing.

Condé Nast Publications was purchased in 1979 by S. I. Newhouse and became a division of Newhouse's empire, which also included newspapers, book publishers, and cable television companies. Newhouse expanded its magazine titles by purchasing Street & Smith Publications, Inc., a publisher of sports magazines (1959); *Gentleman's Quarterly* (1979); *Tatler*, a British monthly (1983); *Gourmet* (1983); *Details* (1988); *Architectural Digest* (1993); and *Bon Appétit* (1993). The company revived the *Vanity Fair* title in 1983, which had been merged with *Vogue* since 1936, and launched *Conde Nast Traveler* in 1987 and *Allure* in 1991.

In mid-2005, the company launched *Domino*, a shelter magazine aimed at first-time homeowners. It followed the surprising success of *Lucky*, which the company started in 2001. The women's magazine, which called itself "the magazine about shopping," told readers how and where to buy clothing, beauty items and household products. *Advertising Age* named it the "Magazine of the Year" in 2003 after it surpassed one million subscribers during its first two years.

Further Reading

Maier, Thomas. *Newhouse: All The Glitter, Power, and Glory of America's Richest Media Empire and The Secretive Man Behind It*. New York: St. Martin's Press, 1994.

Meeker, Richard H. *Newspaperman: S.I. Newhouse and The Business of News*. New Haven: Ticknor & Fields, 1983.

Nourie, Alan, and Barbara Nourie, eds. *American Mass-Market Magazines*. Westport, CT: Greenwood, 1990.

Seebohm, Caroline. *The Man Who Was Vogue: The Life and Times of Condé Nast*. New York: The Viking Press, 1982.

Tebbel, John William, and Mary Ellen Zuckerman. *The Magazine in America, 1741–1990*. New York: Columbia University Press, 1991.

DAVID E. SUMNER

CONSUMER REPORTS

Since 1936, *Consumer Reports* has tried to give consumers unbiased assessments of the products they buy. Unlike most media operations, *Consumer Reports* accepts no advertising in an effort to ensure its objectivity. No free product samples are accepted from manufacturers. *Consumer Reports* does not allow its reviews to be used for the sale of products. In fact, the magazine aggressively works to prevent advertisers from using positive *Consumers Reports'* assessments as a blurbs or endorsements.

Consumer Reports' mission is to "test, inform and protect." The magazine and its popular web site ConsumerReports.org are published by Consumers Union, a nonprofit organization based in Yonkers, New York, that works to create a fair and safe marketplace for all consumers. Its precursor organization was known as Consumer Research, whose leaders included engineers Arthur Kallet and Frederick Schlink.

In 1926, Schlink organized a consumers club in White Plains, New York. It distributed a mimeographed list of approved products as well as a list of products to avoid because they were of inferior quality or had made false advertising claims. In 1928, he helped found Consumers Research, which published the *Consumers Research Bulletin*. Borrowing the commercial model of a respected engineering journal, it accepted no advertising. In 1933, Schlink and Kallet published a book entitled *100,000,000 Guinea Pigs: Dangers in Everyday Foods, Drugs and Cosmetics*. The book warned consumers of the dangers they faced in a largely unregulated marketplace.

But Consumers' Research was beset by labor problems in 1935. Several employees formed a labor union and were promptly fired by Schlink. Forty employees of Consumers Research went on strike. Schlink refused to negotiate with them.

In 1936, the striking workers started their own organization known as Consumers Union, and Kallet was appointed director. Initially, its publication was called *Consumers Union Reports*. The focus was on inexpensive consumer products such as milk, stockings or fans because the organization could not afford to buy and test more expensive products. The publication's circulation was about four thousand.

But the magazine was able to rate automobiles in its early days thanks to the generosity of Lawrence Crooks, a wealthy man with a passion for cars. He bought the cars himself or borrowed cars from his friends for testing purposes. Crooks headed up the Consumers Union auto testing division until 1966.

In 1942, Consumers Union changed the name of its magazine to *Consumer Reports* to underscore the fact that it serves not just union members but all consumers in the United States. Its circulation rapidly increased in the years after World War II as consumer products returned to the shelves because years of war-time rationing. Circulation was four hundred thousand in 1950, a four-fold increase from 1942. The magazine's circulation by 2005 was about four million, making it one of the nation's largest-circulated magazines.

Consumer Reports is the flagship of a small media empire. In addition to the magazine and the subscription-based website, there's a health newsletter and related website, the *CR Money Adviser Newsletter*, television and radio programs, auto price services and the New Car Buying Kit. There is even a web site aimed at children called ConsumerReports.org 4 Kids. The overall organization employs more than 450 people.

Consumers Union operates the world's largest nonprofit educational and consumer product testing facility at its National Testing and Research Center in Yonkers. At the center, autos, appliances, electronics, foods, baby and child, health and family, and recreation and home improvement products are tested. The magazine also gathers marketplace intelligence by way of reader surveys and through more than 150 anonymous shoppers.

Consumers Union goes to bat for consumers on such issues as food safety, financial services, product safety and health issues through its three advocacy offices in Washington, D.C., San Francisco, and Austin, Texas. Specialists testify before state and federal legislative and regulatory organizations.

The magazine has been highly decorated over the years for its service and investigative journalism. *Consumer Reports* has won many prestigious journalism awards, including the National Magazine Award, the Pulitzer Prize of magazine journalism. It won its first of three National Magazine Awards in 1974 with a three-part series that examined the contamination of the U.S. water supply.

Along the way, Consumers Union and its *Consumer Reports* have ruffled many feathers for its no-holds-barred reporting and testing. In 1939, an article in *Readers Digest* attacked Consumers Union for damaging the U.S. economy. *Good Housekeeping* accused the organization of exacerbating the economic depression. Consumers Union was even placed on the list of subversive organizations by the House Un-American Activities Committee during the height of the McCarthy Era in the 1950s.

Some corporations have been upset by candid analyses of its products in the pages of *Consumer Reports*. The organization has been sued for product disparagement fifteen times during its existence, although Consumers Union has prevailed in all cases. For example, automaker Suzuki sued after the magazine found that the Suzuki Samurai rattled and turned over easily in turns. After eight years of litigation, Suzuki settled. No money was awarded to Suzuki, although there was a clarification and an acknowledgment by *Consumer Reports* that Suzuki was committed to safety.

In 2004, the magazine prevailed in a lawsuit brought by Sharper Image, which charged that published test results of its top-selling air purifier unfairly disparaged the product. A judge ruled that the retailer had to reimburse the magazine for its attorney's fees. The magazine estimated it spent more than $500,000 defending itself. Consumers Union President James Guest said dismissal of the Sharper Image suit sent a clear message that there's a steep price to be paid when corporations unfairly attempt to stifle criticism.

Undaunted by the lawsuits and criticism, the magazine remains committed to its mission of looking out for the consumers' interests. It will continue to warn consumers of potentially dangerous products marketed by manufacturers and to alert them to false advertising claims. The magazine's stock in trade is its impartial reporting and its unwavering commitment to independence.

Further Reading

Anonymous. "It's Our Anniversary." *Consumer Reports*, January 1996: 10–13.

Harvey, Mary. "Consumers Union of United States." *Magazine Management* 29, no. 5 (April 15, 2000): 60.

Kallet, Arthur, and F. J. Schlink. *100,000,000 Guinea Pigs: Dangers in Everyday Foods, Drugs, and Cosmetics*. New York: Vanguard Press, 1933.

Parloff, Roger. "The Ionic Breeze Is No Match for Consumer Reports." *Fortune* 150, no. 12 (December 13, 2004): 56–58.

ConsumerReports.org. http://consumereports.org/main/content/aboutus.jsp.

EDMUND LAWLER

COPYRIGHT AND PHOTOGRAPHY

For most of copyright's history, copyright meant just what the term would literally imply: the legal "right" to prevent others from making "copies" of a work. Copyright was originally a trade regulation in the book publishing industry, but the law now applies to a dizzying array of works, including photographs. [For more details, see the entry entitled "Copyright, The Legal Issues of".] The story of copyright's expansion involves changes in technology, economics, and ideology. The story of photography and copyright fits this pattern well.

In the first federal copyright statute, passed in 1790, copyright protected only "books, maps, and charts." Congress added "prints" (but, importantly, not paintings, drawings or sculptures) in 1802 and music in 1831. Those were the only works protected by copyright when photography's invention was made public in 1839. With this technological advance, however, photography soon joined the list of protected works. Congress added photography in 1865, and yet it did not add any other visual arts at the same time. By itself, the invention of photography was not enough to get Congress to protect it. Rather, the economic interests of the photography industry were crucial. In an era in which pioneering photographers like Mathew Brady were capturing images of the Civil War and the West, Congress wanted to encourage the use of photography to capture history as it was happening. In short, the development of the technology of photography, along with the development of an important economic interest seeking protection, led to legal protection.

The question of copyright protection for photographs was not unequivocally answered in 1865, however, since the Constitution places limits on Congress's power; Congress may grant copyright only to "authors" as that term is understood in the Constitution. Therefore, one of the fundamental questions that arises is whether a photograph is an original, intellectual conception of a human "author" or simply a direct transcription of nature. If it is viewed as the latter, Congress may not protect it through copyright law.

Two cases, one from the nineteenth century, the second from the twentieth, illustrate the problem and demonstrate the way in which changes in the ideological conception of the relationship between photographer and photograph effected broader copyright protection for photographs.

In the nineteenth-century case, well-known photographer Napoleon Sarony sued a lithographer who had made numerous copies of a carefully posed portrait of Oscar Wilde. The lithographer argued that a photograph is "a reproduction, on paper, of the exact features of some natural object, or of some person," and is thus "not a writing of which the producer is the author." The essence of the argument was that Sarony wasn't the author of the photograph, nature was; and copyright could thus not protect the photograph. The U. S. Supreme Court did not disagree as a general matter, but instead concluded in 1884 that Sarony authored the particular portrait of Wilde because Sarony had, "entirely from his own original mental conception, ... [posed Wilde] in front of the camera, selecting and arranging the costume, draperies, and other various accessories ..., arranging the subject so as to present graceful outlines, arranging and disposing the light and shade, [and] suggesting and evoking the desired expression ...." [*Burrow-Giles Lithographic Company v. Sarony*, 111 U.S. 53 (1884)] In short, Sarony (who did not actually operate the camera and was thus more similar to a modern-day movie director) was the photograph's "author" because he prepared the scene before the photograph was taken. The Court was thus able to sidestep the metaphysical question of whether an "ordinary photograph" was simply a reproduction of nature.

During the twentieth century, the legal system answered that question firmly in favor of the view that virtually all photographs are "authored" by a photographer, not by nature. In 1963, Dallas dressmaker Abraham Zapruder was taking home movies of President Kennedy's motorcade when Kennedy was shot. The film consisted of a series of photographic images (frames), which in sequence made up the film. In a case involving a book with copies of some of Zapruder's frames [*Time Incorporated v. Bernard Geis Associates*, 293 F. Supp. 130 (S.D.N.Y. 1968)], one of the questions the court had to address was whether Zapruder was, in the legal sense, an "author" of the images. In contrast to Sarony, Zapruder had obviously not prepared the scene prior to taking his "photographs." What he had done, and what the court considered sufficient to make him an "author," was to select "the kind of camera (movies, not snapshots), the kind of film (color), the kind of lens (telephoto), ... the time [at which the pictures] were to be taken, and ... the spot on which the camera would be operated." Using this rationale, virtually every photograph involves some choice by a human being. Recognizing the grave importance to society of broad access to the Zapruder frames, the court eventually ruled that the unauthorized use of them in a book constituted "fair use" and was thus not copyright infringement. Nonetheless, protection for photography had come a long way from its focus on the scene-preparing activities of Sarony. In some sense, by protecting choices such as type of film, lens, camera and photographer placement, courts have implicitly accepted the modern notion of photography as not merely a representation of nature but rather as a photographer's personal stamp on nature.

Recent case law involving different types of works suggests that Zapruder's frames are right on the border of copyrightability, and it may well be that, over time, choices of the sort Zapruder made will not be protected. For now, however, copyright law recognizes "authorship" in nearly all photographs.

In summary, the technological development of photography and the economic interests of photographers led Congress to provide copyright protection for photography, but it was the gradual acceptance of an ideological assumption about human "authorship" of photographs that led to the wide protection for photography in today's law.

Further Reading

Burrow-Giles Lithographic Company v. Sarony, 111 U.S. 53 (1884).

Edelman, Bernard. "The Law's Eye: Nature and Copyright" (translated by David M. Thomas and Theodore Trefor) In *Of Authors and Origins: Essays on Copyright Law*, edited by Brad Sherman and Alain Strowel, 79-91, Oxford: Clarendon Press, 1994.

Edelman, Bernard. *Ownership of the Image: Elements of a Marxist Theory of Law* (*Le Droit saisi par la Photographie*), trans. Elizabeth Kingdom, London: Routledge & Kegan Paul, 1979.

Farley, Christine Haight, "The Lingering Effects of Copyright's Response to the Invention of Photography." *University of Pittsburgh Law Review* 65 (2004): 385-456.

Gaines, Jane M. "Photography 'Surprises' the Law: The Portrait of Oscar Wilde." In Gaines, Jane M., *Contested Culture: The Image, The Voice, and the Law*, 42-83, Chapel Hill, N.C.: The University of North Carolina Press, 1991.

Time Incorporated v. Bernard Geis Associates, 293 F. Supp. 130 (S.D.N.Y. 1968).

ANUJ C. DESAI

COPYRIGHT, THE LEGAL ISSUES OF

Copyright is the legal mechanism by which authors are given control over the reproduction of their intellectual creations. Most legal issues that arise in current copyright disputes fall into three broad categories: subject matter (is something protected by copyright?); ownership (who owns the rights?); and infringement (do certain activities violate the rights of the copyright owner?).

These three issues, though legally distinct, have had connections throughout the history of copyright. The scope of subject matter covered by copyright and the type of activities that constitute infringement have both expanded over time. Originally, copyright protected only books, whereas today its coverage includes newspapers, music, movies, plays, paintings, choreographed dances, architecture, boat hull designs, and semiconductor chips. In addition, the original conception of copyright was as a trade privilege consisting of a single right, the "right" to make a "copy"; and that too has expanded, with the law now providing copyright owners not only the right to copy, but also the right to make what the law refers to as "derivative" works (about which more later), and the right to display and/or perform one's works publicly. Much of this expansion occurred because important economic interests demanded it. But, the expansion has also been intertwined with ownership issues and, in particular, with an ideological change from viewing copyright as a publisher's right to viewing it as an author's right.

Like many aspects of American law, American copyright law derives from English law. Anglo-American copyright law is conventionally treated as having begun with the 1710 Statute of Anne, but the notion of copyright as a means of controlling the reproduction of texts dates back to regulations of the book trade in the early sixteenth century. With its roots primarily in what was known as the "stationer's copyright," the pre-eighteenth century copyright belonged to printers and publishers, not authors. The stationer's copyright was a right recognized among members of the Stationers' Company, a trade group consisting of bookbinders, publishers, and printers. As a legal matter, the stationer's copyright was simply an internal regulation within the publishing industry, but it invariably amounted to an exclusive right to print a book because, under the licensing regime in effect at the time, the right to use a printing press was restricted primarily to members of the Stationers' Company.

The 1710 Statute of Anne was similarly designed primarily as a means of regulating the book trade. Though the Statute of Anne did for the first time establish a broadly available government-granted copyright, the principal changes from the stationer's copyright were designed primarily to loosen the Stationers' monopolies in the book industry rather than to grant rights to authors.

By the end of the eighteenth century, however, copyright was increasingly conceived of as an author's right. This ideological assumption about initial copyright ownership was taken up by the drafters of the first state copyright statutes during the Confederation period and then by the framers of the United States Constitution in 1787. The Constitution empowers Congress to "promote the Progress of Science and useful Arts, by securing for limited Times to Authors … the exclusive Right to their … Writings." Publishers were not even mentioned, and the constitutional language incorporated the now-common utilitarian rationale that exclusive rights will induce authors to create works for the promotion of the public good.

Still, the author-centered approach had virtually no impact on the breadth of legal rights until well into the nineteenth century. The first federal copyright law, passed in 1790, provided only the exclusive right to "print[], reprint[], publish[] [and] vend[]," rights which were all provided by the Statute of Anne and the stationer's copyright before it. It was only during the nineteenth century that copyright developed into protection for the intellectual "work" rather than simply the text of a book.

Key to this expansion was what the law today calls the right to make "derivative works." One important figure in this transformation was Harriet Beecher Stowe: Stowe lost a seminal 1853 case based on an unauthorized German translation of her bestseller *Uncle Tom's Cabin*. Around the same time, numerous theatres produced plays based on the book, all without Stowe's permission or compensation. In 1870, Congress responded to these inequities by granting literary authors new rights, including a right of translation and a "right to dramatize." These changes would not have made sense under the seventeenth- and eighteenth-century conception of copyright as a book publisher's privilege to print a text, but once the focus shifted to an author's right in her intellectual "work," denying a novelist the right to compensation for a translation or dramatization of her book seemed unjust.

Similarly, the fair use doctrine, which is today celebrated as one of the principal safeguards against unbridled copyright protection, initially developed as a means to expand, rather than contract, copyright. When copyright meant only a publisher's right to print a specific text, fair use was unnecessary. It was clear that everything except an exact printing of the copyrighted book was permitted. But once it became the intellectual work that the law protected, questions arose as to the legality of creating an abridgement of a work. It was in this context that courts in the middle of the nineteenth century developed fair use to determine when an abridgement of a particular work constituted copyright infringement.

During the twentieth century, Congress changed copyright law numerous times, including two major revisions, in 1909 and 1976. As copyright law became important to an increasing number of industries, these changes incorporated compromises among various interest groups affected by the law, from satellite television providers to semiconductor producers, from public libraries to the construction industry, from vessel hull manufacturers to ballet companies. What began as a book trade privilege has grown to become the means of legal protection for vast segments of our economy, covering virtually anything that can be characterized as an intellectual work.

Further Reading

Abrams, Howard B. "The Historic Foundation of American Copyright Law: Exploding the Myth of Common Law Copyright." *Wayne Law Review* 29 (1983): 1119–1191.

Bracha, Oren. *Owning Ideas*. S.J.D. Thesis, Harvard University, 2005.

Bugbee, Bruce W., *Genesis of American Patent and Copyright Law*. Washington, D.C.: Public Affairs, 1967.

Feather, John. *Publishing, Piracy and Politics: An Historical Study of Copyright in Britain*. London: Mansell Publ'g Ltd., 1994.

Ginsburg, Jane C. "A Tale of Two Copyrights: Literary Property in Revolutionary France and America." *Tulane Law Review* 64 (1990): 991–1023.

Goldstein, Paul. *Copyright's Highway: The Law and Lore of Copyright from Gutenberg to the Celestial Jukebox*. Stanford, CA: Stanford University Press, 2003.

Kaplan, Benjamin, *An Unhurried View of Copyright*. New York: Columbia University Press, 1967.

Litman, Jessica. "Copyright Legislation and Technological Change." *Oregon Law Review* 68 (1987): 275–361.

Patterson, Lyman Ray. *Copyright in Historical Perspective*. Nashville, TN: Vanderbilt University Press, 1968.

Rose, Mark. *Authors and Owners: The Invention of Copyright*. Cambridge, MA: Harvard University Press, 1993.

Samuels, Edward. *The Illustrated Story of Copyright*. New York: St. Martin's Press, 2000.

Sherman, Brad, and Strowel, Alain. *Of Authors and Origins: Essays on Copyright Law*. Oxford: Clarendon Press, 1994.

Vaidhyanathan, Siva. *Copyrights and Copywrongs: The Rise of Intellectual Property and How It Threatens Creativity*. New York: N.Y.U. Press, 2001.

Walterscheid, Edward C.. *The Nature of the Intellectual Property Clause: A Study in Historical Perspective*. Buffalo, NY: William S. Hein & Co., Inc., 2002.

Woodmansee, Martha, and Peter Jaszi, eds. *The Construction of Authorship: Textual Appropriation in Law and Literature*. Durham, NC: Duke University Press, 1994.

ANUJ C. DESAI

COSMOPOLITAN

Cosmopolitan of the twenty-first century has no resemblance to its namesake founded in the late nineteenth century. Dramatic transformations in format and style succeeded at various points in the magazine's history, enabling *Cosmopolitan* to create a new or substantially different readership when its circulation or advertising mired in a period of long decline. The original *Cosmopolitan* was a monthly literary magazine from March 1886 to early 1889. It published serial fiction, short stories of adventure and romance, poems, and translations of European writers. The magazine achieved a small circulation of twenty thousand to twenty-five thousand copies, not enough to return a profit for the three different publishers that owned *Cosmopolitan* during its first years, which included missing two editions in the summer of 1888.

John Brisben Walker, a wealthy real estate magnate from Denver who previously had worked for newspapers in the Midwest, bought *Cosmopolitan* in 1889 when its publisher was about to kill the title. Walker retained the literary format, but added nonfiction articles, primarily travelogues and summaries of current events. Most important, Walker spent lavishly on quality woodcut illustrations and the newly feasible photographs made possible by the half-tone engraving process.

Walker gradually reduced fiction and poetry to add more nonfiction articles to *Cosmopolitan* on important political and social issues. He was fascinated by transportation, too, and *Cosmopolitan* treated readers to the latest developments in railroads, automobiles, subway systems, and aviation. Walker promoted higher education for women, resolution of racial problems, and a belief that modern technology would create a better world. *Cosmopolitan* editions containing articles, illustrations, and photographs of the Columbian Exposition in Chicago in 1893 and St. Louis World's Fair in 1904 testify to the publisher's fascination with themes of progress.

Cosmopolitan soared in circulation, distributing 350,000 copies a month during the late 1890s when it briefly was the largest quality general magazine in the nation. Walker, however, had a desire to become an automobile magnate, and he sold *Cosmopolitan* to William Randolph Hearst in 1905 to obtain the money necessary for his venture into manufacturing cars, which later bankrupted him.

Hearst quickly transformed *Cosmopolitan* to a magazine version of his sensationalist newspapers. A series of articles in 1906, "The Treason of the Senate," was a late entry into what became known as muckraking journalism, a label specifically derived from the angry reaction by President Theodore Roosevelt to the *Cosmopolitan* series that exposed bribery and corruption by senators whose actions were favorable to cartels and other powerful economic interests. *Cosmopolitan* continued its exposé journalism for several years.

With a diminution of public interest in muckraking journalism and with evidence that fiction was more popular with readers, Hearst again transformed *Cosmopolitan* in 1912. It became a fiction magazine that also featured classy illustrations by famous contemporary artists, including Charles Dana Gibson. Serial fiction and short stories focused on romance, marital infidelity, and other rather risqué themes for the era. The serials supplied complete novels over many months, a method to retain subscribers and to keep single-copy purchasers buying the magazine month after month. Journalistic articles eventually appeared infrequently, while nonfiction essays on political and social issues replaced them. Circulation reached one million copies a month by 1915. Artful cover illustrations throughout the 1910s into the 1920s depicted sophisticated young women, fashionably dressed and affluent.

Cosmopolitan combined with *Hearst's International* magazine in 1925 for efficiency, because both magazines delivered similar material to readers. This resulted in a rather cumbersome cover masthead for the dual titles; by the 1930s, *Cosmopolitan* was in larger type than *Hearst's International*, which was dropped from the cover in 1952.

Stories by Fannie Hurst, Somerset Maugham, Sinclair Lewis, and P.G. Wodehouse were commissioned for a middle-class readership. Near the end of the 1920s, editors also added melodramatic and adventure stories. The magazine endured the Great Depression, attaining a monthly circulation of nearly two million copies by the start of World War II. Notable writers—among them Pearl Buck, Agatha Christie, A. J. Cronin, Edna Ferber, Ellery Queen, Rebecca West—published their work in *Cosmopolitan* and noteworthy persons—Albert Einstein, Eleanor Roosevelt, Bernard Shaw—published essays on contemporary issues during the 1930s. Cover illustrations portrayed young women enjoying the amenities of city life at galleries, restaurants, and parks.

Another transformation occurred early in the postwar years when *Cosmopolitan* shifted to primarily nonfiction articles aimed at the many young mothers who stayed home to care for the children of the Baby Boom generation. The magazine introduced how-to articles on childrearing, housekeeping, budgeting, recipes, and other subjects, while also providing advice columns. Cover photographs substituted for the artful illustrations that had been a *Cosmopolitan* trademark.

Celebrity coverage also was important. Articles and interviews with movie stars and personalities from television programs were regular items. Because of intense competition from several other magazines also directed toward women readers from middle-class households, *Cosmopolitan* faltered for an extended period, and its circulation fell below two million copies by the early 1960s.

Loss of readers meant loss of advertisers. The magazine, which since the 1930s had routinely published 140 to 180 pages a month, experienced a dramatic decrease in revenue. Executives drastically reduced the number of copies distributed for newsstand sales to control costs. To reverse the downward trend, Hearst Corporation executives hired Helen Gurley Brown, author of a best-selling book on attitudes about sex among single women, to remake *Cosmopolitan* in 1965. Sex, sexuality, and advice about beauty, careers, fashion, and other subjects of interest to women in their twenties and thirties were the mainstay of *Cosmopolitan* from that point forward.

Cosmopolitan thrived for years on this formula. Also, cover photographs and lengthy profiles of celebrities, along with ever more sexually provocative photographs in advertisements and articles, appealed to a substantial number of women readers. International editions of the magazine proved popular in Britain and Europe. Circulation surpassed three million copies a month and remained near that number into the twenty-first century. Advertisers again flocked to the magazine, and occasionally the magazine exceeded three hundred pages.

Further Reading

Endres, Lathleen L., and Therese L. Lueck. *Women's Periodicals in the United States, Consumer Magazines.*.Westport, CT: Greenwood Press, 1995.
Zuckerman, Mary Ellen, *A History of Women's Magazines in the United States, 1792–1995.* Westport, CT: Greenwood Press, 1998.

JAMES LANDERS

COX, JAMES M. AND COX ENTERPRISES, INC.

As a boy, James M. Cox (March 31, 1870–July 15, 1957) plowed the fields from dawn to dusk dreaming of one day working for a newspaper. The sixth and last child of Eliza and Gilbert Cox, he was born at home in Jacksonburg, Ohio. His childhood reading included the *Cincinnati Commercial Gazette*. Cox moved to Middletown to live with his sister and brother-in-law (Annie and John Q. Baker) until he completed the state two-year teacher-training program. He taught in one-room schoolhouses for a few years and supervised a night school in Middletown where one of his students was a former slave. On Saturdays, he delivered Baker's newspaper, *The Weekly Sentinel*. When Baker began publishing daily, Cox joined the staff as the sole reporter and the local correspondent for the *Cincinnati Enquirer*. The *Enquirer* hired him full-time after he telegraphed them news of a fatal train wreck. Cox impressed his colleagues with his accurate, fair reporting but he was fired when he displeased a railroad-tycoon pal of the publisher.

Cox, who had a strong sense of public service, combined journalism and politics in his career. He left Cincinnati to serve as private secretary from 1894 to 1897 for Democrat Paul Sorg, the representative from the 3rd Congressional District of Ohio. In 1898 he purchased the *Dayton Evening News* and renamed it the *Daily News*. He replaced boilerplate (romantic cliffhangers from a national distributor) with hard news. Ironically, Cox and his staff ignored one of the century's most intriguing stories—the Wright Brothers' flying machines in nearby fields—because it seemed too preposterous to be true. Other newspaper acquisitions followed: in 1903, the *Springfield Daily News*; in 1923, the *Miami* (Florida) *News*; in 1939, the *Atlanta Journal*; in 1949, the *Dayton Journal and Herald*; and in 1950, the *Atlanta Constitution*. In politics, Cox represented Ohio as a Democrat in the U. S. House of Representatives from 1909 until 1913. He served as Ohio governor from 1913 to 1915, and again from 1917 to 1921. In 1920, the Democratic Party nominated him to run for president with his running mate Franklin D. Roosevelt. They were defeated that year by another influential newspaper publisher from Ohio, Warren G. Harding.

The Cox newspaper chain entered the broadcasting field with AM radio stations in Dayton in 1934 and in Atlanta five years later. Cox launched the first television station in the South and the first FM station both in Atlanta in 1948. The Cox company kept acquiring newspapers and started a pioneer cable TV operation in the 1960s. Eight years later, the corporation acquired Manheim Auctions, an automobile sales branch that grossed over $1 billion in 1997.

Cox Communications, Inc., merged into Cox Enterprises, Inc. in 1985. In the early twenty-first century, descendants of James Cox helped to manage the Cox empire from its Atlanta headquarters. True to its print roots, Cox Newspapers included seventeen daily and twenty-five non-dailies. The corporation also provided telephone services, direct mail-order, and customized newsletter outlets as well as interactive Internet services. Digital Domain, an enterprise Cox shared with partners, won the Oscar for special effects in the movie, *Titanic*, in 1998. Cox, like other media giants, had diversified its portfolio to remain viable in a rapidly changing technological world.

Further Reading

Cebula, James E. *James M. Cox: Journalist and Politician.* New York: Garland, 1985.

Glover, Charles E., *Journey Through the Years: The Story of Cox Enterprises, Inc.* Atlanta: Longstreet, 1998.

Grant, Philip A. "Congressional Campaigns of James M. Cox, 1908 and 1910." *Ohio History* 81 (Winter 1972): 4–14.

Hooper, Osman Castle, *History of Ohio Journalism, 1793–1933.* Columbus, OH: Spahr and Glenn, 1933.

Hynds, Ernest C. *American Newspapers in the 1980s.* New York: Hastings, 1980.

Kobre, Sidney, *Development of American Journalism.* Dubuque, IA: Brown, 1969.

Mott, Frank Luther. *American Journalism: A History of Newspapers in the United States Through 250 Years, 1690–1940.* New York: Macmillan, 1941.

Squires, James D. *Read All About It: The Corporate Takeover of America's Newspapers.* New York: Random House, 1993.

PAULETTE KILMER

CREDIBILITY GAP

Every president has faced opponents who believe that the commander-in-chief has misrepresented the facts, twisted the truth, and manipulated the situation to achieve political advantage. For Lyndon B. Johnson, however, the distrust became so widespread that the term "credibility gap" came to characterize his administration. The phrase represented an accumulation of a wide variety of reporters' grievances against the president, some of which had started as minor irritants when Johnson entered the Oval Office. Journalists came to see these grievances as signs of the president's pathological need for secrecy, coalescing around the issue of Vietnam.

On May 23, 1965, David Wise penned an article for the *New York Herald-Tribune* on the differing rationales presented by the White House for American military intervention in the Dominican Republic the month before: was it to save lives, or to prevent a Communist takeover? The article's opening lines suggested that "For the past two days the Johnson administration has been grappling with what might best be described as a credibility problem of its own making. . . . The administration is discovering, . . . as other administrations have in the past, that when the gap between a government's actions and its words becomes discernible, it is in trouble." The now-unknown headline writer paired two words to create the historic phrase by entitling the article "Dilemma in 'Credibility Gap.'" According to the historian Eric Goldman, this was the first use of the term in print.

Wise cites the etymological ancestor of the phrase in John F. Kennedy's 1960 campaign charge that America faced a "missile gap" against a better-armed, better-pre-pared Soviet Union. Journalistic lore suggests that during the Vietnam War, correspondents in Saigon had coined the term "*credibility* gap" to characterize the military's press briefings, known derisively as the "Five O'Clock Follies." The expression worked its way stateside, where it was widely used among correspondents before hitting print. Although the *New York Herald Tribune*'s headline seems to mark its first published appearance, the term's "principle popularization" came from Murrey Marder's news analysis in the *Washington Post* on December 5, 1965, which focused on the "creeping signs of doubt and cynicism about Administration pronouncements, especially in its foreign policy. . . . The problem could be called a credibility gap. It represents a perceptibly growing disquiet, misgiving, or skepticism about the candor or validity of official declarations."

The phrase gradually found more frequent usage in news reports and political debates, particularly concerning Vietnam. By November of 1966, for example, the *New York Times* concluded an editorial by suggesting that "when it comes to the war in Vietnam, the most disturbing escalation is in the credibility gap." In March of 1967, journalistic opinion-leader Walter Lippmann penned a two-part series for the *Washington Post* and giving speeches highlighting the charges, and the next month a panel on National Educational Television considered the issue. In September of 1967 an article in *The Progressive* by William McGaffin and Erwin Knoll traced the origins of "the Gap" to the 1964 presidential campaign, during which "he told the American people, 'we are not about to send American boys nine or ten thousand miles to do what Asian boys ought to be doing for themselves.'" Before the end of that year, media stories delighted in a Credibility Gap game, complete with an "Administration pack of lies," created by "two angry professors."

Johnson and his aides bristled at both the term and its connotations. They insisted that the administration's policies on Vietnam remained consistent, with only changes of implementation; redefining the role of American military personnel and committing more troops simply represented steps in discharging the fundamental policy of combating aggression. They complained that the articles often used comments, such as the 1964 campaign promise, completely out of context, ignoring the discussion that framed the remarks. Staff members and supportive journalists pointed to various reasons for inconsistent statements, including the tensions between remaining Kennedy staffers and those added by Johnson, the complexity of the issues involved, "loose talk" among some aides, adaptations to specific audiences, and a hypercritical press corps. They redoubled efforts to court favorable journalists, debated how best to help the public understand what was at stake in Vietnam, and developed extensive memoranda both refuting the charges and pointing to the credibility gaps of others, including Lippmann and Robert F. Kennedy. After supporters argued that Bill Moyers' tendencies toward self-aggrandizement led to media mistrust, the president replaced him as press secretary with George Christian—a move leading James Reston to quip that Moyers had been "badly wounded at Credibility Gap." Sympathetic journalists bemoaned the "vilification—even obscenity" of the vituperative attacks based on "inconsequential nit-picking on matters of national security," resulting in a "'Credibility Gap' cliché [that] lacks substance." A few, such as Philip Potter of the *Baltimore Sun*, acknowledged Johnson's penchant for secrecy but counseled him on the benefits of developing a thicker presidential skin.

Thus the White House files on the credibility gap grew as both the articles and the refutations burgeoned. In January of 1968, three aides warned that "unless checked now, the Credibility Gap will be a major campaign issue"—but by that point, it was too late. Between Vietnam and the press, Lyndon Johnson found the credibility gap too wide a chasm to cross, and he withdrew from the presidential campaign. Although Johnson retired, the term "credibility gap" did not. It has entered the contemporary American lexicon, haunting every subsequent president as well as other politicians, business leaders, academics, and, yes, journalists. From international relations to environmental issues to sports, the term "credibility gap" has became what Doris Graber would call a condensation symbol, stirring up "vivid impressions" that "arouse emotions" and "supply instant categorizations and evaluations."

Further Reading

"Confusion on Vietnam." *New York Times*, November 7, 1966, 46.

"Credibility and the Press." *Washington Star*, January 5, 1967, in Ex PR 18, box 359, Lyndon B. Johnson Library, University of Texas, Austin.

"'Credibility Gap' Fun for Skeptics." *New York Times*, November 26, 1967.

Goldman, Eric F. *The Tragedy of Lyndon Johnson*. New York: Alfred A. Knopf, 1969), 409.

Graber, Doris. *Verbal Behavior and Politics*. Urbana: University of Illinois Press, 1976, 289–293.

Johnson, Lyndon B. Library, University of Texas, Austin. The LBJ Library includes credibility gap files in Ex FG 1, boxes 14 and 16; George Christian's files; and Fred Panzer's files, box 340 (9).

Lipppman, Walter. "The Credibility Gap—I." *Washington Post*, March 28, 1967, A-17.

Lippmann, Walter "The Credibility Gap—II." *Washington Post*, March 30, 1967, A-21.

Marder, Murrey. "Credibility Gap: Greater Skepticism Greets Administration Declarations." *Washington Post*, December 5, 1965, A21.

McGaffin, William and Erwin Knoll, *Anything But the Truth: The Credibility Gap and How the News is Managed in Washington*. New York: Putnam, 1968.

McGaffin, William and Erwin Knoll. "The White House Lies," *Progressive*, September 1967.

Potter, Philip. "Johnson's Credbility Gap: Public Relations and Disputed Questions of National Survival," *Baltimore Sun*, January 16, 1967, 1A, 9A.

Reston, James. "Washington: On Disposable Press Secretaries," *New York Times*, December 16, 1966, 46.

Smith, Howard K. in *Washington Post*, December 19, 1966, in Ex FG 1, box 13, Lyndon B. Johnston Library, University of Texas, Austin.

Smith, Smith, remarks at a UPI breakfast, April 24, 1967, transcript in CF FG 1, box 16, Lyndon B. Johnston Library, University of Texas, Austin.

Telephone interview with Henry Trewhitt of the *Baltimore Sun* by the author, May 19, 1978. Milwaukee, Wisconsin.

"The President and the News." NET panel of Ben Bagdikian, Douglas Kiker, Al Otten, and Philip Potter; see memorandum of April 19, 1966, Ex PR 18, Box 358, Lyndon B. Johnston Library, University of Texas, Austin.

Turner, Kathleen J. *Lyndon Johnson's Dual War: Vietnam and the Press*. Chicago: University of Chicago Press, 1985.

Wise, David. "Dilemma in 'Credibility Gap." *New York Herald Tribune*, May 23, 1965, 15.

Wise, David. *The Politics of Lying: Government Deception, Secrecy, and Power*. New York: Random House, 1973, 22–23, 290–291.

KATHLEEN J. TURNER

CROLY, JANE CUNNINGHAM

Jane Cunningham Croly (Dec. 19, 1829–Dec. 23, 1901), who wrote under the pen name "Jennie June," was one of the first American women to earn a living as a journalist and was an architect of the woman's club movement that expanded woman's sphere beyond the home and into her community. Croly worked as an editor, publisher, reporter, and columnist during a nearly fifty-year career in magazines and newspapers.

She used her forum to promote the rights of women to work yet she herself was ambivalent about suffrage and believed women's first calling was to the home. The mother of six children, Croly needed to work and often was the main financial support for her family. Her columns, books and articles were pivotal in popularizing the club movement, which began in the 1860s, as a purposeful and creative outlet for nineteenth century women. Croly believed that women had an obligation to be involved in the domestic aspects of their communities and often wrote in national magazines and New York newspapers on the need for women and their clubs to take responsibility for "municipal housekeeping."

Croly was born in Leicestershire, England, on December 19, 1829. In 1841, she moved with her family to New York State and moved to New York City in 1853 to seek work as a writer. She created a column called "Parlor and Side-Walk Gossip" that appeared first in the *Sunday Times and Noah's Weekly Messenger* but quickly began being distributed to newspapers throughout the country. She married fellow journalist David G. Croly in 1856 and together they moved to Rockford, Illinois, where he became the founding editor of the *Rockford Daily News*. After a year, they returned to New York City where David found work as an editor on the *New York World* and Jennie worked as the manager of the newspaper's fledgling woman's department. During her decade there, she worked steadily while she also gave birth to six children. Years later, Croly reminisced that despite pregnancy and childbirth, she never was away from the office for more than two weeks (with the exception of when she was traveling abroad). Despite this highly unusual role as a working mother, Croly maintained a very traditional philosophy for her readers, advocating always that a woman's best place was indeed in the home. For Croly, however, the home was defined more broadly to include the community where a woman lived and she argued quite passionately in her writing that women needed to clean up their cities and attend to the civic needs to women and children within their towns and cities.

Croly worked as the chief staff writer for the popular *Mme Demorest's Mirror of Fashions* beginning in 1860 and stayed with the magazine through several metamorpheses. She also was, for a brief period, co-owner and editor of *Godey's Lady's Book.* She founded the General Federation of Women's Clubs that united hundred of clubs in the United States and abroad. She authored the massive *History of the Women's Club Movement in America,* which was published in 1898. Croly died in New York in 1901.

Further Reading

Blair, Karen. *The Clubwoman as Feminist: True Womanhood Redefined, 1868–1914.* New York: Holmes and Meier, 1980.

Croly, Jane Cunninghmam. *History of the Women's Club Movement in America.* New York: Henry G. Allen, 1898.

Gottlieb, Agnes Hooper. *Women Journalists and the Municipal Housekeeping Movement, 1968–1914.* Lewiston, NY: Edwin Mellen Press, 2001.

Haught, Nancy I. "Jane Cunningham Croly (1829–1901): Journalism's Ambivalent Advocate of Women," unpublished master's thesis, University of Oregon, 1982.

AGNES HOOPER GOTTLIEB

CRONKITE, JR., WALTER L.

Whether reporting on the assassination of President John F. Kennedy in 1963, or the 1968 Tet Offensive in Vietnam, or the landing of the first man on the moon in 1969, in national moments of great despair and extraordinary triumph, Walter Cronkite (Nov. 4, 1916–) was the journalist that Americans most trusted to give them news they needed to know. David Halberstam observed that Cronkite was "the right man at the right time" and television was "the right instrument" to take the nation through the tumultuous second half of the twentieth century.

Cronkite was born in St. Joseph, Missouri, the only child of dentist Walter Leland Cronkite and housewife Helen Lena Fritsche Cronkite. The family moved to Kansas City where he had a "perfectly ordinary childhood," he recalled. There he hawked issues of the *Kansas City Star* on street corners and remembered running home to tell the neighborhood the news that President Warren Harding had died in 1923. He became fascinated reading about the lives of foreign correspondents in *American Boy* magazine. When he was ten his family moved to Houston, and there his interest in reporting and politics deepened when a local reporter, Fred Birney, spoke to Cronkite's class at San Jacinto High School in Houston. Cronkite became editor on the school newspaper,

the *Campus Cub*, and won the news writing competition of the Texas Interscholastic Press Association relying on Birney's caution "to use adjectives and adverbs with caution lest they imply editorial opinion." He also worked as an unpaid copy boy and cub reporter on civic affairs for the *Houston Post.* "Seeing an occasional paragraph in print," Cronkite remembered, "was better than gold." He could not "imagine anything more exciting than the heavy odor of printer's ink and pulp paper and melting lead. The unique clanking of the linotype machine and the shaking rumble of the big presses" completed his conversion to a career in journalism.

Cronkite became a campus correspondent for the *Houston Post* while a student at the University of Texas in Austin. He also did a daily five-minute sportscast on KNOW, the campus radio station, and became a state capital reporter for the Scripps-Howard newspaper chain. But he dropped out of school after his junior year to work full-time as a general assignment reporter at fifteen dollars a week for the *Houston Press.* His editor Roy Roussel made sure Cronkite became "a stickler for accuracy."

In 1936 Cronkite became the news and sports editor at KCMO, a small 100-watt radio station in Kansas City for twenty-five dollars a week. Cronkite began dating the station's continuity writer, "a gorgeous redhead," named Mary Elizabeth Simmons Maxwell. Although "overworked and underpaid" when he returned to print journalism in 1939 at the United Press office in Kansas City office, he saved enough money "to pay the organist for a single song" when he married "Betsy" on March 30, 1940. They had three children and at her death were wed fifteen days short of sixty-five years.

Cronkite's wire service experience was perfect preparation for his years at CBS News. "We had a deadline every minute because there was a paper going to press every minute," he remembers. "It was a blistering, relentless battle." He learned to write "fast, fact by fact." Because of intense competition from Associated Press, there was "a powerful incentive to be first" and "to be right." After the Japanese attack on Pearl Harbor, Cronkite was shipped out with a naval task force to report the battle for the North Atlantic and the allied invasion of North Africa. Cronkite was the first war correspondent to arrive in New York and his firsthand reports on the first sustained allied success of the war proved a sensation on both sides of the Atlantic. A Paramount newsreel featured Cronkite's eyewitness account. By the end of 1942, Cronkite was in London, reporting the cross channel bombing war between the British and Germans. Early in 1943, he was one of eight pool reporters who boarded B-17 Flying Fortresses and B-24 Liberators of the U.S. Eighth Air Force at the start of their bombing campaign against Germany. German anti-aircraft fire and fighter planes engaged the American squadron when it came in sight of the Dutch coast. Several planes and crews were lost. "The shelling was so thick," Cronkite remembers one crew member saying, "you could get out and walk on it." Cronkite's lead was admittedly "purple." It began "I've just returned from an assignment to hell, a hell at

17,000 feet, a hell of bursting flack and screaming fighter planes."

Cronkite's growing reputation brought him to the attention of CBS News and Edward R. Murrow. Murrow offered Cronkite a job with the network, but Cronkite after some uncertainty decided to stay at United Press. He reported stories on the Eighth Air Force and reported the D-Day invasion in June 1944 while embedded with Ninth Air Force engineers on a bluff just behind Omaha Beach, which saw some of the bloodiest fighting of the war. Cronkite barely escaped death when, reporting from London, a German V-1 struck a hundred yards from his flat on Buckingham Gate Road. Dozens were killed in the raid. In September 1944, Cronkite accompanied the U.S. 101st Airborne in their liberation of the Netherlands. His glider narrowly evaded German fire and nosed into the ground at Eindhoven. Two days later American forces joined Field Marshal Bernard Montgomery and Britain's 21st Army Group. Cronkite reported on the German counter-offensive, begun on December 17 in the Ardennes Forest. Sixty thousand men were killed in the ten-day Battle of the Bulge. When it was over, Cronkite wrote, Hitler's army had been smashed and lay "smoldering in the snow." Cronkite accompanied Allied forces in the liberation of Amsterdam.

Cronkite covered the Nuremberg trials of twenty-one Nazi war criminals for United Press after the war. He reported the start of the Cold War as U.P.'s Moscow Bureau Chief. Cronkite returned to Washington in 1948, where he reported national news for a group of Midwestern radio stations. In July 1950, he accepted Murrow's offer to report the Korean War for CBS News. He never got the chance. The network's application for a television station in the nation's capital was approved by the Federal Communications Commission, and Cronkite was tasked with the responsibility of setting up its news operation. "I didn't know anything about TV," Cronkite recalled, "but neither did anyone at the network."

Cronkite quickly realized that he could "absorb the news of the day" and go on the air without a script. Within a year he was reassigned to New York. He began appearing regularly on the network's first public affairs programs, *Man of the Week*, *It's News to Me*, and the popular *You Are There*. Cronkite's reputation was established in 1952 with network coverage of presidential nominating conventions in Chicago. Cronkite "anchored," the first time the term was used for a journalist, the gavel to gavel coverage. Cronkite considered it "a marvelous experiment in news collection and distribution."Only 9 percent of all American homes had televisions when Cronkite came to CBS. By the time he began anchoring the network's nightly news show on April 16, 1962, that number had grown to more than 90 percent. Initially, the *CBS News with Walter Cronkite* was a fifteen-minute broadcast that ran second in the ratings behind NBC's *Huntley-Brinkley Report*. Cronkite also served as the show's managing news editor and long argued with CBS management that "the nation was too large and complicated" for a quarter hour nightly newscast. On September 2, 1963, CBS became the first network to move to a half hour news format. Cronkite marked the occasion with a famous interview of John F. Kennedy in which the president acknowledged the administration's deepening commitment to South Vietnam, while noting "in the final analysis" it was the job of the Saigon government and not the United States to resist Communist attacks from North Vietnam.

At 12:30 on November 22, 1963, CBS broke into its early afternoon soap opera with a CBS News Bulletin. Cronkite's voice could be heard saying, "In Dallas, Texas, three shots were fired at President Kennedy's motorcade in downtown Dallas. The first reports say that President Kennedy has been seriously wounded by this shooting." This was the first news the nation had of the assassination attempt. Finally, at 2:38 p.m. the American public watched apprehensively as Cronkite was handed a wire service report. "President Kennedy died at one p.m. Central Standard Time," he reported. Taking off his glasses, he looked up at a studio clock, and said, "some thirty-eight minutes ago." Putting his glasses on again, he briefly shuffled some papers on his desk, fighting to keep his emotions in check. Some observers believe that this broadcast transformed Cronkite from "America's anchorman" to "America's clergyman" in times of crisis.

Five years later, Cronkite again served as the national conscience. It came after the TET offensive in January 1968 during which North Vietnamese forces launched bloody attacks on many of South Vietnam's most important cities. Cronkite flew to South Vietnam to report on fighting there. His February 27 prime time special report, detailing growing American casualties in the conflict, included a closing comment. It was the first time Cronkite had publicly stepped away from his role as anchor to become a commentator. "We've been too often disappointed by the optimism of American leaders both in Vietnam and Washington to have faith any longer in their silver linings," he said. "For it seems now more certain than ever that the bloody experience of Vietnam is to end in a stalemate. For every means we have to escalate, the enemy can match us, and that applies to invasion of the North, the use of nuclear weapons, or the mere commitment of 100 or 200 or 300,000 more American troops to the battle. And with each escalation the world comes closer to the brink of cosmic disaster." (February 27, 1968). Cronkite called for a negotiated settlement to end the conflict and a phased reduction of American forces. President Lyndon Johnson, watching the telecast from the White House, reportedly turned to his aide George Christian and said, "If I've lost Cronkite, I've lost middle America." Weeks later, Johnson announced he "would not seek and would not accept" the nomination of his party to serve another term as president.

Cronkite's signature story was the American space program. The space race began on October 4, 1957, when the Soviet Union sent Sputnik, an artificial satellite into space. "If the Sputnik isn't a threat to our own immediate security, it is to our sense of security," Cronkite reported. In April 1961, the Soviets sent cosmonaut Yuri Gargarin into space. On May 5, 1961, Cronkite stood beside a CBS trailer at Cape Canaveral, Florida to report America's first manned space flight. Alan Shepard's fifteen-minute suborbital flight aboard Mercury's Redstone rocket was "high drama," Cronkite told viewers, "A failure would have been a major Cold War defeat." The success assured the nation "we have a place in space." On May 25, 1961, President Kennedy committed the nation "to landing a man on the moon and returning him safely to the earth" by the end of the decade. On February 10, 1962, John Glenn became the first American astronaut to orbit the earth. Cronkite became a cheerleader for the live space launches and was unapologetic in his enthusiasm. An estimated worldwide audience of three hundred million watched coverage of the July 16, 1969, launch of Apollo 11. Its moon landing four days later, and Neil Armstrong's words,"Tranquility Base here. The Eagle has landed," left Cronkite speechless. "Whew, boy," he exclaimed, taking off his glasses, smiling broadly, while shaking his head and wiping away the tears.

Cronkite's nightly news program had made him "the most trusted man in America," according to annual polling in the 1970s. He put that popularity to one final test in the century's greatest political scandal. Five men had been arrested on June 17, 1972, for breaking into Democratic National Headquarters in Washington, D.C.'s Watergate Hotel. Although White House press secretary Ron Ziegler called the story "a third rate burglary," it was later reported by Bob Woodward and Carl Bernstein in the *Washington Post* that the Committee to Re-elect President Richard Nixon had been implicated in the incident. For months, the *Post* was largely alone in aggressively pursuing ties between the Watergate episode and growing evidence the White House may have been involved in covering up its complicity in the crime. Cronkite assigned a four-member team of reporters to investigate. On the eve of the national election in 1972, he hosted a CBS news special "The Watergate Affair" that claimed "a high level campaign of political sabotage and espionage without parallel in American history." After winning re-election, Nixon's top aides warned CBS executives the network would "pay" for its opposition to the president. Instead, the CBS story helped legitimize press attention to the controversy. The *Post*'s managing editor Ben Bradlee believed, "When the great white father decided this was a story, it was magic. It gave us a big boost." By January 1973, several members of the Watergate conspiracy were convicted for their crime. Congressional investigations and impeachment hearings followed. Nixon was forced to resign the presidency on August 9, 1974.

Cronkite's retirement from the nightly news on March 6, 1981, at the age of sixty-five, prompted many calls for him to reconsider. He felt he had been "fighting deadlines since I was 16-years-old" and assured viewers "I'll be back from time to time with special news reports and documentaries." Cronkite's summer series, *Universe*, ended after thirteen weeks. CBS seemed eager to promote Cronkite's replacement, Dan Rather, and may well have felt Cronkite's continuing presence overshadowed their new star. Although he was made a CBS board member, Cronkite was disappointed by his reduced role at the network. Eventually, he helped organize a production company that developed award-winning documentaries on cable television. His first love, how-

ever, remained reporting the news. He particularly deplored what he saw as the increasing tabloid tendency of broadcast journalists in the 1980s and 1990s. "We need to emphasize breaking news developed within a 24-hour news cycle," he told Larry King in 1996. "This is what directly affects our futures and our lives. What doesn't affect us directly, but is only interesting, is fluff." Viewers were turning away from network news, he observed in 2004, because too much time was spent airing a reporter's "personal opinion" about "stories that have little significance" in the hope of "getting a bigger rating."

Further Reading

Boyer, Peter J. *Who Killed CBS? The Undoing of America's Number One News Network*. New York: Random House, 1988.

Cronkite, Walter. *A Reporter Remembers*. New York: Simon & Schuster Audio-book, 2000.

——. *A Reporter's Life*, New York: Random House, 1996.

James, Doug. *Walter Cronkite: His Life and Times*. Brentwood, TN: JM Press, 1991.

Murray, Michael D. *The Political Performers: CBS Broadcasts in the Public Interest*. New York: Praeger, 1994.

Westman, Paul. *Walter Cronkite: The Most Trusted Man in America*. Minneapolis: Dillon Press, 1980.

BRUCE J. EVENSEN

CROWTHER, FRANCIS BOSLEY

In their lead on the death of Bosley Crowther (1905–1981), the *New York Times* film critic for twenty-seven years, the paper lauded him as long being "the most influential commentator in the country on the art and industry of motion pictures." The claim is not an exaggeration. Crowther was a staunch advocate of the Hollywood's socially conscious film makers from 1940 through 1967, a strong opponent of McCarthyism and the blacklisting of supposed Hollywood communists, and a determined ally of the personal films of post-World War II European cinema.

The year that Bosley Crowther was born to F. Bosley and Eliza Leisenring Crowther in Lutherville, Maryland, the village of six hundred, distinguished by large Victorian homes set in oak groves, surrounding the Maryland College of Women, was in its fifty-third year. Many of the community's lawyers, doctors, and merchants would take one of four stages that daily departed for Baltimore, ten miles to the south. It was in this community of self-conscious respectability with its emphasis on moral responsibility that Crowther saw his first film. When he was five he vividly remembered a traveling exhibition by Lyman B. Howe, who supplemented his pictures with sound produced from a gramophone behind a screen. Crowther's seventy-year romance with the cinema had begun.

The family's income allowed Crowther to develop his skills as a writer, first at Woodberry Forest School in Woodbury, Virginia, and later at Princeton University. Crowther served a twelve year apprentice at the *New York Times* as general reporter, feature reporter and rewrite man before realizing his dream of becoming the paper's film critic. He would bring acute powers of observation, a genuine love of movies and a highly developed skill as a writer to the job, reviewing two to three movies a week and fifty longer Sunday articles a year.

From his first reviews, Crowther showed himself a champion of the serious-minded film maker. Crowther anointed Charlie Chaplin's parody on Adolph Hitler *The Great Dictator* as "the most significant film ever produced." Its devastating mimicry" of "the most hated man alive" was of "transcendent significance" and made it the best film of 1940. As chairman of the New York Film Critics in 1940 he championed the cause of *The Grapes of Wrath*, praising John Ford's sympathetic depiction of Dust Bowl "Okies" as "one of the few great sociological pictures of all time." When Orson Welles was viciously attacked by the Hearst press over the making of *Citizen Kane*, Crowther argued that "suppression of the film would have been a crime." He was among the first to praise it as perhaps "the most sensational film ever made in Hollywood" (*New York Times Directory of the Film*, 72).

He celebrated Billy Wilder's *The Lost Weekend*, a bleak portrayal of alcoholism and delirium tremens, as "motion picture art of unsurpassed honesty" (*New York Times*, December 3, 1945). William Wellman's *The Ox-Bow Incident*'s depiction of mob violence offered "realism as sharp and cold as a knife" (*New York Times*, May 10, 1943). *The Best Years of Our Lives*, William Wyler's canvas of beleaguered servicemen home from war, was "superlative entertainment" because of its "quiet and humanizing thoughtfulness" (*New York Times*, November 22, 1946). *Crossfire*'s attack on anti-Semitism was "a frank and immediate demonstration of the brutality of religious bigotry" (*New York Times*, July 23, 1947). John Huston's *The Treasure of the Sierra Madre* was "ruthlessly original and realistic" in its depiction of human greed (*New York Times*, January 24, 1948).

At a time in which Hollywood's five major vertically integrated studios dominated the production and exhibition of major motion pictures, Crowther diligently sought out foreign films that he could promote. He praised Noel Coward's war-time drama *In Which We Serve* (1942) for its "eloquence" (*New York Times Directory of the Film*, 76). Laurence Olivier's *Henry V* was "rich in theatrical inventiveness" (*New York Times*, June 18, 1946) .Watching Roberto Rossellini's account of the Italian resistance movement was "a real experience" because of its "elegant arrogance" (*New York Times*, February 26, 1946). Marcel Carne's *Children of Paradise* captured "the melancholy masquerade of life" (*New York Times*, February 2, 1947). Vittorio De Sica's *The Bicycle Thief* (December 3, 1949) was "an absolute triumph" in its depiction "of modern city life" and the "almost unbearable compassion and candor" of the director's *Umberto D* demonstrated De Sica's "genius as a director of realistic films" (*New York Times*, November 8, 1955) .Akira Kurosawa's *Rashomon* was "striking in its cinematic and architectural artistry" (*New York Times*, December 27, 1951). Readers were encouraged to see Ingmar Bergman's *The Seventh Seal*, "a piercing and powerful

contemplation of man's passage on the earth" (*New York Times*, October 14, 1958). Frederico Fellini's *La Dolce Vita* was "a fertile and fierce" examination of "a society in sad decay" (*New York Times* (*New York Times*, April 20, 1961).

Crowther criticized Wisconsin Senator Joseph McCarthy and the House Committee on Un-American Activities for their widely publicized work of purging Hollywood from Communist influence. He saw the determination of a Western sheriff in *High Noon* to stand against mob sentiment as "thrilling and inspiring" (*New York Times*, July 25, 1952). Crowther praised the rise of the auteur movement and personal film making in the late fifties and sixties following the collapse of the Hollywood studio system. Francois Truffant's semi-autobiographical *The 400 Blows* was "a small masterpiece" by a "fresh, creative talent." Jean-Luc Godard's *Breathless* was "a pictorial cacophony" suggesting "the tough underbelly of modern metropolitan life" (*New York Times*, February 8, 1961). Michelangelo Antonioni's *Blowup* said "something savagely real about emotional commitment" in a pop culture world.(*New York Times*, December 19, 1966). Stanley Kubrick's *Dr. Strangelove* was a "clever and incisive satire" of America's military establishment, but in the end Crowther wondered "what this picture proves" (*New York Times*, January 31, 1964). Of the widely acclaimed *Bonnie and Clyde* he was even more disdainful, ridiculing it as "sentimental claptrap" that was "pointless" and "lacking in taste" (*New York Times*, April 14, 1967).

Critics charged that Crowther's enthusiastic praise of traditional Hollywood hits such as *Gigi* (1958), *West Side Story* (1961), and *My Fair Lady* (1964) and distaste for new work by counter-cultural film makers showed he was increasingly out of step with modern movie goers. When he was named critic emeritus of the *New York Times* in 1968 Crowther observed that across seven thousand films he had sought to celebrate movies that "stimulate and expand human experience" (*The Great Films: Fifty Golden Years of Motion Pictures*, forward). It was the responsibility of film lovers of his generation, he argued in his last book, *Reruns: Fifty Memorable Films* (1978) to pass on the great movies to the next generation as if one was handling a family treasure. That affection for films and respect for his craft made Bosley Crowther one of the most significant critics in film's first century.

Further Reading

Beaver, Frank Eugene. *Bosley Crowther: Social Critic of the Film, 1940–1967*. New York: Arno Press, 1974.

Bosley Crowther Papers. Brigham Young University.

Crowther, Bosley. *The Great Films: Fifty Golden Years of Motion Pictures*. New York: Putnam, 1967.

Crowther, Bosley. *Hollywood Rajah: The Life and Times of Louis B. Mayer*. New York: Henry Holt, 1960.

Crowther, Bosley. *The Lion's Share: The Story of an Entertainment Empire*. New York: Dutton, 1957.

Crowther, Bosley. *Movies and Censorship*. New York: Public Affairs Pamphlets, 1962.

Crowther, Bosley. *Reruns: Fifty Memorable Films*. New York: Putnam, 1978.

Crowther, Bosley. *Vintage Films: Fifty Enduring Motion Pictures.* New York: Putnam, 1977.

Los Angeles Times, March 8, 1997.

New York Times, March 8, 1997.

The *New York Times* web site has 328 of Crowther's movie reviews online.

The New York Times Directory of Film. New York: New York Times, 1971.

BRUCE J. EVENSEN

C-SPAN

C-SPAN (Cable-Satellite Public Affairs Network) went on the air to 3.5 million households March 19, 1979, from a Crystal City apartment as the U.S. House of Representatives began televising its proceedings. In the first speech covered, Rep. Al Gore (D-Tenn.) welcomed the cameras, two years after the House had approved them and Brian Lamb, a former Pentagon press aide and *Cablevision*'s Washington bureau chief, had won cable industry support for his idea of a public affairs television network based in the nation's capital. For the first time, people outside the Beltway could watch their government in action—without interruption and without editorial comment.

Several major trends in media, technology, and politics in the 1970s culminated in C-SPAN's arrival. The emerging cable industry, pressed to offer viewers quality programming beyond what they could get for free via local broadcasters, gained a key competitive foothold in 1972 with the Federal Communication Commission's (FCC) "open skies" approval of domestic satellite distribution. In Washington, the longtime debate in the House between members hoping to "expand the gallery" via television coverage and those worried cameras would be disruptive and do little to illuminate the actual legislative process progressed in favor of lawmakers dissatisfied with the limitations of commercial network news coverage of Congress. Meanwhile, Lamb, a critic of what he had come to regard as the inherently undemocratic nature of the Big Three commercial network television oligopoly, was drumming up interest among cable operators for alternative public affairs programming produced in Washington and delivered to local cable by satellite.

Lamb helped found C-SPAN in 1979 and from its inception into the twenty-first century served as both CEO and anchoring presence. While the absence of on-air "personalities" is an essential characteristic of C-SPAN's programming strategy, Lamb remained the network's most well-known face and his early life experiences, especially in Indiana and Washington, D.C., and his populist critique of commercial broadcast television's coverage of government and politics, were primary influences on C-SPAN and its unique brand of public service television.

Lamb was born October 9, 1941, in Lafayette, Indiana, son of a tavern-keeper and later wholesale beer distributor. He developed an interest in broadcasting and journalism early, and initially hoped to become an entertainer. While an undergraduate at Purdue University, Lamb started an "American Bandstand"-inspired dance party show for a local UHF television station. He graduated in 1963 with a BA in Speech, enlisted in the Navy and in 1966 was assigned to the Defense Department's public affairs unit at the Pentagon and to the White House as a social aide to President Lyndon B. Johnson. In Washington, Lamb began his education into the practice of national politics and the problematic nature of the interaction between the government and the press.

Following a brief, disillusioning foray into partisan political activity as a field staffer for the Richard Nixon-Spiro Agnew campaign in late 1968, Lamb, who has never joined or contributed to a party or a candidate, returned to Washington in 1969, working as a freelance audio reporter for UPI and later as press secretary to Sen. Peter Dominick (R-Colo.) before joining the Office of Telecommunications Policy (OTP) in the Nixon Administration in 1971. Lamb's boss at OTP, Clay "Tom" Whitehead, provided strong support for the FCC's 1972 "open skies" decision that authorized domestic communications satellites and enabled a crucial technological breakthrough for cable television operators seeking to offer customers more than local broadcast programming.

Lamb left OTP in 1974, began a biweekly newsletter called *The Media Report* and was hired as Washington bureau chief for *Cablevision* magazine that December. Convinced the "Big Three" commercial television oligopoly was undemocratic in nature, and enthusiastic about the potential of the emerging cable-satellite networks, Lamb's ensuing campaign to sell the cable industry on the idea of a new public affairs network coincided with mounting dissatisfaction in Congress with network news coverage of the legislative process. After the House voted in October, 1977, to televise its proceedings, Lamb made a hand-shake deal with then Speaker Thomas "Tip" O'Neill (D-Mass.) to provide gavel-to-gavel floor coverage. That December, the cable industry incorporated C-SPAN as a nonprofit cooperative, with twenty-two industry executives contributing $425,000 in start-up money. When the House turned on its cameras in March, 1979, C-SPAN went on the air. The Senate followed suit by allowing TV coverage and in June 1986, C-SPAN2 went on the air.

C-SPAN's growth since its origins in 1979 was impressive. Initially, it operated with only four employees, shared a spot with the Madison Square Garden Channel on RCA's Satcom I satellite, and broadcast part time, whenever the House cameras were on. By 2006, C-SPAN employed about 275 people at its modern broadcast facilities and corporate headquarters located two blocks from the U.S. Capitol. By then, the network was comprised of three, twenty-four-hour cable television networks (C-SPAN, C-SPAN2, and C-SPAN3) available to more than eighty-eight million homes; C-SPAN Radio broadcasting via a 50,000-watt FM-radio station in Washington and also available on satellite radio; and eleven web sites offering free live and on-demand audio and video to a worldwide audience. Although C-SPAN did not subscribe to the audience rating services used by commercial networks, a commissioned 2004 national survey indicated that 20 percent of the U.S.

cable and satellite viewing audience (an estimated 34.5 million people) watched C-SPAN at least once or twice a week, and 90 percent of the network's viewers were also voters. In addition, by 2006, legislative TV channels influenced by C-SPAN had emerged in a number of state capitals and also internationally.

The network's slow and steady growth from cable niche to media institution frequently referenced by politicians and late-night comedy shows alike has been driven by a mission-level commitment "to allow the American television audience the opportunity to see public policy and political events as they happen, in their entirety, and without commentary." C-SPAN's programming philosophy is grounded in unedited and unfiltered long-form, gavel-to-gavel coverage; camera angles and production values intended to minimize distraction and provide a "you are there" viewing experience; and a "no stars" concept of on-air talent that is unique among national television news and public affairs operations. The network's independent and determinedly noncommercial editorial approach depends upon a similarly unchanging financial model and system of corporate governance. The network receives no funding from the government, carries no advertising and obtains its operating funds from those cable systems and other distributors that choose to offer C-SPAN to their customers. On average $.05 of each cable subscriber's monthly bill goes to fund C-SPAN, whose annual operating budget has averaged about $40 million in early years of the twenty-first century. The network's board of directors, consisting of cable industry executives, oversees business operations and is not involved in editorial decisions concerning programming.

Lamb was C-SPAN's first on-air host and his detached but revealing interviewing technique became part of the network's signature programming style. His on-air duties included regular turns hosting the daily "Washington Journal" morning call-in program and later the weekly "Q&A" interview show, which in 2004 succeeded the popular "Booknotes." Lamb salary as C-SPAN's CEO was $250,000 a year.

"We have a saying around here [that] if you care who wins you shouldn't be here. It's just not our role. We're in the business of showing everything," Lamb said.

While long-form coverage of the House and Senate, and regular viewer call-in opportunities, remained integral to C-SPAN's purpose, the network's programming lineup and its window on the public affairs domain came to extend well beyond the Congress and the federal legislative process. The network covered a wide array of public policy-related events both inside and outside of Washington and representing a broad spectrum of ideological viewpoints. During presidential campaign years, C-SPAN crews produced extensive ground coverage from New Hampshire and Iowa as well as, since 1984, gavel-to-gavel coverage of the major party nominating conventions, which had received increasingly limited attention from national network news. C-SPAN 's international programming included live coverage of the weekly Prime Minister's Questions sessions in the British Parliament. As C-SPAN expanded, it devoted substantial resources and airtime to special series on American presidents and authors as well as to question-and-answer sessions involving high school students and leaders from a variety of fields. The network became known for its focus on nonfiction books through the "BookTV" weekend programming on C-SPAN2 as well as the popular "Booknotes," a nonfiction author-interview program that Lamb hosted for 801 weekly installments before the series ended in 2004.

Created by cable as a public service, C-SPAN's long-term prospects remained closely linked to the interests of the industry. The network's position in the local cable channel lineup, or indeed whether the C-SPAN networks were offered at all, was the decision of the local cable operator, who had to make channel space available and typically forego advertising revenue in order to offer C-SPAN. In an era of industry consolidation and the emergence of sprawling Multiple System Operators (MSOs) such as Comcast and Time-Warner, increasing bottom-line business considerations inevitably make cable's valuation of C-SPAN subject to the pressures of cost-benefit analysis. "Who knows what will happen ten years from now? Right now there's a total commitment on the part of the cable television industry and the satellite providers, but what happens if the economic model changes down the road?" Lamb said in a 2003 interview. However, if the quarter century since C-SPAN's arrival on the small screen demonstrated anything, it was that there was an equally committed national audience for the brand of long-form, unfiltered coverage of the political process and government "in the raw" that C-SPAN pioneered and has made its programming signature.

Further Reading

Ebner, Michael H. "Bringing Democracy to Television," http://www.indiana.edu/~oah/nl/99aug/lamb.html, (1999–) (accessed April 13, 2007).

Elving, Ronald D. "C-Span gets Pushy," http://archives.cjr.org/year/95/5/c-span.asp, (Sept./Oct. 1995) (accessed April 13, 2007).

Frantzich, Stephen, and John Sullivan. *The C-SPAN Revolution.* Norman: University of Oklahoma Press, 1996.

Hazlett, Thomas W. "Changing Channels," http://reason.com/9603/fe.LAMB.text.shtml (March 1996) (accessed April 13, 2007).

Lamb, Brian. "Debunking the Myths," http://www.c-span.org/about/company/debunk.asp?code=DEBUNK2, (Jan. 6, 1997) (accessed April 13, 2007).

CHRISTOPHER LONG

D

DALLAS MORNING NEWS

In the world of Texas journalism, the *Dallas Morning News* is an anomaly, a newspaper born as a satellite publication in a gamble on future economic and population growth. Its unlikely appearance on the barren North Texas landscape was the single greatest predictor of steady and robust growth of the metropolitan area.

The *Morning News* was founded in 1885 as an expansion outpost of *The Galveston News*, which began publishing in 1842 and had become the most powerful newspaper in the state. A charter member of the Associated Press, the Galveston paper was one of the first to use rotary web presses and statewide rail distribution.

The idea of growing a satellite newspaper was initiated by Alfred Horatio Belo, who had become majority owner of the Galveston paper in 1865, succeeding longtime publisher Willard Richardson. In 1882, Belo sent associate George B. Dealey to North Texas, where he scouted locations in Waco, Fort Worth, Sherman, and Dallas, which had become the fifth largest city in the state with a population of ten thousand.

Several dailies were publishing at the time, but Dealey gathered $25,000 in stock subscriptions from local businessmen eager to import the prestige of the flagship *Galveston News*. Belo named Dealey publisher, setting the stage for a rapid swing of publishing influence from the Texas coast to the thriving commercial district on the Trinity River.

When Belo established his publishing outpost, Texas was considered a strong Dixie state, a post-Civil War territory mired in "the South's defeatist moonlight-and-magnolia nostalgia." Belo, Dealey and their Dallas investors knew that moving the state into modernization would require northern business strategies. The *Morning News* was a catalyst for helping the state transcend its regional frontier identity to become a gateway to the west.

The *Morning News* was a booster paper, one that "encouraged growth, business expansion, and civic improvements." It took its role as moral and social guardian very seriously, aggressively fighting the Ku Klux Klan and promoting the benefits of peace and prosperity on the nation's southern border. The paper campaigned against gambling, prize fighting, and legalized prostitution while pushing a local agenda that included improved municipal and health services, civic involvement, and agriculture diversification.

During the early decades of the twentieth century, the *Morning News* was an icon of progressive economic and technological growth. In 1922, it established one of the nation's first radio stations with the founding of WFAA (Working for All Alike), which became the first 50,000-watt clear channel station in the Southwest in the 1930s. Dealey's son, Walter, obtained the first broadcast license in Texas, saying, "If we put in a sending station now, it will be comparable to when the *Galveston Daily News* established a branch paper in Dallas. Back then the idea was to ship the news by wire. The time has come to ship the news by wireless."

In 1991, after more than one hundred years of publication, the *Morning News* purchased and closed its remaining rival, *The Dallas Times Herald*, and became the paper with monopoly power in the Dallas market. Since 1986, the newspaper has won eight Pulitzer Prizes.

Further Reading

Acheson, Sam. *Dallas Yesterday,* Dallas: Southern Methodist University Press, 1977.
——. *35,000 Days in Texas: A History of the Dallas News and Its Forebears,* New York: Macmillan, 1938.
Cox, Patrick. *The First Texas News Barons,* Austin: University of Texas Press, 2005.
Sharpe, Earnest. *G.B. Dealey of the Dallas News,* New York: Henry Holt, 1955.
Thometz, Carol Estes. *The Decision-Makers: The Power Structure of Dallas,* Dallas: Southern Methodist University Press, 1963.

FREDERICK R. BLEVENS

DANA, CHARLES A.

Charles A. Dana (Auguse 8, 1819–October 17, 1897) was one of the towering figures of nineteenth-century journalism. As the editor of the influential *New York Sun*, Dana molded the newspaper into a lively, well-written sheet that appealed to the urban working class population. Dana's *Sun* was an example of a new independent press of the Gilded Age that was political, but not overtly partisan. Historians have described newspapers like the *Sun* as "personal journalism," in which the content is a reflection of the editor's personality and views, rather than political partisanship or the independent and objective presentation of a more modern professional paper.

Little in Dana's early life presaged a career in journalism. Born in 1819 into a poor family in New Hampshire, Dana had a difficult childhood and was forced to live with an uncle in Buffalo through his teenage years. His success as a student, however, offered Dana an opportunity to study at Harvard, beginning in 1839. He managed to complete only a year and a half of classes before dropping out due to lack of financial resources. While at Harvard, Dana was attracted to Transcendentalism and its dedication to social reform. In 1841, Dana joined the experimental community of radicals and intellectuals at Brook Farm, in rural Massachusetts, and taught school there. He also wrote for the *Harbinger*, a weekly newspaper dedicated to Fourierism, a type of Christian socialism that promoted producer-owned cooperatives and respect for the working man. Although the Brook Farm community broke up after a short time, Dana met his wife, Eunice MacDaniel Dana, there and continued to correspond with former members.

Dana got his start in New York journalism in 1846 with the assistance of Horace Greeley, another friend from the days at Brook Farm. Impressed with Dana's intellect and skill as a writer, Greeley hired Dana as a reporter for the *New York Tribune*, one of the most influential and widely circulated papers in the nation. Dana became the paper's city editor in early 1847. In 1848, as political unrest and class warfare broke out across Europe, Dana arranged a deal to cover the uprisings for several New York papers. Although his experiences in Europe did little to change his sympathy for the laboring classes, Dana returned to America in early 1849 with less enthusiasm for radicalism and a greater appreciation of gradual reform. Dana became the managing editor of the *Tribune* and acted as Greeley's second in command. Many journalists of the time considered Dana to be nearly as important as Greeley in maintaining the *Tribune's* excellence during the 1850s. Greeley and Dana were influential voices in Whig/Republican politics during that decade, but quarreled over the slavery question as the Civil War neared, with Dana being much less willing to compromise with the South. Dana resigned from the *Tribune* in 1862.

Dana's connections in the Republican Party led him to a position in government service during the Civil War. He was initially appointed to a commission investigating wartime corruption. While investigating conditions in the Army on the western battlefields, Dana developed close ties with General Ulysses S. Grant and became one of the general's most ardent supporters. With Grant's assistance, he was later appointed Assistant Secretary of War, a position he held to the end of the conflict.

Dana had always occupied the more radical wing of the Republican Party and this remained true through the postwar period. Rather than setting up shop in New York again, Dana accepted an offer from a group of Chicago businessmen to edit a paper to rival the *Chicago Tribune*. The *Chicago Republican* under Dana promoted suffrage rights for black Americans, demanded punishment for the leaders of the Confederacy, and expressed a growing opposition to President Andrew Johnson's reconstruction policies. The newspaper also reflected the pro-business orientation of its backers and promoted development and industrial growth in the city. Dana edited the newspaper for ten months and

then left for unknown reasons, although the paper's owners were likely uncomfortable with his political views.

Dana's rise to prominence in journalism truly began when he bought the *New York Sun*, the first "penny paper," from Moses Beach in 1868. The *Sun* had long been popular among the artisans and working men of the city, most of whom were Democrats. If anyone was surprised that a prominent Republican would buy this paper, they had forgotten about Dana's early involvement with social reform and his long advocacy of workers' rights. Dana edited the paper with a constant independence from party and it continued to reflect his personal views, which turned increasingly Democratic. The *Sun* was no sure backer of Democratic candidates, however. Dana offered only lukewarm support to many of them and backed a Greenback-Labor candidate over the Democrat Grover Cleveland in 1884. He broke totally with the party after William Jennings Bryan won the 1896 nomination. He also became more conservative on the question of labor rights by the end of his career, due in part to his attitudes about immigrants.

The *Sun* served as a model for a successful paper under Dana. He hired skilled writers to produce clear and concise copy and expanded the definition of news to include more human interest stories. The paper was famous for its playful "casual essays" on interesting topics. Dana also revamped the paper's outward appearance, cleaning up the type font and reducing the number of columns per page. Dana believed that advertising was a waste of newsprint and hoped to someday publish the *Sun* entirely from subscription revenues. Although this was never possible, advertisements were limited as much as possible. By 1874, the *Sun* had the largest circulation among New York daily newspapers. The paper's popularity was undercut later in the century by competition for the working class reader from Joseph Pulitzer's *New York World*. Readers were turned away by his weak support for the Democratic Party and circulation dropped rapidly. Dana remained committed to using the paper to express his own views and remained editor until he passed away on October 17, 1897.

Further Reading

Rosebault, Charles J. *When Dana was the Sun*. New York: McBride and Co., 1931.

Steele, Janet E. *The Sun Shines for All: Journalism and Ideology in the Life of Charles A. Dana*. Syracuse, NY: Syracuse University Press, 1993.

Stone, Candace. *Dana and the Sun*. New York: Dodd, Mead and Co., 1938.

ROBERT RABE

DAVIS, ELMER

Elmer Davis (June 13, 1890–May 18, 1958) worked as a reporter, novelist, and radio commentator before heading the Office of War Information (OWI) (1942–1945) during World War II. His main OWI achievement was to prod the army and navy to release news more quickly and completely.

Otherwise, the well-intentioned Davis had an impossibly difficult job. Internal and external disputes about the content of American propaganda undermined the OWI's effectiveness and led to drastic budget cuts in mid-1943. After the war, Davis returned to radio and campaigned against anti-Communist witch hunts.

Davis was born January 13, 1890, in Aurora, Indiana, where his father worked as a bank cashier and his mother taught high school. Although Davis liked to poke fun at his "hick" first name, he was an outstanding scholar. He earned nearly all A's at Franklin College, near Indianapolis, and received a Rhodes scholarship.

For a decade beginning in 1914, Davis wrote for the *New York Times*, where his notable stories included the sailing of industrialist Henry Ford's peace ship for Europe in 1915. During World War I, Davis covered developments in Austria (see *New York Times*, May 26, 1918, 13) and after the war, continued to cover international affairs including the Washington Naval Conference in late 1921 and early 1922 (see *New York Times*, Oct. 4 and 9, 1921; Nov. 27, 1921; and Feb. 2, 1922, 1). In the 1920s and 1930s, Davis worked as a free-lancer and fiction writer. During the 1930s, his byline occasionally appeared in the *New York Times* and he commented on political developments on the radio (see *New York Times*, July 1, 1932, 17; Nov. 8, 1932, 28; Dec. 28, 1933, 17; March 7, 1937, 65; and Sept. 24, 1938, 10).

Davis's big break came in 1939, when Hitler's armies invaded Poland, and England and France declared war on Germany. CBS hired Davis to provide news analysis. Davis previously had substituted for the network's H.V. Kaltenborn, but nothing could have prepared him for his start as a full-time commentator. He described his first nineteen days as "an endlessly unrolling strip of time, punctuated at irregular and unpredictable intervals by brief blank spots of sleep."

He moved easily from the printed page to the microphone, becoming a celebrity just as radio was cementing its role as the dominant medium for fast-breaking news. Listeners associated Davis's flat, reassuring Midwestern voice and lean prose with the early news of the war, and they liked Davis, Edward R. Murrow speculated, because of his friendly, down-to-earth manner.

President Franklin D. Roosevelt responded to demands for consolidation of America's many war information outlets by announcing the creation of the OWI in June 1942, but only after he had been assured Davis would accept the job. Davis espoused a strategy of bolstering American morale and weakening the enemy by disseminating truth. However, he lacked the authority to force government agencies to release information. Some reporters and civilians complained the army and navy gave out too many half-truths and held up bad news; conservative congressional critics alleged the OWI pursued a Democratic, progressive agenda. Davis, who lacked administrative experience, let the squabbling get out of hand. In a report to the president, he said the OWI's Domestic Branch had been a "cocktail" of dissimilar views; by the time they began to blend, "Congress poured most of the contents of the shaker down the drain."

Davis joined ABC after the war. In his final years he wrote two notable books of commentary: *Two Minutes Till Midnight* (1955), in which he described the dangers of atomic war but concluded it would be preferable to Soviet domination, and *But We Were Born Free* (1954), in which he prescribed courage and the Constitution as antidotes to McCarthyism.

Further Reading

Burlingame, Roger. *Don't Let Them Scare You: The Life and Times of Elmer Davis.* Philadelphia: J.B. Lippincott, 1961.

"Davis, Elmer." *Current Biography: Who's News and Why, 1940.* New York: H.W. Wilson, 1940, 224–226.

Davis, Elmer. "Broadcasting the Outbreak of War." *Harper's,* November 1939: 579–588.

———. *But We Were Born Free.* Indianapolis: Bobbs-Merrill, 1954.

———. "OWI Has a Job." *Public Opinion Quarterly* 7 (1943): 5–14.

———. *Two Minutes Till Midnight.* Indianapolis: Bobbs-Merrill, 1955.

Roshco, Bernard. "A Giant Named Elmer." *American Journalism Review* 13 (Dec. 1991): 35–37.

Sweeney, Michael S. *Secrets of Victory: The Office of Censorship and the American Press and Radio in World War II.* Chapel Hill: University of North Carolina Press, 2001.

Winkler, Allan M. *The Politics of Propaganda: The Office of War Information 1942–1945.* New Haven, CT: Yale University Press, 1978.

MICHAEL S. SWEENEY

DAY, BENJAMIN

Benjamin Day (April 10, 1810–December 21, 1889) founded the *New York Morning Sun*, the first successful penny newspaper in America, in 1833. As its publisher for the next five years, he introduced new ideas for the content, sales, and distribution of newspapers, ideas that had wide-ranging implications for the rise of a mass-circulation press in New York and other major cities.

Born April 10, 1810, in West Springfield, Massachusetts, Day was the son of Henry Day, a hatter, and Mary Ely, a descendant of one of the signers of the Mayflower Compact. At fourteen, Benjamin Day was apprenticed to printer Samuel Bowles, founder of the *Springfield Republican*. After five years of learning the printer's trade at the Republican, Day left for New York City, where he found work at the *Evening Post* and the *Journal of Commerce*. In 1832, he started his own print shop, a decision that turned out to be a first step toward publishing his own newspaper.

As Day himself described it in a speech in 1851, the idea of launching a paper was prompted by a slump in his printing business caused by the New York cholera epidemic of 1832. Models for the content, pricing, and distribution of a new kind of newspaper already existed in England, and a short-lived attempt to introduce such a paper in New York was made in early 1833. Possibly because of the failure of that venture, the *Morning Post*, Day later claimed that he had little faith in his own project but nevertheless proceeded with it, and on September 3, 1833, the first issue of the *Sun* was published. Its prospectus promised to "lay before the public, at a price within the means of everyone, ALL THE NEWS OF THE DAY, and at the same time afford an advantageous medium for advertising."

It was readily evident that the four-page newcomer was different from the existing political and mercantile papers, the "six-pennies." Its price was one cent, and instead of being sold through subscriptions and delivered to the reader's home, the *Sun's* primary means of distribution was street sales. Under the so-called "London plan," carriers bought copies of the paper from Day at a discount and then sold them directly to readers, keeping what they were paid.

Just as Day's method of distribution borrowed ideas from the British capital, so did the *Sun's* content. Day by and large eschewed the political and economic news that dominated the pages of the six-pennies and instead offered human interest items from the city's police court. That such content had relatively little news value was evident from the fact that the *Sun* at times clipped "London Police" stories from English papers when there was not enough time to gather it locally.

As press historian Sidney Kobre noted, the primary purpose of the *Sun* in its early years was to entertain rather than inform, and that purpose was obvious in the paper's most notorious story, the moon hoax. Published in 1835, it consisted of a series of articles ostensibly reprinted from a Scottish scientific journal that claimed that an astronomer had discovered human-like beings on the moon. After Day's competitors exposed the hoax, the *Sun's* editors remained coy about the stories' veracity, and they repeatedly noted the stories had provided good entertainment for readers. The hoax had also boasted the *Sun's* circulation to nineteen thousand, according to Day, supposedly making the New York penny paper the largest in the world. A year after the moon hoax, circulation had increased even further, reaching thirty thousand. The episode suggested that entertaining readers could be more profitable than merely giving them the "facts."

A publisher rather than an editor, Day relied on skillful writers such as George Wisner and Richard Adams Locke to provide the editorial content of his paper. He still exerted a degree of influence over the content, however, insisting that the *Sun's* editorials be politically neutral and that each issue contain literary items such as essays and poems. As the head of a thriving business enterprise, Day also concerned himself with making advertising revenue more stable by insisting on payment in advance, and he made sure that the paper's growing circulation was made technically possible by purchasing a steam-driven press.

In 1838, Day sold the *Sun* to his brother-in-law, Moses Y. Beach, a move he later regretted. For the next twenty-five years, he involved himself in several publishing enterprises, including another penny paper called the *True Sun* and a literary weekly entitled *Brother Jonathan*. Day retired during the Civil War and lived the rest of his life off his personal wealth. He died in New York City December 21, 1889.

Further Reading

Bjork, Ulf Jonas. "'Sweet Is the Tale'": A Context For the New York Sun's Moon Hoax." *American Journalism* 18, no. 4 (2001): 13–27.

Bradshaw, James Stanford. "Day, Benjamin Henry." In *Biographical Dictionary of American Journalism*, edited by Joseph P. McKerns, 171–173. New York: Greenwood Press, 1989.

"Day, Benjamin Henry." In *The National Cyclopædia of American Biography*, vol. 13, 307–308. New York: James T. White & Company, 1906.

Kobre, Sidney. *Foundations of American Journalism*. Westport, CT: Greenwood Press, 1970.

O'Brien, Frank Michael. *The Story of the Sun*, New York: 1833–1928. New York: D. Appleton and Co., 1928.

Thompson, Susan. *The Penny Press: the Origins of the Modern News Media, 1833–1861*. Northport, AL: Vision Press, 2004.

Whitby, Gary L. "Horns of a Dilemma: The *Sun*, Abolition, And the 1833–34 New York Riots." *Journalism Quarterly* 67, no. 2 (1990): 410–419.

ULF JONAS BJORK

DAY, DOROTHY MAY

Among U.S. history's most influential advocacy journalists and activists, Dorothy Day (November 8, 1897–November 29, 1980) is best known for her leadership of the pacifist and social justice-oriented Catholic Worker movement and its tabloid newspaper, the *Catholic Worker*. She co-founded both, with Peter Maurin, in New York City in 1933 as an immediate response to the Great Depression's widespread poverty and homelessness. The movement sponsored soup kitchens around the United States and abroad, an immediate solution, and the penny paper sought to inspire long-term solutions through thoughtful reporting and commentary.

As editor of the *Catholic Worker* from 1933–1980, Day recruited a staff that included Michael Harrington, Tom Cornell, James Forest, and other leaders in peace and social justice activism. She published wood engravings by the masterful Fritz Eichenberg and liturgical art by Ade Bethune and solicited editorial contributions from Thomas Merton, Eileen Egan, Martin Buber, Daniel and Philip Berrigan, and others. And Day focused the paper, which she wisely kept as a lay enterprise, consistently on issues of peace and social justice, successfully negotiating the shoals of the Catholic hierarchy's disapproval. She maintained the *Catholic Worker*'s stalwart pacifism through the Spanish Civil War, World War II, the Korean War, and the Vietnam War. During World War II, Catholic bishops sometimes banned the *Catholic Worker* and its salespeople were even beaten in the streets. Circulated plummeted from a pre-war high of about 190,000 to about 50,500 (November 1944). But Day prevailed with her historic peace witness and in 1983 the American Catholic Bishops praised her peace advocacy, placing it in the same category as that of Mohandas Gandhi and Martin Luther King, Jr., as a legitimate model for Catholics. Since her death, a movement within the Catholic Church to petition for the declaration of her sainthood has even grown.

As an advocacy journalist, Day viewed journalism as another form of activism, on a par with public speaking, leafleting, civil disobedience, and other forms of advocacy as a means to remake society. She herself was arrested and imprisoned several times through her practice of civil disobedience to protest war, experiences she recounted in her writings. As Robert Ellsberg, a former *Catholic Worker* editor, has observed, Day's life was seamless; there was no separation between what she believed and how she lived. She lived in voluntary poverty for more than fifty years at the New York City Catholic Worker house of hospitality on the Lower East Side, sometimes sharing her room with destitute women and wearing the dresses she obtained from the common clothing bin.

Such experiences gave her writing great power. Besides enterprising reportage and a regular column for the *Catholic Worker*, she also wrote several compelling books based on her *Catholic Worker* experiences as well as free-lance articles for *America, Commonweal*, and other publications. She often wrote literary journalism, journalism that tries to inform at a deep level using literary techniques such as characterization and scene-setting, in order to illuminate timeless truths about human existence.

Before converting to Roman Catholicism in 1927 after the birth of her only child, Tamar, Day was a deeply involved activist of the Old Left who wrote for such publications as the Socialist *Call*, Max Eastman's *The Masses*, and the *Liberator*. After her conversion she sought to combine traditional Roman Catholic piety with her longtime advocacy of justice for the masses. In so doing, she forged a distinctive and influential brand of journalism and editorial leadership. Although she was a divorced, single mother, and Catholic convert, she managed to start a successful radical movement and newspaper during the thirties, in the Catholic Church, then a decidedly conservative, hierarchically clerical institution (especially in regard to gender roles). Indeed, in the December 19, 1980, issue of *Commonweal*, the historian David J. O'Brien called her "the most significant, interesting, and influential person in the history of American Catholicism." Her papers are kept at Marquette University in Milwaukee, Wisconsin.

Further Reading

Coles, Robert. *Dorothy Day: A Radical* Devotion. Reading, MA: Addison-Wesley, 1987.

Day, Dorothy. *By Little and By Little: The Selected Writings of Dorothy Day*, ed. Robert Ellsberg. New York, NY: Alfred A Knopf, 1983.

——. *The Long Loneliness: The Autobiography of Dorothy Day*. New York, NY: Harper and Row, 1952.

——. *On Pilgrimage*. New York: Catholic Worker Books, 1948.

——. *On Pilgrimage: The Sixties*. New York: Curtis Books, 1972.

Forest, Jim. *Love Is the Measure: A Biography of Dorothy Day*, rev. ed. Maryknoll, NY: Orbis Books, 1994.

Klejment, Anne, and Alice Klejment. *Dorothy Day and "The Catholic Worker": A Bibliography and Index*. New York and London: Garland, 1986.

Klejment, Anne, and Nancy L. Roberts, eds. *American Catholic Pacifism: The Influence of Dorothy Day and the Catholic Worker Movement*. Westport, CT: Praeger, 1996.

Miller, William D. *Dorothy Day: A Biography*. New York: Harper and Row, 1982.

——. *A Harsh and Dreadful Love: Dorothy Day and the Catholic Worker Movement*. New York: Liveright, 1973.

Piehl, Mel. "Dorothy Day." In Dictionary of Literary Biography series, vol. 29, *American Newspaper Journalists, 1926–1950,* edited by Perry J. Ashley, 89–96. Detroit: Gale Research Co., 1984.

Roberts, Nancy L. "Dorothy Day" (evaluative essay). In *A Sourcebook of American Literary Journalism: Representative Writers in an Emerging Genre*, edited by Thomas B. Connery, 179–185. Westport, CT: Greenwood, 1992.

——. *Dorothy Day and the* Catholic Worker. Albany: State University of New York Press, 1984.

——. "Dorothy Day: Editor and Advocacy Journalist." In *A Revolution of the Heart: Essays on the Catholic Worker*, edited by Patrick G. Coy, 115–133. Philadelphia: Temple University Press, 1988.

Nancy L. Roberts

DENVER POST

When the *Denver Post* was founded in August 1892 as a weekly, it had to compete against more than fifty other daily, weekly, and monthly publications. More than a century later, although the media scene had changed dramatically, what with online, broadcast and print alternatives, the *Post*'s main daily competition had become its business partner. The *Denver Post* and the *Rocky Mountain News* entered into a Joint Operating Agreement in 2001 that formed the Denver Newspaper Agency, which handles business operations for both newspapers. That marked the end of a long, ruthless battle between the *Post* and the *News* that included sensationalism and name calling in the early years and absurdly low-priced subscriptions—about a penny a day—in later years. But the competition over the years also has led to some outstanding journalism, such as the coverage of the school shootings at Columbine High School. In 2000, both newspapers won Pulitzer Prizes for their coverage—the *Post* for reporting and the *News* for photography. It was the fifth Pulitzer Prize for the *Denver Post* (during the 1960s, for example, the *Post* won two Pulitzers for Editorial Cartooning). Under the Joint Operating Agreement, both newspapers maintained separate and independent news-editorial staffs, and vowed to continue to compete journalistically.

Three years after the founding of the *Post*, Harry Tammen and Frederick Bonfils purchased the then-daily *Evening Post* for $12,500 and declared war against its four rival dailies. Its yellow journalism featured use of red headlines, lurid stories, editorial crusades, and promotional stunts. The *Post* managed to outlast all rivals, except for the *News*, which was bought in 1926 by Scripps-Howard Newspapers. The morning *News* and afternoon *Post* each tried furiously to put the other out of business. But for many years, the *Post*, declaring itself "The Voice of the Rocky Mountain Empire," held the dominant position in the market. The

Post was sold in 1980 to the Times Mirror Co. for $95 million and became a morning newspaper the following year. But its circulation declined until William Dean Singleton's MediaNews Group bought it in 1987, also for $95 million. Both newspapers competed fiercely for circulation. Thanks to the low subscription prices, both the *Post* and *News* claimed the largest circulation gains in the country in 2000, with neither gaining a clear lead. While the *News* reportedly had been losing millions of dollars, the *Post* reported profits of $192 million in the 1990s when U.S. Attorney General Janet Reno approved the Joint Operating Agreement in January 2001. The two newspapers continued to publish competing newspapers Monday through Friday, but the *News* oversaw publication of a single newspaper on Saturdays and the *Post* oversaw a single Sunday edition. In 2002, Greg Moore was named editor of the *Denver Post*, making the *Post* the largest circulation daily newspaper at the time to be run by an African American. Publisher William Dean Singleton, who has been criticized by journalists in the past for closing newspapers, is often credited with improving the *Post* financially and journalistically. The *Post*'s daily circulation, Monday through Friday, averaged about 268,000 in 2005, a drop of about 150,000 in the five years since the Joint Operating Agreement was approved. Its Sunday circulation was about 736,000, up by about 150,000 in the five years since the disappearance of its Sunday rival.

Further Reading

Anton, Mike. "Battle of Wits, Words Made History." *The Rocky Mountain News* (May 12, 2000): 5A.

Fowler, Gene, Timber Line: *A Story of Bonfils and Tammen*, Garden City, NY: Garden City Books, 1951.

Hornby, William H., *Voice of Empire: A Centennial Sketch of the Denver Post*, Denver: Colorado Historical Society, 1992.

Kreck, Dick. "A 108-Year-Old Street Fight: Newspapers Share a Long, Colorful History." *The Denver Post* (May 12, 2000): A-16.

Hosokawa, Bill. *Thunder in the Rockies: The Incredible Denver Post*. New York: William Morrow & Co., 1976.

Morton, John, "Life after the War," *American Journalism Review* 22, no. 6 (July/August 2000): 88.

Prendergast, Alan, "Peace Comes to Denver," *Columbia Journalism Review* 39, no. 2 (July/August 2000): 16–20.

Sherman, Scott, "The Evolution of Dean Singleton," *Columbia Journalism Review* 41, no. 6 (March/April 2003): 32–41.

KRIS KODRICH

DETROIT FREE PRESS

Detroit. Lansing, Michigan. London, England. All three have shared the *Detroit Free Press'* masthead in its history. On May 5, 1831, the first edition of *The Democratic Free Press and Michigan Intelligencer* was printed and distributed with three-week old political news from around the state and country. The four-page paper was divided into five columns per page. In November 1832, the paper was renamed *The Democratic Free Press*. Three years later the name was changed yet again to the *Detroit Daily Free Press*. In 1847, the *Detroit Daily Free Press* started a paper in Lansing, primarily for the coverage of state news, but it failed. Later the paper became the *Lansing State Journal*, owned by Gannett Company, Inc. Fifty years after the founding of the *Free Press* in Detroit, a London edition of the paper debuted. At its peak, two hundred thousand copies were sold but the London paper folded in 1899.

Meanwhile, the success of the *Free Press* in the United States is the result of a team effort. John Pitts Sheldon, former *Detroit Gazette* publisher and later *Free Press* editor, was credited with giving birth to the Detroit paper. Wilbur Fisk Storey, who bought the paper for $3,000 in February 1853 and sold it in 1861 for $30,000, nurtured it to adolescence. Henry N. Walker, editor/owner of the paper from 1861 to 1905, and William E. Quinby, who bought controlling interest in the paper in 1872, brought the paper to maturity.

A mature newspaper included a Sunday edition, the state's first, and a unionized staff. With the unions came strikes and the strikes resulted in shutting down the presses of the newspaper from three days to nine months. For example, a strike in 1955 lasted 47 days while one strike in 1964 went on for 134 days. The strike that began in November 1967 did not end until August 1968.

In July 1995, about twenty-four hundred members of the Newspaper Guild and Teamsters went out on strike against the Detroit newspapers. Unlike the strikes during the earlier years, the paper hired replacement workers and continued to publish throughout the nineteenth-month strike. The papers, however, lost more than $140 million in canceled subscriptions and advertisements.

Work stoppages aside, the *Free Press* was destined to become links in the largest newspaper chains in the United States. First, it was a part of Knight-Ridder newspapers, then a part of a joint operating agreement (JOA) with the *Detroit News* and finally a part of Gannett Company, Inc.

John Shively Knight bought the *Free Press* in 1940 with a $100,000 down payment on the morning of May 1, 1940, and a promise to pay the balance after advertisers paid their bills that afternoon. Thirty-four years later Knight Newspapers Inc., merged with Ridder Publications Inc., and became the nation's largest newspaper group, Knight Ridder.

The 1989 JOA, approved by the Justice Department so Detroit would not become a market with one editorial voice, allowed the printing, advertising, and circulation arms of the *Free Press* and *News* to merge while keeping the editorial staffs separate to compete.

At the time of the JOA application, both Detroit papers, owned by the richest newspaper chains in the country—Gannett and Knight Ridder, had a circulation of more than six hundred thousand. By 1994, however, the *Free Press'* circulation dropped from 626,434 to 551,650. By 2005, it had dipped to 370,875.

Nevertheless, in 1998 the *Free Press* staff left its building on West Lafayette Boulevard, which had been its home since 1925, and moved into the *News* building. To keep the staffs physically separate, the main entrance for the *Free Press* staffers was off West Fort Street and the editorial departments were on different floors of the building.

In August 2005 the staff division blurred again temporarily as Knight Ridder sold the *Free Press* to Gannett and Gannett sold the *News* to MediaNews Group Inc. Under the terms of the purchase agreements, the *News* would become a morning publication and the papers would no longer publish joint weekend editions. The *Free Press* would become the lone paper printed on Sunday.

What Edward Douglas Stair, *Free Press* principal owner in 1919, said about the paper then still rang true for many Detroit citizens in the early twenty-first century: "it represents permanence and worth of the highest sort."

Further Reading

Angelo, Frank. *On Guard: A history of the Detroit Free Press.* Detroit: Detroit Free Press, 1981.
"Bitter showdown in Motown." *Time*, Jan.17, 1983.
Lutz, William W. *The News of Detroit: How a Newspaper and a City Grew Together.* Boston: Little, Brown & Company, 1973.
McCord, Richard. *The Chain Gang: One Newspaper versus the Gannett Empire.* Columbia: University of Missouri Press, 1996.
www.gannett.com/go/press/pr080305.htm (accessed April 19, 2007).

S. L. COMBS

DETROIT NEWS

If James E. Scripps' wife, Hattie, had not been so persistent and encouraging, the *Detroit News* would not have been printed more than 130 years ago. Originally named the *Evening News*, Scripps first published 10,000 copies of the four-page tabloid newspaper on Aug. 23, 1873. It cost 2 cents a copy, 3 cents less than the cost of the other four papers already publishing in Detroit, Mich. Scripps wanted to publish an affordable paper for the city's working people and the first year, with his lower price per copy, he lost $5,000. By the end of the second year, the paper earned $21,000 in profits. Later he dropped the price to 1 cent and started publishing on Sunday. By 1892 the *Detroit News* had become the nation's eleventh largest evening newspaper with a circulation of 36,360.

Scripps, who had served a frustrating elected term in the Michigan Senate with none of his 24 proposed bills passing, died on May 29, 1906. He left the newspaper and the commercial radio station, WWJ, in trust to his son-in-law, George G. Booth (husband of his daughter Ellen) and his son, William E., who was serving as the newspaper's treasurer. (Booth's father operated two Canadian newspapers.)

In the 1930s, the newspaper was known for campaigning against crime in the city and state with countless stories and bold headlines about arrests and convictions of criminals.

Two major riots widely covered by the *Detroit News* ripped Detroit apart and helped speed it to becoming one of the nation's poorest and most segregated cities. The 1943 riot lasted 36 hours and the *News* reported that in its ashes there were 25 blacks killed (17 by police), nine whites killed, 675 people injured (416 hospitalized), 1,893 arrested. Property loss totaled $2 million. During the 1967 riot, *News* employees could see the billowing smoke from the riot area through the newspaper windows, three miles away on West Lafayette Boulevard. It took seven days for the smoke to clear with the help of federal troops sent by President Lyndon B. Johnson. Thirty-three blacks and 10 whites were killed during the riot that resulted in $60 million in property damage.

Like the city, the newspaper had its own growing pains. In 1920 the circulation was 232,852 and jumped to 322,835 in 1930. It had a high of 830,000 when it was purchased in 1986 for $717 million by Gannett Co. Inc., but dropped to 359,057 in 1994, and 263,703 in 2005.

Over the years, the paper had its share of labor problems. Unionized workers went on strike and shut down the *Detroit News* (and the *Detroit Free Press*) from Nov. 16, 1967 through Aug. 8, 1968. The next major strike, however, would not silence the presses. After 2,400 employees walked off their jobs on July 13, 1995 at the *News* and *Free Press*, the papers continued to publish using replacement workers. The strike lasted about 19 months and cost the papers more than $140 million in lost subscribers and advertisers.

The *News* made journalism history on March 19, 1972 with a Page One editorial that said the nation's largest evening paper would no longer accept and print display advertisements for X-rated films. It also would no longer print reviews or stories about X-rated films. Other major newspapers during this period also stopped advertising this type of entertainment.

To rescue the nation's fifth largest newspaper market at the time from becoming a one-newspaper town, the Justice Department approved a joint operating agreement (JOA) for the *Detroit News* and the *Detroit Free Press*. In 1989, the papers, owned by the Gannett Company, one of the wealthiest newspaper chains in the nation, merged their business functions (printing, circulation and advertising) but kept their news staffs separate and competing. About 16 years later, Gannett switched news staffs.

On Aug. 3, 2005, Knight-Ridder Inc., sold the *Detroit Free Press* to Gannett and Gannett sold the *Detroit News* to MediaNews Group Inc. The new JOA partners agreed to allow the *News* to become a morning paper and to discontinue joint weekend publications. The *News* published Monday through Saturday.

Further Readings

Angelo, Frank, *On Guard: A history of the Detroit Free Press.* Detroit: Detroit Free Press, 1981.
Lutz, William W., *The News of Detroit: How a Newspaper and a City Grew Together.*Boston, Little, Brown & Company, 1973.
McCord, Richard, *The Chain Gang: One Newspaper versus The Gannett Empire.* Columbia, Mo., University of Missouri Press, 1996.
www.gannett.com/go/press/pr080305.htm (accessed April 13, 2007).

S.L. COMBS

DIGITAL INFORMATION TECHNOLOGIES

Digital information technologies have had a profound effect on the collection, creation, and distribution of news and information. These technologies can create the five basic modes of news—text, graphics, photographic images, audio, and video—in a single format, based on programmable computer language, for use in a variety of devices, including computers, television sets, telephones, and other receiving instruments.

Digital technologies either coexist with or replace analog technologies. Analog technologies transform media, such as audio and video, into electronic or mechanical patterns. For example, analog video cameras scan a picture one line at a time and convert the colors into electrical signals for broadcasting. Digital technologies generate, store, and process data by using computer language based on codes and variations of the numbers zero and one. For example, a digital video camera allows a news outlet to broadcast the images, translated into a series of zeros and ones, via a television set or a computer.

Although news organizations had used large, mainframe computers for accounting and circulation in the 1960s, news organizations started to depend upon digital technologies for news operations, making it easier to compile, condense, correct, and create the news. For example, computers made it faster to write and edit stories at a newspaper and made it easier to eliminate jobs in the physical production of the newspaper because typesetters were no longer needed.

Reporters also found that digital technologies could assist in reporting the news. Philip Meyer and the *Detroit Free Press* surveyed African Americans after the 1967 riots in the city. Using an IBM mainframe computer, Meyer found that contrary to conventional wisdom those with a college education were equally as likely to have joined the riot as high school dropouts. The story earned a Pulitzer Prize in 1968 and launched computer-assisted reporting.

In 1973, the Associated Press introduced a computer-based system that enabled large bureaus, such as New York, Washington, D.C., and Chicago, to collect and transmit news to its members. Although the AP system only provided textual material via computer, newspapers started the transition to the use of digital information in the newsroom in the late 1970s and 1980s, particularly when IBM introduced its personal computer in 1981 and Apple unveiled the Macintosh computer in 1984. Five years later, reporters and editors founded the National Institute for Computer-Assisted Reporting at the University of Missouri to train journalists in the use of computer programs to report the news.

The transition from analog to digital images for both photography and video began in the 1960s when the National Aeronautics and Space Administration converted to digital signals for its space probes. In 1991, Kodak and Nikon released the first professional digital camera system. This technology eliminated the need to process film, which often took the photographer away from a story and could force an earlier deadline. Although a debate continues over whether digital images attain the quality of film, the new technology for cameras allowed photographers to stay at a scene and to file directly from the location with a computer.

Audio engineers have introduced a variety of digital technologies—some of which have influenced news and information. In the mid-1980s, Philips and Sony developed digital audiotape, or DAT, which provided high-quality recordings and saw increased use in the production of news programming. Despite the belief that this technology would gain widespread acceptance, consumers moved instead to compact discs, or CDs, and Sony ended production of DAT recorders in 2005.

The development of the Moving Pictures Experts Group-1, Layer 3, or MP3 technology, in the late 1990s helped launch Apple's iPod, a popular storage device for audio and video. The MP3 technology allows users to download music, but also audio and video of news programming. The iPod, which was introduced in 2001, ushered in a variety of devices that can receive text, images, audio, and video. Wireless telephones and personal digital or data assistants are among other devices that can receive news through digital formats.

Television news and entertainment have experienced a significant transition to digital technologies. In 1996, the U.S. Congress mandated that all broadcast channels had to change to digital television by 2006 and eliminate their existing analog transmissions entirely three years later. Analog television uses magnetic waves to transmit and display broadcast pictures and sound, while digital television uses technology based on computer programs to provide dramatically improved pictures and sound. Digital television also provides data, such as textual material and graphics that can be viewed either by a television set or a computer. As digital transmission began in the late-1990s, many news organizations introduced digital video cameras and editing facilities. These technologies provide higher-quality pictures and sound.

As a result of the ability to produce a variety of media forms by digital means, some news organizations have moved toward convergence, a process of reporting a story for print, audio, video, and the World Wide Web. For example, the *Tampa Tribune* and WFLA-TV, both owned by Media General, moved into the same building in 1999. The two outlets shared resources in what is generally considered one of the most extensive experiments in convergence. Not only did print journalists appear on television, but they also learned television fundamentals at WFLA and the University of South Florida. Moreover, television reporters learned print skills, and photojournalists learned how to use both still and video cameras. Perhaps more than at any time in the past, journalists found that they were expected to be able to work with a variety of formats.

The World Wide Web and News

The Internet, a principal outlet for the transmission of digital information, has dramatically transformed the content and the delivery of news. The Internet has three main components: electronic mail, Usenet, and the World Wide Web. Even though electronic mail and Usenet have had some impact on news, the World Wide Web has caused the most change. In the 1960s and 1970s, a variety of scientists developed the digital technologies to link computers into networks capable of communicating instantaneously. For example, the Advanced Research Projects Agency, later the Defense Advanced Research Projects Agency, enabled scientists to communicate via electronic mail in 1972. Timothy Berners-Lee, a British scientist, developed the basic structure for the Web in 1989 and sent out his plans publicly so that individuals could refine and use the program. In 1993, Marc Andreessen and Eric Bina, graduate students at the National Center for Supercomputer Applications at the University of Illinois, created the browser, Mosaic, which made it much easier for individuals to navigate through the Web. The browser laid the foundation for Netscape and other browsers.

At first, media organizations seemed reluctant to embrace the Web as a place to display news stories, mainly because it was believed that the sites would not generate significant revenues. Moreover, television broadcast organizations found it exceedingly difficult to provide news stories because their reports required significantly more time to download than textual material and images.

In 1996, Microsoft launched a joint operation with NBC for a cable news outlet, MSNBC, based in Fort Lee, New Jersey, and a web site, msnbc.com, based at Microsoft headquarters in Redmond, Washington. Despite much fanfare, MSNBC remained mired as the third most popular news channel behind Fox and CNN. NBC took over as the majority holder of the news outlet in 2005, but Microsoft and NBC continue to operate msnbc.com together. It was not until 1998 when Matt Drudge, an Internet gossip columnist, revealed that President Bill Clinton engaged in a sexual affair with a White House intern that the Web got noticed in mainstream America. By 2000, every national news outlet and most local news operation had opened a web site.

A variety of digital software programs, an expansion in computer ownership, and a growth in the capacity of online services made it easier to provide news on the Web. Most of the web sites provided news content for free, but charged for archived material and other special services. A few outlets, such as the *Wall Street Journal*, charged a monthly fee for access to the site. Others, such as the *New York Times*, charged for specific content, such as columnists. Advertisers saw a growing market online, particularly for younger readers and viewers, and started to move campaigns to web sites.

The Project for Excellence in Journalism, a joint project of Columbia University and the Pew Charitable Trusts, viewed journalism on the Web as both positive and negative. "This is an exciting possibility that offers the potential of new audiences, new ways of storytelling, more immediacy, and more citizen involvement," the 2004 report said. "(But) the move to the Web may lead to a general decline in the scope and quality of American journalism, not because the medium isn't suited for news, but because it isn't suited to the kind of profits that underwrite newsgathering."

Newspapers found it easy to create templates for web sites, using such off-the-shelf software programs as Microsoft's Front Page, Macromedia's Dreamweaver, and a host of other programs. Graphics and photographic images could be easily created with such software programs as Macromedia Flash and Fireworks, and Adobe Photoshop. Many specialty software programs could enhance a text-and-image site with relative ease. Another computer program, RSS, or Really Simple Syndication, allowed a computer user to track news sites with constant updates and links to specific locations. The *New York Times* began to use RSS in 2002, and it became the standard for aggregating news content three years later when most Internet browsers included the software.

Broadcast outlets faced greater problems in using the World Wide Web. Simply put, an audio or video story has far more digital information than textual story or image. Nevertheless, radio outlets moved aggressively on to the Internet. A former professor at the Massachusetts Institute of Technology, Carl Malamud, is generally credited with creating the first Internet radio station, Internet Talk Radio, in 1993. He used a digital technology known as multicast backbone, or Mbone, which enables individuals to transmit to other computers. Today, radio and television outlets use a digital technology known as streaming, which means that the media are delivered with only a few seconds delay from an actual live feed. Also, the stream does not actually remain on the computer, but simply passes through as the listener or viewer uses it. Windows Media, RealAudio, and MP3 are the three most popular programs for streaming audio and video.

The popularity of the iPod and similar portable storage devices for audio and video enabled two new technologies to gain popularity. Podcasting, a word created by combining iPod and broadcasting, became widely available in 2005. It should be noted that the name itself is a misnomer since neither an iPod nor an over-the-airwaves broadcast is required to listen to a podcast. The editors of the *New Oxford American Dictionary* declared podcasting the 2005 word of the year. The dictionary defined the term as "a digital recording of a radio broadcast or similar program, made available on the Internet for downloading to a personal audio player." Many news outlets, including newspapers and magazines, created podcasts for individuals to download interviews and other news programs. A vodcast is a video podcast or a video-on-demand broadcast. The first vodcasts appeared in 2005 via iTunes and the Dutch national broadcasting outlet, VPRO. In late 2005, Nova, the science program from the Public Broadcasting System, became the first U.S. broadcasting outlet to offer a vodcast.

An individual can select a specific vodcast offered by a news organization either to watch live or to view later. Even though video downloads have become far more accessible, the broadcasts often lack the quality of material offered on broadcast television. That happens because the vodcasts and other video technologies on the Internet must reduce the size of the broadcast through a process called compression. Compressing a file means that a typical television program, which contains thirty separate scenes each second, will be converted to a file that contains fifteen frames per second. As a result, the audio and visual qualities of the broadcast suffer. Evolving digital technologies, such as iTunes, have improved the quality of news broadcasts over the Internet, but the download times for such programming take significantly longer than compressed videos.

The Advantages and Disadvantages for News Providers and Consumers

Digital information technologies have enabled news providers a greater ability to provide information in a variety of ways on a continuing basis to news consumers. Alternatively, news consumers no longer must depend on news outlets based solely on geographical proximity or time. Simply put, news consumers can read and view literally thousands of web sites throughout the world for information at any time of the day. A news consumer can read only the headlines or dig down to the original documents of an investigation. News consumers can create their own publications, known commonly as "The Daily Me," to focus mainly or solely on the topics in which the individuals have interest.

Even though the technology has made it possible to expand news content, the new systems and programs also have created more pressure on news organizations to provide instantaneous coverage. As a result, factual errors and credibility problems have happened. In an article for the *Harvard International Review*, Reuters Global News director Stephen Jukes outlines some of the basic problems news organizations face in the world of providing news and information every minute of every day. First, he notes that speed causes many errors. Jukes cites two prominent examples: the instantaneous, but often inaccurate, reporting immediately after the U.S. Supreme Court ruled on the 2000 U.S. presidential election. Also, he notes that many television outlets showed Palestinians celebrating the attacks of September 11, 2001. He further comments that the material lacked proper context in that most Islamic countries condemned the attacks.

Second, he points out that as news budgets have dwindled freelance journalists have become major sources of information for news organizations. Because of an increasing dependence on freelancers, it has become difficult to validate the accuracy of the material provided. He notes that news organizations must be significantly more diligent to determine whether the material is accurate. "Digital images are notoriously easy to manipulate," Jukes writes. "There is a new burden of responsibility to verify that the material being offered for purchase is genuine and has not been doctored for propaganda purposes."

Digital technologies, particularly the Internet, have created a significant shift in the reading and viewing of news. Newspapers have seen a significant decline in readership and advertising revenues as more people go to the World Wide Web for their news. Television news also has seen a significant decline in viewers, although it remains unclear whether it is because of increased competition from cable and satellite programming or the World Wide Web or both.

The Pew Research Center for the People and the Press found that online journalism has had a profound influence on U.S. reading and viewing habits. In 2005, an estimated 70 percent of all U.S. adults, or about ninety-seven million people use the Internet for news. Of this number, an estimated 11 percent depend mainly on the Internet for news. That's an increase from 5 percent only three years earlier, and people between the ages of eighteen and twenty-nine have been responsible for the most significant increase.

Digital technologies also enable the individual to play a role in the transmission and creation of news and commentary through Web logs, or blogs, which appear on the Web. The technologies for creating blogs have become increasingly simple to use, enabling anyone with a computer and an Internet connection to provide information, graphics, commentary, and other news for public use. As a result, the number of blogs has grown into the millions throughout the world since they started in 1997.

These technologies became evident during a series of disasters, including the Indian Ocean tsunami in 2004, the London bombings, and Hurricane Katrina in 2005. A flurry of citizen-produced content included blogs of eyewitness accounts, digital photography, and amateur video. But the mainstream media, such as the *New Orleans Time-Picayune*, also turned to the Internet when the newspaper could not print newspapers as a result of Hurricane Katrina. The online traffic of www.nola.com almost tripled in the aftermath of the storm as the news organization provided blogs, photos, and neighborhood forums for evacuees to share information and to reach relatives.

Although the digital revolution has produced significant changes in news, this revolution has occurred primarily in the developed world. Although much discussion has occurred about the so-called "digital divide" in the United States, computer access has grown significantly so that more than 60 percent have Internet access at home.

The same may not be said in many developing countries throughout the world. The vast majority of Web pages exist in English, and the developed world still dominates the use of digital technologies for news and information. Nevertheless, the access of people in the developing world to digital technologies has grown significantly. The World Internet usage shows that while Africa represents 14 percent of the world's population, only 2.3 percent of the continent's 915 million people use the Internet. Despite lagging significantly behind the rest of the world in overall use, Africa saw a four-fold increase between 2000 and 2005.

Asia and the Middle East also have smaller percentages of users when compared with overall populations, while North America, Latin America, Australia, and Europe have larger percentages of Internet users when compared with overall populations. Nevertheless, Internet use almost parallels analog telephone access in many developing countries, which have far fewer telephones than the developed world. Therefore, some experts believe that digital telephones may increase access to and the use of Internet news in the developing world.

Further Reading

Abramson, Albert. *The History of Television 1942 to 2000*. Jefferson, NC: McFarland, 2003.

Hafner, Katie, and Matthew Lyon. *Where Wizards Stay Up Late: The Origins of the Internet*. New York: Touchstone, 1996.

Jukes, Stephen. "Real-Time Responsibility: Journalism's Challenges in an Instantaneous Age," http://hir.harvard.edu/articles/1016/ (accessed April 9, 2007).

Project for Excellence in Journalism. "The State of the News Media 2006," http://www.stateofthenewsmedia.com/2006/ (accessed April 9, 2007).

Wade, Robert Hunter. "Bridging the Digital Divide: New Route to Development or New Form of Dependency?" *Global Governance*, 8, no. 4 (2002): 443–467.

Whittaker, Jason. *The Cyberspace Handbook*. London: Routledge, 2004.

Winston, Brian. *Media Technology and Society: A History From the Telegraph to the Internet*. London: Routledge, 1998.

CHRISTOPHER HARPER

DIGITAL PHOTOGRAPHY

Digital photography—or the recording of photographs with electronic pixels as opposed to film—is the standard practice for capturing journalistic images. In the mid-2000s, close to 100 percent of U.S. newspapers were using digital cameras. Not unlike most digital adaptations in the media, these numbers grew quickly during a short span of about five to seven years. Although digital imaging dates to 1945 with the invention of electronic analog computers, it developed slowly until the 1960s when NASA's exploration of space provided a push in development due to its desire to use digital cameras to document the solar system. Kodak is credited with inventing several cameras in the mid-1970s that "converted light into digital pictures." In 1979, *National Geographic* photographer Emory Kristof was the first to use an electronic camera while photographing life at the bottom of the ocean.

The 1980s were a time of digital experimentation for photojournalists as manufacturers introduced some of their first systems. Sony released the Mavica electronic still camera in 1981, and in 1986, Kodak released the first megapixel sensor and subsequently introduced a system for recording images on disc. During this time the Associated Press also was instrumental in pushing newsrooms toward a digital workflow. The 1982 establishment of the first satellite color photo network improved the speed and quality of AP photos and marked the end of analog transmission. In 1987 the AP introduced a high-speed collection and delivery network for photos that used satellite circuitry and digital technology. In 1990 the organization began delivering photos via satellite to computer terminals at newspapers.

However, newsrooms in the 1980s and into the early 1990s still were primarily using film to record images. Although digital preparation of photographs for publication (or imaging) was gaining momentum (with AP transmissions and the first release of Adobe Photoshop in 1990), most images produced by photographers in the newsroom became digital by using a scanner to digitize a film negative, slide, or printed photo.

The 1991 release of the first professional digital camera system by Kodak and Nikon enabled a larger number of photojournalists to embrace this form of picture-taking. Throughout this decade technology developed quickly and competition drove down the cost of digital cameras. A 1997 a survey of 225 U.S. photo editors indicated that almost all newspapers were digitally imaging photos (or electronically preparing them for publication) at this time, and about 30 percent were using digital cameras to create at least some of the original photographs. Six years later—in 2003—a survey of members of the National Press Photographers Association documented that digital camera use was at 95 percent in American newspapers and moving rapidly toward 100 percent. The mid-2000s was the time when photojournalists' transition to digital cameras and imaging became complete.

The Major Changes

Photojournalists working at the time of the transition from film to digital indicate four common effects from this evolution. They are speed and ease in the gathering and editing processes, improved quality and display of images, increased content (and competition) from citizen journalists, and the need to deal with new ethical considerations. Most of these anecdotal observations are supported by a 2003 study where photographers gauged the advantages and disadvantages of digitization. The study noted that photographers described the most fundamental disadvantage of digitization as limited storage for the increased number of images they are creating.

Speed and Ease of the Gathering Process

Gone were the days of portable, makeshift darkrooms in hotel room bathrooms. Digital photography provided the photojournalist with freedom from chemical processing (which also was better for the environment) and the additional time that comes along with that. Without digital cameras, photographers missed images or sent less-than-timely photos from events just to make deadline, knowing that the processing of negatives would take at least an hour. In addition, with digital cameras there were no more worries about airport x-ray machines, the effects of temperature on film, changing film every thirty-six frames, opening the back of the camera every thirty-six frames and letting in dust, and simply carrying film.

These changes also translated into speed of publication. Digital technology allowed photojournalists to transmit their images from remote locations anywhere in the world with wireless cell phones. They could shoot and transfer files right out the camera onto a live server and onto a network. Images could be immediately transmitted and published online during an event or moments after it.

Improved Quality and Presentation of Images

The freedom from film and processing allowed photographers to concentrate more on shooting. This was probably one of the best benefits. Photographers could stay longer at events translating into better, timelier images for a print publication. (For instance, at a sporting event the photographer could supply his publication with the celebration at the end of a big game as opposed to action from the first half.) In 2003 it was found that photographers were shooting significantly more photos with digital cameras, about eleven photos per assignment overall. The difference was most apparent in sports, where the number of photos taken was about 50 percent more than when film was used. Photographers said this increase was due to an increase in time, ease of shooting and the fact that taking more photos did not translate into a greater financial cost.

Photographs also improved in technical quality at this time due to the viewing screen on the back of the digital camera and the overall image resolution quality. The camera screen allowed photographers to quickly check their lighting, exposure, and composition and to compensate accordingly. This self-selection process also made photojournalists more involved in the picture-editing processes for their publications—whether online or in print. They also became more perceptive in their conversations with picture editors.

As the editor of *News Photographer* magazine observed in November, 2006:

> Everyone has a digital camera now... Of course, the product is different—but now you see pictures from the London Tube bombing, prisoner abuse in Iraq, a plane crashing in someone's yard, the house fire that's out before the fire department and photographers get there.... The Father's Day edition of The Indianapolis Star published the stories of 11 fathers, written by family members. All the photographs were from the families. Anyone with a digital camera, a laptop and an Internet connection now can show a picture to the world..."

As digital cameras became more accessible, so did the number of people taking journalistic photos. The ability for anyone to make and submit a photograph on deadline changed the way professional journalists' gathered news and saturated the market with images. It also changed professionals' relationships with non-professionals, placing them on more of an even playing field.

Online, searchable digital album sites that provided ways for an individual with an Internet connection and digital camera to display and share images also influenced photojournalism. Sites such as flickr.com and buzznet.com became resources for editors looking for particular news photos. Some news organizations set up their own online photo-sharing communities from which to garner images for publication.

Digital photography and the Internet have made the number of images by both professional and amateur shooters increase dramatically since the early 2000s.

Dealing with New Ethical Considerations

Ethical considerations have become a serious issue in photojournalism with digital photography and imaging. Although pre-digital techniques such as burning (or exposing more light to a part of a photographic print) were among a multitude of ways to manipulate images in a darkroom, the ease and quickness of digital changes, as well as the questionable ethical uses of these techniques caused many who once thought still photographs to be unchangeable (and therefore the truth) to doubt that belief.

Additionally, advances in computer technology made the alteration of photographs and other images mostly impossible to detect. The publication of digitally manipulated photos in major publications such as *National Geographic, Time* magazine and the *Los Angeles Times* further encouraged public doubt of journalistic images. In 1982 National *Geographic* digitally relocated pyramids on a photo to make the image fit the cover proportions. (The editor in this instance said the intention was not to deceive his readers. In fact, the cover carried a caption: 'This Picture is a Fake.") *Time* digitally darkened a June 1994 Los Angeles Police Department photo of former football star O.J. Simpson during coverage of his trial for the murders of Nicole Brown Simpson and Ron Goldman. (The magazine referred to the image on the contents page "photo illustration." Eventually, the editor did apologize to his readers for this manipulation.) *Los Angeles Times* photographer Brian Walski used his computer to combine elements of two photographs of a U.S. soldier and Iraqi citizens, taken moments apart, in order to improve the composition. The image was distributed across the Tribune Company's wire service as a single image. Both the *Hartford Courant* and *The Chicago Tribune* used the photograph prominently in their papers in April 2006. When a *Courant* employee noticed the manipulation shortly after publication, Walski was fired, and apologies from the papers followed. (Walski also admitted his lapse in judgment and accepted responsibility for it.)

The ease of image manipulation in the digital age makes trust and high ethical standards 100 percent necessary for photojournalists. Public faith in the veracity of photography is almost as old as photography itself, and as digital techniques advance, it is only fair to insist that photojournalists work to maintain this long-developed trust.

Further Reading

Bellis, Mary. "History of the Digital Camera." InventorsAbout. com. 11 August 11, 2004, Nov 9, 2006; http://inventors. about.com/library/inventors/bldigitalcamera.htm (accessed April 7, 2007).

Dunleavy, Dennis. "A Bird's View of History: The Digital Camera and the Ever-Changing Landscape of Photojournalism." *The Digital Journalist,* February 2006.

Fahmy, Shahira, and C. Zoe Smith, "Photographers Note Digital's Advantages, Disadvantages," *Newspaper Research Journal* 24, no. 2 (Spring 2003): 82–96.

Kobre, Kenneth. "The Long Tradition of Doctoring Photos." *Visual Communication Quarterly* 2 (1995): 14–15.

Mitchell, William J. *The Reconfigured Eye: Visual Truth in the Post-photographic Era.* Cambridge, MA: MIT Press, 1992.

Roberts, Paula, and Jenny Webber. *Visual Truth in the Digital Age: Towards a Protocol for Image Ethics.* Australian Institute of Computer Ethics Conference. Lilydale, Australia, July 1999.

Wheeler, Thomas H. *Phototruth Or Photofiction?: Ethics and Media Imagery in the Digital Age.* Mahwah, NJ: Lawrence Erlbaum Associates, 2002.

LAURA RUEL

DIX, DOROTHY

Mrs. Elizabeth Meriwether Gilmer (November 18, 1870–December 16, 1951), better known as Dorothy Dix, was probably the most celebrated "sob sister" (the term referred to journalists, usually women, who specialized in sentimental stories) in newspaper history with a readership totaling sixty million. At the peak of her professional career, she was both the highest paid and most recognized female journalist in the world.

Born on the Tennessee-Kentucky border in 1870, she eventually migrated to New Orleans, Louisiana, where, after writing short articles for the *New Orleans Picayune*, she was promoted in 1896 to write her own column, "Sunday Salad." Since at the time it was often considered unladylike for a woman to use her read name with a newspaper column, Mrs. Gilmer had little choice but to create a *nom de plume.* "I had always liked the name Dorothy, for some reason. The next thing that popped into my mind that began with a D was Mister Dicks. So I chose that and spelled it Dorothy Dix."

The focus of the column hinged on attitudes about women. Dix believed that both men and women held many misconceptions. She wrote: "It is foolish for girls to think that they have the same chances of marrying that their mothers and grandmothers had. Now, for the girl who is sitting around waiting for some man to come along and marry her, it is a catastrophe to be passed by. She becomes the sour and disgruntled old maid, eating the bitter bread of dependence, the fringe on some family that doesn't want her. Or else she has to take any sort of poor stick of a man as a prop to lean on . . . learn a trade, girls. Being able to make a living sets you free. Economic independence is the only independence in the world."

The column's rapid success, however, also called for a change in its name and it only seemed natural that the column be named after the writer. Thus, "Dorothy Dix Talks" was born. By 1901, Mrs. Gilmer had been hired by William Randoph Hearst and found a home at the *New York Journal.* Initially, she interviewed celebrities and politicians before covering a crime beat and she quickly gained fame for her coverage of murders. Letters seeking her advice did not abate, however, and she continued to write her advice column. By 1917, the Wheeler syndicate asked her to write only the column, which she did, and it became a daily feature of the syndicate. To fill in the extra columns, she began to run letters from her readers, with answers, of course.

Dix's fame was clearly worldwide, and the Australian political term, a "Dorothy Dixer,' came to be known as a type of question that a politician could answer in a way that either supported his party or criticized the opposition. Dix eventually returned to New Orleans, and later to Pass Christian, Mississippi. She died in 1951.

Further Reading

Dorothy Dix Collection. F.G. Woodward Library, Austin Peay State University, Clarksville, TN.

Hermann B. Deutsch, "Dorothy Dix Talks"In *Post Biographies of Famous Journalists*, edited by John E. Drewry, 31. Athens: The University of Georgia Press, 1942.

LLOYD CHIASSON JR.

DORR, RHETA CHILDE

Rheta Childe Dorr (November 2, 1866–August 8, 1948) combined her skills as a writer with her interests as a feminist to engage in advocacy journalism for the general circulation press. She employed the techniques of investigative journalism to uncover women's working conditions, then used her position within the woman's movement to bring about protective legislation. She worked around government restrictions and newspaper hiring practices to travel abroad and succeeded in reporting on some of the most significant events of her time.

Dorr was born in Omaha, Nebraska, one of five children of Lucie N. and Edward P. Childe. After attending the University of Nebraska for two years, she went to New York City, where she sold occasional poems and stories to newspapers. In 1892 she married John Pixley Dorr and moved to Seattle where he was in business. They had a son, Julian, in 1896, but the couple soon clashed over Rheta's independent ways. They separated in 1898, and Rheta returned to New York with her son.

Rheta Childe Dorr had continued working as a correspondent during her marriage and shortly after returning to New York, the American Press Association hired her to write a weekly column on fashion. She gradually established herself in the competitive news industry, and in 1902 landed a job as the women's page editor for the New York *Evening Post*. In addition to the usual columns on food and fashion, Dorr wrote about reforms to which she was deeply committed, including woman suffrage, improved women's working conditions, and attempts by women to organize labor unions. At the same time, her position in several organizations positioned her ideally to work as an advocacy journalist. In 1904, she became chair of the Committee on Industrial Conditions of Women and Children for the General Federation of Women's Clubs, and the following year, became a member of the newly established New York Chapter of the Women's Trade Union League.

Dorr launched her career as a foreign correspondent in

1906 when she made a deal with the *Post*, the Boston *Transcript* and *Harper's Weekly* to cover the coronation of King Haakon of Norway. Once she had completed her assignment, she traveled through Europe, including Copenhagen, where she reported on the meeting of the International Woman Suffrage Alliance.

When Dorr returned to the United States, she went undercover for nearly a year to observe firsthand women's working conditions. She wrote a compelling series that eventually appeared in *Hampton's Magazine* and became the basis of her first book, *What Eight Million Women Want* (1910). She also became more active in the suffrage movement and from 1913 to 1914, was editor of the *Suffragist* for the militant National Women's Party.

When the United States declared war on Germany in 1917, she traveled to Russia as a fully credited war correspondent for the New York *Evening Mail*, one of just a handful of women to attain such accreditation. Her reports about the women's regiment, the "Battalion of Death," extolled the courage of the volunteer fighters, but in the end denounced the Bolshevik revolution as mismanaged and futile.

Dorr continued writing as a foreign correspondent for several papers after the end of World War I and published several books based on her experiences. She remained a feminist till the end of her life.

Further Reading

Beasley, Maurine H., and Sheila J. Gibbons. "War Correspondence." In *Taking Their Place: A Documentary History of Women and Journalism,* 2nd ed. State College, PA: Strata Publishing, Inc., 2003.

Cardinal, Agnes, Dorothy Gillman, and Judith Hattaway, eds. *Women's Writing on the First World War.* Oxford: Oxford University Press, 2002.

Dorr, Rheta Childe. *What Eight Million Women Want.* Boston: Small, Maynard & Co., 1910.

——. *Inside the Russian Revolution.* New York: MacMillan, 1917.

——. *A Woman of Fifty.* New York: Funk and Wagnalls, 1924.

Gottlieb, Agnes Hooper. *Women Journalists and the Municipal Housekeeping Movement 1868–1914.* Lewiston, NY: Edwin Mellen Press, 2001.

Schlipp, Madelon Golden, and Sharon M. Murphy. "Rheta Childe Dorr: Freedom Fighter." In *Great Women of the Press.* Carbondale: Southern Illinois University Press, 1983.

ELIZABETH V. BURT

DOUGLASS, FREDERICK

"The Liberator became my meat and my drink. My soul was set on fire. It sent a thrill of joy through my soul that I had never known before." Frederick Douglass'(1818–February 20, 1895) introduction to the abolitionist press helped transform a runaway slave into a leading spokesman, and eventually, an editor, on behalf of African American freedom. His journey from slave to statesman is a remarkable and unexpected story of the moral force of an individual life and the power of his press.

"I never met a slave who could tell his birthday," Douglass wrote in an 1845 autobiography. Slaves knew their ages, he said, "about as well as horses knew theirs." Plantation documents would later reveal that Frederick Augustus Washington Bailey was born in Talbott County on Maryland's Eastern Shore to Harriet Bailey, a slave. Douglass would later suspect that his father was his white master, Aaron Anthony. When he was six, Douglass was assigned the responsibility of being a companion and caretaker for the son of plantation owner Col. Edward Lloyd. He witnessed his Aunt Hester strung up and forced to stand on her toes and lashed for disobedience "until red blood came dripping to the floor." Two years later he became the household slave of Hugh and Sophia Auld, where he was taught to read the Bible, attended black churches, and began reading the abolitionist press. "From that moment," he later wrote, "I understood the pathway from slavery to freedom."

When he turned fifteen, Douglass learned the trade of ship's caulker as an urban slave in Baltimore. He was able to save enough money to buy a book, *The Columbian Orator*, committing his favorite speeches to memory and impassioned delivery. Douglass courted Anna Murray, a free black domestic servant, and with her help in 1838 escaped on the Underground Railroad to the North, posing as a sailor. The two married in New York City and settled in the whaling port of New Bedford, Massachusetts, where Frederick hoped to find work as a ship's caulker under the alias "Frederick Douglass." White shipbuilders would not work with him, and he was forced to earn money as a common laborer.

In the summer of 1841, Douglass attended a meeting on Nantucket Island of the American Anti-slavery Society, organized by leading abolitionist William Lloyd Garrison, publisher of *The Liberator*. Asked to speak, Douglass proved to be a sensation. "I appear before you as a thief and robber," he told the crowd. "I stole this head, these limbs, this body from my master and ran off with them." At Garrison's urging, Douglass became a leading spokesman for the abolitionist cause. In 1843 the two men left on a six-month tour of anti-slavery meetings in New England, Ohio, Indiana, and Illinois. Crowds were fascinated but incredulous. They had a hard time believing any man so articulate could have been a slave. In 1845, Douglass' abolitionist supporters published his 144-page autobiography, *Narrative of the Life of Frederick Douglass, Written by Himself*, that sold thirty thousand copies on both sides of the Atlantic and was eventually translated into French, German, and Dutch.

Douglass became so famous after the book's wide distribution that he lived in England between 1845 and 1847 to avoid capture by his slave master. His freedom was bought by English admirers for $600. After twenty months abroad, Douglass returned to the United States and in December 1847 moved with Anna to Rochester, New York, a community swept up in religious fervor and reform agitation. There, he launched on December 3, 1847 *The North Star*, an abolitionist paper that took its name from the famous star that slaves followed north to find their freedom. The paper would be widely circulated in the United States and Europe. His July 28, 1848, issue advocated political rights for all Americans. "We hold woman," Douglass wrote in an editorial, "to be justly entitled to all we claim for man." In 1848 he supported the Free Soil Party in its opposition to the extension of slavery into territories that had yet to come into the Union. In 1849 Douglass wrote the party had "subjected this vile abomination of slavery to wide-spread exposure." Two years later Douglass broke with Garrison and other abolitionists by embracing the political platform of Free Soilers. He merged the *North Star* with the *Liberty Party Paper* to establish *Frederick Douglass' Paper.*

During the 1850s, Douglass became increasingly hostile to the slow pace of reform efforts. On July 4, 1852, he reported "the character and conduct of this nation never looked blacker to me." White Americans "may rejoice" at their day of independence, Douglass wrote. "I must mourn." Douglass urged violent opposition following passage of the Fugitive Slave Act that obligated Northerners to capture and return runaway slaves. John Brown, an Ohio farmer, was violently opposed to the extension of slavery into the territory of Kansas. Douglass became his admirer. In 1859 the two men met to consider Brown's plan to lead a slave insurrection after capturing the federal arsenal in Harper's Ferry, Virginia. Douglass considered joining the conspiracy but in the end declined. After the failed raid on October 16, Brown was tried for treason. Douglass wrote, "Posterity will owe everlasting thanks to John Brown. Slavery is a system of brute force that must be met with its own weapons." After Brown's execution on December 2, Douglass argued that only violence could bring down the slave system. "John Brown has initiated a new mode of carrying on the crusade of freedom," he predicted.

The election of Abraham Lincoln, the Republican Party presidential candidate in 1860, pushed southern states into succession. Douglass saw the coming conflict as an opportunity to end "the social degradation" of slavery by lifting African Americans "to a place of common equality with all other men." In the first two years of the fighting, Douglass agitated for the North to end slavery and to enlist black volunteers. Lincoln's Emancipation Proclamation went into effect January 1, 1863, abolishing slavery throughout the South. In August of that year Douglass became the first African American to visit the White House and meet an American president. "I felt big there," Douglass remarked afterward. His job now became the recruitment of black soldiers. His writing and speeches helped enlist the black community in the conflict. "Now or never," Douglass exhorted them. "I urge you to fly to arms and smite with death the power that would bury the government and your liberty in the same hopeless grave. He who would be free must themselves strike the first blow."

Two hundred thousand black soldiers and sailors served, one-tenth of the Union force. Two of Douglass' sons, Charles and Louis, were among the volunteers. Louis became a Sergeant Major in the 54th Massachusetts colored regiment after leading an assault on Fort Wagner guarding Charleston Harbor. As the war wound down, Douglass continued to agitate for a peace that would secure the rights of African Americans. He argued that there should be "no peace but an abolitionist peace. Liberty for all. Chains for none." At the close of the war, Douglass successfully lobbied for passage of the Thirteenth, Fourteenth, and Fifteenth amendments to the U.S. Constitution, abolishing slavery and granting African Americans full citizenship rights, including the vote.

Between 1870 and 1874 Douglass published the *New National Era* from Washington, D.C., where he promoted the uplift of the black community. He moved his family to Cedar Hill, a fashionable fourteen-room house in the Anacostia hills overlooking Washington. In 1874 he became president of the Freedman's Savings Bank, designed to assist the economic development of former slaves. He remained active in the Republican Party until his death. President Rutherford B. Hayes appointed Douglass the U.S. Marshal for the District of Columbia in 1877. James A. Garfield named Douglass the district's Recorder of Deeds in 1881. Benjamin Harrison appointed Douglass ambassador to Haiti in 1889.

Anna Douglass died in 1882 and two years later Douglass created controversy by marrying a white woman, Helen Pitts, who was twenty years younger than Douglass. In his remaining years, Douglass castigated fellow Republicans for failing to stop the state sanctioning of segregation in the South. He fought for a federal anti-lynching law and preached non-violence to blacks frustrated by a lack of racial progress. At his passing, admirers in United States and Europe remembered his clarion call to agitate for social justice. "Without struggle," he had long maintained, "there is no progress."

Further Reading

Foner, Philip Sheldon. *The Life and Writings of Frederick Douglass.* New York: International Publishers, 1950.

Gates, Jr., Henry Louis. *Frederick Douglass Autobiographies.* New York: The Library of America, 1994.

Huggins, Nathan Irvin, and Oscar Handlin. *Slave and Citizen: The Life of Frederick Douglass.* Boston: Little, Brown, 1980.

Lampe, Gregory P. *Frederick Douglass: Freedom's Voice, 1818–1845.* East Lansing: Michigan State University Press, 1998.

McFeely, William S. *Frederick Douglass.* New York: Norton, 1991.

Quarles, Benjamin. *Frederick Douglass.* Washington: Associated Publishers, 1948.

BRUCE J. EVENSEN

DOW JONES & COMPANY

Charles Henry Dow and Edward Davis Jones were reporters for a financial news agency on Wall Street in New York City after each had worked briefly for different newspapers in Rhode Island. As friends and colleagues, Dow and Jones discussed plans for a full-service news agency that would provide bulletins throughout the day on financial items and offer news articles on the activities of bankers, brokers, financiers, and other members of the Wall Street business community. However, their employer was not interested in anything other than bulletins. Dow and Jones, aged thirty-one and twenty-six respectively, along with Charles Bergstresser, began their own news agency on Wall Street in November 1882.

Dow Jones & Company attracted a sizable number of subscribers who received carbon copies of handwritten bulletins and news briefs from messengers throughout each business day. Dow Jones soon issued its first daily two-page news summary, published at the end of business hours. In mid-1884, the company created a list of representative stocks to compute an average closing price to reflect daily stock market activity; this list, gradually including more stocks from various manufacturing sectors, became the Dow Jones Industrial Average in 1896. Dow Jones also arranged to trade information from other important financial centers with news agencies in those cities, which gave subscribers additional essential information.

Dow Jones decided to publish a daily newspaper devoted to national and international financial news. The afternoon *Wall Street Journal* appeared in July 1889. The four-page newspaper published Monday through Saturday, except on days the stock exchanges were closed. It primarily served several thousand subscribers in New York, but newspapers also were shipped by railroad to cities in the northeast and south to Washington, D.C. A morning edition started in 1898; the afternoon edition ceased in 1934 and the Saturday edition closed in 1953.

Jones retired in 1899, as did Dow in March 1902. Clarence W. Barron, the owner of a financial news agency in Boston whose firm was part of the news cooperative with Dow Jones, bought the company. *Barron's*, a weekly financial publication, began in 1921.

Throughout its existence, Dow Jones & Company survived and thrived by editorial and technological innovation, enabling it to collect revenue from a variety of customers and advertisers. Its "ticker" service to banks, brokerages, and other premium clients started in 1897. The first regional edition of the *Wall Street Journal* rolled off presses in 1929, providing timely delivery by using material received from New York by teletypewriter; during the early 1960s, electronic facsimile transmission and satellite relay to a network of printing facilities allowed same-day delivery of the *Journal* in many major cities.

Profitable and dynamic, Dow Jones responded quickly to new media opportunities. It invested successively in suburban newspapers, international financial publications, a radio news service, a cable-television news network, and online news services.

Dow Jones remained an influential and prosperous entity during the early years of the twenty-first century.

Further Reading

Rosenberg, Jerry M. *Inside The Wall Street Journal: The History and the Power of Dow Jones & Company and America's Most Influential Newspaper*. New York: Macmillan Publishing, 1982.
Wendt, Lloyd. *The Wall Street Journal: The Story of Dow Jones & the Nation's Business Newspaper*. Chicago: Rand McNally & Company, 1982.

JAMES LANDERS

DRUDGE REPORT

The Drudge Report, an Internet web site created by Matt Drudge, began in 1996, and was delivered by e-mail and by America Online before finding its primary home at *www.drudgereport.com*. After 1998, a banner headline usually anchored the page, focusing on the top news of the moment. Below the banner were dozens of secondary headlines that usually linked to news stories from web sites of news organizations around the world. The stories linked from the page were as diverse as any newspaper, touching on politics, breaking news, crime and celebrity gossip. The site also linked to dozens of newspapers and columnists. Drudge and his employees updated the site dozens of times each day.

By 2006, Drudge was reporting twelve million hits a day on his site. A study by Comscore found that during the first three months of 2005, the site had 2.3 million unique visitors who visited an average of 19.5 times. The *New York Times* reported that on election night in 2004, more people logged onto the Drudge Report than its own web site. The Drudge Report is often cited as the most well-read blog in the United States.

Matt Drudge was born on October 27, 1966, and grew in Takoma Park, Maryland, where he fell in love with journalism while delivering papers for the *Washington Star*. After working a variety of odd jobs in California, Drudge launched his Drudge Report from a basement apartment in Hollywood. In his early days, he often found news from entertainment sources, and even admitted to digging in the trash to find Nielson ratings that he would be the first to report. Drudge developed a reputation for being right, and first, just enough to earn a regular following of readers. In his autobiography, he says he was the first to name Bob Dole's vice-presidential nominee in 1996 ("a source close to Dole called from a houseboat anchored off San Diego"); first to report Jerry Seinfeld would ask for a million dollars a week or leave his show ("based on a tape recording of Seinfeld's rant leaked to Drudge"); and first to report the merger of Microsoft and NBC (after someone overheard a network executive's conversation in an elevator).

Drudge's biggest scoop came on Saturday, January 17, 1998, when he reported that *Newsweek* magazine held a story alleging President Bill Clinton had an affair with White House intern Monica Lewinsky. Over the next four days, Drudge continued to dole out persistent updates that proved to be accurate; and readers, journalists, and political insiders swarmed to his web site. On Sunday, January 18, Drudge reported Lewinsky had been subpoenaed to give a deposition in the Paula Jones case and he posted Lewinsky's resume. On Monday, Drudge reported news of an affidavit Lewinsky submitted denying any "sexual relationship with President Clinton" and reported that NBC News had obtained a copy of the affidavit. On Tuesday, Drudge reported that Ken Starr, the independent counsel probing the case, was investigating obstruction charges against the president after investigators obtained "intimate taped conversations" of Lewinsky discussing details of her alleged sexual relationship with Clinton. All were bone fide Drudge scoops. On Wednesday, January 21, Drudge reported another bombshell: Lewinsky kept a "garment with Clinton's dried semen on it." The next day, Drudge appeared live on NBC's *Today* show, reporting his scoop on a program that could not confirm the details on its own.

By Wednesday, January 21, the mainstream media finally caught up to Drudge. And in a business that values being first, Matt Drudge established himself as a new player in political journalism. As his memoir makes clear, he did as many reporters do everyday: he worked the phones, tracked down multiple sources, and received tips based on his original reporting that advanced the story.

Drudge's performance in covering the Lewinsky story earned him both scorn and accolades. Some media analysts decried the loss of editors as gatekeepers. Others criticized Drudge's conservative political leanings. He's also made several high-profile mistakes. One of his biggest came during the 2004 presidential election when he erroneously reported that Democratic candidate John Kerry had an affair with an intern.

Drudge was sued for libel in 1997 in a case that raised several potentially groundbreaking legal issues, including whether online speech should be held to a different standard for libel than print publications and just who in cyberspace is considered a publisher under the law. The lawsuit was the result of a story Drudge posted on August 10, 1997, in which he reported that "one influential Republican, who demanded anonymity," claimed court records alleged that Sidney Blumenthal, who was to begin work as a White House aide the next day, had beaten his wife. Within a day, Drudge retracted the story and apologized. Blumenthal filed a $30 million defamation lawsuit against Drudge. Howard Kurtz, the *Washington Post's* media reporter, called the suit "potentially ruinous" and concluded Drudge "doesn't have a terribly strong legal defense." Blumenthal also issued subpoenas to find the identities of Drudge's sources, raising for the first time the question of whether Drudge would qualify as a journalist under a myriad of reporter's shield laws.

After four years of meandering through the courts, Blumenthal dropped the lawsuit and even reimbursed Drudge's attorney for travel costs. Drudge declared victory for the cyber-journalist once again.

Drudge operates in a new medium with different rules, where anyone with motivation and a web site can become a disseminator of news. Some point to the lack of editorial oversight or any ethical cannon of fairness to suggest that Drudge is a threat to journalistic standards. But Drudge is a pioneer in online journalism and political blogging. He says transparency is the greatest strength for this new breed of journalism.

"Everything I print from my apartment, everything I publish I believe to be true and accurate. I put my name on every single thing I write," Drudge told the National Press Club in 1998. "I'll make mistakes. I'll retract them if I have to; apologize for it; try to make it right. But as I've pointed out, the main organizations in this country have let us down every once in a while and end up in trouble with editors. So I don't maintain that an editor is salvation. There won't be editors in the future with the Internet world, with citizen reporting just by the nature of it. That doesn't scare me."

Further Reading

Blumenthal v. Drudge, 992 F. Supp. 44 (D.C. Cir. 1998).

Comscore Networks. "Behavior of the Blogosphere: Understanding the Scale, Composition and Activities of Weblog Audiences," http://www.comscore.com, August 2005.

Davis, Lanny J. *Truth to Tell*. New York: The Free Press, 1999.

Drudge, Matt. *Drudge Manifesto*. New York: New American Library, 2000.

Godwin, Mike. "The Drudge Retort: Is Matt Drudge Guilty of Libel?" *Reason*, February 1998.

Grossman, Lawrence K. "Spot News: The Press and the Dress," *Columbia Journalism Review*, November/December 1998.

Isikoff, Michael. *Uncovering Clinton: A Reporter's Story*. New York: Crown Publishers, 1999.

Kurtz, Howard. "Blumenthals Get Apology, Plan Lawsuit," *The Washington Post*, August 12, 1997.

Kurtz, Howard. "Clinton Aide Settles Libel Suit Against Matt Drudge – at a Cost," *Washington Post*, May 2, 2001.

Kurtz, Howard. "Clinton Scoop So Hot It Melted," *The Washington Post*, January 2, 1998.

Kurtz, Howard. "Cyber-Libel and the Web Gossip-Monger," *The Washington Post*, August 15, 1997.

O'Neil, Robert M. "The Drudge Case: A Look at Issues in Cyberspace Defamation," *Washington Law Review*, July 1998.

Sullivan, Andrew. "Scoop," *The New Republic*, October 30, 2000.

Toobin, Jeffrey. *A Vast Conspiracy*. New York: Random House, 1999.

JASON M. SHEPARD

EDES, BENJAMIN

Benjamin Edes (October 14, 1732–December 11, 1803), along with his partner John Gill, printed one of the most important anti-British newspapers in pre-revolutionary America, the *Boston Gazette*. Edes and Gill took over the *Gazette* from printer Samuel Kneeland and published their first issue of Massachusetts's second oldest paper on April 7, 1755. They continued to print the paper together until the British occupied Boston in 1775.

Born in Charlestown on October 14, 1732, Edes learned the printing trade as an apprentice in Boston. In 1754, Edes and Gill opened their own print shop and printed a prospectus for a new paper, the *Country Journal*. Before they could print their first issue, Kneeland offered the *Gazette* to the pair since Gill had served as an apprentice in Kneeland's shop and had married the printer's daughter. The pair called their paper the *Boston Gazette, or Country Journal*. In 1756, they altered the name, substituting *and* for *or* in the nameplate. It continued to operate under that name until the American Revolution.

Edes was the principal member of a group called the Loyal Nine, which organized following Parliament's passage of the Stamp Act in March 1765. The act required newspapers and other important documents to be printed on stamped paper. The Loyal Nine, along with similar ones in other cities, soon became known collectively as the Sons of Liberty. Realizing the power of the press, Edes turned his into a mouthpiece of opposition to the tax and Britain. The Loyal Nine organized a series of protests that led to anti-Stamp Act riots in August.

The repeal of the Stamp Act did not diminish Edes' involvement with the Patriot cause. He took the lead in the printing partnership, turning the *Gazette* into a mouthpiece of revolution. Fellow Boston printer Isaiah Thomas called Edes a "warm and a firm patriot." John Adams, who wrote under pseudonyms in the paper, said that Edes, Gill, and Samuel Adams spent hours in the *Gazette* office "cooking up paragraphs, articles, occurrences, &c., working the political engine."

After the Battles of Lexington and Concord in April 1775, publication of the paper ceased. Edes escaped the city with his printing wares and resumed publication of the *Gazette* in Watertown in June. There he also published works for the provincial congress of Massachusetts. In November 1776, after British troops left Boston, Edes returned to the city to publish the *Gazette*, and the partnership with Gill, who went in hiding when Boston was occupied, was dissolved. In 1779, Edes formed a partnership with his sons, both of whom began papers that folded. Edes continued to publish the *Boston Gazette* until 1798.

Inflation, depreciation of paper currency, and his sons' failed newspaper attempts soon left Edes with little capital. His monetary woes, coupled with the rise of new printing offices in Boston and old age, ended the *Gazette*'s run. Edes died on December 11, 1803. According to Thomas, "No publisher of a newspaper felt a greater interest in the establishment of the United States than Benjamin Edes; and no newspaper was more instrumental in bringing forward this important event than *The Boston Gazette*."

Further Reading

Copeland, David A. *Debating the Issues in Colonial Newspapers*. Westport, CT: Greenwood Press, 2000.

Davidson, Phillip. *Propaganda and the American Revolution, 1763–1783*. Chapel Hill: University of North Carolina Press, 1941.

Schlesinger, Arthur M. Prelude to Independence: The Newspaper War on Britain 1764–1776. New York: Alfred A. Knopf, 1957.

The Boston Gazette: 1774. Introduction by Francis G. Walett. Barre, MA: The Imprint Society, 1972.

Thomas, Isaiah. *The History of Printing in America*. New York: Weathervane Books, 1970, originally published 1810.

DAVID A. COPELAND

EL DIARIO/LA PRENSA

From coverage of the Great Depression to the Bay of Pigs fiasco in Cuba, from the Sandinista Revolution in Nicaragua to the terrorist attacks of September 11, 2001, *El Diario/La Prensa* (1913–) has provided Spanish-speaking readers in New York with news and analysis of critical world events. The oldest Spanish-language newspaper in New York, *El Diario/La Prensa* continues to offer a different perspective on the news. Its editors admit the newspaper slants its coverage in favor of Latinos and Hispanics, who make up one-fourth of the city's eight million residents. And New York's opinion leaders and politicians take notice. "*El Diario* is one of the primary ways that the Latino community finds out what's going on in the world," New York Mayor Michael Bloomberg told CBS-2 TV in June 2003 for a special report on the newspaper's ninetieth anniversary.

Founded as a weekly in 1913 by Rafael Viera, *La Prensa* became a daily newspaper in 1918. On its ninth anniversary as a daily, *La Prensa* wrote that it wants to be a mirror for the Hispanic community as well as a source of news about readers' native countries. In 1963, it merged with *El Diario*, which had been started in the 1950s to serve the growing population of immigrants from the Caribbean. The newspaper was widely appreciated for its "human relations department," which helped the new immigrants get help in education, health and social services. Among the celebrities to be interviewed in the *El Diario/La Prensa*'s pages were the actresses Dolores del Rìo, Mario Moreno "Cantinflas," and Marìa Fèlix. The newspaper closely followed the singing career of Guadalupe Victoria Yoli Raymond, better known as "La Lupe." A former editor, Manuel de Dios Unanue, was gunned down in a New York restaurant in 1992 by a member of a Colombian drug cartel who was later convicted. Unanue had published a book about the inner workings of the Medellin Cartel in 1988.

The circulation of *El Diario/La Prensa* is about fifty thousand, just edging its chief rival newspaper, *Hoy*, with which it has been locked in a tight battle for circulation since *Hoy*'s founding in 1998. *Hoy* was found to have inflated its circulation figures by 46 percent in 2003. The National Association of Hispanic Publications routinely names *El Diario/La Prensa* as one of the best Hispanic daily newspapers. *El Diario/La Prensa* is owned by Impre-Media LLC, which was formed in 2004 and also owns *La Opinion* of Los Angeles and *La Raza* in Chicago. In 2006, *El Diario/La Prensa* had about fifty journalists in the newsroom, and they were supplemented with freelancers as well as correspondents based in Latin America. *El Diario/La Prensa* made its own news in its ninetieth anniversary year when its top editor, Gerson Borrero, resigned that position but stayed as a columnist to protest the newspaper owners' decision not to publish a column by Cuban President Fidel Castro. The newspaper owners later apologized for killing the column. "Mistakes must be admitted so we can learn from them," said a letter to readers signed by Publisher Rossana Rosado along with Douglas Knight and John Paton of the Canadian company Knight Paton Media, one of the investors in ImpreMedia.

Further Reading

Borrero, Gerson. "Some Good Always Comes Out of the Bad," *Gotham Gazette* (November 2003), http://www.gothamgazette.com/citizen/nov03/spanish_eldiario.shtml (accessed April 9, 2007).

Gersh Hernandez, Debra. "Spanish-Language Papers Vie for Readers," *Presstime* (March 2004): 19.

"*La Prensa* Cumple Hoy su Noveno Año de Servicio, como Diario, a la Colonia Hispana," *La Prensa* (June 4, 1927), http://www.eldiariony.com/especiales/90/detail.aspx?id=638537&SectionId=46 (accessed April 9, 2007).

Ruiz, Albor. "*El Diario* Apologizes for Muzzling Castro," *New York Daily News* (October 23, 2003): 3.

KRIS.KODRICH

EL NUEVO HERALD

With its vibrant Cuban influence, vigorous international tourism and commerce, steamy nightlife, and tropical postmodern architecture, Miami presents a cultural mix befitting a true Latin American capital residing at the southern edge of the United States. The *Miami Herald* tried to capture and reflect this diversity over the years but never quite got it right. Finally, it started another newspaper. *El Nuevo Herald* (1987–) traces its roots to a Spanish-language insert named *El Herald* that began in 1976, and renamed *El Nuevo Herald* in 1987. It merely provided translations of some *Miami Herald* stories. In 1998 the newspaper was transformed into its own entity with its own stories, style, and viewpoint. As the newly transformed newspaper's first editor-in-chief, Carlos M. Castaneda, described his aim to *Columbia Journalism Review* in 2000, "I want stories that affect the pockets and the hearts of people." Alberto Ibargüen, who oversaw both Knight-Ridder newspapers as chairman of the *Miami Herald* Publishing Company, had been pushing to make *El Nuevo Herald* more independent since he arrived in Miami in 1995 as *El Nuevo Herald*'s editor. "We covered Miami, Cuba and Latin America. Those were our three stories, in politics, arts and sports," he told the *Harvard International Journal of Press/Politics* in 1999.

According to the 2000 census, about 57.3 percent of 2.3 million people living in Miami had Hispanic or Latino roots. Only New York and Los Angeles had larger Spanish-speaking markets. It was not always that way. Only about one hundred thousand Hispanics lived in Miami in 1960, but with Fidel Castro in power in Cuba, thousands more Cubans began streaming into Miami. Traditionally a liberal newspaper, the *Miami Herald* was not much to the liking of the conservative anti-Castro exile community. *El Nuevo Herald* has been able to keep a tight focus on the Cuban community. "It's a different world that they cover," Martin Baron, the *Miami Herald*'s executive editor, told Nieman Reports in 2001.

With a circulation of eighty-nine thousand in 2005, *El Nuevo Herald* was among the largest-circulation U.S. daily newspapers in Spanish. The National Association of Hispanic Publications recognized *El Nuevo Herald* as the best U.S. Spanish-language daily newspaper in 2005. The journalism staff for *El Nuevo Herald* then numbered about 67, compared with 379 for the *Miami Herald*, which had a circulation of about 312,000. The content of *El Nuevo Herald* focused extensively on Latin American issues and culture, covering Hispanic soccer stars and singers with the style of a celebrity magazine; performers like Gloria Estefan and Ricky Martin were featured. Meanwhile, its local news coverage centered heavily on the exile community and the newspaper's conservative, anti-Castro politics aim to please. For example, *Nieman Reports* found that the coverage of the return of Elian Gonzalez to Cuba in 2000 was covered much differently in the two newspapers, with *El Nuevo Herald* taking an anti-Castro stand in both its news and op-ed pages. The day federal agents removed Elian from the home of his Miami relatives, *El Nuevo Herald* featured a headline "Que Verguenza!" ("How Shameful!") and an accompanying photograph showing the boy with a gun-pointing agent.

Further Reading

Clary, Mike. "Would You Create Another Newspaper to Compete with Your Own? In Miami, the Herald Did." *Columbia Journalism Review* 39, no. 1 (May/June 2000): 56–58.
Gutierrez, Barbara. "*El Nuevo Herald* Provides a Latin American Take on the News." *Nieman Reports* 55, no. 2 (Summer 2001): 37–39.
McEnteer, James. "In Miami, Mañana Is Now." *The Harvard International Journal of Press Politics* 4, no. 3 (1999): 113–121.

KRIS KODRICH

ENTERTAINMENT PRESS

The relationship of journalism to the entertainment media changed in important ways with the rise of movies in the early twentieth century. For the local newspaper the key relationship was the review (really preview) of the upcoming movie, as well as profiles of stars and the regular revenue from advertising movie schedules. *Variety* started with reviews in 1907. The *New York Times* commenced in 1913. Nearly all newspapers in 1915 reviewed D.W. Griffith's *The Birth of a Nation*.

Early on, audiences needed the guidance of film reviewers on two levels. The simple consumer reporting aspect of the review was vital. Does the reviewer recommend the new film or not? At the same time, the art form was still new and film fans were learning how to interpret the emerging syntax of film. Yet remarkably as the narrative form—with stars—became what is now called the Classical Hollywood Cinema, by 1920 journalistic assessment of a film was formalized. Although audiences have grown slightly more sophisticated, film reviewers are still doing what reviewers did in the 1920s. Movie reviewing is a standard journalistic beat.

Carl Sandburg, for example, wrote movie reviews between 1920 and 1928 for the *Chicago Daily News*. Consider the one he wrote for the now classic Keaton's *The General*. Published January 18, 1927, it reads little different that what one might read seventy-five years later:

"If they'll put Buster Keaton at the head of the armies next time there's a war his maneuvers will bring that war to a pleasant, painless and prompt conclusion, because the belligerents will simply die laughing…. *The General*, we are told, is based upon historical fact and treats in a lighter vein an incident during the Civil War known as 'the Andrews railroad raid,' which occurred in the spring of 1862 when a band of Union soldiers invaded Confederate territory and captured 'The General,' one of the South's crack railroad engines. Buster plays the part of Johnnie Gray, the young railroad engineer who piloted 'The General,' and Marion Mack is Annabelle Lee, his sweetheart…. Annabelle

…happens to be in the baggage car when the raid takes place and is carried off into the enemy country—Johnnie in hot pursuit—neither of glory nor his sweetheart, but of his beloved engine. How this pursuit covers him with honor; jumps him into the rank of commissioned officer and throws him into the arms of his adored one must be seen to be appreciated."

Sandburg ended with his recommendation: "The [photo] play is chuck full of hilarity, pathos and thrills, such as when Johnnie chases himself with a loaded cannon; attempts to burn down a bridge and gets on the wrong side of the fire; shoots a cannon into the air and with fool's luck hits the dam that floods the river and puts the enemy to rout…. If you want a good laugh, don't miss The General."

Newspapers and the Hollywood Tradition

Film reviewers write for newspapers and their work is primarily read to help the reader decide whether or not to see a particular movie. They are journalists. A secondary purpose of a film review is to help the reader to appreciate film as an art as Sandburg shows us. Film reviewers present their own opinions as a tool for others' use.

Part of the difficulty inherent in film reviewing is that it is simultaneously a form of consumer reporting (what is the film about? who's in it?), a statement about the worth of a film (is the movie good or not?), a teaching opportunity (how is this film an example of film comedy?). When these things come together, as Sandburg demonstrated, it is journalism that enlightens, entertains, and is useful in deciding whether or not to go see the movie.

The reviewer must select just enough of the most important plot points and present them in a way that makes the thrust of the narrative clear. The well-written review is enjoyable to read, and the informal prose of the good writer is as subjective as can be. Style is a remarkably personal element, and one which is due at least as much to personal talent as to technical skill. Entertainment lies in how the information is expressed.

Where many reviewers run into trouble with their readers is in the evaluative section of their review. What are the criteria? Usually the reviewer seeks a good story, acting that is seamless with the characters, and a twist that makes this film story just slightly more complex and clever that the average narrative film.

For example, James Agee, who reviewed for the *Nation* and *Time* in the 1940s, wrote intensely personal and seemingly casual columns. His first column for the *Nation* set out his goals: "I would like so to use this column about moving pictures as to honor and discriminate the subject" and thereby serve "you who are reading it. It is my business to conduct one end of a conversation, as an amateur critic among amateur critics." Agee presented himself as a participant in a discussion rather than an authority laying down the objective truth about films, and that was part of his skill. His columns read like a post-movie chat with a friend; they are the answer to "So, what did you think of the film?" More importantly, he saw himself as a devotee or admirer of cinema rather than as someone laying down immutable laws about what was good or bad. Agee presented himself as a film lover writing for other film lovers, not primarily as an arbiter of taste.

Classic Reviewing

Bosley Crowther was the nation's foremost film reviewer as he penned review after review from 1938 to 1967. His career presented a classic case of the reviewer in the pre-television age. Throughout his nearly thirty years of movie reviewing, the *New York Times* editors considered Crowther just a specialized reporter with a beat he learned on the job. Crowther's movie reviewing career started in college where he served as an editor of the *Daily Princetonian*, and in his senior year, 1928, won a national essay contest sponsored by the *New York Times*. For his writing performance, Bosley was offered a job on the city beat. In 1933, Brooks Atkinson asked Crowther to join the Drama Department. He spent five years covering the theater scene in New York and then in 1938 changed desks and began writing for the Movie Department. Two years later he became the chief film critic for the *Times*. During his tenure, Crowther wrote an average of about 150 reviews a year. His beat required two or three reviews each week plus a lengthy Sunday column in which he would comment on the movie scene in general. In 1967—at age sixty-two—after nearly thirty years on this beat, Crowther stepped down from his position as chief critic. Crowther had a national, even international, profile at the *New York Times*, and his career set an example for many other critics whose reviews appeared in hundreds of newspapers across the country.

Radio

As Crowther and other newspaper reviewers tended their craft in the 1930s, national radio became a factor with which journalists had to reckon. Although radio stations were often owned by newspapers and seen as direct competitors, radio on the local level never developed reviewers per se. Radio more often offered gossip, and two women gossips dominated the airwaves.

Hedda Hopper started as a movie and radio actress. She failed at both professions. What came next? In 1939, on CBS, she launched *The Hedda Hopper Show*. Louella Parsons had achieved success for rival NBC, and Hopper came to challenge her. Hopper's ratings were not tremendous but good enough for sponsor Sunkist to keep her on CBS until 1947 and then picked up by NBC until 1951. She also did a five-minute chat show with Hollywood's big names. Gossip was never in short supply on these broadcasts, and the stars and their films got plugs galore. She would report almost any rumor, but to her credit, she was quick to confess her mistakes, and spent much of her time on the radio making amends. She played a game with the studios and her listeners, getting leaks from studio public relations departments that had been calculated to increase the box-office. Unlike her rival Parsons, Hopper did not start her gossiping in the

newspapers. She started out in radio and was so successful in programs on both CBS and NBC during her airwaves career; she then became a nationally syndicated newspaper columnist.

Louella Parsons had a style all her own. She gushed and came over the radio as sweet as honey. If you listened closely, you could almost hear her breathless praise. But she was known to drip venom, too. Louella did try her hand at acting, but she was meant to be a Hollywood gossip. During the town's heyday, she was probably the best known film industry chronicler in the land. She started her famous career writing for the Hearst newspapers. She was learning with NBC what would work on the radio. Indeed, she took to radio in reaction to the model Hedda Hopper initiated in 1939. In 1945, ABC signed her to do a fifteen-minute show on Sunday nights, following Walter Winchell on ABC. The duo gave ABC its top-rated half hour. Thereafter for seven years, Parsons had a steady audience and fought Hopper for the title of "Queen of Radio Gossips." Only the coming of television ended their "orchestrated feud" in 1952.

Newspapers and Reviewing Radio Entertainment

Radio stations carried their own entertainment to be reviewed. From the creation of NBC in November 1926 and CBS three months later, U.S. newspapers carried brief descriptions of programming. So with the networks came examples such as Ben Gross who pioneered a regular column about broadcasting in the *New York Daily News*, which he continued for forty-five years. Newspapers across the United States added columns about schedules, programs, and celebrities during radio's network era in the 1930s and 1940s. Yet the reviewing never developed. For example, a Gallup poll of radio reviewing in newspapers that appeared in *Fortune* in the April, 1939, came to the following conclusion. Question: Do you read the columns in the newspapers about the radio stars and programs? Answer: 1/3rd "Yes", "1/3rd occasionally," and 1/3rd "Never." Yet the third who read about radio in newspapers were addicted. Yet there was never a prestige to radio show reviewing that there was to what such critics as Bosley Crowther wrote about movies in print.

But gossip was an important part of radio programming. Everyone wanted to know the truth about celebrities—whether movie or radio stars. Radio made the gossip genre part of broadcasting that would continue with television.

Television

The coming of television changed a newspaper/radio reviewing mix. Newspapers reviewed TV shows in the same manner as movies. Jack Gould, for example, was a TV reviewer for the *New York Times* from 1947 to 1972, complementing Crowther's film reviews for much of that period. Early on, newspaper writers had to view the live shows in rehearsal or at the same time as the audience. With the coming of videotape in the late 1950s, the networks could send the entertainment programming on tapes to newspaper reviewers ahead of time so they could truly review the shows like film critics.

The big change came with reviewing in a specific magazine, *TV Guide*; with reviewing films on television with Gene Siskel and Roger Ebert; and then with TV gossip in the Parsons and Hopper tradition with *Entertainment Tonight*. When the average television fan wanted a review, they read *TV Guide*. Walter Annenberg—inspired by a Philadelphia area television magazine called *TV Digest*—conceived the idea of publishing a national television feature magazine, which he would then wrap around local television listings. Annenberg purchased *TV Digest*, along with the similar publications in other cities such as *TV Forecast* from Chicago, and *TV Guide* from New York. He combined their operations to form *TV Guide*. The first issue—covering the week April 3–9, 1953, featured Lucille Ball and Desi Arnaz's real life son, Desi Jr. As TV spread to 99 percent of American homes, Annenberg expanded the magazine by creating new regional editions and purchasing existing television listings publications in other markets.

Reviewing came when Annenberg and his aide, Merrill Panitt (who would go on to become *TV Guide's* editorial director), realized that in order to achieve the circulation necessary to make their publication a truly mass medium, they needed to go beyond the fan magazine approach that had been typical of most earlier television and radio periodicals. They therefore created a magazine that was both a staunch booster of the American system of television, yet at times also one of the most visible critics of the medium's more egregious perceived shortcomings. In fact, *TV Guide's* greatest accomplishment under Annenberg may have been the magazine's success in walking the fine line between encouraging and prodding the medium to achieve its full potential without becoming too far removed from the prevailing tastes of the mass viewing public.

As a consequence, *TV Guide* became extremely popular, widely read, and very influential among those in the television industry. A large number of distinguished authors wrote articles for the magazine over the years, including Margaret Mead, Betty Friedan, John Updike, Gore Vidal, and Arthur Schlesinger, Jr. Many of these writers were attracted by the lure of reaching *TV Guide's* huge audience. At its peak in the late 1970s, *TV Guide* had a paid circulation of nearly twenty million copies per week. In 1988 Annenberg cashed out and sold *TV Guide* to Rupert Murdoch's News Corporation in 1988 for approximately $3 billion—at the time, the largest price ever commanded for a publishing property. Murdoch then changed the tenor and influence of the magazine by using it to boost his Fox Television Network.

Because of television, Roger Ebert became perhaps the most recognizable film reviewer of the last quarter of the twentieth century. Although his column for the *Chicago Sun-Times* won the first Pulitzer Prize given for film reviewing, most movie fans associated him with his TV show. Partnered with *Chicago Tribune* reviewer Gene Siskel—and after Siskel's death, with critic Richard Roeper—Ebert's show with its trademark thumbs up or thumbs down should be credited with turning the TV set into a reviewing machine with clips, not descriptions.

They played TV parts: Siskel was the tall, thin one who looked and acted like a dower university professor, while Ebert, rolly-poly, played the curmudgeon, lover of Hollywood, and was willing to say filmgoing was not so serious, but great fun.

They started on the local PBS Chicago outlet WTTW in September 1975. When the two critics disagreed, sparks often flew to the delight of viewers. After two seasons, the successful series was retitled *Sneak Previews* and appeared biweekly on the PBS network. By its fourth season, the show became a once-a-week feature on 190 outlets and achieved status as the highest rated series in the history of public broadcasting.

The two stars left PBS in 1981 to launch *At the Movies* for commercial television under the banner of Tribune Entertainment, a syndication arm of the *Chicago Tribune*. Basically utilizing the same format as *Sneak Previews*, the significant change came as the reviewing was shortened for advertisements. In 1986, citing contractual problems with Tribune Entertaiment, Siskel and Ebert departed for Disney, a major studio. The series became simply *Siskel & Ebert*. It set the standard offering reviews—with clips—for more than four thousand films over twenty-two years.

In his defense of television film reviewers, Ebert pointed out the show was the first national venue to discuss the issue of film colorization, the benefits of letterbox, video dubbing and the technology of laser disks. And, in May 1989, extolling the virtues of black and white cinematography, they videotaped their show in monochrome—the first syndicated program to do so in twenty-five years. Ebert argued their appeal came from their disagreements—two friends who had seen a movie and discussing their differences of opinion. In February 1999, an era ended when Siskel died unexpectedly. But the standard and principles of the genre had been set.

In 1981 a new type of show began: *ET* (*Entertainment Tonight*) This Paramount studio syndicated show about movies and television continued the tradition of Parsons and Hopper. *ET* provided the latest gossip from the entertainment world in what seemed like a newscast. For more than generation, *ET* has aired in first-run syndication (in November 2000 it aired its five thoudsandth show), maintaining consistently high ratings. The brainchild of Al Masini, otherwise known for creations such as *Lifestyles of the Rich and Famous*, *ET* was an "infotainment" magazine presenting news-style coverage focused on the world of entertainment—but from a Paramount point of view. Rather than receive the show physically (on tape via courier), local stations could tape the satellite broadcast of the show and air it at their convenience anytime that same day. This meant that the show had the "up-to-the-minute" feel of a newscast.

ET looked like a newscast (complete with two anchors, a man and woman who introduced stories from a desk in a studio) and emphasized freshness with such features as "today's" celebrity birthdays. For Paramount studio, the program's producer, it meant free public relations for Paramount movies and TV shows, being made across the lot. By the start of the second season, Mary Hart was a star and would remain the show's hostess into the twenty-first century. *ET* thus took news gathering seriously (the Associated Press cites the show as a source, and Hart has been inducted into the Broadcasting and Cable Hall of Fame) but recognized that the "puff" pieces were what made the show attractive. The successful *ET* formula became a proven gossip strategy for the late twentieth and early twenty-first centuries.

Further Reading

Adkins, Gale. "Radio-Television Criticism in the Newspapers: Reflections on a Deficiency." *Journal of Broadcasting*, Summer 1983.

Agee, James. *Agee on Film: Reviews*. Boston: Beacon, 1964.

Arledge, Roone. *Roone: A Memoir*. New York: HarperCollins, 2003.

Altschuler, Glenn C., and David I. Grossvogel.. *Changing Channels: America in TV Guide*. Urbana: University of Illinois Press, 1992.

Barbas, Louella. *The First Lady of Hollywood: A Biography of Louella Parsons*. Chapel Hill: University of North Carolina Press, 2005.

Broddy, Larry. *Turning Points in Television*. NewYork: Citidel Press, 2005.

Ebert, Roger. "All Stars or, Is There a Cure for Criticism of Film Criticism." *Film Comment*, May/June 1990.

Eells, George. *Hedda and Louella*. New York: Warner Library, 1973.

Gould, Lewis L. Editor. *Watching Television Come of Age: The New York Times Reviews by Jack Gould*. Austin: University of Texas Press, 2002.

Haas, Ealasaid. "A Peculiar Form of Journalism: A Peculiar Form of Journalism: The Art of Film Reviewing," master's thesis, Stanford University, 2001.

Laurent, Lawrence. "Wanted: the Complete Television Critic." In *The Eighth Art*. New York: Holt, Rinehart and Winston, 1962.

Orlik, Peter B. *Critiquing Radio and Television Content*. Boston: Allyn & Bacon, 1988.

"Radio Industry." *Fortune*, April, 1939.

Register to the Bosley Crowther collection: MSS 1491 Harold B. Lee Library. Departmenrt of Archives and Manuscripts. Brigham Young University.

Seldes, Gilbert. *The Public Arts*. New York: Simon and Schuster, 1956.

Shayon, Robert Lewis. *Open to Criticism*. Boston: Beacon Press, 1971.

Smith, Ralph Lewis. *A Study of the Professional Criticism of Broadcasting in the United States*. New York: Arno Press, 1973.

Variety Radio Directory, 1938–1939.

Watson, Mary Ann. "Television Criticism in the Popular Press." *Critical Studies in Mass Communication*, March, 1985.

Westin, Av. *Newswatch: How TV Decides the News*. New York: Simon and Schuster, 1982.

DOUGLAS GOMERY

ESPIONAGE ACT OF 1917

Congress passed the Espionage Act on June 15, 1917, little more than two months after the United States entered World War I. In May, President Woodrow Wilson had argued that it was "absolutely necessary to the public safety" and "for the protection of the nation" that the government have the "authority to exercise censorship over the press" (*New York Times*, May 23, 1917, 1).

The Espionage Act had two provisions related to censorship. One made it a felony to attempt to thwart recruiting or enlistments into the U. S. armed services, or to try to cause insubordination in the armed forces, or to communicate false information in an effort to hinder the work of the military. Violators could be imprisoned for up to twenty years and/or fined $10,000. The second provision gave the postmaster general the authority to ban from the mail material deemed to be treasonable or seditious. It imposed a maximum penalty of either $5,000 or five years in prison. Albert Burleson, who was postmaster general, used his power to deny access to the mails aggressively and often capriciously during the war.

In subsequent months, additional legislation and presidential executive orders strengthened the power of the government over the press. (In addition, several states also enacted legislation similar to, or even more severe than, the federal Espionage Act, and many of these measures remained in force long after the war ended.) On October 6, 1917, Congress passed the Trading-with-the-Enemy Act which increased the president's authority to censor international communications and which invested the postmaster general with immense power over the foreign language press in America. Shortly after this act, President Wilson created by executive order a Censorship Board, of which the postmaster general was a member, to further strengthen the censorship of messages in an out of the country. (President Wilson had already taken control of the Transatlantic Cable in an executive order in April, 1917). On May 16, 1918, an amendment designed to strengthen the Espionage Act became law. Known as the Sedition Act, it outlawed "disloyal, profane, scurrilous, or abusive language about the form of government of the United States, or the Constitution…, of the military or naval forces…, or the uniform of the army or navy…, or any language intended to bring the form of government of the United States, of the Constitution…, or the flag of the United States, or the uniform of the army or navy… into contempt, scorn, contumely, or disrepute." For many people, this amendment to the Espionage Act recalled the appalling Sedition Act of 1798, even though it was more restrictive than the earlier law. Whereas the earlier law had forbidden criticism of specific individuals (e.g., the President and members of Congress), the latter legislation prohibited criticism of the government itself.

More than two thousand people were indicted under the Espionage Act and more than one thousand were convicted. German-language newspapers, socialist and pacifist publications, and Irish-American papers were among those that fell under suspicion. In August, 1917, the government let it be known that it was on the lookout for "anti-American utterances" and would suppress pro-German publications (*New York Times*, August 19, 1917, 13). In September, five people who worked at the *Philadelphia Tageblatt* were arrested and required to post $10,000 bail for allegedly distorting war news to favor Germany. Burleson suspended the second-class mailing privileges of the paper and those of the *Philadelphia Sonntagsblatt*. In October, in Newark, officials seized the *New Jersey Freie Zeitung* (founded in 1858), and arrested the paper's owners and editors. Other German-language publications also suffered during the war.

Socialists and pacifists fared no better. The post office barred several issues of *The Masses*, described by the *New York Times* as "Max Eastman's anarchist magazine." In November, a federal grand jury indicted Eastman, John Reed, and five other members of the *Masses* business or editorial staff for conspiracy under the Espionage Act. (*New York Times*, November 20, 1917, 4). News dealers pulled back from distributing *The Masses* for fear they would be prosecuted under provisions of the Trading-with-the-Enemy Act. Also excluded from the mails were many other publications including the *American Socialist*, the *International Socialist Review*, and *Appeal to Reason*. In early 1918, Victor Berger, the former Wisconsin congressman and editor of the *Milwaukee Leader*, was charged with "obstructing recruiting, encouraging disloyalty, and interfering with the prosecution of the war" (*New York Times*, March 10, 1918, 1). He was sentenced to twenty years in federal prison although the U. S. Supreme Court later overturned the conviction in 1921. In late June, 1918, Eugene V. Debs, the socialist leader who had four times run for president, was arrested in Cleveland for violating the Sedition Act. The *New York Times* reported that Debs had told his audience that "they were fit for something better than cannon fodder" (*New York Times*, July 1, 1918, 1). Debs went to prison in Atlanta and from there ran for president in 1920, receiving more than nine hundred thousand votes. In 1921, President Warren Harding commuted Debs' sentence to time served.

Irish-American newspapers came under suspicion for publishing propaganda that attempted to undermine relations between the United States and the Allies. The *Gaelic American*, the *Irish World*, the *Freeman's Journal*, and the *Bull* were among the papers denied mailing privileges. The *Gaelic American*, a New York weekly sympathetic to Sinn Fein, was investigated on charges that the paper had attacked the United States Secret Service by claiming that it worked to promote the interests of England (*New York Times*, November 10, 1917, 8). The *Irish World* came under attack for its criticism of English policy toward Palestine; *Freeman's Journal* similarly came under suspicion for hostility toward England. The *Bull's* editor, Jeremiah O'Leary, was charged with publishing articles and cartoons that advocated rebellion against England; he suspended publication of the paper after it was barred from the mail (*New York Times*, October 17,1917, 9).

The Espionage Act and more generally the repression during World War I stimulated much consideration about how to protect civil liberties. In July, 1917, the Civil Liberties Bureau was created and the following October became known as the National Civil Liberties Bureau. The U. S. Supreme Court upheld the constitutionality of the Espionage Act after the war in such notable cases as *Schenck* (1919) and *Abrams* (1919), although in the latter case Justices Oliver Wendell Holmes and Louis D. Brandeis dissented and began to argue for a broader interpretation of the First Amendment using the idea of "clear and present danger." It was an important step that eventually led to stronger legal protections for free speech.

Although the Sedition Act was repealed on March 3, 1921, the original Espionage Act was left intact and throughout the twentieth and into the twenty-first centuries, it remained one of the primary statutes the U.S. government used to combat espionage and the unauthorized release of national defense secrets. In 1955, Senator Hubert Humphrey noted, though, that the 1917 act had never really been studied to make sure that it was adequate to meet the needs of a more modern era of "hydrogen bombs, radar, and guided missiles." During the Cold War, the Espionage Act helped to create what Senator Daniel Patrick Moynihan called a "culture of secrecy." In 1971, the Richard M. Nixon administration attempted, unsuccessfully, to use it to prevent the *New York Times* from publishing the Pentagon Papers. During the subsequent war on terrorism, and as late as 2006, the U. S. government continued to threaten journalists who published classified material with prosecution under the Espionage Act.

Further Reading

Chafee, Zechariah, Jr. *Free Speech in the United States*. Cambridge, MA: Harvard University Press, 1964, originally published 1941.
Moynihan, Daniel Patrick. *Secrecy: The American Experience*. New Haven, CT: Yale University Press, 1998.
Murphy, Paul L. *World War I and the Origin of Civil Liberties in the United States*. New York: W. W. Norton, 1979.

STEPHEN VAUGHN

ETHICS

Since the first newspaper in America (*Publick Occurrences*) appeared in 1690 in Boston, journalists and news organizations have been criticized and their actions and behaviors have been scrutinized by the public, the government, and peers. With the ratification of the First Amendment of the Bill of Rights in 1791, journalism and freedom of the press became more a part of U.S. democracy and American citizens gradually came to expect the press to have certain obligations to the public. These included truth-telling, social responsibility, and a commitment to inform the public as fairly and accurately as possible—ideals expressed during the late 1880s, when journalism started to become more of a profession than a trade. The topic of "journalism ethics" surfaced in publications at this time, and from that point forward critics increasingly examined and evaluated the ethical behavior of newspaper publishers, editors, and reporters.

Publications in colonial America during the early eighteenth century began setting the basic foundations for the newspapers of the future by publishing information concerning matters of public interest. Publishers and those who worked for them had their own ideas about what a newspaper should be and what, if any, standards should be maintained. Because each paper had its own goals, it is difficult to generalize about newspaper standards or principles of behavior. "News" stories were often biased or opinionated. The idea of objectivity did not appear to be an important factor in decisions about what information went into the news pages.

Journalism played an important part in the American Revolution, and because of its role, it gained in stature. Essays by pamphleteers and political statements in newspapers articulated principles of the newly emerging republic. Many people simply assumed they knew what constituted virtue, truth, and liberty. Journalists who followed these self-evident values were thought to be able to exercise "a corrective influence on government, manners and morals." (Robert Fortner, *Journalism History*, 1978). Thomas Jefferson, who drafted the Declaration of Independence, wrote in 1787, in what has become an often-quoted line: "If it were left to me to decide whether we should have a government without newspapers or newspapers without government, I would choose the latter."

But the early press in America often failed to pursue virtue, truth, and liberty. George Henry Payne, in his *History of Journalism in the United States*, commented in 1924 that "manners of men [were] rude, and ... journalism developed ... as more or less illegitimate or 'poor white' brother of literature." Most newspapers in the early Republic were influenced by political parties and their reporting was strongly biased in favor of the party that sponsored them. Criticism and commentary on public issues often included personal attacks on public officials.

During the 1830s, the Penny Press, which appealed to the common man of the Jacksonian era, challenged the influence of the partisan newspapers. Sensational news articles sold papers, and, because of their low cost, the Penny Press newspapers were widely accessible to citizens. Here was news for the masses, not just the privileged. Many scholars hardly considered this new style of journalism an improvement. The historian Frank Luther Mott said of the Penny Press that its sins included "bad taste; coarseness, which sometimes became indecency, overemphasis on crime and sex; and disreputable advertising."

Some researchers see the origins of the ideal of objective or neutral reporting emerging as a reaction to the sensationalism of this period. For instance, in 1835, a fabricated story, known today as "The Moon Hoax," was published in the *New York Sun*. The *Sun* ran a series of fabricated articles that described life on the moon. The public was enthralled, then outraged, when the stories were proven to be false. Critics denounced not only these stories but more broadly the press as a whole. Novelist James Fenimore Cooper criticized newspapers vigorously between 1837 and 1845. In 1838, he wrote in the *American Democrat* that "the entire nation breathes an atmosphere of falsehoods," and that the press "as a whole owes its existence to the schemes of interested political adventurers."

Because of the proliferation of story "faking" and a variety of other concerns, Philadelphia journalist and former newspaper editor Lambert Wilmer published in 1859 *Our Press Gang: A Complete Exposition of the Corruption and Crimes of the American Newspaper*, the first book of press criticism published in the United States. Wilmer hoped to transform journalism by pointing out its "great abuses" and wrote in the introduction to *Our Press Gang*:

> Our journalism is both tyrannical and slavish; it succumbs to every powerful influence, and it is bold and independent only when it attacks the weak and defenseless.... Remember, my countrymen, that nothing is easier than lying, especially among newspaper editors; for it is an art which they have studied, and which they thoroughly understand.

Wilmer's book listed fourteen charges against U.S. newspapers. They included immoral behavior by journalists, misusing power, misleading the public, advocating "villainy and imposture," fostering immorality and vice, interfering with the court system, accepting favors or gifts, and invading privacy.

Wilmer's work was noteworthy, and it marked the beginning of a century of criticism of the press. Fred Fedler, a historian of journalism ethics, concluded that between 1850 and 1950 journalists were often portrayed as ruthless and dishonest—generally accurate descriptions, according to Fedler.

In response to the increasing criticism of the press, some journalists began to emphasize the importance of ethical guidelines. One was George Childs, who became the editor of the *Public Ledger* in Philadelphia in 1864. He stressed accuracy in reporting as did his managing editor, William McKean. The historian George Payne said in 1924 that McKean should be given the credit "for the system of editorial ethics put forth as guiding principles" of the newspaper, which included the following: "Always deal fairly and frankly with the public." The guidelines highlighted the values of rights and justice, and were titled "The Constitutional Principles of a Great Newspaper." Payne believed that other papers, including the *New York Sun* and *Baltimore Sun*, contributed to "a developing democracy" and were dedicated to democratic values.

Following the Civil War, the public came to expect more immediacy in news stories. Newspapers continued to receive more revenue from advertisers and readers, thereby depending less on political party subsidy; more of them became "independent." Indeed, independence became an important principle for nineteenth- and twentieth-century journalists.

During the late nineteenth century, advertising in the press became a growing ethical issue. Many publishers and editors began to realize the importance of keeping the news and editorial pages separate from advertising to avoid conflicts of interest. Such efforts met with limited success, however. In his 1924 textbook *The Ethics of Journalism*, Nelson Crawford noted that those who placed advertising in newspapers and asked special favors in return were following common practice and undoubtedly had given little thought to ethical concerns. Crawford wrote that financial independence was linked to ethical standards, yet there was the danger that the journalist may come to believe his news organization was merely a commercial enterprise, rather than a public trust.

In the meantime, journalism was slowly moving toward becoming a profession and not merely a trade. Journalism education became a vital part of this development. Between 1875 and 1879 Cornell University offered a certificate of journalism, and between 1878 and 1884, the University of Missouri offered courses, too. Although there was little indication that these classes covered ethical behavior, the courses covered the history of journalism and the basic skills of reporting—important steps toward creating a profession with genuine standards and principles.

The establishment of the Institute of Journalists in 1889 was another important stride toward professionalization. Its goal was to improve the image of the journalists and it was an outgrowth of idealistic young men in an organization called the National Society of Journalists. Despite such efforts, though, sensationalism remained an obvious problem. Headlines were often overdone and misleading, and the newspapers were plagued with "yellow journalism" and deception.

Yellow journalism, or "gee-whiz" journalism, became a major issue during 1890s with the events leading up to and including the Spanish-American War. At the center of events were two competing New York City newspapers, William Randall Hearst's *Journal* and Joseph Pulitzer's *World*. The papers faked interviews, reported misleading information, and printed half-truths. Other ethical problems of yellow journalism included the suppression and coloring of news. The public seemed to have an appetite for all this nonsense, however, because both newspapers attained paid daily circulation of several hundreds of thousands of copies.

Historians agree that Hearst, and also Pulitzer, led the yellow journalism movement with their circulation war. Indeed, the Spanish-American War in 1898 has often been called "Hearst's War." But other newspaper publishers also tried to involve themselves in the affairs of state as they attempted negotiate with the leaders of other countries. In their efforts to create news and become part of the stories they reported, they engaged in practices that today are usually considered unacceptable and unethical even if they are still commonly practiced.

Because of the surge in yellow journalism, some journalists believed that ethical standards might be raised by having a full curriculum in journalism, not just occasional classes. The proponents of journalism education believed that the right curriculum would encourage self-reflection or self-examination, and ultimately improve moral reasoning by members of the press. Efforts to improve university education in journalism took a step forward in 1893 when Joseph French Johnson presented a curriculum to the Wharton School of Business at the University of Pennsylvania, but it died after Johnson left for New York University. The University of Illinois started a four-year curriculum for journalism students in 1904. The first separate school of journalism was created at the University of Missouri in

1908. Joseph Pulitzer left $2 million to Columbia University to create a college of journalism four years later.

Meanwhile, efforts to raise the standards of journalism came from within the profession itself. As Hearst and Pulitzer engaged in yellow journalism, Adolph S. Ochs bought the *New York Times*. Ochs believed journalists should have the courage to tackle the news without fear, and his methods differed from those of Hearst and Pulitzer. He wrote in the *New York Times* in August 1896 that he was not going to humor the public with the sensational tactics of other newspapers. Instead, his paper would present the news in a timely manner, and the editorial pages of the *Times* would be a forum for all. He banned comics and discouraged photographs. Ochs emphasized unbiased, truthful content in his news pages. Once he dropped the cost of his paper to a penny, the *Time's* circulation grew.

Despite the work of Ochs and other outstanding newsmen, journalism as a whole lacked a clear set of guiding principles at the beginning of the twentieth century. Henry Watterson, the longtime editor of the *Louisville-Courier Journal*, lamented:

"Journalism is without any code of ethics or system of self-restraint and self-respect. It has no sure standards of either work or duty. Its intellectual landscapes are anonymous, its moral destination confused. ...The journalist has few, if any, mental perspectives to fix his horizon; neither chart of precedent no map of discovery upon which his sailing lines and travel lines have been marked." Watterson did not believe all newsmen were tainted, but he was concerned that no code existed to state general press standards.

Joseph Pulitzer's son, Ralph Pulitzer, made an effort to improve standards at the *New York World*. He believed accuracy in the news was all-important and that faking was not allowable. Therefore, in 1908, Pulitzer created the *New York World's* Bureau of Accuracy and Fair Play, trying to rid the news of inaccuracies and "fakers."

If such journalists as Pulitzer thought a code would advance the profession, others, such as H.L. Mencken, were more pessimistic. In a 1914 *Atlantic Monthly* article, Mencken wrote that all codes were "moonshine" because "if American journalism is to be purged of its present swinishness and brought up to a decent level of repute—and God knows that such an improvement is needed—it must be accomplished by the devices of moral, not by those of honor."

Other commentators were less cynical than Mencken and saw evidence of progress in the early twentieth century, however limited it might have been. In his *History of American Journalism*, published in 1917, James Melvin Lee discussed journalism's social readjustment. Writing about what he saw as "a trend of the times," Lee believed that by 1900 most newspapers had begun to make "ethical advances" and that an era of "moral awakening" had started. When Leon Flint published *The Conscience of the Newspaper* in 1925, he saw a trend toward professionalism and social responsibility or "better service to the public." However, at the end of his "Codes and Ethical Standards" chapter, he asked: "Is it too much to hope that before long even the most hard-headed editor will get over being skittish and jumpy when somebody mentions ethics and an ethical code?" And, in his "Professional Training" chapter, Flint wrote that college journalism courses and curriculum should aim to teach ideals.

During the first quarter of the twentieth century, the journalism education not only emphasized the need for clear standards but better opportunities for women reporters. Sigma Delta Chi, a professional journalism fraternity, was started in 1909 at Depauw University, and Theta Sigma Phi, an honorary and professional fraternity for women in journalism was begun at the University of Washington. In 1912, the American Association of Teachers of Journalism was created. Both groups had professional responsibility as their mantra.

Discussions of ethical behavior became more prominent in newsrooms and in academia. In 1911, Will Irwin wrote a series for *Collier's* in which he said that "The newspaper should be a gentleman." In the series' eighth article, "All the News That's Fit to Print," Irwin listed four principles of journalism and wrote that reporters' behaviors had improved despite the earlier yellow journalism. Why? Because more reporters and editors had college degrees. He pointed out that young people on the staffs of newspaper, the future editors, had formulated a code of sorts.

- Don't print information one hears at a friend's house or at the club.
- Don't publish anything without the permission of the informer.
- Don't pretend to be someone you are not; in other words, "Don't sail under false colors."
- Be respectful and sensitive to your sources.

Other areas related to journalism—advertising, photography, and press agentry—came under renewed ethical scrutiny at the beginning of the twentieth century. Advertising was particularly troublesome for many reformers. In 1904, the National Federation of Advertising Clubs of America was created, and one of the organization's goals was to suppress deceptive advertising. The organization was renamed the Associated Advertising Clubs of America and later "of the World." In 1911, its members agreed to follow "The Ten Commandments of Advertising." The first commandment was "Thou shalt have no other gods in advertising but Truth." Irwin's series in *Collier's* gave examples of advertisers playing one paper against another. He wrote that honest and ethical publishers differentiated between advertising and editorial content. The Postal Act of 1912 made this procedure mandatory if newspapers were to get second-class mailing rights, which were based on percentages of editorial, or non-advertising, content.

It should be noted that early in the twentieth century a type of reporting called "muckraking" came into existence. This method of reporting led to more in-depth, investigative pieces. The muckrakers scrutinized seemingly every aspect of American political and economic life, and did not neglect the ethical problems brought to journalism by false advertising and the commercialization of the news.

Photography, one of the most important new communication technologies of the nineteenth century, created important ethical problems for journalists. In 1897, the *New York Tribune* was the first major newspaper to publish halftones. Before halftones, newspapers used woodcuttings, and when cameras came into use in the mid-nineteenth century, reproductions of photos in newspapers only showed black and white tones. Therefore, in the late 1800s it was a common practice that obituary photos were often "faked" by using the image of someone who looked similar to the person who had died. Obituary photos were not the only photos to be faked. Photography also raised concerns about the invasion of privacy. The production of half-tones and then photographs in newspapers led to more realism, more truth in the news pages. By 1910, most newspapers adopted the reproduction process, and hand-engraving was on its way out.

The growth of the public relations profession posed serious ethical challenges. Publicity agents, or press agents, were abundant by the 1920s—although some form of press agentry had been visible since the 1840s. By 1924, according to Crawford, large newspapers received dozens, perhaps hundreds, of publicity releases a day from publicity people.

Crawford, who also worried about the influence of advertising, warned of propaganda disguised as news. Good journalists should be trained to spot such propaganda. Crawford believed that some of journalism's problems and inaccuracies stemmed from ignorance and "intellectual and spiritual fear." He stressed social responsibility, argued that objectivity was a "sound ethical rule," and warned that suppressing information because of a private interest was not acceptable. Students of journalism should be taught at the outset that news stories were no place for opinion; opinion belonged on the editorial pages.

Early Codes

Although editors had written guidelines for journalistic behavior earlier, the first official journalism code, the Kansas Newspaper Code of Ethics, was written in 1910 by a group of editors in the state. It was one of the codes written during the early 20th century that was created by an "elite" group working within journalism, according to one writer (J. Edward Gerald, *Social Responsibility of the Press*, 1963). A division existed among the writers of the codes about whether they were enforceable. The ethical codes of the medical and legal professions were relatively easy to enforce (one was simply expelled from the profession), but journalism was more complicated (how did one deny a citizen the opportunity to write for a newspaper?).

The debate over enforcing journalism codes often raised the old question of whether working for the press was a trade or a profession. Codes of ethics for journalists did not become common until "newsmen spoke of a 'profession' of journalism," according to a former dean of the College of Communication of the University of Illinois, Theodore Peterson. Even then, no pressure was applied on newspapers to adopt codes.

Codes continued to be written. For instance, in 1922 the Oregon Editorial Association adopted a resolution that stated newspapers in Oregon would avoid sensationalism in the news. In 1922, the American Society of Newspaper Editors (ASNE), under the leadership of Casper S. Yost of the *St. Louis Globe-Democrat*, was organized in New York City. In 1923, the organization, more than one hundred members strong, adopted the Canons of Journalism at its annual meeting. The code, written mostly by *New York Globe* editor H. J. Wright, continued to epitomize the ideals of journalism into the early twenty-first century. Ethical issues covered in the code included responsibility, freedom of the press, independence, sincerity, truthfulness and accuracy, impartiality, fair play, and decency. Over the next fifty years, newspapers throughout the United States adopted the ASNE code and many state press associations also created their own similar codes. Sigma Delta Chi, later renamed Society of Professional Journalists, adopted the ASNE code in 1926 and kept it for almost fifty years, when it then created its own code.

It should be noted, however, that this important code had its critics. In 1929, the *New Republic* pointed out that the last sentence of the Canons of Journalism showed its weakness: "Lacking authority to enforce its canons, the journalism here represented can but express the hope that deliberate pandering to vicious instinct will encounter effective public disapproval or yield to the influence of a preponderant professional condemnation." In other words, for a code that was not enforceable, the only guiding principle remained the journalist's own moral compass.

In 1933, professors from Bryn Mawr College published a seven-part article titled "Measuring the Ethics of American Newspapers" in *Journalism Quarterly*. Looking for similarities in journalism codes of ethics, the authors of the Bryn Mawr study conducted the first known analysis of ethical codes of national and state journalism associations. They found that, in general, the codes they examined defined a newspaper's fundamental function as "being a disseminator of information." However, the study pointed out conflicts of interest with many codes' guidelines—and this is where ethical decision making came into play. For instance, the study found that the news function may conflict with public welfare and with privacy rights. The publicity function may conflict with the news function by bias or distortion. The amusement function may conflict with public welfare because of the risk of sensationalism. It should be noted, too, that by the 1930s, two positions on objectivity had also emerged: the first, objectivity was impossible, and the second, using "just the facts" would lead to relative objectivity.

Ethics and the Beginning of Broadcast Journalism

Legislation passed in 1910 and 1912 put the governing control of radio broadcasting under the U.S. Secretary of Commerce. The 1927 Radio Act created the foundations for the regulation issues of censorship, ownership, and political utilization. Extending the 1927 Radio Act, the 1934 Communications Act gave the Federal Communications Commission more power. All this regulation, however, allegedly served only the government and station owners, not the public; the FCC was criticized for not being watchful of the public's interest.

In 1923, the National Association of Broadcasters was formed. In 1929, this organization created both a Code of Ethics and a Standards of Commercial Practice. These codes were voluntarily imposed, of course.

During the 1930s, hope persisted that the professional development of radio would progress toward higher standards in commentary and news programming. Yet economic factors affected broadcast journalists ability to serve the public, and advertising sometimes affected the content of the newscast. And there was propaganda. During World War I, wireless broadcasting came under the control of the U.S. Navy. During World War II, the government asked that news organizations provide news, information—and propaganda—to help the war effort.

Fifteen years after World War II, nine in ten homes had television sets. Newscasters were celebrities. Entertainment's invasion into the news was a concern, and low ratings led to cancellations of news programs. Fred Friendly, who worked for CBS News from 1950–1966 and was a close friend of Edward R. Murrow, explained that, "Because television can make so much money doing its worst, it often cannot afford to do its best" (Friendly, *Due To Circumstances Beyond Our Control*, 1967). In 1966, Friendly resigned as president of CBS News when the network chose to run an episode of *I Love Lucy* instead of an important congressional hearing on the Vietnam War. Years before, Murrow had warned Friendly that entertainment was threatening the ability of broadcasting to honor its obligation to be socially responsible.

Twentieth-Century Society and the Press

During the 1930s and the early1940s, interest in journalism ethics waned. During World War II, the U.S. Office of Censorship asked for voluntary censorship among the media. Because of their support of the government through the airing or publishing of propaganda during the two world wars, news organizations seemed to lose a sense of independence.

After World War II, though, freedom of the press became a renewed concern to the government as did the fact that news organizations no longer seemed as government-friendly as previously. As news outlets took seriously their obligation to inform the public, some critics charged that antagonism toward established institutions was becoming a standard of professional journalism. There were also well-founded concerns that with the growth of news organization consolidation, economic factors were becoming the driving motivation behind reporting.

These concerns led to the creation of the Commission on Freedom of the Press. Robert M. Hutchins, the chancellor of the University of Chicago, and thirteen other men, mostly university professors, formed the Commission and Henry R. Luce, the publisher of *Time, Life* and *Fortune* magazines, supplied $200,000 for the seventeen meetings the commission held and the research it did. Published in 1947, the Commission's report, "A Free and Responsible Press," stated that the press was failing to meet the needs of society because it gave into the public's whims and pressures from owners. A short, yet wide-ranging report, it recommended the creation of an agency to assess and report annually on press performance in the areas of freedom and responsibility. It should be noted that the ethics committee of the ASNE at that time polled its members about the establishment of press councils; the majority of the editors did not favor them.

Lee Brown, in his 1974 book, *The Reluctant Reformation: On Criticizing the Press in America*, discussed the concept of the press council and argued that better discourse between society and the press could benefit society. Brown's work came a year after The Twentieth Century Fund had announced that it would fund a national press council. A task force set up by the Fund recommended "that an independent and private national news council be established to receive, to examine and to report on complaints concerning the accuracy and fairness of news reporting in the United States as well as to initiate studies and report on issues involving the freedom of the press." The National News Council, created in 1973, was funded privately and accepted complaints from the public against the news media. The charges were studied by the Council, which then reported its findings. The Council never really had any concrete support from the news media and it ceased operation in 1984.

However, many local state councils were created, and three state councils continue to exist today in Washington, Hawaii, and Minnesota. The first local council was started by Houstoun Waring of the *Littleton Independent* in Colorado in 1946.

The newspaper ombudsman position came into existence during the late 1960s. An ombudsman handles reader complaints and explains how the process of newsgathering and reporting works. In 1967, A. H. Raskin of the *New York Times*, writing in the *New York Times Magazine*, supported the use of ombudsmen when he wrote that every newspaper should have a "Department of Internal Criticism." According to the Organization of News Ombudsmen, the first U.S. newspaper ombudsman was appointed in June 1967 in Louisville, Kentucky, to assist *The Courier-Journal* and *The Louisville Times* readers. Today, many major American and international news organizations have ombudsmen.

Many United States cities in the 1960s and 1970s had magazine publishers who observed press behavior. One example was the *Chicago Journalism Review*, the first journalism review owned and operated by working journalists. Most of these efforts soon died out, though. Many news organizations do have their own media critics today, and many magazines continue to observe the behavior of the press—just as they did more than century ago.

The Twenty-First Century

When Brown examined press criticism in *The Reluctant Reformation*, he believed that the press was unable to keep up with the demands of society and concluded that the press was under attack by the public. Citizens had too often come to think that the news media's reporting was unfair, partial, and slanted.

In the twenty-first century, the same problems exist even though journalists have codes of ethics for guidance. Several national organizations have provided codes, including the American Society of Newspaper Editors, National Press Photographers Association, Radio-Television News Directors Association, Society of American Business Editors and Writers, and the Society of Professional Journalists. Many other regional publications have their own in-house codes. These efforts still remain guidelines, not rules and the most important principle in them is truth-telling. With all the new technology available for gathering and spreading the news, new codes and standards are constantly being formulated.

Although ethical reasoning is being taught in some journalism programs, surveys continue to report that the public believes the press lacks credibility. And there is no shortage of critics. In a *New York Times Book Review* article (July 31, 2005), Richard Posner argued that "the news media have also become more sensational, more prone to scandal and publicly less accurate." The author went on to describe news media that pander to political polarization, sensationalism, and entertainment. The struggle to ensure that journalism lives up to its best values has been a constant theme in American history and will remain so in the future so long as the nation's democratic ideals remain alive.

Further Reading

Branson, Craig. "A Look at the Formation of ASNE," http://www.asne.org.

Bleyer, Willard G. *Main Currents in the History of American Journalism.* Boston:Houghton Mifflin Co., 1927.

Brown, Lee. *The Reluctant Reformation: On Criticizing the Press in America.* New York: D. McKay, 1974.

Christians, Clifford. "An Intellectual History of Media Ethics." In *Media Ethics: Opening Social Dialogue*, edited by Bart Pattyn, 15–46. Leuven, Belgium: Peeters Publishing, 2000.

Crawford, Nelson A. *Ethics of Journalism.* 1924. A reprint of the first edition. New York: Greenwood Press, 1969.

Dicken-Garcia. Hazel. *Journalistic Standards in Nineteenth Century America.* Madison: University of Wisconsin Press, 1989.

Fedler, Fred. "Actions of Early Journalists Often Unethical, Even Illegal." *Journal of Mass Media Ethics* 12, 1977: 160–170.

Flint, Leon N. *The Conscience of the Newspaper.* New York: D. Appleton-Century Co., 1925.

Fortner, Robert S. "The Self-Conscious Image and the Myth of an Ethical Press." *Journalism History* 5 (1978): 46–49.

Gerald, J. Edward. *The Social Responsibility of the Press.* Minneapolis: University of Minnesota Press, 1963.

Hausmann, Linda W. "Criticism of the Press in U.S. Periodicals, 1900–1939: An Annotated Bibliography." *Journalism Monographs,* 4 (August 1967).

Irwin, Will. *The American Newspaper.* Reprint of *Collier's* January to June 1911 magazine series with comments by Clifford

F. Weigle and David G. Clark. Ames: The Iowa State University Press, 1969.

Kingsbury, Susan, and Hart, Hornell. "Measuring the Ethics of American Newspapers." *Journalism Quarterly* 10, nos. 2–8 (1933).

Lee, James Melvin. *History of American Journalism*, 2nd ed. Boston: Houghton Mifflin Co., 1923.

McKerns, Joseph P. "Media Ethics: A Bibliographical Essay." *Journalism History* 5, (1978): 50–53, 68.

Milton, Joyce. *The Yellow Kids: Foreign Correspondents in the Heyday of Yellow Journalism.* New York: Harper & Row, 1989.

Mott, Frank. *American Journalism.* New York: Macmillan Co. 1950, originally published 1941.

Payne, George Henry. History of Journalism in the United States. D. Appleton and Co., 1924.

Shuman, Edwin L. Practical Journalism: A Complete Manual of the Best Newspaper Methods. New York: D. Appleton and Co., 1905.

Sloan, William David, and Startt, James D. *The Media in America: A History,* 3rd ed. Northport, AL: Vision Press, 1996.

Time-Life Books. *Photojournalism.* New York: Time-Life Books, 1971.

Wilmer, Lambert A. *Our Press Gang.* New York: Arno Press, 1970, originally published 1859.

Yost, Casper S. *Principles of Journalism.* New York: D. Appleton & Co., 1924.

LEE ANNE PECK

ETHNIC/IMMIGRANT PRESS

Although Benjamin Franklin began the first ethnic newspaper in 1759, in the German language, other groups have established their own publications, many in the nineteenth century, along with other media, to meet the challenges and opportunities of America. Several groups started their papers as a result of what the majority society was doing to them. For instance, African Americans in 1827, began *Freedom's Journal,* in New York, stating, "We wish to plead our own cause; too long have others spoken for us." The cause was slavery and its abolition. The Jewish press began in 1823, also in New York, because Jews were beleaguered by missionaries trying to convert them to Christianity. Then too, in 1828, the Native American press began with the *Cherokee Phoenix,* as Native Americans were pushed off their land by the American government and embarked on their Trail of Tears to the Oklahoma territory, arriving in 1835, after suffering many deaths along the way.

Other publications were established in part to keep alive, in the minds of immigrants, the idea of the homeland and returning to it someday. Immigrants came to America for its promise of economic gain. Living in America proved advantageous for them. At first many groups—for example, Arab, Romanian, Lithuanian, and Mexican—insisted they would return to their homelands. Their various ethnic press editors believed that. The uncertainty, the puzzling difficulties of Americanizing, however, soon gave way to being able to work and live in the United States, and whole communities came into being, fashioned around such ethnic institutions as houses of worship, clubs, and other associations.

In their travels, immigrants had experiences that opened doors to assimilation. They pushed carts, later bought horses to do so, and then peddled their way around the country. Upward mobility became the by-product of such simple trading, as people succeeded and joined the middle-class. The basic elements required no advanced training or even much language skills. Often merchants created a base, a village of refuge, where they could improve their literacy by learning to read an ethnic newspaper.

At the same time, many forces in any given community felt the pull of American life and the diminishing influence of their homeland settlement. Some people were exhorted to modify their heritage, to Americanize. This usually took the form of sermonizing in English, publishing textbooks for learning English, teaching about American customs, traditions, and even naturalization procedures; giving lessons on American history, explicating the complexities of social and economic life, such as how to protect the sanctity of the family, or how to uphold the honor and integrity of the ethnic group. The ethnic group's press interpreted America for them, bringing distinctive elements of American life and values to the immigrants' attention, and thereby providing guidance.

Without question there was cultural ambivalence. While the press kept the homeland alive in the minds and hearts of an immigrant group, it also pressed them to modify their traditional ways. Some groups came from the old country bearing religious and political differences that added greater diversity to America. At the same time, the press enticed readers in the homeland to join their brethren with information about life in America, for some newspapers and magazines found their way abroad.

Many publications appeared in the United States, courtesy of an ethnic group's fraternal societies, houses of worship, political organizations, and cultural associations. The press was sponsored early on by institutions within the ethnic community. Therefore, such efforts carried specific religious, political, or nationalistic overtones.

The ethnic press became a mirror reflecting the wide diversity in the ethnic group's society, and it actually defined what that society was. Often between four to eight pages in length, the newspapers' functions broke down as follows: surveillance of the society in the United States and in their homeland, acting as a forum for opinions, serving to advertise products and services of the ethnic groups' businessmen (and sometimes women), transmitting the heritage of the group, immigrant success stories, features including fiction and poetry.

The establishment of these print media made a contribution to American life as well. For example, as the first Jewish publication, *The Jew,* used Hebrew fonts; so too did *Kawkab Amrika* introduce Arabic characters to America, using the slow but traditional method of setting type by hand.

Populations climbed extraordinarily. The Chinese population in California grew from eight hundred in 1849, at the time of the Gold Rush, to twenty-five thousand in 1852, and to twenty thousand in San Francisco alone by 1870.

Consequently, the Chinese press developed, often defending its readers from the vicious stereotypes in words and illustrations found even in the best mainstream newspapers and magazines. During the late nineteenth and early twentieth centuries, the numbers of immigrants from southern and eastern Europe grew rapidly, sometimes at a rate of more than one million per year. Each group developed its own press. Similarly, as the number of Latinos, Southeast Asians, and other ethnic groups increased during the late twentieth century, media emerged that accommodated their needs.

Contemporary Ethnic Media

Overall, almost all people, whatever their origin, use ethnic media regularly for news and for surveillance of their local, national, and international environment. However, they also use mainstream media. The educated immigrants who move to America and who understand English use general media right away. Those who come knowing little or no English usually learn the language and begin using both ethnic and general newspapers, as well as online news sources. Generally speaking, the longer that immigrants are in this country, the more they use mainstream media. It is inaccurate to suggest that the ethnic press ghettoizes a community.

In the late twentieth and early twenty-first centuries, foreign-language newspapers flourished, thanks to burgeoning immigrant population. In some cities, the circulation of some ethnic media rivaled those of established English-language publications. For example, *La Opinion* in Los Angeles had a circulation approaching two hundred thousand, and was the third largest newspaper in the city behind the *Los Angeles Times* and the *Daily News*. The Tribune Co. which owned the Times, also had a 49 percent ownership of *La Opinion*.

Ethnic media played an important role in bringing different groups into mainstream American life. Local news—politics, sports, traffic—was important, and ethnic websites addressed local issues. A goal of all ethnic media was to enable people to function in America, and if they became citizens, to be effective voters. Even in cases of rapid growth of ethnic newspapers, such as Asian Indian, readers were not immune from the influences of conventional media. For example, African Americans chose to use ethnic newspapers and other media but they also used mainstream media. Such groups could not be characterized as self-isolated from the rest of American communication. Yet for those who are illiterate, ethnic broadcasting played more prominently in their lives. Then, too, it must be recognized that some groups, such as the Chinese, preferred their own media, particularly television. Asian Indians favored web sites to connect with one another and their American-based publications paled besides those from India which found their way to the United States.

Rather than fragment American society, ethnic newspapers and broadcasting media usually urged participation in American life. They were indispensable for building inclusive national communication and represented a distinctive genre with solid footing no other media can replicate. They differed from the majority press by advocating, standing up for their individual communities. They often used a journalism style that was geared toward creating strong community relationships. They offered a forum for finding solutions to community problems. Ethnic media alerted audiences to the threats from the at-large society, whether it was scapegoating, discrimination, stereotyping, or passing xenophobic legislation.

In 1996, an effort began to coordinate the nation's ethnic media when the nonprofit Pacific New Service established New America Media (NAM). It was the United States' first national collaboration of ethnic news organizations. By 2007, NAM brought together more than seven hundred ethnic media outlets into a subscription-based service. Its web site (http://news.newamericamedia.org/news/) offered readers a remarkably diverse pool of news, editorials, and analysis. NAM sponsored its own awards, casually termed the "Ethnic Pulitzers."

Further Reading

Kessler, Lauren. *The Dissident Press: Alternative Journalism in American History.* Beverly Hills, CA: Sage Publications, 1984.

Miller, Sally M., ed. *The Ethnic Press in the United States: A Historical Analysis and Handbook.* Westport, CT: Greenwood Press, 1987.

New America Media (http://news.newamericamedia.org/news/) (accessed April 9, 2007).

BARBARA S. REED

FAIRNESS DOCTRINE

The Fairness Doctrine was a regulatory policy enforced by the Federal Communications Commission (FCC) from 1949 to 1987. It imposed a duty on all broadcast licensees to actively seek out controversial issues of public importance and provide fair and balanced coverage by giving opposing viewpoints a reasonable opportunity to be expressed. In practical terms, the Fairness Doctrine compelled television and radio broadcasters to allow differing positions reasonable airtime on controversial issues of public importance.

The purpose of the Fairness Doctrine was to ensure balanced information. At the time the doctrine was adopted, broadcasting licenses were relatively scarce due to the limited availability of radio and television frequencies and the relatively high demand for their use. The reality of this scarcity led the federal government to take the view that broadcast licensees were "trustees" of public discourse and therefore obligated to include contrasting viewpoints in the coverage of controversial events. As such, the Fairness Doctrine was meant to countervail any attempts by broadcasters to use their monopoly-type power over the distribution of information by requiring presentation of opposing viewpoints.

In 1967, two corollary doctrines were adopted and expanded the scope of the Fairness Doctrine. The first, the "personal attack rule," required broadcast licensees to provide airtime for victims of personal attacks made during a broadcast. Specifically, broadcast stations had to notify each person or group personally attacked on air of what was said as well as an opportunity to respond. The second, the "political editorial" rule, mandated that if a broadcaster endorsed or opposed a specific candidate for public office, the broadcasters had to notify the other candidate(s) within twenty-four hours and provide reasonable opportunities for the non-endorsed political candidates to respond. However, neither of these corollaries, nor any other Fairness Doctrine provision should be confused with the "Equal Time" Rule, which mandates that all qualified candidates for a given office get equal access to broadcast facilities if one candidate gets such "use."

In 1969, the Supreme Court upheld the constitutionality of the Fairness Doctrine against challenges by broadcasters that it violated the First Amendment. In *Red Lion Broadcasting Co., v. Federal Communications Commission*, a radio station permitted a preacher to make disparaging statements against an author who had written a book critical of then Republican presidential candidate Barry Goldwater. The author demanded free airtime from the radio station so that he could rebut the public charges leveled against him. The radio station refused to allocate free rebuttal airtime and a Fairness Doctrine challenge ensued.

Broadcasters argued that the Fairness Doctrine's requirements unduly interfered with their First Amendment right to use their allotted frequencies to express or not express whatever speech they wanted. The Court disagreed, stating that the purpose of the First Amendment was to produce an informed citizenry "capable of conducting its own affairs" and that in order to serve that goal, the rights of the viewers and listeners had to be elevated above the rights of the broadcasters.

Significantly, the Court emphasized the fact that broadcasting was an inherently scarce resource due to the limitations of the radio and television spectrums. The Court reasoned that it was entirely consistent with the purpose of the First Amendment to view broadcast licensees as privileged proxies for society at large and therefore obligated to program in the public interest.

Five years later, the Supreme Court seemed to contradict the rationale of Red Lion by nullifying a Florida law involving a right of political candidates to respond when their record was attacked in a newspaper. In *Miami Herald Publishing Co. v. Tornillo*, the court concluded that the law violated the First Amendment. The Court found no constitutional difference between a government regulation forbidding certain speech and a government regulation compelling certain speech like the statue at issue. The opinion made no reference to *Red Lion*.

During the Ronald Reagan administration, a more pro-industry FCC sought to repeal the Fairness Doctrine. In a 1985 report, it viewed the doctrine as having a chilling effect on free speech and it questioned the scarcity rationale. It noted that broadcast reporters faced with the onerous task of actively finding contrasting viewpoints for every controversial issue raised in a news story tended to simply avoid covering controversial issues altogether. Two years later, the FCC formally repealed the regulation.

In the 1987 determination, FCC concluded that the doctrine had the "net effect of reducing, rather than enhancing, the discussion of controversial issues of public importance." In addition, the underlying rationale for the policy was no longer applicable since advances in technology has resulted in a proliferation of new information resources such as cable channels, VCRs, satellite television and the Internet.

Even within the radio industry, the number of radio stations grew by 30 percent from 1974 to 1985. During this same time period FM service increased by 60 percent.

Indeed, when the Fairness Doctrine was first promulgated in 1949, 2,881 radio stations and 98 television stations existed in the United States. By 1989, there were more than 10,000 radio stations and almost 1,400 television stations on air. According to the FCC, the significant increase in the number of media outlets has largely negated the government's fear that a few partisan broadcasters would monopolize the distribution of information. A federal appeals court upheld the FCC's power to repeal the doctrine, concluding that the commission did not require Congressional approval to make this decision.

Although the commission abolished the bulk of the Fairness Doctrine in 1987, it retained the political, editorial and personal attack rules until 2000, when the FCC repealed them. Attempts to revive the Fairness Doctrine have occurred periodically. In 1987, Congress passed a bill codifying the Fairness Doctrine that was ultimately vetoed by President Reagan. In 1993, a similar bill seeking restoration of the Fairness Doctrine did not pass Congress. The repeal of the Fairness Doctrine may have led to the growth of partisan news programming as evidenced by the popularity and rise of media outlets and/or figures such as Fox News, MSNBC, and talk show hosts such as Rush Limbaugh.

Further Reading

Conrad, Mark. "The Demise of the Fairness Doctrine: A Blow for Citizen Access." *Federal Communications Law Review*, 41, (1989) 161–187.

Report on Editorializing by Broadcast Licensees, 13 F.C.C. 1246 (1949).

Candidates for Public Office; Equal Opportunities Requirement, 47 USC sec. 315(a).

Red Lion Broadcasting Co. v. F.C.C., 395 U.S. 367, 89 S. Ct. 1794 (1969).

Miami Herald Publishing Co. v. Tornillo, 418 U.S. 241, (1974).

Report Concerning the General Fairness Doctrine Obligations of Broadcast Licensees, 102 F.C.C.2d 143, 146, 161 (1985).

Federal Communications Commission News, Report No. MM-263, August 4, 1987.

Syracuse Peace Council v. Federal Communications Commission, 867 F.2d 654, 660 (DC Cir, 1989).

No author, *What Happened to the Fairness Doctrine*, http://www.pbs.org/now/politics/fairness.html (accessed April 13, 2007).

Zuckman, Harvey L., Corn-Revere, Robert L., Frieden, Robert M., Kennedy, and Charles H. *Modern Communications Law*. St. Paul, MN: West (1999).

MARK CONRAD

FEDERAL COMMUNICATIONS COMMISSION

The Federal Communications Commission (FCC) is an independent regulatory body created by an act of Congress on June 19, 1934. The Commission was established to regulate broadcasting and wired communication services in the United States. In 2007, the Commission had about two thousand employees and an annual budget of approximately $280 million. It is charged with the oversight of the nation's broadcast, satellite, and telecommunications services.

With the passage of the Communications Act of 1934, the newly formed FCC merged the regulatory responsibilities of the Federal Radio Commission (FRC) and the Interstate Commerce Commission into one agency that was given the task of "establishing rapid, efficient, Nation-wide, and world-wide wire and radio communication service." While the FRC was never intended to be a permanent regulatory body, the FCC was created for just that purpose. The Communications Act describes the administration, formation, and powers of the FRC. Five regulatory commissioners are appointed by the president and confirmed by the Senate. Each commissioner serves a five-year term and no more than three commissioners can be members of the same political party. One commissioner is appointed chairperson and is responsible for setting the agenda for the FCC. The commissioners supervise all the FCC activities, delegating responsibilities to various bureaus and offices with the commission.

The 1934 act has been amended considerably since its passage. Many of the alterations have been in response to the numerous technical changes in communications that have taken place during the FCC's history, including the introduction of television, satellite and microwave communications, cable television, cellular telephone, digital broadcasting, and PCS (personal communications) services. As a result of these and other developments, new responsibilities have been added to the commission's charge. For example, the passage of the Cable Act of 1992 and the Telecommunications Act of 1996 required revisions to the 1934 act. But the flexibility incorporated into the general provisions has allowed the agency to survive for more than seventy years. In 1996 Congress mandated that the Commission develop policies that would accelerate technological innovation and competition within various segments of the communication industry.

The Federal Communications Commission's bureaus and offices are organized by function. For example, responsibility for oversight of electronic media (radio, television, and cable) is largely in the responsibility of the Media Bureau. The Wireless Telecommunications Bureau oversees cellular and PCS phones, pagers, and other non-broadcast radio services. Other bureaus include the International, Enforcement and Wireline Competition Bureaus. Each bureau is subdivided into divisions charged with conducting rulemaking proceedings, engineering, and industry analysis.

Congress provided the FCC with the ability to promulgate rules and regulations as a means of administering the communication policy. Normally the FCC will gather information about a subject before developing policy. After reviewing comments, the FCC may determine that regulation is needed and will release a Notice of Proposed Rulemaking. During this period, the FCC will gather responses and comments about the proposed rule. After comments have been gathered, the bureau in charge of the specific issue may make a recommendation to the commission that the proposed rule be adopted or modified. The commissioners then vote on the proposal and a simple majority vote is needed for a proposal to pass. Rules and regulations adopted by the FCC have the same force as law and are subject to judicial review.

Generally, the commission is concerned with licensing, engineering and technical considerations, and while it is charged with regulation of media, it is barred from making content decisions about broadcast programming. However, Congress can stipulate that the FCC enforce specific policies passed as congressional legislation. For example, it has specifically authorized the FCC to enforce a ban against indecent and obscene programming on radio and television stations. This issue gained prominence as programming became more provocative. Cable programming, often seen as more controversial, is not required to meet the same standards as over-the-air broadcasting, since cable networks are not licensed. This disparity between the two services caused confusion with the viewing public and difficulties for the FCC as it tried to apply enforcement standards for broadcast outlets. Another area where Congress has specifically authorized FCC action is that of children's television programming.

In its seventy-year history, the Federal Communications Commission has changed its regulatory policies as the entertainment business has grown from radio to include television, cable and now satellite communication. Early FCC policy tended to be proscriptive, spelling out detailed rules about station performance, record-keeping requirements, and license renewal procedures. Among early commission concerns were issues of fairness and balance in programming, overcommercialization, and abuse of network power over its affiliates.

In the early 1980s, the FCC changed direction and adopted a deregulatory stance, using "marketplace competition" as an alternative to formulaic regulation. During that period, it quickly did away with many earlier policies, including the highly controversial "Fairness Doctrine." Since then, the number of radio and television licenses has multiplied to more than eighteen thousand full service and low-powered broadcasting stations.

With the increase in the numbers of broadcast stations and as competition in the entertainment industry has spawned numerous new technological alternatives for consumers, the importance of individual stations has decreased. Early commission policy had stressed the importance of "localism" as a goal for individual licensees. However, as the industry has transformed over the last three decades, radio stations have become highly formulaic, often automated services and television stations have become outlets for national programming as opposed to developers of local content. The FCC instituted low-power stations, a new classification of broadcasters, to help reinvigorate the idea of localism.

When Congress passed the Telecommunications Act of 1996, it directed the FCC to evaluate commission rules biannually, encouraging the FCC to eliminate unneeded regulatory policies. Over the past few years, the FCC has taken steps to further loosen requirements for broadcast license ownership and cross-media consolidation. These policy initiatives have been met with little success, however, as court rulings have reversed FCC policy and directed the Commission to re-examine its proposals.

Technology continues to drive change in the communication and entertainment industries and the FCC must develop policies that will ensure broadcasting will survive in the twenty-first century. Currently, the Federal Communications Commission has adopted several strategic goals designed to accelerate the acceptance of digital broadcasting and broadband information services in the United States.

FRITZ MESSERE

FEMINIST JOURNALISM

Newspapers and magazines, as well as, more recently, cable television shows, radio broadcasts, documentary film, and now Internet sites produced by, for, and about women have been crucial mechanisms by which women can critique and resist dominant conceptions of women, and celebrate alternative and even oppositional visions of womanhood. As important as "feminist" journalism is, the term is slippery. One reason is that, until the 1960s, such journalism outlets rarely used the term feminist; even now only scholarly journals regularly title themselves "feminist." Feminist journalists may advocate social and political platforms that technically do not refer to women's rights or that do not refer to women exclusively. Even self-identified feminist newspapers and magazines vary in their commitment to distinctively feminist principles for content and production. Meanwhile, conventional women's pages and women's magazines have covered feminism and arguably have feminist potential. Nonetheless, feminist journalism here refers to outlets that consistently advocate expansive political, social, and cultural roles for women that transcend or resist ones encouraged by mainstream media and that expose gender oppression (assumed to be associated with oppression by sexual orientation, class, race, ethnicity, and religion). Largely women-run, feminist news media enable women to exchange news they cannot find in mainstream media and to develop journalistic and media skills, albeit skills that have little purchase in mainstream media, given that they involve commitments to different conceptions of professionalism and journalism ethics.

Feminist newspapers and magazines have had a crucial journalistic mission: to teach women how to take up their lives as "new women," often, with a specifically feminist identity. The papers explain how these new women might dress, name, and judge themselves. These institutions have small audiences. They are rarely profitable—nor are they intended to earn profits. Moreover, because of the exhaustion of volunteers and lack of financial, intellectual or journalistic assistance, they usually are short-lived; those underwritten by large national women's organizations tend to be the most successful.

Women's Rights Journalism

Historically, feminist journalism in the United States was an outgrowth of efforts (usually in the East Coast, especially New York) on behalf of other causes, such as abolition and moral reform, as well as ones specifically important to women, such as health and dress reform, and especially suffrage. In 1828 Frances Wright, an abolitionist who had been active in a socialist commune, began editing the *Free Enquirer*, where she advocated equal rights for women, universal suffrage, abolition, liberalizing of divorce laws, birth control, and free education. *The Female Advocate* (1832), published by a minister and his wife, and *American Woman* (1845) bemoaned vice and prostitution. Indeed, limitations on women's participation in the abolition and temperance movements inspired several women's rights periodicals. *The Lily* (1849–1856) was initially proposed by Amelia Bloomer because local temperance leaders limited women to fundraising and attending lectures. *Lily* promised to work for the enfranchisement, and emancipation of women not only from unjust laws but also "from the destructive influences of Custom and Fashion." Elizabeth Aldrich's *Genius of Liberty* (1851–1853), "Devoted to the Interests of American Women," was among several pre-Civil War papers promoting the "enlargement of the sphere of women." In 1852, Anna Spencer began the *Pioneer and Woman's Advocate* on behalf of "Liberty, Truth, Temperance, Equality." Also in Providence (Rhode Island), Paulina Wright's *The Una* (1853–1855) addressed suffrage, marriage, coeducation, and women's work (especially as physicians).

Especially in the early stages of the movement, many women suffrage journals either began with a different scope or expanded their scope to embrace multiple feminist issues. *The Revolution* (1868–1870) took up the cause of women victimized or abused by men, including prostitutes, and demanded changes in marriage and divorce law. *The New Northwest* (1871–1888), produced in Oregon by Abigail Duniway (and three of her six children) was "A Journal for the People, Devoted to the Interests of Humanity, Independent in Politics and Religion. Alive to all live Issues. Thoroughly Radical in Opposing and Exposing the Wrongs of the Masses." *The Farmer's Wife* (1891–1894) in Topeka, Kansas, advocated suffrage as well as Populism, prohibition, veterans' pensions, industrial protectionism and "social purity."

By the 1890s, when suffrage editors narrowed their focus to getting the vote, journals emerged for other causes. *Lucifer the Lightbearer* (1885–1906) advocated free love and anarchy. Representing a loose-knit coalition of working girls' clubs *Far and Near*'s (1890–1894) farewell editorial claimed to have eliminated some constraints, asserting: "There is no such thing as absolute failure for any conscientious effort." Among publications with broad political ambitions with respect to women's political and economic freedom and socialism was *The Socialist Woman*, started in Girard, Kansas in 1907, before eventually moving to Chicago as *The Coming Nation* (1913–1914). The well-known feminist novelist and social activist Charlotte Perkins Gilman published *The Forerunner* (1909–1916), writing nearly all its copy.

These efforts dramatized, sustained and nurtured the community of new women. Not only did the early women's rights editors form a community among themselves—writing, reprinting and borrowing from one another, they also offered a heroic model for later feminists. *Chrysalis* (1977–1980) republished selections from Susan Anthony and Amelia Bloomer. The feminist collective publishing *New Women's Times* (1975–1984) in Rochester, New York, often invoked Anthony's name.

Second-Wave Feminism

Mainstream media and counter cultural movements of the 1960s, and their periodicals, marginalized and ignored feminist issues. Radical leaders—and radical editors of publications such as *The Rat* and the *Village Voice*—were seen as conspicuously sexist. One co-founder of *off our backs*, among the best-known and certainly the longest surviving second-wave periodical in the United States, accused the *New York Guardian* of blacking out feminist news. The 1970s, therefore, gave rise to hundreds of feminist periodicals. Some lasted only for a year or two, or even only for an issue or two, when the economic, physical, and time burden of production outweighed passion and zeal for exchanging information. One highly incomplete archive, at the University of Southern California, holds more than three hundred U.S. lesbian and feminist periodicals published since the early 1970s. There have been feminist magazines for Christians; Jews (*Lilith*, published since 1976 and named for Adam's first companion, who, since she was not taken from his bone, was his equal); ecofeminists; and witches or "goddess-minded wimmin"). Various professions—nurses, lawyers, sociologists, clerical workers, teachers, business executives—maintained their own publications. In the 1970s, *Prime Time* reached older women; *La Wisp* discussed peace. *Union Wage* advocated labor issues; *Red Star* (originally *Hammer Sickle Rifle*) represented the Red Women's Detachment of the Marxist-Leninist Party; *Coyote Howls* was a highly sophisticated San Francisco-based newspaper for and by prostitutes.

Second-wave publications were highly innovative in attempts to boost funding and/or circulation. *New Directions for Women* (1972–1993) used Ford Foundation money to send issues free to prisons and mental hospitals, and federal grants to train minority women and displaced homemakers in publishing. Evolving distinctively feminist ways of working often was equally important, although developing collective, noncompetitive modes was never easy. They disdained professionalism, which smacked of hierarchy and elitism. *Notes from the First Year* was initially conceived as an unedited summary from consciousness-raising discussions. These writers did want control over their news and to be centrally involved in making news. In particular, second-wave feminists experimented with alternative formats and with innovative organization, often nonhierarchical collectivities. Sometimes jobs and titles were rotated; some collectives dispensed with titles and bylines. As a matter of political education, a few charged men more for an issue than women.

The publication *off our backs*, begun in 1970, published news of feminist and lesbian activism. The publication nearly died in 1980 when a member embezzled $5,000 from its Washington, D.C., collective. Exemplifying feminist journalism's explicitness regarding activism and advocacy, and disdain for conventional journalistic principles, *off our backs* announced mission involved global social justice and equality for women: "We intend to be just; but we do not intend to be impartial....[W]e ourselves are committed to a struggle and we will take stands to further the cause of that struggle." Still published in 2006, *oob* was the longest continuously running feminist publication in the United States.

Changes in the lesbian press encapsulate much of the trajectory of feminist journalism, from marginalization, to extreme experimentation with different ways of doing journalism, to a split between those emphasizing style and flash to attract readers, and those remaining strongly provocative, albeit, with smaller circulation. *Curve*, a glossy magazine founded as *DENEUVE* in 1991, covered entertainment, politics, and relationship issues (from columnist "Fairy Butch"). *Curve's* web site claimed that it was read by "over a quarter million well-educated, sophisticated, upwardly mobile gay women." In the mid-1970s, many separatist (that is, anti-male) lesbian magazines began, with some of them representing criticism of the feminist press as heterosexist: lesbian volunteers for *off our backs* split to form *Furies*. *Lesbian Tide* (1971–1980) rejected information from straight people or gay men; others referred to "wimmen" to avoid the word "men." Their names hinted at their strident spirit and political independence: *Amazon, Dyke, Lesbian Feminist, Sinister Wisdom, So's Your Old Lady*; many incorporated lavender into the name.

Most feminist outlets have accepted some advertising, but limit the kind of advertising they will carry; thus few attracted much advertising revenue. A few declined any advertising, such as *No More Fun and Games* (1968–1973), which looked to nontraditional money-making schemes, including film showings and poster sales; its radical "cell" also questioned all "phallic social structures," including heterosexual sex and the nuclear family.

Nonprint and Third-Wave Feminism Journalism

Broadcast feminist media are much more difficult to sustain than print editions because they cannot be produced by just a couple of women with help from family or a few volunteers. Some Pacifica stations broadcast a feminist "magazine." Women's International News Gathering Service (WINGS) produced news programs by and about women around the world. These were used by noncommercial radio stations, especially as part of feminist radio programs, but could also be heard on the Internet and on audio cassettes.

Most feminist radio shows featured music, but some local stations aired a weekly or monthly show with feminist and/or lesbian news.

Experiments in feminist television were even rarer: television production was even more difficult, more complex, and more expensive than radio. In 1996, wanting "public awareness of feminist positions, a forum for feminist thought and analysis of national policy issues, and a vehicle for recording women's herstory," the National Organization for Women (NOW) discussed possibilities for feminist television. Although the proposal stalled, feminists did use public access cable channels. For example, starting in 1994, *New Directions for Women* was produced by a New Jersey women's collective and cable-cast on public access channels in four states. So, public access was a way to express feminist positions on sex crimes, career and workplace issues, same-sex marriage, childrearing, and marital and domestic issues.

The Internet was a more accommodating space for feminist journalism, especially when the goal was not financial. Many feminists migrated to the Internet, sometimes as an adjunct to other media formats, and increasingly substituting for them. Some sites were highly self-conscious about their politics. *The Women's Space* provided news and commentary from a perspective it described as "radical feminist" and "distinctively and unapologetically woman-centered." According to the site, it offered "information and encouragement to women and girls and to men and boys who would like to be women's allies." To showcase a distinctive, self-critical feminist politics, this "Internet community" said it wanted to enlarge the space for radical feminist/lesbian separatist thought and to explore theories that even its membership opposed.

Most of the emerging opportunities for third-wave feminist journalism emphasized sassiness, edginess, or at least humor, even at the same time that they aimed to sustain a visionary global women's network. They tended to be less cutting edge with respect to political vision than to style. *BUST*, "for women with something to get off their chests," describes itself as the Voice of the New Girl Order. Unlike second-wave feminists, who refused to answer to "girls," third-wave feminists were apparently defined as, to quote *BUST*, "today's sassy girls who know that *Vogue* is vapid, *Glamour* is garbage, and *Cosmo* is clueless." Similarly, *Bitch*, whose slogan is Feminist Response to Pop Culture, critically examined images of femininity and feminism available in media. *Fierce* advertised itself as a "revolutionary magazine" for all women over twenty-one (and young, smart, edgy chicks over eighteen): *Hip Mama*, begun in 1993, took on the "true challenges and rewards" of creating a "progressive" family, from raising draft dodgers, "guerrilla mothering," to teen parents. *On The Issues: The Progressive Woman's Quarterly* asserted that "women's lives, women's thinking, women's votes, women's power matter." Published by a social psychologist who founded a women's medical center, it covered surgical alteration of genitals, the drug industry, domestic violence, as well as paganism and eco-feminism.

Conclusion

In the early twenty-first century, print media continued to be relatively easy to produce. Relative to television or radio broadcasting, or film, they required little capital investment, few technical skills, or access to complex, expensive technologies. These could be, and usually were, produced by a few people without professional journalism backgrounds. Feminist newsletters, pamphlets, journals, and magazines often embraced primitive production values on principle. Meanwhile, they greatly encouraged reader submissions. Moreover, because politically alternative print media required little money to produce, and did not need to charge much (especially since the goal is not making a profit), people could work for the sake of the project, unconcerned with appeasing advertisers. But because distribution was not free, feminists needed to be innovative in subsidizing and pricing their publications to make them accessible.

Personality and political rifts dealt fatal blows. Some feminist media died when participants were diverted by other causes, new jobs, or families. But the major problem, as well as the final straw, was nearly always that production and distribution costs exceeded revenues. For example, several periodicals emerged, but then died, to serve large and obese women, as part of what *Radiance* (1984–2000) called the "worldwide size acceptance movement." Although major bookstore chains and supermarkets may have carried *Ms.*, other feminist periodicals could only be found at independent and/or feminist bookshops, a dying breed. Internet sites, which might have avoided most of these problems, were often beset by technical issues.

Taken as a whole, these outlets not only enabled and encouraged women to experiment with mechanisms for organizing, producing, and distributing feminist news, but also help women adopt and celebrate new identities, to find one another and to legitimate and win status for their causes.

Further Reading

Endres, Kathleen L., and Theresa L. Lueck, eds. *Women's Periodicals in the United States: Social and Political Issues.* Westport, CT: Greenwood Press, 1996.

Steiner, Linda. "The History and Structure of Women's Alternative Media." In *Women Making Meaning: New Feminist Directions in Communication*, edited by Lana Rakow, 121–43. New York: Routledge, 1992.

LINDA STEINER

FIRST AMENDMENT CASES

Although the First Amendment has been part of the Constitution since 1791, the U.S. Supreme Court did little to interpret and apply it until early in the twentieth century. The Court has since developed a huge and important body of First Amendment jurisprudence, much of which has shaped the legal rights of the press. The Court has also held press freedom to be part of the "liberty" protected by the Fourteenth Amendment (*Gitlow v. New York*, 1925). For simplicity's sake, in the remainder of this entry, we will use "First Amendment" to encompass both First and Fourteenth amendment cases.

The first of the Supreme Court's major First Amendment decisions came in 1919 in *Schenck v. United States*, a decision upholding the conviction of a Socialist for violating the Espionage Act by sending pamphlets to draftees allegedly urging them to resist conscription. *Schenck* illustrated and foreshadowed a difficult problem: what standards will provide principled, reasonably consistent and predictable results that appropriately reconcile press freedom and competing interests? Courts do not apply the First Amendment literally. Rather, the amendment's directive to "make no law" has been interpreted to strongly protect the press in some contexts but to provide little or no protection in others. Publication receives more protection than the act of gathering news. The press gets more protection in print and Internet form than in broadcast form.

The Supreme Court has long emphasized that it particularly disfavors censorship. An early landmark was *Near v. Minnesota* in which the Court voided a Minnesota statute that permitted courts to permanently restrain the publication of newspapers or periodicals found to have been "malicious, scandalous and defamatory." The state used the statute to end the publication of Near's vicious and often anti-Semitic newspaper. But the Supreme Court noted that "it has been generally, if not universally, considered that it is the chief purpose of the guaranty [of freedom of the press] to prevent previous restraints upon publication." Forty years later, the Court reiterated its disapproval of prior restraint when asked by the Nixon administration to uphold injunctions stopping the *New York Times* and *Washington Post* from publishing information from the so-called Pentagon Papers (*New York Times v. United States*). The government insisted that publication of the papers—classified documents on the history of U.S. involvement in Viet Nam—would seriously harm national security. The Court held that the government had failed to provide the enormous justification necessary for prior restraint, even though several justices suggested that the newspapers might be criminally prosecuted after publication occurred.

Subsequently, the Court has rejected the use of prior restraint to stop reporters from publishing potentially prejudicial information about criminal defendants (*Nebraska Press v. Stuart*), from identifying juvenile offenders (*Smith v. Daily Mail, Oklahoma Publishing Co. v. District Court*), and from disclosing their own secret grand jury testimony after the proceedings have concluded (*Butterworth v. Smith*). However, the Court also has permitted public school officials to censor student publications in high schools (*Hazelwood School District v. Kuhlmeier*), and has upheld the CIA's requirement that agency employees submit to lifelong censorship of anything they wish to publish about the agency or intelligence gathering (*Snepp v. United States*).

Regulation or punishment of the press aside from prior restraint is an entirely different matter. Such steps still face difficult First Amendment barriers, though, especially when law is deployed because of the content or viewpoint being expressed. The press is, of course, subject to laws of general applicability as long as it is not singled out discriminatorily. For example, the press can be taxed. But if the government singles out the press for special taxation not uniformly applied to others, the courts are likely to find a First Amendment violation (*Grosjean v. American Press; Minneapolis Star v. Minnesota Commissioner of Revenue*).

Libel and invasion of privacy suits are the most common examples of attempts to punish the press. Regarding libel, the Supreme Court has given the press powerful First Amendment protection. In *New York Times v. Sullivan* and a series of subsequent cases, the Court has held that a) people suing the press for libel must prove the libel was false; and b) depending on whether they are public or private figures, plaintiffs must prove that the defendant either lied, seriously doubted the truth, or acted unreasonably. Imposing such requirements is essential, the Court has asserted, to guarantee that citizens and the press are not afraid to speak out on public issues.

Sullivan was an excellent case in point. Sullivan, an elected police commissioner, sued the *Times* after it ran an editorial advertisement/fundraising appeal from civil rights activists criticizing the police force he supervised. The ad contained factual errors and the *Times* acknowledged that it had not checked its accuracy. A jury awarded a half-million dollars. But the *Times* convinced the Supreme Court that the libel suit was little more than a disguised sedition prosecution designed to silence government critics.

The Court has not been nearly as active in the realm of privacy law. It has spoken most clearly regarding false light invasion of privacy, which involves highly offensive distortion or fictionalization that need not be defamatory. The Court simply borrowed and applied the *Sullivan* standard: false light plaintiffs must prove the defendant knowingly or recklessly distorted facts or made them up (*Time, Inc. v. Hill*).

The Court has taken a more cautious and nuanced approach when addressing cases involving the disclosure of highly personal facts about people. The first such case the Court heard involved a broadcaster who had reported the name of a murdered sexual assault victim. A reporter had obtained the name from open court records during the assailant's trial. The Court ruled that the First Amendment prohibits liability for invasion of privacy where the information comes from court records open to the public (*Cox Broadcasting v. Cohn*). In a second case, a newspaper, using information mistakenly made available by law enforcement, published the identity of a sexual assault victim while her assailant was at large. The victim suffered great psychological distress, and sued the newspaper (*Florida Star v. B. J. F.*). Publication of a sexual assault victim's identity could be the basis for liability, the Court found, but not in this case. The First Amendment provides substantial protection where the press reports legally obtained, truthful information regarding a matter of public significance—all of which applied here. Like-

wise, when a suit was brought under anti-wiretapping laws against a radio talk show host who broadcast a recording of an illegally intercepted cell phone conversation, the First Amendment saved the broadcaster—but barely. Had the conversation not been found to involve a matter of public interest, the outcome would have been different (*Bartnicki v. Vopper*).

As for other types of privacy—using someone's name or likeness for commercial purposes without consent, or physically intruding in a private space—the Court has remained largely silent. What it has said suggests little, if any, First Amendment protection (*Zacchini v. Scripps-Howard Broadcasting Co.; Hanlon v. Berger; Wilson v. Layne*).

With one notable exception, the Supreme Court has declined to recognize special First Amendment rights to gather information or have access to government proceedings. The exception is a strong First Amendment right of the press and public to attend criminal trials and pretrial hearings (*Richmond Newspapers Inc. v. Virginia; Globe Newspaper Co. v. Superior Court; Press-Enterprise v. Superior Court (I); Press-Enterprise v. Superior Court (II)*). Otherwise, the Court has reiterated that the press has no more First Amendment right to gather news than any other member of the public, and has thus upheld restrictions on press access to prisons and jails (*Pell v. Procunier; Saxbe v. Washington Post; Houchins v. KQED*). Likewise, the Court has rejected journalists' pleas for a First Amendment right to withhold confidential information from grand juries (*Branzburg v. Hayes*). In passing, the Court rather cryptically noted that "news gathering is not without its First Amendment protections." Thus far, however, those protections remain unclear.

The Supreme Court has long accorded different degrees of First Amendment protection to different media. In the print context, the Court will nearly always require the government to prove it has a compelling interest and is using the least speech-restrictive means when it wishes to regulate content. But for over-the-air broadcasting, the Court has permitted the government to impose a legal obligation to cover public affairs fairly, require access for political candidates on the same terms, provide free reply time for victims of personal attacks and for candidates broadcasters have editorially opposed, and confine indecent material to late-night hours (*Red Lion Broadcasting Co. v. FCC; CBS v. FCC; FCC v. Pacifica Foundation*). None of these regulations are constitutionally permissible for print media. More recently, the Court has granted the Internet protection equivalent to that of print (*Reno v. ACLU*). The Court seems to have concluded that cable television, too, merits print-like First Amendment protection (*U.S. v. Playboy Entertainment Group*).

Further Reading

Bartnicki v. Vopper, 532 U.S. 514 (2001).
Branzburg v. Hayes, 408 U.S. 665 (1972).
Butterworth v. Smith, 494 U.S. 624 (1990).
CBS v. FCC, 453 U.S. 367 (1981).
Cox Broadcasting v. Cohn, 420 U.S. 469 (1975).

Dienes, C. Thomas, Lee Levine, and Robert C. Lind. *Newsgathering and the Law*, 3rd ed. Newark, NJ: LexisNexis Matthew Bender, 2005.

FCC v. Pacifica Foundation, 438 U.S. 726 (1978).

Florida Star v. B. J. F., 491 U.S. 524 (1989).

Franklin, Marc A., David A. Anderson, and Lyrissa Barnett Lidsky, *Cases and Materials [on] Mass Media Law*, 7th ed. New York: Foundation Press, 2005.

Gitlow v. New York, 268 U.S. 652 (1925).

Globe Newspaper Co. v. Superior Court, 457 U.S. 596 (1982).

Grosjean v. American Press, 297 U.S. 233 (1936).

Hanlon v. Berger, 526 U.S. 808 (1999).

Hazelwood School District v. Kuhlmeier, 484 U.S. 260 (1988).

Houchins v. KQED, 438 U.S. 1 (1978).

Lewis, Anthony. *Make No Law: The Sullivan Case and the First Amendment*. New York: Random House, 1991.

Minneapolis Star v. Minnesota Commissioner of Revenue, 460 U.S. 575 (1983).

Near v. Minnesota, 283 U.S. 697 (1931).

Nebraska Press v. Stuart, 427 U.S. 539 (1976).

New Times v. Sullivan, 376 U.S. 254 (1964).

New York Times v. United States, 403 U.S. 713 (1971).

Oklahoma Publishing Co. v. District Court, 430 U.S. 308 (1977).

Pell v. Procunier, 417 U.S. 817 (1974).

Press-Enterprise v. Superior Court (I), 464 U.S. 501 (1984).

Press-Enterprise v. Superior Court (II), 478 U.S. 1 (1986).

Red Lion Broadcasting Co. v. FCC, 395 U.S. 367 (1969).

Reno v. ACLU, 521 U.S. 844 (1997).

Richmond Newspapers Inc. v. Virginia, 448 U.S. 555 (1980).

Saxbe v. Washington Post, 417 U.S. 843 (1974).

Schenck v. United States, 249 U.S. 47 (1919).

Smith v. Daily Mail, 443 U.S. 97 (1979).

Snepp v. United States, 444 U.S. 507 (1980).

Time, Inc. v. Hill, 385 U.S. 374 (1967).

U.S. v. Playboy Entertainment Group, 529 U.S. 803 (2000).

Wilson v. Layne, 526 U.S. 603 (1999).

Zacchini v. Scripps-Howard Broadcasting Co., 433 U.S. 562 (1977).

ROBERT E. DRECHSEL

FIRST LADIES

From the days of Martha Washington to the present, the wives of Presidents of the United States have drawn attention from the press. Referred to as first ladies from the middle of the nineteenth-century to the present, they have been both idealized and criticized. While journalists frequently have applauded their performances as in the case of the stylish Jackie Kennedy, at times they have been vilified, like Hillary Rodham Clinton for allegedly attempting to assume too much authority. They have been turned into targets for political attacks on their husbands' administrations as well as portrayed as symbols of their spouses' success. Study of press coverage illustrates societal ambivalence over women assuming power customarily held by men.

The position of first lady is not mentioned in the United States Constitution, but presidents' wives, in response to intense press coverage of their activities, have developed their role until today it is an important element in the American presidency. In recent decades first ladies have employed sophisticated White House communication strategies to promote administration aims including web sites used by Hillary Rodham Clinton and Laura Bush. Their public communication has been aimed in particular at women voters, at a time when family values, as personified by the president's own family, appear on political agendas.

As journalists follow the activities of first ladies today, they cover modern versions of the position as defined by the first two women to hold it, Martha Washington and Abigail Adams. Martha Washington saw herself chiefly as an official hostess for her husband, George, while Abigail Adams gave political advice to her husband, John. With Washington functioning as a traditional supportive spouse and Adams as a quasi-policy maker within the administration, the two women set the stage for a debate over the position of the president's wife that continues today. Should a first lady simply preside over the White House and take care of her husband? Or should she play an active role in the political process, as did Eleanor Roosevelt? Is there a happy medium between these two approaches? In what way does a first lady establish the style or tone of an administration? First ladies since Washington and Adams have tried to deal with these questions in the light of a press that has been eager to both praise and censure, usually in line with its own political orientation and shifting ideas on women's position in public life.

Early First Ladies

Both Washington and Adams confronted hostile press reports that contended the way they conducted themselves gave disturbing indications of their husbands' unsuitability for leadership of the new nation. Washington, referred to as "Lady Washington," was criticized for riding in an elegant coach bearing the Washington crest and pulled by six white horses. Opponents viewed this as evidence that George Washington wished to be a monarch rather than an elected president. Adams' efforts to assist her husband met virulent attacks from editors opposed to his Federalist Party. They referred to her sarcastically as "Mrs. President," ridiculed John Adams for being influenced by her and compared the couple to "Darby and Joan," comic figures in a popular ballad.

Even Dolly Madison, whose social skill made her one of the most popular first ladies in history, was not immune from criticism. When the anti-Federalist Thomas Jefferson, a widower, succeeded John Adams as president, Madison filled in as White House hostess. A vicious rumor made its way into a Federalist newspaper that she was Jefferson's mistress. When her husband, James Madison, was elected president himself in 1808 as the candidate of Jefferson's Democratic-Republican Party, Dolly Madison won public esteem. She staged White House receptions attended by both political figures and the general public at large that prompted The *National Intelligencer*, a Washington newspaper with a national circulation, to give her favorable notice. At her death in 1849 President Zachary Taylor referred to her as the nation's "First Lady," and the term came into common use with the production of a play by that name based on Madison's life in 1911.

Unlike Madison, numerous presidents' wives in the nineteenth century suffered from ill health and avoided the public eye. An exception was youthful Julia Tyler, who eloped with President John Tyler in 1844. She cultivated a reporter who fawned on her in the *New York Herald* claiming her beauty and accomplishments surpassed those of Queen Victoria. Unlike the political party press of Washington's day, the *Herald* represented the penny press, a new kind of newspaper aimed at ordinary readers, which saw president's wives as good news copy.

Mary Todd Lincoln, the unstable wife of Abraham Lincoln, received initial adulation as a "Republican Queen," following Lincoln's election in 1860 as the first Republican president. Improved printing technology allowed illustrated newspapers to show her wearing expensive gowns at White House receptions, while newspaper correspondents who flocked to Washington during the Civil War publicized her comings and goings, which included shopping trips, in telegraphed dispatches. The press soon castigated her for excessive spending while the nation was in the midst of bloody conflict. Of Southern background, she also was accused of being disloyal to the Union. Unfortunately, she took no steps to counter criticism by letting reporters know of her visits to the wounded.

The clothing and personal style of presidential wives were prominently featured in news from Washington when a group of enterprising women correspondents established careers in the capital in the 1870s. Columns on White House social life became staples supplied to newspapers across the country. Correspondents focused attention on Lucy Hayes, wife of President Rutherford B. Hayes, known as "Lemonade Lucy," because of her refusal to serve alcoholic beverages. Although women journalists generally applauded her stand on temperance, they were less pleased when she declined to support woman suffrage. Emily Edson Briggs, who wrote as "Olivia" for the *Philadelphia Press*, contended Hayes could not "hear the groans of our sex."

As press photography developed, photographs of first ladies and articles about them became highly prized for newspapers and magazines. In 1886 when Grover Cleveland became the first president to marry in office, the press eagerly spied on him and his bride, Frances Folsom, who was twenty-one years younger, in their honeymoon cottage. It was apparent that president's wives were turning into national celebrities.

Press Attention Increases

Journalistic interest in first ladies increased after women got the right to vote in 1920. Before that first ladies who wished to avoid much personal contact with reporters were able to do so. The press was slow to discover the extent to which Edith Wilson, the second wife of President Woodrow Wilson, covered up the true extent of his incapacity following a stroke. The *London Daily Mail* that disclosed the "startling" news in 1920 that she actually had been acting president by deciding who and what should be bought into her husband's sickroom.

It was Eleanor Roosevelt who greatly enhanced interaction between the first lady and Washington reporters. As the wife of Franklin D. Roosevelt, the only individual ever elected president four times, Eleanor Roosevelt held White House press conferences only for women reporters from 1933 until 1945 when her husband died in office. By refusing to admit men, she forced news organizations to hire women to cover her. A journalist herself and an influential member of the Roosevelt administration, she wrote a daily newspaper column, "My Day," billed as a diary of her activities, and was a frequent contributor to women's magazines as well as a paid radio commentator. While her press corps portrayed her favorably, newspapers opposed to Roosevelt's Democratic party criticized her for pursuing her own career, traveling extensively, speaking up on behalf of African Americans and other deprived groups, and trying to mettle in men's affairs.

Roosevelt made such an impact on the position of the first lady that ever since her day the press has tended to judge first ladies on whether they choose to follow her model of activism or play a less visible role. Roosevelt's immediate successors, Bess Truman and Mamie Eisenhower, both chose the traditional route, avoiding comment on public affairs, although they maintained cordial relations with individual press women. Like Roosevelt, they frequently were featured on women's pages, standard features of newspapers of the day that covered women's fashions, clubs and social events. Women's pages gave special attention to White House entertaining and first ladies' ceremonial activities.

Jackie Kennedy, the glamorous wife of President John F. Kennedy, revolutionized media attention to first ladies. Appearing on television, she presented an image of sophisticated elegance as she attracted a record audience of viewers for a special tour of the newly restored White House in 1962. Frequently photographed for newspapers and magazines, her regal bearing as a young wife and mother charmed world leaders and the general public alike. But, she had a love-hate relationship with White House women reporters contending they invaded her privacy.

Lady Bird Johnson, who followed Jackie Kennedy, established successful press relations by hiring an experienced press secretary, Elizabeth Carpenter. She planned numerous events for reporters making sure they were on hand to cover Johnson as she pushed her beautification campaign to improve the environment by planting flowers and screening junkyards. Johnson was more acclaimed for her press relations than her successors, Betty Ford, wife of President Gerald Ford, and Rosalynn Carter, wife of President Jimmy Carter.

Betty Ford gave a televised interview in which she said that she would not be surprised if her teenage daughter had had an affair. The remark created an initial outcry from conservative voters, although others praised Ford for her candor especially in disclosing details of her own breast cancer. Rosalynn Carter was given the unflattering term, "steel magnolia," by journalists on grounds she concealed her own ambitions to influence her husband's policies behind a façade of Southern womanhood.

Recent First Ladies

Both Republican Nancy Reagan and Democrat Hillary Rodham Clinton drew criticism from the press in different ways. During Ronald Reagan's two terms as president (from 1981–1989), Nancy Reagan, who said she had no agenda other than helping her husband, was accused of being preoccupied with her wardrobe and aloof from the public. Critics contended she exercised power behind the throne, spearheaded a "Just Say No" drug campaign that ignored complex issues, and insisted an astrologer be consulted in scheduling her husband's trips.

Hillary Rodham Clinton was known to be a top advisor to President Bill Clinton with influence like that of a co-president. Placed in charge of developing a health care system, she was unsuccessful in carrying out this task. She soon found herself the object of much hostility in part because of Whitewater and other scandals associated with the Clinton administration. Repeatedly Rodham Clinton was compared in print to Lady Macbeth. Journalists questioned her ambiguous status as both a wife and a presidential aide and debated whether stories about her belonged on the lifestyle pages, the successors to the old women's pages, or on the front pages even though she was not an elected official. They were uncertain how to deal with a new model of a first lady, one who had personal political ambitions that led to her election as Senator from New York State in the year 2000 and presidential candidacy in 2008.

Like first ladies of the late twentieth century, Laura Bush was assisted by a professional staff of about twenty, including a press secretary and other media advisors, when she served as first lady. Relatively noncontroversial like her mother-in-law, Barbara Bush, she played a relatively traditional role in presiding over the White House and promoting education, although she spoke out on behalf of women in Afghanistan. Yet, as in the case of her predecessors, media scrutiny of the role of the first lady continued, providing a kind of ongoing referendum about the position of women in American society. Through the years the media spotlight has been both kind and cruel to first ladies as journalists have evaluated their performances.

References and Further Reading

Allgor, Catherine. *Parlor Politics*. Charlottesville: University Press of Virginia, 2000.

Anthony, Carl Sferrazza. *First Ladies: The Saga of the Presidents' Wives and Their Power, 1789–2000*. Vols. 1 and 2.: Morrow, 1990, 1991.

Baldrige, Letitia. *A Lady First: My Life in the Kennedy White House and the American Embassies of Paris and Rome*. New York: Viking, 2001.

Beasley, Maurine H. *First Ladies and the Press: The Unfinished Partnership of the Media Age*. Evanston, IL: Northwestern University Press, 2005.

Boller, Paul E., Jr. *Presidential Wives: An Anecdotal History*. New York: Oxford, 1989.

Bush, Barbara. *Barbara Bush: A Memoir*. New York: Scribner, 1994.

Caroli, Betty Boyd. *First Ladies*. Expanded ed. New York: Oxford, 1995.

Carpenter, Liz. *Ruffles and Flourishes*. Garden City, N.Y.: Doubleday, 1970.

Carter, Rosalynn. *First Lady from Plains*. Boston: Houghton Mifflin, 1984.

Clinton, Hillary Rodham. *Living History*. New York: Simon and Schuster, 2003.

Eisenhower, Julie Nixon. *Pat Nixon: The Untold Story*. New York: Simon and Schuster, 1986.

Feinberg, Barbara. *First Ladies: Changing Expectations*. New York: Franklin Watts, 1998.

Ford, Betty, with Chris Chase. *The Times of My Life*. New York: Harper & Row, 1978.

Gerhart, Ann. *The Perfect Wife: The Life and Choices of Laura Bush*. New York: Simon and Schuster, 2004.

Gould, Lewis L., ed. *American First Ladies: The Lives and Legacy*. New York: Garland, 1996.

Gutin, Myra G. *The President's Partner: The First Lady in the Twentieth Century*. Westport, CT: Greenwood, 1989.

Johnson, Claudia T. (Lady Bird). *White House Diary*. New York: Holt, Rinehart and Winston, 1970.

Marton, Kati. *Hidden Power: Presidential Marriages That Shaped Our Recent History*. New York: Pantheon, 2001.

Mayo, Edith P., ed. *The Smithsonian Book of the First Ladies: Their Lives, Times and Issues*. New York: Holt, 1996.

Reagan, Nancy, with William Novak. *My Turn: The Memoirs of Nancy Reagan*. New York: Random House, 1989.

Rosebush, James S. *First Lady: Public Wife*. Lanham, MD: Madison, 1988.

Smith, Nancy Kegan, and Mary C. Ryan. *Modern First Ladies: Their Documentary Legacy*. Washington, D.C.: National Archives and Records Administration, 1989.

Troy, Gil. *Mr. and Mrs. President: From the Trumans to the Clintons*, 2nd ed. rev. Lawrence: University Press of Kansas, 2000.

Truman, Margaret. *First Ladies: An Intimate Group Portrait of White House Wives*. New York: Fawcett Columbine, 1995.

Watson, Robert P. *The Presidents' Wives: Reassessing the Office of First Lady*. Boulder, CO: Lynne Rienner, 2000.

Weidenfeld, Sheila Rabb. *First Lady's Lady. With the Fords at the White House*. New York: Putnam, 1979.

MAURINE H. BEASLEY

FLEET, THOMAS

Thomas Fleet (1685–1758), colonial Massachusetts printer, newspaperman, and editor of the *Boston Evening Post*, developed a reputation for wit, style, and most importantly, journalistic impartiality in an era of partisan presses. His newspaper was regarded as the best then published in New England.

Fleet was born in Shropshire, England, in 1685. He became an opponent of the High Church in that country and in 1712, he moved to Boston where he established a printing house on Pudding Lane. Early in his career, he printed tracts and sermons by the Puritan minister Cotton Mather, whose work was a staple of Fleet's business for the next fifteen years. In addition, Fleet, married to Elizabeth Goose, printed the stories told to his children by his mother-in-law as "Mother Goose's Melodies for Children," first published in December 1719. From 1729–1731, Fleet served as printer for the Massachusetts House of Representatives. In 1732 Fleet became publisher of the *Weekly Rehearsal*, assuming its editorship in April 1733 with the statement "the publisher of this paper declares himself of no Party, and invites all Gentlemen of Leisure and Capacity, inclined on either side, to write any thing of a political Nature, that tends to enlighten and serve the Publick." In August 1735, he renamed the *Weekly Rehearsal* the *Boston Evening Post*.

An Anglican, Fleet was highly critical of the Great Awakening; indeed, his candor led many clergy to label his newspaper heretical. Fleet's antagonism toward the Great Awakening evangelists led to increased criticism of his newspaper, forcing him to retreat from his stridency toward a more neutral posture in all areas.

Fleet understood the importance of a free and unfettered press. In 1724, under attack for printing an accurate account of Sir Robert Walpole being taken into custody, and threatened with a prosecution for seditious libel that never materialized, Fleet defended himself by maintaining the truth of what he had printed. In May 1738 Fleet reprinted an account of the Zenger Trial under the heading "The Liberty of the Press."

As a printer and editor, Fleet periodically declared himself and his paper impartial. "I am of no Party," he wrote in March 1741," but act purely as a *Printer*, and would as soon serve one Side as the other." A shrewd businessman, Fleet believed the key to success and longevity as a newspaperman lay in the ability to accommodate a diversity of interests. Fleet realized that an open press would necessarily have more patrons, more advertisers, and therefore generate more income than a partisan press. This early notion of journalistic of impartiality, or perhaps objectivity, was firmly rooted not so much in ethics as in economics.

Fleet and his newspaper earned a sterling reputation among his contemporaries. Fellow printer Isaiah Thomas called Fleet "the most enterprising journalist in Boston," and his *Boston Evening Post* the "best newspaper then published in Boston." He characterized Fleet as "industrious and economical; free from superstition; and possessed a fund of wit and humor, which were often displayed in his paragraphs and advertisements." Thomas Fleet died on July 21, 1758. The ownership and editorial responsibility of the *Boston Evening Post* went to his sons Thomas Jr. and John Fleet, who published the newspaper until its forced closure in 1775.

Further Reading

Apfelbaum, Charles and Lois Apfelbaum. *Early American Newspapers and Their Printers, 1715–1783.* Valley Stream, NY: Appletree Press, 1980.

Botein, Stephen. "'Meer Mechanics' and an Open Press: The Business and Political Strategies of Colonial American Printers." *Perspectives in American History* 9 (1975): 127–225.

Copeland, David A. *Colonial American Newspapers: Character and Content.* Dover: University of Delaware Press, 1996.

Duniway, Clyde. *The Development of Freedom of the Press in Massachusetts.* Harvard Historical Studies XII. Cambridge, MA: Harvard University Press, 1906.

Levy, Leonard W. *Freedom of Speech and Press in Early American History.* New York: Harper and Row, 1960.

Mott, Frank Luther. *American Journalism, a History: 1690–1960.* New York: Macmillan, 1962.

Sloan, William D. and Julie H. Williams. *The Early American Press, 1690–1783.* Westport, CT: Greenwood Press, 1994.

Thomas, Isaiah. *The History of Printing in America.* Ed. Marcus A McCorison. Barre, MA: Imprint Society, 1970.

JAMES L. MOSES

FOOTBALL JOURNALISM

Football journalism, like the sport itself, emerged in the Northeast over the final third of the nineteenth century. The earliest games were played by Princeton, Yale, Harvard, and a small number of nearby universities (Rutgers, Columbia, Pennsylvania, Stevens, Tufts), many of whose graduates were socially and professionally prominent citizens of New York, Boston, and Philadelphia. The activities of their alma maters were thus worthy of attention from those cities' newspapers. The large-circulation newspapers in New York in the late 1880s and early 1890s played the key role in creating the conventions of football journalism soon adopted throughout the country. Their accounts of the championship games played by Harvard, Yale, and Princeton, the so-called Big Three, were widely syndicated and imitated in local coverage, a process of diffusion that transformed the extracurricular activities at a handful of Northeastern universities—at a time when just 2 to 4 percent of American males attended college—into a truly national popular spectacle by the end of the century.

The Daily and Weekly Press

From the inaugural contest between Princeton and Rutgers in 1869, and into the early 1880s, the coverage of intercollegiate football matches was meager and almost exclusively local. With the formation of the Intercollegiate Football Association in 1876 by Harvard, Yale, Princeton, and Columbia, an end-of-the-season championship game was established, to be played on Thanksgiving Day on the grounds of one of the competing schools. Transplanting the contest in 1880 to New York, as the site most convenient for the students from all of the association's schools, set the stage for the game's transformation. Football became a beneficiary of the newspaper revolution in New York in the 1880s and 1890s, led by Joseph Pulitzer and William Randolph Hearst. After purchasing the *World* in 1883, Pulitzer increased its football coverage and enhanced it with all of the innovations he brought to the modern newspaper—sensationalism, lavish illustration, Sunday supplements, a separate sports section, an even more sensationalistic evening edition. The *World*, in turn, influenced the coverage in rival papers, including the *New York Herald* and the *Journal* after Hearst acquired it in 1895, to up the ante in sensationalism.

Hearst also introduced the star reporter to the sports pages, when he hired Richard Harding Davis and Stephen Crane to cover big games in 1895 and 1896.

The most distinctive aspect of football journalism as it acquired its own conventions in this formative period was its divided attention to the contests themselves and the socially distinguished spectators who attended them. From its beginnings as a college game, football had a very different place in the American sporting landscape from baseball (or certainly boxing), and newspaper coverage emphasized its association with the social elite. At the same time, the most striking aspect of the game accounts was the purplish prose and extravagant allusions and metaphors more typical of journalism pitched to the lower classes. Newspaper coverage from this period established football, with its star players and concept of team play, as heroic, even epic or mythic, combat, securing the game's cultural power at a time of great anxiety over the enervating impact of modern life.

As sports coverage in daily newspapers increased by 50 percent over the first two decades of the twentieth century, the conventions of football journalism became fully established throughout the country. The game was promoted and popularized by such writers as Walter Camp who selected football's All-American teams until his death in early 1925. Coverage of football more than doubled again in the 1920s, as sports in general and football in season became primary reasons for male readers to buy newspapers. Professional football was first organized in 1920, in what soon became the National Football League, but the pro game remained a comparatively minor affair by latter-day television era standards through the 1930s, even in the cities that fielded teams in the NFL; and elsewhere it was all but ignored into the 1950s. Football journalism thus developed largely in response to intercollegiate football.

Intersectional rivalry was intense in the 1920s and 1930s, as football teams in the Midwest, Far West, and South carried the banner of their cities, states, and regions into combat with the Eastern establishment and each other. Syndicated sports columnists for the major newspapers—including Walter Eckersall, Damon Runyon, Lawrence Perry, and preeminently Grantland Rice—became famous national "experts" on the national football scene, but the most important voices in each newspaper were their own writers. It has long been conventional to think of the sports writing of this era as belonging to either the "Gee Whiz" or the "Aw Nuts" school: the extravagant mythmakers were led by Grantland Rice, whose christening of the 1924 Notre Dame backfield as the Four Horsemen is one of the most famous leads in sports journalism history but was also typical of this style. Rice carefully cultivated his friendship with Notre Dame Coach Knute Rockne, helping to make Rockne and the Fighting Irish national icons. Rice named University of Illinois running back Red Grange "the Galloping Ghost," helping to launch Grange's career in films and his future with the Chicago Bears and the National Football League. Nay sayers among sportswriters included such well-known figures as Runyon, Ring Lardner, and W.

O. McGeehan. This distinction addressed only the famous columnists. In the broader world of sports journalism, debunking was limited to metropolitan newspapers. Local sportswriters and columnists were always boosters of the home team, whether they indulged in the colorful allusions and metaphors of the Rice school or wrote in a plainer style. Beginning in the 1940s, Red Smith of the *New York Herald Tribune* set a new standard for sports journalists in writing directly but also artfully, in an understated way, about football and other sports.

The 1920s and 1930s also saw a thriving African American press, ethnic press, Jewish and Catholic press—voices from outside the football mainstream clamoring to get in. The coverage of black-college football in newspapers such as the *Chicago Defender* and *Pittsburgh Courier* mirrored the reporting and commentary in the mainstream newspapers. The black press also maintained a constant challenge to segregation and to discrimination in "mixed football" that was all but ignored in mainstream newspapers. The Jewish and ethnic papers covered "our boys" wherever they played: the Polish or Italian or Bohemian or Jewish players at colleges throughout the land. The Catholic press had its own schools to follow: Fordham, St. Mary's, Duquesne, Villanova, Georgetown, Boston College, and preeminently Notre Dame among a dozen others. The black press selected its annual All-America teams from the black colleges; several of the ethnic and religious papers named All-Polish, All-Italian, All-Jewish, or All-Catholic All-Americans. In celebrating their own, however, all of these papers campaigned for inclusion in the American mainstream.

The Periodical Press

During the period between the two world wars, football journalism also thrived in popular magazines. The great general-interest weeklies, the *Saturday Evening Post* and *Collier's*, led the way, with celebrity profiles and "inside dope" appearing in virtually every issue during the season. Magazine journalists overwhelmingly celebrated college football, with the exception of the writers in the intellectual journals, who tended to be highly critical of "professionalism" in the supposedly amateur sport. Much of the football journalism in popular magazines was written "by" or "with" the famous football coaches of the day, for whom such publication provided a lucrative side income (as the coach's weekly television show would later do). Ghostwriters and publicity directors at the colleges actually wrote much of this material, which helped make heroes of top coaches. In 1937, Francis Wallace inaugurated in the *Saturday Evening Post* what became another staple of football journalism, the preseason preview. In the late 1930s, the photojournalism of *Life* and *Look* brought new attention to the pageantry of big-time college football and to the larger social world—Homecoming weekends, alumni reunions, small-town passions for high-school football—in which the sport was deeply embedded.

From football's beginnings through the 1950s, the print

media wielded power and influence in the world of football that journalists would never have again. The large-circulation newspapers in New York in the 1880s and 1890s played a key role in transforming college football into a national spectator sport. Beginning in the 1920s, radio was a powerful force in binding fans to their local teams, while newsreels contributed importantly to the celebrity of football heroes and did much to establish bowl games and the Army-Navy game as major cultural events. University administrators found that promoting sports was big business. One hundred thousand seat stadiums were built in the roaring twenties transforming college football into civic spectacle.

If through the early 1950s print journalists in particular dictated how the public thought about football, during the era that followed, television was much more powerful as a medium, although its influence was more diffused. In a super-saturated media world, no single voice or collection of voices could have the power of the daily and periodical press before the coming of television.

Football Journalism in the Age of Television

Two key factors, television and the cultural revolution of the 1960s, radically changed football journalism. In the 1960s, public relations specialist Pete Rozelle, working as Commissioner of the National Football League, helped bring the sport to the top tier of television attractions, by signing a national contract with the CBS television network, by merging with the rival American Football League, and by creating, starting in 1967, the Super Bowl. When Rozelle became league commissioner in January 1960, professional football had ten teams playing twelve-game schedules in half-filled stadiums. Several of the teams had no television contracts. At his retirement in 1989, twenty-eight teams of the National Football League were playing a sixteen-game schedule before packed houses and record ratings, culminating in Monday Night Football and Super Bowl Sunday, major cultural events.

Television, of course, had a major impact on such sports as football but it also changed journalism. One of its early victims was the general-interest magazine, as *Collier's* ceased publication in 1957, the *Saturday Evening Post* in 1968, *Look* in 1971, and *Life* in 1972. As magazines increasingly became specialized, *Sports Illustrated*, which began publication in 1954, became one of the most successful publications of the second half of the twentieth century. Initially uncertain about its product and audience—wary of popular team sports and striving to be a "literary" journal for upscale readers—the magazine found its bearings by the late 1960s under the legendary editor, André Laguerre, as a magazine that covered all sports, including football, often with literary distinction. In addition to its football "experts" such as Tex Maule (an early champion of the professional game), writers such as Dan Jenkins and Frank Deford brought the perspectives and distinctive styles of the best magazine journalists to their writing on football.

Under Laguerre and for another decade after he retired in 1974, *Sports Illustrated* was essential reading for serious football fans.

Sports Illustrated's place in the world of the sporting media was challenged by ESPN, the all-day, all-sport cable television network that debuted in 1979. With television's arrival in the 1950s, the daily press had continued to be the principle source of sporting news through the 1970s. Newspaper football coverage changed at the end of this period for a different reason: the general shift in journalism after Watergate and the turmoil of the 1960s to more critical coverage of "the Establishment." By the late 1970s, football reporters in the daily press were no longer ignoring the personal failings of the athletes and coaches they covered, and they were paying keen attention to the ethical and financial aspects of the game. This shift created a particular dilemma for sportswriters and columnists in college towns, where athletic departments and many readers expected them to continue playing the traditional booster role.

ESPN had a major impact on both *Sports Illustrated* and the sports departments of daily newspapers. As football fans and sports fans generally relied more and more on ESPN and its signature program, *SportsCenter*, for late-breaking scores, highlights, and features, print publications had to redefine their roles. *Sports Illustrated* tried to hold readers through in-depth reporting and a willingness to tackle controversial issues (although by the late 1990s it was publishing fewer such stories and trying harder to capture younger readers with busy graphics and quickly digestible articles). Newspaper journalists wrote less about the games—their readers had likely already seen the highlights on *SportsCenter* and maybe the games themselves, as the airwaves became saturated with both college and professional football in the 1980s—and more about athletes' off-field behavior and the business practices of local franchises. ESPN, in turn, strove to assert its "journalistic" against its "entertainment" side, through tougher interviewing and investigative stories. In 1998, it also launched its own print publication, *ESPN The Magazine*, to compete directly for *Sports Illustrated*'s readers, though with an emphasis on attracting eighteen to thirty-four-year-old males, the demographic most coveted by advertisers. *Sports Illustrated* responded by entering the cable market in a joint venture with CNN.

The competition between ESPN and *Sports Illustrated* points to the future of football journalism: newspapers and magazines struggling to remain essential, as television and the new electronic media become increasingly pervasive. Magazines such as *Esquire*, *The New Yorker*, and the *New York Times Magazine* continue to publish occasional, high-quality football journalism, and books by journalists such as H. G. Bissinger's *Friday Night Lights* (1990) and David Maraniss's biography of Vince Lombardi, *When Pride Still Mattered* (1999), signaled new possibilities for serious football nonfiction. But football in the new century increasingly belonged to the worlds of television and the Internet, rather than to the traditional print media.

Further Reading

Levine, Peter. *Ellis Island to Ebbets Field: Sport and the American Jewish Experience.* New York: Oxford University Press, 1992.

Lipsyte, Robert. *SportsWorld: An American Dreamland.* New York: Quadrangle Books, 1975.

McChesney, Robert. "Media Made Sport: A History of Sports Coverage in the United States." In *Media, Sports & Society,* edited by Lawrence A. Wenner. Newbury Park, CA: Sage Publications, 1989.

Nugent, William Henry. "The Sports Section." *American Mercury,* March 1929.

Oriard, Michael. *King Football: Sport & Spectacle in the Golden Age of Radio & Newsreels, Movies & Magazines, the Weekly & the Daily Press.* Chapel Hill: University of North Carolina Press, 2001.

——. *Reading Football: How the Popular Press Created an American Spectacle.* Chapel Hill: University of North Carolina Press, 1993.

Woodward, Stanley. *Sports Page.* New York: Simon & Schuster, 1949.

MICHAEL ORIARD

FORBES

Offering coverage that ranged from commerce and high finance to technology and lifestyle trends, *Forbes* was a personality driven business magazine aimed at both established executives and middle-level managers who aspired to success in the business world. A biweekly, it celebrated the pursuit of profit and the cut and thrust of capitalism without apology.

The publication was founded in 1917 by Scottish immigrant Bertie Charles "B.C." Forbes and was the first modern business magazine in the nation. Primarily reported and written by founder Forbes himself, it soon gained a reputation for its colorful focus on "doers and doings" in American private enterprise. This emphasis on the personalities behind the business headlines remains today. The vibrant writing, however, was based on sound journalism, and the magazine soon earned a reputation for solid reporting and sharp business savvy. For example, *Forbes* warned readers about the impending stock market crash of October, 1929, months before it occurred.

Inspired by this periodical's success, during the 1930s other publishing companies started competitors, most notably *Business Week* and *Fortune.* In response, *Forbes* broadened its coverage of U.S. industry and, during the 1940s, at the urging of B.C. Forbes's second son, Malcolm, introduced a celebratory annual feature on the country's leading corporations. The idea eventually developed into the acclaimed *Forbes 500* issue.

By the late 1950s, after an unsuccessful run for the governorship of New Jersey, Malcolm was playing a larger role in the magazine's affairs, and he assumed complete control of the family-owned parent company, Forbes, Inc., in 1964. In the sometimes bland world at the top echelons of American business, Malcolm stood out for both his eccentricity

and *joie de vivre.* He became famous for extravagant parties at his chateau in France, a brief romance with Elizabeth Taylor, a documentary film he financed about a motorcycle odyssey across China, and late in life, an appetite for the pleasures to be found in the darker corners of New York City's *demimonde.*

Malcolm Forbes's buoyant personality seemed ideally matched to the outspoken persona of the magazine. He initiated an enormously successful advertising campaign around the motto: "Forbes: Capitalist Tool." With similar bravado, he used the family yacht *Highlander* to entertain advertisers on lavish evening cruises on the Hudson River.

In 1982, *Forbes* launched its famous "Forbes Richest 400" list. The compendium of profiles of the richest individuals in the United States was an instant hit. It celebrated the material apex of the American Dream, earned the magazine untold free publicity, and became a highly anticipated annual feature.

At the time of Malcolm's death in 1990, his son, Malcolm Stevenson (Steve) Forbes Jr., assumed the roles of CEO of the company and editor-in-chief of *Forbes.* Under his direction, *Forbes FYI,* a quarterly lifestyle supplement, debuted in 1990, and two years later, *Forbes ASAP* (1992–2002), a technology quarterly supplement, also appeared. In 1998, the company launched an English-language international edition, *Forbes Global Business and Finance.* Other country-specific editions in local languages (e.g., *Forbes Korea, Forbes China, Forbes Russia*) followed.

Eight decades after its debut, *Forbes* magazine continued to prosper. Still faithful to its founder's belief in laissez-faire capitalism, as well as to his journalistic focus on business news and personalities, its paid circulation in 2004 stood at more than 810,000.

Further Reading

Bodine, Paul S. "Forbes" *International Directory of Company Histories,* vol. 30. Chicago: St. James Press. Gale Research Co. 2000.

Forbes Magazine, http://www.forbesinc.com/company/

Winans, Christopher. *Malcolm Forbes: The Man Who Had Everything.* New York: St. Martin's Press, 1990.

Heller, Robert. "The Battle for U.S. Business." *Management Today.* Aug. 1984.

Kuczynski, Alex. "Changing of the Guard, and Coverage, at *Forbes* Magazine." *New York Times,* October 12,1998.

DAVID ABRAHAMSON
ILENE ROSENBLUM

FORUM

A monthly magazine with a title that embodied its purpose, *Forum* dedicated itself to presenting the pro-and-con arguments on issues of the day for the first twenty years of its existence. Relying on an editor who decided what subjects should be covered and on contributors recognized as authorities or experts, *Forum* was considered a valuable resource for colleges and universities for most of the 1890s, and faculty often required students to read articles in the magazine for classroom discussions.

Forum started in March 1886. It achieved a respectable circulation of thirty thousand copies a month several years onward under editor Walter Hines Page (1891–1895). Page recruited well-known authorities and experts whose celebrity status would attract more readers. Page also had an ability to anticipate the emergence of important national and international issues, which added a greater degree of timeliness to *Forum* articles.

Articles on economics, education, literature, racial relations, religion, science, and social problems filled *Forum*'s pages. The magazine presented perspectives on cartels, a federal income tax, labor unions, and immigration.

Forum distinguished itself from 1898 through 1900 with numerous articles on the issue of imperialism while Congress and the public debated whether to annex the islands of Guam, the Philippines, and Puerto Rico acquired by victory in the Spanish-American War. Among the articles were "Isolation or Imperialism" (September 1898), "Shall We Keep the Philippines?" (November 1898), and "Do We Owe Independence to the Filipinos?" (June 1900, when Filipino nationalists fought against U.S. governance).

Readership declined, however, and *Forum* distributed only about fifteen thousand copies a month early in the twentieth century. The magazine switched to quarterly publication in 1902, and relied mostly on a staff of editors to write articles in various subjects. Readership did not increase.

Monthly publication resumed in 1908 when *Forum* expanded its format to include fiction, poetry, and reviews. Early work by Sherwood Anderson, H.L. Mencken, and Edna St. Vincent Millay appeared. Readership gradually increased.

The 1920s saw the return of pro-and-con articles on important contemporary issues, while retaining fiction and poetry. Subjects of interest included communism, religious fundamentalism, and military preparedness. Again, well-known contributors wrote articles. Circulation reached ninety thousand copies a month at the end of the decade.

Although moderately popular, *Forum* never was profitable, a condition worsened by the national financial crisis of the 1930s. The publisher bought *Century* magazine, an esteemed but weak publication, and merged it with *Forum* in mid-1930 in an effort to make the magazine more attractive to advertisers by adding an upper-class element.

Forum and Century provided many informative articles on possible cures for the nation's economic situation during the Great Depression, an era when advertising revenue fell dramatically and many readers stopped buying the magazine.

Circulation had fallen to about thirty-five thousand copies a month in mid-1940, prompting the sale of *Forum and Century* to *Current History* magazine. Another transfer of ownership ensued a few years later, another name change

and reappearance under its original title, and then *Forum* ceased to exist in January 1950.

Further Reading

Tebbel, John, and Mary Ellen Zuckerman. *The Magazine in America: 1741–1990*. New York: Oxford University Press, 1991.

JAMES LANDERS

FOX NEWS

9:31 a.m. Baghdad Time. April 7, 2003. Members of the U.S. Army's Third Infantry Division have arrived in central Baghdad and embedded Fox reporter Greg Kelly was with them. "This is a statue of Saddam Hussein on his horse," reported the voice of Brian Wilson from the Fox News (1996–) Channel desk in New York. "We have been led to believe that U.S. forces may be about to blow up this statue." At that moment, the statue suddenly disappeared from the screen and loud cheering could be heard. "Well, it looks like it just got blown up, ladies and gentlemen. Oh, my gosh." Moments later, Muhammad Saeed al-Sahhaf, the Iraqi Information Minister also known as "Baghdad Bob," was telling reporters that "no American troops have entered the center of Baghdad. We have surrounded and slaughtered them." As Sahhaf spoke, Fox on a split screen replayed Saddam Hussein's statue "being blown to smithereens."

What the rival Cable News Network (CNN) was calling the "War in Iraq," Fox was reporting as "Operation Iraqi Freedom," the words the George W. Bush administration was using to justify its preemptive strike into the Middle Eastern nation. Fox's war reporting would solidify its place in cable news. In 2002, the then six-year-old cable news network surpassed CNN in sustained viewership. In June 2004, surveys showed that one in four Americans claimed to "regularly watch" Fox News; higher viewership than any over the air or cable network. By the spring, 2006, the network's one-and one-half million prime time watchers was higher than the combined totals of CNN, CNBC, and MSNBC. The network's growing popularity led to charges that its "conservative bias" tilted stories in the direction of the Republican Party. Fifty-two percent of all Fox News viewers described themselves as "conservatives." One-third of all Republicans claimed to regularly watch the network while only one in four Democrats watched. And only one in four Democrats said they believed "all or most" of what they saw on Fox News, the lowest number for any news network. Former President Bill Clinton charged that the network had done "a hatchet job on me." Political activist Robert Greenwald, producer of the documentary "Outfoxed: Rupert Murdoch's War on Journalism," claimed, "Fox is not a conservative network, it's a Republican network." And one research team described "a Fox News effect" that had pushed the electorate to the right just enough to elect George Bush in 2000 and to sustain Republican Party strength in 2004.

When Fox News Channel went on the air October 7,

1996, the morning after the first Bill Clinton–Bob Dole presidential debate, few people took it seriously and it was not even carried in New York, where its signal originated. Australian-born Rupert Murdoch, who had made millions in British tabloids, had for a year been planning to compete with the established, sixteen-year-old CNN. CNN founder Ted Turner said he was "looking forward to squashing Rupert like a bug." Murdoch hired Roger Ailes, a political consultant to Richard Nixon, Ronald Reagan, and George H.W. Bush. Ailes, who had successfully launched CNBC as a financial news network, watched CNN closely and thought "they were boring and looked like a network that had never had any competition. We started with 25 percent of the resources of CNN. Not a single person predicted we'd be alive a year later." Fox positioned itself "as David going up against the Goliath of the liberal news media," observed one media researcher. "It was a brilliant master stroke." Fox initially interested many Americans "who believed the networks were liberal and Democratic-leaning," concluded another university professor. Shepard Smith, a ten-year veteran at Fox, saw a network "producing newscasts for people in small-town America who felt they weren't being served by news that had a New York attitude."

From its inception, Fox looked different than its competitors. Its screen was busier. It scrolled headlines at the bottom of its frame, plastered notes in the corners and relied on exploding graphics as a bridge to shows and segments. "Viewers hadn't seen anything like it," says Terry Anzur of NBC News. Soon, other networks broke out computer-generated graphics to dress up their broadcasts. Newsbreaks began with an ominous tolling bell and the title card "Fox Alert." Ailes understood the importance of not only doing news "but building shows around personalities that have strong opinions about the news." These personalities included Geraldo Rivera, Bill O'Reilly, Sean Hannity, Neil Cavuto, and John Gibson as daily hosts of news interview shows with a decided point of view. The network's motto was, "We report. You decide," but one media critic maintained that "all too often Fox both reports and decides."

ABC News White House correspondent Brit Hume joined Fox News in December 1996 and became managing editor of its nightly *Special Report*. In May 1998, Hume was joined by Washington insiders Fred Barnes and Morton Kondrake, who left *The McLaughlin Group*, to do news analysis for Fox during the Clinton impeachment controversy. In December 1999, the network achieved its highest ever rating when it conducted a live forum with six Republican presidential contestants. In October 2000, for the first time Fox News tied CNN in the monthly ratings and *The O'Reilly Factor* beat CNN's highest rated show *Larry King Live* in household ratings. Researchers at the University of California-Berkeley and Stockholm University analyzing George W. Bush's razor-thin win over Al Gore in the contested 2000 presidential election concluded that Fox may have been responsible for increasing Bush's vote total by two hundred thousand nationwide and by ten thousand in the battleground state of Florida, enough to "likely have been decisive in the close election."

The network's viewership increased after the terrorist attacks on September 11, 2001. Fox beat CNN in both daytime and prime-time ratings across the board. In November 2003, veteran network correspondent Chris Wallace became the host of *Fox News Sunday* to compete with NBC's *Meet the Press* and CBS's *Face the Nation*. In September 2004, Hume, Wallace, Barnes, and Kondrake, joined by political correspondents Tony Snow, syndicated columnist Charles Krauthammer, Martha MacCallum, the *Weekly Standard*'s Bill Kristol, Fox News contributor Mara Liasson, and others, had a larger audience in their coverage of the Republican National Convention than any of the networks. It was the first time a cable news network had beaten a broadcast news network in special events coverage. In April 2006, Snow left Fox to become press secretary to President Bush. By the end of 2006, the network reached ninety million American households and was seen in fifty-five countries worldwide. The network's radio news operation, begun in 2003, grew in two years to a sixty-station full service network, staffed by Fox News personalities. A deal struck with Clear Channel Communications and Sirius Satellite radio gave Fox worldwide reach.

In the early twenty-first century, critics divided sharply over how to evaluate the significance of Fox News. The Pew Center for the People and the Press found that the network's "vitality" came from its unparalleled recognition of the "political polarization" of the American electorate and in their "news viewing habits."

Further Reading

Anderson, Brian C. "Fox News: Enraging Liberals for Ten Years," *Los Angeles Times*, October 4, 2006.

Collins, Scott. *Crazy Like a Fox: The Inside Story of How Fox News Beat CNN.* New York: Penguin Press, 2004.

Friedman, Jon. "Why Fox Remains No. 1 in Cable News," *MarhetWatch*, Oct. 6, 2006.

"News Audiences Increasingly Politicized," Pew Research Center for the People and the Press, Survey Reports, June 8, 2004.

"Outfoxed: Rupert Murdoch's War on Journalism," a documentary film produced by Robert Greenwald, 2004.

"Roger Ailes Interview," *Washington Journal*, C-Span, August 16, 1999.

BRUCE J. EVENSEN

FRANK LESLIE'S ILLUSTRATED NEWSPAPER

Frank Leslie's was the nation's first successful illustrated newspaper (1855–1922) and a major force in pictorial journalism in the last half of the nineteenth century. The paper was founded as a sixteen-page weekly in December 1855 by Frank Leslie, an energetic engraver and journalistic entrepreneur who pioneered news illustrations as a better way of understanding the world.

Leslie was born Henry Carter in Ipswich, England, in 1821. As a child Carter was interested in art and wood engraving, a passion his father, a successful manufacturer, discouraged. Undeterred, young Henry submitted sketches to London publishers as "Frank Leslie," which soon became his professional name. After a stint at the *Illustrated London News*, Leslie immigrated to New York in 1848, where he made illustrations for P.T. Barnum. In 1852, he became the chief engraver for *Gleason's Pictorial Drawing-Room Companion*, a feature-oriented magazine in Boston. Restless and ambitious, Leslie soon returned to New York to establish his own publishing firm. His first magazine was a monthly, *Frank Leslie's Ladies' Gazette of Fashion and Fancy Needlework*. Using income from this and another magazine, *Frank Leslie's New York Journal of Romance*, he established *Frank Leslie's Illustrated Newspaper* as a popular—and sometimes lurid—periodical filled with eye-catching illustrations. "His plan," one of his journalists later noted, "was to give exact illustrations of the current events of the day, and in this way make them a prime agent in the instruction of the people." For ten cents a week, Americans could see—thanks to wood-block engraving—images of people and places they would not otherwise encounter.

One of *Leslie's* strengths was speed—getting images to the public faster than the competition. Instead of one engraver taking a week or more to produce a full-page engraving, Leslie broke the image into sections and used teams of engravers to turn out full-page pictures overnight. Like Barnum, Leslie had a keen sense of what the public wanted, and the paper illustrated crime reports, disasters, sports, and other sensational stories to attract readers. *Leslie's* also mounted popular crusades, including an exposé of New York's "swill milk" in the late 1850s that boosted the paper's circulation and prompted new dairy regulations. By 1857, the paper's success inspired Fletcher Harper to start a rival—and more respectable—illustrated paper, *Harper's Weekly*. Both papers prospered during the Civil War, with *Leslie's* circulation climbing as high as one hundred sixty thousand.

Leslie died in 1880, his publishing empire overextended and in debt. His flamboyant and savvy second wife, Miriam, revived *Leslie's* in 1881 by scooping the competition with the first illustrations of President James Garfield's assassination. She sold the weekly in 1889. The new owners, W.J. Arkell and Russell B. Harrison, continued *Leslie's* emphasis on images. "The eye cannot wait to compass a column of description when, with a glance, it can traverse Africa in a picture, explore Egypt in another...," they wrote. Although circulation rose during the Spanish American War and World War I, *Leslie's* continued to lose readers. The paper ceased publication in 1922, its nineteenth-century visual style a victim of a newer journalistic form, news photography.

Further Reading

Brown, Joshua. *Beyond the Lines: Pictorial Reporting, Everyday Life, and the Crisis of Gilded Age America*. Berkeley: University of California Press, 2002.

Mott, Frank Luther. *A History of American Magazines, 1850–1865*. Cambridge, MA: Harvard University Press, 1938.

JOHN M. COWARD

FRANKLIN, BENJAMIN

When he composed a seriocomic epitaph for his future gravesite, a young colonial tradesman wrote about the body of "B. Franklin, Printer" lying there like an empty, deteriorated book cover, but hoping to appear again someday on a new and corrected edition. Benjamin Franklin (January 17, 1706–April 17, 1790) often looked ahead and considered not only what would improve himself, but also what would foster progress in government, human knowledge, and everyday life. He made celebrated contributions to the world as a statesman, scientist, and inventor, but never lost his pride in his initial occupation. His last will and testament, made at the end of his long and illustrious life, began, "I, Benjamin Franklin, of Philadelphia, printer...." He relied on his skill with words and knowledge from print culture to became a moral leader and democratic philosopher who personified America's Enlightenment.

Early Life and Career

As a boy in a large Puritan family of modest means in Boston, Franklin had little schooling, but ample curiosity and a love of reading. Two books particularly impressed him, one by Daniel Defoe about civic improvements and another by Cotton Mather about doing good. At the age of twelve, Franklin entered the printing trade in Boston as an apprentice to his twenty-one-year-old brother James. Benjamin wrote news ballads and hawked them in the streets until his sagacious father Josiah warned him that verse-makers were usually beggars. The son took the advice and, with *The Spectator* (published in England by Joseph Addison and Richard Steele) as a model, started prose writing, a skill that he described in his autobiography as a principal means of his advancement.

Using the pseudonym "Silence Dogood," Franklin submitted humorous essays to his brother's newspaper, *The New-England Courant*, in 1722. The two brothers and other contributors made the *Courant* a forum for witty criticism of public officials and Puritan leaders. When the Massachusetts legislature reacted by jailing James for a month, his apprentice refused to cooperate when questioned and, taking over the paper, republished a *London Journal* essay saying that a free people have a right to free expression. Eventually, finding himself in conflict with his older sibling as well as the government, Benjamin ran away to Philadelphia where he worked for Samuel Keimer, an eccentric printer who also quarreled with him.

After some misadventures in London where he had gone to buy printing equipment to start his own business back in the colonies, Franklin returned to Philadelphia in 1726 with resolutions to make his life better by practicing frugality, honesty, and industry and by praising rather than defaming others. He then initiated a personal project to achieve moral excellence by putting more virtues on his list and developing a private liturgy for himself. Franklin's efforts, which he later chronicled in his autobiography, failed from time to time, but, as he expected, he found that the self-discipline made him happier and that a person could do well in the world by doing good.

Franklin grew rich with reliable job printing and a successful newspaper, the *Pennsylvania Gazette*. Keimer started the paper to beat Franklin into journalism, but the publication did not prosper. Writing under pseudonyms in Philadelphia's only other paper, Andrew Bradford's *American Weekly Mercury*, Franklin broke one of his resolutions by ridiculing Keimer and was soon able to buy the *Gazette* for a small sum. The newspaper took popular positions under Franklin and proved to be more entertaining and skillfully edited than the *Mercury*.

The *Gazette* and the sayings in his *Poor Richard's Almanack*, Franklin wrote in his memoirs, provided the common citizen with morally instructive reading. He also said that he kept personal libel out of his paper. When Franklin had something particularly controversial to say he usually did not endanger the good will his paper had generated. A number of his more stinging or risqué essays appeared in pamphlets or in essays published in other newspapers without his name. Some of the pieces were not identified as his until more than two centuries later.

Franklin's stealthy writings included hoaxes that made fun of rigid religious or legal thinking. His "The Speech of Miss Polly Baker," for example, has a brassy woman, who was repeatedly prosecuted for having children out of wedlock, convince a court not to punish her again by making clever, logical arguments and citing the biblical command to "increase and multiply." One of her judges marries her the next day. The tale, which readers often believed was true, was reprinted on both sides of the Atlantic for several decades before he admitted authorship.

Conventional morality could be too much strain at times for Franklin. (One example was his son William, who became Royal Governor of New Jersey in 1763, being born out of wedlock in about 1731.) Generally, however, he was concerned with being an upright citizen and earned the respect of others with his commitment to personal rectitude and public-spirited projects. He was a stern family patriarch and, for both profit and the public good, set up a network of printing offices that stretched across British North America.

Thinking Philadelphia could be improved with joint efforts, Franklin orchestrated the creation of a library, fire company, defense association, college, hospital, and insurance company. He held offices in Pennsylvania and became a deputy postmaster general for North America. His electrical experiments, inventions, and writings made him an international celebrity and won him the respect of scientists in Europe and elsewhere. No American on the eve of the Revolution was better known or more admired.

Franklin on the World Stage

Franklin's extraordinary intellect, dedication to service, and a pleasing personality made him one of the most famous individuals of his time. To many he represented what a person from an ordinary background could achieve with opportunity and the right ideas. To some political opponents and later scholars, however, he could seem like a wily poseur. Maintaining principles at all times was not easy, but Franklin did take seriously his beliefs in freedom, democracy, morality, and the betterment of humanity.

Thinking he had grown wealthy enough and hoping to devote himself to science, Franklin retired from active involvement in his printing business in 1748. His pen remained active, however, as he became embroiled in public controversies and sketched out a vision of a democratic future at a time when the prevailing form of government was monarchy.

Franklin lived in England for most of the twenty years before America declared independence. He represented the Pennsylvania Assembly and later other colonies in arguing for their causes. The experience became frustrating as his often moderate positions and sometimes self-serving actions made him distrusted on both sides of the Atlantic, but he wrote many pointed and sometimes sardonic newspaper essays defending America and warning about the consequences of British policies.

Sent to France to negotiate for assistance after the American Revolution broke out, Franklin set up a press at his residence to print diplomatic materials, propaganda, and amusing essays for his French friends. One of his publications was *Information for Those Who Would Remove to America*, which was published in both English and French for readers interested in moving to the new nation. The essay offered practical advice about employment and portrayed the country as a land of opportunity, plain virtues, and mutual forbearance. Franklin charmed the French with his natural, down-to-earth demeanor and was lionized as a new world sage.

Franklin was a calming presence at the Constitutional Convention in 1787, particularly at the end when he wrote a widely reprinted speech on the need to approve a document that might be imperfect, but that was nevertheless necessary and as close to perfect as the delegates could make it. He asked the delegates to doubt their own infallibility as far as the flaws were concerned and to realize that any form of government was a blessing to the people if well administered and that any system would collapse into despotism when the people become corrupt enough to need it.

Franklin often worried about democratic debate and the associated journalism becoming too heated and demeaning. In an essay published by the *Federal Gazette* in 1789 as Congress was completing its work on the Bill of Rights, he explained that he thought press freedom meant a right to express opinions on public matters, but should not mean a liberty to make false statements damaging to an individual's reputation.

Another matter of particular concern at the end of Franklin's life was slavery. He was elected president of a Pennsylvania abolition society in 1787 and wrote a series of public pleas on the subject. His last newspaper essay, written a month before his death, was a parody of arguments for slavery that showed how the same arguments could be used to justify enslaving whites.

Benjamin Franklin was an advocate of freedom and responsibility who, perhaps more than anyone, defined what America should be. He not only talked about what could be done, but also demonstrated what was possible in a democratic environment. Not without reason, Thomas Jefferson, who followed in his footsteps, called the Philadelphia printer the greatest man of the age.

Further Reading

Conner, Paul W. *Poor Richard's Politicks: Benjamin Franklin and His New American Order.* New York: Oxford University Press, 1965.

Franklin, Benjamin. *The Autobiography of Benjamin Franklin: A Genetic Text.* Edited by J. A. Leo Lemay and P. M. Zall. Knoxville: University of Tennessee Press, 1981.

Franklin, Benjamin. *The Papers of Benjamin Franklin.* Edited by Leonard W. Labaree et al. New Haven, CT Yale University Press, 1959.

Frasca, Ralph. *Benjamin Franklin's Printing Network: Disseminating Virtue in Early America.* Columbia: University of Missouri Press, 2006.

Lemay, J. A. Leo. *The Life of Benjamin Franklin.* Philadelphia: University of Pennsylvania Press, 2006.

Sappenfield, James A. *A Sweet Instruction: Franklin's Journalism as a Literary Apprenticeship.* Carbondale: Southern Illinois University Press, 1973.

Smith, Jeffery A. *Printers and Press Freedom: The Ideology of Early American Journalism.* New York: Oxford University Press, 1988.

Smith, Jeffery A. *Franklin and Bache: Envisioning the Enlightened Republic.* New York: Oxford University Press, 1990.

Tourtellot, Arthur B. *Benjamin Franklin: The Shaping of Genius, The Boston Years.* New York: Doubleday, 1977.

Wood, Gordon S. *The Americanization of Benjamin Franklin.* New York: Penguin Press, 2004.

JEFFREY A. SMITH

FREEDOM OF INFORMATION ACT

The twentieth century witnessed a profound change in national policy and institutions. Beginning during the so-called Progressive Era of 1901–1917 and then, more substantially, during the New Deal of the 1930s, the role and responsibilities of the federal government radically expanded. New federal agencies were established whether to regulate banking and business practices—the Food and Drug Administration, Federal Reserve Board, Federal Trade Commission, Federal Communications Commission, National Labor Relations Board—or to promote formerly private initiatives—old age pensions, unemployment compensation, subsidies to farmers, home mortgages, loans to small businesses. At the same time, an increase in federal spending stimulated key sectors of the nation's economy. In the years after 1945, the federal role and spending (particularly in the military area) expanded further to include loans and grants to college students, aid to mothers and dependent children, funding of scientific research, prohibition of racial and sexual discrimination, affirmative action. Federal programs and spending—their administration and priorities—had become important public policy concerns.

Paralleling the federal government's expanded domestic role the nation's international role also expanded, dating from U.S. involvement in military conflict during the World War II years of 1941–1945 and then in an extended non-military conflict with the Soviet Union during the so-called Cold War. One byproduct was the creation of new institutions (the Central Intelligence Agency, CIA, in 1947 and the National Security Agency, NSA, in 1952) and the extension of the role of the Federal Bureau of Investigation (FBI), after 1936 from law enforcement to include the non-criminal monitoring of "subversive" (after the 1980s "terrorist") activities. These new "national security" threats required that presidents and the U.S. intelligence agencies conduct policy in secret. On the one hand, President Franklin Roosevelt in 1941, by executive order, imposed classification restrictions on information relating to military and foreign policy while President Harry Truman in 1951 extended classification restrictions to all federal agencies and departments. On the other hand, beginning with Truman and extended under Dwight Eisenhower, presidents claimed a constitutional right of "executive privilege" to withhold information from Congress (and thus the public). Concurrently, presidents and other federal officials more actively promoted their programs, ushered in by President Franklin Roosevelt's effective use of press conferences and "fireside chats" (nationwide radio addresses) to influence public opinion and advance his administration's policies.

In response to the increasing importance of decisions in Washington, D.C., many of the nation's newspapers either established Washington bureaus or relied increasingly on the wire services (notably, the Associated Press and United Press International) for coverage of developments in the nation's capital. Yet, while the federal government's role impacted significantly on the lives and fortunes of American citizens, these very institutional changes rendered it increasingly more difficult for the public (and journalists) to learn about federal priorities and decisions. By the 1950s, reporters, and even members of Congress and congressional committees, confronted major difficulties in learning about federal actions, as federal officials acted to control information, actions that for a time acquired legitimacy in the security-conscious atmosphere of the Cold War years.

Congress first addressed the problem of an expanded federal bureaucracy in 1946 when enacting the Administrative Procedure Act. Intended to promote congressional oversight, this act mandated Congress's right of access to federal agency records. Federal agencies and departments, moreover, were required to publish in the *Federal Register* the plans and methods whereby "the public may secure information or make submittals or requests" for federal records although federal officials could impose restrictions to preclude the release of information when "in the public interest" or for "good cause." Some federal agencies, notably the FBI, immediately exploited these loopholes to preclude the release of any of their records. The scope of these denials became a major public policy issue during the 1950s, triggered in particular by the Eisenhower Administration's expanded use of "executive privilege" claims and the "culture of secrecy" that had evolved in the early Cold War years.

In response, beginning in 1955, a subcommittee of the House Committee on Government Operations, headed by Congressman John Moss, held hearings on government secrecy policy. Moss's efforts to curb executive secrecy languished until the 1960s. Then, the relaxation of Cold War tensions, and the re-emergence of a more liberal and skeptical political climate (captured by the increasingly more militant civil rights and anti-Vietnam war movements), culminated in the enactment of legislation, signed into law by President Lyndon Johnson on July 4, 1966 and to become operational a year later, the Freedom of Information Act (FOIA).

The FOIA established the principle of the public's "right to know," but at the same time recognized the need for some secrecy in the conduct of the nation's business and to safeguard both privacy rights and sensitive security information. While federal officials were required to conduct a full search and release all relevant records responsive to a specified FOIA request, certain information was exempted from disclosure—if the information was classified, violated an individual's privacy rights or "trade secrets," or revealed an agency/department's "sources and methods" or "internal rules and procedures." This legislative attempt to balance disclosure and secrecy interests ultimately rendered the FOIA of limited value as agency officials (notably in the FBI and CIA) broadly interpreted these exemption provisions to withhold information. By the early 1970s, the extent of these withholding actions, in the charged political climate created by recent revelations of the Richard Nixon Administration's abusive secrecy policies and questionable political uses of the intelligence agencies, led to congressional enactment in November 1974 (overriding the veto of President Gerald Ford) of a series of key amendments to the 1966 FOIA. The amended Act, which took effect on February 19, 1975, required federal officials to respond to FOIA requests within a specified time period, to set copying fees at normal commercial rates, and to report annually to Congress on their processing of FOIA requests. In addition, the courts were empowered to conduct *in camera* reviews to ascertain whether agency "national security" withholding claims were proper while successful litigants challenging agency/departmental withholding claims were entitled to payment of their legal fees.

The amended FOIA, however, did not open all federal records to interested requesters—or necessarily promote the public's "right to know." For, while federal officials were required to release all records relating to a specific request, that option was available to those who could identify relevant records. This requirement would either foreclose research into secret programs or necessitate that requesters know how federal officials filed and maintained especially sensitive records. Second, the privacy and trade secret exemptions precluded the release of an individual's or corporation's records to anyone else. Records on individuals, however, could be released if the individual was deceased, but even then information collected by a federal agency

about the individual's moral character could be withheld. Federal officials, moreover, tended to interpret the FOIA's exemption provisions broadly, even capriciously. While these exemption claims could be challenged, the costs of litigating discouraged many requesters (unless, like journalists, they could command the financial resources of a large corporation). Finally, requesters were required to pay copying fees of ten cents per page—an onerous burden in those cases where an identified file numbered thousands of pages.

Variances in presidential policies also influenced the quality of released records—as some presidents (Ronald Reagan, George W. Bush) either issued executive orders extending classification restrictions or encouraged federal officials to risk having their exemption decisions challenged in court. Other presidents (Jimmy Carter, Bill Clinton) issued less restrictive classification orders or encouraged federal officials to release records even if withholding was permissible under the act if such releases would not harm security interests.

The history of the FOIA's implementation highlights another access problem, involving the role of the courts. This problem is graphically captured by a specific case involving records of the CIA—a case that indirectly underscores both the value and limitations of the FOIA.

In 1975, the Senate Select Committee on Intelligence Activities (the so-called Church Committee), as part of a more extensive review of CIA operations, uncovered specific CIA programs to fund first the research involving and then the production and uses of mind-altering drugs and poisonous toxins. The committee, however, was unable to document the scope of these programs and how extensively the agency had used these drugs and toxins. CIA officials had first informed committee investigators that records relating to these programs had been destroyed in 1973 while in October 1975 congressional testimony the CIA officer who had headed the Agency's poisonous toxin program, Sidney Gottlieb, admitted that a comprehensive written record had never been created about this program "because of the sensitivity of the area and the decision to keep any possible use of materials like this recordless." A subsequent FOIA request, triggered by the Church Committee's public revelations of these programs, contradicted Agency officials claims of incomplete extant CIA records. Obligated under the FOIA to conduct a full search of all relevant CIA files (which were intentionally compartmentalized), CIA officials located extant records that had been filed in the Agency's financial accounts relating to the Agency's contracting out research to universities and private firms. These released financial records contradicted Agency officials' testimony that these research programs had been limited in scope. When the requesters filed suit to secure the release of the names of the contracted parties, however, CIA officials rebuffed this request—even though information relating to this program had by then been declassified. CIA officials did not then claim that this information could be withheld under the FOIA's personal privacy and sources and methods exemption provisions. They instead cited a provision of the 1947 National Security Act creating the CIA that affirmed the CIA Director's responsibility "for protecting intelligence sources and methods from unauthorized disclosure." Ruling on this suit in 1985, the Supreme Court held in *CIA v. Sims* that the CIA had the right to withhold this information because the 1947 Act "vested in the Director of Central Intelligence very broad authority to protect all sources of information from disclosure."

The Supreme Court's deference to executive "national security" claims accompanied a companion lobbying effort by the Reagan Administration in 1981 and 1982 to convince the Congress to exempt all CIA and FBI records from the FOIA's disclosure requirements. These lobbying efforts failed. Nonetheless, Congress did adopt more limited restrictions in 1984 and 1986—in 1984 exempting CIA "operational files" from release under the FOIA's mandatory search and disclosure requirements and in 1986 authorizing the FBI, in the case of a request pertaining to an ongoing (i.e., not closed) investigation, to deny that any such records existed.

The FOIA, nonetheless, has proved to be an invaluable research tool for journalists, individuals who were the subjects of agency/departmental files, and academic researchers. Its complicated history, moreover, provides insights into public attitudes about governmental accountability, deference to the presidency and the intelligence community, and the contesting principles of openness and secrecy.

Further Reading

Dorsen, Norman, and Stephen Gillers, eds. *None of Your Business: Government Secrecy in America.* New York: Viking Press, 1974.

Fisher, Louis. *The Politics of Executive Privilege.* Durham, NC: Carolina Academic Press, 2004.

Hernan, Peter, and Charles McClure. *Federal Information Policies in the 1980's: Conflicts and Issues.* Norwood, NJ: Ablex Publishing, 1987.

Melanson, Philip. *Secrecy Wars: National Security, Privacy, and the Public's Right to Know.* Washington, D.C.: Brassey's, 2001.

Mollenhoff, Clark. *Washington Cover-Up.* Garden City: Doubleday, 1962.

Moynihan, Daniel. *Secrecy: The American Experience.* New Haven, CT: Yale University Press, 1998.

Theoharis, Athan, ed. *A Culture of Secrecy: The Government Versus the People's Right to Know.* Lawrence: University Press of Kansas, 1998.

ATHAN G. THEOHARIS

FREEDOM'S JOURNAL

Controversy raged over the status of slaves and free blacks in the North throughout the late eighteenth century. In 1799 the New York legislature finally freed at age twenty-eight the sons born to slave mothers after July 4, 1799 and, at age twenty-five, their daughters born after that date. That meant that between 1824 and 1827 those children would be free to vote and live as New York citizens, joining the small population of free blacks who enjoyed full legal privileges.

Blacks were less than 10 percent of the total population in 1800, but that was too many for some white New Yorkers. When another law passed in 1817 freeing in1827 all slaves born before 1799, the impending change and fears that free blacks would vote against Democrat-Republicans fed a reactionary frenzy. Stepping up efforts to block free blacks' rights, the New York legislature in 1821 dropped property-holding requirements for white voters but raised the required holding for black voters to $250—a prohibitive amount for most people.

New York City had become a settling place for free Northern blacks. As July 4, 1827 (emancipation day) neared, racial tensions rose. Against this backdrop, Samuel Cornish, a black Presbyterian minister, an educated and respected leader, and a voice for emancipation and equal rights—began *Freedom's Journal* (1827–1829) on March 16, 1827, a weekly, to serve the city's black community. John Russwurm, his co-editor, held a college diploma from Bowdoin (1826).

The first volume, third issue of *Freedom's Journal*, stated an aim to avoid controversy but said the paper arose from a need to mobilize behind the Constitution and the ballot to defend the rights of free African Americans. "Daily slandered, we think that there ought to be some channel of communion between us and the public, through which a single voice may be heard, in defense of five hundred thousand free people of colour. ... we believe that the time has now arrived, when the calumnies of our enemies should be refuted by forcible arguments."

Between its beginning and July 4, 1827, *Freedom's Journal* called for immediate abolition of slavery, spoke out against racism, and called for the creation of an organization to collect money to buy freedom for slaves. It advocated an end to protectionist tariffs as a precursor to ending slavery, emphasized education for blacks, denounced drunkenness in multiple articles, and published news about racial laws and racist incidents throughout the North and South.

Cornish aimed to unite and energize the black community. The *Journal* addressed local issues, voiced community needs, and thoroughly informed readers on issues of race, slavery, emancipation, law, and the national economy. Articles even advised parents on childrearing. But with the parental voice came a thunder of condemnation—for racism, slavery, and eventually for the American colonization movement that would keep slavery alive by freeing some slaves and sending them to Africa.

Cornish's decision to publish an outspoken African American newspaper amid severe attacks on free blacks—even lynchings—was a daring choice. The paper was viciously attacked while white press editors stood by.

In six months, Cornish resigned and left Russwurm in charge. Under Russwurm the editorial tone became more conciliatory toward colonization. Readers began to complain. Cornish returned, but could not revive the readership. He finally closed it and launched a monthly, *The Rights of All.* It survived six months, going out of business after the October 9, 1829, issue. It claimed close to a thousand subscribers and dozens of subscription agents in the United

States, England, Canada, and Haiti. One agent, David Walker, published four important articles known as "Walker's Appeal," supporting slave rebellion as self defense. The pamphlet version was banned in the South. *The Rights of All* also reported on black organizations in New York City and Connecticut, took uncompromising stands against colonization and extensively covered race riots in Cincinnati and resulting flight of blacks to Canada.

Freedom's Journal is an important newspaper in American journalism history in its clear and uncompromising voice for abolition, as an educational paper, as a civic record, and as a voice for the urban black community. It was a brave and stabilizing force during frightening times for free Africans Americans. Awareness of its rich content requires revision of existing literature that glorifies white idealists but overlooks black voices, leaders, and publications. William Lloyd Garrison, publisher of the abolitionist paper, *The Liberator*, beginning in Boston in 1835, has been criticized for ranting about slavery in the south but ignoring black newspapers in the North.

Cornish returned to co-publish another newspaper in the coming decade, *The Colored American. Freedom's Journal* (March 16, 1827–March 28, 1829), *and The Rights of All* (May 29–Oct. 9, 1829) are easily researched through Donald M. Jacobs' detailed index of all issues. Two hundred pages list the contents of both papers—a monument to Jacobs' team and a living monument to the breadth and quality of these papers. *Freedom's Journal* and *The Rights of All* reveal rich social history of African Americans in the North and South during this time.

Further Readings

Gross, Bella. "Freedom's Journal and the Rights of All." *Journal of Negro History* 17, No. 3 (Jul., 1932), 241–286.

Hutton, Frankie. *The Early Black Press in America, 1827–1860.* Westport, CT: Greenwood Press, 1993.

Jacobs, Donald M., Heath Paley, Susan Parker, and Dana Silverman, eds. *Antebellum Black Newspapers; Indices to New York Freedom's Journal (1827–1829), The Rights of All (1829), The Weekly Advocate (1837), and The Colored American (1837–1841).* Westport, CT: Greenwood Press, 1976.

Penn, I. Garland. *The Afro-American Press and Its Editors.* New York: Arno Press, 1969.

Sagarin, Mary. *John Brown Russwurm; The Story of Freedom's Journal, Freedom's Journey.* New York: Lothrop, Lee & Shepard: 1970.

Carmen E. Clark

FRONTIER PRESS

Historian Frederick Jackson Turner, the son of a pioneer Wisconsin newspaper editor, sat patiently through four long academic presentations before getting his turn to face an exhausted audience during a history discussion the evening of July 12, 1893, at the Columbian Exposition in Chicago. Because of his tired audience, Turner may not have read his entire paper, but "The Significance of the Frontier in American History" influenced all subsequent writing about American history for several generations. Turner presented a *theory* of American history to a field that had been dominated by chronological narratives.

With a nostalgic tone tied to the Census Bureau's 1890 declaration that the frontier had been filled in, Turner said settling the frontier had defined the American nation's character and spirit. "Much has been written about the frontier from the point of view of border warfare and the chase," Turner said, "but as a field for the serious study of the economist and the historian it has been neglected." By the end of the following century, Turner had come under attack because his frontier defined the character of white men with scant attention to the native peoples, Spanish descendents, and women who peopled the American West. He had seen the frontier as a process as much as a place.

And he celebrated conquest. Like his contemporaries, Turner defined progress as the advance of civilization to displace the savagery of nature and, by implication, native peoples. The frontier was "the meeting point between savagery and civilization," and it forced national social, economic and political institutions to adapt to expansion and change. Each advance required the development process to begin anew. "This perennial rebirth, this fluidity of American life, this expansion westward with its new opportunities, its continuous touch with the simplicity of primitive society, furnish the forces dominating the American character." The United States, Turner said, provided a case study in the world's progress from savagery to civilization.

Although Turner and his students neglected the role of newspapers in this social evolution, newspapers were integral to the first discussion of manifest destiny, which provided the rationale for the United States to exert jurisdiction over other European descendents for control of the entire North American continent. John Louis O'Sullivan, editor of the *United States Magazine and Democratic Review*, wrote in a summer 1845 edition that the hand of "Providence" would join with technology—railroad and telegraph —to unite the nation. While railroads will make travel faster, O'Sullivan wrote, "the magnetic telegraph will enable the editors of the 'San Francisco Union,' the 'Astoria Evening Post,' or the 'Nootka Morning News' to set up in type the first half of the President's Inaugural, before the echoes of the latter half shall have died away beneath the lofty porch of the Capitol, as spoken from his lips." Newspapers celebrated this sense of progress and destiny—often to the point of encouraging wars against the native peoples who controlled adjacent land.

Historians of the American West often use newspapers as sources but seldom study the role of newspapers in social and economic development. "Just as the six gun, the windmill and barbed wire were regarded as the principal tools in the conquest of the Great Plains, so the frontier newspaper may be regarded as another important instrument in the civilizing of the West," historian Oliver Knight wrote in 1967. "We do not have any generally accepted theories about newspaper functions, as we do about railroads, mining and stockraising, and hence nothing to challenge our understanding of a primary institution on the frontier," journalism historian William H. Lyon lamented in 1980.

Frederick Jackson Turner's frontier began at Massachusetts Bay and moved west and the first "West" was in settlements across the mountains. The westward movement of the printing press has been thoroughly documented by Douglas C. McMurtrie, a printer who set out in the 1920s and 1930s to update Isaiah Thomas's 1810 history of printing in the United States. Unfortunately, only one volume on the Middle and South Atlantic states was completed in what McMurtrie planned four-volume study, but he published dozens of pamphlets, articles and books containing "firsts," such as the first newspaper and the first printing press in states and territories. In the process, he traced the westward paths of many editors and their presses.

Generalizing about frontier editors and their relationships to their communities can be difficult. Some printers received a stake from former employers or other publishers in the family as a start their own publication farther west. Early on, Benjamin Franklin helped young printers establish newspapers in early frontier outposts. Sometimes a successful publisher wanted to repeat the expierence in a nearby town. Once they were established, newpaper editors often advocated the sorts of reform that would stablilize a town, such as good schools, clean water, sewage treatment, and livestock vaccination. Some editors fought desperately for their own parties to win local elections to yield lucrative printing contracts. Failing that, they'd move to another town.

As colonial settlers violated the king's laws about moving west of the Allegheny Mountains, they took printing presses with them—along with motives and aspirations as varied as those their forebears brought with them from the Old World. Some sought freedom and independence in a new territory or escape from home; a few sought adventure; others sought wealth; and some, of course, sought to convert the heathen sinners or natives who were there ahead of them. In all cases, a printing press could come in handy.

Newspapers went with towns, of course, where enough people lived to place advertisements and purchase subscriptions. Town settlers encouraged a printer to establish a business and publish a newspaper as evidence the town could become a thriving city. To increase an editor's stake in a town, founders would occasionally give the editor some lots to sell to support his business. Such editors often boosted their towns with overly optimistic stories and encouraging subscribers to purchase copies to send to friends and relatives back East. Editors also sent their newspapers to other publications throughout the nation as "exchanges" in the hope that positive articles would be reprinted. The editor, in turn, would reprint articles from eastern papers for readers eager for news from back home.

While large metropolitan newspapers increased their capital investments, smaller publications could still be operated by one person who worked as both editor and printer standing at a type case and operating a hand press, such as the Washington hand press patented by Samuel Rust of New York in 1821. When folded in half, one sheet became a four-page publication. A printer-editor or slave-apprentice could make 250 impressions an hour of two side-by-side pages with a Washington hand press. Rust made his press portable with innovations, like hollowed out legs, which made the bulky machine lighter to transport than its cast iron competitors. Another common cast iron press was the Ramage, introduced by Rust's competitors, and operated on a similar principle. These simple presses served many small Western towns from Minnesota to Texas until well after the Civil War.

The dependence of frontier editors upon town boosterism or political patronage demonstrated that the 1833 birth of the penny newspapers in New York City did not kill the party press in the hinterlands. Political patronage supported newspapers throughout the West as new communities grew. Sometimes this dependence was the result of difficult economic circumstances. Economic conditions forced editors to seek political patronage just to keep their presses running, but some editors aligned with politicans or political parties, which often put them on even shakier ground. In Washington Territory, editors often depended upon federal patronage, primarily in the form of contracts for the printing of laws, journals and reports.

Editors promoted settlement, hoped for political patronage and state printing contracts, faced transportation and communication difficulties, pleaded with advertisers and subscribers to pay their bills (sometimes in kind with eggs, meat or whiskey), and engaged in vituperative debates with other editors. A few editors risked life and limb when they editorialized on some issues. For example, the target of vitriolic attacks by the editor of the *Missouri Argus* beat to death the proprietor of that paper. One ongoing editorial feud carried over into a concurrent court battle and ongoing street fight between the Missouri editors. A few Minnesota editors also carried their fights into the street, as they doggedly attacked political corruption. Of course, corruption ran rampant among the opposition's politicians and hardly ever on the editor's own side.

Some publications counted on local printing contracts. Governments printed official documents, such as notices of public auctions and land sales. Governments also required public notices to be published in the official newspaper of the county or city before some business and legal transactions could be completed. The registration of livestock brands, for example, required such publication. With printing contracts at stake, rivalries often broke out between towns and among political factions within towns. Newspapers joined the fights when towns, such as those on the Kansas frontier, competed for railroad lines and train stations.

Nonetheless, some editors were fiercely independent. Itinerant printer Legh Freeman became involved in land-speculation and town-promotion schemes. At times, Freeman's wife and family ran the paper while he traveled and sent home columns about his stereotypical fantasy life as a frontier scout. Like the mythic mountain man Jim Bridger whom Freeman may have interviewed early in life, the editor tried to stay ahead of advancing civilization. This wanderlust was illustrated when he operated the "press on wheels," the *Frontier Index* newspaper, which jumped from town to town just ahead of the Union Pacific Railroad across Nebraska, Colorado, Wyoming, Utah, and Montana. In 1868, a mob seeking revenge for a vigilante hanging in Bear River City, Wyoming, went to the *Frontier Index* office after burning the jail and releasing prisoners. Editor Freeman was said to have left town, as he wrote, "so fast you could have played checkers on his coattails." Before the attack, Freeman disclaimed rumors that he was a member of the vigilantes, but he endorsed them, saying the vigilantes were so successful that "honest men can now walk our streets in safety, provided they keep sober and are armed to the teeth."

Digging out the lives of ordinary journalists can still yield new information about frontier newspapers and Western society. Mark Kellogg, an obscure reporter in Dakota Territory, became a national figure and a subject of continuing historical interest when he died at the Battle of the Little Big Horn in 1876. Historians are still putting together the obscure pieces of Kellogg's seemingly contradictory life. Kellogg worked as a Copperhead journalist and candidate for public office in LaCrosse, Wisconsin, in the 1850s. He published an 1872 campaign paper for Horace Greeley in Brainerd, Minnesota, where he again ran for office. A printer and telegrapher, Kellogg sent dispatches from railroad construction camps and towns in Minnesota and Dakota Territory to the *St. Paul Pioneer* and other newspapers.

People in remote areas eagerly awaited delivery of newspapers from more settled areas back home and they pointed to the publication of a local paper as evidence that their town will be among those that survive. Competing newspapers in small towns worked out novel ways to get their exchanges ahead of the competition, thereby making the local paper appealing to those who didn't get the papers from New York, Denver, Chicago, San Francisco, or Atlanta. In these ways, newspaper served as a link between urban and rural life.

Each town type—cattle towns, mining towns, farming towns, seaports—faced different circumstances. In Rocky Mountain mining towns, for example, high prices for individual issues and pleas for patronage became necessary in camps where no one felt permanent enough to pay for a subscription. Health, sanitation, law and order were common subjects for boom town editors. Colorful editors in mining camps thrived on strident personal journalism at the very time large, metropolitan newspapers became reliant upon standardized, straight news. Newspapers of the Southwest faced the unique situation of conflicts between U.S. and Mexican cultures and governments in addition to the conflict with Native Americans found in every Western state. Cultural barriers and language differences required some newspapers to reach Spanish-speaking readers.

Spanish-language media have been neglected as a subject for study, even though the first mechanical press in the New World appeared in Mexico City in 1535—a century before the first English-language press at Harvard College—and Spanish publications reporting events were soon peeled off the press. Regular periodicals, however, appeared contemporaneously with their English counterparts in the East, but different circumstances resulted in fewer successful newspapers.

Editors often became local celebrities, in part, because their patrons believed the press to be necessary to the region, the party or the cause. Among those who celebrated the frontier was the West's most famous journalist who spent about three years in Nevada. Yet Mark Twain personified the rugged individualist in the image he left behind. After heading to Nevada to avoid the Civil War and to prospect for silver and gold, Samuel Langhorne Clemens failed as a miner but acquired a job writing feature stories for the *Virginia City Territorial Enterprise*. While there he adopted the *nom-de-plume* Mark Twain and played the role of an archetypal frontier reporter, but his brief stint as an editor was a dismal failure. "I moralize well, but I did not always practice well when I was a city editor; I let fancy get the upper hand of fact too often when there was a dearth of news." Perhaps because of later pretensions to high society, Mark Twain revealed little about his Nevada career other than the anecdotes relayed in his second book, *Roughing It*.

William Wright, alias Dan De Quille, roomed with Twain for a year on the Comstock, and the two men stole material from each other. The fact that De Quille remains more obscure today—in sharp contrast to their relative reputations on the Comstock—may be attributed to the fact that De Quille failed to collect and republish his writing.

Edgar Wilson Nye (Bill Nye) of Wyoming was a more typical, but more obscure writer than Twain, followed Twain's lead in Western experience and on the national lecture circuit. Like Twain, Nye was a popular national figure, but his writing in Wyoming newspapers and his later books of humor were of much less lasting quality. While poking fun at themselves, Twain, Nye, and others created a stereotype of frontier editors as rough-and-tumble fighters who would resort to six guns or as humorists who never let the facts get in the way of a good story.

Some Western lore had its roots in newspapers. The *Tombstone Epitaph*, for instance, promoted the Earps in their feud with the Clanton family, whose bloody gunfight near the O.K. Corral provided heroes and fodder for pulp fiction, film, and television. By contrast, one individual, Jesse James, perpetuated his own myth through newspapers, even while remaining in hiding from the law.

Competing towns on the Kansas frontier perpetuated stories of conflict between homesteaders and the open range as the towns fought over railroads, cattle drives, and long-staying homestead families. Like other town leaders, editors in Kansas cattle towns at the end of the trail drives in the 1870s boosted town development by competing for cattle drives and railroads, but conflicts arose when farmers and some businesses wanted long-term settlement instead of rowdy cowboys and foreign cattle trampling crops and infecting local cattle. Local politicians and their respective newspapers argued over herd laws restricting the movement of cattle and quarantine statues requiring trail herds to remain in isolation before moving through areas with other livestock. As waves of immigrants settled in the countryside, editors changed their positions on law and order and abandoned their opposition to herd laws.

The lure of free land provided opportunities for urban malcontents to leave the growing cities while, at the same time, it forced employers to improve conditions for workers who would be tempted to move westward. On the frontier, meanwhile, the settler sometimes became an individualist who exhibited anti-social behavior and an antipathy to political control, as the Populist movement showed Turner and his contemporaries.

As the first of the "progressive historians," Turner reconciled Protestant predestination with social Darwinism, and nostalgia for a vanishing frontier with scientific history. Turner's assumptions permeate frontier journalism. Early journalism historians easily accepted some of these assumptions of progressive history because newspaper editors on the frontier often shared the beliefs of farmers, town builders and railroad tycoons that they were advancing the cause of civilization by promoting settlement of the North American continent.

Further Reading

Barnard, Sandy. *I Go With Custer: The Life & Death of Reporter Mark Kellogg*. Bismarck, North Dakota: Bismarck Tribune Company, 1996.

Bennion, Sherilyn Cox. *Equal to the Occasion: Women Editors of the Nineteenth Century*. West Reno: University of Nevada Press, 1990.

Benson, Ivan. *Mark Twain's Western Years*. New York: Russell & Russell, 1966.

Blankenburg, William B. "The Role of the Press in an Indian Massacre, 1871," *Journalism Quarterly* 45 (1968): 61–70.

Burd, Gene. "The Ghost Town Newspaper: An 'Autopsy' Approach to Frontier Press," *Journalism History* 8:3-4 (Autumn-Winter 1981): 99–103.

Cloud, Barbara L. *The Business of Newspapers on the Western Frontier*. Reno: University of Nevada Press, 1992.

Chiu, Herman B. "Power of the Press: How Newspapers in Four Communities Erased Thousands of Chinese from Oregon History," *American Journalism* 16 (1999): 59–77.

Cronin, Mary M. "Mixing Protest and Accommodation: The Response of Oklahoma's Black Town Newspaper Editors to Race Relations," *American Journalism* 19 (2002): 45–64.

Dary, David. *Red Blood and Black Ink: Journalism in the Old West*. Lawrence: University Press of Kansas, 1999.

Dyer, Carolyn Stewart. "Economic Dependence and Concentration of Ownership Among Antebellum Wisconsin Newspapers," *Journalism History* 7:2 (Summer 1980): 42–46.

Dykstra, Robert R. *The Cattle Towns*. Lincoln: University of Nebraska Press, 1968.

Ellison, Rhoda Coleman. "Newspaper Publishing in Frontier Alabama," *Journalism Quarterly* 23 (1946): 289–301.

Endres, Fred F. "'We Want Money and Must Have It:' Profile of an Ohio Weekly, 1841–1847," *Journalism History* 7:2 (Summer 1980): 68–71.

Fatout, Paul. *Mark Twain in Virginia City* Bloomington: Indiana University Press, 1964.

Finerty, John. *War-Path and Bivouac or The Conquest of the Sioux* Norman: University of Oklahoma Press, 1962, originally 1890.

Garcia, Hazel Dicken. "Letters Tell the News (Not 'Fit to Print'?) About the Kentucky Frontier," *Journalism History* 7:2 (Summer 1980): 49–53, 67.

Gilluly, Sam. *The Press Gang: A Century of Montana Newspapers, 1885–1985*. Helena: Montana Press Association, 1985.

Hage, George S. *Newspapers on the Minnesota Frontier 1849–1860*. St. Paul: Minnesota Historical Society, 1967.

Halaas, David Fridtjof. *Boom Town Newspapers: Journalism on the Rocky Mountain Mining Frontier, 1859–1881*. Albuquerque: University of New Mexico Press, 1981.

Heuterman, Thomas H. *Movable Type: Biography of Legh R. Freeman*. Ames: The Iowa State University Press, 1979.

Heuterman, Thomas H., and Jerilyn S. McIntyre, ed, *Journalism History, Special Frontier Issue.* 7 (Summer 1980).

Huntzicker, William E. "Media." In David Wishart, editor, *Encyclopedia of the Great Plains,* edited by David Wishart, 501–505.. Lincoln: University of Nebraska Press, 2004.

Karolevitz, Robert F. *Newspapering in the Old West: A Pictorial History of Journalism and Printing on the Frontier*. Seattle: Superior Publishing Co., 1965.

Karolevitz, Robert F. *With a Shirt Tail Full of Type: The Story of Newspapering in South Dakota*. Brookings: South Dakota Press Association, 1982.

Knight, Oliver. *Following the Indian Wars*. Norman: University of Oklahoma Press, 1960.

Knight, Oliver. "The Frontier Newspaper as a Catalyst in Social Change," *Pacific Northwest Quarterly* 58:2 (April 1967): 74–81.

Limerick, Patricia Nelson. *The Legacy of Conquest: The Unbroken Past of the American West*. New York: W.W. Norton, 1987.

Lingenfelter, Richard E., and Karen Rix Gash. *The Newspapers of Nevada: A History and Bibliography, 1854–1979*. Reno: University of Nevada Press, 1984.

Lomicky, Carol S. "Frontier Feminism and the Woman's Tribune: The Journalism of Clara Bewick Colby," *Journalism History* 28:3 (Fall 2002): 102–111.

Lyon, William E. *The Pioneer Editor in Missouri 1808–1860*. Columbia: University of Missouri Press, 1965.

Malone, Michael P. *The Battle for Butte: Mining and Politics on the Northern Frontier, 1864–1906*. Seattle: University of Washington Press, 1981.

Martin, Asa Earl. "Pioneer Anti-Slavery Press," *Mississippi Valley Historical Review* II (March 1916): 509–528.

Martin, Douglas D. *Tombstone's Epitaph*. Albuquerque: University of New Mexico Press, 1951.

McMurtrie, Douglas C. "The Pioneer Press in Montana," *Journalism Quarterly* 9:2 (June 1932): 170–81.

McMurtrie, Douglas C. "Pioneer Printing in North Dakota," *North Dakota Historical Quarterly* VI, 3 (April 1932): 221–230.

McMurtrie, Douglas C. "Pioneer Printing in Wyoming," *Annals of Wyoming* 9, 3 (January 1933): 729–742.

Murphy, James E., and Sharon M. Murphy. *Let My People Know: American Indian Journalism*. Norman: University of Oklahoma Press, 1981.

Rankin, Charles E. "Type and Stereotype: Frederic E. Lockley, Pioneer Journalist." *American Journalism* 14 (1997): 182–204; and in *Frontier and Region: Essays in Honor of Martin Ridge*, edited by Robert C. Ritchie, and Paul Andrew Hutton, 56–81. Albuquerque: University of New Mexico Press, 1997.

Saum, Lewis O. "Colonel Custer's Copperhead: The 'Mysterious' Mark Kellogg," *Montana, the Magazine of Western History* XXVIII:4 (October 1978): 12–25.

Savage, William W. Jr. "Newspapers and Local History: A Critique of Robert R. Dykstra's The Cattle Towns," *Journal of the West* 10 (1971):. 572–577.

Schmitt, Jo Ann. *Fighting Editors* .San Antonio, Texas: The Naylor Company, 1958.

Stiles, T.J. *Jesse James: Last Rebel of the Civil War.* New York: Alfred A. Knopf, 2002.

Stratton, Porter A. *The Territorial Press of New Mexico 1834–1860* Albuquerque: University of New Mexico Press, 1969.

Turnbull, George S. *Influences of the Newspapers on the Economic, Social, Cultural and Political History of Pioneer Oregon to 1859.* Seattle: University of Washington, 1932.

Turner, Frederick Jackson. *The Frontier in American History.* Tucson: The University of Arizona Press, 1986, originally 1920.

Twain, Mark. *Roughing It.* New York: Signet, 1962.

Wade, Richard C. The Urban Frontier: Pioneer Life in Early Pittsburgh, Cincinnati, Lexington, Louisville, and St. Louis. Chicago: University of Chicago Press, 1950.

Watson, Elmo Scott. "The Indian Wars and the Press, 1866–1867," *Journalism Quarterly* 17 (1940): 301–312.

Wheeler, Keith. *The Chroniclers.* Alexandria, VA: Time-Life Books, 1976.

Whisenhunt, Donald W. "The Frontier Newspaper: A guide to Society and Culture," *Journalism Quarterly* 45:4 (Winter 1968): 726–728.

WILLIAM E. HUNTZICKER

FRONTLINE

Long after commercial television networks ended serious news documentaries, public television's *Frontline* carries on the heritage of *See It Now, CBS Reports,* and *NBC White Papers. Frontline* launched its first season in January 1983 and returned to produce about two dozen documentaries each year since. A wide array of independent producers generated individual programs under the guidance of a Boston-based staff led by an executive producer for the series. Some producers produced many programs for the series, of course, but the mix of talents shifted each year, and shifted significantly over the course of almost a quarter century. Diverse producers reflecting a range of interests and styles kept the program vibrant over its long life span.

Frontline enjoyed a level of independence rare in American broadcasting, even public broadcasting. Part of its independence derived from the respect commanded among independent producers and the public broadcasting leadership by *Frontline's* Executive Producer Peter Fanning, who nurtured and protected the series from its beginning. Fanning's philosophy combined a delicate balance of independence for the individual producers with central guidance and strong professional standards. Individual producers enjoyed less independence than the *Point of View* series on PBS, but more than they would expect in a network newsroom. Award-winning programs resulted from the collaboration of Fanning and individual producers.

Fanning himself gave credit to the leadership of *Frontline's* primary producing station, WGBH in Boston, which enjoyed resources beyond those of other public television stations and an equivalent resolve to use them in the public interest.

The circumstances of its birth also contributed to *Frontline's* high degree of independence. Ravaged by the Richard Nixon administration, public affairs, and other national programming on public television enjoyed a revival during the Jimmy Carter years. The Carter administration provided more money for public broadcasting, stipulating that much of it go to national programs, particularly public affairs. To insulate the programming from political interference, the Corporation for Public Broadcasting placed the money under an independent programming czar, Lewis Freedman, a respected producer who had worked in both commercial and public broadcasting. Freedman proposed a signature documentary series for public television and, with Fanning, projected a six million dollar annual budget. Freedman's national program fund would provide five million of those dollars if public television stations would collectively promise the remaining one million. Freedman guaranteed funding for five years, with the program fund's portion going down each year and the stations' portion going up. This arrangement freed *Frontline* of the need to shop around for underwriting from corporations and foundations and the uncertainty of year-to-year funding. Fanning had five years to prove the worth of the series. More than two decades later, the stations collectively provided the core funding for the series and the insulation that went along it.

A white South African, Fanning produced programming in his native land for the BBC and other broadcasters. In 1977 he settled at WGBH as producer of *The World,* a series that produced fifty documentaries on international topics, and eventually morphed into *Frontline.* Under the banner of *The World,* Fanning and WGBH refused the entreaties of the State Department, and caused a diplomatic crisis, by broadcasting "Death of a Princess," about the beheading of an adulterous member of the Saudi royal family. In a sense, the decision of Fanning and WGBH to stand up to the very government that provided much of public broadcasting's funding demonstrated a maturity for the still young institution and established the working philosophy for *Frontline.*

Seeking to combine "credible, thoughtful reporting with powerful narrative," *Frontline* has helped drive the national and international news agenda since its first broadcast, an exposé on gambling that shook the National Football League and shocked its fans just before the 1983 Super Bowl. The initial program documented the gambling activities of a major team owner, suggesting fixed games and murders to cover them up. Later that first season, *Frontline* investigated poverty in Washington on the eve of President Ronald Reagan's State of the Union address, exposed the workings of the Vatican bank, and took on the hot button issues of abortion and gun control.

NBC anchorwoman Jessica Savitch served as on air reporter for the NFL documentary and host for the series during its first two years. Her compelling on-air style and national prominence helped give credibility to the new series, but the strength of its reporting made it an institution even after her death.

Twenty-two years later, in 2005, *Frontline's* shocking "Ghosts of Rwanda" documented how America and the world stood by and did nothing as the Rwandan government butchered eight hundred thousand people in one hundred days.

During the program's first two decades, *Frontline* was honored repeatedly by the major award competitions in television for investigations into topics such as "Remember My Lai?"(1989) "Who profits from drugs" (1989), "High crimes and misdemeanors" (1990), "Innocense Lost/when children testify" (1991), "Clarence Thomas and Anita Hill" (1992), "The best campaign money can buy?" (1993), "The Kervorkan File" (1994), "Waco, the inside story" (1995), "The choice '96" (1996) "Murder, money and Mexico" (1997), "Hunting for bin Laden" (2001), "Inside the Terror Network" (2002), and "Truth, War and Consequences" (2004).

While its style remains proudly investigative, not all *Frontline* programs rake muck. Its producers investigate "values" as much as they focus on "whistle blowers and wrongdoing." It has, for example, explored the lives of Jesus Christ, William Shakespeare, Thomas Jefferson, and Pope John Paul II.

By the early twenty-first century, *Frontline* had built an extensive web presence to support its investigations, providing a full library of programs, additional background and forums for viewers and educators. In collaboration with KQED, the public television station in San Francisco, the *Frontline* staff now offers a second series called *Frontline World*, consisting of short pieces (about ten minutes) from an array of reporters around the world. A television series first, *Frontline World* is also a web resource and an active participant in promoting international understanding through related educational efforts and a fellowship program.

Further Readings

Bullert, B .J. *Public Television Politics and the Battle over Documentary Film*. New Brunswick, NJ: Rutgers University Press, 1997.

Jarvik, Laurence. *PBS, Behind the Screen*. Rocklin CA: Prima Publishing, 1997.

Stewart, David. *The PBS Companion: A History of Public Television*. New York: TV Books, 1999.

JACK W. MITCHELL

GALE, ZONA

Zona Gale (August 26, 1874–December 27, 1938) was one of those women of the late nineteenth century who saw education and journalism as opportunities for independence. The only daughter of a former schoolteacher and a retired locomotive engineer, she grew up in Portage, a small town in central Wisconsin. She was one of the first generation of midwestern women to attend a public university, and in 1895 received her Bachelor's Degree from the University of Wisconsin. Gale had written fiction throughout her childhood and college years, and while still a student, was approached by a reporter from the Milwaukee *Sentinel* who asked her to write two articles on university societies. Encouraged by her mother to follow up on this opportunity, she moved to Milwaukee upon her graduation to look for a job with a newspaper.

The twenty-one-year-old Gale faced a formidable task, for though women were making their presence known in the newspaper industry toward the end of the nineteenth century, they represented less than 5 percent of fulltime editors and reporters at this time. She was persistent, however, and landed a job at the *Evening Wisconsin* covering society events at a salary of $15 a week. During the next four years, she reported for the *Evening Wisconsin*, switched over to the Milwaukee *Journal*, and, in 1899, received her Master's Degree in Letters from the University of Wisconsin. During the same period, she took several breaks to seek newspaper work in Chicago and New York, occasionally receiving an assignment and publishing a "special." At the same time, she was active in the woman's club movement (which encouraged self-development and social reform) and woman suffrage, serving in June of 1900 as the chairwoman of the local press committee of the General Federation of Women's Clubs, which was to hold its biennial convention in Milwaukee.

Ambitious for a job at a major newspaper, she left Milwaukee for New York, where she got a job at Joseph Pulitzer's sensational *Evening World*. Here, she thrived, covering stories on murder trials, scandalous family disputes, and factory strikes. She also investigated social conditions, including women's working conditions and poverty in city tenements. Both her writing style and the types of stories she covered won her a certain acclaim, for the *World* was soon promoting her stories under a byline (at a time when few newspapers identified their writers), and on several occasions even used her name in the story's headline.

At the same time, Gale had started writing fiction again and published several stories in newspapers and magazines. When she sold two stories to *Success* for $125 each and then a third for $65 in 1903, she left her full-time job at the *World* to write on a freelance basis. In the next few years she published her fiction in a number of popular magazine, including *The Smart Set, Ainslee's*, and *Harper's*, while continuing to publish occasional pieces for the *World*. In 1906 she published her first novel, *Romance Island*, and in the next five years published twenty-three short stories and another novel, *The Love of Pelleas and Etarre*, as well as a collection of short stories about a fictional midwestern town, *Friendship Village*. Much of this work was criticized as sentimental, but it charmed readers seeking the comfort of good old-fashioned American small towns seeped in wholesome traditional values.

In October 1911, after winning a $2,000 first prize for best short story in a competition run by the *Delineator*, Gale returned to Portage to care for her aging parents. Here, she continued to publish fiction as well as freelance articles in a wide range of magazines, including the *New York Times Sunday Magazine*, the *Nation, New Republic*, and *Ladies Home Journal*. In this period, her work strongly reflected her developing feminism, social awareness, and commitment to the reformist ethos. She wrote about woman's rights, suffrage, prohibition, education reform, progressive Wisconsin politics, and the peace movement, and her work was sometimes rejected on the grounds that it was too advanced for the times. In 1915, for example, the editor of *Atlantic Monthly* rejected a short story about a racially mixed neighborhood because he could not imagine presenting it to his readers.

In 1920, Gale published her twelfth novel, *Miss Lulu Bett*, the story of a small-town spinster blossoming into independent womanhood. The following year she wrote the script for a play by the same title, and received the Pulitzer Prize for drama in 1921. This brought her celebrity, and in the following years, she was often approached by aspiring writers for advice on how to get work published. She was generous with her advice (be persistent and keep writing) and maintained her support of journalism education by serving on the boards of professional journalism organizations such as Theta Sigma Phi and educational institutions such as the University of Wisconsin. She remained a prolific writer, turning out several short stories and magazine articles every year and a novel every two years, until her death from pneumonia in 1938.

Further Reading

Burt, Elizabeth V. "Rediscovering Zona Gale, Journalist." *American Journalism 12:4* (Fall 1995): 444–462.

Derleth, August, *Still Small Voic: The Biography of Zona Gale*. New York: D. Appleton-Century Company, 1940.

Simonson, Harold P. *Zona Gale*. New York: Twayne Publishers, 1962.14.

Roberts, James P. *Famous Wisconsin Authors*. Oregon, WI Badger Books, 2002.

Williams, Deborah Lindsay. *Not in Sisterhood: Edith Wharton, Willa Cather, Zona Gale and the Politics of Female Authorship*. New York: Palgrave, 2002.

ELIZABETH V. BURT

GALLICO, PAUL WILLIAM

During the "Golden Age" of American sports no one was more responsible for making star players celebrities or in seeing sport as a civic spectacle than Paul Gallico (July 26, 1897–July 15, 1976) of the *New York Daily News*, who continued his search for romance and the heroic ideal as a writer of magazine fiction, books, and motion picture screenplays.

Gallico freely admitted that creating and cultivating sports "legends" was a "meal ticket" few sports writers could pass up, and during the Jazz Age few were better at it than this unlikely son of an Italian concert pianist and his Austrian wife. Paolo Gallico and Hortense Erlich had hoped their son would follow his father into music, but Paul, who was born in New York City, preferred sports. After graduating Columbia in 1921, where the six foot, three inch Gallico had been an oarsman on the university rowing team, Gallico married Alva Taylor, the daughter of *Chicago Tribune* columnist Burton Lester Taylor. This led to a job at the *Tribune*'s sister publication, the *New York Daily News*, as a movie critic even though Gallico "didn't like movies." When his reviews made that apparent, the paper's publisher Joseph Medill Patterson fired him. Managing editor Philip Payne "hid" Gallico in the sports department where he "served time" writing "color and crowd stuff" for the paper's Sunday edition. The paper's Sunday edition had a circulation of one million, the largest in the nation, because of its ability, Gallico learned, "of making readers an eyewitness to the big news of the day."

Gallico won notoriety through a stunt. In August 1923 he boxed a round with Jack Dempsey. His account of a bloody lip, knockout, and "terrific headache" delighted readers and his publisher. As sports editor of the *Daily News*, beginning in 1923, Gallico wrote about golfing with Bobby Jones, hitting against Dizzy Dean, swimming against Johnny Weissmuller, racing against Cliff Berege, and flying acrobatics with Al Williams.

Gallico acknowledged his writing on sports in the 1920s involved "an appalling amount of purple ink," but he saw it as his job "to impress and excite the reader." To his generation of "gee-whiz" sports writers, athletic competition was "played for high drama" in which "everything went." Storytellers told readers "we were going to war. It was our side against theirs." Readers, Gallico reasoned, were ready for these "delicious idiocies" and eager for "passionate devotions." The adulation of the athlete, Gallico found, "to the point of almost national hysteria," reflected a post-war generation's appetite "for alter egos that lifted us above our humdrum lives." If perpetrating "sentimental tosh" made the sports writer the bane of the serious-minded, it commended him to circulation managers who saw the "poetry" in playing sport to the limit. It made both the athlete and the sports writer a star. Finally, sports writers could "afford to drive a motor car and have a home in the country."

Beginning in 1932, Gallico began publishing magazine fiction. Fourteen short stories appeared in the *Saturday Evening Post* and another in *American Magazine*. Gallico left the *Daily News* in 1936 to pursue a range of writing assignments. Twenty-six reminiscences about Jazz Age sports appeared in *Cosmopolitan* and were later published in the best-selling *Farewell to Sport* (1938). Pieces for *Collier's*, *Good Housekeeping* and *Readers Digest* quickly followed. *The Snow Goose* (1941) won honorable mention in the O. Henry Memorial Prize competition. *Lou Gehrig: Pride of the Yankees* (1942) became a huge Hollywood hit.

In the summer of 1944, Gallico became war correspondent for *Cosmopolitan*. After the war he lived in England, Liechtenstein, and Monaco, marrying and divorcing four times, including two baronesses. His forty-one books and eleven screenplays tended to embrace an essential psychological simplicity in which he wrote about the world not as it was, but as he hoped it would be.

Further Reading

Chicago Tribune, July 17, 1976.

Chapman, John. *Tell It to Sweeney: The Informal History of the New York Daily News*. Garden City, NY: Doubleday, 1961.

Evensen, Bruce J. *When Dempsey Fought Tunney: Heroes, Hokum, and Storytelling in the Jazz Age*. Nashville: University of Tennessee, 1996.

Gallico, Paul. *Confessions of a Story Writer*. New York: A.A. Knopf, 1946.

——. "The Golden Decade." In, *Sport U.S.A.: The Best of the Saturday Evening Post*, edited by Harry T. Paxton. New York: Thomas Nelson, 1961.

——. *Golf Is a Friendly Game*. New York: A.A. Knopf, 1942.

——. *Farewell to Sport*. New York: A.A. Knopf, 1938.

——. *Further Confessions of a Story Writer: Stories Old and New*. Garden City, NY: Doubleday, 1961.

——. *The Golden People*. Garden City, NY: Doubleday, 1965.

——. *Lou Gehrig: Pride of the Yankees*. New York: Grosset & Dunlap, 1942. *New York Times*, July 17, 1976.

Holtzman, Jerome. *No Cheering in the Press Box*, New York: Holt, Rinehart and Winston, 1974.

Nugent, Henry. "The Sports Section," *American Mercury* 16, March 1929.

"Paul William Gallico," in *Current Biography: Who's News and Why, 1946*. New York: H.W. Wilson, 1947.

Paul Gallico Papers. Special Collections. Columbia University. New York, NY.

BRUCE J. EVENSEN

GANNETT CENTER FOR MEDIA STUDIES

The Gannett Center for Media Studies (1984–1998) was established at Columbia University as the first institute for advanced study of media and technological change in the United States, and perhaps the world, in 1984–1985. Organized as an operating program of the Gannett Foundation, a philanthropy made possible by earnings from the Gannett Company's media properties, and later renamed The Freedom Forum, the Media Studies Center developed a respected, advanced fellowship program for academics and media professionals, a technology studies program and laboratory as well as publications, high profile conferences and other activities. Announced at a news conference at Columbia University in spring 1984, the center opened its doors on two levels of the Columbia journalism building in early 1985 with dedication ceremonies later that spring. The center operated at Columbia until mid-year 1996 when it moved to the IBM Building in midtown Manhattan and was subsequently phased out by the foundation late in 1998. The center was notable as a joint venture between a university and a foundation and for its generous funding, some $51 million in its twelve years at Columbia alone.

Aimed at the advancement of new knowledge about media and technological change, the center connected higher education and media industries, directed its work at journalism and communication education, media and communication organizations and industries as well as the general public. The center was well publicized and its director and fellows were widely quoted in media reports for more than a decade. One media critic called it "one stop shopping for reliable information on almost anything about the media." It was said that the center conferred status on journalism education and the news and entertainment media through a variety of interrelated activities that drew senior, mid-career and younger scholars and professionals to the Columbia campus. Among those who held semester and full year fellowships from media industries included famous editors, broadcasters, media executives, commentators, industry researchers, and others; from the academy came scholars from several fields including journalism and mass communications, history, political science, economics, law, and others engaged in media research. The center was often cited as a bridge between academe and industry and was hailed by many for fostering mutual respect between the two. Columbia's president Michael I. Sovern called it "a place for journalism to catch its breath," and Cornell's president Frank L.H. Rhodes, the center's advisory board chairman, said its evident success, well documented in many sources, was the result of "high minded goals, first rate programs with substantive outcomes, a driving ambition to be useful and a reputation for integrity and independence," in spite of its quasi-corporate sponsorship.

The genesis of the Gannett Center was the 1947 Hutchins Commission Freedom of the Press that called for "centers of intelligence" for mass communication industries and also was inspired by the work of Columbia's

famed Bureau of Applied Social Research, headed by sociologist Paul Lazarsfeld for more than three decades before its closure in 1971. During its twelve years at Columbia the center produced many research studies and published the quarterly *Gannett Center Journal*, later the *Media Studies Journal*. Known for its intellectual products which included notable studies of presidential campaign coverage, media systems abroad, and journalism education, it was also the well spring for some 150 books about the media including well-known, popular volumes as well as scholarly tomes on topics that included biography and memoirs, media history, media industries and issues, media influence and impact, media laws and ethics, as well as media technology and international media. The flow of books, developed by fellows continued long after the center was phased out, including one that appeared as late as 2005. In its scholarly work and fellowship program, the center championed "different ways of knowing," which meant welcoming varied research methods from social science inquiry to history, law, and cultural studies and less formal journalistic accounts too.

The center's extensive program of national and international conferences drew former presidents of the United Sates, other chiefs of state, government ministers, heads of media companies and other luminaries as well as notable intellectuals, working professionals and ordinary citizens. Conferences were notable for their connections between the academy and industry with all sessions integrating the two. The center also had an extensive public scholarship effort that involved popular media including television and networks, radio programs, newspaper and magazine coverage, and other outlets, which drew on its staff and fellows for information, analysis and comment.

Other activities included a summer leadership institute for journalism school deans and other administrators, an annual seminar series for PhD students, technology seminars for media professionals and other tailored events for various educational and industry group as well as high level delegations for Congress, parliamentary groups from several countries as well as various study groups and commissions.

A pioneer both in the study of technology and its applications, the center helped develop software, a pilot electronic newspaper and extensive online operations including pioneering Internet websites and other work. Preparation of media education and media industries for the consequences of the onrushing digital age was a major center priority. As the first institute of advanced study for media—not a graduate program or industry training institute—the Gannett/Freedom Forum Center demonstrated the utility and value of a media think tank, protected from the stresses of daily work life and routines. Other institutions concerned with media and journalism subsequently adopted many of the ideas developed at the center. And, according to former fellows, the influence of the institution individuals touched by it is incalculable.

The center's demise was a calculated decision of the Freedom Forum, the successor to the Gannett Foundation, which chose to spend its resources elsewhere. It was also said that the center as an intellectual enterprise was at odds with the foundation's corporate culture and had also suffered from strained relations with the Columbia Journalism School, where many faculty scorned research. In the end, though, the decision to dismantle the center was largely economic. The Freedom Forum preferred to close the center rather than seek other sources of funding or bequeath it to another institution.

In 1996 when the center's founding director departed for a new assignment, the program in a new venue and with new leadership shifted its focus from research and advanced study to more direct service for media professionals. Most of the efforts for higher education were phased out as was technology studies and most publications. The center's parent foundation had financial difficulties for a time and focused its efforts on the Newseum, a museum of news, first in Arlington, Virginia, and later in Washington, D.C.

Further Reading

Dennis, Everette E., and David L. Stebenne. "Requiem for a Think Tank: The Life and Death of the Gannett Center at Columbia, 1984–1996," *Harvard International Journal of Press/Politics,* vol. 8, no. 2, Spring 2003, 11–35.

EVERETTE E. DENNIS

GANNETT, FRANK

Frank Gannett (September 15, 1876–December 3, 1957) launched the Gannett Company, one of the world's largest newspaper chains, in 1906 when he purchased a half-interest in the *Gazette* in Elmira, New York. In 1912, he bought the *Ithaca Journal* and then in 1918, he purchased two newspapers in Rochester, NewYork, and merged them together to form the *Times-Union*. Gannett relocated his company to Rochester headquarters.

From these modest New York roots, his company prospered. At the time of his death, the Gannett Company had grown to include twenty-two newspapers, four radio stations, and three television stations. In the years since his death, Gannett was transformed into a public company with holdings of ninety daily newspapers operating in forty-one states, the District of Columbia, U.S. territories, and in Europe, Canada and Asia. By 2006, the conglomerate also included twenty-two television stations, more than nine hundred non-daily publications and more than one hundred web sites.

Gannett was born in Bristol, New York, on September 15, 1876. His father, at first a farmer in rural upstate, ultimately owned several hotels. The young Gannett attended Cornell University, where his interest in journalism flourished at the college's newspaper and as a local correspondent for the *Ithaca Journal* and the *Syracuse Herald*. After his graduation from Cornell in 1898, Gannett was hired as the city editor of the *Ithaca Journal* and worked his way through the ranks of that paper. By 1906, Gannett was ready to transition from newspaper management to newspaper ownership in a partnership, the Empire State Group.

By the time he bought out his partners in 1923 and renamed the group the Gannett Company, the company owned six newspapers in New York.

Gannett concentrated his newspaper accumulations in the Northeast, where he bought medium sized journals in one-newspaper towns. He shied away from big cities where competition for advertising could be fierce. Gannett earned a reputation as a chain owner who allowed the local editors autonomy. He also established the company's spirit of innovation that allowed *USA Today*, the flagship newspaper of the Gannett chain, to transform late twentieth century journalism more than thirty years after his death. Gannett was an investor who helped in the development of teletype technology. His newsrooms relied on shortwave radio to facilitate swift reporting of breaking news. His printing presses at the Rochester newspapers were adapted for color in 1938, presaging the major technological advance that *USA Today* spawned when it debuted in 1982. The Gannett Company created the Gannett National Service in 1943 to provide its local newspapers with enterprise, news stories and regular information from Washington, D.C.

At the time of his death at age eighty-one from the effects of a fall, Gannett was remembered as a religious man who eschewed religious and racial intolerance. Mourners recounted that he put his principles behind his newspaper policies by refusing to carry advertising for alcohol.

Further Reading

"A Brief Company History," http://www.gannett.com/map/history.htm (accessed April 9, 2007).
"Frank Gannett: Newspaper Publisher 1876-1957," *Notable American Unitarians*, http://www.harvardsquarelibrary.org/unitarians/gannett.html.(accessed April 9, 2007).
Newsmen Attend Gannett Service," *New York Times*, 7 December 1957, 21.
Prichard, Peter. *The Making of McPaper: The Inside Story of USA Today*. Kansas City: Andrews, McMeel & Parker, 1987.

AGNES HOOPER GOTTLIEB

GARRISON, WILLIAM LLOYD

William Lloyd Garrison (December 10 or 12, 1805–May 24, 1879) remains both iconic and controversial in the American anti-slavery movement and abolitionist press. His newspaper, *The Liberator*, was the leading and longest running abolitionist newspaper of the nineteenth century. In it, he minced no words shaming and condemning slave holders, churches, and clergy taking neutral positions on segregation and slavery. In his orations, organizational involvement, and newspaper he demanded immediate liberation and full rights for all held in slavery.

Born in Newburyport, Maryland, in 1805, William Lloyd Garrison grew up in poverty, raised by his mother after his father abandoned the family. He was indentured at thirteen to Ephraim W. Allen, publisher of the *Newburyport Herald*, to learn the printing trade. Over time he moved from setting type to writing and editing, and then to editor of the *Newburyport Free Press*, which failed within a year. Garrison went to Boston, eventually became editor of the *National Philanthropist*, and then moved to Bennington, Vermont, in 1828 to co-edit *The Journal of the Times*. There he met Benjamin Lundy walking a New England circuit and speaking against slavery. Lundy lured him to Baltimore the next year to co-edit *The Genius of Universal Emancipation*, the national newspaper of the American Colonization Society, in its new office.

Garrison abandoned the colonization strategy of sending free blacks to Africa for immediate emancipation. Lundy and Garrison were soon jailed and Garrison convicted of libel over Garrison's lambaste of a local ship owner and his captain in a November 1829 column, "Black List." He accused them of transporting slaves to New Orleans. Serving a jail sentence in lieu of fine, he wrote poetry, letters to local officials and newspapers, and a pamphlet about his case. He was freed early when a New York philanthropist, Arthur Tappan, read his pamphlet and paid the fine. Garrison left Maryland before the second libel suit came to judgment.

Garrison began *The Liberator* in Boston on January 1, 1831, under the slogan, "My country is the world; my countrymen are all mankind." Through *The Liberator* he aimed to build anti-slavery activism, influence, and fervor in the North—particularly in New England—and to advocate for the needs and interests of free blacks. He spurned politics and legal initiatives to speak from moral high ground, also supporting women's rights and opposing the use of alcohol. The paper became the organ of the New England Anti-Slavery Society in 1832 and the voice of the American Anti-Slavery Society when it formed in 1833. Although it performed important organizational work, *The Liberator* was especially known for publishing Garrison's deeply felt convictions.

Garrison was a pacifist who decried the Nat Turner slave rebellion in 1831, for which free blacks criticized him. Regardless, because of the *Liberator's* outspoken anti-slavery views, pro-slavery proponents blamed the paper for the Turner affair and other violent acts. Indeed, *The Liberator* grew in infamy from that start. The Vigilance Association of Columbia, South Carolina offered a $1500 reward for the identity of anyone circulating *The Liberator*. Georgetown, D.C., instituted a fine of $20 or thirty days to anyone of color leaving the post office with a copy. North Carolina indicted Garrison for felonious acts, and Georgia offered a $5,000 reward for information leading to Garrison's conviction for violating state law.

Garrison co-founded the abolitionist New England Anti-Slavery Society in 1832, and *The Liberator* boldly called for action and increasingly assailed anti-slavery moderates who, Garrison believed, did not go far enough. Garrison was dragged from his office in 1832 before addressing the Women's Anti-Slavery Society and nearly stripped naked. It was not the only time Garrison faced physical violence. In 1833, co-founded the American Anti-Slavery Society in Philadelphia, and that year, returning from England and headed for a meeting, he met a mob planning to tar and feather him. Another mob in 1835 intending to tar and feather a British anti-slavery visitor almost got him instead. Unbowed, Garrison published a humorous account of that incident, and in the *Liberator's* recurring column, "Refuge of Oppression," he satirized his enemies by republishing snippets from pro-slavery papers, speeches, and articles.

The Liberator circulated from Boston throughout New England, the nation, and the world for thirty-five years, through January 1, 1866—twelve days after the Thirteenth Amendment was ratified. It fueled anti-slavery zeal from afar, but it also aided Boston's sweeping racial reform, which far surpassed gains in other Northern cities. Despite Garrison's pacifism, he was blamed for slave rebellions and violent acts. He was jailed, attacked by mobs, burned in effigy, his office damaged, and bounties put on his head. His readers of color were threatened with fines or imprisonment from Georgetown, D.C., into the deep South. Although *The Liberator's* circulation is estimated at less than three thousand, a large number of readers were black—75 percent in 1834.

Critics today point to racial and cultural paternalism in Garrison's view that free blacks should elevate themselves to dominant cultural standards. *The Liberator* acknowledged leaders of color but largely ignored Boston's everyday black citizens, churches, and urban black publishers, including two failed black Boston newspapers. Garrison was an icon to early anti-slavery historians. More recent studies have accused Garrison of egotistically factionalizing anti-slavery forces in the late 1830s and weakening their growing voice. Controversy grew around Garrison as friction developed within the anti-slavery societies. He had defended female activists and proposed suffrage for both women and emancipated slaves. By 1837 he openly challenged churches to integrate and make public anti-slavery stands. He denounced the Constitution as a pro-slavery document and adamantly opposed getting into electoral campaigns.

In 1840 the American Anti-Slavery Society spawned two groups: the Liberty Party, which began electoral activity, and the American and Foreign Anti-Slavery Society, which banned women from membership. The Liberty Party started *The Abolitionist* in 1842. Garrison became president of the American-Anti-slavery Society in 1843 and held the office until 1865. He continued publishing *The Liberator*, writing most of its content and scrounging money to keep it afloat.

Garrison became convinced that the North and South must dissolve their union rather than live under constitutional slavery. In 1844 *The Liberator* adopted the slogan, "No Union With Slave-holders." He condemned 1850 revisions to the Fugitive Slave Act, directing abolitionists to harbor runaway slaves. In 1851 when Frederick Douglass proposed revising the U.S. Constitution to outlaw slavery, Garrison flew into attack, permanently embittering their relations. He publicly burned a Constitution in 1854.

Garrison finally supported the Republican Party platform to bring the vote to women and free blacks in 1859 but did not support Lincoln's War until the Emancipation Proclamation was issued. When the war ended and the

Thirteenth Amendment passed, he stopped publishing *The Liberator*—declaring its mission accomplished. Garrison's four sons and one daughter extended his integrationist and egalitarian fervor and his journalistic tradition.

Further Reading

Fanuzzi, Robert. 2003. *Abolition's Public Sphere*. Minneapolis: University of Minnesota Press.

Mayer, Henry. 1999. "William Lloyd Garrison: The Undisputed Master of the Cause of Negro Liberation." *Journal of Blacks in Higher Education* 23,105–109.

———. 1998. *All on Fire: William Lloyd Garrison and the Abolition of Slavery*. New York: St. Martin's Press.

Walter M. Merrill and Louis Ruchames, eds. *To Rouse the Slumbering Land, 1868–1879: The Letters of William Lloyd Garrison*, vol. 6. Cambridge, MA: Harvard University Press, 1981.

Nord, David Paul. 1986. "Tocqueville, Garrison and the Perfection of Journalism," *Journalism History*, 13:56–64.

CARMEN E. CLARK

GERMAN-LANGUAGE PRESS IN AMERICA

In the heyday of the immigrant press around 1910, the most numerous group of newspapers were those published in German. According to the *Ayer's* directory, more than 460 German-language dailies and weeklies were issued in 1916, appearing in 36 different states and in more than 270 cities and towns. In circulation, they ranged from German America's flagship, the *New-Yorker Staats-Zeitung*, which reported an edition of 138,000, down to the *Anzeiger* of Providence, Rhode Island, which laid claim to 300 readers. This huge press served an immigrant group that numbered more than 2.3 million, according to the 1910 census. If their American-born children were included in the ethnic community often referred to as German America, it grew to almost 8 million members.

Early Papers, 1732–1865

The German immigrant press was not only voluminous, it also had a pedigree that predated the founding of the United States itself. In 1732, Benjamin Franklin was involved in launching the first German-language paper in the English colonies, the *Philadelphische Zeitung*. The choice of Pennsylvania as the site of that venture was no coincidence, as that colony had a considerable number of German immigrants within its borders. Franklin's paper only lasted two issues, however, and the first German paper of any duration did not appear until 1739, when *Der Hoch-Deutsch Pennsylvanische Geschichts-Schreiber* was founded by Christopher Sauer, an immigrant from the Wittgenstein region who had learned the printer's trade in America.

Evidence of the need for a diversity of opinion among the Pennsylvania Germans was the appearance in 1762 of a competitor for Sauer's paper, then run by his son and renamed *Germantauner Zeitung*. The newcomer, the

Wochentliche Philadelphische Staatsbote, would soon side with those advocating a break with Great Britain, while the *Zeitung* supported the Loyalists. During and following the American Revolution, German-language newspapers were also established in regions where Pennsylvania Germans were settling, such as Maryland and Ohio.

The origins of the huge number of German-language around the turn of the last century lie, however, in growing immigration from Germany to America after 1830. In the 1820–1829 decade, an average of 575 people left Germany for America each year. The following decade, that number rose to 12,000, and it reached 38,000 between 1840 and 1849 as political turmoil in Germany increased.

The arrival of so many new immigrants made the ground fertile for new newspaper ventures, and prospective publishers were also aided by frequent calls for new papers in locations where existing ones did not reflect the opinion of all members of the growing ethnic community. Newspapers with political aspirations also benefited from the emergence in the 1820s of an American party system that viewed the press as an essential tool in politics and established a patronage system for financing newspapers loyal to party principles. Beginning a practice that would endure for most of the nineteenth century, U.S. political leaders of the Jacksonian era were also persuaded by the journalists of the foreign-language press that non-English papers were indispensable when it came to reaching immigrant voters.

Finally, the early 1830s also witnessed the arrival of a small but significant group of intellectuals who fled after participating in failed revolutions in Europe and now made new careers in journalism in German-America. These men would be intimately connected with the newspapers that appeared after 1830 in cities with major German settlements, such as Buffalo, New York, Cincinnati, Pittsburgh, and Cleveland.

The diversity of the German-American press increased further when another group of intellectuals, often sympathetic to liberal reform, arrived in the wake of the revolutions of 1848. As the "forty-eighters" entered the editorial offices across German-America, they changed the political alignment of German-language journalism away from the largely passive Democratic allegiances that were a legacy of the Jacksonian era toward a more active involvement in politics and loyalty to the newly formed Republican Party. With ideals of the failed revolutions still vivid in their minds, many of these newcomers championed radical policies that would, in time, give rise to a substantial German-American working-class press. Opposition to the views of the "forty-eighters" would, in turn, lead to the establishment of numerous conservative papers, swelling the ranks of the German-language press further. On the eve of the election of 1856, one editor estimated the number of papers to be a little over 100; four years later, it had grown to 144.

The Heyday of German American Journalism

The German immigrant press continued to grow after the Civil War, nourished by a steady influx of immigrants that in the ten years following the war averaged more than 100,000 per year. In 1876, the number of papers stood at 448, and four years later another 100 had been added. Cities such as New York, Philadelphia, Chicago, Cincinnati, Milwaukee, and St. Louis each had five or more German-language dailies.

Although published in a foreign language, German - American papers had a great deal in common with their English-language counterparts, to which they often looked for ideas. Like the "American" papers, the German immigrant press moved away from political partisanship and funding following the Civil War, choosing instead to rely on advertising. Technological innovations such as rotary presses and linotype machines also made it possible for circulations to keep pace with the growth in readership. Changes in content were also inspired by developments in American journalism in general. In St. Louis, for instance, Austrian immigrant Joseph Pulitzer filled the pages of the *Westliche Post* with crime and accidents, a technique he would go on to apply as a publisher of English-language papers in both St. Louis and New York.

During this heady time, Carl Schurz, one of several immigrants able to pursue a successful career in American politics, listed four functions of the German American press. First, it explained America to the immigrants; second, it promoted cooperation among German-Americans (something Schurz himself clearly had benefited from when his countrymen had gone to cast their ballots); third, it informed Germans in the United States about Germany; and fourth, it taught the immigrants about the "open-handed generosity" of the United States. Each of these functions was clearly reflected in the papers' content, which offered readers news and editorials about American society and politics, stories chronicling the daily lives of fellow immigrants and celebrating their achievements and organizations, news items from Germany, and pieces generally lauding life in the new country.

Decline, 1893–2005

As German-American journalists noted the ever-growing number of papers in the last decades of the nineteenth century, many of them assumed that the immigrant community, its institutions and its newspapers would survive forever in America. Change, however, was imminent. Annual immigration had averaged more than 130,000 in the 1880s, but in the early 1890s it began to fall off, and after 1893 and until 1924 it would never exceed 50,000. As a result, the number of German-born immigrants began to decline after 1890: it went from 2.78 million in the 1890 census to 2.66 ten years later. The press felt the drop in the number of foreign-born German-Americans almost immediately. The number of papers peaked in 1893–1894 and then began to decline.

The decline took place despite the fact that the number of second-generation German Americans was still growing and would continue to do so for another twenty years. The children of the original immigrants, were not, however a particularly lucrative audience for the German-language press, as they overwhelmingly turned away from the German language.

While the German-American press thus had begun to decline two decades before World War I, there is little doubt that the outbreak of war in Europe and America's eventual entry into that war as Germany's enemy had a devastating effect on newspapers published in German in America. Around the turn of the century, German-American journalism had, to a large extent, become a matter of promoting and defending the ethnic community, and that commitment entailed, by necessity, ties to the original homeland of community members. Moreover, as the war began, many German-American papers saw it as their duty to counter what they saw as a preponderance of Allied viewpoints in the American press, assuming that the United States would remain neutral in the conflict.

With U.S. entry into the war, German-language newspapers became conspicuous targets in the surge of patriotism and anti-German hysteria that followed the declaration of war. Buffeted by a concerted propaganda by the U.S. government intended to "sell the war" to the American public by demonizing the German enemy and by repressive measures that threatened editors who interfered with the war effort with jail and fines and mandated translations of foreign-language content, the German-American press saw its numbers fall further. Financial difficulties worsened the situation, as the war drove up the price of newsprint public opinion made readers decline to renew their subscriptions and advertisers withdraw their patronage.

The result was that the war years hastened the decline of the German-language press, cutting its numbers in half between 1917 and 1920. Although the 1920s would witness a growth in total circulation, the number of papers continued to fall in that decade, and the press was soon dealt other severe blows, first by the end of unrestricted immigration in the mid-1920s, followed by the onset of the Great Depression, and then the titanic struggle to defeat German fascism during World War II. By the early 2000s, the number of German-language newspapers, by then all weeklies, numbered fewer than ten.

Further Reading

Bergquist, James M. "The German-American Press." In *The Ethnic Press in the United States: A Historical Analysis and Handbook,* edited by Sally M. Miller, 131–159, New York: Greenwood Press, 1987.

Bergquist, James M. "The Val J. Peter Newspapers: The Rise and Decline of a Twentieth-Century German-Language Newspaper Empire." *Yearbook of German-American Studies* 29 (1994):117–128.

Conolly-Smith, Peter. *Translating America: An Immigrant Press Visualizes American Popular Culture, 1895–1918.* Washington, D.C.: Smithsonian Books, 2004.

Geitz, Henry, ed. *The German-American Press.* Madison, WI: Max Kade Institute for German-American Studies, University of Wisconsin-Madison, 1992.

Miller, Daniel, and Don Heinrich Tolzmann. *Early German-American Newspapers.* Bowie, MD: Heritage Books, 2001, 1908.

Saalberg, Harvey. "The *Westliche Post* of St. Louis: German-Language Daily, 1857–1938." *Journalism Quarterly* 45 (1968):453–456.

Shore, Elliott, Ken Fones-Wolf, and James P. Danky. *The German-American Radical Press: The Shaping of a Left Political Culture.* Urbana: University of Illinois Press, 1992.

Sonntag, Mark. "Fighting Everything German In Texas, 1917–1919." *Historian* 56, no. 4 (1994): 655–670.

Waldenrath, Alexander. "The German Language Newspress in Pennsylvania During World War I." *Pennsylvania History* 42, no. 1 (1975): 25–41.

Wittke, Carl. *The German-Language Press in America.* Lexington: University of Kentucky Press, 1957.

ULF JONAS BJORK

GITLOW V. NEW YORK

Gitlow v. New York, 262 U.S. 652 (1925) is a Supreme Court of the United States decision that provided the intellectual bridge from a limited interpretation of the First Amendment to judicial precedents nationalizing protection for speech and press freedom. Until *Gitlow*, the words of the First Amendment—"Congress shall make no law . . . abridging the freedom of speech, or of the press . . ."—were viewed as applying only to federal power, not to actions by states or localities.

Seen in one light, the Supreme Court's action merely held that Benjamin Gitlow, as business manager for a radical socialist newspaper, *The Revolutionary Age*, was properly convicted for violating New York's criminal anarchy statute. Gitlow and his colleagues were prosecuted under language making it a crime to utter, teach, or advocate violent overthrow of government or the assassination of government officials. The newspaper's publication of "The Left Wing Manifesto," a diatribe containing exhortations such as "'. . . The Communist International calls the proletariat of the world to the final struggle!'" The majority of the Supreme Court read these words as unlawful calls to violent action. By a 7–2 vote, the Court upheld Gitlow's conviction.

Justice Edward Sanford wrote for the Court's majority, concluding that the publication was a direct and dangerous call to action that went beyond advocating abstract doctrine or predicting future industrial strife. Some of the newspaper's words were denounced as direct incitement to violence. The majority ruled that the New York Criminal Anarchy Statute was a constitutional exercise of a state's police power to outlaw words endangering society (*Gitlow*, 666–667).

Justice Oliver Wendell Holmes, Jr., joined by Justice Louis D. Brandeis, dissented, arguing that this publication was not a clear and present danger to government. Expression of opinion and incitement differed only in the speaker's enthusiasm for the result. Holmes wrote: "Eloquence may set fire to reason. But whatever may be thought of the redundant discourse before us, it had no chance of starting a present conflagration" (Gitlow, 673).

Despite the Court's upholding the convictions of members of the Left Wing Faction of the American Socialist Party, Justice Sanford added a judicial aside which helped lead to nationalizing the First Amendment. "For present purposes," Sanford wrote, "we may and do assume that freedom of speech and press—which are protected from abridgement by Congress—are among the fundamental liberties protected by the due process clause of the Fourteenth Amendment from impairment by the States" (*Gitlow*, 666). The Fourteenth Amendment, ratified in 1868 in an attempt to protect freed slaves from repressive state government actions, was used by Justice Sanford to empower use of the First Amendment and other portions of the Bill of Rights against state misconduct for generations to come. The first judicial offspring of *Gitlow v. New York* was the now-legendary decision in *Near v. Minnesota* (1931) .

In *Near*, the Supreme Court ruled that pre-publication censorship was forbidden by the First Amendment, and that its command applied not only to federal actions but also to actions by states. *New York Times v. Sullivan* (1964), the Court's sweeping decision protecting news media against punitive use of civil libel laws by state courts, gave new force to the First Amendment, as applied to the states through the Fourteenth Amendment. That judicial leverage was provided by *Gitlow v. New York.*

Further Reading

Chafee, Jr., Zechariah. *Free Speech in the United States*, Cambridge, MA, Harvard University Press, 1941.

Kalven, Jr.., Harry. *A Worthy Tradition: Freedom of Speech in America*, Jamie Kalven, ed., New York, New York University Press, 1988.

White, G. Edward. *Justice Oliver Wendell Holmes: Law and the Innner Self* (New York: Oxford University Press, 1993.

Gitlow v. New York, 268 U.S. 652 (1925).

Near v. Minnesota, 283 U.S. 697 (1931).

New York Times v. Sullivan, 376 U.S. 654 (1964).

DWIGHT L. TEETER, JR.

GODDARD, MARY KATHERINE

Mary Katherine Goddard (June 16, 1738–August 12, 1816), a member of a prominent family of printers and newspaper publishers, was the first printer of the Declaration of Independence with the names of the signers attached. She served as postmaster of Baltimore during and after the Revolutionary War, giving her a claim to being the first woman to hold a federal position in the United States. She also edited and published the *Maryland Journal*, a Baltimore newspaper considered one of the best of the Revolutionary period.

Goddard was born on June 16, 1738, in either Groton or New London, Connecticut, the daughter of Sarah Updike Goddard, an exceptionally well-educated woman for her day, and Giles Goddard, a physician and postmaster. She was associated in printing and publishing with her mother and brother, William Goddard, who established the first print shop and newspaper in Rhode Island, the *Providence Gazette.* In 1762 the mother and sister moved from New London to Providence to assist him, running William Goddard's business on their own when he left to open similar shops, first in Philadelphia and then in Baltimore. In 1768 the two women moved to Philadelphia (where the mother died) to manage the print shop that published the *Pennsylvania Chronicle*.

In 1774 Goddard joined her brother in Baltimore taking over his printing office and newspaper, the *Maryland Gazette*, while he was traveling in an attempt to establish a new postal system. Less erratic than he, she made the *Gazette* a strong voice for the Revolution. To keep the paper alive during the difficult days of the Revolution, she started a paper mill, engaged in barter with subscribers, fought for press freedom, and printed "extraordinaries" (extra editions) on newsworthy events such as the battle of Bunker Hill. As Baltimore's chief printer, she was authorized by the Continental Congress, which had been forced by the British to flee from Philadelphia to Baltimore, to print the first official copy of the Declaration of Independence with the names of signers in January 1777.

In 1775 she was appointed postmaster, a position commonly held by a newspaper publisher. She held the post until 1789 when she was dismissed against her will on grounds the position might involve more traveling than a woman could undertake. Two hundred leading citizens petitioned without success that she be retained. In 1784 she and her brother quarreled, resulting in her departure from the printing office and newspaper. Goddard greatly resented being forced out at a time when both the publishing operation and the post office, which she had overseen during a period of economic duress, had become profitable.

Unlike most women of the day, Goddard never married, supporting herself in later years running a bookshop. She died in Baltimore on Aug. 12, 1816, freeing a slave, Belinda Starling, who had helped her. Her life demonstrated the tribulations confronting a woman in publishing at a time when women had few legal rights.

Further Reading

Beasley, Maurine H. "William Goddard." In *American Newspaper Journalists: 1690–1872*, edited by Perry J. Ashley, vol. 43, 248–255. Detroit: Gale, 1985.

Henry, Susan. "Sarah Goddard, Gentlewoman Printer," *Journalism Quarterly* 57 (Spring 1980): 23–30.

Hudak, Leona. *Early Women Printers and Publishers, 1639–1820*. Metuchen, NJ: Scarecrow, 1978.

Miner, Ward. *William Goddard: Newspaperman*. Durham, NC: Duke University Press, 1962.

Schilpp, Madelon Golden, and Sharon M. Murphy, *Great Women of the Press*. Carbondale: Southern Illinois University Press, 1983.

Thomas, Isaiah. *The History of Printing in America*, vol. 1. Worcester, MA: Isaiah Thomas Jr., reprint New York: Burt Franklin, 1964.

MAURINE H. BEASLEY

GODEY'S LADY'S BOOK

Established in 1830 in Philadelphia, *Godey's Lady's Book* (1830–1898) was one of the most popular and widely-circulated magazines of nineteenth-century America. The monthly issues of the *Lady's Book* burst with short fiction, poetry, travel essays, art criticism, "how-to" articles for homemakers, and moral instruction for its intended female audience. The magazine published the period's most significant female authors, including Lydia Sedgewick, Eliza Leslie, Anne Stephens, and Lydia Sigourney. Male authors like Edgar Allen Poe, T.S. Arthur, and Nathaniel Parker Willis also graced the pages of *Godey's Lady's Book*. *Godey's Lady's Book* circulated approximately one hundred thousand copies by the time of the Civil War and demonstrated the lasting viability of the "woman's magazine" for the first time. Many other magazines imitated the *Godey's* format or adapted their content to include more material for female readers.

Louis A. Godey, the founder and publisher of the magazine, established the *Lady's Book's* friendly and direct mode of address, speaking to readers as a congenial, if somewhat paternalistic, companion. The magazine's reputation in the literary world emerged under the editorial direction of Sara J. Hale. Hale, editor of Boston's *Ladies' Magazine*, sold her magazine to Godey in 1837 and assumed control over the *Lady's Book*. Hale had a sharp eye for quality material and better contacts among notable authors; the *Lady's Book* enjoyed its best years in the 1840s and 1850s. Hale also held a more expansive view of the place of women in society, advocating education for women and urging intelligent readers to consider careers in teaching and other professions.

Godey's Lady's Book was perhaps most popular because of its lavish illustrations. Godey employed as many as 150 women to hand-color the magazine's engraved fashion plates, which were featured in each issue during the magazine's prosperous years. The plates accompanied essays on current trends in fashion and were frequently cut from the magazine and hung in middle class parlors. The plates have attracted the attention of historians seeking clues about idealized conceptions of dress and behavior among Victorian women. Less studied are the wood cut illustrations and fine art steel engravings that were designed to cultivate appreciation for the arts.

Some academic debate exists about the legacy of *Godey's* and similar periodicals. They have often been seen as the epitome of the mawkish and sentimental culture that filled women's lives with frivolous stories and normative advice literature that tended to limit women to a separate, domestic sphere. Certainly politics and social issues had no place in Godey's magazine and the idealized vision of women evident in the magazine's text and images did little to challenge dominant gender roles. However other scholars have pointed out that *Godey's* offered women like Hale and Sedgeick an unprecedented place in the literary marketplace and allowed female writers a rare forum to express their views while promoting a community of readership among women for the first time.

Godey's success began to trail off in the years after the Civil War. Editress Hale ended her remarkable career in 1877 at the age of eighty-nine. The magazine changed ownership in the 1880s and finally folded in 1898.

Further Reading

Douglas, Ann. *The Feminization of American Culture*. New York: Doubleday Anchor, 1977.

Lehuu, Isabelle. *Carnival on the Page: Popular Print Media in Antebellum America*. Chapel Hill: University of North Carolina Press, 2000.

Mott, Frank Luther. *A History of American Magazines*, vol 1. Cambridge, MA: Harvard University Press. 1930.

Okker, Patricia. *Our Sister Editors: Sarah J. Hale and the Tradition of Nineteenth-Century American Women Editors*. Athens: University of Georgia Press, 1995.

ROBERT RABE

GODKIN, E.L.

The Irish-born founder of *The Nation* and longtime editor of the *New York Evening Post* was widely known as America's national scold, a journalist whose "sympathy was not so highly developed as his gift for antipathy," as the *New York Times* put it. Yet his influence on both local and national affairs vastly exceeded his publications' meager circulation. One of his editors wrote that "no man in this country has ever exerted so wide an influence with an editorial pen and remained as unknown a personality."

A clergyman's son, Godkin (October 2, 1831–May 21, 1902) earned a law degree in England and began writing for several London publications, covering the Crimean War for the *Daily News*. In 1856, he came to America as the paper's roving correspondent; simultaneously, he studied for the U.S. bar and briefly practiced law in New York even as he continued filing his dispatches and writing occasional editorials for the *New York Times*.

In 1865, a group of abolitionists headed by Frederic Law Olmstead, the prominent architect and co-designer of New York's Central Park, asked Godkin to edit a new publication, a weekly review called *The Nation*, whose purpose was to advocate for "the elevation of the Negro" in the Reconstruction South, while also serving as the best critical journal in both literary and political affairs.

Although *The Nation's* circulation under Godkin (who assumed financial control several months later) never exceeded twelve thousand, it became a must-read journal and its commentaries were followed closely by political leaders and the American intelligentsia; its earliest contributors included most of the leading scholars and writers of the period.

In 1881, Godkin sold the magazine to Henry Villard, the railroad magnate who had just purchased the *New York Evening Post*. As a result, *The Nation* became the *Post's* weekly edition, republishing material that already had appeared in the daily, and Godkin became the paper's associate editor as part of a triumvirate, including Carl Schurz and Horace White. Two years later, Schurz resigned—prompted by Godkin's strident resistance to labor unions—and Godkin assumed control.

"My notion is, you know, that the *Evening Post* ought to make a specialty of being the paper to which sober-minded people would look at crises of this kind, instead of hollering and bellowing and shouting platitudes, like the *Herald*, the *Times*," he wrote to W.P. Garrison, his successor as editor of *The Nation*. Before long, the paper was known, in one prominent New Yorker's words, as "that pessimistic, malignant and malevolent sheet—which no good citizen ever goes to bed without reading." (In fact, the *Evening Post's* circulation was barely above that of *The Nation's*—but, like the magazine, it was read by the city's movers and shakers.)

Godkin's was a laissez-faire, intellectual liberalism, based on opposition to tariffs, strong support for civil-service reform, and a vigorous crusade against corrupt Tammany Hall; Godkin also steered a politically independent course, pulling the paper's support from the national Republican Party in favor of Grover Cleveland. In 1890, Godkin's nine-column exposé of Tammany Hall led to several libel suits against Godkin, none of which prevailed; but the paper's crusade gave birth to the reform movement headed by Charles Parkhurst, which temporarily overthrew the Tammany regime in 1894.

Godkin also was a fierce opponent of jingoism, and reacted with dismay during the period leading up to 1898 as the William Randolph Hearst and Joseph Pulitzer papers sought to plunge the United States into war with Spain. "A yellow journal," he wrote, "is probably the nearest approach, in atmosphere, to hell, existing in any Christian state." As always, Godkin expressed his opinions with an absolute certainty of his rightness, and without any equivocation or moderation.

Ill health forced Godkin to retire at the end of 1899, and he died in 1902. William James wrote that Godkin was "certainly the towering influence in all thought concerning public affairs, and … his influence has certainly been more pervasive than that of any other writer of the generation."

Further Reading

William M. Armstrong. *E.L. Godkin and American Foreign Policy, 1865–1900,* New York: Bookman Associates, 1957.

Alexandra Villard de Borchgrave & John Cullen. *Villard: The Life and Times of an American Titan,* New York: Nan A. Talese/Doubleday, 2001.

Joseph Logsdon. *Horace White, Nineteenth-Century Libera*. Westport, CT: Greenwood, 1971

Frank Luther Mott. "The Nation," *A History of American Magazines, Vol. III, 1865–1885*. Cambridge, MA: Belknap Press/Harvard University Press, 1957.

Allan Nevins, *The Evening Post: A Century of Journalism*. New York: Boni and Liveright, 1922.

New York Times, May 22, 1902, 8, 9.

ERIC FETTMANN

GRAHAM, KATHARINE

Katharine Graham (June 16, 1917–July 17, 2001) was publisher of the *Washington Post* from 1969 to 1979, as well as The Washington Post Company's chairman of the board from 1973 to 1993 and its chief executive officer from 1973 to 1991. As such she was the first woman to head a Fortune 500 Company. She vigorously supported the *Post's* 1971 decision to publish both the Pentagon Papers (after the *New York Times* was stopped from publishing documents illegally smuggled out of the Pentagon) and, shortly after, the two *Post* investigative reporters who pursued the "Watergate scandal."

Graham was born on June 16, 1917, in New York City to Agnes Ernst Meyer and Eugene Meyer, a businessman. Her father purchased the *Washington Post* at a bankruptcy sale in 1933. Graham attended Vassar for two years, and graduated from the University of Chicago in 1938. She worked briefly as a reporter for the *San Francisco News* and later joined the staff of the *Post*, working in the editorial and circulation departments. She married Harvard Law School graduate Philip L. Graham in 1940. Graham clerked for Felix Frankfurter. After World War II, when Meyer was named the first president of the World Bank, he made his son-in-law publisher of the paper. She said in her memoir *Personal History* (1998), which won the Pulitzer Prize for Biography in 1998, that she agreed with her father that "No man should work for his wife." During the 1950s, Meyer acquired two television stations, one in Washington, D.C., the other in Jacksonville, Florida, and purchased the *Washington Times-Herald*. He transferred ownership of the *Post* to Philip and Katharine Graham.

After Meyer's death in 1959, the couple acquired *Newsweek* in 1961. Philip Graham told *Newsweek* correspondents in London that journalism is "a first rough draft" of history, one, he added, "that will never be completed about a world we can never really understand." While her husband was publisher Katharine Graham stayed home to raise their four children, including Donald Graham, who years later succeeded her as publisher and then chairman and chief executive officer. Profoundly shy, her public role was long limited to hosting social events.

The Grahams' marriage was strained and perhaps heading for divorce. After years of suffering manic depression Philip Graham committed suicide in 1963 (conspiracy theorists suggest he was murdered, but there is no evidence to support this assertion). Katharine Graham elected not to sell the paper. Instead she vowed to overcome her unfamiliarity with business and her profound timidity and insecurity, and to take over as publisher. She cultivated a habit of listening to the men important to her, including Ben Bradlee, whom she named managing editor and then executive editor, and Nebraska financier, Warren Buffett, a major *Post* shareholder and director who consistently gave her sound financial advice and support. As her corporate guru, Buffett was particularly helpful when the pressmen went out on a 139-day strike in 1975, a strike that Graham described as her biggest crisis. By all accounts, she survived that crisis and managed to break the power of the pressmen's union. Thus the Washington Post Company grew from a family business into a diversified corporation with newspapers, magazines, and television, cable and educational services holdings worth more than $1 billion.

The impact of the *Post*'s investigative reporting of an attempted burglary of the Democratic National Committee's offices in Washington's Watergate complex is well-known. The trail led directly to the White House, and eventually led to the resignation of President Richard Nixon. Graham was steadfast in her support of the reporters' work, despite a campaign against the *Post*. Nixon tried to prevent license renewal of the company's television stations in Florida, and Attorney General John Mitchell personally singled out Graham for attack.

This is not to say she was always courageous or that she and/or the *Post* lacked critics. In her autobiography, Katharine Graham described how her husband worked overtime during the Bay of Pigs operation to protect the reputations of some Yale friends who had backed the venture. But in a 1979 book called *Katharine the Great*, Deborah Davis went further to allege, among other things, that Bradlee and Philip Graham had collaborated with the Central Intelligence Agency, and that Philip Graham was the main contact in a CIA project to infiltrate U.S. media. Davis also identified—wrongly, it turns out—a Harvard classmate of Bradlee as a CIA agent and as the Watergate reporters' source, Deep Throat. After a number of people criticized the book and Bradlee documented thirty-nine errors, Harcourt Brace Jovanovich disavowed the book and shredded twenty thousand copies. A small company, National Press in Bethesda, Maryland, republished the book, however, in 1987.

After Graham died, the liberal commentator Norman Solomon wrote in a widely republished column that the *Post* had mainly functioned as a "helpmate to the war-makers" in the White House, State Department, and Pentagon. He said it used classic propaganda techniques to accomplish this: evasion, confusion, misdirection, targeted emphasis, disinformation, secrecy, omission of important facts, and selective leaks. This more conservative side of Graham emerged, for example, in a well-publicized speech she gave at CIA headquarters in 1988: "We live in a dirty and dangerous world. There are some things the general public does not need to know and shouldn't. I believe democracy flourishes when the government can take legitimate steps to keep its secrets and when the press can decide whether to print what it knows."

Not a feminist, although she came to respect some feminists and even to invest in *Ms.* magazine, Graham essentially ignored the second-wave women's movement. She was taken by surprise when women writers for the *Post*-owned *Newsweek* filed a federal sex discrimination suit. But certainly Graham became increasingly willing to understand and use her power, and to take on additional powerful positions. She was the first woman to serve as a director of the Associated Press; and the first to be named to the board of the American Newspaper Publishers Association. Before she died, Graham compiled essays about Washington, published posthumously.

Graham never remarried, although she was occasionally linked with some powerful men. One of her closest friends was Meg Greenfield, a *Post* columnist. She died on July 17, 2001, from head injuries sustained when she fell while attending a conference of media executives in Idaho.

Further Reading

Davis, Deborah. *Katharine the Great: Katharine Graham and the Washington Post*. Bethesda, MD: National Press, 1987, originally 1979 by Harcourt Brace Jovanovich.

Felsenthal, Carol. *Power, Privilege, and the Post: The Katharine Graham Story*. New York: Putnam's, 1993.

Gerber, Robin. *Katharine Graham: The Leadership Journey of an American Icon*, New York: Portfolio, 2005.

Graham, Katharine. *Personal History*. New York: Vintage Books, 1998.

——, ed. *Katharine Graham's Washington*. New York: Knopf, 2002.

LINDA STEINER

GREELEY, HORACE

Horace Greeley (February 3, 1811–November 29, 1872) was an American newspaper editor, who published diverse opinions and literary content, and who was a popularly appointed leader of nineteenth-century social and political movements. The New York *Tribune*, the crowning achievement of his career, was one of the most important newspapers in U.S. history. Greeley used the *Tribune* to influence the policies of both the Whig and Republican parties by supporting protective tariffs, the abolition of slavery, and improvements in national infrastructure. In 1872, he ran unsuccessfully for president as a candidate for both the Democratic and Liberal Republican tickets. Although he died a broken man, he was one of the most influential journalists of him time.

Early Life

Greeley was born in the farm town of Amherst, New Hampshire, the third of seven children. His parents were of Scottish-Irish descent. His father, Zaccheus Greeley, owned a small farm and suffered economic hardship during the panic of 1819. Although Horace received irregular schooling until age fifteen, he developed a voracious appetite for books and read constantly. In 1826, he began working as an apprentice at The *Northern Spectator*, a weekly newspaper in rural East Poultney, Vermont. When the paper failed, he moved briefly to Erie County, Pennsylvania, and in August 1831, at the age of twenty, he gathered his possessions and traveled to New York City where, with only $10 in his pocket, he worked as a newspaper compositor and found refuge in the meetings of Workingmen, a group organized to advocate for the rights of laborers.

In January 1833, Greeley and fellow worker Francis V. Story opened a printing office that began issuing the *Morning Post*, among the first of a new group of cheap newspapers dubbed the penny press. Dr. Horatio D. Shepard had supported the venture after developing an idea to restructure the news industry by offering the masses entertaining information at a low price. Most publishers sold penny press newspapers at a high volume with heavy amounts of advertising revenue, but Greeley persuaded Shepard to fix the price of the *Morning Post* at two cents, covering much of the remaining expenses through lottery advertisements, a decision that Greeley's competitors taunted him about for years to come. The *Morning Post* failed in less than three weeks, but Greeley and Story lost only $50 or $60 on their experiment.

In 1834, Greeley founded the *New-Yorker*, a weekly literary and news journal that featured politics, social issues, and the arts and sciences. The publication demonstrated Greeley's editorial skills, but for seven years, he had to supplement his income by writing regularly for The *Daily Whig* and by editing campaign sheets for the Whig Party, which, prior to the founding of the Republican Party, opposed Andrew Jackson's Democrats and represented various liberal causes. By the end of its third year of publication, the *New-Yorker*—a weekly literary paper—reached a circulation of 9,500 copies, but it sustained a total loss of $7,000. Although the paper failed to make a profit, it raised Greeley's public profile and he published it until September 20, 1841.

On July 5, 1836, Greeley married Mary Y. Chency, a Connecticut schoolteacher whom he had met at a New York boardinghouse for Grahamites, a group devoted to healthy dietary practices. Their marriage was an unhappy one due in part to the premature deaths of five of their eight children. One of the Greeley daughters reportedly died because Mary ("Molly") neglected her while obsessing over another child.

As Greeley shunned the sensational content of penny press publications, his acclaim as a political journalist helped form relationships with influential Whigs. He was twenty-eight when he first met Thurlow Weed, editor of the *Albany Evening Journal*. Weed was one of New York's most powerful insiders, and he took an interest in acquiring Greeley's services after reading the *New-Yorker*. He approached Greeley in 1837 about editing a new journal, the *Jeffersonian*, to promote the gubernatorial campaign of his friend William H. Seward. Greeley accepted the offer, for which Weed paid him a $1,000 salary, and began issuing the paper in February 1838. Greeley filled the *Jeffersonian* with political news and Congressional speeches, aiming to persuade readers with reasoned debate, rather than typical stories of crime and vice.

The *Jeffersonian* was short-lived in part because Seward's election made publication no longer necessary, but Greeley's connection with Weed helped him in turn launch the *Log Cabin*, a campaign weekly he first issued May 2, 1840, to promote William Henry Harrison's successful presidential bid. Greeley offered the newspaper at a discount to clubs, a promotional tactic that helped increase readership and would later contribute to the success of the *Tribune*. He was also credited with popularizing the catchy slogan "Tippecanoe and Tyler, Too" and for advancing the "Log-Cabin Candidate" in published songs, speeches, letters, and assorted pro-Harrison propaganda. At its peak, the *Log Cabin* reached an astonishing circulation of eighty thousand copies a week.

The New York *Tribune*

After Harrison's election, Seward and Weed encouraged Greeley to issue a daily paper that would reach Manhattan's working-class audience with a range of content, from local and national news to the advocacy of political ideas that would help advance the Whig agenda. On April 10, 1841, Greeley first issued the New York *Tribune* by merging the staffs of the *Log Cabin* and the *New-Yorker* and expanding the scope of the publications. He edited the *Tribune* for more than thirty years, and during much of that time, the newspaper was the greatest single journalistic influence in the country. It covered the stories of the day, but more importantly, it blended information with interpretation and a sincere, passionate belief in the general benevolence of humanity. As he had done with the *Log Cabin*, Greeley did not write down to his readers; rather, he opened the *Tribune*'s pages to contributions from a range of writers, many of whom identified themselves with a Transcendentalist movement promoting social harmony.

Greeley and the Republicans

Throughout the 1850s, slavery dominated national political debates. Greeley's abolitionist beliefs intensified as the Civil War approached. At first, he had opposed slavery as morally deficient and economically regressive, and he supported movements to prevent its extension. He opposed the Mexican War (1846–1848) and approved of the Wilmot Proviso (1846), which called for the restriction of slavery in territories gained from the war. In 1854, he denounced the Kansas-Nebraska Act, which allowed newly admitted states to decide by the doctrine of popular sovereignty whether they would allow slavery in their borders or ban it, and he sided with the free-soil movement, a politically organized group dedicated to the rights of homesteaders in new territories, which after 1852 evolved into the Republican Party. By 1856, Greeley wrote unequivocally about ending slavery in all states at any cost. In 1860, he attended the Republican national convention in Chicago, and although he initially supported Edward Bates, a candidate from Missouri, he swayed delegates to defeat his former partner William H. Seward, with whom his relations had deteriorated. With Greeley's support, the Republicans nominated Abraham Lincoln.

Greeley expected Lincoln to reward him for the *Tribune*'s help in the presidential election. But when Lincoln decided not to appoint him to a cabinet position, Greeley reacted with scorn and in turn incessantly criticized the administration during the Civil War, costing him previously loyal *Tribune* subscribers. An editorial about the 1860 secession crisis in particular haunted Greeley for the rest of his life because it expressed ambivalence about the possibility of war. Addressing secessionists on Dec. 17, 1860, Greeley wrote that the new administration posed no real threat to their rights: "But if ever 'seven or eight States' send agents to Washington to say 'We want to get out of the Union,' we shall feel constrained by our devotion to Human Liberty to say, Let them go!"

Greeley and the Civil War

By January 1861, it was clear that Greeley's belief in peaceable secession was ill founded. He recanted his earlier capitulations to the South and began publishing a series of famous "stand firm" editorials. The *Tribune* announced "The Nation's War Cry: 'Forward to Richmond!'" on June 26, 1861: "The Rebel Congress must not be allowed to meet there on July 20. By that date the place must be held by the National Army.'" Greeley was away from the newspaper at the time the article was written, and he left managing editor Charles A. Dana in charge. In fact, Fitz-Henry Warren, the *Tribune*'s Washington correspondent, had written the editorials. Whether or not the *Tribune*'s stand had any influence on events on the battlefield, Greeley was left with a heavy conscience after the rout of the Union Army in the first battle of Bull Run.

Greeley pressured Lincoln constantly to emancipate the rebel slaves. His most famous editorial on the subject "The Prayer of Twenty Millions," was published August 20, 1862, urging the president to use the Second Confiscation Act to allow Union commanders to free the slaves of rebel masters. Lincoln had already decided privately to issue the Emancipation Proclamation, but, perhaps fearing that it might push the Border States into the Confederacy, he responded to Greeley that as president his first task was to preserve the Union, whether that meant keeping or abolishing slavery. Lincoln issued the Emancipation Proclamation on September 22, 1862, shortly after Greeley wrote to him, but he did so primarily because the Union Army had just won the battle of Antietam, a strategic victory for the timing of the edict. The *Tribune* celebrated the president's public conversion to the abolitionist cause with extensive coverage of the event, and readers assumed Greeley had worked his influence on national policy.

Greeley reluctantly supported Lincoln for reelection in 1864. His humanitarian hatred of war led him to advocate through the *Tribune* peace negotiations of any sort, often to the embarrassment of the administration. In 1864, Lincoln sent Greeley on what turned out to be a futile mission to Canada to meet with Confederate emissaries. In a final effort to appease his most devoted critic, the president planned to appoint Greeley to the position of U.S. postmaster, but he was assassinated before the order could be filled.

Greeley wrote a two-volume history of the Civil War entitled *The American Conflict* (1864–1866). After the war, he favored universal suffrage and advocated amnesty for all Southerners. He joined the Radical Republicans in Congress in supporting equality for the freedmen and in advocating President Andrew Johnson's impeachment. At the same time, Greeley recommended Jefferson Davis's release from prison, and in 1867, he even signed Davis's bail bond, a magnanimous act that cost the *Tribune* thousands of readers. Poor health slowed Greeley's ability to attend his daily newspaper duties, and by 1868, his eccentricities were increasingly attributed to either an unsatisfied desire for elected office or insanity.

Presidential Candidate

Greeley supported General Ulysses S. Grant during the first years of his presidency but came to resent what he considered Grant's subservience to Republicans who wanted to punish the South. Greeley also grew disaffected with Grant's indifference to civil service reform and the corruption of his administration. In 1871, Greeley began encouraging a dissident movement of Republicans, along with Senators Carl Schurz, Lyman Trumbull, and Charles Sumner, who opposed Grant's military-based Reconstruction efforts and his expansionist foreign policy.

In May 1872, the newly formed Liberal Republican Party nominated Greeley for president. His campaign took an unexpected turn in Baltimore on July 10, 1872, when the weakened and desperate Democratic Party also nominated him as its candidate. The Democrats adopted the Liberal Republican platform, the only time in U.S. history when a major party endorsed the candidate of a third party; however, many Democrats refused to support a man who had spent his life opposing their principles.

Greeley resigned his *Tribune* editorship and delivered speeches across the country to stress the need for national reconciliation, but both campaigns quickly degenerated into a mudslinging melee, epitomized by the anti-Greeley cartoons of Thomas Nast in *Harper's Weekly* and the anti-Grant cartoons of Matt Morgan in *Frank Leslie's Illustrated Newspaper*. While Greeley partisans branded Grant a dictator and a drunk, the president's forces depicted the editor as an opportunist, a traitor, and a fool. The persistent assaults on Greeley's character took such a mental and physical toll on him that toward the end of his campaign, he complained, "I have been assailed so bitterly that I hardly knew whether I was running for the presidency or the penitentiary."

Grant won the 1872 election in a landslide. Greeley won just six of thirty-seven states and 44 percent of the popular vote. Greeley's defeat was accompanied by personal tragedy when in early October his wife, Molly, fell sick and died later that month. Still campaigning, Greeley had returned to his *Tribune* office, but managing editor Whitelaw Reid, who worried about Greeley's deteriorating health and the negative effect it might have on the newspaper's circulation, forced him to relinquish the post. Weeks later, Greeley, suffering a fatal physical and mental breakdown, spoke with Reid a final time and cried: "You son of a bitch, you stole my newspaper." According to Reid, Greeley's final words were: "I know my redeemer liveth."

After the election, Greeley was interned in an asylum in Pleasantville, New York. Exhausted, disheartened, and ill, Greeley died November 29, 1872. At his funeral on December 4, 1872, critics who had made sport out of him and admirers alike mourned the loss of a humanitarian spirit and the nation's best-known editor. A large gathering of common people and local, state, and national leaders, including

President Grant and Chief Justice Salmon Chase, attended the event. Abolitionist Henry Ward Beecher, brother of *Uncle Tom's Cabin* author Harriet Beecher Stowe, eulogized Greeley as "a man who died of a broken heart." The *Tribune* paid tribute to Greeley with special editions and memorial biographies. He was sixty-one years old.

Further Reading

Cross, Coy F. *Go West Young Man! Horace Greeley's Vision for America*. Albuquerque: University of New Mexico Press, 1995.

Fahrney, Ralph Ray. *Horace Greeley and the Tribune in Civil War*. Cedar Rapids, IA: The Torch Press, 1936.

Greeley, Horace. *The American Conflict: A History of the Great Rebellion in the United States of America, 1860–'65*. Chicago: G. & C.W. Sherwood, 1864-66.

Greeley, Horace. *Recollections of a Busy Life*. New York: Arno, 1868.

Hudson, Frederic. *Journalism in the United States, from 1690 to 1872*. New York: Harper & Brothers, 1873.

Isley, Jeter Allen. *Horace Greeley and the Republican Party*. Princeton, NJ: Princeton University Press, 1947.

Lunde, Erik S. *Horace Greeley*. Boston: Twayne Publishers, 1981.

Parton, James. *Life of Horace Greeley*. New York: Mason Brothers, 1855.

Seitz, Don C. *Horace Greeley, Founder of The New York Tribune*. Indianapolis, IN: The Bobbs-Merrill Company, 1926.

Stoddard, Henry Luther. *Horace Greeley, Printer, Editor, Crusader*. New York: G. P. Putnam's Sons, 1946.

Van Deusen, Glyndon G. *Horace Greeley, Nineteenth-Century Crusader*. New York: Hill and Wang, 1953.

GREGORY A. BORCHARD

GULF WAR I

The first war presented live from start to finish on the world's television screens was the Persian Gulf War (1990–1991) between Iraq and a coalition of nations headed by the United States. This conflict was marked by innovative technology both on the battlefield and in newsrooms. Tight control of press access to the combat zone proved a public relations triumph for the U.S. military and suggested that a majority of Americans approved of wartime press restrictions. This article briefly outlines the war and its immediate aftermath, news gathering technologies used to cover the war, press censorship, controversies involving the news media, and an assessment of the news media's performance during the conflict.

Gulf War Outline of Events

In the summer of 1990, Iraq quarreled with its oil-producing neighbors about export quotas and prices. Despite possessing the second largest petroleum reserves in the world (Saudi Arabia has the largest), Iraq was cash poor after its inconclusive border war with Iran (1980–1988) and massive arms buildup. Iraq had the fourth largest national military in the world, with a million troops in uniform and modern weaponry. Iraqi President Saddam Hussein was upset with

Iraq's fellow Arab neighbors, Kuwait, and Saudi Arabia, because their trading practices depressed world oil prices and because they would not forgive Iraq's war debts. Iraq also claimed historical sovereignty over Kuwait.

On August 2, Iraq invaded Kuwait with a large force of troops and tanks, ostensibly to keep oil prices high by controlling Kuwait's oil fields. Six days later, Iraq formally annexed Kuwait. Fearing the Iraqi thrust would continue, Saudi Arabia requested protection from the United States, which rushed airborne troops and warplanes to the Saudi frontier. During the next five months of military stand-off, the American "Desert Shield" force was increased to 440,000 troops, 3,500 tanks, and 2,500 warplanes—half of all U.S. forces worldwide. U.S. President George H.W. Bush fashioned a United Nations coalition that pitted Iraq against most of the world. The multinational ground force represented twenty-eight countries, expanded to thirty-seven by war's end. U.S. forces were joined by 43,000 British troops, 16,000 French troops, and 32,000 troops from the Arab states, for a combined total of more than a half million troops, against an Iraqi complement of a million men and 4,230 tanks. The U.N. Security Council issued a dozen resolutions condemning the invasion and authorizing use of force to expel Iraq. In retaliation, Hussein threatened missile strikes against Israel and reprisals against hostages.

A parallel invading army of journalists and communication technology into Saudi Arabia, Israel, and Iraq accompanied the immense allied war machine. Citing security and personal safety factors, the U.S. military set up mandatory press pools in the combat zone. An initial spate of hard news on the invasion, allied deployment and weaponry, and Iraqi maltreatment of Kuwaitis gave way to feature stories on weaponry, allied soldiers' life in the harsh desert, intercultural encounters, and patriotism at home. News from Washington, D.C., focused on the political coalition and reputed Iraqi atrocities in Kuwait. Unlike previous U.S. wars, news from the enemy perspective also was available through Cable News Network (CNN), which labeled its reports as having been censored by the Iraqis.

After Iraq ignored a U.N. ultimatum, the United States launched the air phase of Operation Desert Storm on January 16, 1991, against military targets in Kuwait and Iraq. Initial strikes disabled Iraq's air defenses. CNN carried live images of the air war in Iraq's capital of Baghdad to millions of television viewers worldwide. An average of two thousand allied sorties per day reported 80 percent accuracy. After eleven thousand sorties, the allies claimed air supremacy. Hussein was not cowed by the devastation, repulsed last minute efforts to end the conflict diplomatically, and promised the "mother of all battles." When an allied ground invasion appeared imminent, Hussein ordered the destruction of Kuwaiti oil fields. Fires burned for a year.

Iraq launched al-Hussein Scud missiles from mobile launchers against Israeli cities and allied positions in Saudi Arabia. Most of the Scuds were shot down by an American antiaircraft weapon system, the Patriot missile. A few Scuds got through and killed some Israeli civilians and twenty-three U.S. soldiers in a barracks. Fearing that Israeli retaliation would drive Arab nations from the coalition, the United States rushed Patriots to Israel's defense.

Five weeks of allied bombing and missile strikes blinded the Iraqis and forced them to dig in. The ground offensive began on February 23, 1991, with a press blackout. The allies' flanking maneuver swept wide into the desert around principal defenses along the Kuwaiti-Saudi frontier and surprised Iraqi units from the side and rear. Many Iraqis deserted or surrendered, but many others were killed. Allied fears that the enemy would follow past practices and use its chemical weapons proved unfounded.

Because the United States and its allies quickly and decisively defeated Iraqi ground forces, the blackout was lifted in less than a day. On the evening of February 25, U.S. warplanes decimated a large convoy of enemy vehicles moving on Highway 6 toward Basra, Iraq. The carnage raised questions in the American press about the morality of pursuing a routed enemy.

On February 27, Iraq announced that it would comply with all twelve U.N. resolutions, and Bush ordered a cease-fire. American commander General Norman Schwarzkopf gave his now famous "mother of all press briefings" in which he reported a nearly vanquished enemy, low U.S. casualties, and misinformation released to the news media to trick the enemy into defending against an amphibious assault. The military thus succeeded in using and controlling the news media to win both the strategic conflict in the field and the public opinion war back home.

Despite the overwhelming victory, the press criticized Bush and the Pentagon for not continuing the war long enough to destroy Hussein and his Republican Guard divisions, which were used during the next month to quell civil unrest in fifteen Iraqi cities by Shiites and Kurds, the Iraqi ethnic groups repressed over the years by the Sunni Arab minority. More than two million refugees fled Hussein's avenging crackdown. The allies eventually responded to appeals for aid by enforcing protective no-fly zones in the north and south, but the Shiites and Kurds felt betrayed by the allies.

News Gathering during the Gulf War

To prepare and file stories, correspondents in the gulf wielded their own technological arsenals, including electronic mail, digital photography, facsimile, satellite imaging, laptop computers, and portable telephones. As transmission speed increased, however, there was less time for reflection and interpretation. Not to be outdone by the media, military briefers at the Pentagon's Joint Information Bureau (JIB) in Dhahran, Saudi Arabia, dazzled television viewers with their own advanced transmission system, which provided perhaps the definitive images of the war: video pictures beamed continuously by intelligent ordnance (so-called "smart" bombs and missiles) as they raced toward their targets.

During and after the war, television generally was regarded as the preeminent medium for immediate and compelling coverage of news events. Transmitted by a portable satellite uplink, CNN's Bernard Shaw, John Holliman, and Peter Arnett narrated from Baghdad's Rasheed Hotel as bombs from F-117A Stealth aircraft and Tomahawk cruise missiles exploded in the distance. Their dramatic reportage made CNN the "network feed" of choice and put the ten-year-old cable news service on an equal footing with the American networks, NBC, ABC, and CBS, which relied on a common feed of information and pictures from the press pools. Early continuous, commercial-free, "real-time" coverage by all U.S. television networks gave way to special reports and segments of regular news programs. Military and foreign affairs experts were employed as on-air consultants.

Newspapers and news magazines had to redefine themselves to avoid being preempted by "real-time" broadcasts. While producing interpretive and background reports, the writers and editors had to keep in mind what readers already knew from watching television. Circulation gains for all print media covering the war showed they kept the news fresh. However, print's long-term viability for breaking news was questioned. Schwarzkopf, Bush, and Hussein admitted they kept up to date by watching CNN.

Gulf War Censorship

The highly effective press censorship scheme used during the Gulf conflict was borne of the recommendations of a 1984 government commission on press war coverage, named for retired Army Major General Winant Sidle, a former press officer during the Vietnam War. Since Vietnam, new wireless transmission technologies had made field censorship of news stories impractical. To control the flow of news, the government would have to keep journalists out of the theater of operations. The Sidle Commission's eight recommendations featured temporary imposition of media pooling in combat zones, security screening of all news copy and pictures, and voluntary media compliance with security guidelines. News organizations were permitted to file formal protests to the Pentagon's Joint Information Bureau over specific exclusions, but adjudication of these protests caused delays that amounted to de facto censorship. The Sidle procedures were tried out briefly and unsatisfactorily for the press during the U.S. military's invasion of Panama in 1989. Defense Secretary Richard Cheney and his assistant for public affairs, Louis A. Williams, promised to do better the next time.

The JIB chose 192 reporters and photographers, assigned to twenty-four official press pools, to represent all 1,400 news personnel that came to cover the Gulf War. Williams intended to open the war zone later, but he was overruled because the flood of Western journalists made the Saudis nervous. Military escorts accompanied the pool reporters; though the escorts rarely interfered, their presence probably inhibited soldiers' candidness. There was grumbling and infighting in the pools, but most journalists cooperated rather than lose their places in the pools. The military censors controlled unfavorable reportage by delaying

its release until its news value was lost. Some journalists later complained that the pool system unfairly favored the national media.

There were challenges to the pool system in U.S. federal court. In *The Nation Magazine v. U.S. Department of Defense* (1991), attorneys for *The Nation* maintained that the pool system, military escorts and the security review violated the First and Fifth Amendment rights of the press. The judge dismissed the case in April, 1991. Other challenges by Agence France-Presse, and the American Civil Liberties Union failed for lack of commitment by the large news organizations, especially the networks and national newspapers. Censorship never became a public issue. Opinion polls after the war showed that Americans were satisfied with the news coverage they got.

Controversies during the Gulf War

Interservice rivalries were debated in the press during the five and a half months of Desert Shield stalemate. On September 16, 1990, a *Washington Post* headline, "U.S. to Rely on Air Strikes if War Erupts," oversold air power, according to General Colin Powell, Chairman of the Joint Chiefs of Staff. He assured President Bush of the necessity of land invasion. The source of the *Post* story, General Michael Dugan, lost his job. Air power alone would be reconsidered by the next U.S. President, Bill Clinton, to cope with humanitarian crises in the former Yugoslavia.

The American public had unprecedented access to the enemy's perspective during Desert Storm. CNN's intermittent, live video broadcasts from Baghdad were transmitted at first via telephone landlines and later by a portable satellite telephone. Arnett exposed intelligence failures that led to U.S. air strikes against an infant formula factory and a bunker occupied by civilians. A debate raged for months after the war whether Arnett's reports were news or propaganda because they had been censored by the Iraqis. Bush and others criticized Arnett and CNN. Senator Alan Simpson of Wyoming accused Arnett, who won a Pulitzer Prize in 1966 for his war correspondence in Vietnam, of being one of the journalists who lost the Vietnam War for the United States. Arnett countered that reports from the allied side were censored, too. Investigations after the war verified Arnett's claims.

As during the Vietnam War, the news media struggled to balance the war and peace stories, with inevitable criticism from both sides. There were demonstrations worldwide for peaceful resolution to the Persian Gulf crisis. Unlike Vietnam, the demonstrators did not try to justify Saddam Hussein's actions and appeared to support passivism in general rather than the enemy in particular. *A Line in the Sand*, an acclaimed ABC news special broadcast during Operation Desert Shield, explained that the U.S. government had fostered the Hussein regime in Iraq and had missed obvious warning signs of its invasion of Kuwait. The press also conveyed concerns that economic sanctions and the bombing campaign hurt Iraqi civilians more than their rulers. On the whole, however, the news media were swept up in the patriotic fervor and helped the government to sell the war to the U.S. public. The war was good business: print circulations, broadcast audiences, and corporate profits ballooned, despite advertising suspensions during critical periods.

Some reporters complained about the pool system restrictions and went out on their own, including crews headed by CBS' Bob McKeown and ABC's Forrest Sawyer. Most pool jumpers were detained by the allies, but CBS reporter Bob Simon and his crew got lost and were captured by Iraqi troops. Released unharmed by the Iraqis after the cease-fire, Simon's harrowing personal story elicited little sympathy from the public, which seem to view Simon as a rule breaker instead of an enterprising journalist. The episode laid the groundwork for Victoria Clark, a senior spokesperson for Secretary of Defense Donald Rumsfeld in the administration of President George W. Bush, to propose "embedding" journalists in military units in the Iraq War of 2003.

News Media Performance during the Gulf War

According to several national polls during and after the war, the American public gave the news media high marks for their war coverage and felt greater respect for journalism as an institution than before the war. Upstart CNN dominated as the preferred news source. Among the broadcast television networks, ABC got most favorable rating. Statistics show the Gulf War story overwhelmed other news of the period by a wide margin, particularly on television. Most people approved of censorship by the military and liked CNN's reports from Baghdad, even though they were censored by the Iraqi military. Few people objected to the news media's obvious jingoism.

Live television coverage of the Gulf War put the war correspondents in an ironic dilemma. Instantaneous, compelling images brought the audience close to events, but removed journalistic judgment from the news and reduced time for analysis and presentation of context. The press pools isolated the correspondents from the war, which weakened their ability to hold the government and military accountable.

Despite dress rehearsals of the Pentagon's press restrictions during U.S. invasions of Grenada (1983) and Panama (1989), the U.S. news media were unprepared to deal with censorship during the Gulf War. Most journalists in Saudi Arabia were dissatisfied with the press pools, but they accepted the necessity to manage their overwhelming numbers in the war zone. Their reluctant consent to the military's rules during the Persian Gulf War weakened their ability to resist government censorship during future conflicts. By failing to join legal challenges, the elite press and the television networks seemed to resign themselves to the American public's apparent tolerance for restricted flow of information during wartime.

Further Reading

ABC News. *A Line in the Sand: An ABC News Special on the Persian Gulf Crisis Hosted by Peter Jennings* (video recording). Oak Forest, IL: MPI Home Video, 1990.

Barnett, Brooke. *The Iraq Wars and the War on Terror.* Westport, CT: Greenwood Press, 2005.

CBS News. *Desert Triumph: The Complete Story of the Persian Gulf War* (video recording). New York: CBS Fox Video, 1991.

Clark, Ramsey. *The Fire This Time: U.S. War Crimes in the Gulf.* New York: Thunder's Mouth Press, 1992.

Cumings, Bruce. *War and Television.* London: Verso, 1992.

Freedom Forum. *The Media at War: The Press and the Persian Gulf Conflict.* New York: Gannett Foundation, 1991.

Greenberg, Bradley S., and Galer Gantz, eds. *Desert Storm and the Mass Media.* Cresskill, NJ: Hampton Press, 1993.

Kennedy, William V. *The Military and the Media: Why the Press Cannot Be Trusted to Cover a War.* Westport, CT: Praeger, 1993.

McCain, Thomas A., and Leonard Shyles, eds. *The 1,000 Hour War: Communications in the Gulf.* Westport, CT: Greenwood Press, 1994.

Nyang, Sulayman S. *A Line in the Sand: Saudi Arabia's Role in the Gulf War.* P.T. Books, 1995.

Yetiv, Steven A. *The Persian Gulf Crisis.* Westport, CT: Greenwood Press, 1997.

RUSSELL J. COOK

HAGERTY, JAMES C.

The son of James A. Hagerty, for many years chief political correspondent for the *New York Times*, James C. Hagerty (May 9, 1909–April 11, 1981), the future reporter and presidential secretary (1953–1961) to President Dwight D. Eisenhower, grew up in New York City in the Bronx. He attended Blair Academy in New Jersey, and upon graduation in 1928 began work with the New York Stock Exchange. The market crash and subsequent Depression sent him back to school and he graduated from Columbia University in 1934. Thereafter he worked for the *Times*, as a member of the city staff and then as legislative correspondent and deputy bureau chief in Albany, resigning in 1943 to become press secretary to Governor Thomas E. Dewey. He handled press relations for Dewey's campaigns for the presidency, in 1944 and 1948. When General Eisenhower ran for the presidency in 1952 it was with Hagerty as spokesman and press adviser, which led in January 1953 to appointment as press secretary to the president.

During the Eisenhower terms, Hagerty was nationally prominent and often quoted concerning the manifold activities of his chief. During Eisenhower's illnesses—a heart attack in 1955, ileitis in 1956, a stroke in 1957—the press secretary handled relations with the media, managing with aplomb the daily statements of medical details. During the president's international travels, before the heart attack but especially in Eisenhower's last years in office, Hagerty supervised the releases.

As press secretary the erstwhile reporter for the nation's most prominent newspaper ably performed his White House duties, for he understood the ins and outs of news gathering from his own experience. Because of his chief's two full terms, Hagerty found himself with much to do, which he accomplished in the usual reportorial way. "In at 8:15..." was the opening pronouncement of entries in his diary that he kept, unfortunately for journalism history, only for the years 1954 and 1955; inexplicably he ceased his entries early in 1956, presumably because daily work made diary keeping impossible.

Hagerty's handling of the office of press secretary differed from his predecessors for three reasons. The first was his chief's introduction of television at press conferences in 1955, which Hagerty joyously welcomed. He knew that Eisenhower, who had met hordes of reporters over the years, would do well. Television by the mid-1950s had come of age

as a medium. And the next year, 1956, was an election year; the time for introduction of televised press conferences was right. In addition to this marked innovation in the White House, Hagerty was important for his closeness to the president, who tried out ideas on him and sought advice about political courses. Hagerty also undertook special political tasks, such as serving as Eisenhower's go-between with the Senate in the difficult business in 1954 of obtaining censure of Senator Joseph R. McCarthy of Wisconsin. When Eisenhower left the presidency Hagerty returned to New York as vice president of the Columbia Broadcasting Companies. He retired in 1971 after suffering a stroke, and spent his last years in Bronxville, New York, with his wife, the former Marjorie Lucas.

Further Reading

Ferrell, Robert H. *The Diary of James C. Hagerty: Eisenhower in Mid-Course, 1954–1955*. Bloomington: Indiana University Press, 1983.
Los Angeles Times, April 12, 1981, A5.
The New York Times, April 12, 1981, 35; and April 13, 1981, D10.

ROBERT H. FERRELL

HALBERSTAM, DAVID

David Halberstam (April 10, 1934–) was a *New York Times* correspondent during the 1960s who was best known for his reporting on the Vietnam War. Since the 1970s, he authored sixteen books, most of them on history and sports. Halberstam's most recognized books include *The Best and Brightest* (1972), about U.S. leaders of the Vietnam War; *The Powers that Be* (1979), about the rise of modern journalism, specifically CBS, the *Los Angeles Times*, TIME Inc., and the *Washington Post*; and *The Reckoning* (1986), comparing U.S. and Japanese automakers Ford and Nissan. Those books were essentially his trilogy on twentieth-century American power.

Halberstam was born in New York City to Blanche Levy Halberstam, a schoolteacher, and Charles A. Halberstam, an Army surgeon. The family moved to Texas, Minnesota, Connecticut, then to Yonkers, New York, where Halberstam graduated high school in 1951. He enrolled at Harvard University and after earning a Bachelors degree, he pursued daily newspaper work in the South, then the battleground of the civil rights movement. Halberstam worked ten months for a small newspaper in Mississippi. In 1956, he joined the staff of the *Nashville Tennessean*.

In 1960, Halberstam joined the *New York Times* Washington bureau. Soon he was dispatched overseas, first to the Congo in 1961, then in September 1962 to Vietnam, where U.S. military advisers assisted South Vietnamese soldiers fighting Communist-backed forces from the north. Halberstam reported on what he witnessed in the field. His grim reports contradicted optimistic reports from the South Vietnam capital Saigon.

President John F. Kennedy criticized Halberstam's reporting and urged editors of the *New York Times* to reassign the correspondent to another post. The *Times* instead backed Halberstam. Furthermore, he was told to cancel a scheduled vacation in order to stay in Asia so as not appear that the *Times* capitulated to Kennedy. Halberstam returned to the United States at the end of 1963. In 1964, he shared a Pulitzer Prize for International Reporting. He returned overseas to report from Poland, and later Paris, then he returned home and resigned from the *Times* in 1967. Halberstam joined the staff of *Harper's* magazine and stayed until 1971.

In 1972 he published *The Best and Brightest*. Halberstam described the United States entanglement in Vietnam and criticized leaders of the Kennedy and Lyndon B. Johnson administrations for this involvement. For this and future books the author's writing style was supported by exhaustive research: hundreds of interviewers with the main and secondary players were synthesized into a novel-like narrative. Sources were friendly and hostile. Fans praised Halberstam's storytelling and richly detailed narrative style. Critics however called his reporting and writing selective and judgmental.

Most of Halberstam's books were bestsellers. Five of them were sports-oriented, including *The Breaks of the Game* (1981); *The Amateurs: The Story of Four Young Men and their Quest for an Olympic Gold Medal*, and *October 1964* (1994). Books that chronicled social history included *The Fifties* (1993) and *The Children* (1998). In 2001, Halberstam wrote *War in a Time of Peace: Bush, Clinton, and the Generals*. *Firehouse* (2002) told the stories of a dozen New York City firefighters who tried to save lives during the September 11, 2001, terrorist attacks.

Halberstam's 1965 marriage to actress Elzbieta Czyzewska ended in 1977. Halberstam married Jean Sandness Butler in 1979 and they had a daughter, Julia.

Further Reading

Halberstam, David. *The Best and the Brightest*. New York: Random House, 1972.
——, *October, 1964*. New York: Villard Book, 1994.
——, *The Powers That Be*. New York: Knopf, 1979.
——, *The Reckoning*. New York: Morrow, 1986.
——, *War in a Time of Peace: Bush, Clinton and the Generals*. New York: Scribner's, 2001.

WAYNE DAWKINS

HAPGOOD, HUTCHINS

When Hutchins Hapgood (May 21, 1869–November 19, 1944) joined the staff of the New York *Commercial-Advertiser* in 1897, he was twenty-eight-years-old and had spent most of his time to that point studying philosophy and literature at Harvard and in Germany, and a very brief stint teaching English at Harvard. But he was eager to observe urban life and produce "human documents," as he put it, about the lives of the immigrant and working class and he believed that the *Commercial Advertiser* under Lincoln Steffens would allow him to do just that. Over the next twenty-five years or so he would work primarily as an editorial writer and columnist for three other New York City newspapers, as a drama critic for a Chicago newspaper, write seven books, and develop a theory of nonfiction writing that today is commonly called literary journalism.

Hapgood was born in Chicago on May 21, 1869, and grew up in Alton, Illinois, one of three brothers, all of whom, like their father, had graduated from Harvard. Although the elder Hapgood was an affluent and highly successful businessman and manufacturer, he instilled in his sons that they had a moral responsibility to serve a greater good. Thus, all the three brothers were filled with the reformist spirit of the Progressive Era and they championed many of the ideas of the time but did so in different ways. Hutchins's oldest brother, Norman, for instance, was at the center of the muckraking movement when he was an editor at *Colliers* and at *Harper's Weekly*, while youngest brother William experimented with employee ownership at his Indianapolis canning company.

Norman Hapgood was working as a drama critic at the *Commercial Advertiser* when Hutchins joined the staff, but it was Abraham Cahan, a writer, editor, and a founder of the *Jewish Daily Forward*, who introduced Hutchins to New York City's East Side Jewish community. Hapgood immersed himself in the East Side Jewish subculture, even learning Yiddish, and in his articles he regularly brought readers into the streets, cafes, shops and homes of Russian Jewish immigrants, punching holes in immigrant stereotypes as he carried out a type of ethnographic, documentary reporting and writing. Much of this work was collected and published in 1902 as *The Spirit of the Ghetto: Studies of the Jewish Quarter in New York*, with a second printing in 1909. Two different publishers brought out editions of the book in 1965 and 1967.

Hapgood also wrote about Bowery low-life, first at the *Commercial-Advertiser* and then at the *Morning Telegraph*. His mostly romanticized depictions of bums, thieves, and street people were collected and published under the title *Types from City Streets* (1910). Three other books, *The Autobiography of a Thief* (1903), *The Spirit of Labor* (1907), and *An Anarchist Woman* (1909) are all interesting but not totally successful attempts by Hapgood to use the in-depth interview and immersion as tools to produce fully developed and realistic portraits or "autobiography of an unconventional kind," as he described his approach in an article for a 1905 article for *Bookman*, "A New Form of Literature."

While Hapgood's ideas about a "new form of literature" resonate today, they were perhaps too visionary for his day and they had little influence on his contemporaries. When he died in 1944, years after he had stopped working as a journalist, in addition to *The Spirit of the Ghetto*, he was probably best remembered for his advocacy of "free love," for co-founding the Provincetown Players, and for his association with a lively group of writers, artists, radicals, and freethinkers who prominently appear in his autobiography, *A Victorian in the Modern World*.

Further Reading

Connery, Thomas B., "Hutchins Hapgood and the Search for a 'New Form of Literature'." *Journalism History* 13, no. 1, (Spring, 1986): 2–9.

Connery, Thomas B. "Hutchins Hapgood." In *A Sourcebook of American Literary Journalism*, edited by Thomas B. Connery, 121–129, Westport, CT: Greenwood, 1992.

Hapgood, Hutchins. *The Spirit of the Ghetto: Studies in the Jewish Quarter in New York*. Cambridge, MA: Belknap Press, 1967.

Hapgood, Hutchins. *A Victorian in the Modern World*. New York: Harcourt, Brace, 1939.

Maraccio, Michael D. *The Hapgoods*. Charlottesville: University Press of Virginia, 1977.

THOMAS B. CONNERY

HEARST, WILLIAM RANDOLPH

William Randolph Hearst (April 29, 1863–August 14, 1951) was one of America's wealthiest and most powerful newspaper publishers who used his empire to crusade mostly for progressive causes, a consummate politician who held White House aspirations, an extravagant spender who built one of the United States' most fabled homes, and the inspiration for a film classic.

Born on April 29, 1863, Hearst was the only son from the marriage of George Hearst, a self-made California multimillionaire and later U.S. Senator, and Phoebe Apperson, a Missouri schoolteacher. Hearst's childhood was not solely that of privilege. As his father's fortune rose and sunk, he was alternately the child from a mansion on the hill or the boy confined to public school because his father had gone broke. However, during his late teenage years, Hearst's father's fortune became vast and stable on the footings of a successful mining venture and Hearst joined the sons of privilege at St. Paul's School in Concord, New Hampshire, and then Harvard University.

While at Harvard, Hearst became interested in journalism, particularly after his father acquired the *San Francisco Examiner*, a failing Democratic paper. With the encouragement of his father, Hearst became the editor-in-waiting and undertook a careful study of New York newspapers, in particular Joseph Pulitzer's innovative and vastly successful *World*. Of less interest to Hearst were his academic studies

and so, at Harvard's choice, he left the university without completing his degree and returned to San Francisco to assume the helm of the newspaper in the spring of 1887. He immediately imported all of Pulitzer's techniques and gave his paper a national scope by arranging for the exclusive use of *New York Herald* articles via cable. Hearst's efforts paid off in substantial circulation increases but at a tremendous financial cost to the family's fortune. The paper probably did not become financially remunerative for many years, but it gave the young Hearst a reputation of journalistic success that was noted in New York's Park Row.

As Pulitzer had done when leaving St. Louis for New York, Hearst left San Francisco in 1895 and dove into New York journalism by buying a failing newspaper, the *New York Journal*. In one of those odd twists of history, the paper had once been a financially successful enterprise launched by Albert Pulitzer, brother of Joseph. Since its sale to other investors, however, it had fallen on hard times. In a few short months, the thirty-two-year old Hearst enlisted flamboyant advertising techniques, lured away from Pulitzer many of his best editors with promises of high salaries, paid unheard of fees to famous writers, including Richard Harding Davis and Stephen Crane, and dropped the price of the paper to a penny. The circulation shot up from 20,000 to 150,000 and, although still a long way from the *World*'s circulation, the *Journal* had all the makings of overtaking it. Pulitzer was befuddled by this young imitator who now threatened his franchise in exactly the same manner Pulitzer had when first encountering the stodgy world of New York newspapers a dozen years earlier. Having grown complacent at the reigns of the money-churning *World*, Pulitzer became locked in a battle for survival against an adversary who seemed to have unrestricted access to his family's fortune though his widowed mother.

The competition between the two reached its apex in the late 1890s during one of the most notorious epochs of American journalism. The competition grew so frenetic that each paper abandoned restraint and published stories so extreme, so "newsworthy," and so outrageous that they were not to be believed. Often they were not. The excesses gave birth to the term "Yellow Journalism" drawn from popular color comics featuring Yellow Kids published by the two newspapers.

An insurrection against Spanish rule in Cuba became the proxy for the journalism war between the *World* and the *Journal*. Each paper outdid each other in stunts and inflammatory coverage fanning the call for war to assist the Cubans. When the *U.S.S. Maine* mysteriously blew up in Havana Harbor on February 15, 1898, killing more than 250 American sailors, Hearst's *Journal* urged the nation to avenge the murder of the Americans, transported members of Congress to Cuba on Hearst's private yacht, and spared no expense to publish an additional six to eight pages a day of articles, interviews, maps, illustrations, and cartoons on the Cuban crisis.

By the time war was declared by the United States in late April, the competition between the *Journal* and the *World* had grown into a twenty-four-hour a day affair. This gave rise to the creation of the "Lobster Trick," the nickname for a shift of reporters and editors who came to work at 1:00 a.m. to start producing the almost hourly editions of the evening newspapers. Pulitzer could not out "Yellow" Hearst nor match his spending. The *Journal* and its evening edition reached a daily circulation of a million copies and Hearst became a national figure.

His actual power in instigating the war has been exaggerated and the most famous tale of Hearst's telegram to Frederic Remington telegram—"You furnish the pictures, and I'll furnish the war"—has likely been proven apocryphal. Nonetheless, Hearst used his fame and his newspaper to begin a career in politics that lead first to his election to the House of Representatives in 1902 and a string of vain efforts at higher office that included New York City Mayor, New York governor, and even the Democratic presidential nomination. Though he would not attain other political office than his two terms in the House, Hearst remained an influential force in politics. Candidates for all sorts of offices kowtowed to the publisher.

Hearst's political future and financial life were threatened by his virulent opposition to the U.S. entry into World War I. The Wilson administration tried to gather information to prove disloyalty or even treason. The government investigative heat caused editors and reporters to quit and his public vilification—the *New York Times*, for instance, referred to him as the "spokesman for the Kaiser"—wiped out profits and endangered both his newspaper empire and his public life.

In the 1920s, with the war and the controversy behind him, the growth of the Hearst media empire was on the march again and he was undoubtedly the most famous newspaper publisher in the United States and certainly the most powerful. He owned twenty newspapers in thirteen cities. One out of four families read a Hearst newspaper and countless others read Hearst-produced features and columns syndicated to local papers. Though he teetered near financial collapse from his overextension, a bond issue, heavily promoted by his newspapers, and his eventual inheritance of the family fortune, following his mother's death, staved off disaster. In time Hearst vast newspaper empire, his movie studio, and his very successful magazine division that included *Good Housekeeping* and *Cosmopolitan* became immensely profitable.

Hearst lived on a scale whose lavishness was news making. He owned a castle in Wales and built his own on a 240,000-acre ranch at San Simeon, California. With more than 165 rooms, the Hearst Castle was filled with great art treasures and crowded with movie stars, writers, and other glitterati. (It is today a state park.) Hearst became involved in an affair with film actress Marion Davies, popular in great measure because she was a creation of Hearst newspapers, magazines, and movies. As the two became increasingly open about their relationship, Hearst's wife Millicent Veronica Willson, a former chorus girl, retreated to New York and built an independent life of philanthropy.

In 1932, Hearst played a key role in securing Franklin Roosevelt's 1932 presidential nomination after initially opposing him. Following the election, Hearst became an opponent of both FDR and the New Deal, renouncing decades of strong support for Progressive causes. The 1930s also brought a new financial crisis to Hearst's publishing empire. This time the government prohibited another round of bond sales to readers. A court ordered reorganization triggered the sale of many newspapers, closed his Hollywood studios, and even forced the humiliating sale of many of his treasured antiques and art works.

As World War II approached, the economy's recovery from the Depression helped restore financial health to the company. Hearst, however, advised against entering the war but used his papers to support the war effort after the Japanese attack on Pearl Harbor in December, 1941. After the war, Hearst's last editorial campaign was as a strong anti-Communist.

Ironically, Hearst, who was one the first newspaper publishers to recognize the importance of motion pictures, was immortalized in mythical fashion in a now-classic film by Orson Welles. *Citizen Kane*, which is biographical in spirit but not fact, so shaped the public's perception of the publishing magnate that one of Hearst's biographers called his book *Citizen Hearst*. Hearst tried vainly to stop the release of the film.

Hearst died on August 14, 1951, in Beverly Hills, California, leaving in trust for his family the Hearst Corporation whose restored financial health made it one of the five largest privately held companies at the end of the twentieth century.

Further Reading

"Career of Hearst Marked by Power, Increased Wealth, Crusading and Controversy," *New York Times*, Aug. 15, 1951, 20.

Nasaw, David. *The Chief: The Life of William Randolph Hearst*. Boston: Houghton Mifflin, 2000.

Proctor, Ben. *William Randolph Hearst: The Early Years*. New York: Oxford University Press, 1998.

Robinson, Judith. *The Hearsts* New York: Avon, 1992.

JAMES MCGRATH MORRIS

HEATTER, GABRIEL

Gabriel Heatter (September 17, 1890–March 30, 1972) employed a booming voice to bring his uniquely optimistic view of the day's news to the Mutual Broadcasting System in the mid-twentieth century. Greeting listeners with the declaration, "There's good news tonight!" he was one of the most popular of the radio commentators.

Others were known for their strident views or unruffled delivery. Heatter often wept on the air when relating a story, and his political leanings were difficult to decipher from his fifteen-minute broadcasts. He offered earnest reactions rather than analysis, and his simplistic views often mirrored those of the lower- to middle-class Americans who were at the core of his daily audience of twelve million to fourteen million listeners.

Heatter, born in New York City, came to broadcasting in middle age. His most valuable trait was his voice, deep and rich even in childhood. In his teens he began working for newspapers, and his print career included jobs with the weekly *New York Record* and the daily *Brooklyn Times* and *New York Journal*. He had written for trade publications and had published magazine opinion pieces when, at age forty-two, he was invited to argue against socialism on radio station WMCA. The management, impressed by his delivery, invited Heatter to broadcast essays regularly. Within six months he was working at New York's WOR and soon was a regular commentator for Mutual.

His coverage of the Lindbergh kidnapping trial in 1935 and the execution of convicted kidnapper Bruno Hauptmann the following year gained national attention. When the execution was delayed by nearly an hour, Heatter filled the time without a script, a feat of ad-libbing that critics hailed and listeners rewarded with a large and loyal following. At his peak he was heard on nearly two hundred stations across the country and earned $400,000 a year.

After he became a national star, Heatter worked from a studio in his home on New York's Long Island. He broadcast commentaries nearly every day for the next twenty-five years. His outlook and delivery—once described as a cross between a bassoon and a Chinese gong—distinguished him on the air. Aside from the major news, he presented stories that supported his optimistic view of life. He favored emotional drama, including tales of heroism and faith.

During World War II, Heatter began opening his broadcast with a good-news story—and the cheery salutation—as a way to keep up morale. Enough bad news followed that he was nicknamed "the voice of doom." Still, Heatter offered optimistic predictions based on his feelings rather than facts and colored his broadcasts with his own emotions. Critics considered his style far too dramatic and personal, but millions tuned in to hear his reassuring voice.

Heatter hosted two uplifting human-interest shows, *We, the People* in the late 1930s and *A Brighter Tomorrow* after the war. He moved to Miami Beach in 1951 and left Mutual in 1961, although he continued to broadcast locally before retiring in 1965.

Further Reading

Fang, Irving E. *Those Radio Commentators*. Ames: Iowa State University Press, 1977.

"Gabriel Heatter, 81, War Newscaster, Dies." *Los Angeles Times*, March 31, 1972.

"Gabriel Heatter, Radio Newsman, Dies." *New York Times*, March 31, 1972.

Heatter, Gabriel. *There's Good News Tonight*. Garden City, NY: Doubleday, 1961.

DOUGLASS K. DANIEL

HEMINGWAY, ERNEST

Ernest Hemingway (July 21, 1899–July 2, 1961) won the Nobel Prize for Literature in 1954 and is remembered for being a fiction writer. But Hemingway was also a journalist. He covered high school sports for his school newspaper, and worked as a reporter for the *Kansas City Star*

for seven months in 1917–1918 before he went to Italy as an ambulance driver for the Red Cross. Near the end of his life he was writing "The Dangerous Summer," a long article on bullfighting for *Life* magazine. In between his work appeared in the *Toronto Daily Star* and *Star Weekly, Esquire, Vogue, Fortune, PM, Collier's, Holiday, Ken, New Republic, True, Life,* and *Look*, and had filed dispatches for the North American Newspaper Alliance. He covered the Greco-Turkish War, the Spanish Civil War, and the Second World War, submitting by-lined dispatches from Madrid to Rangoon.

Hemingway was born July 21, 1899, in Oak Park, Illinois, the son of a physician. His early life was filled with outdoor adventures in the vicinity of his family's cottage in the Michigan woods. During the last year of World War I, he was injured on the Italian front. After a brief period of work in Chicago and Toronto, he lived in Paris and began writing fiction and poetry while serving as the European correspondent for the *Toronto Daily Star*. His early stories were often fictionalized accounts of his newspaper dispatches. His literary reputation was established with *The Sun Also Rises* (1926) and *A Farewell to Arms* (1929), *For Whom the Bell Tolls* (1940), *The Old Man and the Sea* (1952), and other novels and short stories.

Hemingway continued writing journalism and fiction in such places as Key West, Florida, Havana, Cuba, and Ketchum, Idaho. He continued to blend reporting and fiction in such works as *Death in the Afternoon* (1932) and *Green Hills of Africa* (1935). Hemingway's newspaper and magazine journalism has been collected in *Hemingway: The Wild Years* (1962) and *By-Line: Ernest Hemingway, Selected Articles and Dispatches of Four Decades* (1967).

His early experience writing for the *Kansas City Star* taught him discipline and influenced his mature writing style. Although he was a competent reporter when assigned to the police and hospital beats, he was better suited to narrative journalism and feature writing, which enabled him to write more subjectively. His European dispatches were often personal accounts and observations focusing on the process of reporting. His growing literary fame shaped his reportorial persona, and in his later work he typically was at the center of the story. Always Hemingway seemed to push the boundaries between fact and fiction, offering personal impressions in his journalism and then recreating characters and events in his fiction.

Hemingway often made light of his journalism and considered it inferior to fiction. He deemed it unfair to compare work written against a deadline with his carefully-crafted literary prose. And yet Hemingway is often seen as an icon of journalistic dash, mettle and romance, famous not only for his economical sentences but also for his ability to witness and report extraordinary events from bullfights to battles.

Further Reading

Ashdown, Paul. "Ernest Hemingway." In *A Sourcebook of American Literary Journalism*, edited by Thomas B. Connery, Westport, CT: Greenwood, 1992.

Baker, Carlos. *Ernest Hemingway: A Life Story.* New York: Charles Scribner's Sons, 1969.

Bruccoli, Matthew J. *Ernest Hemingway, Cub Reporter.* Pittsburgh: University of Pittsburgh, 1970.

Fenton, Charles A. *The Apprenticeship of Ernest Hemingway.* New York: Viking, 1954.

Kobler, J.F. *Ernest Hemingway, Journalist and Artist.* Ann Arbor: UMI Research Press, 1985.

Stephens, Robert O. *Hemingway's Nonfiction: The Public Voice.* Chapel Hill: University of North Carolina, 1968.

White, William, ed. *By-Line: Ernest Hemingway, Selected Articles and Dispatches of Four Decades.* New York: Charles Scribner's Sons, 1967.

Zimmerman, Gene Z., ed. *Hemingway: The Wild Years.* New York: Dell, 1962.

PAUL ASHDOWN

HIGGINS, MARGUERITE

Marguerite Higgins (September 3, 1920—January 3, 1966), a twentieth-century combat correspondent whose heroic professionalism under fire opened the profession to other women, covered World War II, the Korean War, and the Vietnam War. She was the first woman to win a Pulitzer Prize for International Reporting when she was among a team of *New York Herald-Tribune* reporters to be honored for their war coverage in 1951.

Higgins was born on September 3, 1920, in Hong Kong. Her father, Lawrence Daniel Higgins, who had been an American pilot in World War I, was working there for a steamship company. Her mother, Marguerite de Godard, was French. The family moved to Oakland, California, when Higgins was three. Higgins attended the University of California, Berkeley, on scholarship and there got her start in journalism at the college newspaper, the *Daily Californian*. She was the senior editor of that paper when she graduated from the university with honors in 1941.

After graduation, she moved to New York to become a news reporter. When she failed to find work, she talked her way into Columbia University's master's degree program in journalism even though all the allotted slots for women were taken for the class of 1942. She joined classmates Flora Lewis (who later became a noted *New York Times* foreign correspondent and columnist) and Elie Abel (who ultimately became dean of the Columbia University Journalism program after a broadcasting career). Higgins had been earlier turned down for a position at the *New York Herald-Tribune*, but as a student she was hired to work as a campus correspondent for the newspaper. After she graduated from Columbia, she began work for the news staff at the *Herald-Tribune*. Higgins married a philosophy professor from Harvard, Stanley Moore, but the marriage ended in divorce.

With the United States at war and manpower scarce, Higgins transferred in 1944 to the *Herald Tribune's* London bureau. From there, she moved to Paris. She spent the rest of the decade in Europe covering World War II and its aftermath. She made a name for herself in the final days of the war in Europe when she arrived at the Dachau concentration camp in southern Germany before the Allied troops. The German SS soldiers who ran the prison surrendered to Higgins and her colleague. They collected German weapons and then Higgins announced to some thirty thousand prisoners in French, German, and English that they were free.

At age twenty-five, in 1945, she was appointed chief of the *Herald-Tribune's* Berlin bureau and covered the Berlin airlift and the Nuremberg war trials. Higgins was disappointed when the *Herald-Tribune* editors decided to transfer her to Tokyo as the newspaper's Far East correspondent in 1950, but found herself in the middle of a war zone just days after her arrival when North Korean troops marched across the South Korean border and headed toward Seoul. After a few weeks, American Lieutenant General Walton H. Walker ordered Higgins and all American women to leave Korea, saying, "This is just not the type of war where women ought to be running around the front lines." Higgins disagreed and appealed to General Douglas MacArthur, who rescinded the order the next day. Higgins' work in Korea earned her the coveted Pulitzer Prize.

In her first book, *War in Korea: The Report of a Woman Combat Correspondent* (1951), she explained that she considered it a "personal crusade" to be able to cover the war for her newspaper. She viewed it as a crossroad for women correspondents and that if she had backed down, it would have proven to the world that women were a handicap to newspapers. Instead, her coverage opened doors to newspapers for other women. She was one of the earliest correspondents to cover Vietnam. She also spent ten weeks trekking through the Soviet Union for her book, *Red Plush and Black Bread*, published in 1955.

She was married in 1952 to Major General William E. Hall, whom she had met in Berlin where he was an Army intelligencer office during the Soviet blockade. Her first child, a girl, died shortly after her premature birth in 1953. Her son, Lawrence Higgins Hall, was born in 1958 and a daughter, Linda Marguerite Hall, in 1959.

She relocated to Washington, D.C., and covered the State Department for the *Herald-Tribune*. She wrote a regular column on international issues. In 1963, Higgins left the *Herald Tribune* and joined the staff of *Newsday* in Long Island as a columnist based in Washington. Her column was syndicated.

She had, throughout her career, regularly visited Vietnam. Her book, *Our Vietnam Nightmare*, outlined her belief that America's interference in the area was at the root cause of many of its problems. During her tenth trip to Vietnam in late 1965, Higgins fell ill with a rare tropical disease, leishmaniasis, which is transmitted through a bite by a sand fly. She died on January 3, 1966, at the age of forty-five. She is buried in Arlington National Cemetery.

Further Reading

Belford, Barbara. *Brilliant Bylines: A Biographical Anthology of Notable Newspaperwomen in America.* New York: Columbia University Press, 1986.

Biographical History, Marguerite Higgins Papers: An Inventory of her papers at Syracuse University, http://library.syr.edu/digital/guides/h/higgins_m.htm (accessed April 9, 2007).

Higgins, Marguerite. *War in Korea: The Report of a Woman Combat Correspondent.* Garden City, NY: Doubleday, 1951.

Higgins, Marguerite. *News is a Singular Thing.* Garden City, NY: Doubleday, 1955.

May, Antoinette. *Witness to War: A Biography of Marguerite Higgins, the Legendary Pulitzer Prize-Winning War Correspondent.* New York: Penguin Books, 1983.

Murray, Peter Noel. "Marguerite Higgins: An Examination of Legacy and Gender Bias." PhD dissertation, University of Maryland, College Park, MD, 2003.

AGNES HOOPER GOTTLIEB

HUMOR

Humor in American journalism dates back at least to Ben Franklin's *Dogood Papers* of the early 18th century. Although the humor and satire were unusual for colonial journalism when Franklin's writings appeared in the *New England Courant* (1723–25), in the early twenty-first century, they are regularly seen in newspapers in print and online, including such publications as *The Onion, Bean Soup Times,* and *Comedy Zine.* Each of these publications satirized the news of the day, as Franklin had done earlier. In the late twentieth and early twenty-first centuries, though, news reports themselves became the humorist's target in addition to the news itself. Parodies of television news reporting could be also seen on such programs as *Saturday Night Live* and *The Daily Show.*

Adding humor to reporting is a challenging task and can be of high literary quality. In 1904, General Henry Van Ness Boynton, long-time Washington, D.C., correspondent for the *Cincinnati Commercial Gazette,* suggested that the "real business of journalism" was "to record or to comment, not to create or interpret." To that he added a caveat: carefully describing events to offer complete purity was not necessarily the ideal in journalism. As such, he offered a framework for considering the place of humor in journalism. To connect with readers, listeners, and viewers, journalists over time have made use of literary tools found in fiction and poetry, including storytelling, alliteration, and metaphors. Exaggeration might typically appear in columns along with what in humor is referred to as a reverse—a writing technique setting the audience up for one thing then delivering the opposite of what is expected.

Ben Franklin helped to set the tone for using humor. Many of Franklin's colonial crime reports in the *Pennsylvania Gazette,* for example, were laced with digs at government, written caricatures of politicians, and comic engravings that lampooned proposed laws. His reports became formulas for other journalists because Franklin seemed to suggest that humor was an important tool for journalists to learn because of its ability to persuade.

In the early and mid-1800s, Samuel Clemens (a.k.a. Mark Twain) defined a new level of humor in journalism. He delivered commentary about the government with such sentences as: "It could probably be shown by facts and figures that there is no distinctly American criminal class except Congress." While often bitingly accurate with his humor, Twain also liked to make up stories, many of which appeared as news in the *Hannibal Journal,* which was run by his brother. Twain is famous for saying, "Truth is more of a stranger than fiction," and "When in doubt, tell the truth." While attempting to make a living at silver mining in Nevada, he found more financial success from the humorous sketches he sold to the Virginia City, Nevada, *Territorial Enterprise.* The newspaper later unsuspectingly hired the young Samuel Clemens as a reporter. It was there that he took his now-famous pen name.

In 1867, shortly after Twain was hired, he penned the national sensation, "The Celebrated Jumping Frog of Calaveras County." Soon after, the *Sacramento Union* scooped up Twain's humorous letters and articles about Hawaii, New York City, Europe, and the Middle East. Looking back on his life and work, Twain said, "When I was younger, I could remember anything, whether it has happened or not." That idea—that memoir, personal essay, and creative nonfiction have their place as news alongside reportage about current events—was taken to heart by many other journalists.

Prominent humorist James Thurber was acclaimed by literary critics as Mark Twain's successor. As a writer and also managing director of the *New Yorker* between 1927 and 1933, Thurber wrote and drew about the frustrations average people faced along with the overwhelming pressure of everyday modern life. Thurber had a special gift with the humor technique of heightening hysteria through exaggeration. He helped make the *New Yorker* home to another humorist of the day, Dorothy Parker, who began as a caustic theatre critic but holds legendary status today in journalism for her humorous and often biographical short romance stories-as-news, and her biting book reviews written under the byline, "Constant Reader."

Will Rogers was the first humorist to make it big on the radio. He reached a nationwide network audience and wrote more than four thousand syndicated columns. He famously asserted, "I never met a man I didn't like." Rogers was named "Ambassador at Large of the United States" by the National Press Club. Damon Runyon and Ring Lardner were sports columnists who developed a nationwide fan following because of their use of satire in disparaging what Lardner saw as the "blissful asininity" of hero worship. Runyon's work later captured the "Good Time Charlies" of New York's Broadway crowd, where "all of life is six to five against." In the second half of the twentieth century, Mike Royko in Chicago and Jimmy Breslin in New York won Pulitzer Prizes for nationally syndicated columns relished for their humorous celebration of the common sense of America's common men and women.

There were, of course, many others who became known for their humor. Robert Benchley was a humorist and columnist at *Vanity Fair,* the *New Yorker,* and *Life* magazine, whose opinions on theater and drama in the 1930s and 1940s reflected the jaded views of the Algonquin Round Table. "Defining and analyzing humor," Benchley once wrote, "is a past-time of humorless people." Benchley observed that "it took me 15 years to discover that I had no talent for writing, but I couldn't give it up because by that time I was too famous." Art Buchwald was a Pulitzer Prize winning political satirist whose column for the *Washington Post* was syndicated to more than three hundred newspapers. Erma Bombeck was a humorist whose column of surviving suburbia appeared throughout the 1960s and 1970s. "The grass is always greener," Bombeck famously wrote, "over the septic tank." Marriage has no guarantees, she warned her readers. "If that's what you're looking for, go live with a car battery."

Mad magazine used satire and parody to cover current events. It first appeared in 1952, and was directed at the pre-teen set, the first magazine for that audience to deal with contemporary affairs in a humorous form. During the 1960s, *Mad* dealt with the Vietnam War, civil rights, and offered spoofs on popular television programs dealing with race relations.

During the 1970s, *National Lampoon* was directed at teens and young adults. It continued the model set by *Mad* by using humor to bring awareness to current events, cultural foibles, and politics. The audience turned out to be a new information-hungry generation delighting in the unusual. The magazine's "True Facts" column, edited by John Bendel, focused on "odd" news, which showed readers the human condition in ways that made them laugh as well as think, if only a little.

The youth-oriented parodies of the news made popular by *Mad* and the *National Lampoon* had their counterparts on television in the late twentieth and early twenty-first centuries as evidenced by the popularity of *Saturday Night Live* and the *Daily Show with John Stewart* which satirized such sober news programs as *Meet the Press*, *60 Minutes*, *CNN Headline News*, and the *CBS Evening News*, among others. Whatever the format, using humor effectively has always been a difficult thing for journalists to master, but it remains one of the most powerful means of commenting on the events of the day.

Further Reading

Grauer, Neil A. *Remember Laughter: A Life of James Thurber.* Lincoln: University of Nebraska Press, 1994.

Lee, Judith Yaross. *Defining New Yorker Humor.* Jackson: The University Press of Mississippi, 2000.

DEBRA A. SCHWARTZ
RALPH RIVAS

HUNTLEY, CHET

Chester Robert Huntley (December 10, 1911–March 20, 1974) grew up in a succession of small Montana towns and went on to become half of the most successful team of network news anchors in television history. Chet Huntley joined NBC News in 1955 and, within a year, he teamed up with David Brinkley to cover the Republican and Democratic national political conventions. After the team attracted the largest share of the television convention audience, the network replaced John Cameron Swayze's evening news broadcast with the nightly fifteen-minute The Huntley-Brinkley

Report on October 29, 1956. The program expanded to half an hour in 1963.

Born December 10, 1911, in the living quarters of a Northern Pacific Railroad depot in Cardwell, Montana, Huntley's father worked for the railroad and the family lived in Saco, Scoby, Willow Creek, Logan, Big Timber, Norris, Whitehall, Bozeman, and Reedpoint. Huntley also spent time on his grandfather's sheep ranch, and he lovingly and nostalgically described his Montana childhood in a memoir, *The Generous Years: Remembrances of a Frontier Boyhood* (1968). He attended Montana State College in Bozeman and the University of Washington in Seattle, where he began his broadcast career at a local radio station KPCB in 1934. For writing and reading the news, he was paid $10 a month plus laundry service, and he sometimes traded sponsor accounts for food.

In 1938, he started with CBS Radio in California in 1951 and moved to ABC. As a commentator, Huntley won $10,000 in a libel suit against a viewer who labeled him a communist after he had criticized Senator Joseph McCarthy's careless anticommunist charges. Huntley never collected the damages, saying he just wanted the woman to leave him alone. An NBC talent search lured Huntley to NBC, where officials hoped his solemn demeanor and deep voice would compete with CBS's successful Edward R. Murrow.

In his New York office high in NBC's Rockefeller Plaza tower, the conservative, independent Huntley kept memorabilia from his Montana boyhood, including his father's roll-top desk, guns, and western art. In 1967, he crossed the picket lines of striking American Federation of Television and Radio Artists, saying reporters should not be represented by the same unions as entertainers. His partner, Brinkley, honored the strike.

On the *Huntley-Brinkley Report*, Huntley read the national and world news in New York and Brinkley reported from Washington. Huntley's most controversial moment may have been his narration of pictures showing an attack on the U.S. embassy in Saigon during the Tet Offensive of 1968. Television news, at that time, did not normally spill blood on the living room floor. News reports were heavily edited and they did not come live. Film had to be flown from Vietnam to somewhere else, usually Tokyo, where it was processed and transmitted to New York. The only time unedited pictures went directly on the air came during the Tet offensive when, during his news program, Huntley provided narration for pictures going directly out over the air as the pictures were received. His report erred in saying enemy troops had taken the U.S. embassy, but the pictures did show firing on the embassy grounds.

Huntley was accused of a conflict of interest because he raised livestock. Critics jumped on him when he provided commentary on agricultural issues without disclosing his interests. He even introduced a product line, "Chet Huntley's Nature Fed Beef," from his farm in 1964, but he quickly dropped the enterprise.

Huntley described himself as a "classic liberal," meaning "an open-mindedness, a feeling that ideas are not dangerous and let's consider them all." He often expressed disappointment that his critics failed to acknowledge NBC's contribution to racial integration. He became a spokesman for network news reporters responding to attacks by Vice President Spiro Agnew in 1969 and the Richard Nixon administration attacked back, hoping to associate his name in the public with the "liberal media." Saying he did not want to "keel over" at the office, Huntley retired from NBC in 1970 and started building Big Sky, a ski resort northwest of Yellowstone Park in Montana.

After leaving NBC, Huntley continued in broadcasting as a station owner and radio commentator while seeking corporate support for his Big Sky project. He had envisioned an environmentally friendly development near Bozeman that would boost Montana's ailing economy, but he faced opposition from environmentalists and Nixon administration officials.

Huntleys first marriage to Ingrid Rolin ended in divorce in 1959; they had two daughters. While watching Brinkley in Washington from his New York monitor, Huntley noticed a weather broadcaster, Tippy Stringer, in the background. He asked Brinkley for an introduction; they were later married. Huntley died from abdominal cancer March 20, 1974, at Big Sky, Montana, three days before the resort opened.

Huntley earned a number of national broadcast awards, including two Overseas Press Club Awards, an Alfred I. DuPont Award, and a George Polk Memorial Award. Huntley and Brinkley as a team won eight Emmy and two Peabody awards.

Further Reading

Beaubien, Michael P., and John S. Wyeth Jr. *Views on the News: The Media and Public Opinion: The Chet Huntley Memorial Lectures.* New York: New York University Press, 1994.

Brinkley, David. *David Brinkley: 11 presidents, 4 wars, 22 political conventions, 1 moon landing, 3 assassinations, 2000 weeks of news and other stuff on television and 18 years of growing up in North Carolina.* New York: Alfred A. Knopf, 1995.

Ferretti, Fred. "Chet Gets Ready to Say, Good-by, David." *New York Times,* July 5, 1970, Section 2, 13.

Huntley, Chet. *The Generous Years: Remembrances of a Frontier Boyhood.* New York: Random House, 1968.

Johnston, Lyle. *"Good Night, Chet": A Biography of Chet Huntley.* Jefferson, NC: McFarland & Company, 2003.

Kaufman, Michael T. "Chet Huntley, 62, Is Dead; Gave the News to Millions." *New York Times,* March 21, 1974, 4A.

WILLIAM E. HUNTZICKER

HUNTLEY-BRINKLEY REPORT

Chet Huntley and David Brinkley hardly knew each other when NBC teamed them to provide the network's coverage of the 1956 political conventions. Lagging behind CBS in news ratings, network officials were delighted at the chemistry between the two men and, beginning October 29, 1956, teamed them nightly on *The Huntley-Brinkley Report* (1956–1970) to replace John Cameron Swayze's *Camel News Caravan.* The fifteen-minute news program

struggled for two years, before edging out CBS's *Douglas Edwards with the News* for the number one spot—a position it held continuously until 1967—five years after Walter Cronkite replaced Edwards.

For most of its nearly fifteen years, *The Huntley-Brinkley Report* led in the ratings until it ended with Huntley's retirement on July 31, 1970. In 1963, after CBS expanded its evening news program with Walter Cronkite to thirty minutes, the *Huntley-Brinkley Report* also expanded to thirty minutes and featured an interview with President John F. Kennedy.

The Huntley-Brinkley Report's distinctive theme music—the second movement of Beethoven's Ninth Symphony—and characteristic sign off became icons of television news. Brinkley broadcast from Washington, and Huntley read the national and world news from New York. To provide cues for technicians to switch between the sites, the men used their first names as a signal. Huntley said, "David," and the feed switched to Brinkley in Washington. To end the program, they signed off with "Good night, Chet." "Good night, David." "And good night for NBC News."

With a well-respected staff experienced in radio, they wrote new rules for television, emphasizing pictures and narrative over sound. Although Huntley carried most of the program with news outside of Washington, Brinkley's strong television presence made viewers feel they divided the program equally.

Of course, they covered major events of the Cold War, civil rights, and space exploration. Television cameras watched in 1957 as a nicely dressed fifteen-year-old African American girl with books under her left arm emerged from a school bus at Central High School in Little Rock, Arkansas. National Guardsmen lined the street to enforce the governor's pledge that black children would never enter the school, despite a federal court order for integration. Mobs threatened reporters, especially television reporters, as well as the blacks seeking to integrate public accommodations, schools and voting booths throughout the South. Television helped an eloquent Rev. Martin Luther King Jr. demonstrate the strong contrast between his nonviolent means and white police forces.

Two days after President Kennedy's assassination in November 1963, NBC was the only network broadcasting live from the Dallas police department when assassin Lee Harvey Oswald was being transferred from the city to the county jail. As Oswald approached the camera, a man stepped forward and shot him. Millions watched Oswald collapse in pain. It was a first: murder—live on television. Television reached its largest audience to date with more than half of the 93 percent of the homes tuned in as the nation grieved the president's death over the next few days.

Pictures from Vietnam brought war images into living rooms. At the time of the Tet Offensive in 1968, the *Huntley-Brinkley Report* aired combat footage as it arrived from Tokyo where the film had been developed. Huntley narrated the report without seeing the pictures in advance, giving the impression of a live broadcast.

Huntley's retirement in July, 1970 (he died in 1974), ended the *Huntley-Brinkley Report*, but Brinkley continued at NBC for another decade before going to ABC with a weekly Sunday morning program. He retired in 1996 and died in 2003.

Further Reading

Barnouw, Erik. *Tube of Plenty: The Evolution of American Television*, 2nd Rev. Ed. New York: Oxford University Press, 1990.

Bliss, Edward Jr. *Now the News: The Story of Broadcast Journalism*. New York: Columbia University Press, 1991.

Brinkley, David. *David Brinkley: 11 presidents, 4 wars, 22 political conventions, 1 moon landing, 3 assassinations, 2000 weeks of news and other stuff on television and 18 years of growing up in North Carolina*. New York: Alfred A. Knopf, 1995.

Donovan, Robert J., and Ray Scherer. *Unsilent Revolution: Television news and American Public Life*. New York: Cambridge University Press, 1992.

Frank, Reuven. *Out of Thin Air: The Brief Wonderful Life of Network News*. New York: Simon & Schuster, 1991.

Johnston, Lyle. *"Good Night, Chet": A Biography of Chet Huntley*. Jefferson, NC: McFarland & Company, 2003.

Trotta, Liz. *Fighting for Air: In the Trenches with Television News*. New York: Simon & Schuster, 1991.

WILLIAM E. HUNTZICKER

HUTCHINS COMMISSION: THE COMMISSION ON FREEDOM OF THE PRESS

The Commission on Freedom of the Press, whose investigations and research led ultimately to the 1947 publication of its report, *A Free and Responsible Press: A General Report on Mass Communication: Newspapers, Radio, Motion Pictures, Magazines, and Books*, provided the most authoritative document of the twentieth century dealing with what became the widely accepted philosophical framework for the daily workings of the U.S. press. When, in 1963, Frederick S. Siebert, Theodore Peterson, and Wilbur Schramm published *Four Theories of the Press: The Authoritarian, Libertarian, Social Responsibility, and Soviet Communist Concepts of What the Press Should Be and Do*, they explained four normative theories to illustrate the press's position in relation to its political environment. Reference to the commission's report in the book helped to establish the report as the origin of the normative concept of social responsibility of the press in the United States.

The Commission's Origin

The idea for an inquiry into the status and future of the freedom of the press originated between Time Inc. publisher Henry R. Luce and University of Chicago Chancellor Robert M. Hutchins in December 1942. World War II and the fight against fascism had stimulated much thinking about the meaning of democracy and how to protect it, as had the appearance of such new media as radio and motion pictures. In 1943, Hutchins and Luce selected seventeen people to serve as commissioners and advisors on the Commission on Freedom of the Press, later known as the Hutchins Commission. The commissioners were Hutchins, Zechariah Chafee Jr., John M. Clark, John Dickinson, William E. Hocking, Harold D. Lasswell, Archibald MacLeish, Charles E. Merriam, Reinhold Niebuhr, Robert Redfield, Beardsley Ruml, Arthur M. Schlesinger, and George N. Shuster. Advisors were John Grierson, Hu Shih, Jacques Maritain, and Kurt Riezler. Staff members included Llewellyn White and Ruth A. Inglis, who wrote the commission's reports on radio and motion pictures, respectively. On December 15, 1943, the group met for the first time in New York City. There was no formal agenda for the commission, but its members clearly understood that their role was to examine the role of journalism in a democracy.

Although the Foreword to the commission's report indicates that Hutchins chose the commissioners, an examination of the correspondence between Luce and Hutchins shows that Luce played a significant role in the selection process. It is not surprising that most of them shared Luce's education, values and jingoistic ideology. Eleven had graduate degrees from Luce's alma mater, Yale, or from Harvard, or from Columbia. More than half of them taught at the University of Chicago, where Hutchins was chancellor. Others were professors at Harvard or Columbia. Several of them were consultants or staff members of New Deal agencies. Many were government officials or former government employees and were dedicated, if not outspoken, proponents of Franklin D. Roosevelt's administration.

Although the commission was harshly criticized for excluding journalists, Hutchins and Luce considered including several journalists as potential commission members in the initial selection process, including Walter Lippmann, Kent Cooper, and William Paley. Others considered for membership included advertising executive Chester Bowles, Federal Communications Commission Chairman Lawrence Fly, Walter Millis, Frank Luther Mott, George H. Soule, Marshall Field, Eugene Meyer, and Chester Rowell. The only involvement by a journalist in the commission's work came in the fall of 1946, when Hutchins sent Lippmann a copy of the report, to which Lippmann responded with a brief critique.

The Report

The commission's last meeting was held from September 15 to 17, 1946. Its 133-page report, *A Free and Responsible Press*, said that the press is free for the purpose of serving democracy and that a press that shirks its democratic duty will lose its freedom. The report said freedom of the press faced various threats: the increasing concentration of ownership; lack of public access to media; excessive attention to the sensational at the expense of vital information; and the public's willingness to consume the sensational while at the same time condemning its production. The press's faults, the report said, had become serious public dangers, because "the preservation of democracy and perhaps of civilization may now depend upon a free and responsible press."

The commission reached its conclusions after considerable debate over whether the government should regulate the press. Additional laws were not now appropriate, it said, but legal restrictions were virtually inevitable unless the press improved. To avoid government intervention, the press would have to become more competent and professional, and elevate public tastes instead of pandering to them.

As commission members discussed limits to government control of the press, they considered the creation of a citizens' organization to promote press freedom. In the end, the only recommendation the commission made for such a body was a press council. After prolonged discussions, the commission concluded that legal restrictions on the press would be easily abused and should only be a last resort.

Reaction to the Report

Even before publication of the report, the Hutchins Commission came under fire from the press. It conducted meetings in secret, broadly defined the press to include radio, magazines, television and motion pictures, and excluded journalists from the commission, raising the hackles of newspaper executives.

Predictably, the report met with rejection. Journalists argued that the commission had overlooked journalism's long commitment to serving democracy and had overemphasized the dangers confronting press freedom.

The commission's report was run as a supplement in the April 1947 issue of Luce's *Fortune*. Although Luce would later publicly praise the commission's efforts, he published the report with an editorial expressing his disappointment in the commission's work.

It was nearly two decades later, when *Four Theories of the Press* became a landmark in journalism scholarship, that the report came to be considered a directive for "moral order"—a call for American journalists to help impose democratic ideals on the world.

Further Reading

Bates, Stephen. *Realigning Journalism with Democracy: The Hutchins Commission, Its Times, and Ours*. Washington, D.C.: The Annenberg Washington Program in Communications Policy Studies of Northwestern University, 1995.

Blanchard, Margaret. "The Hutchins Commission, The Press and the Responsibility Concept." *Journalism Monographs* 49, 1977.

Chafee, Zechariah, Jr., *Government and Mass Communications: A Report from the Commission on Freedom of the Press*. Chicago: University of Chicago Press, 1947.

———. *A Free and Responsible Press: A General Report on Mass Communication: Newspapers, Radio, Motion Pictures, Magazines, and Books*. Chicago: University of Chicago Press, 1947.

"Dangers to Press Freedom." *Fortune*, April 1947, 2–5.

Fackler, P. Mark. "The Hutchins Commissioners and the Crisis in Democratic Theory." PhD dissertation, University of Illinois-Urbana, 1982.

Hocking, William Ernest. *Freedom of the Press: A Framework of Principle: A Report from the Commission on Freedom of the Press*. New York: Da Capo Press, 1972, originally 1947.

Inglis, Ruth A., *Freedom of the Movies: A Report on Self Regulation from the Commission on Freedom of the Press*. New York: Da Capo Press, 1972, originally 1947.

Leigh, Robert D., ed. *A Free and Responsible Press: A General Report on Mass Communications — Newspapers, Radio, Motion Pictures, Magazines and Books*. Chicago: University of Chicago Press, 1947.

McConnell, Jane S. "The Emergence of 'Social Responsibility': The Movement To Make The Media Safe For Democracy." PhD. dissertation, University of Iowa, 2000.

McIntyre, Jerilyn S. "Repositioning a Landmark: The Hutchins Commission and Freedom of the Press." *Critical Studies in Mass Communication* 4 (1987): 136–60.

Peoples Speaking to Peoples: A Report on International Mass Communication from the Commission on Freedom of the Press. Chicago: University of Chicago Press, 1946.

Siebert, Frederick S., Theodore Peterson, and Wilbur Schramm. *Four Theories of the Press: The Authoritarian, Libertarian, Social Responsibility and Soviet Communist Concepts of What the Press Should Be and Do*. Urbana: University of Illinois Press, 1963.

White, Llewellyn. *The American Radio: A Report on the Broadcasting Industry in the United States from the Commission on Freedom of the Press*. New York: Arno Press, 1971, originally 1947.

JANE S. MCCONNELL

INDIANAPOLIS STAR

For more than sixty years the most widely circulated newspaper in Indiana—with a circulation that peaked at close to a quarter million copies—and twice a Pulitzer Prize winner, the *Indianapolis Star* began publishing June 6, 1903, as a twelve-page morning paper under the leadership of Muncie, Indiana, industrialist George McCulloch, who had made his fortune in the interurban rail business. That first issue, edited in a building that had once housed the *Indianapolis Sun*, included eighteen stories and greetings from President Theodore Roosevelt, whose train had stopped in Indianapolis the night before the first issue appeared. Within four years the *Star* had eliminated two long-standing city morning newspapers, the *Indiana Journal* and the *Indiana State Sentinel*. By 1911, *Chicago Post* publisher John Shaffer, a friend of Presidents William Howard Taft and Warren G. Harding, had taken over as both editor and publisher, serving in those functions until he died in 1943. During his leadership, the "Businessman's Paper" led campaigns for social and economic reforms. Roy W. Howard was the paper's first sports editor. The writer Janet Flanner became the paper's first movie reviewer in 1916. Another woman, Anna Nicholas, was an editorial writer for the paper's first twenty-five years. Other veterans of the staff included Elmer Davis and Raymond Gram Swing.

Newspaper and radio station owner Eugene C. Pulliam bought the *Star* for $2.4 million in 1944, and led the paper in a spirited battle with two afternoon competitors, the *Indianapolis News* and the *Indianapolis Times*. Pulliam changed the paper's slogan from "Fair & First" to "Where the Spirit of the Lord is, there is Liberty," which it has remained. In 1948, Pulliam merged the *Star* and the *News* in Indianapolis Newspapers, Inc., with the papers sharing advertising, production and a building. The *Times* shut down in 1965. Three decades later, the *Star* and the *News* combined their newsroom operations. When the *News* ceased operations in 1999, the *Star* became the city's only daily newspaper. Over the years it pulled back from its broader state reach. In 1996 the *Star* and WTHR, Channel 13, joined to share news content and to promote each other. Although always proclaiming its independence, since its founding the *Star* has endorsed only Republican presidential candidates, except Progressive Theodore Roosevelt in 1912 and Democrat Lyndon B. Johnson in 1964.

The *Star* has won two Pulitzers, the first for a 1974 series on police corruption in Indianapolis, and the second for a 1990 series on Indiana doctors who had been convicted of malpractice on multiple occasions, but continued to practice. The second series was facilitated by the use of computer-assisted journalism. Lawrence S. "Bo" Connor was city editor on the first Pulitzer story, and managing editor during the second. But the *Star* generated unfavorable publicity in 1976 when it attacked the Indiana chapter of the ACLU and the Jewish Community Relations Council, which had fought the city's plans to install a manger scene as part of local holiday decorations.

The Gannett Corporation bought the *Star* in 2000, a year after the death of Eugene S. Pulliam, the last member of a three-person trust that had controlled the paper, and who had taken over the paper from his father in 1975. The selling price for Central Newspapers, of which the *Star* was a part, was $2.6 billion. The first Gannett publisher, Barbara Henry, who came from the *Des Moines Register*, had once worked for the *Indianapolis News*. The paper cut staff, streamlined operations, and opened a $72 million printing facility. A third of the newsroom staff left the paper in the first four years of Gannett ownership, but the churn had started during the last year of Pulliam ownership, when new editor Tim Franklin vowed to make the *Star* one of the best newspapers of its size in the country. The paper won George Polk Awards in 2000 and 2001.

With no significant local print competition remaining, the *Star* must face alone the problems with which other newspapers are struggling, the development of the Internet as an information source, and the decline in the number of readers. In the meantime, it remains a dominant Indianapolis institution.

Further Reading

Carrington, John O. "The Foreign Policy of the Indianapolis Star, 1918–1939." PhD dissertation, University of Kentucky, 1958.

Davis, Andrea M. "Star Takes Next Major Step in Era of Change: Local News Reorganization Adds to Upheaval." *Indianapolis Business Journal* 23, no. 25 (September 2, 2002).

Houseman, Gerald L. "Antisemitism in City Politics: The Separation Clause & the Indianapolis Nativity Scene Controversy, 1976–1977." *Jewish Social Studies* 42, no. 1 (Winter 1980): 21–36.

King, Mason. "Staying on a Star Trek: New Editor Franklin Survives Gannett Transition."*Indianapolis Business Journal* 21, no. 23 (21 August 2000).

Murphy, Beth. "Indianapolis Star," In *Encyclopedia of India-napolis*, edited by David J. Bodenhamer, and Robert G. Barrows, 807–808, Bloomington: Indiana U. Press, 1994.

Pulliam, Russell. *Publisher Gene Pulliam: Last of the Newspaper Titans*. Ottawa, IL: Jameson Books, 1984.

Robertson, Lori. "Indianapolis 500." *American Journalism Review* 26, no. 1 (February/March 2004): 24–33.

OWEN V. JOHNSON

INTERPRETATIVE REPORTING

The notion that news articles should provide analysis or perspective to explain the significance of the information being reported received serious attention during the 1920s. Scholars and critics commented that the daily flow of news seemed disconnected or unrelated to any relevant or influential factors. Noted intellectuals, including philosopher John Dewey and sociologist Robert E. Park, argued that newspapers simply funneled information to citizens without caring whether it enabled them to better understand events and issues. Walter Lippmann, an editor and essayist, also noted the superficiality and standard formula of news articles, and proposed that journalists should learn to identify the causes and effects of circumstances that affected society.

These criticisms and suggestions eventually led to the development of interpretative reporting, a form of journalism different from objective reporting—or, in newsroom parlance, straight reporting. Interpretative reporting gave journalists who had expertise or experience in certain subjects the authority to evaluate information for its relevance and significance, and allowed journalists to discuss the unstated reasons for actions, decisions, policy proposals, and public statements. Conversely, objective reporting limited journalists to reporting only information that could be attributed specifically to sources of information, who then were responsible for opinions and statements.

By the 1930s, with the advent of the Great Depression and attendant intense political debate about the role of government in the nation's economic system, some journalists accepted the fact that news needed more analysis and perspective. At an annual conference in 1933, the membership of the American Society of Newspaper Editors approved a resolution urging editors to "devote a larger amount of attention and space to explanatory and interpretive news" to describe economic, political, and social factors affecting legislation and public policy. Soon, the rise of fascism and militarism in Germany, Italy, and Japan joined the list of news items considered appropriate for interpretative reporting.

Initially, news columnists in Washington, D.C., practiced interpretative journalism. Whether writing for a news service, a news syndicate, or a major metropolitan newspaper, columnists had the latitude to explain the barter, compromise, and machination inherent in the legislative process. The New Deal era offered columnists many opportunities to describe congressional responses to various controversial proposals by President Franklin D. Roosevelt and the effects of political infighting on a range of policy issues. Editors believed that readers would accept the subjective judgments of columnists because of their expertise in political matters and journalistic prominence.

The next step for interpretative reporting involved the creation of week-in-review sections in Sunday editions of several major metropolitan newspapers. Editors would select a newsworthy subject, combine information on the subject from separate news articles published during the previous week, and correlate the material to explain or interpret the developments; this method applied to all newsworthy items chosen for week-in-review treatment. These presentations allowed editors to arrange the information according to their judgment of its relevance and significance. For the most part, week-in-review sections consisted of information on national and international items from news services.

The Associated Press began distributing a weekly review of news in 1935, which became a regular feature in many small- and medium-size newspapers that did not have the newsroom resources of metropolitan newspapers to create their own summary. The weekly review of news was an established feature by the 1950s.

Another significant step was the gradual expansion of interpretative reporting to some state capital bureaus. Like their counterparts in the nation's capital, reporters who covered the statehouse and legislature described the political factors affecting legislation. By writing about the tradeoffs and power brokers associated with lawmaking, reporters gave their readers a useful perspective on the legislative process.

These efforts to broaden the scope of news presentations were evolutionary and hardly readily adopted by most editors, who wished to avoid accusations of bias they were certain would result from ignoring the tenets of objective reporting. Apparently, the traditionalist viewpoint prevailed: an article in *Journalism Quarterly*, an academic journal, decried the lack of interpretative reporting in most newspapers during the early 1940s.

Much interpretative journalism was limited to subjects generated by distant journalists, not local reporters. Even by the 1960s, local reporters rarely had an opportunity to interpret events and issues in their home areas. Curtis D. MacDougall, a journalism scholar, concluded that most editors believed interpretative reporting was safer the farther it was from the newsroom. Editors were aware that hometown readers were more familiar with local events and issues, which made news interpretation riskier.

Resistance to interpretative reporting by traditionalists was not without merit. The historian Frank Luther Mott criticized some interpretative articles for reading more like editorials than news. An article in *Nieman Reports*, a journal for journalism practitioners and scholars, also stated that too much opinion was present in interpretative articles. When a journalist, rather than a specific source, became responsible for judgments and conclusions, the line between advocacy and interpretation was difficult to distinguish.

The limitation of straight reporting was the focus of debate among journalists when Senator Joseph R. McCarthy, a Wisconsin Republican, began a crusade during the early 1950s to expose Communist influence in the federal government. Reporters assigned to cover McCarthy knew full well that the senator was inconsistent when citing the number of federal employees or officials he accused of being Communists or Communist sympathizers, but the journalistic standards of the day expected reporters to write exactly what a public official said, not what was said before. McCarthy's manipulation of numbers was so blatant, however, that editors at some newspapers receiving the text from news services occasionally inserted previously cited numbers for background so readers could see the senator's inconsistency.

1960s: Breakthrough

Interpretative reporting finally found a place on the pages of many newspapers, and on network television news programs, from the late 1960s onward. Several long-term, dramatic events and issues eroded the resistance of traditional editors, who continued to restrict interpretative reporting into the 1970s. Among these newsworthy items were civil rights activism, cultural transformation, environmental awareness, racial tension, the Vietnam War, and the Watergate scandal. Each of these items required analysis and perspective, and many had a profound impact on local communities, which brought interpretative reporting closer to home.

Interpretative reporting gained some credence when the *New York Herald-Tribune* emphasized it in its daily news columns during the early 1960s when the newspaper fought an ultimately failing battle to survive against another upscale competitor, the *New York Times*. The *Herald-Tribune* editor, formerly with *Newsweek*—itself a practitioner of interpretative journalism, employed the style to illustrate discrepancies between official government statements and actual policy decisions in foreign affairs.

The *Times*, too, published more interpretative articles as it dawned on editors there that newspapers should offer more than straight news to combat competition from increasingly popular television news programs, which provided immediate news coverage. Some editors at other newspapers also realized that newspapers should publish more interpretative articles to enhance value to readers.

Newsmagazines had an influence, too. Although some newspaper editors occasionally criticized the interpretative style seen in *Time* and *Newsweek* for being too opinionated, these editors recognized the advantages of providing perspective for readers.

Another contributor to interpretative reporting was Philip Meyer, a reporter for local Knight-Ridder newspapers and later a national correspondent for the organization. Meyer demonstrated the potential for news interpretation based on meticulous research of data pertinent to crime, education, and other social issues. Meyer's book, *Precision Journalism*, became a resource for journalists.

Both the Vietnam War and Watergate scandal proved the worth of interpretative reporting. Journalists in Vietnam sought to contrast the optimistic reports and statements of U.S. government officials and military commanders with appraisals of the situation in the countryside at various points during the war. Throughout the Watergate scandal, statements by the Nixon administration warranted scrutiny when compared to information gathered by Congress and evidence submitted by prosecutors.

These years also saw the rise of interpretative reporting on television. Network correspondents offered immediate analysis of statements made by public officials at news conferences or in speeches to ascertain inaccuracies and inconsistencies.

Debate about the dangers associated with interpretative reporting versus its utility lessened considerably by the late 1970s. Articles and opinion pieces about the subject appeared infrequently in journals and magazines directed toward editors and other journalists.

Some newspapers now devote several pages to interpretative journalism in Sunday editions and some have an entire section designated for it.

Although it is not the contentious issue it once was, interpretive journalism continues to raise concerns of bias. Political conservatives and liberals alike perceive, although from different perspectives, the subjective presentation and selection of information by news media organizations.

Interpretative reporting also continues to cause concern among some journalists. Many newspapers require the display of an inset headline, usually "news analysis," with an interpretative article. The purpose is to alert readers that the article may represent the perspective of the reporter.

Further Reading

Blankenburg, William and Ruth Walden. "Objectivity, Interpretation and Economy in Reporting." *Journalism Quarterly* 54, Autumn 1977.

Dewey, John. *The Public and Its Problems*. Chicago: Swallow Press, 1954.

Landers, James. "The *National Observer*, 1962-1977: Interpretive Journalism Pioneer." *Journalism History* 31, Spring 2005.

Lippmann, Walter. *Public Opinion*. New York: Harcourt, Brace and Company 1922.

MacDougall, Curtis D. *The Press and Its Problems*. Dubuque, Iowa: Wm. C. Brown Company, 1964.

——. *Interpretative Reporting*. New York: Macmillan Company, 1972.

Park, Robert E. "News as a Form of Knowledge" in *On Social Control and Collective Behavior: Selected Papers*, edited by Ralph H. Turner. Chicago: University of Chicago Press, 1967.

Schudson, Michael. *Discovering the News: A Social History of American Newspapers*. New York: Basic Books, 1978.

JAMES LANDERS

INVERTED PYRAMID

The inverted pyramid news story has been the standard format for news writing for more than a century. It is most widely used for newspaper writing, especially what is seen as "hard news," but has also been adapted for use in broadcast and Internet news production. Many journalists and journalism educators see the inverted pyramid form as the most effective means of presenting news information to readers. It is also believed by many to be a successful means for maintaining objectivity in news writing because of its emphasis on the presentation of facts.

The concept behind the inverted pyramid format is relatively simple. The writer prioritizes the factual information to be conveyed in the news story by importance. The most essential pieces of information are offered in the first line, which is called the lead (or summary lead). This usually addresses the so-called "five W's" (who, what, when, why, and where). Thus, the reader is able to ascertain the key elements of the story immediately. The writer then provides the rest of the information and supporting contextual details in descending order of importance, leaving the least essential material for the very end. This gives the completed story the form of an inverted pyramid, with the most important elements, or the "base" of the story, on top.

Journalists like this form of news writing for several reasons. The formulaic nature of the style makes it easy to produce quickly. Once a reporter masters the basic format, the preparation of routine news stories under deadline pressure becomes an easier task. Much of the early training of journalists consists of practicing the inverted pyramid style. It is also considered to be a service to readers, who may be thought of as too busy to read entire stories or, more cynically, too naive to prioritize the information on their own. By presenting the news in the inverted pyramid style, readers are given the essential facts even if they fail to read to the end. The ability to write a strong and arresting lead, in order to grab the attention of readers has long been a valued skill. Editors also like the inverted pyramid form because it simplifies the task of copy editing. If a story is too long to fit the news hole, it can be shortened by taking copy from the bottom, where the least essential information will be. Finally, the inverted pyramid is based entirely on the presentation of facts, which makes it more objective, and therefore more acceptable in modern journalism. The writer's interpretation and opinion are less likely to be evident when a story adheres to the inverted pyramid format.

The inverted pyramid began to appear in American newspapers in the late nineteenth century, and by World War I had become a standard form. Earlier news writing was more likely to be chronological in nature. The writer would begin a story by setting up the situation, establishing background, providing contextual information, and introducing the characters, much as in the writing of fiction. Facts were then narrated as they occurred, regardless of their relative significance. In many cases, the most important information would come at the very end of the story where it could be missed by readers who did not read to the bottom of the page. Although this form of writing remains popular in magazine journalism and some types of newspaper feature writing, it lost favor as a means of presenting hard news.

Scholars have attempted to explain the origination of the inverted pyramid style, but these efforts have not been conclusive. Recent scholarship has argued that the inverted pyramid was not devised by journalists, but emerged from the model provided by news dispatches written by Secretary of War Edwin M. Stanton during the Civil War. Stanton's dispatches during the war, and especially the initial announcement of President Abraham Lincoln's assassination, were among the very first pieces of writing to display the inverted pyramid form. By contrast, the first Associated Press account of Lincoln's shooting, written by Lawrence Gobright, was written in a classic narrative form. Stanton's dispatches ran in Civil War-era newspapers and may have influenced the development of new writing forms after the war, although the lag between the end of the war and the adoption of the inverted pyramid form as a journalistic standard raises questions about the timing and processes of this influence.

Several other explanations for the emergence of the inverted pyramid have been posited over the years. One of the most durable is technological in nature. According to this theory, news correspondents learned to organize their dispatches this way when they began to use the telegraph to transmit stories from the field back to their editor. Given the unstable nature of early telegraph technology, according to the argument, journalists realized that they needed to present the most vital information at the onset of the transmission in the event that the telegraph line went dead or the message was otherwise disrupted. Only the least important information would be lost if the line failed halfway though the transmission. Although this explanation has been a hallmark of journalism history textbooks for generations, it has little basis in fact. Reporters began to take advantage of the telegraph in the 1840s, and used it extensively through the Civil War years. However, scholars have found few, if any, examples of inverted pyramid stories published before the 1870s and even as late as 1910 they remain a minority. A variation on this explanation involves the high transmission rates that accompanied the telegraph in the early years. According to this theory, stingy editors demanded that their correspondents save money by writing their stories in the efficient inverted pyramid style. This also fails to account for the time gap between the advent of telegraph reporting and the adoption of the inverted pyramid. Another theory considers the Associated Press the originator of the inverted pyramid style. Because the AP wants to sell its news to a large and diverse group of members, it must attempt to remove partisanship and bias from the stories it offers. Adoption of the inverted pyramid, with its basis in factual information, standardized the AP's product and made it palatable for any and all member newspapers. Timing is again a problem with this explanation because the wire services began operating before the Civil War and were highly successful in the late nineteenth century when the inverted pyramid was barely in use. It also fails to account for the unabashed partisanship of many newspapers that bought AP service in the late nineteenth century.

Content analyses of American newspapers demonstrate that the inverted pyramid first became a standard during the Progressive Era, which coincided with the beginning of academic journalism education and the widespread adoption of professional ideals and standards. Early journalism educators adopted the inverted pyramid style as the most efficient presentation of news and it appears in many early textbooks. Many of the professors, like other progressives, viewed newspaper readers as rational minded citizens who valued the primacy of fact and were best served by objective news models. Occupational ideals at the time also tended to promote the idea that the journalist's role was to provide information, not influence opinion. In an era when objectivity assumed a new importance, the model of facticity and impartiality provided by the inverted pyramid assumed primacy in newsrooms across the country. The emergence of this style of news writing, then, is best seen as a reflection of cultural and professional ideals and attitudes about the nature of journalism and the public it serves, rather than merely the result of technological changes.

The inverted pyramid has been the target of many critics over the years. On one hand, many see it as boring, an outdated convention that restricts the creativity of journalists and their ability to tell compelling and complicated stories. Several generations of journalism students have chafed under the constraints of the form. Moreover, as the very notion of objectivity has been challenged, reliance on a form of journalism so closely associated with a "just the facts" mindset can seem limited. Other critics have blamed the inverted pyramid for turning journalists into stenographers who merely take down and repeat information, which leaves them susceptible to manipulation by politicians or public relations campaigns and leaves no room for interpretation. The so-called "new journalism" of the 1960s and 1970s challenged the boundaries of acceptable writing style and paved the way for an increase in alternative narrative structures, including in some cases a return to the older chronological approach. Since the 1970s, newspapers and other media outlets have been more likely to make use of different styles and many journalism textbooks offer a wider variety of approaches to writing styles. Variations on the inverted pyramid form, however, remain dominant in hard news presentation, even in many Internet news presentations.

Further Reading

Mindich, David T. Z. *Just the Facts: How "Objectivity" Came to Define American Journalism*. New York: New York University Press, 1998.

Schudson, Michael. *Discovering the News: A Social History of American Newspapers*. New York: Basic Books, 1978.

ROBERT A. RABE

INVESTIGATIVE JOURNALISM

Investigative journalism digs beneath the surface of everyday news events to expose corrupt local officials, bad schools, poor health care, exploited children, environmental pollution, innocent people on death row, business policies that cheat or harm consumers, unfair tax laws, and many other social and government problems. Researchers James S. Ettema and Theodore L. Glasser have called investigative reporters "custodians of conscience" because they bring to the public's attention violations of cherished American values. Reporters who specialized in this type of journalism defined it in the 1970s as original reporting about important public issues that reveals hidden information.

Because they are original reporting, individual investigative projects can take weeks, months, or even years to complete. Investigative reporters must be expert at patiently sifting through public records, conducting dozens of interviews, analyzing data, and recording their personal observations. Sometimes they go undercover. Always they work to give clear, convincing evidence through extensive documentation. Investigative reports are carefully crafted narratives designed to evoke enough outrage in readers that they will demand reforms.

A Long Tradition

Modern investigative reporting evolved from a strong tradition in American journalism of exposing government and social problems. Since America's colonial period, newspapers have sought to attract readers and change society for the better by exposing hidden information about public affairs as a check on government leaders and other powerful members of society. Indeed, revolution in the American colonies in the eighteenth century grew from complaints about British rule fueled by newspaper exposés. The colonies' first newspaper, *Publick Occurrences Both Forreign and Domestick*, published by Benjamin Harris in September 1690, exposed atrocities by Britain's American Indian allies during King William's War. Editor James Franklin, Ben Franklin's older brother, challenged Boston officials by revealing their inability to protect British shipping from pirates operating off the Massachusetts Bay Colony's coast. Later, Samuel Adams and his colleagues associated with the *Boston Gazette* stirred opposition to British rule by exposing atrocities committed by British soldiers stationed in Boston. By 1770, newspapers, particularly those in Boston, routinely stirred public outrage at British rule by revealing the alleged deception of colonial rulers.

After independence, American newspapers, emboldened by partisanship, sought to expose the graft, corruption, and scandal of their political enemies. Secret treaties, sexual misdeeds, and hidden political agendas ended up on the front pages of American newspapers. Republican Benjamin Franklin Bache, Ben Franklin's grandson, caused a sensation in 1795 by publishing a financial exposé of the Federalist government in Washington that may have been the first example of investigative reporting based on a leaked government document. Despite the Federalists' attempt to stifle criticism with passage of the short-lived Alien and Sedition Acts of 1798, partisan newspapers continued to publish political secrets into the early nineteenth century.

With the introduction of cheap newspapers for a mass audience starting in 1833, editors expanded their targets beyond politics to include other institutions, especially the legal system. Crime coverage became a staple of the penny papers, and when a socially connected clerk murdered the young prostitute Helen Jewett, the leading New York dailies, the *Sun* and the *Herald*, competed to reveal details of the crime, Miss Jewett's background, and the reasons the justice system ultimately failed to convict the accused, Richard Robinson. James Gordon Bennett, owner and editor of the *New York Herald*, went beyond police statements to uncover the sordid details of the murder, while Benjamin Day, proprietor of the *New York Sun*, conducted extensive interviews with court officials and jurors to reveal manipulations of the justice system by Richardson and his attorneys. As exhibited by Bennett and Day, the penny press editors' creed included a commitment to exposing the failures of urban institutions, including churches, the courts, and local government.

Exposure journalism became rare when newspapers and magazines focused their attentions on the American Civil War, but during the later decades of the nineteenth century aggressive original reporting again surfaced. The *New York Sun*, for example, unearthed lobbying scandals and government contractors who milked the treasury. The *Cincinnati Gazette* exposed corruption within the federal Freedmen's Bureau in connection with the founding of Howard University. *Frank Leslie's Illustrated Newspaper* exposed a scheme to allow impure milk to be sold to households in New York City, and the *New York Times* and *Harper's Weekly* teamed up to drive the corrupt city administration of Boss Tweed out of power. The *Times* set a new standard for reliable, incontrovertible evidence in investigative reporting by printing secret Tweed accounting ledgers. When it came to what the profession called "detective reporting," though, few could match the spirited Nellie Bly. She burst into the sensationalist press of New York in 1887 working for Joseph Pulitzer's *New York World*. Her first assignment, given by the *World*'s renowned editor John Cockerill, required her to go undercover into the city's notorious Blackwell's Island, the mental hospital for women. Posing as "Nellie Brown," Bly emerged with a gripping tale of cold baths, withheld medications, and other abuses that ultimately led to the institution's reform. Bly's contemporary, Jacob Riis, took time off from his police reporting duties for New York newspapers to train a camera's lens at the living conditions in New York's Bowery, where recent immigrants crowded together in tenements and alleyways. Publishing his work in books, Riis became the first exposure journalist to use photographs to document social ills. Additionally, the *San Francisco Examiner* crusaded for safer harbor ferries in 1888, and the *Chicago Tribune* exposed unsafe fireworks in 1899.

Exposés also became standard fare for social reformers, who used such reporting to motivate readers to agitate for change. Small weeklies published for workers, political reformers, civil rights activists, and women's rights advocates regularly used exposés to document the need for changes. The African American journalist Ida B. Wells, for example, exposed the largely unnoticed national scourge of mob lynchings. Also, the excesses of capitalist monopolies became ammunition for political reformers, including Henry Demarest Lloyd, who in 1894 published "Story of a Great Monopoly" in the *Atlantic Monthly*, which exposed the illegal and unethical practices of the Standard Oil Company.

Lloyd's work became the model for Ida Tarbell and other reporters at the turn of the century when they set off the muckraking era. Muckraking, a pejorative term coined by an aggravated President Theodore Roosevelt who felt the reporters went overboard, proved a profitable endeavor for national magazines like *McClure's*, *Collier's*, and *Cosmopolitan*, beginning in 1903. Aligned with the Progressive Party, a middle-class political movement that wanted government to regulate big business, muckrakers took aim at industrial trusts, political corruption, and social ills such as child labor and other abusive working conditions. Along with Tarbell, Lincoln Steffens, Ray Stannard Baker, David Graham Phillips, Rheta Childe Dorr, Upton Sinclair, and others produced more than one thousand magazine articles between 1903 and 1917, laying out an array of social ills brought about by corrupt governments, poor living conditions, and greedy corporations. Their articles set the stage for multiple social and political reforms, including a shorter work week, prohibitions against child labor, the Pure Food and Drug Act, and direct election of U.S. senators. When the muckraking era quieted with the beginning of World War I, newspapers picked up the call for reforms through exposure of social and political ills.

During the early twentieth century, the *New York World* exposed police corruption and the violence of the Ku Klux Klan, the *New York Evening Post* revealed inhumane conditions in New Jersey prisons, the *Chicago Herald* revealed the White Sox World Series scandal, and the *St. Louis Post-Dispatch* exposed the federal government's sell-off at bargain prices of U.S. petroleum reserves to oil companies. Though not a dominant characteristic of American newspapers during the early twentieth century, exposure journalism, often in the form of crusades, appeared more or less regularly in the press until about the 1930s, when exposés fell out of favor because of their association with sensationalism and the onset of the Great Depression.

During the 1930s and 1940s, small opinion magazines such as *Nation* and the *New Republic*, books, and a nationally syndicated column by Drew Pearson kept the muckraking tradition alive. the *Nation* and the *New Republic* published exposés spiked by daily newspapers; William Helms, Matthew Josephson, and Cary McWilliams published books on federal government corruption and social ills such as the exploitation of migrant farm workers; and Pearson founded "Washington Merry-Go-Round" in 1932, a syndicated column known for its exposés.

Beginning in the late 1940s, though, reporting in the muckraking tradition infused with the standards of objectivity began to appear in American newspapers. One of the earliest practitioners was Clark Mollenhoff of the *Des Moines* (Iowa) *Register*, who had been inspired by muckraker Lincoln Steffens but who brought to bear an objectivity honed through his training in law school. Mollenhoff, Robert Collins of the *Atlanta Journal* and the *St. Louis Post-Dispatch*, and Jack Nelson of the *Atlanta Constitution* brought the practice of investigative journalism into modern American newspapers during the 1940s and 1950s, reporting about bootleg liquor, prostitution, illegal gambling, race relations, and local government corruption. Mollenhoff and Robert Greene, who formed the first investigative reporting team as an editor at New York's *Newsday*, held seminars for working journalists through the American Press Institute to teach other journalists how to conduct investigations.

The Re-Emergence of Investigative Journalism

Several factors led to increased popularity in investigative journalism in newsrooms from the late 1950s through the 1970s. Mistrust of government, social unrest, new laws, and new technologies led the news media to embrace investigations. Government missteps included manipulations of the press by Wisconsin's red-baiting Senator Joseph McCarthy whose multifarious charges of communist infiltrators were shown to be largely baseless. They also included President Dwight D. Eisenhower's administration's deception of the American people about American spy planes flying over the Soviet Union—a lie accepted as truth by the American press until the Soviets shot down a U.S. spy plane and paraded its pilot, Francis Gary Powers, before television cameras. Additionally, the civil rights movement, violently suppressed and unprotected by local and state government officials in southern states, and the anti-Vietnam War movement that raised questions about America's foreign and domestic policies, further eroded the press's confidence in government leaders. A highlight was when *Washington Post* reporters Robert Woodward and Carl Bernstein, and other members of the press, exposed the Watergate scandal and other corruption in the Nixon administration, leading to President Nixon's resignation in 1974.

The press emerged from the 1960s and 1970s with legal sanctions for investigative reporting. In 1964, the U.S. Supreme Court expanded protections for journalists in a ruling, *New York Times v. Sullivan*, which made it extremely difficult for public officials to sue for libel. This protection was extended to public figures and to reporting methods in later cases. Reporters' investigative tools increased with passage of the Freedom of Information Act in 1966, which established a formal procedure for gaining access to government records, and the Government in the Sunshine Act in 1976, which established the right of access to government meetings.

In the realm of technology, the arrival of television news encouraged print journalists to adopt investigative journalism as a way to retain readers. Television, for its part, broadcast investigative documentaries by journalist Edward R. Murrow and started "Sixty Minutes," a popular magazine show with an investigative flare. Smaller cameras fueled undercover reporting on television and in print. And the tape-recorder, the copy machine, and computers emerged as technologies that could aid journalistic investigations.

As a result of these influences, investigative journalism thrived during the 1960s and 1970s in daily and weekly newspapers, on television, in magazines, and in alternative publications such as *Ramparts* magazine and underground urban newspapers such as the *Berkeley Barb*.

A Service Organization for Investigative Journalists

Beyond the American Press Institute seminars on investigative journalism, there was little interaction among reporters who practiced the craft until the formation of Investigative Reporters and Editors (IRE), a national organization founded in 1975. Reporters from the *Indianapolis Star* teamed up with a former investigative editor turned academic, Paul Williams, and Ron Koziel of the *Chicago Tribune* to establish IRE. They called an organizational meeting, raised funds, and set the organization's agenda with the help of Greene and other noted investigative reporters.

IRE supported the practice of investigative journalism by holding training sessions, bringing journalists together annually to exchange ideas and skills, and promoting the practice in American newsrooms. The organization housed its offices at the University of Missouri School of Journalism, giving it instant credibility, and brought attention to the practice with its Arizona Project in 1976–1977. The project gathered members of the organization in Phoenix, Arizona, to complete the work of their slain colleague, Don Bolles of the *Arizona Republic*. Bolles was murdered because of investigative stories he had written. It was the first time that news organizations had set aside their natural competitiveness to work on a single set of stories.

Beginning with fewer than one hundred members and a shoe-string budget, IRE by the 1990s had attracted a membership of more than thirty-five hundred members and operated with a budget in the hundreds of thousands of dollars. Its training seminars, newsletter, annual conventions, and annual awards led to the institutionalization of investigative journalism in American newsrooms throughout the country. Moreover, the organization spread the techniques of investigation into daily reporting, leading to more thorough reporting on routine government and feature stories. It taught journalists how to write and produce better investigations and trained journalists to enhance their investigations with social science methodologies and computer analyses. During the 1990s, IRE merged with the National Institute for Computer-Assisted Reporting, and reached out to other countries, notably Mexico and Russia, to help establish similar investigative reporting organizations.

Investigative journalism remained popular through the 1980s and 1990s. High-profile investigative teams were set up in newspaper and television newsrooms. Investigative television news programs modeled after "Sixty Minutes" were started on every network and on cable and public television and radio stations. Newsmagazines such as *Time* and *Newsweek* and magazines such as *Mother Jones* and *The New Yorker* regularly published investigative articles.

While investigative journalism remained an important standard for news organizations well into the twenty-first century, starting in the late 1990s institutional pressures and less-than-solid reporting began to erode support for the practice. Important exposés of police misconduct; criminal justice failures; city, state, and federal government corruption; environmental pollution; sexual misconduct by public officials, including President William Clinton; and controversial policies of the George W. Bush administration continued to be produced throughout the 1990s and into the early decades of the twenty-first century. Nevertheless, sloppy and poorly substantiated investigations led to news media embarrassments and high-profile libel suits. Moreover, financial strains in the news business led publishers and news directors to limit investigative journalism, which requires substantial resources if done correctly. By several measurements, investigative journalism entered the twenty-first century a practice besieged. Yet, given its long and distinguished tradition in American journalism and the strength of IRE, it was likely that investigative journalism would remain an integral part of American news organizations.

Further Reading

Adler, Renata. *Reckless Disregard: Westmoreland v. CBS, et al., Sharon v. Time.* New York: Vintage, 1986.

Aucoin, James. "The Re-emergence of American Investigative Journalism, 1960–1975," *Journalism History* 21, no. 1 (1995): 3–15.

——. *The Evolution of American Investigative Journalism.* Columbia: University of Missouri Press, 2005.

Benjaminson, Peter, and David Anderson. *Investigative Reporting.* Bloomington: Indiana University Press, 1976.

Bent, Silas. *Newspaper Crusaders: A Neglected Story.* Westport, CT: Greenwood Press, 1970.

Blevens, Frederick. "The Shifting Paradigms of Investigative Journalism in the 20th Century." *American Journalism* 14, no. 3 & 4 (1997): 257–261.

Clurman, Richard M. *Beyond Malice: The Media's Years of Reckoning.* New York: New American Library, 1990.

Downie, Leonard Jr.. *The New Muckrakers.* New York: New American Library, 1976.

Ettema, James S., and Theodore L. Glasser. *Custodians of Conscience: Investigative Journalism and Public Virtue.* New York: Columbia University Press, 1998.

Greenwald, Marilyn, and Joseph Bernt, eds. *The Big Chill: Investigative Reporting in the Current Media Environment.* Ames: Iowa State University Press, 2000.

Harrison, John M., and Harry H. Stein, eds. *Muckraking: Past, Present, and Future.* University Park: Pennsylvania State University Press, 1973.

Miraldi, Robert. *Muckraking and Objectivity: Journalism's Colliding Traditions.* New York: Greenwood, 1990.

Nord, David Paul. "Newspapers and American Nationhood, 1776–1826." *Proceedings of the American Antiquarian Society* 100, no. 2 (1988): 42–64.

Protess, David L., et. al. *The Journalism of Outrage: Investigative Reporting and Agenda Building in America.* New York: Guilford, 1991.

Serrin, Judith, and William Serrin, eds. *Muckraking!: The Journalism that Changed America.* New York: New Press, 2002.

Shapiro, Bruce, ed. *Shaking the Foundations: 200 Years of Investigative Journalism in America.* New York: Thunder's Mouth Press, 2003.

Tichi, Cecelia. *Exposés and Excess: Muckraking in America, 1900/2000.* Philadelphia: University of Pennsylvania Press, 2004.

Weinberg, Steve. *Telling the Untold Story: How Investigative Reporters Are Changing the Craft of Biography.* Columbia: University of Missouri Press, 1992.

JAMES AUCOIN

JAPANESE AMERICAN PRESS

There is a Japanese expression that a newspaper will emerge wherever three or more Japanese call home. The Japanese American experience partly confirms this saying. The first Japanese language newspapers in the United States were established by Japanese immigrants (Issei) intellectuals who wanted to shape Meiji-era Japan. The political dissidents who created the first Japanese-language newspapers in the 1880s hoped to smuggle them back to Japan. Of many papers, we primarily know of their shifting names, as activists tried to evade Japanese censors. Norio Tamura has written extensively in Japanese on these pioneering papers.

The Japanese American community press emerged soon after to serve the immigrants who transitioned from sojourners to settlers. Newspaper publishers were instrumental in this shift. The most influential individual was Kyutaro Abiko, who established San Francisco's *Nichibei Shimbun (Japanese American News)* in 1899 by merging two papers. Abiko not only advocated that immigrants should become settlers in America, but organized agricultural developments in California. His paper peaked at over twenty-five thousand subscribers in two editions. Other major newspapers were established in immigrant ports of Hawaii and the West Coast. These papers blossomed especially during the Russo-Japanese War (1904–1905) as Issei devoured victorious telegraphed news from home. In addition, papers serialized poetry, memoirs, and fiction from Japan as well as original works by Issei intellectuals. They also ran translations of English and other foreign literature. Smaller newspapers served rural communities, such as Sacramento's *Ofu Nippo*, with local news, advertisements, and annual yearbooks.

Because of acculturation and racist immigration laws, the Japanese American press gradually offered more English language pages for the American-born Nisei (second generation). This became the trend of the 1920s. Nisei James Y. Sakamoto established the first English language Japanese American newspaper 1928. His Seattle weekly was called the *Japanese American Courier*. Other prewar Nisei periodicals included a literary monthly and the weekly newsletter of the Japanese American Citizen's League (JACL). There also was a small bilingual left-wing newspaper called *Doho* that grew out of the Japanese Section of the American Communist Party. Its writers attacked other papers for reprinting propaganda from Japan's official Domei News Service. Most Nisei, though, were still in high school when war uprooted their lives.

Periodically, for example during the early 1920s and during World War II, there have been efforts to control the Japanese-language press in the United States. In 1921 Hawaii Territorial legislator Lawrence M. Judd proposed a Foreign Language Press Control Act, mandating foreign language newspapers submit official translations of all stories. This was primarily to control Japanese newspapers like Hawaii's *Nippu Jiji* and the *Hawai Hochi* that had supported the rights of striking sugar plantation workers. Governor Charles McCarthy signed the act in April. Although it was not enforced, it demonstrated elite suspicion of the Japanese press.

Why authorities wanted to control the *Nippu Jiji* is perhaps better understood by considering its history. Although its origins can be traced as far back as the first Japanese newspaper in Hawaii in 1892, its direct origins were from the *Yamato* (Japan), which started in 1895 as a mimeographed semi-weekly representing the immigration companies. It later became a daily typeset newspaper. In 1906 the paper was renamed the *Nippu Jiji* (the Japan - Hawaii Times). From 1905 to 1941 the main influence on the newspaper was its publisher-editor poet-intellectual Yasutaro Soga (1873–1957). Soga had worked on another early Japanese language newspaper that attacked the exploitation of the immigration companies. Soga's fame was cemented when he defended the interests of Japanese plantation workers who formed the Higher Wages Association. Soga was arrested on February 26, 1909 for "inciting unrest" as one of the leaders behind the 1909 strike. The strike united much of the ethnic community, although planters tried to buy influence by subsidizing Sometaro Shiba's *Hawai Shimpo*, which tried to take over the *Nippu Jiji*. Passions soared, and one union activist physically attacked Shiba during the trial. On August 22, 1909, Soga, two reporters and other union leaders were found guilty of third-degree conspiracy, sent to prison for ten months, and ordered to pay $300. The community celebrated when the *Jiji* staff was pardoned on July 4, 1910.

In January 1919, the *Nippu Jiji* became the first Japanese-language newspaper in Hawaii to establish an English-language section, which consisted of translations of articles and editorials. The paper gradually became more conservative, reflecting Soga's improved ties with territorial elites, and the Japanese Consul General.

The suppression of the Japanese American press during World War II was much more immediate and dramatic. Soga was interned on the night of Pearl Harbor. Like all Japanese-language newspapers in Hawaii, the *Jiji* was closed from 11 December 11, 1941 until January 8, 1942. It re-emerged under the control of Soga's son, Shigeo, and was renamed as the *Hawaii Times* that November. Like many ethnic newspapers, the *Times* gradually declined. It became a Japanese-language weekly in 1982, and ceased publishing three years later.

The treatment of Soga and the *Nippu Jiji* was typical of what happened to the Japanese American Press during World War II. All Japanese-language newspapers were closed on the day of the attack. Many editors were interned, and all papers were restricted. For example, American-born Yasuo Abiko took over the *Nichibei Shimbun* after Pearl Harbor; however, military authorities prohibited it from moving and resuming operations west of the Exclusion Zone. Only Japanese newspapers in Denver and Salt Lake City survived the war.

Most of the 120,000 detained Japanese Americans received their news from mimeographed newspapers published in each concentration camp. These were basically newsletters with official announcements in English and Japanese, although a few developed into professional-looking papers with some independence. Authorities usually preferred more malleable writers over experienced Issei and Nisei reporters. One exception was Bill Hosokawa, who had studied journalism at the University of Washington. After having to go abroad for work, he returned to the United States just before Pearl Harbor, and was detained in the Puyallup Assembly Center, and later sent to the Heart Mountain Relocation Center. He helped the *Heart Mountain Sentinel* to become a leading concentration camp newspaper, one of the only ones to be professionally printed. Although it looked professional and had good writers, critics point out that it supported the administration. For example, it criticized Nisei who resisted being drafted from inside Heart Mountain. Hosokawa, by this time, had already found employment on an Iowa paper. A few years later he was editing the *Denver Post* where he remained for many years. Hosokawa also wrote a column for the JACL's weekly, the *Pacific Citizen*. The war made the JACL the dominant Japanese American association.

Japanese American newspaper publishers struggled to reestablish themselves after being allowed to return to the West Coast in 1945. Finding space, Japanese fonts, and raising capital were Herculean endeavors. While most Americans advanced economically during the war, the forced evacuation bankrupted Japanese America. Publishers and subscribers alike had lost homes, farms and other investments. Some Issei editors and journalists, though, overcame these difficulties—like Shichinosuke Asano, who re-established the former *Nichibei* staff into the *Nichi Bei Times*. Asano used the paper to create a movement to send food to devastated Japan, and led the campaign for Japanese American civil rights. Although the *Nichi Bei Times* and a handful of other papers survived, countless others folded.

The combination of halted immigration, intermarriage, a low birthrate, and so few Nisei who read Japanese took a toll on the ethnic press.

The Asian American activist newspapers and magazines of the 1970s represent a more recent chapter of the Japanese American press history. Many of these newspapers were also short-lived, but contributed to the Pan Asian American ethnic media. Nisei and Sansei (third generation) students influenced by the civil rights movement helped create *Gidra* and other alternative presses to fight the power; such as establishing Asian American Studies programs on campuses, and resisting the gentrification of Los Angeles' Little Tokyo. In the early twenty-first century, the leading Japanese American ethnic newspaper was the *Pacific Citizen*, which came with JACL membership. Many once powerful presses had by then closed because of competition from other print and electronic media. The survivors either continued to provide news to ethnic Japanese or to postwar immigrants, residents, and tourists.

Further Reading

Ichioka, Yuji. *The Issei: The World of the First Generation Japanese Immigrants, 1885–1924*. New York: Free Press, 1988.

Mizuno, Takeya. "The Creation of the 'Free' Press in Japanese American Camps: The War Relocation Authority's Planning and Making of the Camp Newspaper Policy." *Journalism & Mass Communication Quarterly* 78 (2001): 503–518.

Stevens, John. "From Behind Barbed Wire: Freedom of the Press in World War II Japanese Centers." *Journalism Quarterly* 48 (1971): 279–287.

Yanagida, Chiyo. "The Nippu Jiji and the Japanese Language School Issue in Hawaii, 1919–1927." Unpublished MA thesis, University of Hawaii at Manoa, 1996.

Yoo, David. "'Read All About It': Race, Generation and the Japanese American Ethnic Press, 1925–41." *Amerasia Journal* 19 (1993): 69–92.

ANDREW B. WERTHEIMER

JEFFERSON, THOMAS

Thomas Jefferson (April 13, 1743–July 4, 1826) was one of America's most ardent defenders of press freedom as well as one of the nation's most trenchant critics of journalists. Imbued with strong Enlightenment sentiments about the press as the people's friend and the tyrant's foe, he nevertheless was a politician who was stung by criticism and personal attacks. Unlike Benjamin Franklin, James Madison, and Alexander Hamilton, Jefferson did not often write for newspapers himself. Like many prominent English politicians, he made arrangements with journalists to see that the day-to-day work of promoting his political objectives was done. He intervened only at critical points, as when he vehemently opposed the Sedition Act of 1798, a federal law that temporarily outlawed dissent.

Scientist and Sage

At a White House meeting for Nobel Prize winners in 1962, President John F. Kennedy famously quipped that the building had not before had such a gathering of human talent and knowledge except, perhaps, when Thomas Jefferson dined alone. Like Benjamin Franklin, the third president was not only a prominent proponent of democracy in the founding era, but also a voracious reader, an inventor, and an active participant in the growth of scholarly thought and investigation. Jefferson made contributions to philosophy, religion, music, literature, linguistics, architecture, mathematics, meteorology, medicine, paleontology, education, history, law, and government.

His life was also one of odd juxtapositions. The author of the Declaration of Independence, one of history's most renowned statements of human liberty and dignity, owned slaves and may have fathered children with one of them. While living beyond his means like an aristocrat, he championed the rights and judgment of the common citizen. An aesthetician, scholar, and diplomat, he could also be a political pugilist and revolutionary.

Historians who have attempted to understand Jefferson's mind have often turned to a dialogue between his head and his heart that he wrote in a long letter dated October 12, 1786. The head advises him to avoid pain by living a cautious, calculating life of isolation and intellectual pleasure. The heart, in accord with Scottish moral sense philosophy and French beliefs in guidance by *sensibilité*, contends that sublime delight can come from mingling tears with the unfortunate and sharing bread with the hungry. Nature, the heart says, placed the foundation of morals in sentiment rather than in uncertain reasoning. The heart, the apparent winner of the debate, observes that the American Revolution was successful by relying on what was right rather than on what seemed prudent.

Democratic Politician

Jefferson became a lawyer and was a Virginia legislator before the Revolutionary War. His brilliantly argued pamphlet *A Summary View of the Rights of British America* (1774) brought him to prominence in the patriot cause and his drafting of the Declaration of Independence and of republican legislation in Virginia and in Congress secured his reputation as a democratically minded leader. Serving in George Washington's cabinet as secretary of state, he clashed with Secretary of the Treasury Alexander Hamilton over economic priorities and international relations. Their partisans took their disagreements to the press and formed political parties in the 1790s. Hamilton's Federalists were generally pro-British and drew support from the wealthy and the commercial class. Jeffersonian Republicans were often pro-French and were identified with the interests of farmers and laborers. Seeing a need to gain journalistic backing, Jefferson courted a series of printers with government patronage and other inducements.

Jefferson assisted and defended two particularly bold newspaper editors that Washington and the Federalists thoroughly despised, Philip Freneau and Benjamin Franklin Bache. Jefferson and his political ally James Madison convinced Freneau to start a newspaper in Philadelphia,

then the location of the federal government, and solicited subscriptions. Freneau's *National Gazette*, which began publication in 1791, attacked England and its American admirers while praising revolutionary France. The paper published political essays by Madison and accused the Washington administration of having monarchical inclinations. Jefferson did not instruct Freneau on what to say, but did provide him with a job as translator in the State Department and told an irate president that all governments needed the criticism a free press could provide. The *National Gazette* had trouble with subscription payments, however, and ceased publication in 1793 when a yellow fever epidemic struck Philadelphia and Jefferson resigned his cabinet position.

Bache's Philadelphia *General Advertiser*, later renamed the *Aurora*, then became the leading voice of the Jeffersonians in the years before they took control of Congress and the executive branch in election of 1800. Jefferson had a working relationship with Bache, Franklin's grandson, even before the paper was founded in 1790. Bache was eager enough to convey Franklinian and Jeffersonian principles without patronage, but he struggled financially. While serving as vice president in the Adams administration, Jefferson consulted with Bache and worked to procure more subscriptions. His friendship with the often outspoken editor was a subject for derision in the Federalist press.

The Federalists enacted the Sedition Act of 1798 over Republican protests in order to silence Jeffersonian journalists such as Bache. A number of opposition party editors were jailed under the law's provisions prohibiting writings defaming the president (John Adams, a Federalist), the federal government, or either house of Congress (both of which were controlled by Federalists). The statute did not protect Jefferson, the Republican vice president. He denounced the Sedition Act as unconstitutional and went as far as drafting resolutions passed by the Kentucky legislature that said states could pass judgment on federal laws that used powers not delegated by the Constitution. The law expired by its own terms when Jefferson became president in 1801 and he issued pardons to journalists who had been subjected to its enforcement.

Jefferson was reviled by Federalist writers as an atheist with radical ideas and a slave harem. Reacting bitterly at times, he repeatedly insisted that the only exception to press freedom was that journalists could be brought to court for making false statements of fact that injured an individual's reputation. Often, however, he was simply content to celebrate journalism as a necessary means of public enlightenment. Many of his commentaries on the press were in correspondence, but in his inaugural addresses he set forth clearly the democratic theory that republics rest safely on unshackled contests of opinion.

Further Reading

Banning, Lance. *The Jeffersonian Persuasion: Evolution of a Party Ideology.* Ithaca, NY: Cornell University Press, 1978.

Cunningham, Noble E., Jr. *The Jeffersonian Republicans: The Formation of Party Organization.* Chapel Hill: University of North Carolina Press, 1957.

Mott, Frank Luther. *Jefferson and the Press.* Baton Rouge: Louisiana State University Press, 1943.

Smith, James M. *Freedom's Fetters: The Alien and Sedition Laws and American Civil Liberties.* Ithaca, NY: Cornell University Press, 1956.

Smith, Jeffery A. *Printers and Press Freedom: The Ideology of Early American Journalism.* New York: Oxford University Press, 1988.

Smith, Jeffery A. *Franklin and Bache: Envisioning the Enlightened Republic.* New York: Oxford University Press, 1990.

Wills, Garry. *Inventing America: Jefferson's Declaration of Independence.* Garden City, NY: Doubleday, 1978.

JEFFREY A. SMITH

JENNINGS, PETER

A Canadian-born high school drop out who spun records for the radio show "PJ the DJ" did not seem a likely American icon, but that is what Peter Jennings (July 29, 1938–August 7, 2005) became for a generation of viewers who watched his rise from boy anchor to trusted host of television's number one rated network newscast.

Peter's father Charles, a national correspondent for the Canadian Broadcasting Company, honed his son's natural curiosity and powers of observation by having him describe everything he saw in a summer sky. After the boy gave his report, his father asked him to look again, this time describing what he saw in eight equal quadrants of the sky. Whether reporting terrorist killings of Israeli athletes at the 1972 Olympics in Munich, or the space shuttle Challenger disaster in 1986, the fall of the Berlin Wall in 1989, ethnic cleansing in Bosnia, or the events of September 11, 2001, Peter Jennings used his carefully crafted skills of descriptive detail and analytical clarity to become one of the most trusted men in broadcast journalism.

"I always wanted to be in broadcasting," Jennings remembers. "If I hadn't succeeded, I couldn't have done anything else." His sister Sarah remembers Peter as "high spirited" and his parents Charles and Elizabeth having "high expectations" for the Toronto-born, Ottawa-raised Peter Charles Archibald Ewart Jennings. At nine, he hosted his own weekly radio music show for kids, *Peter's Program.* Soon he switched to television to host a teen music and dance show, *Saturday Date,* on CJOH in Ottawa. He began reporting for a small radio station in Brockville, Ontario. At twenty-four, Jennings had developed matinee idol looks and became the anchor for the evening news on CTV, Canada's first commercial television network. Elmer Lower and ABC News executives discovered Jennings in the summer of 1964 when he covered the Democratic National Convention in Los Angeles for CTV. Jennings covered the Republican National Convention that summer in San Francisco as a floor correspondent for ABC News.

ABC News had been a far distant third in the ratings war behind Walter Cronkite at CBS and Chet Huntley and David Brinkley at NBC. The network had had eleven anchors in the four years leading up to the surprise announcement on February 1, 1965, that the twenty-six-year-old Jennings was chosen to anchor the fifteen-minute nightly *Peter Jennings and the News.* Jennings was smooth, but somewhat shallow and admittedly "no Cronkite." In two years, ratings for the network's news program failed to rise appreciably in its target audience of young, urban viewers. Jennings was offered lucrative contracts to become an anchor at ABC stations in Chicago and Los Angeles, but decided "I needed more seasoning." In 1968 he became an ABC foreign correspondent, based in Beirut, Lebanon. It was the Middle East's first American television news bureau. While covering the Middle East, "I learned how to be a newsman," Jennings recalls. "I learned to be skeptical and find sources I could trust. I learned the importance of research and preparation." That preparation paid off in 1972 when Jennings, assigned to cover the Summer Olympics in Munich, reported the kidnapping and killing of eleven Israeli athletes by members of the Palestinian group "Black September." Roger Goodman, vice president of ABC News, thought the Munich coverage was "the beginning of Peter Jennings."

Jennings covered the Yom Kippur War in October 1973 and was criticized by some for being "pro-Palestinian" in the Arab-Israeli struggle. Jennings believed "American reporters are generally very misinformed about the Arab world and don't live in it." Jennings romance with Hanan Ashwari, a spokeswoman for the Palestine Liberation Organization, was duly noted by conservative critics. Jennings eventually married a Lebanese woman, one of four marriages. His 1974 profile of Anwar Sadat won a Peabody Award and helped establish ABC News as a hard-charging leader in international news. On July 10, 1978, Jennings, based in London, was one of three co-anchors named to *ABC World News Tonight.* Frank Reynolds was based in Washington and Max Robinson reported from Chicago. Jennings reputation as a first rate foreign correspondent grew later that year when he interviewed the Ayatollah Khomeini in Paris. On February 1, 1979, Jennings was on a plane accompanying Khomeini when the cleric returned to rule Iran. Later that year Jennings married Hungarian American author Kati Marton. They had two children, Elizabeth and Christopher.

When Frank Reynolds died in 1983, ABC News President Roone Arledge asked NBC's Tom Brokaw to anchor *World News Tonight.* Brokaw stayed to anchor the *NBC Nightly News. World News Tonight with Peter Jennings* was launched on August 9, 1983, and in the twenty-two years that followed, Jennings, Brokaw, and Dan Rather at CBS News became friendly rivals in the network news ratings. Two-thirds of all Americans watched a nightly network news show when the three anchors began their remarkable run. Jennings and ABC were a distant third when the competition began. By 1989 they were in first and Jennings was voted the nation's "most believable source of news." *World News Tonight* would remain the nation's most watched nightly news show for eight years with a peak of fourteen million viewers. Jennings, Rather, and Brokaw reported from the scene of major news stories such as the ending of the Cold War and the smashing of the Berlin Wall in 1989. "We all made each other better," Brokaw believed.

Jennings helped build a first rate staff of correspondents and news producers who shared his insatiable intellectual curiosity and his determination to "dig deeper," said Tom Jarriel, a forty-year veteran at the network. Correspondent Dean Reynolds thought Jennings "a bulwark against the dumbing down of the news." Jennings commitment to long form journalism led to the highly acclaimed documentary series *Peter Jennings Reporting* that focused on AIDs, the tobacco industry, cocaine trafficking in Bolivia, U.S. clandestine aid to Khymer Rouge rebels in Cambodia, genocide in Bosnia, the India-Pakistan nuclear standoff, and the search for the historical Jesus. Jennings was in the central market of Sarajevo on February 5, 1994, when a bombing killed sixty-eight. His dramatic and sustained coverage of the conflict would later prompt the Bill Clinton administration and the United Nations to impose a military force that ended the violence in Bosnia. Jennings twelve-part series on the American Century became a best-selling book. One hundred seventy million Americans tuned in to some portion of Jennings bravura twenty-five-hour performance on New Year's Eve in 1999 when he and ABC's worldwide reporting team welcomed the new millennium.

Jennings will be remembered for more than sixty hours of on air work in the immediate aftermath of the bombings at the World Trade Center on September 11, 2001, that included sixteen hours of continuous coverage on that day. New York Mayor Rudy Guiliani later spoke for many when he said, "Peter Jennings' compassion and eloquence helped many of us to soldier on." Afterward, Jennings explained that nearly forty years in broadcast journalism had helped prepare him for that day. "When everyone is getting worked up, it's my job to really focus, give good information, and sober, quiet perspective."

In 2003, Jennings became an American citizen. He liked carrying copies of the U.S. Constitution in his briefcase and back pocket. He was "fascinated by a country based on a document." His last major foreign assignment was in 2004 when he went to Iraq, came under fire in Mosul, attended the opening of the trial of Saddam Hussein for war crimes in Baghdad, and challenged American leaders on Iraq's prolonged and often violent transition to democracy. The anchor's uncharacteristic absence in the aftermath of a devastating Indian Ocean tsunami in December 2004 and the passing in Rome of Pope John Paul II, led to speculation Jennings might be ill. On April 5, 2005, he announced in a raspy voice on *World News Tonight* that after years of smoking he had been diagnosed with lung cancer. It would be his last broadcast. His passing four months later followed the November 2004 retirement of Brokaw and the March 2005 end of Rather's anchoring responsibilities. It was widely recognized as the end of an era in which three main over-the-air networks had dominated how Americans got their news.

Further Reading

Goldberg, Robert, and Gerald Jay Goldberg. *Anchors: Brokaw, Jennings, Rather, and the Evening News*. Seacaucus, NJ: Carol, 1990.

Jennings, Peter, and Todd Brewster. *The Century*, New York: Doubleday, 1998.

——. *In Search of America*. New York: Hyperion, 2002.

New York Times, August 8, 2005, A1 and B7.

Pratte, Paul Alfred. "Peter Jennings." In Michael D. Murray, ed., *Encyclopedia of Television News*, Phoenix: Oryx Press, 1999.

"State of the Art: TV & Radio News, An Interview with Peter Jennings." *Broadcasting & Cable*, September 27, 1993, 36–40.

BRUCE J. EVENSEN

JEWISH PRESS IN AMERICA

The birth of Jewish journalism in America centered on the theme of defense, reacting to external religious pressures. Under the impact of community growth, however, the press became a community builder, covering internal social values, general politics, and international affairs affecting Jews. The editors were concerned about their people's development, while preserving their heritage.

Early Publications

Many publications established in the 1820s came from the need to respond to the activities of others. The pioneer Jewish publications were *The Jew, The Occident and American Jewish Advocate, The Asmonean, The Israelite, The Jewish Messenger*, and the *Weekly Gleaner*—all antebellum publications. The history of American Jewry deals with the clash between accommodation to American life and the heritage, traditions, and customs of the Jewish historical experience, between those who sought assimilation of and those desiring pluralism in the American Jewish community. Jewish journalism of the antebellum period recounts the record of the struggles and challenges.

The first Jewish periodical in America began publication in March 1823 and ran until March 1825, as a response to Protestant evangelical efforts to convert Jews to Christianity. For some Christians, converting Jews was an evangelical commitment, and numerous associations, societies and organizations sprang up in the 1790s and the early 1800s, including the most active, the American Society for Meliorating the Condition of the Jew (ASMCJ). *Israel's Advocate*, the house publication of the ASMCJ, resulted in the first regularly issued American publication by and about Jews.

The Jew, Being a Defence [sic] of Judaism against all adversaries and particularly against the Insidious attacks of Israel's Advocate, as its full title suggests, devoted itself wholly to attacking the idea of Christian conversion, particularly urged by the ASMCJ. That association had some two-hundred branches from Maine to Georgia and affiliation with six other independent related societies.

Editor of *The Jew*, Solomon Henry Jackson, from London, settled in New York City in 1820, becoming the first Jewish printer in America. *The Jew* ran to twenty pages monthly, and Jackson bound the issues into one volume. Although Jackson was a printer by occupation, he lacked a cylinder press and possessed only a flat bed and Hebrew font type. Yet he contributed to the Jewish community by translating and publishing a Jewish prayer book, as well as the first American edition of the Passover *Haggadah*, or Order of the Service, both in Hebrew and English.

For Jackson, ever watchful of *Israel's Advocate,* the watchdog role was his primary purpose; indeed, other minority presses served the same role. Essentially, *The Jew* covered three subject areas: theological discussions disproving Christianity; an out-and-out attack on the ASMCJ, its motives and methods; and a defense of Judaism and Jews from misinformation created by innuendo or direct statement. By far the greatest amount of space was devoted to the first. Moreover, Jackson completely ignored news of the world as well as news within the Jewish community. For example, information about the Monroe Doctrine, promulgated in 1823, appeared nowhere; nor did news in 1824 of Jewish expulsions from Russian villages.

Furthermore, in terms reminiscent of the first issue of *Freedom's Journal*, the first black newspaper in America, but predating its appearance by four years, Jackson defended his right to respond to attacks as the first law of nature that is inherent in man. Jackson claimed the right to be himself, the right to be different, to perceive his Jewish difference as no less real, worthy, and honorable than any other "difference." Indeed, preserving differences constituted true equality set forth in the Declaration of Independence. Therefore, in the American tradition, retention of distinctive cultures and religions needed to be encouraged.

Jackson ceased publication of the periodical at the end of the second volume. Missionaries ignored him and his publication, and would not react to the feisty Jewish editor. *The Jew* also may have folded for lack of support, because it carried no advertising nor did any society or organization subsidize it. Moreover, the 1825 Postal Act raised rates on any periodical the Postal Service determined to be a magazine, and conceivably they designated it so. Yet, it remains unclear if Jackson produced a publication one might call a newspaper or magazine, because it did not fit either category.

The merit and significance of *The Jew* is that it showed that a Jew with courage could speak, not merely to defend but also to attack strongly those who desired to convert Jews, and as a result threaten the well-being of the Jewish community. Undoubtedly, the publication served as an example to others who followed in the Jewish press.

The second publication for the American Jewish community was *The Occident and American Jewish Advocate.* It enumerated and described Jewish settlements, discussed and debated the quality of Jewish life, and continually defined and encountered the major problems facing the Jewish community in the New World, running 1843 through 1869. The number of Jews in America grew rapidly during this period, from fewer than three thousand (out of a population of more than nine million) in 1820, to forty thousand by 1845, to one hundred-fifty thousand in 1860. Editor Isaac Leeser had emigrated from Central Europe to Richmond, Virginia, and became lay reader or leader of services of a Philadelphia congregation, one of a dozen but all lacking an ordained rabbi. For the first time in their history, Jews could select which ideas and ideals to live by with no one forcing them to do anything. They could commit themselves anew to their Jewish faith, or become Christians, or become secular persons. Therefore, individuals could choose among a variety of identities.

Nevertheless, in 1840, events launched Leeser to national stature, when the Jews of Damascus faced the accusation of ritual murder, resulting in the imprisonment and subsequent torture deaths of many Jews. In the United States, Leeser, to his credit, mobilized others and pushed U.S. President Martin Van Buren to act. That effort showcased what strength the Jewish community had when it came together, so he decided to publish a magazine, modeled after those in Europe, especially *Der Orient*, a Leipzig-based publication.

The Occident became the first instrument to instill a sense of national belonging to broadly dispersed American Jews. News of America's Jewish communities dominated this content. Editorially, Leeser advocated and instructed, implored and demanded. He advocated alterations to the American Jewish community, projecting his plans to institutionalize the Jewish community on a national level. He prescribed new communal institutions as the best defense against missionaries, to guard the vulnerable and the ignorant, while educating for Jewish knowledge and pride. *The Occident* became an effective vehicle to defend American Jews. Leeser waged a fight against Sunday "blue" laws for years. When American Jews were required to observe Sunday closings, they were renouncing traditional Jewish practices such as breaking the Jewish Sabbath to observe the Christian. Leeser argued that such laws violated the Bill of Rights with its freedom of religion clause. He also objected to efforts in some states to connect such holidays as Thanksgiving only to Christianity, and denounced the anti-Semitism of the Know Nothing Party in California.

A nearly four-fold increase in the Jewish population between 1830 and 1840 brought new challenges as Jews began to accommodate themselves to living in America and being Americans. As Jewish immigrants sought to blend in with American life, they wanted more respectable, disciplined, shorter services, in English as well as Hebrew; weekly sermons (on the Protestant model), and a dues structure for all members of their religious congregations. Agitation for reform soon grew into an organized movement to revolt against the unquestioning authority of the past, discarding sacred precepts and basic practices of traditional Judaism, such as Sabbath observance, dietary laws, intermarriage, the belief in a personal messiah, and close identification with other Jews. Leeser realized that such reforms hopelessly divided American Jews.

The Occident also reported on international issues. When the United States negotiated a treaty with Switzerland in the mid-1850s, Leeser campaigned to protect the Jews of Switzerland, who faced discrimination in business. This cause propelled a delegation to call on President James Buchanan. Also, in 1858, a seven-year-old Jewish-Italian child, secretly baptized as a Roman Catholic by his Catholic maid, was abducted from his parents. Despite protests and petitions to both President Buchanan and his Secretary of State, all efforts failed, and the child remained estranged from his biological parents and his faith.

Such concerns resulted in something Leeser had long sought to create: the Board of Delegates of American Israelites, in 1859, the first real national organization of Jews, with delegates from twenty-nine synagogues in thirteen cities. This organization successfully fought the Presbyterian Church's proposal to make Christianity the official American religion, and served the original purpose of issuing formal statements protesting anti-Semitism whether in America or anywhere in the world. Jews inside and outside the United States relied on Leeser's *Occident* to bring them news of Jewish concerns, to prepare the framework for a variety of new institutions, to help preserve a separate identity for American Jews. Leeser's *The Occident*, usually a forty-eight- to sixty-page effort, bound in leather-clad volumes, was a significant magazine at a crucial time in the development of American Jewry and served the community as a major vehicle to propose, to ensure, and then to watch the growth of community institutions.

Because the Jewish community increased substantially during the 1840s, as whole families, rather than isolated individuals, began to arrive in America from Central and Eastern Europe, it was the time when the contemporary American Jewish scene emerged and found its shape and direction. Two publications, weeklies, established in 1849, addressed Jewish New Yorkers, who comprised the leading community. The German-language *Israels Herold*, [*sic*] lasted but three months. The second, in English, was *The Asmonean*, edited and published by Londoner Robert Lyon, who, in 1844, emigrated to New York. Intended for the Jewish population of New York City, it circulated throughout the country. The first issue of *The Asmonean* appeared on October 19, 1849, and every Friday thereafter for almost ten years. The design on the first issues borrowed heavily from the *Irish-American*. While comprehensive Jewish communal and foreign news was probably the main drawing card of *The Asmonean*, Lyon also printed editorial material of a non-Jewish nature, often taken from other domestic and foreign sources. For example, politics occupied a significant place, perhaps because of periodic advertisements from Tammany Hall and the City of New York—including city ordinances. *The Asmonean* was unashamedly biased towards the Democrats. Lyon reported on city elections. He facilitated the workings of a democratic government in the same way that a regular city paper did. Active civically and politically, Lyon was assistant city inspector and served as vice president of the Hebrew Benevolent Society.

Advertising amounted to half of Lyon's twelve-page paper. Regularly Lyon bragged of two hundred thousand subscribers and circulation in every state, north and south. He issued one supplement in German but dropped it almost at once; however, advertisements printed in German appeared frequently. From the beginning, Lyon used his paper to defend and unite, continually and forcefully. *The Asmonean* was always on guard to vindicate the honor of Jews. When New York's general newspapers identified Jews in crime stories, Lyon often questioned the veracity of those accounts. He also editorially opposed the new Maryland constitution requiring a person to "profess Christianity" to hold office. Lyon long advocated a statistical census of Jews in the United States.

The Asmonean reached out to Jewish readers who were facing pressure to assimilate rapidly. Lyon showed what it meant to create and maintain a proper home for Jews living in America. He carried articles about business, the theater, literature, and politics. He developed an excellent financial section, perhaps modeled on the "money page" of James Gordon Bennett's *Herald*. The general physical appearance of papers born after *The Asmonean* indicated the enormous influence of Lyon's paper. Lyon made a living by purveying news. He sought to make Jewish readers more American by acquiring knowledge about the country they now lived in and how it operated. When he suffered a stroke and died in 1858, his publication died with him.

Three other Jewish newspapers were founded before the Civil War, *The Israelite* in Cincinnati, the *Jewish Messenger* in New York, and the *Weekly Gleaner* in San Francisco. These newspapers, like those that preceded them, served diverse communities and became an intercommunal form of communication before the Civil War. They did their part to strengthen identity, defend against outside forces, and assist in accommodating to life in America while discussing the burning issues of the day.

The Civil War saw challenges to Jews in America. Coverage began early, with talk by leaders about the "injurious effects" of the "threatened disruption." Editors spoke of concern about treatment of troops in the Union and Confederate armies. Both had Jewish enlistees, and Jews who rose to higher ranks. While the Jewish press bragged about the spirit and discipline of American armies, latent bigotry appeared, for example, when ex-Senator of Louisiana Judah Benjamin became Minister of War and then Secretary of State of the Confederacy. In addition, one Jewish editor, also a rabbi, fled Baltimore, under threat of a Secessionist mob. Strongly opposed to slavery and defender of the Union, he journeyed to Pennsylvania and took a pulpit in Philadelphia.

Then too, Jews were excluded from the office of Chaplain in both armies; Jews took it as acts of injustice and intolerance. When General Ulysses S. Grant banished Jews from an area encompassing western Tennessee, northern Mississippi, Alabama, and Kentucky, Jewish newspapers editors met with President Abraham Lincoln, who reversed the order. Two other Union generals tried to expel Jews from their various businesses as well as from the army.

Essentially, life remained unchanged for most Jews throughout the Civil War. They created communities, consecrated synagogues, and maintained various organizations and institutions. Other articles spoke of Jewish soldiers, how they distinguished themselves, and about Jewish support for the war—everything from clothing drives to donated funds. At war's end, Jews numbered two hundred thousand in America.

Yiddish Press

The Yiddish-language press began in the 1870s and grew with the increasing population between 1880–1925, when 2.5-million Jews migrated from Eastern Europe to the United States. Poor and persecuted, they left for the freedom and possibilities of America. Unprepared, they needed guidance, and Yiddish newspapers became their teachers. Yiddish, a fusion language like English, combines Medieval German, Hebrew, Slavic, and romance languages using a modified Hebrew alphabet. Some Yiddish papers used an Americanized or Potato Yiddish, trying to reach people using the Yiddish they spoke. Some who were proponents of the Socialist Labor Party started the Workingmen's Party in the 1870s.

The *Jewish Daily Forward*, the largest, most influential, Yiddish-language daily in the world, began in April 1897 in New York. To get the paper published, workers gave a day's pay! Cloak makers, cigar makers, and tailors—ready to give their last cents— created what became the official organ of the Socialist Labor Party. Among the paper's calls for labor union meetings and messages about organizing, were also dramatic stories and rank sensationalism. In the 1930s, the *Forward* boasted a circulation of 275,000, bigger than many other mainstream dailies. Its message was that immigrants and their children could become Americans, and the paper would show them how. Editor Abraham Cahan emigrated from a village near Vilna [now Vilnius], Lithuania. He believed in Marxism and social democracy, and joined the Socialist Labor Party, feeling elated by being in America. He edited the Yiddish paper for half a century. The *Forward* was eight pages and carried more than mere manifestos; it was alive with arguments. Cahan urged readers to organize a union, join it and get others to do so too. Then, the *Forward* urged people to strike. It editorialized for better homes, apartments with fresh air, improved education for children, and elimination of dangerous tenements. The paper explained how to function in America and participate in a democracy.

For the most part, Yiddish papers were papers of transition and assimilation. When *The Forward* began a page in English, for example, one of the first writers for it was British philosopher Bertrand Russell. In addition, it ran an art section, and a theatre page about the rapidly growing Yiddish theater.

Almost all Yiddish newspapers in America died, in part because the immigration laws of the 1920s closed the gates to America, and with World War II, large numbers of Yiddish-speaking Jews in Eastern Europe were killed. In the early 1940s, the Yiddish press became aware of the Holocaust as whole communities disappeared. Also, the big story in January 1949, reported that the Soviet Union liqui-

dation of leaders of the Jewish community along with the closing of Jewish institutions. When twenty-four Yiddish intellectuals were executed, many Yiddish papers ran their pictures. Yet the Yiddish press initially was sometimes for, sometimes against Israel. Editor Cahan visited Israel and his socialist enthusiasm for the farmers led to his support of Zionism.

The Forward became a weekly in 1983, but launched an English-language supplement. In 1990, an English-language *Forward* began, with a separate staff. Jewish newspapers in the new millennium were either independently owned or sponsored by a federation or council of Jewish organizations in an American community. Of great benefit to the Jewish press was the Jewish Telegraphic Agency, begun during World War I, resembling the Associated Press and based in New York. Also, in 1944, the American Jewish Press Association began for English-language Jewish publications in the United States and Canada. In 2007, it represented about 250 entities.

Further Reading

Berlin, George L. "Solomon Jackson's *The Jew:* An Early American Jewish Response to the Missionaries." *American Jewish History.* 71 (September 1981):100–28.

Englander, Henry. "Isaac Leeser." *Yearbook, Central Conference of American Rabbis,* 28 (1918): 213–52.

Grinstein, Hyman B. *The Rise of the Jewish Community in New York: 1654-1860.* Philadelphia: The Jewish Publication Society of America,1945.

Metzker, Isaac. *The Bintel Brief: Sixty Years of Letters from the Lower East Side to the Jewish Daily Forward.* New York: Schocken Books, 1990.

Sarna, Jonathan. *American Judaism, a History.* New Haven, CT: Yale University, 2004.

Soltes, Mordecai. *The Yiddish Press, An Americanizing Agency.* New York: Columbia University, 1925.

Sussman, Lance J. *Isaac Leeser and the Making of American Judaism* (American Jewish Civilization Series).Detroit, MI: Wayne State University Press, 1996.http://www.forward. com/about/history/History (accessed April 9, 2007).

BARBARA STRAUS REED

JOHNSON, LYNDON AND THE MEDIA

Soon after Lyndon Baines Johnson became president, he approached the press pool on the plane flying from his Texas ranch to the nation's capitol. We all succeed or fail together, he told them; give me favorable news coverage, and I'll make you big men in your field. This anecdote represents each side's fundamentally different views of the role of the press in American politics. For Johnson the politician, the offer embodied both the exchange principles on which he had built his career and his belief that news should provide favorable coverage of the government. For members of the media, the offer constituted a bribe.

Johnson had moved onto the national political scene in the 1940s, seeing reporters as instruments to be used to accomplish his ends in certain circumstances and as potential threats to be avoided in others. As a member of

Congress, even as Senate Majority Leader, Johnson maintained a chummy control in his relationship with journalists, attracting attention when he found it advantageous and otherwise avoiding it: in almost all cases, Capitol Hill reporters had a multitude of other sources and stories to pursue.

In November of 1963, John F. Kennedy's assassination catapulted Vice President Lyndon Johnson into the presidency, and the situation changed. The White House tops the news agenda; Johnson could not avoid the spotlight, and collaborations gave way to competitiveness. Moreover, Johnson suffered in comparison to his young, sophisticated, media-savvy predecessor, whose understanding of reporters' self-conceptions as "watchdogs" enabled JFK to maneuver for more positive coverage.

Although initial media coverage lauded Johnson for soothing the jangled nerves of a nation, irritants quickly developed. Members of the White House press corps in particular felt manipulated by Johnson's hinting that his 1964 budget would be a record-breaking $100 billion, maybe even $103 billion, only to unveil a $97 billion budget that was lower than even John F. Kennedy's last budget. They resented breaking news of prospective nominations based on solid leads, only to have Johnson deny that he had even seriously considered those individuals and then name someone else to those posts in what journalists saw as retribution. They chafed at his denials of fast driving and raunchy talking, even though reporters had accompanied him on the careening trips across his Texas ranch. They derided his enthusiastic remarks to American troops claiming a great-grandfather at the Alamo, who turned out to be a great-uncle at the battle of San Jacinto. They disliked his restless experimentation with press conference formats, from jaunts around the White House lawn to barbeques at the ranch. And they particularly resented the last-minute announcements of travel plans (e.g., to his ranch), which disrupted not only their professional routines but also their personal lives. For his part, Johnson could not understand why journalists could not appreciate his efforts to enliven the news process, keep a promised confidence, entertain them as guests rather than reporters, and comprehend that his responsibilities as president constrained advance planning of personal travel. He saw many members of the press corps as arrogant, insensitive easterners who could not understand the burdens of being president. By mid-1965, then, the relationship between Lyndon Johnson and the press exhibited a fair amount of acrimony.

During this early period of Johnson's presidency, Vietnam lurked in the borders of both political and news agendas. Johnson preferred to focus on his visionary Great Society agenda, an ambitious set of domestic programs tackling poverty, disease, bigotry, and ignorance. As conditions worsened in Vietnam, Johnson's deep-seated antipathy toward Communist Chinese aggression led to a quiet redefinition of the role of American troops from advisory to combat, and a gradual increase in their numbers. Johnson rejected aides' proposals for major campaigns to explain these steps, hoping instead to gain public support without

being "too provocative and warlike" (Johnson, *Vantage Point*, 149).

For its part, the mainstream news media initially seemed essentially disinterested in the story of Southeast Asia. Journalists confronted the difficulties of covering a guerrilla war, without clear-cut enemies and front lines, in a country whose language, culture, politics, history, and social upheaval were literally foreign, for an audience at home whom media institutions perceived to be largely uninterested in the subject. With expanded American military involvement came expanded American media coverage. Rising casualty rates, lack of apparent progress, and growing disaffection among journalists gradually transformed this coverage from largely supportive of the administration's policies to increasingly critical—both for doing too much, and for not doing enough in Vietnam.

Moreover, "journalists" now included representatives not only of print media, but also of television. In 1963, NBC and CBS expanded their newscasts from primitive, under-funded, fifteen-minute affairs to more sophisticated, half-hour broadcasts positioned as lead-ins to the prime-time schedule. The growth in both news-gathering budgets and the need for news made Vietnam the first television war. Although photographers consigned much of the footage to a category they wryly called "the wily VC [Viet Cong] got away again," some coverage shocked the nation, as when CBS showed Marines setting a Vietnamese village aflame with cigarette lighters (Halberstam, *Best and Brightest*, 787). When Senator J. William Fulbright opened hearings on the administration's Vietnam policy in January of 1966, television cameras publicized and legitimized the growing dissent.

Burgeoning dissatisfaction among politicians, the public, and press found voice in the expression "credibility gap," encapsulating the distrust of official optimism. The administration's repeated proclamations of progress and predictions of success slammed into a wall of contradictions with the Tet offensive of early 1968. The well-coordinated attacks included an assault on the American embassy in Saigon, and media reports conveyed shock and dismay. Although subsequent events revealed it to be a military victory for the United States, Tet clearly constituted a psychological defeat. Veteran anchor Walter Cronkite would return from Vietnam to declare on air that the war was "mired in stalemate," a pronouncement that stunned the White House. Little more than a month later, Johnson announced that he would not run for re-election.

From Johnson's perspective, he had to fight battles both at home and abroad, and the press bore responsibility for the unsuccessful wager of each. To his dying day, Lyndon Johnson could not "forgive them their press passes" (Carpenter, *Ruffles and Flourishes*, 98).

Further Reading

Liz Carpenter, Liz. *Ruffles and Flourishes*. New York: Doubleday, 1970.

Halberstam, David. *The Best and the Brightest*. Greenwich, CT: Fawcett Publications, 1969.

Johnson, Lyndon B. *The Vantage Point: Perspectives of the Presidency, 1963–69*. New York: Holt, Rinehart, and Winston, 1971.

Landers, James. *The Weekly War: Newsmagazines and Vietnam*. Columbia: University of Missouri Press, 2004.

Turner, Kathleen J. *Lyndon Johnson's Dual War: Vietnam and the Press*. Chicago: University of Chicago Press, 1985.

"Who, What, When, Where, Why: Report from Vietnam by Walter Cronkite." In *The Big Story: How the American Press and Television Reported and Interpreted the Crisis of Tet 1968 in Vietnam and Washington*, edited by Peter Braestrup, 180–89. Boulder, CO: Westview Press, 1977.

Wyatt, Clarence R. *Paper Soldiers: The American Press and the Vietnam War*. Chicago: University of Chicago Press, 1993.

Zarefsky, David. *President Johnson's War on Poverty: Rhetoric and History*. Tuscaloosa: University of Alabama Press, 1986.

KATHLEEN J. TURNER

JOURNAL OF OCCURRENCES

The *Journal of Occurrences* (September 28, 1768–August 1, 1769) was the first news distribution service in the history of American journalism. The *Journal* originated in Boston. The series contained detailed reports of British tyrannical actions and atrocities committed primarily by the troops stationed in Boston. *Journal* articles were written in the form of a diary of events (many imaginary or embellished), but they also contained numerous editorial comments. The authors clearly intended the "Journal of Occurrences" to function as propaganda designed to agitate the Americans against the British.

The *Journal of Occurrences* first appeared in John Holt's *New York Journal* beginning on October 13, 1768. Newspapers from Salem, Massachusetts, to Savannah, Georgia, including the *Boston Evening Post*, reprinted the articles after they appeared in the *Journal*. The authors apparently sent the pieces to Holt to be published in order to preserve their anonymity and to be sure the articles continued to appear. Royal officials, particularly Governor Francis Bernard of Massachusetts, fretted over the impact of the *Journal* and would have arrested the authors if they could have determined who they were.

The focus of the articles was always Boston and Massachusetts, primarily because the main target was the British troops stationed there after September 1768. The diary began on September 28, 1768, the day the troops arrived in Boston, and ended on August 1, 1769. Most of the diary entries dealt with reports of soldiers mistreating the citizens of Boston. For example, the October 13, 1768, issue of the *New York Journal* reported the following: "A Physician of the Town walking the Streets the other evening was jostled by an Officer, when a Scuffle ensued, he was afterwards met by the same Officer in Company with another, both as yet unknown, who repeated his Blows, and as is supposed gave him a Stroke with a Pistol, which so wounded him as to endanger his life." Other reports declared that women were no longer safe and were treated rudely by the soldiers on a regular basis. Overall, the reports chronicled everything from indignities and insults to assaults and attempted rapes in an effort to show how badly the occupying military force was treating the people.

Historians have never identified the authors of the *Journal of Occurrences*. Bernard and other Boston royal officials clearly believed that Samuel Adams and his supporters produced the diary entries. Other possible authors suggested by historians include William Cooper, Boston town clerk; Henry Knox, owner of a Boston bookstore; Benjamin Edes, co-printer of the *Boston Gazette* with John Gill; William Greenleaf, an employee in the print shop of Edes and Gill; Isaiah Thomas, a Boston printer; or Samuel Adams's cousin John. Because the discussion ranged over a variety of topics, the *Journal* probably had multiple authors. Ultimately, the name of the author or authors is less important than the impact of the day-to-day reports of British tyranny and inhumanity. The *Journal of Occurrences* helped set a context in which many Americans believed that the British could not be trusted, a feeling that the Boston Massacre of 1770 reinforced. This change in outlook created by the press was necessary as a basis for the fight for independence that officially began in 1775.

Further Reading

Davidson, Philip. *Propaganda and the American Revolution, 1763–1783*. Chapel Hill: University of North Carolina Press, 1941.

Dickerson, Oliver M. *Boston Under Military Rule (1768–1769) as Revealed in a Journal of the Times*. Boston: Chapman & Grimes, 1936.

Schlesinger, Arthur M. *Prelude to Independence: The Newspaper War on Britain, 1764–1776*. New York: Random House, 1957.

Sloan, Wm. David, and Julie Hedgepeth Williams. *The Early American Press, 1690–1783*. Westport, CT: Greenwood Press, 1994.

CAROL SUE HUMPHREY

KALTENBORN, HANS V.

When President Truman scored his upset victory over Republican challenger Thomas E. Dewey, he mocked the election night certainty of the nation's best-known radio commentator that Dewey would win. "While the President is a million votes ahead in the popular vote," Truman said, imitating the clipped phrases and cultivated tone of radio's best known voice, "we are very sure that when the country vote comes in, Mr. Truman will be defeated by an overwhelming majority."

Truman's humor was not lost on a nation that knew the voice of Hans V. Kaltenborn (July 9, 1878–June 14, 1965) when they heard it. For thirty-six years, this son of a German baron elegantly combined news and analysis in reporting war, peace, and politics during the earliest days of radio's history. Betty Wessels, mother of the Milwaukee-born Kaltenborn, died in childbirth, and he was raised by his father, Rudolph von Kaltenborn who ran a building supply company while struggling with alcoholism. Young Kaltenborn enlisted in the Fourth Wisconsin Volunteers when he was nineteen, hoping to fight in the Spanish-American War, but got no further than Alabama, where he reported in English and German on army life for Wisconsin's *Merrill Advocate*. After the war he served for a year as the paper's city editor. He became the paper's "foreign correspondent" in 1900, bicycling his way across England, France, and Germany, filing stories for a dollar a piece, hoping to get noticed and "make good" (*Fifty Fabulous Years*, 12).

In 1902 Kaltenborn returned to the United States, beginning a twenty-eight-year relationship with the *Brooklyn Eagle*, interrupted between 1905 and 1909 when he took a degree in political science from Harvard. He worked his way up from night and city hall reporter to associate editor and editorial writer. He married Baroness Olga von Nordenflycht, the daughter of a German diplomat in 1910, and liked giving lectures on foreign policy. On April 4, 1922, he broadcast what he later claimed was radio's first editorial over an Army Signal Corps station in New York City. He liked reading his columns over the air on WYCB and by 1924 was a regular commentator on WEAF.

In 1926 and 1927 Kaltenborn toured the Far East and visited the Soviet Union. His growing reputation helped him resign from the *Eagle* in 1930 and become a news editor for the Columbia Broadcasting System, where he saw his commentaries as the work of a "contemporary historian"

(*Europe Now*, xi) whose reporting represented "first drafts of history" (*Kaltenborn Edits the War News*, 2). In 1933 he broadcast from the London Economic Conference and in 1936 he reported on the Spanish Civil War and the Battle of Irun from Hendaye. Interviews with Adolf Hitler and Benito Mussolini, Edouard Daladier, and Neville Chamberlain were followed by 102 broadcasts made over 20 days at the height of the Munich crisis in September 1938 that would lead to the dismemberment of Czechoslovakia and a temporary "false peace" for Europe. Kaltenborn's instantaneous translation of German and French communiqués, received over shortwave, combined with his unscripted, round-the-clock summaries, running from two minutes to two hours, described a world nearing war and saw him at the peak of his powers.

In the spring of 1940 Kaltenborn signed a lucrative contract with the National Broadcasting Company, reporting the war from Britain, Italy, France, Germany, and the South Pacific. His weekly newsreels on the war helped him "guide public opinion"; more than one million theater goers wrote to Kaltenborn asking for his views (Kaltenborn Papers. Box 181). Kaltenborn's purpose in helping to organize the Association of Radio News Analysts was to help broadcast journalism serve as an instrument of informed consent at a time in which world events required American leadership. In the post-war period, Kaltenborn continued to liken a journalist's job with "the duty of public service" (Kaltenborn Papers. Box 1), but his opinionated pieces advocating internationalism seemed increasingly out of favor in the Cold War atmosphere of McCarthyism. Kaltenborn had hoped to repeat his radio success on television but in September 1955, he was forced to retire from NBC. He returned for election night coverage and a brief stint as temporary host of the "Today Show" in 1958.

Critics often carped that Kaltenborn's capacities as a self-promoter and unflagging confidence over the air bordered on arrogance, but historians have generally seen him as an important, leading pioneer in the development of broadcast news and commentary.

Further Reading

Barnouw, Erik. *The Golden Web: A History of Broadcasting in the United States, 1930–1953*. New York: Oxford University Press, 1968.

Bliss, Jr., Edward. *Now the News: The History of Broadcast Journalism*. New York: Columbia University Press, 1991.

Culbert, David Holbrook. *News for Everyman: Radio and Foreign Affairs in Thirties America*. Westport, CT: Greenwood Press, 1976.

Fang, Irving B. *Those Radio Commentators!* Ames: Iowa State University Press, 1977.

Kaltenborn, Hans V. *Europe Now: A First Hand Report*. New York: Didier, 1945.

——. *Fifty Fabulous Years*. New York: Putnam, 1950.

——. *I Broadcast the Crisis*. New York: Random House, 1938.

——. *It Seems Like Yesterday*. New York: Putnam, 1956.

——. *Kaltenborn Edits the War News*. New York: Dunton, 1942.

——. *Kaltenborn Edits the News*. New York: Modern Age Books, 1937.

——. *We Look at the World*. New York: Rae D. Henkle, 1930.

NBC Papers contain many of Kaltenborn's radio and television scripts. Wisconsin State Historical Society. Madison, Wisconsin.

Papers of Hans V. Kaltenborn. Wisconsin State Historical Society. Madison, Wisconsin.

BRUCE J. EVENSEN

KANSAS CITY STAR

On September 18, 1880, the *Kansas City Evening Star* published its first issue. Two newsmen from Indiana, William Rockhill Nelson and Samual Morss came to Kansas City seeking their fortune in a cattle and railroad town on the verge of explosive growth. The *Evening Star* and the city grew together.

Initially, the paper faced competition from three other dailies, but Nelson smartly undercut the competition by charging 2 cents a copy instead of the standard nickel. News coverage was unique. Where other papers focused on national events, the *Star* sought news in local affairs and became a beacon of civic reform. Within a year Morss left town, and Nelson, with his larger than life ideas and ego, set his sights on publishing a "Paper for the People" of Kansas City. As its journalistic reputation grew, it dominated regional politics. In 1901, Nelson bought a morning paper called the *Kansas City Times* and the two papers remained until 1990, when they were combined into one daily called the *Star*.

When Nelson died in 1915, circulation was more than two hundred thousand and growing. In the 1920s, the paper bought its first radio station, published its first comic strip, and ran its first photograph. During the 1930s, Kansas City became a haven for jazz, booze and political corruption. Tom "Boss" Pendergast dominated city news until 1939 when he was convicted of income tax evasion, thus ending the "machine" era.

During World War II, women began to take their places in the newsroom. After the war, circulation and profits soared. Roy Roberts emerged as the new *Star* president and his political power reached national levels. He challenged tax and labor relations laws, infused eight million dollars into a new plant, and purchased Kansas City's first television station. In 1951, the paper won a special Pulitzer citation for covering the 1951 flood. Roberts, a diehard Republican, had a running battle with President Harry S. Truman, who as a young man had worked briefly in the paper's mailroom. Toward the end of the Truman presidency, the *Star* was indicted and found guilty of coercive and monopolistic advertising practices. It was forced to sell both its radio and television stations, and abandon combination advertising and subscription rates. Roberts called it a Truman "inquisition."

The first minorities were hired in the 1960s and charged with writing positive stories about the black community. During the 1970s, the *Star* experienced financial difficulties, but new ownership ignited change, experimentation and expansion with zoned news, sports and business coverage. Capital Cities purchased the newspaper in 1977. The Walt Disney Company briefly owned the paper in 1996 before selling it to Knight Ridder in 1997.

The *Star* launched Project Warmth in the 1980s and since has collected millions of dollars in contributions and winter clothes. The 1990s brought new technology culminating in the *Star* creating an Internet presence at KansasCity.com. A new state of the art printing and distribution plant, located near the *Star's* downtown location, opened in 2006.

During its 125-year history, the *Star* won seven Pulitzer Prizes. It changed ownership five times, purchased in 2006 by McClatchy Company. In its succession of high-profile publishers and editors, the *Star* attempted to retain the goal of its founder: as Kansas City goes, so goes the *Star*.

Further Reading

Palmer, T. C. *Bosses of the News Room: The 10 Men who have directed the News Department of the Kansas City Star and Times since employees acquired the newspapers from the estate of William Rockhill Nelson*. Kansas City: *Kansas City Star*, 2002.

Tully, M. *The Kansas City Star: 125 Years* (Special Section), September 18, 2005.

CAROL KOEHLER

KENDALL, AMOS

Amos Kendall (August 16, 1789–November 12, 1869) was one of the preeminent political journalists of the Jacksonian period, the postmaster general during the controversy over the circulation of abolitionist literature, and an early promoter of telegraphy as an important news-gathering tool.

Kendall was born on August 16, 1789, in Dunstable, Massachusetts, the son of Molly (Dakin) and Zebedee Kendall. He spent his early years in New England, working on the family farm, teaching school, and attending Dartmouth College. During a visit to Washington, D.C., in 1814, Kendall learned of job opportunities in Kentucky. Shortly after arriving in Lexington, he became a tutor in the household of Congressman Henry Clay. Kendall found teaching unfulfilling and spent the next two years mixing work in journalism, politics, and the law.

In 1816, Kendall became co-owner and editor of the *Argus of Western America*. Published in Kentucky's state capital, the *Argus* first championed Henry Clay but shifted allegiance to Andrew Jackson before the 1828 presidential campaign. Because of the journalistic assistance rendered by Kendall, the newly elected President Jackson invited him to become a Treasury Department auditor.

While filling this official post, Kendall joined Jackson's Kitchen Cabinet, an inner circle of presidential advisers, as the administration's chief political communicator. Kendall took the president's rough-hewn ideas and fashioned them into official messages and newspapers articles. When the *Washington Globe* became the administration's new organ in 1830, Kendall arranged for his assistant editor on the *Argus,* Francis Preston Blair, to come to Washington as its editor. Many of Jackson's ideas were funneled through Kendall for publication in the *Globe.*

Jackson appointed Kendall postmaster general in 1835 to manage that troubled agency. As head of the Post Office, Kendall confronted one of the antebellum period's most serious controversies involving press freedom—what to do about abolitionist literature in the mail. Kendall acknowledged that postal authorities had no legal basis for interfering with the abolitionists' mail, but he nonetheless advised that Southern postmasters could refuse to deliver the supposedly provocative publications.

Kendall also used postal operations to strengthen the position of Western newspapers in competition with their Eastern counterparts. For instance, in 1836, he launched postal expresses on major routes partly to rush news to editors on the frontier so they could publish it for their readers before newspapers from eastern cities reached the West.

Serving as postmaster general through the administration of Martin Van Buren, Kendall left public office to pursue personal interests and to attend to his family. In the early 1840s, he published two short-lived Washington newspapers. In 1845, Samuel F. B. Morse, inventor of the telegraph, enlisted Kendall to promote his new technology. As he labored to bring order to the new telegraph industry, Kendall grew concerned about the prospect of the New York Associated Press monopolizing the distribution of the nation's news.

The Civil War prompted Kendall's last foray into political journalism. Between 1860 and 1868, he wrote articles criticizing both the secessionist tendencies in the South and the centralizing tendencies in the North. Kendall died in Washington, D.C., in 1869.

Further Reading

Cole, Donald B. *A Jackson Man: Amos Kendall and the Rise of American Democracy.* Baton Rouge: Louisiana State University Press, 2004.

John, Richard R. *Spreading the News: The American Postal System from Franklin to Morse.* Cambridge, MA: Harvard University Press, 1995.

Stickney, William, ed. *Autobiography of Amos Kendall.* Boston: Lee and Shepard, 1872.

RICHARD B. KIELBOWICZ

KENNEDY, ASSASSINATION OF JOHN F.

The assassination of President John F. Kennedy marked a major turning point in American journalism, as television news gained legitimacy and began to overtake newspapers as the country's primary source of news.

Kennedy was in Texas on Friday, November 22, 1963, to help bring together the state's feuding Democratic politicians, in preparation for the 1964 election. Riding in a motorcade through downtown Dallas, Kennedy was hit by an assassin's bullets at 1:30 p.m. EST. News that something was amiss in the motorcade was reported immediately over local radio stations by reporters near the parade route. Wire service reporter Merriman Smith called in the news from a pool car in the motorcade. As a result, United Press International moved a bulletin on its "A" wire at 1:34 p.m., indicating that three shots had been fired at the president's motorcade. Don Gardiner broadcast the bulletin first to a national audience, breaking into ABC Radio programming at 1:36 p.m. As the pool car sped to Parkland Hospital, Smith continued to dictate the news to UPI editors over the car phone, thus preventing fellow passenger, Associated Press reporter Jack Bell, from doing the same. After arriving at the hospital, Smith dictated the "flash" for which he would later receive a Pulitzer Prize.

At 1:40 p.m., Walter Cronkite broke into CBS's broadcast of the soap opera *As the World Turns.* Viewers could only hear Cronkite's voice and see a bulletin slide because the network did not have a camera in the newsroom. Cronkite was forced to announce the news from a radio booth until a studio camera could be moved into the newsroom and warmed up. Similarly, NBC broke into programming with an audio-only announcement from Don Pardo at 1:45 p.m. Less than thirty minutes after the shooting, and within minutes of one another, all three television networks had anchors on camera. On ABC, Don Goddard reported from a makeshift studio until the network could set up its main television studio for anchor Ron Cochran, while Frank McGee, Chet Huntley, and Bill Ryan reported to NBC's audience. As network technicians struggled to set up lines for video feeds, anchors tried to gather and disseminate information over the telephone in real time. When NBC was unable to put Robert McNeil's telephone report on the air, McGee was forced to repeat McNeil's words as he heard them. The procedure became even more awkward when, unknown to McGee, viewers could suddenly hear McNeil's words for themselves, even as McGee continued to repeat them. On CBS, off camera journalists could be heard giving Cronkite information that viewers had already heard for themselves.

CBS was the first to report Kennedy's death because of a misunderstanding. Correspondent Dan Rather thought he was speaking to another reporter when he said the president had reportedly died. Instead, he was speaking with a CBS radio editor, who understood Rather's information to be confirmed and broadcast it on the CBS radio network. At 2:16 p.m., the report was shared with the CBS television audience, although Cronkite cautioned that it was unconfirmed. At 2:37 p.m., confirmation that Kennedy had died at 2:00 p.m. came in the form of an Associated Press "flash." When Cronkite announced the news, he momentarily lost his composure, regaining it after a brief pause and a clearing of his throat.

As evening fell on November 22, much of television's coverage shifted to Washington, beginning with the arrival of Air Force One at nearby Andrews Air Force base. Viewers watched as the Kennedy's coffin, followed by Mrs. Kennedy, was taken off the presidential plane. Lyndon B. Johnson then gave his first brief remarks to the nation as president. The networks continued coverage through a weekend of solemn ceremonies at the White House and the Capitol. On Sunday, November 24, the hushed tones of television commentators were abruptly interrupted by additional, jarring news from Dallas. When police prepared to transfer suspected assassin Lee Harvey Oswald from the Dallas police station to the county jail, night club owner Jack Ruby shot Oswald dead. The moment was captured by two press photographers. Bob Jackson of the *Dallas Times-Herald* captured Ruby the moment he shot Oswald at point-blank range, an image that would later be recognized with a Pulitzer Prize. Just a split second earlier, Jack Beers of the *Dallas Morning News* snapped the same scene, although it lacked the drama of Jackson's photo. Oswald's murder was the first televised murder in American history and it was seen live on NBC. CBS had chosen not to carry Oswald's transfer live, but did subsequently show videotape of the shooting. ABC did not have a camera at the scene of the shooting.

It would be years before the Kennedy assassination itself would be televised. *Life* magazine outbid CBS News for film Dallas businessman Abraham Zapruder captured of the shooting on an 8mm home movie camera. The magazine subsequently published a few of the less graphic frames of the film.

Newspapers across the country issued extra editions over the four days. The Fort Worth *Star-Telegram* "couldn't print them fast enough" to satisfy readers who "would stand in line to buy one edition, then go to the back of the line to buy a copy of the next one" (Schieffer, *This Just In*, 4). But it was television upon which Americans relied in larger numbers than ever before. The networks stayed on the air throughout the weekend, pre-empting programs and commercials.

It was the most extensive coverage ever given to a single story. NBC was on the air longest—seventy-one hours and thirty-six minutes. At a time when broadcast technology was still in its infancy, each of the three networks committed hundreds of personnel to broadcast the most technically complex coverage ever attempted. NBC deployed more technical equipment than it had for any other broadcast in the company's history—sixteen mobile units and twenty-two videotape recorders which produced some three thousand miles of tape. In New York and Washington alone, NBC used forty-four cameras. The cost was enormous: some estimates put network losses at $40 million.

However, the audience was bigger than ever before, too. It was estimated that some 40 percent of American households tuned into network television coverage over the weekend, with the average home tuning in for at least thirteen consecutive hours. By Monday, the day of Kennedy's funeral, an unprecedented 93 percent of American households and 41.5 million television sets were turned on. The nascent industry was lauded as a national cathedral that allowed Americans to mourn together.

Further Reading

Aynesworth, Hugh. *JFK: Breaking the News, A Reporter's Eyewitness Account of the Kennedy Assassination and its Aftermath.* Richardson, TX: International Focus Press, 2003.

Bliss, Edward. *Now the News: The Story of Broadcast Journalism.* New York: Columbia University Press, 1991.

Huffaker, Bob, et al. *When The News Went Live, Dallas 1963.* Lanham, MD: Taylor Trade Publishing, 2004.

Manchester, William. *The Death of a President, November 1963.* New York: Harper and Row, 1967.

Newseum, the. *President Kennedy Has Been Shot.* Naperville, IL: Sourcebooks, 2003.

Schieffer, Bob. *This Just In: What I Couldn't Tell You on TV.* New York: G. P. Putnam's Sons, 2003.

Semple, Robert. *Four Days in November.* New York: St. Martin's Press, 2003.

Zelizer, Barbie. *Covering the Body: The Kennedy Assassination, the Media, and the Shaping of Collective Memory.* Chicago: The University of Chicago Press, 1992.

DALE CRESSMAN

KENNEDY, JOHN F. AND THE MEDIA

After Democratic Senator John F. Kennedy of Massachusetts was elected president in November 1960 by a razor-thin margin, he decided that he would do everything possible to assure that he would be re-elected by a much larger margin in 1964. To Kennedy, who was relatively unknown before 1960, favorable media coverage would lead to a positive public image, which in turn would result in the high approval ratings that would virtually assure his re-election. This media-savvy political calculator succeeded: public approval stayed well above 50 percent throughout his presidency, and he had the highest approval ratings in the Gallup poll after two years in office—76 percent—of any modern president.

To achieve these ratings, Kennedy worked assiduously—at times obsessively—to obtain favorable coverage for himself and his policies in the news media. Kennedy thought that what appeared in the media would go far toward determining his ability to govern, the likelihood of his being re-elected, and even his place in history. Despite some missteps in media relations, notably a request for voluntary press censorship after the disastrous Bay of Pigs invasion of Cuba in 1961 that angered many journalists, Kennedy was remarkably successful in achieving favorable coverage in most newspapers and magazines, and especially on television.

Contrasts with Kennedy's predecessor, Dwight D. Eisenhower, help to explain his overall success in getting positive coverage. The new president was youthful, good-looking, and photogenic—advantages especially on television and in magazines that emphasized photographs. He spent countless hours granting interviews to journalists representing all major media. He was much more articulate and witty—and thus more quotable—than Eisenhower. A former journalist,

Kennedy flattered reporters by reading many of their stories and frequently offering reactions. He socialized with several journalists who were personal friends, and invited them and many other reporters, editors, and publishers to White House functions. And, like most journalists, Kennedy was a moderate-to-liberal supporter of new government programs, not the moderate-to-conservative critic of federal spending that Eisenhower had been.

The First Television President

Kennedy was the first president to use the relatively new medium of television effectively. He used it above all to have instantaneous, unmediated communication with the American people. As he told a print journalist friend after a well-received, hour-long televised interview in 1962, "Well, I always said that when we don't have to go through you bastards, we can really get our story over to the American people."

Kennedy also used his access to television—free of charge because he was president—to communicate with other holders of power, including the chairman of U.S. Steel when Kennedy was angry about a price hike, the premier of the Soviet Union when Kennedy wanted to convey the unmistakable message that the Soviet leadership would have to remove the nuclear missiles that they had sent secretly to Cuba, and the president of South Vietnam when Kennedy believed that "changes in policy and . . . personnel" were needed.

Whereas Eisenhower had held one televised news conference, Kennedy held sixty-two and, in the process, became a media celebrity as well as a political leader. The young president also made nine televised political speeches, including important ones on Berlin in 1961 and civil rights in 1963 in addition to the address on Cuba in 1962 that solidified his reputation as a forceful leader in the Cold War.

Television networks also gained from Kennedy's frequent appearances in front of the cameras. A Roper poll in 1963 found that, for the first time, more American relied on television than on newspapers as their primary source of news.

Uneasy Relations with Print Journalists

Especially during their first two years in office, Kennedy and his personable press secretary, Pierre Salinger, spent much time trying to influence coverage in newspapers and magazines of the president, his family, his administration, and his policies. Although the administration generally received largely favorable coverage except in conservative Republican media, news stories and commentaries in the mainstream print media were not nearly as free of criticism as the coverage Kennedy typically received on television.

Kennedy knew that reporters and editors insist on reaching their own conclusions about what to include in news stories, and that reporters typically try to provide some balance between positive and negative perspectives. He also was aware that, as he put it, "bad news is news and good news is not news." As a politician deeply concerned about his image, however, Kennedy repeatedly criticized reporters for even minor criticisms in largely positive stories.

At times the president went beyond criticizing. In July 1961, he stopped seeing Hugh Sidey, the main White House correspondent for *Time*, after a critical story in that widely read news magazine. In August 1962, he cut off contact with his friend Ben Bradlee, a leading White House correspondent for *Newsweek*, after Bradlee reportedly said that White House officials "would find one paragraph to quibble about" in largely favorable articles. Most egregiously, in October 1963, Kennedy tried to convince the publisher of the *New York Times,* Arthur Ochs Sulzberger, to remove David Halberstam, whose stories from Saigon frequently had been critical of U.S. policy, from covering the growing war in Vietnam. Sulzberger rejected the president's request.

Like Kennedy, journalists covering the administration sometimes overreached. In April 1963, Hanson W. Baldwin, a *New York Times* military analyst, argued in a magazine article that the administration used "blatant methods" of "management and manipulation of news." Baldwin was right that the administration had limited the flow of news during the Cuban missile crisis and its aftermath. But he failed to note that Kennedy's handling of news may well have contributed to the peaceful resolution of a very dangerous situation. Moreover, all administrations can be faulted for trying to manage the news, especially if the phrase basically refers to seeking favorable coverage.

It seems fair to conclude that Kennedy's diligence and skill in working with journalists contributed to largely favorable coverage and high public approval ratings. And so did his service at a time when most Americans—including most journalists— looked to the president for leadership in waging the Cold War, a time before such troubling developments as the large-scale war in Vietnam and the Watergate crisis badly damaged the presidential-press relationship. Kennedy and his colleagues thus almost certainly received the most favorable coverage of any administration in the second half of the twentieth century.

Further Reading

Baldwin, Hanson W. "Managed News: Our Peacetime Censorship." *Atlantic Monthly* 211:4 (April 1963): 53–59.

Berry, Joseph P., Jr. *John F. Kennedy and the Media: The First Television President.* Lanham, MD: University Press of America, 1987.

Giglio, James N. "JFK: Image and Reality." *New England Journal of History* 52:2 (1995): 66–90.

Halberstam, David. *The Powers That Be.* New York: Knopf, 1979.

Kern, Montague, Patricia W. Levering, and Ralph B. Levering. *The Kennedy Crises; The Press, the Presidency, and Foreign Policy.* Chapel Hill: University of North Carolina Press, 1983.

Prochnau, William. *Once Upon a Distant War; David Halberstam, Neil Sheehan, Peter Arnett—Young War Correspondents and Their Early Vietnam Battles.* New York: Times Books, 1995.

Roberts, Charles. "JFK and the Press." In *Ten Presidents and the Press*, edited by Kenneth W. Thompson, 63–77. Washington, D.C.: University Press of America, 1983.

Salinger, Pierre. *With Kennedy*. Garden City, NY: Doubleday, 1966.

Watson, Mary Ann. *The Expanding Vista: American Television in the Kennedy Years*. New York: Oxford University Press, 1990.

RALPH B. LEVERING

KNOX, FRANK

One of the most colorful characters in the history of American journalism was Frank Knox (January 1, 1874–April 28, 1944), who rode with Teddy Roosevelt's Rough Riders, rose to the rank of major while fighting in France under General John J. Pershing, and served as Franklin Roosevelt's wartime Navy Secretary. In between these periods of public service, he ran for president as a Republican, became his party's vice presidential pick, and crusaded as a newspaper editor and publisher in small towns and large cities during America's Progressive and Interwar eras.

William Franklin Knox was an ardent nationalist born to Canadian parents. William Edwin Knox and Sarah Collins Barnard Cox had moved to Boston before their only son and eldest of six surviving children was born. Knox's father was an oyster dealer and his mother a pious Presbyterian when the family relocated to Grand Rapids, Michigan, when he was seven. At eleven, Knox delivered newspapers and helped out in his father's failing grocery store. He dropped out of high school after his junior year to supplement the family income as a shipping clerk and salesman. Beginning in 1893, Knox attended Alma, a Christian college, studied Latin and Greek, played varsity football, taught gym, and in 1898 married college sweetheart Annie Reid, a small town girl from Michigan.

In May 1898, Knox hurried to Tampa, Florida, enlisting in the First Volunteer United States Cavalry, then being organized by Leonard Wood and Theodore Roosevelt to fight the Spanish after the sinking of the *U.S.S. Maine* in Havana Harbor. Knox became one of the Rough Riders who stormed San Juan Hill on July 1, tearing his pants on a barbed wire fence and taking a bullet through his hat. He suffered sunstroke and a bout of malaria before his discharge.

Knox was a $10 a week reporter on the *Grand Rapids Herald* in 1899, becoming by 1900 its city editor and a year later its circulation manager. Along with friend John A. Muehling he bought the *Lake Superior Journal* in 1902, added the *Sault Sainte Marie Weekly News*, and became the Upper Peninsula's two-fisted defender of lumberjacks and seamen, whose pay was systematically stolen in protected saloons. Knox's "clean-up campaign" included his knock-out of one saloonkeeper, who saw firsthand the power of the press. The windows of Knox's newspaper office were shot out, but he would not be intimidated.

In 1910, Knox was the campaign manager for Chase C. Osborn, who became Michigan's governor. Knox unsuc-

cessfully organized Roosevelt's Bull Moose run for the presidency in 1912 and accepted the invitation of Progressives in New Hampshire to launch a crusading paper in their state. Knox and Muehling sold their papers in Michigan and started the *Manchester Leader*, soon buying the *Union* and *Mirror* to become a dominant voice for New England reformers. Knox deepened his commitment to Republican Party politics, strongly backing the unsuccessful presidential bid of Charles Evans Hughes in 1916. A year later, at the age of forty-three, he enlisted in the First New Hampshire Infantry for service in World War I as an artillery officer. Promoted to major, he came under fire in France with the 153rd Artillery and was mustered out as a lieutenant colonel.

The Republican Party was moving to the right. Knox was the floor manager of Leonard Wood's unsuccessful bid to win the party's presidential nomination in 1920 which Warren Harding won. Four years later, Knox failed to win party endorsement for his New Hampshire gubernatorial bid. In 1927, Knox accepted the offer of William Randolph Hearst to take charge of the *Boston American*, a big money loser. Knox's work propelled him to the lucrative job of general manager of Hearst's nationwide network of twenty-seven newspapers. Four years later, he got his dream job in journalism when he and Theodore T. Ellis, a Worcester, Massachusetts, industrialist, purchased the *Chicago Daily News*.

For nine years, Knox supervised one of the nation's leading newspapers, fighting machine politicians, while often using front page space to write signed editorials excoriating Franklin Roosevelt's New Deal as creeping socialism. Knox sought the Republican Party's presidential nomination in 1936 and settled for second on the ticket behind Alf Landon. They were defeated in Roosevelt's re-election landslide. Knox hailed Roosevelt's pro-British activism at the beginning of World War II and in July 1940 was made Navy Secretary in Roosevelt's coalition cabinet. Republican leaders were shocked. Knox bluntly answered, "I am an American first, and a Republican afterward" (*New York Times*, April 29, 1944, 8).

Knox was a tireless advocate of a two-ocean navy, supervised a quintupling of its tonnage and firepower, and, when he died on the eve of the D-Day invasion to liberate Europe from the grip of Hitler and the Axis powers, the American navy was widely recognized as the most powerful in the world. Knox was buried with full military honors at Arlington National Cemetery with President Roosevelt observing that whether as a soldier, journalist, publisher, or public official, "Frank Knox truly put his country first" (*Chicago Daily News*, April 29, 1944, 1).

Further Reading

Albion, Robert Greenhalgh, *Makers of Naval Policy, 1798–1947*. Annapolis, MD: National Institute Press, 1980.

Archive of past issues of the *Chicago Daily News*. Chicago Historical Society, Chicago, IL.

Beasley, Norman. *Frank Knox, American*. Garden City: Doubleday, Doran & Co., 1936.

"In the Line of Duty," *Chicago Daily News*, April 29, 1944, 1.

Papers of Frank Knox, Library of Congress, Archival Manuscript Collection, Washington, D.C.

Knox, Frank. *The Brotherhood of Courage*. New York: National Association of Manufacturers, 1943.

Knox, Frank. *"We Planned It That Way."* New York: Longmans, Green & Co., 1938.

"The Last Edition," *Chicago Daily News*, March 4, 1978, 1.

BRUCE J. EVENSEN

KOREAN WAR

The Korean War began Sunday June 25, 1950, with the invasion of South Korea by North Korean troops. There was no United States involvement, but there soon would be and with it an American media presence. Actually, one American journalist, Walter Simmons of the *Chicago Tribune*, happened to be in Seoul when the war started, and he filed the first story by an American journalist. He had gone to Seoul to cover talks between the United States and South Korea a week earlier and had remained. The time difference meant that stories about the invasion easily made the Sunday newspapers. There was no other big news that weekend, so the start of the Korean War was front page news in newspapers all over the America.

President Harry S. Truman asked for United Nations armed intervention, and the UN agreed on June 28. Truman then committed U.S. troops to the war under General Douglas MacArthur. American correspondents came from Japan to cover the war. Two of the first and best were Marguerite Higgins of the *New* York *Herald Tribune* and Keyes Beech of the *Chicago Daily News*, who were among the six journalists to share the 1951 Pulitzer Prize for International Reporting for their coverage of the war. The other four were Fred Sparks of the *Chicago Daily News*, Homer Bigart of the *New York Herald Tribune*, and Relman Morin and Don Whitehead of the Associated Press.

Correspondents faced considerable risks throughout the war. During the early months of the fighting, there were 270 journalists who were accredited to cover the war. Before the war was over, 600 journalists had been accredited, but the number in Korea at any one time was probably less than 100. Conditions were particularly dangerous in the early days of the war as the North Koreans ran roughshod over both South Korean and U.S. troops. Six correspondents were killed in the first month of the war, and seventeen were killed in the three years of the war. Conditions were primitive, both in terms of living conditions and communication. At the outset, there was no direct communication from Korea to the United States, and correspondents found the only way to get a story through in timely fashion was to go back to Tokyo to file it.

Higgins was the most celebrated journalist. She saw the first U.S. soldier killed in action and was in considerable personal danger in the early days of the war. She went back to Tokyo when the North Koreans captured Seoul. She returned a few days later with MacArthur on his first visit to the front and got an exclusive interview with him. The *Herald-Tribune* sent Bigart to relieve Higgins, but she refused to leave. She was ordered to leave Korea on the grounds that the U. S. Army did not have facilities for women journalists, but she was able to get MacArthur to overrule that order at the eleventh hour. She also was one of the journalists at Chosin Reservoir when that terrible battle began.

The Korean War was the first war to be covered by television, but not in the way that we have become accustomed to. There were no satellites, and so television journalists found that considerable lapsed between when stories were filed and when they were aired.

The UN forces were forced back to the Pusan peninsula, but MacArthur executed a brilliant amphibious landing at Inchon on September 15. That forced the North Koreans to withdraw from South Korea, and MacArthur led the UN forces into North Korean and was heading for the Yalu River at the Chinese border. Nearly three hundred correspondents from nineteen counties reported the UN advance.

Chinese Enter the War

As UN forces neared the Yalu, the Chinese entered the war. That led to one of the most ferocious battles ever engaged in by Americans troops, the battle of the Chosin Reservoir. It lasted 15 days, with 6,135 Americans killed and 14,000 wounded. Though outnumbered 10 to 1, the American killed 28,000 Chinese. Seventeen Americans received the Medal of Honor for their efforts at Chosin. A disastrous retreat by the UN forces back to the North Korean-South Korea border followed. Some correspondents criticized MacArthur's strategy, and he responded by instituting full censorship. There also was criticism of the failure of U.S. intelligence to deliver adequate information about the Chinese presence near the North Korean border. Until then correspondents had been left to their own devices and were much freer to report than American correspondents had been during World War II. Stringent regulations were imposed in January, covering not only military information but also statements that would injure morale or embarrass the United States.

After the retreat from the Yalu, the war settled into what was very much a stalemate and remained that way for the duration. The big news became the conflict between MacArthur and Truman. MacArthur wanted to expand the war to China, using atomic bombs and also using the Chinese Nationalist Army then on Taiwan. Truman feared this would touch off World War III, and he wanted no part of it. The two had a secret meeting on Wake Island in October 1950, and it was assumed that they had reached an understanding. However, the conflict simmered beneath the surface. It burst out into the open on April 5, 1951, when House Minority Leader Joseph Martin released a letter written to him by MacArthur. MacArthur complained about the restrictions placed upon him. Truman was outraged, and six days later he removed MacArthur from the command.

MacArthur returned to the United States to a hero's welcome. He addressed a joint session of Congress, airing his grievances. The *New York Times* had been trying to get the White House to respond to MacArthur, and after MacArthur's speech, it did. It released the minutes of the Wake Island meeting. Anthony Leviero of the *Times* used that material to write a Pulitzer Prize winning story on the Truman-MacArthur controversy.

Negotiations for a truce began in Panmunjom, Korea in July 1951. They were to continue for two years until an agreement finally was reached to end the fighting. The UN command insisted that reporters be permitted to cover the truce site, but they were not allowed to cover the negotiations. Still reports were issued on the progress of the negotiations, and these stories became at least as important as the war stories.

Dwight D. Eisenhower made bringing an end to the war part of his campaign for president in 1952. He vowed he would go to Korea and did so after he was elected, and a truce was negotiated by the end of his first five months in office.

Assessing the Coverage

The Korean War was easier to cover than World War II because it was in one relatively small country rather than being spread all over the globe. There also was a clearly defined battle line, which would not be the case in the Vietnam War. The dividing line between North and South Korea, the thirty-eighth parallel became the point of reference for much of the coverage. The only significant naval action of the war was the Inchon landing.

MacArthur was succeeded by General Matthew Ridgway, and there was little conflict between the press and the military. In contrast to the coverage of the Vietnam War, there was little complaint about the coverage of the Korean War. From the time the truce negotiations began until the truce was agreed to two years later, the war was very much a stalemate with no major offensives by either side.

Despite this consensus, there was a story that was missed, one that did not get covered until more than forty years after the end of the war. It was about the massacre of several hundred South Koreans by U.S. soldiers in the summer of 1950 at No Gun Ri, south of Seoul. The soldiers believed that among the hundreds of people there were North Korean infiltrators. There were other lesser atrocities witnessed by journalists but not reported because they did not want to be disloyal or harm the war effort. It was the Associated Press that finally reported the massacre at No Gun Ri, and the AP won the Pulitzer Prize for the story in 1999. However, the AP was challenged about the story by the military and ultimately by other media. Robert L. Bateman, in the book *No Gun Ri* (2002), argues that while there was an atrocity, it probably involved only a dozen or so Koreans. There is, of course, no possible way of making a count a half century after the event.

Part of Bateman's argument rests on the absence of eyewitnesses and the heavy part played in the AP story of sources whose veracity might be doubted. Bateman also cited editorials in *Newsweek* and the *Wall Street Journal*

asking how the Pulitzer Prize could be awarded for a story that rested so much on hearsay. It was also pointed out that atrocities against American POWs often went unreported, in part because information about them was no longer available.

Further Reading

Bateman, Robert L. *No Gun Ri: Military History of the Korean War Incident*. Mechanicsburg, PA: Stackpole Books, 2002.

Cumings, Bruce. *War and Television*. London ; New York : Verso, 1992.

Emery, Michael, and Edwin Emery, *The Press and America*. Englewood Cliffs, NJ: Prentice Hall, 1992.

Higgins, Marguerite. *War in Korea*. Garden City, NY: Doubleday, 1951.

Stein, M.L. *Under Fire: The Story of American War Correspondents*. New York: Julian Messner, 1968.

GUIDO H. STEMPEL III

KUPCINET, IRV

For sixty years Irv Kupcinet (July 31, 1912–November 11, 2003) wrote on people and events for the *Chicago Times*, and beginning in 1948 the *Chicago Sun-Times*, stories that were syndicated to more than one hundred newspapers, making him the nation's most durable columnist.

In the city of broad shoulders, Kupcinet's were among the broadest. "Mr. Chicago" was born in Lawndale, a Jewish neighborhood on the city's West Side, to Russian immigrants Max and Olga Kupcinet. As a boy he sat beside his father making deliveries on a horse-drawn bakery truck. He edited the school newspaper at Harrison High and played quarterback. He had a football scholarship to Northwestern University but transferred to the University of North Dakota after a fistfight with the coach's brother. Kupcinet's professional career ended with a shoulder injury in his rookie year with the Philadelphia Eagles. Late in 1935 he took a job as a sports writer for the *Chicago Times* at $32.50 a week. He supplemented his salary by refereeing in the National Football League, including the Chicago Bears 73–0 championship win over the Washington Redskins in 1940. Between 1953 and 1976 Kupcinet was color analyst on the Bears radio broadcasts.

Kupcinet married Esther "Essee" Solomon on February 12, 1939, and honeymooned "covering spring baseball training in Florida." Soon Kupcinet was writing his own sports column, ending it with a short section on "people." On January 18, 1943, that effort was expanded into "Kup's Column." In one thousand words six times a week Kupcinet said that he "followed my town's daily drama, recorded some of its history, checked its blood pressure, and took its pulse." "Kup" (as he became known), often with Essee at his side, became Chicago's "man-about-town" for the next sixty years. He searched for stories on the powerful and the ordinary, in nightclubs and along city streets, writing on presidents and celebrities as well as doormen and waiters. Their names would appear in boldface for three generations of readers from coast to coast. His charity work with cerebral palsy, for the disabled, for wounded veterans and variety clubs helped build friendships with Bing Crosby, Bob Hope, Jack Benny, Frank Sinatra, and scores of others. For fifty consecutive Junes, beginning in 1945, Kupcinet hosted annual Purple Heart cruises on Lake Michigan for soldiers wounded in the war. Walter Winchell was the prototype of the sarcastic, score-settling gossip columnist. Kup was his opposite. His tireless reporting through his unparalleled pool of sources yielded stories that generally brightened a reader's day. "The thing about Kup that was unique," said friend Studs Terkel, "is that he's a decent man." He "knew our secrets and never published them," said long-time Chicagoan Mike Wallace of CBS News. "There was no malice in the man. That's why he was so widely loved."

Kupcinet was a pioneer television talk show host. In 1957 he replaced Jack Paar on NBC's "America After Dark," which eventually became "The Tonight Show." Two years later Kupcinet launched "At Random, "a late Saturday night talk show, produced in Chicago, that offered a seventy-station national network twenty-seven years of extraordinary guest lists. "Kup's Show," as it came to be called, might involve Carl Sandburg and Malcolm X, Milton Friedman, Norman Rockwell and Margaret Mead, Truman Capote and Norman Mailer, or Charles Darwin, grandson of the naturalist, and Sir Julian Huxley debating the population explosion. Federal Communications Commission Chairman Newton Minow appeared on one show to discuss the future of television with the philosopher Mortiner Adler and teamster Jimmy Hoffa. An August 1960 show featured a discussion of the John F. Kennedy–Richard Nixon presidential race that involved Edward R. Murrow and Walter Cronkite from CBS, syndicated columnists Walter Winchell and Drew Pearson, and Jack Bell from the Associated Press. Other shows were spiced with Alfred Hitchcock's explanation of why actors were "temperamental children" and Bob Hope defending American conduct in Vietnam from attacks by Tommy Smothers. The unscripted shows would last three hours and more with viewers holding "Kup's Show" parties to participate in what Kupcinet called "the lively art of conversation." Over the years, the show won fifteen Emmys and a Peabody.

Kupcinet's son Jerry became a director, his daughter Karyn an actress. In 1963 Karyn Kupcinet was murdered in Los Angeles. The case remains unsolved. In 1966 Irv Kupcinet refused a lucrative offer by the Tribune syndicate to move to Hollywood and replace Hedda Hopper. He was determined to keep Chicago as his home. He considered it "the most underrated city in the world." Later he explained, "there's something special about Chicago. It will always be my number one beat." In 1986, the Wabash Avenue Bridge, over which Kupcinet had daily walked to work, was named after Chicago's favorite son. Mayor Richard J. Daley observed that Kup "embodied the city's energy, excitement and optimism. Chicago has been the home of many great writers, but only one of them has been called, 'Mr. Chicago.'"

Further Reading

"The Incomparable 'Kup.'" *Editor & Publisher*, November 17, 2003.

Kupcinet, Irv. *Kup: A Man, an Era, a City*. Chicago: Bonus Books, 1988.

Kupcinet, Irv. *Kup's Chicago*. Cleveland: World Publishing, 1962.

New York Times, November 11, 2003.

BRUCE J. EVENSEN

L

LABOR PRESS

Although a proposal to establish a workers' magazine was circulated by William Manning in 1797, the first U.S. labor papers were not published until the late 1820s. Some fifty labor papers were launched from 1828 to the mid-1830s, most in the industrializing northeastern part of the country. These early papers tended to concentrate on the emerging labor movement's political concerns—winning the right to organize and strike in the face of prosecutions for unlawful association, shorter working hours, free public education, abolition of imprisonment for debt, and similar reforms. Like the movement they served, these were eclectic papers, which opened their columns not only to news of the nascent unions but to the wide range of reform thought sweeping the country as the economy shifted from artisan and local to industrial and national production. (Indeed, many of these early papers were produced by printers who saw the traditions of their craft collapsing around them.) Most of these papers were weeklies or monthlies, but the *New York Daily Sentinel* was published (with a brief stint as a semiweekly) from February 13, 1830, until 1833.

This early labor press depended on the health of the labor movement it served, with papers exploding in periods of organizational ferment and suspending publication when unions were under particularly severe attack. As the Working Men's Party and the independent labor political action these early papers championed flourished, so did the labor press; when the political establishment closed ranks to crush the nascent movement, its press collapsed (although the *Working Man's Advocate* survived until 1849). However, historian Roger Streitmatter argues, this early labor press left a lasting legacy, with many of the ideas it championed becoming law in the 1830s and beyond.

Only in the 1860s did the movement become sufficiently entrenched to preserve its unions, and its newspapers, during economic downturns and repression. While still interested in political reform, the papers issued in this era were increasingly focused on workplace issues and more closely tied to emerging trade unions and to the Knights of Labor. Most unions of any size published a national magazine or newspaper, while union locals typically supported weeklies sponsored by the broader labor movement, which offered space to sponsoring unions to communicate their concerns. These papers combined organizational news with commentary on local and national events, fiction and poetry,

theoretical articles and letters. Labor papers exchanged with each other, and freely reprinted items, forming a sort of alternative public sphere in which the labor movement articulated its concerns and reached out to other publics.

Most of the daily labor papers launched during this period began life as strike papers, issued by striking printers in an era where the tools of production were still within reach. The strike paper sought to replace the newspaper(s) being struck, and so offered an array of news and features aimed at a general public, albeit with a heavier emphasis on labor news and perspectives. These papers typically disappeared once the strike that called them into existence ended, but others eventually became the dominant newspaper in their market (some surviving to this day), usually after the original strikers or unions were bought out. In the 1940s, the International Typographical Union launched a chain of labor dailies through its Unitypo subsidiary, serving small to mid-sized cities where the local publisher refused to recognize the union. The last of these papers were closed down or sold to commercial interests in 1963.

Other genres of labor papers included newsletters issued by union locals, official union publications ranging from weekly newspapers to glossy magazines, newspapers issued by local labor federations or private publishers who made their living serving the labor movement's communication needs, and publications issued by mutual aid societies, political groups and other organizations that considered themselves part of a broader labor movement.

These papers supported their own news services (Federated Press' dispatches from the 1920s through 1956 are now available on microfilm; it was one of four services available to labor papers when it suspended operations), and were part of an expansive communication agenda that also saw unions and other workers' organizations launch radio stations, experiment with television broadcasting, and distribute motion pictures.

While many papers were issued directly by unions, readership was dominated by independent papers issued in behalf of the movement. English-language pro-labor papers were often published by printers or journalists looking to make a living in the service of the cause. A prominent example was *John Swinton's Paper,* issued weekly from 1883 to 1887 by the well-known reform journalist. Like most of its contemporaries, *Swinton's* was an eclectic paper which gave voice to the Knights of Labor, trade unionists, and advocates of labor politics alike. Foreign-language labor papers were typically published by cooperative societies, jointly owned by union locals, mutual aid and other immigrant societies, and socialist organizations.

In many cities, publishers issued weekly newspapers endorsed by local unions but run as private businesses. Mutual aid societies and socialist parties also published daily, weekly, and monthly newspapers, providing news and viewpoints often excluded from the general press. Chicago's immigrant working-class communities supported publications ranging from newspapers quite similar (language aside) to mainstream dailies to militant papers deeply enmeshed in the lives of the ethnic communities that published them. These papers were often issued by publishing cooperatives in which local unions, mutual aid societies, socialist groups, and individual supporters with the necessary means would invest, and which were held accountable to the movement through regular stockholders' meetings at which editorial policies were discussed and editors elected. On occasion these cooperatives voted for dramatic changes in policy. The shareholders of the Finnish daily *Socialisti* reaffiliated their paper to the International Workers of the World (IWW), and the *Chicagoer Arbeiter-Zeitung* left the ranks of the Socialist Labor Party to become the world's first anarchist daily in 1884, and in 1910 affiliated to the Socialist Party.

By World War I most cities of any size supported at least one labor newspaper, and many supported scores of papers published in the dozens of languages spoken by the largely immigrant U.S. working class. Some papers adhered to socialist or other political ideologies, others to a broadly working-class perspective independent of formal political alliances, and others still were the organs of particular unions or mutual aid societies. Many papers were launched by working printers, combining entrepreneurial or cooperativist impulses with broader commitments to visions of a mobilized working class that typically sought to promote labor's interests in the political process. During the first Red Scare after World War I, these papers became the targets of government repression or harassment.

While organizational independence often supported a more vibrant press, it could also create difficulties. The Chicago Federation of Labor (CFL) battled a succession of self-avowed labor papers that allied themselves with a handful of unions uncomfortable with its progressive stance and labor racketeers who sometimes gathered advertising through strong-arm tactics. Chicago's *Union Labor Advocate* began life in 1901 as the CFL's official organ, renting space in the Federation's headquarters and receiving a stipend for publishing the minutes of its meetings. The privately owned monthly magazine carried endorsements from several unions, articles promoting the CFL's reform agenda, and advertisements from union-friendly merchants. But the CFL's increasingly radical stance inevitably clashed with the publisher's economic interests and in 1910 the Federation severed its ties to the paper because of the *Advocate's* sale of its editorial columns in state elections. In 1911 the *Union Labor Advocate* regrouped as a weekly newspaper, gaining the endorsement of the Building Trades Council

before its decision to align itself with newspaper publishers in the 1912 newspaper lockout completely discredited it with most unionists. Henceforth, the Chicago Federation refused to endorse any privately owned publication as its organ, ultimately launching its own *The New Majority* (later *Federation News*) in 1919.

Outright ownership by local labor councils was unusual, however. More typical were local papers such as the *St. Louis/Southern Illinois Labor Tribune,* launched in 1937. Always privately owned (the original owner was a beer distributor; the paper in 2006 was owned by a public relations firm), the paper was endorsed by the American Federation of Labor whose affiliated locals subscribed to the paper for their members. In 2006, more than one hundred union locals in the metropolitan area have the weekly mailed to their members. In other cities, the local paper was jointly owned by the union locals that endorsed it, or by a printer with close ties to local unions.

Circulating in an environment more conducive to specialized publications, the foreign-language labor press was more prolific than its English-language counterparts, and more likely to serve as readers' primary source of news. Nine of the fifteen daily labor newspapers published in 1925 were foreign-language titles, published in such languages as Czech, Finnish, Lithuanian, Serbian, Slovene, and Yiddish. Chicago's Polish-language *Dziennik Ludowy* (a weekly and later a daily, with a short-lived Detroit edition) received financial support from the International Ladies Garment Workers Union, the Laborers, Meatcutters, Machinists and Amalgamated Clothing Workers, all of which had substantial Polish memberships, and switched its affiliation from the socialists when the Chicago Federation of Labor launched its own labor party in 1919.

English-language union dailies published in the twentieth century include the *Butte* (Montana) *Daily Bulletin, Chicago Daily World, Daily People, Milwaukee Leader, New York Leader, Nome* (Alaska) *Industrial Worker, Seattle Union Record,* as well as a host of strike papers. The *Butte Bulletin* was a continuation of a weekly strike newspaper, launched in 1918 in response to the mining interests' dominance of the local press. Its founders were members of the electricians and typographical unions, its readers predominantly miners, and its mission was to break the mine operators' grip on their community. The *Bulletin* survived three years as a daily, and two more as a weekly, before it succumbed to a lack of advertising. The Chicago and New York papers continued Socialist Party papers of different names, while the *Milwaukee Leader* also began life as a Socialist paper before local unions—which had always endorsed it as their official organ—took over ownership after founder Victor Berger's death. With the notable exception of the *Milwaukee Leader,* these English-language papers typically lasted for five or six years; foreign-language dailies, more firmly rooted in their communities and less subject to competition, were often longer-lived, and some continue weekly publication to this day, though often retaining more of their ethnic than their labor character.

But the daily was never the dominant form for the labor

press. Instead, most papers were weeklies or monthlies, published by a myriad of organizations and containing a mix of content as eclectic as the movement they served. The editors of these papers were, for the most part, drawn from the ranks of the movements they served, even if many had spent several years on union staffs or otherwise separated from the jobs they once shared with their readers. Much of the content was written by rank-and-file workers, and labor papers rarely spoke with a single voice. Even national newspapers, such as the railroad unions' jointly published *Labor* (which circulated 750,000 copies every week in the 1940s) sought to offer a distinctive working-class voice, from its initial advocacy of nationalization of the rail industry to its long decline alongside the rail unions it existed to serve.

Garment workers unions published their journals in multiple languages, reflecting the largely immigrant character of the workers they organized, while the carpenters union was one of several to charter separate language branches, which often issued their own publication or endorsed another labor-aligned newspaper published in their language and encouraged members to subscribe to it for official union news as well as broader labor and other coverage.

The Industrial Workers of the World, too, published dozens of papers in the 1910s and 1920s, issued in several languages by its industrial unions, the General Executive Board, local branches, and, in the case of its Finnish-language daily *Industrialisti,* a publishing cooperative. These publications ranged from the mimeographed *Agricultural Workers Bulletin* (containing short reports on job conditions throughout the harvest region alongside lengthy theoretical articles on the evolution of agriculture as an industry) to an illustrated monthly magazine, the *Industrial Pioneer.* *Industrialisti* continued publishing until 1975 (although as a fortnightly in its final years), and the IWW continues to publish the *Industrial Worker* and several local newsletters, as well as to maintain a vibrant web presence.

The working-class press's period of peak influence ran from the 1880s through the 1920s, when it was decimated by a combination of the Great Depression (which wiped out many of the mutual aid associations that supported it), laws slashing the number of new immigrants, press consolidation that reduced the economic and social space for alternative publications, and post-war repression. There was a resurgence during the two decades of rivalry between the American Federal of Labor (AFL) and the Congress of Industrial Organizations (CIO), but these publications were more closely aligned to the needs and policies of union officials. In 1940, Levine documented 646 English-language labor newspapers being published in the United States (including three dailies), with a combined circulation of more than 6.5 million copies. In 1956, the U.S. Labor Department listed more than 800 labor newspapers, many of them issued by union locals or regional councils and circulated only within their ranks.

By the early twenty-first century, most unions had turned their official publications over to public relations staffs, few of whom ever worked in the industries whose members they serve. The glossy monthlies they produced were often bet-

ter designed and written than their predecessors, but rarely offered much room for the voice of the rank and file or the expansive social vision that once was found in many labor papers. The American Federation of Labor and the secessionist Change to Win coalition do not issue their own periodicals, and the AFL-CIO had cut off its financial support to the International Labor Communications Association. Many local labor newspapers had closed, victim to deindustrialization and decimation of the ranks of the industrial unions which supported them. Although hundreds of union locals still published often feisty bulletins for their members, several labor federations sponsored substantial publications such as *The* (Peoria, IL) *Labor Paper* or the Duluth *Labor World,* and publications such as *Labor Notes* sought to offer rank-and-file workers a broader working-class vision, the American labor press was in decline. However, a new generation of activists turned to public access television and the Internet, reviving an effort to bring working-class voices and concerns to the general public that dates back to the very origins of the labor movement itself.

During the labor press's earlier, most ambitious period, many of these publications related to their readers in ways quite different than the general circulation press. Labor editors were, for the most part, drawn from the ranks of the movements they served, sharing their linguistic and ethnic diversity, social and economic circumstances, and aspirations. Their newspapers were an integral part of the working-class communities they served, not only reporting the news of the day or week, but offering a venue where readers could debate political, economic, and culture issues. The working-class press stemmed from an alternative press ideology, one that sought to erase distinctions between newspapers and readers and to involve its supporters in every aspect of the newspaper, from management and editorial decisions to reporting. These papers thus not only served otherwise unmet informational needs, they also served as examples of a more democratic media practice which provided working-class communities with forums in which they could debate pressing issues, shape a common response, and mobilize their participation in the broader society. They were building blocks in a public sphere that perhaps no longer exists, a political process that implicitly recognized a multiplicity of interests and provided spaces in which they could come together—simultaneously preserving their distinct identities and taking their place in the broader polity.

Further Reading

Bekken, Jon. "The Working-Class Press at the Turn of the Century," in William Solomon and Robert McChesney (eds.), *Ruthless Criticism: New Perspectives in U.S. Communication History.* Minneapolis: University of Minnesota Press, 1993.

Bekken, Jon. "A Paper for Those Who Toil: The Chicago Labor Press in Transition." *Journalism History* 23(1), 1997.

Godfried, Nathan. *WCFL, Chicago's Voice of Labor, 1926–1978.* Urbana: University of Illinois Press, 1997.

Hoerder, Dirk, ed. *The Immigrant Labor Press in North America, 1880s–1970s,* 3 vols. Westport, CT: Greenwood Press, 1983.

Labor Press Project, http://faculty.washington.edu/gregoryj/labor-press/ (accessed April 17, 2007).

Pizzigati, Sam, and Fred J. Solowey, eds. *The New Labor Press: Journalism for a Changing Union Movement*. Ithaca,NY: ILR Press, 1992.

Schofield, Ann, ed. *Sealskin & Shoddy: Working Women in American Labor Press Fiction, 1870–1920*. Westport, CT: Greenwood Press, 1988.

Rodger Streitmatter, Roger. "Origins of the American Labor Press." *Journalism History 25(3)*, 1999, 99–106.

JON BEKKEN

LADIES' HOME JOURNAL

"Never underestimate the power of a woman." It is the registered trademark that has worked well for the *Ladies' Home Journal (LHJ)*. First used by the magazine in the 1940s, the slogan captured the American woman's can-do attitude. Since then, the slogan has woven its way into American culture, appearing on everything from stationery to t-shirts, from baseball caps to canvas bags, from blogs and web sites to the pages of popular publications.

The *Ladies' Home Journal* is one of the oldest, continuously published magazines in the United States. It had a modest beginning—as a column in the weekly newspaper, *Tribune and Farmer*. From there it grew to a page, then an eight-page supplement, and finally in December 1883, a distinct publication. The publisher was Cyrus H. K. Curtis, who went on to acquire the *Saturday Evening Post*; the editor was his wife, who used her maiden name, Louisa Knapp.

The couple had developed an editorial formula tailor made to the middle-class American female reader of the late nineteenth century. In January 1884, Knapp promised to deliver "a pure and high-toned family paper." The magazine offered the non-fiction that married women needed to carry out their domestic responsibilities—childrearing advice, cooking information, and practical suggestions on running a household—and the escapism that matrons craved—short stories and serialized novels written by some of the most popular writers of the day, including Ella Wheeler, Louisa May Alcott, and Harriet Beecher Stowe. The magazine was an immediate success.

The success of the Journal could have put Knapp at odds with readers. Here was the editor of a magazine advancing the domestic role of women. Yet, Knapp was a working woman—a working mother. Nonetheless, Knapp never presented herself as an independent career woman. According to a story that originally appeared in the New York-based *Journalist* but was reprinted in the *Ladies' House Journal*, Knapp was "very domestic" and did her work at home—in her library.

Tensions were eliminated in 1890 when Curtis hired a new editor, Edward W. Bok, who took the *Ladies' Home Journal* to even greater heights during his twenty-nine-year tenure. Bok built on Knapp's successful editorial formula. He continued the editorial mix of domestic advice with escapism in fiction. The *Ladies' Home Journal* under Bok offered the best writers of the day. Sarah Orne Jewett, Mrs. Burton Harrison, William Dean Howells, James Whitcomb Riley, and Bret Harte, all wrote for the *Journal*. Also, the *Journal* had never looked better. Bok hired some of the finest illustrators of the day—Kate Greenaway, Charles Dana Gibson, Maxwell Parrish, Howard Charles Christy, and others—to do the front covers and inside drawings of the magazine.

The non-fiction of the *Ladies' Home Journal* under Bok was a strange conglomeration. On the one hand, he invited the leading female reformers of the day, including Frances Willard, Jeanette Rankin, and Anna Howard Shaw, to contribute essays, even as he disavowed the growing women's club movement of the late nineteenth and early twentieth centuries. Nonetheless, Bok attempted to enlist the support of the mighty Woman's Christian Temperance Union in his battle against patent medicine. Although many prominent male politicians contributed articles, Bok's *Journal* opposed women's suffrage—indeed writers emphasized that the vote was counter to everything in woman's true nature. Under Bok's direction, the *Ladies' Home Journal* attained great stature within the publishing community for high quality editorial material, an enormous circulation (exceeding one million) and advertising success.

After Bok retired in 1919, subsequent editors, H.O. Davis, John E. Pickett, Barton W. Currie, and Loring A. Shuler, found it difficult to break free of the editorial formula that seemed to work so well. Good fiction remained the hallmark of the magazine. Dorothy Parker, Booth Tarkington, Pearl Buck, Edith Wharton, Agatha Christie, H.G. Wells, and others contributed to the magazine. The magazine continued to hire some of the finest illustrators of the day. Non-fiction always provided the newest and best ways for women to carry on their domestic responsibilities. These editors did, however, add "celebrity" to the editorial mix. Actress Dorothy Gish, actor John Barrymore, and many other media personalities of the day wrote essays for the magazine.

By the Depression, the *Ladies' Home Journal* suffered from a malaise. In 1935, Curtis Publishing, still the owner of the magazine, tried an innovative approach to the editor's job. The company hired a husband-and-wife editorial team, Bruce and Beatrice Blackmar Gould, who brought a new energy and fresh editorial vision to the magazine. For twenty-seven years, the pair crafted an editorial package that, while reflecting the changing times, always valued women's domestic responsibilities. Thus, during World War II, the *Ladies' Home Journal* provided feature stories on women heroines who helped the war effort both in the United States and abroad, fiction that reinforced patriotic themes, and photographs and illustrations designed to inspire during even the darkest days of the conflict.

The more conservative America of the 1950s seemed made to order for the *Ladies' Home Journal* brand of journalism. The Goulds provided the best in fiction, advice for both the newlywed and experienced matron, celebrity interviews and essays, and fine photography and illustrations.

The Goulds also introduced one of the magazine's most popular columns, "Can This Marriage Be Saved."

But in the 1960s the nation and the women were changing. In 1962, the Goulds retired, allowing a new generation to deal with social changes and financial difficulties within Curtis Publishing. The Goulds' successor, Curtiss Anderson, did try to adjust to the changing times, even offering a special issue in 1964 in which Betty Friedan, who had just published *Feminine Mystique,* wrote about the "Fourth Dimension Woman." The next month, however, the *Journal* was back to its old message with the wife of Stuart Udall, then secretary of the Department of Interior, defending homemaking.

Anderson did not last long at the *Journal.* In 1964, he was replaced by Davis Thomas, whose tenure was even briefer. In 1965, Curtis Publishing hired John Mack Carter, the well-regarded editor of *McCall's,* another women's magazine, to guide the *Ladies' Home Journal* through financial and social challenges.

Financially, Curtis Publishing was in trouble. Facing increasing competition, advertising decreases and revenue losses (the publishing house finished in the red in 1961), Curtis sold the *Ladies' Home Journal* to Downe Communications in 1968.

To meet the social changes, Carter's *Journal* became more progressive, dealing with both the Civil Rights movement and the Vietnam War in its own style. In 1968, Mrs. Medgar Evers, widow of the slain Civil Rights activist, offered her perspective on a "Black Christmas." The magazine also demanded a full accounting of the prisoners of war and those missing in action. The *Journal* still had clout among its readers—more than sixty thousand signed petitions were sent to Congress demanding something be done.

Carter and the *Ladies' Home Journal* came face to face with the feminist movement on March 18, 1970, when some one hundred feminists from the National Organization for Women, the Feminists, Media Women, the Redstockings and the New York Radical Feminists "occupied" the magazine's editorial offices for eleven hours. They demanded a chance to put out a "liberated" issue of the periodical, the replacement of Carter with a woman, an all-woman editorial staff, an end to "exploitative" advertising in the periodical, and day care for employees. The event, which was extensively covered at the time and has become at least a footnote in most feminist histories of the period, did have results. The *Ladies Home Journal* issued an eight-page supplement entitled "The New Feminism."

Even before the siege, however, the *Ladies' Home Journal* was taking note of the women's movement, running stories on working women and discrimination in the work force. After the siege, the *LHJ* provided more "liberated" coverage, although the magazine could hardly be considered feminist. The Boston Women's Health Collective did provide an article on rape; feminist writer Letty Cottin Pogrebin wrote a column about working women;

and the magazine premiered its "Women of the Year" TV program.

Carter left the *Ladies' Home Journal* in 1973 and was replaced by his long-time editorial associate Lenore Hershey. It was a seamless transition. Hershey's *Journal* kept many of the innovations that Carter had introduced and acknowledged the diversity of women's experiences. Along with the mainstay editorial fare of food, fashion, and family, Hershey introduced a regular column by financial adviser Sylvia Porter and hosted a conference on Women in the Workforce, co-sponsored by AT&T.

In 1981, Hershey retired, replaced by Myrna Blyth, former executive editor of *Family Circle.* Under Blyth, the magazine was sold twice: in 1982 to Family Media for $15 million and in 1986 to Meredith Corporation for $92 million. Meredith, which also published *Better Homes and Gardens,* remained the owner of the *Ladies' Home Journal* well into the twenty-first century.

Under Blyth, the magazine addressed many issues facing American women—abortion, rape, drugs, balancing home and work, dealing with the challenges in the workplace. Nonetheless, the magazine never lost sight of its primary focus, giving its readers practical advice and information about food, fashion, family, and celebrities.

In 2002, Myrna Blyth retired. In 2004, she published *Spin Sisters: How the Women of the Media Sell Unhappiness and Liberalism to the Women of America,* a controversial, unflattering account of leading women in the media generally.

In 2006, Diane Salvatore, former executive director of *Marie Claire* and editor of *YM* teen magazine, was the editor of the *Ladies' Home Journal.* The magazine had a new mission— "heart, home and family." But that mission did not differ markedly from the editorial formula that had worked so well for the magazine for more than a century. The *Ladies' Home Journal* remained a place where women readers could find advice on running their homes and dealing with their families—and find some escapism from the stress of their lives. It continued to be a magazine that would "never underestimate the power of a woman."

Further Reading

Damon-Miller, Helen. *Magazines for the Millions: Gender and Commerce in the* Ladies' Home Journal *and the* Saturday Evening Post, *1880–1910.* Albany: State University of New York, 1994.

Holme, Bryan, ed. *The Journal of the Century.* New York: Viking Press, 1976.

Hunter, Jean E. "A Daring New Concept: The Ladies' Home Journal and Modern Feminism." *NWSA Journal,* Autumn 1990.

Scanlon, Jennifer, *Inarticulate Longings:* The Ladies' Home Journal, *Gender and the Promises of Consumer Culture.* New York and London: Routledge, 1995.

Steinberg, Salme Harju, *Reformer in the Marketplace: Edward W. Bok and the* Ladies' Home Journal. Baton Rouge: Louisiana State University, 1979.

KATHLEEN L. ENDRES

LANGE, DOROTHEA

Dorothea Lange (May 26, 1895–October 11, 1965) was one of America's most influential documentary photographers. She is best remembered for chronicling conditions of destitute farm families and migrant workers during the Great Depression. Lange was born Dorothea Nutzhorn on May 26, 1895, in Hoboken, New Jersey, into a family of German immigrants. At age seven she was stricken with polio that left her with a slight limp. When Dorothea was twelve, her father deserted the family, and she later dropped Nutzhorn and adopted her mother's maiden name Lange. After graduating from Wadleigh High School for Girls in 1914, Lange decided to become a photographer. She attended New York Training School for Teachers from 1914 to 1917, but spent most of her time learning the craft of photography from photographers Arnold Genthe and Clarence H. White.

In 1918 Lange moved to San Francisco and found employment as a photofinisher and freelance photographer. The following year she opened a portrait studio and continued to work as a portrait photographer for the next sixteen years. During the early 1930s she became interested in photographing the people she saw from her studio window whose lives were affected by the Depression. She turned her camera to the human suffering she witnessed and photographed breadlines, unemployed men seeking work, and labor strikes. In 1934 her photographs were exhibited at the studio of photographer Willard Van Dyke.

In 1935 Lange was hired by the Rural Rehabilitation Division of the California State Emergency Relief Administration to photograph the migrant laborers who came to California. Later that year Lange was hired as a photographer for the Resettlement Administration (later known as the Farm Security Administration) to create images for government publicity to promote New Deal agricultural relief programs. In 1936 Lange made her most notable photograph, *Migrant Mother*, taken at a migrant workers' campsite in California which depicts a woman and her children living in squalor in a pea picker's camp. The image was widely circulated in newspapers and magazines, and became a symbol for the plight of the rural poor. Lange worked for the Resettlement Administration until 1939, when she was dismissed due to budget cuts and a contentious relationship with her boss, Roy Stryker. The same year, Lange published a book of her photographs titled *An American Exodus: A Record of Human Erosion,* with her second husband, economist Paul Schuster Taylor, supplying the text.

In 1941 Lange became the first woman to win a Guggenheim Fellowship in photography, but was unable to complete it because of the nation's entry into World War II. Beginning in 1942, Lange was hired by the War Relocation Authority to photograph the internment camps where Japanese-Americans were held. From 1943 to 1945 she found employment with the Office of War Information in San Francisco. During the 1950s, Lange worked as a staff photographer for *Life* magazine, and produced several photographic essays including "Three Mormon Towns" (1954) and "Irish Country People" (1955). From 1958 to 1963 Lange again worked as a freelance photographer, accompanying her husband on U.S. aid missions around the world. In 1964 Lange was diagnosed with cancer of the esophagus, and she died on October 11, 1965.

Further Readings

Meltzer, Milton. *Dorothea Lange: A Photographer's Life.* New York: Farrar, Straus, and Giroux, 1978.

Ohrn, Karin Becker. *Dorothea Lange and the Documentary Tradition.* Baton Rouge: Louisiana State University Press, 1980.

Partridge, Elizabeth. *Restless Spirit: The Life and Work of Dorothea Lange.* New York: Viking, 1998.

Partridge, Elizabeth, ed. *Dorothea Lange: A Visual Life.* Washington, D.C.: Smithsonian Institution Press, 1994.

Riess, Suzanne. *Dorothea Lange: The Making of a Documentary Photographer.* Berkeley: University of California, Bancroft Library, Regional Oral History Office, 1968.

Taylor, Paul Schuster, and Dorothea Lange. *An American Exodus: A Record of Human Erosion.* New York: Reynal and Hitchcock, 1939. Rev. ed. New Haven, CT: Yale University Press, 1969. Reprint. New York: Arno Press, 1975.

MICHELE KROLL

LARDNER, RING

Veteran Jazz Age editor Stanley Walker saw two competing camps of sports writers emerging in America's prosperity decade. The "Gee Whiz!" crowd greatly outnumbered its competition by creating "pasteboard heroes" through writing "overblown sagas" that "godded up" athletes. The "Aw Nuts!" school of sports writers denigrated the "fine fetish" of playing sport to the limit (Walker 1934, 123–124). The undisputed leader of sports writers who made a living dampening the public adulation of sports heroes was Ring (Ringgold Wilmer) Lardner (March 6, 1885–September 25, 1933).

The sports writer nationally known for disparaging the "blissful asininity" and "anile idolatry" of hero worship was the spoiled son of a privileged family in Niles, Michigan. (Lardner 1922, 459) Ring was the youngest of nine children born to Henry Lardner, a businessman who made his money in real estate, and Lena Bogardus Phillips, a rector's daughter who wrote poetry, played the piano and organ, and loved the arts. Ring was named after a relative, Cadwalader Ringgold, a navy admiral who fought pirates in the West Indies, and explored the Antarctic and Western Pacific.

Ring was a casual student under private tutors. He studied mechanical engineering at the Armour Institute in Chicago, but quit to write and produce comic operas for the Niles Opera House during the 1903 season. The collapse of his father's finances forced him to find work as a substitute mailman and gas company meter reader. He had little ambition and had not prepared for a career. When his brother Rex became a reporter for the *Niles Daily Sun*, Ring talked his way into a job as "sporting editor" of the *South Bend Tribune*. He made twelve dollars a week and a dollar a game as official scorer at South Bend Class B baseball games.

Chicago's best known baseball writer Hugh Fullerton helped launch Lardner's career as a big city sports reporter in 1907 for the *Chicago Inter-Ocean*. Lardner's arrival in the nation's second city coincided with mounting municipal excitement over their baseball teams and America's new "national past-time." The White Sox had defeated the Cubs in the 1906 World Series and the Cubs swept the Detroit Tigers in the series the following year. William Randolph Hearst hoped to make his *Chicago Examiner* the city's number one morning paper by boosting baseball. He hired Lardner, who faithfully followed the Cubs and Sox through an extraordinary 1908 season that saw Big Ed Walsh win thirty-nine games for the South Siders, while Tinkers to Evers to Chance led the Cubs to their second consecutive World Series win. Lardner expanded his sports reporting in the *Chicago Tribune*, the city's dominant morning paper, in 1909 and 1910. He grew more interested in the players than the play and began writing "Pullman Pasttimes" as managing editor for the *Sporting News* in 1911, where he developed sketches that amusingly re-created club-car conversations he had had with the sport's most colorful characters.

Lardner married Ellis Abbott of Goshen, Indiana on June 28, 1911, and attempted to amuse readers that year as sports editor of the *Boston American* by using humor to blunt the sting of the 107-loss season of the National League Braves, who finished fifty-four games out of first place. In 1912, Lardner returned to work for the *Examiner* and in the following year on June 3, 1913, he took over the column "In the Wake of the News" at the competing *Tribune*. There, freed from the responsibilities of covering a team, Lardner used his powers of wit and irony and whimsically used vernacular in helping to raise sports journalism to the level of literary art. H.L. Mencken and F. Scott Fitzgerald celebrated Lardner's deft touch with language. A young Ernest Hemingway was an early imitator. A biographer writes that Lardner would become "one of the most copied and parodied writers of his time" (Bruccoli 1992, xii).

Widely quoted Lardner lines included, "The Del Ray motordome at Los Angeles burned to the ground with a great saving of life" (Elder 1956, 106) and a parody on family relations, "Are you lost daddy I asked tenderly. Shut up he explained." (Rosmond and Morgan 1962, 28) Of one heavyweight contender he told readers, "I don't care if he win or lose, only I kind of figure that he can't" (*Chicago Tribune*, July 4, 1919). His famous dialogues include an apocryphal exchange between a batter who had just struck out and disconsolately returns to the dugout. The manager asks, "Has he got anything?" The player answers, "He ain't got nothin'." The manager replies, "Looks like he must have somethin'" (Lardner, Jr., 83).

Lardner's fictional pieces on baseball busher Jack Keefe began appearing in the *Saturday Evening Post* in 1915. The stories were compiled in the popular 1915 book *You Know Me Al*. Additional compilations of Keefe tales appeared in *Treat 'Em Rough* (1918) and *The Real Dope* (1919). Lardner's sports reporting were nationally distributed through the Bell Syndicate, beginning in 1919, including his coverage that year of a World Series he suspected was being thrown by the White Sox. After watching Chicago's "alleged" pitcher Lefty Williams give up four runs in a third of an inning in the deciding game, Lardner suggested "William" might be the "illegitimate son" of a Duke of Normandy, whose real name was "Robert the Devil." Lardner predicted "it is probably the last world serious I will ever see" (Bruccoli 1992, 608–609). Eight players were later banned for their role in baseball's biggest scandal.

Beginning in 1920 Lardner largely abandoned baseball for other sports and wider features that would appear in the *Saturday Evening Post*, *Collier's*, *American Magazine* and the *New Yorker*. Several collections of short stories were published, and he collaborated with George S. Kaufman and others on Broadway plays. After a long illness from heart disease, Lardner died an early death, leaving friend Fitzgerald to famously write, "Ring got less percentage of himself on paper than any other American of the first flight" (Fitzgerald 1933, 255). Mencken thought Lardner unsurpassed in his ear for the vernacular and considered his work a lasting "mine of authentic Americana" and "an incomparable service to etymology" (*Chicago Tribune*, September 26, 1933, 16).

Further Reading

Bruccoli, Matthew J., ed. *Ring Around the Bases: The Complete Baseball Stories of Ring Lardner*. New York: Charles Scribner's Sons, 1992.

Bruccoli, Matthew J., and Richard Layman, eds. *Ring W. Lardner: A Descriptive Bibliography*. Pittsburgh: University of Pittsburgh Press, 1976.

Caruthers, Clifford M., ed. *Letters of Ring Lardner*. Washington, D.C.: Orchises, 1995.

Caruthers, Clifford M. ed. *Ring Around Max: The Correspondence of Ring Lardner and Max Perkins*. DeKalb, IL: Northern Illinois University Press, 1973.

Elder, Donald. *Ring Lardner*. Garden City, NY: Doubleday, 1956.

Friedrich, Otto. *Ring Lardner*. Minneapolis: University of Minnesota Press, 1965.

Geismar, Maxwell. *Ring Lardner and the Portrait of Folly*. New York: Thomas Y. Crowell, 1972.

Geismar, Maxwell, ed. *The Ring Lardner Reader*. New York: Charles Scribner's Sons, 1963.

Fitzgerald, F. Scott. "Ring," in *The New Republic* 76, October 11, 1933, 254–255.

Hilton, George W., ed. *The Annotated Baseball Stories of Ring Lardner, 1914–1919*. Stanford: Stanford University Press, 1995.

Hodermarsky, Mark. *Baseball's Greatest Writers*. Dubuque: Kendall/Hunt Publishers, 2003.

Lardner, Ring. "Ring Lardner Himself," *Saturday Evening Post* CLXXXIX, April 28, 1917, 37, 45.

Lardner, Ring. "Sport and Play." In *Civilization in the United States: An Inquiry by Thirty Americans*, edited by Harold E. Stearns, 459–461. New York: Harcourt, Brace, 1922.

Lardner, Jr. Ring, *The Lardners: My Family Remembered*, New York: Harper & Row, 1976. *New York Times*, September 26, 1933.

Papers of Ring Lardner. Newberry Library. Chicago, Illinois.

Patrick, Walton R. *Ring Lardner.* New York: Twayne Publishers, 1963.

Rosmond, Babette, and Henry Morgan, eds. *Shut Up, He Explained.* New York: Charles Scribner's Sons, 1962.

Seldes, Gilbert, ed. *The Portable Ring Lardner,*.New York: Viking Press, 1946.

Walker, Stanley. *City Editor.* New York: Frederick A. Stokes, 1934.

Yardley, Jonathan. *Ring: A Biography of Ring Lardner,* New York: Random House, 1977.

BRUCE J. EVENSEN

LATINO PRESS

Partly native, partly immigrant, partly bilingual, and partly Latin American, the Latino press is the oldest of the presses of people of color in the United States. This is not surprising, since the first printing press and the first newspaper on the American continent were established in Mexico. The first Latino newspaper, *El Misisipí* (1808–1810), was founded in New Orleans during the Napoleonic Wars. The four-page bilingual newspaper was published primarily in Spanish and focused its coverage and commentary on the European conflict and its impact on Latin America. Little is known about *El Misisipí* as there is only one existing copy.

In the Southwest, more than one hundred Latino newspapers were published between 1846 and 1900, most of them in New Mexico, Texas, and California. Spanish-language newspapers and inserts were the financial engine behind the establishment of English-language newspapers because some local and state governments paid newspaper businesses to publish translations of new laws into Spanish. Some of these sections were used as mere instruments of symbolic conquest with no ties to the Latino communities they pretended to serve. In some instances, they were even boycotted and rejected by those communities. This was the case of the Santa Barbara newspaper *The Gazette* (1855–1858) and its Spanish-language section *La Gaceta.*

By contrast, newspapers controlled by Latino journalists during this era served as instruments to resist the subordinate status of Latino communities of color, which were physically subjugated and openly denied equal political, legal, and social status. *El Clamor Público* (1855–1859) of Los Angeles, for example, defended the rights of Latinos and forcefully denounced lynchings and other forms of extralegal violence against Latino communities in California. Like pioneer African American journalists (such as Samuel Cornish and Frederick Douglass), the editor of *El Clamor Público,* Francisco P. Ramírez, was a democratic idealist who believed in a notion of democracy that was inclusive (not limited by race) and comprehensive (not limited to electoral politics).

Nineteenth-century newspapers were also essential in the formation of an early pan-Latino identity because they were edited by and directed toward Spanish-speaking people from different backgrounds. In New York, Cubans, Puerto Ricans, and Spaniards established the first Latino newspapers, while in California, Latino newspaper editors were from Peru, Chile, Mexico, Spain, Colombia, and California. This common identity became political when some Latino newspapers resisted the expanding United States empire. Again, *El Clamor Público* is an early example; the newspaper opposed U.S. intervention in Latin America and private military expeditions into Mexico and Central America. Later, in New York, after the Spanish-American War ended and Puerto Rico was taken by the United States, Luis Muñoz Rivera's bilingual newspaper, the *Puerto Rico Herald* (1901–1904), was an important voice against the Foraker Act, which imposed a U.S.-controlled governing body in the island.

The first half of the twentieth century saw the emergence of contemporary Latino newspapers. Two of the oldest newspapers still published today in the United States were established then: *La Prensa* (1913) in New York and *La Opinión* (1926) in Los Angeles. *La Prensa*, established by Spaniards in New York City, was generally sympathetic to Latin American revolutionary movements and Spain's Republic. After the World War II, *La Prensa* became responsive to the needs of the growing Puerto Rican population in the city. The paper was finally merged with *El Diario de Nueva York* in 1961 to become *El Diario/La Prensa*, a forceful advocate for the rights of a diverse group of Latinos in New York City—Puerto Ricans, Dominicans, Cubans, and Central and South Americans. In Los Angeles, *La Opinión* was established in 1926 by Ignacio Lozano, owner of San Antonio's *La Prensa* (1913). Both *La Prensa* of San Antonio and the early *La Opinión* were thought of as addressing the needs of an exiled community of Mexicans. Eventually the Lozano family closed *La Prensa* in 1957, and *La Opinión* changed its focus to primarily address the needs of a growing and diverse Latino community in Southern California.

The Latino press was instrumental in the fight for the civil rights of Latinos. Ignacio López, editor of *El Espectador* (1933–1961) in California's San Gabriel Valley, is considered one of the pioneer Latino editors in this regard. Like his African American counterpart, Charlotta Bass of the *California Eagle*, López used *El Espectador* to fight for the equal rights for Latinos to housing, schools, and public places, particularly movie theaters and swimming pools. The paper organized boycotts and lawsuits to achieve these goals. Later, during the 1960s, the Chicano press emerged, predominantly but not exclusively in the Southwest, as an underground press of the civil rights struggle of the 1960s and 1970s. Publications such as *El Malcriado* (1964) of the United Farm Workers and *La Raza* (1967–1973) of El Barrio Communications Project were openly political and deeply involved with the groups and communities they covered.

During the last thirty years, fueled by rapid migration from Latin America, English-language newspapers became more interested in the Latino market. The *Miami Herald* started a Spanish-language section in 1976 called *El Miami Herald*, predominantly with Spanish-language translations of English-language articles. After years of confrontations between the *Herald* and a segment of the Cuban-American exile community over the coverage of Cuba, the newspaper decided to have a separate publication in Spanish, *El Nuevo Herald* (1987), first distributed as an insert of the English-language paper and later independently. Since then, *El Nuevo Herald* has become one of the most powerful Latino newspapers in the country, with a daily circulation of almost ninety thousand copies. Meanwhile, on the West Coast, in the mid-1980s the *Los Angeles Times* launched a monthly bilingual insert, *Nuestro Tiempo*. In 1988, the format was changed to Spanish-only due to low advertising revenue, and the project was closed once the *Times* bought 50 percent of *La Opinión*'s stock in 1990. This began a new partnership between the two media companies, which lasted fourteen years. During those years, *La Opinión* continued functioning independently of the *Times*. In 2004, the partnership between the papers was dissolved. *La Opinión*'s circulation is now one hundred twenty-five thousand copies.

That same year, the Tribune Corporation, owner of the *Los Angeles Times*, launched *Hoy* as a national newspaper with some local content produced and distributed in New York City, Chicago, and Los Angeles. Meanwhile, CPK Media Holdings, the new owners of *El Diario/La Prensa*, joined *La Opinión*'s Lozano family to create a Latino newspaper chain called ImpreMedia. Since then, ImpreMedia has bought *La Raza* of Chicago, *El Mensajero* of San Francisco, and *La Prensa* of Orlando, transforming itself into the largest Latino newspaper chain in the country.

Further Reading

Cortés, Carlos E. "The Mexican-American Press." In *The Ethnic Press in the United States: A Historical Analysis and Handbook*, edited by Sally M. Miller, 247–260, New York: Greenwood Press, 1987.

Del Olmo, Frank. "Chicano Journalism: New Medium for New Conciousness." In *Readings in Mass Communication*. 2nd ed., edited by Michael C. Emery and Ted Curtis Smyth, 306–312, Dubuque, Iowa: William G. Brown, 1974.

Fitzpatrick, Joseph P. "The Puerto Rican Press." In *The Ethnic Press in the United States: A Historical Analysis and Handbook*, edited by Sally M. Miller, 303–314, New York: Greenwood Press, 1987.

Goff, Victoria. "Spanish-Language Newspapers in California." In *Outsiders in 19th-Century Press History: Multicultural Perspectives*, edited by Frankie Hutton and Barbara Straus Reed, 55–70, Bowling Green, OH: Bowling Green State University Popular Press, 1995.

Gutiérrez, Félix F. "Francisco P. Ramírez: Californio Editor and Yanqui Conquest." *Media Studies Journal* 14, no. 2 (Spring/Summer 2000):16–23.

Gutiérrez, Félix. "Spanish-Language Media in America: Background, Resources, History." *Journalism History* 4, no. 2 (Summer 1977): 34–41, 65–67.

Rodríguez, América. *Making Latino News: Race, Language, Class*. Thousand Oaks, CA: Sage, 1999.

JOSÉ LUIS BENAVIDES

LAWSON, VICTOR FREMONT

Victor Lawson (September 9, 1850–August 19, 1925) helped invent the modern American newspaper by neither writing nor editing the *Chicago Daily News*, but by creating a publication that took its communal responsibilities seriously, while emphasizing the importance of international and cooperative news-gathering that gave readers the news they needed to know.

Chicago was a cholera-infested frontier town of twenty-eight thousand when Lawson was born to Norwegian immigrants who had come to the city to make money in real estate speculation. Iver Lawson and Melinda Nordvig Lawson were able to send their son to Phillips Academy in Andover, Massachusetts, but the Great Chicago Fire of 1871 all but wiped out the family's holdings and ended Iver Lawson's public career as city alderman and state senator.

After his father's death in 1872 Lawson began managing the *Skandinaven*, a daily Norwegian-language newspaper in which his father had been a partner. In December 1875 Lawson allowed friend and former schoolmate Melville E. Stone to rent eight square feet of space in the *Skandinaven* office to turn out the first issues of the *Chicago Daily News*. Six months later, Stone could not pay the struggling paper's $50 wire service bill. Lawson bought out Stone's two partners and the two men began a collaboration that made journalism history.

By the end of 1876, the *Daily News* at fourteen thousand was Chicago's widest circulating afternoon newspaper. Stone edited the paper and supervised its staff. Lawson established its business principles and overall direction. The two men positioned the paper not in service to any particular class of readers but instead ceaselessly searched for stories that interested readers who had a shared interest in the life of the city and its future. The paper's price, only a penny, put it within reach of every laborer and businessman who took pride in the paper's editorial advocacy of improving city streets, sewers, schools and public utilities. Neighborhood news celebrated the city's growth and growing diversity. The paper was among the first to effectively court women readers with short stories, household hints, fashion reports, and family news that Lawson was certain women liked to read.

Lawson married Jessie Bradley in 1880 after the two met while singing in the choir of a local Congregational church. The circulation of the *Daily News* soared to one hundred thousand by 1885, facilitating the couple's philanthropies that included construction of community centers, the completion of a sanitarium to serve the city's poorest children, the building of dormitories for young men new to the city, financial and editorial support for the city's expanding charities, and seed money for the eventual establishment of the Chicago Theological Seminary. The Lawsons were strict Sabbatarians who banned liquor from their home and liquor ads from the *Daily News*. Throughout the paper's 102-year history, it did not publish on Sundays.

Lawson had firm ideas about news and advertising. He shared Stone's enthusiasm for accuracy and impartiality and established a fixed ad rate. He insisted that advertising be listed as advertising and not news. To do otherwise "risked one's reputation with the public" (Lawson's Papers. Letters dated February 28, 1878, and February 11, 1879). In 1888, the year Stone sold his interest in the paper to

Lawson, the circulation of the *Daily News* reached two hundred thousand, second largest in the nation. Lawson had launched a morning newspaper, *The News*, in 1881. When he sold it in 1914, it was worth $2.3 million. Soon after Lawson died in 1925, the *Daily News* sold for an unprecedented $13.5 million. By this time, nearly half a million of the city's three million residents were regular readers of the *Daily News*. Lawson's reputation was now international. He was a champion of cooperative news-gathering, who had established the City News Bureau in 1890 to assure professional police reporting, and he had become president of the Associated Press in 1894, eventually creating a network of twelve hundred newspapers that voluntarily shared the news on a non-profit basis. Other newspapers followed Lawson's lead in establishing foreign news bureaus after 1898, but few could match his lead in developing reporters and columnists. Eugene Field, George Ade, Ben Hecht, Finley Peter Dunne, and Carl Sandburg were among those who learned their craft at the *Daily News*. The paper would receive its first Pulitzer Prize for Reporting in the year of Lawson's death.

Few men foresaw the future of journalism as clearly as Victor Lawson. His emergence as a young publisher with communitarian concerns in America's late Gilded Age helped transform twentieth century news-gathering into a cooperative enterprise evoking municipal pride while enhancing international awareness.

Further Reading

Abramoske, Donald J. "The Founding of the *Chicago Daily News*." *Journal of the Illinois State Historical Society* 59, 1966, 341–353.

Baker, Ray Stannard. "Interesting People: Victor F. Lawson," *American Magazine* LXIX, November 1909, 64.

Chicago Tribune, August 20, 1925, 1, 2.

Dennis, Charles H. *Victor Lawson: His Time and His Work*. New York: Greenwood, 1968, originally 1935.

Gramling, Oliver. *AP: The Story of News*. New York: Farrar and Rinehart, 1940.

Moses, John, and Maj. Joseph Kirkland. *The History of Chicago*. Chicago: Munsell, 1895.

Nord, David Paul. "The Business Values of American Newspapers: The Nineteenth-Century Watershed in Chicago." *Journalism Quarterly* 61, 1984, 265–273.

Nord, David Paul. "The Urbanization of Journalism in Chicago." *Journal of Urban History* 11, August 1985, 411–441.

Papers of Victor F. Lawson, Newberry Library, Chicago, Illinois.

Pierce, Bessie Louise. *A History of Chicago: The Rise of a Modern City, 1871–1893*. Chicago: University of Chicago Press, 1957.

Rosewater, Victor *History of Cooperative News-Gathering in the United States*. New York: D. Appleton, 1930.

Schwarzlose, Richard Allen. *American Wire Services: A Study of Their Development as a Social Institution*. New York: Arno Press, 1979.

Smith, Henry Justin. *A Gallery of Chicago Editors*. Chicago: Chicago Daily News, 1930.

Stone, Melville E. *Fifty Years a Journalist*. New York: Greenwood, 1968, originally 1921.

BRUCE J. EVENSEN

LEE, IVY LEDBETTER

Ivy Ledbetter Lee (July 16, 1877–November 9, 1934) is considered to be one of the fathers of modern public relations. The son of a minister, Lee was born in Georgia in 1877 and attended Princeton University where he studied under Woodrow Wilson and was fully indoctrinated in the ideals of America's Progressive Era that emphasized the importance of facts and the ability of people to rationally draw their own conclusions.

Lee began his career as a reporter covering general assignments and Wall Street for the *New York Journal*, *World* and *Times*. Lee left newspapering in 1904 and worked two years as a freelance writer and publicist before opening a publicity firm in 1906 with fellow reporter George Parker. The firm was the fourth publicity agency founded in the United States.

Lee and Parker envisioned an approach to serving clients that radically differed from the flimflam press agentry that characterized public relations work at the time. The former reporter understood that news workers needed information and timely service in order to adequately cover his clients.

In 1906, Lee issued a now-famous Declaration of Principles outlining how his firm would operate. In part, it read: "This is not a secret press bureau. All our work is done in the open. We aim to supply news. This is not an advertising agency; if you think any of our matter ought properly to go to your business office, do not use it. Our matter is accurate. Further details on any subject treated will be supplied promptly, and any editor will be assisted most cheerfully in verifying directly any statement of fact" (Hiebert 1966, 48).

Two years later, *Editor & Publisher* observed Parker & Lee had established its credibility among editors and was "never sensational, never libelous, always trustworthy, and always readable."

Lee's early clients included the mine owners during the 1906 anthracite coal strike and the Pennsylvania Railroad. Among other innovations, Lee convinced the railroad's publicity-shy officials to reverse their long-standing policy to avoid publicity about train accidents. Instead, Lee gave reporters complete access to all the facts about an incident—and even took reporters to accident sites at the railroad's expense.

During 1914, while serving as the assistant to the railroad's president, Lee served as part-time consultant to his most famous client, John D. Rockefeller, Jr. Lee had been recommended by Arthur Brisbane to help the Rockefellers respond to attacks stemming from the suffocation deaths of thirteen women and children during a bitter coal strike in Colorado.

Hired a full six weeks after the so-called "Ludlow Massacre," Lee recommended that the coal operators launch a program to communicate factually their side of the strike to opinion leaders. News interest in the controversy had already waned, so Lee produced a series of nineteen bulletins during the year that were mailed to as many as forty thousand prominent individuals nationwide, including newspaper editors. The intensive effort helped stem the tide of negative public opinion as the strike collapsed at the end of the year.

After working during 1915 on the staff of the Rockefellers, Lee opened his own publicity firm in 1916 and immediately attracted a stable of prominent clients—public utilities, banks, investment companies, shipping interests, mining firms, and foreign cartels. Among his first assignments was promoting ridership on New York's subway system. His "Elevated Express" and "Subway Sun" posters were popular artifacts in New York City's culture from 1918 to 1932.

Lee continued his work for the Rockefellers until his death in 1934, and encouraged the family to be more open about its activities. Contrary to popular accounts, Lee never recommended that John D. Rockefeller Sr. give away dimes to children. However, he helped recraft the image of the once-despised oil baron into one of a kindly philanthropist. Lee also was instrumental in promoting some of John D. Rockefeller Jr.'s most important initiatives: the Rockefeller Foundation's new medical school in China, the restoration of Colonial Williamsburg, and the building of Riverside Memorial Church and Rockefeller Center in New York.

Lee's initial work for the Rockefellers, which he conducted secretly in order to avoid publicity for his railroad employer, thrust Lee into the public spotlight when he and the Rockefellers became the target of a pro-labor investigation by the U.S. Commission on Industrial Relations. Lee's two appearances before the federal investigators—in January and May 1915—resulted in widespread visibility for both him and the power of publicity agents. Upton Sinclair later vilified Lee as "Poison Ivy" in his attack on American journalism, *The Brass Check* (1920).

Controversy followed Lee throughout his career. In the 1920s, Lee was attacked for his belief that United States should recognize the Communist regime in Russia. Later, as a result of his work for a Belgian chemical company and the German Dye Trust just prior to his death in 1934, Lee was investigated for being a Nazi propagandist. In both cases, he was absolved of any wrongdoing.

Lee never used the term "public relations." Instead, he practiced what he called *publicity*, which he defined as "everything involved in the expression of an idea or of an institution—including the policy or the idea expressed" (Lee 1925, 8). Nonetheless, Lee was among the first to articulate the importance of two-way communication between organizations and the public as well as a counseling role in modern public relations. According to Lee, the modern publicist: "… is going to become much more than a mere press agent. As he develops, he will see that his job cannot be done if he is merely to have policies determined and then be told that he must "put them over." … If he has personality, brains and judgment, he is going to be able very soon to show the heads of the corporation that the policy of the corporation is the vital thing, rather than the mere information that is put out to the public" (Lee 1925, 26–27).

Lee staunchly denied claims that he could get newspapers to publish anything he wanted—claims made during the early 1920s, when *Editor & Publisher* and *Printer's Ink* waged vigorous campaigns to discourage editors from using "free publicity" materials. He argued that information had to be *newsworthy* in order for information to gain coverage. Whereas "improper" propaganda failed to disclose the source of information, "proper" publicity was honest, acknowledged and responsible (Lee 1925, 33, 37).

Further Reading

Goldman, E.F. Two-*Way Street: The Emergence of the Public Relations Counsel*. Boston: Bellman, 1948.

Hallahan, Kirk. "Ivy Lee and the Rockefellers' Response to the 19131914 Colorado.

Coal Strike," *Journal of Public Relations Research, 12* (2003), 264–315.

Hiebert, Ray Eldon. *Courtier to the Crowd: The Story of Ivy Lee and the Development of Public Relations*. Ames: Iowa State University Press, 1966.

Lee, Ivy. *Publicity: Some of the Things It Is and Is Not*. New York: Industries Publishing Company [privately published, 1925].

Marchand, Roland. *Creating the Corporate Soul: The Rise of Public Relations and Corporate Imagery in American Big Business*. Berkeley: University of California Press, 1998.

Sinclair, Upton. *The Brass Check. A Study of American Journalism.* Pasadena, CA: Author, 1920.

KIRK HALLAHAN

LEGISLATIVE BRANCH REPORTING: THE CONGRESS

Congress has traditionally gone to great lengths to accommodate reporters, only to see its share of news coverage diminish over time. For over a century, Congress stood at the center of Washington news as the most open branch of the federal government. Steadily since the 1930s the focus of the Washington press corps has shifted towards the presidency. The one hundred senators and four hundred and thirty-five representatives engaged in significant legislative activities can rarely command the media attention a president receives at routine events. Reporting about Congress has decreased on the national level, producing fewer front-page and evening news reports, but the proliferation of cable news channels and online newsletters have offered senators and representatives a myriad of other opportunities for public visibility.

As elected officials, members of Congress have usually been eager for press attention to inform and impress their constituencies, promote their legislative initiatives, and build their national reputations. Members issue press releases, hire press secretaries, hold press conferences, stage photo opportunities, conduct public hearings, and give interviews to reporters—on and off the record. The legislative branch has been a particularly fertile field for uncovering otherwise suppressed information about the government. Legislative bodies are rarely able to hold secrets, since those determined to withhold information are usually balanced by others with a compelling reason to release it. Reporters appreciate the abundance of sources and daily stories on Capitol Hill, although their editors discourage them from filing "railway timetable" accounts of when a bill has left a subcommittee and where it is likely to stop next.

Reporting on the national legislature began with the First Congress in 1789. The House of Representatives, then the only part of the federal government directly elected by the people, provided a public gallery and welcomed reporters to observe its proceedings from the start. Senators, at that time elected by state legislatures, considered public scrutiny unnecessary and met entirely in closed session. Persistent complaints from newspaper editors finally led the Senate to construct a public gallery and the open its sessions to view in 1795. The first reporters who covered Congress acted essentially as stenographers who recorded debates verbatim or summarized them without comment. The newspapers' practice of underwriting the reporting of debates followed the federal government from New York to Philadelphia in 1790, and to Washington, D.C., in 1800.

During the first three decades in Washington, the *National Intelligencer* dominated Congressional reporting. The paper's publishers, Joseph Gales and William Seaton, also served as public printers, and government printing contracts subsidized their coverage of the Congressional debates. The *Intelligencer* was mailed free to newspapers around the country, where exchange editors could clip and reprint those portions of the debates most relevant to their readers. It was not uncommon for speeches by Daniel Webster, John C. Calhoun, and Henry Clay, along with many lesser lights, to occupy prominent space in the nation's newspapers. Most senators and representatives therefore took pains to correct the transcripts of their remarks before publication. In 1825, Gales and Seaton began privately publishing the *Register of Debates*, a forerunner of the *Congressional Record*, the daily verbatim accounts of Congressional proceedings that the Government Printing Office has published since 1873.

A single newspaper from the national capital could suffice during the "Era of Good Feelings," when only a single political party functioned. As political unity unraveled in the 1820s, various factions launched their own newspapers in Washington to promote their presidential candidates and legislative agendas. At the same time, regional differences were growing more pronounced. During the tariff debates in 1827, merchants from New England and planters from the South sent local editors to spend the Congressional session in Washington to report on bills that would affect their particular economic interests. Since these out-of-town journalists at first sent their reports back to their papers by letter, they became known as correspondents.

Contending for limited space in the public galleries, the correspondents sought equal access with the reporters of debate on the floor of the House and Senate chambers. But members of Congress distinguished between the neutral reporters, who simply recorded their speeches, and the correspondents, who analyzed and criticized what they said.

They denied the correspondents privileges of the floor, but in 1841 Kentucky Senator Henry Clay persuaded the Senate to reserve the front row of the gallery above the presiding officer for the press. Once the House of Representatives moved to its current chamber in 1857, it too established a press gallery.

The inventor Samuel F. B. Morse publicly tested the telegraph in the Capitol in 1844, after running wires from Washington to Baltimore. Baltimore newspapers were the first anywhere to publish telegraph dispatches, reporting on votes taken in Congress. Some of the leading newspapers then pooled their resources and created the Associated Press, to utilize the new means of communication. Political news filled the wires, but high telegraph tolls encouraged shorter reports and newspapers shifted away from reproducing Congressional speeches verbatim.

Mid-nineteenth century newspaper reporting was overtly partisan, with prominent politicians often owning the newspapers for which the correspondents reported. Since newspapers could usually afford to pay their Washington correspondents only for the months that Congress was in session—about half the year—many of the correspondents took part-time assignments as committee clerks in the House and the Senate, while still filing their dispatches. Reporters who moonlighted as clerks got inside sources of news, and the members of Congress who hired them could count on favorable publicity. An exception to the prevailing partisanship was the Washington correspondent for the Associated Press, who knew that his dispatches went to newspapers of all political leanings and therefore stuck to the facts and avoided editorializing. The trend toward objective reporting accelerated during the latter nineteenth century as commercial advertising weaned newspapers off of political patronage. The more that newspapers separated their news and editorial pages, the more unseemly it became for Washington correspondents to clerk for the Congress.

The Press Galleries and Their Standing Committees of Correspondents

Admission to the Congressional press galleries was determined at first by the Vice President in his role as President of the Senate, and by the Speaker of the House. As politicians, they sought favor with the press and admitted anyone who claimed to be a reporter. By the 1870s lobbyists were posing as reporters and the exposure of their activities in several scandals threatened to discredit the press corps as a whole. The leading correspondents then approached the Congressional leadership with an offer to reform the press galleries. Officially sanctioned by the House and Senate, the journalists elected a Standing Committee of Correspondents that set rules for admission and judged the credentials of those applying for press passes. The first rules defined a legitimate reporter as someone who filed telegraph dispatches to a daily newspaper. As intended, the rules eliminated lobbyists from the press galleries, but they also shut out most women and minorities. Women drew assignments for social reporting, which while popular did not justify the costs of telegraphy. Women reporters mailed their stories to their papers, so the Standing Committee denied them accreditation. Similarly, since the black press consisted entirely of weeklies—and the mainstream daily papers did not hire African Americans—black reporters found themselves ineligible for press gallery membership.

Not until World War II did appreciable numbers of women gain access to the Congressional press galleries. They took the place of men who had gone overseas as war correspondents or combatants. Although the men reclaimed many of these jobs after the war, the ranks of women reporters expanded over the following decades. No African American reporter sat in the press galleries until 1947, when the Senate Rules Committee ordered the Standing Committee to give press credentials to Louis Lautier, Washington correspondent for the National Negro Publishers Association, on the ground that one of his client papers was the *Atlantic Daily World*, the sole black daily at the time. The integration of the press galleries by race and gender matched the diversification of membership in Congress and ensured that issues concerning women and minorities would receive greater media coverage.

The authority of the Standing Committee of Correspondents to define legitimate journalism also created barriers against new technology. Newspaper reporters denied press passes to the writers for the muckraking magazine of the Progressive era, and also to the first radio broadcasters of the 1920s and 1930s. In 1939 Fulton Lewis Jr., a newspaper reporter turned radio commentator, protested this exclusion to his friends in Congress, who responded by creating a separate Radio Gallery. Congress also established a Periodical Press Gallery—for magazines and newsletters—and a Press Photographers Gallery. Each new gallery elected its own self-governing Standing Committee of Correspondents, which had jurisdiction over the corresponding galleries in the Senate and House.

Since the major radio networks operated the first television networks, the Radio Correspondents' Galleries converted effortlessly into the Radio and Television Correspondents' Galleries in 1953. By the 1990s, the Standing Committees of Correspondents of each of the galleries had more difficulty grappling with the implications of digital electronics and the Internet. Telegraph operators and bulky tickertape machines that had long been staples of the press galleries were removed as reporters began to send dispatches and follow breaking news online. Applications for press gallery credentials came from Internet news operations that ranged from large media organizations to single-person web logs (or blogs). This posed the problem of separating the professional journalists among them from the amateurs and advocates for special interests.

In 2005 the Standing Committee of Correspondents for the newspapers' press gallery reconciled its rules to the new media. To be admitted, reporters must work for a news services whose principal business was the selling of news content to daily news publications, and be full-time, paid correspondents who required on-site access to Congressio-

nal members and staff. They could not engage in lobbying, paid advocacy activities, advertising, publicity or promotion work for any political party, corporation, or government agency.

The Changing Impact of Technology

During the era when the Capitol represented the center of national journalism, correspondents timed their arrivals and departures in Washington with each session of Congress. In the nineteenth century the executive branch did not produce sufficient news to justify the expense of posting a correspondent at the capital all year. For the months that Congress was in adjournment, newspapers relied on reporters for the wire services and the local Washington papers to provide news coverage from the capital.

Beginning with Theodore Roosevelt, presidents held informal and formal press conferences, and the first pressroom was opened in the West Wing in 1902. Despite mounting presidential competition, Congress remained the best source of information in Washington, since its members were often willing to share news that the administration was not ready to release. As late as 1932, reporters ranked assignments at the Senate as more rewarding than those at the White House. The following year, Franklin D. Roosevelt and the New Deal changed all that. The dynamic new president courted the press corps to win public support for his programs. Covering that multitude of programs provided Washington reporters with year-round employment.

Roosevelt took advantage of radio to speak to the public directly, over the heads of reporters, editors, and publishers. Many members of Congress were equally anxious to use the new medium, although the more seasoned political speakers had trouble standing still before a microphone and addressing an unseen audience. Radio networks offered airtime to senators and representatives, but they spoke in a multitude of voices, which put them at a disadvantage against the sole voice of the president.

The arrival of television provided Congress with additional opportunities and handicaps. Television affected the way Congressional candidates campaigned, and eventually caused oratory to devolve into sound bites. Television aired Harry Truman's State of the Union message to a joint session of Congress in 1947, but it could not broadcast the debates in either the House or Senate. House Speaker Sam Rayburn also instituted the "Rayburn Rule" that barred television cameras from all House committee hearings, a ban not lifted until 1972. The Senate permitted the televising of its hearings, which elevated a number of senators into presidential contenders. The televised hearings of a special committee to investigate organized crime in 1950 made a national celebrity out of the committee's chairman, Tennessee Senator Estes Kefauver. Wisconsin Senator Joseph R. McCarthy similarly courted the cameras at his investigations into alleged Communist subversion in the government, but in 1954 the televised Army-McCarthy hearings revealed his bullying tactics and contributed to his censure by the Senate. Television coverage of a Senate investigation into labor racketeering, as well as the presidential primaries and the first televised presidential debate, may have enabled a backbench senator, John F. Kennedy, to win the presidency in 1960.

With more Americans getting their news from television than any other source, the networks struggled to find more interesting ways of presenting the news from Congress. When Southerners conducted a lengthy filibuster against the Civil Rights Act of 1964, CBS assigned correspondent Roger Mudd to broadcast from the Capitol steps each day that the filibuster lasted. Although Mudd balanced interviews with proponents and opponents of the bill, those conducting the filibuster realized that his daily accounts were dramatizing their obstructionist tactics. They persuaded the Capitol Police to move the reporter and camera crew off the steps to the lawn across the Capitol plaza. Thereafter it became commonplace for television correspondents to broadcast from that vantage, positioning the Capitol dome prominently behind them.

The House of Representatives finally permitted televising of its debates in 1979, and the Senate followed in 1986. The Cable-Satellite Public Affairs Network, C-SPAN, provided regular outlets for the broadcasts. Not only citizens but reporters could now follow the debates from a distance, and the Congressional press galleries emptied out except during moments of high drama.

As the national news coverage of Congress eroded, legislators counted on local and regional news coverage to keep their constituents informed and boost their chances of re-election. The wire services and other news services assigned regional reporters to cover the Congressional delegations from one or more states in a particular region. By the 1970s, this system raised charges of an unduly cozy relationship between the regional reporters and their key Congressional sources. Dependent on the members from their regions, reporters largely refrained from criticizing their regular sources. By the end of the twentieth century, news services had cut back sharply on regional reporting and had also reduced "building coverage" (the stationing of a reporter at a single government agency on a regular basis). Reporters shifted to covering such broad issues as education, science, and military policy, which they followed wherever the story led. This resulted in fewer journalists and broadcasters coming daily to the Capitol. Some members of the digital-age generation of reporters boasted they could cover the news as adequately by electronic messaging and web sites as by attending press conferences and collecting press releases. But veteran journalists warned that a remote approach would miss the personal observations, inside tips, and general familiarity with legislative procedures on which Congressional reporting had so long depended.

Further Reading

Blanchard, Robert O., ed. *Congress and the News Media.* New York: Hastings House, 1974.

Cook, Timothy E. *Governing with the News: The News Media as a Political Institution.* Chicago: University of Chicago Press, 1998.

Marbut, F.B. *The News from Washington: The Story of Washington Reporting.* Carbondale: University of Southern Illinois Press, 1971.

Povich, Elaine S. *Partners & Adversaries: The Contentious Connection Between Congress and the Media.* Arlington, Virginia: The Freedom Forum, 1996.

Ritchie, Donald A. *Press Gallery: Congress and the Washington Correspondents.* Cambridge, MA: Harvard University Press, 1991.

Ritchie, Donald A. *Reporting from Washington: The History of the Washington Press Corps.* New York: Oxford University Press, 2005.

DONALD A. RITCHIE

LEHRER, JAMES

Jim Lehrer (May 19, 1934–) is executive editor and anchor of PBS' highly acclaimed long-running *The Newshour with Jim Lehrer,* and previously co-anchor with Robert MacNeil of its predecessor, *The MacNeil-Lehrer NewsHour. The MacNeil-Lehrer NewsHour* was the first hour-long news program on television in the early 1980s and set the standard for balanced, in-depth news reporting on TV. Lehrer moderated ten televised debates of presidential and vice presidential candidates between 1988 and 2004, including all three presidential debates in 2000. Lehrer was also the author of many novels.

James Charles Lehrer was born May 19, 1934, in Wichita to Fred and Lois Lehrer, who owned and operated the Kansas Central Bus Lines and later managed the San Antonio and Beaumont, Texas, Trailways lines during the Depression. Lehrer served as a sports reporter and editor for the student paper, the *Jefferson Declaration,* at San Antonio's Thomas Jefferson High School, and developed an enduring admiration for the work and life of journalist-novelist Ernest Hemingway.

During his two years at Victoria College, a small junior college near Beaumont, Lehrer served as editor for the student newspaper: *The Jolly Roger.* He also retained his parents' love for buses, working during his junior college years as a ticket agent; he has actively collected bus memorabilia ever since. Lehrer's 1992 memoir, *A Bus of My Own,* takes its name from his souvenir 1946 Flexible Clipper passenger bus.

Initially rejected by the University of Missouri School of Journalism because of their unfamiliarity with Victoria College, Lehrer performed well enough on qualifying examinations to have his English and foreign language requirements waived. He earned a bachelor in journalism (BJ) from the Missouri school in 1956.

The son and brother of U.S. Marine Corps veterans, Lehrer served three years as an infantry officer in the Marines. During a decade of newspaper work in Dallas beginning in 1959, Lehrer progressed from night desk rewriter to reporter to city editor—first for *The Dallas Morning News,* then the *Dallas Times Herald.* His stories included an investigative series on the Communist Party in Texas, coverage of the assassination of President John F. Kennedy, and interviews with Elvis Presley and Van Cliburn.

Lehrer also wrote the inscription for the JFK Open Tomb Memorial, two blocks from the assassination site in Dallas. It begins: "The joy and excitement of John Fitzgerald Kennedy's life belonged to all men. So did the pain and sorrow of his death. When he died on November 22, 1963, shock and agony touched human conscience throughout the world...." During his newspaper years, Lehrer also wrote *Viva Max!*, a novel about a modern-day attack on the Alamo, that was made into a 1970 film starring Peter Ustinov, Harry Morgan, and Jonathan Winters.

Guest spots as an interviewer for Dallas public TV station KERA opened the door for Lehrer to become their executive director of news and public affairs in 1970. He hosted KERA's *Newsroom*, a nightly news and public affairs program funded by the Ford Foundation. The experimental news format featured Lehrer in a swivel chair surrounded by a circle of reporters in desks, whom he would debrief live regarding stories on which they were working. The program ended with the news team responding to viewer feedback collected by volunteers fielding phone calls and opening mail. Some of *Newsroom's* investigations were controversial; Lehrer noted that Dallas newspaper reporters "brought us stories they could not get in their own papers" and KERA aired them.

In May 1972 Lehrer moved up to a public affairs coordinator post with PBS in Washington, D.C., where he later teamed up with Robert MacNeil on the short-lived *America '73* weekly PBS documentary funded by the National Public Affairs Center for Television (NPACT). The Lehrer and MacNeil team later coanchored gavel-to-gavel daily coverage of the U.S. Senate Watergate hearings, and Lehrer alone President Richard Nixon's impeachment inquiry. Both received positive ratings and public acclaim, leading to the October 20, 1975, premier of the *Robert MacNeil Report*, live from WNET in New York City, with Lehrer serving as Washington correspondent.

The thirty-minute program went national within six months and featured interviews with prominent guests at both locations regarding one contemporary news event. "We decided as an article of faith and practice that all guests were in fact guests." Lehrer said of *Report* in *Bus of My Own*. "We would help them get their positions or opinions out in a coherent and understandable form, so the audience could decide weight and merit."

The highly acclaimed program continued in its twin-host format for over two decades, was broadened to examine a handful of stories each evening, and garnered more than thirty awards for excellence in journalism. It was renamed *The MacNeil-Lehrer Report* in 1976, then *The MacNeil-Lehrer NewsHour* in 1983 and expanded to one hour—becoming the first sixty-minute news program on television. The program became *The Newshour with Jim Lehrer* in 1995 when MacNeil retired.

The two veteran TV newsmen are partners in MacNeil/Lehrer Productions, coproducer of *Newshour*, which also created two award-winning productions hosted by Lehrer: *The Heart of the Dragon,* a twelve-part documentary series on life in the Peoples Republic of China; and *My Heart, Your Heart* a one-hour expose on heart disease inspired by Lehrer's heart attack, surgery, and lifestyle changes.

Because his impartial manner and calm demeanor was recognized across the political landscape, Lehrer was asked frequently to moderate televised debates in all the U.S. presidential campaigns from 1988 to 2004. He also hosted the Emmy Award-nominated program *Debating Our Destiny: Forty Years of Presidential Debates.*

Known for his meticulous plotting and research, Lehrer is an active author and playwright. His novels included a series of mysteries featuring a fictional lieutenant governor, The One-Eyed Mack. Among Lehrer's works are: *Viva Max!* (1970), *Kick the Can* (1988), *Crown Oklahoma* (1989), *The Sooner Spy* (1990), *Lost and Found* (1991), *Short List* (1992), *Blue Hearts* (1993), *Fine Lines* (1995), *The Last Debate* (1997), *White Widow* (1999), *Purple Dots* (1998), *The Special Prisoner* (2000), *No Certain Rest* (2002), *Flying Crows: A Novel* (2004), and *The Franklin Affair* (2005); plays *The Will and Bart Show, Silversides Thruliner, Cedar Chest, Chili Queen,* and *Church Key Charlie Blue*; and memoirs *We Were Dreamers* (1975) and *A Bus of My Own* (1992).

Lehrer's work earned multiple Emmys, Peabody Awards, the University of Missouri Journalism School's Medal of Honor, the William Allen White Foundation Award for Journalistic Merit, and the presidential National Humanities Medal in 1999. He and novelist wife, Kate, lived in Washington, D.C., and owned an 18th-century farmhouse close to the Antietam battle site that helped inspire Lehrer's thirteenth novel, *No Certain Rest.*

Further Reading

Lehrer, James. *A Bus of My Own*. New York: G. P. Putnam's Sons, 1992.
——. *We Were Dreamers*. New York: Atheneum, 1975.

KEVIN C. LEE

LERNER, MAX

Max Lerner (December 20, 1902–June 5, 1992) juggled two professional careers, one as an educator and scholar, the other as a newspaper columnist and pundit. Born the youngest of four children to a poor Russian Jewish family, he was brought to America as a five-year-old and took eagerly to schooling. In New Haven, Connecticut, where the family ran a small dairy, he rose before dawn to deliver milk from a horse-drawn cart before attending high school and returned home to wash bottles. Upon graduation in 1919, he won a scholarship to Yale where he won four prizes. Warned he could not make a career teaching English literature because the field was closed to Jews, he entered Yale Law School, but quit in his first year to apply for a fellowship in a graduate economics program at Washington University in St. Louis, transferring after earning his MA to the newly founded Robert Brookings Graduate School of

Economics and Government in Washington, D.C. There he studied with a phalanx of mostly Progressive "institutional economists." He was especially enamored of the writings of Thorstein Veblen, who had attacked "conspicuous consumption" and the machinations of the "captains of industry."

After receiving his doctorate in 1927, Lerner helped edit the *Encyclopedia of the Social Sciences* (1927–1932) and then in the 1930s became a popular teacher at Sarah Lawrence, Harvard, and Williams. He began publishing a steady stream of law review articles, essays, and book reviews, as well as widely read and admired introductions to editions of classic texts in political theory. He also made his mark as a spokesman for the non-Communist left, writing *It Is Later Than You Think* (1938), a manifesto calling for a transition to "democratic collectivism" to rescue the country from the buccaneer capitalism that he blamed for bringing on the Great Depression. While at Williams, he served as managing editor of *The Nation* (1936–1938) until he was fired by the publisher for supporting President Franklin Roosevelt's controversial 1937 proposal to "pack" the Supreme Court with additional justices who would sustain New Deal legislation.

In 1943, after a brief stint in a war information office, Lerner became chief opinion writer for the maverick New York tabloid *PM* (1943–1948). *PM* was the brainchild of Ralph M. Ingersoll, formerly a close associate of Henry R. Luce, who set out to produce an innovative daily that would be run by its staff, fight for the powerless, and accept no advertising, relying for revenue solely on circulation. Lerner joined the paper after Ingersoll was drafted and wrote for it until it finally went under in 1948. By then, he had won a devoted following. He became a columnist for the short-lived *New York Star* (1948–1949) and then in subsequent years, wrote some six thousand columns for the *New York Post* (1949–1970s) the city's leading liberal paper until it was bought from Dorothy Schiff by Rupert Murdoch in 1976 and moved to the right. In 1949, he was appointed to the faculty of newly established Brandeis University and remained there until 1973. While at Brandeis, he held an endowed chair and became Dean of the Social Sciences. He commuted between New York and Boston and crisscrossed the country on lecture tours, sparring with right-wing polemicists on radio and television. His magnum opus, *America as a Civilization,* a thousand-page tome, appeared in 1957. Although some critics complained that it was too eclectic, it was generally well received. *Time* magazine noted that having once been a radical critic of America, he had now developed a "crush" on the country.

As a columnist, Lerner saw himself following in the footsteps of three pioneer contributors to Joseph Pulitzer's *New York World*: Heywood Broun, William Bolitho, and Walter Lippmann. Although not as crusading as Broun, as good an aphorist as Bolitho, or as influential in shaping American thinking on world affairs as Lippmann, Lerner turned his column into a window on the world that reflected his readers' concerns and helped them frame their liberal point of view. Though he was mainly preoccupied by politics, he liked to write about whatever struck his fancy. "In American journalism," he noted, "there are exclusively political commentators and general ones. I fall into the latter category." Occasionally, he wrote about his family, his travels, and the latest Broadway play. In the 1950s, he championed the work of Alfred Kinsey on sexual behavior. In the 1960s he defended and befriended Hugh Hefner, and later became a frequent guest at Hefner's "Playboy Mansion West." Until the 1980s, he was a staunch supporter of liberal causes and felt honored to have made the Nixon White House's "enemies list."

The turmoil caused by the war in Vietnam, compounded by the rise of the New Left of the 1960s and 1970s, made him more conservative. In 1967, he reluctantly turned against American involvement in the war, but radical assaults on the country and its universities triggered by war protest struck him as dangerous and deluded. More and more, he found himself agreeing with other liberal centrists who were turning neo-conservative, until, to the horror of many of his long-time readers, he announced he had voted for Ronald Reagan in 1980.

Lerner had a lifelong love of literature, especially poetry, and in his prime his prose could be sparkling, captivating, and brimming with insight. And although his books mostly drew a limited readership, he often gave them catchy titles, including *Ideas Are Weapons* (1939), *Ideas for the Ice Age* (1941), *The Mind and Faith of Justice Holmes* (1943), and *The Unfinished Country* (1959)—the last a phrase borrowed from the novelist Thomas Wolfe. His admirers included a host of other writers, including Wolfe, Noel Coward, Norman Cousins, Edward Albee, and Tennessee Williams. In his later years, Lerner's columns suffered from clichés and name dropping, and one of his books—*Ted and the Kennedy Legend* (1980)—was a pot boiler, more an effort to cash in on the senator's misfortune and celebrity than a serious think piece.

Lerner married twice (the second time to one of his former Sarah Lawrence students) and had six children. He was a devoted father and a loving husband to his second spouse—the latter, however, "in my fashion": he had many affairs and espoused and practiced sexual liberation, seeing *Eros* as the life force that also sustained his intellectual creativity.

Further Reading

Lakoff, Sanford. *Max Lerner: Pilgrim in the Promised Land.* Chicago: University of Chicago Press, 1998.

Lerner, Max. *America as a Civilization: Life and Thought in the United States Today.* New York: Simon and Schuster, 1957.

——. *Actions and Passions.* (New York: Simon and Schuster, 1949.

——. *Public Journal.* New York: Viking, 1945.

——. *The Unfinished Country.* New York: Simon and Schuster, 1959.

Milkman, Paul. *PM: A New Deal for American Journalism.* New Brunswick, NJ: Rutgers University Press, 1997.

SANFORD LAKOFF

LIBEL

The law of libel, once used to prosecute and jail journalists who dared criticize government and once regarded as beyond the reach of First Amendment protection, still poses a significant threat to the press. But the danger is far from what it used to be. The U.S. Supreme Court has given the press substantial First Amendment protection even when it disseminates false, defamatory information. The primary risk for journalists today lies largely in the possibility of expensive and complex civil—not criminal—litigation and enormous monetary damage awards. However, the likelihood of winning a libel suit against the press in the United States is small in most cases.

Libel is the publication of false information that damages someone's reputation. The "someone" can be a person, business or organization, but it cannot be the government. Such was not always the case. Just seven years after the First Amendment became part of the Constitution, Congress adopted a sedition act, which made it a crime to publish: "[a]ny false, scandalous and malicious writing...against the government of the United States, or either house of the Congress..., or the President, with intent to defame..., or to bring them, or either of them, into contempt or disrepute; or to excite against them, or either of any of them, the hatred of the good people of the United States." The administration of President John Adams used the law to prosecute and jail a number of journalists, all of whom happened to be Adams' critics.

The law expired in 1801, but the idea that seditious libel could be used to punish government critics lived on. Again, during World War I, Congress passed a seditious libel law that could be—and was—used to prosecute people for a stunning range of statements. The law made it a crime, punishable by up to twenty years in prison, during wartime to criticize the form of government, the constitution, the U.S. military, even the uniforms of soldiers, and the Supreme Court upheld convictions (*Abrams v. United States*). The law expired in 1921 but it was never held unconstitutional. Meanwhile, many states had passed so-called "criminal syndicalism" or "criminal anarchy" statutes and used them aggressively to prosecute people and publications who advocated overthrowing the government.

In 1931, the Supreme Court grappled with yet another method of controlling government critics. Minnesota adopted a statute that permitted abatement of "malicious, scandalous and defamatory newspapers, magazines and other periodicals" as public nuisances. In other words, such publications could be ordered to cease publication permanently unless they could prove that what they had published was true and they had published with good motives and for justifiable ends. Otherwise, further publication would result in a contempt citation, which could be enforced with fines and jail terms. The state used the statute to silence *The Saturday Press*, a virulent and anti-Semitic critic of local government and officials in the Twin Cities.

The Supreme Court by 5–4 vote struck down Minnesota's statute as an unconstitutional form of censorship (*Near v. Minnesota*). In the process, the Court cast doubt on the very concept of seditious libel, although it reiterated that there would be no First Amendment obstacle to individual libel suits brought by the public officials targeted by the newspaper. As recently as 1952, the Supreme Court upheld an Illinois law that made it a crime to publish or disseminate anything that "portrays depravity, criminality, unchastity, or lack of virtue of a class of citizens, of any race, color, creed or religion which said publication or exhibition exposes the citizens of any race, color, creed or religion to contempt, derision, or obloquy or which is productive of breach of the peace or riots" (*Beauharnais v. Illinois*) The white supremacist defendant had handed out racist leaflets in Chicago.

Meanwhile, the law of civil libel remained unchanged and quite favorable for plaintiffs. It was a so called "strict liability" wrong. The basic rules were these: the person claiming libel would have to show that he or she had been identified and defamed by a publication, but actual reputational harm need not be proved. Defendants were held responsible regardless of their blameworthiness—even if the libel were the result of an unavoidable accident. Defendants had a chance only if they could prove one of a handful of defenses. Common defenses were proof of truth, the privilege to accurately report what transpired during official government proceedings, or the privilege to express an opinion with a basis in fact.

All of this changed in 1964 when the Supreme Court decided *New York Times v. Sullivan*. L. B. Sullivan, an elected city commissioner responsible for the police in Montgomery, Alabama, sued the *Times* and several signatories of an editorial advertisement the *Times* had run as a fundraising effort by civil rights activists. The advertisement offered a number of examples of police misconduct and harassment of civil rights protestors, and declared that demonstrators had been met with an "unprecedented wave of terror." Several of the examples contained seemingly minor factual errors, but the *Times* had run the ad without checking its accuracy. Although not named in the advertisement and not even serving as police commissioner when some of the purported incidents occurred, Sullivan sued, claiming that generalized criticism of the police generally reflected on him specifically. A jury awarded him $500,000, and more suits were pending.

The U.S. Supreme Court saw the case as a seditious libel prosecution disguised as a civil libel case. Declaring that it considered the Sedition Act of 1798 to have been "inconsistent with the First Amendment," the Court then found Alabama's civil libel law unconstitutional because it raises "the possibility that a good-faith critic of government will be penalized for his criticism...." The solution, the Court concluded, was to turn the law of libel upside down. It removed libel from the category of unprotected expression. No longer would critics of government officials have to prove the truth of their allegations. Henceforth, the First Amendment would require public officials to prove what the Court called "actual malice"—that the defendant either knew the allegations were untrue or recklessly disregarded whether they were true. In other words, public officials would have to prove the actual state of mind of the critic, and they would have to do so with evidence that was "clear and convincing." Further, the Court noted, failure to have investigated a claim would not inherently constitute actual malice, nor would refusal to retract. This was a standard Sullivan could not satisfy.

Within seven years, the Court had expanded this First Amendment protection to libel of public figures who were not government officials (*Curtis Publishing Co. v. Butts*) and, ultimately, to all libels involving matters of public interest (*Rosenbloom v. Metromedia*). But in 1974, the Court concluded that it had gone too far, and concluded that if states wished to, they could relax the "actual malice" standard for libel plaintiffs who were neither public officials nor public figures—as long as states did not retreat to the old standard of strict liability (*Gertz v. Robert Welch, Inc.*). Almost all states have since selected negligence—requiring proof that the libel occurred because of the defendant's failure to use due care. But the Court continues to require all plaintiffs to prove the falsity of the libels of which they complain.

Although the developments in libel law since *New York Times v. Sullivan* have certainly helped defendants, they have also made libel law extremely complex and often excruciatingly expensive regardless of the outcome. Proving actual malice or even negligence requires extensive and expensive gathering of evidence. And because most jurisdictions have made it easier—though not easy—for private figures to win, many cases involve struggles over whether the plaintiff is a public figure or private figure—a determination one judge has famously compared to nailing a jellyfish to a wall.

For the rare plaintiff who prevails, the financial rewards can be substantial. Juries can award damages as compensation for reputational harm, for proven out-of-pocket financial loss, and for punishment. Journalists particularly fear the latter, because awards can run into the millions. Ironically, the amount of time and energy focused on issues of public figure-private status or proof of actual malice and negligence have tended to deflect attention from what concerns plaintiffs most: having the record set straight. Yet efforts at reforming libel law to place greater emphasis on correcting errors have made little headway.

Today's Internet world is creating new problems for American journalists. Libel law in the United States is unique in the high degree of protection it grants to the press. Plaintiffs therefore are increasingly seeking to sue in countries with libel law more favorable to them. Now that the Internet makes the circulation of libel far beyond the boundaries of the United States far easier than in the past, plaintiffs in other countries are claiming that libels originating on Web sites in the United States should be actionable in countries where they are received. Courts are just beginning to grapple with the issue.

Further Reading

Beauharnais v. Illinois, 343 U.S. 250 (1952).

Bezanson, Randall P., Gilbert Cranberg, and John Soloski. *Libel Law and the Press: Myth and Reality*. New York: Free Press, 1987.

Curtis Publishing Co. v. Butts, 388 U.S. 130 (1967).

Friendly, Fred. *Minnesota Rag: Corruption, Yellow Journalism, and the Case That Saved Freedom of the Press*, reprint ed. Minneapolis: University of Minnesota Press, 2003.

Gertz v. Robert Welch, Inc., 418 U.S. 323 (1974).

Lewis, Anthony. *Make No Law: The Sullivan Case and the First Amendment*. New York: Random House, 1991.

Near v. Minnesota, 283 U.S. 697 (1931).

New York Times v. Sullivan, 376 U.S. 254 (1964).

Rosenbloom v. Metromedia, 403 U.S. 29 (1971).

Sack, Robert D. *Sack on Defamation: Libel, Slander and Related Problems*, 3rd ed. New York: Practising Law Institute, 1999.

ROBERT E. DRECHSEL

LICENSING

Governments sometimes require that journalists or media organizations obtain legal permission to do their work. Having to meet official standards in order to operate means that freedom of expression will be compromised and perhaps largely curtailed. In America, print publications have been free of such constraints since the early eighteenth century, but broadcast stations have had to obtain federal licenses since the early twentieth century. Radio and television licenses have rarely been lost for violations of laws and regulations, but the possibility has made owners at least cautious about some practices and programming.

Print Publications

Printing presses were used in England for more than half a century before Henry VIII established the first secular licensing power with a royal proclamation in 1530. The restraint applied only to religious publications and was exercised by church officials. In 1538, after his rejection of papal authority caused religious and political upheaval, Henry issued another proclamation that imposed licensing and censorship on all printing and assigned enforcement duties to his Privy Council. He also developed the practice of giving particular printers a monopoly for certain types of works.

As later monarchs expanded the use of exclusive privileges to publish books on subjects from law to Latin, some printers were rewarded for their behavior while others were driven by economic need or personal principles to produce forbidden material. The Stationers Company, an organization of prominent printers and booksellers that was chartered in 1557, was given the tasks of maintaining monopolies and granting permission for publication. The company policed the use of presses with searches and fines for illegal printing. In practice, however, the degree of repression in licensing and post-publication punishment varied with the situations and individuals involved.

During the tumultuous seventeenth century, as the royal prerogative power used to restrict printing fell under assault, prepublication controls were denigrated as unwise and oppressive and were eliminated. Yet sometimes a similar authority was claimed by colonial officials in the early eighteenth century. One of the last attempts to require government approval failed in 1723 when Massachusetts legislators tried to stop James Franklin from printing his sarcastic *New-England Courant* newspaper without permission. Franklin refused to submit to control and a grand jury would not indict him.

When Franklin's brother Benjamin and other delegates met at the Constitutional Convention in 1787, licensing and censorship were only a distant and unpleasant memory. States had constitutional protections against government interference with the press and the framers of the federal Constitution seemed to agree that the new national government would have no power over publication. The First Amendment, which was ratified in 1791, said that Congress shall make no law abridging freedom of the press.

Congress later occasionally has used national security rationales to write laws to punish dissenting journalists and the military has imposed battle zone censorship of news stories at times, but the United States never has had any full-fledged scheme of domestic licensing and censorship for the print media. Tradition, the power of publishers, and the language of the Constitution seem to have precluded such a possibility. When Woodrow Wilson asked Congress for authority to censor the nation's newspapers during World War I, for instance, he was turned down after members emphasized the importance of the First Amendment and editorials denounced the idea as suitable for a despot.

Broadcast Media

The fledgling broadcast industry of the early twentieth century did not have the same status as the long-established print press. The Radio Act of 1912 required broadcasters to have a license issued by the secretary of commerce. Fearing the misuse of the new medium during World War I, President Wilson used wartime authority provided in the law, a power that was continued in later communication statutes, to close or take over nearly all of the nation's civilian broadcasting facilities for the duration of the conflict. Members of his cabinet wanted the federal government to own the country's radio stations after the war, but the idea was rebuffed by Congress.

The 1912 law did not allow the secretary of commerce to deny a license to any American citizen or to solve signal interference problems. The Radio Act of 1927 set up the Federal Radio Commission (FRC) to regulate the industry as interstate commerce and to control the times, spectrum frequencies, and power levels of broadcasts. The statute recognized that radio stations had freedom of expression, but required them to operate in the public interest, convenience, or necessity and prohibited any obscene, indecent, or profane language on the airwaves. The law also provided that if one legally qualified candidate for a public office used a station, then the others would have an equal opportunity and that the stations could not censor the statements.

The Communications Act of 1934 retained the main features of the 1927 statute, but added wire communication to the responsibilities of the FRC which was renamed the Federal Communications Commission (FCC). Both laws assumed that broadcasters are protected by the First Amendment and yet are subject to public interest obligations because the limited electronic spectrum they use belongs to the people. Although some scholars and broadcasters have contended that the FCC should be little more than the "traffic cop" of the airwaves, the agency has at times created and enforced various content requirements and restrictions.

The 1927 and 1934 laws determined that not everyone can have a license. Federal regulations have set character and capability qualifications for broadcast licensees and have limited the number of stations one person or company can own. Franklin Roosevelt, who faced overwhelming opposition from wealthy publishers, tried unsuccessfully to prevent newspapers from owning radio stations. In the competitions for lucrative television licenses during the Dwight Eisenhower administration, newspaper applicants with conservative credentials did much better than those that did not. In 1975 the FCC banned the formation of new newspaper and broadcast station combinations.

During the last two decades of the twentieth century, Congress, the FCC, and the courts made a number of decisions to deregulate broadcasting. One of the rationales was that marketplace forces should determine more of what the industry does. Content restrictions were loosened or discarded and limits on the number of stations a person or company could own were expanded. License periods were extended and renewal procedures were streamlined. The FCC, however, retained its indecency standard and struggled to define its meaning while continuing its enforcement.

Further Reading

Benjamin, Louise Margaret. *Freedom of the Air and the Public Interest: First Amendment Rights in Broadcasting to 1935.* Carbondale: Southern Illinois University Press, 2001.

Clegg, Cyndia S. *Press Censorship in Jacobean England.* Cambridge: Cambridge University Press, 2001.

Powe, Lucas A., Jr. *American Broadcasting and the First Amendment.* Berkeley: University of California Press, 1987.

Radio Act, Pub. L. No. 62-264 (1912); Radio Act, Pub. L. No. 69-632 (1927); Communications Act, Pub. L. No. 73-416 (1934).

Siebert, Fredrick S. *Freedom of the Press in England, 1476-1776: The Rise and Decline of Government Control.* Urbana: University of Illinois Press, 1952.

Smith, Jeffery A. *Printers and Press Freedom: The Ideology of Early American Journalism.* New York: Oxford University Press, 1988.

JEFFERY A. SMITH

LIEBLING, A.J.

With both a personality and a writing persona that alternated between *bon vivant* self-indulgence and a more serious, somewhat darker world view, A.J. Liebling (October 18, 1904–December 28, 1963) is credited with helping to invent modern media criticism. Whether he was passionately describing the gustatory glories of French cuisine as a Paris correspondent or pointing out journalistic and ethical lapses in the mainstream press in his long-running *New Yorker* column "The Wayward Press," Liebling could be counted on for telling and original insights, a flair for evocative description, and, not least, a touch of sometimes sly and *noir*-ish humor.

Abbott Joseph Liebling was born in the Upper East Side of Manhattan on October 18, 1904, to Joseph Epstein, a Jewish immigrant who arrived in New York in the 1880s and became a prosperous furrier, and Anna Slone, a well-educated woman from San Francisco. Liebling grew up in a privileged household, attended by governesses and enrolled in good schools in New York City, where he was recalled as a "pudgy, precocious and intellectual" boy. Entering Dartmouth College in 1920, Liebling—who described himself as "an agnostic of Jewish origin"—was expelled in 1923 for failure to attend chapel. Shortly thereafter he enrolled in Columbia University, graduating in 1925 with a bachelors degree in Literature. Somewhat archly he would later claim, however, that the school encouraged "colorless, odorless, and especially tasteless" writing.

Liebling's influences as a master of nonfiction prose were varied, but it can be argued that one of the most important was the way he made people think about those who lived in New York City. As noted critic Joseph Epstein wrote, Liebling defined the essence of a New Yorker as "something other than somebody who is put upon by high rents, rudeness, human squalor, and an urban scene that is not so much distracting in its variety as it is jarring in its tumult."

After graduation from Columbia, Liebling remained close to his roots in New York, initially working as a sports reporter for the *New York Times*. He was fired after eight months, however, when he gave the name "Ignoto" to a basketball referee whose real name was, in an untypical lapse of reporting rigor, unknown to Liebling. Soon afterwards Liebling embarked on what would become a life-long pursuit of "the good life." Convincing his father in 1926 to pay for a year in Paris, he went abroad to study at the Sorbonne. But his real mission, it soon became obvious, revolved around ardently devoting himself to the wonders of French cooking. His love affair with food soon developed into the book, *Between Meals*.

Liebling returned to the United States in 1927 and worked for a variety of newspapers. But his three years with the *Providence Journal* and then the (Providence) *Evening Bulletin* as a reporter and feature writer ended when he resigned from the *Bulletin* in 1930 because a fellow staff member was fired to make room for an advertiser's son. Returning to New York City, he worked for the *World Telegram* for four years, but, after writing more than a thousand feature articles, his request for a raise was denied—and, clearly feeling underappreciated, he left that paper as well.

In 1935, Liebling was hired by editor Harold Ross of the *New Yorker*, and it was there he remained for the rest of his working life. Finding his true calling at last, he wrote about what interested him, including profiles ranging from national political figures such as Earl Long and General George Marshall to unknown professional boxers. Liebling's avid interest in boxing manifested itself not only in the *New Yorker* but also in his books, *The Sweet Science* and *The Honest Rainmaker*. He is generally credited with raising the writing about boxing to the level of literary art. In *The Sweet Science*, his ability to use pugilism as a means to reveal philosophical insights about both human nature and society remains widely admired to this day.

In addition to his success as media critic (he penned the oft-quoted phrase "freedom of the press is guaranteed only to those who own one"), Liebling earned a strong reputation as a foreign correspondent. He reported on World War II for the *New Yorker*, filing from London. He accompanied troops in North Africa and, after landing under fire on the Normandy beaches on D-Day, participated in the liberation of Paris.

As a testament to his reportorial and writing talents, Liebling's work has been collected into seventeen books. Some articles drip of his slyly sarcastic style, while others manage to convey his lust for life. All provide readers with sharp insights reflected through the prism of his engaged and questioning intellect. Throughout his career, Liebling focused on the written medium, revering print journalism and seeking, in his "The Wayward Press" column in the *New Yorker*, to elevate its standards of language and logic. Serving in the self-appointed dual roles of literary critic and ethics watchdog, his columns did occasionally border on the polemic—but even rivals conceded that they were always masterfully written. In particular, he feared the advent of economic consolidation of the media industry and the disappearance of varied array of daily newspapers.

Liebling died in 1963 at the age of fifty-nine from complications of viral pneumonia. Two days after his death, an editorial ran in the *New York Times* that closed by saying, "His death stills a pen that could inspire as well as wound. The press will be duller for the loss of his barbs."

Further Reading

Epstein, Joseph. "A.J. Liebling: The Minnesota Fats of American Prose." *Bookworld*. October 10, 1971.

Liebling, A.J. *The Most of A.J. Liebling*. Selected by William Cole. Simon and Schuster: New York, 1963.

Liebling, A.J. *The Press*. New York: Ballantine Books, 1963.

Liebling, A.J. *Sweet Science*. New York: Viking Press, 1956.

Sokolov, Raymond. *Wayward Reporter: The Life of A.J. Liebling*. New York: Harper & Row, 1980.

DAVID ABRAHAMSON
LOKA L. ASHWOOD

LIPPMANN, WALTER

Most journalism historians consider Walter Lippmann (September 23, 1889–December 14, 1974) to be the premier political analyst of twentieth century journalism. A prolific columnist, editor, and author of magazine articles and books, he influenced presidents from Woodrow Wilson to Richard Nixon and did as much as any newspaper columnist to inform public opinion. At the peak of his career, many readers considered Lippmann's column to be the most important political commentary in print. Regardless of whether or not one agreed with him, Lippmann was required reading for anyone who was serious about politics or foreign affairs.

Lippmann's early life seemed to place him on the track to academia rather than a career in journalism. He was born in New York City on September 23, 1889, the only child of a successful clothing manufacturer. In his boyhood, Lippmann developed what would become a lifelong appreciation for strong leaders, such as Theodore Roosevelt, who acted decisively to attain their goals. He attended private schools in New York and enrolled in Harvard in 1906. There he encountered some of the leading intellectuals of the day, including George Santayana and William James, and took an active part in the academic community of the campus. At Harvard he developed a keen sense of social responsibility and leaned toward non-radical socialism. He organized a reading group that quickly turned into an activist organization working for social and educational reform on campus. Lippmann also honed his skill as a writer by publishing articles in college magazines and came to believe that he could have the greatest impact in the world of ideas through his mastery of the written word.

Bored with academic life, he turned down the opportunity to attend graduate school at Harvard and instead took a job as a cub reporter for the *Boston Common*. He also worked for a short time as a research assistant to the muckraker Lincoln Steffens. In 1913 he published his first book, *A Preface to Politics*, which drew on Freudian theory and the application of the principles of scientific management to political organization while arguing for a strong government and active regulation of business. In 1914, Lippmann was one of the intellectuals and writers who established the *New Republic*, a moderate leftist magazine that featured some of the most astute political commentary of the time. Lippmann's writing on foreign policy attracted the attention of readers like President Wilson and further enhanced his growing reputation. His second book, *Drift and Mastery*, published in 1914, announced his break with socialism and signaled his disillusionment with his radical circle.

The First World War shaped many of Lippmann's early attitudes about human nature and the role of mass communication in society. Believing that American national interests were threatened by German aggression, he wrote interventionist editorials and pressed Wilson to be more forceful. When the United States entered the war, Lippmann became an assistant to Secretary of War Newton Baker. In 1917 he worked on a committee that prepared strategies for postwar negotiations, including what would become President Wilson's Fourteen Points. The experience heightened his interest in geopolitical strategy and diplomacy and established him as an insider in the highest levels of government for the first time. Lippmann also worked on the American propaganda offensive and interviewed German prisoners of war to help study the effect of propaganda on troop morale.

He found that few of the captives could articulate the causes of the war or the German war aims, a discovery that led him to question the capacity of the public to understand the complexity of modern society. The wartime suppression of dissent, the failure of the Paris peace negotiations and the postwar Red Scare distressed Lippmann and forced him to reconsider some of his core beliefs about government and the public. His 1920 book, *Liberty and the News*, co-written with Charles Merz, severely criticized the *New York Times* for emotional and inaccurate coverage of the recent war. Rather than providing facts, the authors wrote, the *Times's* stories reflected the values of the paper's owners to the detriment of public understanding.

Lippmann returned to the *New Republic* for a time after the war, but he felt uncomfortable with the magazine's ideology and quarreled with some of the other writers. In the fall of 1921, he was offered a job as assistant director of the editorial page at Ralph Pulitzer's *New York World*, what many regarded as the city's best liberal daily. Lippmann was attracted to the paper's crusading editorial page and the potential to reach a much wider audience; the salary of $12,500 a year was enticing too. He accepted the position and agreed to begin in January, 1922.

Several free months before starting at the *World* gave him the opportunity to complete his next book, an analysis of the formation of public opinion and the role of communication in society. *Public Opinion*, published in 1922, reflected Lippmann's lost faith in traditional democratic theory in the face of the modern world. Rather than making rational decisions based on facts, Lippmann believed that most people responded with emotion and personal bias, the "pictures in their heads" as he phrased it. At the same time, the press failed to present a comprehensive and accurate account of the issues of the day; "truth" and "news" were not the same thing. In *Public Opinion*, he called for an expert class who would have the time and intellectual capacity to study current affairs and recommend policies that would ensure effective governance. This conclusion left Lippmann open to charges of being elitist and anti-democratic, but the book remains one of the classics of public opinion theory.

Lippmann's reputation continued to grow during his years in the editorial department at the *World*. Although the *World* was traditionally a Democratic organ, Lippmann maintained some influence with the Republican administrations of the 1920s. He joined the *New York Herald-Tribune* in 1931 and began writing the "Today and Tomorrow" column that would be his primary vehicle for most of the rest of his career. The column was an instant success and Lippmann became a household name; at its peak the column was syndicated in more than two hundred papers. Lippmann initially underestimated Franklin D. Roosevelt, but later, recognizing the need for strong governmental action to end the Great Depression, he supported the New Deal. Despite his increasing conservatism, Lippmann understood that a new approach was necessary to rescue capitalism and believed that Roosevelt's programs were good for the country. As war threatened in Europe, Lippmann urged armed neutrality and a realistic assessment of the nation's true strategic interests. By 1941 he was an interventionist and argued for increased aid to Great Britain. He visited England and France as a war correspondent.

Lippmann's 1943 book *U.S. Foreign Policy* outlined his new belief, one that would carry though the Cold War, in military power, realism, and the rejection of his earlier Wilsonian internationalism. Where many early Cold Warriors wanted to challenge the Soviet Union on every front, he accepted the idea of a postwar Soviet sphere of influence and believed that the two powers could coexist, though he continued to support a strong military and preparedness. The Soviet position, to Lippmann, was essentially one of defense. He argued that America's true interest was in a strong Europe and disdained the tendency to fight proxy wars in Asia, Africa, and Latin America. Lippmann was an early critic of Senator Joseph McCarthy and similar anti-Communist crusaders, but he never brought the full weight of his reputation to bear against them. Although he rarely watched television and held the medium in low regard, the aging writer was a surprise ratings hit in a series of CBS interviews aired between 1960 and 1965. Lippmann signed a new contract and moved his column to the *Washington Post* and *Newsweek* in 1963.

The 1960s saw Lippmann back firmly in the Democratic fold. He admired John F. Kennedy's energy and talent, though he was willing to be critical of the young President's missteps. Lyndon B. Johnson actively courted Lippmann's favor and the columnist responded with initially positive commentary. The social welfare legislation in Johnson's Great Society program appealed to him and the new civil rights laws were a step toward alleviating the racial discrimination that had somewhat belatedly come to his attention. His respect for Johnson was destroyed, however, when he came to believe that the President was deceiving him about his plans to escalate the Vietnam War. Lippmann saw the war in southeast Asia as a diversion that undermined the nation's real interests and a distraction that weakened the push for social reform at home. In the final years of his career, Lippmann was an ardent critic of Johnson's war and engaged in a semi-public sniping match with the President. Lippmann was so disillusioned with the Democrats and the chaos of America in the late 1960s that he endorsed Richard Nixon in the 1968 election. Failing health forced Lippmann to stop writing in 1971, although he continued to travel and visit friends when he could. He died of a heart attack in New York on December 14, 1974. Lippmann was married twice and had no children.

Further Reading

Childs, Marquis, and James Reston, eds. *Walter Lippmann and his Times*. New York: Harcourt, Brace, and Co., 1959.

Lippmann, Walter. *Public Opinion*. New York: Harcourt, Brace, 1922.

Riccio, Barry D. *Walter Lippmann: Odyssey of a Liberal*. New Brunswick: Transaction Press, 1994.

Rossiter, Clinton, and James Lare, eds. *The Essential Lippmann: A Political Philosophy for Liberal Democracy*. New York: Random House, 1963.

Steel, Ronald. *Walter Lippmann and the American Century*. Boston: Little, Brown, 1980.

ROBERT A. RABE

LITERARY JOURNALISM

Literary journalism aims to be factual while using the techniques commonly associated with literary writing, particularly literary fiction—all in service of illuminating a larger or "literary" truth about human existence. It has sometimes been called "creative nonfiction," "artistic nonfiction," "the nonfiction novel," and "the news story."

Perhaps the best brief definition of literary journalism was provided by Stephen Crane, one of its late nineteenth-century practitioners, when he described his goal: to give the reader the "feel of the facts." Literary journalism has also been called "new journalism," especially by Tom Wolfe, Norman Mailer, Truman Capote, and other literary journalists of the 1960s and 1970s and beyond, who sought, by using this term, to differentiate themselves from their predecessors.

Literary journalism is a vibrant prose tradition that dates back at least to Daniel Defoe in mid-seventeenth-century England, whose *A Journal of the Plague Year* is a factual, painstakingly reported, literary account. Many scholars, such as Avis Meyer, also point to the great English essayists such as Richard Steele, Joseph Addison, Jonathan Swift, and Ben Johnson as important figures in bridging the gap between journalism and literature. Certainly Addison and Steele's *Tatler* and *Spectator* established in early eighteenth-century England the informative or persuasive periodical essay as a major form. Indeed, Addison and Steele's work influenced colonial American newspaper editors such as James Franklin and his brother Ben, who tried to craft journalism that was factual, interesting, and written with literary panache. Nineteenth-century British writers such as Charles Lamb, William Hazlitt, and Charles Dickens are also important precursors.

In the nineteenth and twentieth centuries, literary journalism developed in the United States as a recognizable, ongoing genre, as Thomas B. Connery notes in his path-breaking 1992 essay, "Discovering a Literary Form." Outstanding practitioners of the form who emerged during the nineteenth century include Samuel Clemens (Mark Twain), Richard Harding Davis, George Ade, Abraham Cahan, Julian Ralph, Stephen Crane, Theodore Dreiser, Hutchins Hapgood, Walt Whitman, Lincoln Steffens, and William Hard. They published in a variety of magazines such as *Harper's* and *Arena* and in many newspapers.

Twain's journalism, for example, was substantial and influential, with a distinctively literary quality that made good use of the American vernacular. In fact, he wrote many of his most humorous pieces for newspapers, an outlet with fewer constraints than the genteel nineteenth-century book publishing industry. "Among his contemporaries," Jack A. Nelson writes in *A Sourcebook of American Literary Journalism: Representative Writers in an Emerging Genre*, "Twain's wit, his style, his pithy observations and mordant insights, along with his frontier-honed skill at cutting through sham, hypocrisy, pretense, and show to get at the bare-boned reality of a thing, made his work sought after then and makes it readable and pertinent yet" (p. 41).

Stephen Crane's *New York Tribune* sketches are masterpieces of characterization and description. In "The Men in the Storm" (1894), he paints a stark contrast between middle-class pedestrians heading home during a fierce winter storm with "an absolute expression of hot dinners in [their] pace" and a group of homeless men waiting to get into a shelter, for whom "these things were as if they were not." Ultimately, Crane's narrative says something about the harshness of nature, a frequent theme in his other literary journalism ("The Open Boat," 1897) and in his naturalistic fiction (*Maggie: A Girl of the Streets*, 1893).

Crane and others were writing in a period pivotal to the development of literary journalism, about 1890–1910. During this time, massive social and cultural changes may have sparked the advance of this alternative to conventional journalism, as they did during the 1930s and 1940s and during the 1960s and 1970s. Put simply, in times of crisis, journalism—particularly literary journalism that aims to transcend the limits of "objective" conventional journalism—seems to thrive.

The 1930s and 1940s brought the Great Depression, World War II, and the development of atomic weapons. Not surprisingly, this was a rich period in literary journalism's development as writers experimented with different ways to report on the nuances of the day's important stories. One was James Agee, who developed a kind of documentary prose-poetry to tell the story of Alabama sharecroppers. His *Let Us Now Praise Famous Men*, illustrated with Walker Evans's photographs of the sharecropper families and their surroundings, informs at the level of literature.

Another important figure in this period was Ernest Hemingway, who forged a unique prose style highly influenced by his career as a reporter at the *Kansas City Star*. He seemed always mindful of the newspaper's style-sheet admonitions to "use short sentences, use short first paragraphs, use vigorous English." Despite Hemingway's disavowal of the value of his time as a reporter for his subsequent writing, it was this very experience that led him to create a signature lean and powerful writing style—for both his literary journalism and his subsequent literary fiction.

The challenges of the 1930s also formed the crucible of Depression-era advocacy journalism, sometimes with a decidedly literary bent, as shown by the work of Dorothy Day and Meridel LeSueur. In her reportage, columns, and commentary for the *Catholic Worker*, Day demonstrated the skills that could have led her to a successful fiction writing career. Instead, she crafted literary journalism that dramatized the plight of the poor and homeless in New York City. Her contemporary Meridel LeSueur also found inspiration in the story of the struggles of the masses; her "Women on the Breadlines" remains a masterpiece of Depression literary journalism in its sensitive evocation of the impact of poverty.

At the end of World War II, John Hersey's *Hiroshima* (originally published as a special issue of the *New Yorker* in 1946), addressed the crucial issue of the day, the development of the atomic bomb, and raised the question of whether using such a weapon against civilians was ever justifiable. Britain's Rebecca West examined law and civilization in works such as *Black Lamb and Grey Falcon* (1941), a study of Yugoslavia on the eve of World War II, and her two books on the Nuremburg treason trials. George Orwell, another British author, wrote powerful studies of the European working poor and the Spanish Civil War, among other works of literary journalism.

In the twentieth century, owing to newspapers' adoption of "objectivity" as a professional norm, magazines have assumed preeminence as a repository of literary journalism—among them the *The New Yorker, Texas Monthly, Harper's, Atlantic Monthly, Rolling Stone,* and *Esquire*. The *New Yorker*, founded by Harold Ross in 1925, has nurtured a long list of literary journalists, including E.B. White, James Thurber, Lillian Ross, Janet Flanner, A.J. Liebling, Martha Gellhorn, John Hersey, and Joseph Mitchell.

Other practitioners of the so-called New Journalism of the 1960s, 1970s and beyond include Truman Capote, Norman Mailer, Tom Wolfe, Joan Didion, Michael Herr, Hunter S. Thompson, Gay Talese, Gloria Steinem, Tracy Kidder, Jane Kramer, Susan Orlean, John McPhee, and Mark Singer. The period of the Vietnam War, in particular, saw political, social, and cultural change that found expression in many singular book-length works of literary journalism, among them Capote's *In Cold Blood* (1965), Mailer's *The Armies of the Night* (1968), Wolfe's *Radical Chic and Mau-Mauing the Flak-Catchers*(1970), Didion's *Slouching Towards Bethlehem* (1968), and Herr's *Dispatches*(1977).

This period saw considerable discussion and debate about the limits of literary journalism, with traditionalists such as Hersey and Ross arguing that professional journalistic norms of accuracy and factual verifiability forbade the use of techniques such as interior monologue. How, they asked, could a responsible reporter really expect that a source remembers what he or she was thinking at a particular time? Others such as Mailer maintained the literary journalist's right to claim such insight and even called what they were doing "New Journalism."

In a fascinating study of "The Politics of the New Journalism," scholar John J. Pauly notes, "The very term *New Journalism* proved singularly effective at calling out opponents into symbolic combat...offering "a double dare to the establishments of Journalism and Literature. It challenges the authority of Journalism's empire of facts, and the sanctity of Literature's garden of imagination" (p. 110).

In the early twenty-first century, such debates were long forgotten as literary journalists such as Richard Rhodes, Adrian Nicole LeBlanc, Tracy Kidder, and Susan Orlean continued to push the boundaries of that borderland between fact and fiction, literary journalism. Today magazines remain frequent forums for their efforts, but full-length books of literary journalism also are proving highly popular. In fact, where once reporters at the end of the day and on breaks used to have a novel going in the desk drawer, today's journalists frequently have a book-length work of literary journalism in their computers that they try to work on in their spare time. This, too, says something about the institutionalization of literary journalism today as a distinctive genre in its own right.

Further Reading

Connery, Thomas B. "Discovering a Literary Form." In *A Sourcebook of American Literary Journalism: Representative Writers in an Emerging Genre*, edited by Thomas. B. Connery, 3–37. Westport, CT: Greenwood Press, 1992.

——. "Research Review: Magazines and Literary Journalism, An Embarrassment of Riches." In *The American Magazine: Research Perspectives and Prospects*, ed. David Abrahamson, 207–216. Ames: Iowa State University Press, 1995.

Fishkin, Shelley Fisher. *From Fact to Fiction: Journalism and Imaginative Writing in America*. Baltimore: Johns Hopkins University Press, 1985, 3–10.

Hartsock, John C. *A History of American Literary Journalism: The Emergence of a Modern Narrative Form*. Amherst: University of Massachusetts Press, 2000.

Kerrane, Kevin, and Ben Yagoda, eds. *The Art of Fact: A Historical Anthology of Literary Journalism*. New York, NY: Simon and Schuster, 1997.

Kramer, Mark. "Breakable Rules for Literary Journalists." In *Literary Journalism: A New Collection of the Best American Nonfiction*, edited by Norman Sims and Mark Kramer. New York: Ballantine, 1995.

Pauly, John J. "The Politics of the New Journalism." In *Literary Journalism in the Twentieth Century*, edited by Norman Sims, 129. New York: Oxford University Press, 1990.

Sims, Norman. "The Art of Literary Journalism." In *Literary Journalism: A New Collection of the Best American Nonfiction*, edited by Norman Sims, and Mark Kramer, 3–19. New York: Ballantine, 1995.

——. "Introduction." In *The Literary Journalists*, edited by Norman Sims, 3–25. New York: Ballantine, 1984.

——, ed. *Literary Journalism in the Twentieth Century*. New York: Oxford University Press, 1990.

Weber, Ronald. *Journalism, Writing, and American Literature*, Occasional Paper No. 5, Gannett Center for Media Studies (now Freedom Forum), April 1987, 1–15.

NANCY L. ROBERTS

LLOYD, HENRY DEMAREST

Known as the "millionaire socialist," Henry Demarest Lloyd (1847–1903) was a journalist, nonfiction writer, and social reformer who unwittingly made Ida M. Tarbell's 1904 muckraking study *The History of the Standard Oil Company* famous. For it was Tarbell's better-publicized work which validated Lloyd's 1893 path breaking *Wealth Against Commonwealth* and helped set the stage for the U.S. Supreme Court-ordered breakup of John D. Rockefeller's monopoly in 1909.

Lloyd was born in New York City in 1847, the son of a Dutch Reformed Church minister and of a mother who was a direct lineal descendant to one of the first Dutch settlers in New York. His stern Calvinistic upbringing provided Lloyd with the moral consciousness of a reformer and a dislike for any organized ideology. Well educated, Lloyd studied to be a lawyer but turned to reporting as a result of the 1872 Liberal Republican movement, which nominated *New York Tribune* editor Horace Greeley in an unsuccessful bid for president. Lloyd obtained work as a business reporter for the *Chicago Tribune* in the wake of the city's disastrous 1871 fire and soon excelled at editorial writing.

Given leeway by publisher Joseph Medill, Lloyd became an advocate for Chicago's rebirth as the Midwest's leading city, but it was his interest in an obscure Ohio oil company, Standard Oil, and its one-time produce clerk chief executive, Rockefeller, which gave him national prominence. Lloyd expanded on an 1878 *Tribune* editorial to produce an 1881 *Atlantic Monthly* article that raised the then obscure Standard Oil to national prominence and became a starting point for every subsequent late nineteenth-century monopoly investigation. Married to the only daughter of one of the *Tribune*'s major owners, his wife's wealth allowed Lloyd to retire from the *Tribune* in 1885 and devote himself full time to writing and public speaking. For the remainder of the decade, he specialized in national magazine articles on reform, attacking laissez-faire capitalism, unregulated commodities trading, and the railroads and other monopolies. His support of the anarchists following the 1886 Haymarket Square bombing led to his exclusion from Chicago's upper-class society and his entrance into an independent political circle with thinkers such as Jane Addams, William Dean Howells, Eugene V. Debs, and Booker T. Washington.

Lloyd began researching *Wealth Against Commonwealth* in 1889. He discovered that the Standard Oil Company was crushing all of its competition and overcharging its customers in what Lloyd called a "tribute." In an era before corporate public relations, Standard Oil and Rockefeller refused to provide any information or even acknowledge *Wealth*, so Lloyd's work had the effect of a one-sided or *ex parte* prosecution when it was published in 1893. Nonetheless, *Wealth* made Lloyd the leading reform journalist in the era before muckraking and influenced an entire generation of American social thinkers.

Lloyd's anti-monopoly writings and independent politics led him to Populism. He ran unsuccessfully for a Congressional seat as a People's Party candidate in Chicago in 1894. By the mid-1890s, Lloyd had moved closer to socialism, but he saw in Populism an opportunity to overthrow what Lloyd saw as American plutocracy. It was with great personal dismay that Lloyd witnessed the demise of the People's Party at their 1896 St. Louis national convention as they embraced pro-silver Democratic presidential candidate William Jennings Bryan. Lloyd subsequently argued that socialist Eugene Debs would have been the party's best candidate, but Lloyd and others could not convince Debs to attend the convention.

Lloyd wrote several other books on cooperatives, social reforms in New Zealand, and political philosophy. He also became involved in the issue of public ownership of municipal utilities as the result of a controversy involving public transportation in Chicago. He died in 1903 as Ida

Tarbell was completing her series of Standard Oil articles for *McClure's*.

Further Reading

E. Jay Jernigan. *Henry Demarest Lloyd*. Boston: Twayne, 1976.

Richard Junger. *The Journalist as Reformer: Henry Demarest Lloyd and Wealth Against Commonwealth*. Westport, CT: Greenwood Press, 1996.

John L. Thomas. *Alternative America: Henry George, Edward Bellamy, Henry Demarest Lloyd, and the Adversary Tradition*. Cambridge, MA: Belknap Press, 1983.

RICHARD JUNGER

LOCAL NEWS

"News" is often defined as information that has one or more of these basic attributes: it is timely; it has social importance; it involves prominent people or institutions; it has broad impact; it is unusual in generally interesting ways; and it has proximity to the audience. Of all those characteristics, when it comes to "the local," it is the latter—nearness to the audience—that trumps all. Consider: A small-town newspaper would put a story about the local Spelling Bee on the front page while omitting entirely news about political strife in an African nation, or would publish multiple front-page stories about the search for a new high school principal when no other news outlet in the world would even be interested. Some news outlets at the turn of the twenty-first century were entirely devoted to "proximity" news. Examples include weekly newspapers (and some dailies), "city magazines" or regional magazines, local radio stations, and city-focused web sites.

"Local news" can take many different forms, and the attributes of that information can vary widely from medium to medium and from market to market. But in general, local news is information published by a news outlet that would be of interest only to people in a distinct and relatively small geographic region—that is, a neighborhood, a city, a county, a school district, or a loosely aligned region. Although local news is a significant part of regional television and radio newscasts, as well as regional magazines, newspapers by far generate the greatest amount of local news coverage in America.

Local news often can be divided into categories, or "beats," which facilitate routine coverage. Among the most common local news beats are "cops and courts," or routine coverage of crime and punishment; "local government," or coverage of the deliberations and decisions of municipal, county, and regional government bodies; "schools," or coverage of the doings of educational institutions; "business," coverage of the local economy; and "local sports," with emphasis on scholastic and youth leagues. Most news outlets also have general assignment reporters, or "G.A.'s," who focus on "breaking local news," such as traffic accidents, structure fires, natural disasters, and public appearances by celebrities. Local news includes many so-called "features," generally manifest in coverage of the social activities of a community—festivals, fairs, fundraising events, school graduations, and the like—or profiles of community residents with interesting anecdotes or activities.

The forms of local news also vary considerably. Many newspapers publish what some journalists call "micronews," or simple listings of information, such as deed transfers; marriages and divorces; bowling scores; school lunch menus; calendars of local events; and, of course, notices of the milestones of life: birth announcements, honor-roll listings, school graduations, marriage engagements, wedding announcements, anniversaries, promotions and retirements, and death notices. "Local briefs" are short articles that describe noteworthy events or developments, such as fatal vehicle accidents, announcements by local government bodies, upcoming community events, and notable accomplishments of local people. Full-length articles can range from coverage of routine government activity (i.e., city council meetings, public-works hearings, audits of government financial records) to hard-hitting investigative work—in fact, from 1985 to 2005, thirteen of the twenty-three reports that won the Pulitzer Prize for investigative reporting were local news stories, mostly about corruption at local institutions.

Although generally producing fewer and less-detailed local-news stories, broadcast news outlets nonetheless do provide a substantial amount of local news—although critics and researchers alike have noted that broadcast local news, particularly TV news, is much more focused on accidents, disasters, and serious crime than on routine or mundane community information. However, broadcast outlets are the most common sources for "live" information such as local weather forecasts, current traffic conditions, vote-tallies on election nights, and high-school football scores on game nights. Local and regional TV and radio stations also are the primary providers of severe-weather warnings and related information—for example, in the rural regions of the northern states, overnight snowstorms invariably cause children and parents to tune in to radio or TV stations early the next morning to see if the schools will be delayed or closed for the day. Many awards for broadcast journalism excellence—including the Emmy Awards—are given for in-depth local news coverage.

Historically, local news always has been a part of the American news media. Several examples could be found in the only edition of the 1690 proto-newspaper *Publick Occurrences, Both Forreign and Domestick*. After an introduction justifying the need for the Boston newspaper, the editor begins the accounting of news by discussing the quality of the local corn crop raised by "the Christianized Indians" and reporting about a "very Tragical Accident" in which a widower hanged himself "in the Cow-House" using "a Rope, which they had used to tye their Calves withal...." Later items focus on outbreaks of illness in the region, conflagrations in Boston, developments in the war against the French near Quebec, and the comings and goings of various sea vessels. Years later, the first true American newspaper, the *Boston News-Letter* published in 1704, also included quite a bit of local news: the arrival of ships, obituaries of local people, summaries of sermons given in local churches, and like sundries. A focus on local crime and violence was later a hallmark of Benjamin Day's *New York Sun* and other penny-papers of the mid-nineteenth century. In fact, the emphasis of local news coverage in American media is often attributed to the penny press—as historian Michael Schudson wrote in *Discovering the News*, "for the first time, [the press] printed reports from the police, from the courts, from the streets, and from private households." By the late-nineteenth century, when cities were on the rise and the American public became increasingly urban, newspapers committed considerable resources into local news coverage, particularly coverage of local crime and corruption. In the twentieth century, radio's audio-only delivery became a significant carrier of local news during working hours and "drive time." As television stations became more numerous in the mid-twentieth century, many stations committed more resources to local news teams, and many adopted promotional slogans that capitalized on their local-news focus, slogans such as "We're your hometown news team" and "Live. Local. Latebreaking,"

Local news coverage was more than just a journalistic consideration—it also figured prominently in the business practices of news companies. Historian Phyllis Kaniss, in her book *Making Local News*, argued that the emphasis on local news that developed during the penny press era was tied to urbanization. As cities grew in size, it became more difficult for residents to get local news via gossip and word-of-mouth, so they were willing to buy such information via newspapers. And as the nineteenth century progressed, newspaper publishers with a vested interest in the cohesion of "the city" used local news coverage to create a sense of "community" among the increasingly diverse and fragmented urban population. With the rise of broadcast news media in the mid-to-late twentieth century, newspapers increasingly turned to local news coverage as a way to compete for the public's attention and for advertising dollars. Later, detailed local news coverage became the primary focus of suburban newspapers as large metropolitan newspapers provided less coverage of routine government action and of micronews, for which the public demonstrated considerable interest.

One journalistic practice to come out of that public interest was "localizing," by which local news outlets reported on local aspects of state, national, and international news. Common examples "localizing" included stories about local government projects that are to be funded by state or federal budgets, or stories about local residents who are implicated in national or international news stories (e.g., victims of plane crashes, soldiers killed in military actions, athletes competing in national or international competitions). In fact, "localizing" is such a dominant practice in American news media that many times it is done even when national or international developments are unlikely to affect the community. For example, when the U.S. government announces plans to close military bases, news outlets in military communities that would be unaffected by the

cuts would run stories about how the federal action will *not* affect the community.

The public's desire for local information did not seem to abate in the early twenty-first century. An extensive survey of the newspaper industry in 2001 by the Readership Institute of the Media Management Center at Northwestern University found that "Intensely local, people-centered news" ranked "at the top of the list of content items with the greatest potential to increase overall readership of the newspaper."

Although the public seems to have had a strong interest in local news, attitudes about local news among journalists and journalism scholars is quite mixed, and has led to many professional disagreements. Among journalists, the more routine aspects of local news coverage are often viewed with boredom and sometimes even contempt. Many journalists find little professional satisfaction in covering school board meetings and county fairs or doing profiles of local people who grow extraordinarily large vegetables. Coverage of daily police reports, Little League Baseball games. and the like often fall to interns and entry-level reporters rather than veteran journalists. Journalism educators essentially ghettoize local news by focusing on "big time" journalism as positive examples of "good journalism"—such as the coverage of huge news events by major news outlets such as CNN, *The New York Times*, and *Newsweek*—and then point to "the small-town papers" for negative examples, such as sloppy editing, emphasis on "trivial" matters, and a lack of "hard hitting" news. Similarly, role models for aspiring reporters were usually nationally recognized journalists who rarely did local news coverage. Media critics and scholars also helped to undermine the importance of local news, since so many of them lamented that the working media's emphasis on arguably trivial local news left little space for national and international news. Moreover, journalism scholars often focused their research on the activities of the "marquis names" of journalism—that is, the major national news outlets. And while local news coverage was often recognized by high-profile journalism awards, much of that recognition went to relatively large news organizations that covered extraordinary events, rather than for extraordinary coverage of relatively banal events by mid-sized or small-market newspapers and news stations. For example, the Pulitzer Prize for "breaking news reporting" was usually awarded for local coverage of events on the scale of the Columbine High School massacre in suburban Denver in 1999 (for which the award went to the *Denver Post*), the federal raid to remove Cuban refugee Elian Gonzalez from his Miami relatives in 2000 (for which the award went to the *Miami Herald*), and the attacks on the World Trade Center on September 11, 2001 (for which the award went to the *Wall Street Journal*).

Yet many journalism professionals and scholars also championed local news and news outlets that emphasized local coverage. In particular, a number of American journalists embraced what came to be called "community journalism," or journalism that was unabashedly and zealously committed to local news coverage. "Community journalism" was most often seen as the bailiwick of relatively small (and often rural) news outlets, such as suburban weekly newspapers, small-town daily newspapers, rural radio stations, and regional television news stations based in small cities. Journalism educator Ken Byerly, author of the 1961 textbook called *Community Journalism*, is generally credited with coining the term, which he perhaps best described as the notion that "A dogfight on Main Street is more important than a revolution in Bulgaria." According to the *Editor & Publisher Yearbook*, an annual listing of the world's newspapers, about 95 percent of U.S. newspapers have circulations of less than fifty thousand and as such were considered "community newspapers." Those newspapers made up the bulk of the membership in most state press associations, but also of some national and international journalism groups such as the National Newspaper Association and the International Society of Weekly Newspaper Editors. Many high-profile professional organizations often ran special local-news training sessions for community media at regional and national conventions. College courses in "community journalism" were offered at several journalism schools in America, and a handful of universities created special programs to focus on "community journalism" education and research, such as the Huck Boyd National Center for Community Media at Kansas State University, the Carolina Community Media Project at the University of North Carolina-Chapel Hill, and the Institute for Rural Journalism and Community Issues based at the University of Kentucky. And in 2004, a group of journalism educators (including this author) formed a community journalism interest group for the Association of Educators in Journalism and Mass Communication in an effort to encourage more training and research focused on local-news journalism.

In addition to these endeavors, local news had previously been a topic of scholarly research. Both "local news" and "community journalism" was at least part of many research projects from the mid-twentieth century forward. (In particular, the research team of Phillip J. Tichenor, Clarice N. Olien, and George A. Donahue were renowned for several foundational studies of local news outlets published in the late-twentieth century.) While such research was too varied to summarize in this article, one common finding in many studies was that "local news" could influence audiences in significant ways, from the political activism to attitudes about race and gender, to perceptions of crime and public safety in their communities. Another common finding was that news outlets that emphasize local news often differed from "national" news outlets in substantial ways, from the professional practices of the journalists to audience attitudes toward their local and regional news products.

In the early twenty-first century, local news was no longer provided exclusively by traditional news media. On a basic level, people can use the Internet to get local news related to places they plan to visit or places where they have previously spent some time — thus extending the interest in "proximity" beyond physical location. But the most noteworthy development may be news production rather than news consumption. Using the Internet, so-called "citizen journalists" are also providing information about the goings on in their communities, from accounts of simple activities such as block parties and community-service projects to photographs and eyewitness accounts of major disasters such as hurricanes and wildfires. Through a variety of online communication formats including e-mail, amateur news sites, and "blogs," people can document local news that might not be covered by local news media, "break" news before newspapers and newscasts, and provide "micro-local news" information published on mainstream news Web sites that was submitted by readers and was generally unfiltered. Indeed, the Internet showed the potential to overtake newspapers as the dominant source of local news in America.

Further Reading

Byerly, Ken. *Community Journalism*. Philadelphia: Chilton. 1961.

Coulson, David, Riffe, Daniel, Lacy, Stephen, and St. Cyr, Charles. "Erosion of Television Coverage of City Hall? Perceptions of TV reporters on the Beat." *Journalism & Mass Communication Quarterly 78*, 1 (Spring 2001): 81–92 .

Donohue, George A., Olien, Clarice N., and Tichenor, Phillip. J. "Structure and Constraints on Community Newspaper Gatekeepers." *Journalism Quarterly 66*, 4 (Winter 1989): 807–812.

Kaniss, Phyllis. *Making Local News*. Chicago: University of Chicago Press. 1991.

Lauterer, Jock. *Community Journalism: the Personal Approach,* 3rd ed. Chapel Hill: University of North Carolina Press. 2005.

Moy, Patricia, McCluskey, Michael, McCoy, Kelley, and Spratt, Margaret. "Political Correlates of Local Media Use." *Journal of Communication 54*, 3 (September 2004): 532–546.

Outing, Steve. Improving citizen journalism. *Poynteronline*, May 5, 2005. http://www.poynter.org/column.asp?id=31&aid=82055 (accessed April 9, 2007).

Poindexter, Paula, Smith, Laura, and Heider, Don. Race and "Ethnicity in Local Television News: Framing Story Assignments and Source Selections." *Journal of Broadcasting & Electronic Media 47*, 4 (December 2003): 524–536.

Schudson, Michael. *Discovering the News: A Social History of American Newspapers*. New York: Basic Books. 1978: 22.

BILL READER

LOS ANGELES TIMES

The growth of the twentieth-century century metropolis, Los Angeles, was in no small way aided and abetted by the *Los Angeles Times* and its four-generation Otis-Chandler dynasty. In eight decades a sleepy goat herding village of twelve thousand inhabitants was transformed into America's second largest city, and a former third-rate partisan rag was transformed into one of America's top five daily newspapers.

The *Los Angeles Times* began publishing in December 1881 as a four-page daily that was primarily advertising content. A few months later Harrison Otis, a printer and Civil War lieutenant colonel, settled in Los Angeles and began working at the paper for $15 a week. He later bought a share of the paper. In 1886, Otis with $18,000 bought out his partner and took control of the *Times*.

Harry Chandler left New Hampshire for southern California's warmth in order to heal his pneumonia-damaged lungs. Chandler sold fruit to farmhands and prospered. His next venture was buying newspaper circulation routes, including the *Times'* entire fourteen hundred-member list at that time. Chandler became Otis's business manager, and son-in-law.

The Otis-Chandler duo approached empire-building differently. Otis was blustery and welcomed fights with real and imagined foes. Otis attacked political adversaries in adjective-laden editorials and he violently resisted union labor. Chandler avoided fights, yet he strategically used the newspaper as an instrument of an expanding economic order.

Otis co-founded the Los Angeles Chamber of Commerce, which recruited thousands of midwestern farmers to head West for sunshine and cheap land.

As Los Angeles' population swelled to more than 102,500 by 1900 and then to 319,200 a decade later, its inhabitants needed a reliable water supply. Otis and Chandler became silent partners in a group that bought land then diverted its fresh water from the Owens Valley, two hundred miles west of Los Angeles. Otis and Chandler were stridently anti-union. Their *Times* competed against unionized city dailies. In 1910, the *Times* building was rocked by a pre-dawn bombing that killed twenty-one workers. The *Times* pinned the crime on "unionites" who had "committed one of the worst atrocities in the history of the world" (*Los Angeles Times*, Oct. 3, 1910, I4). Two union activists were convicted after a sensational trial in which Clarence Darrow served as the defendants' lawyer. The attack hardened Otis's and Harry Chandler's resolve to keep their newspaper and most of the city free of union activity.

Harrison Gray Otis died in 1917 and much of the *Times's* shrill editorial voice left with him. Harry Chandler became chief executive of the Times Company. His considerable influence in Los Angeles resulted more from cunning than from bluster. Harry Chandler profited from a real estate syndicate he arranged with a handful of partners. Their customers were tens of thousands of new arrivals that the *Times* beckoned to come west. Like the growing movie and aircraft industry, the *Los Angeles Times* prospered. From 1921 to 1923, the *Los Angeles Times* led all American newspapers in display and classified advertising lineage and later hit highs of four million classifieds in 1964 and five million in 1977. In 1935, the *Times* emerged as a high-circulation U.S. daily at 186,423, up 20,000 from 1930. The newspaper went on to hit circulation highs of 757,776 in 1962 (fourth highest among American dailies) and 1,043,000 in 1980 (second).

Despite business success, the *Los Angeles Times* in the first half of the twentieth century was a journalistic disgrace. Its editors ignored an oil company swindle in the late 1920s that fleeced 40,000 Southern Californians of $150 million. The *Times* was co-conspirator in a smear campaign against Upton Sinclair, the celebrated muckraking journalist and socialist who ran for governor in 1934. The *Times* ran stories that branded Sinclair a "radical Socialist" and that linked him to a "huge Communist army in America" (*Los Angeles Times*, October 4, 1934, A4; and Oct. 5, 1934, A1). The *Times* newsroom in the 1930s looked the other way and coddled two mayoral administrations and their complementary police chiefs.

Harry Chandler's son, Norman, ascended to vice president and general manager in 1936 after a lengthy apprenticeship. In 1941, he advanced to president and general manager. When Norman's father died in 1944, he assumed the role of president and publisher. Norman was bland compared to his deal-making father, yet the son led like a patriarch. His newspaper and company was standard bearer for the Southern California status quo. Norman Chandler's wife Dorothy Buffum Chandler became a director of the *Times* in 1948. She was a shaper of Los Angeles civic life. "Buff" Chandler's relentless fundraising resulted in the Music Center of Los Angeles County, the rescue of the Hollywood Bowl from a wrecking ball, and the elevation in status of the Los Angeles Philharmonic.

The *Los Angeles Times* of the 1940s and 1950s Norman Chandler-era was closely identified with the California Republican Party. Its political stories "read like memos to and from the GOP National Committee," said a March 2006 *Los Angeles Times* account. Kyle Palmer, the *Times'* political editor, was known for his staunch support of Richard Nixon, the U.S. Senator and then two-term vice president under Dwight Eisenhower.

Commercially, the *Times* was prosperous. It was the dominant morning newspaper in a fast-growing metropolis. The *Times* battled the Hearst-owned morning and afternoon papers for the circulation, but led in advertising. In the late 1940s, Chandler's company launched the *Los Angeles Mirror*, a politically independent afternoon tabloid catering to working-class readers. In the late 1950s, Otis Chandler, Norman's son, was nearing the end of his seven-year apprenticeship for future leadership of company. Otis Chandler was keenly aware of the paper's journalistic shortcomings because unlike his father, he worked as a reporter and editor.

In 1958, Norman Chandler signaled major change at the *Times* when he replaced editor L.D. Hotchkiss with Nick Williams, a long-time night editor who seemed like an ordinary foot soldier, but actually was a well-read newsman and authority on southern California life. "I want the Times to be fair," Chandler instructed his new editor, "and I want it to dig, investigate and report what it learns." Dorothy Chandler was determined to change the image of the paper too. She groomed her son Otis to be the next leader of the empire. Although Otis Chandler was not the first choice of the more conservative Chandler family members, he was installed as publisher in 1960. Norman Chandler became chairman of Times Mirror Co.

Otis Chandler signaled that a new day had dawned at the

Los Angeles Times when in 1961 the newspaper published a five-part series critical of the ultraconservative John Birch Society. The *Times* withstood fifteen cancellations and consternation from Chandler family members who had well-heeled Birchers as friends. Journalistically, the *Times* in the Otis Chandler era applied East Coast standards in order to upgrade the newspaper. Top editors such as Robert Donovan and Edwin Guthman recruited talent for the Washington bureau. National and foreign bureaus opened and then expanded. Frank McCullough nurtured investigative reporting. Paul Conrad, an acerbic editorial cartoonist, was added to the opinion pages.

The *Times* won six Pulitzer Prizes during the twenty-year Otis Chandler era. Bill Thomas succeeded Nick Williams as editor in August 1971. Chandler improved the marketing of the newspaper and added zoned editions in the expanding southern California suburbs. The first computer operated by a newspaper in the United States was installed at the *Los Angeles Times*, and offset printing soon replaced linotype production.

During a two-decade run of journalistic and publishing triumphs, Otis Chandler suffered a blow. In the early 1970s, he was implicated the GeoTek oil- and gas-drilling scandal. Chandler's friend Jack Burke was convicted for defrauding investors. Chandler, who received thousands of dollars in finder fees from GeoTek, was fined by the Securities and Exchange Commission. The embarrassing details were initially reported in the *Wall Street Journal* instead of in Chandler's newspaper.

Chandler stepped down as publisher in 1980 and Tom Johnson, the first non-family member, led the paper. In 1990, circulation topped 1,225,000, making the *Los Angeles Times* America's largest daily metropolitan newspaper. In the 1990s, Mark Willes, a cereal company CEO with no publishing experience, became CEO of the Times Mirror Company. In June 2000, Times Mirror was acquired by the Tribune Company of Chicago. That $6.4 billion merger ended 119 years of hometown ownership. If in the quarter century following Chandler's retirement there were changes in leadership, the *Times* reputation for quality journalism continued. Between 1981 and 2006, the *Times* had won twenty-seven of its thirty-seven Pulitzer Prizes.

In August 2005, Dean Baquet was promoted to editor of the *Times*, one of the few blacks to ever lead a major metropolitan U.S. newspaper. Despite declining circulation, Baquet vowed to make the newspaper a compelling read and sharpened its focus on coverage of southern California and the entertainment industry. In June 2006, the *Times* had a showdown with the administration of President George W. Bush: The newspaper published details on how the United States attempted to track overseas bank transfers by suspected terrorists. Despite government officials' protests and threats, the *Times'* editors explained that U.S. citizens had a right to know what their government was doing.

Further Reading

Bellows, Jim. *The Last Editor: How I Saved The New York Times, The Washington Post and the Los Angeles Times from Dullness and Complacency.* Kansas City, MO: Andrews McMeel Publishing, 2002.

Dawkins, Wayne, "Newsmaker: Dean Baquet." *The Crisis* [NAACP], September/October 2005.

Halberstam, David. *The Powers That Be.* New York: Knopf, 1979.

King, Peter H., and Arax, Mark. "As Dynasty Evolved, So Did Power in L.A." *Los Angeles Times,* March 26, 2006.

McDougal, Dennis. *Privileged Son: Otis Chandler and Rise and Fall of the L.A. Times Dynasty.* Cambridge, MA: Perseus Publishing, 2001.

Talese, Gay. *The Kingdom and the Power.* New York: Bantam Books, 1970.

The full run of *Los Angeles Times* articles can be accessed electronically by using ProQuest Historical Newspapers.

WAYNE DAWKINS

M

MACNEIL, ROBERT

Robert MacNeil (January 19, 1931–) was a reporter for Reuters, the BBC and NBC, then co-anchor and executive editor for twenty years with Jim Lehrer of PBS' award-winning *The MacNeil-Lehrer NewsHour* (previously *The Robert MacNeil Report*). *NewsHour* was the first television news program to devote large blocks of time to detailed reporting on a few issues.

Robert Breckenridge Ware MacNeil was born in Montreal, Canada, January 19, 1931, to Robert and Peggy Mac-Neil, and raised in Halifax, Nova Scotia. His two middle names were drawn from American forbearers on both sides. His father, a World War II naval commander decorated for his heroics, was frequently absent from home. MacNeil traces his love of language to his well-read parents. He is known as Robin to friends, associates, and viewers of *News-Hour*, which he and co-host Lehrer ended each evening by exchanging their signature salutes: "Goodnight Robin," "Good night Jim."

In high school and Dalhousie University in Halifax, MacNeil developed an interest in theater. Backstage following his performance as Cassio in *Othello*, a Canadian Broadcasting Corporation producer offered him work in live radio dramas. He was a regular on CBC radio, and later secured a role in a daily radio series. He moved to Ottawa where he wrote and broadcast a weekend review of news for radio station CFRA, and attended Carelton College (now University), earning a BA in English in 1955.

MacNeil moved to London in June 1955 to pursue playwriting, then took a job with the newly founded Independent Television News (ITV) for three months before moving to Reuters. Beginning as a subeditor, he worked his way up to the Reuters Central Desk. MacNeil also began writing and broadcasting stories from London for the CBC in Toronto.

As London correspondent for NBC, MacNeil covered the British government, then dozens of stories in Europe and Africa—including the August 1961 German erection of the Berlin Wall, during which he was briefly arrested and held in East Berlin.

During the Cuban Missile Crisis, NBC directed Mac-Neil to use his Canadian passport to fly to Havana, where he and four other journalists were arrested and confined to the Capri Hotel. Tapping into phone lines, the group called Reuters. After his release, MacNeil bought a box of cigars at the airport in Havana that subsequently were delivered to John Kennedy via the president's press secretary, Pierre Salinger.

In March 1963 he moved to Washington to cover the State Department and White House. When the shots that killed Kennedy were fired in Dallas, MacNeil sprinted from the press bus behind the president, up the Grassy Knoll in search of a perpetrator, then into a building to look for a phone, the Texas School Book Depository. MacNeil asked a man descending the steps where he might find one. Historian William Manchester, who reconstructed a second-by-second account of the assassination in *The Death of a President*, strongly believes it was Lee Harvey Oswald that MacNeil encountered.

Later, with interns keeping a hallway pay phone open, MacNeil regularly updated NBC on the president's condition from in the emergency room of Parkland Hospital. He would give a sentence of detail over the phone and Frank McGee would repeat MacNeil's updates live over the air to Americans watching the unfolding tragedy. He also covered the assassinations and funerals of Martin Luther King Jr. and Robert Kennedy, and the 1968 Chicago Democratic Convention. His 1982 book, *The Right Place at the Right Time*, details his reporting during those cataclysmic years.

MacNeil covered Barry Goldwater and Lyndon B. Johnson in the 1964 election, then anchored and reported for *The Scherer-MacNeil Report,* a Saturday news program that garnered high ratings. He also anchored local newscasts and developed documentaries on topics such as electronic surveillance and gun control legislation. MacNeil returned to London as a feature news reporter, doing longer international pieces for the BBC's *Panorama*, a show he described as imminently superior to any news program on U.S. television.

MacNeil's critical exposé on the role of television in U.S. politics, *The People Machine*, was published in 1968. He returned to Washington to cover the 1972 elections for PBS with Sander Vanocur. Jim Lehrer later replaced Vanocur and the duo covered the ensuing Senate Watergate hearings, programming that attracted high ratings, large donations for public broadcasting, and an Emmy Award.

On New York's WETA, *The Robert MacNeil Report* with Jim Lehrer reporting from Washington premiered in October 1975. PBS quickly began distributing the show nationally and renamed it *The MacNeil-Lehrer Report*. Consistent with MacNeil's BBC sensibilities and Lehrer's print reporter background, the co-hosts placed news values over production, and strove for fairness. *MacNeil-Lehrer* devoted a half hour of noncommercial airtime to one news story with up to four guests explaining different views on the topic. The conversations were shot in the round, with guests seated at a horseshoe desk. The program's audience grew and attracted corporate underwriters.

MacNeil-Lehrer expanded to sixty minutes in 1983 and became the *NewsHour*. It routinely included live interviews from its studios in New York and Washington with high-ranking policy makers and internationally known experts. Over the next two decades, the highly acclaimed program appeared on over three hundred stations and earned more than thirty awards for excellence in broadcast news. The co-hosts formed MacNeil-Lehrer Productions, which produced the program and features, such as MacNeil's *The Story of English*. With producer William Cran, MacNeil traced the history of the language from its roots to its role as a global language in the 1986 series that ran on the BBC, PBS, and Australian Broadcasting, and earned Peabody and Emmy awards. MacNeil and Cran's *Do You Speak American?* was adapted into a PBS documentary that premiered in January 2005. MacNeil retired in October, 1995.

MacNeil is author of novels *Burden of Desire* (1992), *Voyage* (1995), *Breaking News* (1998), and memoir *Word-struck* (1992). His 2003 *Looking for My Country: Finding Myself in America* describes his search for a chosen nationality. MacNeil became an American citizen in 1997.

Further Reading

Lehrer, James. *A Bus of My Own*. New York: G. P. Putnam's Sons, 1992.

MacNeil, Robert. *Looking for My Country: Finding Myself in America*. New York: Nan A. Talese, 2003.

——. *The People Machine: The Influence of Television on American Politics*. New York: HarperCollins, 1968.

——. *The Right Place at the Right Time*. New York: Little Brown, 1982.

KEVIN C. LEE

MAGAZINE PUBLISHERS

When the earliest magazines appeared in America in 1741, they were very similar to their English counterparts and were often little more than compilations of articles lifted from British publications. The first American magazine publishers—Benjamin Franklin and Andrew Bradford—were not unlike their readership: members of the colonies' cultural and intellectual elite. Doctors, lawyers, ministers, and educators were the original readers of magazines, and it was this audience that Franklin catered to with *The General Magazine and Historical Chronicle for All the British Plantations in America*, a monthly reflecting his personal views of the issues of the time. The debut of Franklin's magazine, however, fell three days short of Bradford's introduction of *The American Magazine or a Monthly View of the Political State of the British Colonies*, which narrowly won the honor of being the first American magazine.

In the end, neither magazine flourished—a lack of advertising and the mechanical difficulties of production made early publishing a costly and largely recreational undertaking—but the concept enjoyed a measure of success. With individual publishers handling the writing and editing responsibilities, periodicals were constantly started throughout the remainder of the eighteenth century. Though they rarely lasted more than a few months, they could claim to be significant and important forums for political and intellectual discourse. Matthew Carey's *American Museum* published Thomas Paine's *Common Sense*, and as editor of *The Royal American*, Joseph Greenleaf printed the first important engravings, most done by Paul Revere.

At the close of the eighteenth century, editor Joseph Dennie's *Port Folio* established itself as a leading periodical into the early 1800s. Dennie (1768–1812) was among the first to resemble a modern editor, soliciting popular contributors like John Quincy Adams and investing in newly available copper plate engravings. While he was successful in attracting an impressive two thousand subscribers, he had yet to make financial gains. *Port Folio* did, however, remain a popular monthly for eight years. For a time it held violently Federalist views, to the point that Dennie was indicted on—and later acquitted of—charges of seditious libel.

The Rise of the Commercial Model

It was not until the end of the nineteenth century that periodicals became sources of profit. Two of that century's most significant monthlies were *McClure's* and *Munsey's*. Publisher Samuel Sidney "S.S" McClure was a showman who worked his way up from a poor Irish background. His sensational magazine contained historical and scientific discourse, as well as profiles of famous personalities. Pages of eyewitness coverage of the Spanish-American war particularly boosted his readership, as did the heavily used tactic of exposing political corruption, also known as muckraking. By marketing his publication at the low price of ten cents, McClure attracted a large audience.

In order to compete, other publications had to lower their prices as well. *Munsey's* popularity increased when publisher Frank Munsey took its price down to ten cents in 1893. He paid good rates to his contributors and published quality fiction work, such as Hall Caine's *The Christian* in 1896, and later, various works by O. Henry. But what *Munsey's* really sold was a Victorian version of sex, a concept that was quickly spreading its way throughout publications of the time. *Munsey's* pages were full of nude and half-dressed women, spreads that played a significant role in the periodical's success.

Along with the continued proliferation of general monthlies, weekly periodicals began to emerge in the nineteenth century. One of the most notable was the *Saturday Evening Post*, which began in 1821 and did not cease publication until 1969. Charles Alexander and Samuel Coate Atkinson, two Philadelphia publishers, nurtured the four-page, pictureless magazine through its early years; publisher Cyrus

H.K. Curtis and editor George Horace Lorimer would later make it one of the most successful magazines in America. Curtis realized that large circulations attracted advertisers, and consequently kept newsstand and subscription rates at low prices. With a secured audience of consumers, advertisers were willing to pay, and magazines became dependent on them for revenue.

Using his understanding of mass marketing, Curtis made *Ladies' Home Journal*, the first modern women's service magazine, extremely popular after he acquired it in 1883. Like *McClure's* and *Munsey's*, *Ladies' Home Journal* maintained a high readership thanks to its low issue price, and editor Edward William Bok was able to relate to women in a way that made the publication uniquely accessible. Under his leadership, *Ladies' Home Journal* evolved into a service magazine by providing advice and feedback to readers, a formula that has become the norm among magazines.

Curtis's second major triumph was with the *Saturday Evening Post*, which he acquired in 1897 and entrusted to editor George Horace Lorimer. Though languishing at the time, the work of Curtis and Lorimer made the magazine a prominent general weekly across the country by 1909, reaching an all-time circulation high by 1959 with 6.2 million readers. With the success of magazines such as *Ladies' Home Journal* and the *Saturday Evening Post*, other publishers were pushed to design new periodicals to reach ever-expanding audiences.

Though publisher William Randolph Hearst (1864–1951) began his career in newspapers, purchasing the *San Francisco Examiner* in 1887, he launched his first magazine, *Motor*, in 1903. In 1905 he bought *Cosmopolitan* from John Brisben Walker; formerly focused on domestic and foreign affairs, the publication became more sensational under Hearst's leadership. He acquired *Good Housekeeping* in 1911, *Harper's Bazaar* in 1912, and *Town and Country* in 1925. By the time of his death in 1951, Hearst had established a media empire that continues to flourish. One of Hearst's contemporaries, lawyer Condé Nast, first gained publishing experience as advertising manager of *Collier's*. Nast (1873–1942) bought *Vogue* in 1909 and quickly made it an elite fashion publication. A century later, Condé Nast Publications still proclaims itself a harbinger of style.

Not all of the twentieth century publications were focused around specific topics. The first issue of *Reader's Digest*, published in 1922 by DeWitt and Lila Bell Wallace, compiled previously printed articles, much like the first magazines in the eighteenth century. Wallace intended his magazine to promote an influential America, and carefully selected and edited pieces to convey a can-do tone of optimism. Since this attitude echoed middle class sentiment of the time, *Reader's Digest* was hugely successful.

Recognizing the allure of condensed information, Henry Luce and his partner Briton Hadden (February 18, 1898–February 27, 1929) both Yale graduates with some journalism experience, published the first issue of *Time* in 1923. Again appealing to a mass market of readers, *Time* presented the weekly news in convenient subdivisions that were entertaining and accessible. Luce also started *Fortune*

in February 1930, successfully targeting entrepreneurial readers amidst the economic chaos of the Great Depression. Luce then introduced *Life* in 1936, which depicted America though abundant photography that became known worldwide. *Life*, along with its competitor, *Look*, epitomized the nationally marketed general interest publications of the early twentieth century. *Sports Illustrated*, launched by Luce in 1954, grasped the importance of sports in the national consciousness.

Specialization and the Future of Magazines

In the years following World War II, general interest magazines gave way to the rise of special interest publications. With Americans prospering financially, they had more time to devote to hobbies, and a consequent interest in reading about their leisure activities. From a publisher's perspective, competition with the new medium of television made it increasingly difficult to guarantee advertisers that readers would see their pages. (One exception was *TV Guide*, first published in 1953 by Walter Annenberg and uniquely positioned to garner television's readership). Special interest magazines were an ideal solution—advertisers could be sure that narrowly defined target audiences would be reached. Also, because it was becoming cheaper and easier to produce magazines, special interest publications with smaller circulations could still profit. Ziff-Davis Publishing took advantage of this idea. In the 1960s, in an attempt to target recreational activities, Ziff-Davis launched titles like *Car and Driver*, *Boating*, *Skiing*, and *Popular Photography*. Capitalizing on the benefits of the loyal readerships and satisfied advertisers of special interest publications, Ziff-Davis later published titles such as *PC Magazine* and *Electronic Gaming Monthly*.

Special interest magazines continued to flourish in the 1970s, with an emphasis on self-awareness and self-improvement. *Psychology Today* was founded in 1967 by Nicholas Charne, and *Ms.* was founded by Gloria Steinem in 1971. A feminist woman's magazine that rejected superficial components common in women's service journalism, *Ms.* exemplified the continued diversification and specialization of the publishing industry. Niche magazines remain the standard today, with some nine hundred new titles being created each year, though few become smash hits. One such hit is *Maxim*, which came to the United Sates in 1997 after publisher Felix Denis founded it in London. In less than two years, *Maxim* became the leading men's magazine, focusing on topics like sex, sports and beer—and effectively capturing a young male audience.

In addition to understanding target readership, what can aid publishing success is a demonstrated understanding of the changing functionality of the magazine. No longer purely a print medium, magazines are expanding their niche identities through unique websites for their publications. For example, Rodale publishing has a home site linking readers to sites specially designed for each of its nine special interest publications like *Men's Health*, *Prevention*, *Organic Style*, and *Runner's World*. These web pages serve as an extension of their printed counterparts, and allow for increased reader interaction as well as additional advertising space. In some cases, a publication's web page can take on a life of its own. *O, the Oprah Magazine*, founded and based completely around the titled celebrity, utilizes its web space as a forum where readers can sign up for activities in their local communities as well as participate in nationally orchestrated campaigns.

This kind of international accessibility that embraces the individual nature of readers will undoubtedly increase the importance of online publishing, particularly as an extension of print publications. Additionally, as titles become ever-specialized and increase in number, the quantity of publishers decreases with ongoing conglomeration. Ziff-Davis and Time Mirror are just two of the publishers absorbed by larger corporate entities in recent years, and major publishers such as Hearst, Time, and Condé Nast act as publishing empires within a larger net of company affiliations.

With the advent of the World Wide Web, many magazine publishers have seen opportunities to move beyond the traditional print form to serve their audiences better with more information, in more timely fashion, and often in an interactive mode. Still in its early stages of development, the early results have led to optimism. With the special loyalty that many magazine readers feel for "their" publications, the future of the magazine publishing as an industry is regarded by most observers as a very promising one.

Further Reading

Abrahamson, David. *Magazine-made America: The Cultural Transformation of the Postwar Periodical*. NJ: Hampton Press, Inc., 1996.

Compaine, Benjamin M. *The Business of Consumer Magazines*. White Plains, NY: Knowledge Industry Publications, 1982.

Elson, Robert T., Curtis Prendergast and Geoffrey Colvin. *The world of Time, Inc: The Intimate History of a Publishing Enterprise, 1923–1980* (vols. 1–3). New York: Atheneum, 1986.

Janello, Amy, and Brennon Jones. *The American Magazine*. New York: Harry Abrams, 1991.

Mott, Frank Luther. *A History of American Magazines* (vols. 1–5). Cambridge, MA: Harvard University Press, 1938.

Peterson, Theodore. *Magazines in the Twentieth Century*. Urbana: University of Illinois Press, 1956.

Richardson, Lyon N. *A History of Early American Magazines, 1741–1789*. New York: Nelson and Sons, 1931.

Tebbel, John W. *The American Magazine: A Compact History*. New York: Hawthorn Books, Inc., 1969.

Tebbel, John W. and Mary Ellen Zuckerman. *The Magazine in America, 1941–1990*. New York: Oxford University Press, 1991.

DAVID ABRAHAMSON
CHRISTINA BRYZA

MAGAZINES, MEN'S

Although magazines created by men appeared in America as early as the 1740s, magazines for men, designed specifically to speak to definable male gender interests, did not fully emerge until the late- nineteenth and early twentieth

centuries. Focusing originally on participatory sports but soon evolving to cover such lifestyle subjects as fashion, grooming, leisure pursuits, spectator sports, and sex, these magazines have consistently played a significant role in defining both the sociocultural role of males and the nature of masculinity in American society.

It can be argued, however, that the genre has an earlier, albeit indirect, history. A number of early eighteenth-century periodicals were in some sense aimed at an elite segment of the new nation's male population, cultivated men of high intelligence and substantial means. Most notable were Benjamin Franklin's *General Magazine* (1741), Andrew Bradford's *The American Magazine* (1743), and Isaiah Thomas's *The Royal American* (1774), which proclaimed itself to be "the first distinctive American magazine." These publications covered the pressing issues of the day: government, finance, technology, and commerce.

By the early 1800s, specialized publications began to focus on vocations open largely to men; in effect, the first trade magazines. Appealing to professions with mostly male members such as lawyers, physicians, musicians, scientists, farmers, and academics, periodicals with such titles as *American Law Journal* (1808), *American Farmer* (1817), and *American Journal of Science* (1818) developed small but devoted followings. About the same time, comic magazines proved popular with many men. The most famous was *Salmagundi*, edited by Washington Irving, of *The Legend of Sleepy Hollow* fame.

By the mid-nineteenth century, American magazines clearly had begun to define themselves explicitly by gender. Magazines for male audiences became counterparts to such successful specialized women's magazines as *Godey's Lady's Book* and *Peterson's Ladies' National Magazine*. For example, *Graham's Magazine* featured landscapes and battlefield scenes, while the *Western Review* offered articles on botany and Indian fighting.

Not until the late nineteenth and early twentieth centuries did what might be generally recognizable today as men's magazines emerge. Here, by way of providing a useful definition, both quantitative and qualitative criteria apply. For example, most students of the magazine form agree that for a periodical to have a gender-specific readership more than 60 percent of its audience must be of one gender. In the qualitative realm, the central subject of the publication must be one that, at any given sociocultural historical moment, most people would agree is customarily of specific interest to one gender.

Using these criteria, the first two categories of genuine men's magazines were outdoor periodicals (often called "sporting journals") and publications promoting a certain, often urbane, masculine lifestyle. The former genre—devoted to hunting, fishing, horse racing, bicycling, and other out-of-doors activities—included titles which wielded substantial political influence. *Forest and Stream* (1873) was a major factor in the establishment of the Audubon Society, while *Appalachia* (1876) was instrumental in the passage of the Act of Congress creating the national forests. By the turn of the century, more than fifty such magazines were being published, and with each new technological development, periodicals appeared to serve the new, largely male interest. The invention of the internal combustion engine in the early twentieth century, for example, soon such fostered titles as *Motor* and *Motor Boating*. The successors to the sporting journals of the late nineteenth century still flourish today. Magazines such as *Sports Afield*, *Field and Stream*, and *Outdoor Life* cover many of the same topics, while a wealth of publications, similarly targeted at male readers, concentrate on such leisure-active pursuits as boating (e.g., *Yachting*, *Sail*, *Boating*), automobiles (*Car and Driver*, *Road & Track*, *Hot Rod*), and private aviation (*Flying*, *Pilot*, *Soaring*).

Most observers agree that the founding of *Esquire* in 1933 marks a point of origin for men's lifestyle magazines. Founded by Arnold Gingrich, within its pages were men's fashion spreads and scantily clad pinups, as well as both fiction and nonfiction by such contemporary literary lights as Ernest Hemingway, F. Scott Fitzgerald, and William Faulkner. By the mid-1950s, a number of other magazines were employing a similar editorial formula. One of the more successful of the era was *Argosy*; which claimed to be "The Complete Men's Magazine," and to have a circulation of more than one million. It featured the work of such authors as Edgar Rice Burroughs, Horatio Alger, Louis L'Amour, and Dashiell Hammett. Many of today's most popular men's interest magazines came into existence in the 1950s and 1960s. *Sports Illustrated* (1954) benefited from the fact that television soon turned spectator sports into a national obsession. *Playboy* (1953), and its later competitor *Penthouse* (1969) tapped into a new appetite for guilt-free ribaldry and idealized female nudity. In a more serious vein, the *Advocate* (1967) spoke to political, social, and cultural issues that concerned gay men.

The 1960s and early 1970s saw a major transformation of the American consumer magazine publishing industry what with the decline of many large mass-market, general-interest publications such as the original *Life*, *Look* and the *Saturday Evening Post* and the emergence of a wide variety of smaller "special-interest" magazines focused on specific leisure and recreational subjects and aimed at specialized audiences. Competition from television and apparent mismanagement played a role in the demise of many mass-market magazines, while new publishing technology and a major shift in national advertising toward segmented marketing favored the development of smaller, more specialized magazines. Magazine publishing became an exercise in "niche marketing"—and one of the most promising and profitable niches men and their interests.

Hundreds of magazines fall under the "men's interest" category. With topics ranging from fitness to fashion, cigars to sex, as well as all manner of material pursuits, the market brims with options. To give some idea of the diversity of subject matter, one need only to look at a sample of some top men's magazines. Sex, fashion, music, cars, and shopping defined the most financially successful cluster of men's magazines during most of the 1990s. The field at the time was led by four publications: *GQ*, *Arena*, *Esquire*, and *FHM*.

At the upper end of the market, *GQ* and *Esquire* magazines were most popular among slightly older readers. *FHM* and *Arena* appealed to younger fashion-conscious men with an interest in popular music.

Esquire and *GQ* offer refinement and variety for professional men looking for a broader scope of information. Topics such as upscale fashion, business, health, fitness, sports, fiction, entertainment, family life, and tips on improving one's sex life are cast in a way to appeal to a somewhat more sophisticated audience—or, as is often the case in magazine publishing—a group of readers who wish they were so.

Men's Health, *Men's Fitness*, and *Men's Journal* are designed to help men obtain a well-rounded, healthy lifestyle in body, mind, and spirit. They also discuss exercise and diet techniques, and provide columns to aid emotional and mental well being. In addition, leisure activities and sports are popular topics.

Details, one of the nation's leading magazines for men interested in the latest styles and trends, is diffuse in focus, covering fashion, business, technology, food, entertainment, travel, politics, celebrities, women, careers, and grooming. Also growing in popularity is *Black Men*, a lifestyle magazine for African Americans. With an editorial mix of sex and relationship articles, sports, business, personal finance, grooming, and community news, it also includes pictures of beautiful women.

Cargo, *Stuff*, and *Blender* all celebrate consumptive materialism and offer articles targeted at a very specific readership. Younger and perhaps less accomplished professionally than their elder brethren, The audience of these publications is likely to be younger and less accomplished professionally than their elder brethren, and more likely to be interested in electronic gadgets, hip hop, celebrity, music, and entertainment.

Similar to the category above but targeted at slightly older readers, *Playboy*, *Penthouse*, and *FHM* appeal slyly to "what every man wants." Articles featuring large photographs and little text—known in the trade as "pictorials"—prominently display numerous women models in varying states of undress ranging from scantily clad to nude. There are also features on sports, fashion, and exotic automobiles, and all devote substantial space to bawdy jokes and humor.

Such salaciousness is not necessarily what every man wants, and there is also a market for men interested in religion and/or marriage. *New Man*, a Christian magazine, introduces another view of masculinity and Christianity. Its stated goal is to help Christian men apply God's truth to five major areas of life: spiritual, intellectual, physical, social, and emotional. Correspondingly, *Marriage Partnership* is a magazine to help men sustain strong marriages and partnerships by offering advice on problem solving, cooperative decision making, and sharing activities.

One important constant in the men's interest category over the years has been change. And one of the most important new men's magazines—indeed, it created a whole new category of publication colloquially know as the "laddie magazines"—is *Maxim*. Founded in 1997, this monthly magazine targets post-pubescent young men and was originally established in London and then brought to the United States. Its mildly transgressive blend of soft-core titillation and sophomoric humor have propelled its circulation well past the two million, and as further evidence of its success with male readers, its newsstand sales alone far surpass that of *GQ, Esquire,* and *Men's Journal* combined. *Maxim's* editorial formula is hardly subtle. Atop each cover a line proudly proclaims the six topics on which the publication focuses: sex, sports, beer, gadgets, clothes, and fitness. While this list is not notably original in the broader context of both historical and contemporary men's periodicals, what sets *Maxim* apart—and no doubt is key in its meteoric success—is the playfully juvenile and assertively unapologetic tone with which the magazine approaches these topics. The editors claim that the resulting attitude is that of a "smart, funny guy in a bar," but it could perhaps be argued that a better description might simply be "boys behaving badly."

Evidence suggests that the lessons of *Maxim*'s success have not been lost on other men's magazines. A number of them, including such venerable stalwarts as *Playboy* and *Esquire,* have taken steps to lighten their editorial mix, intentionally seeking to appeal to the *Maxim* (read: younger) reader. The result has been a move toward shorter articles, unsophisticated humor, and a coarser editorial tenor. Publishers of men's periodicals hope that by repositioning their publications along the line of *Maxim,* they too will reap similar financial rewards.

Such is the state of the American men's magazine at the start of the new century. It is a strikingly diverse category of publications, with a magazine for almost every male interest. As with many contemporary American media, entertainment values tend to dominate over journalistic ones. But then this is hardly a new phenomenon. Most males, young or not so young, have read men's magazines as a diversion, as a respite from daily cares, or perhaps as an escape into fantasy. In the end, it is the readers who select the magazines they want, and for men, it is clear that the choices are abundant.

Further Reading

Abrahamson, David. *Magazine-Made America: The Cultural Transformation of the Postwar Periodical.* Cresskill, NJ: Hampton Press, Inc., 1996.

Abrahamson, David; Bowman, Rebecca Lynn; Greer, Mark Richard; and Yeado, William Brian. "A Quantitative Analysis of U.S. Consumer Magazines: A Ten-Year Longitudinal Study." *Journal of Magazine and New Media Research,* 5:1 (Spring 2003).

Beale, Claire. "Men's Titles Set to Come of Age." *Marketing,* February 1994: 12(1).

Fahey, Maryjane. "The Magazine for Magazine Management." *Folio,* March 2004.

Handy, Bruce. "Bosom Buddies: Today's men's magazines all share a common interest. Can you tell?" *Time,* February 1999: 76(1).

Loeb, Marshall. "Sex, Sports, Beer, Gadgets, Clothes: The Magic and Menace of *Maxim.*" *Columbia Journalism Review* May 2000: 68.

Mott, Frank Luther. *A History of American Magazines.* Cambridge, MA: Harvard University Press, 1968.

Murphy, David. "Sporting Chances." *Marketing* June 1998: 29(2).

Tebbel, John. *The American Magazine: A Compact History.* New York: Hawthorn Books, Inc., 1969.

DAVID ABRAHAMSOM
KIM WEISENSEE

MAGAZINES, NEWS

The emergence of news as a commodity in American magazines during the last dozen years of the nineteenth century was a direct response to keen competition among general periodicals. Many editors and publishers of magazines, most of them from a newspaper background, believed news articles could serve a significant editorial purpose and attract a sizable readership. By the early years of the twentieth century, articles on current events and issues received as much space, and sometimes more, as did popular fiction and poetry in numerous monthly general magazines.

Competition among monthly general magazines, a separate category from women's magazines and literary magazines, had begun in earnest late in the nineteenth century. Technology of the era—high-speed printing presses, web-fed paper, and half-tone photographs—had combined with cheap postal rates and a nationwide railroad network to permit inexpensive mass production and distribution.

Also, an abundance of manufacturers and producers needed to advertise nationally, which caused a tremendous surge in revenue. Consumer products streamed from manufacturers to distributors and retailers, and national brands used magazines to advertise apparel, candy, canned vegetables and meat, cereal, rolled-film cameras, patent medicines, shoes, soaps, and soups. National advertising expenditures soared tenfold to a half-billion dollars by during the last third of the nineteenth century.

Demographics and economics created a vast readership for magazines. The national population almost doubled between 1880 and 1910. The population clustered more in cities, which enabled magazines to distribute copies quickly. At the same time, the national economy transformed from primarily agricultural to industrial, which resulted in a significant rise in the number of workplace managers, proprietors, administrators, and professional occupations. Men in these positions earned appreciably more money than factory workers and laborers, and they could afford to buy magazines.

Quality general magazines, heretofore written for an elite readership, seldom had a circulation exceeding fifty thousand copies a month. Suddenly, several became periodicals for a nascent middle class of Americans whose incomes and collective curiosity propelled the aggregate circulation of general magazines into the millions by the early 1900s. "Editors locked up their ivory towers and came down into the market place," wrote Frank Luther Mott, the esteemed historian in *A History of American Magazines, 1885–1905.* New or transformed national magazines emphasized current events and issues to attract a broader readership, including

American, Arena, Century, Collier's Weekly, Cosmopolitan, Everybody's, Forum, Literary Digest, McClure's, Public Opinion, Outlook, and *World's Work.* These modern magazines contained articles and commentary on international items, science, medicine, education, transportation, municipal governance, and social concerns.

The marketplace rewarded those magazines that emphasized journalism and penalized those that did not sufficiently do so. *Cosmopolitan,* a failure as a literary magazine, was revived in 1889 as a general magazine emphasizing journalism. By the turn of the century, *Cosmopolitan* circulation had grown from 20,000 copies monthly in 1889 to 75,000 copies in 1891 and to 350,000 copies by 1900. *McClure's,* a startup in 1893, reflected the fascination of editor-publisher Samuel S. McClure with everything modern and attained a circulation of 369,000 by 1900. Conversely, *Century,* a general magazine that reluctantly, but never fully, embraced journalism, suffered a decline in circulation from 198,000 copies at the start of the 1890s to 125,000 copies by the early 1900s.

The late 1880s through the early 1900s have become a demarcation for magazines in the United States, an era when a higher proportion of articles about economic, political, and social issues appeared in monthly general periodicals. Editors and publishers realized that many Americans wished to learn about the factors causing great changes in society and their lives. Weekly general magazines devoted to news entered the marketplace in force during this period, too, their rapid distribution made possible by subscribers and buyers concentrated in urban areas.

Prior to the 1890s, some general magazines regularly published a certain number of articles regarding political and social issues of contemporary relevance among more prevalent literary fare. Most of these articles on contemporary issues were commentaries or treatises rather than reports or analyses. Thus, although the articles were about relatively recent subjects, which usually meant publication several months afterward, they were not necessarily journalism; adherence to factual information and mention of specific events were not elements of most.

Magazines and many newspapers appeared in a variety of page sizes—folio, small folio, quarto, octavo—until well into the twentieth century, so it was sometimes difficult to separate magazines from national non-daily newspapers by specific physical format. *Harper's Weekly,* for example, looked like some newspapers of the era and the editors described it as a newspaper, but scholars have regarded it as a magazine because it offered a sizable amount of current events, accompanied by superb illustrations from the late 1850s into the early 1900s. Its subtitle declared it was a "Journal of Civilization," and it recorded momentous events of the Civil War, helped expose municipal corruption in New York City, and documented social turmoil in the last years of the nineteenth century.

Magazine journalism, in the sense of timeliness, began with articles from contributors who were not journalists but instead were experts or otherwise regarded as knowledgeable on certain subjects. Some of the important monthly general magazines of the late nineteenth century published articles by current and former government officials, diplomats, scholars, prominent businessmen, and members of the American intelligentsia. Sometimes these contributors submitted unsolicited material and an editor used the article on a space-available basis; later, editors commissioned articles from contributors.

Gradually, because of meteoric increases in subscriptions and single-copy sales for periodicals that emphasized journalism, the larger monthly general magazines began to employ paid correspondents to ensure a reliable supply of timely articles on contemporary events and issues.

Although the gradual emphasis on news in general magazines occurred from the late 1880s into the early 1900s, a turning point that demonstrated the commitment to timeliness by major monthly general magazines was the Spanish-American War in 1898. Until the war, an article about a specific event of major importance usually did not appear in a general magazine until several months afterward, which represented the time it took to commission an article, receive the manuscript, and schedule it for publication. Evidence of this interval was seen in *Cosmopolitan,* which addressed a serious diplomatic crisis between Britain and the United States from July to November 1895, six months after it had begun, and *Century,* which dealt with the same crisis eight months after its resolution.

However, the outbreak of war between the United States and Spain coincided with a period of intense competition among some of the larger monthly general magazines, which resulted in publication of war-related articles within a month or two of the official war declaration. The much shortened interval represented efforts by editors to rush anything remotely related to the war into print. *McClure's* published "An American in Manila" only one month after U.S. Navy warships had destroyed a Spanish naval squadron in the bay; the article itself pertained to life in Manila a few years earlier. *Cosmopolitan,* a quality general magazine of the era, also managed to print "Havana Just Before the War" a few weeks prior to the invasion of the island by U.S. troops in July 1898. During autumn 1898, just two months after the conclusion of combat in Cuba, *McClure's* presented articles about the capture of Santiago and other battles.

Collier's Weekly also demonstrated that news could be published within a couple weeks of actual events. Its photographs and articles about the war in Cuba established the magazine's reputation with the public for coverage of current events. Later, *Collier's* provided articles on the two-year Filipino insurrection against American occupation, a dramatic series written by Frederick Palmer, a staff correspondent.

With a sense of immediacy developed during the war with Spain, magazines engaged in the intense debate about national policy regarding what to do with the newly acquired Spanish colonies of the Philippines, Puerto Rico, and Guam. Articles and commentary in *Arena, Atlantic Monthly, Century, Cosmopolitan, Forum, McClure's,* and *Outlook,* among others, coincided with the debate in

Congress and the attempt by Democrats to make imperialism an issue in the presidential election campaign of 1900.

Magazines also presented serious commentary on news events and issues. *Forum*, although never a major magazine since it began monthly publication in 1886, presented opinion essays on important contemporary subjects, and published articles on political, economic, and social issues. Colleges and universities used it in classrooms.

Collier's and *Outlook*, with a distribution of 125,000 copies, exemplified the contemporary standard for political reportage and commentary by weekly general magazines during the early 1900s. *Collier's* and *Outlook* focused on presidential candidates, commented on the platforms of the political parties, and identified various issues as significant for the nation. Readers across the nation received timely reports. Women's magazines, too, reported on events and issues pertinent to their readership. Governmental reform, public sanitation, the safety of food and medicine, civic involvement by women, and access to higher education were among the subjects.

The concept of the newsmagazine, devoid of literary work, had evolved by the start of the twentieth century. News sustained *Literary Digest*, a weekly first produced in 1890. The magazine provided a roundup of newspaper articles on specific subjects, summaries of select articles of a timely nature, and a section of articles that blended original reporting with edited material from other publications, including magazines. *Public Opinion*, a weekly that first appeared in 1886, reprinted dozens of news items from around the nation arranged by subject, although each item usually consisted of a brief paragraph, not a full story.

World's Work, a monthly that began in 1900, opened each edition with a news summary now familiar to readers of weekly journals of opinion. Original articles commissioned by editor Walter Hines Page presented information on topics he believed of importance, interest, and relevance. *World's Work* was a prototype of the newsmagazine with its arrangement of articles by specific departments.

Several magazines became crusaders for economic and social justice early in the twentieth century. Exposés in these magazines served the agenda of reformers. *McClure's* started the investigative journalism trend in January 1903. Soon, a slew of magazines competed for readers by presenting exposés on life insurance companies, investment scams, church ownership of tenements, patent medicine ingredients, contaminated food products, political corruption, price-fixing in certain industries, and predatory practices by financiers and industrialists. *American, Arena, Collier's, Cosmopolitan, Everybody's, Forum, Public Opinion*, and *World's Work* were among the notable periodicals engaged in muckraking.

Circulation soared for some of these magazines from 1903 to 1907: *American* reached 300,000 copies; *Collier's* attained 568,000; *Everybody's* leveled off at 750,000 copies.

The muckraking era ended abruptly. Interest among Americans waned. Several popular magazines lessened their news content in response. By the start of World War I and into the 1920s, fiction made a comeback in general magazines. *Collier's* had resorted to boosting its fiction component to rebuild circulation.

By the 1920s, *Literary Digest* dominated the weekly magazines devoted to current events and commentary. Other magazines attracted readers with lively commentary on events and issues. *Common Sense, Dial, Nation, New Republic*, and *Survey* were quality journals of opinion. The appearance of *Time*, a weekly newsmagazine, in 1923 and its phenomenal success signified the viability of news as a sole editorial component unaccompanied by commentary. *Business Week* applied a similar formula upon its debut in 1929. Although *Time's* two longstanding competitors, *Newsweek* and *U.S. News & World Report*, added commentary columns to the news, the weekly newsmagazines concentrated their efforts toward immediacy of coverage about events and developments in economic, political, and social issues. All three attracted an impressive number of readers.

The Depression era and World War II resulted in an expansion of news coverage in all major magazines directed toward specific readership categories, such as women's, rural, and general. Items of importance and interest to each readership category were the focus of articles that accompanied the usual fare of features and miscellany. *Life* and *Look* published news photographs, some of which were stand-alone and others to accompany articles.

The 1950s and 1960s were a continuation of news coverage by all major categories of magazines. Articles dealt with dramatic cultural and social changes, civil rights activism, Vietnam War, space exploration, Cold War tension, and a variety of other topics. *Esquire, New Yorker, Rolling Stone* and others created new narrative styles to attract readers in their twenties and thirties who appreciated livelier, descriptive writing. This same period saw the demise of many general magazines, however. Television diverted public attention and advertising dollars from these periodicals.

Specialized periodicals, those that catered to a niche readership, became a growth industry in magazines from the 1970s onward. Articles and commentary about events and issues pertinent to readers with specific interests broadened the definition of news by providing information on items within very narrow parameters. Niche magazines produced a higher number of magazines available to Americans during the early years of the twenty-first century than ever before. News, in its broadest sense, remained a key element for most of the magazines that served niche readerships.

Further Reading

Cooper, John Milton, Jr. *Walter Hines Page: The Southerner as American, 1855–1918*. Chapel Hill: University of North Carolina Press, 1977.

John, Arthur. *The Best Years of the Century: Richard Watson Gilder, Scribner's Monthly and the Century Magazine, 1870–1909*. Urbana: University of Illinois Press, 1981.

Mott, Frank Luther. *A History of American Magazines, Volumes 2, 4, and 5: Sketches of Magazines*. Cambridge, MA: Harvard University Press, 1957 and 1968.

Nourie, Alan, and Barbara Nourie. *American Mass-Market Magazines.* New York: Greenwood Press, 1990.

Tebbel, John, and Mary Ellen Zuckerman. *The Magazine in America, 1741–1990.* New York: Oxford University Press, 1991.

Wilson, Harold S. *McClure's Magazine and the Muckrakers.* Princeton, NJ: Princeton University Press, 1970.

JAMES LANDERS

MANCHESTER UNION LEADER

The *Manchester Union Leader* (aka *New Hampshire Union Leader*) was a paper that became well known for reflecting the conservative views of its publisher William Loeb (December 26, 1905–September 13,1981), and it became nationally prominent in 1972 for its attacks on Maine's Democratic Senator Edmund Muskie. During the mid-1970s, Loeb changed the paper's name to the *Union Leader* to emphasize the fact that it was the only statewide daily newspaper in New Hampshire.

The *New Hampshire Union Leader* was first published in 1863 as the *Manchester Daily Union.* Publisher James M. Campbell reported only on national news. In 1880, under the direction of Stilson Hutchins, the paper began coverage of local news across the entire State. Always a paper with a sharp political edge, the *Daily Union* began as a staunch supporter of the Democratic Party, a loyalty it continued until 1912, when publisher Rosencrans Pillsbury refused to support William Jennings Bryan for President. One year later, Pillsbury merged the *Union* with its chief rival, the *Manchester Leader.* The new editor, Frank Knox (January 1, 1874–April 28, 1944), led the *Manchester Union Leader* through a period of prosperity and political independence for the next three decades until his death in 1944. (Knox was long active in the Republican Party and became Alf Landon's vice presidential running mate in 1936. Knox's other paper, the *Chicago Daily News* was strongly anti-FDR and the New Deal. In 1940, though, Knox became Secretary of the Navy in Roosevelt's cabinet.)

In 1946, the man whose name remains synonymous with the newspaper, Loeb, purchased control of the paper. Under his direction, the *Manchester Union Leader* embarked on an aggressive conservative political agenda, endorsing such candidates as Barry Goldwater, Richard Nixon (1960, 1968), and Ronald Reagan, while blasting anti-Vietnam war candidates Eugene McCarthy and George McGovern as killers responsible for the deaths of American soldiers. He once called McGovern a communist and referred to him as "George McDovern." Never one to confuse party loyalty with conservative politics, Mr. Loeb withdrew his support of Nixon in 1972 because of Nixon's "softness" on China.

Most notoriously, in 1972, Loeb attacked Democratic front-runner Edmund Muskie as a political opportunist too unstable to be trusted with the nuclear bomb. During the primary campaign, Loeb published fifteen stories unfavorable to Muskie and twenty-eight editorials supporting Muskie's chief opponent, Sam Yorty, primarily with anti-Muskie rhetoric. Loeb went so far as to attack Muskie's wife by reprinting an unfavorable article about her from *Newsweek* magazine. Muskie responded to the attacks by mounting a platform outside the *Union Leader* to denounce Loeb; unfortunately, Muskie broke down when talking about the attack on his wife and appeared to some in the audience to be crying. The incident made national headlines and appeared on the nightly news. While he did win the primary, he did so with a smaller-than-expected margin and his candidacy was weakened to the point that opponent George McGovern received the nomination. The incident propelled Loeb onto the national stage and with him the *Manchester Union Leader.*

Loeb continued his controversial career for the next decade. The *Manchester Union Leader* became known for Loeb's eccentric practices of writing editorials on the front page and printing all the letters-to-the-editor he received. When Loeb died in 1981, his wife, Nackey S. Loeb (February 24, 1924–January 8, 2000), continued her husband's conservative politics, once calling President Bill Clinton a "disgrace." Mrs. Loeb computerized the editing and typesetting of the paper, expanding its sports, business, and consumer coverage. She also devoted the newspaper to community affairs and charitable activities.

Subsequently, the *Union Leader* became less controversial under the editorship of Joseph McQuaid, son of William Loeb's editor-in-chief, Bernard McQuaid. The newspaper remained profitable and a vocal presence in national politics, especially because the New Hampshire primary is the first in the nation, and can influence candidates who seek their party's nomination for the residency.

In April, 2005, the newspaper was renamed the *New Hampshire Union Leader.* It had a daily circulation of approximately 63,000 readers and a Sunday circulation of some 83,000 readers. The Sunday edition was known as *The New Hampshire Sunday News.* An electronic version of the newspaper was available at UnionLeader.com, and a complete edition of the newspaper could also be obtained for a fee on the Internet. The newspaper was independently owned by the Union Leader Corporation until October, 2000, when, upon the death of Publisher Nackey S. Loeb, ownership was transferred to the Nackey S. Loeb School of Communications, Inc. Through this transfer, the *Union Leader* has been able to remain an independent outlet for news.

Further Reading

Veblen, Eric P. *The Manchester Union Leader in New Hampshire.* Hanover, NH: University Press of New England, 1975.

RICHARD KATULA

MAPS AND THE NEWS

Journalism provides the public with one of its most valuable sources of information about other places and to that end, journalists have used maps to communicate with readers for many years. Francis Galton prepared the first weather map, published in *The Times* of London on April 1, 1875. It is now a standard in newspapers worldwide. American journalists used maps as a central reporting technique in covering one of the seminal events of the nineteenth century—the Civil War. Maps displayed the relative location and movement of troops as well as the terrain and vegetation influencing the outcome of battles. In the twenty-first century, most Americans have become familiar with the "red states" and "blue states" that make maps synonymous with American presidential elections.

Improvements in technology gave the press the ability to use maps more frequently. In the late nineteenth century, photoengraving technology made it possible for newspapers to increase their use of graphics although such publications as Joseph Pulitzer's *New York World* and William Randolph Hearst's *New York Journal* took advantage of these developments to sensationalize the news. Aside from weather maps, the use of news maps by newspapers was rare before the twentieth century. The *New York Times* began to expand its use of news maps in the 1930s, but not until 1940 did it average using one non-weather map per issue. (The London *Times* reached that average in 1920.) Other papers in the United States were slower to use maps. Not until 1970 did the *Christian Science Monitor* average using a news map each day, and as late as 1985, the *Wall Street Journal* used news maps on average only every other day (Monmonier 1989, 55). The arrival of film technology and then television increased the use of visuals in news reporting. Maps were a staple of newsreel coverage of World War II, for example. With the spread of television during the 1950s, news maps were seen regularly by millions of viewers. As color television became more common during the 1960s and 1970s, maps became more sophisticated.

Television surely provided an impetus for newspapers to use images more often and new technology made it possible for them to do so. During the 1970s, a major advance occurred in newspaper production with the adoption of photocomposition, or computer-generated "cold type." Improvements in offset printing and the use of electronic color-separation scanners made it possible for mid-sized and large dailies to use color during the 1970s and 1980s. More recently journalists have turned to Geographic Information Systems (GIS) software to take their mapping communication to a higher level. GIS software not only enables journalists to display data from the U.S. census and similar government sources, but to also map data of their own creation. Reporters from the *Miami Herald* were among the first journalists to use GIS, mapping structural damage from Hurricane Andrew in 1992. GIS not only revealed the spatial pattern of hurricane damage, but also revealed its connection with poor construction and lax building inspections which added significantly to the damage. Their work earned the Pulitzer Prize for the *Herald* and introduced journalists to the discovery qualities of GIS and cartographic analysis. Since 1992, print and broadcast media in San Diego, Charlotte, Providence, Philadelphia, Chicago, and Washington have been among the numerous news outlets to employ GIS and mapping to examine such topics as school busing, lead poisoning, property assessments, drunk driving, and the Florida ballot controversy in the 2000 presidential election.

A properly selected and constructed map is an indispensable tool for any journalist addressing the questions of *where* and *why*. It is important to understand what type of map works most effectively in an article and what form of data is most appropriate for conveying the message. A good map is a visually striking, highly efficient means of communication, if principles of map design and data presentation are observed.

Location can be defined in absolute and relative terms, and maps effectively convey both. A news article utilizing the visual qualities of a map enables the reader to see, for example, the size and location of Iraq relative to Israel, Saudi Arabia, and Syria, and to better understand the results of U.S. military activity in Iraq. Mapping the location of the Kurdish concentration makes it immediately apparent why Turkey closely monitors events in northern Iraq. More locally, a map displaying the proposed path of new power lines in a city tells readers whether their neighborhood is to be affected. A map depicting a spatial cluster of robberies tells readers not only the exact location of the crimes, but also how close the problem is to their residence. To borrow from the old cliché, if a picture is worth a thousand words, maps are worth many more.

Mapping information can often provide answers to a second important question: *why*? Effective maps demonstrate clusters or other spatial concentrations which help to explain why events or phenomena occur where they do. This ability to display spatial patterns makes the map a far more effective means of communication than a list or table of information by location. Lists require the reader to have a well-developed mental map of the areas being described. For example, only a small portion of the reading public has the ability or knowledge to recognize the meaningful spatial patterns in the alphabetized list of corruption convictions shown in Table 1.

In contrast to an alphabetized list, a map of the same information reveals patterns of corruption in the continental United States that suggest possible reasons why this crime occurs more frequently in some states rather than others. Many of the states in the cluster spanning from New York to Illinois have long histories of urban corruption synonymous with big city machine politics. Is this tradition still at work? The swath of public corruption convictions along the U.S. southern and coastal border raises the specter of a drug connection. Lastly, the lack of public corruption in northern New England and much of the West is striking. Are officials in these regions more honest than elsewhere? If so, why? Maps reveal patterns and raise questions which are virtually indiscernible in an alphabetized list. These inherent qualities invariably make their use far more effective in telling a story.

Selecting the Appropriate Map Technique

While maps may greatly enhance a message, selecting the proper type of map to display data is crucial to their effectiveness. Among the cartographic techniques available to a writer, choropleth, dot distribution, graduated symbol and

Table 1 Federal Public Corruption Convictions by State, 1995–2004

Alabama	157	Hawaii	55	Mass.	190	New Mexico	23	South Dakota	40
Alaska	39	Idaho	49	Michigan	199	New York	790	Tennessee	190
Arizona	60	Illinois	596	Minnesota	67	N. Carolina	156	Texas	569
Arkansas	64	Indiana	123	Mississippi	212	N. Dakota	55	Utah	29
California	871	Iowa	37	Missouri	168	Ohio	515	Vermont	12
Colorado	59	Kansas	40	Montana	51	Oklahoma	83	Virginia	224
Connecticut	76	Kentucky	240	Nebraska	11	Oregon	21	Washington	107
Delaware	31	Louisiana	310	Nevada	46	Pennsylvania	515	West Virginia	57
Florida	813	Maine	25	New Hampshire	12	Rhode Island.	27	Wisconsin	96
Georgia	207	Maryland	88	New Jersey	348	South Carolina	81	Wyoming	11

Source: U.S. Department of Justice

contour (isoline) maps are the most common and easily understood by readers.

To determine which of these forms best fits an article, journalists who have used maps effectively in the past have considered three criteria: scale, geographical unit and the discrete or continuous character of the data surface. Scale refers to the amount of local detail the writer wishes to display on a map. The map scale increases proportionately to the local geography displayed. Thus large scale maps display a small amount of the earth's surface, but in much greater detail than small scale maps. Conversely, a global map would be considered a small scale display because, although it portrays a large surface, very little detail can be communicated about any particular location. Each of the map types illustrated in Figure 2 varies in its effectiveness as a large or small scale map. Graduated symbols are par-

ticularly problematic in smaller scale formats. There is a tendency for the symbols to overlap one another to such an extent that they obliterate the pattern on the map. Dot distribution maps are better suited to larger scales. On small scale maps, such as a global or national depiction, there is insufficient space to avoid severe over-lapping of the dot symbols.

Journalists have used contour and choropleth maps frequently in their work because both map types are effective in large or small scale displays, are sufficiently familiar to readers and usually contain patterns that are easily discerned.

The contour, or isoline, map is especially familiar to readers of the daily weather map. In this type of map, isolines—lines of equal value—are used to communicate the continuous change in values across an area. In an isoline

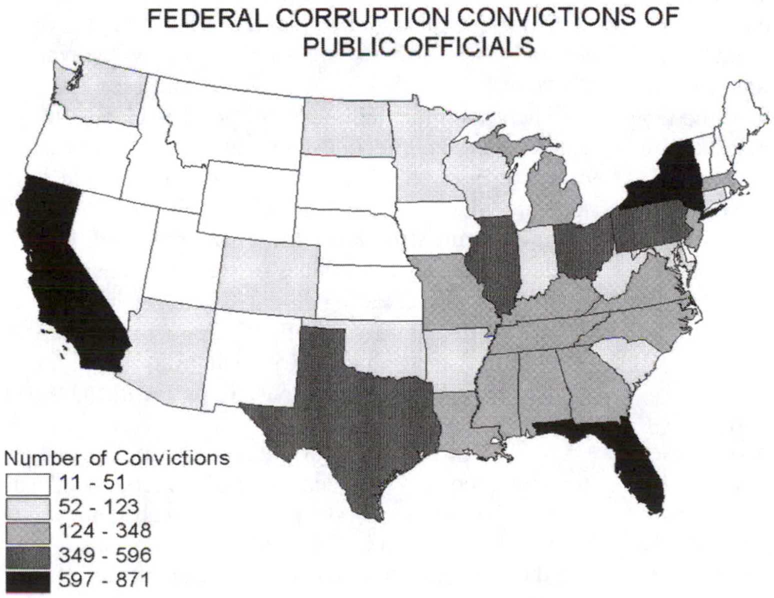

FEDERAL CORRUPTION CONVICTIONS OF PUBLIC OFFICIALS

Number of Convictions
11 - 51
52 - 123
124 - 348
349 - 596
597 - 871

Figure 1 Federal Corruption Convictions of Public Officials.

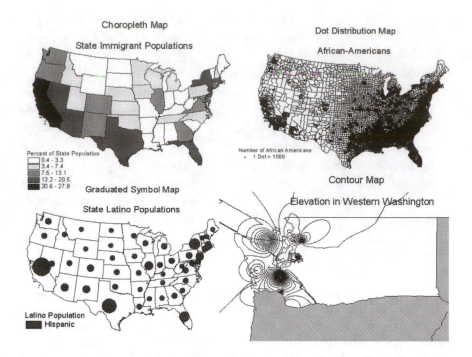

Figure 2 Types of Maps.

map the reader is able to determine the quantitative value at any point on the surface by assessing the distance between contours and noting the values of these isolines. The key is to recognize that contour/isoline maps are only suitable for data that are geographically continuous, i.e., values which change continuously from point to point within the area displayed on the map. Examples of geographically continuous data include precipitation, temperatures, terrain and population density. In each case, these data are based upon points rather than areal units.

When a writer wishes to compare geographical units such as states, countries or counties, the choropleth map is the ideal means of communication. Choropleths are areas of equal value, meaning that values are assumed to be the same throughout a spatial unit and are limited to the boundaries of that territory. Choropleth values are therefore geographically discrete. They are geographically confined to that spatial unit and are equal in value throughout the territory. A presidential candidate either wins a state's entire electoral allotment by carrying a plurality of its popular vote, or receives none if he/she fails to do so. Given these discrete qualities, a choropleth map has historically been the most effective means of communicating U.S. presidential election results.

Proper Map Construction

Choropleth maps have been used often in news reporting, but not always correctly. Among the most common misuses has been the failure to properly shade the geographical units displayed on the map. In constructing a choropleth map, the writer must remember that a reader's eye will naturally gravitate towards the shade or color of greatest intensity, assuming (correctly) that intensity is related to quantity.

Choropleth maps become unreadable or misleading if this principle is not observed. Consider the map in Figure 3.

This map in Figure 3 fails to use a logical monochromatic scale, leading the reader to assume that the greatest concentration of guns available to children is in mid-Southern states. In fact, states in the Southwest and Southeast are far more dangerous to children. This misimpression was created because the shade depicting the greatest value was among the lightest on the map, while mid-level values are shaded much more intensively. Whether in gray tone or color, it is imperative that a progressive monochromatic scale be directly related to the values being mapped. It is also important that the shade patterns used in a choropleth map be easily distinguishable. In Figure 3 it is not immediately apparent, for example, that Maryland and New Jersey have markedly different numbers of guns available to children.

There are other principles of good map design that are applicable to an effective choropleth map. In addition to an effective map title, legends must also have a clear title to indicate what numerical units are being displayed on the map. In Figure 3 no legend title was provided, leaving the reader to wonder if the values represent numbers of guns or children. A close reading of text should not be necessary to make that distinction. An effective choropleth map should be able to "stand alone" in it readability. Applying these principles to Figure 3, its revised continental U.S. version might appear as Figure 4.

A final and highly important consideration in using maps for news reporting has been the need to recognize the difference in the message produced by data in absolute versus per capita form. A map is a highly effective means of answering the question "how much is found at each location?" but the spatial variation in quantity can change significantly

Access to guns

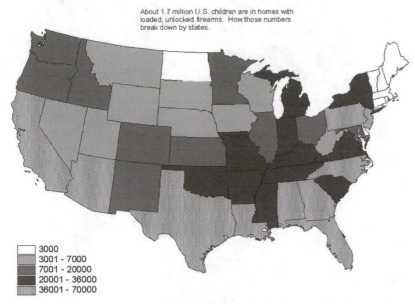

About 1.7 million U.S. children are in homes with loaded, unlocked firearms. How those numbers break down by states.

☐	3000
	3001 - 7000
	7001 - 20000
	20001 - 36000
	36001 - 70000

Figure 3 A Misleading Choropleth Map.

according to whether absolute or per capita values are used. The failure to recognize this distinction can produce maps that convey little more than population size. For example, the spatial pattern of corruption convictions shown in Figure 1 may primarily be a function of the population sizes of each of the forty-eight continental states. This is often the case when mapping the absolute amount of a phenomenon. In some instances absolute volume is the message of the story. But consider the different message produced by reexamining the corruption story through a map of the data in per capita form (Figure 5).

California, which has more corruption convictions among its public officials than any other state, virtually disappears in significance when its population size is taken into account in Figure 5. The populations of the Dakotas and Montana are among the smallest in the United States, but apparently the proportion of their public officials who were convicted for corruption was among the highest in the country. In 2005, much attention focused on the effectiveness of the government's response to damage from Hurricanes Rita and Katrina. Figure 5 might lead to interesting speculation as to whether there is any connection between

Figure 4 A More Meaningful Choropleth Map.

Children at Home with Loaded Guns

Number of Children Living with Loaded Guns
☐	0 - 5000
	5001 - 15000
	15001 - 34000
	34001 - 53000
	53001 - 200000

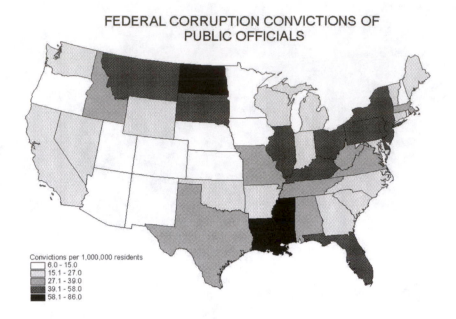

FEDERAL CORRUPTION CONVICTIONS OF PUBLIC OFFICIALS

Convictions per 1,000,000 residents
- 6.0 - 15.0
- 15.1 - 27.0
- 27.1 - 39.0
- 39.1 - 58.0
- 58.1 - 86.0

Figure 5 A Per Capita Map of Corruption Convictions.

government hurricane response and the high concentration of per capita official corruption in Louisiana and Mississippi—a pattern that is only revealed by mapping the data in relation to the size of each state's population.

In 2007, there were a number of commercially available mapping packages, products developed by ESRI being predominant. In addition to using them, modern journalism enterprises had ample opportunities to employ graduates of geography and Geographic Information System programs. There was an exponential growth in the number of individuals with GIS and computer mapping skills, and the news media were well-positioned to take advantage of their capabilities.

Further Reading

Bosse, David (compiler). *Civil War Newspaper Maps, A Cartography of the Northern Daily Press.* Westport, CT: Greenwood Press, 1993.

Herzog, David. *Mapping the News.* Redlands, CA: ESRI Press, 2003.

Monmonier, Mark S. *Maps with the News: The Development of American Journalistic Cartography.* Chicago: University of Chicago Press, 1989.

ROBERT M. PIERCE

MARCH OF TIME, THE

The newsreels of *The March of Time* (1935–1951) projected *Time* magazine's fast-paced, syncopated, self-important ethos onto movie screens across the nation and the world. Newsreels, in general, borrowed from stagecraft, radio and, most notably, cinema. *The March of Time* films of the 1930s and 1940s bridged a gap between the brief, unconnected collages offered by traditional newsreels and long, textured, interpretive narratives of serious documentary films.

The March of Time made its debut on American movie screens on February 1, 1935, a dozen years after the founding of *Time* magazine. Drawing on the reportorial resources of *Time* and the visual sensibilities of another Luce product, *Life* magazine, *The March of Time* aspired to journalism — but it sometimes filled the role of slick propagandist for the particular Americanism of *Time* owner Henry Luce.

The March of Time grew out of a similarly themed radio show. Roy Edward Larsen, originally *Time's* circulation manager and later a major stockholder in the company, first experimented with a broadcast version of *Time* in 1928. At first, Larsen described the ten-minute show, which featured at least one "hair raising" story per broadcast, as "newscasting." But he soon invented a new term—"newsacting"—which was more accurate because the broadcasts contained numerous dramatic recreations of news events. In 1931, CBS promoted the show nationally and rechristened it *The March of Time*, after a Harold Arlen song of the same name.

The radio version of *The March of Time* would provide a narrative template for the film version, while its dramatic and unique visual style owed much to *Life*. Larsen had almost total control over its operations after *The March of Time* was incorporated as a separate company under the control and ownership of *Time*. The multimedia empire Luce created represented an early example of the corporate synergy that characterizes the modern media.

A *New York Times* review of the first episode of *The March of Time*, published Feb. 2, 1935, asserted that it bore approximately the same relationship to the newsreel "as the weekly interpretive magazine bears to the daily newspaper." The purpose of the newsreels, according to their editors was to show the news as "live dramatic events that unfold on the screen as they actually took place." When necessary, the producers acknowledged, they would not hesitate to recreate or re-enact stories (*The New York Times*, February 2, 1935, 10).

One hundred and sixty *March of Time* documentaries were produced during its sixteen-year run. The first episodes, billed by the producers as "a new kind of pictorial journalism," contained two or three reels. At ten minutes per reel, they were far longer than typical newsreel subjects and allowed for far more analysis and interpretation. In 1938, each episode covered only a single subject, allowing for even more depth. As British filmmaker John Grierson observed, "It gets behind the news . . . and gives perspective to events. Not the parade of armies so much as the race in armaments."

The March of Time was popular, profitable, and generally well-regarded by critics, but re-enactments of current or historical events and melodramatic narration by Westbrook Van Voorhis—known as the "Voice of Time"—made it difficult to say if it represented a legitimate form of journalism. (In one episode, Ethiopian King Haile Selasse was portrayed by a *Time* office boy.)

That the series attempted to influence on public perception and opinion was undeniable. By 1936, each episode was screened in over five thousand theatres in thirty-two hundred cities around the world. Over the course of its sixteen-year history, *The March of Time* informed, amused, and sometimes inflamed. In only the third episode, the series earned the enmity of Louisiana Governor Huey Long by describing him as a "demagogue" and his administration as a "decidedly un-American dictatorship."

The report on Long bore the stamp of *The March of Time*'s creative director, Louis de Rochemont, who had long argued that staging scenes and using actors was no different than rendering an occurrence in words, as legitimate print journalists did every day. The Huey Long segment mixed actual footage of the governor with re-enactments of his "more obnoxious behavior" by an impersonator. While the film disclosed the re-enactment, it is doubtful that a day or two after its screening audience members could remember what was real and what was made up. In addition, the Long segment was edited to marry alleged Long statements to footage of the governor or the actor who impersonated him. The result may well have been devastating, but it also pointed up the manipulative power of *The March of Time* formula.

Other controversies followed. In 1938, several exhibitors refused to show an episode entitled "Inside Nazi Germany" because of threats by American Nazi groups. Another episode, which used elaborate re-enactments to highlight the grandiose character of the Dominican Republic's dictator-president caused an international incident.

Social Impact

With their depth, striking imagery, high production values, and authoritative tone,

The March of Time films gave viewers vivid contexts and frames of reference for world events, government policies, and political leaders. And, because of the series' huge reach, senators, C.E.O.'s, and assorted other public figures were all too happy to appear before *The March of Time* cameras.

The March of Time tended to turn its cameras on complex processes rather than sensational occurrences. Episodes explored the operations of the Tennessee Valley Authority (which brought electricity to the rural South), the rise of right-wing radio priest Father Coughlin, and, internationally, political intrigues in the Soviet Union.

During World War II, *The March of Time* focused on both the battlefield and the war room and its style had a profound influence on director Frank Capra's popular and effective "Why We Fight" series, which sought to explain the larger purposes and ramifications of the war to soldiers and civilians.

Many critics felt the series began to lose its energy and sense of innovation in 1942, as the somber atmosphere of a nation at war removed some of the unpredictability and edge from the series. In addition, de Rochemont left the company, taking his unique aesthetic sensibility with him. The rise of television helped spell the end of the series. It ceased production in 1951. There were two later, short-lived incarnations on television. Time marched on but *The March of Time* had ended.

Further Reading

Alexander, William. "*The March of Time* and the World Today." *American Quarterly*, vol. 29, no. 2 (Summer, 1977): 182–193.

Bohn, Thomas W. and Lichty, Lawerence W. "*The March of Time*: News as Drama," *Journal of Popular Film*, Volume 2, No. 4 (Fall, 1973): 373–387.

Fielding, Raymond. *The American Newsreel: 1911–1967*. Omaha: The University of Oklahoma Press, 1972.

Fielding. *The March of Time: 1935–1951*. New York: Oxford University Press, 1978.

Grierson, John. *Grierson on Documentary*. New York: Praeger, 1971.

"The Screen." *New York Times*, Feb. 2, 1935, 10.

MIKE DILLON

MARKHAM, EDWIN

Industrializing America was becoming "a modern Babylon," Edwin Markham (1852–1940) wrote in 1906, where children were "barred from school, dragged from play and sleep and rest, and set tramping in grim, forced march to the mills and mines and shops" while privileged parents "give our children books and beauty by day and fold them into white beds at night" (Weinberg 1961, 362).

Charles Edwin Anson Markham's own childhood began in Oregon City in the Oregon Territory. He was the sixth child and fifth son of Samuel Markham and Elizabeth Winchell Markham, Campbellites who believed in the unity of all believers yet knew only division within their marriage. The couple divorced and his father died before Edwin was five. In 1856, Edwin and a sister moved with their mother to a ranch near Suisun City, northeast of Oakland, where

Mrs. Markham would marry and divorce two more times. Markham attended Vacaville College, where he graduated with a teaching degree in 1870.

Markham became an Oakland area teacher and administrator. Markham's poetry appeared in *Commonweal*, *Scribner's*, and *Century* magazines and on January 15, 1899, the *San Francisco Examiner* published his poem "The Man with the Hoe," based on a painting by Jean Francois Millet. Markham saw himself in the stooped image of the hoeman, old before his time, the "emptiness of ages in his face." His hoeman is a "symbol of betrayed humanity." He bore "the burden of the world on his back" and his suffering represented "the awful degradation of man through endless, hopeless, joyless labor." The poem, translated into forty languages, earned Markham $250,000. Collections of his poetry, published in 1899 and 1901, solidified Markham's reputation as a major poet and defender of the working man.

Markham's articles, first appearing in *Cosmopolitan* in 1906, helped build public opposition to child labor. More than 1.7 million children under fourteen years of age worked in 1900, nearly half of them in factories, mines, textile mills, and tenement workshops that enveloped them in "an eternity of petty movements," while leaving victims "stunted, slow and sad, their lives emptied of passion and poetry" (Weinberg 1961, 363, 365). Markham wondered how an "age of enlightenment" could justify "children robbed of childhood" "crowded into caverns of our industrial abyss," where they were subjected to pneumonia and maiming for a 22-cent daily wage all so that "a few more millions may be heaped up" by those already wealthy (Markham 1961, 362, 364, 366).

Championing the Child Labor Federation and other political action organizations, Markham and fellow muckrakers fought for state and federal intervention. By 1907, two-thirds of all states had passed legislation banning child labor. A federal law followed in 1916. By then, Markham had become a revered national figure who advocated cooperative action to assure "industrial freedom" for every man, woman and child. (The Markham Book. Entry for October 21, 1899. Box 3455. Markham Papers. Library of Congress.)

Further Reading

"Edwin Markham," in Scot Peacock, ed., *Contemporary Authors*, vol. 160, Detroit: Gale Research, 1998.

Edwin Markham Archives, Horrmann Library, Wagner College, Staten Island, New York. There is also a collection of Markham's statements on social justice in "The Markham Book" in his papers at the Library of Congress, Washington, D.C.

Evensen, Bruce J. "The Media and Reform, 1900–1917." In *The Age of Mass Communication*, edited by Wm. David Sloan. Northport, AL: Vision Press, 1998.

Filler, Louis. "Edwin Markham, Poetry, and What Have You." *Antioch Review* 23, 1963–1964.

——. *The Unknown Edwin Markham: His Mystery and Its Significance*. Yellow Springs, OH: Antioch Press, 1966.

Markham, Edwin. *Lincoln and Other Poems*. New York: McClure, Phillips, 1901.

——. *The Man with the Hoe and Other Poems*. New York: Doubleday & McClure, 1899.

——. "The 'Hoe-Man' in the Making." *Cosmopolitan*, September 1906.

——. "Spinners in the Dark." *Cosmopolitan*, July 1907.

Markham, Edwin, Benjamin B. Lindsey, and George Creel. *Children in Bondage*. New York: Hearst's International Library, 1914.

New York Times, March 8, 1940.

Stidger, William L. *Edwin Markham*. New York: Abingdon Press, 1933.

Weinberg, Arthur, and Lila Weinberg, eds. *The Muckrakers*,.New York: Simon and Schuster, 1961.

BRUCE J. EVENSEN

MASSES, THE

The wit and satire that leavened *The Masses'* (1911–1917) socialist critique of American society made it the most compelling publication among the lively radical press that preached cultural rebellion during the decade before World War I. Piet Vlag, a Dutch-born anarchist and chef of the Rand School for Social Sciences restaurant, founded the monthly magazine in January 1911 in bohemian Greenwich Village as an organ of the cooperative store movement. Wealthy socialist insurance executive Rufus Weeks financed the first year, although the staff and contributors of the cooperatively owned nonprofit venture set policy at monthly meetings. When Vlag quit publishing in August 1912 after Weeks withdrew his subsidy, the *Masses'* artists agreed to continue publication because it was a vital venue for publishing their satirical political cartoons and drawings of working-class urban life, vanguard of the "Ashcan School." The cooperative elected as its unpaid editor the absent Max Eastman, a charismatic socialist speaker and writer who was finishing his dissertation in philosophy at Columbia University.

"We are going to make *The Masses* a *popular* [italics in original] Socialist magazine—a magazine of pictures and lively writing," the revived magazine announced in its inaugural issue of December 1912. *Masses'* abstention from dogma and its buoyant, experimental tone gave it a broader reach than other radical periodicals; the unifying theme of the eclectic periodical was its iconoclastic commitment to free expression. Causes it championed informed the prewar radical agenda that marked Americans' shift from Victorianism to modernism: modern art and literature, the new field of psychology, the sexual revolution, and socialism in the broadest sense. It criticized institutional religion, marriage, militarism, censorship, and big business. The magazine served as a vibrant forum for the burgeoning feminist movement by advocating woman suffrage, birth control, female sexual fulfillment, and the independent "New Woman" in nonfiction articles and poetry and short stories culled by fiction editor Inez Haynes Irwin.

The Masses' greatest legacy may be its satirical line drawings by contributors including Cornelia Baxter Barns,

Robert Minor, Boardman Robinson, John Sloan, and Art Young. Minor's lampoon of puritanical censor Anthony Comstock was a quintessentially *Masses* social critique: A pompous lawyer who casts a mother before a judge intones, "Your Honor, this woman gave birth to a naked child!" More serious was Mary Heaton Vorse's reportage on the Lawrence, Mass., textile workers' strike and Eastman's militant suggestion in 1913 that "black citizens arise and demand respect in the name of power." More often the magazine ignored race issues and occasionally was guilty of offensive racial caricatures. *The Masses'* biggest flaw may have been that contributors cared more about personal emancipation than political reform and lacked the intellectual discipline to effect real social change. Despite its title, *Masses* readers were disaffected middle-class intelligentsia who found their alienation from American culture valorized in its pages, in which its privileged contributors romanticized outsiders such as prostitutes and criminals. The magazine's great paradox was the tension between its sophisticated creators' ardent individualism and its championing of the proletariat.

Authorities felt sufficiently threatened by *The Masses* to attempt suppressing it. Magazine distributors refused to carry it, and editors faced a criminal libel suit that stemmed from a July 1913 story and cartoon that accused the Associated Press of suppressing news about an unprecedented military tribunal convened to punish strike supporters in the West Virginia coalmines. Radical luminaries rallied at Cooper Union to support the magazine, and two years later the government dropped the case. The U.S. Post Office effectively killed *The Masses* by refusing it mailing privileges in August 1917 because of its criticism of the draft and American entry into the war. Although the magazine won a court injunction against the ban, the federal government charged several contributors with conspiracy to incite mutiny in the military and obstruct the draft, crimes punishable under the Espionage Act of 1917 by up to ten thousand dollars in fines and twenty years in prison. Codefendants Eastman, Young, managing editor Floyd Dell, business manager Merrill Rogers, and poet Josephine Bell approached their April 1918 trial with the same insouciance that colored the magazine. A single juror's refusal to convict caused a mistrial, and a second conspiracy trial that October won acquittals for co-defendants Eastman, Dell, Young, and John Reed, who trekked back from covering the Russia Revolution for the event. Meanwhile a federal Court of Appeals had reversed the injunction against the post office ban on mailing *The Masses*. Contributors regrouped in February 1918 to launch a successor, *The Liberator*, but it proved a pale, staid successor.

Further Reading

Eastman, Max. *Enjoyment of Living.* New York: Harper, 1948.

Fishbein, Leslie. *Rebels in Bohemia: The Radicals of The Masses, 1911–1917.* Chapel Hill: University of North Carolina Press, 1982.

May, Henry F. *The End of American Innocence: A Study of the First Years of Our Own Time, 1912–1917.* New York: Knopf, 1959.

Jones, Margaret C. *Heretics & Hellraisers: Women Contributors to The Masses, 1911–1917.* Austin: University of Texas Press, 1993.

O'Neill, William. *Echoes of Revolt: 'The Masses,'' 1911–1917.* Chicago: Quadrangle Books, 1966.

Zurier, Rebecca. *Art for "The Masses": A Radical Magazine and Its Graphics, 1911–1917.* Philadelphia: Temple University Press, 1988.

"The Masses," http://www.spartacus.schoolnet.co.uk/ARTmasses.htm (accessed April 19, 2007).

Linda J. Lumsden

MCCLURE'S MAGAZINE (1893–1929)

"Capitalists, workingmen, politicians, citizens—all breaking the law, or letting it be broken. Who is left to uphold it? There is no one left; none but all of us." (*McClure's Magazine*, January 1903, 336) These fighting words from Ulster-born Samuel Sidney McClure initiated Progressive-era agitation in which muckraking reporters used a journalism to expose how industrializing America threatened the rights of its most vulnerable citizens. In January 1903, Ida Tarbell's article on the Standard Oil Trust, Lincoln Steffens's attack on municipal lawlessness, and Ray Stannard Baker's story of suffering among coal miners opened a new era in the magazine's battle against corrupt power and encouraged competing magazines to take public service seriously and join in the struggle.

During the last two decades of the nineteenth century, the nation's population increased 50 percent, national wealth doubled, and consumer goods reached $25 billion annually. High-speed presses, halftone photoengraving, rural free delivery, and reduced postal rates made magazines attractive for advertisers. With $7,300 in seed money from Phillips and his syndicate, McClure marketed his monthly magazine at fifteen cents, less than half the price of *Harper's, Century, Scribner's,* and the *Atlantic Monthly*. Initially, he aimed to bring the best in biography, science, and fiction to a wide readership, but the enterprise began badly and the magazine lost $80,000 during its first year and half. His enthusiasm undiminished, McClure remained determined to offer "noble entertainment" and "worthy knowledge" to "uplift, refresh and encourage all who read it" (McClure Papers. Correspondence. Box 3. Folder 7. Lilly Library. Indiana University). By late 1894, *McClure's* circulation began its rise from forty-five thousand to eighty thousand with sixty pages of advertising per issue. *Cosmopolitan, Munsey's, Godey's,* and *Peterson's* soon joined *McClure's* in offering mass marketed monthlies for subscription costs of a dollar a year.

McClure sustained circulation gains with writers who could "seize hold of new, complex ideas" while "studying them down to the bottom and putting them in readable prose." (Lyon 1963, 116) A heavily illustrated seven-part series on Napoleon, and a two-volume work on Abraham Lincoln, raised readership in December 1895 to three hundred thousand. *McClure's*, which publicized inventors and ran lengthy interviews with Thomas Edison and Alexander Graham Bell, was among the first publications to appreciate

Marconi's work in wireless, the Wright Brothers early experiments in manned flight, and the social significance of the horseless carriage. Acquisition editor Viola Rosebore promoted high quality fiction by publishing the work of Stephen Crane, Jack London, O. Henry, Rex Beach, Bret Harte, Willa Cather, Booth Tarkington, and Hamlin Garland.

McClure presented "the latest in politics, finance, education, health and science" told in a way that would capture a national following (Wilson 1970, 104–105). In spring, 1901, McClure directed his staff to investigate the role of trusts in American business practices. Tarbell took the lead, gathering information on Standard Oil, the largest of all trusts, the company that had been responsible for driving her father and other competing oilmen into bankruptcy. Her path-breaking series first appeared in 1902, and exposed John D. Rockefeller's top secret "Cleveland Plan," a monopoly built on illegal rebates and drawbacks. It served as a template for investigative journalism in *McClure's* and among its competitors, and eventually led to action by the U.S. Supreme Court in 1911 that broke up the Standard Oil trust. In 1904, Burton J. Kendrick followed Tarbell by exposing fraud within the life insurance industry. During the same period, Baker attacked racism, mob violence, and lynching. Samuel Hopkins Adams investigated miscarriages of justice across the South and the role of unsanitary conditions in promoting contagious diseases. Steffens, in the meantime, exposed municipal mismanagement from St. Louis to New York City.

At the height of its influence, *McClure's* suffered twin defeats in 1906 that greatly influenced its future. President Roosevelt had been an early and enthusiastic supporter of its reform-minded journalism, but in April he criticized "muckrakers" for what he saw as their determination to dig up dirt on people in public life. Although not intended as a direct attack on *McClure's*, the widely publicized remarks put many Progressive Era publications on the defensive. McClure's visionary plans to launch another popular magazine, a book reprint business, and his long absences from New York, further alienated his staff. John Phillips and Tarbell, who were heavily financially invested in the magazine, offered to buy him out. When he refused, they bolted, taking Baker and Steffens with them. Together they launched a competing magazine, the *American Chronicle*. *McClure's* would never again reclaim its status as the nation's leading progressive publication.

Between 1906 and 1911 McClure rebuilt his staff and attempted to continue the magazine's commitment to investigative journalism. He made Willa Cather his managing editor. George K. Turner's articles on the links between political corruption, organized crime, and prostitution led in 1910 to a Congressional ban on the transportation of women across state lines for purposes of prostitution. Other articles advocated conservation, public health, and penal reforms. In the fall of 1911, McClure lost control of the magazine but the publication continued for another eighteen years. In its final days it was a women's magazine pushing consumerism behind front covers of Gibson Girls, and offering "reckless, irrepressible youth" ads for "modern rouge that stays on

no matter what one does!" (*McClure's Magazine*, January 1923, inside back cover).

In old age, McClure reconciled with key members of his staff and they warmly remember the days in which their work set a standard of excellence in journalism's effort to cultivate a civil society that would protect its most vulnerable members.

Further Reading

Baker, Ray Stannard. *American Chronicle: The Autobiography of Ray Stannard Baker*. New York: Charles Scribner's Sons, 1945.

Evensen, Bruce J. "The Evangelical Origins of the Muckrakers." *American Journalism*, Winter 1989.

Evensen, Bruce J. "The Media and Reform, 1900–1917." In *The Age of Mass Communication*, edited by Wm. David Sloan. Northport, AL: Vision Press, 1998.

Filler, Louis. *The Muckrakers: Crusaders for American Liberalism*. New York: Harcourt, Brace, 1939.

Lyon, Peter. *Success Story: The Life and Times of S.S. McClure*. New York: Charles Scribner's Sons, 1963.

McClure, S.S. *My Autobiography*. New York: Frederick Ungar, 1963.

McClure Publishing Company Archives, Special Collections Department, University of Delaware Library, Newark.

Moers, Ellen. "The Tradition of McClure's." *Commentary*, April 1964.

Papers of Samuel Sidney McClure, Manuscripts Department, Lilly Library, Indiana University, Bloomington.

Steffens, Joseph Lincoln. *The Autobiography of Lincoln Steffens*. New York: Harcourt, Brace, 1931.

Tarbell, Ida. *All in a Day's Work*. New York: Macmillan, 1939.

Wilson, Harold S. *McClure's Magazine and the Muckrakers*. Princeton, NJ: Princeton University Press, 1970.

BRUCE J. EVENSEN

MCCORMICK, ROBERT RUTHERFORD

Robert Rutherford McCormick (July 30, 1880–April 1, 1955) was the iconoclastic publisher, editor, and persona of the *Chicago Tribune* for much of the first half of the twentieth century. Known for his staunch conservatism and near paranoid control of his newspaper, McCormick made the *Tribune* into one of the largest circulating newspapers in the United States and a leader in advertising revenue. Simultaneously, he was attacked for journalistic excesses eclipsed only by rival press lord William Randolph Hearst.

McCormick was the grandnephew of inventor Cyrus Hall McCormick and the grandson of Joseph Medill, *Tribune* editor and publisher from 1874 to 1899. A graduate of Yale University and the Northwestern University law school in 1907, McCormick helped found the prestigious Chicago law firm of Kirkland and Ellis. He served briefly as a Chicago alderman and sanitary district board member, assuming partial control of the *Tribune* in 1911 in time to thwart its sale by other family members to the competing *Chicago Daily News*. Editor James Keeley almost cost McCormick and his family the *Tribune* the following year in a libel suit by accusing Illinois U. S. Senator William Lorimer of buying his political office. Evidence discovered by the competing *Chicago Inter Ocean* exonerated the *Tribune* and the *Tribune*'s coverage influenced the passage of the Seventeenth Amendment permitting direct election of senators in 1913.

McCormick served as an officer in the American Expeditionary Force in France during World War I. At six feet, four inches tall, men naturally followed him and he earned the Distinguished Service Medal for his leadership. Beginning in the 1930s, his rank led many to call him the "Morning Colonel" in contrast to the "Evening Colonel," *Daily News* publisher and Spanish-American War veteran Frank Knox. McCormick's suburban Chicago estate in Wheaton was named Cantigny after the French city and site of American soldiers' first European offensive. Before his death, McCormick endowed a museum dedicated to the U. S. Army's First Infantry Division, and his name is well known to military historians.

McCormick shared *Tribune* managerial duties with his cousin, Joseph Medill Patterson, from the departure of Keeley in 1914 until Paterson left to supervise the *New York Daily News* in 1925. McCormick bought an AM radio station in 1924 and had it renamed WGN for "World's Greatest Newspaper," the newspaper's masthead moniker along with a flag. WGN was first to broadcast major sporting events such as the World Series and provided live coverage of the Scopes Monkey Trial in 1925 at a cost of $1,000 per day for telephone lines alone. McCormick provided weekly commentaries as part of the Saturday-evening "Chicago Theater of the Air" Mutual Network broadcast from WGN from 1940 until his death. He purchased or established timberlands, paper mills, and shipping facilities in Canada to guarantee the *Tribune* an unfettered supply of newsprint. McCormick headquartered his various enterprises in Tribune Tower, a 462-foot skyscraper constructed near Lake Michigan in 1925 in what was described as a "military-Gothic" style. After a visit to his office by gangster Al Capone, the paranoid McCormick had an escape passage installed along with hidden inside doors, trapping unsuspecting employees until McCormick freed them with a button at his desk. His limousine was armor plated as well.

McCormick's *Tribune* was victorious in two precedent-setting law cases. One involved Chicago Mayor William Hale Thompson and led to a 1923 Illinois Supreme Court decision upholding the right of citizens and journalists to criticize government officials. The second was filed by automobile manufacturer Henry Ford after the *Tribune* called him an anarchist in a 1916 editorial. A jury found for Ford in 1919 but awarded him only six-cents in damages, strengthening the right of journalists to state true opinions. McCormick also helped pay the legal fees of Jay M. Near, a Minnesota editor whose newspaper was suppressed by state officials. The 1931 U. S. Supreme Court *Near v. Minnesota* decision established specific procedures before government could exercise prior restraint of the press. McCormick had a passage from the decision carved into the granite walls of the Tribune Tower lobby. In gratitude, the American Newspaper Publishers Association named him permanent chairman of its press freedom committee.

A Republican, isolationist, opponent of organized labor, and anti-communist, McCormick was one of the staunchest critics of Democratic President Franklin D. Roosevelt and his New Deal even though the two had been fellow preparatory school students. As McCormick came under increasing pressure from Roosevelt's supporters, his editorial policy became so monolithic that writers who ignored his personal directives found themselves banished to menial duties. To embarrass Roosevelt indirectly, the *Tribune* revealed that American forces knew the position of the Japanese fleet in advance of the 1942 Battle of Midway, alluding to the breaking of the main Japanese code, one of the greatest military secrets of World War II. The Justice Department investigated but failed to prosecute the *Tribune* for the indiscretion, testing the wartime limits of the First Amendment. McCormick relished confounding his critics, and readers bought his newspaper even if they did not agree with it. Anthropologist Robert Ardrey claimed that the secret of Chicagoans vitality was reading the *Tribune* at breakfast. "We hit the ceiling . . . [then] we hit the street on a dead run." *Tribune* drama critic Burton Rascoe labeled McCormick, "the greatest mind of the Fourteenth century."

The *Tribune* began losing circulation during McCormick's final years and he predicted that the paper would cease within ten years of his death. McCormick opposed President Harry Truman's Fair Deal and the post-war Marshall Plan to aid European recovery. However, claiming to have been asleep at the time, McCormick denied any involvement in the *Tribune*'s "Dewey Defeats Truman" 1948 headline debacle. Embittered by Republican Party failures, McCormick supported a new political party, the "American," in the 1950s. He purchased the faltering *Washington Times-Herald* in 1949 only to sell the paper to the competing *Washington Post* in 1954, using some of the profits to buy a personal jet. Wisconsin Senator Joseph McCarthy's famed 1950 list of fifty-seven "card-carrying Communists" was based largely on a series of *Tribune* articles. Childless in two marriages, McCormick often brought his dogs to his office, where they would lick visiting employee's shoes. One of the last major practitioner of personal journalism, McCormick died of heart disease in 1955 and was buried in his World War I uniform in the garden of his Cantigny estate.

Beyond Cantigny, which houses his papers, McCormick was survived by the McCormick-Tribune Foundation, which supports civic, educational, and journalistic causes, the McCormick Tribune Freedom Museum, opened as the first museum dedicated to the First Amendment in 2006, and the McCormick Convention Center, one of the Colonel's many personal causes. In true McCormick spirit, the convention center, located on the Lake Michigan site of the 1933–1934 World's Fair, violates a covenant dating back to the 1850s and long advocated by the *Tribune* that Chicago keep its lakeshore "forever open, clear and free."

Further Reading

Chicago Tribune, April 1955, 1, 2; December 1979, G31.

City of Chicago v. Tribune (1923).

Ford v. Chicago Tribune (1919).

Smith, Richard Norton, *The Colonel: The Life and Legend of Robert R. McCormick, 1880–1955.* New York: Houghton Mifflin, 1997.

Waldrup, Frank C. *McCormick of Chicago.* New York: Prentice-Hall, 1966.

Wendt, Lloyd. *Chicago Tribune: The Rise of a Great American Newspaper.* Chicago: Rand McNally, 1979.

RICHARD JUNGER

MCNAMEE, GRAHAM

Graham McNamee (1888–1942) was the most recognized voice of the Roaring Twenties, remembered for a play by play presence that evoked the excitement and spontaneity of the moment that set a standard of announcing excellence in infant radio.

Graham McNamee was the only child born to Annie Liebold and John Bernard McNamee in Washington, D.C., where his father worked as legal adviser to the Interior Department. When he was six, the family moved to St. Paul, Minnesota, where McNamee's father became counsel for the Northern Pacific Railroad. The youth's father wanted him to be a lawyer, his mother, a pianist and singer at local churches, pushed him into voice lessons. Graham was awkward socially and turned his nervous energy to baseball, football, basketball, and semi-pro hockey. After high school, he drifted into jobs as railroad clerk and door-to-door salesman for the Armor Meat Packing Company.

When McNamee's father died in 1912, he moved with his mother to Weehawken, New Jersey, so McNamee could pursue voice training and a singing career in nearby New York. It was a struggle. McNamee found New York "overcrowded with ambitious singers" (McNamee 1926, 13). McNamee took and gave singing lessons and sang as a soloist in area churches before moving to New York, where he led a precarious life singing in light and grand opera. The highpoint came when the baritone debuted as a concert singer at New York's Aeolian Hall on November 22, 1920.

By the summer of 1923 McNamee, who had married soprano Josephine Garrett on May 3, 1921, walked into the American Telephone and Telegraph office on lower Broadway, hoping to audition for a singing role on the radio. WEAF was then one of five hundred radio stations serving barely one million receiving sets nationwide. It had broadcast the 1922 Chicago–Princeton game from Stagg Field and boasted an experimental network that extended to Boston, Washington, and Providence. McNamee was hired as a part-time singer and staff announcer, "coaching and rehearsing artists," and charged with "the handling of temperamental singers" (McNamee 1926, 37). He was "more shaky than the fighters" (38) when broadcasting Harry Greb's fifteen-round defeat of Johnny Wilson for the middleweight crown on the evening of August 31, 1923, but fan letters thought otherwise. McNamee solidified his growing reputation six weeks later in calling three mammoth Babe Ruth home runs that vaulted the New York Yankees to their first World Series championship against the arch rival New York Giants.

McNamee "got quite a thrill" (McNamee 1926, 44) in reporting big sporting events, an enthusiasm quickly communicated to listeners in a freely flowing style that searched for the hidden detail that made the moment. There was little advertising in early radio, allowing McNamee long periods of improvisation. Although he would go on to broadcast to millions he imagined his listeners individually, seeking to make each feel "that he or she is there with me in the press stand" (McNamee 1926, 52–53) seeing and feeling what McNamee was experiencing. Sports writer Heywood Broun spoke for many when he said McNamee was unsurpassed in giving listeners a vivid sense of movement and emotion. McNamee had raised announcing, he thought, to "the kingdom of art" (McNamee 1926, vii).

McNamee broadcast from the Republican and Democratic national conventions in 1924 and reported the return of Charles Lindbergh to the United States in 1927. But he was best known and is most remembered for his sports broadcasting. Annual gatherings of the Kentucky Derby, Indianapolis 500, and Rose Bowl were incomplete without McNamee's call of the contest. Few could forget McNamee's reporting on Ruth's called shot home run at Wrigley Field against the Chicago Cubs on October 1, 1932. But what he saw as the greatest moment in sports history had come in the same city five years before. An estimated worldwide audience of one hundred million was listening in on September 22, 1927, when McNamee, reporting for the newly created National Broadcasting Company, called the heavyweight championship fight between Jack Dempsey and Gene Tunney. In the middle of the seventh round with Dempsey, the fan favorite behind in points, the audience heard McNamee suddenly say, "Dempsey comes back with a hard right to Tunney's face. Ohhh. Dempsey comes on with a right. He's got Tunney against the ropes. There's another right landing on the champion's jaw. There's another right and Tunney is down. Tunney is down." Ten men were so overcome with listening excitement they dropped dead of heart attacks. They did not live to discover that Tunney survived the "long count" when Dempsey didn't go to a neutral corner and that Tunney won the fight.

Such was the power of Graham McNamee's voice on the public imagination. The rise of commercial radio in the thirties with its proliferation of stations would tighten formats by creating schedules that diminished McNamee's impact. Two years after his divorce in February 1932, he married Ann Lee Sims. By this time he was widely recognized as an important force in the development of early radio and for generations that followed the prototype sports broadcaster.

Further Reading

Banning, William Peck. *Commercial Broadcasting Pioneer: The WEAF Experiment, 1922–1926.* Cambridge, MA: Harvard University Press, 1946.

Barber, Red. *The Broadcasters.* New York: Dial Press, 1970.

Chicago Tribune, May 10, 1942.

Douglas, George H. *The Early Days of Radio Broadcasting.* Jefferson, NC: MacFarland Publishing, 1987.

Evensen, Bruce J. *When Dempsey Fought Tunney: Heroes, Hokum, and Storytelling in the Jazz Age.* Knoxville: University pf Tennessee Press, 1996.

McNamee, Graham. *You're on the Air.* New York: Harper & Brothers, 1926.

New York Times, May 10, 1942.

National Broadcasting Company Papers. State Historical Society of Wisconsin, Madison.

Towers, Wayne M. "World Series Coverage in New York City in the 1920's." *Journalism Monographs* 73 (1981).

BRUCE J. EVENSEN

MEDILL, JOSEPH MAHARRY

"Cheer up, Chicago!" the city's biggest booster said in the aftermath of a devastating fire that wiped away fifteen city blocks, killing 250, while leaving 100,000 homeless. "Chicago," Joseph Medill (April 6, 1823–March 17, 1899) assured his readers, "shall rise again!" For forty-four years, Medill oversaw Chicago's rise from the world's cholera capital to the nation's second city, his *Tribune* becoming one of the most important American newspapers west of the Hudson River.

Joseph Maharry Medill was born on a farm near St. John, New Brunswick, to William Medill and Margaret Corbett Medill. When he was nine, his Scotch-Irish parents moved their family to a cooperative farm community near Massillon, Ohio. The opening of the Ohio and Erie Canal in 1832 had made Massillon one of Ohio's largest wheat markets, but a fire ruined the family's fortunes, broke his father's health, and forced Medill to abandon plans for college, while looking after three younger brothers and two sisters. Medill solicited subscriptions for Horace Greeley's *New York Tribune*, studied law, and was admitted to the Ohio Bar in 1846. As a newlywed he drifted into journalism through his father-in-law's country weekly, the *Tuscarawas Advocate*, in New Philadelphia, Ohio. His wife Katherine taught him typesetting. Starting in 1849, Medill published newspapers in Coshocton and Newark, Ohio, bringing his brothers into the business, while kindly rejecting payments in chickens and trousers.

Medill was a Free Soil Whig, rejecting extension of slavery into territories won in the Mexican War. He bitterly opposed the Compromise of 1850 that strengthened the Fugitive Slave Law, requiring all U.S. citizens to return runaway slaves. The North should never be "forced to enforce slavery," Medill told his readers. "Involuntary servitude," he wrote, "is inconsistent with all principles civil or religious." He changed the name of the *Coshocton Whig* to *Coshocton Republican* and had fist fights with local Democrats sympathetic to slavery. In 1851 Medill founded the *Daily Forest City* in Cleveland and a year later created the *Cleveland Leader* after a merger with a Free Soil paper. He tried to prevent General Winfield Scott from running on a pro-slavery platform in 1852 when the Whigs decisively lost the presidency to Democrat Franklin Pierce.

Congressional passage of the Kansas-Nebraska Bill in January 1854, repealing the Missouri Compromise of 1820 and leaving it up to every state whether it would enter the nation slave or free, mobilized Medill to action. He urged Whig editors to join him in creating a new political party, the "National Republican Party," that would be dedicated to the gradual suffocation of slavery by preventing its spread to new states coming into the Union. Greeley was encouraging. "If you can get the name Republican started in the West," he wrote, "it will grow in the East." At a March 1854 meeting in the *Leader* office the new party's platform began to take shape. "No more slave states. No more slave territory. Slavery is sectional. Liberty is national."

In April 1855 Medill brought his wife, two daughters, and three brothers to Chicago after buying an interest in the *Chicago Tribune*. Medill thought Chicago had the makings of "a great city." By then it had grown to 64,000 settlers, third in the West behind Cincinnati and St. Louis, but still it was "a quagmire of mosquito marshes" on the foot of Lake Michigan. Eight years before only sixteen thousand people had lived in the city when the *Tribune* had begun life as a xenophobic, anti-immigrant paper in a third floor loft. As managing editor, Medill told his readers that the paper's know-nothing days were over. He added prohibition, a protective tariff, and a pro-business sentiment to his editorial opposition to slavery. "Not one in fifty" Chicagoans, he wrote, had "opened their eyes" to the business and manufacturing center Chicago would soon be.

Abraham Lincoln introduced himself to Medill in the fall of 1855, arriving at the *Tribune*'s downtown office at 51 Clark Street to personally take out a subscription in the paper. Medill had widely publicized Lincoln's remark after the passage of the Kansas-Nebraska Act that "slavery is founded in the selfishness of man's nature, opposition to it in his love of justice." Lincoln had considered retiring from politics before becoming a leading orator in the growing anti-slavery movement. Medill was among those urging Lincoln, a long-time Whig, to switch to the Republican Party. In advance of the Republican nominating convention in 1856 he finally did, winning 110 ballots in an unsuccessful bid for vice-president. Two years later, Medill was among state Republican leaders promoting Lincoln in his senatorial bid against incumbent Stephen A. Douglas, author of the Kansas-Nebraska Act. On June 17, 1858, the *Tribune* reported the beginning of the campaign with Lincoln's now famous words, "A house divided against itself cannot stand. I believe this government cannot endure permanently half-slave and half-free. It will become all one thing or all the other."

Medill urged a series of Lincoln-Douglas debates that projected Lincoln's views across the nation. Seven in all were held. On the eve of the second in Freeport, Illinois, on August 21, Medill advised "Friend Lincoln" in a private letter to "put a few ugly questions at Douglas." Hadn't Douglas "destroyed the principle of self-government in the territories and states" by forcing slavery on the North. Medill urged Lincoln to be "bold, defiant and dogmatic, fighting the devil with fire," exposing Douglas as "a brazen and lying rascal" by "giving him hell." That evening, Lincoln got Douglas to admit that territories and states did have the right to ban slavery. Douglas would narrowly win the Illinois Senate race, but his "Freeport Doctrine," as it came to be known, split the Democratic Party when he became their presidential nominee in 1860. Medill puffed Lincoln for president, getting the Republican Party to schedule its nominating convention for Chicago. Medill was in charge of seating arrangements. He packed the gallery with *Tribune* men who had uncharacteristically been given the day off with pay. They shouted their support for Lincoln, and on the third ballot, Lincoln won.

That November, Medill reported that "Honest Old Abe" had been elected president and that Republicanism had been "triumphant over fraud, fusion, cotton, disunion and treason." Before Lincoln could take the oath of office, southern states had already formed the Confederacy. Two of Medill's three brothers would be killed in the four-year Civil War that followed. Medill championed the Union and the sentiments expressed by Lincoln in his Gettysburg Address in 1863. In the November 21 *Tribune* Medill wrote that "More than any other single event will this glorious dedication" encourage "a deeper resolution" for those who fought in the war and the nation that stood with them.

Medill and the *Tribune* had a record press run of 53,000 copies on April 10, 1865, announcing Robert E. Lee's surrender of the Confederate Army at the Appomattox Court House in Virginia. An estimated 20,000 people gathered before the *Tribune* office in the streets of Chicago to celebrate. An impromptu parade took four hours to pass the building. Five days later, the *Tribune* reported the "terrible news" that President Lincoln had been assassinated at Ford's Theater in Washington, D.C.. Medill found it "almost impossible to comprehend." Medill would later write that "Lincoln was so great where men are rarely great, in his simplicity, his integrity, and his purity of patriotic purpose."

The post-war period was difficult for Medill. He saw the great cause of the Civil War—equal rights for all men—receding and his grip on the *Tribune* slipping. He believed President Andrew Johnson obstructed efforts to secure the rights of freed slaves and "should be impeached and ejected from office." Medill had been turned out of his own his leadership role at the paper when a well-connected competitor Horace White bought majority control of the *Tribune*. Medill's 20 percent share of the paper encouraged him to hang tough. Nearly half of Chicago's 112,172 residents were reading the *Tribune*, generating revenues of $400,000, four times the annual average of the next nearest paper.

By 1870 Chicago's population soared to three hundred thousand, but the city had been hastily constructed in pine and stucco. On October 8, 1871, Medill warned that "There has been no rain for three weeks. A spark might set a fire that would sweep from end to end of the city." That night it happened. The Great Chicago Fire swept from the city's west side through its downtown and near north corridor in walls of flame more than one hundred feet high. Survivors fled into Lake Michigan to take cover. Half the city's population was made homeless. The "fireproof" *Tribune* was one of seventeen thousand buildings lost. An emergency press, shipped from Baltimore, allowed the resourceful Medill to resume publishing on October 11 with his personal promise "this once beautiful city shall rise again." Chicago did, starting the next month, with Medill as its mayor.

Medill insisted on building codes to rationalize reconstruction in the city. It became home to the modern steel skyscraper. His Chicago Public Library system became a great source of civic pride. However, when he recommended Sunday saloon closings, the city's Irish and German citizens rebelled. Medill served only one term as mayor, bought out White, and returned to lead the *Tribune* to unprecedented profits in the Gilded Age. Medill and the *Tribune* were no friend of organizing labor which helped push the city's population to half a million in 1880 and more than one million in 1890. Following the Haymarket Square riot in 1886, the paper reported in August that "dangling nooses wait for the dynamite fiends" convicted of setting off a bomb at a labor rally that killed eight police officers. Medill succeeded in boosting Chicago into hosting the World's Columbian Exposition in 1893. A final triumph was the *Tribune*'s exclusive report in May 1898 that America's "New Navy" under the command of George Dewey had destroyed the Spanish fleet in Manila Bay. President William McKinley received the news by telephone from *Tribune* editor James Keeley.

When he was near death, Medill apocryphally reported, "My last words shall be: What is the news." His daughters Kate and Elinor had married newspapermen and their sons Robert McCormick and Joseph Medill Patterson would lead the *Tribune* well into the twentieth century. The paper's extraordinary influence in municipal affairs and leading voice in national politics had been the crowning achievement and lasting legacy of Joseph Medill.

Further Reading

Bennett, James O'Donnell. *Joseph Medill: A Brief Biography and an Appreciation*. Chicago: Chicago Tribune, 1947.

Chicago Tribune. *A Century of Tribune Editorials, 1847–1947*. Chicago: Chicago Tribune, 1947.

Kinsley, Philip. *The Chicago Tribune: Its First Hundred Years*, vols. 1 and 2. Chicago: Chicago Tribune, 1943 and 1945.

Papers of Joseph Maharry Medill, Chicago Tribune Archives, Chicago, Illinois.

Tebbel, John W. *An American Dynasty: The Story of the McCormicks, Medills and Pattersons*. New York: Doubleday, 1947.

Wendt, Lloyd. *Chicago Tribune: The Rise of a Great American Newspaper*. Chicago: Rand McNally, 1979.

BRUCE J. EVENSEN

MEET THE PRESS

The leading political talk show program in the United States has been on the air for well over a half-century. As of 2007, *Meet the Press* was the longest running network program still on the air. The original studio set from the prominent NBC News program sits in the Smithsonian

Institution and its programs are preserved in the Library of Congress.

Meet the Press was first telecast from the nation's capital on November 6, 1947. President Franklin D. Roosevelt's Postmaster General, James A. Farley, was the program's first guest and the moderator at that time was Martha Rountree. Lawrence E. Spivak also sat-in as moderator on occasion and eventually took over. He was succeeded by Ned Brooks. Over the years, some prominent NBC News network correspondents including Bill Monroe, Garrick Utley, and Chris Wallace performed this function as well. Marvin Kalb and Roger Mudd were moderators in 1984–1985, before Mudd left to teach in Virginia and Kalb departed network television to teach at the John F. Kennedy School of Government at Harvard University.

The prominent weekly program has aired in many different time slots and network locations: late nights on Wednesday evenings, then Monday night, and Saturday, before finally settling on the current schedule early on Sunday morning. The distinguished political newsmaker program started with a format of one news source and usually one moderator, often joined by a group of four interviewers. The press panel of questioners has included both print and broadcast journalists. Some of the best-known national journalists have appeared often. David Broder of the *Washington Post* appeared as a panelist more than three hundred times, more any other non-NBC News staff person. Journalists May Craig and Robert Novak also made more than two hundred appearances. When the occasion called for it, the guests included journalists in the news, including author Bob Woodward. In the early twenty-first century, the program sometimes featured one interviewer and a single guest, or a few guests appearing separately, although occasionally expanding to meet a special occasion. In 2006, for example, Congressional candidates from Ohio and Missouri visited the program just prior to national elections.

The program had as guests all U.S. presidents and every secretary of state since it was first initiated, as well as prominent international heads of state including David Ben-Gurion, Indira Gandhi, Madame Chiang Kai-shek, Ferdinand Marcos, Fidel Castro, and Pakistani President Pervez Musharraf. Former Senate Republican leader, Bob Dole of Kansas, appeared on *Meet the Press* more than two dozen times, and, in fact, on Easter Sunday morning, 1990, he broke the previous record of twenty-five appearances held by Senator and later Vice President, Hubert Humphrey of Minnesota.

The National Broadcasting Corporation (NBC) program, offered over the web via MSNBC, has always been credited for having high journalistic standards, set early by the program's founder Spivak. He created the basic imprint and philosophy underlying *Meet the Press* and contributed to it until his retirement in November, 1975. He drew upon his Harvard education and experience as an editor and publisher of the *American Mercury*. The program has been the center of controversy on more than one occasion. Whittaker Chambers, for example, named Alger Hiss as a Communist working in the State Department, thus contributing to the post-World War II Red scare. The theme of government secrecy and reporting methods have also been frequent program topics.

Long-time contributors to the program commented on the late Lawrence Spivak's counsel to Tim Russert when he first took over the program in 1991. Spivak recommended to always prepare thoroughly and to try to retain something of an adversarial tone, to ensure that the guests are totally candid in relating the most accurate and up-to-date information on a topic in the news. Russert, who was credited with resurrecting and even elevating the status of the program, joined NBC News in 1984.

When he joined the NBC network, Russert oversaw the weekday morning *Today* program for a period of time. His supervision included arrangements to have the program staff travel abroad to cover important international events. While with *Today*, he arranged the first televised meeting with Pope John Paul. Russert's law degree and his exposure to the inner workings of national politics, by virtue of having worked as a special counsel to the U.S. Senate from 1977 to 1982, gave him credentials to host *Meet the Press*. He became NBC News' Washington Bureau Chief and took over as moderator of *Meet the Press* on December 8, 1991. Russert initiated a feature for the program that would permit the use of video clips from previous, historic appearances by such well-known figures as Martin Luther King Jr. *Meet the Press* also became the first network program broadcast using high definition television.

Further Reading

Rick Ball, and NBC News. *Meet the Press: 50 Years of History in the Making.* New York: McGraw-Hill, 1998.

Michael D. Murray. "The World of Change in TV News: A Conversation with Garrick Utley." *American Journalism*, 14, 2, (Spring 1997): 10–17.

Rudolph, Ileane. "Bless This Press: 'Meet the Press'." *TV Guide* (Nov. 8, 1997): 37–39.

Tim Russert, "Meet the Press: 50 Years of History." C-SPAN, November 3, 1997. Available from C-SPAN Archives, Videoape 94704.

Garrick, Utley. *You Should Have Been Here Yesterday: A Life in Television News.* New York: Public Affairs, 2000.

Michael D. Murray

MENCKEN, HENRY LOUIS

Henry Louis Mencken (September 12, 1880–January 29, 1956), journalism's lead provocateur in America's Jazz Age, was an icon for a generation of skeptics who deplored hypocrisy, self-righteousness, and self-serving men in politics. His newspaper career began at the *Baltimore Morning Herald* in 1899, and he moved up quickly to become Sunday editor of the *Herald* in 1901, and city editor in 1903. When the *Herald* closed in 1906, Mencken moved to the *Baltimore Sun*, and for the rest of his life was on the staff of the *Sun* or *Evening Sun*.

Mencken's magazine career started at the *Smart Set*, where he began reviewing books in 1908. He and George

Jean Nathan were co-editors of the literary magazine from 1914 to 1923, bringing it from obscurity to center stage in American letters. Noted for satire and promoting unknown writers, the magazine's discoveries included F. Scott Fitzgerald and Aldous Huxley. Mencken and Nathan founded the *American Mercury* in 1924, and Mencken was sole editor from1924 to 1933. As a critic of American culture, Mencken may have attained his highest pique in this period. The editors dedicated the *American Mercury* to exploring American life, their goal being "a realistic presentation of the whole gaudy, gorgeous American scene."

Mencken's first book, *George Bernard Shaw: His Plays* (1905), gained little notice. More substantial material soon followed with *The Philosophy of Frederick Nietzche* (1907); the *Prejudices* series, a collection of essays, in a series of six volumes (1919–1927); and *Treatise of the Gods* (1930). The scholarly *American Language* (1918) was both a critical and a commercial success, and remains in print. Mencken published revised editions in 1921 and 1923, an expanded volume in 1936, and supplements in 1945 and 1948. He published memoirs in a series of three volumes: *Happy Days, 1880–1982* (1940); *Newspaper Days, 1899–1906* (1941); *Heathen Days, 1890–1936* (1943).

The farcical Scopes Trial in July 1925 in Dayton, Tennessee, was a national embarrassment, which meant it was a moment of glory for Mencken. Putting a teacher on trial for teaching evolution gave Mencken the chance to enhance his reputation for South-baiting, a sport he relished. His nationally syndicated commentaries regularly skewered the South as a bastion of religiously inspired ignorance where yokels guarded the gates of stupidity. The trial brought to life his stereotypes of the South and rural America—a culturally barren, bigoted landscape, populated by hillbillies and led by hucksters. He appointed himself chief antagonist to the prosecution, which included William Jennings Bryan, despised by Mencken and a prominent figure among Christian fundamentalists. Mencken left Dayton before the trial ended, missing the dramatic moment when Clarence Darrow called Bryan to the stand to testify as an expert on the Bible. Mencken had a hand in staging the drama, having talked Darrow into defending John Scopes and having the *Baltimore Sun* post Scopes' bail.

For Menken, Dayton and the trial were emblematic of larger ills in American culture. His attack on the South was an assault on what he saw as a Puritanism that infected American culture with its suffocating moralism that was hostile to art and ideas. He linked the Puritanism with a Christian fundamentalism that thrived on illiteracy and ignorance. Mencken's antipathy to Bryan illustrated a larger criticism of American democracy's essential foible: that because "all men are created equal" their thoughts and abilities must be equal. With more than a little implied elitism, Mencken saw in Bryan's radical egalitarianism an unchecked democracy that would devolve to mob rule, reined by ignorance and impulse.

Mencken's fondness for German culture resulted in more serious collisions with public sentiment. Prior to World War I, he praised German idealism and ambition while condemning British Puritanism. His byline disappeared from *Sun* newspapers during the war. A minor controversy erupted in the early 1930s over anti-Semitic passages in *Treatise on the Gods*. Like many Americans, he did not foresee the true menace of the Nazis and dismissed them as counterparts to American Klansmen, ignorant but not necessarily evil. In the late 1930s, Mencken's hold slipped on the skeptical imagination, as liberal intellectuals, a substantial part of his audience, found themselves at odds with his isolationist, anti-Franklin D. Roosevelt positions, which opposed both Nazism and any action against it. His earlier German sympathies accelerated his decline in influence after World War II.

As a critic and writer, Menken had an extraordinary influence on American literature during his era, but still considered himself primarily a journalist. His impact on journalism endured, leaving the gold-standard and stereotype of the profession—the verbally raucous cynic, deft with language, and sharp with criticism.

Further Reading

William Manchester. *Disturber of the Peace: The Life of H.L. Mencken*, 2nd ed. Amherst: University of Massachusetts Press, 1986.

Terry Teachout. *The Skeptic: A Life of H.L. Mencken*. New York: Harper Collines, 2002.

Fred C. Hobson. *Mencken: A Life*. New York: Random House, 1994.

Fred C. Hobson. *Serpent in Eden: H.L. Mencken and the South*. Chapel Hill: University of North Carolina Press, 1974.

ED CAUDILL

MEYER, EUGENE

Eugene Meyer (October 31, 1875–July 17, 1959), a wealthy financier and public official, purchased the *Washington Post* at a bankruptcy sale in 1933 and laid the foundation for it to become one of the nation's most important newspapers. Although *The Post* did not attain this stature until his daughter, Katharine Graham, took over following the death of both her father and her husband, Philip S. Graham, Meyer's vision for the newspaper led to its ultimate success.

Meyer was born in Los Angeles, California, on October 31, 1875, to Eugene Meyer, a prosperous Jewish immigrant from Alsace-Lorraine, France, and Harriet Newmark Meyer. He attended the University of California for one year and then enrolled in Yale University where he graduated in two years with a Phi Beta Kappa key at the age of nineteen. After working in his father's international banking firm and studying finance in Europe, he bought his own seat on the New York Stock Exchange in 1901 when he was twenty-six. Investing in copper, oil, chemicals and automobile financing, he soon became a director of a number of corporations. In 1910 he married Agnes Elizabeth Ernst, a strong-willed, intellectual woman of Lutheran background who had worked as a New York newspaper reporter. In addition to Katharine, the couple had four other children.

By the time he was forty he was worth $40 million

dollars and able to undertake unpaid public service. Starting in 1917 he held posts under seven Presidents of the United States: Director of the War Finance Corporation during World War I; member of the Federal Farm Loan Board (1927); governor of the Federal Reserve Board (1930–1933); first chairman of the Reconstruction Finance Corporation (1932); and first president of the World Bank (1946).

At the age of fifty-eight, he bought *The Post* for $825,000 with encouragement from his wife, who occasionally wrote for it. Meyer revitalized the dying newspaper, giving it a vigorous editorial page, improving news coverage and redesigning its appearance. He expressed his journalistic philosophy in a credo published on the front page of *The Post* on March 5, 1935: "The first mission of a newspaper is to tell the truth as nearly as the truth may be ascertained….As a disseminator of news, the paper shall observe the decencies that are obligatory upon a private gentleman."

Although the newspaper continued to lose money after he bought it, under Meyer's leadership circulation and advertising both soared. By 1943, circulation had tripled to 162,000. In 1946, Meyer stepped down as editor and publisher to head the World Bank, naming his son-in-law, Philip Graham, to succeed him. Meyer returned to the newspaper six months later as chairman of the board. In 1954 he purchased the *Times-Herald* and consolidated it with the *Post*, giving his newspaper a monopoly in the morning field and assuring its financial success. Meyer remained board chairman until his death in Washington on July 17, 1959. He and his wife established the Agnes and Eugene Meyer Foundation to improve social conditions in Washington, DC.

Further Reading

Bray, Howard. *The Pillars of the Post: The Making of a News Empire in Washington*. New York: Norton, 1980.

Graham, Katharine. *Personal History*. New York: Knopf, 1997.

Meyer, Agnes E. *Out of These Roots: The Autobiography of an American Woman*. Boston: Little Brown, 1953.

Roberts, Chalmers M. *The Washington Post: The First 100 Years*. Boston: Houghton, 1977.

Mifflin, 1977; revised and enlarged as *In the Shadow of Power: The Story of the Washington Post*. Cabin John, Md.: Seven Locks Press, 1989.

Pusey, Merlo J. *Eugene Meyer*. New York: Knopf, 1974.

MAURINE H. BEASLEY

MILWAUKEE JOURNAL

Milwaukee already had four German-language daily newspapers and two English-language dailies when the *Milwaukee Daily Journal* published its first edition in mid-November 1882. Four weeks later, it had a new owner when its editor, Lucius W. Nieman, bought half the shares. The *Journal* gradually attracted a sizable readership by offering shorter news articles, lively headlines, and a focus on crime, domestic disputes, fires, labor turmoil, and political

scandals. Reporters also thoroughly covered the legislature in Madison, where the *Journal* favored the Democrats. During the era of progressive Republican leadership by Governor Robert M. La Follette in the early 1900s, the *Journal* frequently condemned his rhetoric for its radical tone, although the newspaper also endorsed some of his reform proposals for state government.

The newspaper won its first Pulitzer Prize in 1919 for public service, a recognition of its lengthy campaign to expose German propaganda and pro-German attitudes in German-language newspapers in Wisconsin. At the same time, the *Journal* steadfastly promoted Americanism to overcome ethnic allegiances in Milwaukee. A second Pulitzer Prize was awarded in 1935 for editorial cartoons, a third in 1953 for international reporting, a fourth in 1967 for public service involving coverage of water pollution problems, and a fifth in 1977 for local reporting for a series on issues affecting the elderly.

A poll of newspaper publishers in 1952 placed the *Milwaukee Journal* among the top ten dailies in the nation, as did a *Time* list for 1964. Much of the praise for the *Journal* related to its printing quality from the 1930s to 1970s. Its color presses produced sharp tones for advertisements and news photographs, and its black-and-white sharpness was superior.

Another distinction arose from the transition to employee ownership that began in 1937. Harry J. Grant, publisher since 1919 and part-owner of Journal Company, wanted to ensure the newspaper remained locally owned. He persuaded the other owners to sell their stock to create a trust agreement for employees to buy units of ownership held during their employment. Eventually, 90 percent of Journal Company was owned by employees. This arrangement resulted in an unusual situation in late 1961: *Journal* union workers, most of them unit owners, went on strike over pay and the installation of automated equipment that would eliminate jobs. The strike lasted nearly a month.

Journal Company, which by now owned local television and radio stations, bought the morning *Milwaukee Sentinel* in July 1962 after the Hearst Corporation announced its closing during a strike. Later, the company—Journal Communications—continued to add new holdings in community newspapers, commercial printing operations, radio and television stations, and telecommunications. At the start of the twenty-first century, the company had six thousand employees. However, similar to other afternoon newspapers across the United States, the *Milwaukee Journal* steadily lost readership from the 1970s onward and merged with the *Sentinel* in April 1995. Journal Communications also offered shares for public sale in 2003 to raise capital for expansion.

Further Reading

Portrait of a Paper, the Milwaukee Journal: 75th Aniversary-Year, the Milwaukee Journal. Milwaukee Journal, 1958.

JAMES LANDERS

MOODY, DWIGHT LYMAN

Dwight Lyman Moody (1837–1899) was America's best-known nineteenth-century revivalist, in part, because of his effective use of the press. Moody was among the first to see the role mass media could play in promoting the gospel. He helped to perfect an organizational structure and publishing campaign that allowed him to reach an estimated audience of one hundred million across America's Gilded Age.

Moody was the sixth of nine children born to Betsy and Edwin Moody, a farm family living in the Connecticut River valley of East Northfield, Massachusetts. His father died when Dwight was four, leaving the boy with only four years of formal schooling before he went to work on neighboring farms. His stubborn independence won him a job at his uncle's Boston shoe store when he was seventeen. Mandatory church attendance was a condition of his employment. In September, 1856, Moody arrived in Chicago, then the nation's fastest growing city, hoping to make a fortune selling boots and speculating in real estate.

Moody was drawn to Christian service by his involvement with the Young Men's Christian Association, an organization dedicated to meeting the spiritual and social needs of young men new to the city. "Crazy Moody" was seen as a nuisance by Chicago editors for barging into newspaper offices insisting they publicize efforts aimed at aiding young men and the poor. As chief librarian and president of Chicago's YMCA, Moody started his own newspaper. Two hundred thousand copies of *Everybody's Paper* circulated annually throughout the city, focusing on religious news often ignored by the city's daily press. The Civil War accelerated these efforts. Moody spent seven stints at the front as a member of the United States Christian Commission, helping to distribute one and a half million Bibles to Union soldiers, in addition to 1.3 million hymnals and 40 million pages of tracts.

Moody's sphere of influence widened after the Civil War. His full-time involvement in evangelical outreach led him to coordinate and oversee the distribution of five tons of religious literature annually, much of it in gospel wagons that ranged across large and small settlements of the American Midwest. He also oversaw the activities of the YMCA's publications committee which annually issued five million pages of tracts and papers including the association's *Heavenly Tidings*, and the *Watchman*, which commanded such wide acceptance that it was later adopted by the national YMCA as its official organ. In October 1867, Chicago's YMCA building, the first in the nation, opened its doors to nightly speakers and socials that were publicized at train stations and trolley bus lines across the city. Moody considered the association's publications crucial in "taking Christianity to the lost and not waiting for them to come to us" (*Chicago Tribune*, October 5, 1867). The opening of the YMCA's library to the public in April, 1869, provoked civic celebration. For the first time in municipal history, all the city's daily and weekly newspapers could be found in a single place, plus thirty-five of the leading newspapers from across the nation. The holdings eventually became the core collection of the Chicago Public Library.

Beginning in June, 1873, Moody began a series of highly successful, widely publicized revival meetings that made him the best known evangelist in the Anglo-American world. Starting in York and the north of England he developed a mass media campaign that relied heavily on the twin powers of prayer and publicity in to get out the gospel. He forged an alliance with R.C. Morgan, veteran editor of *The Christian*, a widely circulated evangelical newspaper that publicized Moody's meetings across Great Britain and Ireland. Moody told ministers in Carlisle that the press helped to create "a spirit of excitement among the people" by "encouraging people to expect a blessing of unusual magnitude" (*Carlisle Daily Journal*, November 18, 1873). In Edinburgh and Glasgow, this sense of civic spectacle helped bring the believer and the simply curious to his meetings in record numbers. Critics attacked Moody's man-made means of marketing the gospel. He responded, "It seems to me a good deal better to advertise and have a full house than preach to empty pews." Moody believed the press was a place where the sacred and the profane were daily served to a persuadable public. The modern church competes with the world for the attention of the people," he said. What the church needed to learn was how to use the press "to ask people to come in" (*The Christian*, October 23, 1873).

Moody's organizational acumen extended to issuing press releases, granting exclusive interviews, and reserving seats, tables, and inkwells for reporters. A trained staff answered reporters' questions, helped them get their stories out, and granted them special access to proceedings that drew capacity crowds in Dublin, Manchester, Sheffield, Birmingham, and Liverpool between September, 1874, and February, 1875. Local churches could no longer contain the crowds who gathered at his municipal meetings. The *London Morning Post* observed that the vast crowds that came to the city's Agricultural Hall to see what all the excitement was about were themselves "a sight worth going many miles to see" (March 10, 1875). More than two-and-a-half million people attended the 285 meetings of Moody's Greater London Campaign. Even the oppositional *Vanity Fair* considered the crowds "the greatest multitudes ever gathered in this generation" (April 3, 1875).

Moody returned to America as "God's man for the Gilded Age," embarking on a series of revival meetings between October, 1875, and April, 1877, in Brooklyn, Philadelphia, New York, Chicago, and Boston that generated column inch after column inch of stenographic, front-page coverage. Christian households across the United States kept scrapbooks of these press accounts as a chronicle of civic pride and spiritual history. Many newspaper publishers saw Moody's meetings as a way of stimulating circulation at a time of acute financial crisis in the nation and within the newly independent newspaper business. Times were tough in America's centennial year, admitted *Chicago Daily News* editor Melville Stone. Attempts to fend off intense and highly personal competition for readers made it "war in the mud with mud to the neck" (*Chicago Daily News*, September 20, 1876). The press helped make Moody a spiritual celebrity, observed *Chicago Times* publisher Wilbur Storey. Moody provided a form of entertainment that Storey called "saucepan journalism" (December 31, 1876). A sauce contained many ingredients designed to tickle the palate, and newspapers discovered that Moody's meetings, played as civic extravaganzas, did precisely that.

Newspapers competed with one another in publishing bound volumes of Moody's meetings, each claiming to be the most authoritative. The *Boston Globe* helped to establish its reputation through its coverage of Moody's meetings and aggressively marketed early and weekend editions of the paper across New England. This, as elsewhere, made Moody's campaigns regional news with excursion trains offering discount rates to tourists who came to the city both for a look at Moody and to do some shopping. Using a door-to-door canvass, a network of volunteers made available to communities and neighborhoods Moody's *Tabernacle News*, which was a reprinting of crusade coverage as it had appeared in cooperating dailies. During the 1860s, Moody had to begin his own newspaper to get out Christian news. By the end of the 1870s, he had demonstrated how popular religion could use the mass media to spread the gospel.

In the remaining two decades of his life, Moody opened four schools in Massachusetts and Chicago to prepare men and women for Christian service. As part of this initiative, he formed the Bible Institute Colportage Association, which distributed one and a half million Christian pocketbooks across the country by the end of the century. Moody was the writer of seven of the first eleven books in a list that grew to include ninety titles, many sold door-to-door by Moody's student army for a third of the price of standard paperbacks. This mass distribution of Christian literature, aided by Moody's brother-in-law, Fleming Hewitt Revell, helped to create the Christian publishing industry and charted a course that evangelical leaders would use during the twentieth century to reach the world through the written word. At his death on the eve of that century, editorial writers observed that no man had spoken to more men and women during his lifetime. The communication strategy Moody devised would be used to reach millions more in the century that followed.

Further Reading

Curtis, Richard. *They Called Him Mister Moody*, Garden City. NJ: Doubleday, 1962.

Daniels, W.H. *Moody: His Words, Work, and Workers*. New York: Nelson and Philips, 1877.

Dorsett, Lyle W. *A Passion for Souls: The Life of D.L. Moody*. Chicago: Moody Press, 1997.

Evensen, Bruce J. *God's Man for the Gilded Age: D.L. Moody and the Rise of Modern Mass Evangelism*. New York: Oxford University, 2003.

Findlay, Jr., James F. *Dwight L. Moody: American Evangelist, 1837–1899*. Chicago: University of Chicago, 1969.

Gundry, Stanley. *Love Them In: The Proclamation Theology of D.L. Moody*. Chicago: Moody Press, 1976.

Moody, D.L. *New Sermons, Addresses and Prayers*. St. Louis: N.D. Thompson, 1877.

Moody, William R. *D.L. Moody*. New York: Macmillan, 1930.

Pollock, J.C. *Moody: A Biographical Portrait of a Pacesetter in Modern Mass Evangelism*. Grand Rapids, SD: Zondervan, 1963.

BRUCE J. EVENSEN

MOTHER JONES

Mother Jones, founded in 1976 to promote progressive, democratic-socialist ideals, was named after the early twentieth-century labor organizer Mary Harris, who used the name as she traveled America stirring up protests over working conditions. Its *modus operandi*, founders Adam Hochschild, Paul Jacobs, and Richard Parker decided, would be muckraking—investigative journalism with a reformist streak.

Investigative journalism had seen a rebirth in American journalism by 1976, two years after the *Washington Post* had exposed the Watergate scandal that drove President Nixon from office. The magazine's founders and its business manager, Mark Dowie, gambled that there would be an audience for a muckraking national magazine that exposed corporate America. Throughout the years, the magazine's editors have expanded its coverage to politics and international human rights issues. In 2004, they started an annual Mother Jones 400 investigation of the four hundred largest donors to political campaigns.

A nonprofit entity, the Foundation for National Progress, raised funding for the magazine through grants and donations and published the magazine in a glossy format six times a year. In the newsroom, progressive management practices allowed employees to elect the publisher and the managing editor. By its twenty-fifth anniversary in 2001, the crusading publication had a circulation of 165,000.

In a twenty-first century media environment of chain newspapers and conglomerates of media properties, *Mother Jones* remained independent, its muckraking articles often leading to follow-up articles in dailies and on network television news programs, spreading the magazine's influence beyond its paid readership. Two projects published by the magazine became classics after winning National Magazine Awards for excellence in reporting. Dowie, who reported stories in addition to his business duties, had a hand in both. In 1977, the magazine published Dowie's exposé of Ford Motor Company's decision to continue marketing its popular Pinto sedans despite a known defect in the design of its gas tank that caused cars to explode in rear-end collisions. Another attention-getting article appeared in 1979, when the magazine devoted its November issue to a series of articles reported by Dowie and other writers who revealed corporate dumping of unsafe products on Third World countries, sometimes with federal government complicity. The magazine's editors and publishers embraced advocacy, and saw muckraking as a strategy for igniting social activism for progressive causes. A popular enticement to subscribers was an activists' guide, *Raising Hell: A Citizens' Guide to the Fine Art of Investigation.*

The magazine's activism caught the federal government's attention, as well, and the Internal Revenue Service launched an investigation into its nonprofit status in 1979–1980. The IRS claimed that the magazine was required to pay taxes on the income from its advertising. *Mother Jones* staffers countered that the IRS investigation was a political vendetta against the magazine. They won the dispute, but it was an expensive legal fight.

Corporate advertisers largely avoided the magazine's pages, turned off by its aggressive muckraking. Consequently, the magazine relied primarily on paid subscriptions, donations, and fund-raising efforts. An investigative fund financed through donations from readers and set up within the Foundation for National Progress provided support for the magazine's muckraking projects.

Because of its alternative financial structure, *Mother Jones* became arguably the most successful American general interest magazines edited with a progressive perspective in the late twentieth century. It attracted readers with good writing, solid reporting of sensational subjects, and attractive graphics. Yet, its attempt to balance progressive social activism with commercial success sometimes strained the organization.

The magazine's management became embroiled in a public squabble in 1986 with social activist Michael Moore, a former alternative newspaper publisher who was recruited to be editor of the magazine. Within less than a year, he was fired, partly for refusing to publish an article critical of the Sandinista regime in Nicaragua. Moore, who would go on to produce successful documentaries, claimed in his film, *Roger and Me*, that he was fired because the articles he published did not have enough commercial appeal. The split with Moore was emblematic of the ideological differences among the New Left and progressives that strained relations at the magazine throughout its history. To more radical activists, the magazine betrayed its ideals beginning in the 1980s by becoming bland and moderate to attract readers.

Mother Jones co-founder Hochschild, though, countered the magazine's critics in a twenty-fifth-anniversary retrospective, arguing that the magazine's values had remained constant over the half-century of its existence. The magazine also moved to keep pace with changing technology. During the 1990s, it moved quickly to embrace the Internet, becoming the first general interest magazine to establish a web presence with MOJOwire.com, its online version.

Further Reading

Armstrong, David. *A Trumpet to Arms: Alternative Media in America.* Boston: South End Press, 1981.

Downie, Leonard Jr. *The New Muckrakers.* New York: New American Library, 1976.

Hochschild, Adam. "The First 25 Years," *Mother Jones* 23, no. 3 (May/June 2001): 50–53.

Peck, Abe. *Uncovering the Sixties: The Life and Times of the Underground Press.* New York: Pantheon Books, 1985.

Tichi, Cecelia. *Exposés and Excess: Muckraking in America, 1900/2000.* Philadelphia: University of Pennsylvania Press, 2004.

JAMES AUCOIN

MOTION PICTURES

The press has been a favorite Hollywood subject since the silent era. The movies have depicted enduring tensions within journalism while also portraying (sometimes fancifully) key figures and events in journalism history.

Silent films helped fix the clichés of hard-drinking journalists in frenetic newsrooms pursuing fabulous exclusives. However, the most influential work in the genre's history was Ben Hecht and Charles MacArthur's 1928 Broadway farce *The Front Page* and the 1931 movie version of the play. The authors drew liberally and exaggeratedly upon their Chicago newspaper backgrounds in telling of a reporter who tries to leave journalism and his tyrannical editor for marriage and an advertising career. When a huge story breaks, the reporter is inexorably sucked back into the world he has been desperately trying to escape. *The Front Page* established familiar themes such as the disreputable-but-thrilling world of journalism versus the respectable-but-dull world of home and family. It simultaneously criticized and celebrated the tabloid press's scoop-mad mentality.

By appearing at the dawn of sound pictures, *The Front Page* surely influenced numerous other fast-talking newspaper films during the Depression. Some of these movies were melodramas such as *Five Star Final* (1931), which depicted a ruthless tabloid driving a married couple to suicide. Offering a more humorous take were screwball comedies such as *It Happened One Night* (1934), *Libeled Lady* (1936), *Nothing Sacred* (1937), and *His Girl Friday* (1940). The last film was a remake of *The Front Page* and it turned the reporter character into a woman (played by Rosalind Russell) who was her editor's (played by Cary Grant) ex-wife and his equal in wit and cunning. Such strong women were common in screwball films, but they were the focus of critique in Frank Capra's *Mr. Deeds Goes to Town* (1936) and *Meet John Doe* (1941). The female reporters in those films found salvation only by forsaking their cynicism and devoting themselves to the male heroes and the populist causes the men embodied. The latter film showed the press complicit in a neo-fascist plot to take over America.

The best known journalism movie of the era remains *Citizen Kane* (1941), in which a press baron's megalomania subsumes his youthful pledge to serve the public interest and leads to his ruination. Director and co-writer Orson Welles insisted that the movie was not solely inspired by William Randolph Hearst, but the parallels still were such that the Hearst press sought unsuccessfully to kill the film.

Meanwhile, lobbying from press associations helped prompt Hollywood to produce more laudatory portraits of journalism. Ronald Reagan depicted "jet propelled" reporters who helped local police in his first movie *Love Is On the Air* (1937) and later in *Nine Lives Are Not Enough* (1941).

More famous films included *Dispatch from Reuters* (1940), which starred Edward G. Robinson depicting the wire service founder, Paul Julius Reuter, as a champion of press freedom, and *The Story of G.I. Joe* (1945), in which Burgess Meredith dramatized Ernie Pyle's battlefield reporting. In postwar films such as *Gentleman's Agreement* (1947) and *Call Northside 777* (1948), conscientious, professional reporters far removed from the *Front Page* stereotype uncovered anti-Semitism and municipal corruption. However, the film noir era also saw movies as scathing toward the press as any seen to that point. In A*ce in the Hole* (1951), a reporter scored a scoop by keeping a man trapped in a cave; in *Sweet Smell of Success* (1957), a Walter Winchell-like columnist destroyed lives and careers. *Deadline, USA* (1952) showed a crusading newspaper exposing a murderous gangster, but the triumph was bittersweet: The newspaper promptly folded. (The story was inspired by the death of the *New York World*.)

The Vietnam and Watergate era was marked by "conspiracy" movies in which government, big business and other institutions covered up terrible truths. The prime journalistic example was *All the President's Men* (1976). In portraying Woodward and Bernstein's Watergate exposés, the filmmakers recreated the *Washington Post* newsroom in meticulous detail and bathed it in light in contrast to the murky darkness of official Washington. Some have criticized the film for exaggerating the press's role in the Nixon administration's downfall; others have praised it for vividly portraying how methodical investigative reporting can expose power's abuses. The flipside was *Network* (1976), in which a television network turned its news anchor into the "Mad Prophet of the Airwaves" as a ratings gimmick, only to have him assassinated on the air when his ratings dipped. Here the news media (and TV more broadly) were enmeshed in the conspiracy instead of outside it; they were a force for evil instead of light.

Post-1980 movies have reiterated many of the themes of earlier films. Reportorial irresponsibility led to death and ruined reputations in *Absence of Malice* (1981). Overseas correspondents sought to make sense of Third World conflicts in *The Year of Living Dangerously* (1983), *Under Fire* (1983), *The Killing Fields* (1984), and *Salvador* (1986). Journalists engaged in *Front Page*-like exploits in *The Paper* (1994) and *True Crime* (1999), in both movies freeing innocent individuals from behind bars. Television news was the focus of gentle but pointed critique in *Broadcast News* (1987) and of dark satire in *To Die For* (1995), whereas *Up Close and Personal* (1996) transformed the lurid life of television anchor Jessica Savitch into an uplifting story of romance and professional principle, changing names and incidents as needed.

Other movies stayed closer to the real-life facts. *Shattered Glass* (2003) showed how young *New Republic* writer Stephen Glass fabricated more than two dozen stories before he was finally discovered and banished. *Good Night, and Good Luck* (2005) depicted Edward R. Murrow and CBS News taking on Senator Joseph McCarthy, and *Capote* (2005) told of how Truman Capote wrote the non-

fiction classic *In Cold Blood* by befriending—and exploiting—the killers of a Kansas family.

Over the years, journalists often have complained how Hollywood has depicted their profession; those depictions frequently have not jibed with how journalists like to see themselves. Nevertheless, motion pictures have made journalism seem exciting and important. Even negative portrayals of the press have underscored ideals of proper professional practice by dramatically illustrating the consequences of deviating from those ideals. The movies imply that even if journalism has lost its way, it can find its way again, and journalists can do the right thing and serve their proper role in American democracy.

Further Reading

Barris, Alex. *Stop the Presses!: The Newspaperman in American Films*. South Brunswick, NJ: A.S. Barnes, 1976.

Ehrlich, Matthew C. *Journalism in the Movies*. Urbana: University of Illinois Press, 2004.

Good, Howard. *Outcasts: The Image of Journalists in Contemporary Film*. Metuchen, NJ: Scarecrow, 1989.

———. *Girl Reporter: Gender, Journalism, and the Movies*. Lanham, MD: Scarecrow, 1998.

———. *The Drunken Journalist: The Biography of a Film Stereotype*. Lanham, MD: Scarecrow, 2000.

Ness, Richard R. *From Headline Hunter to Superman: A Journalism Filmography*. Lanham, MD: Scarecrow, 1997.

Saltzman, Joe. *Frank Capra and the Image of the Journalist in American Film*. Los Angeles: Norman Lear Center, University of Southern California, 2002.

Vaughn, Stephen, and Bruce Evensen. "Democracy's Guardians: Hollywood's Portrait of Reporters, 1930–1945," *Journalism Quarterly*, 68 (Winter, 1991), 829–838.

MATTHEW C. EHRLICH

MOYERS, BILL

Admired by some for his courage, his independence, and his intellect and condemned by others as a liberal partisan, Bill Moyers (June 5, 1934–) generated a level of respect and of controversy reminiscent of broadcast pioneer Edward R. Murrow. Like Murrow, Moyers' reporting led conclusions. Like Murrow, Moyers' work embodied a strong sense of morality, of justice, and democracy. Like Murrow, Moyers took on powerful interests and generated powerful reactions. Like Murrow, Moyers provided a unique voice in American journalism. His education for the Baptist ministry, his lingering southwest accent, and his deep concern for the moral and the spiritual blended comfortably with his intellectual approach to journalism.

Born in Hugo, Oklahoma, in 1934 and graduated from the Southwest Baptist Theological Seminary in Fort Worth in 1959, Moyers began his career as a newspaper reporter in Texas. He soon joined the staff of Senator Lyndon Johnson and developed a close relationship with the future president, to whom he became a special assistant in 1963 and press secretary from 1965–1967. He split with Johnson over the Vietnam War in 1967 and moved to New York as publisher of Long Island's *Newsday*. Political differences with the

Moyers, Bill

paper's owner ended that relationship in 1970, and Moyers tried his hand at television, beginning with his *Bill Moyers' Journal* on PBS, a mix of interviews, commentary, and investigative documentaries. His series of "Essays on Watergate" brought particular acclaim. They brought together neatly his instincts for investigative journalism, and his concern for ethics and the health of democracy.

After five years at PBS, Moyers attracted the admiration of CBS founder, William Paley, who personally recruited Moyers for his network. Paley insisted on a wide latitude for Moyers as principal correspondent for the documentary series, *CBS Reports*. As with Murrow, Paley's support waned when serious journalism conflicted with the bottom line. While Moyers enjoyed considerable freedom, he received little air-time, and, after two years, he returned to *Bill Moyers' Journal* at PBS. Three years later, CBS lured him back in a new role, commentator on the *CBS Evening News* and host of several series on the network, none successful enough to retain their place on the CBS schedule.

In 1986, Moyers cast his lot permanently with public television. With his wife, Judith Davidson, he formed Public Affairs Television, Inc. His production company attracted funding from private foundations and produced a range of specials and series for PBS that solidified his reputation as a television personality able to bring big ideas to the small screen and ask provocative questions about public and private life.

Public Affairs Television began with ten hours of programming discussing the U.S. Constitution in its two hundredth anniversary year. Constitutional scholars representing a range of political views discussed the core document of American democratic government. His *World of Ideas* series interviewed intellectuals seldom seen on television. Novelists, sociologists, philosophers, and radical critics joined Moyers "conversations about democracy." Moyers brought to public attention Robert Bly's ideas about masculinity with "A Gathering of Men." The seminary graduate developed a particular rapport with Sarah Lawrence College professor Joseph Campbell in a series of conversations about "The Power of Myth," attracting critical acclaim and surprisingly large audiences. The Campbell series generated a book, *Joseph Campbell and the Power of Myth* (1988), which sold 750,000 copies and remained on the *New York Times* best seller list for more than a year. Other best-selling books based on his television work followed, including *The World of Ideas* (1989), *The World of Ideas II* (1990), and *Healing the Mind* (1992).

Moyers returned to weekly current affairs television toward the end of his career with the series *Now, with Bill Moyers*, which exemplified the values and interests that had guided his life in journalism, particularly the integrity of democracy and the threat posed by manipulative leadership. Broadcast during the George W. Bush administration, the Moyers programs came under attack from Republicans and the management of the Corporation for Public Broadcasting. While that strong criticism did not drive Moyers out of television, his seventieth birthday did, as he chose

to devote his remaining years to a biography of Lyndon Johnson.

As he left *Now*, Moyers said, "I'm going out telling the story that I think is the biggest story of our time: how the right-wing media has become a partisan propaganda arm of the Republican National Committee. We have an ideological press that's interested in the election of Republicans, and a mainstream press that's interested in the bottom line. Therefore, we don't have a vigilant, independent press whose interest is the American people." His journalistic career exemplified the vigilance and independence about which he despaired.

Further Readings

Jarvik, Laurence. *PBS, Behind the Screen*. Rocklin CA: Prima Publishing, 1997.
Moyers, Bill. *Listening to America: a Traveler Rediscovers his Country*. New York: Harpers Magazine Press. 1971.
——. *A World of Ideas: Conversations with Thoughtful Men and Women about American Life Today and the Ideas Shaping our Future*. New York: Doubleday, 1989.
——. *Healing and the Mind*. New York: Doubleday, 1993.
——. *Moyers on America: A Journalist and his Times*. New York: Anchor Books, 2005.
Stewart, David. *The PBS Companion: A History of Public Television*. New York: TV Books, 1999.

JACK W. MITCHELL

MS. MAGAZINE

Ms. is a monthly magazine devoted to feminist issues that began publication in 1971, during the heyday of the second-wave of the American women's movement. It was launched by a small group of feminist journalists, including the well-known activist Gloria Steinem. Since its inception, the magazine has promoted the concept of *sisterhood*, echoing the radical feminist belief that women everywhere share common problems that link them to one another through time, superseding class, race, religion, and other differences. The founders of *Ms.* sought to establish a universal sisterhood of readers on the basis of gender, and to create a publication that would embrace women everywhere.

The first issue of *Ms.* appeared as an insert in the December 1971 issue of *New York* magazine, a glossy urban monthly whose editor had supported Steinem's early career as a political writer. The preview issue generated eighty-five thousand subscription requests and the founding editors were subsequently able to secure $1 million in start-up funding from Warner Communications. The first stand-alone issue of *Ms.* appeared a few months later; the cover designated it as the "Spring 1972" issue. The editors used a seasonal—rather than a monthly—date because they feared that the magazine would linger on newsstands. Instead, the first issue sold out its initial press run of three hundred thousand copies in just eight days.

In the early and mid-1970s, *Ms.* struck a chord with many American women who were tired of the predictable format of women's magazines, which tended to recycle sto-

308

ries on cooking, marriage, childrearing, and fashion. By contrast, the *Ms.* preview issue featured articles on abortion, sexism in the English language, and the epiphanies of housewives who "converted" to feminism. The magazine continued to offer hard-hitting journalism, covering such revolutionary topics as rape, domestic violence, sexual harassment, lesbianism, prostitution and pornography, and international women's issues. No other popular magazine offered American women a greater range of voices and perspectives than *Ms.*, a reality that attracted five hundred thousand subscribers and an estimated pass-along readership of three million.

By the end of the 1970s, however, tensions within the women's movement and the commercial pressures associated with mainstream publishing began to take their toll. Some feminist critics lambasted the magazine for concentrating on issues affecting white, middle-class feminists, and shying away from topics more relevant to women of color and poor women. At the same time, *Ms.* faced stiff new competition from magazines like *Working Woman*, which chipped away at the feminist magazine's readership and advertising base. Many large corporate advertisers abandoned *Ms.* in this period, as they found some of the newer magazines more amenable to advertiser influence over editorial content.

In 1987, the foundering magazine was purchased by an Australian media company whose editors gutted the feminist content. Readership declined precipitously, and the magazine was sold again in 1989 to Lang Communications. Lang turned the magazine into an advertising-free, subscriber-supported publication and appointed the radical feminist Robin Morgan editor-in-chief. Steinem penned a major exposé for the revamped *Ms.* and feminist writers such as Andrea Dworkin and Alice Walker returned to its pages. By the third issue, the circulation figures exceeded the break-even point of 75,000.

In 1998, *Ms.* was purchased by Liberty Media, a consortium of investors including Gloria Steinem. In 2001, the Feminist Majority Foundation, led by Eleanor Smeal, a former president of the National Organization for Women, assumed ownership of Liberty Media and became the publisher of *Ms.*

Further Reading

Bradley, Patricia. *Mass Media and the Shaping of American Feminism: 1963–1975.* Jackson: University of Mississippi Press, 2003.

Farrell, Amy Erdman. *Yours in Sisterhood: Ms. Magazine and the Promise of Popular Feminism.* Chapel Hill: University of North Carolina Press, 1998.

Heilbrun, Carolyn G. *Education of a Woman: The Life of Gloria Steinem.* New York: Ballantine Books, 1995.

McCracken, Ellen. *Decoding Women's Magazines: From Mademoiselle to Ms.* New York: St. Martin's Press, 1993.

Steinem, Gloria. *Outrageous Acts and Everyday Rebellions.* New York: Holt, Rinehart and Winston, 1983.

Thom, Mary. *Inside Ms.: 25 Years of the Magazine and the Feminist Movement.* New York: Henry Holt, 1997.

CAROLYN BRONSTEIN

MUCKRAKING

Muckraking means the search for and the exposure of political or commercial corruption, but many people associate muckraking with digging dirt to sensationalize, making "muckraking" one of the most misunderstood words in the history of American journalism.

This misunderstanding is historically situated. Theodore Roosevelt had been a great friend of muckraking journalists in the early years of his Progressive Era presidency, when they had worked together to expose official and corporate misconduct. By April 1906, Roosevelt wearied of reporting that reminded him of the man with the muck-rake in John Bunyan's *Pilgrim's Progress*, who never looked up but "continued to rake to himself the filth of the floor" (Weinberg, xvii). Ever since, some readers have said that reporting that goes to any lengths to attract a following is modern "muckraking." The men and women who diligently worked to make journalism an instrument in creating a more civil society at the start of the twentieth century would likely be astonished at the comparison.

"The fact that he lumps us is a bad sign," Lincoln Steffens wrote Upton Sinclair, when social critic Edmund Wilson began muckraking the muckrakers in 1932 (Winter and Hicks 1938, 928). Differing historians since then have seen the muckrakers as liberal social reformers or conservative advocates of middle class interests; as moral crusaders or self-interested defenders of the status quo; as journalists who strove to achieve an unselfish consensus based upon Protestant ethics or tools of special interests who were attempting to protect their positions when threatened by the changes brought by industrialization and immigration. Many of these writers have seen muckrakers as driven by a morality of absolutes that appeared threatened by the nation's new concentration of wealth and the rise of corrupt political machines that mismanaged many of its cities.

The diversity of views on who the muckrakers were and what they achieved reflects the variety of individuals drawn to journalism during America's Progressive period. The first two decades of the twentieth century would see the creation of organizations dedicated to the professionalization of journalism. A journalist's training and associations became informed by codes of conduct that emphasized the high calling of the profession, its constitutional obligations, its social responsibility, and its potential role in helping to create a civil society that encouraged the self-actualization of all its citizens. As their investigative reporting filled the pages of popular magazines and leading newspapers of the period it operated on the sunny optimism that readers were fundamentally rational and that when given the news they needed to know they would make the political decisions necessary that encouraged the creation of a more just society.

Muckrakers often used common story-telling strategies in trying to achieve their purposes. They had a fundamental faith in facts that could be mounted to expose hidden situations that created victims. Muckrakers worked to incite a response in behalf of those victims by identifying those responsible. Proposed remedies were often related to the creation of a good society based on communal responsibility. The Progressive impulse widely shared among muckrakers was that journalism placed a central role in making self-government possible. Their achievements in corporate, regulatory and electoral reform would be a source of inspiration and controversy for generations of journalists and journalism educators who followed them.

Early Muckraking

Lincoln Steffens, Ray Stannard Baker, and Mark Sullivan were among those claiming to be the first muckrakers, but Ida Tarbell's work on the Standard Oil trust for *McClure's Magazine* preceded theirs, even though she considered herself more an historian than a muckraker. Muckraking pieces had appeared in local newspapers across the country in the late nineteenth century, many of them taking on the morally earnest manner of Nellie Bly's 1887 undercover expose of Blackwell Island's insane asylum for women in the pages of Joseph Pulitzer's *New York World* or the bleak intensity of photojournalist Jacob Riis's depiction of ghetto life in 1890 New York. The rise of the ten- and fifteen-cent, mass marketed magazines coincided with the maturing of a democratic marketplace in which newly literate, often immigrant, urban readers, and an emerging white collar professional class sought stories explaining the new America then coming into view. Circulation extended to once rural America that was now within reach of national advertisers who saw in muckraking magazines a means of expanding their market.

The Arena, founded in 1889, was a forerunner of what was to come. *Forum* and *Outlook* ran investigative pieces probing the emerging social and political environment. *McClure's Magazine*, first introduced at the height of a financial panic in June 1893, initially struggled to win circulation. Tarbell's skillfully written series on Abraham Lincoln, often drawn from original sources, pushed readership to three hundred thousand by the end of 1895. Those numbers were not sustained until the aftermath of *McClure's* January 1903 edition that famously featured Tarbell's third installment on corrupt practices of the Standard Oil trust, Lincoln Steffens depiction of urban venality in "The Shame of Minneapolis," and "The Right to Work," Ray Stannard Baker's harrowing account of union violence in the anthracite coal fields of Eastern Pennsylvania. In an unusual editorial introducing the articles, S.S. McClure wrote, "Capitalists, workingmen, politicians, citizens—all breaking the law, or letting it be broken" (*McClure's Magazine*, January 1903, 336). This would be the clarion call for the many muckrakers who followed, each urging their readers to redress grievances in behalf of society's most vulnerable citizens.

Tarbell's nineteen-part series on the Standard Oil trust led to a criminal investigation of the company and its court-ordered break up. Steffens series on urban corruption would take him to St. Louis, Chicago, New York, Philadelphia, and Pittsburgh and built nationwide public opinion for municipal

reform. Baker's muckraking of labor and business alliances that gouged consumers led to exposés on the beef trust and the fruit industry. His examination of illegal railway rebates would lead to passage of the Hepburn Act that enabled the Interstate Commerce Commission to oversee rail rates. Tarbell, Steffens, and Baker along with *McClure's* editor John S. Phillips bought a controlling interest in the *American Magazine* in 1906 to further their muckraking agenda. Baker published a series of articles indicting mob violence while appealing to the social conscience of his readers to end the scourge of racism in America.

By mid-decade muckraking had established itself with a growing circle of magazines dedicated to financing a journalism of exposure. *Collier's, Cosmopolitan, Everybody's, Hampton's, Pearson's,* and *Success* were regularly producing pieces devoted to detective work designed to uncover hidden abuses in public life and to mobilize public opinion to win legislative remedies. The enthusiasm spread to *Atlantic Monthly, Ladies Home Journal,* and other high priced publications that previously had prided themselves on editorial content designed to attract the more cultivated classes. Walter Lippmann has observed that the muckraking movement was propelled by "real causes of dissatisfaction" that had been produced by America's rapid industrialization (*Drift and Mastery*, 5). Baker believed that journalism was creating "an awakening sympathy for the world's down-trodden and oppressed" (*American Chronicle*, 92).

Mature Muckraking

Outstanding examples of mature muckraking and its legislative consequences include the six-part exposé on the patent medicine industry that Samuel Hopkins Adams wrote for *Collier's*, beginning on October 7, 1905, and Upton Sinclair's scathing summary of conditions in Chicago's stockyards, written in the same year for the weekly socialist newspaper, *Appeal to Reason*. Adams launched a five-month investigation that carefully chronicled the health effects posed by patent medicines and the complicity of the newspaper and advertising industries in pushing more than 250 products that were more dangerous than the diseases they purported to cure. Sinclair's seven-week undercover investigation of Chicago's meatpacking industry described appalling working conditions where meat was stored in great rooms of "dirt and sawdust" and "dried rat dung" (*The Jungle*, 161–162). The scandals created by these series forced Congress to pass the Pure Food and Drug Act in 1906 making the federal government more responsible for the health and safety of its citizens.

George Kibbe Turner was one of the Progressive Era's most effective muckrakers. *McClure's* reprinted twelve million copies of his October 1906 account of Galveston's recovery from a killer hurricane that had destroyed half the Texas town. The publicity promoted a decade-long debate in which three hundred cities experimented in non-partisan commission forms of government. Turner's April 1907 article for *McClure's* uncovered a citywide conspiracy in Chicago that netted liquor, prostitution and gambling interests \$135 million annually. Turner's reporting led to the creation of a vice commission to clean up the city, a pattern repeated in communities across America. His 1909 attack on the white slave trade that preyed upon New York's tenement population led to a grand jury investigation of Tammany Hall and Congressional passage of the Mann Act on June 25, 1910, that prohibited the transport of women across state lines for immoral purposes. Forty-five states soon passed laws punishing third-party profits from procurement and prostitution.

The muckraking career of Charles Edward Russell was similarly successful. He took on the beef trust with a series of articles in 1904 for *Everybody's*. Over the next decade he would write for *Cosmopolitan*, *Hampton's* and *Pearson's*, his targets including slum landlords, election graft, railroad fraud and race relations. His examination of prisoner abuse within the Georgia penal system for *Everybody's* in June 1908 led to a special session of the state legislature. Later that year, his attacks on Trinity Church in New York forced one of the nation's wealthiest and most visible churches to clean up its tenements and stop preying upon the poor. Muckrakers widely shared Russell's conviction that their work required the gathering of evidence, the marshaling of facts and the "discovery of innumerable and indispensable details" that proved one's case (*Lawless Wealth*, 285–287).

Muckrakers were drawn to defend the most vulnerable members of society from the most powerful. This was particularly true of their opposition to child labor, a scourge that saw by 1900 more than 1.7 million children under fourteen years of age laboring in factories, mines, mills, and urban sweatshops across the nation. Edwin Markham's powerful indictment of this predatory practice first appeared in *Cosmopolitan* in September 1906. Investigative pieces by John Spargo, Robert Hunter, Marie Van Vorst, and William Hard followed, telling the stories of scores of children subjected to maiming and pneumonia for a 22-cent daily wage. Outraged public opinion passed legislation banning child labor in two-thirds of all states by 1906. A federal ban followed in 1916. Joined by Mary Alden Hopkins and Rheta Childe Dorr, muckrakers were able to extend labor protection to men and women as well. Pieces on plant safety and working conditions, appearing in *Hampton's* and *Everybody's*, led forty states to adopt Workmen's Compensation laws by 1917, an increase of twenty-seven states in just five years. Their cause was magnified by Abraham Cahan's heart wrenching reports in the pages of the *Jewish Daily Forward* of 146 ghetto residents killed in the Triangle Factory fire on March 25, 1911.

Muckraking's Legacy

Not every muckraker felicitously followed Russell's admonition to "never give credence to any claim without complete investigation" (*Lawless Wealth*, 286). William Randolph Hearst used David Graham Phillips nine-part series on the U.S. Senate to charge his political opponents with "treason" ("The Treason of the Senate," *Cosmopolitan*, March 1906, 187–190), opening muckrakers to criticism they were not

taking their social responsibility seriously. Their lasting legacy, however, according to Will Irwin, a contemporary who muckraked the muckrakers, far exceeded their shortcomings. It was highlighted by Thomas Lawson's meticulous work on the stock market and insurance industries; William English Walling's muckraking reports on racial prejudice; and C.P. Connolly's warning against those who put private interest before the public good. When Frank Norris wrote of life in the mines and Louis Brandeis muckraked insurance fraud they were following the muckraking article of faith that an enlightened understanding of social injustice would lead to a just society. Ernest Crosby's thoughtful probing of machine politics asked readers and regulators to do their parts in reforming abuse of power. Georgine Milmine and Judson Welliver's exposure of the growing materialism of religious institutions and Louis Eberle and Henry Beach Needham's attacks on special interests helped civic reformers to win changes in the law. According to William Kittle, journalism now was big business and muckrakers would hold it responsible to police special interests, including itself, "to better serve the public good" ("The Making of Public Opinion," *Arena*, July 1909, 33–35).

A movement championed by America's most widely read popular magazines spread to newsrooms large and small across the country. In Osceola, Wisconsin, a small town editor sided with a local farmer in his fight against the extractive policies of Weyerhauser. The land belonged to the people, Alfred Roese argued, and not the corporations, and it was the job of journalism to make sure that the people's rights were ensured. The nation's pre-eminent small town editor, William Allen White, called this Progressive impulse muckraking's greatest achievement because it sought "to lift men and women to higher things, to a more abundant life" by "widening the public sense of evil-doing." This was critical because "cruelty becomes intolerable" as citizens "become aware that it exists" (*The Old Order Changeth* 1910, 17–31).

Muckraking receded as a public preoccupation when the nation prepared for war and in the Jazz Age that followed. The confidence that journalism serves the public interest by giving citizens the news they need to know faded in the years after Watergate as journalism became corporatized and seemed to be always seeking stories on celebrity and scandal. From Enron to Firestone, however, modern journalists who assiduously uncover the facts to expose the hidden situation, carefully chronicling victims and victimizers, appropriate the strategies their muckraking forerunners once used with relentless energy in working to make America a more civil space where all individuals were really free to realize their full potential.

Further Reading

Baker, Ray Stannard. *American Chronicle: The Autobiography of Ray Stannard Baker*. New York: Charles Scribner's Sons, 1945.

Evensen, Bruce J.."The Evangelical Origins of the Muckrakers." *American Journalism* 6, 1989.

——. "The Media and Reform, 1900–1917." In *The Age of Mass Communication*, edited by Wm. David Sloan. Northport, AL: Vision Press, 1998.

——. "Progressivism, Muckraking and Objectivity." In *Fair & Balanced: A History of Journalistic Objectivity*, edited by Steven R. Knowlton, and Karen L. Freeman. Northport, AL: Vision Press, 2005.

Filler, Louis *Progressivism and Muckraking*, New York: R.R. Bowker, 1976.

Fitzpatrick, Ellen F., ed. *Muckraking: Three Landmark Articles*. Boston: Bedford Books, 1994.

Harrison, John M., and Harry H. Stein, eds. *Muckraking*. University Park: Pennsylvania State University Press, 1973.

Lippmann, Walter. *Drift and Mastery: An Attempt to Diagnose the Current Unrest*. New York: Mitchell Kennerley, 1914.

Miraldi, Robert, ed. *The Muckrakers: Evangelical Crusaders*. Westport, CT: Greenwood Press, 2000.

——. *Muckraking and Objectivity: Journalism's Colliding Traditions*. New York: Greenwood Press, 1990.

Russell, Charles Edward. *Lawless Wealth*. New York: B.W. Dodge & Co., 1912.

Sinclair, Upton. *The Jungle*. New York: Doubleday, Page, 1906.

Stein, Harry H. "American Muckrakers and Muckraking: The 50-Year Scholarship." *Journalism Quarterly* 56, 1979.

——. "American Muckraking of Technology Since 1900." *Journalism Quarterly* 67, 1990.

Swados, Harvey. *Years of Conscience: The Muckrakers*. Cleveland: World Publishing, 1962.

Weinberg, Arthur, and Lila Weinberg, eds. *The Muckrakers*. New York: G.P. Putnam's Sons, 1964.

Wilson, Harold. *McClure's Magazine and the Muckrakers*. Princeton, NJ: Princeton University Press, 1970.

Winter, Ella, and Granville Hicks, eds. *The Letters of Lincoln Steffens*. New York: Harcourt, Brace, 1938.

BRUCE J. EVENSEN

MURDOCH, RUPERT

"I'm willing to ignore or take on conventional wisdom," Rupert Murdoch (March 11, 1931–), owner of News Corporation, told investors at their October 20, 2006, meeting. "We try to invest in new businesses, rather than overpaying for already established ones. We're patient as these efforts find new footing. We're always thinking about the next generation of new revenue sources." In fifty years that strategy had taken Murdoch from ownership of the *Adelaide* (Australia) *News* to a media empire of more than eight hundred businesses in more than fifty countries with assets in the range of $55 billion. Murdoch's holdings included Fox News, America's most watched cable news network, and the *New York Post*, its fifth most widely read newspaper. On April 13, 2005, Murdoch told the nation's newspaper editors that like many he had "grown up in a highly centralized world where news and information were tightly controlled by a few editors," and late in life "as a digital immigrant" he saw the revolution in "how people get information, where they get it, and who they get it from" as the most significant change in human history over the past several hundred years.

Keith Rupert Murdoch was born in Melbourne, Australia, to Sir Keith Murdoch, a celebrated World War I correspondent who became chief executive of *The Herald* and *Weekly Times*, based in Melbourne, and Dame Elisabeth Joy Greene Murdoch, who remained into her nineties a strong influence on her famous son. Murdoch studied economics and political science and sold advertising for a student newspaper at Oxford University in England, prior to his father's death in 1952. He learned Britain's newspaper business by working as an editor on Lord Beaverbrook's London *Daily Express*. Returning to Australia in 1954, Murdoch expanded the family's newspaper holdings two years later when he spent $400,000 to purchase a Sunday newspaper in *Perth*. In 1960 he spent $4 million to acquire the Sydney *Daily* and *Sunday Mirror*, converting the tired tabloid into Australia's widest selling newspaper. "Competition was so fierce," ace reporter Steve Dunleavy remembers, reporters would do anything to get a story." So did headline writers. "Tennis star shocks priest," *Mirror* readers were promised. "Banned sex books," were "free for some." A prowler reportedly insisted on "stripping women naked." A Sydney schoolgirl, the *Mirror* revealed, kept "an orgy diary."

For the serious-minded, Murdoch created Australia's first national newspaper, *The Australian*, launched in Canberra on July 14, 1964. Three years later, his newspaper, magazine, and television holdings were worth an estimated $50 million. Murdoch used that money in 1969 to make a big splash in British publishing, buying *News of the World* with its six million mainly working class readers and acquiring *The Sun*, a $5-million-a-year tabloid loser, which would go on to earn one million pounds weekly for Murdoch's News Corporation. Murdoch's formula for depicting bare-breasted babes called "sunbirds," great train robbers, doped horses, and violated victims made him the scourge of Fleet Street. He was called "the Dirty Digger" for "vandalizing" the British press. His censure by the Press Council made for good publicity and further stimulated sales. *The Sun*'s circulation soared from eight hundred thousand to two million in a year and to four million in seven years, eclipsing the *Daily Mirror* as Britain's leading tabloid. In late 1970, Murdoch became part owner of London Weekend Television.

Murdoch's first acquisition in the United States was his $19.7 million purchase of the *San Antonio Express-News* in 1973. He successfully competed with the Hearst paper in town by tall tale telling that had worked well elsewhere. Readers were warned that "armies of insects were marching on San Antonio" and that police had recovered a "handless body." Shock and sentiment became a Murdoch staple. There was the story of "an uncle who tortures pets with hot forks" and the army's decision "to poison 350 puppies." Murdoch took this formula on a national stage later that year by introducing the super market *Star* to compete with the *National Enquirer*. Murdoch's "American Women's Weekly" parlayed stories on the sex lives of the rich and famous with a pinch or two of Hollywood gossip into a circulation of four million by 1980. Murdoch charged critics with "elitism."

On November 20, 1976, Murdoch paid $30 million to acquire the *New York Post*, America's oldest daily newspaper that had been begun 175 years before by Alexander Hamilton. Under Dorothy Schiff the paper had achieved standing in the liberal community for its support of the trade union movement and social welfare programs and its early opposition to Joseph McCarthy. Schiff's columnists included Eleanor Roosevelt, Drew Pearson, Eric Severaid, and Max Lerner, and they had helped push the paper's circulation to half a million until New York's print union strikes made the paper a money loser. Under Murdoch, *Post* stories were short and headlines loud. A July 1977 power blackout became "twenty-four hours of terror" leading to "a city ravaged." When competing *Daily News* columnist Jimmy Breslin began corresponding with the "Son of Sam" who was sought by police for several shootings, Murdoch had *Star* reporter Steve Dunleavy get in on the act. His "Open Letter to Son of Sam" was a personal appeal asking the killer to surrender to the *Post*. Every day Murdoch insisted on a new angle—the Mafia had ordered Son of Sam's contract killing; "no one" was "safe from Son of Sam"; Son of Sam would strike on the anniversary of his first killing; a "gunman sparked a Son of Sam chase," even when the gunman wasn't Son of Sam. The *Post*'s single word headline *"Caught!"* following the arrest of David Berkowitz by New York City police on August 10, 1977, pushed the *Post*'s circulation to more than one million.

Critics charged Murdoch and the *Post* fed working-class readers "sex, scandal, and sensation" with a twist of "upscale gossip." The paper's executive editor, Steven Cuozzo, claimed Murdoch's "common touch" had "broken the elite media's stranglehold on the national agenda." The *Post*'s irreverent humor was a hit with its readers. Characteristic was the famous April 15, 1983, headline "Headless Body in Topless Bar." By November 1, 2006, the *Post*'s 704,011 circulation had overtaken the *New York Daily News* and *Washington Post* and brought the paper even with the *Los Angeles Times* for fifth in the nation. At a time of declining circulation in the newspaper industry, Murdoch's *New York Post* was only one of three newspapers in the nation's top twenty-five dailies to post a circulation increase.

Murdoch's "pyramiding of power" won him control of the *Village Voice* in 1977 and *The Times* of London in 1981. Soon, the *Boston Herald* and the *Chicago Sun-Times* were added to Murdoch's growing portfolio. In 1985 Murdoch became a naturalized U.S. citizen to satisfy legal requirements that only American citizens could own television stations in the country. He purchased the Twentieth Century Fox film studio, merged it with Metromedia television stations, and created Fox Broadcasting. Murdoch's British-based satellite network Sky Television merged with British Satellite Broadcasting in 1990, pushing Murdoch's assets by 1991 to $24 billion. On October 7, 1996, Murdoch's Fox News Channel was ready for launch, guided by former Republican Party consultant Roger Ailes. The network's handling of the Clinton impeachment solidified its appeal to conservative viewers. Its war reporting in the aftermath of the September 11, 2001, terrorist attacks helped to make it the nation's most watched cable news network, much to the irritation of Ted Turner and the Cable News Network. Liberal critics charged Fox was "blatantly biased." Murdoch claimed Fox's large audience appreciated "its independence." By the beginning of 2007, thirteen of the fourteen highest rated programs in cable news were on Fox News.

Murdoch had six children from three marriages and by 2006, they had begun to position themselves to have a stake in Murdoch's estimated $55 billion media empire. Increasingly that empire was digital. Seventy million Americans had visited a social networking site by July 2005, when Murdoch's News Corporation paid $580 million for MySpace.com. It had been started two years before for the teen and twenty-something crowd. Within a year, MySpace was receiving fifty million visitors monthly and was responsible for an extraordinary four and a half percent of all American Internet visits. News and information, Murdoch believed, had irrevocably become interactive "for the computer proficient and the self-empowered." Technology in the new media environment, he was convinced, was "liberating us from old constraints, lowering key costs, easing our access to new customers and markets, and multiplying the choices we can offer."

Further Reading

Chenoweth, Neil. *Virtual Murdoch: Reality Wars on the Information Highway.* London: Secker & Warburg, 2001.

Cuozzo, Steven. *It's Alice!: How America's Oldest Newspaper Cheated Death and Why It Matters.* New York: Times Books, 1996.

Kiernan, Thomas. *Citizen Murdoch.* New York: Dodd, Mead & Co., 1986.

Leapman, Michael. *Arrogant Aussie: The Rupert Murdoch Story.* Seacaucus, NJ: Lyle Stuart, 1985.

Page, Bruce. *The Murdoch Archipelago.* New York: Simon & Schuster, 2003.

Rohm, Wendy Goldman. *The Murdoch Mission: The Digital Transformation of a Media Empire.* New York: J. Wiley, 2001.

Shawcross, William. *Murdoch.* New York: Simon and Schuster, 1992.

BRUCE J. EVENSEN

MURRAY, JAMES

Jim Murray (December 29, 1919–August 16, 1998) was among the most widely acclaimed sports columnists of the second half of the twentieth century. From 1961 to 1998 he entertained readers of the *Los Angeles Times* with humor and a literary style that earned him a Pulitzer Prize and enshrinement in the Baseball Hall of Fame.

James Patrick Murray was born December 29, 1919, in Hartford, Connecticut. His grandparents raised him after his parents divorced. In the early 1940s Murray started as a general writer for the *Hartford Times* while attending Trinity College until his graduation in 1943. Murray wrote for the *New Haven Register* before moving west in 1944 and joining the *Los Angeles Examiner*. In 1945 he married Geraldine Norma Brown with whom he would have four children. After four years at the *Examiner* as a general writer, he became *Time* magazine's Hollywood correspondent. In 1953 *Time* editor Henry Luce asked Murray to help develop a sports magazine. *Sports Illustrated* debuted in August 1954 with Murray serving as the West Coast Editor. His six years at *SI* covering California sports catapulted Murray into a prime position at one of the nation's largest newspapers; in 1961 he became sports columnist for the *Los Angeles Times*.

Writing every day enabled Murray to display his talents. His staccato style accentuated his biting one-liners. His columns brimmed with metaphors and hyperbole, such as "Willie Mays' glove is where triples go to die." Some of Murray's best work was about his personal life. When he lost his left eye because of a detached retina in June 1975 he told his readers, "I lost an old friend the other day" (*LA Times*, July 1, 1979). He wrote about a woman that stole his heart. Murray describes the beautiful girl then reveals, "When I say she's a perfect '10', I mean she's 10-10-10...*I am her grandfather!*" (*LA Times,* December 28, 1980) His sense of humor is legendary, but he could write about emotional subjects as well. When his wife died in 1984 he wrote, "If there was a Hall of Fame for people, she would be No. 1. She was a champion at living" (*LA Times*, April 3, 1984).

Murray skewered social injustices. He railed against the Masters golf tournament for its segregationist policies. When an African American was allowed to play in 1975 Murray wrote, "They finally got around to the Emancipation Proclamation" (*LA Times*, April 10, 1975) Murray, however, refused to be an advocate. He believed in writing the truth instead of preaching to his readers. Murray maintained, "Satire is the best weapon in a writer's arsenal to attack injustice" (*Jim Murray*, 215).

Murray won America's Best Sportswriter a record fourteen times. He entered the National Sportscasters and Sportswriters Hall of Fame in 1977. He won the Red Smith Award for sports writing in 1982. He received the JG Taylor Spink Award for baseball writing and was inducted into the Baseball Hall of Fame in 1988. In 1990 Murray became only the second sports writer to win the Pulitzer Prize for commentary.

In 1996 Murray married his second wife, Linda McCoy-Murray. Murray died on August 16, 1998. As he grew older he penned many columns on aging, but, as Jim Murray wrote, "That's the nice thing about sports, you can be Peter Pan" (*Jim Murray*, 17).

Further Reading

Murray, Jim. *Jim Murray: An Autobiography*. Macmillan: New York, 1993.
——. *Jim Murray: The Last of the Best*. Los Angeles Times: Los Angeles, 1998.
——. *The Jim Murray Collection*. Taylor Publishing Company: Dallas, TX, 1988.
——. *Jim Murray: The Great Ones*. Los Angeles Times: Los Angeles, 1999.

JAMIE Q. TALLMAN

MURROW, EDWARD R. AND THE MCCARTHY ERA

Although Edward R. Murrow's challenge of Senator Joseph McCarthy on his March 9, 1954, *See It Now* broadcast has taken on mythic proportions, the program was not the first condemnation of McCarthy by a member of the news media. Murrow himself had challenged McCarthy on several previous occasions and numerous print journalists had been doing so since 1950. McCarthy enjoyed support from the conservative press, Republican politicians and much of the public, but at the time of Murrow's famous broadcast, McCarthy had begun to encounter criticism from previously supportive sources.

Murrow's broadcast was not undertaken without serious risk to Murrow's reputation and to CBS. Both were entangled in the era's red-baiting and blacklisting, giving them reason to fear reprisal from program sponsors and Congress. What made the March 9 program remarkable was its departure from the day's typically cautious news programming.

The Press and McCarthy

McCarthy was not the first U.S. politician to exploit the nation's Cold War-era fear of Communism; but he was a media demagogue from the beginning. Critics argue that the McCarthy-era press contributed to McCarthy's success by publicizing his accusations without reporting on the veracity of his charges. Fear of offending officials and readers coupled with a lack of recognition of the meaning and significance of McCarthy's campaign led to the failure of the press to provide readers with complete information.

McCarthy had powerful allies in the media and he also used his understanding of the press to his advantage. He held morning press conferences to announce afternoon press conferences in which he promised to reveal startling new information thus grabbing the afternoon headlines without providing any actual information. Often the afternoon press conferences would never take place. He timed other announcements for evening deadlines of morning publications leaving little time for reporters to investigate his charges. Because McCarthy was a U.S. senator, newspapers generally categorized his announcements as news and reported what he said without verifying or interpreting the information for their readers. Most newspapers failed to use their editorial pages to take a position on the senator or his methods. The influential Hearst chain and Colonel Robert McCormick's *Chicago Tribune* and *Washington Times-Herald* were champions of anti-Communist efforts and supported McCarthy's contributions to that cause.

A small but prominent set of newspapers and columnists did voice strong opinions about the senator's campaign from the beginning. Among the senator's critics were the *Milwaukee Journal*, the *Capital Times* of Madison (Wis.), the *Washington Post*, and the *Christian Science Monitor*. Such columnists as Drew Pearson, Joseph Alsop and Stewart Alsop, and radio commentator Elmer Davis were among McCarthy's critics. Murrow, too, was an early opponent.

Murrow and CBS: World War II to McCarthyism

In 1950, Murrow was among the nation's most dominant broadcast newsmen. Hired by CBS News in 1935, Murrow headed to London in 1937 to establish the network's radio news operations in Europe. Sensing the coming political and military crises emanating from Nazi Germany, he hired former wire service reporter William Shirer and gradually recruited a group of talented reporters, later dubbed "the Murrow boys." Murrow and his team helped transform radio news by moving it from the studio to on-the-spot reporting.

Murrow's reports from the rooftop of the Broadcasting House in London during the 1940 Battle of Britain earned him acclaim from the public and from his journalism peers. He combined rich descriptions of his observations with live "sounds of war" to place his audience at the scene. The Overseas Press Club honored his work as the best foreign radio news reporting of 1940 and when he returned to New York in December 1941, leading political and media figures lavished praise on him at an elaborate banquet CBS threw for its star reporter. Later reports on combat missions he flew over Berlin with the Royal Air Force and the liberation of Buchenwald cemented his reputation as a reporter who took news seriously and delivered it to his listeners in detailed and descriptive fashion.

After a postwar stint in CBS management, Murrow returned to broadcasting in September 1947 with "Edward R. Murrow and the News," a weekday evening radio report that would run for twelve years. He had a reputation for keeping his political views out of his reporting and committed himself to providing his audience with the facts and allowing them to form their own opinions. Yet he did not hesitate to offer commentary and interpretation. He held individual civil liberties in high regard and saw a clear distinction between proper government investigation and the excesses of McCarthyism. About the 1947 investigations of the House Committee on Un-American Activities, for example, Murrow said Congressional committees typically restricted themselves to what people did "rather than what individuals think." In 1950, he pointed out that McCarthy had yet to produce any evidence against those he accused.

Privately Murrow was a committed anti-Communist. Yet neither he nor CBS escaped the red-baiting and blacklisting of the day unscathed. Nervous about his commentary on McCarthyism, Campbell Soup dropped its sponsorship of his radio report during the summer of 1950. Also that summer, a group of former FBI agents published *Red Channels*, a compilation of alleged Communist Party members or sympathizers working in the media. It listed six current CBS employees, including one of the Murrow boys, making the network fearful of dropped sponsorships and new

regulations and timid in its programming and hiring decisions. By the end of that year, CBS circulated an in-house loyalty oath in an effort to guard against additional allegations. Murrow, a member of the CBS board of directors, reportedly expressed concerns in private, but publicly did not protest.

See It Now debuted in November 1951. A collaboration between Murrow and Fred Friendly, a producer Murrow first worked with in 1947, the program distinguished itself by examining issues in-depth and offering a point of view. For the most part it steered clear of McCarthyism and other controversial issues. In December 1951, Murrow contrasted McCarthy's complaint about a smear campaign directed against the senator with footage of earlier accusations leveled by McCarthy. Murrow closed the program by commenting that the senator's perception appeared to depend on who was being attacked. McCarthy was still on the ascent at that time, however, and Murrow's commentary did not generate the notice his later attack would.

"A Report on Senator Joseph R. McCarthy"

In late 1953, *See It Now* began to adopt a more aggressive documentary flavor. In October, "The Case of Lt. Milo Radulovich" aired; the first of two thinly disguised challenges to McCarthy. Radulovich was judged a security risk and asked to resign from the Air Force Reserves because his father and sister were accused of having Communist sympathies. When Radulovich refused, an Air Force board ordered his separation from the service. The program, featuring interviews with Radulovich, his father and sister and citizens of his hometown, came across as an editorial defense of the lieutenant. Murrow ended with a personal appeal: "And it seems to us that—that is, to Fred Friendly and myself—that this is a subject that should be argued about endlessly." The Air Force declined to comment on air. A few weeks later, however, it reversed its decision regarding Radulovich.

Following the Radulovich program, McCarthy's investigative team revived the reporter's involvement twenty years earlier with a summer seminar for Americans in Moscow. Murrow responded with the story of a showdown in Indianapolis between the American Legion and a group of people who planned to start a chapter of the American Civil Liberties Union, interweaving footage of the Legion protest with the ACLU's meeting in a Catholic church. Neither the Radulovich nor Indianapolis stories mentioned McCarthy's name, but Murrow's message was clear: The excesses of McCarthyism were stripping individuals of their rights as American citizens.

The political tide began turning against McCarthy in early 1954 during his investigation of the Army, especially following his attack on Ralph Zwicker, a decorated general. McCarthy's Senate colleagues stepped up their criticism and much of the conservative press turned its back on him. In his radio report on the Zwicker hearing, Murrow grew bolder in his criticism of McCarthy and was ready to challenge him on television. McCarthy still enjoyed significant support, but Murrow and Friendly believed he had become vulnerable.

Murrow and Friendly approached the McCarthy program cautiously, deciding to tell the story using McCarthy's own words and waiting until a strategic time arrived to move forward with it. Murrow's reputation as a straightforward reporter helped insulate him, as did the popularity of *Person to Person*, a weekly celebrity interview program he launched in October 1953. Yet to challenge a U.S. senator openly on television seemed a risky proposition.

Murrow opened the March 9 broadcast by briefly noting its controversial content and offering McCarthy the opportunity to respond in kind. The program then launched into clips of McCarthy on the attack. These clips alternated with shots of Murrow seated in the studio reading from a script—pointing out contradictions and correcting the senator's errors. Murrow abandoned any pretense of objectivity; helping to account for the program's impact. In his closing comments, Murrow condemned McCarthy for repeatedly abusing his investigatory powers and called on Americans to take responsibility for protecting the nation's tradition of freedom. He concluded with these now-famous words: "The actions of the junior Senator from Wisconsin have caused alarm and dismay amongst our allies abroad, and given considerable comfort to our enemies. And whose fault is that? Not really his. He didn't create this situation of fear; he merely exploited it—and rather successfully. Cassius was right. 'The fault, dear Brutus, is not in our stars, but in ourselves.'"

Still fearful of antagonizing sponsors and Congress, CBS had not advertised the program but did not interfere with its production. Many network affiliates did not air it. A small audience of approximately 2.4 million households tuned in. Among those who did watch, reaction tilted heavily in Murrow's favor. CBS and its affiliates logged thousands of calls and letters between the show's conclusion and the end of the month—the large majority supportive of Murrow. The following week's *See It Now* continued the anti-McCarthy theme with its coverage of Annie Lee Moss's appearance before the McCarthy committee. Murrow added little editorial commentary but the lack of clear evidence presented during the hearing made Murrow's point.

McCarthy's response on the April 6 *See It Now* was a poor though professionally produced performance. He devoted little time to refuting the March 9 program, spending most of the program reviewing the spread of Communism and painting Murrow as a Communist sympathizer. He called Murrow "a symbol, the leader, and the cleverest of the jackal pack which is always found at the throat of anyone who dares to expose individual Communists and traitors."

Despite the positive reaction to the March 9 broadcast, CBS executives grew nervous given a subsequent grassroots campaign building on McCarthy's response and the propensity of *See It Now* to continue tackling controversial issues. CBS President William Paley eventually moved *See It Now* to a different time slot and reduced the number of annual broadcasts. It was cancelled in 1958.

Murrow's presence at CBS became increasingly tense and uncomfortable—for network executives and for Murrow. Murrow continued his radio program until 1959 and in 1960 joined *CBS Reports*, a news program produced by Friendly. Until the end, Murrow pushed television toward advocacy journalism. One of the last programs he was involved in was "Harvest of Shame," a powerful documentary on the treatment of migrant workers for which he provided impassioned editorial commentary. Murrow parted with CBS in 1961 and took the top job at the United States Information Agency. He died in 1965.

Further Reading

Baughman, James L. *Same Time, Same Station: Creating American Television, 1948–60*. Baltimore: Johns Hopkins University Press, 2007.

Bliss, Edward, Jr., ed. *In Search of Light: The Broadcasts of Edward R. Murrow, 1938–1961*. New York: Alfred A. Knopf, 1967.

Doherty, Thomas. *Cold War, Cool Medium: Television, McCarthyism, and American Culture*. New York: Columbia University Press, 2003.

Fried, Richard M. *Nightmare in Red: The McCarthy Era in Perspective*. New York: Oxford University Press, 1990.

Merron, Jeff. "Murrow on TV: *See It* Now, *Person to* Person, and the Making of a 'Masscult Personality'." *Journalism Monographs*, no. 106, July 1988.

Oshinsky, David M. *A Conspiracy So Immense: The World of Joe McCarthy*. Oxford and New York: Oxford University Press, 2005.

Persico, Joseph E. *Edward R. Murow: An American Original*. New York: McGraw-Hill Publishing Company, 1988.

JULIE B. LANE

NATION, THE

The first issue of *The Nation* appeared on July 6, 1865, the debut of a small-circulation opinion magazine that would promote progressive politics and provide a steady stream of significant criticism on literature and arts for more than 140 years. Its founding rooted in the successful abolitionist movement, the magazine quickly moved beyond its original intent to focus on reconstruction issues to report and comment on a wide range of social and political topics.

The magazine's considerable influence through the years derived not from a large, diverse circulation, but instead from who was writing it, reading it, and quoting it—prominent intellectuals and politicians of each new generation. Each week, the magazine, published on newsprint with few illustrations, offered commentary on the important issues of the day and extensive reviews of books, art, music, and science.

The idea for the magazine came from Frederick Law Olmsted, America's most prominent landscape architect at the time, who took his idea for an intellectual weekly to journalist Edwin Lawrence Godkin, then editor of the *New York Evening Post*. When Olmsted became distracted by professional responsibilities, Godkin pushed forward, attracting the necessary financial backing. Forty investors led by a Philadelphia minister, James Miller McKim, and George L. Stearns and Charles Eliot Norton, both of Boston, founded the company that would publish the magazine; Godkin became the founding editor. All had been prominent in the abolitionist movement before the Civil War. The first issue was a small quarto of thirty-six pages that provided a mix of editorials, commentary, poetry, book reviews, art criticism, and scientific essays.

Throughout its history, the magazine published North America's and Europe's luminaries in literature, academics, and the arts. The magazine carried articles and commentary by Sinclair Lewis, H.L. Mencken, Willa Cather, W.E.B. DuBois, Upton Sinclair, Lionel Trilling, James Thurber, Jean-Paul Sartre, Ralph Nader, Hunter S. Thompson, Martin Luther King Jr., James Baldwin, Carlos Fuentes, and Alice Walker, among many other well-known writers and intellectuals.

Nevertheless, the magazine struggled financially throughout its history and had a succession of owners. Circulation fluctuated tremendously, too, ultimately reaching 178,000 in 2005.

Godkin's Purchase

Political disputes among investors during the magazine's early years resulted in Godkin's purchase of the magazine, but financial strains ultimately led him to sell the publication to the *New York Evening Post* in 1881. For the next thirty-three years, *The Nation* was issued as a weekly edition of the *Post*, an arrangement that ended in 1918 because of political differences with the *Post*.

When the magazine merged with the *Post*, Godkin was succeeded in the editorship by his long-time assistant editor, Wendell Phillips Garrison, son of abolitionist journalist William Lloyd Garrison. Hammond Lamont, Paul Elmer More, and Harold deWolf Fuller, all Harvard graduates, successively edited the magazine until its break with the *Post*, when Oswald Garrison Villard, a noted Civil War journalist and grandson of William Lloyd Garrison, became editor. The U.S. Post Office briefly suspended the magazine from the mails in 1918 when Villard printed an article that accused U.S. labor unions of promoting war for their workers' benefit. Villard remained editor until 1933 and part-owner until 1935, when the magazine was sold to a Wall Street financier and philanthropist, Maurice Wertheim. Editorial management shifted to noted liberal journalists Freda Kirchwey, whose father was dean of the Columbia University Law School; conservationist Joseph Wood Krutch, and social critic Max Lerner. Two years later, Wertheim broke with his liberal editors over the Roosevelt administration and sold the magazine to Kirchwey.

Kirchwey's Leadership

In its early years under Godkin, *The Nation* took a progressive stand on racial issues, but adopted a conservative outlook on politics. The magazine consistently supported industry in its sometimes violent disputes with unions, attacked the feminist movement, and opposed socialism. Under its next distinguished editor and owner, Villard, the magazine's political views shifted to the left, showing enthusiastic support for President Roosevelt's New Deal during the Great Depression. Under Kirchwey, the magazine settled firmly within the liberal, progressive political camp. Throughout its history, the magazine had provided a strong voice for civil rights, and that voice was amplified under Kirchwey's editorship. In 1951, Kirchwey enticed Carey McWilliams, the magazine's West Coast editor and author of several muckraking books, to join the magazine's management. She named him editor in 1955, a position he held for twenty years.

During the 1950s, Kirchwey, McWilliams, and their staff faced the greatest challenge in the magazine's history because of its support for those persecuted during the nation's hysteria over Communism. Many subscribers abandoned the magazine because it was perceived as being pro-Communist. The magazine survived, like it had during previous periods of financial struggle, through donations from loyal readers. It re-emerged during the 1960s, under McWilliams's editorship, as a fierce voice for civil rights, feminism, and opposition to the Vietnam War. McWilliams periodically published lengthy muckraking pieces—exposés of the Federal Bureau of Investigation and Central Intelligence Agency, among others.

Several Publishers

After Kirchwey, the magazine went through several publishers. Kirchwey sold *The Nation* to George Kirstein, a former insurance executive, in 1955. After publishing the magazine for ten years, Kirsten sold it to James J. Storrow Jr., a Boston businessman for $150,000. In 1978, the magazine sold to a limited partnership headed by philanthropist Hamilton Fish, who became publisher, and Victor S. Navasky left *The New York Times Magazine* to become editor. New York businessman Arthur Carter invested in the magazine in 1985–1986, taking over as publisher. In 1994, Navasky became publisher after organizing a partnership to buy Carter's stake in the magazine, naming Katrina vanden Heuvel editor. Navasky put the magazine on firmer financial ground by attracting new readers, increasing circulation from twenty thousand to 178,000 by the time he turned over general management duties to vanden Heuvel in 2005. The magazine in 2006 was owned by The Nation Company, a limited partnership, which involved a number of investors, including vanden Heuvel, Navasky, Alan Sagner, Peter Norton, Frank Davis, and actors Paul Newman and Robert Redford.

Further Reading

Alpern, Sara. *Freda Kirchwey: A Woman of The Nation.* Cambridge, MA: Harvard University Press, 1987.

Horowitz, Irving Louis. "Shaping the Nation Magazine," *Sewanee Review* 113, no. 4 (2005): 648–654.

Navasky, Victor. *A Matter of Opinion.* New York: Farrar, Straus and Giroux, 2005.

——. *The Education of Carey McWilliams.* New York: Simon and Schuster, 1978.

Mott, Frank Luther. *A History of American Magazines: 1865–1885.* Cambridge, MA: Harvard University Press, 1938.

"The Century Just Past," *The Nation* 270, no. 2 (January 10/17, 2000): 3–4.

Vanden Heuvel, Katrina, ed. *The Nation, 1865/1990.* New York: Thunder's Mouth Press, 1990.

JAMES AUCOIN

NATIONAL ASSOCIATION OF BLACK JOURNALISTS

The National Association of Black Journalists (NABJ) became the largest organization of journalists of color during the late twentieth century. It emerged as a result the newsroom desegregation movement that started in reaction to the 1968 Kerner Commission report. As black journalists began to integrate white newsrooms, they found that they had to struggle against tokenism and advocate for more accurate and inclusive coverage of blacks in the press. Until the advent of NABJ, black journalists waged these struggles largely in isolation.

NABJ was formed on December 12, 1975, by forty-four journalism professionals meeting in Washington, D.C. Its founders included prominent Philadelphia journalists Chuck Stone of the *Philadelphia Daily News*, Acel Moore of the *Philadelphia Inquirer,* Joe Davidson and Claude Lewis of the *Philadelphia Bulletin* as well as DeWayne Wickham of the *Baltimore Sun*, Les Payne of *Newsday*, Marica Gillespe, editor of *Essence* magazine, and ABC News anchor Max Robinson. NABJ was an outgrowth of the Philly-based Association of Black Journalists (ABJ), whose constitution NABJ used to craft its own organizing document. Stone was elected as the organization's first president. In 1976 NABJ held its first convention in at Texas Southern University, the second of the nation's historically black colleges or universities with a school of communications, after Howard University, and the first in the western part of the United States.

NABJ's objectives included improving the ties between blacks working in white newsrooms and blacks working in the black press, sensitizing members of white media to the racism inherent it its coverage and hiring practices, increasing the white media's balanced reporting of blacks and the concerns of the black community, and increasing employment opportunities for black journalists in the mainstream media.

During the 1990s NABJ reached its apex in terms of influence, prestige, and membership numbers. Its members helped to shape coverage of some of that decade's biggest stories, including the Los Angeles riots and the trial of O. J. Simpson. The start of the twenty-first century found the organization still strong, with approximately 3,300 members, and the model for similar ethnic journalism organizations. However, its critics contended that the organization's successes in changing the way race was handled in news coverage made the organization complacent and unable to cope with what they believed was the more subtle institutionalized racism that was often reflected in newsrooms. Other critics argued that the organization's demand for more inclusive, nuanced coverage of racial issues was even a danger to journalism.

The significance of NABJ lay in the fact that it was an organization whose members confronted white media's treatment of blacks and newsroom practices that contradicted journalism's belief in impartiality and objectivity.

NABJ could claim victories in its struggle for more complex, comprehensive coverage of blacks; there were significant improvements in that area by the early twenty-first century when compared to what NABJ's forty-four founders saw at the organization's creation. The fact that a significant number of blacks became editors, producers, and managers was a testament to the organization's continued advocacy for the cause of newsrooms that reflected the nation's diversity.

Further Reading

Dawkins, Wayne. *Black Journalists: The NABJ Story.* Newport News, VA: August Press, 1997.

——. *Rugged Waters: Black Journalists Swim the Mainstream.* Newport News, VA: August Press, 2003.

Newkirk, Pamela. *Within the Veil: Black Journalists, White Media.* New York: University Press, 2000.

CALVIN L. HALL

NATIONAL INTELLIGENCER

From 1800 until 1828, the Jeffersonian Republicans dominated American politics. During that time, the *National Intelligencer* (1800–1864) functioned as the semiofficial newspaper of Democratic-Republican presidents from Thomas Jefferson to John Quincy Adams. At the request of President-elect Jefferson, Samuel Harrison Smith founded the tri-weekly *National Intelligencer* in the new capital of Washington, D. C. The first issue appeared on October 31, 1800, and the paper continued to be published until 1864. Smith broke new ground in news reporting by establishing ongoing detailed reports of the actions of Congress. By 1802, Smith had gained confirmed access to both the House and Senate. Both Federalist and Republican newspapers reprinted his reports. By the time Smith retired in 1810, most press outlets in the country published the *Intelligencer* reports of the doings of the national legislature on a regular basis.

Smith was succeeded at the helm of the *National Intelligencer* by Joseph Gales, Jr., and his brother-in-law William Winston Seaton. These two editors continued the effort to give complete and accurate reports of the debates of Congress. Gales covered the work of the House while Seaton reported on the activities of the Senate. From 1812 until 1829, they held the exclusive right to report the debates in Congress and published the only lengthy records of the actions of the national legislature. During the presidencies of James Madison and James Monroe, the *National Intelligencer* continued to be the primary source of information about the national government and newspaper editors throughout the country depended on it for news from Washington, D. C.

During the War of 1812, Gales and Seaton tried to provide detailed reporting as best they could. When the British threatened an invasion of the Chesapeake Bay area in 1813, both volunteered for service in the militia. They took turns on active duty so that one of them could continue to publish the newspaper. They even began publishing the paper on a daily basis. Although smaller in size and content, the *National Intelligencer* did not miss an issue in 1813. When the British finally attacked in 1814, the entire staff of the newspaper turned out for military service. The paper suspended publication for a short time, but resumed in a much smaller size on August 31, 1814. While burning Washington, the British destroyed all the records and much of the equipment of the newspaper office. Because of this loss, the paper appeared irregularly for several weeks. Nearly a month passed before Gales and Seaton restored their paper to its regular appearance and publication schedule. The *National Intelligencer* once more appeared in its normal size and format on September 26. From that point until the 1864, the *Intelligencer* continued its coverage of politics in the nation's capital.

Following the War of 1812, the *National Intelligencer* continued to speak for the Republican administration until the 1820s when the Republicans split into the Democrats and the Whigs. Gales and Seaton sided with the Whigs and afterward their political influence declined as evidenced in 1829 when they lost their government printing contract. They had supplemented their income by printing official government documents for the Senate from 1819 to 1826 and for the House from 1819 to 1829. Although Gales and Seaton continued to publish the *National Intelligencer* until the 1860s, the paper never regained its position of dominance.

Further Reading

Ames, William E. *A History of the National Intelligencer.* Chapel Hill, University of North Carolina Press, 1972.

CAROL SUE HUMPHREY

NATIONAL OBSERVER

A stepchild of the *Wall Street Journal*, the *National Observer* (1962–1977) began its somewhat brief life in February 1962 for pragmatic and idealistic reasons: because the printing presses at regional facilities that produced the weekday *Wall Street Journal* sat idle two days a week; and because Bernard Kilgore, president of the newspaper's parent company Dow Jones, believed that a weekly national newspaper would attract a sizable readership.

The original mandate from Kilgore to *National Observer* editors was to identify the most important news of the week, review relevant articles in newspapers and magazines, then write original articles that would explain the significance of pertinent actions and events. Editors recruited writers whose style would make the *National Observer* more interesting and readable than local newspapers.

Soon, however, the *National Observer* generated its own ideas for articles on important subjects and interesting people. Correspondents monitored the news, decided which subjects to develop, and conducted their own interviews and research for original stories. In some ways, the weekly newspaper was similar to a newsmagazine in its approach to focusing on major events and issues, except that its broadsheet format allowed longer stories and bigger illustrations.

There was plenty of news for the *National Observer* to cover from the 1960s into the 1970s: civil rights activism, environmental concerns, feminism, racial tensions, urban decay, the Vietnam War, Watergate scandal, and youth culture. *National Observer* correspondents traveled around the nation, Asia, and Europe to develop stories.

Articles paid special attention to cultural and social changes rippling through American society. *National Observer* coverage anticipated the ultimate significance of certain changes in family life, schools, and popular culture. Many articles focused on ordinary people whose lives were, or would be, affected by conflict and controversy. *National Observer* correspondents described rural towns, inner-city neighborhoods, college campuses, and workplaces.

The weekly newspaper also offered well-written feature articles on people and places. Its descriptive, lively features were on the front page, inside pages, and often on the back of the single-section publication, where text and illustrations might occupy most of the page. Color was added in 1975 to make the newspaper more appealing.

Readers responded to the *National Observer*. Circulation reached 230,000 copies during 1963, about 90 percent went by mail to subscribers and the other to newsstand buyers. At its peak in 1975, *National Observer* distributed 512,000 copies a week, short of its goal of 700,000 copies. Its usual circulation was 430,000 to 460,000 copies.

Advertisers did not find the *National Observer* a good buy, because its readership was much smaller than any of the three weekly newsmagazines and its demographics for age and income were similar to the newsmagazines, thus making it inefficient to advertise. *National Observer* ceased publication in July 1977, having lost an estimated sixteen million dollars during its fifteen years.

The newspaper was a Pulitzer Prize finalist in 1967 for civil rights coverage, and it won a Pulitzer Prize in 1974 for commentary on public affairs.

JAMES LANDERS

NATIONAL POLICE GAZETTE

Journalist George Wilkes and attorney Enoch Camp patterned the *National Police Gazette* after Great Britain's crime news sheets for constables. Wilkes designed his weekly, which was often referred to as *The Police Gazette* for working white men. Like most newspapers, *The Police Gazette*, which was started in 1845, reported crimes to teach people lessons about citizenship as well as to sell papers.

Police Gazette agents sold subscriptions in barbershops, saloons, and firehouses all over the country during the nineteenth century. Although Wilkes said his staff covered everything personally, he probably recycled items from other newspapers via an exchange system wherein editors swapped issues to attain news and fillers from remote areas. Sometimes journalists from major New York dailies covered sensational murders for the *Gazette*.

Richard Kyle Fox took over as editor in 1877 and revived the declining paper by adding sports stories and theater gossip to the staple of crime scoops. Kyle's gung-ho support eventually helped win respect for boxing, which was illegal. The ample coverage of matches of bare-handed fisticuffs and blood sports, including cock and dog fighting, shared pages with bizarre contests, such as fights involving kangaroos. Fox's innovative competitions and large woodcuts of pretty actresses pleased readers.

In *Objectivity and the News*, Dan Schiller explained that *The National Police Gazette* used stereotypes in reporting news. The editor depended on authority figures so greatly that factual articles were often cast along class, gender, or racial lines. For example, on June 2, 1883, an illustration and an article, "The Mongolian Curse," denounced Chinese heathens for "luring even little girls into their opium dens on Mott Street."

Indeed, the pink *Gazette's* intricate woodcuts impressed competitors and graphically depicted lynching as a gory fable in which virtuous whites avenged the honor of "ruined" maidens and dusky perpetrators stoically accepted their fate. For instance, in the June 2, 1878, edition, "the best of the yeomanry of the county, physically and probably in reputation" put on flowing black masks in the woods. Then, the three-hundred vigilantes wounded the deputy, blinded the sheriff in one eye, and stormed the jail to exact "an awful vengeance." First, they slashed a black man who, crazed with fear, had shot fatally a deputy—butchering him "like a hog" and "[flinging] the sickening mess into the privy." Next, they hanged four blacks accused of ravishing three street walkers at the "house of ill repute." Ironically, the doomed prisoners "showed the nerve and coolness of a hero."

Established dailies clipped items from the *Gazette*. Moreover, police departments used it and similar publications, like *The Detective*, to track down offenders. Police science was in its infancy. The national system for identifying suspects via fingerprinting was not established until after 1900.

Kyle's portrayals of career women, blacks, Jews, the Chinese, and those considered elite, like professors and doctors, as enemies of manhood made him a multimillionaire. Nevertheless, for a decade before he died in 1922, the *Gazette* faded as daily tabloids prospered. In 1932, Harold Rosswell bought it and later sold it to a Canadian company.

Further Reading

Brown, Joshua. *The Social and Sensational News of the Day: Frank Leslie, The Days' Doings, and Scandalous Pictorial News in Gilded Age New York, New-York Journal of American History* (formerly *New-York Historical Society Quarterly*), 66 (Fall 2003) 2.

Gabor, Mark. *The Illustrated History of Girlie Magazines: From the National Police Gazette to the Present*. New York: Harmony Books, 1984.

Reel, Guy Smedley, "This Wicked World: The 'National Police Gazette,' Richard K. Fox, and the Making of the Modern

American Man, 1879–1906," PhD dissertation, Ohio University, 2003.

Schiller, Dan. *Objectivity and the news: The Public and the Rise of Commercial Journalism*, Philadelphia: University of Pennsylvania Press, 1981.

Smith, Gene, and Jayne Barry Smith, ed. *The Police Gazette*. New York: Simon and Schuster, 1972.

Van Every, Edward. *Sins of New York: As 'Exposed' By the Police Gazette*. New York: Stokes, 1930.

Welky, David. "'We Are The People!' Idealized Working-Class Society in The National Police Gazette 1880–1900." *Mid-America* 2002 84(1-3):101–127.

PAULETTE D. KILMER

NATIONAL PUBLIC RADIO (NPR)

An afterthought in the campaign to gain federal funding for public television, public radio has become a force in American journalism greater than anyone had imagined at its beginning. Its primary national network, National Public Radio, has led the way. Public radio began in state universities as educational radio in the 1910s and 1920s, but had largely languished since. Suddenly and unexpectedly infused with federal money by a quiet amendment to the Public Television Act of 1967, educational radio stations made the critical decision to create National Public Radio (NPR) as a network to centrally produce quality programming beyond the capability of individual stations. Unlike its television counterpart, the Public Broadcasting Service (PBS), which was denied the power to produce programs, public radio stations empowered National Public Radio to assemble its own Washington-based production staff, a decision that allowed NPR to create a consistent and definable national sound and identity for public radio.

Like PBS, National Public Radio set out to provide an "alternative" to commercial broadcasting, but unlike public television it dabbled only fleetingly with the idea of serving the specialized needs of diverse audiences from ghetto children to would-be French chefs to home restorers. Public radio came to understand that it existed in a commercial radio environment in which any successful station must serve a specific type of listener consistently. Public radio could not change audiences every half hour as television might. It demanded consistency, but for political and public service reasons, it could not simply target a specific audience and ignore everyone else. Public radio needed to be for everyone, so it built its consistency on a philosophy of inclusiveness, a service ostensibly for everyone even if only a select group of persons chose to listen. NPR defined itself as a more democratic medium than commercial radio, a common meeting place where persons of all backgrounds and points of view listened to one another, including the generally unheard voices of those marginalized by their station in life or by the unpopularity of their views.

While sincerely pursuing those "alternative" goals, NPR ultimately became a leader in quality mainstream journalism. NPR programming found its audience among highly educated people, graduates of the universities that created educational radio in the first place. National Public Radio continues to provide an "alternative" to commercial radio, but it is an alternative built on quality news, the sort of news commercial broadcasting largely abandoned in its quest for lower costs, larger audiences, and maximum profit. As journalistic standards of commercial broadcasting declined, NPR found itself upholding those very standards to which it had initially tried to provide an alternative.

Initial Service

NPR initiated its service in April 1971 with a live broadcast of hearings on the Vietnam War by the Senate Foreign Relations Committee chaired by Senator J. William Fulbright, a war critic. That first editorial decision suggests NPR's initial self-image, but, unlike one of its progenitors, Pacifica Radio, NPR never assumed a radical persona.

The next month, the network offered its first daily program *All Things Considered*, ninety minutes of features reflecting its alternative self image. The title deliberately avoids the word "news," and the programs initial mission statement promised only "some news" in the daily program. Rather, the program would consider "all things," particularly those not found in other media. It would "consider" all things thoughtfully, thoroughly, and tentatively, seeing complexity and tolerating ambiguity. Joined by several co-hosts over the years, host Susan Stamberg came to personify the program and NPR as an organization. More interested in people and literature than she was in news events, happier asking questions than providing authoritative answers, she made an unconventional anchor for an unconventional program.

For their first six years, National Public Radio and *All Things Considered* survived in relative obscurity and strict austerity imposed by the hostility of the Nixon administration to public broadcasting, if not to public radio. A rebellion among public radio stations, some seeking a stronger NPR, some seeking a larger role for stations in program production, but united to their discontent with the status quo, brought in a new regime in 1977 headed by Frank Mankiewicz, press secretary to Robert Kennedy, campaign manager for George McGovern, syndicated columnist, author, television commentator, and scion of Hollywood's Mankiewicz brothers, Herman and Joseph. He satisfied those seeking a stronger NPR and disappointed those seeking a larger role for stations. He set out to find more money for NPR and to raise its low public profile. His seven-year presidency cemented NPR's role as leader of public radio and redefined NPR as a "news" organization in the generally accepted meaning of that word. He said he defined "alternative" as doing what the other guys do but doing it better. And that is just what NPR did. Mankiewicz created a conventionally structured news department and hired newspaper editor Barbara Cohen (now Cocheran) to head it. He brought in highly connected Washington insiders like Cokie Roberts, who covered the Congress of which her mother was a member, her father had been a leader, and her brother a power broker. Public radio became "must listening" for Washington politicos.

Morning Edition

The *Morning Edition* (of *All Things Considered*) began under Mankiewicz and Cohen in November 1979, but its purpose and sound differed from its eight-year-old parent. *Morning Edition* was un-apologetically a "news program. Its host, Bob Edwards, worshiped the legacy of Edward R. Murrow and brought to the program his hero's slow, resonantly voiced authority. In part because of its morning time slot, *Morning Edition* emphasized news from abroad, where news happens while Americans sleep. It focused as well on American government and politics, which greatly interested Mankiewicz and those around him. While different in tone and emphasis from its afternoon edition, *Morning Edition* continued to consider a much wider range of topics than most broadcast news. It had business and sports, of course, but also examined the arts, culture, and the world of ideas. Over time, *All Things Considered* evolved in the direction of *Morning Edition* to the point that today it might be considered the afternoon edition of *Morning Edition.*

In spite of his many contributions to the development of National Public Radio, Mankiewicz was forced from his position in 1983, when the public radio system and Congress discovered he had led NPR into near bankruptcy. Cuts to federal funding for public broadcasting by the Reagan administration triggered the crisis, but NPR's mismanagement of the cuts exacerbated it. The debacle led to a new funding system for National Public Radio in which public radio stations paid the bills and set directions for NPR. The stations, in turn, depended increasingly on listener support and private contributions. What had begun as an enterprise funded totally by governments—primarily state for the station and federal for National Public Radio—now needed to please audiences to pay the bills. And audiences valued NPR news far more than any other service provided by public radio.

Building on the inherited strength in news, NPR's subsequent presidents—Doug Bennet, Delano Lewis, and Kevin Klose—and a series of news vice presidents each put more resources into news and each pushed it further toward the goal of journalistic excellence, at the expense of the idiosyncratic. Each president, more than his predecessor, committed to the highest standards of journalism as defined by professional journalists. Gone were the last vestiges of NPR as an "alternative" voice, except in terms of quality.

The growing strength of NPR news coincided with the declining investment in news by other broadcast organizations more committed to the bottom line than public service. Many newspapers, too, cut their news budgets in the name of profitability. NPR opened expensive news bureaus abroad as commercial broadcasters and newspapers closed theirs. NPR staffs thirty-six overseas bureaus and offices, which provide about one-third of its news output. In the events leading up to and during Gulf War of 1991, NPR fielded the largest staff of any radio organization in the world and among the largest of any media. NPR's serious news coverage, particularly international news, spurred audience growth and retention with each major news event since the 1991 Gulf War. At the turn of the twenty-first century, *Morning Edition* and *All Things Considered* ranked second and third in audience size among all radio programs, commercial or non-commercial. More than thirty million people listened to public radio stations every week, twenty-five million of them to NPR programming.

Success has led to further success, as listeners and other nongovernmental funding sources sought to preserve and improve what many of the perceived to be the best hope for quality broadcast journalism in the United States. A $200 million bequest from an heir to the McDonald's hamburger empire provided the most dramatic example of a broader impulse to preserve and expand this unique institution dedicated to not-for-profit public service journalism.

Further Readings

Engelman, Ralph. *Public Radio and Television in America.* Thousands Oaks, CA: Sage Publication, 1996.

Looker, Thomas. *The Sound and the Story: NPR and the Art of Radio.* Boston: Houghton Mifflin, 1995.

McCauley, Michael. *NPR: The Trials and Triumphs of National Public Radio.* New York: Coulmbia University Press, 2005.

Mitchell, Jack. *Listener Supported: The Culture and History of Public Radio.* Westport, CT: Praeger, 2005.

NPR Archive. http://www.npr.org/templates/archives/rundown_archive_hub.php (accessed April 4, 2007).

JACK W. MITCHELL

NATIVE AMERICAN JOURNALISM

Native American journalism was born in the removal crisis of the 1820s, when the federal government increased pressure on tribes of the southeastern United States to move to Indian Territory. The Cherokees fought back in court, and also in the court of public opinion. In 1826, Cherokee leaders dispatched Elias Boudinot on a speaking tour of eastern cities, where he met with sympathetic crowds. His speech, published as "An Address to the Whites," called for a new view of Indians. "The term *Indian* is pregnant with ideas the most repelling and degrading," Boudinot said. But Boudinot assured his audience that the Indian condition was rapidly improving. Boudinot cited his own experience: "I have had greater advantages than most of my race; and I now stand before you delegated by my native country to seek her interest, to labour for her respectability, and by my public efforts to assist in raising her to an equal standing with other nations of the earth." Boudinot's fundraising effort on behalf of the Cherokees raised $1,500, enough to buy a press and pay a Boston foundry cast type in two languages, English and Cherokee. By February 1828, editor Boudinot and his printers in New Echota (now Georgia), had created something new and remarkable: the *Cherokee Phoenix, and Indians' Advocate*, a bilingual tribal newspaper, the first of its kind in the world.

Educated in missionary schools and fully acculturated into white society, Boudinot believed American Indians had little choice but to surrender their traditions. "There are, with regard to the Cherokees and other tribes, two alternatives; they must either become civilized and happy, or sharing the fate of many kindred nations, become extinct," Boudinot said, echoing a popular nineteenth-century idea. He and other prominent Cherokees saw the *Phoenix* as a crucial part of the civilizing process. Boudinot used the newspaper to publish the laws of the nation—written laws themselves being evidence of tribal advancement—and to document "the manners and customs of the Cherokees, and their progress in Education, Religion and the arts of civilized life…." These topics—all designed to inform Indians and boost the public standing of the tribe—fulfilled the mission of the *Cherokee Phoenix*, a mission that has been emulated in various forms by Native newspapers ever since. In the 1840s and 1850s, the leaders of the Five Civilized Tribes (the Cherokee, Creek or Muskogee, Choctaw, Chickasaw, and Seminole) founded several newspapers in Indian Territory, including the *Cherokee Advocate* in 1844. Like the *Phoenix*, the *Advocate* was a bilingual newspaper, "devoted to the physical, moral, and intellectual improvement of the Cherokee people." After suspensions during the Civil War, the *Advocate* was reestablished in 1870 under the leadership of William Penn Boudinot, Elias Bouidnot's son. The *Advocate* continued until 1906, becoming one of the long-running Indian newspapers in history.

Other Indian Territory newspapers included the bilingual *Choctaw Intelligencer*, founded in 1850. The *Intelligencer's* editors, a white minister named John P. Kingsbury and an educated Choctaw named Jonathon Edwards Dwight, wrote that their paper was "designed to be an advocate of genuine morality, sound education, and Temperance, and a source of information in regard to agriculture, …[and] history, Indian traditions, manners and customs…." Although the *Intelligencer* succeeded editorially, it struggled financially—like many early Native papers—and closed in 1852. Another Indian Territory paper, the semimonthly *Cheyenne Transporter*, was founded by Indian school officials at the Cheyenne and Arapaho Agency in 1879, but soon became an independent publication. The *Transporter* vigorously supported Indian education, but it also promoted Indian boarding schools, institutions that weakened family ties and destroyed tribal traditions. Nevertheless, the *Transporter* defended Indian land claims against Kansans and other "Boomers" who were encroaching into the Territory, an editorial position that threatened the paper's financial stability. It folded in 1886.

Outside of Indian Territory, many nineteenth-century Indian publications were published by missionaries in search of converts. In 1835, Baptists established the *Siwinowe Kesibwi*, or *Shawnee Sun*, at Shawnee Mission, Kansas, the first newspaper published entirely in a Native American language. Jotham Meeker, a missionary who had trained as a printer, worked out a Shawnee writing system and published a four-page, two-column monthly which continued, sometimes irregularly, for several years. In Massachusetts

in 1838, Christian activists established a similar paper, *The Oregonian, and Indian's Advocate*. The thirty-two-page monthly was published by the Oregon Provisional Emigration Society, a group that advocated Christian settlement in the West. That task, in turn, required the improvement of the Indians, a fact the paper's motto made clear: "Our Object the Elevation of the Indian Race—Our Means a Christian Settlement in Oregon." Under that banner, the *Oregonian* was sympathetic to Indian rights, even as it sought to spread Christianity and undermine Native traditions. The society's plan was to "treat [Indians] as men, and give them the blessings of civilization and religion…."

These were high ideals, too high to be helpful to many Indians. Yet this dilemma—whites using the press on behalf of Indians—was a key part of Native journalism. In the last decades of the nineteenth century, for instance, white activists founded several Indian reform publications. Albert Meacham's monthly journal, *The Council Fire*, was established in 1878 in Philadelphia and was "devoted to the civilization and rights of the American Indian." Like many other "friends of the Indians," Meacham believed in assimilation for Indian people, unaware of the cultural damage that would soon result from such policies. A similar publication, *The Indian's Friend*, was founded in 1888, also in Philadelphia, by the Women's National Indian Association. Not surprisingly, its motto followed the Christian idealism of the era: "To Aid in Civilization, Teach Industry, and Give Religious Instruction to the Indians of Our Country."

Indian journalists reasserted their voices in the twentieth century, led by a new generation of leaders. One of the most outspoken was Dr. Carlos Montezuma, a Mojave-Apache man who earned a chemistry degree at the University of Illinois and trained as a physician at Northwestern. Born in Arizona and raised by several white benefactors, Montezuma founded *Wassaja: Freedom's Signal for Indians* in 1916. Like Elias Boudinot, Montezuma was a highly assimilated individual and he used his four-page monthly to argue against paternalistic and demeaning federal Indian policies. Reservation life, he argued, damaged the competitive spirit of Indians. *Wassaja* also lashed out at other would-be friends of the Indian, including "missionaries, philanthropists, anthropologists, sociologists, psychologists, archeologists, artists, and writers." Montezuma repeatedly attacked the Bureau of Indian Affairs and called for its abolition. A similar militancy appeared in the white-operated *Indian Truth*, a publication of the Indian Rights Association, founded in 1924 in Philadelphia. In its first issue, *Indian Truth* exposed the legal abuses in Oklahoma that cheated Indians out of oil royalties. Editor Matthew Sniffen also used the publication to attack Indian Commissioner John Collier, whose "traditional" Indian policies Sniffen opposed.

The battle over sovereignty and self-determination was joined again in the turbulent 1960s. Perhaps the leading journal of the so-called Red Power movement was *Akwesasne Notes*, established by the Mohawks in Hogansburg, New York. Editor Jerry Gambill, a Canadian aboriginal, set an aggressive editorial tone and eventually built the publication's circulation to more than eighty thousand. His militancy soon produced a backlash. The paper's office was attacked with brick and bottles, and the post office harassed the paper by delaying its second-class mailing privileges. Gambill was arrested and jailed for illegal entry into the U.S. Nevertheless, *Akwesasne Notes* was an effective outlet for radical Indian voices at a crucial time in American history.

By the 1970s, the need to control their own media messages prompted Native journalists to move into broadcasting. In the West and in Alaska, areas with widespread Native populations, Indians began operating non-profit as well as commercial radio stations. The first commercial Indian-owned-and-operated radio station was KMDX-FM in Parker, Arizona, which went on the air in late 1977. The station was unable to generate a strong advertising base, however, and closed in 1978. A more successful Indian-oriented station was the Catholic-owned KNOM, a nonprofit station that reached thousands of indigenous Alaskans. Staffed entirely by volunteers, the award-winning station went on the air in 1971 in Nome, where it continues to broadcast.

Native journalists established several important independent Indian papers the last years of the twentieth century. These include Paul DeMain's bi-weekly *News from Indian Country*, which covered national Native news from the Lac Courte Oreilles Ojibwe Reservation in Wisconsin. In Oklahoma, the *Native American Times* provided national coverage as the largest independently owned Native American newspaper. The reservation-based but independent *Navajo Times* covered the nation's largest tribe from Window Rock, Arizona.

At the beginning of the twentieth-first century, Native American journalism continues to develop. The Cherokees, for instance, revived the *Phoenix* as a monthly tabloid edited by Dan Agent. Another successful Native newspaper, *Indian Country Today*, was founded as a weekly in 1981 by the Lakota writer Tim Giago. *Indian Country Today* flourished, becoming the largest weekly in the South Dakota and eventually expanding its coverage. In 1998, the Oneida Nation of New York purchased the paper and expanded its operations to include quarterly magazines and a web site, indiancountry.com, one of many popular sources of Native American information on the Internet. One of the most innovative online outlets is Reznet, an award-winning Native student newspaper founded by Dennis McAuliffie, Jr. and based at the University of Montana.

Further Reading

Littlefield, Daniel F. Jr., and James W. Parins. *American Indian and Alaska Native Newspapers and Periodicals, 1826–1924*. Westport, CT: Greenwood Press, 1984.

Littlefield, Daniel F. Jr. and James W. Parins, eds. *American Indian and Alaska Native Newspapers and Periodicals, 1925–1970*. Westport, CT: Greenwood Press, 1986.

Littlefield, Daniel F. Jr. and James W. Parins, eds. *American Indian and Alaska Native Newspapers and Periodicals, 1971–1985*. Westport, CT: Greenwood Press, 1986.

Murphy, James E., and Sharon M. Murphy. *Let My People Know: American Indian Journalism, 1828–1978*. Norman: University of Oklahoma Press, 1981.

Perdue, Theda, ed. *Cherokee Editor: The Writings of Elias Boudinot*. Knoxville: University of Tennessee Press, 1983.

JOHN M. COWARD

NBC NEWS

The National Broadcasting Corporation was first established as a radio experiment by RCA and its founder David Sarnoff in 1928, although the network had actually signed-on the airwaves, in pre-experimental mode, two years earlier. Sarnoff was known historically as the young Marconi Company employee who, in 1912, claimed to be the lone telegraph operator picking up distress calls from the sinking of the *Titanic*. He was later dubbed a "visionary" for predictions of radio success. At the outset, NBC almost immediately began to offer a glimpse at news of the day, including coverage of Charles Lindbergh's transatlantic flight in 1927 and reporting of election results over two developing radio networks, dubbed Red and Blue, of NBC. It divested the Blue Network in 1941 but the year before that managed to cover the Republican National Convention. With great initiative, it covered the D-Day invasion, when it pre-empted entertainment programming in 1944, and even broadcast interviews from the scene. Television News development began slowly at NBC but the stage had clearly been set.

Beginning in the late 1940s and 1950s, the television network began programming talk shows that had evolved from radio into solid public affairs formats. "Garroway at Large," broadcast nationally from the network's Chicago affiliate, WNBQ, served as a springboard for Dave Garroway hosting of the "Today" show that would evolve into a major audience attraction over the NBC network, "live" from New York. The network was also experimenting with formats in concert with their affiliate stations. One public affairs series "Portrait of America," focusing on different homes and families also emanated from Chicago and set a positive tone for investigation into domestic challenges facing the nation in post-World War II America. "Meet the Press," the longest continuously scheduled program on network television, also went on the air from the nation's capital with Martha Rountree at the helm on November 6, 1947.

The Nightly News on NBC began in 1949 with the effort known as the "NBC Newsreel." Shortly after that, a bow-tied John Cameron Swayze, who started as a newspaper reporter in Kansas City and then worked in radio news and broadcast management, began "hop-scotching the globe for news" on the NBC "Camel News Caravan" over a twenty station hook-up. This occurred long before the term "anchorman" had been coined for television use. Swayze also hosted "Watch the World," a weekly half-hour of news topics designed to be of interest to high school students. He wore a fresh flower in his lapel every day and emerged as a well-known figure nationally at a time when television was starting to catch-on as an advertising medium. R. J.

Reynolds Tobacco Co., maker of Camel Cigarettes, was the show's highly valued sponsor. NBC became the first network to air weekend news that same year.

An innovation of Sylvester "Pat" Weaver, the "Today" show began in 1952. It was produced by the entertainment division of the network but it included regular news with reports and news-film provided on both the hour and half-hour. The development of that particular program had a powerful indirect effect on news development at the "Peacock Network." It more than doubled the number of news writers at the NBC Network, for example, and it began contributing to a process of changing the orientation of television news away from radio to a visual medium that included information and film that made the entire enterprise more serious from a journalistic point of view, and eventually, more lucrative. It also forced a move by network employees toward union representation with Reuven Frank, a writer on the "News Caravan," destined to achieve a great many innovations as head of the news division, installed as the first shop steward.

NBC first became highly competitive in news in the next decade under the careful supervision and watchful eye of network President Robert Kintner, who served in that position from 1958 to 1965. Kintner was formerly President of ABC-TV and was often quoted by his NBC network news staff at that time for pushing the concept of "CBS Plus 30," meaning that under his leadership, the network would always attempt to improve on the performance of the perceived TV news leader of the early era—the network of Edward R. Murrow and Fred W. Friendly, CBS—by offering thirty more minutes than its competitor in its coverage of special events. At Kintner's insistence, NBC emerged from the 1956 presidential campaign by supporting the development of the Huntley-Brinkley news program. As a result, NBC became very highly regarded for its innovative commitment to news, pubic affairs and documentary programming. It grew in popularity and ratings.

NBC stations covered many important news events in the 1950s, including national political conventions. The week before the 1952 conventions in Chicago, and long before nonstop air flights, NBC News sent John Cameron Swayze to California to broadcast from both Los Angeles and San Francisco as a way to inaugurate network television's extension to the West Coast. At the conventions, live coverage was allowed from the meeting rooms of the national committee. NBC News correspondent Frank Bourgholtzer was treated to a "live" on-air tour of the White House with President Harry S. Truman serving as his guide. The president, who previously showed little use for television, played "The Missouri Waltz" on the piano. Soon afterward, the death of Soviet Dictator Joseph Stalin created the interest for international coverage and a few praiseworthy NBC News Specials entitled, "Before and After Stalin" and "The Road to Spandau," which won a Sigma Delta Chi Award for excellence in television writing.

By 1955 NBC had initiated the documentary series "Project XX," a reference to the twentieth century, with a focus on history. It followed in the footsteps of "Victory at Sea" a skillful adaptation of newsreel footage in the account of U.S. Naval operations during World War II. Although not produced by the news division, "Project XX" also won high praise and had the added, indirect effect of bolstering the network's status among critics and members of the general public who were beginning to get accustomed to information via television. Among the most celebrated from that series were "Mark Twain's America" and "The Real West," starring Gary Cooper. Both relied on historical authenticity to re-tell, with great visual skill and superior writing, some often told stories from American history.

The second of the so-called "Great Debates" between John F. Kennedy and Richard M. Nixon emanated from NBC station WRC-TV on October 7, 1960. It was produced by NBC News Vice President Julian Goodman and moderated by Frank McGee. By the middle of the 1960s, NBC News' largest bureau outside of the United States was located in Saigon and dedicated to covering the war in Vietnam. Key correspondents included Garrick Utley, John Cochran, and Ron Nessen, who would later become President Gerald Ford's press secretary. By 1974, NBC had the largest number of news affiliates, 210, compared to 194 for CBS, the former leader.

The co-anchors of NBC's dominant evening news team emerged in the nineteen fifties and lasted almost fifteen years. David Brinkley, based in Washington, D.C., and Chet Huntley from New York City appeared together on the "Huntley-Brinkley Report," and became well-known for their status during a network news build-up to over three-hundred staffers accentuated by their nightly news sign-off: "Good night, Chet. Good night, David. Good night, for NBC News." The program began on October 15, 1956, when the two were teamed-up for the first time during political convention coverage. Their partnership caught-on quickly and lasted until Huntley's retirement in July, 1970.

An independent thinker from Montana, Chet Huntley had a deep baritone voice and been viewed as a somewhat straight-laced contributor of sufficient television presence to add depth to the program. Brinkley, originally from North Carolina, was credited for providing that nightly newscast with excellent writing and a tongue in cheek approach to the key events and people of the day, particularly those involving political stories and politicians who took themselves a little too seriously. Brinkley appeared as a sort of younger brother to Huntley's senior, more somber approach.

David Brinkley eventually left NBC to join ABC News in 1981 where he hosted that competing network's popular Sunday morning public affairs program, "This Week with David Brinkley." As a long-time symbol of NBC News however, he also produced the outstanding "David Brinkley's Journal," first inserted as a segment into the evening news—and then in an expanded, documentary format, which he always insisted on writing himself. "David Brinkley's Journal" won Emmy Awards in both 1962 and 1963 as the best public affairs series on television. NBC moved to a thirty-minute nightly news format in1963, right along with the "CBS Evening News with Walter Cronkite."

Brinkley and Huntley achieved great popularity and a

research organization in 1965 found them to be more easily recognized by the general public than movie stars Cary Grant, James Stewart or the British rock and roll phenomenon from that decade and beyond—The Beatles. Television comedian Milton Berle and legendary crooner, Frank Sinatra, sang "Huntley-Brinkley" to the classic tune "Love and Marriage" at the inauguration of John F. Kennedy. Their ratings gave them a great deal of attention and in the face of that the celebrated news team upheld some important standards for that network including the adamant refusal to wear matching on-air blazers—coats with an NBC logo with the classic network chimes that had been suggested by a network manager. Ironically, except on very rare occasions involving "hard news" events, Brinkley also refused to interview movie stars and other popular entertainment celebrity figures, as a matter of principle, news values, and personal pride.

In addition to Brinkley and Huntley a large number of important broadcast journalists began their careers as NBC News correspondents including Pauline Fredericks, Nancy Dickerson, Frank McGee, Edwin Newman, Irving R. Levine, Sander Vanocur, and John Chancellor, who hosted "Today" and is remembered for inadvertently blocking an isle at the 1964 Republican National Convention and being ushered out while announcing: "This is John Chancellor, somewhere in custody." He eventually took-over the anchor position from Brinkley for the "NBC Nightly News." The network also established a dozen early international television news bureaus situated in Athens, Bonn, Cairo, Havana, Hong Kong, Leopoldville, London, Moscow, New Delhi, Ottawa, Paris and Tokyo. This gave broadcast news a newly found stature and increasing sense of importance, almost on a par with the nation's newspaper press.

Under Robert Kintner, NBC was determined to be at the scene of the action whenever news took place and whatever the cost. White House correspondent Robert MacNeil was in the presidential motorcade in Dallas, Texas on November 22, 1963, when President John F. Kennedy was assassinated. He quickly followed the police investigating the shooting up the grassy knoll adjacent to the crime scene after the shooting and then reported from Parkland Hospital on Kennedy's death. Since the NBC News chief, Robert Kintner, had cancelled all commercials during the Kennedy funeral and all related events—the murder of Kennedy's alleged assassin, Lee Harvey Oswald, was carried over the airwaves "live," as it happened. NBC News' reporter Tom Pettit reported: "He's been shot. Lee Harvey Oswald has been shot." And network television viewers watched that scene unfold as the assailant, Jack Ruby, was grabbed by Dallas police officers and had his gun removed.

Long-form network news documentaries of the "NBC White Paper" series became some of the most hard-hitting and highly regarded of the 1960s under the direct supervision of Irving Gitlin and Fred Freed. Those programs initially addressed civil rights issues and then evolved into major investigations extending well beyond U.S. borders including those focusing specifically on the Cold War leadership of the Soviet Union, revisiting an earlier theme in "The Death of Stalin" and the follow-up program entitled, "The Rise of Khrushchev." Documentaries explored foreign policy issues, some of them historical in nature such as "The Decision to Drop the Bomb" and the "Bay of Pigs Invasion," while others took a close look at politics such as "The Year of the Mayors," and "The Hill Country: Lyndon Johnson's Texas."

NBC News was identified with many "firsts" with respect to female reporters. The first major female news correspondent, Pauline Frederick became known for her reports from the United Nations from 1953 to 1974. The first major female TV news anchor, Barbara Walters, started her network news career at NBC's "Today" show. Connie Chung anchored NBC News at Sunrise and co-anchored a magazine program, "American Almanac" with Roger Mudd. Catherine "Cassie" Mackin was the first woman to serve as a network television political floor correspondent and did so for NBC during presidential nominating conventions of the nineteen seventies. She covered politics on a par with Tom Brokaw, who became Walters' replacement at "Today." He then covered the Watergate scandal as Chief White House Correspondent for NBC in 1973. Brokaw became anchorman of "NBC Nightly News" three years later and was in the anchor seat in 1985 when General Electric purchased RCA, and with it, NBC Television. Tom Brokaw broadcast "live" from the scene of the fall of the Berlin Wall in 1989, as well as anchoring nightly news in conjunction with coverage of the September 11, 2001, terrorist attacks on New York and Washington, D.C.

Katie Couric was broadcasting "live" on NBC's "Today" show the morning when the attack first occurred—she gained a popular following before being recruited to the evening news anchor position at network competitor, CBS News. Couric was replaced on NBC's "Today" show by Meredith Vieira, who worked previously in news at CBS and ABC before joining, "The View," a daytime talk program created by Barbara Walters. The NBC network's key public affairs series is the multi-part magazine program, "Dateline NBC," hosted by Stone Phillips and Ann Curry. The network's continuing top interviewer and host of "Meet the Press" is Tim Russert, who previously served as counselor to former New York Governor Mario Cuomo and chief of staff for the late New York Senator Daniel Patrick Moynihan. Topping the list of the NBC network's correspondents in 2007 were Andrea Mitchell and Lisa Myers. Brian Williams anchored the "NBC Nightly News." He previously hosted "The News with Brian Williams" on MSNBC, the joint all-news cable channel of Microsoft and NBC.

Further Reading

Frank, Reuven. *Out of Thin Air: The Brief Wonderful Life of Network News.* New York: Simon and Schuster, 1991.

Murray, Michael D. "A Passion for Politics: A Conversation with Tom Brokaw," *American Journalism*, 17, 3 (Summer 2000): 109–17.

———. "Creating a Tradition in Broadcast News: A Conversation with David Brinkley," *Journalism History*, 21, 4 (Winter 1995): 164–169.

———. "The World of Change in TV News: A Conversation with Garrick Utley," *American Journalism*, 14, 2 (Spring 1997): 10–17.

———, ed. *Encyclopedia of Television News*. Phoenix: Oryx Press, 1999.

Yellin, David G. *Special: Fred Freed and the Television Documentary*. New York: MacMillan,1972.

MICHAEL D. MURRAY

NEAR V. MINNESOTA

The United States Supreme Court has been robust, but not absolute, in its protection of the press against governmental attempts to censor unwelcome news or opinion through the issuance of injunctions that result in prior restraint. An injunction is a court order that restrains a person from doing something. When the injunction restrains the press before publication, it is called a prior restraint. Prior restraints against journalists and broadcasters raise constitutional questions because the First Amendment states that "Congress shall make no law . . . abridging freedom of speech or of the press."

Near v. Minnesota (1931) was the first prior restraint injunction decided by the Supreme Court. The case raised several issues. Do the Constitution and America's free press traditions always forbid prior restraint injunctions? Can the U.S. Constitution's First Amendment shield the press from state and local laws as well as from federal laws that would, if enforced, create a prior restraint?

Jay Near and his partner, Howard Guilford, published the *Saturday Press*, a small weekly newspaper in Minneapolis, Minnesota. They defamed local officials on several occasions in their attempts to publicize city government corruption. They wrote that "a Jewish gangster was in control of gambling, bootlegging and racketeering in Minneapolis, and that law enforcing officers and agencies were not energetically performing their duties." Rather than suing for libel after publication, the prosecutor obtained a state court injunction based on a local nuisance abatement law. The statute forbade "any publication whatsoever which is malicious, scandalous or defamatory."

Chief Justice Charles Evens Hughes brought together a bare 5–4 majority of Supreme Court justices to overturn the injunction. Under the Constitution's Fourteenth Amendment due process clause, Hughes said, states cannot make or enforce local laws that abridge a citizen's federal constitutional rights. The First Amendment applies to state, as well as federal laws and checks the power of all branches of government, not just Congress. Hughes reviewed the English roots of America's First Amendment approach. The famous British jurist, William Blackstone, had written that, "The liberty of the press is indeed essential to the nature of a free state; but this consists in laying no previous restraints upon publications, and not in freedom from censure for criminal matter when published." Hughes said that "In determining the extent of the constitutional protection, it has been generally, if not universally, considered that it is the chief purpose of the guaranty to prevent previous restraints upon publication." The injunction against the Saturday Press, Hughes ruled, violated the First Amendment liberty of the press that is protected against infringement by the states through the Fourteenth Amendment.

It is important to note that *Near v. Minnesota* did not provide absolute protection against all prior restraints. Hughes said the Constitution might not prevent prior restraint of material that would incite violence, or endanger troops during wartime. The specific circumstances under which a prior restraint against the press would be constitutional remains unsettled. Courts have restrained the press from writing about some aspects of trial coverage. Some elements of privacy law also allow prior restraint injunctions. In the Pentagon Papers case, *New York Times Co. v. United States* (1971), the Supreme Court remained split. In a narrow unsigned, or *per curiam* opinion, the Supreme Court ruled only that the government had failed to meet the heavy burden of proof necessary to support a prior restraint. The door was left ajar for future officials to meet that burden and to argue against unfettered publication.

Further Reading

Friendly, Fred W. *Minnesota Rag*. New York: Random House, 1981.

Near v. Minnesota 283 U.S. 697 (1931).

New York Times Co. v. United States 403 U.S. 713 (1971).

JEREMY COHEN

NEOCONSERVATIVE JOURNALISTS

The phrase "neoconservative journalists" is perhaps as difficult to define with precision as is the term "neoconservative." Neoconservatism generally is viewed as a movement of American intellectuals who began thinking of themselves as conservatives in the late 1960s, though their background had been in the left politics of New York City and some had been Trotskyites. While neoconservatism has been characterized by James Q. Wilson, an academic who frequently has contributed to neoconservative journals, as "a mood, not an ideology," nevertheless this movement to the right can be seen as based on a number of unambiguous issues: an instinctive opposition to the prevailing intellectual establishment, referred to as the "new class"; support for an assertive American foreign policy; belief in American exceptionalism; qualified support for American-style capitalism and free markets; opposition to the emerging welfare culture of the Great Society; defense of strong families and criticism of the cultural forces believed to be weakening them; and support for various meritocracies that were seen as being undermined by the New Left of the 1960s. Neoconservatives were distinguished from more traditional American conservatives, by both themselves and others, principally by a secular approach to politics, a lack of devotion to the past, and a willingness to get heavily involved in partisan politics by attempting to exert intellectual influence. The term neoconservative was coined somewhat pejoratively by Michael Harrington in 1973 to describe his former fellow travelers who were moving away from the left.

The paradigmatic first generation neoconservatives were Irving Kristol, often referred to as "the godfather of neoconservatism," and Norman Podhoretz. Having honed their polemical skills in the left-intellectual circles of mid-century New York, opinion journalism came naturally to them as a profession. Podhoretz became editor of *Commentary*, a publication of the American Jewish Committee, in 1959, and eventually turned it into a vehicle for his emerging political views. Kristol started *Public Interest* with Daniel Bell in 1965, originally as a publication squarely within the liberal New Deal tradition of progressive government. But the editors soon were impressed with what Nathan Glazer called "the limits of social policy," and began to take the magazine in a more conservative direction, questioning the capabilities of government to solve a multitude of social problems. In addition to *Commentary* and *Public Interest*, other publications that often put forward neoconservative views have been *The American Spectator, The American Enterprise, Policy Review, The New Criterion, First Things, Crisis, Forbes, Fortune, The American Scholar, The Weekly Standard, The National Interest, Public Opinion, Society, Foreign Affairs* and *The Washington Quarterly*. These journals of opinion, targeting a relatively small but educated and influential readership, formed the battleground of neoconservative polemics and dovetailed with efforts in the emerging world of conservative think tanks, such as the American Enterprise Institute, the Hoover Institution and Heritage Foundation. It was generally understood within the precincts of these journals that they were not in competition with each other, but rather served together as an echo chamber that more effectively propelled ideas out into the mainstream public discourse. The polemical style generally involved setting up the 1960s counterculture as nemesis, and defending the status quo against disintegrating change. The "new class" of teachers, journalists, government bureaucrats and other knowledge workers was not seen as precisely the same thing as the counterculture, but was allied to it in the sense of seeking to vest enormous new powers in the state. This was nothing but a power grab by people who had emerged victorious in the academic meritocracy yet could not compete financially with the business class, in the view of neoconservatives. Kristol, indeed, attempted to ally neoconservative polemics with business, an effort that bore fruit with substantial funding for the journals and think tanks.

Neoconservatives thus brought their organizational skills, and a penchant for political hardball, to a body of conservative ideas that in the 1950s had been considered disenfranchised and scattered to the four winds. Political power arrived with the election of Ronald Reagan in 1980. Reagan had been brought into the world of opinion journalism by William F. Buckley's more traditionally conservative *National Review*, but he was also believed to be very much under the influence of neoconservatives. Enjoying access to a conservatism come to power, many neoconservatives became rather prominent public figures in the

1980s, including Jeanne Kirkpatrick, William Bennett, Midge Decter, Joshua Muravchik, R. Emmett Tyrrell, Jr., Hilton Kramer, Arnold Beichman, Richard John Neuhaus, Gertrude Himmelfarb, Michael Novak, and many others. Several neoconservative public figures of the day, politicians such as Daniel Patrick Moynihan, and academics such as Nathan Glazer, Donald Kagan and Seymour Martin Lipset, were not employed primarily as journalists, but virtually all were in the habit of publishing articles regularly in the non-academic journals of opinion that defined the neoconservative universe of ideas.

Though most neoconservatives were intellectuals with roots in the academy, they took naturally to political power, and soon found themselves as part of a schism in Reagan conservatism, set against antagonists referred to as "paleoconservatives." Paleoconservatives, traditionalists anchored in an old right sensibility long pre-dating the 1960s, claimed that the neoconservatives were interlopers who sought only power and brought nothing new to the conservative movement in the way of ideas. The paleocons fired away at their neocon adversaries from publications such as *Chronicles of Culture, Southern Partisan*, and *Intercollegiate Studies Review*. As a power struggle, this became a mismatch. Neoconservatives carried the day both in the Reagan administration, where Bennett's selection in 1981 over M.E. Bradford as head of the National Endowment for the Humanities was seen as significant, and in the world of mainstream conservative journalism, embodied principally by Buckley, Jr.'s *National Review*. When Buckley, in 1991, gave it as his view that the work of Patrick J. Buchanan and Joseph Sobran, a former editor of *National Review*, could be seen by reasonable people as anti-Semitic, it was viewed as a final plighting of the troth between Buckley and neoconservatism.

Much of the polemics involving neoconservatives and their role found its way to a discussion of anti-Semitism. Though many neo-conservatives, such as Kirkpatrick and Bennett, were not Jewish, perhaps the majority were, and had roots in the New York Jewish intellectual scene of the mid-twentieth century. David Brooks, op-ed columnist for the *New York Times* and a second generation neoconservative, has put forth the view that the word neoconservative has become code for Jewish, and that to discuss any issue of the day using that category was equivalent to sending veiled anti-Semitic messages. Critics replied that Brooks' formulation was a tactic for preempting debate by stigmatizing one side with ad hominem motives. Exchanges of this sort normally got around to neoconservative support for Israel, which was seen by critics as being without reservation and in lockstep with the far right of the Likud Party.

Brooks wrote in the post-September 11, 2001, environment, when the neoconservatives escaped anonymity in mainstream America and their movement became a household word. The anti-terrorist policy of George W. Bush was generally thought to have been largely a neoconservative formulation, shaped by administration figures believed to have been especially influential with Vice President Cheney and Secretary of Defense Donald Rumsfeld, such people as Paul Wolfowitz, I. Lewis Libby, Douglas Feith, and John Bolton. The public build-up to the invasion of Iraq was spurred on by second-generation neoconservative journalists William Kristol, Charles Krauthammer, and Robert Kagan, who extolled the virtues of a benevolent American hegemony in the world, and used the term "empire" quite freely. As Iraq remained the central focus of the Bush administration well into its second term, neoconservatism came to be identified closely with an aggressive American foreign policy. With American fortunes in Iraq appeared to falter, the term became largely pejorative again, though in a different sense than that intended originally by Harrington, who lamented the movement away from a focus on public welfare within the nation's borders.

By the end of year one in the second term of the second Bush administration, neoconservatism seemed to stand principally for the concept of "moral clarity," for being able to distinguish the exemplary ideals and history of the United States from those of less virtuous actors on the world stage, and for being committed to spreading those ideals around the globe, by military means if necessary. Thus ripened, the movement's true godfather, some claimed, was Leo Strauss, a German émigré and professor of political philosophy at the University of Chicago from 1949 to 1973. Educator to several prominent neoconservatives, Strauss emphasized that the west must develop such moral clarity and be prepared to fight for its vision, or it will perish.

Historians will perhaps view American neoconservatives, many of them from recently immigrated families, primarily as a force for reinvigorated American and Israeli nationalism. Uninterested in drawing the usual lessons from the first half of the twentieth century about the perils of nationalism, they advocated a strong military, aggressively deployed. Toward that end and others, they made groundbreaking use of opinion journalism, and forged improbable alliances of their intellectual capabilities with corporate capital and Christian Zionists.

Further Reading

Clarke, Jonathan, and Stefan Halper. *America Alone: The Neoconservatives and the Global Order.* Cambridge and New York: Cambridge University Press, 2004.

Dorrien, Gary. *The Neoconservative Mind: Politics, Culture and War of Ideology.* Philadelphia: Temple University Press, 1993.

Gerson, Michael. *The Neoconservative Vision: From Cold War to Culture Wars.* Lanham, MD: Madison Books, 1996.

GORDON JACKSON

NEUHARTH, ALLEN H.

Allen Neuharth (March 22, 1924–), as chairman of the Gannett Company, founded the national newspaper, *USA Today*, in 1982. As publisher of *USA Today*, Neuharth has been credited with transforming the face of the modern newspaper to include color, computer graphics, and a breezy writing style.

Neuharth was born on March 22, 1924, in Eureka, South Dakota. His father died when he was two and school had to take a back seat to helping the family survive during the Great Depression. He worked on his grandfather's farm, picking up cow chips to be used for fuel. Then, Neuharth gravitated to the news business as a youngster when he worked as a newsboy delivering the *Minneapolis Tribune*. He abandoned that calling because a job as a butcher boy, sweeping up and helping to slaughter the animals, paid better. He returned to journalism, however, as a teenager when he became editor of the *Echo*, a weekly quarter-page in the *Alpena Journal* that served as the local high school paper. Neuharth served in the U.S. Army in World War II in the U.S. 86th Infantry Division in France, Germany, and the Philippines. He returned to the United States after the war and attended the University of South Dakota, where he ultimately became the editor of the university newspaper.

Neuharth's first professional position demonstrated an entrepreneurial leaning—he and a colleague from university founded *SoDak Sports*, a weekly newspaper dedicated to South Dakota sports. It went bankrupt within a year.

Neuharth then traveled across the country to write for the Knight newspaper chain's *Miami Herald*. He climbed the executive ladder to the assistant managing editor position and then transferred to the Knight paper in Michigan, the *Detroit Free Press*. He joined Gannett Newspapers in 1963 as general manager of the chain's flagship newspapers in Rochester.

At Gannett, Neuharth was an integral part of the steady expansion of the chain. He became president in 1970. During his tenure (he retired as president, chief executive pfficer, and chairman in 1989), Gannett revenues expanded 1,450 percent. In 1979, for example, Gannett owned seventy-eight daily and twenty-one weekly newspapers, seven television and more than a dozen radio stations, a number of outdoor advertising plants, and the Louis Harris & Associates research firm.

Neuharth's lasting contribution to journalism, however, took the form of his vision to create a national newspaper that appealed to a generation of readers who had spent their leisure time watching television. When *USA Today* debuted on September 15, 1982, the newspaper's cluttered front page included its now well-known "Newsline" index along the left margin, a graph, color photos and a promo for its national weather map. It featured stories that were short, contained on that page and written in an informal, chatty style. It focused on "usable" news for consumers. Critics, many of whom were in more traditional journalistic enterprises, dismissed *USA Today* as "McPaper," classified it as junk food journalism, and underestimated its influence.

USA Today used its thorough and national approach to sports to lure many readers to its five-day a week newspaper. Its marketing strategy also tapped in to the increasingly mobile business community by circulating heavily in airports and hotels.

Neuharth estimated that the company lost about $400 million on the venture before *USA Today* became a journalism powerhouse with circulation exceeding two million.

Neuharth retired from his management positions at Gannett in 1989 when he turned sixty-five. He published an autobiography, *Confessions of an S.O.B.*, in 1989. His editorial column for *USA Today* continued into the new millennium.

Further Reading

Neuharth, Al. *Confessions of an S.O.B.* New York: Doubleday, 1989.

Prichard, Peter. *The Making of McPaper: The Inside Story of USA Today.* Kansas City: Andrews, McMeel & Parker, 1987.

AGNES HOOPER GOTTLIEB

NEW-ENGLAND COURANT

Sustained, critical journalism began in the British colonies of North America with this weekly paper. Earlier dissent from government policy had been fleeting, such as Benjamin Harris's single issue of Publick Occurrences (1690). The first newspapers to last, such as Boston's News-Letter (1704), did not question authority. In the summer of 1721, printer James Franklin and apprentice Benjamin, set a new course. James, age 24, and Benjamin, age 15, used their small print shop to challenge the status quo.

The *New-England Courant* (1721–1727) was usually a single sheet of paper, with two columns of news printed on each side. Varied type sizes and a standing wood cut made its only visual appeal. The paper's circulation of 500 or so was at the practical limit of print shops in the colonies. Two series in the early years of the paper made the greatest mark on the American press.

The "Silence Dogood Papers" were written secretly by Benjamin and, according to his *Autobiography*, slipped under the print shop door and accepted by his brother as a reader contribution. Benjamin, pretending to be a gossipy widow, was finding his voice by aping the graceful essays he had found in British journals such as the *Tatler* and the *Spectator*. Fourteen installments into this series of 1722, James discovered the author and the essays stopped.

The *Courant*'s ridicule of public health measures against small pox was far riskier. alf of the population of Boston contracted this disease in 1721, and one of seven townsfolk died. Puritan ministers of the town, such as Increase Mather, called for the novel practice of inoculation, believing (correctly) that localized exposure would strengthen the body's defenses. The *Courant*, after calling for contributions "Sarcastick, Ludicrous, or otherwise amusing" in the second issue, joined prominent Anglicans in the town who scoffed at clergy who, "By teaching and practicing what's Orthodox/ Pray hard against *Sickness*, yet preach up the Pox!" James Franklin claimed to be impartial, but he printed 21 major stories ridiculing inoculation to two essays that seemed to endorse the practice.

In a sea of trouble, the *Courant* survived for more than five years (no issues have been found after the summer of 1726). James Franklin, "the Wicked Printer," was cursed by the Rev. Mr. Mather and answered back with the first American publication of "Cato's Letters" from England, a call for exposure of public wrongs as "a Duty which every Man owes to his Country." Massachusetts jailed the printer for a month in 1722 after the *Courant* accused the authorities of leisure in the pursuit of pirates. The following year, the colony attempted to keep James Franklin out of the public prints by asserting the right to license anything he published. The printer evaded this by creating the pretense that Benjamin was the publisher. This fiction saved the paper but lost the apprentice. The apprenticeship broken, Benjamin took sail for Philadelphia in 1723. The rough and tumble on the *Courant* provided invaluable lessons for the man who would become the most important printer of the colonial era.

Further Reading

http://www.ushistory.org/franklin/courant/index.htm

Leonard, Thomas C., *The Power of the Press: The Birth of American Political Reporting.* New York: Oxford University Press, 1986.

Miller, Perry, intro. *The New-England Courant: A Selection of Certain Issues* Containing Writings of Benjamin Franklin or Published by Him during his *Brother's Imprisonment. Reproduced from copies of the originals owned by the Massachusetts Historical Society in honor of the 250th anniversary of his birth.* Boston: American Academy of Arts and Sciences, 1956.

THOMAS C. LEONARD

NEW REPUBLIC

"The popular will cannot be taken for granted, it must be created," Herbert Croly said in starting the *New Republic* (1914–), a journal of opinion dedicated to promoting Progressivism in America. Croly, the son of two journalists, saw the publication's purpose as "less to inform or entertain" but instead to "start little insurrections in the realm of their convictions." His friend and the publication's cofounder Walter Lippmann was more pragmatic. "The *New Republic*," he wrote, "was founded to explore and develop and apply the ideas which had been advertised by Theodore Roosevelt when he was a leader of the Progressive Party." Those ideas, Max Eastman wrote in *The Masses* on May 29, 1915, were rooted in the belief that "fundamental democratic progress comes by telling, and persuading and showing how," instead of his certainty that "in the real world privilege can only be uprooted by power." During its high water mark in the early Cold War period under editor Henry A. Wallace, the *New Republic* reached a circulation of one hundred thousand and counted in its contributors and readers leading American liberals.

The first issue of the magazine, published November 7, 1914, and running thirty-two pages, sold only 875 copies, but within a year that number grew to 15,000. Croly's 1909 book *The Promise of American Life* argued for a planned economy and an interventionist foreign policy, a "new nationalism" that reflected Theodore Roosevelt's progressive agenda. Heiress Dorothy Payne Whitney appreciated Croly's social activism and shared his certainty that a strong central government and individual liberty could coexist in a middle ground between socialism and unfettered capitalism. She encouraged Croly to start a magazine that she would finance to promote these views.

The *New Republic* under Croly and Lippmann helped to redefine twentieth-century American liberalism, which previously had been associated with the doctrine of laissez faire, and it quickly became a leading voice of left-of-center intellectuals. The magazine sought to be on the cutting edge of new ideas. In the April 17, 1915 issue, it was Lippmann who first introduced Sigmund Freud to many Americans, pointing out that Freud's theories challenged "the very essence of what we call ourselves." Over the years, the *New Republic* published articles by many other prominent leaders and writers including Charles Beard, a Progressive Era historian; Jane Addams, founder of the U.S. settlement house movement; Bertrand Russell, philosopher and social activist; H.G. Wells, a science fiction and socialist writer; Walter Weyl, a leader in the trade union movement; Virginia Woolf, leading humanist and modernist writer; John Maynard Keynes, a Cambridge economist; Waldo Frank, a social and political reformer; and Randolph Silliman Bourne, a public intellectual and pacifist.

The *New Republic* initially opposed American entry into World War I, but supported intervention after the sinking of the *Lusitania* on May 7, 1915, and President Woodrow Wilson's April 2, 1917, request to Congress that it declare war on Germany. Eastman complained the *New Republic* had become Wilson's mouthpiece. Norman Thomas, writing in the *New Republic* on May 26, 1917, urged the journal "strategically situated as you are, to assist the cause of conscientious objectors." Lippmann was appointed assistant to Newton Baker, Wilson's secretary of war. He oversaw the drafting of a Fourteen Point Program that became the basis of Wilson's post-war peace plan.

Croly railed against the policies of Republican presidents in the 1920s and held out hope for the Russian Revolution. Ernest Poole, a product of a New York settlement house, visited Russia and had his pieces published in the *New Republic*. Even after Croly's death in 1930, his successor Bruce Bliven editorially urged Joseph Stalin as late as 1938 to organize his surviving "opponents" into a legal political opposition. The advice was not heeded. However, the advice of Edmund Wilson, the magazine's associate editor between 1926 and 1931 was taken seriously. Wilson developed a reputation as America's foremost literary critic by promoting the work of Princeton classmate F. Scott Fitzgerald, as well as novelist Ernest Hemingway, and the socially responsible writing of Upton Sinclair, John Dos Passos, Sinclair Lewis, and Theodore Dreiser, and social critic of Southern society, novelist William Faulkner. He was ably aided in this work by the magazine's long-time literary editor Malcolm Cowley and Wilson's wife, author, and drama critic, Mary McCarthy.

Bliven supported the presidential candidacy of socialist Norman Thomas in 1932 but became a keen supporter of Franklin Roosevelt's New Deal. That support extended to Roosevelt's war-time vice president Henry A. Wallace, who was fired from his job as Commerce Secretary in September 1946 when he opposed President Harry Truman's Cold War policies toward the Soviet Union. Wallace became editor of the *New Republic* and predicted that the Truman Doctrine, designed to limit Soviet penetration of Western Europe, would lead to "a century of fear." Wallace left the magazine in December 1947 to unsuccessfully run for president as a candidate of the Progressive Party. He was replaced as editor by Michael Whitney Straight, whose eight years of stewardship saw the magazine's circulation shrink by two-thirds to thirty thousand, leading one 1950s critic to claim the *New Republic* had become "that faint voice of the left." In 1963, seven years after leaving the magazine, Straight admitted that he had a covert relationship with Soviet agents while working for the U.S. State Department in the 1940s.

Although buoyed by the film criticism of Delmore Schwartz, the theater criticism of Eric Bentley, and the drama criticism of Robert Brustein, editor Gilbert A Harrison was unable to return the magazine to its former influence. In 1975, Harvard lecturer Martin Peretz began his long and controversial control of the publication. Peretz had been a New Left supporter of Democrat Eugene McCarthy but broke with other liberals over their support of Third World liberation movements and careened idiosyncratically through the 1980s, opposing President Ronald Reagan's domestic policies but strongly supporting his aid to Contra rebels in Nicaragua. Peretz backed both Gulf Wars but by June 2004 announced the magazine's "regret" that it had supported toppling Saddam Hussein. The Iraqi president "was a threat," *The New Republic* reported, "but he was not an urgent enough threat to require war." Peretz remained adamant in his support of Israel and terse in his opposition to those on the Left who had defected to the Palestinian cause. "Nonviolence is foreign to the political culture of Arabs generally and of the Palestinians particularly," Peretz wrote on March 19, 1986.

Peretz positioned the *New Republic* with the policies of the Democratic Leadership Council in the 1990s, seeing Bill Clinton's election as "the best chance in a generation to bring reform and renewal." It strongly endorsed the Al Gore-Joseph Lieberman ticket in 2000 and was an ardent exponent of Gore's initiative to curb global warming. The magazine steadfastly opposed President George W. Bush's tax policy and social security reform package. It long argued for abortion rights and gay marriage.

Widely publicized revelations that the magazine's associate editor Ruth Shalit had been fired for plagiarism in 1995 and that features writer Stephen Glass was discharged three years later for fabricating stories helped erode the magazine's credibility. Circulation stood at sixty thousand in 2003.

Further Reading

Conklin, Groff, ed. *New Republic Anthology, 1914–1936.* New York: Dodge Publishing, 1936.

Levy, David W. *Herbert Croly of the New Republic: The Life and Thought of an American Progressive.* Princeton, NJ: Princeton University Press, 1985.

Seideman, David. *The New Republic: A Voice of Modern Liberalism.* New York; Praeger, 1986.

Stettner, Edward A. *Shaping Modern Liberalism: Herbert Croly and Progressive Thought.* Lawrence: University of Kansas, 1993.

Straight, Michael. *After Long Silence.* New York: W.W. Norton, 1983.

Wickenden, Dorothy, ed. *The New Republic Reader: Eighty Years of Opinion and Debate.* New York: Basic Books, 1994.

BRUCE J. EVENSEN

NEW YORK DAILY NEWS

"Dead!" In "Second Coming" type, a special edition of the *Daily News*, "New York's picture newspaper" captioned on January 13, 1928, a front-page photograph of Ruth Snyder's final moment in Sing Sing Prison's electric chair. A miniature camera strapped to the ankle of photographer Tom Howard captured the electrocution as "the helmeted head of the murderess," her "face masked, hand clutching, the electrode strapped to her right leg." A record number of New Yorkers would read about it—1.5 million. It was an extraordinary moment for a newspaper that seemed near its own death barely a decade before. Instead, the *New York Daily News* had a long and prosperous life as a leader of the tabloid press and one of the makers of modern American journalism.

While convalescing from wounds and a gassing at Mareuilen-Champagne-Marne, Captain Joseph Medill Patterson, grandson of the *Chicago Tribune*'s famous publisher, met in London with Lord Northcliffe, Britain's World War I propaganda director. Northcliffe, who as Alfred Harmsworth in civilian life, had popularized the tabloid with the *Daily Mail* and the illustrated half-penny *Daily Mirror*. Patterson and Northcliffe shared the certainty that America might be "ready for a new kind of newspaper" that "thought visually" while capturing the energy of urban America by "telling stories in a flash." Patterson's cousin Robert McCormick agreed to fund the experiment with *Chicago Tribune* money.

New York's *Illustrated Daily News* began life with a bare-bones staff and borrowed presses in a squared corner of the old *Evening Mail* office on June 26, 1919. Patterson urged his young staff to "think in terms of pictures" all the time while targeting women readers with stories that had "the romance and drama" of everyday life. The first edition sold eighty-three thousand copies, but three weeks later barely ten thousand papers sold, with three in four newsstand editions going unsold. The paper's crime coverage was expanded to include daily pictures of crime scenes. Patterson's daily edict "to print pictures of New York girls involved in romance" failed to win new readers. A publicity campaign directed to "letting people know that the *News* is on the earth and what it really is" failed as well. By the fall, Patterson's experiment seemed at an end. After a million dollars in losses, the *Tribune* appeared poised in the fall of 1919 to put the paper's thirty-five member staff out of their misery.

Patterson took a series of early morning subway rides to see what riders were reading. Patterson had hoped to attract women readers between seventeen and thirty years of age with contests, serials and tall tales of romance and mystery. He was struck how commuting males of all ages had their papers opened to the sports page. His fear had been that the paper's shoestring operation "couldn't compete with other papers in sports anymore than we can with the stock market." As an experiment Patterson authorized the paper's photographic department "to take more and better pictures" of major sporting events and to publish them "before anyone else." By the end of the year the paper's circulation improved to fifty-seven thousand. By June of 1920 the paper was perfecting "picture scoops" that played sports and celebrity to the limit. Circulation surged to one hundred thousand. A real breakthrough came on September 7, 1920, when staff photographer Lou Walker fit a telescopic lens on a light sensitive Graflex camera to capture heavyweight champion Jack Dempsey's knockout of Billy Miske in a title bout. A record press run followed. Patterson was amused to see that competitors who had castigated the *News* for its "common pandering to the meretricious tastes of the masses" eagerly copied the paper's style and its pictures in a feeble effort to steal the paper's circulation.

The paper's expanded sports coverage, cleaner look and increased reliance on pictures and contests boosted circulation to 275,000 by the end of 1920. Within three years its Sunday circulation of one million would be the nation's largest. Five thousand posters strategically placed around the city teased readers with photo stunts and hot pink headlines. The paper's "bulldog edition" immodestly asked its competitors in full-page headlines "How does the *Daily News* do it?" Subway tours now showed businessmen were hiding copies of the disreputable *Daily News* inside the socially respectable *New York Times*. By April 1925 the paper's sports section, run by "gee-whiz" journalist Paul Gallico and determined to "impress and excite the reader" by "playing athletic competition for high drama," had swelled to eight full pages. Advertisers who had once shunned the *Daily News* "because it wasn't good for selling anything but corsets" now came calling to Emmet J. Gordon, the paper's business manager, who told them to wait their turn.

The *Daily News* cultivated consumption in America's prosperity decade by appealing to first and second generation Jews, Italians, Irish, Germans, Poles, Chinese, Greeks, Spaniards, and Egyptians who read the paper, its market analyst Sinclair Dakin found, "as a right of passage" into American society. These garment workers, East Side salesmen, pushcart peddlers, and union men wanted "grapefruit for breakfast, to own their own home, to have money in the bank, and a better future for Sweeney juniors."

The *Daily News* eagerly embraced Franklin Roosevelt's New Deal. Patterson ordered his editors to tell the story of the Great Depression with the same passion they had shown in establishing the paper's reputation as a friend of the working class. Patterson pushed for preparedness and a bigger navy on the eve of Pearl Harbor and after the war saw the *Daily News* gain a daily circulation of 2,400,000 and a Sunday circulation of 4,500,000, twice the totals of any other American newspaper. These gains were not sustained after Patterson's death in 1946. The paper lost 240,000 readers in the 1950s and 900,000 on Sundays. Some of its readers graduated to the *New York Times*, which had a daily circulation gain of 139,000 during the decade and 184,000 on Sundays. Others moved to the suburbs. Long Island's *Newsday*, guided by Patterson's daughter Alicia, enjoyed a circulation of 330,000 by 1961.

The *Daily News* building at 220 East 42 Street, designed by Raymond Hood, became a national landmark and the model for Superman's *Daily Planet* where Clark Kent fought for "the American way." Pulitzer Prize winning cartoonist C.D. Batchelor and his successor Bill Gallo became local favorites with a national following. The paper would win ten Pulitzer Prizes in all, including one in international reporting for its 1959 series by Joseph Martin and Philip Santora that disclosed the brutality of the Batista regime in Cuba and the prediction by the authors that Fidel Castro, leader of a revolutionary movement, would soon come to power. The *Daily News* won praise and readers for its reporting on the November 1963 assassination of President John F. Kennedy and the first moon landing in July 1969. Writers Jimmy Breslin, Pete Hamill, Mike Lupica, Juan Gonzalez, and Jami Bernard contributed to the paper's solid reputation during the final third of the twentieth century along with famous photos and headlines that included managing editor William Brink's header on October 30, 1975, that read "Ford to City: Drop Dead." President Ford would later say that his decision not to offer New York City financial aid and that headline probably cost him the state of New York in the closely-contested 1976 presidential election he narrowly lost to Jimmy Carter.

British media millionaire Robert Maxwell kept the financially strapped *Daily News* in business in the early 1990s. The paper's purchase by Mort Zuckerman in 1993 placed it on firmer financial footing. The paper's August 18, 1998, headline "Liar, Liar" when President Bill Clinton admitted to "inappropriate behavior" with a White House intern that nearly cost him the presidency became a classic. Its July 18, 1999, headline "Lost!" announced the crash of a private plane off Martha's Vineyard that killed John F. Kennedy, Jr. and two companions. By 2006, the paper's eight hundred thousand daily circulation made it the nation's seventh most widely read paper. Its claim to being "New York's Hometown Newspaper" and "The Eyes, the Ears, and the Honest Voice of New York" harkened back to a long history in which the *Daily News* was widely perceived as Gotham's "people's paper."

Further Reading

Alexander, Jack. "Vox Populi." *New Yorker*, August 6, 1938, 27–32.

Hannigan, William. *New York Noir: Crime Photos from the Daily News Archive*. New York: Rizzoli, 1997.

O'Sullivan, Shawn, ed. *New York Exposed: Photographs from the Daily News*. New York: Abrams, 2001.

Papers of Joseph Medill Patterson, Chicago Tribune Archives, Chicago, Illinois.

Papers of Joseph Medill Patterson, Donnelley Library, Lake Forest College, Lake Forest, IL.

Schneider, Walter E. "Fabulous Rise of the *N.Y. Daily News*." *Editor and Publisher*, June 24, 1939, 5.

BRUCE J. EVENSEN

NEW YORK HERALD

For most of the nineteenth century, the *New York Herald* (1835–1924) was among the most important and popular newspapers in the United States. It pioneered the use of innovative newsgathering techniques and became a great American *news*paper—one concerned primarily with reporting current events in a straightforward, non-partisan way, rather than serving as a polemical mouthpiece for a political party or cause. Incredibly, for all but six of its eighty-nine years as an independent newspaper, the *Herald* was owned and run by just two people: the James Gordon Bennetts, father and son.

The elder Bennett (1795–1872) was a native of Scotland who rejected his family's push to study for the priesthood and headed for America after reading Benjamin Franklin's autobiography. Arriving in New York in 1822, he began writing for several papers before purchasing the *New York Courier*, only to quickly resell it. A second attempt at running a paper, the *New York Globe*, lasted only one month.

In 1835, with just $500 in his pocket, Bennett launched the *Herald*, a one-cent rival to Benjamin Day's *New York Sun*. He had no illusions about the challenge—or his ability to meet them. "Shakespeare is the great genius of the drama, Scott of the novel, Milton and Byron of the poem —and I mean to be the genius of the newspaper press," he wrote.

He discarded the sarcastic police reports which had proved so popular in the *Sun* in favor of comprehensive news articles told straightforwardly; his editorial comments were independent with no real hint of partisan bias. The *Herald* boasted more foreign news, business coverage (indeed, the paper's stock market reports were the forerunner of the modern financial pages) and what Bennett called "theatrical chit-chat" than its rivals. The writing was livelier and, as time went on, grew more sensational.

That was never more true than in the spring of 1836, when Bennett and the *Herald* leapfrogged to the head of the New York newspaper world with its coverage of the murder of Ellen Jewett, a local prostitute. Never before had a crime been covered so thoroughly; Bennett himself even played detective and became convinced of the accused killer's innocence (he was later acquitted). From then on, lurid crime news became of the *Herald*'s most popular features.

Bennett's instinct was to provide his readers what they wanted—not what he thought they should want. "An editor must always be with the people—think with them—feel with them—and he need fear nothing, he will always be right" he wrote. He eschewed the formalities and pruderies of contemporary newspaper writing in favor of a sparkling, often risqué style. And he brought about major innovations in illustration—the most famous example being the full page of woodcuts of Andrew Jackson's funeral.

Rival editors initially despaired at Bennett's success: Henry Raymond of the *New York Times* wrote that "I wish the Devil would come 'round every evening to tell me what the people of New York want to read, as he does Bennett." Others demonized him: The *Philadelphia Public Ledger* wrote that of Bennett's refusal to use a carte de visite because he had one "engraved on his face: We should say that the job was done not by the printer's devil but the devil's printer; perhaps by the old gentleman himself." Even the staid *New York Times* published a cartoon attack on Bennett "the Satanic," the only time a cartoon has appeared on the paper's front page.

It was about this time that Bennett's rivals launched what came to be known as the "moral war" against the *Herald*; a widespread demand, aided by business officials and religious leaders, that the public boycott the paper because of its "reckless depravity" and "moral leprosy." But all the indignation had little effect; though it lost some circulation, by 1840 it was the most widely read newspaper in the world.

Bennett had supported compromises on slavery, and even took a soft line towards southern secession, in hopes of avoiding a civil war. When the conflict finally broke out, the *Herald* shifted course and became a firm backer of the Union cause. Yet it was widely viewed as a "soft peace" or even Copperhead organ; still, the paper's reporting remained non-partisan and provided the most comprehensive news of the war. Reporters followed Bennett's instructions to "Get the names of the dead men on every battlefield as soon as you can … But that alone is not enough. Get the names of the wounded. Find out their condition and, if possible, ask them if they have any message they wish relayed to their relatives. Get the facts, and get them quickly." Generations of battlefield reporters who followed would follow this same formula.

In 1867, Bennett turned over the reins to his twenty-five-year-old playboy son and namesake, who took control with little journalistic training. Born to a life of wealth and privilege, James Gordon Bennett Jr. (1841–1918) proceeded to run the paper—largely in absentia—for more than half a century, during which its fortune alternately rose (thanks largely to his journalistic instincts and flair for sensational stunts) and ebbed (due mainly to his personal eccentricity and erratic behavior).

Bennett, Jr. spent his boyhood in Paris at the insistence of his mother, who could not bear to see the way New York society vilified her husband and his scandalous, though wildly popular, newspaper. Indulged and pampered, he won a reputation as a playboy with a special taste for yachting.

But Bennett Jr. improved on his father's legendary formula for journalistic success and drove the paper at his own frenzied pace and adapted its pages to his own peculiar notion of news. Like his father, he believed beating his rivals on both speed and content. Yet he was not content to sit back and wait for news to happen. And, also like his father, he did not believe in an impersonal style of journalism. "I make news," he told his editors. "If I want the *Herald* to be turned upside down, it must be turned upside down." In 1869, he sent the British correspondent Henry Stanley to Africa to search for Dr. David Livingstone, a missionary believed to be missing. Their meeting more than two years later produced one of the most famous dispatches in journalistic history:

"Preserving a calmness of exterior before the Arabs which was hard to simulate as he reached the group, Mr. Stanley said: 'Dr. Livingstone, I presume?' A smile lit up the features of the pale white man as he answered: 'Yes, that is my name.'"

In 1874, the *Herald* stunned New York by devoting its entire front page to a story under the headline: "Escaped Animals Roam Streets of Manhattan." The article terrified the populace, which remained largely indoors that day; most people had not read to the end of the story, which admitted that it was a complete fabrication designed to call attention to conditions at the Central Park Zoo. He also financed a disastrous Arctic expedition by George W. DeLong which ended with the deaths of the noted explorer and most of his men.

But Bennett's paper also scored legitimate news beats. And it became a social crusader, distributing free ice in the slums during the hot summers and providing free food and medical care to the poor.

In 1877, following a social scandal in which he reportedly urinated into the fireplace at his fiancée's home and then was horsewhipped by her brother, Bennett returned to Paris, where he remained in self-exile for the rest of his life. But he continued to run the *Herald* with the same firm control, spending a fortune in daily cables with precise instructions.

In 1883, he formed a company with the mining magnate John Mackay to build a new transatlantic cable, breaking Jay Gould's monopoly; four years later, he established a Paris edition of the *Herald*, which became the leading English-language paper in Europe and which survives today as the *International Herald Tribune*. At age seventy-three, he married for the first time, wedding the daughter of Paul Reuter, founder of the news agency.

There were setbacks for the paper under Bennett, though. The paper could not compete with the yellow journalism of the Hearst and Pulitzer papers even if their sensationalistic approach owed much to Bennett's father's own style. To make matters worse, Hearst instigated prosecution of the *Herald* for running ads for houses of prostitution; Bennett was forced to pay a $31,000 fine. He also made disastrous business decisions, raising advertising rates even as circulation fell and retaining agate-type ads when other papers had discarded them; the result was a huge loss in display advertising. Moreover, he funneled the paper's profits to his own bank account.

The paper continued to slide and was losing money when Bennett died in 1918. It was sold to Frank Munsey, who merged it with the *Sun.* His repeated attempts to buy the *New York Tribune* from the Reid family were rebuffed, so he sold them the *Herald* instead. The two papers were merged in 1924 as the *New York Herald Tribune,* which lasted until 1966.

Further Reading

[James Gordon Bennett, Jr.], *New York Times,* May 15, 1918.

Campbell, W. Joseph. *The Year That Defined American Journalism: 1897 and the Clash of Paradigms.* New York: Routledge, 2006.

Oliver Carlson. *The Man Who Made News: James Gordon Bennet.* New York: Duell, Sloan and Pearce, 1942.

Crockett, Albert Stevens. *When James Gordon Bennett Was Caliph of Baghdad.* New York: Funk & Wagnalls, 1926.

Kluger, Richard. *The Paper: The Life and Death of the New York Herald Tribune.* New York: Alfred A. Knopf, 1986.

O'Connor, Richard. *The Scandalous Mr. Bennett.* Garden City, NY: Doubleday & Co., 1962.

Seitz, Don C. *The James Gordon Bennetts, Father and Son.* Indianapolis: Bobbs-Merrill, 1928.

ERIC FETTMANN

NEW YORK MAGAZINE

Founded in 1968, *New York Magazine* pioneered a hip, gossipy brand of urban journalism that appealed to the refined sensibilities of the kinds of people who read the venerable *New Yorker*—with which it was designed to compete—as well as the trendy Andy Warhol crowd that was building a new club and art scene downtown. Like the *New Yorker,* *New York Magazine* operated on the premise that Manhattan was the center of the universe.

The weekly magazine reflected the melded sensibilities of the two partners who founded it. Milton Glaser, a preeminent designer, gave the magazine its modern look while editor Clay Felker infused it with a "new journalism" ethos by tapping maverick writers working in that genre, notably Tom Wolfe, whose counter-culture classic, *The Electric Kool-Aid Acid Test,* began as an article in *New York.* Prior to the founding of the magazine, Felker had been the editor of a Sunday supplement for the doomed *New York Herald-Tribune,* where he nurtured writers such as Wolfe, Jimmy Breslin, and Gail Sheehy.

But *New York,* which fed the narcissism of its young, upscale readership, was driven by a revolutionary consumer ethos as well as a journalistic one. In the words of early associate Michael Wolff, Felker proposed that "you are what you buy." *New York,* Wolff explained, "wasn't so much a guide to the city as it was a guide to being cleverer, hipper, more in-the-know." In other words, *New York's* readers were among the first yuppies.

As New York the city sank towards its graffiti-covered, crime-ridden, bankrupt nadir of the 1970s, *New York* the magazine thrived by celebrating the city's virtues at the same time it produced radical chic exposés on race and class

inequities that were far more cutting than those published in the city's newspaper press. Felker told *Folio Magazine* in 2004 that as the city drifted into crisis under the pressure of poor political leadership and white flight, "we felt that the thing to do was to talk about what was good about the city, point out what was wrong and how to deal with it."

New York was also in the forefront of niche marketing and branding. In the 1960s, television was the prime arena for broad-based mass entertainment. As television ascended, it eclipsed general circulation magazines like *Life, Colliers,* and the *Saturday Evening Post.* In order to compete, many magazine entrepreneurs identified affluent market segments and created products that spoke directly, and exclusively, to them. *New York* was such a magazine. It gave its hipper-than-thou, affluent readers articles that spoke to their interests, ambitions, and vanities.

Once Felker and Glaser demonstrated their formula, city papers began popping up in urban centers all over the United States. According to analyst Miriam Greenberg, "these urban lifestyle magazines, as they might be called, are consumer magazines that fuse the identity and consumption habits of their readers with the branded 'lifestyle' of a given metropolitan region. . . ." In fact, *New York* was itself an accessory. Reading it did not make one cool; having it on one's Jens Rimson-designed coffee table did.

The influence of *New York* went far beyond the new wave of city magazines it spawned. In its wake followed niche publications that catered to runners, cyclists, knitters, vegetarians, pot smokers—whoever had the interest, and the money, to make the magazine appealing to advertisers seeking to reach them.

Felker attempted to turn *New York* into a national magazine in the 1970s, an effort that squandered much of the publication's cultural and financial capital. The drive to take the publication national led Felker to join forces with a corporate firm whose clients demanded that the magazine be made more advertiser-friendly—i.e., more mainstream and less controversial. Disgusted, writers like Breslin, who called the magazine "too dilettantish," stopped contributing.

In 1977, Australian magnate Rupert Murdoch gained control of the magazine and Felker was forced out. Murdoch diluted *New York's* editorial content, diminishing its appeal to young readers, who in any case had far more lifestyle-oriented media products to choose from than they did in 1968. In 1991, Murdoch sold *New York* to Primedia, which in turn sold the magazine to current publisher Bruce Wasserstein in 2004.

The magazine has waned in prominence and influence since those heady early days, in large part because of the many imitators it inspired in New York City and elsewhere. But its core ethos—snob appeal—survives. The headline over a recent cover story was, "Filthy Stinking Rich."

Felker, though, believed the magazine he founded had lost its way. "You get the feeling that they are scrambling around to do special issues to sell advertising," he told *Folio* in 2004. "It's not very consistent."

Further Reading

Barack, Lauren. "Clay Felker on Running *New Yor.,*" *Folio*. January 1, 2004.

Greenberg, Miriam. "Branding Cities: A Social History of the Urban Lifestyle Magazine." *Urban Affairs Review*, Vol. 36, no. 2 (November 2000): 228–263.

Schlosberg, J. "The Glittering World of City Magazines." *American Demographics*, July 1986: 22–25.

Wolff, Michael. "35 Years: The Story of New York." *New York Magazine,* April 7, 2003.

MIKE DILLON

NEW YORK POST

In 2006, the *New York Post*, part of the Rupert Murdoch media empire, was a tabloid known for its sensational headlines, sports and celebrity gossip sections, and conservative perspective. The *Post* had the eighth-largest newspaper circulation in the United States (about 650,000 daily circulation), ranking fourth in New York City behind the *Wall Street Journal*, the *New York Times,* and the *New York Daily News.*

The newspaper has an illustrious past, having been founded by former Treasury Secretary Alexander Hamilton in 1801 as the *New-York Evening Post*, making it one of the oldest newspapers published in the United States. Hamilton raised $10,000 for this second effort at a Federalist publication, his first being the *Gazette of the United States*. From the start, the *Post* attacked the Republican policies of the Thomas Jefferson administration and served as the leading voice of the Federalists. In fact, Hamilton himself helped launch the paper by writing an eighteen-part series, under the pseudonym Lucius Crassus, that attacked Jeffersonian policies. When Hamilton was shot and killed in a duel with Vice President Aaron Burr in 1804, the *Post* put a black border around the front-page report.

For most of its history, the *Post* had a distinctly progressive voice. One of its editors in the nineteenth century was William Cullen Bryant, who from 1829 to 1878 led the newspaper as a strong opponent of slavery, as an ally to President Abraham Lincoln, and as a supporter of the emerging trade union movement. In the late 1890s, department stores in New York City pulled their advertising from the *Post* in a boycott because of the newspaper's editorial stand in favor of free trade.

The New York newspaper wars never abated. In 1898, the *Post* accused the "yellow journals" such as William Randolph Hearst's *New York Journal* of "fomenting" the Spanish-American War. When the war's outcome soon proved favorable, the *Journal* reprinted the *Post* accusation with an in-your-face headline: "Some People Say the Journal Brought on This War. How Do You Like It as Far as It's Gone."

In 1900, Oswald Garrison Villard became the owner of the *Post* following his father's death. He was a founding member of both the National Association for the Advancement of Colored People (NAACP) and the American Civil Liberties Union (ACLU) and supported women's suffrage and equal rights for African Americans. Largely educated in Germany, Villard was a pacifist who opposed U.S. participation in World War I, upsetting his patriotic readers and forcing him to sell the *Post*.

By the end of World War I, the *Post*'s great days of influence were over and hard financial times were coming. The *Post* converted to a streamlined tabloid in 1942 and remained a supporter of progressive politics. For example, it was the only New York City daily to support Democrat Adlai Stevenson over Republican Dwight Eisenhower in the presidential elections of 1952 and 1956.

The *Post* moved away from being a liberal stalwart upon its purchase by the Australian-born Murdoch in 1977. He soon divested the newspaper because of federal regulations limiting cross-media ownership; Murdoch had just started the Fox television network and needed his flagship TV station in New York City. After Murdoch became a U.S. citizen in 1985, which loosened restrictions upon his ownership of U.S. media, his News Corporation reacquired the financially struggling *Post* in 1993.

Murdoch imported a sensationalist style of tabloid journalism from his British newspapers, including *The Sun*, which had the leading circulation in Britain. On the newsstand, the *Post*'s front page screamed its daily headline in big, black letters. The most famous example remains "Headless Body in Topless Bar." In recent times, the *Post* called a former General Mills executive who eliminated jobs a "cereal killer."

The *Post* hemorrhaged money in its war with the *Daily News* for tabloid supremacy, in part because Murdoch started a price war with the *Daily News* in 2000 by cutting its price from 50 cents to a quarter. Over several months, circulation climbed by some fifty thousand. The *Post* also became edgier in content. For instance, just a week after the terrorist attack of September 11, 2001, the *Post* was one of five news organizations sent anthrax-contaminated letters. A subsequent *Post* front page showed a female *Post* employee with an upright middle finger and the headline "ANTHRAX THIS."

Further Reading

Auletta, Ken. *Backstory: Inside the Business of News*. New York: Penguin Press, 2003.

Burns, Eric. *Infamous Scribblers: The Founding Fathers and the Rowdy Beginnings of American Journalism*. New York: Public Affairs, 2006.

Campbell, W. Joseph. *Yellow Journalism: Puncturing the Myths, Defining the Legacies.* Westport, CT: Praeger, 2001.

Copeland, David A. *Colonial American Newspapers: Character and Content*. Newark: University of Delaware Press, 1997.

Nevins, Allan. *The Evening Post: A Century of Journalism*. New York: Russell & Russell, 1922.

PAUL PARSONS

NEW YORK SUN

America's first successful penny newspaper (an earlier experiment folded after just three weeks), the *New York Sun* (1833–1950) was also the first paper to employ newsboys as sales agents and the first to use a steam-powered press, rather than a hand-cranked one, to mass-print its copies. Its most important contribution, however, was to make newspapers of the 1830s accessible to the poorly paid common laborers of the day—both through its affordable price and its fresh, lively approach to news writing.

Benjamin H. Day was just twenty-two years old when he founded the *Sun* on Sept. 3, 1833, in an effort to supplement his declining job-printing business. The paper was but four pages (it was decades before more were added) and, unlike its competitors, featured short, bright stories about anything that proved interesting, whether socially significant or not, rather than lengthy political essays or even political news. Its most notable feature, styled after those in the London papers, was the police report: humorous and sardonic snippets from the day's session in magistrates court. It was compiled by George Wisner and became immensely popular—as did the *Sun* itself. By 1837, the *Sun's* circulation —spread by the then-unknown practice of employing carriers in the streets—totaled more than that what four years earlier had been the circulation of all other New York dailies combined. The paper seemed truly to reflect its slogan, "It Shines for All."

In 1835, the paper's circulation had tripled overnight when a writer named Richard Adams Locke produced what became one of the greatest "fakes" in newspaper history: an account of "telescopic observations" showing that a race of bat-like creatures inhabited the moon. His series ran for more than a week before the hoax was disclosed by a rival reporter in whom a drunken Locke had confided. The *Sun's* circulation exceeded nineteen thousand, the largest in the world, so Day claimed.

In 1837, scared off by losses during a financial panic that year and competition from rival penny dailies, Day sold the paper to his brother-in-law, Moses Y. Beach, under whose guidance the *Sun* continued to hold its circulation lead among U.S. papers for another fifteen years (except for a seventeen-month period during the Civil War, when it was published as a religious paper by a rich young man who paid Beach $100,000 to do so). And it was Beach who in 1848 hosted the meeting of leading newspaper publishers at which the Associated Press was founded.

Charles A. Dana, backed by politicians Roscoe Conking and William Evarts, bought the paper in 1868 and ushered in the paper's glory era. His formula was innovative, but simple: "The newspaper must be founded upon human nature. It must correspond to the wants of the people. It must furnish that sort of information which the people demand, or else it can never be successful." Yet he did this without pandering to his readers, or indulging in sensationalism. As one of his biographers, Frank O'Brien, put it, Dana "had the indefinable newspaper instinct that knows when a tomcat on the steps of City Hall is more important than a crisis in the Balkans." Dana himself (or possibly his city editor, John Bogart—no one knows for certain) put it best in the classic definition: "When a dog bites a man, that is not news. When a man bites a dog, that is news." Dana's formula was successful and, by 1876, he had tripled the paper's circulation,

yet he refused to publish a paper that was larger than four pages. In 1897, as per his instructions, the *Sun* famously published an obituary for him that was only one sentence long: "Charles Anderson Dana, editor of the *Sun,* died yesterday afternoon."

In 1897, Dana's successor, E.P. Mitchell, handed an editorial writer named Francis Pharcellus Church a letter from an eight-year-old girl asking if Santa Claus existed and instructed him to compose an answer for the paper. The result, with its classic assurance that "Yes, Virginia, there is a Santa Claus," is probably the most famous newspaper editorial ever written. Less than a decade later, Will Irwin composed another classic, "The City That Was," in the wake of the San Francisco earthquake. Other notable *Sun* writers of the period included the swashbuckling war correspondent Richard Harding Davis and the pioneer reform photographer, Jacob Riis.

In 1916, the paper passed to Frank Munsey, whose stated mission was to consolidate existing newspapers out of existence. Four years later, the Morning *Sun* was merged into the *New York Herald*; the Evening *Sun,* which remained was a pale imitation of the legendary paper of Dana's day. Munsey died in 1925 and left the paper to the Metropolitan Museum of Art, which sold it to William T. Dewart.

Although 1949 was to prove the high-water mark for circulation among New York's daily newspapers, it was the beginning of the end for the *Sun,* which had staggered along. Two years earlier, the paper had achieved its second-highest circulation in history, a total of 314,156 copies sold daily. But from that point on, sales begin to slip precipitously; by the fall of 1949, the *Sun* had lost fifty-three thousand copies—a 17 percent drop. Declining ad sales, combined with increased costs and a reluctance to invest in new technology prompted Dewart to sell the paper to Scripps-Howard, which merged it with the *New York World-Telegram.* The year 1949, though, brought the paper recognition for one of its greatest editorial accomplishments: a Pulitzer Prize for Malcolm Johnson's series exposing corruption on the docks, which was adapted by Budd Schulberg into the classic motion picture *On the Waterfront.*

A harsh, but no doubt realistic, obituary for the paper was written by John S. Knight, then-publisher of the *Chicago Daily News* and the *Detroit Free Press:* "The *Sun* became just another good newspaper with dull, factual reporting and complete market coverage, but wholly lacking in sparkle, imagination and impact" —a telling indictment of a paper once known for its emphasis on just those qualities. Moreover, he added, "The death of the *Sun* is a graphic illustration of what can happen to any newspaper when it lives with a cash register in the place where its editorial heart belongs."

In 2002, a new daily paper calling itself the *New York Sun* and continuing the edition numbers from where they left off in 1950, made its debut. Although it revived the original paper's nameplate logo and continued numbering its issues from where the original paper left off more than a half-century earlier, there was no connection.

Further Reading

Dana, Charles A. *The Art of Newspaper Making*. New York: D. Appleton, 1895.

Hudson, Frederic. *Journalism in the United States From 1690 to 1872*. New York: Haskell House, 1968, original published 1873.

Liebling, A.J. "Dismally," *The Press*. New York: Ballantine Books, 1975, originally in *The New Yorker*, January 28, 1950.

"Light That Failed." *The Washington Post*. Jan. 5, 1950.

Mitchell, Edward P. "Mr. Dana of 'The Sun'." *McClure's Magazine,* Oct. 1894.

O'Brien, Frank M. *The Story of The Sun*. New York: Harper, 1923.

Porter, Russell. "World-Telegram Acquires The Sun; Two Merge Today." *New York Times,* January 5, 1950.

ERIC FETTMANN

NEW YORK TIMES

"The first time the editors saw that photograph, we knew that we were seeing a freeze-frame of a world-altering moment," observed Howell Raines, executive editor of the *New York Times*, of a picture taken moments before United Airlines flight 175 struck the south tower of the World Trade Center on the morning of September 11, 2001. The picture would be a part of the paper's extraordinary coverage of events on that day and would win its 1,100 member news department an unprecedented six Pulitzer Prizes, two George Polk Awards, and honors from the Overseas Press Club and the American Society of Newspaper Editors, while re-establishing the *New York Times*, then in its one hundred and fiftieth year, as the newspaper of record in the United States. No newspaper is more significant in deciding what is the news of the day and none is more influential in setting the news agenda for print and broadcast journalists across the country. And no American newspaper has been more important in the development of journalistic standards and practices than the *New York Times*.

"We do not mean to write as if we were in a passion unless that shall really be the case," wrote Henry Jarvis Raymond, publisher of the *New-York Daily Times* wrote on September 18, 1851 in the paper's first issue, "and we shall make it a point to get into a passion as rarely as possible." Raymond and *Times* co-founder George Jones, an Albany banker, had learned the newspaper business from Horace Greeley, publisher of the *New York Tribune*, and within two years exceeded his circulation by a pattern of careful and conscientious reporting. "There are few things in the world which it is worthwhile to get angry about," Raymond told his readers, "and they are just the things anger will not improve." Raymond, a Whig, was an early supporter of the Republican Party, helped write its 1856 platform, reported the first battle of Bull Run at the beginning of the Civil War, and defended the *Times* office with a Gatling gun in July 1863 against anti-draft rioters who blamed it for supporting "this black Republican war." One hundred nineteen people were killed and thousands injured before federal troops ended the uprising. Raymond was elected to the House of Representatives in 1864, where he worked for national reconciliation. His strong opposition to Radical Republican reconstruction in the South, alienated him from the party. Exhausted by overwork, Raymond died suddenly on June 18, 1869 at the age of 49.

Raymond's war "to end venality in public affairs" became the basis of the *Times* determined campaign to smash the Tweed Ring. Beginning in September 1870, *Times* editor Louis J. Jennings, a no-nonsense Englishman, ably assisted by managing editor John C. Reid and chief political correspondent John Foord, published proof that Tammany boss William M. Tweed and his political organization had bilked New York City of an estimated $100 million. The *Times* turned down a five million dollar bribe to stop the series. When Tweed was convicted for his crime, the *Times* celebrated "the end of Irish Catholic despotism that rules the City of New York, the Metropolis of Free America." The two decades that followed, however, nearly saw the end of the *Times*. Jones was disgusted with the scandals of the Grant administration and steered the paper toward political independence. In 1876, the paper was alone in not taking sides in the aftermath of the disputed presidential election between Rutherford B. Hayes and Samuel J. Tilden. Charles Ransom Miller, who became the paper's editor on April 13, 1883, dropped the paper's price to two cents, hoping to compete with the *New York Sun* and the *New York World*, and endorsed Grover Cleveland, a Democrat, for president in 1884. Jones died in 1891 with many expecting the "Old Gray Lady" to quickly follow.

The *Times* circulation had sunk to 9,000, when Adolph S. Ochs, publisher of the *Chattanooga Times*, bought a controlling interest in the paper on August 18, 1896, with $75,000 in borrowed money. Ochs brought his background in printing to give the *Times* a brighter look. An illustrated Sunday magazine was launched on September 6. Agate type was banned and the space between lines widened. The "Saturday Review of Books" began appearing on October 10. The paper made a major commitment to business and financial reporting. On October 18, "News Condensed" began appearing on the front page for readers commuting to work. A week later, the paper's famous motto, "All the News That's Fit to Print," first appeared. Ochs aimed to distinguish the *Times* from its yellow press competitors, Joseph Pulitzer's *New York World* and William Randolph Hearst's *New York Journal*. The paper's fifty half-tone photographs of Queen Victoria's Jubilee procession on July 4, 1897 sold out. Circulation soared to 25,000. When Ochs cut the paper's price to a penny on October 10, 1898, readership tripled within a year. The *Times* began the new century with a circulation of 102,000 readers, surpassing the storied *New York Sun*.

Ochs hired managing editors Henry Lowenthal and Carr Van Anda to give the *Times* unparalleled reporting on local and state government. Louis Wiley was brought in to run the business office and plan for plant expansion. Frederick Mortimer ran "Topics of the Times" devoted to lively reporting on science and the arts. Ochs promised his readers the *Times* would report the news "impartially, without fear or favor." The paper published its first edition from the $2.5 million Times Tower on January 2, 1905. Two years later, a lighted ball began its annual descent to Times Square to mark each new year. Those years would see major stories carefully chronicled by America's new newspaper of record. The *Times* sponsored Robert Peary's race to the North Pole in September 1909 and used the wireless to report the sinking of the *Titanic* in April 1912. The *Times* won its first Pulitzer Prize in June 1918 for its reporting on World War I. The following year it was the only newspaper in the world to print the entire Treaty of Versailles. The *Times* had an exclusive on the best-remembered story of America's Jazz Age. It signed aviator Charles A. Lindbergh to give *Times* readers a first-hand account of his May 1927 crossing of the Atlantic. On November 6, 1928, thousands gathered to watch 14,800 bulbs installed on the side of Times Tower flash the news bulletin that Hebert Hoover had defeated Al Smith for president.

When Ochs died on April 8, 1935, the *Times* was firmly established as America's leading newspaper, circulating to half a million daily readers and three-quarters of a million on Sundays. Ralph Pulitzer spoke for many when he said the *Times* under Ochs had demonstrated that "the life-blood of a newspaper is the news." Arthur Brisbane observed that Ochs had "made the *Times* a permanent and useful institution," while encouraging other publishers to take their public service seriously. Ochs's 44-year-old son-in-law Arthur Hays Sulzberger promised to continue the paper's pattern of "honest and impersonal journalism," while analyzing events that seemed to threaten another world war. Lester Markel directed "News of the Week in Review" for the Sunday *Times*; Washington bureau chief Arthur Krock offered signed columns on the editorial page; and Anne O'Hare McCormick joined the paper's editorial board and introduced a column on international affairs. A lead editorial on June 15, 1938, written by Charles Merz warned America's "way of life" was threatened by German aggression in Europe and Japanese actions in Asia. In August 1940, James Reston reported the Nazi blitzkrieg on London. Critics charged *Times* reporting was "interventionist." On December 8, 1941 the paper reported "the sudden and unexpected attack on Pearl Harbor" had "plunged the United States and Japan into active war."

Byron Darnton and Robert Post were *Times* reporters killed covering the war. Harold Denny and Otto Tolischus became prisoners of war. Tolischus was tortured by the Japanese. Drew Middleton, Hanson Baldwin, Harold Denny, Herbert Matthews, and the publisher's nephew, Cyrus Sulzberger, covered the conflict. William L. Laurence received two Pulitzer Prizes for his reporting on the Manhattan Project and its aftermath. He was the only journalist to witness the dropping of the atomic bomb on Nagasaki. The *Times*' Clifton Daniel, soon to become President Harry S Truman's son-in-law, reported in August 1945, "the hitherto secret details of the grisly race between Germany and the Allies to find a weapon so destructive that it would insure absolute victory." In the years following the war, the *Times* came under heavy criticism for correspondent Walter Duranty's

failure to report Joseph Stalin's Ukrainian genocide in the 1930s and the paper's avoidance of Hitler's "final solution" that exterminated six million European Jews. The paper initially opposed the creation of a Jewish state in Palestine and only supported it in May 1948 as part of a two state solution brokered by the United Nations. Under executive managing editor Turner Catledge, the *Times* was attacked by Radio Moscow in March 1952 as a "tool of the monopolies" in its distortion of the "peaceful policies of the Soviet government." A Senate committee in January 1956, led by Mississippi Senator James Eastland, investigated allegations the *Times* staff had been penetrated "by one hundred Communist Party members." The *Times* editorially charged that "if the real purpose of the present inquiry is to demonstrate that a free newspaper's policies can be swayed by Congressional pressure, then we say to Mr. Eastland and his counsel that they are wasting their time."

One famous example of *Times* - government cooperation occurred on the eve of the Bay of Pigs, the April 17, 1961 invasion of Fidel Castro's Cuba by Cuban rebels who had been trained in South Florida by the Central Intelligence Agency. Reporter Tad Szulc knew the day of the invasion but Washington bureau chief James Reston ordered it withheld. After the invaders were slaughtered on the beach, President John F. Kennedy quipped that had the *Times* reported what it knew he would have called off the attack and avoided "a colossal mistake." Two years later, Kennedy was rebuffed by the *Times* new publisher, 37-year-old Arthur Ochs "Punch" Sulzberger, when he asked that *Times* reporter David Halberstam be transferred out of South Vietnam. Halberstam's reporting on a growing American "quagmire" received a Pulitzer Prize. In December 1966, Harrison E. Salisbury was rebuked by the Lyndon B. Johnson administration after he traveled to Hanoi and reported American warplanes were bombing non-military targets. His reporting encouraged press skepticism toward the war.

The *Times* also made history in court. In *Times v. Sullivan*, the U.S. Supreme Court ruled in March 1964 that public officials could not sue newspapers for libel unless they proved the press maliciously disregarded the truth. In February 1970, *Times* reporter Earl Caldwell refused to appear before a federal grand jury to disclose confidential sources used in his story on the Black Panthers. The U.S. District Court ruled that reporters were constitutionally protected from revealing confidential sources unless the government could show a "compelling interest." The case led to the founding of the Reporters Committee for Freedom of the Press and the fight for shield laws to protect reporters and their sources. On June 30, 1971 the Supreme Court ruled (*New York Times v. U. S.*) that the *Times* could continue publishing the Pentagon Papers over the objections of the Nixon administration. The series revealed a classified account of U.S. involvement in the Vietnam War. Richard Nixon's effort to prevent further government leaks would lead to the Watergate scandal and his resigning the presidency in 1974. Reston wrote no public figure had "studied the press so carefully and understood them so little."

On January 28, 1986 the space shuttle *Challenger*

exploded 74 seconds after liftoff. All seven astronauts were killed. The following year the *Times* received a Pulitzer Prize for reporting that revealed serious design flaws had doomed the spacecraft. The paper won awards for Bill Keller's coverage of perestroika under Soviet leader Mikhail Gorbachev; Nicholas Kristoff's account of a government crackdown on student protesters in Beijing's Tiananmen Square; and the courageous coverage of John Burns during the civil war in Bosnia and his reporting of the Taliban movement in Afghanistan. Under Arthur Salzberger, Jr. the *Times* offered unprecedented coverage in the aftermath of the September 11, 2001 attacks on the World Trade Center. Its special section "A Nation Challenged," attempted to analyze the worldwide roots and consequences of Islamic terrorism. The section included biographical sketches of 2,600 people killed in New York City on September 11, 2001, including 343 New York firefighters, 23 police officers, and 37 Port Authority employees.

The reputation of the *Times* suffered a series of blows under executive editor Howell Raines and Bill Keller. For eight years, Raines had served as the paper's editorial page editor and was a strong proponent of advocacy journalism. His perceived inability to keep his opinions off the paper's front page alienated many on the *Times* staff, including conservative critics on cable television and in the blagosphere. Raines was forced to resign his post after admitting he had twice promoted staffer Jayson Blair for racial reasons and encouraged editors to overlook Blair's repeated fabrications. Keller was criticized for "allowing to stand unchallenged" reporting in the *Times* from "unnamed American officials" and "intelligence experts" who appear to have erroneously claimed Iraqi President Saddam Hussein was seeking weapons of mass destruction. That claim, first appearing in the *Times* on September 7, 2002, would be used by the George W. Bush administration to justify its pre-emptive war on Iraq.

In May 2005, the paper's weekday circulation of slightly more than one million was the third highest in the nation. Its Sunday circulation exceeded 1.5 million. Its online edition was one of the most popular stops on the web, averaging more than 500 million page-views a month among more than 10 million unique visitors. Although critics continued to condemn the paper for its "liberal bias" and no newspaper was more scrutinized by American print and broadcast journalists, the *New York Times* remained the ultimate agenda-setter in deciding what was the news of the day.

BRUCE J. EVENSEN

Further Reading

Berger, Meyer, *The Story of the New York Times: The First Hundred Years, 1851–1951*, New York: Simon and Schuster, 1951.

Diamond, Edwin, *Behind the Times: Inside the New York Times*, New York: Villard Books, 1993.

Frankel, Max, *The Times of My Life and My Life with the Times*, New York: Random House, 1999.

Goulden, Joseph C., *Fit to Print: A.M. Rosenthal and His Times*, Seacaucus, NJ: Lyle Stuart, 1988.

Krock, Arthur, *Memoirs: Sixty Years on the Firing Line*, New York: Funk & Wagnalls, 1968.

Mnookin, Seth, *Hard News: The Scandals at the New York Times and Their Meaning for American Media*, New York: Random House, 2004.

Tifft, Susan E. and Alex S. Jones, *The Trust: The Private and Powerful Family Behind the New York Times*, Boston: Little, Brown, 1999.

NEW YORK TIMES V. SULLIVAN

In *New York Times v. Sullivan* (1964), predicated on a libel suit involving the 1960s civil rights movement and the activities of Rev. Dr. Martin Luther King Jr., the United States Supreme Court ruled in 1964 that the nation has a profound and long-standing commitment to the principle that debate on public issues should be uninhibited, robust, and wide-open. As a result, public officials must expect that their work will be scrutinized closely and even criticized by the public. Frequently cited as a special protection for journalists, *New York Times v. Sullivan* was one of the boldest and most important statements protecting the right of free expression to criticize and promote improvement in their government for all citizens, not just journalists.

The case began as an advertisement, "Heed Their Rising Voices," which appeared in the *Times* on March 29, 1960. In the ad, a group identified as the "Committee to Defend Martin Luther King and the Struggle for Freedom in the South" and headed by A. Philip Randolph, a well-known African American editor, labor organizer, and radical, cited the U.S. Constitution and Bill of Rights in defense of civil rights protesters in the South who were "being met by an unprecedented wave of terror by those who deny and negate that document which the whole world looks upon as setting the pattern for modern freedom." The ad contained several factual errors, some minor such as the song protesters sang on the steps of the Alabama State Capital in Montgomery, but others more serious. The primary contention in the ad was that the Montgomery police department intimidated protesters with shotguns and tear-gas, assaulted, and falsely arrested Dr. King, and "bombed his home almost killing his wife and child." Montgomery police City Commissioner L.B. Sullivan alleged that the statements defamed him as the official in charge of the Montgomery Police Department and filed suit, although he was never identified by name in the ad.

Civil libel suits such as Sullivan's, brought by public officials against the press, were not uncommon before 1964. For instance, former President Theodore Roosevelt won a jury verdict of six cents and his dignity against a Michigan newspaper in 1913 for accusing him of being "not infrequently" drunk. Chicago Mayor William Hale Thompson unsuccessfully sued the *Chicago Tribune* for libel for accusing him of bankrupting the city during the 1920s. Before the *Sullivan* case, libel law applied equally to public officials and private citizens, and there was a strong common law tradition that prominent persons, such as public officials, had more of a reputation to lose and therefore deserved greater damages when libeled. A Montgomery County, Alabama, jury agreed, finding against the *Times* for $500,000 even though only thirty-five copies of the *Times* containing the ad were circulated in the county, and the state supreme court upheld the verdict.

Scholars have suggested that the U. S. Supreme Court granted certiorari to the *Times* case because the John F. Kennedy and Lyndon B. Johnson presidential administrations and Congress had become involved in the civil rights protests by 1963, but the Supreme Court had failed to make any definitive statement on the issue. A decision reversing the Alabama courts would send a strong message to both whites and blacks battling each other in the South. Writing for the court in its unanimous decision ruling for the newspaper on March 9, 1964, Associate Justice William Brennan held that the First Amendment did apply to the case even though the libel was published in an advertisement and not a news story. Brennan then considered whether the *New York Times* knew the ad to be false, a quality he called "knowing falsehood." Since its reporters had been present and witnessed some of the protest activities in question, there was no reason for the newspaper to suspect falsity. Next, Brennan posited whether the newspaper or the advertisement's creators had been so careless in their behavior so as not to examine carefully the truth of the ad to know that it was false. This quality Brennan called "reckless disregard of the truth." Again, the advertisement was substantially true even though it contained inaccuracies and exaggerations. Citing a case involving the NAACP the previous year, Brennan noted that the protection of the Constitution does not turn upon "the truth, popularity, or social utility of the ideas and beliefs which are offered." Explaining that even false statements can sometimes contribute to public debate, Brennan stated that erroneous statements are inevitable and must be protected if the freedoms of expression are to have "breathing space" to survive.

The distinction of what was called actual malice versus traditional malice or negligence had been established in some states before 1964. For instance, the Kansas Supreme Court ruled in 1908 that litigants in cases "of public concern, public men, and candidates for office" had to prove actual malice. Nineteenth-century Michigan jurist and scholar Thomas M. Cooley held in an 1881 case involving the *Detroit Free Press* that the open discussion of public ideas was "embodied in the good sense of the common law." Brennan also borrowed from the philosophy of Alexander Meiklejohn, a First Amendment scholar, who argued in 1948 that freedom of speech and press were protected in the Constitution to permit democracy to function, and so-called political speech, the kind in the "Raising Voices" advertisement, required protection by the courts. In turn, Meiklejohn and Brennan were influenced by the Marketplace of Free Ideas doctrine of John Milton and John Stuart Mills.

Although the *Times* decision imposed the actual malice standard on all federal and state courts, a large number of issues were left undecided by the decision, including a definition of what determined a public official, whether public officials included other types of public persons, how long an individual remained a public figure, whether at least some public officials had a right to private lives, and what constituted knowing falsehood or reckless disregard of the truth. These issues were addressed in subsequent Supreme Court cases.

In spite of increasingly more conservative Courts with less emphasis on individual rights, *New York Times v. Sullivan* remained a strong precedent in the early twenty-first century. In subsequent years, the Court cited or upheld *Times* in diverse cases ranging from the advertising of public issues, liquor, and lawyers to campaign fund raising, hate crimes, and consumer information, evoking a principle Associate Justice Oliver Wendell Holmes described in a 1919 minority decision, "the ultimate good desired is better reached by free trade in ideas."

Further Reading

Atkinson v. Detroit Free Press, 46 Mich. at 385, 9 N.W. at 525 (1881).
City of Chicago v. Tribune, 307 Ill. 595, 139 N. E. 86 (1923).
Coleman v. MacLennan, 78 Kansas at 723, 98 P. at 285 (1908).
New York Times v. Sullivan, 376 U. S. 254.
Rosanova v. Playboy Enterprises, 411 F. Supp. at 443 (1978).
Strom, Peter W., and Paul L. "Rough Rider Clears Name in the U. P." *Michigan Bar Journal*, 80 (May 2001): 59.

RICHARD JUNGER

NEW YORK TIMES V. U.S. (1971)

In *New York Times v. U. S.*, more popularly known as the Pentagon Papers case, the U. S. Supreme Court ruled in 1971 that the government could not prevent publication of a previously top-secret, government-funded study titled, "History of the United States Decision-Making Process on Vietnam Policy." However, the decision was on the immediate publication of the study and did not establish any definitive, long-term constitutional principles on prior restraint, or the government suppression of a publication. This ambiguity left open the possibility of future prior restraint cases, a prospect that was realized in 1979 with *U. S. v. The Progressive*.

The case began around 1970 when Dr. Daniel Ellsberg, a former marine and an economist working for the Rand Corporation, a military policy analysis company, photocopied thousands of classified documents related to a history of the Vietnam War that Rand was preparing for the government. Ellsberg had spent two years employed by the State Department in Vietnam during the 1960s, and with other civilian State and Defense Department employees working in that country came to the conclusion that the war could not be won. He tried unsuccessfully to have several sympathetic U. S. senators, including Arkansas Democrat J. William Fulbright, release the papers on the U. S. Senate floor, where they would have been privileged. (Eventually, after some of the documents had appeared in the *New York Times*, Democratic Alaska Senator Mike Gravel did release 4,100 pages on the Senate floor on June 29, 1971.)

In 1971, Ellsberg contacted the *New York Times* and

began leaking documents to it. The newspaper did not identify Ellsberg as its source, but the FBI investigated the leak and Ellsberg was forced to hide until he surrendered to authorities on June 28. The first story based on the documents appeared on Sunday, June 13, 1971, on the front page of the *New York Times*, one column away from a wedding photograph of President Richard M. Nixon and his daughter Tricia. Although Nixon did not read the article at that time, it detailed how the previous four presidential administrations, going back to President Harry S. Truman, had made commitments to support non-Communists in Vietnam even though intelligence and other analysts warned that a Communist insurgency in the country could not be stopped. Presidential aide H.R. Haldeman called the article and a related one published the following day "gobbledygook" in a tape-recorded, White House conversation with Nixon, "but out of the gobbledygook, comes a very clear thing: you can't trust the government; you can't believe what they say; and you can't rely on their judgment." In another conversation, Nixon told Attorney General John Mitchell in reference to the then unknown Ellsberg, "Let's get the son-of-a-bitch in jail."

That evening, Attorney General Mitchell warned the *Times* against further publication of the documents, and a Washington, D.C., court granted a restraining order when another article appeared the following day, justifying the delay on national security grounds until the documents could be reviewed properly. This was not the first time the federal government had restrained a major American newspaper. In June 1863, Union General Ambrose Burnside ordered troops to stop the presses of the *Chicago Times* for published comments against military conscription, an order remanded three days later by President Abraham Lincoln, and there were other restraints against Civil War newspapers, obscene publications in the Victorian Era, and radical publications during World War I. Following the court order, Ellsberg released additional documents to the *Washington Post* and *Boston Globe*, which were also enjoined, and with the new technology of photocopy machines, the prospect of copied documents appearing in dozens of newspapers prompted the Supreme Court to hear the case in a rare Saturday-morning session on 26 June 1971.

The government contended that the First Amendment did not ban prior restraint, a position the *Times* and *Post*'s lawyers choose not to contend. They later defended their decision not to argue such a fundamental Constitutional principle given that a losing decision would have prevented the Pentagon Papers from being declassified and released to the public at all. The government cited the 1931 *Near v. Minnesota* prior restraint case, in which the Court ruled the First Amendment's protection was not "absolutely unlimited," and that certain military information such as troop numbers or recruiting activities could be restrained although a heavy burden of proof rested with the government. It pointed also to other, common prior restraints such as in advertising, labor relations, corporate, and copyright law.

The newspapers argued that the First Amendment was meant to protect historical documents, information not related to the actual military situation at the time. The Vietnam study was historical in nature and most of the information it contained came from 1945 to 1967. The newspapers held also that government's system of classifying national security documents related to Vietnam had been haphazard and arbitrary, based more on political necessity than national security, a position the government did not dispute seriously.

Given the gravity of the case, all nine justices wrote individual opinions. Chief Justice Warren E. Burger and Justice Harry Blackmun, Nixon appointees, and Justice John Marshall Harlan II supported the government's position. Justices Hugo Black, William O. Douglas, William J. Brennan, and Thurgood Marshall, all strong supporters of civil liberties, opposed the government. The deciding votes belonged to Justices Byron White and Potter Stewart. Justice White, a John F. Kennedy appointee, often sided with Burger, Blackmun, and Harlan in limiting the scope in civil liberties cases. In his decision, he encouraged a criminal prosecution of the newspapers for publishing classified information in violation of the law, but he did not believe the government had met the strong burden of proving substantial harm based on *Near v. Minnesota*.

Justice Stewart held that publication of the documents would not "result in direct, immediate, and irreparable harm to our Nation, or its people." The United States, in contrast to the United Kingdom, did not have an official secrets act automatically classifying national security documents at the time, so, as Justice Stewart explained, the "awesome responsibility" of making such designations rested with the Executive Branch, with the only effective check on such a power "an enlightened citizenry—in an informed and critical public opinion which alone can here protect the values of democratic government." "I should suppose," White summarized, "that the hallmark of a truly effective internal security system would be the maximum possible disclosure." With Stewart's and White's votes, the newspapers prevailed, six to three, and most jurists and legal scholars refer to their opinions in cases involving national security and press freedom.

Dr. Ellsberg was tried on a variety of criminal charges including espionage, but government misconduct, including a bungled attempt to assassinate him, led to a mistrial and the charges were dropped eventually. In subsequent cases involving leaked national security information however, the government was more careful and intelligence experts such as Victor Marchetti and Samuel Morrison were censored or prosecuted in the 1970s and 1980s.

The forty-seven volumes of documents released to the newspapers and in the Senate are a public document, but the complete set of Pentagon Papers remain sealed at the Lyndon B. Johnson Presidential Library in Texas. The Pentagon Papers case remains one of the most telling chapters in the story of the poor relationship between the press and President Richard M. Nixon.

Further Reading

Near v. Minnesota, (1931), 283 U.S. 697.

New York Times v. U. S. (1971), 403 U. S. 713.

Rudenstine, David. *The Day the Presses Stopped: A History of the Pentagon Papers Case.* Berkeley: University of California Press, 1998.

RICHARD JUNGER

NEW YORK TRIBUNE

The New York *Tribune* was founded in 1841 by Horace Greeley (1811–1872), a visionary journalist who, throughout the nineteenth century, used his newspaper to address many of the nation's most compelling political and social issues. Greeley edited the *Tribune* until his death and made it one of the leading newspapers of the penny press era by blending daily events with a range of literary content and advocacy of progressive causes. In 1872, Greeley ran unsuccessfully for the presidency. During the race, his health failed, causing him to lose control of his paper to managing editor Whitelaw Reid (1837–1912). In 1922, the Reid family merged the newspaper with the *New York Herald*, a rival of the *Tribune*, forming the *New York Herald Tribune*. The *Herald Tribune* struggled until operations closed in 1966, but the Paris edition of the newspaper survived. In 2003, the *New York Times* purchased the last vestiges of Greeley's empire, which is still published as the *International Herald Tribune*.

Horace Greeley and the *Tribune*

Horace Greeley, the creator of the *Tribune*, was born in Amherst, New Hampshire. After working as a printer, he moved to New York City and met Horatio David Sheppard, the chief exponent of a marketing scheme first advanced in the early 1830s and later known as the penny press. In 1833, Greeley and business partner Francis V. Story began printing the *Morning Post*, among the first of the new, cheap publications to use Sheppard's model of high circulation and a one-cent per copy price. The paper failed in less than three weeks, but Greeley and Story lost only $50 or $60 on their experiment.

In 1835, James Gordon Bennett, Sr. (1794–1872), a Scottish immigrant and penny press maverick, asked Greeley to go into partnership with him in starting the *New York Herald*. In a departure from traditional practice, Bennett spent $500 to launch the paper, which he based on large circulation rates and advertising, rather than subsidies by political interests or payments from a small number of subscribers. Accordingly, the *Herald* was characterized by its accounts of crimes, scandals, and natural wonders such as mermaids and sea monsters, capturing the attention of a large leadership. Greeley on principle rejected the *Herald*'s reliance on sensational content and declined the venture. Bennett never forgave Greeley, and their rivalry led to life-long editorial antagonisms. At one point, the *Herald* dubbed Greeley "the most unmitigated blockhead concerned with the newspaper press."

Greeley instead experimented with various publications, writing primarily for newspapers affiliated with the Whig Party, all the while accruing financial losses. After achieving popular success with The *New-Yorker*, which showcased his talents as a literary editor, and the *Log Cabin*, a campaign paper that promoted William Henry Harrison's presidential bid, Greeley borrowed $1,000, used about $1,000 of his own, and mortgaged his printing shop for a total capitalization of less than $3,000 to issue the *New York Daily Tribune*. The newspaper was first published April 10, 1841, attracting five hundred subscribers. By the end of its second month, circulation reached eleven thousand, which at the time utilized the full capacity of the *Tribune*'s presses. The content was alert, cheerful, and aggressive, and attacks on the *Tribune* from penny press rivals only increased the newspaper's sales.

The initial success of the *Daily Tribune* allowed Greeley to publish the *New York Weekly Tribune*, which was first issued Sept. 2, 1842, and thereafter once a week on Saturdays for a subscription price of $2 a year or $1 a year when "clubs" of twenty members bought it. The *Weekly Tribune* featured an eclectic array of content, wider in scope than the *Daily Tribune*. Readers were drawn to its extensive coverage of issues that directly interested them, including farming reports and market prices, as well as political campaigns and the endeavors of great literary and intellectual figures. Greeley's audience acquired a personal affection for him, and although the *Tribune* office was always based in Manhattan (it relocated in 1845 after a fire and again in 1863 after it was destroyed in New York City's infamous draft riots) it was said that settlers, farmers, and homesteaders in the Midwest, read the newspaper "next to the Bible."

In lieu of the *Weekly Tribune*'s editorial quality, Greeley raised the price of the *Daily Tribune* to 2 cents per issue. Although the *Daily Tribune* did not sell in nearly the same quantities as the *Weekly Tribune*, which ranged from fifty thousand to one hunded thousand copies in the 1850s, it reached a peak of sixty thousand during the Civil War and thereafter sold between thirty and forty-five thousand issues. After May 1845, Greeley also issued a *Semi-Weekly* edition of the *Tribune*, which reached a steady circulation of fifteen to twenty-five thousand newspapers.

As part of the ongoing rivalry between Greeley and Bennett, the *Tribune* in 1847 challenged the *Herald* to determine by an investigation of an impartial committee, which newspaper led the industry. The *Herald* accepted the challenge and won by a narrow margin with a total circulation of 28,946 to the *Tribune*'s 28,195. However, by 1860, the *Tribune*'s combined daily, weekly, and semi-weekly sales reached almost three hundred thousand, leading other newspapers in composite numbers.

Part of the reason for the success of the *Tribune* was the tone of its editorials. It covered the stories of the day, but more importantly, it blended information with interpretation and Greeley's passionate belief in the general benevolence of humanity. Greeley opened the *Tribune*'s pages to numerous contributors, including many transcendentalists, and he was also among the first editors to publish bylines, which attracted talented writers to his staff. Henry Jarvis Raymond (1820–1869), who in 1851 founded the *New York Times*, assisted Greeley in the department of literary criticism, fine arts, and general intelligence during the *Tribune*'s earliest days. In 1846, Greeley hired Charles A. Dana, and for the next fifteen years, the nationally recognized literary figure served as the *Tribune*'s chief editorial assistant. In 1849, George Ripley began conducting for the *Tribune* the first regular literary and book review department in a U.S. newspaper, which continued under his supervision for more than thirty years.

Greeley's vision for the *Tribune* might not have survived without the assistance of Thomas McElrath, who invested $2,000 in the newspaper during an early financial crisis. According to Greeley, McElrath made him a voluntary and wholly unexpected business deal for the struggling but hopeful enterprise. His presence at the *Tribune* was much less outspoken than Greeley's, and during the ten years that the *Tribune* was issued by Greeley and McElrath, the latter never once indicated that the radical opinions it expressed on abolitionism, the death penalty, socialism, and other frequent aberrations from traditionally conservative Whig doctrine were injurious to the interests of the publishers. The *Tribune* popularized the ideas of French communitarian Charles Fourier (1772–1837), advocated homestead legislation, supported women's rights, attacked the exploitation of wage labor, denounced monopolies, and backed the temperance movement; however, the only time McElrath expressed dissatisfaction with Greeley's work was when the latter dipped into the newspaper's treasury to help a friend who was, in McElrath's opinion, beyond help.

The *Tribune* and the Civil War

Historians credit Greeley with helping found the Republican Party. In 1854, he suggested the party name, and in February 1856, he attended its national organizational meeting in Pittsburgh, using the *Tribune* to support candidate John C. Fremont in the presidential contest. In 1860, he attended the Republican national convention in Chicago, and swayed delegates to support the nomination of Abraham Lincoln.

Greeley expected Lincoln to reward him for the *Tribune*'s help in the presidential election, but when Lincoln decided not to appoint the editor to his cabinet, Greeley reacted with scorn and incessantly criticized the administration during the Civil War. Greeley published one of his most famous editorials, "The Prayer of Twenty Millions," in the *Tribune* August 20, 1862, urging the president to use the Second Confiscation Act to allow Union commanders to free the slaves. Lincoln issued the Emancipation Proclamation shortly after Greeley wrote him, but he did so primarily because the Union Army had just won the battle of Antietam, a strategic victory for the timing of the edict. The *Tribune* celebrated the president's decision with extensive coverage of the event, and many readers undoubtedly assumed that Greeley had influenced national policy.

After the war, the *Tribune* promoted universal suffrage and advocated amnesty for all southerners, including Jefferson Davis. It supported General Ulysses S. Grant during the first years of his presidency, but Greeley came to resent what he considered to be Grant's subservience to Republicans who wanted to punish the South.

In May 1872, the Liberal Republican Party, a group of Republican dissidents in the North, nominated Greeley for president. In July 1872, he was also nominated by the Democratic Party, which adopted the Liberal Republican platform. Greeley resigned his *Tribune* editorship to campaign. The *Tribune*'s competitors attacked Greeley's campaign in print, and Grant's popularity in the North contributed to a Republican landslide. Greeley's defeat was accompanied by personal tragedy. In October his wife Mary ("Molly") became ill and died. Still campaigning, Greeley had returned to his *Tribune* office, but managing editor Whitelaw Reid, who worried that Greeley's deteriorating health might hurt the newspaper's circulation, forced him out.

The *Herald Tribune*

Whitelaw Reid had graduated from Miami University of Ohio in 1856, and while working as a reporter during the Civil War, he formed a friendship with Greeley. By 1869, Reid was managing editor of the *Tribune*, and after Greeley's death, Reid gained financial as well as editorial control of the paper, maintaining its status as a nationally leading newspaper. In 1881, Reid strengthened his position by marrying the daughter of millionaire Darius Ogden Mills (1825–1910). He was appointed the U.S. minister to France from 1889–1892 and ambassador to the United Kingdom from 1905–1912.

After Reid's death in 1912, his son Ogden Mills Reid (1882–1947) and Ogden's wife Helen Rogers Reid (1882–1970) were unable to adapt the *Tribune* to changes in the newspaper industry that demanded higher production costs and greater entertainment value. In 1922, the Reid family merged the *Tribune* with the *Herald*, which by then was also struggling, to form the New York *Herald Tribune*. Ogden Reid ran the *Herald Tribune* until his death in 1947, and in 1959, the Reid family sold their remaining interests to John Hay Whitney (1904–1982), heir to a family fortune from Standard Oil, tobacco, transportation, and real estate.

The *Paris Herald Tribune* and *International Tribune*

In 1959, control of both the *Paris Herald Tribune* and the *New York Herald Tribune* was transferred to John Hay Whitney, who had inherited more than $30 million in 1927, and by 1964, was worth an estimated $250 million, partly through success of investments and his venture capital firm, J.H. Whitney & Co. Whitney had served as an ambassador for President Eisenhower, dabbled successfully in Broadway and film finance, worked with Nelson Rockefeller in the motion picture section of the wartime Office of the

Coordinator on Inter-American Affairs, was an early backer of *Newsweek*'s Vincent Astor, and was the brother-in-law of CBS founder William Paley. Whitney reportedly invested $40 million into the *Herald Tribune*.

Managerial indecision and major strikes by the typesetters union in 1962 and 1966 led to a drop in demand for the *Herald Tribune*, and Whitney Communications Corporation closed the New York edition of the newspaper in 1966, selling 50 percent of the *Paris Herald Tribune* to the *Washington Post*. In a desperate attempt to salvage three dying newspapers, Whitney created the *New York World Journal Tribune*, an awkward afternoon edition that combined remnants of the *Herald Tribune*, Hearst's *Journal American*, and the Scripps-Howard *World-Telegram & Sun*; however, the *World Journal Tribune* survived only eight months.

In 1967, the New York Times Company bought a 33 percent stake in the *Paris Herald Tribune*, renaming it the *International Herald Tribune*. In 1991, the *Times* and *Washington Post* jointly acquired the Whitney family's remaining shares of The *International Herald Tribune,* later establishing an alliance with the *Frankfurt Allgemeine Zeitung.*

In 2003, the *Times* bought the *Washington Post*'s shares of the *Herald Tribune* for $65 million, bringing a tenuous close to the relationships of three nineteenth-century editors: ownership of the *Tribune*, which had been founded in reaction to the sensationalism of James Gordon Bennett Sr. was transferred, along with the last vestiges of the *Herald*, to the *Times*, a newspaper founded by Henry Raymond, one of Horace Greeley's first assistant editors, who had shunned both the scandalous and altruistic content of his rivals.

Further Reading

Brown, Francis. *Raymond of the Times*. New York: Norton, 1951.

Cortissoz, Royal. *The Life of Whitelaw Reid*. New York: Scribner's, 1921.

Crouthamel, James. *Bennett's New York Herald and the Rise of the Popular Press*. Syracuse, NY: Syracuse University Press, 1989.

Greeley, Horace. *Recollections of a Busy Life*. New York: Arno, 1868.

Hudson, Frederic. *Journalism in the United States*. New York: Harper & Brothers, 1873.

Kluger, Richard. *The Paper: The Life and Death of the New York Herald Tribune*. New York: Knopf, 1986.

Maverick, Augustus. *Henry J. Raymond and the New York Press*. New York: Arno, 1870.

Parton, James. *Life of Horace Greeley*. New York: Mason Brothers, 1855.

Pray, Issac. 1853 *Memoirs of James Gordon Bennett and His Times*. New York: Arno Press, 1835, 1970.

Robertson, Charles. *The International Herald Tribune: The First Hundred Years*. New York: Columbia University Press, 1987.

Seitz, Don C. *Horace Greeley, Founder of The New York Tribune*. Indianapolis, IN: The Bobbs-Merrill Company, 1926.

———. *The James Gordon Bennetts, Father and Son*. Indianapolis, IN: Bobbs-Merrill, 1928.

Van Deusen, Glyndon G. *Horace Greeley, Nineteenth-Century Crusader*. New York: Hill and Wang, 1953.

GREGORY A. BORCHARD

NEW YORK WORLD

Probably no other newspaper in American journalism combined the simultaneous extremes of the *New York World* (1860–1931) during the twenty-eight years it was owned by Joseph Pulitzer: a "newspaperman's newspaper" that combined great, crusading reporting and a highly literate editorial page with over-the-top sensationalism that would personify the era of "yellow journalism." The *World* was a trend-setter and one of the most innovative newspapers ever published; it revolutionized the practice of journalism in America, mostly for the better. It left a legacy of brilliance that within a dozen years won ten of the prizes named for its most illustrious owner.

The *New York World* was born on June 14, 1860, on the eve of the Civil War, as a religious paper published by Albert Cummings, founder of the *Philadelphia Evening Bulletin*. It eschewed advertising from theaters and lotteries, refused to publish news of criminal cases and divorces, stressed moral reforms and Sunday sermons—and lost money rapidly. Even acquiring James Watson Webb's *Courier and Enquirer* did not help; the paper was sold to leading Democratic political figures, banker August Belmont and New York mayor Fernando Wood. Manton Marble was installed as editor, and the religious content was replaced by general newsgathering.

During the Civil War, the *World* was New York's leading Copperhead paper: It railed against African-Americans, advocated a soft peace with the south and denounced President Abraham Lincoln's "infamy." In May, 1864, the paper was suppressed for three days (along with the *Journal of Commerce*) by General John Dix after it printed a phony story about a purported presidential proclamation ordering a new draft call. Marble assumed control in 1869, but the paper—which had become New York's fifth-largest—could not compete with Charles A. Dana's *Sun*. In 1876, Pennsylvania Railroad magnate Thomas Scott bought the *World* and he unloaded it three years later to the notorious financier Jay Gould, who also began hemorrhaging money.

Joseph Pulitzer, the Hungarian immigrant who had made a terrific success with the *St. Louis Post-Dispatch*, bought the paper in 1883 and immediately revamped its formula: He invested in a top-notch staff, published more pages in each issue with bigger headlines and larger illustrations than had ever before been seen. He introduced political cartoons and, later, color comics. And he knew the kind of news he wanted covered: the more sensational, the better. Horrific crimes, sex scandals, disasters—these were the *World's* new fodder. Pulitzer had no apologies for those who deplored his idea of news copy. "The daily journal is like a mirror," he said. "Let those who are startled by it blame the people who are before the mirror, not the mirror, which only reflects their features and actions."

Overnight, that formula reversed the paper's fortunes: In four months, he had doubled the circulation to 40,000; within a year, it was 100,000. Four years later, he was selling 250,000 copies, and a decade after taking control, the

World had a combined morning and evening circulation of one million and was making a $500,000 annual profit.

Pulitzer and his editors—including John Cockerill and Morrill Goddard—did not simply wait for news to happen. They sponsored crusades against the "monkey kings of Wall Street," the "Broadway Boodlers" (a phony streetcar franchise), police brutality, abuse of immigrants on Ellis Island and the New York Central Railroad. The paper's most memorable crusade was its successful campaign to raise money to build the pedestal for the Statue of Liberty; from then on, the statue became the *World's* official logo. The paper also became an advocate for working class families, and it played an important role in the acculturation and socialization for newly arriving immigrants. The paper sponsored community benefits, sponsoring a corps of doctors to provide free medical care to the poor as well as free coal in the winter and ice in the summer. And the *World* launched its own news-making stunts in the person of young Elizabeth Cochrane, who—under the pen name "Nellie Bly"—exposed conditions at insane asylums by having herself committed (one of the first examples of undercover reporting) and then traveled around the world on a seventy-two-day jaunt that made her a worldwide celebrity.

Overwork shattered Pulitzer's nerves; that, and his blindness, forced the publisher to exile himself from New York and delegate authority to his editors, although he remained in constant contact with them, communicating through an elaborate series of telegraphed codes. By 1897, the *World* faced a new threat: William Randolph Hearst, the brash San Francisco publisher, had come to town and purchased the moribund *Evening Journal*. He had made a lengthy study of Pulitzer's methods and resolved to copy them—and go them one better, even to the point of wooing away, at one point, the entire *Sunday World* staff. The two papers went head-to-head following the destruction of the battleship *Maine* in Havana harbor, outdoing each other in agitating for war—and then covering the ensuing conflict with unrestrained jingoism. E.L. Godkin, editor of the *New York Evening Post* (Pulitzer's favorite newspaper, ironically) lamented that "nothing so disgraceful as the behavior of these two newspapers has been known in the history of American newspapers."

For Pulitzer, the most important page of his paper was the one on which the editorials appeared. He lavished more care on that than on any other section. It was meant to set the tone of the paper and fulfill his promise, made in the first issue he took control, that the *World* would be "dedicated to the cause of the people rather than the purse potentates" and would "fight all public evils and abuses and battle for the people with earnest sincerity."

Following Pulitzer's death in 1911, the paper continued on the course he had set, under such brilliant editors as Frank I. Cobb and Herbert Bayard Swope. Indeed, this era established the *World's* lasting legacy, featuring editorials by Walter Lippmann, columns by Franklin P. Adams and Heywood Broun, music criticism by Deems Taylor, cartoons by Rollin Kirby and poetry by Dorothy Parker and such great crusades as an investigation into the revived Ku Klux

Klan. Beginning in 1925, however, the paper began losing money; by 1930, it was bleeding to the tune of $1.6 million a year. The following year, Pulitzer's sons convinced a judge to let them break their father's will, which forbade them to sell or close the paper (and also had endowed both the Pulitzer Prizes and a School of Journalism at Columbia University); after a feverish last-minute battle by the paper's staff to purchase control, it was sold to Scripps-Howard and merged with the *New York Telegram*. To the many journalists who had worked for it, and for its loyal readers, it was the passing of an era—one they would always refer to as, literally, "the end of the *World*."

Further Reading

Barrett, James Wyman. *Joseph Pulitzer and His World*. New York: Vanguard Press, 1941.

Juergens, George. *Joseph Pulitzer and the New York Worl.*, Princeton. NJ: Princeton University Press, 1966.

Kahn, E.J. *The World of Swope*, New York: Simon and Schuster, 1965. "Scripps-Howard Buy World as Court Permits Sale and Pulitzers Fulfill Contract." *New York World final news edition,* February 27, 1931.

"The New York World." *Washington Post,* February 26, 1931.

"The World Printed With the Telegram; Employees End Fight." *New York Times,* February 28, 1931.

ERIC FETTMANN

NEW YORKER

The *New Yorker* was among the most significant American magazines of the twentieth century. It has consistently published outstanding work, and nurtured outstanding practitioners, in journalism, fiction, humor, graphic arts, criticism, and essays. Beyond that, the magazine pioneered and established new and influential approaches in all those forms.

The magazine, a weekly, was founded in 1925, by editor Harold Ross, a thirty-two-year-old Colorado native and former newspaper reporter, and publisher Raoul Fleischman, a wealthy New Yorker. A prospectus, written by Ross, accurately described the early issues (which, except for the distinctive typeface, would probably not be recognizable to current readers):

> The *New Yorker* will carry each week several pages of prose and verse, short and long, humorous, satirical and miscellaneous.
>
> The *New Yorker* expects to be distinguished for its illustrations, which will include caricatures, sketches, cartoons and humorous and satirical drawings.
>
> The *New Yorker* will be the magazine which is not edited for the old lady in Dubuque. It will not be concerned with what she is thinking about.

To contribute to the magazine, Ross recruited such well-known figures as the writers Robert Benchley, Dorothy Parker, Alexander Woolcott, and Franklin P. Adams, and the illustrators Ralph Barton, John Held, and Rea Irvin. Irvin also joined the staff as art director and designed the magazine's display typeface, which was named after him.

Irvin's picture of a top-hatted dandy (later dubbed Eustace Tilley) looking through a monocle at a butterfly adorned the cover of the first issue and, for some seven decades, was reprinted each year on the anniversary issue.

The first issue's print run of thirty thousand copies sold out. Circulation struggled in the summer of 1925, but was on the upswing by the end of the year and the magazine was turning a profit by 1927. A few years later, circulation was at one hundred thousand and the *New Yorker* was firmly established.

The content and nature of the magazine changed dramatically in its first decade. At the beginning, the *New Yorker* was resolutely and somewhat archly dedicated to humor. By 1935, it was a uniquely distinguished and well-rounded publication, publishing short fiction by the likes of John O'Hara, Sally Benson, Irwin Shaw, John Cheever, and Kay Boyle; reportage by Joseph Mitchell, A.J. Liebling, and Janet Flanner (her dispatches were printed under the pen name "Genet"); humor by James Thurber, S.J. Perelman, and Frank Sullivan; light verse by Ogden Nash; essays by E.B. White; and cartoons by Charles Addams, Peter Arno, Helen Hokinson, William Steig, and Thurber.

Several factors explained the change. One was an important early hire by Ross, the editor Katharine Angell. (She later married E.B. White and took his last name.) Where the rough-hewn Ross was interested almost exclusively in journalism and humor, Angell had training in, and commitment to, literature, and she continually pressed her boss to broaden the magazine's horizons. To his great credit, he was open to her suggestions. Second, when the full impact of the Great Depression began to be felt, it would have been very difficult to sustain the resolutely facetious tone of the early days. Finally, there was what could be called directed good fortune. All of the people named in the paragraph above were mainly or completely unknown when they found their way to the *New Yorker's* offices. Under the guidance of Ross, Angell and other editors, they emerged as singular artists and craftspeople of the highest level.

In journalism, the early *New Yorker* pioneered two separate genres. the *New Yorker* invented the term "Profiles" for its series of extensively reported and finely written personality pieces. In the late 1930s, Ross noted that "After the *New Yorker* started, other magazines got onto the fact that it was possible, notwithstanding libel laws, personal taste, etc., it was possible to write history about living people." Indeed, today "profile" is a general term for any article about a person. Probably the most celebrated *New Yorker* profile in the early years was Wolcott Gibbs's piece on Henry Luce, the founder of *Time* magazine, which was written entirely in a parody of Time-ese.

The *New Yorker's* "Reporter at Large" consisted of lengthy investigations of pretty much anything that interested the reporter. Morris Markey, an ex-newspaperman was responsible for the department from 1926 to 1936; in the first year alone, he reported on the Tombs prison, a boxing match, Bible-thumping churches, a Harlem dance hall, and an East Side speakeasy. In later years, the Reporter at Large was written by a stable of New Yorker staffers includ-

ing Liebling, Mitchell, Meyer Berger, St. Clair McKelway, and John McNulty. In their immersion reporting, frequent first-person approach, and stylistic excellence (and occasional experimentation), the pieces prefigured the "New Journalism" of the 1960s and 1970s.

Also notable was the section of unsigned pieces at the front of the magazine, The Talk of the Town. Leading it off was Notes and Comment, an editorial almost always written in the unmistakable voice of E.B. White; there followed three or four generally whimsical sketches of New York life, written in the first person plural. In the early years, Talk was mostly written by Thurber. Later, such *New Yorker* stalwarts as Brendan Gill, John Updike, and Ian Frazier wrote extensively for the section.

The *New Yorker's* reputation as a source of excellent journalism, already strong by the beginning of the 1940s, was cemented by its World War II coverage. This was directed by a young editor named William Shawn, who sent more than a dozen correspondents, including Liebling, John Lardner, John Hersey, Robert Shaplen, Walter Bernstein, Joel Sayre, E.J. Kahn, and Edmund Wilson, to cover the war in Europe and the Pacific. The culmination of the coverage was Hersey's epic "Reporter at Larger" on the bombing of Hiroshima, which Ross and Shawn considered so important that they devoted an entire issue to it in August 1946. The article, later published as a book, was selected by a New York University School of Journalism panel as the most significant piece of American journalism of the twentieth century.

Harold Ross died in 1951 and was succeeded by Shawn, who maintained the *New Yorker* as a weekly dedicated to publishing the best literature, journalism and humor. Noteworthy articles or series published under Shawn's editorship, all of which became books, included: Joseph Mitchell's "Joe Gould's Secret"; Rachel Carson's "Silent Spring" (which finished number two in the NYU rankings); Lillian Ross's "Picture"; Truman Capote's "In Cold Blood"; Hannah Arendt 's "Eichmann in Jerusalem"; Mary McCarthy's "The Stones of Florence"; James Baldwin's "The Fire Next Time"; and Anthony Lewis's "Gideon's Trumpet." In addition, Calvin Trillin and John McPhee joined the staff, and proved themselves worthy successors to Liebling and Mitchell.

The *New Yorker* also developed a reputation as a home for the highest-quality criticism. Its staff reviewers over the years included Dorothy Parker on books; Lewis Mumford on architecture; Edmund Wilson on books; Michael Arlen on television; Whitney Balliett on jazz; Kenneth Tynan on theater; Harold Rosenberg on art; Liebling on the press; and, most famously, Pauline Kael as film critic from 1967 to 1991.

In the late 1960s and the 1970s, spurred by Shawn's opposition to Vietnam War, the *New Yorker* became much more politicized than it had ever been before. Jonathan Schell's 1967 Reporter at Large piece, "The Village of Ben Suc," chronicled the destruction of a South Vietnamese village. Schell went on to become the chief writer at Notes and Comment, which he used as an antiwar platform.

Until 1985, the *New Yorker*, was a publicly held corporation. That year the magazine was purchased by Advance Publications, a media company owned by the Newhouse family. In 1987, the chief executive, S.I. Newhouse Jr., dismissed Shawn and replaced him with Robert Gottlieb, the editor-in-chief of the book publisher Alfred A. Knopf.

Five years later, at Newhouse's request, Gottlieb resigned. He was replaced by Tina Brown, the British-born editor of *Vanity Fair* magazine. The *New Yorker* was as famous for its conservative style as for its liberal politics, but under Brown, the changes came fast and furiously. She included photographs and color illustrations in the *New Yorker* for the first time, and, maybe even more daringly, put authors' names at the beginning of articles instead of at the end, where they had been ever since the beginning in 1925. In terms of content, Brown was much more interested than Shawn or Gottlieb in breaking news, and she put a high premium on journalistic scoops (as well as celebrity profiles, her critics pointed out). Under her editorship, the magazine published numerous outstanding pieces, including Mark Danner's "The Truth of El Mozote," about an investigation into a massacre in a remote Salvadoran town, and Philip Gourevitch's reports on the Rwandan genocide, which were published as the book *We Wish to Inform You That Tomorrow We Will Be Killed with Our Families* (1998).

Brown resigned in 1998 and was replaced by David Remnick, a staff writer for the magazine and a former reporter for the *Washington Post*. Under Remnick the magazine emphasized foreign affairs and political journalism more than ever before. Especially notable has been the work of Seymour Hersh in covering the United States' war on terrorism. Hersh won National Magazine Awards in both 2004 and 2005, the latter for pieces including his exposé on prisoner abuse at Abu Ghraib prison in Iraq.

The *New Yorker* had lost money in the Tina Brown era—as much as $30 million in a single year, according to press reports. But the magazine appeared to right itself financially under Remnick—passing the one million mark in circulation for the first time in 2004 and, according to company executives, turning an annual profit for the first time in two decades.

Further Reading

Adler, Renata. *Gone: The Last Days of the New Yorker.* New York: Simon & Schuster, 1999.

Botsford, Gardner. *A Life of Privilege. Mostly.* New York: St. Martin's Press. 2003.

Corey, Mary F. *The World Through a Monocle: The New Yorker at Midcentury.* Cambridge, MA: Harvard University Press, 1999.

Davis, Linda H. *Onward and Upward: A Biography of Katharine S. White.* New York: Harper & Row, 1987.

Gill, Brendan. *Here at the New Yorker.* New York: Random House, 1975.

Kahn, E.J. *About the New Yorker and Me: A Sentimental Journey.* New York: Putnam, 1979.

Kunkel, Thomas. *Genius in Disguise: Harold Ross of the New Yorker.* New York: Random House, 1997.

Kunkel, Thomas, ed. *Letters from the Editor: The New Yorker's Harold Ross.* New York: The Modern Library, 2000.

Lee, Judith Yaross. *Defining New Yorker Humor.* Jackson: The University Press of Mississippi, 2000.

Mehta, Ved. *Remembering Mr. Shawn's New Yorker: The Invisible Art of Editing.* Woodstock, NY: The Overlook Press, 1998.

Ross, Lillian. *Here But Not Here: A Love Story.* New York: Random House, 1998.

Thurber, James. *The Years with Ross.* Boston: Little, Brown and Company, 1959.

Yagoda, Ben. *About Town: The New Yorker and the World It Made.* New York: Scribner, 2000.

BEN YAGODA

NEWHOUSE PUBLISHING

The largest privately owned media conglomerate in the United States, the Newhouse group, began inauspiciously in 1922, when Samuel I. Newhouse, a young, inexperienced businessman, purchased half-ownership of the *Staten Island Advance*, a ten-thousand-circulation daily on Long Island, New York, that was losing money. By 2006, the group of publishing and cable companies controlled by the Newhouse family owned more than twenty-eight dailies and weeklies in ten states, most of them monopoly newspapers in their respective cities; forty magazines, including some of the most profitable and prestigious in the United States, including *The New Yorker*, *Vanity Fair*, *Wired*, and *Vogue*; business journals and newspapers in more than forty cities; a cable television operation, Bright House Networks with more than two million subscribers, and part ownership in the Discovery Channel and Time Warner Telecom; two news services, Newhouse News Service and Religion News Service; and Internet operations, including Wired.com. *Forbes* magazine estimated the total worth of the media properties in 2003 at fifteen billion dollars. In terms of size and wealth, the companies ranked within the top ten among newspaper chains, magazine chains, and cable systems in the country. It remained a secretive company, with family members firmly in control throughout the conglomerate.

Newspapers

Newhouse built his media empire and fortune in the newspaper business. His business plan was to create one-newspaper towns, giving his papers a monopoly on advertising in his newspapers' circulation areas. He bought dailies in a single city and merged them into one, creating newspapers such as *The Newark Star-Ledger* in New Jersey and *The Syracuse Herald-Journal* in New York. In other cities, he purchased his newspaper's competitors and closed them down, which is what he did in Harrisburg, Pennsylvania. For his twenty-fifth wedding anniversary in 1959, he purchased the Conde Nast magazine group, taking ownership of *Vogue* and the group's other upscale lifestyle magazines. He placed his elder son, S.I. Newhouse Jr. in control. Two years earlier, he had acquired the Street & Smith magazine group.

Magazines a Sideline

But to Samuel Newhouse, magazines remained a sideline business. He focused his attention on his newspapers properties, which to him held the potential for greater profit. Newhouse expanded his newspaper chain rapidly from 1930 to 1970, mostly using company assets and incurring little debt. He purchased controlling interests in the *Long Island Press* and the *Newark Ledger* in 1932 and 1934, respectively. In 1939, he acquired two Syracuse, New York, papers from William Randolph Hearst and the *Newark Star-Eagle*, which he merged with the *Ledger*. During the 1940s, Newhouse bought papers in Syracuse, New York, the *Jersey Journal*, and newspapers in Harrisburg, Pennsylvania. During the next decade, he bought *The Oregonian* in Portland, the *St. Louis Globe-Democrat*, and the *Birmingham News* and *Huntsville Times* in Alabama, paying record prices for each. His family's holdings expanded during the 1960s with the acquisition of the *New Orleans Times-Picayune* and the *New Orleans States-Item*; the *Oregon Journal*; three Springfield, Massachusetts, newspapers; the *Mobile Register* and the *Mobile Press* in Alabama and the *Mississippi Press-Register* in Pascagoula; and the *Cleveland Plain-Dealer*. During the 1970s, Newhouse bought eight newspapers and *Parade* magazine from the Booth newspaper chain. *Parade* was the largest magazine supplement in the country.

His management style was to allow the Newhouse newspapers to remain in local control because he had little interest in running day-to-day operations. His interest, though, was in profits, and under his control, the Newhouse newspapers gained a reputation for penny-pinching and poor quality. Because of his reputation, Newhouse's bids for the distinguished *Washington Post, New York Times*, and *The New Yorker* magazine met with haughty rejections.

During the 1960s and 1970s, the Newhouse family also purchased five television stations and four radio stations, and expanded their magazine holdings. Additionally, S.I. Newhouse Jr. made great strides in turning the Conde Nast magazines into highly profitable enterprises.

Sons Take Control

When the senior S.I. Newhouse died in 1979, control of the companies passed to his sons, S.I. Newhouse Jr. and Donald Newhouse. S.I. Newhouse Jr. took over the magazines, and Donald Newhouse managed Advance Publications. Largely under the leadership of S.I. Newhouse Jr., the conglomerate closed less-profitable newspapers, including the *St. Louis Globe-Democrat*, the *Syracuse Herald-Journal*, and *Mirabella* magazine, bought fewer papers, expanded its magazine holdings, and moved into book publishing and cable.

About a year after the senior S.I. Newhouse's death, his sons bought the prestigious Random House book publishing company, sold five televisions to Times Mirror Publishing Company, and invested in cable television systems.

As owner of Random House, the Newhouses led the book publishing industry into focusing on blockbuster best-sellers and cutting back on publishing high quality literature, which usually returned low profits. Later in the 1980s, the Newhouses acquired Fodor's Travel Guides and the Crown Publishing Group and relaunched *Vanity Fair* as a glossy celebrity magazine under the editorship of Tina Brown, who focused the magazine on culture and politics. Winning what the elder Newhouse dreamed of but could not obtain, the Newhouse brothers bought *The New Yorker* in 1985, firing its legendary editor William Shawn, who had molded the magazine's editorial content since 1952. The takeover of *The New Yorker*, one of America's most respected magazines noted for publishing premium fiction and nonfiction, met with scorn from the journalism community. Newhouse publications, from its newspapers to its magazines, suffered under a reputation for shameless commercialism and shoddy quality, and there was fear that the quality of the esteemed *New Yorker* would erode. But the Newhouses held firm, reveling in their triumphant acquisition.

As for their foray into book publishing, the Newhouses' made their mark, then left. They sold Random House and the Crown Publishing Group in 1998 to the German publishing giant, Bertelsmann, focusing their interest on their newspapers and magazines and moving aggressively into cable and the Internet. The Newhouses entered a partnership with Time Warner Cable in 1995 to expand their cable system and purchased Fairchild Publications, which included *W, Jane*, and *Women's Wear Daily*, from the Disney Corporation in 1999. They broke off their partnership with AOL Time Warner in 2002. That same year, the Newhouses purchased the *Modern Bride* magazine from Primedia.

Legal Troubles

The Newhouse media companies have been threatened twice by legal troubles. Before he died, Samuel Newhouse had constructed a complicated financial structure designed to avoid income and inheritance taxes. After his death, the Internal Revenue Service demanded about one billion dollars in taxes and penalties and the U.S. Justice Department launched a fraud investigation against the Newhouse family when it insisted it owed no more than forty-nine million dollars. Because the Newhouse conglomerate has succeeded largely by avoiding debt, paying the IRS's demands would have severely hampered the family's ability to expand its companies. The conflict revolved around the value of the senior Newhouse's holdings when he died, which the family set at ninety-one million dollars and the IRS assessed at $962 million. The case ended up in U.S. Tax Court, and when it was over, the Newhouses had won.

The second legal tangle proved even more threatening to S.I. Newhouse, Jr. His father had purchased the *Cleveland Plain-Dealer* in 1967 for the record price of $54.2 million, and the Newhouses continued to operate it in competition with Cleveland's other daily, the *Cleveland Press*. Then, in 1982, the *Press* abruptly closed. Allegations surfaced in lawsuits that the Newhouses had paid the *Press*'s owner, Joseph Cole, more than twenty-two million dollars for a largely worthless subscription list so he would shut down the paper, giving the *Plain-Dealer* a monopoly on news and advertising in Cleveland. Those charges led the U.S. Justice Department to launch a criminal antitrust investigation that could have landed S.I. Newhouse Jr. in prison. Though a federal district judge had found evidence of an alleged antitrust conspiracy, the Justice Department granted S.I. Newhouse Jr. immunity for his testimony before a grand jury. Ultimately, the Justice Department declined to bring charges against anyone.

The 1990s

Emerging unscathed by the legal troubles, the Newhouses entered the 1990s well placed to become one of America's leading media conglomerates. They continued to acquire media properties, buying, among others, *Wired* magazine, and then, in 2006, purchasing its online news service, Wired.com. They launched new magazines, including several in foreign countries. At their newspapers, they installed new publishers and editors, brought in new printing presses, added newsroom employees, built expensive new office buildings, and urged publishers to improve the papers' coverage in the communities they served. Previously lackluster dailies became winners of state press awards and Pulitzer Prizes, some for the first time since becoming Newhouse properties.

Within three generations, the Newhouse family went from near-poverty to be in charge of one of the largest and richest media conglomerates in the United States. With headquarters in Manhattan, New York, and across the river at the *Newark Star-Ledger*, the Newhouses controlled a media conglomerate that eclipsed the wildest dreams of its ambitious founding father, Samuel I. Newhouse. At the same time, the national spotlight shined on a family that had cultivated their privacy.

Further Reading

Brown, Tina. *Life's a Party*. North Pomfred, VT: David & Charles, 1984.

Kahn, E.J. Jr. *Year of Change: More About The New Yorker & Me*. New York: Viking Penguin, 1988.

Lent, John. *Newhouse, Newspapers, Nuisances*. New York: Exposition Press, 1967.

Loomis, Carol J. "The Biggest Private Fortune: Media Magnates Si and Don Newhouse Control a $7.5 Billion Empire," *Fortune* 16 (August 17, 1987): 60–67.

Maier, Thomas. *Newhouse: All the Glitter, Power, and Glory of America's Richest Media Empire and the Secretive Man Behind It*. New York: St. Martin's, 1994.

Meeker, Richard H. *Newspaperman: S.I. Newhouse and the Business of News*. New Haven, CT: Ticknor & Fields, 1983.

JAMES AUCOIN

NEWHOUSE, SAMUEL I.

Samuel Irving Newhouse (May 24, 1895–August 29, 1979) was born Solomon Neuhaus on May 24, 1895, to poor Russian and Austrian immigrants on New York's Lower East Side. Adopting the Americanized name of Newhouse and his nickname, Sammy, Newhouse sold newspapers on the streets of New York until he graduated from secretarial school. His first full-time job was to assist a prominent Long Island attorney, who owned the *Bayonne Times* in Bayonne, New Jersey, where he was introduced to newspaper work. He also earned a law degree while at the paper and practiced law for a brief period.

The Long Island attorney, Hyman Lazarus, financially backed Newhouse's first newspaper purchase in 1920, the *Fitchburg Daily News*, a struggling Massachusetts paper, which they sold within months. Finding a newspaper closer to home, Newhouse, with Lazarus's backing and six hundred dollars he borrowed from relatives, bought controlling interest in the *Staten Island Advance*. It would become the first newspaper in what would ultimately be one of the larger newspaper, magazine, and broadcasting chains in the nation.

Newhouse viewed newspapers as commercial investments and showed little interest in their content or their social role. He methodically bought newspapers throughout the country, leaving their control in the hands of local publishers and editors but keeping tight reins on their finances. Throughout his career, Newhouse-owned newspapers generated bountiful profits but little recognition for quality. Newhouse's business plan consisted of establishing monopoly newspapers through acquisitions, mergers, and fierce competition—and to pay cash for every property as much as possible. It was genius strategy for someone who wanted to make a lot of money from newspapers—and he did. Initially, he purchased controlling stakes in the *Long Island Press* and the *Newark Ledger*, but later purchased papers outright. In 1939, he bought two Syracuse, New York, dailies and merged them to form the *Syracuse Herald-Journal*. In relatively quick secession over the next four decades, he bought dailies in New Jersey; Harrisburg, Pennsylvania; Portland, Oregon; St. Louis; Birmingham, Huntsville, and Mobile, Alabama; Pascagoula, Mississippi; New Orleans; Springfield, Massachusetts; and Cleveland, Ohio. In 1959, he purchased the Street & Smith magazines and Conde Nast magazines.

In the mid-1960s, Newhouse donated fifteen million dollars to Syracuse University for its School of Communications, which put his name above the door. Both of his sons, S.I. Newhouse Jr. and Donald Newhouse, had attended the university's journalism program.

At the time of his death in 1979, he owned twenty-two newspapers through Advance Publications, Inc., six television stations, four radio stations, five national magazines, and twenty cable TV stations.

Control of his media empire passed to his sons. S.I. Newhouse Jr. took over the magazines, Donald Newhouse managed the newspapers and broadcast outlets, and they worked together to continue to grow the companies. In 2006, Samuel I. Newhouse's legacy was a media company that owned newspapers in ten states; forty magazines; business publications; cable systems serving more than two million subscribers, and Internet properties—an empire worth an estimated fifteen billion dollars in 2003, according to *Forbes* magazine.

Further Reading

Lent, John. *Newhouse, Newspapers, Nuisances.* New York: Exposition Press, 1967.

Loomis, Carol J. "The Biggest Private Fortune: Media Magnates Si and Don Newhouse Control a $7.5 Billion Empire." *Fortune* 16 (August 17, 1987): 60–67.

Maier, Thomas. *Newhouse: All the Glitter, Power, and Glory of America's Richest Media Empire and the Secretive Man Behind It.* New York: St. Martin's, 1994.

Meeker, Richard H. *Newspaperman: S.I. Newhouse and the Business of News.* New Haven, CT: Ticknor & Fields, 1983.

JAMES AUCOIN

NEWHOUSE JR., SAMUEL I.

Samuel I. Newhouse Jr. was born on November 8, 1927, in Staten Island, Long Island, New York, to Mitzi and Samuel I. Newhouse, who was building what would become one of America's largest and more successful media conglomerates. After high school, he attended Syracuse University, majoring in journalism and working on the college newspaper. Leaving before obtaining a degree, S.I. Newhouse Jr. joined his father at Advance Publications, drifting through several jobs but failing to find his niche. He took leave from the company to spend two years in the Air Force and then returned to the family business. In 1959, the elder Newhouse tapped him to run the Conde Nast magazine group, which Newhouse had acquired that year. His younger brother, Donald Newhouse, remained at Advance's headquarters in Newark, New Jersey, to continue to learn newspapers and broadcasting.

When S.I. Newhouse Jr. arrived in the executive offices of *Vogue*, he was thirty-two years old and shy, having spent his adulthood in the shadow of his highly successful father. Nevertheless, working out of the Manhattan headquarters, he thrived on the challenges of the competitive New York magazine world. Mentored by the able Conde Nast editorial director, Alexander Lieberman, he developed into a capable publisher, and magazines his father had considered a sideline in his sprawling media company became highly profitable. S.I. Newhouse Jr. had learned well from his father that media properties were above all commercial businesses.

When the elder Newhouse died in 1979, S.I. Newhouse Jr. and his brother, Donald, took over the company, which by then had acquired dailies in ten states, five national magazines, nine TV and radio stations, and other media properties. Observers inside and outside the company believed Donald would take over from his father, but to the surprise of many, S.I. Newhouse Jr. emerged as the dominant partner.

In 1980, the Newhouses purchased the prestigious Random House book publishing company, gaining a national prominence the elder Newhouse had never achieved, and sold off the company's five television stations. Moreover, four years later S.I. Newhouse Jr. engineered the company's purchase of *The New Yorker*, stunning the journalism world. Because of the Newhouses' reputation for putting profits before quality, admirers of the magazine worried that its vaulted tradition of fine reporting and writing would be lost among the money-changers. He drew criticism in 1985 for firing the magazine's esteemed editor, William Shawn, who had directed the magazine for thirty-two years.

S.I. Newhouse Jr. showed talent for finding products that could keep the company's audience demographics attractive to advertisers. He started and acquired magazines, for example, that appealed to younger readers, including the financially troubled *Wired* and its online news service, Wired.com.

S.I. Newhouse Jr. and his brother, Donald Newhouse, inherited a successful media company and turned it into a high-profile empire, fully capable of competing with the powerful mega media companies of the early twenty-first century. By the mid-1990s, it had become the largest, wealthiest privately held media company in America, primarily because of Samuel I. Newhouse Jr.

Further Reading

Felsenthal, Carol. *Citizen Newhouse: Portrait of a Media Merchant.* New York: Seven Stories Press, 1998.

JAMES AUCOIN

NEWS ANCHORS

CBS-TV producer/director Don Hewitt is said to have coined the term "anchor man" to describe Walter Cronkite's work as lead reporter at the 1952 Democratic and Republican National Party Conventions. Since then the expression has grown to include "anchor woman" as well as the less gender-specific "anchorperson." The idiom itself alludes to the "anchor leg," or fourth runner in a relay race. The anchor of a relay team is said to be the most competitive runner, able to catch and pass all other challengers. Such a metaphor fits nicely with the notion of a radio or TV "news team" and their alacrity at being first to break a major story before their rivals.

While many use the terms "newscaster," "newsreader," and "news anchor" interchangeably, broadcasters in other countries draw sharp cultural distinctions. The term "news anchor" is only specific to news presenters in the United States and Canada. Other nations—most notably Great Britain, Ireland, Australia, China, Romania, Columbia, and the Philippines—refer to their main on-air presenters as newsreaders or newscasters. Here are the differences: A TV news*reader* is a pleasant looking/sounding actor, not engaged in news gathering or educated in the conventions of journalism, whose sole role and talent lies in delivering news messages in an authoritative and often dramatic or entertaining style. A news*caster* is similar to the above except he or she is a qualified, working journalist engaged in compiling and writing news as well as presenting it. Both terms were coined in the 1980s to distinguish trained journalists—news*casters*—from trained actors—news*readers*. Both the BBC (British Broadcasting Corporation) and RTÉ (Radio Telefís Éireann, Ireland's broadcast service) have moved to using news*casters* almost exclusively.

A news anchor in North America is a television personality and "information host" that may write and/or edit portions of a news program, and most often introduces pre-produced stories. The anchor rarely develops a news story as a field reporter might, though occasionally news anchors are sent on assignment where they employ journalistic newsgathering and newswriting techniques. At times the anchor is called upon to ad lib—speak without the use of notes or prompter—during "breaking news" situations. An example would be ABC-TV's Peter Jennings (deceased) who remained on the air for twenty-four-hours commentating upon and describing the aftermath of the September 11, 2001, terrorist attacks on the World Trade Center in New York City and the Pentagon in Washington, D.C. Anchorpersons frequently interview politicians and prominent newsmakers, and moderate panel discussions as well.

In the early twenty-first century, during a time of worldwide media conglomeration, TV news anchors are viewed quite differently than they were during the so-called Golden Age of television from the 1950s to the 1970s. News anchors are no longer idealized journalists, reporters steeped in the hardscrabble newspaper tradition that spoke truth to power and gave voice to the disenfranchised. They are instead TV celebrities, archetypes of the status quo, corporate faces used to attract advertisers and promote network news "products," such as high revenue producing morning television and primetime "news magazine" programs.

In today's postmodern world—one that values participatory technology and eschews traditional broadcasting's hierarchical, one-way, appointment-based, "command and control" model—it is doubtful that future TV anchorpersons will hold the persuasive cultural power that once did Edward R. Murrow, Walter Cronkite, or Chet Huntley and David Brinkley during the early second half of the twentieth century.

Further Reading

Shedden, David. "Early TV Anchors," http://poynteronline.org.

BOB PONDILLO

NEWS AND TERRORISM

Terrorism is the "systematic use of coercive intimidation against civilians for political goals." The goals of terrorist action are political, and are sometimes unclear, but generally include spreading anxiety and alarm among immediate victims and their families, as well as the wider public. Group terrorism can be understood as the breakdown of conventional channels of mobilization, participation and expression, with violence used as a mechanism of last resort to polarize conflict. At its worst, widespread terrorism turns into open civil war seeking to undermine and overthrow political targets, for example, the Irish Republican Army, and its activities for generations in Northern Ireland. State terrorism involves coercive intimidation initiated by government authorities against civilian populations, representing "terrorism from above" that is most common among repressive regimes, for example, the death squads used during the 1980s to suppress dissent in El Salvador, Nicaragua, Guatemala, and Chile; Saddam Hussein's gassing of the Iraqi Kurds; or more recently the use of the Fifth Brigade by Robert Mugabe against the Ndebele in Zimbabwe.

Despite the best intentions of journalists to provide news which is, as Joseph Pulitzer once suggested, drastically independent of government and public opinion, there is frequently a "domestic prism" which shapes much foreign news, including that about terrorism. The "local angle" is always important in news. Thus terrorism news frequently reinforces government positions, and minimizes global perspectives concerning how issues should be defined, especially those of terrorist organizations whose policies oppose those of the United States and its Allies. Decades of research by multiple scholars supports this view, which is quite different from arguments that any news about a terrorist action benefits simply because they create events which prompt press coverage of them. Government broadly defined as the executive branch, and Congress, along with politically relevant interest groups, culture and public opinion all play their roles in the framing of news about international issues, terrorism included. The result of what might be called a "domestic prism" for U.S. citizens is that they have, in regard to global terrorism, spent years in what arguably might be described as a Platonic cave of unreality.

There are two types of frames about terrorism, ones from a divided society, such as the battle for control in Northern Ireland, involving extensive terrorist actions on the part of the Irish Republican Army, and counterterrorism on the part of the British Government, or the conflict between Israel and the Palestinians in Israel/Palestine. These offer the possibility for contested interpretations of terrorism events between opposing sides, if few opportunities for deliberation arising in the wake of horrendous acts of violence by terrorists and others engaged in frame contestation concerning what is described in the Western press (but not in the Arab nor the Muslim press, which should be the subject of future scholarship) as retaliation, or counterterrorism.

Consensual terrorism news frames occur in a united society, one in which political actors, public opinion, and news organizations are all agreed that a terrorist attack has occurred and is unjustified. This happened in the case of September 11, 2001, when the United States was attacked by the terrorist organization, al-Qaeda. Such frames can be powerful. They can create a strong rally-round-the-flag effect, which bolsters a weakened presidency. They can instill fear that another such act can occur, accompanied by a desire for retaliatory action. They can offer support for military censorship policies, and support press self-censorship efforts, as, for example in regard to a retaliatory war against Taliban-led Afghanistan in the winter of 2001. At that time, President George W. Bush inaugurated a harsh rhetoric, picked up by news organizations, and continued through two midterm (2002, 2006) and one presidential election (2004). He starkly contrasted American virtue with the vices of its enemies, and, ultimately, with those of his Democratic political opponents, whose lack of vision and weakness would endanger American lives, and, by implication benefit terrorists. Thus, on November 8, 2001, Bush argued at Atlanta's World Congress Center, prior to launching an attack on Taliban-led Afghanistan, that:

> We value life; the terrorists ruthlessly destroy it.
>
> We value education; the terrorists do not believe women should be educated.
>
> We value the right to speak our minds; for the terrorists, free expression can be grounds for execution....

Given the emergence of an agreed-upon terrorism frame, even if opposition politicians and journalists have doubts or disagreements with a policy, if the United States is perceived to be vulnerable, as was the case following constantly repeated television portrayals of Americans under attack on September 11, 2001, they will probably suppress explicit criticism out of concern for damaging public morale or fear of a public backlash. The consensual or one-sided news framing that followed the September 11, 2001, attacks left little room for democratic deliberation and debate. In the age of global media, however, it is important to point out that even the reach of competing global frames was possible. Thus information about September 11, 2001, that was withheld from the American public penetrated its news media via reports of debates in the British House of Commons. CNN reported information about U.S. operations in Afghanistan early in the war that had been similarly withheld from U.S. audiences by utilizing news coverage from Al Jazeera.

The post-September 11, 2001, news frame was one of vulnerability. The Bush administration argued that international threats to American security drastically increased after that time, building on a growing threat during the 1990s, thereby justifying their ongoing "War on Terrorism" frame. Did independent evidence of indicators of terrorist incidents that could be used for comparison with the way that the mass media depicted these events support this conclusion? An analysis of international terrorism incidents and numbers of casualties between 1969 and 2002 reveals, not surprisingly, that the terrorist threat has been long-standing and widespread. When one examines all news stories about terrorism in *The New York Times* and on network news during this same period, they suggest that the international threat against American security actually receded, rather than rose, during the 1990s.

It is not possible to review all of these data here, but it is important to note that the end of the Cold War in the late-1980s and early-1990s generated a significant peace-dividend, so much so that the threat of international terrorism around the world declined. The U.S. State Department estimated that, far from a growing global threat, in fact the 1990s witnessed *a substantial fall in the number of incidents of international terrorism*. The number of terrorist incidents plummeted by almost half; down from 666 incidents at the peak of 1987 to 348 incidents during 2001, its lowest level since statistics were first collected by the U.S. government in 1968. Nor was this just a statistical aberration or change of classification: similar trends were confirmed in a RAND-MIPT series. During the 1990s fewer countries confronted significant terrorist threats, the number of terrorist groups fell, and fatalities from international terrorism declined. The main factors driving this development can be found in the global spread of democratization that facilitated greater autonomy or self-determination for many ethno-political groups, and the end of some of the most repressive state regimes. In addition, counter-terrorism measures may also have become more effective.

The trends in U.S. TV news followed the real-world decline. The average number of stories about terrorism on the U.S. network news was four stories per week during the 1980s; this dropped to two stories per week during the 1990s, when international coverage in general was sharply reduced on U.S. TV news. (Coverage in *The New York Times,* however followed a slightly contrary trend, increasing from just over two stories about terrorism per day to about two-and-a-half stories per day during the 1990s.) Of course, it could be that incidents of international terrorism fell while cases of local terrorism grew on American soil, but, in fact, the FBI also documented falling levels of domestic terrorism. Incidents monitored by the FBI, however, dropped from twenty-three cases per annum during the 1970s down to only five cases per annum during the 1990s. During the 1970s many domestic incidents were attributed to radical left-wing groups, anti-war extremists, and Puerto Rican separatists, including the Weather Underground, Armed Forces of Puerto Rican Liberation (FALN), the Black Liberation Army, and the Symbionese Liberation Army. The fortunes of these groups declined in the mid-1980s, due to law enforcement initiatives and changes in the political culture. During the last decade, the overall number of domestic incidents remained low, although some right-wing anti-government and racist fringe radicals, militia and "patriot" groups became more active in the United States, such as Aryan Nation, along with some environmental extremists and animal rights activists.

Data developed concerning terrorist incidents during the 1990s makes it clear that Americans have not been made aware of one important subset of these concerns—who experienced terrorism, and where, in the world. Comparative analysis of the State Department data indicates that terrorist incidents were far more frequent in Africa and Latin America, than they were in the United States. Thus, although spectacular terrorist acts affected Americans during this period, only 15 international terrorist attacks took place from 1996 to 2000 within North America, compared with 151 incidents in Africa, 159 in the Middle East, 251 in Asia, 309 in Western Europe, and 637 in Latin America A comparison of the total casualties produced by international terrorist incidents also shows only 7 casualties within North America from 1996 to 2000, compared with 253 hurt in Latin America, 404 in Asia, 945 in Western Europe, 1,754 in the Middle East, and a remarkable 6,411 casualties in Africa.

News coverage in the United States during the 1990s reflected the "local angle"—spiking when terrorist incidents occurred which affected American citizens on U.S. soil. A comprehensive study from an earlier period, comparing the number of terrorist incidents from 1968 to 1980 recorded in a RAND database against news coverage of these events by the three main American television networks, reached a similar conclusion, estimating that only between 15 to 18 percent of terrorist acts were ever reported. The study also found that the *New York Times*, while more comprehensive, still covered only one-third of all such incidents. Following the general pattern of international news coverage, U.S. networks covered terrorist events in Africa and Latin America the least, and in North America and the Middle East the most. The neglect of U.S. media coverage of terrorism in countries such as Colombia, Peru, Sri Lanka, and the Philippines persisted during this era despite the existence of widespread armed conflict, major violations of human rights, and substantial civil unrest. Throughout this period, the reality, if not the press coverage, was of sporadic outbreaks of group conflicts and terrorist acts that particularly afflicted many other parts of the world other than the United States, including Africa, Asia, and Western Europe.

American citizens had long been directly affected by terrorism prior to September 11, 2001, but to a far lesser degree than in many parts of the world. Prior to September 11, 2001, Americans experienced a largely mediated form of international terrorism, which contributed to insularity and a lack of understanding of the problem. After the attacks of September 11, a consensual news frame emerged, along with press self-censorship, government censorship of news, and divisive political rhetoric. The frame stressed the strategically and ethically unhelpful emotion of vulnerability. However, media existed—national and transnational news organizations, and bloggers—that could construct information helpful to global citizens, in the United States and elsewhere, as they attempted to work in a multilateral fashion to remove the causes of global terrorism.

Further Reading

Entman, Robert. *Projections of Power: Framing News, Public Opinion, and U.S. Foreign Policy.* Chicago: University of Chicago Press, 2004.

Pippa Norris, Montague Kern, and Marion Just, eds. *Framing Terrorism: the News Media, the Government and the Public.* New York: Routledge, 2003.

Nacos, Brigitte L. *Terrorism and the Media: From the Iran Hostage Crisis to the Oklahoma City Bombing.* New York: Columbia University Press, 1994.

Paletz, David L., and Alex P. Schmid, eds. *Terrorism and the Media.* Newbury Park, CA: Sage, 1992.

Weimann, Gabriel. *Terror on the Internet: The New Arena, the New Challenges.* Washington, D.C. : United States Institute of Peace Press, 2006.

Weimann, Gabriel, and Conrad Winn. *Theater of Terror: The Mass Media and International Terrorism.* New York: Longman, 1994.

MONTAGUE KERN

NEWSPAPER GROUPS

Newspaper chains—more commonly referred to as newspaper "groups" by researchers and industry insiders—first appeared in the United States in the late nineteenth century. Within one hundred years—by the end of the twentieth century—the newspaper group had become the chief form of newspaper organization in the United States, with more than 80 percent of daily newspapers affiliated with groups and the top two dozen groups accounting for 69 percent of total U.S. daily newspaper circulation.

The growth of newspaper groups reflects broad changes within the newspaper industry (in economics, technology, partisanship), in media more generally (with the rise of competition by other news and information sources), and in U.S. business (with the rise of large-scale business organization).

While the growth of newspaper groups can be seen as a logical business development, many critics have warned that group ownership inevitably undermines a newspaper's quality. They contend that newspaper groups' absentee owners often ignore local community concerns while focusing instead on profits. Critics thus conclude that newspaper groups are not generally committed to the full and frank discussion of issues envisioned by the free speech and press guarantees in the First Amendment to the U.S. Constitution.

Newspaper groups increased steadily throughout the twentieth century:

1910: 13 newspaper groups, 62 daily newspapers, 2.9 percent of US newspapers.

1920: 31 groups, 153 dailies, 7.5 percent of US newspapers.

1960: 109 groups, 560 dailies, 31.9 percent of US newspapers.

1986: 127 groups, 1,158 newspapers, 69.9 percent of U.S. newspapers.

The advent of newspaper groups is best understood within the context of changes within the newspaper industry in the nineteenth century. In the early 1800s, most newspapers were small (four-pages) weeklies with limited circulation. Partisanship fueled the press generally, both in terms of content (an emphasis on political essays and advocacy) and finances—with support from the party faithful in a variety of forms (e.g., donations, printing contracts, etc.). By 1900, the small-format weekly had given way to much larger daily newspaper (with eight pages or more daily, twenty-four or more on Sunday). Competition was intense; most U.S. cities had two or more daily newspapers papers (and metropolises a half dozen or more). The definition of news itself had evolved, too. Editors limited much of their advocacy to the editorial page; the rest of the paper was turned over to reports on the day's events (gathered by a growing corps of reporters) in politics, business, sports, arts, and society. Circulation grew alongside the population; new technology in type-setting and printing presses allowed circulations in the tens and hundreds of thousands. Competition also drove costs upward, as well; newspapers vied with one another with circulation promotions, contests and prizes. By 1900, the newspaper in many U.S. cities was a big business.

Like other business executives of that era, newspaper publishers looked for ways to make their business more efficient economically. In the last third of the nineteenth century, newspaper production and distribution costs had spiraled, driven by labor costs (printers, reporters), paper (for the many-paged, large circulation dailies), buildings, and real estate.

Start up costs, less than $1,000 early in the nineteenth century, had risen to well over $500,000 for many big city newspapers. *Printers' Ink,* an advertising trade journal, estimated in 1890 that most big-city newspapers had operating budgets exceeding $400,000 annually.

The pioneer in developing newspaper groups in the United States was Edward Willis Scripps, an editor-publisher of modest origins. A shrewd strategist and demanding manager, Scripps demonstrated that economies of scale were possible within a geographically dispersed group of newspapers. Starting in the Midwest in the late 1870s– first, as a reporter and circulation worker at his brother James' newspaper in Detroit, and then as editor and later owner of the Cleveland *Press*—Scripps established more than fortry newspapers during his lifetime. Scripps generally focused on the Midwest and West, avoiding New York and the eastern seaboard. As historian John Tebbel writes, "Scripps did not invent the chain idea, but he was the first American publisher to make it work."

Underlying Scripps' operation was a low-cost strategy that kept expenses at individual newspapers well below the market norm. Scripps paid low wages to inexperienced reporters, opted for cheap offices, used the cheapest paper that could be run through his old presses, and generally avoided costly circulation competition with established newspapers.

Additionally, Scripps' newspaper group provided further efficiencies that allowed him to start and run newspapers that could compete fairly well with others while still operating well below market norms. Early in his career, Scripps required each of his newspapers to share news and features. This practice ultimately led to the creation of an international telegraph news service (United Press Association) and a news features service (the Newspaper Enterprise Association, or NEA). The costs for each were spread across the growing Scripps Concern; in turn, each Scripps newspaper had a relatively inexpensive supply of breaking news (from United Press) and news features, cartoons, columns and other human-interest content from NEA. The creation of a newspaper group provided the foundation for United Press and the Newspaper Enterprise Association; they in turn facilitated low-cost start ups and expansion.

Each Scripps newspaper also received the benefit of the group's ability to hire highly qualified auditors, accountants as well as circulation advisers and editors to provide support and ideas. The Scripps Concern's financial strength provided a safety net for Scripps newspapers during times of crisis. When the 1906 earthquake stopped newspaper production in San Francisco, the Scripps Concern's quick support meant that the Scripps *Daily News* was the first newspaper back in business. When advertisers resorted to boycotts against Scripps papers in San Diego, Seattle, Cincinnati, and Denver, the group's collective resources provided a vital financial backup and assured continued publication.

The growing Scripps newspaper group also served as a training ground for prospective editors and managers; some energetic reporters were promoted to editorships, while circulation managers moved into broader business management. Scripps preferred to promote from within; he wanted editors and managers who understood his business methods, and he also saw this as a way to motivate even entry-level employees to work for the broader organization.

Scripps demonstrated that the members of a newspaper group could provide substantive support to one another, thus lowering costs generally and making those papers more efficient than many of their competitors. Several other newspaper industry figures noted Scripps' success and created their own groups. One of the best known of these figures was William Randolph Hearst. By the 1920s, Hearst had twenty-eight newspapers in major U.S. cities, including New York, Chicago, San Francisco, Detroit, and Boston. Like Scripps, he recognized the importance of leveraging the enterprise of all of his newspapers to the benefit of all; his news service (International News Service) and King Features Syndicate provided news and human interest content to all of his newspapers.

With Hearst came the first major complaints about the impact of newspaper chains. While Scripps and his papers had kept a fairly low profile (indeed, Scripps was practically a recluse), Hearst and his papers were attention-seeking, self-serving, sometimes shocking, and frequently erratic. Scripps' critics primarily were big business interests who objected to his support for the working class and Progressive reform measures. In contrast, Hearst's critics objected to his willingness to use his national newspaper group to promote his political career and the film career of his mistress. Hearst, unlike Scripps, demonstrated that a vast media empire in the hands of one person might not be in the interests of journalism.

In the 1910s and 1920s, Frank Munsey's efforts to create a newspaper group added further to the criticism of such broad ownership. In Munsey's case, the concerns centered on his bottom-line focus, and particularly on his willingness to close or merge newspapers. Concluding (correctly) that the industry was overextended, Munsey proceeded to buy and consolidate papers in an effort to create efficient and profitable organizations. As Tebbel notes, Munsey's "unsentimental attitude" about newspapers profoundly irritated members of the profession. When Munsey died, noted editor William Allen White said that Munsey had "contributed to the journalism of his day the talent of a meat packer, the morals of a money changer, and the manners of an undertaker. He and his kind have about succeeded in transforming a once noble profession into an 8 percent security."

Other newspaper groups emerging in the early decades of the twentieth century included Gannett, Newhouse, Knight and Ridder. The first Gannett newspaper was the Elmira, New York, *Gazette*, purchased by Frank Gannett in 1906. In the next few decades, Gannett emerged as a strong regional group. Further expansion starting in the 1960s made it into the largest U.S. group, with 99 daily newspapers in 2000. Samuel Newhouse's first newspaper was the Staten Island *Advance* (1922); by 1963, he owned 26 newspapers. Newhouse had a two-pronged management strategy of cutting production costs and valuing local autonomy. Newhouse cut production costs by promoting automation, which created substantial labor problems for his newspapers (including extensive litigation and a dramatic multi-year strike in Portland, Oregon).

At the same time, Newhouse granted great editorial autonomy to his newspapers, figuring that local editors knew best how to serve their communities. This policy had a mixed outcome; some editors produced a high quality journal while others were less public-service oriented. The Knight group began in the 1930s when John S. Knight acquired the Akron, Ohio, *Beacon Journal*, and the Ridder group began with Herman Ritter's *Staats Zeitung*. (The two companies merged in 1974, and the combined Knight Ridder was the second largest U.S. newspaper publisher in 2000, with thirty-two dailies; it was bought and dismantled in 2006 by McClatchy). McClatchy was a small California-based group (Sacramento, Fresno, Modesto) dating from the nineteenth century: its remarkable expansion outside of California came only in the late 1970s and reached a major point in 2006 with the acquisition of Knight Ridder.

Fueling concern over the rise of newspaper groups was the over-all decline in the total number of U.S. dailies. When E.W. Scripps was establishing his group in the late nineteenth and early twentieth century, the general newspaper market was still expanding—and Scripps' small newspapers attempted to secure readers that other newspapers had not been serving. Once the industry began to contract, however, newspaper groups seemed to some to be a problem.

One clear twentieth-century trend was the decline of daily newspapers. In 1920, there were slightly more than 2,000 daily newspapers; by 1950, the total was 1,772. Although some groups had consolidated newspapers, the major impetus for newspaper closures was the fact that cities (and their advertisers) could not support as many newspapers as they had in earlier years. In two periods—during

the 1930s depression and again after World War II—several economic challenges forced closures. Between 1937 and 1939, ninety-eight dailies died or merged with other newspapers, because of increased operating costs and declining revenues. In the late 1940s, when wartime wage and price controls ended, newspapers faced spiraling costs and limited or declining revenues. Elizabeth Neiva reports that composing room costs at a typical 50,000–100,000 circulation daily newspaper rose by 98 percent between 1945 and 1948. In the 1950s and 1960s, newspapers faced increasing competition for readers' attention and for advertising revenues. Advertisers contributed further to newspaper failure; in two or three newspaper towns, they regularly dropped their advertising with the newspaper that lagged in circulation. Suburban newspapers, reflecting the changing dynamic of U.S. cities and neighborhoods, also undermined the preeminence of some metropolitan newspapers. The pressures were many and great.

As the total number of newspapers declined, the number of groups increased. By 1960, there were more than one hundred newspaper groups in the United States, but only three had a significant national presence: Hearst, Scripps-Howard, and Newhouse. Hearst had four million circulation, Scripps Howard three million, and Newhouse two million. In the next few decades, Hearst and Scripps-Howard's newspaper presence eroded (while the parent companies remained active in other media), while Newhouse and particularly Gannett would flourish in the latter third of the twentieth century.

The greatest growth of newspaper groups occurred after 1960; between 1960 and 1980, 587 daily newspapers were sold to newspaper groups. Several factors contributed to group growth in this era. First, several existing groups (such as Gannett) went from private to public ownership; in turn, they used the capital raised in this process to buy newspapers. (Public ownership also allowed groups to raise money for new technology.) Second, newspapers were profitable investments but barriers to entry were high; as such, it was easier to buy an existing newspaper than to start one. Contributing to newspaper profits was the very substantial drop in production costs in the 1970s, as publishers converted from "hot type" to photocomposition and offset presses. Third, high gift and estate taxes—coupled with high buyout offers from groups—meant that many independent (often family) owners sold. In some families, heirs of recently deceased owners simply could not generate enough cash to meet high inheritance taxes (which were based in part on the high prices groups were willing to pay for acquisitions). As Neiva notes, "Even those families who had been in the newspaper business for generations were unable to resist the immense sums that newspaper executives dangled in front of them." In some instances—such as that of the Bingham family in Louisville, Kentucky—sales to groups also stemmed from heirs who squabbled over profits and management control. Fourth, some family-owned newspapers were suffering from inept management. As Neiva notes, a 1953 Harvard Business School study demonstrated that many U.S. publishers had "little knowledge of, and considerable contempt for, the skills normally associated with running a business." As Stephen Lacy and Todd F. Simon note, professional management by a group could easily outperform independents.

The impact of public ownership was remarkable. Gannett went public in 1967; between 1971 and 1978, the company acquired forty-seven daily newspapers. Other groups recognized the economic potential of going public; between 1969 and 1972, twelve other newspaper companies went public and joined Gannett in trying to buy additional newspapers. Neiva writes that by 1977, "the acquisition trail had become a superhighway as newspaper groups swallowed other newspaper properties at the rate of one every four to five days." By 1987, four of the five largest newspaper groups were publicly held. (Gannett was not the first newspaper group to go public, but it clearly demonstrates the vast expansion made possible by that process. The trend was started by Dow Jones, publisher of the *Wall Street Journal*, in 1963, followed by Times Mirror Co. in 1964.)

By 1978, the ten largest newspaper groups (Knight Ridder, Gannett, Newhouse, Tribune Co., Scripps Howard, Dow Jones, Hearst, Times Mirror, Cox, and Thomson) had total circulation of 23.8 million, or 38.6 percent of the total market. By 1986, the twelve largest groups accounted for more than 47 percent of U.S. daily circulation.

Independent or family ownership declined sharply after 1960. Critics noted this decline, fearing that there would be far fewer voices—and thus a paucity of debate about public issues and policy. Even in the 1950s, A.J. Liebling worried about "the diminishing number of newspapers and their concentration in the hands of a group of wealthy individuals who share the same point of view." Echoing those concerns in more recent decades, Ben Bagdikian warns about the dangers of a smaller and smaller number of owners—a cartel—controlling the news. Bagdikian argues that newspaper groups often cut news budgets and provide homogenized wire service material to readers in an effort to increase profits—a process he refers to as the "Howard Johnsoning of the news" (Neiva 1996, 40). It is this concern over a lack of difference in opinion and views that has worried many; as George H. Douglas writes, it is "still impossible to escape the conclusion that the best and healthiest newspapers in America have been single, independent newspapers with their own stubborn and individual charm."

Are newspapers associated with groups inevitably worse than the "independent" or family owned newspaper? James L. Baughman writes that group ownership is no guarantee of a decline in quality. Some papers improved under group ownership—particularly when the group was one such as Knight Ridder which made editorial quality a high priority. Baughman adds that some "well heeled outsiders" were often "more than willing to see their papers challenge the excesses of local elites with which a hometown owner might have identified." Other groups, such as Gannett, were known for a cash-flow mentality that eroded local news coverage.

Just as group ownership was no guarantee of disaster, local family ownership was no guarantee of quality. Benjamin M. Compaine writes, "There are cases where some have complained of deterioration when a chain buys a local newspaper, but there are also cases of noticeable improvement when certain chains buy a newspaper. The difference seems not so much determined by group or independent, but by the motives and interests of the owners." Compaine observed that it is difficult to idealize local independent ownership in the case of William Loeb's vitriolic reign as owner and publisher of the Manchester, New Hampshire, *Union Leader*.

Several commentators have noted that newspaper groups can possess several distinct advantages that can benefit news. First, newspaper groups can leverage group resources to improve news, through special news agencies or by creating a new national organization. Compaine writes that "a group owner may offer a local newspaper access to better national reporting and features, as well as help in advertising sales." Second, their size and scope mean that they can hire excellent managers and staff; as such, they can offer career training and advancement. Third, groups tend to have larger staffs than independent local newspapers.

Research that supports the argument that group newspapers, by the nature, are inferior to independent or family newspapers appears inconclusive. Lacy and Simon argue that there appear to be "few, if any, systematic effects due to group ownership" and not all of these are negative. They conclude, "Perhaps the best summary of group ownership effects is to say that some groups perform well by journalistic standards and some do not, just as some independent newspapers perform well and others do not."

Further Reading

Baughman, James L. *The Republic of Mass Culture: Journalism, Filmmaking, and Broadcasting in America since 1940*, 3rd ed. Baltimore: Johns Hopkins Press, 2005.

Compaine, Benjamin M. *The Newspaper Industry in the 1980s: An Assessment of Economics and Technology*. White Plains NY: Knowledge Industry Publications, 1980.

Douglas, George H. *The Golden Age of the Newspaper*. Westport, CT: Greenwood Press, 1999.

Lacy, Stephen, and Todd F. Simon. *Economics and Regulation of United States Newspapers*. Norwood, NJ: Ablex, 1993.

Neiva, Elizabeth M. "Chain Building: The Consolidation of the American Newspaper Industry." *Business History Review*, 70, 1 (Spring 1996): 4.

Tebbel, John. *The Compact History of the American Newspaper*. New York: Hawthorn Books, 1963.

GERALD J. BALDASTY

NEWSPAPER PUBLICITY ACT OF 1912

An obscure amendment to the 1913 post office appropriations act established the first important federal controls aimed at the press's business operations. Known as the Newspaper Publicity Act, the regulations, still in effect, required newspapers and magazines using the highly subsidized second-class mail privilege to identify their owners and stockholders twice a year in their publications and to label advertisements that resembled news stories and editorials. In addition, the act forced daily newspapers to publish accurate circulation figures along with their ownership statements.

The U.S. Supreme Court unanimously affirmed congressional authority to enact such legislation in *Lewis Publishing Co. v. Morgan*, a 1913 case instigated by the American Newspaper Publishers Association, which challenged the law's constitutionality on First Amendment grounds. The justices dismissed the First Amendment argument, ruling that the federal government had the right to place restrictions on the press's business operations as long as the press accepted special privileges from the government—privileges like the second-class mail rate.

Soon after the Supreme Court's decision, the industry recognized the intrinsic business advantages of supporting the press regulations and urged strict enforcement of the law. In fact, publishers asked postal officials to audit the circulation statements filed with the Post Office Department and, when they refused, the industry formed the Audit Bureau of Circulations. In later years, weekly newspaper and magazine publishers persuaded Congress to extend the circulation requirement to them.

The Newspaper Publicity Act was fitting legislation for the Progressive years, an era known for its emphasis on government as a regulator and publicity as a disinfectant for industrial and social ills. While publishers often used publicity to expose wrongdoing in other institutions, many resisted public exposure of their own business dealings. They had good reason to squirm for the press during this time period was guilty of many of the wrongdoings that reformers ascribed to businesses generally.

Newspaper and magazine publishers commonly lied about their circulation, adapted their editorial policies to favor advertisers, and printed advertisements disguised to resemble news stories and editorials. Others concealed the identity of their publications' owners and stockholders to hide conflicts of interest. And still others were not "publishers" at all, but actually manufacturers who created advertising sheets to look like news publications in order to qualify for the highly subsidized second-class mail privilege. In 1911 a government commission estimated that second-class mail paid less than one-fifth of the Post Office Department's delivery costs.

Professional press and advertising associations, organized in the late nineteenth century, frequently discussed how responsible members of the industry could protect themselves and the public from the irresponsible segments. Three common abuses—hidden ownerships, disguised advertisements, and circulation liars—dominated their discussions.

Hidden ownership fell within two groups. The first group—corporate magnates and politicians secretly owning newspapers and magazines to influence public opinion—captured the public's attention and sparked much political debate. Publishers, advertisers, and government officials, however, worried much more about the second category—merchants camouflaging advertising sheets to

resemble legitimate publications in order to qualify for the second-class mail subsidy. In 1897 postal officials estimated that up to 85 percent of the publications in the second-class category did not deserve the subsidy.

Many of these publications were full of reading notices—disguised paid advertisements. Calling them the "worst feature" of the commercial press, historian James M. Lee asserted that "it was possible to insert at a higher cost almost any advertisement disguised as a bit of news." Not only did reading notices tout ordinary products, like baking powder and vegetable shortening, they also promoted the political agendas of such businesses as oil, insurance, railroad, and private utilities. And they provided a lucrative source of revenues for publishers facing fierce competition for readers and advertisers.

Lying about circulation became commonplace, and advertisers resented the obfuscation. To them, a publication's paid circulation was a commodity—one that should be measured accurately before purchase like any other service or product. Publishers who refused to reveal circulation figures or who lied about them were thieves, robbing not only advertisers and honest publishers but also the federal government in its efforts to weed out "illegitimate" publications from the postal privilege. By the time the Newspaper Publicity Act became law, an alliance had formed between advertisers and some publishers with a common objective: to run the circulation liars out of business.

Attached as a rider to the postal appropriation bill, the regulations had relatively smooth sailing through Congress. Democratic representative Henry Barnhart, a weekly newspaper publisher, sponsored the ownership and advertising provisions. In explaining his support to House colleagues, Barnhart said, "I would have the reading public know who it is and what it is that fills the editorial columns, and when this is known the reliability of the editorial opinion disseminated may be easily and safely measured." Providing bipartisan support, Republican Senator Jonathan Bourne Jr. shepherded the regulations through the Senate. "I deem it just as important for the public to be protected from false news, as for it to be protected from impure foods," he asserted, "and there is just as much justification for requiring a paper to carry the names of its owners, as for requiring that a can of fruit shall bear the name of the concern that packed it."

Supporters expected much from the press regulations. Reformers believed it would open up the sometimes-tainted editorial processes to readers, helping them to become informed consumers of the press. Publishers and advertisers, on the other hand, saw the regulations as a way to legitimatize their fledgling industry by exposing the "illegitimates" to ridicule while publicizing the "legitimates" as "government-certified" publications.

Like many Progressive reforms, though, the Newspaper Publicity Act fell short of expectations—a victim, in part, of the reformers' naïve faith in the power of publicity, industry's success in co-opting the regulatory process, and the government bureaucracy's reluctance to assume new responsibilities. But, for perhaps the first time, policymakers considered the press a business, subject to public scrutiny and, to a lesser extent, government regulation, the First Amendment notwithstanding.

Further Reading

Kielbowicz, Richard B. "Postal Subsidies for the Press and the Business of Mass Culture, 1880–1920." *Business History Review* 64 (Autumn 1990): 451–488.

Lawson, Linda. *Truth in Publishing: Federal Regulation of the Press's Business Practices, 1880–1920.* Carbondale,: Southern Illinois University Press, 1993.

Lee, James M. *History of American Journalism*, 2d ed. Garden City, NY: Garden City Publishing Co., Inc., 1923.

Stoker, Kevin, and Brad L. Rawlins. "The 'Light' of Publicity in the Progressive Era: From Searchlight to Flashlight." *Journalism History* 30, no. 4 (2005): 177–188.

Cases, Government Reports and Statutes Cited

Newspaper Publicity Act, Public Act 336 of Aug. 24, 1912, 37 Stat. 539 at 553-54(1912).

Lewis Publishing Co. v. Morgan, 229 U.S. 288, 33 S. Ct. 867, 57 L. Ed. 1190 (1913).

U.S. Congress. *Report of Commission on Second-Class Mail Matter.* House Document 559. 62nd Cong., 2d sess.,1912.

LINDA LAWSON

NEWSPAPER READERS

Since 1704 when the first weekly newspaper was published in the colonies, to the twenty-first century when over a thousand dailies flood the market, editors have always tried to satisfy readers' needs and reach high circulations. Readers throughout time, however, have been sometimes elusive, even unpredictable in their often social newspaper usage. Historians have reconstructed past readers from circulation figures, subscription lists, surveys, letters to the editor, and visual images, while market researchers have tried to understand contemporary readers' purchasing practices and reading habits.

During the colonial era, news was mainly transmitted by word of mouth or through personal correspondence. As settlement expanded, however, colonists demanded public access to news. The *Boston News-Letter* (1704), the first paper to survive its initial number, was followed by many more so that by 1760, forty-eight newspapers had been published in the colonies. Most of these targeted an elite male, mercantile, commercial, or political readership, who wanted news about shipping, business, and international affairs culled largely from London newspapers. By the 1730s, newspaper exchange among printers encouraged the spread of local news and, with it, a nascent inter-colonial consciousness. Some Boston papers of the 1720s and 1730s such as the *New-England Courant* that published Benjamin Franklin's "Silence Dogood" letters, however, featured literary essays, poems, and satire that appealed to general readers, including women. Estimates show that for one out of every five or six Bostonians living in 1740, one copy of a Boston paper was printed each week.

Colonial readers would find mostly European news, especially on government, warfare, or diplomatic relations and less on local affairs in America. Beginning in the 1740s, readers increasingly responded to content through their letters to the editor that were sometimes printed. They also showed how much they valued the news when they personally annotated papers or bound them for safekeeping.

Little increase in newspaper production occurred until after the Revolution, during which time inflation dented subscription rates, intimidation of Loyalist printers curtailed publishing, and fighting disrupted news flow. Still, the Continental Congress that provided for an army printer to keep troops informed, endorsed patriot newspapers. Only after peace was established in 1783, did the number of papers, now produced in the interior as well as along the coast, soar. Among the increasingly literate in the new Republic, educated women were recognized as newspaper readers. They engaged the typically partisan paper so eagerly, that by the 1830s, female readership was common in the Boston region. Still, only one in three households subscribed to papers at the beginning of the nineteenth century. News reading, however, was communal, often taking place in taverns or post offices, where papers were read out loud or otherwise shared.

As the nation grew, so too did newspaper offerings. By 1825, there were about 800 newspapers, mainly weeklies—more than twice the number in England—and by 1840, there were 1,631. During this time the daily became more commonplace and, with it, the urban "penny press" that issued cheap papers affordable to all, filled with diverse, often sensational fare. In 1850, one paper circulated per every 4.5 inhabitants of New York City. Promotional prizes now lured subscribers, and well-stocked newsstands attracted transients. Newspaper reading was still social in that it was largely oral and took place in public settings. Newsboys shouted papers' front-page headlines, a graphic feature emerging in the 1850s. Sociable readers mailed illegally annotated papers, to distant family and friends as letter-like greetings, or to announce deaths or marriages.

With the onset of the Civil War, newspaper reading, in New England at least, prevailed over every other types of reading because patriotism was high, and breaking events directly affected embattled loved ones. Papers carried long lists of those who had been killed or wounded. Some people abandoned books altogether for the newspaper. Despite readers' obsession with news, advertisements, rather than readers' payments, ironically, became the major revenue source for papers just after the Civil War era. Advertisers even had some say in content. By 1870, some papers hired advertising managers, which reflected the growing strength of the Industrial Revolution and the rise of a consumer culture. Around the turn of the twentieth century, publishers undertook market research on readers to lure advertisers.

Still, high circulations remained the object of cheap, mass-audience newspapers with a distinctly public, urban ethos, such as Melville Stone's *Chicago Daily News,* which reached a two hundred thousand figure by 1895, and Joseph Pulitzer's *New York World,* and William Randolph

Hearst's *New York Journal* which were known for their sensationalistic, "yellow journalism." During the 1880s, the number of foreign-language papers rose 45 percent, while evening editions for working people increased 112 percent. By 1890, 77 percent of a sample of cotton textile workers' families reserved some income for newspapers and books.

A one-household-to-one-newspaper circulation ratio existed by 1900 that would continue for six decades. Systematic studies of periodical readers' habits began at the century's turn and continued with increasing sophistication until the century's end as publishers quested for more readers. Despite marketing research to increase circulation, readers—such as those who sent Chicago editor James Keeley letters between 1912 and 1917—responded to news in unpredictable ways informed by their own communities. Farm Security Administration photographs commonly show news readers during the 1930s and 1940s interacting with family and friends. Depression-era sharecroppers even papered walls with news, now illustrated with half-tones and photographs, to insulate their homes and, sometimes, purportedly to repel ghosts.

During the 1970s, newspaper circulation began to drop so that by the new millennium, U.S. readers were purchasing half the number of papers consumed per capita in Japan, Sweden, and Finland. Researchers in the 1970s and 1980s responded with focus-group studies, and the industry, with more reader-centered news. "Audiotex" services of the 1990s, such as CityLine, provided customized daily news via phone to meet individual clients' tastes. With computerization enabling publishers to construct vast "list-building" databases, subscribers could now have their names and personal information sold, as fair game, to other marketing enterprises. The "free" delivery of newspaper content via the Internet and other electronic avenues led publishers away from circulations to estimated readerships to gauge their papers' reach—partly to convince advertisers of audiences vastly exceeding dwindling numbers of copies sold. Despite the optimistic picture that resulted, nothing promised to reverse the trend that the United States was becoming no longer a nation of newspaper readers.

Further Reading

Bogart, Leo. *Press and Public: Who Reads What, When, Where, and Why in American Newspapers*, 2d ed. Hillsdale, NJ: L. Erlbaum Associates, 1989.

Henkin, David M. *City Reading: Written Words and Public Spaces in Antebellum New York*. New York: Columbia University Press, 1998.

Leonard, Thomas C. *News for All: America's Coming-of-Age With the Press*. New York: Oxford University Press, 1995.

Nord, David Paul. *Communities of Journalism: A History of American Newspapers and Their Readers*. Urbana: University of Illinois Press, 2001.

Project for Excellence in Journalism, and Rick Edmonds. "Newspapers: Audience." In *The State of the News Media 2006: An Annual Report on American Journalism* (New York: Columbia University Graduate School of Journalism, 2006), via http:www.stateofthenewsmedia.org/2006.

Zboray, Ronald J. and Mary Saracino Zboray. *Everyday Ideas: Socioliterary Experience Among Antebellum New Englanders*. Knoxville: University of Tennessee Press, 2006.

———. "Political News and Female Readership in Antebellum Boston and Its Region." *Journalism History* 22, no. 1 (Spring 1996): 2–14.

RONALD J. ZBORAY
MARY SARACINO ZBORAY

NEWSREELS

During their heyday in the 1930s and 1940s, newsreels operated in a nether region between cinema and journalism and in some respects served as a forerunner to television news. Because of their light regard for accuracy and lack of context and proportion, newsreels constituted a problematic new form of visual media, but they also opened windows on the world in an age when travel was cumbersome and beyond the means of most Americans.

Newsreels were typically shown before feature films, although some movie houses showed them exclusively. These mini-documentaries brought audiences images of current events, but many lacked any sense of journalistic professionalism or integrity. In 1935, Edgar Dale, one of the authors of the Payne Fund Studies (analyses of motion pictures by social scientists during the early 1930s), concluded that newsreels were disjointed and heavily emphasized celebrities and sports. In 1972, Raymond Fielding, in his book, *The American Newsreel: 1911–1967* (1972), wrote that in contrast to newspapers, which often presented in-depth and penetrating coverage of civic issues, "the coverage most valued by [newsreel producers] featured scenes of raw violence, sensation and catastrophe."

If newsreels focused on the doings of celebrities, sporting events, sensational trials and oddities, they also did cover significant events such as wars, elections and coronations. Some were clearly products of corporate publicity offices or government propaganda agencies. In addition, many newsreels "recreated" events, a fact typically not disclosed to audiences. The tone was most often sensational. The Hearst Corporation's entry into the field in 1914 was trumpeted by the headline: "Whizz! Bang! Smash! Startling News Pictures of the World's Biggest Happenings Every Week!"

Roots of the Medium

Crude newsreels, called "actualities," were among the first fare offered by nickelodeons in the early days of the twentieth century. In the infancy of film, the medium was truly the message. Before narrative fiction films appeared, audiences were enthralled by brief moving images of just about anything, from a street scene in Paris, to crowds in the surf at Atlantic City, to an onrushing locomotive (audiences reportedly gasped and jumped out the way).

Thomas Edison presented the first commercially successful "actuality" in 1896, and Pathé Films, which would remain a dominant player in the medium for decades, produced and released the first true newsreel screened in the United States a few years later. William McKinley was the first American president to be in a newsreel and there were early films on many other topics including George Bernard Shaw, Patriot Day parades, and more. Vitagraph, Fox Movietone News, Paramount News, and *Time* magazine's "The March of Time" were familiar names to American movie audiences.

Silent newsreels presented images of World War I with varying degrees of accuracy. In 1923, Will H. Hays, then head of the Motion Picture Producers and Distributors of America, urged that airmail be used to circulate newsreel footage of President Warren G. Harding's funeral. The first major sound newsreel captured Charles Lindbergh's takeoff from Long Island on his path-breaking transatlantic flight. A 1934 newsreel captured the assassination of King Alexander of Yugoslavia.

As the popularity of newsreels grew, the death-defying newsreel cameraman became an icon of popular culture. Tales of cameramen who would risk anything to get a shot were common in fiction films (including Buster Keaton's silent masterpiece, "The Cameraman") and even in the newsreels themselves. It was dangerous, and sometimes deadly, work. With the coming of sound, even the commentators became famous. The voice of Fox's Movietone News, Lowell Thomas, was as familiar to listeners as that of President Franklin Roosevelt, who reached out to the American public via radio in his "Fireside Chats." In a typical Fox newsreel, Thomas would narrate four stories, or "reels." H. V. Kaltenborn, who was famous for his radio commentary, was also a noted newsreel narrator. With their fast-paced, sensational style, the newsreels created indelible impressions. Footage of the airship *Hindenburg* exploding, accompanied by Herbert Morrison's hysterical narration — "Oh! The humanity!" — became an enduring cultural touchstone.

But the explosion of the *Hindenburg* also revealed the medium's ability to blow stories out of proportion. Morrison, whose words were also broadcast the next day on the NBC radio network, described the episode as "one of the worst catastrophes in the world." It was hardly that. In fact, only a small minority of the ninety-six passengers on board were killed.

The potent combination of word and image (sound effects were often added in the editing room) featured in the newsreels could excite the emotions of audiences and in one case led to the lynching of a pair of kidnapping suspects. The apparent power of newsreels to move and to convince viewers alarmed critics.

Cultural Influence

In the 1930s and 1940s, newspapers (which because of technological limitations published relatively few photographs) and radio brought the American public detailed news about national and world events, but the newsreel allowed moviegoers to see the people and places they could only read or hear about. Presidents, kings, debutantes, movie stars, daredevils, scientists, gangsters, and freaks passed by in an endless parade.

During World War II, newsreels allowed Americans to bear witness to the attack on Pearl Harbor, although several days after the events had actually taken place. Later wartime newsreels showed audiences carefully edited combat footage from the Pacific and European theaters. Most wartime newsreels can only be described as propaganda. At war's end, however, the newsreels brought people sound and images of the awesome power of the nuclear bombing of Japan. The horrifying images of the Nazi concentration camps helped Americans understand the true dimensions of the Holocaust.

With their swelling musical scores and breathless narration, newsreels imparted a sense of drama to news that could rarely be conjured in print or perhaps even on radio. In addition, newsreels were a popular medium of publicity and promotion. Movie studios used them to generate interest in their stars, and political and business leaders used them to burnish their images. A newsreel obituary of John D. Rockefeller completely whitewashed his aggressive and illegal business tactics and presented him as a kind of elfin sage, a benefactor of humanity. Hollywood, meanwhile, brought its full resources to bear in a smear campaign against novelist and radical California gubernatorial candidate Upton Sinclair, who, despite initial popular support, lost the 1934 election amid a wave of anti-Communist propaganda in newspapers and newsreels.

Sometimes newsreels were suppressed or censored. In 1937, Paramount cameramen filmed strikers being beaten and killed by police and hired thugs during the Republic Steel strike, but Paramount did not release the film until it was forced to by an investigating committee headed by Senator Robert LaFollette. Newsreel companies were also accused of editing African American soldiers out of World War II documentaries.

Although the public embraced newsreels, many critics in journalistic and academic circles remained wary of them. Newsreels, the critics argued, trivialized world events, framed social issues in ways that benefited their corporate producers, and sometimes perpetuated outright frauds. Newton Meltzer believed that, with some exceptions, newsreels were too shackled by the genre conventions of Hollywood to truly be considered journalism. In 1945, he wrote in *Hollywood Quarterly* that "the escapism that characterizes the screen's fiction dominates its treatment of news as well. Newsreels will not be *news* until they are freed from the superficial formula that has cursed them for nearly four decades, and turned into a useful and representative social document." Oscar Levant was less kind, commenting: "The newsreel: A series of catastrophes, ended by a fashion show."

The widespread availability of television after World War II crippled the movie industry as a whole and newsreels in particular. While early network news broadcasts were crude and brief, viewers tuned into shows like Edward R. Murrow's "See it Now" and "Person to Person" on CBS to see reports from the war zones of Korea, scenes of flooding on the Mississippi and interviews with national and world leaders. The niche that newsreels had occupied for two decades was usurped by television, whose new stars came not from the world of newsreels, but from radio and print journalism. Nevertheless, newsreels struggled on before vanishing completely in 1967 with the death of the Universal Newsreel.

During and after the height of their popularity, however, newsreels resonated in popular culture. They served as convenient expository devices in narrative films, and the most famous newspaper movie of all, *Citizen Kane*, opens with a "News on the March" newsreel reporting the death of fictional character Charles Foster Kane (based loosely, of course, on the press lord William Randolph Hearst).

Philosopher and journalist Walter Lippmann pointed out that the media serve as the prime conduits between "the world outside and the pictures in our heads" of that world. Successful collaboration between media communicators and media audiences in the construction of reality melds the conventions of the former and the expectations of the latter. This the newsreels, which were not quite cinema, not quite journalism, did with noisy aplomb.

Further Reading

Auerbach, Jonathan. "McKinley at Home: How Early American Cinema Made News." *American Quarterly*, Vol. 51 (Dec. 1999), 797–832.

Barnouw, Erik. *Documentary: A History of the Non-Fiction Film.* New York: Oxford University Press, 1974.

Dale, Edgar. *The Content of Motion Pictures.* New York: Macmillan, 1935.

Fielding, Raymond. *The American Newsreel: 1911–1967.* Norman: The University of Oklahoma Press, 1972.

Hochberg, Joel. "The Vanishing Newsreel." *Film in Review,* June-July, 1959: 345–362.

Meltzer, Norman. "Are Newsreels News?" *Hollywood Quarterly,* vol. 2 (April 1947): 270–272.

Mould, David H. "Historical Trends in the Criticism of the Newsreel and Television News, 1930–1955." *Journal of Popular Film and Television,"* vol. 12, no. 3 (Fall 1984): 118–126.

MIKE DILLON

NEWSWEEK

For most of the first three decades of its existence, *Newsweek* seemed to exist primarily as the alternative newsmagazine for people who disliked *Time*. Not until the Washington Post Company bought *Newsweek* in 1961 did the newsmagazine begin to create its own editorial identity, thereby attracting a readership on the basis of its writing style, format, and attention to contemporary culture and society.

News-Week started in February 1933, during *Time's* tenth year. Several wealthy investors and a former *Time* editor believed the nation needed another weekly publication dedicated to summarizing important events and issues, without the obvious viewpoint and odd writing style of the first newsmagazine.

News-Week essentially copied the format of its senior competitor by arranging articles in separate departments according to subject matter and rewriting stories from a variety of newspapers and news services, although it also had several correspondents to obtain original material. Editors perhaps disdained *Time's* unique style and tone, but a lack of lively writing in *News-Week* prevented it from becoming a serious competitor for many years. However, the newsmagazine's pages creatively displayed photographs and had a clean, readable design.

Having exhausted its initial investment capital, nearly bankrupt and in distant second place in readership and advertising, *News-Week* merged in October 1937 with *Today*, also a weekly in financial difficulty, and emerged as *Newsweek*. The combined circulation of the two weak weeklies was about three hundred thousand copies. The principal owner of the new venture was Vincent Astor, a member of a nationally prominent and rich family.

For the next twenty-five years, *Newsweek* concentrated on making sure it covered the same major news events and issues as *Time*, rarely daring to develop articles on original subjects. Its articles on national and international subjects were somewhat lengthier, though, and the newsmagazine consistently furnished pertinent background details. *Newsweek* did have a viewpoint, but stated its opinions each week in an editorial column written by the editor. Competent, concise coverage of various domestic and international crises, political controversies, and other newsworthy events attracted readers. Circulation increased steadily, surpassing a million copies during the early 1950s and adding another half-million by the early 1960s, which put *Newsweek* at about half *Time's* readership.

More readers brought more advertisers to *Newsweek*. Although profitable, *Newsweek* was the perennial second-place newsmagazine with readership demographics too similar to *Time*, and sometimes had difficulty persuading national advertisers to buy space, especially with the rise of network television as a competitor for ad revenue. *Newsweek* lacked the resources to expand its staff of correspondents. Subsequent to the death of its chief financial supporter, Vincent Astor, *Newsweek* was placed on the auction block in 1960 when the Astor Foundation decided to sell the newsmagazine.

The Washington Post Company bought *Newsweek* for $15 million in 1961. Almost immediately, editors sought to establish an identity for the newsmagazine, which adopted a mainstream liberal perspective on the news, both in terms of selection and tone. *Newsweek* wrote about the growing influence of right-wing ideologues in national politics, paid consistent attention to the civil rights struggle in the South, profiled political and civic activists who sought to transform the social system, and generally developed articles on its own that appealed to a younger readership than *Time*—while covering the week's top news.

Newsweek hired more correspondents, opened additional news bureaus in the United States and overseas. It also added liberal columnists, among them Walter Lippmann and Stewart Alsop, and the "Periscope" page offered brief items on politics and national affairs based on insider information from Congress, the White House, and federal policy makers. Editors adopted a narrative writing style for most articles, using scene-setting opening paragraphs and strong summary ending paragraphs. *Newsweek* articles were descriptive and informative, and editors continued to display quality photographs from news services, contract photographers, and staff photojournalists, occasionally as the dominant element on a page.

The 1960s through mid-1970s were good years for *Newsweek* and the other newsmagazines. Public interest in long-running events and issues—civil rights, racial tensions, Vietnam War, cultural and social transformation, Apollo space program, and Watergate scandal—enabled the newsmagazine to build a loyal readership while it provided a weekly summary and perspective. *Newsweek* won national awards for cover articles on racial issues and a postwar retrospective on Vietnam.

Vietnam War coverage further separated *Newsweek* from its direct competitors. *Newsweek* was the first newsmagazine to cite moral concerns related to American tactics in southern Vietnam that relied on artillery and bombs; articles mentioned incidents involving civilian casualties and predicted further harm to noncombatants from American firepower. *Newsweek* also questioned fundamental elements of American strategy, especially the deployment of large infantry units for operations in the countryside and the failure of intensive aerial bombardment to stop the flow of supplies and soldiers from northern Vietnam. A special edition in summer 1967 devoted forty-eight pages to the effects of the Vietnam War on American society.

Numerous articles on popular culture set *Newsweek* apart from its competitors. Trends in movies, music, and television programs warranted one- or two-page articles and occasionally received cover-story treatment, which occupied six or more pages. Articles on fashion and lifestyle habits among younger adults revealed the nontraditional patterns that emerged among the first wave of the Baby Boom generation. *Newsweek* articles on such subjects were neither condescending nor patronizing, but treated developments as meaningful and appropriate.

Other innovations of the era included publishing credit lines with articles that identified correspondents and editors who produced the information and a weekly "My Turn" column devoted to an opinion or observation from a reader.

Newsweek attained a circulation of nearly three million copies by the mid-1970s, which was two-thirds *Time*'s total. Of more importance, however, was the belief on Madison Avenue that *Newsweek* had become a better buy than *Time*. Advertising agencies perceived *Newsweek* as a "hot" item that attracted younger, affluent readers who were eager consumers. Full-page color advertisements aimed at youthful consumers by car manufacturers, cigarette companies, liquor brands, cosmetics, and apparel makers appeared in the newsmagazine. During the early 1970s, *Newsweek* sold about three thousand pages of ads a year, approximately a hundred above *Time*. (Because of the circulation difference, *Newsweek*'s advertising rates were lower than *Time*'s and its annual revenue was less.)

Extra ad revenue allowed *Newsweek* to add pages for national and international news coverage. Additional correspondents, who gathered information, and editors, who wrote the articles, generated the material necessary to fill the expanded weekly editions. At its peak during the mid-1970s, the newsmagazine employed almost two hundred people at the newsroom in New York City and bureaus in the United States, Europe, and Asia. These prosperous years financed the inclusion of color photographs and spot-color ink for highlights in weekly editions that contained an average of just over a hundred pages total, about half of which was news.

The glory years for *Newsweek*, and for the weekly newsmagazines, began to wane during the 1980s. The availability of news and lifestyle programs on cable television networks, the abundance of magazines offering lifestyle and popular culture fare, and the adoption of interpretive journalism by many newspapers diverted readers from the weeklies. The total number of copies remained virtually the same while the adult population increased. *Newsweek*'s circulation stagnated, staying at slightly more than three million copies, into the twenty-first century. The number of editorial personnel decreased to about one hundred seventy early in the twenty-first century.

As a consequence of competition from a variety of sources, which resulted in one-third fewer advertising pages by the mid-1990s, *Newsweek* experimented with different formats to attract and retain readers. It tried special theme editions on a variety of subjects, hoping to appeal to people in their twenties and thirties. It reduced the number of pages for national and international news to make room for so-called soft news, which usually meant anything not connected to politics, government, and other traditional news items. "Periscope" expanded from a single page of brief news items to multiple pages of short items on a variety of subjects, which included news, celebrities, popular culture, and lifestyle. Some editorial experiments worked, others did not—and *Newsweek* had six chief editors within a span of a dozen years.

To adapt to an intensely competitive multimedia environment, *Newsweek* created an online edition for the MSNBC web site, itself a joint venture of the cable news network operated by Microsoft Corporation and the National Broadcasting Company. The online edition has a special section that focuses on a different subject each day and has daily updates other articles written especially for the e-zine.

The print edition of *Newsweek* continued to display excellent page design, photographs, and illustrations in the early twenty-first century. Articles typically were shorter than in the past, and boxed or inset text is a common device to deal with minor topics within a general subject.

JAMES LANDERS

NIEMAN, LUCIUS W.

Four weeks into his job as the first managing editor of the newly founded *Milwaukee Daily Journal* in December 1882, Lucius W. Nieman (December 13, 1857–February 1, 1935) at age twenty-five became half-owner and editor-publisher when one of the founders decided to sell his stake in the unprofitable new newspaper. For the next fifty-three years, Nieman controlled the soon-renamed *Milwaukee Journal* during its ascent from a small competitor against several other newspapers to the dominant daily in a major industrial city.

Nieman was in the right place at the right time in Milwaukee because of his ability and intelligence. Nieman, born in rural Wisconsin, learned to be a typesetter at a weekly newspaper at age twelve, then at age fifteen got a job placing columns of type into page forms for the printing press at the daily *Milwaukee Sentinel*. He wanted to be a reporter, but needed formal education and enrolled in Carroll College in Waukesha about twenty miles west of Milwaukee. Within two years, the *Sentinel* hired him to report city news, and subsequently sent him to cover the legislature in Madison; by his twenty-first birthday, Nieman was *Sentinel* city editor.

Ambitious and astute, Nieman decided he should be more than a mere editor. His opportunity came when local Democrats founded the *Daily Journal* to compete against the Republican *Sentinel* and recruited Nieman to direct the newsroom. The newspaper's shaky start allowed him to buy into ownership and implement the journalism he considered necessary for Milwaukee, a city of brothels, bars, gaming houses, and corrupt government.

Nieman represented a generation of newspaper editors during the late nineteenth century whose campaigns for municipal reform and community improvement appealed to citizens. Nieman wrote or ordered written articles on unsanitary water supplies, lack of fire safety codes, governmental corruption, police corruption, and other urban maladies common to American cities. Not much was accomplished, except that Nieman had established the *Journal* as a voice for civic improvement.

Despite a consistent editorial campaign by the *Journal* against a notoriously corrupt mayor, Milwaukee voters re-elected the mayor several times. Finally tired of him after ten years in office, voters elected Socialists to run city government in 1910. The *Journal* disliked the Socialists and had tried to convince voters not to elect the slate; Nieman preferred traditional political parties. Nieman soon decided the Socialist programs were hardly radical, instead being primarily limited to placing municipal services under governmental control and more responsive to public needs, and the *Journal* endorsed some Socialist goals.

The *Journal* did succeed with an important reform on the state level. After years of campaigning for nonpartisan municipal elections, Nieman's editorials and persistent news coverage aided in the passage by the legislature of a law that required local candidates to run without formal political party affiliation. This legislation freed municipal government from party dominance, effectively separating state and local government.

Nieman was not enamored of the Progressive Republicans led by Gov. Robert M. La Follette, who challenged the status quo for several years during the early 1900s, enacting legislation affecting railroads and other powerful industries. *Journal* editorials selectively favored or opposed measures proposed by Progressives, and alternatively praised or criticized La Follette. Nieman was a political moderate who was uncomfortable with La Follette and the Progressives.

The *Journal* itself formally aligned with the Democrats until 1896 when Nieman refused to support presidential nominee William Jennings Bryan, who sought free coinage of silver. Nieman thereafter professed political independence.

Thorough neighborhood news coverage and close attention to local events and issues made the *Journal* the top newspaper in a four-newspaper town by the early 1900s. The gap between it and competitors widened appreciably from that point forward. The *Milwaukee Journal* survived as the sole afternoon newspaper for the city and nearby suburbs; a state edition circulated to almost every community in Wisconsin. The lone competitor, the Hearst-owned *Milwaukee Sentinel*, remained a distant second for several decades as the city's morning newspaper.

Nieman much preferred the newsroom to the business office. He spent long days supervising editors and reporters, reviewing page proofs, and planning news coverage. As the newspaper grew to a sizable business, Nieman appointed a succession of managers to direct the operation of the *Journal*. Each adhered to Nieman's policy of paying for new equipment and additional office space through revenue or cash reserves, not by borrowing from banks or other lenders. Nieman believed indebtedness made the newspaper vulnerable to outside pressure.

A Sunday edition began in 1911. Advertising revenue increased steadily until World War I and circulation surpassed one hundred thousand in 1915.

As editor, Nieman directed a campaign during World War I to expose propaganda favorable to Germany published by German-language newspapers in Wisconsin. This was a daring effort in a heavily German community and state. Nieman received threats, the newspaper lost some readers and advertisers, but won a Pulitzer Prize for the numerous articles that revealed propaganda.

Printing quality also contributed to the success of the *Journal*. Nieman regularly invested in new presses to improve color capability, which appealed to advertisers and readers alike. Profits enabled the *Journal* to construct a multi-story building for all departments and a set of new printing presses in central Milwaukee in 1924—an accomplishment paid for without loans.

Hard work and the pressure of leadership affected Nieman's health to the point that he appointed Harry J. Grant publisher of the *Journal* in 1919. Nieman continued as majority owner of Journal Company until his death sixteen years later, although he was not actively involved in the daily newspaper.

Nieman had married Agnes Wahl of Milwaukee in November 1900. Upon his death in 1935, she inherited 27.5 percent of Journal Company stock and his niece the other 27.5 percent. His will stipulated sale of all 55 percent within five years. Grant arranged for an employee-ownership plan, which allowed the Journal Company to remain a locally owned, privately held entity for nearly seventy years.

Further Reading

Portrait of a Paper, the Milwaukee Journal: 75th Aniversary Year, the Milwaukee Journal. Milwaukee Journal, 1958.

JAMES LANDERS

NIGHTLINE

ABC's late night news program, *Nightline*, began in 1980 and has been providing critically-acclaimed coverage of the day's top news stories ever since. *Nightline* has been anchored throughout its first twenty five years by award-winning journalist Ted Koppel, whose personal signature as host and interviewer established the program as a journalistic force.

The Iran hostage crisis of November 1979 was the trigger for ABC coverage that led to the establishment of *Nightline*. ABC initially covered the hostage crisis with daily late night updates entitled, *"The Iran Crisis: America Held Hostage."* ABC's early evening news anchor, Frank Reynolds, initially handled the late night anchoring duties as well, but as the crisis wore on, it became clear that he would not continue to anchor two nightly broadcasts. The logical host for the late night hostage updates was Ted Koppel, ABC's chief diplomatic correspondent, who was a frequent contributor to the special reports.

As the hostage crisis wound on, frequently with few new developments, ABC News President Roone Arledge convinced the network executives to leave the 11:30 time slot in the hands of the news division and to use it to cover the top story of the day. The new program, *Nightline*, premiered in March 1980 with Koppel as host. It provided ABC with a counter-programming strategy to late night entertainment on CBS and NBC, and helped elevate ABC as a primary source for news coverage.

The format for *Nightline* was to have a setup correspondent package that frames the key news issue of the day. Veteran *Nightline* correspondents Chris Bury, Dave Marash, John Donvan, and Michel Martin usually presented these setup reports. The anchor then followed by interviewing key newsmakers or analysts. This was where Koppel's acclaimed interviewing skill won praise for *Nightline*. Koppel always maintained a professional demeanor, but was quick to point out a guest's flawed logic or weak evidence. Koppel frequently interviewed two guests with opposing views at the same time, but demanded the discussion remain civil and on topic. The program concluded with a brief perspective or closing statement by the anchor.

Nightline normally ran for thirty minutes, but has on occasion been longer when breaking news developments dictated. In the spring of 1983, ABC expanded *Nightline* to a full hour and covered multiple topics during each program. Ratings for the second half hour were poor, however, and ABC affiliates convinced the network to return to the half-hour format in January, 1984.

Nightline has been at the forefront of coverage of every major news story, including the terrorist attacks of September 11, 2001, the fall of the Iron Curtain, Middle East developments, AIDS, the Clinton impeachment, and presidential campaigns. Virtually every major newsmaker of the era has been interviewed by Koppel as part of *Nightline*, including U.S. presidents, international diplomats, and celebrities. Koppel conducted a good deal of his reporting on location, including his work as an imbedded reporter with the Army's Third Infantry Division as it fought its way from Kuwait to Baghdad in 2003.

The program did not rely solely on outside events to set its agenda, and frequently enterprised stories or even series on topics that were not spot news items of the day. For example, *Nightline* presented a week-long series in 1985 on apartheid in South Africa, a journalistic venture of which Koppel later said he was most proud. Another series of note was called "Crime and Punishment," an in-depth set of reports about America's prison system. *Nightline*'s periodic presentations on race relations in America, "America in Black and White," have followed that topic for over a decade.

Nightline altered its normal format on occasion to conduct broadcast "town meetings" with a live studio audience, discussing such topics as health care. *Nightline* also hosted occasional programs that critiqued the role and performance of the media.

Nightline was recognized repeatedly for its journalistic work, winning numerous Emmy, Peabody, duPont-Columbia, Overseas Press Club, and Sigma Delta Chi awards. Media critics praised *Nightline* for its depth of coverage and balance.

As with most news programs, *Nightline* itself occasionally became the subject of controversy. In May, 2004, *Nightline* produced a program entitled "The Fallen," in which the photographs of all U.S. servicemen and women killed in Iraq and Afghanistan were displayed while Koppel read their names. No other reporting or commentary was provided in the program. Sinclair Broadcast Group ordered its eight ABC affiliate stations to not run the program, claiming that *Nightline* was pushing a political agenda to undermine the U.S. war effort in Iraq. In the late 1980s, *Nightline* was also criticized by the liberal watchdog group, Fairness and Accuracy in Reporting, for too often interviewing news sources with conservative perspectives.

For all of *Nightline*'s journalistic success, however, the program's future with ABC was often clouded. The television news landscape, particularly for evening programming, changed radically during the late twentieth and early twenty first centuries, with *Nightline* facing competition for news viewers from Fox News Channel, MSNBC, and CNN. Early in *Nightline*'s run, there was no network news competition in the time slot and CNN was in its infancy.

By 2006, fewer than four million viewers tuned in to *Nightline* on an average evening, compared to more than six million each night during the mid-1990s. Those numbers placed ABC a distant third place when compared to network rivals NBC and CBS, both of which programmed entertainment talk programs opposite *Nightline*.

ABC executives tried to recruit comedian David Letterman for the late night time slot in 2002 before Letterman eventually renewed with CBS. This flirtation was apparently done without the knowledge of Koppel or the *Nightline* staff. ABC later was believed to have discussed bringing NBC's entertainer Conan O'Brien to replace *Nightline*, but O'Brien opted to stay at NBC.

Koppel announced in spring of 2005 that he would leave ABC and *Nightline* when his contract expired in December, 2005. Leaving with Koppel was long-time executive producer, Tom Bettag. The departure of Koppel and Bettag further fueled speculation that *Nightline* would not be retained at ABC.

Further Reading

Bliss, Edward Jr. *Now the News: The Story of Broadcast Journalism.* New York: Columbia University Press, 1991.

Busiek, Dave. "Holding the Line." *Communicator,* April, 2004: 28–32.

Koppel, Ted, and Kyle Gibson. *Nightline: History in the Making and the Making of Television.* New York: Times Books, 1996.

McConnell, Bill. "Koppel: Will Work for Integrity." *Broadcasting & Cable,* April 4, 2005: 6.

JEFFREY M. MCCALL

NILES WEEKLY REGISTER

Niles Weekly Register (1811–1849), a leading weekly news magazine with a national circulation, began in 1811 with the idealistic motto of publishing accounts of "The Past, The Present, For the Future." As an indexed and relatively comprehensive summary of events from 1811 to 1849, the *Register* is considered the paper of record for its age and has long been a favorite resource for historians. Its usual printing run was 16 book-sized pages, but it often included appendices and extra pages. Two volumes of the *Register* appeared each year and over the lifetime of the publication, its seventy-five volumes exceeded thirty thousabd pages. The *Register* was supported by subscription only and it did not contain advertising.

Hezekiah Niles (1777–1839) founded the *Register* in 1811 in Baltimore. After 1836, his son, William Ogden Niles, ran the *Register* and said that like his father, he would edit the it "without fear or favor, partiality or affection." In 1839, the publication was sold to Jeremiah Hughes, a Whig partisan. Hughes' illness in 1848 resulted in the *Register's* sale to a Philadelphia printer named George Beatty. Its last partial volume was printed in 1849.

Hezekiah Niles was the son of Quakers who had nationalist ideas for economic independence that paralleled those of contemporary Whigs like Senator Henry Clay and economist Matthew Carey. His *Register* influenced a younger generation of writers and publishers such as Horace Greeley and impressed others so much so that towns in Ohio and Michigan were named for him.

Niles' original vision of a news magazine was far ahead of its time. He believed strongly in accuracy and "magnanimous disputation," or rather, fairness and balance in the editorial agenda. Although his own editorials favored the Whig party and its "American system," Niles made a point of including the widest variety of viewpoints from other newspapers, which he received through postal exchanges.

Niles' concept of news embraced the broadest scope of human experience. His *Register* kept close track of economics, technology, science, medicine, geography, archaeology, the weather, and many stories of human interest. There was, for example, a dog who rescued another dog from a river. There was the case of a blind woman restored to sight, and another of a slave who killed himself rather than be sold at the slave market. Niles printed many items about ballooning and predicted that someday man would build machines to fly (although he doubted that steam engines could propel them). Riverboat steam engine disasters were standard fare, and it is interesting that while early accounts were short on facts and long on adjectives, this changed as the publication matured and Niles began stressing facts over emotions.

Niles Weekly Register regularly reproduced documents of historical interest. These included a memoir by Daniel Boone about the opening of the Kentucky frontier, a 1791 report on manufacturing by Alexander Hamilton, and an 1808 Treasury Department report on roads, canals and public works known as "internal improvements."

The *Register* was far more authoritative and comprehensive than its competitors during the partisan press era, although its unique position was lost with the advent of steam printing, the telegraph and the Associated Press in the late 1830s and 1840s. The *Register* was not only a forerunner of objectivity and the broad vision of news, but also a voice of moderation and conscience concerning issues such as slavery and the development of economic independence. As early as 1820, the far-sighted Niles feared a civil war and worked to reconcile Northern and Southern interests.

Further Reading

Earle, W.H. "Niles' Register, 1811–1849:† Window on the World." *Journal of the War of 1812 and the Era 1800 to 1840*, vol. 1 no. 5 (Fall, 1996).

Kovarik, William. "To Avoid the Coming Storm: Hezekiah Niles Weekly Register as a Voice of North-South Moderation, 1811–1836." *American Journalism* (Summer, 1992).

Luxon, Norval. *Niles Weekly Register: News Magazine of the Ninteenth Century.* Baton Rouge.: Louisiana State University Press, 1947.

Schmidt, Phillip R. *Hezekiah Niles and American Economic Nationalism: A Political Biography.* New York: Arno Press, 1982.

Stone, Richard G. Stone. *Hezekiah Niles as an Economist.* Johns Hopkins University Studies in Historical and Political Science, Series L1 No. 5. Baltimore: Johns Hopkins Press, 1933.

WILLIAM KOVARIK

O

OBITUARIES

Jane Treat, granddaughter of Connecticut's deputy governor, opened her bible one spring Sunday—and became the subject of American journalism's first obituary. It was 1704. Sitting outside, reading the scriptures, she was struck "by a terrible flash of lightning." *The Boston News-Letter* recorded this event in its next edition (June 5–12), telling readers her death had been instant, that the lightning strike left her body "much wounded, not torn but burnt," and that in life she was a model of piety and sobriety. Although death reports had previously appeared in American journalism, the story of Jane Treat qualifies as the earliest obituary because it offers also an appraisal of character, an essential determinant in the achievement of obituary classification.

The pioneering newspapers of the American colonies displayed a preference for obituaries ripe with religious expression and lamentation. As republican sentiment grew, however, so too did the courage of the obituary writers. By 1775, therefore, *The Virginia Gazette* obituary of Attorney General Peyton Randolph concentrated more on his life as a statesman than on his spiritual inclinations (November 10). Obituary publication had become soundly established by the middle of the following century; the first edition of the *New-York Daily Times* (forerunner of the *New York Times*) on September 18, 1851, devoted nearly an entire column to it. Fourteen years later, the *New York Times* recorded the assassination of a president in a succession of front pages dominated by the mood of an obituary. Using the latest available technology, the first of these (April 15, 1865) displayed a speed of response that newspapers today would find difficult to match, printing in full a series of cables from Washington. The most prominent despatch was the War Department's 1:30 a.m. cable, just four hours after John Wilkes Booth had shot Abraham Lincoln at Ford's Theatre. This communiqué appeared under eight decks of headlines, the sixth of which declared: "No Hopes Entertained of His Recovery." This unhappy diagnosis was proved correct in the next day's edition, when the editorial column was dedicated to an obituary that spoke of "a man so gentle, so kind, so free from every particle of malice or unkindness" whose violent death had "shocked the public heart beyond expression."

Obituary writing can often reveal prevailing social attitudes. In this vein, *The New York Times* in 1882 published an account of remarkable racial insensitivity, rejoicing at the death of a Native American chief. It began with news of a battle in the Chihuahua region between Mexican troops and "renegade Apaches" in which Chief Loco, described as "head of the entire [Apache] nation," had been killed. Then came the obituary, more a celebration of a death than an acknowledgment of a life, maintaining that he had mistreated his wives, played poker to excess, and that the Apaches would henceforth "go to pieces." That outcome, according to the obituary, would be "an excellent thing for the entire frontier." Employing a crude pun on the chief's poker habit, the headline confronting New Yorkers on that June 21 morning was: "Loco's Chips Passed In."

Obituaries associated with military exploits have generally inspired, over the decades, a much more gracious style of writing. Early examples of this are found in the four columns which *The Boston Post* allocated to General William Tecumseh Sherman (February 16, 1891) and in the Atlanta *Constitution* tribute to Judge Robert Falligant, Savannah branch president of the Confederate Veterans' Association (January 4, 1902). The *Constitution* recalled that at the Battle of Cold Harbor in 1864, the young Lieutenant Falligant fought courageously "all the day until night had drawn its sable mantle over the carnage."

American journalism's engagement with the obituary art has long been characterized by an egalitarian character. *The Washington Post*, for instance, records the lives and deaths of teachers and tradespeople as well as those of prelates and politicians. It was doing this as far back as the 1890s, as demonstrated in the *Post*'s obituary of a local grocer, George C. Cornwell (March 17, 1892), which observed that "when the dread messenger came" the veteran shopkeeper was "still at the helm" of his business enterprise. At the celebrity end of the demographic spectrum, obituaries can offer a permanent memorial in print to fame found and fame lost. *The San Francisco Chronicle* declared that the death of Jean Harlow, while "the platinum blonde" was shooting the film *Saratoga*, had "stunned the movie colony" (June 8, 1937) and blamed the self-destruction of comedian W.C. Fields on "a diet of olives floating in alcohol" (December 26, 1946). On November 24, 1943, the *Chronicle*'s obituary page recounted the rise and fall of Charles Ray. He was a star of the silent films, commanding $11,000 a week "as one of the kings of the screen," but then lost millions on a grandiose production "so bad his friends slunk away without speaking to him." At his death, aged fifty-two, he had been reduced to working as a film extra of "the $7.50 a day variety."

As newspapers have grown in size since the 1980s, introducing magazine and lifestyle sections, so too have obituary pages developed in both scope and column space. They have proclaimed the perfidy of serial bank robber "Fast Eddie" Watkins (in Cleveland's *Plain Dealer* on March 15, 2002), the bleak history of mobster John Gotti (branded as "a narcissistic tyrant" by *The New York Times* on June 11, 2002), and the determination of Alabama's desegregation activist Rosa Parks (who "launched the modern civil rights movement," said *The Washington Post* on October 25, 2005). The obituary itself, in capturing such lives in all their permutations rather than death in its uniformity, has become recognised as a valid instrument of history. It has grown from mourning the pious dead to appraising the infamous dead and offering enlightenment on existences heroic, obscure, misguided, and eccentric. There are reasons, accordingly, for acknowledging it as a rich and mature enactment of the journalism craft.

Further Reading

Ball, John, and Jill Jonnes, eds. *Fame At Last*. Kansas City: Andrews McMeel, 2000.

Hume, Janice. *Obituaries in American Culture*. Jackson: University Press of Mississippi, 2000.

Johnson, Marilyn. *The Dead Beat*. New York: HarperCollins, 2006.

Siegel, Marvin, ed. *The Last Word*. New York: William Morrow, 1997.

Starck, Nigel. *Life After Death*. Melbourne: Melbourne University Press, 2006.

Whitman, Alden. *The Obituary Book*. New York: Stein and Day, 1971.

———. *Come to Judgment*. New York: The Viking Press, 1980.

NIGEL STARCK

OBJECTIVITY IN REPORTING

During the first half of the twentieth century, the concept "objectivity" came to signify an amalgam of related principles considered indispensable to good journalism. Even as the concept was increasingly treated as a central component of a set of journalism principles, press coverage of some events raised doubts about whether objective reporting could assure quality news coverage. In the last half of the century, the concept was debated perhaps more than any associated with journalism.

Precise definitions of journalistic objectivity are rare, and various shadings of a general concept appear in much literature. One meaning, however, at its core since first use of the word in journalism sources is avoidance of bias. Being objective requires journalists to avoid even the hint of their own opinions in news copy and everything else that might make it appear biased, one-sided, or unbalanced. In the early American party press, "impartiality" included a meaning later associated with objectivity, as some argued that newspaper content should show no partiality toward any political party. Of course, most papers during this period were strongly partisan.

Beginning in the 1830s American penny press era, news was increasingly treated as a product to be sold, and jour-

nalists increasingly sought qualities for which the public would pay. Objectivity emerged as one such quality that came to be defined during the next century as thorough and accurate reporting of verifiable facts with fairness and balance, without prejudice, and without journalists' personal involvement in what is reported as news.

Objectivity means, as Donald McDonald wrote in 1971, both a goal and a process. Journalists are to be objective in gathering and presenting news, and the product (news report) is to be recognizably objective. For example, a balanced report is recognizable, presumably, because it includes clearly differing, preferably opposite, viewpoints. Views differ about origins of journalistic objectivity. Throughout press history, people have stressed the need for accuracy in print, and much of what journalistic objectivity signifies has long existed in concepts of accuracy, truth, and fairness. Some principles bound up with its meaning very likely evolved from oral culture. Scholars who have stressed past practices and ideas later associated with objectivity in gathering and disseminating information suggest the concept existed long before the word. The first such research focused on the American penny press era, but subsequent scholarship emphasized earlier objective practices in the United States and England. Journalism historian William David Sloan says colonial American standards for handling information were transferred to reportage when newspapers began in the colonies. Sociologist and media historian Michael Schudson, probably the first American scholar to publish a historical account of a journalism principle, defined objectivity in a 1978 book as separation of facts from values and located its rise in post-World War I America.

References to the word objectivity as a core journalistic principle were not found in a search of sources about journalism published before the twentieth century—and are rare before 1930. Editor Henry Watterson, from at least 1873, used "objective point" to mean focus, goal, and purpose in writing a news story, a meaning unrelated to journalistic objectivity. The word emerged amid influences of at least four trends around the turn of the twentieth century. First, evidence indicates that journalistic objectivity as later understood was shaped by late nineteenth-century interests in scientific methods. Criticisms of the press and discussions of its function and responsibility published around the turn of the twentieth century rejected partisanship and stressed elements—including truth and accuracy– encompassed by objectivity. Ronald Shilen, in a 1955 doctoral thesis, traced Americans' preoccupation with science and scientific method as the foundation of the concept of objectivity as used by the 1950s. Second, a societal shift from an individualist- to collectivist- orientation affecting American society in the era seems embodied in this journalistic concept. When nineteenth-century critics identified good journalism, they cited praiseworthy traits of individual journalists and newspapers, but early twentieth-century discussions increasingly treated journalists as a collective—for which objectivity became a precept. Third, the Progressive Era at the turn of the twentieth century, when reformers sought to assure that social institutions would responsibly serve society, gave impetus to principles, such as objectivity and journalism ethics codes, to assure the press would better serve the public. Fourth, excesses like yellow journalism in the same years enhanced the appeal of principles that, if applied by all journalists, could prevent such excesses.

Early Uses, Rise, and Decline

One of the earliest published references to objectivity as a core journalistic principle appeared in a 1902 article that said, without elaboration, yellow journalism lacked "objective truth." A 1911 textbook by Charles G. Ross defined objective reporting as absence of editorializing. A version of the concept of objectivity is implied in a definition of news quality as "freedom from bias and taint." Summary reports of proceedings of the first conference on the press (1912) and the first canons of journalism adopted by the American Society of Newspaper Editors (1923) used the word impartiality, not objectivity.

The word "objectivity" rarely appears in American journalism texts published between 1911 and 1933, including a 1913 textbook and 1918 anthology by journalism educator Willard G. Bleyer. An exception is Nelson A. Crawford's 1924 text where the word appears twenty-one times in the first five chapters and in three subsequent chapter titles. The author, who refers to the scientific method's general societal influence, calls objectivity "the primary" journalism "ideal" and implies it included "balance and proportion" and excluded interpretation, sensationalism and partisan and newspaper bias. The 1932 revision of Bleyer's 1913 textbook implies objectivity meant absence of both reporters' opinions and newspaper policy influence. The word was not found in a Robert Miller Neal's 1933 textbook that thoroughly covers journalists' work, but a version of the concept is implied in instructions for removing bias and opinion from news stories.

While some people treated objectivity as essential to journalism early in the century, others raised doubts. Maynard Wilson Brown, in a 1936 dissertation, concluded that Americans were not prepared for World War I because prewar correspondence from abroad adhered to observable facts and did not interpret European conditions. Interpretation would have been seen as tainting news with reporters' opinions.

Some commentators have speculated that the 1929 stock market crash led to the first serious doubts about objectivity because inadequate reporting of economic conditions left Americans unprepared for the ensuing crisis. But the 1947 Hutchins Commission Report—albeit practically ignored for two decades because it advocated that journalists interpret news—may have marked the beginning of the end of unquestioning faith in objective reporting. That report delineated press failings and suggested five requirements be met to assure more responsible media. Most discussions of objectivity's decline, however, point to inadequate reporting of Senator Joseph McCarthy's early 1950s efforts to identify communists in America. Journalists later said they believed they could report only McCarthy's observable actions and words—as objectivity required. Identifying inadequacies in such reporting for informing the public about McCarthy's efforts revealed that flaws in journalistic objectivity transcended that episode.

Since 1960, many have dissected objectivity as an inadequate journalistic principle. In addition to criticizing it for deterring full reporting of what the public needs to know, many have argued that no journalist can be objective because everyone's perceptions are colored by cultural values and unique experiences and viewpoints. Moreover, subjectivity enters a journalist's work at every stage—from deciding what is newsworthy and selecting what to report, to determining what information to gather, to choosing what element of an event or issue is most significant and how to emphasize it. Also, many gatekeepers are involved in every story's development, and these journalists who rewrite and edit copy, develop headlines and layout, and determine where to place items among other news of the day, greatly influence what ultimately gets disseminated as news. Further, some have argued that journalistic objectivity itself has been subverted. For example, some agree with sociologist Gaye Tuchman who argued in the 1970s that objectivity had become, along with other journalistic standards, a shield protecting media from criticism more than serving the public.

Objectivity has never fallen completely out of favor despite continued debates about its usefulness and origins and the various shadings of its meaning. Although some dismiss objectivity as unattainable, most journalists and educators associate it with accuracy, balance, and fairness, and call it a goal for which all journalists should strive if only because attempts to reach this ideal—even if unattainable—improve the methods used and the end product.

Further Reading

Bleyer, Willard G. *Newspaper Writing and Editing*. rev. ed. Boston: Houghton Mifflin, 1932.

Brown, Maynard Wilson. "American Public Opinion and European Armaments, 1912–14." Doctoral thesis, University of Wisconsin, 1936.

"Canons of Journalism," adopted by the American Society of Newspaper Editors in 1923.

Commission on Freedom of the Press. *A Free and Responsible Press: A General Report on Mass Communication*. Chicago: University of Chicago Press, 1947.

Connolly, Charles B. "The Ethics of Modern Journalism." *Catholic World* 75, no. 30 (July 1902): 453–462.

Crawford, Nelson A. *The Ethics of Journalism*. New York: Knopf, 1924.

Irwin, Will. "The American Newspaper: A Study of Journalism in Its Relation to the Public." *Collier's Weekly* 46 (January 21; February 18; March 4, 11, 1911); 47 (April 1, 22; May 6, 27; June 3, 17; July 1, 8, 29, 1911).

Knowlton, Steven R. and Karen L. Freeman, eds. *Fair & Balanced: A History of Journalistic Objectivity*. Northport, AL: Vision Press, 2005.

McDonald, Donald. "Is Objectivity Possible?" *The Center Magazine* 4, no. 5 (September/October 1971). Santa Barbara, CA: Center for the Study of Democratic Institutions.

Neal, Robert Miller. *Newspaper Desk Work*. New York: D. Appleton and Co., 1933.
Ross, Charles G. *Writing of News: A Handbook*. New York: Henry
  Holt, 1911.
Schudson, Michael. *Discovering the News: A Social History
  of American Newspapers*. New York: Basic Books, Inc.,
  1978.
Shilen, Ronald. "The Concept of Objectivity in Journalism in
  the United States." Doctoral thesis, New York University,
  1955.
Sloan, William David. "Neutrality and Colonial Newspapers."
  In *Fair & Balanced: A History of Journalistic Objectivity*,
  edited by Steven R. Knowlton and Karen L. Freeman, 36–
  50, Northport, AL: Vision Press, 2005.
Tuchman, Gaye. *Making News: A Study in the Construction of
  Reality*. New York: Free Press, 1978.
Watterson, Henry. "The American Newspaper." An Address to
  the Indiana Press Association, Indianapolis, May 1, 1873. In
  Henry Watterson *The Compromises of Life*. New York: Fox,
  Duffield & Company, 1903, 225–259.

HAZEL DICKEN-GARCIA

OCHS, ADOLPH S.

"It will be my earnest aim that the *New York Times* give the news, all the news…impartially, without fear or favor, regardless of sect, party or interest" in a "clean, dignified, and trustworthy" manner, so that the *New York Times* will become known for its "honesty, watchfulness, earnestness, industry" and "common sense."

This page four statement of principles by an obscure thirty-eight-year-old southern publisher in taking over the debt-ridden, circulation starved *New York Times* on March 19, 1896, was politely ignored by many who thought the Old Gray Lady had drawn her last breath. Chattanooga's Adolph Ochs (March 12, 1858–April 8, 1935) had borrowed money to buy the three-penny *New York Times,* which served only nine thousand remaining readers. Ochs was thought to lack the resources to compete with Joseph Pulitzer, William Randolph Hearst, and the other well-known papers in New York's crowded and intensely competitive newspaper landscape. On Ochs' extraordinary watch the circulation of the *New York Times* surged to a half million daily and three-quarters of a million on Sundays. Its quality and influence made the paper an American institution and the nation's journal of record.

Ochs's Bavarian-born parents were culturally and politically active. Julius Ochs was fluent in six languages. Bertha Levy had hastily fled Germany after the failed Revolution of 1848. Adolph Simon Ochs was the first of six children. He was born in Cincinnati on the eve of the Civil War and was raised in Knoxville, where his mother was a strong Southern sympathizer. At eleven, Ochs worked as an errand boy at the *Knoxville Chronicle*. By fourteen he had become a printer's devil at the paper. At seventeen, he had moved to the composing room of the *Louisville Courier-Journal*. Returning to Knoxville, he worked in the *Tribune*'s composing room, as a reporter, and as assistant business manager. As a nineteen-year-old, Ochs became advertising manager for the struggling *Chattanooga Daily Dispatch*.

When the paper folded, Ochs borrowed $250 and became, at age twenty, the publisher of the *Chattanooga Times*.

Over the next eighteen years, Ochs perfected a news management style that "conducts our business on business principles," Ochs wrote on July 2, 1878, making the paper "the indispensable organ of business, commercial, and productive interests." Ochs avoided political partisanship. He told long-time editor L.G. Walker, "your only policy is no policy—except to be right." Ochs became a town and regional booster, promoting construction of an opera house, a ship channel, a parks movement, and personally served on the city school board, while strongly supporting its chamber of commerce. Ochs put two brothers to work at the *Chattanooga Times*, moved the paper into a $150,000, gold-domed headquarters, where it enjoyed the self-congratulatory title, "Builder of Chattanooga." On February 28, 1883, Ochs married Effie Wise, daughter of Cincinnati rabbi Isaac M. Wise. Their daughter, Iphigene Bertha Ochs, was born in 1892.

A nationwide bank panic in 1893 found Ochs badly over-extended and cash poor. He hoped buying the ailing *New York Mercury* in 1895 would produce the working capital he needed. When the deal fell through in the fall of that year, he turned the day-to-day operation of the *Chattanooga Times* to his brother Milton and focused his energy on acquiring the ailing *New York Times*, which then needed a savior. Editor Charles R. Miller was mired in $300,000 debt with operating losses of $1,500 a day. Ochs privately admitted that it took the "supreme gall of a country newspaperman himself burdened by debt" to pull off the deal, but on August 18, 1896, with $75,000 in borrowed money, Ochs became publisher of the *New York Times*.

Along with managing editor Henry Lowenthal and business manager Louis Wiley, Ochs worked out a plan to resuscitate the *New York Times*. He immediately made a major commitment to stronger financial and business reporting by the paper. The debut on September 30, 1896, of an "Arrival of Buyers" column would grow to two thousand listings daily, eventually making the *New York Times* the Bible of the business class. Wall Street reporters were goaded into putting more "life" in their stories. The initiative stimulated circulation and raised ad rates. Robust reporting on real estate, the courts, schools, city hall, and state government was leavened by Frederick Mortimer's "Topics of the Times," starting on September 8, 1896, where readers found news on science, the arts, and social change. A Sunday Supplement had been launched two days earlier, hinged on deepening readers understanding of current events. The Saturday Book Review section was strengthened. Letters to the editor was expanded to become an open forum on anything that had appeared in the *Times*. Ochs brightened the look of the paper—banning agate type, widening the space between lines, and sharpening reproduction.

Critics complained that the *New York Times* under Ochs pandered to Wall Street interests. Joseph Pulitzer's *New York World* charged that Ochs seemed resigned "to record the dying and the dead." Ochs, however, understood that the sensational yellow journalism of the *World* and William Randolph Hearst's competing *New York Journal* created an opportunity for "serious-minded journalism" done well. On October 18, 1896, Ochs introduced a front page "News Condensed" summary for busy readers who needed to know the news at a glance. One week later, Ochs editorially charged that it was the responsibility of the *New York Times* to report "all the news that's fit to print." On February 10, 1897, the slogan began its stay on the newspaper's masthead. Ochs purpose was to make "reading the *Times* a stamp of respectability."

Times circulation rose from nine thousand to twenty-five thousand in the first year of Ochs's leadership. Ochs slashed the price of the paper to a single penny on October 10, 1898, and within a year circulation and advertising tripled. By 1900, the *Times* circulation of 82,000 surpassed the *Tribune* and the *Sun* and threatened the *Herald*. A year later, circulation soared to 102,000 and ad lines increased from four to five million. By 1912, circulation and ad revenues had doubled again. On the eve of the Great Depression, they doubled once more.

By 1901, Ochs was a wealthy man. He bought the *Philadelphia Times* and put his brother George in charge. A year later that paper merged with the *Philadelphia Ledger*, and eleven years later was sold at a considerable profit to Cyrus Curtis. Ochs also owned the *Nashville American*, but by 1904 he decided to devote all his time and energy to the *New York Times*. In that year the *New York Times* moved from Park Row to a $2.5 million skyscraper on Longacre Square in mid-Manhattan, which the city then renamed Times Square. Ably assisted by new managing editor Carr Van Anda, the *Times* outpaced its competition in reporting the scientific revolution and its impact on exploration, aviation, and transportation. This included front-page play on October 18, 1907, of Guglielmo Marconi's transatlantic "wireless message joining two worlds" and the *Times* exclusive report on September 7, 1909, by Commodore Robert E. Peary that he had reached the North Pole. While newspapers in New York and London distrusted the accuracy of initial wireless reports that the *Titanic* had sunk on its maiden voyage, the *Times* beat its competition and confirmed on the morning of April 16, 1912, that more than twelve hundred passengers "had gone with the ship to the bottom." The paper's World War I reporting won a Pulitzer Prize. When the paper reported on May 22, 1927, that Charles A. Lindbergh had flown the Atlantic, the *Times* had exclusive rights to tell his story.

At his death in 1935, Ochs's son-in-law Arthur Hays Sulzberger became publisher of the *New York Times*. By this time, Ochs had secured his reputation as one of the most consequential publishers in press history. He heartily believed "in the educational value of a newspaper to give complete, accurate, non-partisan news of events of interest to intelligent readers." Columbia University President Nicholas Murray Butler thought no man had done more "to make journalism a positive public servant." Karl Bickel, president of United Press, concurred. Ochs had "set standards in decency, honesty, and accuracy" that had "changed the whole trend of American journalism."

Further Reading

Davis, Elmer. *History of the New York Times, 1851–1921*. New York: New York Times, 1921.

Faber, Doris. *Printer's Devil to Publisher: Adolph S. Ochs of the New York Times*. Hensonville, NY: Black Dome, 1996.

Johnson, Gerald W. *An Honorable Titan: A Biographical Study of Adolph S. Ochs*. Westport, CT: Greenwood Press, 1970, originally 1946.

Papers of Adolph S. Ochs are in the American Jewish Archives in Cincinnati, OH; University of Tennessee Library, Knoxville; and Yale University Library, New Haven, CT.

Stolberg, Benjamin. "The Man Behind the *Times*." *Atlantic Monthly* 138, Dec. 1926, 721–730.

Tifft, Susan E., and Alex S. Jones. *The Trust: The Private and Powerful Family Behind the New York Times*. Boston: Little, Brown, 1999.

BRUCE J. EVENSEN

OFFICE OF CENSORSHIP

President Franklin D. Roosevelt created the civilian Office of Censorship (1941–1945) on December 16, 1941, one week after the United States entered World War II, to prevent military information from reaching America's enemies. Ignoring his penchant for splitting authority among competing offices, Roosevelt made Censorship Director Byron Price "responsible directly to the President" and provided "absolute discretion" to control cross-border communications. The Office of Censorship, with headquarters in the Federal Trade Commission Building in Washington, D.C., screened mail, telephone calls, and telegrams leaving the forty-eight states; intercepted communications that could have harmed war-zone security; and gleaned information that helped catch spies.

Of equal significance, the office had a staff of fewer than two dozen veteran journalists who supervised a voluntary program of suppression by newspapers, magazines, and radio stations inside America's borders. The press and broadcasting censors created and disseminated the *Code of Wartime Practices*, a pamphlet listing sensitive news topics. These included the location of troops, planes, and ships; war industries; weather details that would provide tactical support to the enemy; and movements of the president. Price demanded, and got, censorship immunity for editorial opinion.

Thousands of journalists complied with the voluntary code for a variety of reasons: They shared the patriotism that defined public opinion during America's most popularly supported war; they expected repercussions if violations led to death or destruction; they feared the voluntary program's failure would lead to harsher controls; and they considered Price's system to be sensible and fair, if applied equally to all journalists. Only one American, a radio station manager in New Mexico, deliberately violated the censorship code, briefly, by refusing to provide translations of Spanish-language programs. Hundreds of other violations occurred, but only because journalists had not received, or understood, the *Code of Wartime Practices*.

Attorney General Francis Biddle privately gave Price

the authority to impose mandatory censorship on America's 901 AM radio stations in May 1942. Biddle argued that radio waves do not stop at lines on a map, and thus radio could be regulated like all cross-border communications. Price could have imposed prior restraint and run the broadcasting industry as a government office but decided it was in America's best interests not to do so. As radio successfully policed itself, Price mothballed Biddle's opinion.

Major suppressions included national weather maps through October 1943, when most weather restrictions were lifted; details about radar and other technical advances; and the atomic Manhattan Project. Minor references to atomic research leaked into the press. However, investigative reporter Drew Pearson learned about the development of the atomic bomb as early as 1943 and kept the news quiet at the request of the Office of Censorship. Another reporter, William L. Laurence of the *New York Times*, took leave to work for the Manhattan Project and chronicle the bomb's development. Laurence kept the story secret until after the bombing of Hiroshima, Japan, on August 6, 1945.

Controversy surrounded the censorship of Roosevelt's movements as commander in chief. A group of reporters protested when the president imposed censorship on his cross-country train trip in September 1942 to inspect military installations. However, after Roosevelt lifted the blackout upon his return to Washington, many influential journalists and a majority of the public endorsed the secrecy. Later, journalists grumbled that Roosevelt abused censorship to hide his movements for political or private reasons, as when he secretly talked with former lover Lucy Mercer Rutherford in meetings arranged by his daughter, Anna.

Domestic censorship probably contributed to six civilian deaths in Oregon in May 1945. The War Department had insisted, over Price's protests, that news of the arrival of scores of Japanese balloon bombs in the West be censored. A group of Sunday school picnickers died when one of them kicked a downed balloon, not knowing what it was.

The Office of Censorship argued for the release of information already known to the enemy, or possessing no security value. Despite occasional setbacks, it fostered a spirit of cooperation between the press and the armed forces by pushing the military to make no unreasonable censorship requests, and urging journalists to follow any requests that seemed reasonable. The system worked well, with much of the credit going to Price as well as the unusual degree of unity in World War II.

The office closed on "V-J" day, August 15, 1945, when Japan ceased hostilities. In a message canceling the *Code of Wartime Practices*, Price told journalists, "You deserve, and you have, the thanks and appreciation of your Government."

Further Reading

Doan, Edward N. "Organization and Operation of the Office of Censorship." *Journalism Quarterly* 21 (September 1944), 200–216.

Goodwin, Doris Kearns. *No Ordinary Time: Franklin and Eleanor Roosevelt — The Home Front in World War II*. New York: Simon & Schuster, 1994.

Koop, Theodore F. *Weapon of Silence*. Chicago: University of Chicago, 1946.

Smith, A. Merriman. *Thank You, Mr. President: A White House Notebook*. New York: Harper & Brothers, 1946.

Smith, Jeffery A. *War & Press Freedom: The Problem of Prerogative Power*. New York: Oxford University Press, 1999.

Sweeney, Michael S. "Censorship Missionaries of World War II." *Journalism History* 27:1 (Spring 2001), 4–13.

———. *Secrets of Victory: The Office of Censorship and the American Press and Radio in World War II*. Chapel Hill: University of North Carolina, 2001.

Washburn, Patrick S. "The Office of Censorship's Attempt to Control Press Coverage of the Atomic Bomb During World War II." *Journalism Monographs* 120 (1990).

Winfield, Betty Houchin. *FDR and the News Media*. New York: Columbia University Press, 1994.

MICHAEL S. SWEENEY

OFFICE OF WAR INFORMATION

The Office of War Information (OWI) was the American propaganda agency during World War II. Established in mid-1942, it pulled together a number of predecessor agencies in an effort to provide a coherent story of the war for audiences at home and abroad. But the new organization had difficulties from the start. President Franklin D. Roosevelt, a master propagandist in his own right, was determined to keep control of information in his own hands. Conservative members of Congress believed that the organization was simply a vehicle to ensure a fourth term for FDR, and dismantled the agency's Domestic Branch. Meanwhile, the military was willing to use propaganda if it could help win the war, but only under the rigid strictures of military control.

Propaganda had come of age during World War I. The Committee on Public Information (CPI), headed by journalist George Creel, came to symbolize a fierce campaign to whip up a hatred of all things German in America's drive to defeat the evil Hun. The excesses of that earlier period led some critics to suggest that matters had gone too far. The desire to avoid the mistakes of the CPI ensured that the experience would be less intense the next time it became necessary to create a propaganda agency.

With the outbreak of World War II in 1939, liberal interventionists in the United States argued that the war could bring about a more democratic world order. Even before the Japanese attack on Pearl Harbor in late 1941, they wanted to highlight American values to ensure the survival of democracy in an unstable world. Archibald MacLeish, the noted poet and Librarian of Congress, became head of a new Office of Facts and Figures, which sought to inform the American public about the war, in the fall of 1941. At about the same time, playwright Robert Emmet Sherwood, who also wrote speeches for FDR, established a new Foreign Information Service, which, through the fledgling Voice of America, helped spread the gospel of democracy around the world.

The propaganda effort was chaotic, with those agencies and a number of others competing with one another in their messages and competition for resources. To craft a more systematic and focused message, on June 13, 1942, by executive order, Roosevelt established a new Office of War Information. Its head was Elmer Davis, the well-known CBS radio announcer with the clear, direct delivery and dry humor that reassured his listeners each night.

OWI faced problems from the start. MacLeish, Sherwood, and a number of others who had been active in the early propaganda effort, saw the war as an ideological struggle between the forces of good and evil. They believed in FDR's "four essential freedoms"—freedom of speech and expression, freedom of worship, freedom from want, and freedom from fear—and hoped to trumpet those around the world. But others saw propaganda differently. Secretary of State Cordell Hull was jealous of any intrusions into his domain. He understood that propaganda was related to foreign policy, and was determined to keep control in his own hands. To Davis, he wrote that he assumed that war information activities did not include information relating to American foreign affairs. Secretary of War Henry L. Stimson was intent on winning the war and military necessity took precedence over everything else. He viewed propaganda as a peripheral distraction.

Despite the constraints, propagandists sought to use FDR's liberal pronouncements to publicize the democratic order they hoped would emerge from the war. Sometimes they criticized compromises they felt contradicted the ideological aims of the struggle. They were, for example, angry at the Roosevelt administration's willingness in mid-1943 to work with Italian King Victor Emmanuel III and Marshal Pietro Badoglio, who succeeded Italian dictator Benito Mussolini. One particularly angry broadcast criticized "the moronic little king" and observed that fascism was alive and well in Italy.

Those independent efforts prompted attacks from all sides. Republicans, saw the propaganda agency as a public relations office for the Democratic FDR, Southern Democrats found OWI sympathies for black aspirations objectionable. Representative Joe Starnes of Alabama called domestic propaganda "a stench to the nostrils of a democratic people." In mid-1943, Congress effectively dismantled the Domestic Branch, leaving it just enough money to limp along ineffectively.

The Overseas Branch discovered that it could only be effective if it worked closely under military command. As Davis wrested control of the agency from outspoken propagandists who sought to work on their own, he helped create a Psychological Warfare Branch, attached to Allied headquarters and assisted by OWI. It dropped millions of leaflets that sought to promote the demoralization of the enemy. Later, a Psychological Warfare Division, attached to Supreme Headquarters for the European campaign, issued radio broadcasts as well to try to undermine Nazi morale. At the same time, Voice of America broadcasts attempted to persuade friends and neutrals that an Allied victory was all but assured.

In addition to military propaganda, OWI produced a composite portrait of America that was part of the larger effort to persuade people abroad of the righteousness of the American cause. It highlighted American virtues, showing citizens to be sympathetic, sentimental, and full of common sense, as it sought to counter the image of the United States as a decadent, gangster-dominated society. OWI clung to what it called the "strategy of truth" as an antidote to Nazi propaganda, and reported bad news as necessary, though always with a positive spin.

The Office of War Information ended up making real contributions to the war effort. Military commanders recognized its battlefield contributions. And the pictures of America which the agency produced captured a sense of the American spirit. They were sometimes trite, above all noncontroversial, but they represented the nation's dominant view of the war. OWI's propaganda reflected what the nation considered important as it sought to reconcile its basic values with the requirements of war, even if that meant acknowledging the limitations of the American vision itself.

Further Reading

Shulman, Holly Cowan. *The Voice of America: Propaganda and Democracy, 1941–1945.* Madison, WI: University of Wisconsin Press, 1990.

Steele, Richard W. *Propaganda in an Open Society: The Roosevelt Administration and the Media, 1933–1941.* Westport, CT: Greenwood Press, 1985.

Winkler, Allan M. *The Politics of Propaganda: The Office of War Information, 1942–1945.* New Haven, CT: Yale University Press, 1978.

ALLAN M. WINKLER

OP-ED PAGE

Virtually all newspapers in America have editorial pages on which to publish editorials, opinion columns, and letters to the editor, but the practice of publishing an additional "opposite editorial" or "op-ed" page is much less ubiquitous, found in perhaps only half or fewer of daily newspapers in America. A survey from the mid-1990s indicated that most op-ed pages were found in newspapers with circulations above ninety thousand, and management of the op-ed pages was only separated from management of the editorial page at very large papers. Generally positioned on the odd-numbered page to the right of the editorial page, the op-ed page extends the opinion function of the editorial page by providing space for commentary and analysis, as well as for essays that make counter-arguments to the newspaper's own editorial positions (which lend another meaning to the term "opposite editorial").

Some scholars contend that the op-ed page was pioneered by the New York newspapers in the early twentieth century, perhaps first in the early 1920s by Herbert Bayard Swope of the *New York World*. Swope, then an editor of the paper, saw among his readers considerable interest in "interesting opinion," and according to biographer E.J. Kahn Jr.

in his book, *The World of Swope*, the editor instituted the practice of keeping the page opposite the editorials open for opinion pieces. Early adopters of the op-ed page used the space to run opinion columns by their best writers, but as the practice spread, the page came to be dominated more by opinions from syndicated columnists and notable figures who were not directly affiliated with the newspaper. By the 1970s, editors tried to distinguish their op-ed pages from others, but most adopted the common practice of devoting most, if not all, of their op-ed pages to outside voices. The *New York Times* is widely credited for developing the archetype of modern op-ed pages in September 1970, explaining in an editorial note that the purpose of the page is "to afford greater opportunity for exploration of issues and presentation of new insights" from writers who did not work for the *Times* (although a signature feature of the *Times* op-ed page is its stable of influential columnists). Media critic David Shaw noted in 1975 that the *Chicago Tribune* used its op-ed page to run opinions that countered the *Tribune's* staunchly conservative views, while Shaw's own *Los Angeles Times* opted for more localized opinions of a less intellectual bent than those found in the *New York Times*. In the early 1980s, the *Cleveland Plain Dealer* tried to engage its readers with more local voices by dropping syndicated columnists entirely for a time and recruiting local writers to contribute periodically.

Many editors have noted that one of the greatest challenges of managing a distinct op-ed page is to generate a steady supply of quality submissions in order to fill the daily page. While prominent publications such as the *New York Times* and the *Washington Post* often ask noteworthy people to write op-eds, many newspapers seem to rely on a combination of volunteer writers from the community and unsolicited contributions. Some newspapers create "contributor boards," or groups of diverse people from the community who are asked to occasionally write columns. Some newspapers rely entirely on unsolicited contributions. A few use their op-ed pages for special purposes, such as publishing the submissions of scholastic essay contests or carrying a variety of opinions on a specific theme that is of interest to the community. Flexibility and creativity seem to be the norm for editors trying to fill their op-ed pages. For example, in the 1980s, the *Tennessean* of Nashville, Tennessee, tried to get local academics to write op-eds, but found the essays overly long for the space and generally inaccessible to average readers; the paper then tried to get "movers and shakers" in the community to write, but the editor at the time, Lloyd R. Armour, found those submissions often too short, turgid, and bland. Finally, Armour began running essays written by his own reporters and editors. Other editors will look for longer, well-written letters to the editor as possible op-ed pieces; a few actually pay people in the community to write. Editors sometimes share such strategies with one another via professional conferences and essays in trade journals such as *The Masthead* (the journal of the National Conference of Editorial Writers).

Some journalists and journalism scholars have noted another challenge facing op-ed editors: keeping the page open to "citizen writers" as opposed to politicians, scholars, newsmakers, public relations specialists, and special-interest groups. In a 1994 survey of op-ed editors, researchers found that the editors often gave preferences to submissions from people who were principals in news stories, experts in the topic area discussed, or prominent at the local or national levels. Some editors often will publish polished, mass-distributed op-eds from special interest groups, politicians, and cultural leaders rather than original submissions from local readers. About a third of newspapers that run op-ed pages sell space on the page for "image ads," or advocacy-statement advertisements developed by corporations, special-interest groups, and the like, further limiting the space for essays from "citizen writers."

By the turn of the twenty-first century, many newspapers had expanded the role of the op-ed page to their editorial pages, sometimes surrendering space normally reserved for the newspapers' editorials for essays and letters from contributors and readers. For example, in 1995, the St. Paul, Minnesota, *Pioneer Press* dramatically changed the format of its opinion pages to reduce the frequency of newspaper editorials and use the space for other forms of opinion as needed. Similarly, many newspapers that have just one opinion page per edition will construct them more as op-ed pages than as traditional editorial page. Over time, the term "op-ed" itself has evolved into an adjective denoting all opinion aspects of newspapers, such that some use the term to mean "opinion/editorial" rather than "opposite editorial."

Further Reading

Anderson, Laird B. "Layout and Presentation." In *Beyond Argument: A Handbook for Editorial Writers*, edited by Maura Casey and Michael Zuzel. Rockville, MD: National Conference of Editorial Writers, 2001.

Armour, Lloyd R. "Let the staff write them." *The Masthead 36*, 3 (Fall 1984): 6–7.

Ciofalo, Andrew, and Kim Traverso. "Does the op-ed page have a chance to become a public forum?" *Newspaper Research Journal 15*, 4 (Fall 1994): 51–63.

Rystrom, Kenneth. *The Why, Who and How of the Editorial Page*, 4th ed. State College, PA: Strata, 2004

Shaw, David. "Newspapers Offer Forum to Outsiders." *Los Angeles Times*, October 13, 1975.

BILL READER

O'SULLIVAN, JOHN L.

John Louis O'Sullivan (Nov. 15, 1813–March 24, 1895) was a founder and editor of the nineteenth-century literary magazine *United States Magazine and Democratic Review*, in which he coined the term "manifest destiny" to animate a key concept in United States policy: the drive to expand across North America and beyond.

In 1835, the young O'Sullivan joined with brother-in-law S. D. Langtree to purchase *Metropolitan*, a Washington newspaper supporting Democratic President Andrew Jackson. Aspiring to explain their opinions on democracy, the country's future, and literature to a national audience, however, they sold the paper in 1837 and started *Democratic Review*. In 1841, O'Sullivan assumed full control of the magazine and moved it to New York City, where he practiced law and was elected to the state Assembly. He also edited the *New York Morning News*, a newspaper that he founded with Samuel Tilden, from 1844 to 1846.

As a magazine of literature, *Democratic Review* made its mark by publishing works from writers including Nathaniel Hawthorne, who became a close friend of O'Sullivan, Henry David Thoreau, William Cullen Bryant, and Edgar Allen Poe. As an organ of political opinion, *Democratic Review* left its most consequential imprint when O'Sullivan, writing in the July-August 1845 issue to praise the annexation of Texas, insisted that the United States thwart English, French, and Spanish efforts to block "our manifest destiny to overspread the continent allotted by Providence for the free development of our yearly multiplying millions." The implications of manifest destiny, which meant expansion of not only American territory but also of democracy and economic liberty, its exponents said, dictated the acquisition of the Oregon Territory, California, and Mexican territory in the West, and Cuba. Fifty years later, they cited the concept to urge that America expand into the Pacific and Caribbean basins. Ironically, in pursuing manifest destiny, the United States often resorted to force and conquest—courses that O'Sullivan opposed, believing that his country should seek such a destiny peacefully. In fact, he had written his fateful essay to caution President James K. Polk's administration against waging war on Mexico, a call that the administration did not heed.

O'Sullivan, who sold *Democratic Review* in 1846, also became known for adopting lost causes. He pressed for American purchase and annexation of Cuba and, when the country did not take such actions, supported a former Spanish army officer's attempts to invade and take over Cuba and free the island from Spanish control, bringing O'Sullivan legal trouble (two indictments on charges of violating neutrality laws, but no convictions) and financial setbacks in the late 1840s and early 1850s. Additionally, when the Civil War split the United States, O'Sullivan favored the South and advocated that Northern Democrats should end the war and that Britain should recognize the Confederacy. In 1854, O'Sullivan was named U. S. charge d'affaires and, later, minister resident in Portugal, where he served for four years. He lived the rest of his life overseas and in New York, away from public attention.

Further Reading

Pratt, Julius W., "John Louis O'Sullivan." In *Dictionary of American Biography*, Vol. 14, *Oglethorpe—Platner*, edited by Dumas Malone, 89. New York: Charles Scribner's Sons, 1934.

Sampson, Robert D. *John L. O'Sullivan and His Times*. Kent, OH: Kent State University Press, 2003.

Schlesinger, Arthur M. Jr. *The Age of Jackson*. Boston: Little, Brown and Co., 1945.

MICHAEL GAUGER

P

PACIFICA NEWS

The listener financed Pacifica Foundation began its radio operations in 1949, when it signed on KPFA in Berkeley California. Fifty years later, Pacifica owned and operated additional radio stations in New York (WBAI), Los Angeles (KPFK), Washington (WPFW), and Houston (KPFT) and supplied national programming to about seventy-five other non-commercial "community" or public radio stations throughout the country.

As its name suggests, the Pacifica Foundation seeks to promote a more pacific world, "peace and understanding among nations, races, creeds and colors," to cite its mission statement. Pacifica's founder, World War II conscientious objector Lewis Hill, urged Pacifica to examine the roots of conflict that grow from injustices in our political and economic systems. At the same time, he promised to assemble news from sources "not commonly brought together in the same medium," in order to produce "accurate, objective, comprehensive news" lacking in media driven by the profit motive. In the Cold War era, presenting news from "alternative" sources meshed well with Hill's pacifist agenda.

In its early history, Pacifica gained notoriety for its commentaries and discussions by a wide range of intellectuals, mostly from the left, among them American Marxists Herbert Aptheker and William Mandel, black leaders W.E.B DuBois and Langston Hughes, Socialist Norman Thomas, and the leftist editor of *The Nation*, Carey McWilliams. The regular appearances of future Reagan defense secretary Casper Weinberger on behalf of the California Republican Party did not dissuade critics who saw Pacifica as a subversive organization. In its early history, Pacifica found itself under investigation by the House Un-American Activities Committee and faced revocation of its broadcast licenses by the Federal Communications Commission.

When portable equipment allowed radio to leave the studio in the late 1950s and 1960s, Pacifica became a prime source of pointed documentaries on social and political issues. One reporter's unauthorized trip to North Vietnam during the war produced a documentary controversial not only for its content but for the fact that it was produced at all. It represented, however, a perfect example of the Pacifica goal of promoting "peace through understanding among nations" and of presenting news from sources not normally heard in American media. In the same era, Pacifica broadcast live from Congressional hearings and protest demonstrations of the civil rights, free speech, and anti-war

movements. Some regarded Pacifica as the "voice" of those movements, although the voice could not be heard in most parts of the country.

In the 1970s, Pacifica stations modified their focus, providing voice for a variety of newly conscious identity groups—feminists, ethnic and racial minorities, and gays—on the assumption that understanding among groups leads to peace and that certain voices cannot find expression in the mainstream media. Disputes among those groups and with the Pacifica management sometimes led to ferocious conflicts within the organization, even as it sought to promote peace in the world at large.

Later in that decade, *Pacifica Network News* sought to apply Pacifica's alternative philosophy to a half hour of daily journalism. Reporters provided more depth than commercial radio or television and tackled issues and points-of-view that commercial broadcasting often ignored or minimized. For some *Pacifica Network News* staff, National Public Radio's successful news programs *All Things Considered* and *Morning Edition* provided models to be emulated; for others, NPR served as an example of what happens when an "alternative" medium seeks wide listener acceptance. For most of its history, *Pacifica Network News* endured heated ideological struggles over such issues, of vital importance to those on the inside but often bewildering to those on the outside.

These philosophical differences combined with serious financial problems caused the enterprise to explode in the year 2000. Perceiving themselves under attack from Pacifica management that sought larger audiences and financial stability, news staffers went out on strike. *Pacifica Network News* never really recovered, but the upheaval spawned two new organizations that carry on the Pacifica legacy outside the formal Pacifica structure, *Free Speech Radio* and *Democracy Now*.

Some of the strikers from *Pacifica Network News* created *Free Speech Radio News* to continue producing a daily half hour program of "incisive news and analysis in the service of peace and justice." Produced independently from Pacifica, the freestanding organization sold its product to community radio stations across the country, including those owned by Pacifica. In a sense, the Pacifica news philosophy survived outside of Pacifica when it could not prevail inside.

Other Pacifica staff members, led by veteran Pacifica journalist Amy Goodwin, took their *Democracy Now* program out of Pacifica in the name of saving Hill's philosophy of news. Goodwin had begun *Democracy Now* as a series of daily broadcasts on the Pacifica stations during the 1996 presidential election. The well-received special series remained on the air after the election and became Pacifica's most widely recognized public affairs offering. As producer and host of *Democracy Now*, Goodwin broke new ground with her award-winning coverage of American oil interests in Nigeria. She took the program to Seattle for eight days in 1999, where her broadcast became a center piece for the "Battle of Seattle," between opponents of corporate globalization and police during a meeting of the World Trade Organization.

When Goodman and her *Democracy Now* staff broke with Pacifica during the conflicts of 2000, she found refuge in a community television center, from which she continued to produce the daily program, making it available to Pacifica and other stations as an independent production. The new location in a television facility allowed *Democracy Now* to greatly expand its reach by adding community access cable stations and television satellite direct to home viewers. The program, now co-hosted by Juan Gonzalez, continues to look and sound like a radio program, however. The cameras just eavesdrop on it.

Pacifica itself has since established a level of financial and structural stability that suggest it will continue as a voice of diverse and disadvantaged voices and a creative outlet for partisans of a wide range of cultural traditions, even as the most dynamic examples of its journalistic tradition pursue their alternative approaches from the outside.

Further Readings

Engleman, Ralph. *Public Radio and Television in America, A Political History*. Thousand Oaks CA: SAGE Publications, 1996.

Land, Jeff. *Pacifica's Brash Experiment*. Minneapolis: University of Minnesota Press, 1999.

Lasar, Matthew. *Pacifica Radio: The Rise of an Alternative Network*. Philadelphia: Temple University Press, 1999.

Mitchell, Jack. *Listener Supported, the Culture and History of Public Radio*. Westport, CT: Praeger, 2005.

Pacifica Radio Archive: A Living History. http://www.pacificaradioarchives.org/ (accessed April 5, 2007).

JACK W. MITCHELL

PACIFIST PRESS

Leading historians of the peace movement such as Charles DeBenedetti, Peter Brock, and Lawrence S. Wittner agree that the most central reform movement in United States history is peace advocacy. Since the early nineteenth century when the first organized peace societies developed, both reformers and radicals have worked to realize world peace, often through advocacy writing and editing. They have benefited from First Amendment guarantees of freedom of speech and press in the United States that have protected such communication, even during wartimes when pacifist perspectives were in the minority.

As early as the 1830s, when he made his famous visit to America, Alexis DeTocqueville noted Americans' propensity to organize themselves into associations and social movements that emphasized the publication of pamphlets and newspapers to maintain their cohesion and achieve their goals of changing society. This context is useful in understanding the pacifist press throughout its history.

The pacifist press's perspectives and approaches vary. Peace advocacy can take a variety of forms, for example in its most thoroughgoing approach, embracing absolute pacifism-nonresistance (to the point of non-cooperation with the state, even the withholding of the portion of one's income tax that is thought to support war making activities directly) to a more moderate position of acceptance of "defensive" war. And, a primarily religious perspective characterizes members of the historic peace churches, the Quakers, the Mennonites, and the Church of the Brethren (among others), while another approach distinguishes the many nonsectarian peace advocacy groups such as the American Peace Society (started in 1828), the League of Universal Brotherhood (1846), the Women's International League for Peace and Freedom (U.S. branch, 1915), and the War Resisters League (1923).

All have recognized the potential power of the written word to sway public opinion on issues of war and peace, starting with the very first early nineteenth-century periodicals such as the American Peace Society's *Advocate of Peace*. Harnessing improvements in printing technology and transportation, early nineteenth century peace advocates published millions of pages of tracts, books, and pamphlets devoted to the cause of peace. Their periodical press was equally vigorous and targeted a twofold audience: believers and yet-to-be-converted. Often containing the sermons and speeches that were also printed in tract form, serials such as the American Peace Society's *Advocate of Peace, Calumet,* and *Harbinger of Peace* published in addition annual reports that suggest a spirited, active membership—and one that was frequently represented in other antebellum reform movements such as abolition, women's rights, and temperance.

Other early nineteenth-century leaders include the Connecticut Peace Society's *American Advocate of Peace*, the Pennsylvania Peace Society's *Advocate of Peace and Christian Patriot*, and the *Friend of Peace* of the Massachusetts Peace Society. By the end of 1821, the latter had distributed, along with its auxiliaries, 7,155 copies of the *Friend of Peace*. This was fairly characteristic of the circulation size of the pacifist press in the pre-1850 period, paralleling the typical mainstream magazine circulation. Many copies were passed along to multiple readers, thus boosting real circulation. Pacifist press publishers frequently acknowledged their efforts to get these periodicals into libraries and to opinion leaders (as their often published subscription lists attest).

Typically, content emphasized an Enlightenment-based belief in rationality, that "A few well written remarks on the subject of war may occasion thousands to reflect, and eventually save thousands from untimely death by murderous hands," as the *Friend of Peace* wrote in its August 18, 1819, issue.

With the approach of the Civil War, nonsectarian periodicals such as the New England Non-Resistance Society's *Liberator*, the *Journal of the Times*, and the *Non-Resistant* became prominent. The League of Universal Brotherhood, founded in 1846, sponsored the *Bond of Brotherhood* and *Burritt's Christian Citizen* and the Universal Peace Union (1866) published in succession the *Bond of Peace, Voice of Peace,* and *Peacemaker.*

Less influential at this time were the periodicals of the historic peace churches. The German Baptist Brethren devoted no coverage to their peace testimony until the mid-nineteenth century. The Mennonite press was just developing in the 1850s and in any case, as Mennonites were separatists, it did not try to proselytize outsiders. The few nineteenth-and early twentieth-century Mennonite periodicals started included the *Gospel Herald, Gospel Witness, Herald of Truth,* and the *Mennonite Quarterly Review.*

Meanwhile, the Quaker weekly press started in 1827 with the Philadelphia *Friend* and then the *Friends' Weekly Intelligencer* (1844). However, the amount of original content devoted to peace topics during this period was small. Other Quaker periodicals started during the nineteenth century include the *American Friend,* the *Christian Worker, Friends' Review,* the *Herald of Peace,* the *Moral Advocate,* and the *Messenger of Peace* (published by the Peace Association of Friends in America, a Quaker group founded 1866).

A dynamic subset of the nineteenth-century peace advocacy press included the periodicals of utopian religious communitarians who emphasized peace as one of their tenets, such as the *Circular* of the Oneida Community in upstate New York. Other utopian and religious publications included the *New Harmony Gazette* of the Owenite New Harmony group, the *Shaker Manifesto* of the Shakers, the Adventists' *Review and Herald* and the *World's Crisis,* and the Disciples of Christ's *American Christian Review, Christian Baptist,* and the *Millenial Harbinger.*

Also, the peace departments of many of the major women's organizations such as the Women's Christian Temperance Union published peace advocacy materials in the late nineteenth century. Often these were included as inserts in publications such as the Quaker *Messenger of Peace.*

In the twentieth century, peace advocacy periodicals have built upon this foundation, producing full-color publications and fully harnessing contemporary desktop and digital publishing technology. The historic peace churches continue well-established periodicals such as *Friends Journal* (established 1955); *Mennonite Life* (founded 1946), and *Brethren Life and Thought* (dating from 1955). *Friends Journal,* for example, has a paid circulation of about eighty-five hundred and regularly receives recognition from the Associated Church Press and other professional organizations.

A leader among the religious peace advocacy publications is the *Catholic Worker,* founded in 1933 in New York City by Dorothy Day and Peter Maurin, with a current circulation of about eighty-nine thousand. Since its founding it has advocated pacifism, of a thoroughgoing, nonresistant sort akin to that advocated by Mohandas Gandhi and Martin Luther King Jr. It has also inspired scores of similar, localized newspapers associated with Catholic Worker Houses of Hospitality throughout the United States and also abroad.

Other religious-based pacifist presses include *Fellowship: A Magazine of Peacemaking,* established in 1918 and published by the International Fellowship of Reconciliation, with a 2006 paid circulation of about nine thousand; *Shalom: The Jewish Peace Letter,* published since 1962 by the Jewish Peace Fellowship (2006 circulation, about 3,000); *Peacework: Global Thought and Action for Nonviolent Social Change,* published since 1972 by the New England Regional Office of the American Friends Service Committee; and *Catholic Peace Voice,* issued since 1975 by Pax Christi USA.

As a group, modern peace periodicals vary in perspective and tone, including emphases that range from nonresistant to internationalist and antinuclear. Each war period has generated its own set of pacifist periodicals, with some longstanding examples such as the *Catholic Worker* providing antiwar perspectives on a consistent and continuous basis, since its inception in 1933. During World War I, for instance, Max Eastman's *The Masses* opposed the war, for which the government shut it down under the provisions of the 1917 Espionage Act. During the Cold War, *Liberation* (1956–1977) sought to keep alive pacifist ideals and recruited as editors such peace movement leaders as the minister A.J. Muste, David Dellinger, James H. Forest, Bayard Rustin, and Barbara Deming. Publications such as the *Nation* and *Christian Century,* while not uniformly pacifist, have taken strong antiwar/pacifist positions at various times in history to oppose particular conflicts.

During the Vietnam War, an underground press emerged that included antiwar GI periodicals such as the *Ally* (1968–1974), published in Berkeley, California, and directed toward U.S. troops in South Vietnam. Another was *aboveground,* produced by soldiers at Fort Carson, Colorado. It appeared in nine issues from August 1969 to May 1970, with press runs of from thirty-five hundred to ten thousand copies. According to scholar and former *aboveground* editor Harry W. Haines, some 227 GI underground antiwar newspapers were directed toward U.S. military forces during the Vietnam War. Other influential anti-Vietnam War newspapers included *Ramparts* and *The Guardian.*

Contemporary nonsectarian pacifist press leaders include the bimonthly *Bulletin of the Atomic Scientists,* founded in 1945, with a current circulation of about eleven thousand and aimed at readers interested in the dangers of nuclear power and weapons as well as international relations and the peace movement; *Peace and Freedom: Magazine of the Women's International League for Peace and Freedom,* established in 1941, with a current circulation of about ten thousand; and *The Veteran,* published quarterly by Vietnam Veterans Against the War and aimed toward an audience of veterans, soldiers, and peace activists. Typical of many, *The Nonviolent Activist,* the bimonthly magazine of the War Resisters League (established 1945; circulation, ten thousand), makes its archives electronically available through the organization's extensive web site. The web site also features many other resources, including detailed discussions of tax resistance, local and national antiwar activities, and even an online bookstore.

Such electronic accoutrements are characteristic of many pacifist organizations today, which seem to recognize that they must compete for the attention of sophisticated mass media consumers. Yet this realization is hardly new; since the early nineteenth century pacifist publications have usually shown a solid understanding of their audience and have tried to conform to the best practices, both editorial and technological, of the mainstream media marketplace. It remains to be seen just what influence the new digital technologies will ultimately have on the pacifist press, but certainly pacifists have been attempting to use of them.

Further Reading

Brock, Peter. *Pacifism in the United States: From the Colonial Era to the First World War*. Princeton, NJ: Princeton University Press, 1968.

Curti, Merle. *The American Peace Crusade, 1815–1860*. Durham, NC: Duke University Press, 1929.

DeBenedetti, Charles. *The Peace Reform in American History*. Bloomington: Indiana University Press, 1980.

Haines, Harry W. "Soldiers Against the War in Vietnam: The Story of *aboveground*. In *Voices from the Underground: Volume 1, Insider Histories of the Vietnam Era Underground Press*, edited by Ken Wachsberger. Tempe, AZ: Micah's Press, 1993, 181–198.

Roberts, Nancy L. *American Peace Writers, Editors, and Periodicals: A Dictionary*. Westport, CT: Greenwood Press, 1991.

——. "The Peace Advocacy Press," in *Outsiders in 19th Century Press History: Multicultural Perspectives*, ed. Frankie Hutton and Barbara Reed. Bowling Green, OH: Bowling Green University Popular Press, 1995, 209–238.

——. 'Ten Thousand Tongues' Speaking for Peace: Purposes and Strategies of the Nineteenth-Century U.S. Peace Advocacy Press." *Journalism History*, vol. 21, no. 1 (Spring 1995): 16–28.

Wittner, Lawrence S. *Rebels against War: The American Peace Movement, 1933–1983*. Rev. ed., Philadelphia: Temple University Press, 1984.

NANCY L. ROBERTS

PAINE, THOMAS

Thomas Paine (January 29, 1737–June 8, 1809), citizen of the world and pamphleteer, helped to set flame to the tinder of American dissent against British rule in his pamphlet *Common Sense* and to raise patriot morale to victory in the Revolutionary War through his early *Crisis Papers*. Political leaders have quoted him for centuries; yet, he remains controversial for his ideas and actions in later years. Although he wrote for newspapers, Paine's historical influence intertwines with the pamphlet medium. Thousands of copies of his essays were printed, circulated worldwide, read, shared, revised, and reprinted in a matter of weeks.

In *Common Sense* and the *Crisis Papers*, Paine articulated dissenting views festering in colonial America. He defended natural rights and offered his own vision of a society without Kings, hierarchical religion, slavery, corrupt government, or subjugated women. For his early works and *Rights of Man* (1789), he was immortalized; for his deist vision of a new order he was feared. To this day, presidents and journalists, conservatives and liberals, libertarians and patriots quote his words to epitomize American ideals.

Thomas Paine was born January 29, 1737, in Thetford, Norfolk, England, son of a Quaker stay maker. *The Case of the Officers of Excise* (London, 1772), was his first known publication. In it he argued only higher pay would prevent excise employee corruption. It led to his eventual dismissal as an excise officer. Paine later met Benjamin Franklin in London and immigrated to America in 1774, at thirty-seven, carrying an introductory letter from Franklin. He found writing, printing, and editing work in Philadelphia.

"African Slavery in America," in the *Postscript to the Pennsylvania Journal and the Weekly Advertiser* (1775) was his first significant American publication. Defending natural rights to freedom and signed "Justice and Humanity," it appeared three months after Paine's arrival, and only weeks before opening shots at Lexington and Concord.

Paine soon moved from contributor to editor of Robert Aitken's *Pennsylvania Magazine* (1775–1776). His wildly popular pamphlet, *Common Sense*, emerged in January 1776, published by Robert Bell and later by Thomas Bradford. "The cause of America is, in great measure," Paine began, "the cause of all mankind." Hundreds of thousands of copies circulated within weeks and at least a half million overall, including multiple editions and foreign translations. Philadelphians speculated about who wrote the unsigned pamphlet until Paine was credited. Paine wrote *Common Sense* with the encouragement of Dr. Benjamin Rush, a Philadelphia physician and chemist who had been writing a controversial essay on independence and saw in Paine a talented unknown to present such notions publicly.

A soldier from August 1776 to January 1777, Paine wrote for the *Pennsylvania Magazine* from the battlefield. He is credited with raising morale through his serialized *Crisis Papers*, the first of which began, "These are the times that try men's souls." George Washington ordered it read to his demoralized troops at Valley Forge. Sixteen *Crisis Papers* continued into 1783.

After the Revolution and several appointments in the new government, he went to Europe and then to England, where he wrote *Rights of Man* (1791–1792) in two volumes. Its anti-monarchical defense of the French Revolution was ill-received. Paine left for France heartbeats ahead of his treason conviction in England. Philadelphia printer-publisher Benjamin Franklin Bache published Paine's correspondence in *The Aurora* through the 1790s, a stormy period in American journalism.

Paine was elected to the French National Convention but later imprisoned. There he wrote *Age of Reason*, I and II, and scribbled pleas to George Washington for his release, eventually denouncing him and decrying government corruption in his "Letter to George Washington" (1796).

Paine left America a hero and returned an outcast for his deism in *Age of Reason*, connections to bloody France, and criticism of Washington. William Cobbett crossed the Atlantic to publish a Philadelphia newspaper, *Porcupine's Gazette* (1797–1799), expressly to attack Paine and Joseph Priestley. A newly elected President Thomas Jefferson returned Paine to the United States in 1802; however, Paine was jeered and even Jefferson avoided him. Writing and publishing to the end, Thomas Paine died in New York, June 8, 1809, rejected and impoverished.

Thomas Paine voiced political and religious views underlying the American Revolution and his own dreams of a just society. Little is known of the effects of Paine's translated works although it is known that Spanish versions circulated widely in pre-republican South America.

Further Reading

Foner, Eric. 2004. *Tom Paine and Revolutionary America*. New York: Oxford University Press.

Kaye, Harvey. 2005. *Thomas Paine and the Promise of America*. New York:Hill and Wang.

Larkin, Edward. 1998. "Inventing an American Public: Thomas Paine, the *Pennsylvania Magazine*, and American Revolutionary Political Discourse." *Early American Literature*, 33, 3 1998: 250–276.

Paine, Thomas. 1995 ed. Eric Foner. *Collected Writings: Common Sense, The Crisis, and Other Pamphlets, Articles, and Letters. Rights of Man. The Age of Reason*. New York: Library of America.

Smith, Jeffrey A. 1990. *Franklin and Bache: Envisioning the Enlightened Republic*. New York: Oxford University Press.

CARMEN E. CLARK

PAMPHLETS

Beyond single-sheet broadsides, pamphlets are probably the most widely used and enduring print media in world history; yet, they carry a low-brow reputation through partisan, unsanctioned, or commercial authorship or as simple publications intended for mass audiences. Pamphlets proliferated through small-scale publishing, distribution, and republishing across regions; thus, they can be difficult to collect and catalog. Tracking them can be tedious and imprecise. At the same time, pamphlets have often played an important role in major historical events such as the American Revolution.

Pamphlets are soft-covered booklets of fewer than fifty leaves comprising single signatures (foldings of one sheet) either fastened or unbound. From the pre-Enlightenment era to the twenty-first century, anyone able to pay printing could publish political rants, philosophical essays, gossip and scandal, poetry, sermons, humor, games, or songs as pamphlets. With the rise of science, mass production, consumerism, and public information, pamphlets increasingly bore mainstream societal messages. By the 1930s, the U.S government published pamphlets on many topics. In the twenty-first century, despite the Internet, pamphlets were still used by businesses, government, religious organizations, and in political or educational campaigns.

Although pamphlets pre-date the printing press, the printing press allowed rapid, uniform, and widespread distribution of messages on an unprecedented scale. Merchant ship captains carried them across the Mediterranean, while printers' networks, commerce, and travelers quickly moved pamphlets by the thousands in bundles, within Europe. Pamphlets proliferated in early modern Europe. Printers who had to account for every sheet of paper they used through taxation and numbering may not have used an entire sheet for job printing and could turn scraps into pamphlets, unnoticed. Pamphlet pages could be typeset and stored for ongoing publication.

For the generation that fought the American Revolution and created the U.S. Constitution after independence was won, pamphlets were an important source of ideas. Hundreds of pamphlets writers drew inspiration from such Enlightenment thinkers as John Locke and Montesquieu, from classical Greece and Rome, and from English common law to explain their grievances against Parliament and Crown, to define the ideals of the Revolution, to work out the details of the new state governments, and then, finally, to set out the contours of the new republic's constitution. The pamphlets, often running several thousand words in length, set of chain reaction debates as readers would take up pen to respond at length to arguments with which they disagreed. Colonial newspapers would often reprint the pamphlets and give them wide circulation. Thomas Paine, America's best known pamphleteer, is celebrated today for his pamphlets *Common Sense* and sixteen *Crisis Papers*. The first *Crisis Paper* of December 19, 1776 began with the well-known lines, "These are the times that try men's souls…," and is credited with raising American revolutionary morale.

During the nineteenth and twentieth centuries, pamphlets were used in many areas of life: as religious pamphlets and tracts; as indictments of slavery in the antebellum period; as instructions to immigrant wives about how to live and set up households; as organizing tools for a growing labor movement; as commemorations of important events; and as propaganda defending United States involvement in World War I. Twentieth-century pamphlets instructed Americans of all walks of life about scientific living, public health, and safety; the evils of fascism during World War II; the intolerance of McCarthyism during the 1950s; the virtues of the civil rights movement; and the necessity for ending the Vietnam War.

In the twenty-first century, even with the rapid spread of personal computers, the Internet, and weblogs, pamphlets remained important. Because they were relatively expensive to produce, and small enough to be conveniently tucked into one's pocket and thus highly portable, pamphlets continued to offer a convenient means communication for millions of people.

Further Reading

Bailyn, Bernard. *Ideological Origins of the American Revolution*. Cambridge, MA: Belknap Press of Harvard University Press, 1967.

Newman, Richard, Patrick Rael, and Phillip Lapsansky. *Pamphlets of Protest: An Anthology of Early African-American Protest Literature, 1790–1860.* New York: Routledge, 2001.

CARMEN E. CLARK

PATTERSON, JOSEPH MEDILL

Socialist, isolationist, ultra-nationalist, novelist, playwright, publisher, soldier, social reformer, and political activist, Joseph Medill Patterson (January 6, 1879–May 26, 1946) had many identities during five decades in public life, but the reputation for which he was most proud and best known was as creator and publisher of the *New York Daily News*, America's most successful tabloid newspaper, read by 2.2 million New Yorkers at the close of World War II and 4.5 million on Sundays. Patterson came from a long line of publishers and had a keenly crafted prescience of what readers wanted. That understanding helped to define much of modern journalism—it would be concise, pictorial, and emphasize human interest to attract loyal readers who advertisers were eager to reach.

Patterson was born to publishing. His mother, Elinor Medill, was one of three daughters born to Joseph Medill, the man who had made the *Chicago Tribune* a great newspaper. His father, Robert Wilson Patterson, was managing editor of the *Tribune*, and after Medill's death in 1899, became publisher of the paper. Two years later his son joined him as a $15 a week staff reporter, supplemented by the twenty-two-year-old's $10,000 annual allowance. By that time, Patterson was already a battle-tested foreign correspondent, who reported the Boxer Rebellion for the Hearst Press after a privileged preparation at Groton and Yale University. In 1902 he married heiress Alice Higinbotham. They would have four children.

Patterson quickly tired of the *Tribune*'s conservative editorial policy. In 1903, he opposed corporate interests and traction magnate Charles Yerkes when he successfully ran for a seat in the Illinois state legislature. In 1905, Patterson broke with the paper and backed Democrat Edward F. Dunne for mayor, who made Patterson Chicago's Public Works Commissioner. Nine months later Patterson resigned the post, claiming to the chagrin of his family that he was a convert to Socialism.

Patterson had the money to indulge his causes. After the money panic of 1907, he wrote one novel and three plays that castigated the "desolate" values of the idle rich, ridiculing the "over-refinement" and "inanimateness" of a "dead aristocracy," while publicizing the necessity of the coming socialist state. (See Patterson's *A Little Brother of the Rich* and scripts for the plays "Rebellion" and "Dope.") Patterson's re-conversion to capitalism followed his father's death in 1910. He was made chairman of the Chicago Tribune Co. and along with his cousin, Robert R. McCormick, revitalized the paper by pushing crime news, reform crusades and promotional stunts. Circulation soared to seven hundred thousand and Patterson's genius in features and syndication pushed operating profits to more than $1 million annually on the eve of World War I.

Patterson covered the war's early fighting as the *Tribune*'s foreign correspondent, based in Belgium, Germany, and France. He became a captain in the Rainbow Division of the 149th Field Artillery after the United States entered the war. Patterson fought bravely in the second battle of the Marne, at St. Mihiel, the Argonne, and in the defense of Champagne.

After the war Patterson began planning for a "new kind of newspaper" based on the successes of Lord Northcliffe's *London Daily Mirror* (Patterson to S.N. Blossom, September 9, 1922, Patterson Papers). The *Illustrated Daily News* of New York first appeared on June 26, 1919. Patterson's plan was to produce a paper that "thought visually" in reporting "the rush of big city living" that "tells each story in a flash" (Patterson to Milton E. Burke, acting manager of the *New York Daily News*, May 15, 1922, Patterson Papers). Within three weeks the circulation of the *Daily News* slipped from eighty-three thousand to ten thousand with three of every four newsstand editions going unsold. Undaunted, Patterson built a staff "who think in terms of pictures," demanding his editors inject "romance and drama" in the stories they assigned and printed. The paper's crime coverage was expanded. Reporters were ordered to "hit the paper's themes harder" and "make it snappy, make it local, make it news" (Patterson to William H. Field, July 8, 1919, Patterson Papers). Again and again, Patterson advised editors, "We can't make it too clear and easy for our readers" (Patterson to Arthur L. Clarke, managing editor of the *New York Daily News*, May 5, 1919, Patterson Papers).

Patterson's policy paid off. By the end of 1919, the paper's circulation crept to fifty-seven thousand. By June 1920 it eclipsed one hundred thousand. The paper's earliest readers were women, ages seventeen to thirty, who liked its contests, serials and tall tales of romance and mystery. Patterson expanded the paper's sports coverage to win over men. A twenty-four inch lens was fit on a five-by-seven Graflex camera by staff photographer Lou Walker to get a telescopic view of Jack Dempsey's September 7, 1920, title knockout of Billy Miske. The result was a record press run and the start of "picture scoops" that played celebrity to the hilt. Staff photographer Harry Olen successfully modified photographic plates, making them more light sensitive, creating the most vivid sports stills ever to appear in the press up to that time. This helped push circulation to 275,000 by the end of the year. A Sunday edition was launched three months later and within three years shot to a million circulation, the nation's largest. The daily would surpass that number by 1925. Its front page pictures of beautiful flappers in short skirts led subway-riding businessmen to hide their copies of the *Daily News* inside pages of the socially sanctioned *New York Times*, while on their way to work. Tom Howard's stealth photo of the January 13, 1928, execution of Ruth Snyder in Sing Sing's electric chair became the decade's most sensational photograph.

Patterson advertised the *Daily News* as "the people's paper" and cultivated the look of a people's editor, often appearing at the paper's 42nd Street headquarters at midmorning, munching an Eskimo Pie, while wearing rumpled, washed out trousers and a short sleeve shirt open at the neck. His colloquial editorials written with Reuben Maury and cartoonist Clarence Daniel Batchelor strongly supported Franklin Roosevelt's New Deal, then bitterly opposed his tilt toward Britain at the outbreak of World War II. A six-page sports section, brightly written by Paul Gallico, first-run fiction, contests, and colored comics, featuring "Dick Tracy," "Little Orphan Annie," "Smitty," "Gumps," "Winnie Winkle," and "Gasoline Alley," were widely read by first and second generation East Siders, who "drove trucks, belonged to trade unions, sold goods, ran businesses, believed in God, the United States and life insurance" (Chapman 1961 142–144).

The Depression shifted Patterson's preoccupation from hemlines to hard times. Stories of cutters and out of work garment workers, salesmen and pushcart peddlers solidified the paper's growing reputation as friend of the working man and his family. Patterson personally flew to the Dust Bowl in the summer of 1934, reporting on the impact of the drought on Western farmers and agricultural workers. After divorcing his first wife in 1938, Patterson married Mary King, women's editor at the *Daily News* and fiction editor of the Chicago Tribune-New York News Syndicate.

Early in 1939 Patterson flew to Europe and wrote news stories warning of war. The paper's two million daily circulation in 1940 was twice that of any newspaper in the United States, and Patterson used that power to push for preparedness. He championed building a bigger navy, and after Pearl Harbor he flew to Hawaii and led the call for rebuilding the Pacific fleet. Roosevelt referred to Patterson, McCormick, and Patterson's sister Eleanor "Cissy" Patterson, who published the *Washington Times-Herald*, as the "axis-powers" for their criticism of his conduct of the war. Patterson was particularly wary of Roosevelt's war-time alliance with Joseph Stalin.

Patterson's daughter Alicia continued her father's publishing success by guiding Long Island's *Newsday* in the post-war period. It achieved in suburban reporting what Patterson's *Daily News* had become in the city, a living memorial to its independent creator and enigmatic guide.

Further Reading

Alexander, Jack. "Vox Populi." *New Yorker*, August 6, 1938, 27–32.

Chapman, John. *Tell It to Sweeney: The Informal History of the New York Daily News*. Garden City, NY: Doubleday, 1961.

Chicago Tribune. "J.M. Patterson Dies: Founder of N.Y. Daily News." May 27, 1946, 1, 3, 18.

Hannigan, William. *New York Noir: Crime Photos from the Daily News Archive*. New York: Rizzoli, 1997.

Healey, Paul F.. *Cissy: The Biography of Eleanor M. "Cissy" Patterson*. Garden City: Doubleday, 1966.

Holtzman, Jerome. *No Cheering in the Press Box*. New York: Holt, Rinehart & Winston, 1974.

Lorenz, A.L. "The Joseph Medill Papers: A Publisher's View of the 20th Century." *American Journalism* 14, Spring 1997, 205–208.

O'Sullivan, Shawn. *New York Exposed: Photographs from the Daily News*. New York: Abrams, 2001.

Papers of Joseph Medill Patterson, Chicago Tribune Archives, Chicago, Illinois.

Papers of Joseph Medill Patterson, Donnelley Library, Lake Forest College, Lake Forest, Illinois.

Patterson, Joseph Medill. *A Little Brother of the Rich*. New York: Reilley and Britton, 1908.

———. *The Notebook of a Neutral*, New York: Duffield, 1916.

Schneider, Walter E. "Fabulous Rise of the *N.Y. Daily News*." *Editor and Publisher*, June 24, 1939, 5.

Stewart, Kenneth, and John Tebbel. *Makers of Modern Journalism*. New York: Prentice-Hall, 1952.

Tebbel, John, *An American Dynasty: The Story of the McCormicks, Medills and Pattersons*. Westport, CT: Greenwood, 1968.

Wendt, Lloyd. *Chicago Tribune: The Rise of a Great American Newspaper*. Chicago: Rand McNally, 1979.

BRUCE J. EVENSEN

PEARSON, DREW

"Franklin Roosevelt will go down in history as one of the most idealistic Presidents, but with a positive genius for picking second-rate personalities." The words of Drew Pearson (December 13, 1897–September 1, 1969) appeared in his September 2, 1939, "Washington Merry-Go-Round" at the outbreak of World War II, and were read by an estimated 30 million Americans in 350 communities across the country. They were characteristic of a bluntness and reporting tenacity that made the nationally syndicated columnist and commentator one of the twentieth century's most revered and reviled muckrakers.

"I went into the newspaper business hoping to get into diplomacy," Pearson told an interviewer shortly before his death in 1969 after fifty years as one of the country's best-known journalists. "The motivation behind most of Drew's crusades was his Quaker pacifism," his long-time investigative partner Jack Anderson observed. "Pearson not only fought corruption," Chief Justice Early Warren noted, "but he fought secrecy in government which makes corruption easier." Before his passing, an estimated 60 million readers in 625 of the nation's newspapers followed Pearson's endless stream of exposés and the frequent threats of libel that flowed from them. His home paper, the *Washington Post*, claimed no twentieth-century columnist could match Pearson's "untiring and often merciless skill of investigative political reporting."

Andrew Russell Pearson was born in Evanston, Illinois, the son of Paul Martin Pearson, an English Professor at Northwestern University, and Edna Wolfe. Pearson's family became Quakers after his father accepted a teaching position at Pennsylvania's Swarthmore College when Drew was six. His education at Exeter and Swarthmore, where he received his degree in 1919, encouraged public service and original thinking, based on primary materials, as well as honors work judged by a board of examiners. He edited the school paper, *The Phoenix*. Pearson plunged into post-war relief work in Serbia after graduating. He briefly taught industrial geography at the University of Pennsylvania and economic geography at Columbia University before touring Asia and Europe as a foreign correspondent.

In 1926, a year after Pearson married Felicia Gizycka, daughter of newspaper publisher Eleanor Medill Patterson, he became foreign editor of the *United States Daily*. Three years later, his marriage ended, he became diplomatic correspondent for the *Baltimore Sun*. Along with Robert S, Allen, the Washington Bureau Chief of the *Christian Science Monitor*, Pearson anonymously published two hugely successful books, *Washington Merry-Go-Round* in 1931 and *More Washington Merry-Go-Round* a year later, that captured Depression-era disillusionment with the administration of President Herbert Hoover and key members of Congress. When their identities became known the two were fired and immediately launched a "Washington Merry-Go-Round" column through the United Feature Syndicate.

Pearson strongly supported President Franklin D. Roosevelt's New Deal and bitterly criticized the United States Supreme Court in *Nine Old Men* (1936) and *Nine Old Men at the Crossroads* (1937) for blocking its reforms. He was a constant critic of America's lack of military preparedness in the face of European fascism. In 1932, Pearson attacked the "arrogance" of America's military brass in the "opposition to mechanization." During the first years of the Roosevelt administration, he criticized those who "continue to live in the horse and buggy days of naval warfare." On April 12, 1935, he observed the Navy had become "the President's pet" and was becoming "richer, more cocksure, and less prepared for war." Naval maneuvers, he reported on January 18, 1937, "revealed glaring defects" in the nation's preparedness. Beginning in 1938, Pearson's reach was extended through weekly commentaries on the American Broadcasting Company's radio network. Pearson's sources allowed him on October 21, 1939, to paint a picture of how "petty politics ruled the Navy" and threatened national security. On May 9, 1940, he reported that Vice Admiral Joseph K. Taussig had been "forced to retire" because he had publicly predicted "war with Japan is inevitable." Roosevelt inelegantly called Pearson "a liar." (Later, Harry Truman would later call the reporter "an S.O.B.") Pearson was not deterred. On July 9, 1941, he reported that Naval Intelligence was "closed" to any except "fourth generation bluebloods." After the Japanese attack at Pearl Harbor, he reported, "alibis cannot explain away how both Army and Navy Intelligence had their guard down so carelessly."

After atomic bombs were dropped on Hiroshima and Nagasaki to end World War II, Pearson warned that "the danger of the bomb to future civilization is almost beyond belief." In 1947, Pearson and his second wife, Luvie Moore Pearson, launched "The Friendship Train," a massive relief effort through the United Nations for European civilians. Pearson was a fierce opponent of New Jersey Representative John Parnell Thomas's House Un-American Activities Committee and its well-publicized probe of communists in the entertainment industry. On February 18, 1950, Pearson became the first national commentator to take on Wisconsin Senator Joseph McCarthy's claim that communists

had infiltrated the U.S. State Department. Pearson's careful probing demonstrated that the "harum-scarum senator," though "a shouter," was not credible. When Pearson preached that McCarthy was a danger to civil liberties, a physical altercation between the two men followed. It only intensified Pearson's opposition. The nation needed to know that McCarthy was "mean and vindictive, a very dangerous fellow." President Dwight Eisenhower's failure to confront McCarthy early in his presidency, Pearson believed, "hurt him, hurt the country, hurt the State Department, and hurt American foreign policy."

Pearson was suspicious of John and Robert Kennedy. He had been the first national reporter to claim John Kennedy had not written *Profiles in Courage* for which Kennedy received the Pulitzer Prize in 1957. "There was no one more adept at managing the news than the two Kennedy brothers," Pearson observed. Pearson was an outspoken champion of civil rights and a big backer of President Lyndon Johnson's Great Society. He considered the Civil Rights Act of 1964 an extraordinary achievement and hailed Johnson's anti-poverty program "as a continuation of the New Deal" that was "far-sighted, imaginative, and immensely constructive." Pearson thought that Johnson had been "captured by the military" in fighting communism in Vietnam. "I used to argue with him about Viet Nam," Pearson said, remembering private lunches with the president at the White House, "but not effectively enough."

A cover story in a December 1948 issue of *Time* magazine called Drew Pearson "a querulous Quaker." The *New York Times* noted that "at a time when the power of government and the privilege of high position often favor special interests over the common good," Americans were well served by the "modern muckraking" of Drew Pearson.

Further Reading

Abell, Tyler, ed. [Pearson] *Diaries, 1949–1959*. New York: Holt, Rinehart and Winston, 1974.

Anderson, Jack, and James Boyd, *Confessions of a Muckraker*. New York: Random House, 1979.

Klurfeld, Herma., *Behind the Lines: The World of Drew Pearson*, New York: Englewood Cliffs, NJ: Prentice-Hall, 1968.

Papers of Drew Pearson, 1947–1952, Manuscript Division, Library of Congress, Washington, D.C.

Papers of Drew Pearson, including oral history interview, and audio tapes of radio broadcasts, Lyndon Baines Johnson Library and Museum, Austin, Texas.

Pilat, Oliver. *Drew Pearson: An Unauthorized Biography*. New York: Harper's Magazine Press, 1973.

Weinberg, Steve. "Avenging Angel or Deceitful Devil? The Evolution of Drew Pearson, a New Kind of Investigative Journalist." *American Journalism* 14/3-4 (1997): 283–302.

BRUCE J. EVENSEN

PHILADELPHIA INQUIRER

Established in modest circumstances in 1829 as the *Pennsylvania Inquirer*, the *Philadelphia Inquirer* is typical of U.S. general interest, urban newspapers in its multiplicity of owners and its peaks and valleys of newspaper prosperity, including the struggle in the early twenty-first century to retain readers in new times.

The *Inquirer* prospered during the Civil War, but by 1880 its circulation fell from a high of seventy thousand to just five thousand. Under its third owner, James Elverson, the newspaper was able to pull away from its competitors by shifting its political affiliation to Republican, the city's dominant party, and establishing itself as a "family" paper by expanding coverage to include women's interests. Its gentrification helped secure daily advertising from the city's burgeoning department stores and the success of the strategy enabled the paper to absorb several of its competitors. The paper continued to prosper under the Elverson family until a descendant sold it to Cyrus Curtis, founder of the *Ladies' Home Journal*, in the 1930s. After Curtis defaulted on the Elverson loan, the paper was sold to Moses L. Annenberg in 1936. Annenberg was owner of the *Daily Racing Form* and played a role in the Chicago circulation wars in the 1920s. The purchase of the paper has been interpreted as a move towards family respectability, particularly as it related of his son, Walter. Under Moses Annenberg, the *Inquirer* faced stiff competition, from the *Philadelphia Record*, a Democratic morning paper and frequent critic. Annenberg went to jail in 1939 on a charge of tax evasion and died in 1942. By 1947, the *Record* was out of business, a demise blamed on labor discord.

Under Walter Annenberg, the *Philadelphia Inquirer* represented the likes and dislikes of its owner, even to blacklisting certain individuals. Despite trailing the city's largest newspaper, the *Philadelphia Evening Bulletin,* a labor strike, and revelations that a star reporter had extorted bribes in exchange for silence, the papers profits helped fuel the growth of Annenberg's Triangle Publications.

Sold in 1969 to John S. Knight, the paper became part of the Knight Ridder Inc. newspaper chain. The *Inquirer* enjoyed new resources and success under a famed executive editor, Eugene L. Roberts. Between 1975 and 1990, the newspaper won seventeen Pulitzer Prizes. But in the 1990s the paper faced a decline in advertisers, including the once-reliable department stores, a changing city population, and the challenge of new technologies. The parent company pressured for more coverage of the suburbs, less national and international stories, and staff reductions. Amidst the turmoil of buy-outs and resignations, the *Inquirer* hired, in 2003, its first woman editor, Amanda Bennett. Bennett sought to return the *Inquirer* to its halcyon days by investigative stories, such as one detailing sexual abuses by priests in the Philadelphia Archdiocese.

In 2006, Knight Ridder Inc. sold its newspaper properties to the California-based chain, McClatchy Company. McClatchy sought to sell those newspapers in declining markets, including the *Inquirer*. A group of local business people led by the public relations entrepreneur and Republican activist, Brian J. Tierney, purchased the newspaper in 2006. The group pledged to maintain the newspaper's independence.

Further Reading

Andrews, J. Cutler. *The North Reports the Civil War.* Pittsburgh, PA: University of Pittsburgh Press, 1955.

Jackson, Joseph. *Encyclopedia of Philadelphia*, vols. 1–4. Harrisburg, PA.: The National Historical Assn., 1931–1935.

Morris, Charles, ed. *Makers of Philadelphia.* Philadelphia, PA: L. R. Hamersley, 1894.

Ogden, Christopher. *Legacy: a Biography of Moses and Walter Annenberg.* Boston, MA: Little, Brown, 1999.

"The Philadelphia Inquirer," http://www.philly.com/mld/inquirer, (accessed April 5, 2007).

Wainwright, Nicholas B. "The History of the *Philadelphia Inquirer,* Supplement to the *Philadelphia Inquirer*," *Philadelphia Inquirer*, September 16, 1962.

PATRICIA BRADLEY

PHILLIPS, DAVID GRAHAM

David Graham Phillips (October 31, 1867–January 23, 1911) was one of America's most popular novelists early in the twentieth century, but he also was one of the nation's most highly regarded journalists, working as a reporter and editorial writer for two of the most important newspapers in the country in New York City in the 1890s. He is perhaps most remembered today for his 1906 articles that exposed the corporate connections of members of the U.S. Senate. And it was these articles that caused President Theodore Roosevelt to coin the word "muckrakers" to describe the magazine writers who were exposing corruption in business and government.

After his 1906 articles caused a storm of controversy, Phillips vowed never again to practice journalism and he thereafter stuck to fiction. However, his novels were also controversial. He wrote "muckraking" novels about insurance fraud, Wall Street graft, the press, and politics. One novel, *The Fashionable Adventures of Joshua Craig* (1909), so enraged a violin teacher and poet who felt he had been wronged that he stalked Phillips in New York City and assassinated him on January 23, 1911. The shooting made national headlines (*New York Times*, January 24 and 25, 1911, 1).

Phillips was born in Madison, Indiana, ninety miles from Cincinnati, to a Protestant, Republican family. When Phillips graduated from Princeton University in New Jersey, he aspired to write first for newspapers and then to become a novelist. He achieved both his goals soon enough.

After graduation he went to work for the *Commercial Gazette*, the best newspaper in Cincinnati. He became a star and switched in 1890 to Charles A. Dana's *New York Sun*, known for its talented writers. He worked for the next eleven years in daily journalism. At the *Sun* Phillips covered a wide variety of issues and became nationally known for feature stories he wrote for *Harper's Weekly*. One author credits Phillips with helping to create the modern feature story.

In 1893 he joined Joseph Pulitzer's *New York World*, the nation's largest newspaper. He was made the *World's* London correspondent. Despite a dispute with Pulitzer over whether he should receive bylines, Phillips became the publisher's confidante. In 1896 Pulitzer made him an editorial writer and he wrote all the newspaper's editorials on Europe. Pulitzer also gave him special assignments, including covering the Presidential aspirants in 1899.

In 1901, after publishing his first novel, Phillips left daily journalism. In the next ten years he wrote twenty-three novels and dozens of magazine articles, mostly for the *Saturday Evening Post*. Phillips' novels detailed industrial corruption and showed a newly developed relationship between tycoons and elected officials. His 1905 novel, *The Plum Tree*, muckraked American politics, creating characters that were puppets of industry. Phillips' ideals were generally in line with reform principles.

In 1906, he wrote "The Treason of Senate" for William Randolph Hearst's *Cosmopolitan* magazine. He alleged alliances between politics and industry and implied the need for direct election of U.S. Senators. The articles caused a national sensation and Roosevelt responded by defending the Senate. On April 14, 1906, he criticized the writers who looked too much into the "muck" of society. This was the beginning of the use of the word muckraking to label journalistic exposé.

Further Reading

Filler, Louis. *The Voice of Democracy: A Critical Biography of David Graham Phillips: Journalist, Novelist, Progressive.* University Park: Pennsylvania State University Press, 1978.

Hicks, Granville. "David Graham Phillips: Journalist." *Bookman* 73 (May 1931): 257–266.

Miraldi, Robert. "The Journalism of David Graham Phillips." *Journalism Quarterly.* Spring 1986.

Phillips, David Graham. *The Plum Tree.* Indianapolis: Bobbs-Merrill, 1905.

——, *Treason of the Senate.* Chicago: Quadrangle Books: 1964, originally 1906.

Ravitz, Abe C. *David Graham Phillips.* New York: Twayne Publishers, 1966.

ROBERT MIRALDI

PHOTOJOURNALISM

Photography from its inception may well have been destined to join prose on the pages of newspapers and journals, but the intimate alliance of the two, evident on the front page of every newspaper and nearly every journal in print today, did not happen overnight. The technology that created photography evolved in stages and those stages to a great extent have defined the capabilities and possibilities of photojournalists.

Before the mid-nineteenth century, images in newspapers and other journals appeared far less regularly than today. Before the invention of photography and the attendant printing technology that enabled it to be economically published, news images were illustrations. They were somewhat expensive to produce and had a different role than a photograph. They had to be drawn by an artist who, most likely working from second hand information could not be timely, accurate or objective. After it was drawn, someone had to engrave the image onto wood blocks for printing. This required a publisher to have on hand persons skilled in drawing and engraving, a substantial cost and complexity.

When they did appear, illustrations were special features in a publication and did not serve as reporting tools as much as interpretive devices. Some politically partisan newspapers of the eighteenth and nineteenth centuries, for instance, used illustrations to lampoon their adversaries or to venerate their party leaders. When illustrations sought to present more realistic visualizations of actual events, their credibility was always constrained by their distance from the event and the subjectivity of the artist and the editor. Surprisingly, despite these limitations, illustrations played an increasing role in publishing in the nineteenth century even as photography was introduced and found more and more ways to be applied to journalism.

The introduction of the first widespread photographic technology, the daguerreotype in 1839 (the invention of Louis Daguerre), while not easy to create, offered good quality images and its possibilities were not lost on entrepreneurs and forward thinking persons. As a gesture of goodwill, the French government bought the license in August of 1839 and made it a gift to the world. These dramatic circumstances led to a surprisingly rapid and widespread interest. Within the same year Daguerreotypes were being produced across the Atlantic in the United States.

In 1842, only a few years after the beginning of photography, the first picture news magazine, the *London Illustrated News*, was founded. It was followed in the United States during the 1850s by *Harper's Weekly* and *Frank Leslie's Illustrated Newspaper*. In the nineteenth century especially, the *London Illustrated News* was a successful newsweekly that proclaimed, "Here we make our bow, determined to keep continually before the eye of the world a living and moving panorama of all its activities and influences."

A predecessor of the photo magazine genre, the *London Illustrated News's* bread and butter was images of dramatic events. Fires, wars, maritime disasters, and glamour, again just as today, were among its most popular subjects. The *Illustrated News* appealed to all classes and sold papers—eventually many more than even the *London Times*. It made the paper's founder Herbert Ingram rich, confirming the concept that pictures sell newspapers. Initially, however, there were technological limitations to placing photographs in newspapers. Photographs could not be printed directly onto newsprint. It had to first be traced or drawn and then engraved onto wood blocks just like an illustration. Photography had all the drawbacks of an illustration and numerous difficulties of its own at this early stage in its development and therefore the *Illustrated News* consisted of drawings.

Photography's own technical difficulties up until the 1880s were substantial. The equipment it took to prepare the plate for the exposure, the large camera and the subsequent development all had to be done in a sequence by the photographer. Photographers going to a site to photograph had to show up with a wagon in order to carry their portable lab and heavy camera and tripod.

For decades, action photographs were out of the question. Upon its introduction in 1839, a daguerreotype had an exposure time of thirty seconds. The cameras Matthew Brady used in the 1860s during the Civil War, required exposure times of two to three seconds, still too long to record any action. Action images were still the province of the illustrators.

The impact of photography was proved in the United States during the Civil War. The public was hungry for news and images. Many soldiers had small portraits of themselves made, usually tin types, and sent home. The war photographers created some important images, yet photography was not yet timely and the quality of a photograph could not be widely distributed because the wood block method of printing made it more an illustration. Matthew Brady, a visionary and the man behind many of the most important American photographs of the 1850s and 1860s, had invested heavily in photographing the war and was bankrupted by it. Brady took very few pictures of his own and generally failed to give Alexander Gardner and others credit for the pictures they made. At Gettysburg, Gardner arranged bodies on the battlefield to dramatically tell the story of three days of ferocious fighting in July 1863 that produced more than forty-five thousand casualties.

By the late 1880s, photojournalism still did not really exist. Whatever inherent objectivity a photograph may have had was often lost as images were interpreted by the artists and engravers who prepared them for printing. Cameras were still huge and really only suited for portraiture, landscapes and cityscapes, and they were not easily carried to news where and when it happened.

It was at this time, the late 1880s and 1890s that brought key technical innovations that overcame the impediments of the early years. In 1885 George Eastman introduced a media to record photographic images that was ready to use and developed at a time convenient to the photographer. In 1889 Eastman's company, Kodak, brought to market a roll film which made loading film in a camera easier as well as making it possible to put many exposures on one roll.

The introduction of film triggered a revolution in camera design. Cameras quickly became smaller and the complexity and skill required to create a photograph fell markedly. The cost of photography reached a point that by 1891, Kodak was able to market a relatively inexpensive camera to the mass market that could take one hundred pictures, be sent back to Kodak and then returned with the pictures and the reloaded camera.

With new smaller cameras and film that could be returned to the lab, news photography came closer to reality. The technical solution for printing photographs directly, half tone printing, made it possible by the late 1890s to print photographs easily albeit not with the best quality. After the turn of the century, timely news photography had become a reality and the newspaper business was ready for it. The new photojournalism was both coincidental to and an enabler of a new age of big newspaper empires like that of William Randolph Hearst. Photographs brought drama, realism, and a quicker way to tell international news stories like the sinking of the Titanic, crime dramas and the First World War. Images were soon indispensable to newspapers in the telling of the story of the moment.

Photojournalism also quickly developed a craft and a mission of its own. A pioneering photo essay appeared in 1890. Jacob Riis, a New York journalist who knew poverty first hand, published *How the Other Half Lives* making a case for reform to improve the plight of urban poor. Riis's essay was a forerunner of a type of story that would be done innumerable times in the future. As the technical capabilities of photography improved, ideas about composition, perspective and subject emerged. The Photo Secessionist movement, led by Alfred Stieglitz, urged artistic expression and values in the craft of photography. Outstanding photographers and photojournalists in the early twentieth century were not only adept at managing the technical challenges of photography, but also had a sense of the composition and content of their images. Of the notable photographic artists of the twentieth century, a great number of them had photojournalism on their resumes.

Technical advances in photography seemed to accelerate in the first decades of the twentieth century. Improving printing technologies, films, lenses and cameras were the catalysts for the growing impact of photography on journalism. In 1925, Leica of Germany began to market a precision compact 35mm camera that was capable of taking up to thirty-six high-quality images on one roll of film. The Leica offered professional photographers the possibility of a new relationship to their subject. The bulkier, slower to operate press cameras generally in use at the time made it almost impossible to operate unobtrusively, while the Leica fit in a pocket and could be deployed and shooting in seconds without being very noticeable.

In the 1930s, the celebrated career of Henri Cartier Bresson became closely associated with the Leica. A young, classically trained French artist interested in composition, Bresson discovered photography as his medium of choice when he saw the work of Robert Munkacsi. Bresson acquired a Leica which he unrelentingly carried in the streets of France in search of subjects. Bresson's greatest successes were beautifully composed images of salient and revealing moments of people and life around him. Bresson's self styled "decisive moment" came to be a defining attribute of good news photography.

Bresson and others were still developing ideas about what photography should be. In the early 1930s, a group calling themselves Group f/64 that included Edward Weston, Ansel Adams, Imogen Cunningham, among other mostly west coast American photographers, released a manifesto proclaiming a new regime of what they called straight photography or realism. The group proclaimed, "Group f/64 limits its members and invitational names to those workers who are striving to define photography as an art form by simple and direct presentation through purely photographic methods."

The confluence of artistic endeavor and photojournalism was evident in many of the photo essays of the 1930s. Dorothea Lange and others, created hard hitting natural images of impoverished Americans, many commissioned by New Deal. The proliferation of this new high value image photojournalism found outlets in news magazines. Most notable of these were the business magazine *Fortune* in 1930 and *Life* magazine which appeared in 1936.

Margaret Bourke-White, staff photographer for *Fortune* and then *Life*, had an especially prominent influence on the field. With her press camera she produced series after series of photo essays that defined many of the stories of her day. She was a key talent in the publishing successes of Henry Luce in the 1930s and 1940s providing numerous covers for his magazines.

Life magazine itself was a product of the new availability of high quality photographs in print and it fascinated readers. An invention of Henry Luce and his company, *Life* defined the photo weekly and became a highly influential publication. It employed many prominent photojournalists including White, Robert Capa, Gordon Parks, and Alfred Eisenstaedt as well as many others who at some point in their careers were employed by the magazine.

Life magazine and its competitor, *Look*, ceased publishing as a weeklies in the early 1970s. Their demise marked another phase for photojournalism. In contrast to 1900, imagery in daily life in the late twentieth century had become ubiquitous. From the late 1940s until nearly the end of the century, television was the fastest growing news medium becoming, for instance, the news source of choice in the United States during the Vietnam War and Watergate eras.

The demise of the photo weeklies did not mean photojournalism was any less important. Photography was in fact arguably more vital as print media's need for images to entice readers only grew with the growing competition from television and then cable television. In addition, the number of publications, including niche consumer magazines, grew even as circulation growth stagnated. Many of these publications needed images.

The efficiency of the equipment used in meeting this demand for images increased as photographic technology continued to improve. In the last decades of the twentieth century manufacturers introduced films that were faster and offered more color control and at least five major camera companies offered excellent compact motor driven 35mm single lens reflex cameras that all but completely usurped the other formats.

Film cameras and photojournalists had become especially productive by the 1990s. It is said that Matthew Brady and his teams of photographers created seven thousand images during the entire Civil War. By the end of the twentieth century, a single photographer could easily take hundreds of photographs in a day. But photography and photojournalism once again changed dramatically during the 1990s when the Internet came into wide usage and then professional grade digital photography came into being.

With stagnant circulation but more publications, there was already a great deal of dispersion in print media by the year 2000 when the Internet had already become ubiquitous in many areas and the capabilities of digital photography were about to improve exponentially. The Internet had already become a fourth media channel, albeit increasingly at the expense of broadcast and print. It was also one that was easily accessible to photojournalists equipped with the new high performance digital cameras.

By 2001, technology had increased the resolution of digital cameras to the point where there was an immediate improvement in the ease with which photographers could create high quality images. Cameras could take and store hundreds of images and the qualities of different films could be enhanced by making easy adjustments to the camera or in the editing process later. Extra equipment like film storage containers, portable labs and lighting, and even extra lenses could be discarded and the lap top computer put to use in place of the lab, editing table, and mailbox as images could be conveniently edited and emailed. The change in circumstances was mind boggling. Web publishing, or blogging, lent itself easily to digital photography and added an essentially infinite potential number of reporting channels. The Internet's creation of an accessible media enabled any photographer to report and publish globally, while, at the same time, undermining established media business models and quality standards.

Digital photography presented ethical challenges too. An image can be distributed on the Internet within moments of being taken and it can be done by virtually anyone. New digital technology has only begun to describe new and important ways photojournalism will tell stories to millions in the new millennium.

Further Reading

Barger, Susan, and William White. *The Daguerreotype: Nineteenth Century Technology and Modern Science.* Washington D.C.: Smithsonian Academic Press, 1991.

Baughman, James L. *Henry R. Luce and the Rise of the American News Media.* Baltimore: The Johns Hopkins University Press, 1987, 2001.

Dorfman, John. "Digital dangers: the new forces that threaten photojournalism." *Columbia Journalism Review*, July 2002.

Keller, Emily. *Margaret Bourke-White: A Photographers Life.* Minneapolis, MN: Lerner Publications, 1996.

Panzer, Mary. *Matthew Brady and the Image of History.* Washington, D.C.: Smithsonian Institution Press for the National Portrait Gallery, c1997.

Sinnema, Peter W. *Dynamics of the Printed Page: Representing the Nation in the Pages of* The London Illustrated News. Aldershot, Hants, England: Ashgate Pub., 1998.

PETER W. QUIGLEY

PINKHAM, LYDIA

Lydia Pinkham (1819–1883) was a middle-class housewife who, through a combination of financial necessity, business acumen, and advertising creativity, successfully turned a home remedy into an internationally recognized patent medicine. She was the first woman to use her likeness to market a product and that kindly, respectable, and grandmotherly countenance won the confidence of generations of Americans. Her "Vegetable Compound," which promised relief from a range of "female ailments," was a staple in American medicine cabinets from the 1870s until the 1970s. Lydia Pinkham became a legend in her own time, an icon of American ingenuity.

Born in 1819 in Lynn, Massachusetts, Lydia was the tenth of twelve children of William and Rebecca Estes. At sixteen, Lydia joined the Lynn Female Anti-Slavery Society and later joined the Freeman's Institute. She attended the select Lynn Female Academy and upon graduation, became a schoolteacher. In 1843, she married Isaac Pinkham, whom she had met at the Freeman's Institute. They eventually had three sons and a daughter.

Isaac Pinkham was an ambitious man who failed in a number of get-rich-quick schemes so that by 1875, the family was teetering on bankruptcy. Lydia, who had a strong distrust of doctors, had for some time been treating family ailments with home remedies. She occasionally gave or sold one of these that seemed particularly efficacious for "female complaints" to friends or neighbors. Now the family decided they might try to turn this into a serious business. In 1876, Lydia registered her label and patent for "Lydia Pinkham's Vegetable Compound," with the United States Patent Office. The product contained the herbal medication black cohosh and a substantial alcohol content.

The Pinkhams used picture postcards, a four-page pamphlet entitled *Guide for Women*, and newspaper advertisements to market the product. In 1879, Lydia posed for a photograph that became the company's trademark. At a time when few women let their photographs be published and when no products used the photograph of a woman, the image of this attractive, middle-aged, middle-class, and respectable woman authenticated the medicine in the eyes of the general public. As sales boomed, customers began to write letters of thanks, testifying how the compound had cured their ailments. These testimonials became an important part of the company's advertising strategy and contributed further to the product's credibility. Customers also wrote letters asking Lydia for advice, which she gave in a sympathetic and down-to-earth tone. At first she wrote these letters herself, then she turned the task over to her daughter and daughter-in-law, and eventually to a staff of trained women clerks.

The ads also captured the hard life women were exposed to, whether they be factory girls who were working to support their younger orphaned siblings or pampered middle-class matrons exhausted by the demands of a busy social life. "Female ailments" were one factor that united women of all classes. These ads presented a contrast to the prevailing social view that women were pampered domestic creatures, cared for by their male relatives, and protected from the harsh realities of the world.

Lydia Pinkham died in 1883, five months after suffering a paralytic stroke. The Lynn *Daily Evening Item* published an extra edition to report her death, and the story appeared in newspapers across the nation. Despite the publicity of her death, customers continued to write "Mrs. Pinkham" praising her compound and asking for her advice well into the twentieth century.

Further Reading

Applegate, Edd. "Advertising Patent Medicine: The Rise of Lydia Pinkham" Chap in *Personalities and Products: A Historical Perspective on Advertising in America*. Westport, CT: Greenwood Press, 1998.

Burton, Jean. *Lydia Pinkham is Her Name*. New York: Farrar, Straus and Company, 1949.

Stage, Sarah. *Female Complaints: Lydia Pinkham and the Business of Women's Medicine*. New York: W. W. Norton, 1979.

Washburn, Robert Collyer. *The Life and Times of Lydia E. Pinkham*. New York: G. P. Putnam's Sons, 1931.

ELIZABETH V. BURT

PITTSBURGH COURIER

The *Pittsburgh Courier* was begun in earnest in May 1910 with Robert L. Vann as general counsel and treasurer. There had been an earlier attempt to begin the weekly by Edwin Nathaniel Harleston whose interest was mostly in a literary publication. The first black-owned publication in Pittsburgh had been *The Mystery*, published in the 1840s by Dr. Martin Delany.

Born on August 27, 1879, in Ahoskie, North Carolina, Robert L. Vann's heritage was poor and modest but he managed to become an illustrious, capable attorney and was recognized as a great leader in Pittsburgh and of the *Courier*. His mother, Lucy Peoples was the daughter of ex-slaves. Although Robert L. Vann's paternal heritage is uncertain, his mother gave him the last name of her employer, Albert Vann, who was a prominent citizen in Hertford County.

In 1912 Vann met and befriended Ira Lewis, also a North Carolina native and the two began an alliance that is credited with making the *Courier* a success. Lewis spurred the *Courier* by a focus on securing advertising; circulation figures more than doubled soon after his arrival. Soon Lewis became not only business manager of the *Courier* but also managed Robert L. Vann's unsuccessful bid for an Allegheny County judgeship.

By 1925 the *Courier*, located at 518 Fourth Avenue in Pittsburgh, was using the Associated Negro Press (ANP) news service provided by another prominent black newspaper, the *Chicago Defender* begun by Robert Abbott. The *Chicago Defender* followed the tradition of William Randolph Hearst and was noted for sensationalistic, red bold headlines, provocative reporting and photography. Initially Robert Vann avoided sensationalism and geared his paper on a higher road to end racial injustices and to improve the social condition of blacks.

The *Courier* covered the decade-long Scottsboro case in the 1930s as no other black newspaper. The case concerned the fate of nine black youths, ranging in age from thirteen to twenty, falsely accused of raping two white women on board a moving freight train bound from Alabama to Chattanooga, Tennessee. The case gained national and international prominence and was tremendously controversial, particularly after the Communist Party's International Labor Defense (ILD) provided legal counsel for the boys. In 1931, Vann wrote a stinging editorial in which he made clear that the ILD was probably doing more harm than good in its quest to "get cheap publicity" and had "set about with great hue and cry to give the impression that they were going to release the prisoners here and now." Release was not the case as the youths suffered long and greatly while incarcerated, even after it became clear that they were innocent.

During "Red Scare" of the 1920s, U. S. Attorney General Mitchell Palmer attempted to link black newspapers to communism. The *Courier* escaped government censure and overt criticism at this time. But during World War II, the *Courier* along with other black newspapers became the victims of a major investigation by the federal government. This investigation was initiated by J. Edgar Hoover, then head of the Justice Department's General Intelligence Division (GID). Hoover was strong in his opinion that black newspapers were inciting blacks to riot. Hoover's desire was to reenact the Alien and Sedition acts of 1798 and to use them to shut black papers down. One of the contentious areas was the *Pittsburgh Courier's* Double V-Campaign launched in response to a letter to the editor. The essence of the campaign was that blacks wanted victory abroad over the enemy but also wanted victory at home over injustices, segregation and maltreatment. The campaign was a great psychological boost for blacks and an embarrassment for the government. During the World War II era, the *Courier's* circulation figures reached three hundred thousand.

During this period it was another U.S. Attorney General, Francis Biddle, who listened to reason and saved black newspapers, including the *Courier*, from being shut down with a charge of sedition. John Sengstacke publisher of the *Chicago Defender* stood up to Biddle and persuaded him that black newspapers were printing the truth and moreover had been denied the opportunity to interview top government officials regarding the war and other matters of concern to blacks.

Over the years, but particularly during the World War II era, the *Courier* employed a number of capable male and female reporters and editors, including George Schuyler, Hazel Garland (and eventually her daughter Phyl Garland), Edna McKenzie, Harold Keith, and Evelyn Long Cunningham, who worked initially in the New York office of the *Courier* before moving to Pittsburgh to become a reporter, edition editor and columnist during the heyday of the paper when it published sixteen editions. Cunningham eventually left the *Courier* to work for New York Governor Nelson Rockefeller. Cunningham's work was exemplary as was the work of a number of black professional journalists and editors associated with the *Courier*. Three of them won Polk Awards in Journalism.

John Sengstacke bought the *Courier* in 1967 and the name was changed to *"New" Pittsburgh Courier"* (http://www.newpittsburghcourier.com). The paper was published in 2007 by Rod Doss, a graduate of the University of Pittsburgh and a former advertising manager at the paper whose mission was to inform African American readers in the Pittsburgh area of news that was important to them. The *Courier* was one of about two hundred black newspapers belonging to the National Newspaper Publishers Association, an alliance of contemporary black publishers begun in 1913.

Further Reading

James H. Brewer. "Robert Lee Vann, Democrat or Republican: An Exponent of Loose Leaf Politics." *Negro History Bulletin*, 21, 5 (1958): 100–103.

Bruni, Andrew. *Robert L. Vann of the Pittsburgh Courier: Politics and Black Journalism*. Pittsburgh: University of Pittsburgh Press, 1974.

Lee Finkle. *Forum for Protest: The Black Press During World War II*. Rutherford, NJ: Fairleigh Dickinson University Press, 1975.

Robert I. Vexler, editor and compiler. *Pittsburgh: A Chronological and Documentary History: 1682–1976*. Dobbs Ferry, NY: Oceana Publications, Inc, 1977.

Patrick Washburn. *A Question of Sedition: The Federal Government's Investigation of the Black Press During World War II*. New York: Oxford University Press, 1986.

FRANKIE HUTTON

PLAYBOY

Playboy (1953–) magazine gained prominence as a publication offering quality writing and classy photos of naked women. As such, it drew readership from a wide audience, including adults and teenagers of both sexes. Founder Hugh Hefner put the first issue on the stands in 1953 when he was twenty-seven. Created at a card table in his Chicago apartment, Hefner borrowed $8,000 to finance the magazine and spent $500 to buy the rights to nude photos of Marilyn Monroe, which appeared in the first issue. Within five years, *Playboy* was selling a million copies a month. Within ten years, it was an international empire built on the idea that "respectable men would buy a skin magazine if the nude pictures were surrounded by writing of such high quality that they could plausibly...claim they bought it for the articles." They did.

Perhaps most notable was *Playboy's* penchant for publishing interesting interviews in the question and answer format. They read quickly, and in some cases contained language *Playboy* took a risk by publishing. Vocabulary taboos including the word "crap," for instance, found a place in what became one of the widest read magazines of the late 1960s and 1970s, and continued to sell more than three million copies per month into the twenty-first century.

The journalism in *Playboy* was the "New Journalism," a pioneering sort that mixed fiction techniques with reportage. Articles included vivid description, scene setting, action, and dialog rather than quotations to offer an example of the human condition, or discuss a current event in the less formal manner one would use in the company of friends. The articles represented a new kind of short story, one rooted in journalism rather than fiction. The magazine's editors saw their readership as literate, adventurous, and ready for in-depth articles loaded with the writer's voice.

Playboy's lured readers with not only a sexy female on

the cover but also with a table of contents listed prominent writers and intellectuals. During the late 1960s and early 1970s, magazine carried interviews with and articles by such notable figures as Art Buchwald, Jean-Paul Sartre, Eldridge Cleaver, Gore Vidal, Norman Mailer, Arnold Toynbee, Allen Ginsberg, Arthur Schlesinger, Jr., Woody Allen, William F. Buckley Jr. Marshall McLuhan, Jack Anderson, Walter Cronkite, and many others. There were humor pieces from Jean Shepherd and Robert Morley; Norman Thomas wrote on pacifism in America; and Arthur C. Clarke warned about how artificial intelligence would change our lives.

Playboy could be counted on to condemn censorship and to lampoon the so-called "puritan" sexual values that were at odds with the publication's hedonistic philosophy. The magazine ripened along with the sexual revolution in the United States. Some historians place the magazine's message of sex for fun as the unofficial bible of the sexual revolution. Significantly, the birth control pill and *Playboy's* message—sex is for recreation, not just procreation—arrived at the same historical moment. One of the practitioners of the new journalism, author Tom Wolfe, joked that *Playboy's* highbrow articles were "the magazine's monthly 10 cc. of literary penicillin." At a 1979 reunion of Playmates, Hefner quipped, "Without you, I'd be the publisher of a literary magazine."

In its heyday, *Playboy* was a culturally significant magazine that was followed by many imitators that lacked its literary quality and highly stylized production values. At its peak, the magazine's influence may well have been comparable to such other noteworthy publications as *Esquire* under Harold Hayes and the *New Yorker* under William Shawn.

Further Reading

Meyerowitz, Joanne. "Women, Cheesecake, and Borderline Material: Responses to Girlie Pictures in the Mid-Twentieth-Century U. S." *Journal of Women's History*, 9 (Fall, 1996), 9–35.

Schmidt, Dorothy (Dorcy). "Magazines, Technology, and American Culture." *Journal of American Culture*, 3 (Spring, 1980), 3–16.

Tebbel, John, and Mary Ellen Zuckerman. *The Magazine in America: 1741–1990*. New York: Oxford University Press, 1991.

Wolseley, Roland E. *The Changing Magazine: Trends in Readership and Management*. New York: Hastings House, 1973.

DEBRA A. SCHWARTZ

PM

PM, Ralph Ingersoll's attempt to reinvent the daily newspaper in America, lasted just eight years, from June 18, 1940 to June 22, 1948, but during its short life the New York City-based paper pioneered journalistic innovations that are now commonplace at most newspapers.

Brilliant but erratic, Ingersoll had been the *New Yorker's*

first managing editor, helped develop *Life* for Henry Luce and was editor of *Fortune*. Disenchanted with Luce's conservative politics and determined to found his own publication, Ingersoll quit Time, Inc. in 1939 to start his "new kind of newspaper" (*Time*, April 10, 1939).

Ingersoll wanted to challenge both the limitations of the traditional daily newspaper and what he saw as the political conservatism of the publishers of the day. His vision of an innovative, staff-dominated, liberal daily published without advertising was so compelling that eighteen wealthy investors agreed to give him $1.5 million for the startup, eleven thousand experienced newspaper editors and reporters applied for jobs and sixty thousand people signed up as charter subscribers. President Franklin D. Roosevelt wrote to say, "Your interesting prospectus leads me to believe that you are about to add a notable chapter to the history of our free press" (Hoopes 1985, 222).

Ingersoll assembled an eclectic staff. Dashiell Hammett, the mystery writer, interviewed many of the initial applicants. John P. Lewis, who later became editor when Ingersoll joined the Army in 1942, came from a daily in Buffalo. Margaret Bourke-White, who had shot *Life's* first cover, headed the photo staff. Leo Huberman, a college professor, was labor editor. Theodor Geisell, later known as Dr. Seuss, was a cartoonist. Ben Hecht, who co-wrote the play "The Front Page," was a regular columnist.

At a time when few American newspapers were trying new ideas, Ingersoll's thirty-two-page tabloid introduced a smorgasbord of them. Writers were encouraged to break away from the inverted pyramid to tell stories with beginnings, middles and ends, as well as explanation and background. Routine news was relegated to columns of one paragraph briefs. Editors used large photos throughout the paper and often added charts and graphics to stories. Layouts used wider columns and lots of white space. The paper covered movies, radio, the press, labor, health, and consumer news in depth. It was another 30 years before most of these innovations became standard practice.

Despite a loyal base of 100,000 to 150,000 readers, *PM* had only one profitable year. It was kept alive by Marshall Field III, a liberal department store heir who spent an estimated $5 million to $7 million on *PM* before calling it quits in 1948.

There is no consensus among about why *PM* failed. Among the reasons offered: It lacked features many readers wanted in a newspaper, such as comics, gossip, stock market reports and ads. It reached newsstands after other papers. It betrayed too much predictable bias in its coverage. Infighting between pro and anti-Communists on the staff caused dissension and allowed critics to smear it as a Communist propaganda sheet.

I.F. Stone, who spent five years as one of PM's star reporters and later used the paper's subscriber list to help launch his famous weekly newsletter, called the paper's failure a "gallant defeat, which is more glorious than a victory because it was something original, courageous and different" (Hoopes 1985, 330).

Further Reading

Becker, Stephen. *Marshall Field III*. New York: Random House, 1964.

Cottrell, Robert C. *Izzy: A Biography of I.F. Stone*. New Brunswick, NJ: Rutgers University Press, 1992.

Donohew, Lewis "PM: An Anniversary Assessment." *Columbia Journalism Review*, Fall (1965).

Hoopes, Roy. *Ingersoll: A Biography*. New York: Atheneum, 1985.

Leibling, A.J. *The Press*, 2nd ed. New York: Ballantine Books, 1975.

Mahoney, Patrick R. "PM (1940–1948): A Benchmark of Consumer Journalism." *Media & Consumer*, January (1973).

Margolick, David. "*PM*'s Impossible Dream." *Vanity Fair*, Jan. 1999: 116–132.

Milkman, Paul. *PM: A New Deal in Journalism, 1940–1948*. New Brunswick, NJ: Rutgers University Press, 1997.

Tebbel, John. *The Marshall Fields: A Study in Wealth*. New York: E.P. Dutton, 1947.

Wechsler, James A. *The Age of Suspicion*. New York. Random House, 1953.

GUY T. BAEHR

POLK AWARDS, GEORGE

The George Polk Awards, among the more prestigious honors in journalism, are given annually by Long Island University, which started the program in 1949. Named for the Columbia Broadcasting System (CBS) radio reporter who was murdered while covering the Greek civil war in 1948, the awards recognize about twelve people or organizations involved in print or broadcast journalism in categories such as national, foreign, or local reporting, commentary and book writing; often, a special award is given for career achievements. The criteria for the awards are discovery of an important story, resourcefulness and courage in obtaining information for the story, and skill in telling the story. Journalists and their news organizations submit nominations, which an advisory panel refers to the judges—educators and communicators who are Long Island University alumni or faculty members at the school. The awards ceremonies also recognize journalists who have died in the line of duty.

Of the numerous journalists who won multiple Polk Awards, Seymour Hersh has stood out. Hersh, who was celebrated for his newspaper and magazine reporting on the My Lai massacre, the secret American bombing of Cambodia, diplomat Henry Kissinger's wiretapping, the Central Intelligence Agency's role in the 1973 Chilean military coup, and United States service members' abuse of detainees at Abu Ghraib prison in Iraq, was the first five-time Polk Award winner. Among other multiple winners were Walt Bogdanich, a four-time winner cited for work in both newspaper and television journalism; newspaper writers Homer Bigart, John Kifner, John Darnton, Sydney H. Schanberg, Joseph Lelyveld, Donald Bartlett, and James Steele; television journalists Bill Moyers and Christiane Amanpour; and the magazine *ARTnews*.

Winners have included not only leading journalists and major news organizations, but reporters from small towns or previously unheralded publications, as well. For instance, in 1980, two inmates serving life sentences in prison in Angola, Louisiana, won a Polk Award for covering criminal justice issues and prison life in their magazine. Still other unusual winners have worked in endeavors outside journalism, such as author James Baldwin, literary scholar Henry Louis Gates, and Supreme Court Justice William O. Douglas. Organizations that have been honored with the award include the Center for Public Integrity and the National Security Archive. Among recipients of the award for career achievement are baseball broadcaster Red Barber and newspaper obituary writer Alden Whitman.

The man for whom the awards are named, George Polk, thirty-four, was reporting on the Greek civil war between the fascist government and Communist forces at the time of his murder. Polk's body was found on May 16, 1948, floating in the harbor of Salonika, in northern Greece; his hands and feet were bound, and he had been shot in the head, execution-style. A critic of the government and a $300 million U. S. program of economic and military aid to help the ruling Royalist Party win the war, Polk had reported on government repression, including martial law and executions, and he had alleged that the regime was corrupt, with officials stealing the American money for personal use. Just before his death, he had found evidence of the corruption and was planning to report it in the United States, where he was to return for a Harvard University fellowship; in an interview with the Royalist leader, he threatened to expose the leader's illegal bank account in the U. S. Polk had been last seen on May 9, three days after broadcasting his final report.

The Greek government accused the Communists of Polk's killing and, in a show trial, convicted journalist Gregory Staktopoulos and his mother in April 1949 of complicity in the death; Staktopoulos said he had helped Kremlin-guided Communists slay Polk. (He was sentenced to life in prison yet was freed in 1961 after his sentence was reduced.) The U. S. government and a group of journalists led by columnist Walter Lippmann, the Overseas Writers Special Committee to Inquire Into the Murder of George Polk, supported the Greek verdict and the theory that Communists murdered Polk with the hope that the government would be blamed. Critics pointed to evidence that the Greek rulers were culpable and assailed the committee for accepting the official version of the case. They said the committee's work fell far short of the type of journalism that the Polk Awards were intended to recognize.

Further Reading

Ellis, Sandra L. "George Polk." In *The Museum of Broadcast Communications Encyclopedia of Radio,* vol. 3, edited by Christopher H. Sterling, 1086–1088. New York: Fitzroy Dearborn, 2004.

Hershey, Edward. "A History of Journalistic Integrity, Superb Reporting and Protecting the Public: The George Polk Awards in Journalism," http://www.brooklyn.liu.edu/polk/history.html (accessed April 7, 2007).

MICHAEL GAUGER

POPULAR MUSIC CRITICISM

What came to be regarded as popular music existed long before a popular music criticism. By its very nature, such music—given its simple and spontaneous nature—did not seem to invite a critical discourse, as did what came to be regarded as classical or art music. In the United States, the early music took many forms: broadside ballads, ballad operas, solo songs with instrumental accompaniment, simple arrangements from Italian opera, the songs and performances of Henry Russell, marching band music, minstrelsy, vaudeville, and dance hall and saloon music.

Beginnings

The establishment of the trade magazine *Billboard* in 1894 marks the beginning of a popular music criticism that found expression in the next century in a variety of media. Its advent corresponds with the establishment in New York of a music publishing industry that came to be known as Tin Pan Alley. This industry printed sheet music and aggressively sought to create a national market for its products. Writing about the music often went no further than to serve this end.

The birth of *Billboard* and Tin Pan Alley also correspond to the emergence of a popular music known as ragtime and a debate about its value. That debate foreshadowed later cultural debates regarding jazz and rock-and-roll and the many varieties of popular music they spawned. Ragtime, which enjoyed a national and international vogue between 1897 and 1917, challenged musical and cultural conservatives of the day. They viewed it as any kind of syncopated music and one that threatened social and moral behavior. Ragtime found, however, a powerful voice on its behalf in Hiram K. Moderwell, who, after noting that many well-known foreign musicians had praised it, went on to write about its technical resourcefulness, melody, and rhythm in articles published in *Seven Arts* and *New Republic* in 1915 and 1917, respectively.

The Jazz Era

Jazz emerged as a word in the press for the first time in 1913, and in the 1920s as a major subject of discussion and analysis. Its sources, which included ragtime, and its improvisatory character made it quite different from the music of Tin Pan Alley. Like ragtime it attracted world-wide attention and following and a domestic opposition from those who saw it as subversive. The first writers championing it came from Europe. The Swiss conductor, Ernest Ansermet, wrote what is regarded as the first piece of jazz criticism in 1919. In the United States, the first people to write favorably and analytically about it were literary people such as Carl Van Vechten and people better known as classical musicians and critics, among them the classical music critic of the *New York Herald Tribune* Virgil Thomson. Irving Kolodin, Winthrop Sargeant, Henry Pleasants, and Gunther Schuller sustained Thomson's interest and attention. Classical-music critic Gilbert Seldes published a book, *The Seven Lively Arts*, in 1923, in which he talked about jazz as a significant art and argued for a more ample view by critics of American music and culture, a position taken by John Rockwell in the last quarter of the century.

Writing on jazz increased in the 1930s because of the popularity of the music and a growing inclusiveness in American life represented by the philosophy and programs of the New Deal. Popular music weeklies and monthlies published in both New York and London became important venues for jazz critics. John Hammond of New York contributed articles to the London-based *Melody Maker*. What became an important popular music magazine, *Downbeat*, began in 1934 and published articles by jazz critic Marshall Stearns. George T. Simon wrote for *Metronome*. Leonard Feather moved to the United States from England and emerged as a champion of bop.

Coverage of what still was regarded as jazz—despite its many changes—continued, indeed, perhaps, even expanded after World War II. Newspapers began to employ jazz critics. John S. Wilson joined the *New York Times* in 1952, and in the next decade the *Los Angeles Times* hired Feather. With the advent of rock, critics who had specialized in jazz turned, however, to other careers. Some wrote important books on jazz. Gary Giddins continued to write about jazz for the *Village Voice* in New York even though he did other things for that publication.

Rock-and-Roll, Rock, and Pop

Rock-and-roll arrived in force in the 1950s with the recording "Rock around the clock" by Bill Haley and the Comets, a recording *Billboard* dubbed the best-selling record in the country. Rock-and-roll gave way to rock in the 1960s. Critical writing then came to insist on a distinction between rock and "pop," a term that originated in the United Kingdom as a description for rock-and-roll and the new music styles it engendered. Rock came to be seen as harder, more aggressive, more improvisatory, and more closely tied to African American sources, whereas pop generally has been regarded as softer, more planned or arranged and drawing on older musical traditions such as folk.

Regardless of terminology, all this music and the industry that promoted it should be seen as part of larger social and political changes occurring at the time. African-Americans asserted themselves as members of American society, a gesture that expressed itself through the rock and soul of the 1960s and then the rap or hip-hop of the 1980s and 1990s. Their traditions, which so influenced ragtime and jazz, became central to what continued to be referred to as popular music in both in America and Europe. Demographics and economics supported a vigorous youth culture and a music industry that made youth its principal focus. In the view of Richard Middleton, youth "shifted the cultural politics of popular music, it was from this point on…about physical pleasures—indeed sexuality—and about ideals and choices of life style," or, as Greil Marcus put it more succinctly in a 1997 interview, it was about youth's insistence on "autonomy."

The New Journalism and Criticism

A new journalism blended with and furthered this culture. Steve Jones and others have characterized writing about pop and rock as rather "prosaic" up to the 1960s, with pieces tending to be "factual and statistical." Journalists such as Tom Wolfe and Hunter S. Thompson and novelists such as Norman Mailer and Truman Capote began to employ many of the stylistic characteristics of fiction that proved attractive to music critics. As a contributor to the major rock magazine *Rolling Stone*, Thompson demonstrated the new journalism's potential for propagating rock and pop. "As a literary form," observe Jones and Keith Featherly, "popular music criticism grew up side by side, often page by page with the new journalism."

The musician-critic Lester Bangs exemplified this style. Born in California in 1942, he moved to Detroit and worked for the rock-and-roll magazine *Creem*, which had been established in 1968. As a writer, he did more than perhaps any other—certainly in the view of other critics—to define a style of critical journalism that was based on the sound and the language of rock in such a way to influence a whole generation of younger writers and perhaps musicians as well. He led a rock band, wrote lyrics, sang lead, and played the harmonica. He has been characterized as rock's essential wild man. Other important rock critics included Robert Christgau, the longtime chief rock critic of the *Village Voice* and mentor to many younger writers, and Dave Marsh, active at *Creem* and the biographer of Bruce Springsteen.

Regarded by some as the greatest rock critic of all, Greil Marcus displayed comparable verbal virtuosity. Rockwell regards him as "the most influential writer among American intellectuals to have emerged from the ranks of rock critics." After taking two degrees from the University of California at Berkeley, he wrote on rock for a number of publications. He was an early contributor to *Rolling Stone* and served from 1969–1970 as its recordings editor. He also contributed to *Village Voice*, *Creem*, *New West*, and *Artforum*, wrote several books, and edited *Stranded*, an anthology of essays by twenty rock critics on their favorite rock-and-roll record. Throughout his career, according to Rockwell, Marcus blended aesthetic concerns with "a commitment to moral and political issues that lends his best writing an almost bardic quality."

In the 1970s, mainline newspapers began to include rock criticism. Robert Hilburn started reviewing rock for the *Los Angeles Times* in 1970, and in 1974 Rockwell became chief rock critic for the *New York Times*, a position he held until 1980. Under Hilburn's leadership, the *Los Angeles Times* came to provide the most extensive coverage of popular music of any American newspaper.

Criticism and Access

Magazines and later fanzines served what has been called a gatekeeper role between the producers of music and its consumers. Such publications proliferated, with every music specialty seeming to have its own magazine or magazines. *Rolling Stone* proved to be the most highly regarded and successful. Jann Wenner and Ralph Gleason, a jazz and rock critic, founded the magazine in San Francisco in 1967 where it remained until it moved to New York ten years later. The first magazine expressed much of San Francisco's counterculture and focused on both the visual and musical arts. It attracted a number of writers, including Bangs, who demonstrated on a regular basis a verbal virtuosity matching the music or performances his articles described and analyzed. The early magazine included among its varied offerings lengthy interviews with musicians, their work, and their views. Although some saw a decline in the vitality of the magazine when it moved to New York, Colin Larkin praised the decision of *Rolling Stone* in the 1990s to make music its principal focus and to sustain the standards set by Bangs, Marcus, and others of the magazine's first generation of writers.

Other magazines came into existence to serve just about every musical genre and market. *Crawdaddy* became a major journalistic force in shaping the rock market of the late 1960s. In 1967 *Down Beat* extended its coverage to include rock. The teeny-bop culture had its *Smash Hits* and *Top of the Pops*; the "indie" or independent rock culture, *Spin* and *New Musical Press*; hip-hop or rap people, *Vibe*. Of these, Larkin identified *Living Blues* and *Blues Revue*, *Vibe*, *Spin*, and *Jazz Times* as magazines setting high standards for in the 1980s and 1990s. All, once again, played an important role as gatekeeper between those who marketed and promoted music (the music industry) and audience. This interdependence of industry and press raised questions about magazine's and critic's autonomy and the fulfillment of their role, as Simon Frith puts it, of creating "knowing communities" of performers and audiences.

The advent of the Internet in the 1990s brought an addition and, for many, an alternative to print media. In addition to offering online versions of magazines and fanzines, the Internet made possible a new form of conversation about music: the web log, which allowed unlimited space for anyone who had an opinion to express. For consumers, who sometimes found the cost of magazines and newspapers a challenge to their budgets, this means of securing information and opinion proved attractive.

Further Reading

Bangs, Lester.*Psychotic Reactions and Carburetor Dung*, ed. by Greil Marcus. New York: Knopf, 1987.

Belz, Carl. *The Story of Rock*, 2nd ed., New York: Oxford University Press, 1972.

Christgau, Robert. *Grown Up All Wrong: 75 Great Rock and Pop Artists From Vaudeville to Techno*. Cambridge, MA: Harvard University Press, 1998.

Continuum Encyclopedia of Popular Music of the World, 3rd ed.. London: Continuum, 2003.

Downes, Edward O. D., and John Rockwell, "Criticism." In *The New Grove Dictionary f American Music*, vol. 4, edited by by H. Wiley Hitchcock, and Stanley Sadie, 536–546. New York: Grove's Dictionaries, Inc., 1986.

Draper, Robert. *Rolling Stone Magazine: the Uncensored History.* New York: Doubleday, 1990.

Frith, Simon, Will Straw, and John Street, eds. *The Cambridge Companion to Pop and Rock.* Cambridge University Press, 2003.

Fuld, James J. *American Popular Music 1875–1950.* Philadelphia: Musical Americana, 1955.

Jones, Steve, ed. *Pop Music and the Press.* Philadelphia: Temple University Press, 2002.

Larkin, Colin, comp. and ed. *The Encyclopedia of Popular Music,* 3rd ed., 8 vols. London: Muze UK Ltd., 1998.

Leonard, Neil. "The Reactions to Ragtime." In *Ragtime: Its History, Composers, and Music,* edited by John Edward Hasse, 102–113. New York: Schirmer Books, 1985.

Kernfeld, Barry, ed. *The New Grove Dictionary of Jazz,* 2nd ed., 3 vols. New York: Grove's Dictionaries, Inc..

Marcus, Greil, ed. *Stranded: Rock and Roll for a Desert Island.* New York: Alfred A. Knopf, 1979.

Nicholls, David, ed. *The Cambridge History of American Music,* 3 vols. Cambridge University Press, 1998.

"Pop." In *The New Grove Dictionary of Music and Musicians,* 2nd ed., 29 vols., edited by Stanley Sadie, 101–122. New York: Grove, 2001.

"Popular Music." In *The New Grove Dictionary of Music and Musicians,* 2nd ed., 29 vols., edited by Stanley Sadie, 128–166. New York: Grove, 2001.

Rockwell, John. *All American Music: Composition in the Late Twentieth Century.* New York: Alfred A. Knopf, 1983.

Whitcomb, Ian. *Rock Odyssey: A Musical Chronicle of the Sixties.* Garden City. New York: Doubleday & Company, Inc., 1983.

CHARLES A. WEEKS

POPULIST ERA

Populism was the American political movement that expressed the discontent of farmers and small businessmen with the late nineteenth-century transition from an agrarian to an industrially-based economy. It drew its inspiration from several political traditions. To many, the emergence of the Populist or People's Party in the early and mid-1890s, with its platforms advocating morality, temperance, and individualism, was the essence of populism. However, that party disappeared after some of its principles were absorbed by the Democratic Party and its presidential candidate William Jennings Bryan in 1896. Populism with an upper-case "P" was a mass movement among southern and western farmers during the 1870s and 1880s founded in a belief that land ownership was the essential characteristic of American life and farmers and workers deserved more public respect. In a broader sense, the term populism was based on agricultural reform movements such as the Grange, Greenback, and anti-monopoly organizations that expressed distrust of plutocracy, the elite, or any group that put itself above the masses. Regardless of how the term was defined, many American newspapers and magazines adopted and furthered the movement's objectives and a unique group of publications were launched with the set purpose of supporting Populist programs.

The earliest manifestations of populism in the American mass media occurred with the rise of Jacksonianism in the 1820s and 1830s. America newspaper editors, steeped in the Jacksonian faith of individuality and prejudice against women and blacks, advocated a free-labor system of white men without the encumbrances of privilege and built on small, individualistic producers providing for themselves. "It is true that many among us have become wealthy in a day, and without exertion;" the editor of the *Chicago American* explained in 1836, "but wealth does not necessarily beget what is commonly called 'aristocracy' . . . it is to [our] enterprise that we are mainly indebted for our unexampled prosperity" (*Chicago American,* October 22, 1836, 2). In large cities, the Penny Press became an embodiment of the Jacksonian ideal as artisans, laborers, and other members of the newly emerging middle class made their economic presence felt. Publishers such as James Gordon Bennett sold crime and political news to the new middle class in his *New York Herald* for a penny a copy in contrast to the "Wall Street press," more expensive newspapers catering to the elite. "The banks and corrupt cliques of men control them altogether," Bennett wrote in 1836 (*New York Herald,* September 6, 1836). Many Gilded Age populist newspapers would use the Jacksonian slogan, "Equal rights to all, special privileges to none" as their motto. Democratic editors who embraced the new Republican Party in the 1850s often did so to escape the elitism of a party they felt was beholden to the "Slave Power," and in the pages of northern newspapers, the Civil War was often portrayed as a contest between the "Aristocratic" South and the common-men laborers and factory owners of the North.

Of the coming industrial age, the Chicago-based *Prairie Farmer* warned in 1870, "so silently have these iron coils encircled the country . . . that not until they feel the grinding, crushing condition do [the farmers] become conscious of their condition and their doom" (*Prairie Farmer,* April 16, 1870). The *Prairie Farmer* was the first publication to devote a page to the new Grange movement in 1873. Beginning as an educational and social forum, Grangers evolved into a viable political force in the upper midwest, reaching a membership peak in 1875. In at least four states, "Granger laws" were passed to regulate railroad rates and grain elevators and warehouses. Although the Patrons of Husbandry, as the Grange was called formally, relied on meetings and speeches to advance their cause, many small country newspapers found it advantageous to align themselves with the movement. Their use of ready print, pre-printed inside pages, and boiler plate, pre-composed metal plates, reduced the cost of publishing in smaller markets and made it easier to spread the Granger message.

Grangers were joined by the Greenback Party, a failed third-party effort founded in Indiana in 1872 that used is opposition to "plutocrats" and monopolies to bring farmers and laborers together between 1876 and 1884. Greenbackism, named after Civil War paper money produced by the federal government, held that the government should adjust the currency supply to meet the needs of an expanding economy. The philosophy spread quickly among farmers after the 1873 panic because it advocated inflation, an appealing notion to debtors, but its platform of an eight-hour workday, income taxes, and women's suffrage failed to inspire urban workers due to a lack of coverage in labor and mainstream newspapers. For instance, the *Chicago Tribune* considered greenbackers political extremists, calling them in 1876, "nothing but fanatical . . . leading a forlorn hope for what they believe to be a principle" (*Chicago Tribune*, 31 July 31, 1876, 4). A growing attention to silver as a backing for money detracted from the greenback cause, and monetary policy was hard for many voters to understand in the first place. More than 100 Greenback papers appeared during the 1870s and 1880s, with titles such as *Pomeroy's Democrat*, *Peoples' Press*, *Greenback Journal*, *Louisville Legal Tender*, and *What Cheer Press* but most were tied to an individual campaign or candidate and died thereafter.

The Farmers' Alliance movement, begun in Texas in 1877 as a variant of Greenbackism, spread like a wave across the rural South. By 1888, five state groups combined to form the Southern Alliance with about three million white members. A Black organization called the Colored Alliance had seven hundred thouand members. A northern branch was started in Illinois by agricultural journalist Milton George. Using his own resources through a publication called the *Western Rural*, George's Northern Alliance attracted four hundred thousand members by 1887 and was joined by two other northern groups. Newspapers specifically marketed to farmers began addressing their more radical concerns such as currency, transportation, and the lack of attention paid to them by urban papers. The *Kansas Workman* warned in 1886 that the urban party press "exposes fraud and corruption and the next it lionizes the guilty parties." The *Chicago Tribune*, at the heart of the nation's rail system, editorialized in 1884 against the "feverish railroad building [which] leads to feverish activity in all industries and businesses, and finally the whole fabric collapses with a crash" (*Chicago Tribune*, August 8, 1884, 4). In turn, national financial newspapers opposed farmer organizations, *Dun's Weekly Review* noting in 1889 that cooperatives were absorbing "money which might otherwise go to settle indebtedness with merchants."

With farmers representing much of populism's primary base of support, voters eventually came to view it as a sectional movement. For instance, William Penn Nixon's *Chicago Inter Ocean* successfully tapped into the midwestern market for years. Its Sunday edition sold so widely in the farm belt that it was called "The Farmer's Bible" during the 1870s and 1880s, until it fell on hard times during the early 1890s and came under more urban-oriented control. The *Farmer's Voice* was published in Chicago as well, by the popular Montgomery Ward mail order company, until its radical editor, Lester C. Hubbard, displeased his publisher enough to be fired. the *Searchlight*, published by Kansas Populist Henry Vincent, moved to Chicago in the 1890s. Since more than half of all Americans continued to live in communities of twenty-five hundred or less as late as 1900, a number of dailies allied themselves with the movement and furthered its purposes including the *Topeka State Journal*, *Dakotaian*, *Butte Mining Journal*, and *Leavenworth Times*.

The People's or Populist Party came together in 1889 when the major farm reform organizations met in St. Louis. Although they failed to organize nationally, state groups enjoyed election success in 1890 in Kansas, South Dakota, and to a lesser extent Nebraska, and working through the Democratic Party, the Southern Alliance elected forty-four U. S. representatives. Emboldened by the victories, Georgia radical agitator Tom Watson started *The People's Party Paper* in 1891, the same year several editors formed the National Reform Press Association with more than one thousand members. The NRPA furnished plates of "carefully edited matter" each week to newspapers nationally and served as the main communications agency for the People's Party. A national convention in 1892 resulted in the naming of a former Greenback Congressman, James B. Weaver, as the People's Party presidential candidate. By that date, more than one thousand reform newspapers had appeared in more than two-dozen states identifying themselves as Populist or Farm Alliance. The largest was the *National Economist*, with a circulation of more than one hundred thousand and edited in Washington, D. C., by Dr. C. W. Macune, called the most creative theoretician of the agrarian revolt. Macune proposed one of the most important financial ideas to populism, a banking system for farmers' produce called the sub-treasury system. A dozen significant publications appeared in Kansas alone, including *The Advocate*, the official Alliance journal with an estimated circulation of eighty thousand, the *American Nonconformist*, and the *Kansas Commoner*. Leonidas Polk's *Progressive Farmer*, founded in Winston, North Carolina, in 1886, became involved in a Kansas controversy that led to the selection of William Peffer, an alliance member and editor of the *Kansas Farmer*, as a U. S. Senator. Even though the People's Party attracted a few big city newspapers, such as the failing *Chicago Times* (which called the party "the most remarkable uprising of popular sovereignty in our history" in 1894), to its fold, it failed to finance or sponsor a national newspaper of its own.

The usurpation of a small part of the People's Party platform against the gold standard by the Democratic Party in 1896 brought about a quick decline to populism and its press. As part of its platform, the Democrats supported the unlimited coinage of silver, and the Populists embraced the Democratic presidential candidate, former Nebraska newspaperman William Jennings Bryan. In turn, Georgia editor Tom Watson was named as the vice-presidential candidate. With the victory of Republican William McKinley, the Bryan endorsement effectively killed the Populist Party although it continued to nominate candidates for three more elections. By 1909, more than half of the Populist papers had ceased publication, and those that remained were centered in populist stronghold states such as Kansas, Minnesota, Nebraska, and Texas, where they eventually combined with labor or other reform elements. Chicago's *Prairie Farmer* merged with clear channel radio station WLS in 1928 to form one of the most powerful means of mass communication for agricultural reform interests in the twentieth century, and its editor, Clifford Gregory, was an important influence on New Deal agricultural policy. Broadcasting on Detroit radio station WJR, Catholic cleric Charles Coughlin provided a perspective during the 1930s considered populist by some.

Populism remained a term used by the press well into the twenty-first century as the American industrial economy gave way to one based on service. Journalists described a range of politicians from George McGovern, Jimmy Carter, Jessie Jackson, and Bill Clinton to Ronald Reagan, H. Ross Perot, Pat Buchanan, and Ralph Nader as populists. The label was used to identify talk show hosts, musicians, composers, film directors, organizations, and even clothing such as Banana Republic's "Men's 100% Cotton Twill Populist Pants." A populist media, from alternative or underground publications to hip-hop magazines and "podcast" Internet audio productions, flourished as well. "To be a populist," comedian Ian Shoales explained on National Public Radio in 1992, "all you have to be is popular." Liberal political columnist Molly Ivans confessed in 1996 that she loved the populist's favorite slogan, "Raise less corn and more hell."

Further Reading

O. Gene Clanton. *Populism: The Humane Preference in America, 1890–1900.* Boston: Twayne, 1990.

Lawrence Goodwyn. *Democratic Promise: The Populist Moment in America.* New York: Oxford University Press, 1976.

John D. Hicks. *The Populist Revolt: A History of the Farmers' Alliance and the People's Party.* Minneapolis: University of Minnesota Press, 1931.

Michael Kazin. *The Populist Persuasion: An American History.* Ithaca, NY: Cornell University Press, 1995.

Robert C. Macmath. *American Populism: A Social History, 1877–1898.* (New York: Hill and Wang, 1992.

RICHARD JUNGER

PORNOGRAPHY

While people throughout history have represented sexuality in literature and art, pornography as we know it today did not emerge as a mass industry until the late 1950s, eventually breaking into mainstream distribution outlets and growing to an estimated $10 billion-a-year business in the United States by the end of the twentieth century. Although still proscribed by law in a variety of ways, pornography is increasingly mainstream in contemporary culture.

State and federal law in the United States uses the term "obscenity," not "pornography," to describe sexual material that can be regulated. Obscenity prosecutions in the United States were infrequent and uncontroversial in the eighteenth and early nineteenth centuries. After the Civil War, obscenity became a more public issue, largely due to the work of Anthony Comstock and other crusaders. Obscenity became increasingly politicized in the twentieth century, as literary works such as *Ulysses* were kept out of the country.

In 1957 in *Roth v. U.S.*, the Supreme Court first stated clearly that obscenity was outside the protection of the First Amendment, kicking off a string of cases in which the court wrestled with how to define and regulate obscenity.

The *Roth* case, though, made it much more difficult to prosecute obscenity than had been the case under the 1868 English case, *Regina v. Hicklin.* U. S. Supreme Court Justice William J. Brennan Jr., who delivered the Court's opinion in the *Roth* case, said that "all ideas having even the slightest redeeming social importance" were protected by the First Amendment, unless "they encroach upon the limited area of more important interests." Most barriers to sexual expression in mass media fell after the *Roth* decision and over the next several years, there was considerable disagreement on the Court about how to define obscenity. Not until 1973 did the Court reach a consensus. In the 1973 *Miller v. California* decision, the Supreme Court established a three-part test for identifying obscenity (material that appeals to the prurient interest; portrays sexual conduct in a patently offensive way; and does not have serious literary, artistic, political, or scientific value) and identified contemporary community standards as the measure of evaluation. In decisions since *Miller*, the Supreme Court has upheld the constitutionality of zoning ordinances that restrict adult theaters and the use of racketeering statutes against businesses that sell obscene materials.

A separate category is child pornography—material that is either made using children or, in the digital age, made through the use of technology that makes it appear the sexual activity uses children. The former is illegal (*New York v. Ferber*, 1982); the status of the latter remains uncertain (*Ashcroft v. Free Speech Coalition*, 2002).

"Indecency," a term from broadcasting (over-the-air radio and television), defines a broader category that can be regulated—language or material that, in context, depicts or describes sexual or excretory organs or activities, in terms patently offensive as measured by contemporary community standards for the broadcast medium. The Federal Communications Commission administers indecency regulations.

Obscenity laws tend to be enforced in places where there is political support from citizens. This prosecutorial discretion means material for sale openly in one jurisdiction may not be available in another. However, the availability of mail-order and computer pornography means that graphic, sexually explicit material can be obtained easily anywhere in the United States. As legal prohibitions have lessened, a once-underground industry with ties to organized crime has become a routine business with its own trade magazine, *Adult Video News.* Many large, mainstream corporations are now in the business of distributing erotica or pornography.

The term used most often in the public debate over sexually explicit material is "pornography," which is not rooted in law and has no commonly accepted definition. It is sometimes used as a generic term for commercially produced sexually explicit books, magazines, movies, and Internet sites, with a distinction commonly made between soft-core (nudity with limited sexual activity that does not include penetration) and hard-core (graphic images of actual, not simulated, sexual activity including penetration). In other contexts the term is juxtaposed to erotica, defined as material that depicts sexual behavior with mutuality and respect, while pornography is material depicting sex with domination or degradation. In laboratory studies of pornography's effects, three categories of pornography have been created: overtly violent; non-violent but degrading; and sexually explicit but neither violent nor degrading.

Heterosexual pornography makes up the bulk of the commercial market. There also is a significant amount of gay male pornography available, with a smaller amount of commercially produced pornography for lesbians. Pornography has been distributed using all communication technologies: printing, photographs, film, telephones, video, DVD, and computers. *Playboy* magazine, which debuted in December 1953, was the first sex magazine to break into mainstream distribution channels. Competing magazines followed, and in the 1960s and 1970s pornographic films moved into public theaters. In the 1980s, videos began to swamp other forms of pornography, as the number of pornographic video titles steadily increased (from fifteen hundred new sexually explicit titles released in 1986 to about eleven thousand in 2001) and the circulation of magazines decreased. Computer pornography emerged in the 1990s, and the future legal status of online pornography is unclear after the Supreme Court threw out much of the Communications Decency Act, a controversial part of the 1996 telecommunications law that prohibited not only obscene but indecent material that could be viewed by children.

Pornographic films range from spliced-together collections of homemade footage, to the cheaply made movies that make up the bulk of the market, to the bigger-budget efforts that approach Hollywood production values. Most videos/DVDs are collections of sex scenes strung together with minimal, if any, plot. Oral, vaginal, and anal sex, penetration of women by more than one man at a time, and ejaculations onto women's bodies are standard.

Subgenres of pornography focus on one type of sex, such as anal sex or various fetishes. There are videos that highlight various configurations of interracial sex, usually drawing on racist stereotypes. Although there is sadomasochistic, bondage, and explicitly violent pornography, most of the films on the commercial market do not depict extreme violence, such as beatings or the use of weapons. However, various levels of less brutal violence (hair pulling, slapping, rough treatment) are present in much of the pornography that is typically labeled non-violent.

Up to the 1970s, debates over pornography pitted liberal advocates of sexual freedom against conservative proponents of traditional sexual morality. That changed with the feminist critique of pornography, which emerged out of the larger struggle against sexual violence during the second wave of the women's movement in the 1960s. Feminist critics argued that discussions of the issue should focus not on questions of subjective sexual mores, but on the harm to women, both those used in pornography and those against whom pornography is used.

Journalists have been criticized for failing to cover thoroughly the social, political, and moral issues involving pornography. Since the 1970s, pornography has often been framed simply as a First Amendment issue. Some critics have charged, though, that journalists could do more to incorporate into their work social science research into the effects of sexually explicit materials in mass media.

Further Reading

Cook, James. "The X-Rated Economy." *Forbes*, 122 (September 18, 1978), 81–88, 92.

Dworkin, Andrea. *Pornography: Men Possessing Women*. New York: Perigee, 1981. (Reprint edition, 1989, Plume).

Egan, Timothy. "Technology Sent Wall Street into Market for Pornography." *New York Times*, Oct. 23, 2000, A20.

Lane, Frederick S. *Obscene Profits: The Entrepreneurs of Pornography in the Cyber Age*. New York: Routledge, 2000.

MacKinnon, Catharine A., and Andrea Dworkin. *In Harm's Way: The Pornography Civil Rights Hearings*. Cambridge, MA: Harvard University Press, 1997.

Randall, Richard. *Freedom and Taboo: Pornography and the Politics of a Self Divided*. Berkeley: University of California Press, 1989.

Strossen, Nadine. *Defending Pornography: Free Speech, Sex, and the Fight for Women's Rights*. New York: Scribner, 1995.

Vaughn, Stephen. *Freedom and Entertainment: Rating the Movies in an Age of New Media*. New York: Cambridge University Press, 2006, 64–91, 122–68.

Williams, Linda. 1989. *Hard Core: Power, Pleasure and the "Frenzy of the Visible."* Berkeley: University of California Press, 1989.

ROBERT JENSEN

POST, EMILY PRICE

The 1922 publication of *Etiquette: In Society, In Business, In Politics and at Home* established Emily Price Post (October 27, 1872 or October 3, 1873–September 25, 1960) as the nation's preeminent authority on good manners and social graces. An immediate bestseller, the book launched Post's career as a popular and well-respected media personality. She went on to write monthly columns for magazines, produce a syndicated newspaper column, and broadcast a national radio program.

Born in Baltimore, Maryland, Post was the only daughter of Bruce and Josephine Price. The majority of sources, including the Emily Post Institute, give October 3, 1873, as Post's year of birth though some, notably the *Encyclopedia Britannica*, suggest it may have been October 27, 1872.

Moving with her family to New York at the age of five, Post lived a life of privilege (her father was a wealthy architect), educated by governesses and attending finishing school. As a debutante, she met Edwin Post, a Wall Street banker and fellow member of aristocratic New York society. The couple married in 1892, and Post settled amicably into married life, leading the typical existence of well-to-do society matron.

Post's life took an unexpected turn, however, when an editor from *Ainslie's*, a popular fiction magazine, discovered the humorous letters Post had written to her parents during her travels abroad. The editor encouraged her to take the letters and use them as inspiration for a romantic novel to be published serially in the magazine. The result was *Flight of the Moth.* Published in 1906, the fictional piece gave Post the confidence to pursue writing professionally. Despite the view by some that it was unseemly for a woman of her social stature to pursue writing for money, Post refused to be swayed by such ideas, and persisted in her work. Her writing career stood her in good financial stead after her divorce from Edwin. Able to support herself, Post made no request for alimony.

In 1922, at the age of forty-nine, Post wrote the book that would define her career. Approached by an editor from Funk & Wagnalls to write an encyclopedia of etiquette, Post was initially hesitant, but after reading existing manuals on etiquette and finding their tone infuriatingly condescending, Post agreed to the project. The book became an instant bestseller; it was reprinted eight times within the first year. Post's straightforward, down-to-earth approach resonated with readers. Disdainful of pretension, she believed manners were about making others feel comfortable.

The popular success of *Etiquette* attracted the attention of the media. Post contracted to write a monthly page on etiquette for *McCall's* magazine. She also produced a syndicated daily newspaper column, "Social Problems," which appeared in hundreds of newspapers across the country. And in 1929, she began hosting a radio program on etiquette. Airing three times a week in a coast-to-coast broadcast, the show reached millions of listeners. Post's ability to connect with her audience while providing direct and sensible advice on good manners ensured the show's success, prompting President Franklin Delano Roosevelt to say that the greatest compliment he received when he began his fireside chats was, "You're as good as Emily Post."

Post died in 1960 at the age of eighty-six. At the time of her death, *Etiquette* was in its eighty-ninth printing. The legacy of Emily Post is maintained today through the work of the Emily Post Institute, which addresses issues of civility in contemporary society. Having helped millions navigate the often-confusing terrain of social graces, Emily Post remains firmly entrenched in the American lexicon, synonymous with good manners, graciousness, and decorum.

Further Reading

"Emily Post Institute." http://www.emilypost.com.
Post, Edwin. *Truly Emily Post*. New York: Funk & Wagnalls, 1961.
Post, Emily. *Etiquette: In Society, In Business, In Politic, and at Home*. New York: Funk & Wagnalls, 1922.
———. *The Personality of a House: The Blue Book of Home Design and Decoration*. New York: Funk & Wagnalls, 1930.

SARAH BURKE ODLAND

POSTAL ACTS OF 1792, 1845, 1879

The Post Office performed two services indispensable to newspapers as they developed through the nineteenth century: It aided editors' news-gathering efforts, and it carried publications from print shop to readers. In the late 1800s, postal laws also began adjusting to the expanding role of advertising and magazines in American journalism.

Postal Act of 1792

The Post Office Act of February 20, 1792, the first overhaul of postal laws under the Constitution, represented the nation's earliest communication policy. The act committed the federal government to facilitate the circulation of news by extending several privileges to the press.

The 1792 postal law, modified slightly in 1794, allowed newspapers—regardless of size, weight, or advertising content—to circulate within one hundred miles or anywhere in the state of publication for 1 cent; those mailed outside the state and beyond one hundred miles paid 1.5 cents. Letter postage, in contrast, was divided into nine zones, ranging from a minimum of 6 cents per sheet for delivery up to thirty miles to a maximum of 25 cents per sheet for any distance beyond 450 miles. The privilege accorded the press was striking, especially considering differences in size. The typical newspaper was three to four times the size of a one-sheet letter. Thus, a three-sheet letter mailed beyond 450 miles paid 75 cents when a newspaper could be dispatched for 1.5 cents.

Congress adopted this policy favoring newspapers, most of which had partisan affiliations, to bind the nation together as a political entity. The generation that crafted the first postal policy recognized that the geographic and social diversity of the United States threatened national unity. In *Federalist* No. 84, Alexander Hamilton anticipated the problem as well as the solution for a nation fraying at the edges: "[P]ublic papers will be expeditious messengers of intelligence to the most remote inhabitants of the Union." During debates on the 1792 postal law, lawmakers of various political factions echoed Hamilton's point in supporting low, relatively flat (that is, just two zones) newspaper postage. A few members of Congress, however, expressed concerns that cheap newspaper postage would unleash a flood of city newspapers into the countryside to compete with local publications.

The 1792 law also facilitated the long-distance flow of news by allowing editors to exchange their papers postage-free. Long before the advent of press associations and the telegraph, editors liberally reprinted non-local information culled from newspapers obtained through the mails. The practice, which began in colonial times, was formalized by the 1792 postal law: "[E]very printer of newspapers may send one paper to each and every other printer of newspapers within the United States, free of postage, under such regulations, as the Postmaster General shall provide." Editors made liberal use of this postal privilege. On the eve of the War of 1812, for example, frontier papers borrowed seven times more news than they produced locally. During a thirty-one-day period in 1843, publishers received an average of 364 exchanges. Congress continued postage-free printers' exchanges until 1873; by that time, the telegraph and the press associations using it had matured sufficiently to provide superior nationwide news-gathering services.

Postal policy established in 1792 thus allowed newspaper editors to gather news from anywhere in the nation at no cost and then to disseminate it to readers, also anywhere, at low rates. For political papers, exchanges tied small-town publications to the county seat, state capital, and federal capital. Because of the service's reciprocal nature, papers in state capitals as well as Washington, D.C., obtained a great deal of political intelligence from towns throughout the nation. By exchanging news through the mails on highly favorable terms, hundreds of party papers synthesized a national political community that transcended local orientations. Emulating political parties, countless other antebellum groups—religious denominations, reform interests (e.g., abolitionists, public school advocates), professional societies, and more—began using the nearly uniform newspaper rates and postage-free exchanges to build their national associations. Most notably, antislavery groups capitalized on the postal system to sustain a national (or at least a northern) movement. People who never met face-to-face because of geography and primitive transports formed communities of interest by sharing information in periodicals carried through the mails.

Postal Act of 1845

Although provisions lowering letter postage formed the centerpiece of the Post Office Act of March 3, 1845, Congress did make two changes affecting the press. Postage remained unchanged for all newspapers under 1,900 square inches; larger papers paid higher magazine rates. This size limit responded to demands that postage bear some relation to the size of publications. In fixing the 1,900-inch size limit, however, Congress carefully determined that standard papers would continue to enjoy the lowest rates.

As part of the 1845 postal reform, Congress created a new category of newspaper postage: free delivery for weekly newspapers within thirty miles of the office of publication. This measure aimed to make local papers, especially those in rural areas, more competitive with urban dailies by relieving subscribers of postage. This privilege sparked considerable debate, especially over which regions stood to benefit the most. Petitioners, mainly from rural areas, told Congress that most towns now supported their own publications. Congress withdrew the provision of free local circulation in 1847 because of declining revenues but restored it in a different form in 1851. Whereas the 1845 law had a thirty-mile postage-free zone, the new act permitted most weekly papers to circulate without charge in their county of publication. Some advocates underscored the cultural benefits of protecting the country press from "The poisoned sentiments of the cities, concentrated in their papers," as one congressman put it during the debates. Others simply pointed out that the free in-county provision simply compensated the rural press for the privileges that encouraged the long-distance circulation of city newspapers. Current postal law continues to accord privileges to periodicals that circulate within the county of publication.

Postal Act of 1879

The Post Office Act of March 3, 1879, laid the foundation for modern mail classification by creating the basic mail categories used until the 1990s—first class for letters, second class for periodicals, third class for advertising, and fourth class for parcels. The Mail Classification Act's more narrow purpose, however, was to align postal policy with late nineteenth-century developments in the newspaper, magazine, and advertising industries.

Crude rate classifications devised between 1863 and 1876 unsuccessfully aimed to confine the most favored rate—two cents a pound after 1874—to bona fide newspapers and magazines. Advertising material in the third class paid postage eight times higher than that charged periodicals in the second class. Enterprising advertisers thus began issuing their promotional material just frequently enough to qualify as periodicals, postal administrators complained. Some of these publications had no regular list of subscribers and subsisted entirely on advertising revenue. A series of administrative rulings in the mid-1870s unsuccessfully labored to divert the flood of advertising sheets to the more expensive third class.

To strengthen its hand, the Post Office urged Congress to redefine the primitive second-class mail category so that it clearly excluded advertising circulars. Postal officials fine-tuned the legislation in consultation with leading newspaper and magazine publishers in New York City, Philadelphia, and perhaps other large cities. Despite differences, newspaper and magazine interests closed ranks with one another and with postal authorities against the so-called illegitimate periodicals, publications designed primarily for advertising purposes. The negotiations assured that monthly and quarterly magazines and trade journals would still qualify as bona fide periodicals despite the growing volume of advertising they carried.

Congress intended the Mail Classification Act of 1879 to subsidize informative periodicals in the second class while relegating advertising matter to the much more expensive third class. To qualify for the second class, a publication had to (1) appear at regular intervals at least four times a year; (2) come from a known office of publication; (3) consist of printed sheets without substantial binding; and (4) disseminate "information of a public character, or be devoted to literature, the sciences, arts, or some special industry, and having a legitimate list of subscribers." In addition, the 1879 law specifically excluded from the second class "publications designed primarily for advertising purposes, or for free circulation, or for circulation at nominal rates." Much of the 1879 statutory language still determines publications' postal classification.

When Congress halved second-class postage to one cent a pound in 1885, moderately priced magazines began blanketing the nation, marking the emergence of the modern magazine industry. Many of these new magazines quickly filled with advertising, and postal officials spent decades embroiled in controversies about which deserved the most favorable postal rates. Congress partly resolved the policy controversy with a 1917 law that charged periodicals a dual rate: a lower flat rate on their editorial content and higher postage scaled to distance on their advertising matter. This approach treated advertising on the pages of periodicals more like advertising circulars in the third class. The rate structure for periodicals devised in 1917 remains a cornerstone of postal policy today.

Further Reading

John, Richard R. *Spreading the News: The American Postal System from Franklin to Morse*. Cambridge, MA: Harvard University Press, 1995.

Kielbowicz, Richard B. *News in the Mail: The Press, Post Office, and Public Information, 1700-1860s*. Westport, CT: Greenwood Press, 1989.

Kielbowicz, Richard B. "Origins of the Second-Class Mail Category and the Business of Policymaking, 1863–1879." *Journalism Monographs* No. 96 (1986).

Kielbowicz, Richard B. "Postal Subsidies for the Press and the Business of Mass Culture, 1880–1920." *Business History Review* 64 (Autumn 1990): 451–488.

Kielbowicz, Richard B., and Linda Lawson, "Protecting the Small-Town Press: Community, Social Policy and Postal Privileges, 1845–1970." *Canadian Review of American Studies* 19 (Spring 1988): 23–45.

Post Office Act of Feb. 20, 1792, c. 7, 1 Stat. 232.

Post Office Act of May 8, 1794, c. 23, 1 Stat. 354.

Post Office Act of Mar. 3, 1845, c. 43, 5 Stat. 732.

Post Office Act of Mar. 3, 1879 (Mail Classification Act), c. 180, 20 Stat. 355.

Starr, Paul. *The Creation of the Media: Political Origins of Modern Communications*. New York: Basic Books, 2004.

War Revenue Act, Act of October 3, 1917, c. 63, 40 Stat. 300.

RICHARD B. KIELBOWICZ

PRESIDENCY AND THE PRESS: MCKINLEY TO WILSON

A new relationship emerged between presidents and journalists at the start of the twentieth century, changing how presidents governed and how Americans saw their national leaders in the press. Presidents between 1897 and 1921, especially Theodore Roosevelt and Woodrow Wilson, increasingly turned to daily newspapers and national magazines to appeal for public support of their policies and to overshadow their opponents. The growing availability of news from the president attracted larger numbers of reporters, the nucleus of the modern White House press corps. New practices of managing the press were established, including news releases, daily staff briefings and the first regular presidential press conferences, meeting with the correspondents in a group rather than individually. Daily headlines from the White House helped to create the appearance of authoritative leadership and increased the president's ability to lead public opinion in peace and war.

Earlier presidents had at times used the press, but William McKinley, president from 1897 to 1901, was the first since Abraham Lincoln to seek popular support for a major military campaign, the Spanish-American war. Although not a journalist himself, McKinley was familiar with newspapers from his ten years in Congress and as governor of Ohio. Within days of his inauguration, he attended a meeting of the Gridiron Club and invited Washington, D.C., correspondents to attend an inaugural reception. Later in his first year, he invited them to a holiday party at the executive mansion. These small steps were welcomed by the correspondents, whose relationships with McKinley's immediate predecessors had been distant. David S. Barry, a correspondent for the Republican *New York Sun*, wrote hopefully "there are signs the era of friendliness between public men and newspaper reporters will be restored." However, McKinley remained a target for Democratic newspapers, led by Joseph Pulitzer's *New York World*, which accused him of being a captive of monopolistic trusts, led by wealthy Republican businessman Mark Hanna, who managed McKinley's 1896 campaign against William Jennings Bryan.

As president, McKinley read New York and Washington, D.C., newspapers to help keep track of what was presumed to be popular opinion, and perused a daily scrapbook of clippings from regional newspapers under the title of "Current Comment." Monitoring the press became more urgent as McKinley came under increasing pressure to invade Cuba. Stories of purported atrocities appeared in sensational newspapers such as Pulitzer's *World* and William Randolph Hearst's *New York Journal*. Demands for war peaked in February 1898 after an unexplained explosion sank the U.S. battleship *Maine* in Havana harbor. The crisis drew crowds of correspondents to the executive mansion, where they were handed typewritten statements urging restraint to pass along to their editors, who customarily printed them without identifying the president by name as a source.

Once war was officially declared, a "war room" with maps and twenty telegraph lines was established in the executive mansion, where McKinley tried to centralize the flow of war information. Reporters thronged the halls, but McKinley largely delegated personal contact with the press to his staff and remained personally aloof. In August 1898, he refused the requests of reporters and photographers to witness the signing of the peace protocol on grounds that the press might mar the dignity of the occasion.

Postwar controversies and continued fighting in the Philippines had the effect of keeping the chief executive in the headlines. Sensing the presidency was becoming a news "beat," George Cortelyou, McKinley's chief of staff, set out to make permanent some of the news management practices developed during the war. These included having press statements available on demand; allowing more opportunities to speak with the president personally, even though off the record; treating correspondents from Republican and Democratic newspapers more or less equally; and establishing a priority schedule for releasing official statements and speeches, including the annual Message to

Congress. By early 1901, McKinley's relationship with the press had become so organized he could instruct Cortelyou to distribute the statement he would not seek a third term "by the usual channels." No "usual channels" had existed between the president and the press when McKinley had taken office. Although McKinley's second term was ended by assassination in September 1901, he had established a foundation for systematic use of the press by subsequent presidents, beginning with Theodore Roosevelt.

McKinley had found the press a useful tool to promote the war effort, but Roosevelt made publicity a central feature of his presidency. Roosevelt's outspokenness and distinctive appearance made him a magnet for press coverage throughout his long public career, from flamboyant leader of the "Rough Riders" in Cuba to governor of New York and vice president. Hours after McKinley's funeral, Roosevelt met with leaders of the major press associations to declare new ground rules: He would be open and accessible to reporters who kept his confidences, but those who wrote stories he disliked would be banished.

From 1901 to 1909, Roosevelt met daily, sometimes hourly, with favored correspondents, the "fair-haired boys" from Republican newspapers and occasionally from Democratic ones, presenting them with candid off-the-record comments, news tips and instructions on how to write their stories. "Roosevelt seldom spoke without seeing a picture of how the sentence would look in type, and how it would affect the mind of the readers," wrote Henry L. Stoddard of the *Philadelphia Press*. Although he rarely allowed himself to be quoted directly, Roosevelt easily dominated the headlines, much to the exasperation of his political opponents and GOP party leaders in Congress.

Roosevelt also reached beyond the Washington, D.C., press corps to cultivate reform-minded writers for national magazines, who generally supported his policies despite his critical characterization of them as "muckrakers." The outpouring of publicity helped make Roosevelt the twentieth century's first celebrity president and had the less-desired effect of placing his family in the press spotlight as well. A small bear Roosevelt spared on a hunting trip in Mississippi became the novelty "Teddy bear." The president's rebellious teen-age daughter became "Princess Alice" and the focus of a popular song, "Alice Blue Gown."

Roosevelt's presidency also was marked by an expansion of publicity activities in government agencies. With the aid of forester and fellow reformer Gifford Pinchot, who created one of the first "press bureaus" in the U.S. Forest Service, Roosevelt participated in a series of newsworthy "events" to promote conservation and development of natural resources, including a Mississippi River steamboat cruise and the first national governor's conference at the White House. Congressional opponents were so frustrated at the news coverage they tried unsuccessfully to legislate restrictions on agency promotional campaigns and other publicity practices.

William Howard Taft, president from 1909 to 1913, was as reserved in dealing with the press as Roosevelt had been exuberant. The consequences of Taft's policy of "nonpublicity" showed how much the relationship between presidents and the press had changed under McKinley and Roosevelt. Although Taft had once been a reporter in Cincinnati, Ohio, he did not share Roosevelt's view of the press as a bully audience and source of useful news coverage. Taft discontinued Roosevelt's daily briefings of correspondents, allowed few interviews, and resisted attempts by his military attaché, Archie Butt, to publicize the president. In a letter to journalist William Allen White, Taft wrote: "I am not constituted as Mr. Roosevelt is in being able to keep the country advised every few days on as to the continuance of the state of mind in reference to reform. It is a difference in temperament. He talked with correspondents a great deal. His heart was generally on his sleeve and he must communicate his feelings. I find myself unable to do so." Instead of publicity, Taft said in a rare magazine interview, "what I hope for my administration is the accomplishment of definite results, which will be self-explanatory."

Taft's reticence was a shock to a White House press corps that had come to rely on frequent presidential briefings, advisories, or newsworthy stunts to supply the daily demands of their editors. The correspondents were forced to seek news tips from sources in Congress and also from Taft's critics, including appointees of Roosevelt still in policymaking positions. These holdovers, especially Pinchot, used the news vacuum to publicize their unhappiness with what they regarded as Taft's betrayal of Roosevelt's legacy.

Only after the Democrats won control of Congress for the first time since 1894 and Roosevelt showed increasing signs of running again did Taft seek to make news in his own behalf. He became more accessible to the press and experimented with inviting leading correspondents to group interviews. But Taft's popularity and his presidency had suffered from not meeting the expectations of newsworthy behavior created in the press by McKinley and Roosevelt. Roosevelt's third-party campaign split the Republican Party in 1912, and Democrat Woodrow Wilson was elected president.

Wilson's political experience was limited to two years as governor of New Jersey but as a political scientist he had long viewed the press as a means to create public support for a stronger presidency. As president, he established the first regularly scheduled presidential press conferences open to all correspondents, regardless of political affiliation. These conferences, held twice a week at first, drew one hundred or more correspondents and hangers-on, prompting Wilson to demand self-regulation to control the crowding, a move that led to creation of the White House Correspondents Association.

Correspondents were allowed to question the president freely, but Wilson's responses could be prickly and misleading, as well as off the record. "Of course, I bluffed you," he admitted at a 1914 news conference. Hugh Baillie of United Press International described Wilson's comments as "so artful the meaning of what he said didn't dawn on people until they were outside." Wilson rarely allowed himself to be quoted directly and often was dissatisfied with the resulting stories. "Do not believe anything you read in the newspapers. If you read the papers I see, they are utterly untrustworthy," he wrote to a close friend, Mary Hulbert. Wilson did not enjoy the group encounters with correspondents, and they were discontinued in 1915, ostensibly because of the outbreak of World War I in Europe. Wilson's unhappiness with the press stemmed in part from newspaper coverage of his family life, especially the social lives of his teen-aged daughters. Two daughters, Jessie and Eleanor, were married in the White House within a six-month period in 1913–1914 in the full glare of newspaper and magazine coverage.

Wilson's relations with the press changed abruptly in 1917 when the U.S. entered World War I. The president created the Committee on Public Information (CPI), the twentieth century's first war propaganda agency, and delegated to its director, George Creel, the chore of dealing with the press. Wilson worried that military information might leak to the enemy from the press, but Congress refused to grant him authority to censor newspapers directly. Instead, the CPI warned the nation's editors against using news deemed to be dangerous or unpatriotic. In addition, Wilson's postmaster general denied mailing privileges to hundreds of publications on security grounds. After the Armistice in November 1918, Wilson took 150 correspondents to Europe with him to negotiate terms of the peace, but the resulting news coverage did not prove helpful in persuading Americans to support ratification of the Treaty of Versailles. On returning to the United States, he launched a strenuous but unsuccessful speaking tour to urge its ratification by the Senate and suffered an incapacitating stroke in September 1919 that ended his personal contact with the press corps.

Between 1897 and 1921, presidents McKinley, Roosevelt, Taft, and Wilson had experimented with differing approaches to managing the press to promote or to deflect news coverage. Their successes and failures contributed to making press relations a major feature of the twentieth-century presidency and established a foundation for the modern White House press corps.

Further Reading

Elmer C. Cornwell. *Presidential Leadership of Public Opinion.* Westport, CT: Greenwood Press, 1979, originally 1965.

Robert C. Hilderbrand. *Power and the People: Executive Management of Public Opinion in Foreign Affairs, 1897–1921.* Chapel Hill: University of North Carolina Press, 1981.

George Juergens. *News from the White House: The Presidential-Press Relationship in the Progressive Era.* Chicago: University of Chicago Press, 1981.

Stephen Ponder. *Managing the Press: Origins of the Media Presidency, 1897–1933.* New York: St. Martin's, 1998.

James D. Startt. *Woodrow Wilson and the Press: Prelude to the Presidency.* New York: Palgrave, 2004.

Stephen Vaughn. *Holding Fast the Inner Lines: Democracy, Nationalism and the Committee on Public Information.* Chapel Hill: University of North Carolina Press, 1980.

STEPHEN PONDER

PRESIDENCY AND THE PRESS: HARDING TO HOOVER

The Republican administrations between Woodrow Wilson's and Franklin D. Roosevelt's terms in office are considered transitional presidencies. Warren Harding, Calvin Coolidge, and Herbert Hoover are not remembered as outstanding chief executives. A part of their failures may have been their inabilities to communicate through the press. In the cases of Harding and Hoover, one might not have expected such weaknesses. Harding was a newspaper publisher from Ohio and should have thrived in journalistic circles, while Hoover, as secretary of commerce under Harding and Coolidge, had built a solid reputation partly because he had worked well with the few reporters who covered his office. Hoover also had directed a well-organized, modern, public relations-oriented campaign against Al Smith in the 1928 election. Coolidge, a taciturn, hardworking Yankee, concentrated on his duties in office and was direct in his statements to reporters. His stinginess with words has been exaggerated, but nonetheless he did not like answering questions and his weak press relations were predictable.

The Progressive Era, a time of idealistic reform, was coming to an end as Harding took office. A generation earlier, he had purchased the *Marion Daily Star*, a newspaper near his boyhood home, for $300 and had built it into a success with the help of his wife, Florence. She was more ambitious than he and, at her urging, he entered politics. He served in the Ohio Senate and then as lieutenant governor before being elected to the U.S. Senate in 1914. The Ohio Republican polled 60 percent of the vote in the 1920 presidential election over James Cox, another newspaper publisher and the governor of Ohio. Harding's election represented a rejection of Wilson's hope for U.S. participation in the League of Nations and he promised an era of "normalcy" unencumbered by foreign entanglements, and an end to Progressive politics.

Harding had only personal secretaries, who dealt with reporters, not a formal press secretary. He usually took care of his own press relations, meeting with reporters informally. A handsome man, Harding was one of the first presidents to use newsreels and photo opportunities successfully. He posed and joked at press conferences, because that was how he was most effective, so silent newsreels fit his approach. By the time he took office, newsreels had been in use for twenty-five years with five major companies producing clips viewed in theaters between feature presentations. Newsreels were silent until late 1926. Early, presidential newsreel shots were difficult because cameras were bulky and heavy and setting up was time-consuming and expensive. Indoor newsreel footage required several bright, hot lights. The room temperature could exceed 100 degrees. Despite the 1920s prohibition on the sale and consumption of alcohol, Harding kept a stocked liquor cabinet in the White House and liked to play poker, sometimes with reporters, in the evening. He appointed many strong cabinet officers including Secretary of State Charles Evans Hughes, Secretary of the Treasury Andrew Mellon, Secretary of Agriculture Henry C. Wallace, and Hoover. With these men in place, Harding preferred to leave policy decisions to them and others. Some in his cabinet and "the Ohio Gang," who were informal advisors, took advantage of Harding's lack of interest. His Secretary of the Interior Albert Fall accepted bribes in return for government oil leases in New Mexico and Wyoming. The Teapot Dome scandal began to break as Harding left for a tour of the West Coast in the summer of 1923. Under stress and suffering from high blood pressure, he wanted to get away from the poisoned atmosphere in Washington where once friendly reporters had begun to hound him. He traveled to Alaska by train and then down the coast to San Francisco, where he died of a heart attack. Stephen Early, who later became Franklin Roosevelt's press secretary, was working for the Associated Press and was one of the first correspondents to report Harding's death. Early was suspicious of rosy press reports handed out when Harding was first stricken and stayed up all night waiting for the latest word. Harding was mourned as a hero immediately after his death, but reports of the oil scandal and Harding's adulterous affair with the daughter of a friend in Marion soon sullied his reputation.

Coolidge Sworn In

Vacationing in Plymouth, Vermont, at the time of Harding's death, Coolidge was sworn in as president at his parents' home by his father, a justice of the peace. Coolidge was perhaps the most conservative president of the twentieth century. As governor of Massachusetts, he had used heavy-handed tactics to end a Boston police strike in 1919. He was an honest, straight-forward president whose pro-business attitude and laissez-faire philosophy fit the prosperous 1920s. Voters soon forgot about the Harding scandals to which Coolidge had no connection and Coolidge easily won reelection over John W. Davis in 1924.

Headline writers coined the phrase "Silent Cal" to describe Coolidge's economy of words, but Coolidge held regular press conferences twice weekly and the moniker was an exaggeration. It was not the practice of presidents to field questions extemporaneously in the 1920s. Questions had to be submitted in writing and the president could not be quoted directly. When questions were posed orally, he either answered with a few words or did not respond, but that was typical of the times. As with Harding, no one in the Coolidge White House was designated to be a press secretary. Coolidge understood the need to accommodate newsreel teams and photographers, but did not like posing for shots nor did he appear particularly presidential during photo opportunities. He was a slight man who was usually self-conscious about picture taking.

Not much news emanated from the White House during Coolidge's tenure, but, like the electorate, newspaper publishers tended to be Republican, so Coolidge gained favorable coverage and the support of the preponderance of the nation's newspapers. Harding was the first president

to speak over the radio, but because Coolidge was in office three years longer, he had more radio addresses. In the judgment of many historians, neither man used the new medium effectively.

Nothing typified Coolidge's understated press relations more than his announcement that he would not seek reelection in 1928. While vacationing in Rapid City, South Dakota, in August 1927, almost exactly four years after Harding's death, Coolidge lined up reporters in a classroom of a local high school and handed out slips of paper. Printed on each slip was the statement, "I do not choose to run for President in 1928." He barely elaborated on that statement during the rest of his life.

Coolidge's withdrawal set up one of the classic elections of the twentieth century. Hoover easily won the Republican nomination and Al Smith, the Democratic nod. Hoover was originally from Iowa, though he lived much of his boyhood with his uncle and aunt in Oregon and traveled the world as a mining engineer. Still, voters thought of him as "small town" and Smith, governor of New York, as "big city." Hoover favored Prohibition and Smith opposed it. More importantly to voters of the time, Smith was a Roman Catholic and Hoover a Protestant. Journalists touted the contrasts throughout the election and bigots worried that the Pope would be running the country, if Smith were elected. Moreover, Hoover had been an able food administrator during World War I and an extremely competent secretary of commerce for seven years under two presidents. He had gained the admiration of the public and reporters in 1927 when flooding along the Mississippi River had left thousands homeless. He organized rescue efforts and food distribution flawlessly. He was known as the "Great Organizer." The emphasis on Smith's Catholicism in 1928 ignored the outstanding record Hoover had achieved prior to his election and his immense popularity after World War I. Hoover's inauguration in March 1929 appeared on sound newsreel. More like a home movie, the twenty-minute production had no narrator, so most sound was crowd noise. At the podium the microphone caught Hoover's speech erratically, his voice sounding far away and tinny. Hoover tolerated newsreels at first, but later refused to appear in them when wife Lou Henry told him they made him look much older.

Hoover, Reporters Meet

Three days after taking office, Hoover asked a committee of reporters to have dinner with him and discuss press conference rules. He insisted on retaining the requirement that questions be submitted in writing beforehand with answers given at twice-weekly press conferences, but, in what he considered a generous concession, he agreed to allow reporters to quote him directly. He added the stipulation that any direct quotation be followed by the phrase "in reply to a question from representatives of the press the president stated today." He wanted to make it clear to the public that opinions were being elicited and that he was not just commenting on every issue that came before him. Hoover returned to the practice of specifying a staff member as press secretary, as Wilson had done. George Akerson, an editor from Minnesota, served for two years, and then was replaced by a White House correspondent from Boston, Theodore Joslin. Neither man handled reporters well.

More than two hundred journalists attended Hoover's first press conferences, but, when it became clear that there would be no extemporaneous give-and-take, they stopped appearing. They could pick up a copy of Hoover's written statements later. The press conference, itself, was superfluous. Worse, Hoover favored certain reporters who wrote only positively about him and regarded any reporter who wrote negatively as an enemy. His favoritism rankled.

On October 29, 1929, the stock market convulsed for a second time in a week and by the end of November had lost 60 percent of its value. Fear swept the nation and Hoover did not know how to react. Within a year of the crash, unemployment nationwide reached record levels. Hoover was an ineffective radio speaker and could not reassure the public through the press, because he did not know what to say. He was an organizer, not a speaker. His policies for direct relief to the unemployed relied on voluntarism from the private sector and that effort failed, too.

Reporters, who had been unhappy with his press conferences and his favoritism, were inclined to write negative stories and found willing audiences. Hoover sulked and remained aloof from most of the press, so journalists found other venues for quotations, usually Hoover's political opponents. Hoover was a nineteenth-century man living in a twentieth-century White House. He felt that, as with the journalism with which he grew up in the 1880s and 1890s, reporters either favored a political office holder or wholeheartedly opposed him. There was no such thing as objectivity, in Hoover's estimation, so when criticism was published, he decided that nearly the entire press corps had come to despise him.

Bonus March

When World War I veterans marched on Washington in the spring and summer of 1932 seeking early payment of a bonus they were promised in 1924, they were routed by armed soldiers with bayonets and tear gas and driven from their shanties outside Washington. The Bonus Rout seemed to epitomize the perceived heartlessness of the Hoover Administration. Ironically, because the ex-soldiers erroneously had been labeled Communists by the government and the press, nearly all newspapers supported Hoover for routing the marchers. Actually, General Douglas MacArthur had exceeded his orders in driving the men from Washington, but Hoover never explained MacArthur's actions to the public.

The White House rejoiced when the Democrats nominated Franklin D. Roosevelt in 1932. Hoover remarked privately that Roosevelt, who had suffered an attack of infantile paralysis eleven years earlier, would not be a worthy candidate because of his infirmity. Hoover was so isolated from the press and public that, until late October 1932, he still thought he would win the election. Only after meeting hostile crowds around the country did Hoover realize that he would lose.

Newspapers, which had endorsed Hoover in overwhelming numbers in 1928, remained aloof. Hoover commanded the support of barely 50 percent of the nation's editorial boards. Many had sent staffers to work on his campaign in 1928, but said they could not spare their people in 1932. Hoover, who had always been adored by the public until 1929, could not understand the change of heart. In truth, the Depression was not his doing. He had been in office only seven months, when the crash occurred, but he could not stem the panic that ensued and so he bore the brunt of the ill will of the public and the press. In all likelihood, good press relations would not have saved Hoover in 1932, but his inability to gain favor with reporters drove him into isolation and made the criticism all the more hurtful.

Not only did Franklin Roosevelt's victory in 1932 change the political and ideological balance in the country, but it also changed press-presidential relations. No longer would a president be able to control information flow by requiring written questions in advance and passing out a few statements to reporters. Radio (and later television) became regular tools for dissemination of presidential comments. Press conferences became major productions. Harding, Coolidge, and Hoover represented the last of the presidents who relied on old-fashioned press relations. They did not spend much time worrying about the reporters and imagery. Their policy failures and their lack of rapport with the press corps would only look worse when matched against the performance of their successor, the master of the media, Franklin D. Roosevelt.

Further Reading

Best, Gary D. *The Dollar Decade: Mammon and the Machine in 1920s America*. Westport, CT: Praeger, 2003.

Dean, John W. *Warren G. Harding*. New York: Times Books, 2004.

Ferrell. Robert H. *The Presidency of Calvin Coolidge*. Lawrence: University of Kansas, 1998.

——. *The Strange Deaths of President Harding*. Columbia: University of Missouri Press, 1996.

Liebovich, Louis W. *Bylines in Despair: Herbert Hoover, the Great Depression, and the U.S. News Media*. Westport, CT: Praeger, 1994.

Walch, Timothy, ed. *Uncommon Americans: The Lives and Legacies of Herbert and Lou Henry Hoover*. Westport, CT: Praeger 2003.

LOUIS W. LIEBOVICH

PRESIDENCY AND THE PRESS: FRANKLIN D. ROOSEVELT AND TRUMAN

When Franklin D. Roosevelt died on April 12, 1945, a White House system of communication was already well in place. After twelve years as president, FDR and his administration had made many informational changes that were continued by Harry S Truman and subsequent presidents: a designated press secretary, press conferences on a regular basis, a concerted use all the available media technologies, and an overall administrative system of war communications (World War II not yet officially over). By the end of 1945, the Office of Censorship and the Office of War Information were disbanded, although the openness and availability of documents that had characterized the New Deal would not return to the executive branch.

Press Secretary Stephen T. ("Steve") Early announced Roosevelt's death. Roosevelt had established that his press secretary would have access to the president, an understanding of the issues, a mastery of details, and an astute ability to get along with journalists. Previous presidents had had secretaries who had been former journalists and assisted in a president's press relations, but FDR's first designated press secretary had a title and duties that meant a singular devotion to news.

No one matched Roosevelt in the number of press conferences, almost one thousand, or more than one a week up into his fourth term in office. He found the meetings useful. They were an efficient way to get information out and keep in touch with the public, and also a means to influence the messages about his administration and garner enough public support to pass his programs. By having regular press conferences, the Roosevelt created an expectation of a regular flow of news. And, when he did not meet with the press, the White House correspondents loudly complained. The meetings were mutually useful. With so much news happening, especially during the New Deal and World War II, Washington journalists needed an efficient way to gather news. Roosevelt gave out what he considered to be necessary information, defined the issues, and set the agenda. Roosevelt had the knowledge and the ability to think quickly under pressure, and unless he was ill, he enjoyed the exchange. With Roosevelt's personality and confidence, he could handle most questions, and still keep the correspondents at bay as subordinates. Roosevelt left a legacy not only for his news management at press meetings, but for following the results. One of his secretaries put together a type of internal daily news intelligence report. That type of summation has continued through today and now includes a daily news synopses of the cable, network television, and radio coverage of presidential and administration news and editorials along with editorial cartoons.

Both Roosevelt and Truman used public opinion polling. During Roosevelt's first two presidential election campaigns in 1932 and 1936, polling was in its infancy but by 1940, the he was testing the public's views about the war. Previously, the American newspapers and their editorials had been a major gauge of public viewpoints. During Roosevelt's war years, Gallup polls became the basis for news stories and regular columns. White House communications after Roosevelt increasingly relied on opinion polling with full-time polling advisers to test reactions to policies and legislation before Congress, and even to test potential themes in State of the Union messages.

The White House press bureaucracy, existing prior to Roosevelt, grew with the addition to the many New Deal agencies and their allotted funds for publicity. Now, as an accepted part of government, information officers are in every department and agency to write speeches, meet with journalists, make news releases, arrange interviews, and hold press conferences and briefings, much as was done during the New Deal years. Such a news bureaucracy has extended to Congress, the courts, and even to state and local governments. Overall coordination of agency, department and White House information began with Roosevelt during his second term. Such efforts were more refined during World War II when information could become yet another weapon. Such formalized domestic information offices continued to grow with subsequent presidents from Richard M. Nixon's Office of Telecommunications Policy to George W. Bush's Office of Public Liaison.

The New Deal era was open and flexible, allowing for disagreements among officials to be played out in the media. Yet, once the country was in the war, the president and the rest of the federal government became secretive, focused to the point of intractable, and speaking in one voice to the world. When Roosevelt closed off the information access during World War II, so too did the rest of the executive branch. Such secrecy continued to some extent when Harry Truman became president, then opened up at the end of World War II, only to return during the Cold War and the Korea War.

Immediately after the declaration of war, Roosevelt put into place two information offices: the Office of War Information and the Office of Censorship, both moribund by the end of 1945. Yet, these two offices begot other information agencies that have continued up to today. The United States Information Agency and the Voice of America hired many of the seasoned World War II workers as did the State Department and later the Central Intelligence Agency. More and more presidents want coordinated domestic information and an international and foreign news synchronization.

Roosevelt relied upon all the media of his day to the point of technological artistry. FDR's images appeared in not just photographs and picture magazines, but also in newsreels. Roosevelt's press secretary gave the access, set the numbers, even the distance, and suggested photography and newsreel shots and backdrops. A consistent taboo was the depiction of Roosevelt's legs and reminders of his polio disability.

Roosevelt's word images came in the form of his radio addresses and especially those memorable fireside chats. Roosevelt used common words, giving an air of informality to his presentations. The fireside chats were casual, short, and immensely popular. FDR's press secretary dribbled the news and hinted at topics to build an audience from the print media. When these chats began during the Great Depression, Roosevelt's fresh technique and voice inspired confidence and hope.

Roosevelt's successor Harry Truman struggled to maintain good relations with the press. To many reporters, Truman was the "accidental president" and seemed "a small man in a big chair" following the death in 1945 of Roosevelt, who had been elected four times to the presidency. Truman insisted that the emerging Cold War required the same bipartisan support from the press that had been shown during World War II. The press, however, was eager to re-establish an adversarial role with the president following its general compliance in reporting war news. Jack Bell of the Associated Press thought Roosevelt genuinely enjoyed the give and take of his press conferences but Truman seemed "extremely hostile to his critics." Richard L. Strout of the *Christian Science Monitor* felt Truman lacked Roosevelt's interpersonal skills. As a result, he was "decried and mini-mized" by many White House reporters. Raymond Brandt of the *St. Louis Post-Dispatch* thought the general consen-sus was "that Truman wasn't up to the job."

There was widespread agreement in the press corps that Truman's problems were both stylistic and substan-tive. Arthur Krock, the chief Washington correspondent for the *New York Times*, observed that Roosevelt appeared to open his mind to reporters, creating the impression that he "wanted the news of his administration portrayed in the most favorable possible light." Truman's attitude, instead, seemed to be "take it or leave it." Robert Walsh, a reporter for the *Washington Star*, saw the same attitude and believed it "hurt Truman's image" in the press and with the nation. Another veteran White House reporter saw Truman as "a backwoods preacher laying down the law." This appearance of "arrogance and obstinacy alienated both the Congress and the public." C.L. Sulzberger, the chief foreign corre-spondent for the *New York Times* found Truman "very sin-cere and quite self-confident" with an unfortunate "rural knowledge of the world."

White House observers did not consider Truman well served by his press secretary, boyhood friend Charles Ross, who had won a Pulitzer Prize as Washington bureau chief for the *St. Louis Post-Dispatch*. Ross appears to have shared Truman's distrust of some reporters and his impatience with members of the press. Carroll Kenworthy, editor of the foreign department at United Press, noted that Ross had worked as a news analyst and did not properly appreciate the deadline pressures that drove the wire service reporters and big city dailies. As a result, Truman "very rarely used the news conference as much of a tool to get his ideas across to the public or the Congress." Syndicated columnist Joseph Alsop thought the poor performance of Truman and his press team contributed to the impression they were "over-whelmed by the vast problems of the post-war world." At a time of growing instability in that world, many reporters came to feel that Truman and his press handlers were dan-gerously out of their depth. Robert Riggs, chief Washington correspondent for the *Louisville Courier-Journal*, said the general impression among reporters was that "Truman was not always in command."

Truman's reputation would be rehabilitated by historians who noted his upset election victory in 1948 and the strength of his Truman Doctrine, which prevented the spread of communism in Europe, and Marshall Plan, which suc-ceeded in rebuilding Europe after the war. George Elsey, an assistant to the president and one of Truman's speech writ-

ers, believed Truman saw his job as making tough decisions and "leading public opinion rather than waiting for public opinion to tell him what to do." After he left office, Truman described the president's role as that of "a glorified public relations man" whose principal power lies in persuasion. He was annoyed by members of the "sabotage press" who had "failed to accurately portray our policies to the American people," and "ivory tower potentates," columnists such as Drew Pearson, Walter Winchell, Joseph and Stewart Alsop, and Walter Lippmann, who were more interested in circula-tion, Truman believed, than "serving the national interest." Krock knew Truman better than most White House report-ers and thought "his character curiously combined pettiness with greatness." Truman could make momentous decisions "with an iron backbone," Krock was convinced, "but did not suffer his critics well."

Further Reading

Cantril, Hadley, ed. *Public Opinion, 1935–1946.* Princeton, NJ: Princeton University Press, 1951.

Leuchtenburg, William E.. In *the Shadow of FDR: From Harry Truman to Ronald Reagan.* Ithaca, NY: Cornell University Press, 1983.

Papers of Harry S. Truman. Oral History Interviews. Press Con-ference File. Press Secretary Files. Harry S. Truman Presi-dential Library. Independence, Missouri.

Phillips, Cabell et al., eds. *Dateline: Washington, the Story of National Affairs Journalism in the Life and Times of the National Press Club.* Garden City, NY: Doubleday, 1949.

Truman, Harry S. *Years of Trial and Hope.* Garden City,NY: Doubleday, 1956.

Winfield, Betty Houchin. *FDR and the News Media.* Urbana: University of Illinois Press, 1990; New York: Columbia Uni-versity Press, 1994.

BETTY HOUCHIN WINFIELD

PRESIDENCY AND THE PRESS: DWIGHT D. EISENHOWER

"To think that an old general should come to this," Dwight Eisenhower (1953–1961) said, wearily laughing and wiping his brow. He had just completed cutting campaign commer-cials under the direction of Rosser Reeves, "the dark prince of hard sell," who had sold Anacin to millions of Americans by promising in early television ads "fast, fast relief."

Eisenhower's 1952 Republican Party candidacy for the presidency would be the first pitched for television. Sev-enty million of America's 160 million citizens had watched nominating convention coverage earlier that summer, and the Republican National Committee had assigned Reeves from the Ted Bates Agency the job of selling their candi-date. Bates heard Eisenhower's stump speech in Philadel-phia and thought it "a disaster. He was all over the map. He said sixteen different things. No one could remember what he was talking about." Bates narrowed Eisenhower's focus to "corruption in Washington, lower taxes, and the need for change." Eisenhower carried these campaign themes into his "Eisenhower Answers America" ads and followed them up on the campaign trail with the slogan "I Like Ike" to the strains of an Irving Berlin tune written especially for the general. Adlai Stevenson, his Democratic opponent, never had a chance. Eisenhower, a popular war hero, carried 39 states, won 422 electoral votes to Stevenson's 89 and gained 34 million votes to Stevenson's 27 million. Eisenhower became the nation's first Republican president since the Great Depression.

Eisenhower's nationally telecast inaugural address on January 20, 1953, attempted to rally popular support for his Cold War policy aimed at the quarantine of Communism. "We sense with all our faculties," he told the country, "that the forces of good and evil are massed and opposed as rarely before in history." Eisenhower's television advisor was the Hollywood actor Robert Montgomery and his press secretary was James C. Hagerty, for many years the chief political correspondent at the *New York Times*. Together they worked with Eisenhower in achieving a naturalness in tone and content that, in Eisenhower's words, "will sound good to the fellow digging ditches in Kansas." Eisenhower's inaugural address showed this approach in action. "We have grown in power and responsibility," Eisenhower told his fellow citizens. "We have the power to erase human life from this planet. Freedom is pitted against slavery, brightness against the dark. And we will defend freedom."

While Eisenhower enjoyed for the most part a positive press and a good economy during his presidency, he had his early skeptics. His cabinet was derisively described as "eight millionaires and a plumber." Eisenhower was often portrayed as good-natured, but bland, well-intentioned, but not always in command of the facts. Part of Eisenhower's evasiveness in televised press conferences was intentional. He wanted to appear "non-partisan" and refused to "engage in personalities," often making him appear ambivalent on policy issues. He would profess ignorance of issues he "didn't want to talk about." As Hagerty prepped the president for a March 23, 1955, press conference on whether he would use nuclear weapons to prevent the Chinese from attacking the nationalist Chinese on the island of Formosa, Eisenhower told him, "Don't worry, Jim. If that question comes up, I'll confuse them." Hagerty was a worrier. "One day I sat thinking, almost in despair," Hagerty remembered. "A hand fell on my shoulder and a voice said reassuringly, 'cheer up, things could get worse.' So I cheered up, and sure enough, things got worse." Hagerty would hold bad news to Saturday or Sunday, when the stories figured to get less attention in the press. Good news was released before two o'clock in the East to be sure to lead the nightly network news.

Hagerty won wide admiration of White House correspondents for his thoroughness, honesty, and access to the president. While campaigning for president in Detroit on October 24, 1952, Eisenhower told reporters if elected "I shall go to Korea" in an effort to end a bloody stalemate involving U.S. forces on the peninsula. As president-elect, Eisenhower kept his word, and on December 4, Hagerty arranged photo-opportunities of Eisenhower standing in a chow line with members of the Third U.S. Army Infantry as well as touring installations of the Second U.S. Infantry Division at the fighting front. On July 27, 1953, Eisenhower brokered a cease-fire to end the Korean War. When Eisenhower suffered a heart attack in Denver in 1955, Hagerty rushed to the president's bedside on September 25, the day after. Presidents Chester Arthur, Grover Cleveland, Woodrow Wilson, and Warren Harding went to great lengths to hide their medical problems from the public. Hagerty met with Eisenhower's medical team and then opened the president's oxygen tent to ask him how much he should tell the public in a press conference. It was agreed that the president's personal physician, Dr. Paul Dudley White, would take reporters questions. Some criticized White and Hagertyr for their candor. Their openness helped diffuse charges Eisenhower would not be well enough to seek a second term.

Eisenhower's press conferences were attended by 160 or so reporters who regularly covered the White House. Chief among them were Merriman Smith, the veteran United Press correspondent, whose assigned role was to begin and end each meeting with the reporters. Martin Arrowsmith represented Associated Press and Robert Clark reported for the International News Service. Hagerty was sensitive that wire services reporters were always on deadline and went out of his way to background them on breaking stories. Reporters for major newspaper chains received similar treatment. These included Robert Richards with Copley Newspapers and Kenneth Scheibe at Gannett. Eisenhower's action to send federal troops to Little Rock, Arkansas, in September 1957 to enforce the U.S. Supreme Court's ordered desegregation of the nation's schools was praised by Ethel Payne, who covered the White House for the *Chicago Daily Defender*, a leading African American newspaper. Eisenhower returned to the Oval Office from a vacation in Rhode Island to address the nation on television about his controversial decision. The speech was carefully cast to emphasize the president could not stand by and permit "demagogic extremists and disorderly mobs" from preventing nine African Americans from attending Central High School. Eisenhower's actions and speech helped to diffuse the crisis in Little Rock.

Eisenhower won forty-one states and 58 percent of the vote in his re-election landslide. His second term saw an increase in coverage by the three main television networks and their correspondents, Joseph Harsch at NBC, Martin Agronsky at ABC, and Charles von Fremd at CBS. Eisenhower presided over the creation of the Interstate Highway System during his second term. In 1919 as a Lieutenant Colonel Eisenhower had been involved in supervising the Transcontinental Convoy. During the Cold War he successfully argued for an integrated "communication and transportation system. Without them, we would be a mere alliance of separate parts." Eisenhower also went out of his way to defend CBS correspondent Edward R. Morrow, whose patriotism was questioned after his criticism of Red-hunting Wisconsin Senator Joseph McCarthy. Ike had known Morrow since their days in London during World

War II, he told reporters, and had "always thought of him as a good friend." White House memos and staff meetings show Eisenhower repeatedly urged Republican lawmakers to rein in McCarthy, warning them "he's ambitious. He wants to be president. And he's the last guy in the world who'll ever get there." On December 2, 1954, McCarthy was censured by the Senate.

After the Soviets successfully launched Sputnik on October 4, 1957, putting the first artificial satellite in orbit, Democrats began to criticize Eisenhower for the nation's "missile gap." The Navy's Project Vanguard proved an embarrassing failure, but by January 1958 Eisenhower pointed with pride to the Army's successful Jupiter Project and its launch of Explorer I. On July 29, 1958 Eisenhower announced the creation of the National Aeronautics and Space Administration to oversee the nation's infant space program. Eisenhower would claim in May 1960 that a NASA "weather research aircraft" had accidentally wandered into Soviet air space. It was a lie. On May 7, Soviet premier Nikita Khrushchev showed reporters the downed pilot Francis Gary Powers, who had been captured while on a spy mission to photograph Soviet missile installations. Powers' photographs and plane were also recovered. "I would like to resign," Ike said privately offering Hagerty a grim joke. Publicly, the president never apologized for the incident, and it led the theatrical Khrushchev to bolt their Super Power summit in Paris.

Eisenhower's personal popularity remained high throughout his two terms in office. On January 17, 1961, three days before the end of his presidency he spoke to the nation one last time on television as their commander in chief. His final speech was modeled on George Washington's farewell address to the nation. In it, Eisenhower assured the country that "America today is the strongest, the most influential, and most productive nation in the world." It faced "a hostile ideology global in scope, atheistic in character, ruthless in purpose, and insidious in methods." Then he warned of the "grave implications" and "unwarranted influence of a military-industrial complex" that potentially threatened "our liberties and democratic processes." The final theme of his presidency was the care with which the United States should exercise its power in a troubled nuclear world. "The easiest thing to do with great power is to abuse it," Eisenhower said. An informed citizenry, he was confident, would see that it did not.

Further Reading

Allen, Craig. *Eisenhower and the Mass Media: Peace, Prosperity and Prime Time TV.* Chapel Hill: University of North Carolina, 1993.

Ambrose, Stephen E. *Eisenhower*, 2 vols. New York: Simon & Schuster, 1983–1984.

Diamond, Edwin. *The Spot: The Rise of Political Advertising on Television.* Cambridge, MA: MIT Press, 1984.

Greenstein, Fred. *The Hidden-Hand Presidency: Eisenhower as Leader.* New York : Basic Books, 1982.

Henderson, Philip G. *Managing the Presidency: The Eisenhower Legacy.* New York: Westview Press, 1988.

Melanson, Richard A., and David Mayer. *Reevaluating Eisenhower.* Urbana: University of Illinois Press, 1987.

BRUCE J. EVENSEN

PRESIDENCY AND THE PRESS: NIXON TO CARTER

The liaison between a president and the press is frequently characterized by the opposing forces of mutual benefit and conflicting interests. The president and the press derive mutual benefit in that the president needs to connect with the public, whereas the press needs access to the president to keep their patrons apprised of political events. The conflict in interests lies in the need for the president to control his image and set the agenda for his administration. These opposing forces were particularly evident in the presidency and press relations of the terms served by Richard M. Nixon, Gerald R. Ford, and Jimmy Carter.

Richard M. Nixon

By the time he arrived in the Oval Office, Richard Milhous Nixon had extensive dealings with the press and had experienced both successes and failures. Prior to his election as the president, Nixon had a long record as a politician and had run as a vice-presidential as well as presidential candidate. This background is important to understanding his relationship with the press.

During the 1952 campaign, while running with Dwight D. Eisenhower as a vice presidential candidate, Nixon came under criticism over charges he had received $18,000 in illegal campaign contributions. Nixon countered his critics on television. On September 23 he told television audiences in his famous "Checkers Speech" that the charges against him had been politically motivated and that his kids were keeping "Checkers," a cocker spaniel given to them by a Texas businessman. The performance kept Nixon on the ticket.

Nixon fared less well when he ran for president in 1960 and appeared with his Democratic opponent, Massachusetts Senator John F. Kennedy in a series of televised debates. In the first debate, televised live from Chicago, Kennedy came across as young and witty and Nixon, suffering from a swollen and injured knee, seemed uncomfortable and haggard. Later analysis of the content of the debates shows little substantive difference, but the visuals went in favor of the tanned and relaxed Kennedy. Nixon was to remember the campaign of 1960 with much irritation and blamed the press for favoring Kennedy.

These experiences resulted in two distinct strategies that Nixon used in his dealings with the press. The first was to circumvent press coverage and speak directly to the public. The second was to approach the press itself with a high degree of wariness. We can see the Nixon press strategy of circumventing the press in action in the telethons his campaign utilized both in the 1968 and the 1972 elections. This helped him bypass the press and go directly to the people with his ideas and message. His mistrust of the press led him to engage in a campaign of discrediting the media itself.

As president, Nixon created a special press office for the executive branch and named Herbert Klein, the communications director. He appointed Ronald Ziegler as his press secretary. Ziegler had little experience with the press and over time correspondents turned increasingly to his assistant, Gerald Warren, for information. Ziegler later replaced Klein as communications director during Nixon's second term and Warren then was appointed as press secretary.

After seeing the decrepit state of the pressroom, the president commissioned the construction of a new pressroom in the West Terrace. The West Terrace Press Center allowed reporters to observe visitors to the president's office. Nixon seized the initiative as president, holding his first conference immediately after taking office and five more in the next five months.

The relationship between the press and the president increasingly degenerated as the correspondents grew impatient with the lack of information coming out of the White House. The administration, for its part, blamed the media for displaying excessive liberal partisanship. Two episodes, in particular, serve to illustrate the opposition between the press and the president: the Pentagon papers and the Watergate affair.

The Pentagon papers, commissioned by the secretary of defense and involved the work of numerous scholars, traced the increasing involvement of the United States in Vietnam over a period of three decades. The *New York Times* was able to obtain a copy of this report and began publishing it in serial form. The Nixon administration obtained a temporary restraining order against the *New York Times*, to which the paper vehemently objected although it did suspend its publication. Meanwhile, the *Washington Post* also obtained a copy of the report and began publishing it. The Nixon administration moved against the *Post* also. Eventually, the Supreme Court affirmed the right of the newspapers to publish the Pentagon papers and both the *Times* and the *Post* resumed publication.

Nixon had even less reason to like the press as the *Washington Post* started reporting on the Watergate burglary and the events behind it. The June 17, 1972, break-in at the Democratic National Headquarters in the Watergate office complex in Washington, D.C., created a growing controversy that would doom the Nixon presidency. Other papers, including the *New York Times*, joined the *Post* in reporting that members of the Committee to Re-elect the President had been implicated in the burglary. Televised Congressional hearings in the spring of 1973 probed "what the President knew and when he knew it." The nation was transfixed as a succession of witnesses testified, and eventually it was revealed that taped Oval Office conversations implicated Nixon in a criminal cover-up. This bombshell led to impeachment proceedings against Nixon during which he resigned. This episode made heroes of the two young reporters who first broke the story, Bob Woodward and Carl Bernstein. The long-term effect, however, as one commentator put it, was that after Watergate, every president was guilty until proven innocent in the press.

Gerald R. Ford

Gerald Rudolph Ford, who became president when Nixon resigned, was the only man in American history to serve as president who had never been elected president or vice president. Since both Nixon and his original vice president, Spiro Agnew, had been forced to resign from their offices, Ford was coming into office without a mandate, and possibly without the respect that accompanies the individual elected to the office.

Still, Ford did possess a likable personality that won him much needed good will, even though he was under a cloud due to his loyalty to Nixon. Ford was not a newcomer on the political scene. He had served as the House Minority Leader since 1963 and was generally well-liked by the press for his openness and down to earth candor. As a vice president, he continued a pattern of easy camaraderie with the press, gave many interviews, and frequently talked off the record with reporters.

In Ford's initial address to the American people he assured them that "our national nightmare is over." In a news conference, Ford equivocated on whether he would consider pardoning Nixon of charges stemming from the Watergate investigation. However, on September 8, 1974, in a nationally televised Oval Office speech, Ford gave Nixon a presidential pardon. He told Americans that he firmly believed in "equal justice for all Americans" but that "Richard Nixon and his loved ones have suffered enough." Although Ford hoped the pardon would end "years of bitter controversy and divisive national debate," his decision only extended and deepened the dispute, undermining the fragile confidence the nation had in his presidency. His newly appointed press secretary, Jerald F. terHorst, resigned in protest.

Ron Nessen, who had considerable journalistic experience in network news at NBC, replaced terHorst as press secretary. In his memoirs, Nessen acknowledged rocky relations and mutual distrust in his relations with the White House press corps. Ford became a national laughingstock, cast as a stumbling bumbler by comedian Chevy Chase on the highly popular television show *Saturday Night Live*. Ford struck back, hiring a personal television director and joke writer. He also worked to create a better rapport with the White House press. Unlike Nixon, Ford would usually conduct his press conferences in the East Room in a more relaxed atmosphere and would informally meet with the correspondents.

Ford was dogged by image problems. When he fell down the steps of Air Force One and later injured himself during skiing it seemed to play to public perceptions that he was physically uncoordinated and out of his depth. In reality, he was one of the best athletes ever to occupy the White House. He had been the starting center on the University of Michigan football team, was an ardent golfer, and led a robust life filled with physical activity. But the public would not be persuaded. When, in 1976, Ford referred to Poland as a free country in a televised presidential debate (Poland was actually part of the Communist bloc), his fate was sealed. The pardon, his image, and a debate mistake cost him the election in a razor-thin defeat.

Jimmy Carter

Former peanut farmer and Georgia Governor Jimmy Carter's relationship with the media was complex. To many, Carter owed much to the press, particularly television, for helping him to connect with the American people during his presidential campaign. Once elected, it was the media's consistent and intense attention to the many challenges that faced his presidency that were blamed for Carter's low approval rating and failure to be re-elected.

Carter's candidacy was greatly helped by his image of an honest farmer from Georgia. After the resignations of both Nixon and his vice-president, the perceived honesty and anti-establishment stance of Carter was welcomed by the voters. Carter was well aware of the significance of the media and made a concerted effort to court the press, even hiring a media consultant Gerald Rafshoon.

Once in office, Carter brought with him many Washington outsiders to the political stage, including Joseph Lester Powell Jr., his press secretary. "Jody" Powell, as he came to be known, was only thirty-three and had no journalistic experience. However, he had been with him since Carter's days as governor of Georgia. This long association worked in favor of Powell as it lent more credibility to him. Powell was also generally well-liked by the press correspondents, although the drawn out media attention on the troubles besetting the administration did eventually strain the rapport. Another asset for Carter was Rafshoon, who is credited with advising the president to turn his attention to the regional press and for helping improve his dismal approval ratings. Carter was not helped by other members of his staff, however. Bert Lance, the director of the Office of Management and Budget, resigned under a cloud of suspicion.

Carter did try to use the media to make his case to the public through strategic and clever use of the media, particularly television. He usually held two televised press conferences per month and took advantage of photo opportunities to connect directly with the public. As his approval ratings continued to drop, however, Carter announced that he would cease these conferences and would focus his attention on the regional press.

Two major problems facing Carter that led to these media troubles were the Middle East oil crisis and the Iran hostage standoff. A sharp downturn in oil export from the Middle East led to a serious energy shortage at home, leading to long lines at gas stations and higher prices. The public demanded immediate action, but Carter was slow to move. He did have an energy bill but the public heard little about it. To find a solution to the problem Carter retreated

to Camp David for a ten-day conference with leaders from all walks of life. At the end of the ten days, Carter made a thirty-minute speech outlining his plan. Critics scoffed at the image of a president before a fireplace urging Americans to "turn down their thermostats." The speech produced little momentum for the president's policy.

On November 4, 1979, Iranian militants captured 53 Americans in Tehran and held them hostage for 444 days. Ironically, it was Carter who initially directed the media's attention to this crisis. He had meant to build public support in favor of pressuring the Iranian government for the release of the hostages. But then, as the standoff remained unresolved and the media remained riveted on the issue, it became the greatest burden for the Carter administration. Through the efforts of Algerian negotiators, the hostages were released after President Ronald Reagan was sworn in to office in January, 1981.

In the end, Carter could not overcome his image problem, nor the overwhelming public feeling that double-digit interest rates and double-digit inflation meant that the nation was headed in the wrong direction. In the 1980 election, Carter's opponent, Republican Ronald Reagan was a landslide winner.

Further Reading

Greenberg, David. *Nixon's Shadow: The History of an Image*. New York: W.W. Norton, 2003.

Tebbel, John, and Watts, Sarah Miles, eds. *The Press and the Presidency*. NY: Oxford University Press, 1985.

Hoyt, Purvis, ed. *Presidency and the Press*. Austin: Lyndon B. Johnson School of Public Affairs, University of Texas at Austin, 1976.

Hallin, Daniel C. *The Presidency, the Press and the People*. San Diego: University of California, San Diego, 1992.

Keogh, James. *President Nixon and the Press*. New York: Funk and Wagnalls, 1972.

Rozell, Mark J. *The Press and the Ford Presidency*. Ann Arbor: University of Michigan Press, 1992.

Rozell, Mark J. *The Press and the Carter Presidency*. Boulder, CO: Westview Press, 1989.

SAMAN TALIB

PRESIDENCY AND THE PRESS: REAGAN TO GEORGE W. BUSH

When Ronald Reagan became president in January 1981, a sophisticated media team took over the White House communications operation. The clumsy stonewalling and deceit that marked the Watergate years of Richard Nixon and the inept and isolated Rose Garden strategy of Jimmy Carter during the Iranian hostage crisis gave way to a sunny, television-oriented appeal from the most effective chief messenger since John F. Kennedy died nearly two decades earlier. By 1980, campaigns—especially presidential campaigns—turned on how well candidates used television. This involved the use of both paid advertising and what campaign consultants call "free media"—the candidate's ability to connect with voters on a personal level, especially in his or her nightly appearances on television news. Reagan's skills as a former movie actor and television pitchman helped him present the image of a tough, confident, upbeat leader—seemingly different from his Democratic opponent in 1984, Walter Mondale. Reagan had an actor's natural ability to speak a line without making it seem scripted. For example, in a 1984 presidential debate, he defused a controversy over his advancing age by joking that he would not take advantage of his Democratic rival's "youth and inexperience." Even Mondale had to laugh.

As a candidate and as president, Reagan had an uncanny ability to hit just the right note, even in a crisis—as when he joked to doctors treating him after he had been shot in March 1981, "I hope you're all Republicans." Indeed, some of Reagan's most memorable moments as president were his speeches, most notably his salute at Normandy to the veterans of World War II and his insistent demand that Soviet leader Mikhail Gorbachev "tear down" the Berlin Wall. The live press conference, though, was not Reagan's best forum as he often seemed uninformed. After the early months of his presidency, he appeared less frequently in this setting. On those occasions when Reagan was off-key or appeared adrift—as when he misstated facts in press conferences—few citizens seemed to care as much as the White House press corps did.

More than any other single president, Reagan and his communications team pioneered modern governing through public relations. Michael Deaver, who was Deputy White House Chief of Staff, was among those who worked to manage media coverage of the president. Ed Rollins, a leading political strategist, managed Reagan's successful re-election campaign in 1984. In considering the use of public relations by this administration, though, one should also remember that Reagan, himself, had considerable experience in this area dating back to his days as an information officer in the Army Air Corps during World War II and then later as president of the Screen Actors Guild.

In his struggle with the Democratically controlled Congress, Reagan was aided by an unwitting media. Research has shown that presidents have the advantage over Congress in the battle to dominate the airwaves. The executive branch routinely receives three times more news coverage than does the legislative branch. Moreover, while a majority of news reports of the executive branch are negative in tone, television and newspaper reporters treat the legislative branch even more negatively, regardless of which party controls the White House or Congress.

The media's role in helping Reagan was ironic, given the highly contentious relations between this president and the press. Studies show that Reagan's coverage was mainly negative from the outset, as his efforts to reverse the role of government and alter the strategic balance in the Cold War reversed many years of settled policy. Liberals charged that members of the media were not tough enough on Reagan, even as reporters complained that their stories on his gaffes and foibles did not seem to make any difference with the public. Perhaps the cruelest blow to journalistic egos was the president's nonchalance in shrugging off apparently damaging stories.

Much of Reagan's popularity depended on his technique of going over the heads of the media to appeal directly to the public. But the power of televised rhetoric and personal appeals should not be overestimated. Contrary to some critics, he was not a "teflon president" to whom no bad news would stick. Studies have shown that Reagan's standing in the polls tracked the condition of the national economy. He was unpopular during the recession that began his term and highly popular during the economic expansion that followed. Rather than any magic touch, that explains why voters responded in 1984 to his campaign slogan, "It's morning again in America."

Moreover, when the Iran-contra scandal emerged during Reagan's second term, the president's media magic seemed to evaporate. Growing numbers of citizens were critical of him as details of the scandal unfolded, and polls showed that many doubted his denials of knowledge about the illegal activities involved. But a strong economy is the best teflon for a president, and however unsteady his administration became, voters were still willing to elect Reagan's understudy as president in 1988.

In sharp contrast to his predecessor, George H.W. Bush may have been less comfortable in front of television cameras than any other president. His 1988 campaign demonstrated some effective media moments: a key line, "Read my lips, no new taxes"; well-planned photo opportunities, such as a visit to a flag factory; and effective TV ads that played on public fears of crime by denouncing opponents with coded racial appeals. Lee Atwater is credited with having created some of Bush's most effective publicity in 1988, including the Willie Horton ad which implied that Bush's challenger, Michael Dukakis of Massachusetts, was soft on crime. Horton was an African American and a convicted murderer who had committed rape while on furlough from prison. Once in office, Bush's ability to mobilize public support was hampered by his poor stage presence, occasionally fractured syntax, and a general impression that he viewed media relations as a necessary evil. This caught up with him in the 1992 re-election campaign, when his stumbling performances before the cameras left him unable to sell voters on his stewardship of an economy that was just beginning to emerge from a lengthy recession.

Although Reagan's successor had showed sparks of his predecessor's media effectiveness during his 1988 campaign, Bill Clinton and George W. Bush (and their media teams) turned out to be far more successful students of the man dubbed "The Great Communicator." Just as Reagan had done a dozen years earlier, Clinton drew on his optimistic, media-savvy persona to overcome public doubts about him in securing electoral victory.

As the media environment had changed, the marketing of the presidency now changed as well. Much of this change was the product of necessity. During the 1992 primaries Clinton faced an onslaught of criticism about his past, including allegations of avoiding the draft and smoking marijuana in the 1960s (he claimed he "didn't inhale"), and persistent reports of womanizing. In a last-ditch effort to overcome his negative press on the "character" issue, Clinton introduced America to talk show campaigning. He appeared on Phil Donahue's popular syndicated show and engaged a sympathetic studio audience in conversation about problems facing the country. He donned sunglasses and played the saxophone on the "Arsenio Hall Show." During an appearance on MTV he even answered a query about his preference in underwear (boxer shorts rather than briefs).

In these venues Clinton established one-on-one connections with audience members (and the viewers at home) in a way his opponents, who remained tethered to ten-second soundbites, could not match. His upbeat demeanor and folksy style seemed to encourage forgiveness on the part of voters looking for new leadership after an economic recession. Later this same easy-going manner helped the first Baby Boomer president connect with the informal young adults increasingly drawn to late night TV comedians, cable news, and the daytime talk programs. Such outlets also provided new avenues for bypassing an aggressive press corps.

Like Reagan, Clinton's personal popularity saved his job when things got tough: Although the Republican-led House of Representatives impeached him in 1998 on charges of perjury relating to the Monica Lewinsky and Paula Jones scandals, strong majorities of the public—consistently over 60 percent—sided with the president throughout the year-long controversy. The Senate, reading the public's mood, acquitted the popular chief executive in early 1999.

After the deadlocked and divisive election of 2000, incoming President George W. Bush struggled to win public acceptance. His early efforts to connect with people succeeded mainly on a personal level—many citizens viewed him as a likeable everyman. Research showed that his news coverage was mainly negative. Bush's media image and political fortunes turned around in the wake of the terrorist attacks on New York and Washington, D.C., on September 11, 2001. His public approval ratings skyrocketed in the weeks that followed, and they did not drop back to pre-September 11 levels until near the end of his first term. However, it is not clear that Bush's communications strategy played a major role in this turnaround. As commander-in-chief, his pronouncements about America's resolve to fight Al Queda certainly helped to unify the country. But his immediate reactions were criticized as indecisive, and many critics believed that during the crisis, the president's command presence was outshone by that of New York City Mayor Rudi Giuliani.

Nonetheless, studies found that Bush's network news coverage jumped from stories that were 2 to 1 negative to stories that were 2 to 1 positive following September 11 to the end of 2001. This was mainly due to a "rally 'round the flag effect" that occurs in the wake of international crises. The public and the press both treat the president—any president—as America's unifying leader rather than a divisive politician. As the president benefits from more favorable news coverage, his popularity rises sharply. Studies of recent U.S. military engagements, including the 1991 Persian Gulf War, the

1999 Kosovo crisis, the aftermath of September 11, 2001, and the initial combat phase of the 2003 Iraq war, have all found a shift in the tone of television news toward mainly positive coverage the incumbent president.

The Bush administration also moved to mobilize American and world opinion behind the U.S. war on terrorism. After the attacks on September 11, 2001, the President Bush appointed a former advertising executive, Charlotte Beers, to be Undersecretary for Public Diplomacy. Beers held the post until she resigned in March, 2003. She was replaced by former Morocco Ambassador Margaret D Tutwiler. Karen Hughes, a former Dallas TV reporter and adviser to President Bush, became Undersecretary of Public Diplomacy and Public Affairs, in July, 2005.

The war on the Taliban in Afghanistan, started in late 2001, received high marks from the public and the press, as did the 2003 invasion of Iraq. The latter was launched following administration warnings that Iraqi leader Saddam Hussein was building weapons of mass destruction and its implication that the Hussein regime was connected to the World Trade Center and Pentagon attacks. The Bush administration's decision to "embed" reporters with military units in Iraq helped secure positive news coverage and allowed U.S. audiences to see the rapid advances made by the U.S. military on the road to Baghdad. Likewise, Bush's many appearances before friendly military audiences encouraged people to think of the man who been criticized for avoiding service in Vietnam as a tough president for tough times.

As was the case with the Vietnam War, the American public by 2007 appeared to have soured on military activities that went on longer than expected without a clear exit strategy. Aggressive communication strategies employed to build public support for the Iraq war boomeranged when the administration failed to find either weapons of mass destruction or a credible connection between Saddam Hussein and the attacks of September 11, 2001. Perhaps most importantly, American casualties continued to climb, with no end in sight, long after the president declared "mission accomplished" from the deck of an aircraft carrier on May 1, 2003.

The 24/7 news cycles occasioned by the advent of cable television and online media intensify the problems faced by the modern presidency. Cable news is always on and must always be reporting about something. As a result, stories that even hint of scandal get turned into soap operas that keep viewers coming back for more, and key televised moments get repeated constantly, greatly magnifying their impact. Online commentators are often fervent partisans who do not adhere to traditional media standards of accuracy and balance. So far the online world, and especially the blogosphere, leans far more toward editorializing than reporting, especially as compared to traditional news organizations. But in order to compete with online media, some mainstream news outlets are increasing their offerings of aggressive, largely one-sided commentary.

The increasing cacophony of the modern media may provide future presidents with an advantage over the press in setting the agenda for public policy. Presidents may find it easier to favor more supportive media outlets when the audience for any one outlet is relatively small. Product differentiation concerns may lead media companies to favor more one-sided coverage, as some suggest has been the case in the years since the rise of talk radio and Fox News. Or perhaps the in-your-face new online media environment will overwhelm White House attempts to set the agenda, as reporters and bloggers go in directions of their own choosing.

The only certainty is that a rapidly changing media environment will present future presidents with new challenges, and their success will depend greatly on how well they can turn dangers into opportunities. Meanwhile, journalists will have to explore new methods and practices if they are to keep the public informed about the executive branch while holding the president accountable to the American people.

Further Reading

Bennett, W. Lance. *News: The Politics of Illusion*. New York: Pearson/Longman, 2005.

Campbell, Colin, and Bert A. Rockman, eds. *The George W. Bush Presidency: Appraisals and Prospects*. Washington: CQ Press, 2004.

Cook, Timothy E. *Governing With the News: The News Media as a Political Institution*, 2nd ed. Chicago, IL: University of Chicago Press, 2005.

Cronin, Thomas E., and Michael A. Genovese. *The Paradoxes of the American Presidency*, 2nd ed. New York: Oxford University Press, 2004.

Deaver, Michael, with Mickey Herskowitz. *Behind the Scenes: In Which the Author Talks About Ronald and Nancy Reagan... and Himself*. New York: William Morrow, 1987.

Edwards, George C. III. *On Deaf Ears: The Limits of the Bully Pulpit*. New Haven, CT: Yale University Press, 2003.

Entman, Robert. *Projections of Power*. Chicago: University of Chicago Press, 2004.

Farnsworth, Stephen J., and S. Robert Lichter. *The Mediated Presidency*. Lanham, MD: Rowman & Littlefield, 2006.

Jamieson, Kathleen Hall. *Eloquence in an Electronic Age: The Transformation of Political Speechmaking*. New York: Oxford University Press, 1988.

Kernell, Samuel. 1997. *Going Public: New Strategies of Presidential Leadership*. Washington, DC: CQ Press, 1997.

Kumar, Martha Joynt. "The Contemporary Presidency: Communications Operations in the White House of President George W. Bush: Making News on His Terms." *Presidential Studies Quarterly* 33, 2 (2003): 366–393.

———. "Source Material: The White House and the Press: News Organizations as a Presidential Resource and as a Source of Pressure." *Presidential Studies Quarterly* 33, 3 (2003): 669–683.

Nelson, Michael, ed. *The Presidency and the Political System*. Washington, DC: CQ Press, 2005.

Norris, Pippa, Montague Kern, and Marion Just, eds. *Framing Terrorism: The News Media, the Government and the Public*. New York: Routledge, 2003.

Tulis, Jeffrey K. *The Rhetorical Presidency*. Princeton, NJ: Princeton University Press, 1987.

STEPHEN J. FARNSWORTH
S. ROBERT LICHTER

PRESIDENTIAL RECORDS ACT OF 1978

The Presidential Records Act of 1978 (PRA)—a statute that mandates near total public release of the records of presidents no later than twelve years after they have left office—was the culmination of efforts by members of the United States Congress and the history/archives community to ensure public ownership and access to the records of American presidents. Had it not been for the Watergate scandal and the prolonged battle over custody of President Richard Nixon's papers, including the famed Watergate tapes, the law probably would never have been enacted. While the PRA has never been statutorily amended, several presidential Executive Orders relating to the act remain contested.

For nearly two hundred years the papers of presidents were considered each individual's "personal" property. As such, presidents retained rights to the use of their papers, including the right to donate or dispose of them or restrict public access. Beginning with Franklin D. Roosevelt, presidents began donating their papers to National Archives and Records Administration (NARA) administered presidential libraries.

The Watergate scandal served as the catalyst for enactment of several laws that culminated in the PRA and in public ownership presidential records for every president after President Jimmy Carter. In July 1973, during the Senate investigation into the burglary of the Democratic national committee headquarters at the Watergate hotel in Washington, D.C., in June, 1972, senators learned that President Nixon had made and apparently still retained secretly made tape recordings of conversations held in the White House. They realized that the tapes could possibly reveal the answer to the key question posed by Senator Howard Baker of Tennessee with respect to the burglary and the White House effort to cover it up: "What did the President know and when did he know it?" Congress called for Nixon to turn them over. A two-decade fight over access and control of the Watergate tapes ensued and led to a public outcry over the ownership of presidential papers.

Four weeks prior to leaving office as a result of the Watergate scandal, President Nixon negotiated an agreement (as had his predecessors) to donate his presidential materials to a NARA administered presidential library. But the agreement contained a controversial provision that required destruction of what many considered the most historically important materials, including the White House tapes. Within two weeks Congress stepped in and passed the Presidential Recordings and Materials Preservation Act (PRMPA) a law (44 U.S.C. 2111) that not only protected the Nixon tape recordings from destruction but also directed NARA to take into "protective custody" all the Nixon presidential materials, including his personal papers. The PRMPA provided that the president's "personal and private" papers would be returned to Nixon but the rest would be considered federal property.

The statute also contained an important provision that authorized the establishment of a national commission to study the complex issues surrounding the disposition of the records of not just presidents but all federal officials. On March 31, 1977, the "Public Documents Commission" issued its report calling for federal ownership of all documents produced by the president, members of Congress, as well as federal judges and justices. Congress did not act on the commission's recommendations regarding the papers of members of Congress and federal judges, but it did embrace recommendations regarding public ownership of presidential papers.

The Presidential Records Act (44 U.S.C. 2201-2207) was enacted in 1978 and signed into law by President Carter. The new provisions first applied to the president and vice-president who would assume office on January 20, 1981—that fell to Ronald Reagan and George H.W. Bush. Thereafter, the records of all subsequent presidents and vice-presidents came under the provisions of the PRA.

The PRA accomplished three things: 1) it changed the tradition of handling presidential papers as legal ownership now switched from private to public; 2) it codified into law principles that long existed concerning how presidential papers would be treated and processed by the national archives; and 3) it served to retain for former presidents those constitutional authorities that over the years various federal courts had affirmed rightfully belonged to them (i.e., the right to claim executive privilege).

The PRA defined presidential records to include all documentary materials generated or received by the president and his staff generated "in the course of conducting activities which relate to or have an effect upon the carrying out of constitutional, statutory, or other official or ceremonies of the President." In essence, the definition was meant to cover all materials generated by a president and his staff except "personal records" of the president, a term which is also defined by the statute.

In order to protect the constitutional powers and prerogatives of the president, the PRA provides that "nothing in this Act shall be construed to confirm, limit, or expand any constitutionally based privilege which maybe available to an incumbent or former president" – language that theoretically enables a former or sitting president to claim a privilege and hence bar public release over any presidential document for a period of time. The law also gives the Archivist of the United States independent legal authority and responsibility for the "custody, control, and preservation of, and access to" the president's records. The archivist has an affirmative duty to make such records available to the public consistent with provisions of the act. Time has shown though that this charge is not so easily accomplished.

Once a president's term of office is complete, all official records are transferred to the custody of the Archivist of the United States for processing and permanent retention in a NARA presidential library. For the first five years, the president's records are, in essence, closed while archivists begin processing the papers into defined subject areas or topical record groups. While Congress hoped that this amount of time would be sufficient for processing the majority of a president's records for public access, in the first five years at the Ronald Reagan Presidential Library archivists processed only 9 percent of its holdings; in the case of the William Jefferson Clinton presidential library, less than 1 percent were made ready. The sheer volume of records and often the lack of necessary archival staff means that the processing of records takes much longer than the law anticipated and that in the early twenty first century, there were enormous backlogs. Access to presidential records is granted in accordance with provisions of the Freedom of Information Act (FOIA) and processing requests normally takes three to four years, especially for classified records. While most presidential records can theoretically be accessed five years after a president leaves office, the PRA provides that some records can remain closed for a total of twelve years. After that, the law provides for virtually total public access to a president's papers, excepting only a handful of document types covered by six restrictive exemptions.

The restrictions are designed to ensure that certain types of information are not disclosed prematurely. The most commonly encountered exemptions that one finds referenced on document redaction sheets of the records of a president are the P-1, P-2, P-5, and P-6 exemptions.

The P-1 restriction seeks to protect "classified national security information"; the P-2 restriction applies to information "relating to appointments to Federal office." The P-5 exemption relates to "confidential communications requesting or submitting advice, between the President and his advisers, or between such advisers" and is often of most interest to historians, scholars, and journalists as these records trace the decision-making process in the White House. The P-6 relates to "unwarranted invasion of personal privacy" (the exact definition of "unwarranted" is not clearly defined in statute or at this writing in case law).

While the provisions of law are relatively clear cut, two presidents have issued Executive Orders (EO) relating to aspects of the PRA. In 1989, just four days before leaving office, President Reagan issued EO 12667—the order that established the first policies and procedures for implementing the law. For over a decade the guidance served the public interest well. In November 2001, President George W. Bush issued EO 13233 and nullified the Reagan EO and revised PRA policies and administrative procedures. A coalition of historians, archivists, and government openness advocates sued the government (*American Historical Association v. NARA*) in December 2001 over certain provisions in the Bush issued EO. The plaintiffs claimed that the new procedures locked up some sixty-eight thousand pages of Reagan era P-5 category presidential papers that should have been made public the day Bush took office. The plaintiffs also challenged the constitutionality of aspects of the Bush EO. In time, all but a handful of the sixty-eight thousand Reagan era records were scrutinized by President Reagan's representatives and, as the PRA provides, reviewed by the incumbent president and released to the public. At this writing the validity of certain constitutionally questionable provisions of the EO have yet to be adjudicated.

The PRA seeks to ensure that all the records of a sitting president will, in time, become public. It is from these records that the history and legacy of a president is fashioned. The law makes it clear that former and incumbent presidents are but the temporary gatekeepers of presidential records and firmly establishes the principle of transparency, demonstrating that the American people have a right to gain access to and scrutinize the decisions and actions of presidents and their staff.

Further Reading

Kassop, Nancy. "Not Going Public: George W. Bush and the Presidential Records Act." In *In the Public Domain: Presidents and the Challenge of Public Leadership,* edited by Lori Cox Han, and Diane J. Heith. New York: State University of New York Press, 2005.

Kutler, Stanley I., ed. *Abuse of Power: The New Nixon Tapes.* New York: Free Press, 1997.

Montgomery, Bruce. "Presidential Materials: Politics and the Presidential Records Act." *American Archivist* (Spring/Summer) 2003.

Smith, Nancy Kegan, and Stern, Gary M. "Access to Records in Presidential Libraries: Balancing Legal, Archival, and Public Interests." *The Public Historian,* (Summer) 2006.

Three articles in *RBM: A Journal of Rare Books, Manuscripts, and Cultural Heritage* (Fall) 2002: Nancy Cricco and Peter Wosh, "The Past, Present, and Uncertain Future of Presidential Records"; John Brademas, "Presidential Records;" and Bruce Craig, , "Executive Order 13233: We Dare Not Allow Ourselves to be Bush-Whacked."

R. BRUCE CRAIG

PRICE, BYRON

Byron Price (March 25, 1891–August 6, 1981) gave up a career as executive news editor of the Associated Press in December 1941 to head the newly created Office of Censorship. He guided the news media through an effective system of self-censorship during World War II. His success surprised skeptics expecting a return to the heavy-handed and unpopular policies of the previous world war. Under Price's common-sense administration, journalists avoided news topics that would have provided information to the enemy, and they demonstrated the potential for press-military cooperation. Price's legacy was twofold: a model for wartime censorship that kept citizens substantially informed without compromising security, and a press that emerged from the twentieth century's greatest challenge with its First Amendment freedom intact.

Price was born March 25, 1891, on a farm in Topeka, Indiana, where he performed chores for his parents, John Price and the former Emaline Barnes. He took to journalism early, writing "The Family Record" with a lead pencil for two years starting in 1901. The project also gave him a taste of censorship when his father ordered him to find another hobby. Price nevertheless joined the staffs of his high school and university newspapers as well as the *Journal* in Crawfordsville, Indiana.

He took a job with the United Press wire service after graduating from Wabash College in 1912 but quickly switched to the larger Associated Press. Price took a leave of absence from 1917 to 1919 to serve as an infantry officer in France during World War I. After his return, he served the AP as a political reporter, Washington bureau news editor, columnist, and, beginning in 1937, executive news editor. In his final position, Price supervised the wire service's news production. He encouraged new, creative writing techniques but insisted on accuracy and impartiality. "The Associated Press is my religion," he said.

His long career brought him in contact with hundreds of important national figures, including Franklin D. Roosevelt. When America declared war on the Axis Powers after the Japanese attack on Pearl Harbor, Roosevelt chose Price to ensure information of value did not reach the enemy. The president gave Price virtually a free hand to create and enforce the domestic censorship code (as opposed to the mandatory war zone censorship administered by the armed forces). Price and his staff canvassed military and government offices to create lists of sensitive news topics, which the Office of Censorship printed and distributed to journalists in January 1942. The code had no legal penalties for violations because of the First Amendment prohibition on interference with a free press. Nevertheless, journalists followed the code. Like Price, they viewed wartime censorship as a necessary evil and endorsed it if run intelligently.

Price worked to ensure censorship topics were reasonable. When journalists had a legitimate complaint about too much war news being withheld, he acted as their advocate in negotiations—usually successful—with the army, navy, and White House. Observers considered him above partisan politics. *The New York Times* called Price "an evenhanded, canny and unflappable administrator."

Further Reading

Flint, Peter B. "Byron Price, Wartime Chief of U.S. Censorship, Is Dead." *New York Times,* August 8, 1981, 44.

Kluckhorn, Frank L. "President Appoints Byron Price to Direct Wartime Censorship." *New York Times,* December 17, 1941, 1, 5.

Koop, Theodore F. *Weapon of Silence.* Chicago: University of Chicago, 1946.

"Price, Byron." *Current Biography: Who's News and Why,* 1942. New York: H.W. Wilson, 1942, 681–683.

Price, Byron. "The Censor Defends the Censorship." *New York Times Magazine,* February 11, 1945, 11, 32–33.

——. "Governmental Censorship in Wartime." *American Political Science Review* 36 (October 1942), 837–849.

Records of the Office of Censorship (RG 216), National Archives, http://www.archives.gov/research/holocaust/finding-aid/civilian/rg-216.html.

Sweeney, Michael S. *Secrets of Victory: The Office of Censorship and the American Press and Radio in World War II.* Chapel Hill: University of North Carolina, 2001.

MICHAEL S. SWEENEY

PRINTERS' INK

From its inception in 1888 to its demise in 1972, the advertising trade magazine *Printers' Ink* was one of the most successful and influential journals of its type. The magazine was founded in New York by George P. Rowell, a pivotal figure in advertising in the nineteenth century. Rowell's goal was to provide a weekly periodical useful to publishers, advertisers and the growing body of agency professionals who created and placed ads. Early issues of the magazine, edited by Charles L. Benjamin, provided "how-to" advice, often penned by well-known advertising practitioners, on copywriting and layout, accurate data on ad rates for various publications, and numerous advertisements for newspapers and other periodicals looking to attract the attention of advertisers and agencies. Also frequently included in the approximately thirty page issues were ads for printing and type companies. *Printers' Ink* reflected Rowell's personal distaste for efforts to make advertising scientific through the use of psychology and the social sciences. The periodical instead published articles that promoted the value of careful observation of successful campaigns and instincts developed through on the job experience. To this end, the magazine frequently discussed the pros and cons of specific ad campaigns in its pages. Rowell initiated a series of contests and prizes for the best examples of advertisements. The magazine also warned against the dangers of unbranded and substitute goods. *Printers' Ink* was also a tool in Rowell's long-term crusade to verify newspaper circulations and force publishers to report printing data honestly. At a time when publishers frequently exaggerated circulation figures to boost ad rates, this was a valuable service to the interests of advertisers. *Printers' Ink* enjoyed a circulation of approximately 16,000 during the 1890s, making it the most widely read advertising trade magazine of the day.

In 1908, John Irving Romer acquired the magazine and published it until his death in 1933. While continuing to publish on the practical side of the business, Romer also used *Printer's Ink* to promote and reinforce awareness of professional ideals. As was the case with many fields at the time, advertising professionals sought to develop higher standards and ethical practices to achieve legitimacy among business leaders and counter growing consumer distrust and hostility fueled by deceptive and fraudulent advertisers, including many notorious patent medicine manufacturers. Increasingly wary of the potential for adverse government regulation of advertising, *Printers' Ink* became attentive to political matters. It was an active participant in the "truth in advertising" movement of the 1910s and 1920s that saw the creation of the Better Business Bureaus. Its most significant contribution was the promotion of the *Printers' Ink* Model Statute, a law that made certain types of "false" and misleading advertising illegal; by the early 1920s as many as twenty-five states had some form of this law on their books. During the 1930s, when advertising again faced a growing threat of unwanted government scrutiny and a revived consumer's movement, *Printers' Ink* worked to counter attacks on the industry and inform advertising professionals of the latest news from Washington. During World War II, *Printers' Ink* was an active supporter of the industry's efforts to assist government information programs and publicized the activities of the War Advertising Council. The company issued another periodical called *Printers' Ink Monthly* beginning in 1919. This publication was designed for the advertising agency manager and included information more specifically geared toward the successful operation of a modern agency. The two titles were merged in 1942, after which time *Printers' Ink* sought to cater to this target audience while also retaining its traditional focus.

The last issue of the magazine published under the name *Printers' Ink* came out on September 8, 1967. At that time it was acquired by Decker Communications, who changed the title to *Marketing/Communications*. Decker published it as a monthly though the January 1972 issue and it went out of business in February 1972, reportedly due to lack of advertising revenue.

Printers' Ink remains a highly valuable source of information for historians, and many exceptional studies of the development of advertising in the United States draw upon its contents for contemporary discussions of the issues facing the profession, as well as accurate economic data through the period in which advertising grew into a major force in social and economic life of modern America. The magazine's "Inside Washington" column contains a wealth of information on political and regulatory issues related to advertising. L.D. H. Weld's "Printers' Ink Index" provides voluminous information about billings, spending and placement by medium and long-term economic trends.

Further Reading

Laird, Pamela Walker. *Advertising Progress: American Business and the Rise of Consumer Marketing*. Baltimore: Johns Hopkins University Press, 1998.
Pollay, Richard W. *Information Sources in Advertising History*. Westport, CT: Greenwood Press, 1979.
Pope, Daniel. *The Making of Modern Advertising*. New York: Basic Books, 1983.
Romer, John I., "Legal Repression of Dishonest Advertising." *Printers' Ink,* November 16 (1911): 3.

ROBERT RABE

PRIOR RESTRAINT

A prior restraint is a legal action designed to stop communication. Such controls are distinguished from penalties imposed after the communication has reached others. In either case a restriction exists, but not allowing expression in the first place is usually considered a more serious denial of freedom. The right to speak and to publish has been regarded as necessary for self-fulfillment, self-government, the resolution of conflict, and the advancement of knowledge. Such Enlightenment values are reflected in the nation's founding documents and in the First Amendment in particular. Media organizations are therefore free to make their own decisions about content as long as some exception such as copyright infringement does not apply. The Supreme Court of the United States has stated that prior restraint is unconstitutional as a general rule.

Intentions and Interpretations

Government suppression had a long and inglorious history before the ratification of the First Amendment in 1791. English officials tried to stamp out dissent with laws, censors, and printing monopolies until losing the most general powers for prepublication constraints in the nation's seventeenth-century political upheavals. Colonists, however, still faced occasional attempts to impose prior restraint in the eighteenth century. In 1723, for instance, the Massachusetts legislature ordered the feisty Boston printer James Franklin to submit to censorship, but he did not cooperate and a grand jury refused to indict him. In 1765 Parliament tried to require that American newspapers not be published without paying a stamp tax, but the law proved difficult to enforce and was rescinded in the wake of violent protests.

By the time the Constitutional Convention met in 1787, protecting the right of expression remained a priority. Many in the founding generation, after all, had been outspoken revolutionaries and wanted to preserve for posterity the freedom they had used. Most of the states had constitutional language that described the liberty as unlimited or inviolable. The words placed in the federal Constitution appeared to be an absolute ban on government interference with what the people chose to say or write. Article I, Section 8, says that Congress has the power to make "all laws" for the federal government and the First Amendment says that Congress shall make "no law" abridging freedom of speech or of the press.

Before long, Federalists in Congress passed the Sedition Act of 1798 that outlawed false, scandalous, and malicious statements about Congress, the president, and the federal government. The Sedition Act was a temporary measure ostensibly passed because war with France was anticipated. The Federalists, who were pro-British and who were trying to hold on to power as the Jeffersonian Republicans (who were pro-French) were gaining strength, used the statute to arrest opposition party journalists. Republicans argued that the law being used against them was obviously unconstitutional, but Federalists cited a definition used in Sir William Blackstone's *Commentaries on the Laws of England* (1765–1769). Liberty of the press, the English jurist wrote, meant only freedom from prior restraint, not a right for licentious statements that are unlawful because they are dangerous, offensive, or have a pernicious tendency.

The Sedition Act expired in 1801 when Thomas Jefferson became president, but the debate about the original meaning of the press clause of the First Amendment has continued ever since. Although the oligarchic Blackstone did not accept popular sovereignty, the separation of church and state, and other fundamental features of the United States Constitution, some have assumed that his pronouncement rejecting prior restraint while accepting subsequent

punishment was widely accepted. Others have turned to statements by James Madison, Alexander Hamilton, and other Americans to argue that the founders created a limited government without any power over the press.

The eighteenth-century conclusion about prior restraints did not prevent them from appearing later when rationales for suppression were considered sufficient. Relying on national security arguments, the military has frequently imposed censorship of war coverage and Congress has sometimes passed laws such as the Intelligence Identities Protection Act of 1982 that forbids unauthorized disclosures identifying spies and their sources. Another reason for controls is to maintain order. School officials who have a qualified authority to limit student expression and civil authorities can put narrow, content-neutral "time, place, and manner" restrictions on expressive activities such as a protest if a substantial state interest is involved.

Prior restraints are nevertheless ordinarily unconstitutional. In contrast to many other countries, for instance, the American legal system typically allows the news media to present stories that might affect the outcome of court proceedings. Laws that apply taxes only to the press or that limit the distribution of publications can be challenged as a form of censorship. Material such as obscenity or false advertising, however, can be deemed outside of First Amendment protection and be stopped by an injunction. A right to publish can also be lost if an employee signs a contract not to reveal information.

Major Cases

The Supreme Court's most important pronouncements on prior restraint illustrate the difficulty of reaching a legal consensus when freedom of expression is pitted against fundamental principles. A democracy cannot function without liberty of the press and government is not supposed to silence the people if they are sovereign, but officials are often willing to balance even the most essential and compelling rights against prudential and perhaps personal or political considerations.

The legal thought of the nineteenth and early twentieth centuries frequently followed Blackstone's definition of free expression. Constitutional press guarantees, the Supreme Court said in *Patterson v. Colorado* [205 U.S. 454 (1907)], were mainly to prohibit prior restraints and did not prevent subsequent punishment for statements deemed contrary to the public welfare. The views of the justices, however, became more complicated once scholars challenged their understanding of the press clause and difficult cases arose.

In *Near v. Minnesota* [283 U.S. 697 (1931)], the Supreme Court issued a 5–4 ruling against a state statute allowing the use of injunctions to stop the publication of malicious, scandalous, or defamatory newspapers that were considered a public nuisance. The majority opinion by Chief Justice Charles Evan Hughes quoted Blackstone and Madison rejecting prior restraint, but left off the end of Madison's sentence that said the nation had also made the press exempt from subsequent penalties. The opinion said that the chief purpose of the press clause was to prevent prior restraints and found Minnesota's "gag law" unconstitutional.

The *Near* ruling has been hailed as a victory for freedom of expression and cited in later cases, but Hughes backed away from the bedrock belief that the Constitution's protection against prior restraint is absolute. The chief justice said in dicta that prior restraint could be used to stop interference with a war effort, obscenity, and incitements to violence or the overthrow of government. Hughes and his fellow justices, who had lived through a world war and much radical political strife, were not as willing to trust the marketplace of ideas as the founding generation.

The Supreme Court revisited the issue of prior restraint forty years later in allowing publication of the *Pentagon Papers*, a classified history of the Vietnam War that was leaked to the press. The government argued that the First Amendment did not prohibit stopping information that would cause grave harm, but had difficulty specifying any serious consequences. The press brief questioned both the necessity for a restraint and the authority one would be based upon.

The 6–3 decision came in a brief, unsigned opinion simply stating that officials had not met the heavy burden of justifying a prior restraint. Yet, the case, *New York Times Co. v. United States* [403 U.S. 713 (1971)], did not completely rule out future prior restraints for national security reasons. Each of the nine justices wrote an opinion. Some seemed disposed to accept the government's national security contentions and authority, some appeared willing to consider a prior restraint in some circumstances, and some could see no possibility of officials obtaining such power. In his opinion, his last before his death, the First Amendment absolutist Hugo Black wrote that real security came from the free expression the founders had guaranteed and that the government was using assertions of vague presidential powers without even attempting to rely on a law passed by Congress.

Officials had a federal statute to use in *United States v. The Progressive* [467 F. Supp. 990 (1979)]. A federal district court judge cited the Atomic Energy Act of 1954, a law prohibiting disclosure of nuclear weapon data, in issuing an injunction to stop the publication of a magazine article on the physics of the hydrogen bomb. The author of the article wanted to show that nuclear secrecy was a myth and was used to suppress inquiry on weapons production problems that were being covered up. After other journalists showed that facts involved were available elsewhere and the government encountered skeptical questioning during the oral arguments before an appeals court, the case was dropped and the article was published. The *Progressive* case demonstrated just how difficult it is to contain information even when the government would like to have it suppressed.

Further Reading

Atomic Energy Act, Pub. L. No. 83-703 (1954).

Friendly, Fred W. *Minnesota Rag: The Dramatic Story of the Landmark Supreme Court Case That Gave New Meaning to Freedom of the Press.* New York: Random House, 1981.

Intelligence Identities Protection Act, Pub. L. No. 97-200 (1982).

Morland, Howard. *The Secret That Exploded.* New York: Random House, 1981.

Rudenstine, David. *The Day the Presses Stopped: A History of the Pentagon Papers Case.* Berkeley: University of California Press. 1996.

Smith, Jeffery A. *Printers and Press Freedom: The Ideology of Early American Journalism.* New York: Oxford University Press, 1988.

———. *War and Press Freedom: The Problem of Prerogative Power.* New York: Oxford University Press, 1999.

JEFFERY A. SMITH

PROGRESSIVE ERA

The Progressive Era was the period roughly between 1880 and 1919, during which the United States experienced unprecedented growth and development, which often led to social, political, and economic turmoil. Despite such turmoil, a positive and optimistic spirit infused segments of the American intellectual, political, and social reform communities and spread throughout the general culture and society, including the press. General circulation newspapers and magazines alternately praised the growth of science and industry and conducted exposés and investigations of political and corporate corruption. Reform publications—advocating woman suffrage, civil rights, prohibition, labor reform, and political reform—took up where they left off, calling for sweeping social changes they believed would make America a truly democratic and equitable society. During this period, the press generally expressed an optimistic view of the future, professing its faith in the progress of America, science, civilization, and mankind.

Growth of the Newspaper Industry

The Progressive period was an era in which the United States experienced rapid growth and development—in its population, its cities and towns, settlement of the West, commerce and industry, transportation, and technology. This growth was reflected in the American newspaper industry, which expanded exponentially between 1880 and 1917. In that period, the number of English-language daily newspapers grew steadily from 850 in 1880 to 1,967 in 1900 to 2,200 in 1910. (An additional four hundred dailies of other types, including foreign-language and socialist newspapers were also published in that year.) National circulation also increased, aided by faster printing presses, growing advertising revenue, and better transportation. Daily circulation totals grew from 3.1 million in 1880 to 15.1 million in 1900 and 22.4 million in 1910. In addition to daily newspapers, there was a thriving business in weeklies, bi-weeklies and semi-weekly newspapers. The number of weeklies published increased from 12,000 in 1900 to about 14,000 in 1910. While the majority of these were published in English, there was also a boom in foreign-language publications, which reached their peak in 1917. Nearly half of the 1,325 foreign-language papers in that year were published in German; the rest were published in Polish, Russian, Italian, and Yiddish. These newspapers played an important role in allowing a voice to recent immigrants, many of whom did not read or speak English.

The Progressive Era saw the emergence of giant metropolitan dailies, city newspapers such as the *New York World* and the *New York Journal*, which during the Spanish-American War of 1898 occasionally reached daily circulations of more than one million. In an effort to appeal to all segments of the population, these newspapers continued an earlier trend of differentiating between news "types." They appealed to a range of readers by developing specialty pages and sections devoted to sports, finance, women, entertainment, and society. In an effort to capitalize on the increased leisure time available to the growing middle class and even the working class, many daily newspapers began to publish a Sunday edition. In 1890, about 250 dailies had Sunday editions and this number doubled by the turn of the century.

These years also saw the explosion of special-interest newspapers, from those addressing foreign-language or ethnic audiences to those expressing specific political or social views. These publications represented groups as widely different as the woman suffrage and the anti-suffrage movements, the prohibition movement, the Socialist and Populist parties, African Americans, German-Americans, and the Methodist, Congregational and Roman Catholic churches. Some of these, like the National American Woman Suffrage Association's *Woman's Journal* and the Anti-Saloon League's *American Issue,* were established for the specific purpose of promoting the group's reform and ceased publication once that reform was accomplished. Others, like the NAACP's *Crisis* and the Catholic Church's *Boston Pilot,* continued publication into the twenty-first century.

The growth of newspapers was greatly fueled by a simultaneous growth in the advertising industry. By 1890, advertising was the chief means of promotion of national brand-name products. Department stores bought entire newspaper pages to promote storewide sales or specific items. Advertising agencies, first established in the late 1860s, now began to do more than buy and re-sell bulk newspaper space. They began to design and write ads for customers, as well. During the 1880s, advertising slowly began to replace sales and subscriptions as the chief source of newspaper revenue so that by 1914, 66 percent of newspapers' revenue came from advertising. Some newspaper critics began to fear the influence of advertising on journalism and in 1911, journalist Will Irwin conducted an investigation of major newspapers across the country to discover how often they curbed their reporting to mollify advertisers and political allies. One proposed solution, which had little success, was to create an "adless" newspaper supported by subscribers. Another was to create a non-partisan, adless newspaper funded by city government. Others designed codes of ethics they hoped would erect a wall between the advertising and news function of newspapers.

Developments in Technology

Developments in technology also aided the growth of the newspaper industry. Advances in printing technology brought the invention and adoption of steam-powered rotary presses that in 1890 could print seventy-two thousand eight-page papers—the average size of many dailies at that time—in an hour. Another innovation in printing was the invention of color presses, which allowed newspapers to print color supplements and color comics, a strategy initially used to attract poor and immigrant readers, particularly by what were labeled as "sensational" papers. The *New York World* was one of the first newspapers to do this in 1893 in its use of yellow on the dress of the main character ("The Yellow Kid") in the popular comic strip "Hogan's Alley." Other technological developments introduced during the 1890s included the use of half-tone photographs, which allowed for realistic and sometimes lurid depictions of events, and the linotype, which allowed an operator to rapidly set lines of type at a keyboard similar to that of a typewriter. One linotype operator could do the work of five men and this sped up the process of setting pages significantly.

Major advances in communication technology revolutionized the way reporters collected information and wrote stories. AT&T began to build telephone lines from New York to other cities and states in 1885. As telephone service became available, newspapers were quick to adapt the way they collected news and by 1898 a leading trade publication, *The Fourth Estate,* declared the telephone to be "absolutely essential to the newspaper." Reporters covering breaking news on deadline ("legmen") could now phone their stories into the newsroom where an editor would transcribe their story and prepare it for printing. The wireless was another technology that allowed for instant communication across vast spaces. In 1903, a regular news service opened between New York and London, and in 1909, newspapers started using the wireless on a regular basis.

For those who still relied on footwork, however, advances in transportation also made their jobs easier and more efficient. Elevated railways and underground streetcar services in cities like New York and Boston eased street congestion and made it easier and quicker for reporters to get from one part of the city to another. Automobiles were another invention that eventually made getting from one place to another easier and faster, especially for reporters working in rural areas or traveling from town to town. Motorcars were first introduced in the 1890s and, by 1908, Henry Ford had produced his "Model T," billed as "a motorcar for the multitudes." The development of gasoline-powered trucks also affected the delivery of newspapers so that they could be distributed throughout cities and rural areas to more readers more quickly.

These technological developments also played a role in newspapers in that inventions and technological breakthroughs were often treated as stories and were frequently referred to with awe as miracles, magical, and awe-inspiring. Science and technology were often news makers and became the frequent subject of editorial comment. Automobiles (and later airplanes), which became ubiquitous by the mid-1920s, were initially seen as an oddity, then a fad, then a noisy, smoke-belching danger to all who used the road. Steamships, which by 1892 could carry more than two thousand passengers and cross the Atlantic in five and one-half days, seemed to pose at least two dangers. First, because the larger passenger liners made cheaper fares possible for steerage passengers, more and poorer immigrants could now flood the country. Second, because captains often raced to set a record for their steamship line, ships on the North Atlantic route faced an increased danger of running into icebergs. The sinking of the "unsinkable" Titanic in 1912 provided newspapers with a sensational chance to ponder the dangers of over-reliance on technology while at the same time praising the miracle of the wireless that allowed the sinking ship to call for help and transmit information about the disaster to newspapers on the mainland.

Newspaper Consolidation and Competition

Another development of the period, the consolidation of business interests in chains and monopolies, also affected the newspaper industry. Successful publishers began to acquire multiple newspapers, expanding their influence and power from the regional to the national level. One of the earliest of these, E.W. Scripps, established a chain of afternoon dailies in middle-sized cities through the Midwest. This became the Scripps-McRae League of Newspapers in 1889 and included eighteen papers in states from Ohio to Colorado by 1893. One of the most notorious of chain owners was Californian William Randolph Hearst, who started out in 1887 as the editor of his father's San Francisco Examiner. In 1895, Hearst purchased the New York Journal and by 1920 owned eleven newspapers, at least one magazine, and a press association, the International News Service. While chains made owners wealthy and even encouraged the establishment of new newspapers in some regions, more often they acted to put less powerful newspaper owners or newspapers out of business. One such publisher, Frank Munsey, was infamous for buying newspapers in cities where he already owned one and then either combining them or shutting down his latest acquisition.

Despite consolidation, most cities had several daily newspapers. Chicago and Boston, for example, each had eight dailies in 1900, while New York had nine. Competition for the news, readers, and advertising was fierce and often led to circulation wars. One method of gaining more readers and increasing circulation was to lower prices from the average two or three cents of the period to just a penny. This might lure readers away from a competitor in the short run, but the competitor often responded by lowering its cost as well, and prices usually returned to normal within the year.

Newspapers in competition with each other also promoted stunts to attract readers. In these cases, reporters and editors came up with a gimmick that would peak readers' interest. Though it might not be newsworthy in itself, a stunt might become newsworthy simply because of the attention and publicity it attracted. In the winter of 1889–1890, the World created such a media event when it sent its reporter Nellie Bly (Elizabeth Cochrane) on a fabled trip around the world in 72 days. In addition to publishing regular logs of her adventures, the World published Nellie Bly songs and illustrated board games, sponsored lotteries (to be won by whoever guessed the exact time of her arrival at a specific location), and organized welcome committees when she arrived in major cities along the route. Women reporters often featured in such stunts, playing on societal expectations that women were incapable of physical danger or exertion.

Newspapers also launched crusades or investigations to attract readers. Though publishers' true motivation might be to increase readership and promote themselves as champions of the people, these crusades often had the added benefit of actually bringing about positive change. In 1897, for example, Hearst's New York Evening Journal launched a crusade in support of striking miners in Pennsylvania. The Journal published more than forty articles, editorials, and cartoons in support of the strike and calling for the punishment of local police who fired on miners, killing twenty. Although the police were acquitted, Hearst did arouse sympathy for the plight of the miners, which might have contributed to later improvements in their working conditions. In another crusade, the New York World in 1905 launched an investigation of fraud in the powerful Equitable Life Assurance Society that led to strict regulatory legislation of the insurance industry. Other crusades focused on political corruption. In San Francisco, Fremont Older's San Francisco Chronicle campaigned for civic reform, specifically targeting city machine politics and the corrupt party bosses.

Many crusades, however, were based on flimsy evidence and promoted through lurid headlines, overimaginative illustrations, and sensational claims. Competition among newspapers sometimes led to poorly considered campaigns that backfired for specific publishers or the newspaper industry in general. In 1898, for example, Pulitzer's New York World and Hearst's New York Journal exploited the situation in Cuba and the explosion of the U.S. battleship, the Maine, to promote war with Spain. After the Spanish-American War was over and the bodies were counted, critics blamed the newspapers for jingoism and war mongering. In another instance, Hearst's Journal ran a bitter campaign against President William McKinley's successful bid for re-election in 1900. When McKinley was assassinated in 1901 by an anarchist reportedly carrying a copy of the Journal in his pocket, many held Hearst responsible.

Press Criticism and Improvement

Examples like these led critics to attack any newspapers that used these promotional tactics—reduced prices, stunts, crusades, imaginative headlines, illustrations, cartoons, and color—as sensational or yellow journals. The newspaper industry responded to curb such criticism. Bowing to critics and public pressure, newspapers began to publish corrections of inaccurate information and address readers' complaints on their editorial pages. Press associations, established during the second half of the 1800s mostly by men working in the news industry, sought ways to improve the industry and developed codes of ethics that, unfortunately, were unenforceable. In his last years, Joseph Pulitzer, who had never received a college education himself, began to promote the idea of college training for journalists and at his death in 1911, left an endowment to establish the Columbia University School of Journalism. His endowment also established the Pulitzer Prize, which eventually rewarded journalists for good writing, accurate reporting, courage, and integrity.

Contributions of the Progressive Era Press

Newspapers reached their heyday during the Progressive Era, reaching peak circulations and enjoying a level of competition not seen since in the newspaper industry. They investigated, reported, and interpreted events as well as the important issues of the period. They played an important role in how Americans viewed the world. Immigrants turned to newspapers as a way of learning about this new land. The middle-class looked to newspapers for a reinforcement of lifestyles and values they cherished and clung to in a changing world. Business leaders used newspapers to promote their speculations and business interests and to carry advertisements for their products and promote a spirit of consumerism across the land. Political leaders carried out their campaigns in newspapers and sought their endorsement.

These groups and individuals also found themselves the subject of newspaper stories, sometimes to their detriment. Stories about the "immigration flood" that related immigration to increases in crime provided fuel for the nativist movement that sought to regulate or restrict immigration. Middle-class conservatives felt threatened by stories reporting advances made by the woman's movement and hardened their resistance to such change. Members of the industrial and commercial elite often found themselves at the wrong end of the pen in stories investigating the exploitation of workers, fraud, and corporate corruption. Likewise, public officials found themselves under increased scrutiny in the press.

Newspapers and magazines of the era also served as critics of the status quo and promoted many of the important political and economic reforms of the period. Paradoxically, many mainstream newspapers tended to be conservative in the face of social reform and lagged far behind the more radical reform papers such as those of the woman suffrage and labor movements. Regardless of their position on specific issues, however, newspapers of the Progressive Era were active in the national discussion of controversial issues. They brought these issues to the public's attention, promoted debate by publishing the positions of opposing sides, acted both as a moderator and participant in many of these debates, and generally served as a facilitator of public discussion.

Further Reading

Boyer, Paul et al., eds. *The Enduring Vision.* Lexington, MA: D.C. Heath, 1990.

Burt, Elizabeth V. *The Progressive Era: Primary Documents on Events from 1890 to 1914.* Westport, CT: Greenwood Press, 2004.

Campbell, W. Joseph. *Yellow Journalism: Puncturing the Myths, Defining the Legacies.* Westport, CT: Praeger Publishers, 2001.

Douglas, George H. *The Golden Age of the Newspaper.* Westport, CT: Greenwood Press, 1999.

Gould, Lewis L.. *America in the Progressive Era, 1890–1914.* Harlow, England: Pearson Education Limited, 2001.

Irwin, Will. *The American Newspaper: A Series Appearing in Collier's Magazine, January-July1911,* edited by Clifford F. Weigle. and David C. Clark. Ames: Iowa State University, 1969.

Kessler, Lauren. *The Dissident Press: Alternative Journalism in American History.* Newbury Park, CA: Sage Publications, 1984.

Marzolf, Marion Tuttle. *Civilizing Voices: American Press Criticism, 1880–1950.* New York: Hastings House, 1991.

Mott, Frank Luther. *American Journalism: A History of Newspapers in the United States Through 260 Years: 1690 to 1950,* rev. ed. New York: MacMillan, 1950.

Sloan, Wm. David, ed. *The Media in America: A History,* 5th ed.. Northport, AL: Vision Press, 2002.

Smythe, Ted Curtis. *The Gilded Age Press, 1865–1900.* Westport, CT: Praeger Press, 2003.

——. "The Reporter, 1880–1900: Working Conditions and Their Influence on News." *Journalism History* 7 (1980): 1–10.

ELIZABETH V. BURT

PROGRESSIVE

Founded in 1909 by Wisconsin Senator Robert La Follette as an organ for the independent progressive movement that he was helping to lead, the *Progressive* is best known today for the legal battle over whether it would be permitted to publish an article on the "secret" of the hydrogen bomb.

Initially called *La Follette's Weekly Magazine,* the debut issue promised to "hit as hard as we can, giving and taking blows for the cause with joy in our hearts." "Fighting Bob" La Follette hoped the magazine would not only bolster the progressive cause, but also turn a profit. (Running a political organization and maintaining two households was expensive, and La Follette did not have access to the family wealth or campaign contributions enjoyed by his Senate colleagues.) However, the magazine never attracted the circulation or advertising La Follette had hoped for, and as a result ran at a substantial deficit. At its peak, the weekly reached some forty thousand subscribers, and in 1914 it was scaled back to a monthly tabloid. In 1929, the La Follettes entered into a partnership with Madison [Wisconsin] *Capital Times* publisher William Evjue, expanding the four-page newspaper to weekly publication and renaming it the *Progressive.* Evjue and the La Follettes parted ways during the build-up to World War II, and in 1947 the editors announced that they were suspending publication. Three months later, after distraught readers sent in more than $40,000 in contributions, the *Progressive* was reborn as a monthly magazine issued as a nonprofit venture.

The magazine's early years were dominated by the La Follettes. La Follette's wife Belle co-edited the women's section, and wrote articles condemning racial segregation. His son, Robert Jr. (who succeeded him in the Senate) wrote from Washington on national politics. But La Follette and the progressive movement he sought to spearhead were both on the decline. La Follette's quest for the Republican presidential nomination never gained traction, and his 1924 independent campaign left his health broken (he died eight months later) and his political reputation in tatters.

Evjue shared the La Follettes' roots in Midwestern progressivism, but under his control the *Progressive* increasingly served as the *Capital Times'* regional weekly edition. When the La Follettes resumed control in 1940, they hired political writer Morris Rubin to take the editorial helm—a position he held for the next thirty-three years. Rubin rebuilt the circulation from the five thousand mostly Wisconsin readers he inherited from Evjue with a heavily political magazine, featuring extensive commentary, articles on current events and foreign policy, and an extensive book review section. Committed to "the fight for a genuine program of progressive democracy," the *Progressive* gave space to sitting senators but also to Socialist Party standard-bearer Norman Thomas. It proclaimed its commitment to civil liberties and attacked Senator Joseph McCarthy (who had ousted La Follette Jr. from his Senate seat), but agreed that the government had every right to blacklist Communist Party members. But in the 1950s, the *Progressive* published articles criticizing U.S. nuclear policy, clandestine CIA activities, calling for recognition of China, and championing minority rights.

In 1973, Rubin retired (becoming publisher), and was replaced by Washington editor Erwin Knoll. Knoll's *Progressive* featured more in-depth investigative and explanatory journalism, such as a 1984 report on Central American death squads. But it is probably best remembered for "The H-Bomb Secret: How We Got It, Why We're Telling It," published in November 1979 after several months battling a government injunction against publication. The article, entirely compiled from publicly available sources, was intended to lift the cloak of secrecy Knoll and author Howard Morland believed was stifling a much-needed debate on nuclear weapons policy. The battle cost the *Progressive* a quarter of a million dollars, and while the injunction was ultimately lifted this was not on Constitutional grounds, but rather because the "secrets" at issue were published in other papers while the case was pending. Knoll edited the magazine until his death in 1994, when he was succeeded by Matthew Rothschild, who has in many ways returned the *Progressive* to its roots as a journal of commentary and analysis, although one open to much more radical politics than its founders would have been comfortable with.

Further Reading

DeVolpi, A. et al. *Born Secret: The H-Bomb, the Progressive Case, and National Security.* New York: Pergamon Press, 1981. http://progressive.org/ (includes recent issues, and a pdf of the November 1979 H-Bomb Secret issue), (accessed September 16, 2006).

Thelen, David P. *Robert M. La Follette and the Insurgent Spirit.* Boston: Little, Brown and Co., 1976.
Weisberger, Bernard A. *The La Follettes of Wisconsi,* Madison: University of Wisconsin Press, 1994.

JON BEKKEN

PROPAGANDA AND JOURNALISM

The press has been the target of propagandists from its infancy in America. The first English-language newspaper in the New World lasted only a single issue when Boston's *Publick Occurrences*, appearing on September 29, 1690, criticized the governing council of Massachusetts. Benjamin Harris had published "without authority" and his refusal to serve as propagandist for local authorities meant the colonies would have to wait another fourteen years before another newspaper saw the light of day. John Campbell's *Boston News-Letter*, begun on April 24, 1704, for fifteen years faithfully served as propagandist for civil authority. The colony's governor or his secretary exercised expressed authority to review each issue of Campbell's paper before distribution. This eventually alienated the paper from its public when Campbell continued to support the unpopular administration of Governor Joseph Dudley despite widespread colonial opposition because of his history of maladministration.

Colonial America's most famous printer, Benjamin Franklin, spoke in behalf of printers who were criticized for the opinions appearing in their pages. His "Apologie for Printers," appearing in the June 10, 1731, issue of his *Pennsylvania Gazette*, claimed that printers should not be blamed for the arguments appearing in their papers. "The business of printing has chiefly to do with men's opinions," Franklin wrote, and that meant publishing points of view with which they disagreed. For Franklin, that meant widely circulating "both truth and error," and trusting readers to know the difference.

In the years leading up to the American Revolution, printers were put in the position of propagandist for Loyalist or Patriot forces who saw the press as an instrument of mobilization. Revolutionary leader John Adams divided the country into thirds—one-third favored separation from Britain, one third opposed, and a middle third were undecided. The press became a place where each side tried to persuade the undecided of the rightness of their cause. Adams cousin, Samuel Adams, helped organize the Sons of Liberty, whose Committees of Correspondence spread propaganda throughout the colonies arguing for independence. The so-called "Boston Massacre" of 1770 and the "Boston Tea Party" of 1773 were exercises in political propaganda. Five colonists were killed in a snowball throwing melee with British troops, but the rendering of the episode that most colonists saw was Paul Revere's depiction of soldiers standing as a firing squad and executing defenseless civilians. The tea party was a piece of political theater in which boxes of tea were hurled into Boston harbor to protest the English tax on tea. Newspapers that resisted being mouthpieces for revolutionary forces, such as the *Boston Evening*

Post, operated by Thomas and John Fleet, were silenced. A similar fate awaited publishers of the *Boston Chronicle* and the *Pennsylvania Chronicle*. Patriot printers John Dunlap, James Humphreys, and Benjamin Edes faced the same fate when they resisted publishing the propaganda of Loyalist forces. Other newspapers simply tried to stay in business by printing the propaganda of whichever side seemed winning to be during the six long years of fighting during the American Revolution. Despite a series of setbacks on the battlefield, General George Washington continued to get a good press to prop up the fragile wartime morale.

Propaganda ruled in the party press during the early Republican period. Newspapers could not afford to be neutral. They were financed through competing political parties, the Federalists and the Democratic-Republicans, and were expected to reflect the views of the political interests that supported them. Federalists attacked their political opponents as "anarchists" and Democratic-Republican press charged their political opposition favored "monarchy." The Federalists, led by Secretary of the Treasury Alexander Hamilton, financed a nationwide network of newspapers as a vehicle for expressing their political point of view. Thomas Jefferson, who would become the third president, was the leader of the agrarian forces that heartily opposed in the press the creation of too much power in Washington, D.C. Each side was intemperate in their unbridled use of personal invective in pushing their case. Federalist editors charged Jefferson was a "mulatto," a calumny in the early nineteenth century. Readers were told if Jefferson was elected he would "burn Bibles." Jefferson's allies in the press were no less measured in their political propaganda. They argued that if Jefferson lost the presidential election of 1800 to John Adams, the American experiment in democracy was over. Jefferson narrowly won the election.

The press remained a site of political propaganda well into the administration of Andrew Jackson. By the 1830s the Federalists had faded into history, and the press became the place where competing candidates within the Democratic Party could make their case before the public. When a Pennsylvania publisher who was on Jackson's payroll criticized "Old Hickory" for naming John C. Calhoun as his vice presidential running mate, Jackson suspended payments to the editor who wound up bankrupted. Until newspapers could wean themselves away from economic dependence on political benefactors, they were forced to serve as conduits of political propaganda. Beginning in 1833, the press could increasingly portray itself as resisting propaganda from "private interests" to serve the "public interest." This became a successful marketing strategy in the intense competition to win readers for advertisers, who helped subsidize the astonishing growth of penny papers over much of urban America.

By the late Gilded Age nearly half of all operating costs for the nation's newspapers was paid through advertising. Advertising was a factor in the rise of yellow journalism, initially appearing in the pages of William Randolph Hearst's *New York Journal* and Joseph Pulitzer's *New York World*, a narrative style that relied on sensation and celebrity to stimulate circulation. Hearst, as well as his mentor and eventual competitor, Pulitzer, sold sensationalism and the profits made it irresistible. Hearst, for instance, ran a series of articles blaming Spain for sinking the American warship *U.S. Maine* in February, 1898. Although the stories were of dubious accuracy, some historians have argued that Hearst—and Pulitzer—played an important role in inciting the Spanish-American War with this brand of "propaganda."

The cooperation between journalists and the government entered a new phase during World War I (1914–1918). In April 1917, President Woodrow Wilson appointed controversial journalist George Creel the U.S. Committee on Public Information (CPI), the first large-scale American government propaganda agency. The Committee's goal was to unite American public opinion behind the war, and Wilson and Creel acted on the idea that few people knew how to do that better at the time than journalists. The Committee inundated Americans with information extolling American ideals, vilifying German militarism, and telling citizens what they could do to help win the war. At the same time, the Committee enlisted journalists and others to deliver America's message abroad in more than thirty countries. Creel, who was a former muckraker and a true believer in American exceptionalism, called his book detailing his propaganda war in the war *How We Advertised America: The First Telling of the Amazing Story of the Committee on Public Information that Carried the Gospel of Americanism to Every Corner of the Globe* (1920).

If the word "propaganda" carried negative connotations before the war, its meaning took on even more worrying implications after the war as mass communications became more sophisticated. Webster's dictionary defined propaganda as "the spreading of ideas, information, or rumor for the purpose of helping or injuring an institution, a cause, or a person; and ideas, facts, or allegations spread deliberately to further one's cause or to damage an opposing cause; also, a public action having such an effect." The propaganda work of journalists, advertisers, and others such as the public relations specialist Edward L. Bernays in 1917–1918, led many observers to believe that the government had oversold the war to a public that was too susceptible to emotional appeals. After the war, columnist Walter Lippmann, who had worked in military propaganda in Europe, wrote a powerful critique of modern democracy called *Public Opinion* (1922) and argued that the combination of propaganda and censorship helped to prevent citizens from understanding the real world.

Scholars began to study propaganda systematically after they had seen the results of government media manipulation in World War I. In 1927, Harold Lasswell published one of the first scholarly analyses of modern media manipulation entitled *Propaganda Technique in the World War*. Lasswell said that all war propaganda had certain characteristics: 1) blaming the enemy for starting the war and, if possible, personalizing the enemy (e.g., in World War I, it was the Kaiser); 2) accusing the enemy of unspeakable atrocities, what Lasswell called "Satanism"; 3) giving an illusion of victory and attempting to demoralize the enemy with information whether true or otherwise; 4) explaining to the home front how citizens could contribute to winning the war; and 5) trying to win over neutral countries. In 1935, Yale University psychology professor Leonard Doob explained the difference between education and propaganda in his book *Propaganda: Its Psychology and Technique.* "The educator tries to tell people how to think; the propagandist, what to think," Dobb explained. "The educator strives to develop individual responsibility; the propagandist, mass effects. The educator fails unless he [or she] achieves an open mind; the propagandist unless he achieves a closed mind."

Propagandists were not limited to wartime. During the Great Depression of the 1930s, one of the most popular figures was Father Charles Coughlin, who edited a magazine called *Social Justice*, which boasted circulation at half a million. Every week Coughlin would supplement that circulation with a radio broadcast of his views to 3.5 million Americans in the late 1930s and beyond. Among other things, Coughlin broadcasts attacked President Franklin Delano Roosevelt as a warmonger. St. Louis journalist Marquis Childs, skeptical of Coughlin's verbal attacks and character assassination, took a special interest in the priest's work. Through research, Childs discovered and reported that an article in *Social Justice* bearing Coughlin's byline was a word-for-word translation of a radio speech delivered by Nazi propagandist Joseph Goebbels.

Goebbels, Adolph Hitler, and the Nazis, of course, became masters of using mass media to manipulate vast numbers of people. They used radio, public address systems, film, and public spectacles to create propaganda that was far more disturbing than what had been produced during the Great War. In studying the effects of such propaganda, a powerful effects model of media influence grew out of the Marxist Frankfurt School of intellectuals who tried to explain Germany's willingness to accept Nazism.

American propaganda during World War II was also more effective and complex. After Pearl Harbor, Roosevelt set up the Foreign Information Service (FIS) at the urging of playwright Robert Sherwood. It was based on the idea that the FIS could use mass communication to "tell the world about the aims and objectives of the American government and the American people." Journalists, writers, broadcasters, and others, most of whom were prewar interventionists who believed that words and ideas could be used to fight fascism, joined the new organization. In June, 1942, President Franklin D. Roosevelt combined several government information agencies to create the Office of War Information (OWI) and made broadcast journalist Elmer Davis its director. In 1942, the United States also entered the world of international propaganda with the Voice of America (VOA).

By all accounts, the FIS, the OWI, and VOA were far more sophisticated in their use of psychology and media effects research than had been the case with the CPI in World War I. Many of the people who worked in propaganda for the American government during World War II went on to become leading journalists and scholars in communication research in the postwar world. During the Cold War between the United States and the Soviet Union, enormous resources were devoted to studying propaganda and how to turn world opinion against international Communism. Scholarly research into the power of propaganda proceeded on a massive scale. Research challenged the powerful effects model, contending it overestimated connections between the power of the media and independent thought. In 1955, Elihu Katz and Paul Lazarsfeld, and later Joseph Klapper in 1960, refuted the idea that the media could tell people what to think. Their research led to what became known as the limited effects theory of mass communication. In 1963, political scientist Bernard C. Cohen wrote *The Press and Foreign Policy* in which he argued that even if the media could not tell people what to think, it could perhaps at least tell them what to think about.

By the early 1970s, communication researchers lost faith in the limited effects model. In 1972, a landmark Chapel Hill Study provided the agenda-setting hypothesis about mass communication, which breathed new life into the powerful effects model. The hypothesis held that news outlets have special interests they want to serve, which determine the perspective they report, and the stories they report.

In 1976, George Gerbner first described his cultivation theory of mass communication. It held that television had become the main source of storytelling in society and as such its misuse had created a homogeneous and fearful populace. TV was closing the intellectual commons by reducing the diversity of viewpoints held by the citizenry. Television, he argued, fed people from all strata of society the same thoughts and ideas, thereby allowing an idea with broad appeal to take hold on a mass scale without questioning or thought or vetting. In this way, he argued, television shaped societal values.

Later media effects research in the 1980s and 1990s emphasized how the media "construct" reality, and also how audiences build their own view of social reality as well as their place in it when information is framed certain ways by television, newspapers, and radio. That notion may be extended to the study of online news as well. Key studies in the construction of reality by news outlets included analyses of the U.S. student movement against the Vietnam War in the late 1960s, and opinion formation concerning nuclear power in 1989. During the early 1990s, communication researchers described the agenda-melding function in media effects research, which suggested that the mass media expanded knowledge by exposing people to things that they might not otherwise think about. In so doing, mass communication could help citizens find other people with whom we have common interest.

Most researchers agreed that the spread of digital and web-based technologies in the twenty-first century was creating a new opportunity for propagandists to use media to arouse and mobilize public opinion for a new range of purposes.

Further Reading

Lasswell, Harold D. *Propaganda Technique in World War I.* Cambridge, MA: MIT Press, 1927, 1971.

Rogers, Everett M. *A History of Communication Study: A Biographical Approach.* New York: The Free Press, 1994.

Shulman, Holly Cowan. *The Voice of America: Propaganda and Democracy, 1941–1945.* Madison: University of Wisconsin Press, 1990.

Simpson, Christopher. *Science of Coercion: Communication Research and Psychological Warfare, 1945–1960.* New York : Oxford University Press, 1994.

Vaughn, Stephen. *Holding Fast the Inner Lines: Democracy, Nationalism and the Committee on Public Information.* Chapel Hill: University of North Carolina Press, 1980.

Winkler, Allan M. *Politics of Propaganda: The Office of War Information, 1942–1945.* New Haven, CT: Yale University Press, 1978.

Debra A. Schwartz

PUBLIC RELATIONS AND JOURNALISM

The relationship between public relations and journalism is, and always has been, a symbiotic marriage of convenience, with each discipline depending on, and harboring a healthy suspicion of the other. Editors and reporters depend on public relations professionals for information that would be difficult to uncover independently, and public relations people need journalists as part of their repertoire in getting information on behalf of their clients to the public and opinion leaders.

This relationship starts for many in the academic world. Public relations professionals frequently matriculate in journalism schools, and at the very least, take journalistic writing courses. The skills required for each profession are very much the same. The University of Wisconsin, for example, includes public relations as part of their journalism school, while that university's business school also offers courses in public relations.

Journalists and public relations specialists each provide information to the public, but the manner in which that information is generated makes all the difference. In the case of journalists, the process is often as follows: 1) Determine whether a topic is worthy of exploration. 2) Seek out reliable sources of information. 3) Corroborate the information gained by finding other sources to substantiate it. 4) Find contradicting information from other sources to provide balance. 5) Write or produce the news piece. 6) Submit to an editor for evaluation and editing. 7) Re-write the story for publication.

This process involves reaching out and seeking information in order to inform the public. It includes much research and verification of facts, and often includes opposing points of view.

Public relations professionals, on the other hand, normally are not involved in the investigative process of seeking information, other than fact-finding within their clients' organizations to tell the story accurately. Their fact checking and research are with sources friendly to the client, and not inclined to offering opposing points of view. And, while journalists pull information from around them, public relations people are more prone to push information out to the public—often through willing journalists.

The public relations process can be demonstrated as follows: 1) Work with the client to determine issues of importance to communicate, and become educated on those issues. 2) Determine which elements of the public need that information, i.e., legislators, regulators, constituent groups, or the general public. 3) Produce either background information or fully written press releases to present the information in the desired light, targeted to the desired audience. 4) Select media outlets to help disseminate the information. This may be accomplished via purchased advertising space, events, demonstrations, or through journalists. 5) Measure the effectiveness of the communication.

Journalists often appropriately question the motivations of PR professionals, and certainly the objectivity of the information they receive from PR departments. But, they also realize that without press releases on topics ranging from politicians' positions to recalls on faulty products, they would never be able to collect all the information they need to report. In addition, in an increasingly complex world, the level of technical and intellectual expertise required of journalists and their reading, viewing, and listening publics is very great, and growing daily. Journalists rely in expert testimony, so to speak, from companies and organizations that can put highly complex issues and concepts into terms that laypeople can more easily understand.

In addition, the work loads of radio, television, and newspaper reporters are often overwhelming, so a well written press release that is not overtly promotional, and which addresses both pros and cons of a given issue or event, is often seen as a Godsend to editors and reporters who are unable to do the needed research.

In small town newspapers across America, and in some larger market outlets, press releases from chemical companies, university extension departments, and teachers' unions are printed verbatim, because the editor, reporter, and business manager at those newspapers are often all the same person, and investigative journalism takes a back seat to the challenging logistics of putting out a paper every week.

Many small town newspapers, such as the *Cambridge News* and *Deerfield Independent* in southern Wisconsin, rely on press releases from companies, health agencies, government departments, and non-profits. With a small staff of maybe three people, including the ad salesperson, the ability to seek out information in a journalistic way just is not realistic. In terms of press releases from political campaigns, such newspapers usually use press releases, but often attempt equal treatment, and by supplementing the releases with individual interviews where the editor has the opportunity to probe more deeply

Public relations professionals and journalists do have mutual interests at heart, but there are negotiations that take place for both to achieve satisfactory conditions for the exchange of information. One key element can be the promise of exclusivity on a given story being offered by the PR person. The negotiations which take place can include assurances of certain wording in exchange for making sure the story is the exclusive property of the newspaper, TV, or radio station in question.

Hence, an interview with the American president, or perhaps with a famous or infamous celebrity, will have journalistic limitations accepted under the condition of exclusivity. While failing somewhat in journalistic standards of thorough investigation and openness, these arrangements acknowledge that some information is better than none, and that journalism is in itself a business operating in a marketplace, with competition for stories resulting in decisions that are partly economic in their nature.

The rise of public relations as a profession and as an area for serious research has a long history. Prior to World War I, the field was often associated with press agentry. Willard G. Blyer, who was instrumental in starting journalism education at the University of Wisconsin, believed it was important to understand the close connection between journalism and PR, and to teach people who would work in one or both fields, high professional standards. In addition to his teaching duties, Bleyer himself worked in public relations for the University of Wisconsin for several years, editing its *Press Bulletin*.

During World War I, the United States government began using mass communication systematically for propaganda. Edward L. Bernays, called by some the father of public relations, worked in government propaganda during the war and considered it a laboratory where he learned how modern communication could be used to make appeals to the public. A nephew (by marriage) of Sigmund Freud, Bernays thought that a knowledge of psychology could contribute to more effective publicity. During the 1920s, he wrote about "crystallizing" and "manipulating" public opinion. He utilized the media of the early, mid, and late 20th Century to sell ideas, politicians, and products ranging from an appreciation of ballet to hiring returning servicemen after World War I. He worked on behalf of the American Tobacco Company starting in 1928, but during the 1960s, worked to communicate the dangers of smoking, expressing regret for his previous efforts.

In an interview late in his life, Bernays observed that the public relations function was not just "press-agentry, flackery, and publicity," but should be a "two way street, advising the client on attitudes and actions to win over the public..." and then "educating, informing, and persuading the public to accept these social goods, ideas, concepts, or whatever." The media were necessary to communicate these goals.

Following the end of World War II in 1945, public relations continued to expand and became incorporated into university curricula. With this growth came efforts improve standards of professionalism and ethics. The Public Relations Society of America (PRSA), was chartered in 1947. In 2007, it was the world's largest association of PR professionals with some twenty thousand members and more than one hundred chapters. Within its code of ethics was a statement of professional values which was germane to

those interested the relationship between public relations practitioners and the news media: "We serve the public interest by acting as advocates for those we represent. We provide a voice in the marketplace of ideas, facts, and viewpoints to aid informed public debate.... We acquire, and responsibly use, specialized knowledge and experience. We build mutual understanding, credibility, and relationships among a wide array of institutions and audiences." The key phrases spoke of aiding informed public debate, and using specialized knowledge to build mutual understanding.

If the PRSA had ethical intentions, other critics and organizations have had long-standing and serious doubts about public relations. In 1922, columnist Walter Lippmann in *Public Opinion* warned about the power of publicity to prevent citizens from understanding the real world. In 1961, the historian Daniel Boorstin wrote an influential book entitled *The Image* in which he examined how modern mass media made it possible for public relations and advertising to create "pseudo events" and a celebrity culture. Scott Cutlip, who did much to bring the study of public relations into university curricula and who also wrote one of the most comprehensive histories of the field, entitled his book *The Unseen Power* (1994). In 2006, the Center for Media and Democracy's *PR Watch* (http://www.prwatch.org/cmd/index.html) included the following on their web site: "Unlike advertising, public relations is often hard to recognize. 'The best PR is invisible,' say industry insiders. To spin the news in favor of their clients, PR firms specialize in setting up phony citizens' groups and scientific 'experts' who spin out contrived research." *PR Watch* went on to explained that it exposed "the hidden activities of secretive, little-known...firms... the invisible men who control our political debates and public opinion, twisting reality and protecting the powerful from scrutiny."

The defenders of public relations have argued that in any controversial campaign, people who were on opposite sides of an argument were quick to identify public relations operatives as the people behind their opponents' attack ads, policy decisions, and much of the political process. But still, journalists at best are too often left to face a murky world where they are confronted with a barrage of conflicting "facts" from opposing sides, and must—or at least should—do the hard work of verifying or debunking the information they are provided.

It is understandable, then, why many people have viewed public relations with suspicion. Certainly, the conventional view of a PR person trying to put a positive spin on a difficult situation has been a view that occurred often within the profession. Crisis control was generally the most public face worn by the public relations profession, in part because nothing caused news coverage like a crisis.

Even in attempting to manage the public relations damage of a crisis situation, PR professionals do provide important information to journalists, but in such situations their credibility has often been deeply questioned by members of the news media, and usually with good reason. Whether it has a White House press secretary, a spokesperson for the once powerful but now discredited corporation Enron, or the representative of a coal mine company after a disastrous collapse, the news media become adversarial in their role in crisis situations, and take little of the information provided as credible until they can investigate further.

Responsible public relations professionals have long understood the importance of being truthful. As one authority on strategic communication, branding, and public relations wisely observed: "Public and private sector organizations alike… are reluctant to proactively report anything but 'good news,' and address bad news only when they think they must. It is as if reporting good news… automatically creates a good impression of the organization, whereas even acknowledging bad news does the opposite." However, organizations should focus on transparency, no matter if the news is good or bad. "By telling the truth, even when the truth looks bad, an organization builds credibility with its stakeholders."

As the world of "new media" grows and changes, the ability of public relations professionals to influence the highly fractured and multiplying daily news sources becomes smaller every day. Blogs, special interest sites, and e-magazines have become a source of information to millions of people worldwide. These sources, while often not journalistic in nature, in terms of corroborating information and parsing stories for accuracy, are seen by many as sources of facts. While a PR professional might influence known journalistic news sources, having in impact on thousands of bloggers or other new media sources has become impossible. This developing trend serves as a frustration for both conventional media journalists, and for the public relations professionals with whom they have worked for many generations.

According to research by Nielsen Net Ratings in 2006, only one in three Internet users in the United States used newspaper web sites, but it was unclear where the other two-thirds got their news, or if the one-third who did go to newspaper sites found other news sources that they considered more credible.

As the news media, and communications as a whole, evolved in the twenty-first century, the public relations and journalism industries also faced the need to evolve. Each represented old media, in many ways, and each attempted to incorporate new models of information dissemination. It remained to be seen if their cooperative/adversarial relationship would also change.

Further Reading

Bernays, Edward L. *Crystallizing Public Opinion.* New York, Boni and Liveright [1923].

——. *Biography of an Idea: Memoirs of Public Relations Counsel, Edward L. Bernays.* New York : Simon and Schuster 1965.

Boorstin, Daniel J. *The Image: A Guide to Pseudo-Events in America.* New York, Harper & Row, [2001, 1964, c1961].

Center for Media and Democracy, *PR Watch,* http://www.prwatch. org/cmd/index.html (accessed April 7, 2007).

Cutlip, Scott M. *The Unseen Power: Public Relations, A History.* Hillsdale, NJ: L. Erlbaum Associates, 1994.

"Danielle Blumenthal, Ph. D., on Strategic Communication, Branding, and Public Relations," http://www.geocities.com/ strategiccommunications_prbrand/ (accessed April 7, 2007).

PETER G. WALLACE

PULITZER, JOSEPH

"I want to tell you in simple English that you are a liar and a puppy," corrupt lobbyist Edward Augustine shouted at a twenty-two-year-old Missouri state senator, rushing him with brass knuckles. In their struggle a gun fired, and Augustine was wounded. Joseph Pulitzer (April 10, 1847–October 29, 1911) was convicted of assault with intent to murder. His $405 fine was paid by friends. This episode was an early indication of Pulitzer's eagerness to take on special interests, a trait that helped to make him one of the architects of the modern American newspaper.

He was the oldest son of Philip Pulitzer, a Jew of Magyar descent, and Louise Berger Pulitzer, a Jew who her son would later claim was a Catholic, to escape a Jewish identity he saw as a lifelong liability. He was born in Makó, Hungary, but grew up in Budapest, where his father was a grain merchant. Plagued by poor eyesight and a scrawny build, he was rejected by the Austrian Army, the French Foreign Legion, and the British military. A recruiter in Hamburg, Germany signed Pulitzer to serve in the Union Army. In September 1864, the tall, skinny, near-sighted, German-speaking recruit with the prominent nose arrived in New York. Ridiculed for his appearance and inadequate English, Pulitzer was eager to get out of the military. At war's end he arrived in St. Louis looking for work.

Pulitzer tended mules, loaded cargo, and was a lumberyard bookkeeper before landing a reporter's job on the *Westliche Post*, a German-language daily. The paper's publisher Carl Schurz was impressed by Pulitzer's intelligence and idealism and made him the paper's state capital reporter. His exposés and excessive work habits earned him the derisive nickname, "Joey, the Jew." Pulitzer was elected to the state senate in December 1869 as a Republican and continued his reporting. The deal-making and corruption of political life made a lasting impression. He strongly supported the presidential campaign of Horace Greeley as a Liberal Republican. At twenty-five, Pulitzer became co-owner and managing editor of the *Post*. At twenty-seven, he became a rich man when he bought the competing *Staats-Zeitung*, closed the paper, and sold its Associated Press franchise. Pulitzer thought the Republican Party "deaf and dumb" to the needs of the poor and bolted it in 1876 to support Democrat Samuel Tilden. Convinced Republicans had stolen the closely fought contest, Pulitzer bought the *St. Louis Dispatch* on December 9, 1878, merged it with the *Evening Post*, and on December 12 brought out the first edition of the *St. Louis Post-Dispatch*, promising the paper would follow no party line but "its own convictions" as a sworn opponent of "all frauds and shams."

Pulitzer began his new life with a wife. Kate Davis was a distant cousin of Jefferson Davis, president of the Confederacy. Five of their seven children reached adulthood, becoming heirs to a publishing empire that over 127 years ran ninety newspapers valued in 2005 at nearly $1.5 billion. Pulitzer's publishing philosophy was forcefully expressed in his first days at the *Post-Dispatch*. "If it is a crime to sympathize with the struggle of the poor," he wrote on December 30, 1878, "we plead guilty." In a January 10, 1879, editorial he argued that "Democracy means opposition to special privileges. Republicanism means favoritism to corporations." He was convinced that the exercise of "money power" was "the great issue" before the country. His paper published tax returns to embarrass local business leaders who hadn't paid their "fair share." Insurance and gas companies, bankers and street car monopolists were targeted next.

Pulitzer helped push the circulation of the *Post-Dispatch* from four to twenty thousand through social responsibility and sensationalism. When a lover's triangle erupted in murder it was sure to make the paper's front page. Publishing a young man's suicide note over unrequited love received similar front-page play. Competitors claimed Pulitzer pandered, but he said such stories were "moralizing agents." This criticism intensified on October 13, 1882, when Pulitzer's editor John Cockerill shot and killed a party hack who threatened him with a gun. Public opposition to the incident deepened Pulitzer's determination to enter New York journalism. He left the daily operation of the *Post-Dispatch* in the hands of subordinates. On May 10, 1883, Pulitzer bought the twenty-three-year-old *New York World* from financier Jay Gould for $346,000. The *World* was a wreck. Its circulation of 22,837 placed it at the back of the pack of Lower Manhattan's Park Row papers. "There is room in this great and growing city," Pulitzer wrote, "for a journal dedicated to the cause of the people rather than the purse of the potentates that will serve and battle for the people with earnest sincerity."

Pulitzer's paper took a deep interest in the urban underclass, the living conditions of the immigrant poor, and the rights of union people. Five million immigrants had come to America in the decade before Pulitzer went to work in New York and many of them had stayed in the city. When a young boy was beaten to death at the Elmira Prison for Boys, the *World* launched an investigation, humanizing the victims of abuse by interviewing mothers "whose boys died from the paddlings." On June 23, 1883, the paper published a particularly heartbreaking story of Kate Sweeny, a young immigrant girl, who was suffocated in raw sewage that flooded her basement apartment on Mulberry Street. "Who killed Kate Sweeny?" the *World* wanted to know. "Nobody seems to think it worth an investigation." Pulitzer arranged to have free blocks of ice delivered to the poor in the summer heat. The inside pages of his paper acculturated new Americans on "hints for improving a personal appearance" and "topics of feminine interest," including advice on "what walking costume milady will wear on a cool day." Readers responded to a paper that took an obvious interest in their welfare. Daily circulation climbed to 56,960 in 1884 and 123,295 in 1885.

No symbol better represented the immigrant experience in America than the Statue of Liberty, and it was the Pulitzer and the *World* that played an instrumental part in bringing the statue to America. As early as 1870 it had been agreed that France would provide the statue and Americans the base for the Goddess of Liberty, but pedestal financing stalled. On March 16, 1885, Pulitzer wrote that "it would be an irrevocable disgrace" if America refused to raise the $100,000 necessary to place the 225-ton statue in New York Harbor as "a symbol of our first century of independence." Readers were told that if they contributed money to the pedestal their names would appear in the *World*. More than 120,000 did. The statue was dedicated on October 28, 1886, and became the symbol of the *New York World* masthead. Two years later a huge stained glass window of the Statue of Liberty greeted visitors at New York's latest skyscraper, the golden-domed *New York World* building.

In 1885, Pulitzer hired twenty-two-year-old illustrator Richard F. Outcault to depict working class life in a series of sketches that led to the creation of the modern color comic strip. Outcault's Yellow Kid was a wildly popular troublemaker who first appeared in "Hogan's Alley" on May 5, 1895. Outcault jumped to William Randolph Hearst's *New York Journal* seventeen months later, bringing the Yellow Kid with him, stimulating circulation wars between Pulitzer and Hearst that historians would call "yellow journalism." Pulitzer did not invent the Sunday Supplement, but he raised it to the level of a beloved past-time for readers who slept in on Sundays after an exhausting six-day work week. In the pages of the *Sunday World*, they were introduced to technological changes from the East and tall tales from the West. They learned of confidence men and sports celebrities, the latest in science and the fairest in fashion. They read of the might of the American military and were transported to the elegance of the Paris salon. Reading the *World* became an adventure, an entertainment, a destination.

The *World*'s daily circulation had soared to 217,769 by September 1887 when Pulitzer helped to invent "stunt journalism" through the undercover reporting of Elizabeth Cochrane, who wrote under the pseudonym "Nellie Bly." Bly auditioned for a job at the *World* by getting herself committed to an insane asylum for women on Blackwell's Island to see for herself what became of women there. On October 9, Bly began her extraordinary series on "a human rat trap" that made sane women sick by forcing them to sit unattended for hours at a time, to choke down meals of stale bread and rancid butter, and to accept the humiliation and terror of freezing cold baths or to risk being beaten. Bly's writing in the *World* captured the suffering of the destitute, many of whom, unable to speak English or defend themselves, were victimized by the state. Mobilized public opinion forced city officials on December 18, 1887, to fire or prosecute sadistic staff members and to spend $1 million to improve care for indigent women. On November 14,

1889, Bly left New York on her highly publicized effort to go around the world in eighty days. More than one million readers entered the *World*'s contest to predict when she would return. Thousands gathered to greet Bly on January 25, 1890, seventy-two days, six hours, eleven minutes, and fourteen seconds after she had started.

By 1892, the *World*'s daily circulation of 375,000 was the largest in the nation. Pulitzer was determined to professionalize the training of journalists and began discussions in that year with Columbia University to endow the nation's first school of journalism. Twenty years later Columbia's Graduate School of Journalism became a reality. Veteran publisher Frank Munsey spoke for many when he said, "Pulitzer came to New York as a whirlwind out of the West," and had forever "overturned" America's way of doing journalism. The paper's Sunday edition would soon sell more than half a million copies and be distributed nationwide. Adolph Ochs, publisher of the *New York Times*, called Pulitzer's work "a phenomenon" whose "prodigious success" would be copied by newspapermen for years to come. Pulitzer, however, was not to enjoy his triumph. His health had broken in his late forties. He grew virtually blind and developed an acute sensitivity to noise. The quietest sounds became intolerable. A famous painting by John Singer Sargent during this period captured Pulitzer's vacant stare and pained expression. Eventually he was forced to live on a private luxury yacht, the *Liberty*, in the peacefulness of the open sea.

Pulitzer clearly regretted the excesses he had gone to when competing with Hearst's *Journal*, beginning in 1895. The competition reached a climax when the *U.S.S. Maine* exploded in Havana harbor on February 15, 1898, killing 260 men. The incident became the pretext for the Spanish-American War. Pulitzer and Hearst attempted to outdo each other in reporting alleged Spanish atrocities on Cuba. *World* reporters claimed to have witnessed "skulls slit to the eyes," "ears cut off as trophies," and "mouths gashed to the angle of the jaw to give each face a ghastly grin." Women were reportedly "disrobed and slashed" by Spanish soldiers. Those who "complained had their eyes torn out or were beheaded." The stories stimulated circulation for both papers and their sensationalism threatened to become Pulitzer's lasting legacy. Instead, his will provided for the creation of the Pulitzer Prize to annually reward, beginning in 1917, excellence in journalism and his sons, Joseph Pulitzer II, Ralph, and Herbert soldiered on with the newspapers their famous father had helped to create. Instead of his excesses, Pulitzer is best remembered for his indispensable role in creating the modern American newspaper and its determination to serve the public interest. "Our Republic and its press will rise and fall together," Pulitzer famously said shortly before his death. "The power to mould the future of the Republic," he was certain, "will be in the hands of the journalists of future generations" who must "always fight for progress and reform, never tolerate injustice or corruption" and "always remain devoted to the public welfare."

Further Reading

Baker, Nicholson, and Margaret Brentano. T*he World on Sunday: Graphic Art in Joseph Pulitzer's Newspaper, 1898–1911*. New York: Bulfinch Press, 2005.

Barrett, James Wyman. *Joseph Pulitzer and His World*. New York: Vanguard Press, 1941.

Brain, Denis. *Pulitzer: A Life*. New York: John Wiley & Sons, 2001.

Juergens, George. *Joseph Pulitzer and the New York World*. Princeton, NJ: Princeton University Press, 1966.

Seitz, Don C. *Joseph Pulitzer: His Life and Letters*. New York: Simon and Schuster, 1924.

Swanberg, W.A. *Pulitzer*. New York: Charles Scribner's Sons, 1967.

Wilensky, Harry. *The Story of the St. Louis Post-Dispatch*. St. Louis: St. Louis Post-Dispatch, 1981.

BRUCE J. EVENSEN

PULLIAM, EUGENE C.

Eugene C. Pulliam (1889–1975) was a founder of what became the Society of Professional Journalists, an influential publisher in the Midwest and Southwest, and the grandfather of Vice-President Dan Quayle. He practiced personal journalism, pioneered the op-ed page, and was a stalwart defender of freedom of the press whose outspoken Republican political views migrated from progressive to conservative over the course of his career.

Pulliam was born May 3, 1889, in Ulysses, Kansas, the son of a Methodist home missionary. He entered DePauw University in 1906 (the school gave discounts to the sons of Methodist ministers) where he became campus correspondent for the new *Indianapolis Star*, which he would buy thirty-eight years later. In his sophomore year he helped convert the student newspaper into the *DePauw Daily*, for which he sold advertising to help put himself through school. A year later he joined with nine of his classmates to found Sigma Delta Chi, the professional journalism honorary now known as the Society of Professional Journalists. He left school after his junior year and after a few months joined the *Kansas City Star* as a police reporter and then feature writer. He made William Rockhill Nelson, the *Star*'s, publisher, his lifelong model.

Two years later, after working for a time for his father's ministry, he bought the *Atchison Champion*, with financial assistance from his wife's family. The purchase made him the country's youngest publisher. After three years he sold it and moved to the *Franklin* (Indiana) *Star*, and then the *Lebanon* (Indiana) *Reporter*. So began three decades of buying and selling papers, with fifty-one papers in thirteen states, as well as several radio stations, belonging to him at one time or another, thus earning him the nickname "B.S.C. (buy, sell, consolidate) Pulliam". His biggest purchases came in the 1940s, when he bought the *Indianapolis Star* (outbidding Robert McCormick, Roy Howard, and Samuel Newhouse), the *Indianapolis News*, the *Arizona Republic*, and the *Phoenix Gazette*. His son Eugene S. Pulliam succeeded him as president of Central Newspapers, Inc. One grandson wrote a biography about Pulliam; another—Dan Quayle—was vice-president, 1989–1993, under George H.W. Bush.

Pulliam was a director of the Associated Press, a trustee of the William Allen White Foundation, and a member of the advisory board of the Nieman Foundation. He was a recipient of the John Peter Zenger Award from Arizona State University, a fellow of Sigma Delta Chi, and a recipient of that organization's Wells Key as well as its honorary president on the fiftieth anniversary of its founding, and a member of the Journalism Halls of Fame of Indiana and Arizona. In 1969, General Francisco Franco of Spain presented him with the Order of Isabel the Catholic. In 1974, he created the Pulliam Fellows internships program. He died June 23, 1975, in Phoenix.

Pulliam's politics were idiosyncratic, but powerful. "He was undeniably the most powerful individual in the state," said one head of Indiana's Democratic Party. He was equally influential in Arizona. After first backing Sen. Joseph McCarthy, he turned on him in 1952 when McCarthy questioned James Wechsler, a *New York Post* editor, about Wechsler's politics. He believed that he persuaded Dwight Eisenhower, his fellow Kansan, to run for president, although Eisenhower noted in his diary his hostility towards Pulliam. Despite his generally conservative outlook and his growing Arizona base, he favored Lyndon Johnson over Barry Goldwater in the 1964 presidential race. Four years later he limited coverage of Robert Kennedy in his Indiana papers, giving just brief mention to a speech Kennedy gave on the night of Martin Luther King Jr.'s assassination (Pulliam called King a "rabble-rouser"), a speech that probably prevented serious rioting in Indianapolis. In the late 1960s, he wrote a syndicated column, "Window on the Right," and began to nurture proponents of the New Right.

Eugene Pulliam has been called the last of a breed, men who loved newspapers for their own sake and their power as bully pulpits, rather than as financial investments, and who were outspoken defenders of press freedom. They were entrepreneurs who were motivated not by money, but by their beliefs in Christian morals and human progress. In the process they made a lot of money.

Further Reading

Anderson, Fenwick. "Bricks Without Straw: The Mirage of Competition in the Desert of Phoenix Daily Journalism Since 1947," PhD, University of Illinois, 1980

Bickell, Lara. "Eugene Pulliam: Municipal Booster." In *The Human Tradition in the American West*, edited by Benson Tong & Regan A. Lutz, 137–153, Wilmington, DE: Scholarly Resources, 2002.

Brandenburg, George A. "Star & News Merged in Indianapolis Deal: Pulliam Heads New Company; Announces End of Expansion." *Editor & Publisher* 81, no. 5 (4 September 1948): 5, 42

Buchholz, Michael. "Eugene Pulliam." In *American Newspaper Publishers, 1950–1990*, edited by Perry J. Ashley. Detroit: Gale Research, 1993, 253–261.

Fant, Jr., Gene C. "Eugene Collins Pulliam." In *American National Biography*, vol. 17. New York: Oxford University Press, 1997, 935–936.

Hosenball, Mark. "Pulliam Strings." *New Republic* 199, no. 18 (October 31, 1988): 18–20.

Pulliam, Eugene C. *Is There a Fighter in the House?* New York: Newcomen Society, 1966.

——. *The Menace of Socialism as a Challenge to America.* Columbus: Ohio Chamber of Commerce, 1948.

——. *The People & the Press: Partners for Freedom, An Address.* Tucson: University of Arizona Press, 1966.

——. *The Unchanging Responsibility of the American Newspaper in a Changing Society.* Flagstaff, AZ: Northland Press, 1970.

Pulliam, Russell. *Publisher: Gene Pulliam, Last of the Newspaper Titans.* Ottawa, IL: Jameson Books, 1984.

OWEN V. JOHNSON

R

RADIO

When most people think of "radio news," they tend to associate it with radio's Golden Age, the 1930s and 1940s, or with the rise of national networks like NBC and CBS. It is a common but understandable misconception to think that radio in the 1920s broadcast only music, sermons, and educational talks. Because early radio broadcasts had to be done live, performers and speakers usually did go to the studio. And as a result of technological challenges, coupled with a lack of a budget for developing a news department, most broadcasters found it difficult to cover distant events. But despite this handicap, we can trace news via the "radiophone" (as radio was called in its early days), right back to radio's earliest days.

In the new medium's experimental era, inventor and engineer Lee DeForest, who operated amateur station 2XG in High Bridge, New York, broadcast news reports as early as 1916: in November, he arranged to provide election returns, which he received from the newsroom at the New York American newspaper. Unfortunately, DeForest ended his broadcast before Woodrow Wilson came from behind to win, so the many amateurs who listened in heard the wrong candidate declared the winner. Still, it was a start and got both DeForest and radiotelephony favorable press.

Station KDKA in Pittsburgh is usually given credit for commercial radio's first news milestone, the November 2, 1920, broadcast of the presidential election returns. But while media historians still debate whether KDKA was in fact the first station, or even the first to broadcast election returns, there is evidence that another station did the exact same thing more than two months earlier. In Detroit, in early September, 1920, station 8MK (later WWJ) broadcast the Michigan state election returns (see *Detroit News*, August 30, 1920, p 1: "The News Radiophone to Give Vote Results"). And along with KDKA, 8MK also broadcast the presidential returns in November.

There is good reason why 8MK was so attuned to political coverage: it was the first radio station owned and operated by a newspaper—the *Detroit News*—and some of the reporters from the *News* read their columns on the air. Not every newspaper would be so enthusiastic about radio. Some newspapers saw the new medium as competition and tried to ignore it. The Associated Press briefly forbade its member newspapers from helping radio, promising stiff fines to those who went on the air. But some newspapers, and some wire services, saw the future and decided it would

be good publicity to have news on the air. In Chicago, in mid-January, 1922, the *Tribune* began cooperating with Westinghouse station KYW to provide regularly scheduled news reports (*see Chicago Daily Tribune*, 25 January 1922, p. 4, "Thousands Hear News of World By Radiophone"). The content, according to the newspaper, was summaries of news stories "from all over the world," and it was received with great enthusiasm. This was also the case in cities like Boston, Atlanta, and Los Angeles, where newspapers sent reporters over to a local station to read news several times a night. By December of 1922, there were eighty-three stations owned by newspapers and/or magazines, and many others had a working relationship with a local publication to do at least one newscast each night.

And radio stations did not just rely on their friends at the newspaper. They began to invite political figures, business leaders and advocates for civic organizations to come to the studio and comment on current events. In greater Boston, 1XE (later known as WGI) had well-known economist Roger Babson doing reports on business conditions as early as December, 1921. 1XE was also among the first to get involved with crime news, broadcasting nightly police reports of stolen cars. (The police themselves began to use radio in those formative years—there were two short-lived stations operated by law enforcement, one of which was WLAW in New York and the other KOP in Detroit.) In many cities, especially in the Midwest, radio started to broadcast agricultural reports, stock market news, and the weather forecast, further simplifying the lives of the listeners who needed that information. And of course, nearly every station found ways to give up-dates and scores from the major sporting events.

As technology gradually improved, a few stations found ways to send a "news truck" out to cover events and then bring the information back to the studio. This mobile equipment was costly, but several stations found it got them a lot of good publicity as well as listener approval. WJZ radio (then located in Newark, New Jersey) was one of the earliest to use this approach, making good use of a partnership with the *Newark Sunday Call* newspaper; the *Call* had a news truck, and it helped gather news for WJZ. Other stations did the same when possible, and the public was delighted to see these trucks show up at local events. By the mid-1920s, there was an improved version called the "portable," which contained a portable transmitter that could be assembled on site, enabling the news truck to broadcast from the event.

While we take it for granted today, getting news by radio

had a dramatic effect on American culture in the 1920s. Prior to the advent of broadcasting, nobody expected to receive a news story as it was taking place, nor did anyone expect to hear commentary from newsmakers or reporters. Keeping up with current events meant buying one's favorite newspaper; and when there was breaking news, there would be an "extra" edition. But when the partnership between radio and newspaper began to develop and expand, information could flow more quickly and easily. The availability of radio news was a major benefit for anyone who had trouble reading the newspaper, and it made life easier for people in rural areas who lived far from where newspapers could be bought. But it also affected millions of ordinary Americans who were suddenly able to sit in the comfort of their own living room and listen to experts discussing what was going on in the world. Radio offered immediacy, and newspaper offered the pictures and the analysis. And even before the rise of the networks, radio could offer a shared experience for the entire nation: when President Warren G. Harding died in 1923, stations across the country broadcast tributes to him, and five stations in large cities like Washington, New York, and Chicago linked up via long distance telephone lines to carry President Calvin Coolidge's eulogy.

The availability of experienced print reporters who were willing to broadcast gave radio additional credibility. By 1923, well-respected newspaper reporters like New York's Hans (H.V.) Kaltenborn or Washington, D.C.'s, Frederic William Wile had begun doing regular radio commentary. A new breed of "star" was born. It was not long before magazines were advertising for "eye-witnesses" to cover local news events, and listeners were calling their favorite station asking how they could get hired (see *Radio World*, September 3, 1927, p.17: "Many Seek Jobs As Radio Reporters"). Unfortunately, not every print journalist or politician sounded professional when speaking on the air. This led a few universities to begin offering courses in how to give an effective radio talk. But the public remained enthralled with hearing actual newsmakers, whether they were good speakers or not.

The arrival of national networks like NBC in 1926 and CBS in 1927 only enhanced the availability and the speed of information, as did the subsequent inception of regional networks that concentrated on specific areas of the country. The more radio expanded its news presence, the more major events were covered for a wider audience. Radio brought the American public in-depth reporting about Charles A. Lindbergh's amazing transatlantic flight in 1927, and Lindbergh himself even went on the air to talk about his achievement at a reception held for him in Washington, D.C. In 1928, a team of reporters and commentators covered the primaries of both political parties, as well as the presidential inauguration. And while radio news in the 1920s was still not dominated by the famous anchorman or woman, by decade's end, there were a group of well-known commentators describing and discussing important events.

If the 1920s had shown glimpses of what radio news could achieve, it was during the 1930s that consistent and professional news coverage became a reality. Technological improvements made coast-to-coast broadcasts easier to do, and even news from overseas was reaching the audience in a timely fashion. There was also a new network, Mutual Broadcasting System, which came along in late 1934; it was known mainly for entertainment, but like NBC and CBS, it hired its own reporters and commentators. This enhanced the choices the audience had when seeking out coverage of major events.

An important news milestone of the early 1930s was the creation of a magazine-style program which re-enacted and dramatized the major events of the week. *The March of Time* went on the air via CBS in March 1931, under the auspices of *Time* magazine. The 1930s was also the decade when radio news commentary came into its own. One of the first commentators to do a nightly program on the network was Lowell Thomas, beginning in September 1930. Throughout the decade, listeners could now tune in and hear Thomas and the other such other well-known people as Edward R. Murrow, Dorothy Thompson, Boake Carter, Raymond Gram Swing, and Kathryn Cravens, to name a few.

One reason for the rising importance of news commentators was the resurgence of the battle between the wire services and the broadcasters. For a time, a truce had been declared and radio was able to use newspaper content, but as the Depression affected ad revenues, newspapers were increasingly convinced that radio was hurting their sales. The so-called "Press-Radio War" led to an agreement that pleased the newspapers but caused radio problems: as of March 1934, radio stations were permitted only two newscasts—one in the morning and one in the evening. The newscasts would be provided at a reasonable cost to any stations that wanted them-- they were professionally done, thorough, and accurate. But for stations that had grown accustomed to doing a number of newscasts daily, this was not seen as anything other than an attempt by print journalists to keep radio in a subordinate position. In a few cities, radio fought back, most notably in Boston, where John Shepard 3rd, owner of a regional network, decided to let his staff develop a news service. The Yankee News Service provided as much news as before the Press-Radio agreement, and the existence of this service led radio journalists to fight for and win press credentials just like their print counterparts had. Meanwhile at other stations, and especially at the networks, there was an increased amount of news commentary, since commentators were not part of the agreement. The commentators helped give the audience the perception they were getting as much news as before. Ultimately, the attempt by the wire services to restrict radio news was a failure. Stations found ways to get around it, and listeners were very vocal about wanting to hear more rather than less news, especially with a war looming in Europe, America's on-going economic woes, and other important issues. The Press-Radio agreement came to a merciful end, and radio went back to doing news whenever events warranted the coverage.

Another important news milestone occurred in March 1933, when President Franklin D. Roosevelt began to deliver a regular series of radio talks commonly known as "Fireside Chats." Roosevelt was not the first president to speak on radio (Presidents Harding had done so as early as 1921–1922, and President Coolidge spoke on radio a number of times), but Roosevelt's use of it to reach out to the country during the Depression forged his image as the "radio president" and further illustrated how radio could bring even the biggest newsmakers directly to the listener's home.

Sometimes, something that happened on the air ended up becoming a big news story. In April 1932, a supposedly tame circus lion that was supposed to roar on cue went on a rampage in the WBZ Boston studios, injuring seven people. And of course, there was the Orson Welles' dramatization of *War of the Worlds* for Halloween 1938, which somehow convinced thousands of people that an army of Martians really had invaded. There were also events that started off as puff pieces and ended up as major news events, such as when Chicago announcer Herb Morrison came to New Jersey in May of 1937 to do a story about the airship Hindenburg. Suddenly, the ship burst into flames and Morrison was able to do on-the-scene reporting, which he transcribed so it could be played the next day (audiotape was still not a factor, and programs were either done live or done via transcription).

There were also certain events that captivated the nation, and for the first time, radio was an important part of the coverage. The kidnapping and subsequent murder of aviator Charles Lindbergh's son in the early 1930s was that kind of story. The newspapers did their usual commendable job, but radio was there from beginning to end, covering the entire six weeks of the trial as it occurred, and delivering the final verdict to listeners all over the country. And in 1936, Mutual Broadcasting commentator Gabriel Heatter covered the execution of Bruno Hauptmann, the man convicted of the murder. Listeners came to expect that radio reporters would be able to make even a long court case interesting and understandable.

During the 1930s, a new sort of radio commentary gained popularity—it blended news with religion and politics. Charles Father Coughlin, the Radio Priest, was a fierce proponent of a very conservative view of Catholicism; he was also anti-Semitic who hated President Roosevelt and a number of Roosevelt's policies. Coughlin used his weekly broadcasts not just for Bible preaching but to rant about what he believed was wrong with America and who was responsible for it. In contrast to the emotional arguments made by the radio priest, there were new educational programs where current issues were debated and discussed by some of the best-known experts. One of the most respected shows of this type was *America's Town Meeting of the Air,* which made its debut in 1935.

By the late 1930s, coverage of serious news had expanded, and given the situation in Europe, international news was on everyone's mind. NBC and Mutual beefed up their coverage, but it was CBS that had some of the best on-the-scene reporting. Edward R. Murrow began doing live reports from London, part of a team of reporters covering Europe. In fact, CBS had a staff of fourteen full-time employees in various European cities. And at home, beginning in March of 1938, Robert Trout began broadcasting a nightly show called the *CBS World News Roundup.* Soon, all of he networks would be offering ten- to fifteen- minute nightly news programs.

By 1940, coverage of political conventions had become old hat for the networks, as their team of experienced reporters and commentators was ready to let the audience know about the candidates and their views. But it was in December 1941 that everything changed and news took center stage: when the Japanese attacked Pearl Harbor. It was a Sunday and there was not much news scheduled—mostly religion, soap operas, and sports. But when the news broke and was confirmed, radio news reporters rushed in to work and coverage of World War II began in earnest. News reporters had to contend with military censorship from the Office of Censorship, and the audience had to contend with never getting enough information. But one thing was certain: people wanted to know as much as they possibly could. It was during the war years that the amount of news being broadcast increased dramatically—in 1940, the networks aired 2,396 hours of news; for 1942, it was up to 4,632 hours, and by 1944, the total for the year was 5,522 hours. Network reporters were sent all over the world, putting themselves in danger to provide live coverage from the war zones. And in addition to war coverage, President Roosevelt was in declining health and died suddenly on April 12, 1945. The networks created tributes and retrospectives to him and helped America cope with the tragic loss of a popular president. But when the war ended in May of 1945, radio was also there to describe the jubilation and to discuss such issues as the dropping of the atom bomb and the revelation of what had taken place during the Holocaust. Many of the war correspondents, including Murrow, Trout, and their colleague, Douglas Edwards, would go on to long careers in radio and then TV news.

By the 1950s, radio had regular newscasts and the word "anchor" had entered the radio and TV vocabulary to describe the man (they were all men back then) who was the primary news announcer on a broadcast. Network radio was in transition, as music's Top 40 was becoming the hot format and most of the soap operas and variety shows from radio's Golden Age were moving over to TV. Increasingly network reporters were doing double-duty, being heard on radio as well as being seen on TV. But while TV was becoming dominant for news coverage, radio was still important, especially at the local level, where stations often found it beneficial to maintain a strong news department to keep the community informed.

In the late 1950s, one owner even experimented with an all news format. Gordon McLendon owned a "border station," which was licensed to Tijuana Mexico but heard in much of southern California. XTRA began doing all news as early as 1958, but it had only a two-person staff and mostly relied on wire service reports. The modern all news format did not come into its own until the mid-1960s when a number of AM radio stations that had previously broadcast music decided to devote themselves to twenty-four hours of news, complete with a staff of reporters, writers, and editors. One of the pioneers in the new format was McLendon's Chicago station, WNUS, which became an all-news station in September 1964. Another was WINS in New York, which in April 1965 became New York City's first all-news outlet. Soon, other stations followed, but the progress of all news was slow at first, because it was very expensive to do well. Critics questioned whether listeners would want to hear the same stories over and over, as well as whether advertisers would support the format. In fact, WNUS abandoned all news in 1968 because the management said it was not making enough money. Meanwhile, other stations in large markets like Washington, D.C., and Los Angeles picked up the format, and by the early 1970s, it was getting good ratings and was sufficiently profitable that more AM stations adopted it. The all-news format also reflected changes in American life. More young adults were going to college, more women were entering the workforce, and Americans in general seemed to be working longer hours. Thus the availability of stations which offered news any time, day or night, was a convenience for those who wanted to be informed.

The early 1960s also saw another format that made heavy use of news but added in call-in talk shows. In February of 1960, station KMOX in St. Louis, Missouri, debuted a format called "At Your Service." Created by station General Manager and CBS Vice President Robert Hyland, it featured news, talk, information, sports, and community service. Called by some "full service radio" and by others "news-talk," the format became another AM success story, adopted by hundreds of stations nation-wide. Among the stations that have had the most success with this format is WBZ in Boston, which gradually began to abandon music to concentrate on news and talk beginning in the 1980s; the station fully committed to all-news in 1992, with several issues-oriented call-in talk shows at night, and afterward, was consistently been at the top of the ratings.

During the 1980s there were several dramatic changes in the broadcasting landscape. One was the advent of cable television and the first all-news format on television—Ted Turner's Cable News Network (CNN) went on the air in 1980. It would later be followed by more all-news channels, including Fox News. These television networks also began to provide a service for radio, and today, they have affiliates nationwide. The other major change was at the Federal Communications Commission (FCC), as President Ronald Reagan pushed for deregulation of radio broadcasting. Public service requirements were lessened, as was the amount of news stations were required to broadcast. The deregulation culminated in the end of the "Fairness Doctrine" in 1987. Radio was now free to air programs that only presented one side, without the obligation to let the other side be heard. By the end of the 1980s, partisan talk shows, mostly from the right wing conservative viewpoint, were proliferating; the best known of these was Rush Limbaugh. A liberal alternative, Air America, also emerged.

One other major change in broadcast news occurred during the 1990s, as a result of further deregulation—the Tele-

communications Act of 1996 gave permission to large radio conglomerates to own more stations. Where in the 1940s, two was too many, as NBC had to divest itself of NBC/Blue so that it could keep NBC/Red, by the late 1990s, one company—Clear Channel Communications—owned more than twelve hundred stations. In many cities, deregulation meant the end of local radio, as group owners relied on syndication of national news and talk programs and cut back on local reporting. At the same time, however, AM all-news stations were still prospering in a number of cities and a few news-talk stations could now be heard on the FM band. National Public Radio became known for its in-depth coverage of news, and some of its reporters have been seminal in breaking important stories.

From its earliest days, radio showed itself able to adapt to changing conditions. In a world of the Internet and Ipods, radio may not have the exclusive listenership it once did, but millions of people continue to depend on it in their home, their office, their automobile, and increasingly, on the Internet.

Further Reading

Barnouw, Eric. *A Tower in Babel: A History of Broadcasting to 1933*. New York: Oxford University Press, 1966.

Barnouw, Eric. *The Golden Web: A History of Broadcasting 1933–1953*. New York: Oxford University Press, 1968.

Charnley, Mitchell V. *News By Radio*. New York: MacMillan, 1948.

Halper, Donna L. *Invisible Stars: A Social History of Women in American Broadcasting*. Armonk NY: M.E. Sharpe, 2001.

Hilmes, Michele, ed. *The Radio Reader: Essays in the Cultural History of Radio*. New York: Routledge, 2001.

Sterling, Christopher H., and Michael Keith, eds. *Encyclopedia of Radio*. New York: Routledge, 2003.

Sterling, Christopher H., and John Michael Kittross. *Stay Tuned: A History of American Broadcasting*, 3rd ed. Mahwah NJ: Lawrence Erlbaum, 2002.

DONNA L. HALPER

RADIO ACT OF 1927

The Radio Act of 1927 was signed into law by President Calvin Coolidge on February 23, 1927. It is Public Law Number 632 by the 69th Congress. The Radio Act of 1927 was created to alleviate deficiencies in the Radio Act of 1912. The Radio Act of 1912 did not provide the Department of Commerce, the regulatory body for wireless radio communications at that time, the ability to regulate the power or hours of radio transmission, withhold radio licenses, and perhaps, most importantly, regulate and allocate radio frequencies. The 1927 legislation's purpose was to provide order and stability to a rapidly growing industry.

The radio industry experienced rapid growth during the early to mid-1920s because of the popularity of commercial programming. The development of commercial programming enabled radio stations to make a profit and this served as the catalyst for the rapid growth of radio in the 1920s; hence, the need for additional regulation beyond what the

1912 act could provide. Beginning in 1922, the radio industry made concerted efforts to self-regulate through a series of annual conferences, but failed to create any enforceable policies.

The Radio Act of 1927, superseded the Radio Act of 1912, and contained several significant components that allowed for more efficient regulation of the radio industry. First, the act removed regulatory authority from the Department of Commerce and the Secretary of Commerce and Labor and created a new regulatory agency called the Federal Radio Commission. The commission was comprised of five individuals, appointed by the President, from five geographic zones in the nation.

Second, the Federal Radio Commission was empowered with the authority to allocate radio frequencies and licenses. An amendment to the Radio Act of 1927, the Davis Amendment, mandated that the Federal Radio Commission must ensure that the allocation of radio frequencies, radio licenses, times of operation, station wattage, and wavelength be equally distributed across the designated geographic zones that the Commissioners represented. This requirement was irrespective of the fact that some geographic zones were more heavily populated than others. For instance, rural areas had as many radio stations as urban areas. In 1928, during the first year of the Federal Radio Commission's existence, it required 164 radio stations to justify their existence or be forced to cease all broadcasting. Only eighty-one radio stations survived one of the first regulatory acts of the Federal Radio Commission.

Third, the Radio Act of 1927 created what is referred to as the "public interest standard." The public interest standard is based on the belief that the public at large owns the electromagnetic spectrum, or the radio spectrum, and that individuals are granted the authority, through licensing, to use a portion of the radio spectrum via radio frequencies. Accordingly, since applications for frequencies far outnumber the frequencies available to allocate, the individuals fortunate enough to be granted a license must agree to serve the "public interest, convenience, and necessity" of the community in which they are licensed. The Federal Radio Commission agreed to allow each licensee the ability to program and operate his/her radio station without interference as long as the licensee documented that the "public interest" clause had been met.

Fourth, the Radio Act of 1927 ensured that radio was, indeed, a form of expression and was therefore protected by First Amendment rights. However, under the act, the content of radio programming could not contain obscene, indecent, or profane language. In a related issue, Section 18 of the Radio Act of 1927 required radio stations to give equal time for political candidates so that one candidate would not have access to the medium more than his/her opponent. Finally, the Federal Radio Commission was granted no authority to regulate radio advertising. Because of technological advances and the challenges created by those advancements, the Communications Act of 1934 replaced the Radio Act of 1927.

Further Reading

Aufderheide, Patricia. *Communications Policy and the Public Interest: The Telecommunications Act of 1996*. New York: The Guilford Press, 1999.

Fellow, Anthony R. *American Media History*. Belmont, CA: Wadsworth group/Thomson Learning, 2005.

Messere, Fritz. "Federal Radio Commission … Archives," http://www.oswego.edu/~messere/FRCpage.html (accessed April 8, 2007).

Overbeck, Wayne. *Major Principles of Media Law*. Fort Worth: Harcourt College Publishers, 2002.

JOHN ALLEN HENDRICKS

RATHER, DAN

"How could you sign on to such a policy? You've made us hypocrites in the eyes of the world."

"I don't think it's fair to judge my whole career by a rehash on Iran. How would you like it if I judged your career by those seven minutes when you walked off the set in New York?"

This unexpected eruption between CBS News anchor Dan Rather (Oct. 31, 1931–) and Vice President George H.W. Bush on January 25, 1988, at the beginning of the nightly news marked a turning point in both their careers. Bush overcame the "wimp factor" and went on to become a landslide presidential winner. Rather, who had been at the top of the network news heap, soon slipped behind Peter Jennings at ABC and then Tom Brokaw at NBC. When he was forced to step down as anchor of the *CBS Evening News* on March 9, 2005, amid a major reporting scandal, he had seven million viewers whose age averaged sixty-five and he was vilified for what critics complained was his deliberate effort to prevent Bush's son from winning a second term as president. On June 20, 2006, Rather announced he was leaving the network at which he had worked for forty-four years. It was an inglorious end to one of the most remarkable careers in broadcast journalism history.

Daniel Irvin Rather Jr. was born in Wharton, Texas to Daniel Irvin Rather Sr., an oil field ditch digger, and Byrl Veda Page Rather. He was raised with two younger siblings in the working-class neighborhood of Houston Heights. His father was "a passionate newspaper reader" and during junior high when Rather convalesced at home with rheumatic fever he became an inveterate newspaper reader as well. It was then he decided that he wanted to be a reporter. Bed-ridden, he listened to radio reports of World War II in Europe. "Edward R. Murrow became a hero of mine," he later said. When his parents cashed a war bond, Rather had enough money to attend Sam Houston State Teachers College. He became a sports writer and editor on the school newspaper, wrote ads for KSAN, a 250-watt radio station in Huntsville, Texas, and did play-by-play football, baseball, and basketball. Rather became a stringer for Associated Press, United Press, and International News Service and made eight dollars a week as the college's sports information director.

In 1954, Rather joined the Marines but the Korean War ended before he saw combat. Later that year he was hired to cover city hall, the police beat, and local courts for the *Houston Chronicle* radio station. Rather transitioned to television in 1959, reporting breaking news for KHOU-TV, the CBS affiliate in Houston. He was making enough money to marry Jean Goebel and start a family. The couple would have two children. Rather's professional reputation grew as a result of his unprecedented live coverage in 1961 of powerful Hurricane Carla that killed forty-three people. His round the clock reporting from the Galveston seawall brought him to the attention of CBS news executives. In 1962, as chief of the network's Southwest bureau, based in Dallas, he covered twenty-three states, Mexico, and Central America. This included coverage of violent opposition to the civil rights movement in the South "that changed me dramatically," he said. On November 22, 1963, Rather was in Dallas and reported the shooting of President John F. Kennedy. He was the first of the network reporters to confirm Kennedy's death.

Over the next ten years Rather took on a series of important assignments from CBS News—as White House correspondent in 1963; chief of the network's London Bureau in 1965; as Vietnam War correspondent in 1966; and returning for a second stint as White House correspondent, beginning in 1966. Rather characterized his reporting style as "persistent." He was determined "to stand up to the pressure to intimidate." He told an interviewer, "You want to see my neck swell up, you just tell me where to line up, and what to report."

Rather's determination "to aggressively pursue the story" made him a lightning rod for opponents. He reported being "sucker punched" and "roughed up" on live television while covering the Democratic National Convention in Chicago in 1968. At the height of the Watergate scandal in 1974, he sparred with President Richard Nixon. At a press conference in Houston on March 19, he asked a Watergate-related question that was applauded by those attending. "Are you running for something?" Nixon asked him. Rather smiled, paused, and retorted, "No, Mr. President, are you?" Some viewers charged Rather had been disrespectful and should be fired. Rather later told an interviewer that he saw covering Watergate as high stakes poker. His book on reporting Watergate, *The Palace Guard* (1974), became a best-seller.

Between 1975 and 1981 Rather was chief correspondent for CBS News Special Reports and a correspondent on the hugely popular *60 Minutes*. His most famous story in 1980 saw him grow a beard and go undercover with Mujahadeen rebels in Afghanistan, who were fighting the Soviet invasion of their country. Concerned that Rather would jump to a competing network, CBS replaced retiring newsman Walter Cronkite with Rather to anchor its top-rated *CBS Evening News*, starting March 9, 1981. "I still thought of myself as a reporter first and an anchor second," Rather said, "and that sometimes created trouble." For one week in September 1986, he began signing off CBS broadcasts with the foreboding closing "Courage," which came to be parodied by late night comedians. Rather's most embarrassing moment came on September 11, 1987, when he walked off the set of the *CBS Evening News* when a tennis match threatened to delay the start of his broadcast. Affiliates had to cover seven minutes of dead air until Rather could be persuaded to return to the set. Vice President Bush referred to the incident in his famous dust up with Rather four months later. On January 22, 1991, Rather's newscast was interrupted when AIDs activists stormed his studio.

Highlights of Rather's record twenty-four-year run as network news anchor included his May 1989 reporting of the government crackdown on Chinese student protesters in Beijing's Tiananmen Square and his August 1990 interview with Saddam Hussein in Baghdad on the eve of the first Gulf War. During his coverage of September 11, 2001, he called the attack on the World Trade Center "the Pearl Harbor of terrorism." No story he had ever covered, he believed, "affected Americans as personally" or had "so profoundly changed their lives." Rather also hosted and was a frequent contributor to *48 Hours*, a widely acclaimed network news weekly launched by CBS in 1996.

Rather bristled at conservative critics who had long claimed his antipathy toward the Reagan and Bush administrations reflected a liberal bias. Rather said "those who claim I'm a bomb-throwing Bolshevik want me to report the news the way they want it reported." On September 4, 2004, Rather reported on *60 Minutes II* that CBS had obtained documents indicating President George W. Bush had shirked duties and received preferential treatment years before in the Texas Air National Guard. Critics charged the documents were forgeries and that Rather's report on the eve of a national election was politically motivated. Sixteen days later Rather admitted he could "no longer vouch for the authenticity" of the documents. Four of Rather's co-workers were fired. An investigation found a "myopic zeal to be first on the story." Rather later apologized. The incident led to his departure in 2005 from the nightly news and his separation from CBS News the following year. On July 11, 2006, Mark Cuban's HDNet announced plans for Rather to produce and host a weekly news program *Dan Rather Reports*.

Further Reading

Gates, Gary Paul. *Air Time: The Inside Story of CBS News*. New York: Harper & Row, 1978.

Goldberg, Robert, and Gerald Jay Goldberg. *Anchors: Brokaw, Jennings, Rather*. Seacaucus, NJ: Carol Publishing, 1990.

Rather, Dan, and Mickey Herskowitz. *The Camera Never Blinks Twice: The Further Adventures of a Television Journalist*. New York: William Morrow, 1994.

Rather, Dan. *Deadlines and Datelines*. New York: William Morrow, 1999.

Rather, Dan, and Gary Paul Gates. *The Palace Guard*. New York: Harper & Row, 1974.

Weisman, Alan. *Lone Star: The Extraordinary Life and Times of Dan Rather*. Hoboken, NJ: Wiley, 2006.

BRUCE J. EVENSEN

RAYMOND, HENRY JARVIS

Henry Jarvis Raymond (January 24, 1820–June 18, 1869), oldest of six children born to Jarvis and Lavinia Raymond on an eighty-acre farm near Lima, New York, on January 24, 1820, graduated the new Genesee Wesleyan Seminary (later Syracuse University) at fifteen. He taught school until his father mortgaged the farm to pay for his college education, which he began at the University of Vermont in September 1836.

Raymond's nearly thirty-year journalism career began after editor Horace Greeley published some poetry and prose Raymond sent to the *New-Yorker* while a student. As Raymond approached graduation in 1840, he wrote to Greeley asking for a job. Greeley, in jest, offered to sell him the *New-Yorker*. After campaigning for William Henry Harrison until the election, Raymond traveled to New York City to find a job. At the *New-Yorker,* Greeley was not hiring but welcomed Raymond to spend as much time in the office as he wished. Raymond spent every day there doing whatever he could without pay until Greeley finally hired him after he received an out-of-state job offer.

Uncertain about his future, Raymond asked his former professor, James Marsh, if he should study law or theology. Saying these did not provide the only careers for serving the public good, Marsh suggested journalism, probably influencing both Raymond's career choice and public-service orientation. The press, Marsh said, was not used to its capacity for advancing civilization and needed dedicated people capable of guiding the public. Raymond continued in journalism, and devotion to what he believed the public interest became a life-long principle–epitomized in an 1850 speech stressing work for "social progress" as a duty that included commitment to advancing civilization.

Raymond's work, primarily literary journalism, gradually included reporting after he helped Greeley establish the *New York Tribune* in 1841 and the *New-Yorker* merged with the *Weekly Tribune*. And his occasional political commentary attracted attention. He augmented his income by sending items to the *New York Daily Standard, Cincinnati Chronicle, Bangor Whig,* and *Buffalo Commercial Advertiser*–and writing advertising copy. In October 1843, Raymond moved to the *Morning Courier and New York Enquirer* after James Watson Webb offered a salary Greeley would not match. At some point, he became a manuscript reviewer for Harper publishers and was managing editor of *Harper's Magazine,* 1850 to 1856. Raymond reported on the Franco-Austrian War in 1859, possibly making him the only "great" New York editor of his generation with foreign war correspondence experience as America's Civil War began. And he traveled Civil War battlefields perhaps more than any editor.

Raymond was often uncomfortable with Greeley's views although the two agreed on Whig principles. In 1846, he debated Greeley, who argued in the *Tribune* that only a system advocated by French Socialist Charles Fourier would guarantee fair wages and everyone's right to work. Raymond, in the *Courier,* said reform could be accomplished only through Christianity and on an individual basis. He felt no obligation to reorganize society, he wrote, and called social equality impossible and undesirable. He opposed blaming "haves" for others' plight but did not deny society's responsibility toward "have-nots." He later argued that republican government depended on education and advocated state support to assure equal education for all children.

Raymond is known for establishing and editing the *New York Times,* which was regarded from its beginning as setting a superior journalism standard. Although the *Times* reflected party loyalties, as did other U.S. newspapers during Raymond's eighteen-year editorship, his often eloquent championing of journalism also set a standard. In the late 1850s, for example, he expounded a reporter's right to protect sources, a relatively rare position at the time. And in a partisan era, he wrote in a June 12, 1863, editorial that the press' usefulness depended "entirely on its independence." Each editor must have "complete freedom to express, without dictation from Government or from any class or profession, even his own..., views on public affairs of those for whom to a certain extent he speaks."

Also a politician elected to the New York Assembly in 1850, 1851, and 1862, speaker in 1851 and 1862, and lieutenant governor in 1854, Raymond declined to run for the U.S. Congress when nominated in 1852 but served in the Thirty-Ninth Congress after being elected in 1864. With slavery debates dominating his first New York Assembly term, in 1850, he declared his position—slavery must end and editorially supported William Henry Seward.

After Raymond's second term, in 1851, Webb fired him, apparently for anti-slavery editorializing, and rewrote Raymond's last *Courier* editorial. Raymond moved ahead with plans made with George Jones, whom he had known at the *Tribune,* and issued the four-page *New York Daily Times* at a penny a copy on September 18, 1851, vowing to eschew sensationalism and extreme positions—unless warranted. An increase to two cents on its first anniversary cost one-third of the twenty-five thousand circulation, but advertising filled twenty columns by April 1853 and the offices moved in early 1854 to the Nassau-Beekman street corner. Contemporary James Parton said conduct of the newspaper, more than advertising, brought prosperity.

Prominent in the Whig and Republican parties, Raymond published the Whig *Grapeshot* (1849) and *Campaign Times* (1852), wrote the address for the first Republican national convention in 1856 and worked for a Seward candidacy in 1860. Critical of Abraham Lincoln early on, Raymond became, after the firing on Fort Sumter, New York's strongest journalistic voice for Lincoln. Delegate-at-large and leader of New York's delegation for the 1864 Union Party convention, Raymond chaired the national Union Executive Committee after Lincoln's nomination. His biography of Lincoln, first published in 1864, was expanded under a new title in 1865.

Always a moderate, Raymond once wrote in his journal

that "discretion" accomplishes most in public affairs and said in a speech that extreme conservatism prevents change while radicalism would overthrow great accomplishments. At the 1866 Philadelphia National Union convention, radical Republicans disrupted the continuous success he had enjoyed as a moderate. Three years later, June 18, 1869, Raymond died unattended on the floor inside his home's entryway. The cause was not officially recorded, but he probably suffered a heart attack or stroke.

Further Reading

Brown, Francis. *Raymond of the Times.* New York: W. W. Norton, Inc., 1951.

Davis, Elmer. *History of The New York Times, 1851–1921.* New York: New York Times Company, 1921.

"Extracts from the Journal of Henry J. Raymond," (edited by his son). *Scribner's Monthly* vols. 19–20: (May, July, Sept., 1880): 57–61, 419–424, 703–710; and ibid., vol. 20, 275–280.

Maverick, Augustus. "Henry J. Raymond and the 'Times.'" *The Galaxy* 8: 2 (August 1869): 267–271.

Maverick, Augustus. *Henry J. Raymond and the New York Press.* Hartford, CT: A.S. Hale and Company, 1870; rpt. Arno Press Inc. & The New York Times, 1970.

Raymond, Henry J. *The Life and Public Services of Abraham Lincoln.* New York: Derby & Miller, 1865.

HAZEL DICKEN-GARCIA

READING NOTICES

During the late nineteenth and early twentieth centuries, long before labeled "advertorials" appeared in newspapers and magazines, there were "reading notices," paid advertising disguised as a news column or news story. Advertisers paid the newspapers to sprinkle brand and company names in with the news stories with the intent of attracting readers who might otherwise ignore advertising for the more credible news coverage the newspaper offered.

While newspaper and magazine readers across the United States were subjected to "news" copy that was actually paid advertising, newspaper publishers supported—and even encouraged—this practice because reading notices were far more profitable than traditional display advertising. Advertisers and their agencies supported the practice because the reading notices were perceived as more credible to readers because of the newspaper's supposed objectivity.

At first, the newspapers' attempt to promote a product through what appeared to be news stories was obvious to readers. Over time, however, the practice grew more sophisticated because it became entrenched in the newspaper advertising industry. N.W. Ayer & Sons advertising agency encouraged clients to use reading notices, and *Fowler's Publicity*, an encyclopedia on marketing communications techniques, included instruction on the most effective ways to use reading notices. On the newspaper side, the *New York World* even formed a reading notice department "with a commodious suite of offices …for the use of this important brand of great modern newspapers."

As early as 1891, the National Editorial Association took

offense to the practice of publishing reading notices. The NEA president equated reading notices with committing "fraud" on readers. During this period, however, newspapers of all sizes were publishing reading notices, even the largest and most prominent newspapers of the day, including the *New York Journal*, the *New York Tribune*, and the *New York Times*. The type of companies that promoted their products through reading notices was also quite diverse: everything from household goods to railroads and insurance companies.

Procter & Gamble launched its shortening, Crisco, by promoting it in reading notices that appeared in *Ladies' Home Journal* and several other national magazines. Even Sears, Roebuck & Co. used reading notices to promote its catalog business. The first documented reading notice featured another consumer good, Warner's Safe Cure, a patent medicine. Patent medicines claimed to cure most ills but typically were nothing more than alcoholic concoctions that caused addictions among users, and word about them appeared regularly in reading notices.

Because the content of the reading notices was paid for by advertisers and not vetted according to today's journalistic ethos of objectivity, the information contained in the notice could be harmful. Newspaper readers would read false claims that patent medicines could provide cures without knowing they were reading an ad as opposed to a news story. In 1906, Congress passed the Pure Food and Drug Act, which made it illegal to manufacture or sell any mislabeled or misbranded foods, drugs and medicines. In effect, this legislation shut down the patent medicine industry, but reading notices continued to appear.

Some editors justified the existence of reading notices by claiming that they marked the brand names with stars if the "news" story contained paid advertising. One such *New York Times* reading notice promoted ninety-six different businesses, each with stars beside their names.

The beginning of the end of reading notices came in 1912, when the government passed the Post Office Appropriation Act, which provided a subsidy for newspapers with legitimate news content while prohibiting the subsidy for newspapers containing paid-for editorial content not marked as advertising. Because newspapers have historically relied on the U.S. Postal Service to deliver its product at a subsidized rate, the act had the effect of virtually eliminating reading notices.

In theory, reading notices, and the practice of disguising blatant advertising as editorial content, no longer exists today, although some newspapers have turned some advertising-heavy sections (such as automotive and real estate) over to the advertising departments to write. Advertisers do continue to have other forms of influence over the press, though, by threatening to pull advertising, or by demanding only positive news on their industry or brand.

The closest modern-day variants on reading notices are today's magazine and newspaper advertorials, which are a direct outgrowth of last century's reading notices. The major difference, however, is that advertorials are labeled as advertising content.

A more accurate parallel to the reading notices of last century might be today's pervasive use of brand placements in film and on television, since there is little to no recognition that the content has been supplied either for free or for a charge.

Further Reading

Baker, C. Edwin. (1994). *Advertising and a Democratic Press*. Princeton, NJ: Princeton University Press.

Lawson, Linda (1988). "Advertisements Masquerading as News in Turn-of-The Century American Periodicals." *American Journalism*, v. 5, no. 2, 81–96.

Lawson, Linda (1993). *Truth in Publishing: Federal Regulation of the Press's Business Practices, 1880–1920*. Carbondale, IL: Southern Illinois University Press.

Lesly, Elizabeth (1991). "Realtors and Builders Demand Happy News ... and Often Get It." *Washington Journalism Review*, November.

SUE WESTCOTT ALESSANDRI

RECONSTRUCTION PRESS

An intense struggle between the Republican-dominated Congress and the Democratic-dominated South marked the twelve years after the American Civil War when the Confederate states were brought back into the Federal Union. During the Reconstruction Era from 1865 to 1877, northern Republicans wanted not only to punish the South, but to find a just means of incorporating nearly five million ex-slaves into a society that did not want them. Many in the South wanted to return to a pre-war culture where blacks would have few civil or political rights and whites would rebuild their economy with the cheap labor of the freedmen. Newspapers of this period reflected these tensions.

President Andrew Johnson developed the first proposal for reconstructing the South, a plan that established a lenient set of conditions southern states must meet to return to the Union. Johnson's policy, which Republicans believed gave too much power to former rebels, was unacceptable to Congress. Between 1865 and 1869, Congress passed (over Johnson's vetoes) several Reconstruction acts that continued a federal military presence in the South and set harsher conditions for allowing southern states to return to the Union.

By the end of the war, many northern newspapers had become profitable business enterprises. They made better use of the telegraph during the war and more professional reporting came from the battlefields. Riveting war reporting and detailed pictures and maps of battles sold newspapers. More readers meant more advertising. George P. Rowell, a Boston advertising agent, recognized the importance of circulation to selling advertising space. In 1869, he published the first newspaper directory—*Geo. P. Rowell & Co's American Newspaper Directory*—a compilation of circulation figures and publication frequency for almost five thousand newspapers in the United States and Canada. Newspapers, however, remained primarily political journals. The personal editor, the man everyone in town knew, remained a significant political figure inside and outside of the newspaper office. The editorial page, occupied primarily by Reconstruction politics, remained the most important page in the paper. Consequently, American newspapers played a significant role in defining Reconstruction politics.

The Northern press identified itself with either the Republican (radical or moderate) or Democratic Party. The radical Republican newspapers supported strict Reconstruction policies and favored legislation that improved the economic and political well-being of blacks. Moderate Republican newspapers disagreed with most of Congress' radical legislation but also criticized the South's recalcitrance and continued abuse of blacks. The Democratic press, composed primarily of those newspapers that did not support the Union during the Civil War, criticized Reconstruction legislation, supported general amnesty for former Confederates, and refused to support voting rights for blacks.

In the South, despite shortages of paper, ink, and presses, editors quickly re-established a lively newspaper presence that was shrill and biased. The *Richmond* (Virginia) *Times* noted that were it not for the Democratic newspapers, the military, federal judges, carpetbaggers, and Freedmen's Bureau agents "would have stripped our people as bare as a pack of coyotes devour the carcass of a buffalo." Frank Luther Mott reflected the dominant view of this era held by historians before the American Civil Rights Movement of the 1960s, when in *American Journalism* he depicted Reconstruction as a time of suffering for the southern newspaper that ended only with the termination of the "reign of terror" brought by carpetbaggers. Mott's interpretation viewed Reconstruction as an era of corruption overseen by carpetbaggers, scalawags, and ignorant freedmen. Indeed, most Republican editors and publishers in the South were "scalawags," southern-born Republicans. A number of Republican editors had immigrated to the South well before the war. But fewer than 20 percent of the identifiable Republican editors and publishers were "carpetbaggers"—Northerners who came South after the war.

Mott's "reign of terror" described approximately a dozen incidents of censorship in the early years of Reconstruction. Democratic newspapers continuously criticized the military presence and Reconstruction legislation. Consequently, some Democratic editors were arrested and their newspapers suspended by the military. But, beginning in 1868, when blacks were allowed to vote, several Republican editors were shot and their offices burned by vigilantes in retaliation for encouraging blacks to vote.

Democratic newspapers not only received printing contracts from local and state officials, but enjoyed the support of most white readers and white business owners. Republican newspapers, on the other hand, struggled to survive. Most whites would not subscribe to a Republican paper, white businesses would not advertise in them, and their largest audience—former slaves—could not read. Consequently, Republican newspapers survived primarily on contracts for printing military orders and legal advertising or by acting as the job printer for the local military commander. In March 1867, Congress passed an appropriations act that gave federal printing contracts to two Republican newspapers in each southern state. In states with several Republican newspapers, competition for the contracts was heavy. But, to keep the printing contract, Republican newspapers had to be careful to toe the correct Republican line at all times. General John Pope, the commander of the Third Military District in Georgia and Alabama, took a different tact. He issued an order prohibiting any official from advertising in a newspaper that obstructed Reconstruction. One editor complained that the order had deprived his paper of its "legitimate patronage."

Black newspapers had the most difficult time surviving during Reconstruction. Their primary audience was not only illiterate, but economically unable to support newspapers through advertising. Black Republican newspapers were supported primarily by local equal rights associations, the Freedmen's Bureau, or the Union League, an organization founded in the North and dedicated to instructing blacks in their new freedoms.

Ulysses S. Grant, elected president in 1868, not only supported the Fifteenth Amendment, which gave the vote to black males, but tried to quell the escalating violence by the Ku Klux Klan. Eventually, Grant and the Republicans became exhausted by the continuing violence and Southern recalcitrance and began diverting their attention away from the South. In 1877, when President Rutherford B. Hayes ordered the last troops removed from the South, the Republicans effectively abandoned Reconstruction and Southern blacks. The South returned to the control of whites, blacks lost what few gains they had made, and most Republican newspapers disappeared.

Further Reading

Abbot, Richard H. *The Republican Party and the South, 1855–77.* Chapel Hill: University of North Carolina Press, 1986.

Abbott, Richard H., and John W. Quist. *For Free Press and Equal Rights: Republican Newspapers in the Reconstruction South.* Athens: University of George Press, 2004.

Bond, James E. *No Easy Walk to Freedom: Reconstruction and the Ratification of the Fourteenth Amendment.* Westport, CT: Praeger, 1997.

Current, Richard. *Those Terrible Carpetbaggers: A Reinterpretation.* New York: Oxford University Press, 1988.

Dickerson, Donna. *The Reconstruction Era.* Westport, CT: Greenwood Press, 2003.

Foner, Eric. *Reconstruction: America's Unfinished Revolution, 1863–1877.* New York: Harper & Row, 1988.

Kennedy, Stetson. *After Appomattox: How the South Won the War.* Gainesville: University Press of Florida, 1995.

Mott, Frank Luther. *American Journalism: a History of Newspapers in the United States Through 260 Years: 1690 to 1950.* New York: Macmillan, 1941, 1950.

DONNA L. DICKERSON

REFORM JOURNALISM

If we take the perspective of the founders of the American Republic, then all journalism should be reform journalism. Their perspective may best be seen in the First Amendment to the Bill of Rights, which took the position that all forms of communication, and all ideas—whatever their merit—should be given a chance to be heard. This Amendment to the Constitution gave teeth to the Declaration of Independence's heady assertions that all men were created equal, and had inalienable rights both to liberty and to petition. Such rights were mere rhetoric if freedom to communicate were not guaranteed. So free speech, a free press, a right of assembly, and a right to practice religion without interference were all enumerated in the First Amendment. There was an assumption of tension between a people and their government, an assumption that if there were not free and open communication, a government would inevitably fall into tyranny. So the press was to open itself up to all shades of opinion, function as a kind of common carrier of news and intelligence to keep people informed about the acts of their government and their possible implications for everyday life. The press was an instrument of criticism and reform.

Of course these ideals and expectations have not been borne out consistently in American history. For the first fifty years the American press was a kept press, largely owned by political parties and thus pursuing the agendas of its financial masters. Perhaps the first effort at reform-oriented journalism could be put down to Benjamin Day and his creation of the *New York Sun*, who began a penny paper at a time when more established newspapers charged six cents, and appealed to the "mass of people . . . not . . . interested in newspapers, because the newspapers brought nothing into their lives but the drone of American and foreign politics" (O'Brien 1968, 13–14). Day began to look for daily news, concentrating on disasters, crime and people, and editorializing in favor of improved fire apparatus for New York, and for abolition of slavery. "Before the *Sun* was a decade old, it had many imitators and had altered the whole course of American journalism" (Kobre 1969, 197).

Many other abolitionist newspapers and journals began in the northern part of the United States in the aftermath of the *Sun*, and its attention to spectacle and everyday lives of people led to ever-larger headlines, newspaper hawkers on street corners, and advertising for the masses. During the Civil War, the intense interest in a public that saw regiments of troops raised in virtually every state and territory, and then the carnage of the battlefield, resulted in woodcuts of battles, published first by *Harper's Weekly*, and war correspondents who traveled with the armies and filed stories, including the names of the dead in many cases, via the telegraph. This provided a more sobering view of the war than the reports of glorious victories, which also graced newspapers' front pages.

By the turn of the century, industrialism—which had only gotten underway in the United States by 1850—had become a vital aspect of American life. The United States began to absorb millions of new immigrants from eastern and central Europe, large-scale migration from farms to cities had begun, and people began to trade lives governed by organic time for those driven by the clock. Cities began to absorb thousands of new arrivals, often in substandard living conditions. People became dependent for their daily food on markets and processed foodstuffs rather than on their own labor and talent in growing it. All of this change resulted in another wave of journalism aimed at correcting newly developing problems in everyday urban life.

Both print and photojournalists responded to such developments with exposés of their implications for newly-arrived city residents. Jacob Riis chronicled the situation of the slums in his photographic book, *How the Other Half Lives*, published in 1890, and reform-minded journalist/novelists such as Upton Sinclair tackled the squalid working conditions and hazards in industry (*The Jungle*, published in 1906, dealt with the meat-packing industry). Riis and Sinclair, along with other journalists such as Ida Tarbell, Lincoln Steffens, Nellie Bly, and Ray Stannard Baker, all became known during this period (and especially between 1903 and 1912) as "muckrakers," a name given to them by President Theodore Roosevelt in 1906. This period of reform was inaugurated by *McClure's* magazine in January 2003, and involved other publications such as *Munsey's* and *Cosmopolitan*, as well. The muckrakers took on many of the large industrial trusts of the period, including Standard Oil (by Ida Tarbell), municipal corruption (by Lincoln Steffens), and the abuse of non-union miners by the United Mine Workers in the coal fields of Pennsylvania (by Ray Stannard Baker).

The rise of bolshevism and fascism, along with the collapse of the stock market in 1929, also occasioned another round of reform efforts, especially in the radical press during the Great Depression. These reform efforts were driven by ideology. These publications were often vitriolic and inflammatory, usually had small circulations, and were largely read by their own constituency. So their impact on the social fabric and the conduct of politics was minimal. Nevertheless, they spoke for radical reformations led by the American Communist Party (the *Daily Worker*) and smaller like-minded groups (for instance, *The Partisan Review*, published by the John Reed Club of New York), and by the communists' ideological opposites, such as Father Charles E. Coughlin's *Social Justice*, and *Pelley's*, a publication of William Dudley Pelley's Silvershirts, modeled on the brownshirts of Germany's Nazi Party. *Pelley's* also claimed that it spoke for the leaders of Christianity in America, and was virulently anti-Semitic, but there was never any evidence to back up his claim (see Susman 1970, 170). Coughlin did run for president against Franklin Roosevelt after originally supporting him but then losing faith in the "New Deal." Other similar publications that argued specifically the case of the unions included the Worker's Party's *The New Militant*, the socialist organs *New Masses* and *People's World* (this one out of Berkeley, California), and from black left-wing believers, the *Harlem Liberator*. One major journalistic voice during this period was John L. Spivak, who damned the Roosevelt administration in his book, *America at the Barricades*.

Spivak's critique was not the only book published during this period to point out the suffering of people. John Steinbeck's *Grapes of Wrath* (1939) did as well, garnering Steinbeck a Pulitzer Prize for his portrayal both of the Great

Depression and the exploitation of agricultural laborers. Further evidence was provided by Richard Wright's *12 Million Black Voices* (1941) exposing the realities of lynchings and violence suffered by African-Americans, and photojournalists working for the Works Progress Administration in the 1930s, notably Margaret Bourke-White, Dorothea Lange, Walker Evans, and Roy Stryker. In Washington, D.C., too, the black-edited *Flash!* magazine featured photographs by Robert McNeill depicting the lives of domestic workers in New York City (1937).

In the 1930s, radio journalism began to find its footing, especially toward the end of that decade as war-fever began to develop in Europe and networks (especially CBS) began to report live from European capitals. Although such reports—and those that followed throughout the war—should not properly be thought of as reform journalism, the credibility gained by reporters such as Edward R. Murrow, Eric Sevareid, Howard K. Smith, and Charles Collingwood (see Sterling and Kittross 1990, 214–220), provided the incentive for the developing television services to deliver news after the war and for Murrow to use television to discredit Senator Joseph McCarthy, who chaired the House Un-American Activities Committee that had blacklisted many American film writers, directors and actors, discredited members of the U.S. diplomatic corps, and even accused members of the military of pro-Communist sympathies in the early 1950s.

A seminal work seeking to identify threats to a free press, and to provide solutions for these threats, was *A Free and Responsible Press*, published in 1947 by a Commission on Freedom of the Press (known also as the Hutchins Commission after its chairman). The commission argued that the philosophy that had informed the American approach to a free press (known as classical liberalism) had not protected the press from threats to its freedom and claimed that the clearest threat was concentration of ownership that had resulted from technological change and led to economies of scale that restricted the number of voices in the marketplace of ideas (Commission on Freedom of the Press, 1947, 48–51). The Commission called on several parties (government, radio networks, newspapers and magazines, non-profit groups, and the public) to take action to preserve freedom of the press by adopting various strategies recommended. These strategies were designed to increase the number of voices available to people in society.

If we consider reform journalism to be that which is aimed specifically at correcting abuse or attempting to influence change, then it would not be fair to say that the reporting of the Vietnam War, or the Civil Rights, women's rights, and anti-war movements, of the 1960s and 1970s were truly reform-oriented, even though the reporting of events and perspectives over this period arguably was significant in hastening change. This would also be true of the *Washington Post's* Watergate coverage that undoubtedly influenced the decision of President Richard Nixon to resign in 1974. Such coverage was simply normal journalistic practice that took advantage of the new electronic news gathering capability of television, and persistence—in the case of Watergate. Of course there were reform-minded and polemical publications with clear political agendas during this period, such as *The Nation* (which began publishing in 1865) *Mother Jones* (which began publication in 1976), and *The Progressive* (publishing since 1909), all of which were "left-wing" in political orientation. On the "right" were publications such as the *National Review*, begun by William F. Buckley in 1955, and *Commentary* (begun in 1945).

The social turmoil of this period, especially resulting from the Watergate scandal, resulted in new initiatives to reform journalism. Journalism programs swelled with new students who saw journalism as a way to address problems and new philosophies of journalism began to emerge. Some tried to argue that social science methodologies should be used more fully by journalists (see Philip Meyer, *Precision Journalism*, 2002). Others argued that the "philosophical dimensions of journalism are beginning to compete in public discourse and academic circles with psychological and sociological perspectives which have dominated such discourse since the 1930s" (Merrill and Odell 1983, ix). Certainly issues of ethics began to be prominent in discussions about the activities of journalists, both in professional and academic circles.

Television networks also began to develop new programs that used investigative tools to expose corruption, self-serving, cover-ups, and ethical lapses in government, sports and corporate practices, notably CBS's *Sixty Minutes* that began broadcasting in 1968. This program's producer, Don Hewitt, had been the Director of *See It Now*, the TV vehicle of Murrow's exposé of Joseph McCarthy, and although there was a ten-year hiatus between these programs, was perhaps the closest successor to it.

By the mid-1990s the various strands of reform—including ethics, social responsibility, and investigative journalism—coalesced into a focus called "civic journalism." By 2002, according to the Pew Center for Civic Journalism, "at least one fifth of all U. S. daily newspapers . . . . practiced some form of civic journalism between 1994 and 2001, and nearly all credit it with a positive impact on the community" (2002). One major shift entailed in journalism as a result of doing civic journalism was the use of explanatory story frames rather than conflict story frames, incorporating citizen perspectives and improving community deliberative processes and helping people improve community life. In other words, such efforts were aimed more at solutions than at chronicling problems.

Civic journalism is also referred to as "public journalism," practiced to attempt to re-involve people in public life. The characteristics of this form of journalism included re-evaluating the use of polar conflict as a primary narrative device; recognizing that there is a difference between objectivity and detachment in writing news stories, and between skepticism and adversarialism; and valuing and encouraging public deliberation of issues as principal markers for practicing public journalism (Merritt 2002).

Public or civic journalism emerged from a recognition that people had become disenchanted with public life, seen in low voter turn-outs, lack of attendance at public forums, reductions in participation rates in organizations from PTAs to bowling leagues, and that journalism itself, as practiced under the traditional standards, was partly to blame. It became a way for journalists to reform the public partially by reforming itself. One student of this movement concluded that those who practice public journalism had honorable goals: "They want to ensure that the voice of the public is heard and that not all reporting is top-down; that all communities, even marginalized ones, are listened to so that spin doctors do not control our elections; and that we hear from the middle spectrum of ideas as well as from the polar extremes" (Witt 2004, 51). In the early twenty-first century, civic or public journalism was yet another manifestation of reform journalism.

Further Reading

Bent, Silas. 1970. *Newspaper Crusaders: A Neglected Story.* Westport CT: Greenwood Press, Publishers, originally published by McGraw-Hill Book Company, Inc. in 1939.

Commission on Freedom of the Press. 1947. *A Free and Responsible Press.* Chicago: University of Chicago Press.

Gerald, J. Edward. 1963. *The Social Responsibility of the Press.* Minneapolis: University of Minnesota Press.

Kobre, Sidney. 1969. *Development of American Journalism.* Dubuque, IA: Wm. C. Brown Company Publishers.

Merrill, John C., and Odell, S. Jack. 1983. *Philosophy and Journalism.* New York: Longman.

Merritt, David. "Public Journalism: Where It Has Been; Where It Is Headed." 2002, July 8. The International Media and Democracy Project Website, http://www.imdp.org/artman/publish/article_14.shtml.

Meyer, Philip. 2002. *Precision Journalism: A Reporter's Introduction to Social Science Methods,.* 4th ed. New York: Rowman & Littlefield Publishers, Inc.,originally 1972.

O'Brien, Frank M. 1968. *The Story of the Sun, New York 1833–1928.* New York: Greenwood Press, Publishers, originally published by D. Appleton and Company in 1928.

Pew Center for Civic Journalism. 2002. "Community Impact, Journalism Shifts Cited in New Civic Journalism Study," http://www.pewcenter.org/doingcj/spotlight /index.php.

Roberts, Gene and Hank Klibanoff. 2006. *The Race Beat: The Press, the Civil Rights Struggle, and the Awakening of a Nation.* New York: Knopf.

Spivak, John L. 1935. *America at the Barricades.* New York: Covici.

Susman, Warren I. 1970. "The Thirties." In *The Development of an American Culture,* edited by Stanley Coben, and Lorman Ratner. Englewood Cliffs, NJ: Prentice-Hall.

Tull, Charles J. 1965. *Father Coughlin and the New Deal.* Syracuse, NY: Syracuse University Press.

Witt, Leonard. 2004. "Is Public Journalism Morphing into the Public's Journalism?" *National Civic Review.* (Fall.) 49–57.

ROBERT S. FORTNER

RELIGION AND THE PRESS

From the Anglicans who settled Virginia and the Pilgrims and Puritans of Massachusetts to the present day, religion and religious people helped shape American culture. And for most of the four centuries of American history the press has been a part of that process. However, over the years the relationship between the media and religion has changed in response both to the changing religious climate and to changing journalistic norms.

Religious Journalism: 1690–1835

The first American newspaper, Benjamin Harris's *Public Occurrences Both Foreign and Domestic,* appeared in Puritan Boston on September 25, 1690, a half century after the church set up a printing press at Harvard University as an adjunct to the university's mission to train clergy. In that paper, as in the many other colonial newspapers that followed it, news consisted primarily of items reprinted from other papers and short observations on local life and events, written either by the editor/publisher or contributed by readers; most of each issue, however, consisted of letters or essays in which contributors provided their views on current events and issues.

Although there was little news explicitly about religion, religion infused much of the content. Writers interpreted good news as signs of God's pleasure, bad news as evidence of his wrath. Crime stories, when they appeared, were cast as cautionary tales warning of the consequences of sin. Essayists used arguments grounded in religion to buttress their own position or to attack those with whom they disagreed. Religious journalism—the framing of news, including news about religion, in ways intended to explain, promote and defend a particular faith —was the norm Readers expected a paper to reflect the views of its owner/publisher; an owner who published, without comment or criticism, views with which he disagreed would have been considered morally suspect for not having the courage to defend his own convictions.

However, divergent viewpoints were readily available through competing newspapers, each with its own perspective. On August 7, 1721, the generally Puritan *Boston News-Letter* and the *Boston Gazette,* were joined by James Franklin's *New-England Courant,* which was bankrolled by wealthy Anglicans who saw having their own paper as a way to undermine Puritan hegemony. It was they who provided most of the content during the first few months of publication. As smallpox raged through Boston, the Rev. Cotton Mathers' support for inoculation provided the avenue for their attack. While essays in the *New-England Courant* portrayed support for inoculation as an heretical attempt to wrest from God his rightful control over life and death, essays in the *Boston News-Letter* and *Boston Gazette* by the Rev. Mathers and his supporters responded that inoculation was a gift from God.

Ideas also spread and sometimes had lasting impact as a result of the practice of picking up and commenting on items first published in other newspapers. The Great Awakening, as the period of religious fervor and revivalism that began about 1720, is a case in point. As the Rev. George Whitefield traveled throughout the colonies preaching an experiential and conversionist kind of Christianity markedly different from the dominant Puritan and Anglican strains, newspapers noted his arrival and then carried commentaries supporting or opposing his message. Items about his preaching in one colony were picked up in papers in other colonies, in the process making of Whitefield the first of many American religious celebrities while also creating a climate in which the Baptist and Methodist faiths could flourish

Similarly, both commentary and pick-ups from other papers spread deism and Enlightenment political philosophy throughout the colonies. Widespread republication of John Locke's essay on civil government and Cato's Letter, "Arbitrary Government proved Incompatible with true Religion," paved the way first for Revolution and then for constitutional guarantees of religious freedom. During the Revolution, both patriot and loyalist papers published many essays using religious arguments to justify their cause. After the Revolution, writers continued to use religion in support of their political opinions until industrialization, urbanization and immigration combined to usher in a new model of journalism.

Religion Journalism Takes Root: 1835–1929

In the early 1830s industrialization attracted immigrants, many of them Catholics from Ireland, to the burgeoning cities. That, in turn, unleashed the wave of revivalism and missionary activity that came to be known as the Second Great Awakening as churches responded to the perceived threat to their vision of a Protestant America. Bible, tract, and missionary societies sprang up. Hundreds of Protestant magazines and newspapers promoted efforts to Christianize and Protestantize the nation. In response, Jews and Catholics started their own magazines in an effort to defend their faith against Protestantism, provide news from the old country, and help their immigrant audience adjust to life in America. But by the end of the century, religious journalism became primarily the province of the religious press. Secular media began to practice "religion journalism"—the more neutral reporting of news about religion.

The father of that kind of journalism, James Gordon Bennett, began publishing his *New York Herald* in 1835 as a cheap alternative to the party papers of the era. As a Scot and a Catholic, Bennett wrote from the perspective of an interested, outside observer. Instead of using religious arguments to justify a position or course of action, he reported what members of all religions were doing and what impact it might have on others in ways that were remarkably even-handed by the standards of the day. Although Bennett's irreverent tone and sometimes sensational coverage made him an easy target for criticism, his church histories, favorable mentions of individual acts of charitable and moral behavior and his extensive neutral-to-favorable coverage each May and June of the annual meetings of Bible, tract, and missionary societies eventually became a model for news coverage in the religion sections of secular newspapers and magazines. His thorough but critical attention to church finances, sex scandals involving clergy, meddling by both Protestant and Catholic clergy in politics, and Protestant attacks on Catholics and Mormons foreshadowed the treatment of religion as hard news.

Although few journalists then or now consider him a role mode, newspapers began to follow Bennett's lead by giving more attention to diverse religions and religious viewpoints. *Niles Magazine* occasionally included the Native American viewpoint in critical stories about Protestant attempts to Christianize them. The transcript of Horace Greeley's interview with Brigham Young, published in Greeley's *New-York Tribune* on August 20, 1859, gave thorough and basically respectful voice to the Mormon faith and its leader even though the article ends with Greeley's own opinions about Mormon practices.

During the Civil War, newspapers in both North and South reverted to religious journalism as they attempted to justify their positions on slavery and the war itself. But to meet public demand for information about the war, they also increased in size and frequency of publication. They also began segregating stories by subject type. By 1900 at least four-fifths of all papers had a "church page," usually on Saturday. While that practice apparently met with widespread approval, it led to a division of labor in the reporting of news about religion.

Church pages became the repository for simple stories about local people and events such as announcements of the topics for Sunday sermons; from about 1920 until well into the 1950s some larger papers such as the *New York Times* published synopses of those sermons on a second religion page each Monday. Whether out of their owner/editor's own convictions or in deference to the majority, well-established mainline Protestant churches got most of the coverage. Although most church pages also carried some stories about large, local Catholic churches, smaller and more conservative Protestant churches and those serving racial and ethnic minorities got little attention. Except in major cities with sizeable Jewish populations, stories about non-Christian religions were even rarer.

With religion defined primarily as a local beat, reporters from other beats covered national and international stories about religion, but usually only on those relatively rare occasions when religion inserted itself into issues in such a way that it could not be ignored. But as on the church page, the tendency to frame stories from the perspective of mainstream Protestantism and the penchant for bright, colorful writing that was the vogue from about 1880 through the 1920s made celebrities of evangelists such as Billy Sunday and Dwight Moody. It also produced sensationalized accounts that denigrated minority religions and religious perspectives.

When *Time* magazine began publishing in April 1923, its religion section featured stories about struggles between "modernists" and "fundamentalists" for control of mainline Protestant denominations. In early issues, the magazine clearly sided with the modernists; it treated fundamentalist Christianity as an anachronistic impediment to progress. While some newspaper stories about the 1925 Scopes trial tried to explain conservative Protestant's concerns about

evolution, many treated them as a joke. Until the 1960s, but especially during prohibition and the 1928 presidential election campaign by the Catholic, Al Smith, newspapers and magazines also frequently portrayed Catholicism as a threat to American society.

The Move toward Diversity and Objectivity: 1929–1976

The first impetus toward improving and diversifying religion news coverage occurred in 1912 when the Seventh-day Adventist Church created a publicity bureau to offset criticism of its opposition to blue laws requiring businesses to close on Sunday. By 1920 most major churches and religious organizations had also set up public relations offices; in 1929 they banded together to create the Religious Public Relations Council in an effort to improve church public relations practices and garner more favorable coverage for member churches. To counter anti-Semitism at home and abroad, the National Conference of Christians and Jews started the non-denominational Religious News Service (RNS) in 1934, which was eventually bought by Newhouse Publications and renamed Religion News Service in 1994.

Those efforts increased the amount of coverage on church pages devoted to national-level denominational news, especially from smaller Christian churches. Growing awareness of Nazi Germany's treatment of Jews, fostered in part by RNS efforts, resulted in more favorable coverage of Judaism. But during World War II Jehovah's Witnesses, Quakers and members of other peace churches were generally presented as a threat to the nation.

After the war the Religion Newswriters Association, a professional organization for journalists who cover religion for the secular press, held its first meeting in 1949 at Syracuse University in connection with the opening of the first college-level non-sectarian program in religious journalism as the field was still called. In 1950 George Cornell wrote his first by-lined religion column for Associated Press; a few years later Louis Cassells began covering religion for United Press International.

With those changes, stories exploring religious trends and issues became more common, but for the most part religion news remained much as it had been for a century. In spite of a change in name from "church page" to the more inclusive "religion page," the space continued to be filled primarily with local people and event stories from Protestant churches. Outside the religion page, stories about the civil rights movement of the 1960s and the Vietnam War frequently mentioned religious support or opposition, but few provided much detail. On and off the church pages, Catholicism got generally favorable coverage as a result of both the election of the Catholic John F. Kennedy as president and Vatican II. However, religions new to the American scene such as the Nation of Islam and the Unification Church as well as the many alternative forms of spirituality that sprang up during the era were generally framed by their opponents as dangerous cults.

The Current Climate

Changes in the American religious and political climate in the post-World War II years combined with a sharp increase in chain-owned newspapers and an attendant decrease in two-newspaper towns led to some calls for more objective, substantive coverage of diverse religions. However, the major impetus for change came in the mid-1970s from a confluence of events underscoring the role of religion in the public sphere: the rise of Islamic fundamentalism in Iran, the election of the born-again Jimmy Carter as president, and the birth of the electronic church.

In response, a few papers such as the *Denver Post* abolished its religion section in the early 1980s as part of a move to treat religion more like other kinds of hard news. Many more pumped additional resources into their religion pages. They also developed a more expansive, less institutional definition of religion news and then signaled the change with even more inclusive names such as "Faith and Values" for the space set aside for religion news.

As recently as 1985, the typical newspaper devoted one page each week to religion news. Only two newspapers, the *New York Times* and the *Los Angeles Times,* employed two religion reporters; many staffed the beat only part time. A decade later space for religion news had more than doubled as full-time religion reporters and even staffs of specialists became more common.

By the late 1980s, simple local stories about people and events gave way to lengthy in-depth features of personal religious journeys and forms of spirituality unconnected to any organized religion. The number of stories about mainline Protestantism declined sharply as the number about Evangelical and Fundamentalist Protestantism increased. But in spite of the many stories about conservative Christianity, news in religion sections was no longer overwhelmingly Christian. Stories examining from a variety of perspectives ethical issues, trends and connections between religion and business, science law, politics and popular culture replaced most stories based on news from denominational headquarters. Annual stories of Ramadan, Yom Kippur, and the Summer Solstice became as common as ones about Christmas and Easter. But in spite of all the changes, religion remained primarily a local beat. A division of labor between religion journalists and nonspecialists working other beats continued to produce mangled stories as well as gaps in coverage and a certain disconnect between the image of religion in the religion sections and the image elsewhere in the publication. Religion reporters gravitated to religious sources; for the religion page, they emphasized creating understanding. Off the religion beat, non-specialists relied most heavily on sources from their own beat and framed stores about religion with conflict and controversy remaining the driving news values.

In the weeks after the destruction of the World Trade Center on September 11, 2001, for example, religion journalists generally were able to find sources that would allow them to report in depth on local religious reactions, including reactions from within the Islamic community. Some non-specialists managed to find the sources necessary to explain the variety of strains within Islam in ways that put the beliefs that fueled the attacks into a meaningful context, but many nonspecialists, having little familiarity with Islam or experience reporting about religion, turned to government officials and average citizens whose quotations helped create an impression that "Muslim" is synonymous with "terrorist."

With cutbacks, particularly in international newsgathering since the mid-1980s by newspapers and wire services and also on the religion beat at some papers since about 2000, neither specialists nor non-specialists were able to provide sustained coverage of major issues involving religion, especially from an international perspective. As a result, national news magazines such as *Time* and *Newsweek* provide much of the breaking national and international news with a religion dimension. Quality magazines such as the *New Yorker, Atlantic Monthly,* and *Harper's* have become the repositories for substantive stories that are less time-sensitive.

However, national and international news about religion can also be found in religious publications. Although *Hindus Today* and Muslim publications such as *American-Arab Messenger* circulate primarily within their own religious community, many others such as the secular humanist *Free Inquiry* and the Buddhist *Tricycle* and *Tikkun* are often available in chain bookstores. But because most religious Americans are Christian, most of the approximately one thousand religious magazines are Christian. Of these, the news magazine *World* is most like the secular newsweeklies. Although denominational magazines and those published by missionary and other special-purpose religious organizations often provide information on events and conditions in countries where a church or organization has contacts, other magazines such as the conservative Evangelical Protestant *Christianity Today,* socially-oriented Evangelical Protestant *Sojourners,* mainline *Christian Century,* Catholic lay-edited *Commonweal,* and Jesuit *America* are generally more influential because they are widely read by leaders across the religio-political spectrum.

The Special Case of Broadcasting

Commercial stations have never considered news about religion a priority. A few obtain religion news by purchasing a special feed from wire services such as UPI Radio Network; CBS makes its program, *The World of Religion* available to its affiliates; only a few stations such as WINS in New York have ever produced their own religion news programs. With changes in broadcast law since the late 1970s, many stations have stopped carrying news. At others, the trend has been to provide just headline news. As a result, coverage usually consists of little more than a simple mention of a religious leader or faction in a political story. Anything approaching in-depth coverage occurs only in the case of a major, but easily reported, event such as the death of Pope John Paul II. The only exception is National Public Radio, where Lynn Neary has worked the religion beat since 1993.

Since the early days of broadcasting when some radio frequencies were set aside for non-commercial use, the Moody Bible Institute's radio station WBMI has been the most consistent source for news about religion from a religious perspective. However, since the mid-1970s when a move toward broadcast deregulation paved the way both for ownership of commercial stations by religious organizations and for narrow-casting, WBMI has received stiff competition from M. G. "Pat" Robertson's Christian Broadcasting Network (CBN) Radio Network.

The pattern is much the same on television. As a result of changes in broadcast law in the late 1970s that opened the door for paid religious programming, the networks stopped producing discussion programs featuring mainline Protestant, Catholic, and Jewish clergy. In their place, news and commentary from a conservative Protestant perspective began to appear, first on network and independent stations and more recently on cable channels. Since the late 1970s, Robertson's *700 Club* has been most influential, but the more apocalyptic *This Week in Bible Prophecy* with Jack Van Impe is also widely available.

Unlike newspaper journalists, television journalists are usually general assignment reporters. With the exception of a few years in the 1990s when Peggy Wehmeyer covered religion for ABC, no network has ever employed a religion journalist. Only a few local stations such as WFAA-TV in Dallas and KSL-TV in Salt Lake City have ever had religion reporters although a few have shared one with a local newspaper. Therefore, on commercial television, in-depth reporting of events or issues involving occurs primarily in documentaries such as those produced by Bill Moyers.

On network newscasts since at least the mid-1970s, about 5 percent of all stories at least mention religion. But with the exception of occasional special segments and holiday features, chosen primarily for their visual appeal, most are shorter than thirty seconds. Religion content, for the most part, consists of a simple and often simplistic label attached to a person or a faction. Most of those labels occur in coverage of the Christian Right in American politics or in stories from historic religious trouble spots abroad such as Northern Ireland and the Middle East.

At the local level, there are the obligatory holiday features. Churches and synagogues are sometimes the backdrop for reports on a funeral. Especially since the early 1990s, victorious athletes and accident survivors are shown thanking God for their good fortune. Clergy are sometimes used as sources in stories concerning hate crimes or complaints of civil rights violations, but substantive news about religion remains rare.

Further Reading

Buddenbaum, Judith M. "Network News Coverage of Religion." In *Channels of Belief,* edited by John P. Ferre, 57–78 Ames: Iowa State University Press, 1990.

Buddenbaum, Judith M. *Reporting Religion News: An Introduction for Journalists.* Ames: Iowa State University Press, 1998.

Buddenbaum, Judith M., and Debra L. Mason, eds., *Readings on Religion as News.* Ames: Iowa State University Press, 1999.

Hafez, Kari. *Islam and the West in the Mass Media: Fragmented Images in a Globalizing World.* Cresskill, NJ: Hampton Press, 2000.

Hoover, Stewart M. *Religion in the News: Faith and Journalism in American Public Discourse* Thousand Oaks, CA: Sage, 1998.

McCloud, Sean. *Making the American Religious Fringe: Exotics, Subversives, & Journalists, 1955–1993.* Chapel Hill: University of North Carolina Press, 2004.

Nord, David Paul. *Faith in Reading: Religious Publishing and the Birth of the Mass Media.* New York: Oxford University Press, 2004.

Nord, David Paul. "Teleology and the News: The Religious Roots of American Journalism, 1630–1730." *Journal of American History,* 77 (June, 1990): 9–38.

Said, Edward W. *Covering Islam: How the Media and the Experts Determine How We See the Rest of the World*, 2nd ed. London: Vintage Press, 1997.

Silk, Mark. *Unsecular Media: Making News of Religion in America.* Urbana: University of Illinois Press, 1995.

Sloan, William David, ed. *Media and Religion in American History.* Northport, AL: Vision Press, 2000.

Underwood, Doug. *From Yahweh to Yahoo! The Religious Roots of the Secular Press.* Urbana: University of Illinois Press, 2002.

JUDITH M. BUDDENBAUM

RESTON, JAMES

James Barrett "Scotty" Reston (November 11, 1909–December 6, 1995) chronicled and analyzed eight U.S. presidents plus the American foreign policy establishment from World War II through the Cold War. Reston's platform was the *New York Times*, where he served as correspondent, Washington, D.C., bureau chief, columnist, and executive editor.

Reston was born in Clydebank, Scotland, to Johanna Irving Reston and James Reston. Young James had an older sister. The family immigrated to America in 1920 and settled in Dayton, Ohio. Reston picked up the nickname "Scotty" while caddying at a golf course as a teenager. He enrolled at the University of Illinois, studied journalism, and lettered in golf. After graduation in 1932, Reston's first newspaper job was sportswriter with the *Springfield* (Ohio) *Daily News*.

In 1934, he joined the Associated Press in New York and wrote sports features and a column about the metropolis. In 1937 Reston was transferred to the AP bureau in London to cover sports plus the British Foreign Bureau. At that time, Adolf Hitler and Nazi expansionism consumed Europe. World War II approached.

Reston was hired as a London-based *New York Times* correspondent on September 1, 1939, the day Germany invaded Poland, thus beginning World War II. Reston covered the Nazi siege of London. In mid-1941, he returned to the United States and was assigned to the *Times* Washington bureau and covered the U. S. State Department.

In 1942, months after the United States entered the war, Reston published *Prelude to Victory*, his first book and an emphatic American call to arms. Reston was recruited for the U.S. Office of War Information in London. After a year he rejoined the *Times* at the request of the publisher Arthur Hayes Sulzberger. Reston was tasked with showing the newspaper business to the publisher's presumptive successor, Orvil Dryfoos.

In late 1943, Reston returned to Washington as diplomatic correspondent. While covering the 1944 Dumbarton Oaks Conference, a gathering of allies that planted the seeds for the United Nations, Reston received documents about the gathering leaked by a source in the Nationalist China delegation. Reston's exclusive reports angered diplomatic leaders and press colleagues, but in 1945 he won a Pulitzer Prize for national reporting.

From the late 1940s through the 1950s, Reston was well established as the leading capital correspondent who effectively worked sources and produced scoops. He chronicled and analyzed early Cold War warriors Harry S Truman, Dwight D. Eisenhower, Dean Acheson, John Foster Dulles, Joseph McCarthy, Arthur Vandenberg, and other leading political figures.

Reston's articles were conversational. He employed techniques from his pre-*Times* days as a sportswriter. There was also sometimes a sermon-like quality to his writing; Reston's mother had hoped her son would become a preacher. Many of Reston's articles were labeled "news analysis" because they did not follow traditional news writing conventions, yet his writing did not have the opinionated tone of editorials or signed columns. What Reston introduced was an interpretive writing style that was adopted by journalists and other newspapers in the late twentieth-century.

In 1953, at age forty-four, Reston succeeded Arthur Krock as Washington bureau chief. After twenty years in that post, Krock yielded his chair to the rising star when it appeared that *The Washington Post* was about to appoint Reston as their new editorial page editor. Reston had the blessing of the leaders in New York to recruit young talent that would make the Washington bureau the best in the industry. Reston's recruits became future *New York Times* icons including: Russell Baker, Max Frankel, David Halberstam, Anthony Lewis, Neil Sheehan, Hedrick Smith, and Tom Wicker.

In 1957, Reston won a second Pulitzer Prize for distinguished reporting the previous year on the Dwight D. Eisenhower administration. In 1960 Reston began writing his three-times weekly column, "Washington," which became must-reading for officials and the well-read public. Recurring themes in Reston's columns promoted American ideals and democracy, and for some readers, his commentaries seemed to serve as a national conscience.

By the early 1960s, Reston was a media star similar to the network news anchormen who became prominent in the late 1960s and 1970s. His analytical news writing style was a trademark of his influential journalism career.

Reston was at the center of key public policy clashes between the press and government. He was a fierce defender of press freedom and the people's right to know, yet Reston made exceptions for journalistic restraint if he believed national security truly appeared to be in jeopardy. Reston was instrumental in toning down *New York Times* publication of the failed Bay of Pigs invasion of Cuba in 1961, and in 1962, Reston influenced the decision to delay publication of the Cuban missile crisis story at the request of John F. Kennedy. However, Reston was among the *Times'* leaders who argued for publication in 1971 of the Pentagon Papers, stolen government documents concerning United States involvement in the Vietnam War. Reston's 1967 book, *The Artillery of the Press: Its Influence on American Foreign Policy,* was a collection of his lectures before the New York-based Council on Foreign Relations. Reston also criticized President Richard M. Nixon for stonewalling during the Watergate scandal.

Over the years, Reston held a variety of position at the *Times*. In 1964, he became associate editor in New York and continued writing the column. In 1968, he became executive editor of the *Times*. When the newspaper created the modern op-ed page, he invited non-journalism experts to write on that page about politics, art and culture. He returned to Washington a year later to focus on his column.

Through the 1970s Reston's star began to fade: Network TV news and emerging anchorman stars stole some of that star power. Furthermore, the press-government relationship was more antagonistic because of Vietnam and Watergate. Reston was a skeptical insider among wary Washington officials during World War II, Korea and the early Cold War. Critics now challenged Reston's routines as outdated. He continued writing his columns and observed the Ford, Carter and Reagan administrations. His column ended in 1987 and he retired from the *Times* in 1989 after about a half century of service.

In 1991, Reston published *Deadline: A Memoir*. His family included his wife, Sally (the former Sara Jane Fulton) and three adult sons. When Reston died in December, 1995, *Washington Post* Publisher Katherine Graham eulogized him by saying that he "helped lead postwar America from isolationism to internationalism."

Further Reading

Apple, R. W., Jr. "James Reston, a Journalist Nonpareil, Dies at 86." *New York Times*, December 7, 1995, A1.

Childs, Marquis, and James Reston, eds., *Walter Lippmann and His Times*. New York: Harcourt, Brace, 1959.

Frankel, Max, *The Times of My Life and My Life at The Times*. New York, Delta/Random House, 2000.

Keene, Ann T. *American National Biography,* online, 2001.

Reston, James B. *The Artillery of the Press; Its Influence on American Foreign Policy*. New York: Published for the Council on Foreign Relations by Harper & Row,1967.

——. *Deadline: A Memoir*. New York. Random House, 1991.

——. Papers. University of Illinois Archives, Champaign-Urbana.

——.. *Prelude to Victory*. New York, Knopf, 1942.

——. *Sketches in the Sand*. New York: Knopf, 1967.

Stacks, John F. *Scotty: James B. Reston and the Rise and Fall of American Journalism*. Boston: Little, Brown, 2002.

Talese, Gay. *The Kingdom and the Power*. New York, Bantam Books, 1969.

Tifft, Susan, and Jones, Alex S. *The Trust: The Private and Powerful Family Behind The New York Times*. Boston: Little, Brown and Company, 1999.

WAYNE DAWKINS

REUTERS

"Gentlemen, if I may. A censured press is the tool of a corrupt minority. A free press is a symbol of a free people. Truth is freedom, and without truth there can only be slavery and degradation." Hollywood screenwriters put these words into the mouth of Paul Reuter at the end of the 1940 film, *A Dispatch from Reuters,* that told the story of the man behind the news agency. When the film was made, the Battle of Britain raged. Reuter articulated what the Anglo-American alliance would be fighting for and what they would be fighting against.

The real Paul Julius Reuter was born in Cassel, Germany, the son of a Jewish rabbi. He worked in his uncle's bank in the university town of Göttingen and studied electric telegraphy under Professor Karl Frederich Gauss. On August 6, 1844, the first news received by telegraph appeared in the British press reporting the birth of Queen Victoria's second son. In 1848 Reuter went to work at the Havas news agency in Paris, the future Agence France Presse. Reuter started publishing his own news-sheet in 1849, but the printing press was seized by creditors. Later that year he moved to Aachen on the German, Belgian, Dutch border. In 1850 Reuter used forty-five carrier pigeons to forward stock market and commodity prices from Brussels, where the Belgian telegraph line ended, to Aachen, where the German line began. In October 1851, he set up a telegraph agency based at the London Stock Exchange. Reuter pledged his news agency would be "first with the news." With the help of an eleven-year-old office boy he transmitted stock market quotes and major news headlines between London and the continent using the Dover-Calais submarine cable. It was the beginning of the Reuters News Group that in 155 years of service grew to 15,300 employees in 190 bureaus, providing news and information in 19 languages in 89 countries with annual revenues of $4.4 billion.

In 1858 Reuter began supplying news to London newspapers with a "statement of principles" promising Reuters would "preserve its independence and integrity" in reporting the day's news. A year later Reuters had its first significant scoop, relaying words from the King of Sardinia predicting an imminent war between the French and Austrians. In 1863 London was connected by cable to Crookhaven and Cork. Ships coming from America threw canisters containing news into the sea. Reuter arranged to have the information telegraphed to London. This was how in April 1865, he became the first to report the assassination of President Abraham Lincoln, pushing European financial markets into crisis. When the report was later confirmed, Reuter emerged as Europe's most reliable news source. The Reuters Telegram Company went public later that year.

In the 1870s Reuters expanded in to the Far East and the United States, signing partnerships with Havas and Wolff to create a worldwide news reach. Reuters established bureaus in Alexandria, Cape Town, Bombay, and Valparaiso, Chile, and began transmitting on the Atlantic cable that connected Newfoundland to Ireland.

Reuter retired in 1878, leaving the company's direction to his son, Herbert. Major developments under his leadership included the electronic transmission of news and information using the column printer, which replaced the need for messenger delivery. News into and out of India, Egypt, China, and South Africa became Reuters most profitable hubs. The company in 1900 beat by forty-eight hours the official announcement ending the Boer War. Reuters World War I reporter Herbert Russell believed the company's correspondents considered themselves "independent eyewitnesses on behalf of the nation." On July 1 and 2, 1916, during the battle of the Somme, he reported British troops had "fought gallantly" and had made "good progress into enemy territory," despite the fact the engagement had been like much of the war, a bloody stalemate. Readers were advised British troops had taken "many prisoners. So far the day is going well for Great Britain and France." Correspondent Lester Lawrence claimed with characteristic optimism on March 26, 1918, that the Germans were all but defeated despite their sustained advance on the French front at Osie. "The Germans are paying dearly for every fresh yard of ground," he reported, "until the moment comes for the counter-offensive. The belief of the men is that this is inevitably the last great effort of the Boche, sustained by a recklessness with which the enemy hurls his battalions to certain destruction. He is staking all upon his numbers, and these are being wasted at a rate that cannot be maintained for many days more." Later that year, Reuters was the first news agency to report World War I armistice news to the British Empire.

Between the wars, Reuters was led by the aristocratic Roderick Jones, whose chief editor Herbert Jeans, favored reporters whose personal polish allowed them to easily mix with the important people of the world. In November 1923 management moved in Queen Anne style to larger offices off the Embankment, where they mixed freely with members of the government and affirmed their support for Britain's exercise of imperial power. In 1925, the Press Association, Britain's national news agency, purchased a controlling interest in Reuters. Its services would now be subsidized by the British government in an environment in which Associated Press and United Press were threatening Reuters position of preeminence in parts of Europe and Asia. On the eve of World War II the company's one thousand employees moved into expanded corporate headquarters at 85 Fleet Street.

Reuters robust war reporting was led by the editorial team of Sir Samuel Storey, Walton Cole, and Sidney Mason. They operated under a joint agreement worked out between Sir William John Haley of Reuters and Kent Cooper of Associated Press claiming, "There is acceptance of the right of government to have us withhold news for the common good, but no acceptance of any right of government to say how we shall word what we do transmit." Five Reuters correspondents were killed reporting the conflict, including Stewart Sale, who reported in January 1943 a bombing raid over Berlin. "I looked down on hundreds of points of fire," he reported. "These were incendiaries which had just struck and looked like strings of gems. Others were already an angry red. Most of the pilots thought the flak over Berlin was light. I knew it was bad enough for me." Eight Reuters staff members died in action as members of the British armed forces. Reuters reporters filed stories wherever British forces fought, including Normandy. Marshall Yarrow reported on D-Day, "When I left the fighting area I left something behind me—my face print in the mud of Normandy's beaches." Doon Campbell reported, "The beach ahead was a sandy cemetery of mangled bodies. The big guns of the allied fleet thundered behind me. This was war in its totality: theatrical and terrifying."

During the Cold War, Reuters reporters Ian Fleming and Frederick Forsyth developed reputations and made millions by writing spy thrillers. Peter Jackson achieved an extraordinary exclusive in 1953 by trekking for two weeks into the Himalayas to interview Edmund Hillary, who had just climbed Mt. Everest. Early on a Sunday morning in August 1961, an East German soldier at the Brandenburg Gate told Reuters correspondent Adam Kellet-Long, "Die Grenze ist geschloseen. The border is closed." It was the beginning of a twenty-eight-year standoff at the Berlin Wall. Reuters correspondent Anthony Grey spent two years and two months in jail as a prisoner of Mao Tse-tung's "Cultural Revolution." Helen Womack was an eyewitness to the Soviet withdrawal from Afghanistan. Reuters reporter Bernd Debusmann and photographer Patrick de Noirmont covered the bombing of Baghdad.

Reuters has been criticized for being pro-Palestinian in the continuing Arab-Israeli conflict in the Middle East. The company's Trust Principles continue to claim "independence, integrity, and freedom from bias in the gathering and dissemination of news." In the 1990s, Reuters became a leader in the digital universe. In its 1994 acquisition of TIBCO, Reuters emerged a major player in developing software for the Internet. In that year, Reuters launched its interactive business service and a Financial Television Service. The following year it created a Greenhouse Fund designed to invest in high-tech start-ups. The company's 3000 series, begun in 1996, involved multimedia news packages, a dedicated website and a Netscape Browser. In the years that followed Reuters initiated Business Briefing as an Extranet service, Reuters mobile, PocketReuters, and Newsbreaker, an interactive multimedia news-on-demand product. Reuters Inform followed, a real-time e-commerce report along with Reuters Plus, a daily online, video and text of the latest news. Reuters Messaging was a collaborative venture with Microsoft in 2002 offering high-speed communication in the global financial services industry. In October 2006 Reuters advertised itself as a "global information company" offering the world's "first virtual news bureau" called Second Life, designed to bring financial news and lifestyle stories targeting young adults.

Tom Glocer, Reuters chief executive officer at the end of 2006, reported the company continued to progress "through innovation, new technologies, new audiences, and new ways of presenting the news." That was essentially the strategy their founding father, Paul Reuter, had used 155 years before to make the company a global leader in gathering and disseminating news and information.

Further Reading

Boyd-Barrett, Oliver and Tehri Rantanen, eds. *The Globalization of News.* London: Sage Publications, 1998.
Jones, Sir Roderick. *A Life in Reuters.* London: Hodder and Stoughton, 1951.
Mooney, Brian, and Barry Simpson. *Breaking News: How the Wheels Came Off at Reuters.* West Sussex: Capstone Publishing, 2003.
Read, Donald. *The Power of News: The History of Reuters, 1849–1989.* Oxford: Oxford University Press, 1992.
"Reuters: The Company," http://www.about.Reuters.com (accessed April 9, 2007).
Storey, Graham *Reuters: The Story of a Century of News-gathering.* New York: Crown Publishers, 1951.

BRUCE J. EVENSEN

RICE, GRANTLAND

Henry Grantland Rice (1880–1954) was born to a farm family in Murfreesboro, Tennessee. He was named for his maternal grandfather, Henry Grantland, who had been a major in the Confederate army. The boy and his parents, Bolling Hendon Rice and Beulah Grantland Rice, lived in the grandfather's Nashville home, where he received a baseball, bat and glove that furthered his interest in playing sports. Rice played both baseball and football competitively at Vanderbilt University, while majoring in Latin and Greek. He was a power hitting shortstop, captained the team his senior year, and played semi-pro after graduating before shoulder injuries, sustained in football, forced him to give up his dream of becoming a big league ball player.

Rice stayed close to athletics by becoming sports editor of the *Nashville Daily News* in 1901 for $5 a week. That brief stint led to a writing job at *Forester Magazine* before he became a sports writer at the *Atlanta Journal* in 1902 for $12.50 a week. The *Journal* used Rice's talent and an expanded sports page to compete with the better entrenched *Atlanta Constitution.* The job gave Rice the opportunity to improve his craft by covering prep, college and professional sports. He became an early promoter of Ty Cobb, who was then in the minor leagues. When in 1905 he took a $50-a-week job at the *Cleveland News*, the ambitious Rice had already developed a reputation as one of the hardest working and best sports journalists in the business.

The *Nashville Tennessean* lured Rice back in 1906. A few months earlier, on April 11, 1906, he had married Katherine Hollis from Americus, Georgia. Their daughter Florence, born in 1910, would become a Hollywood actress. Rice covered sports and the theatre for the *Tennessean,* published poetry, and became a scratch golfer. His signed column was the paper's only byline. In 1911, the Rices moved to New York, where Grantland's column "The Sportlight" began appearing in the *Evening Mail*, a venerable paper begun in 1867 by James Gordon Bennett. There Rice was befriended and promoted by the paper's star columnist, Franklin Pierce Adams.

Rice followed Adams to the *New York Tribune* in 1914, the beginning of a national syndication that would make Rice the best known sports writer of his generation. During 1918 and 1919, Rice reported on the advance of the First Army on St. Mihiel, the Battle for Mount Sec and the thirty thousand killed in the Argonne Woods for the Army's *Stars and Stripes*. When Rice returned home, his postwar writing, first in the *Tribune*, and then beginning in 1924 the *Herald-Tribune*, reflected a ceaseless search for athletic heroism. As the unabashed leader of what his editor, Stanley Walker, called the "Gee whiz!" school of sports writers, Rice helped to create the legends of Jack Dempsey, Babe Ruth, Ty Cobb, Walter "Big Train" Johnson, Bobby Jones, Bill Tilden, Knute Rockne and the Notre Dame Fighting Irish, and Red Grange (Rice's "Galloping Ghost"). Rice's frequent golf-playing partner, Ring Lardner, viewed sports figures differently and led the "Aw-Nuts" school of sports writers who cynically deplored "godding up" athletes. Rice, though, understood that World War I had greatly stimulated "the desire for competition of man against man, not man against machine" (*Country Life*, June 1919, 40, 46) Sport for readers was a reflection of everyday life where "the struggle on the field is a repetition of his own struggle in everyday life. He rises or he falls with his hero. It is part of his own experience" (*American Magazine*, May 1924, 41)Red Smith and John Kieran were among those who considered Rice the most influential figure on their generation of sports writers and columnists.

Rice, Lardner, Damon Runyon, Heywood Broun, Paul Gallico, Westbrook Pegler, James P.Dawson, Robert Edgren, Nat Flesicher, Gene Fowler, W.O. McGeehan, Otto Floto, and Warren Brown were among the highest salaried reporters of the Jazz Age, at a time when circulation managers calculated the effect that sports coverage on sales. More than half of all local coverage was devoted to sports in the 1920s, a 50 percent increase from a generation before. If Rice was not the dean of American sports writers as he was often billed (Henry Chadwick long had preceded him), few could match his stature and success. He broadcast the World Series in 1923 and began hosting his own weekly radio show. He formed Sportlight films, producing and narrating short films on sports that won two Academy Awards. After Walter Camp's death in 1925, he took over the selection of *Collier's* All-American football team for the next twenty-seven years. Beginning in 1930, his work became syndicated by the North American Newspaper Alliance.

When he died, obituary writers praised his protean productivity that included twenty-two thousand columns, more than one thousand magazine articles, and such lines as "When the Great Scorer comes / To mark against your name, / He'll write not 'won' or 'lost' / But how you played the game" (*Nashville Tennessean*, June 16, 1908). When Rice died he was more than a sports writer. He was a celebrity, who chronicled tall tales of civic celebration and spectacle that captured the emotion of his era and elevated the stature of the sports writer for generations to come.

Further Reading

Camerer, Dave. *The Best of Grantland Rice*. New York: F. Watts, 1963.

Cooke, Bob. *Wake Up the Echoes: From the Sports Pages of the New York Herald-Tribune*. Garden City, NY: Hanover, 1956.

Grantland Rice Papers. Vanderbilt University. Special Collections Division. Nashville, Tennessee.

Fountain, Charles. *Sportswriter: The Life and Times of Grantland Rice*. New York: Oxford University, 1993.

Harper, William A. *The Way You Played the Game: The Life of Grantland Rice*. Columbia: University of Missouri, 1999.

Hodermarsky, Mark. *Baseball's Greatest Writers*.Dubuque: Kendall/Hunt Publications, 2003.

Inabinett, Mark. *Grantland Rice and His Heroes*. Knoxville: University of Tennessee, 1994.

New York Times, The, July 14, 1954.

Rice, Grantland. "Boxing for a Million Dollars." *American Review of Reviews*, October 1926.

——. "My Greatest Thrill in Twenty-two Years of Sport." *American Magazine*, May 1924.

——. "The Return to Sport." *Country Life*, June 1919.

——. *Sportlights of 1923*. New York: G.P. Putnam's Sons, 1924.

——. *The Tumult and the Shouting: My Life in Sport*. New York: A.S. Barnes, 1954.

BRUCE J. EVENSEN

RIIS, JACOB

Jacob Augustus Riis (May 3, 1849–May 26, 1914) was a lecturer, journalist, photographer, and social reformer whose pioneering book *How the Other Half Lives* (1890) helped launch a crusade to improve living conditions in New York City's tenement house districts. An immigrant who rose to national prominence in progressive reform circles, Riis engaged with some of the most heated issues of late nineteenth and early twentieth centuries, including poverty, immigration, and what it meant to be an American.

Riis was born May 3, 1849, into a middle-class Lutheran family in the historic town of Ribe, Denmark. His father taught Latin and Greek at a centuries-old preparatory academy and occasionally did part-time editorial work for the local newspaper. The father envisioned a literary career for Riis, but the young man became a carpenter. In 1870, inspired by the *Leatherstocking Tales* of James Fenimore Cooper, he left Denmark for America. Arriving in New York City, Riis found a metropolis on the brink of a demographic transformation that would swell its population and give it a distinctly foreign look. In his best-selling rags-to-riches autobiography, *The Making of an American* (1901), Riis recounted how he lived on the edge of poverty, tramping in and around New York, working as a roustabout, laborer, salesman, and reporter for small newspapers.

Two events dramatically altered Riis's fortunes in 1887. He landed a reporting job at the *New York Tribune*, with a beat that included the tenement districts of the city's Lower East Side and notorious Five Points area. That year he also read a four-line news dispatch from Germany announcing the discovery of "flashlight photography," a new technique that made possible nighttime shooting. Riis enlisted the services of two distinguished amateur photographers, Henry G. Piffard and Richard Hoe Lawrence, and the three men set about photographing the tenement districts by night.

On January 25, 1888, Riis delivered a lecture, "The Other Half—How It Lives and Dies in New York," before the Society of Amateur Photographers, using one hundred lantern-slides of New York's slums, the lantern was intended to highlight the work of Piffard and Lawrence, but Riis turned the presentation into a titillating tour of the city's seamier side. In short order, Riis turned the lecture into a newspaper story ("Flashes from the Slums," February 12, 1888, *Tribune*), an article for *Scribner's* magazine (1889), and the book *How the Other Half Lives*. The book launched Riis's career as an influential journalist, lecturer, and reformer.

Although Riis would claim that his title, *How the Other Half Lives*, was original, pure inspiration on his part, "the other half" was an established popular image for nether regions that were best experienced through the works of journalists and artists. The slums of New York City's Lower East Side were teaming with recent immigrants. There was high unemployment, and appalling death rate; few municipal services that reached the poor. Other books had dealt with the city's underside, but none in the manner of *How the Other Half Lives*. Riis's book was the first in America to include snapshots of the slums, and in great measure it was the small grainy photos that helped make the book an instant success.

How the Other Half Lives chronicled the lives of New York's poor, both native-born and immigrants, including blacks, Irish, Italians, Jews, Chinese, and others. By turns Riis reassured, titillated, and challenged his middle-class readers. The book offered something for everyone: statistics for the social scientists, suggestions for the charitable workers, emotional appeals to reformers, and anecdotes, photographs and free-hand sketches for those seeking entertainment. Riis concluded *How the Other Half Lives* with a call to erase the dangerous gap between the classes and races by building a bridge "founded upon justice and built of human hearts." He reiterated that theme in *The Battle with the Slum* (1902), where he proposed "reform by human touch."

Riis followed up *How the Other Half Lives* with additional newspaper work and articles and sketches for prominent magazines. He moved to Charles A. Dana's *Evening Sun* in late 1890, and in March 1892 wrote an article about Italian rag-pickers headlined "Real Wharf Rats, Human Rodents that Live on Garbage under the Wharves." A series of articles for *Scribner's* was collected in Riis's second book, *The Children of the Poor* (1892), and a group of magazine stories and sketches were gathered in *Out of Mulberry Street: Stories of Tenement Life in New York* (1898).

By 1901, Riis was at the height of his powers. That year, his friend Theodore Roosevelt was elected the president; reformers had driven Tammany Hall from city hall; and Riis published his highly popular *The Making of an American*, which sold out two editions in three weeks.

Although Riis is best known for his pioneering photojournalism, during his lifetime he was seen as primarily a writer and a lecturer, and that was how he saw himself. By the time of his death in May 26, 1914, Riis had delivered numerous slide-lectures across the country and written hundreds of newspaper stories, dozens of magazine articles, and fifteen books. However, his work as a photographer represents an intriguing, if brief, chapter in his life.

The technology during the late 1880s was not to the point where newspapers could easily publish photographs. In 1888, the *New York Sun* published a dozen drawings from Riis's photographs from the slums. In 1890, the illustrations in *How the Other Half Lives* were divided between half-tones of poor quality and drawings of the photographs. In 1947, Riis's original photographs were recovered, enlarged, and exhibited in the Museum of the City of New York, thus enhancing his reputation as a photographer.

Riis began taking photographs in early 1888, and in the three years leading up to *How the Other Half Lives*, he supplemented his stock of collected photos with some of his own work. Creating a flash effect by lighting explosive powder in a frying pan, Riis photographed people in tenement apartments, stale-beer joints, police lodging houses, and wharf-side dumps. Yet, it appears that with a couple of exceptions, Riis did not pick up a camera after 1895. Riis modestly called himself a photographer "after a fashion," but he clearly understood the power of photography and knew that, as a rhetorical tool, the camera might be mightier than the pen in his crusade.

Riis's photographs, those he shot himself and those taken for him, revealed different sides of Riis: the sympathetic social reformer, the urban tourist/voyeur, and the master of surveillance, all of whom are both attracted to and repelled by what is on the other side of the lens. The standard view of Riis sees him as an enlightened moral crusader and progressive social reformer who did not always rise above the racial/ethnic stereotyping and "scientific racialism" of his day. In fact, stereotypes permeate Riis's descriptions in *How the Other Half Lives*. His writings also reveal deeply divided attitudes toward the so-called "new immigrants" from eastern and southern Europe, and their prospects for assimilation.

Riis saw himself, and was seen by the American public, as the embodiment of the American Spirit, the quintessential self-made immigrant whose life was a morality tale of complete assimilation and unabashed nationalism. Critics traditionally have seen Riis as intent on turning immigrants into middle-class Americans following his own model. However, there are indications that Riis also valued cultural diversity. Ultimately, in his lectures, writings, and photographs, Riis reveals himself as a more complex figure than the classic progressive reformer he is often made out to be.

Further Reading

Alland, Alexander. *Jacob Riis: Photographer & Citizen.* Millerton, NY: Aperture, 1974.

Gandal, Keith. *The Virtues of the Vicious: Jacob Riis, Stephen Crane, and the Spectacle of the Slum.* New York: Oxford University Press, 1997.

Hales, Peter B. *Silver Cities: The Photography of American Urbanization, 1839–1915.* Philadelphia: Temple University Press, 1984.

Lane, James B. *Jacob A. Riis and the American City.* Port Washington, NY: Kennikat Press, 1974.

Newhall, Beaumont. *History of Photography from 1839 to the Present Day.* New York: Museum of Modern Art; distributed by Doubleday, Garden City, NY, 1964.

Riis, Jacob A. *How the Other Half Lives: Studies Among the Tenements of New York.* 1890. New York: Dover Publications, 1971.

——. *The Children of the Poor.* 1892. New York: Charles Scribner's Sons, 1902.

——. *The Making of an American.* New York: The Macmillan Company, 1901.

——. *The Battle with the Slum.* New York: Macmillan, 1902.

Stange, Maren. *Symbols of Ideal Life: Social Documentary Photography in America, 1890–1950.* New York: Cambridge University Press, 1992.

Stein, Sally. "Making Connections with the Camera: Photography and Social Mobility in the Career of Jacob Riis." *Afterimage* 10 (May 1983): 9–16.

Yochelson, Bonnie. *Jacob Riis.* New York: Phaidon Press, 2001.

——. "What Are the Photographs of Jacob Riis?" *Culturefront* 3 (Fall 1994): 28–38.

JOSEPH P. COSCO

ROBINSON–JEWETT MURDER

The murder of Helen Jewett on April 10, 1836, at a stylish Manhattan house of prostitution sparked America's first mass-media circus. The ruthless competition for readers among the editors of the new penny press—cheap newspapers designed for a mass public and dependent on advertising and circulation rather than political patronage for their profits—led to extravagant coverage of the crime. The unprecedented attention to so unseemly an event delighted thousands of readers, dismayed others, and confirmed the market value of sensationalism and controversy. But the coverage also addressed important questions about equality and justice, and definitively shaped the evolving relationship between readers and their newspapers.

After Jewett was found dead in her bed, her head gashed by a sharp weapon and her bedclothes set afire, police officers arrested her visitor that evening, nineteen-year-old Richard P. Robinson. Despite plentiful circumstantial evidence against the young clerk, the eminent defense team hired by his prosperous employer got him acquitted in a rowdy five-day trial in early June.

The senior and most popular of the penny papers, the *New York Sun*, which was edited by a former labor activist with strong ties to the working class, thrilled its proletarian readers with the radical idea that they had as much right as anyone to form their own opinions about the case. The *Sun's* opinion was clear: casting the affair as yet another example of oppression by the wealthy and powerful, it insisted that Robinson was a brutal rake who exploited an unfortunate woman and used money and influence to elude justice.

Vigorously opposing the *Sun* was James Gordon Bennett, editor of the new and hungry *Herald*, who immediately grasped the potential bonanza in the story. In thunderous prose Bennett trumpeted his own repertorial enterprise, publishing an eyewitness account of Jewett's lavish bedroom, a histrionic description of her "exquisite" corpse, and a confrontational interview with her madam. He hinted darkly at revelations to come and wailed over New York's moral decay. He boasted, justifiably, about the large increase in the *Herald's* circulation, and blasted the *Sun* as incompetent and corrupt. And he insisted that his fearless and independent reporting had uncovered the truth: Robinson was the innocent victim of a conspiracy concocted by the madam and the police.

Many historians (e.g., Schiller) have generally accepted Bennett's claims that his journalism bravely championed a friendless underdog and prevented a miscarriage of justice. Others however argue that the evidence shows Robinson guilty and that Bennett deliberately concocted his titillating yet moralistic defense to counter the working-class (and more accurate) *Sun* with a story more to the taste of the highly desirable middle-class readership, which clearly preferred to see a middle-class young man acquitted of so sordid a crime. Taken together, Bennett's rhetoric and his example left a complicated journalistic legacy: that the duty of the press was to fearlessly ferret out the truth, but that the fortunes of the press depended on its ability to ferret out a "truth" that people would buy.

Further Reading

Schiller, Dan. *Objectivity and the News: The Public and the Rise of Commercial Journalism.* Philadelphia: University of Pennsylvania Press, 1981.

Stevens, John D. *Sensationalism in the New York Press.* New York: Columbia University Press, 1991.

Tucher, Andie. *Froth and Scum: Truth, Beauty, Goodness, and the Ax Murder in America's First Mass Medium.* Chapel Hill and London: University of North Carolina Press, 1994.

ANDIE TUCHER

ROCKY MOUNTAIN NEWS

Rocky Mountain News founder William Byers, despite a spring snowstorm and leaky roof, beat the competing *Cherry Creek Pioneer* by twenty minutes to get the *News* onto Denver's streets in April 1859. The *News*, Colorado's oldest newspaper, has been fiercely competitive ever since. While in 2001 the *News* entered into a Joint Operating Agreement (JOA) with its chief remaining competitor, the *Denver Post*, merging circulation, advertising and other business departments, the newsrooms remained independent and competitive. In his February 26, 2005, column, *News* Publisher John Temple said, "the two newsrooms are still scrapping as if their lives depended on it."

That competitive spirit has existed ever since the *Post* joined the Denver scene in 1892. In fact, the fight even spilled out into the streets near the State Capitol in 1907 in a Wild West duel, when *Post* owner Frederick Bonfils attacked and beat *News* owner Thomas Patterson, who had called Bonfils a "blackmailer" in a cartoon. The fierce newspaper war did in many other newspapers, but in 1926 Scripps-Howard Newspapers bought the *News* and merged it with the *Express*, leaving only the morning *News* and afternoon *Post*. "We believe that a dictatorship of Denver's newspaper field by the *Denver Post* would be nothing less than a blight," said famed newspaper publisher Roy Howard at the time. Each newspaper tried furiously to put the other out of business, with the *News* almost perishing around the time of World War II. It switched to a tabloid format in 1942. Over the years, the newspapers offered various gimmicks to try to outdo the other, from free gasoline in the 1920s to penny-a-day subscriptions in the 1990s. The newspaper war was costly—in seeking government approval for the JOA, E.W. Scripps Co. said the *Rocky Mountain News* had lost $123 million in the 1990s. But circulation had boomed—both the *Post* and *News* claimed the largest circulation gains in the country in 2000, when the *News* had a daily circulation of 426,465 and Sunday circulation of 529,681. But after the JOA, the *News*' daily circulation dropped dramatically, to about 267,000 in 2005. Its Saturday circulation in 2005 was about 591,000. The two newspapers continue to publish competing newspapers Monday through Friday mornings, but the *News* publishes exclusively on Saturdays and the *Post* on Sundays. Both companies agreed to split the profits fifty-fifty under the JOA, but E.W. Scripps Co. and the *News* had to pay $60 million to the *Post* and its owner, Media*News*, to enter the arrangement.

The news staffs of both newspapers vowed to continue the journalistic rivalry that has provided more than a century of colorful reporting. In 2000, both newspapers won Pulitzer Prizes for their coverage of shootings at Columbine High School—the *Post* for breaking news reporting and the *News* for spot new photography. It was the first Pulitzer for the *News*, which won its second Pulitzer Prize just three years later for breaking news photography for its coverage of Colorado's raging forest fires. Tabloid in format Monday through Friday and a broadsheet on Saturday, the *News* is admired for a terse, lively writing style, its reporters who often scoop the competition, and widely read columnists like Mike Littwin and Bill Johnson who do n0t shy away from such controversies as police misconduct. Its sports pages reflect a sports-crazy city that rabidly follows the likes of the Broncos, Avalanche, Rockies, and Nuggets. And its conservative editorials are supplemented by a lively mix of local and national columnists from both the left and right. Beloved *News* columnist Gene Amole, who died in 2002, brought the city to tears with his emotional series of columns chronicling his final battle against illness. The street in front of the *News* building was renamed Gene Amole Way. While Publisher John Temple called Amole the heart of the *Rocky Mountain News*, other *News* jour-nalists hope always to keep in mind his familiar refrain: "Write to express, not to impress."

Further Reading

Anton, Mike. "Battle of Wits, Words Made History." *Rocky Mountain News* (May 12, 2000): 5A.

Kreck, Dick. "A 108-Year-Old Street Fight: Newspapers Share a Long, Colorful History." *The Denver Post* (May 12, 2000): A-16.

Jones, Rebecca, "First with the News: From 1859 to 1999, Denver's Oldest Paper Tells Epic Saga." *Rocky Mountain News* (May 2, 1999): 2N.

Morton, John, "Life After the War." *American Journalism Review* 22, no. 6 (July/August 2000): 88.

Perkin, Robert L. *The First Hundred Years: An Informal History of Denver and the Rocky Mountain News*. Garden City, NY: Doubleday, 1959.

Prendergast, Alan. "Peace Comes to Denver." *Columbia Journalism Review* 39, no. 2 (July/August 2000): 16–20.

Rosen, Jill. "A Piece of Denver Dies." *American Journalism Review* 24, no. 5 (June 2002): 16.

Temple, John. " Newspaper War Lives — Here's Proof." *Rocky Mountain News* (February 26, 2005): 2A.

KRIS KODRICH

ROGERS, WILL

William Penn Adair Rogers (November 4, 1879–August 15, 1935) was an American humorist, newspaper columnist, book author, radio personality, movie actor, stage performer, rodeo star, and early promoter of aviation. Will Rogers was born on a ranch in the Indian Territory, now Oklahoma. His appeal was that of the "regular guy," modest, but able to outsmart politicians and city sophisticates. He had little formal education, attending Scarritt College in Missouri for a year and later running away from Kamper Military Academy, also in Missouri. After working on his family's ranch for three years, he traveled to Argentina and lived among that country's gauchos, then sailed to South Africa to break horses for the British military. There, Rogers, who was part Cherokee, got his start in entertainment as a trick roper billed as "The Cherokee Kid" in Texas Jack's Wild West Show and later performed with Wirth Brothers Circus. In 1914 he moved from the circus to the Broadway stage and vaudeville, often combining stand-up comedy with lariat tricks, and by 1916, he was a Ziegfeld Follies star. His silent movie acting career began in 1918 in *Laughing Bill Hide*, his book writing in 1919 with two volumes of *Rogers-isms*. His McNaught Newspaper Syndicate humor column began in 1922. He also employed his folksy yet insightful style of humor on the speakers' circuit and in *The Saturday Evening Post* and other magazines. He wrote both a daily and a weekly newspaper column and in 1926, added radio commentary, donating much of what he made on the air to various charities. In 1934, Rogers appeared in Eugene O'Neill's stage comedy *Ah, Wilderness!* but gained far wider fame that same year in the movie *Judge Priest* and the following year in the even more popular film *Steamboat Round the Bend*.

Rogers visited most of the nation on the speakers' circuit; appeared in seventy-one movies; enjoyed a large radio audience, sponsored from 1930 to 1935 by Gulf Oil; published six books; and wrote an estimated four thousand "Will Rogers Says" newspaper columns from 1922 until his death in 1935. As an American humor icon, he was the second Mark Twain in that he was almost universally known and loved. He increased his fame abroad with trips to Asia, Central and South America and a round-the-world journey in 1934, the same year he moved to California, where he starred in the Fox film *Life Begins at 40*. Politically, he was a Franklin D. Roosevelt Democrat.

His demise came in August 1935 at Point Barrow, Alaska, during a flying trip with a friend, aviator Wiley Post. Rogers had been a supporter of air travel and in 1927 had been the first U.S. civilian to fly coast to coast.

His fame, compared to that of other humorists, is evident in the many things named for him: a state park, airport, rodeo, band, school, beach, submarine, ranch-style development, hotel, horse race, educational institute, and poetry competition.

Further Reading

Day, Donald, ed. *The Autobiography of Will Rogers*. Boston: Houghton Mifflin, 1955.

Robinson, Ray. *American Original, a Life of Will Rogers*. New York: Oxford University Press, 1996.

Smallwood, James and Steven K. Gragert, eds. *Will Rogers' Weekly Articles*, 5 vols. Stillwater, OK, 1980.

Yagoda, Ben. *Will Rogers: a Biography*. Norman: University of Oklahoma Press, 2000.

SAM G. RILEY

ROLLING STONE MAGAZINE

Rolling Stone, a magazine dedicated to the coverage of rock and roll and the lifestyle and culture that the musical genre embodied, was founded on November 18, 1967, in a rundown printing shop in San Francisco, California, at the height of 1960s counterculture and the Vietnam War. The magazine's title was based on lyrics from the famous Bob Dylan song, "Like a Rolling Stone."

Founder and publisher Jann Wenner was twenty-one when he started the magazine along with music critic Ralph J. Gleason. After dropping out of University of California at Berkeley, Wenner borrowed $7,500 from friends and investors. San Francisco's Summer of 1967 was often referred to as "The Summer of Love," as thousands of hippies flocked to the city for the live music of the Grateful Dead and Jefferson Airplane, the literary musings of counterculture writers Ken Kesey and Alan Ginsberg, the wealth of psychedelic drugs. They fueled the political unrest that was beginning to overtake the nation in the wake of the Vietnam War and assassinations of Robert F. Kennedy and Martin Luther King, Jr. Wenner viewed the launch of *Rolling Stone* magazine as an opportunity to seize upon the cultural zeitgeist

and offered free marijuana paraphernalia with every new subscription to the magazine.

Rolling Stone became known for its in-depth rock and roll reviews and commentary and in-depth political and cultural think pieces that would occasionally run twenty thousand words in the early years of the magazine. It also became known for its raucous, irreverent writers, including Hunter S. Thompson, Joe Eszterhas, Jon Landau, Tom Wolfe, Lester Bangs, Joe Klein, Greil Marcus, Cameron Crowe, and Timothy Crouse, who eventually became journalistic, literary, and creative stars in their own right. Wenner said that he did not want to be identified with the underground newspapers of the time, but *Rolling Stone* did provide longer narrative articles on American politics and social issues. Typical issues included stories on U.S. involvement in the Vietnam War alongside criticism of the latest releases from bands and interviews of rock superstars. In 1971, Thompson published a first shorter version of his best-selling book, "Fear and Loathing in Las Vegas." He later followed up with another, "Fear and Loathing on the Campaign Trail," a scathing send-up of the Nixon campaign in 1972. Despite Thompson's drug-addled, somewhat humorous account, some consider the book to be some of the most truthful political reporting of the past forty years. Furthermore, its seminal pieces on rock music and artists such as Robert Plant, Little Richard, Bob Dylan, and U2, are considered by some to be superior examples of feature writing.

The popularity and influence of *Rolling Stone* moving into the 1970s can still be heard in a 1973 song titled "The Cover of the Rolling Stone" written by humorous children's author Shel Silverstein and performed by Dr. Hook and the Medicine Show that makes clear the only way that a rock band has achieved success is by being placed on the magazine's cover. In 1974, the magazine's circulation was about 325,000. Perhaps 80 percent of its readers were under twenty-five years of age.

Through the years that it has been published, *Rolling Stone* magazine has also become known for its cutting edge photography, from the iconic nude photo of Beatle John Lennon and his wife, Yoko Ono, to the more recent almost-nude shots of teen pop superstar Brittney Spears. Famed photographer Annie Liebowitz has provided some of the magazine's most riveting and recognized photographs of cultural icons throughout the years.

In 1980, the headquarters of *Rolling Stone* moved to New York, where most of the magazine publishing industry resided. By 1998, circulation reached 1.25 million. As of 2006, Wenner, who was still the publisher, operated Wenner Media from his Manhattan office. He also oversaw *Us Weekly* and *Men's Health*. *Rolling Stone* still covered rock music and politics with a liberal slant—although the stories were far shorter than twenty thusand words and most of its readers would most likely not characterize it as revolutionary or as "the voice of a generation." It had become a multi-million-dollar publishing giant with a worldwide readership.

Further Reading

Anson, R. S. *Gone crazy and back again: The rise and fall of the Rolling Stone*. Generation. Garden City, NY: Doubleday & Co., 1981.

Seymour, Corey, "On the Cover of *Rolling Stone*: A Twenty-Fifth Anniversary Special." *Rolling Stone* (December 10, 1992): 147–154.

Draper. R. *Rolling Stone Magazine: The Uncensored History*. Garden City, NY: Doubleday & Co., 1990.

Rolling Stone, http://www.rollingstone.com (accessed April 9, 2007).

SHAYLA THIEL

ROOSEVELT, ANNA ELEANOR

Anna Eleanor Roosevelt (October 11, 1884–November 7, 1962), who used the name Eleanor, made a notable contribution to both print and broadcast journalism during her years as first lady from 1933 to 1945 and subsequently as an United States representative to the United Nations. Married to Franklin D. Roosevelt, the only individual to have been elected president of the United States four times, she pursued a parallel career in public communication, making use of her opportunities as the president's wife to gain material for newspaper columns, magazine articles, books, and radio programs. She also enlarged opportunities for other women in journalism by holding White House press conferences for women reporters only, thus forcing some news organizations to hire women to cover her.

She was born on October 11, 1884, in New York City, to Anna Hall Roosevelt, considered a beauty in elite social circles, and Elliott Roosevelt, the younger brother of Theodore Roosevelt, who served as president of the United States from 1901 to 1909. Her parents separated due to Elliott Roosevelt's drinking and drug addiction and both died before she had her tenth birthday. Sent to live with her maternal grandmother, Mary Ludlow Hall, she received little attention. She was educated privately and at the Allenswood School in England, a finishing school for wealthy young women, which Roosevelt attended from 1899 to 1902.

After making her debut into society, she became engaged to her distant cousin, Franklin D. Roosevelt, and the two were married in 1905. From 1906 to 1916 she bore six children, one of whom died in infancy, and devoted herself to her family while her husband launched a political career. The couple almost divorced in 1918 when she learned of Franklin Roosevelt's affair with Lucy Mercer, her social secretary, but agreed to stay together for the sake of his political aspirations and their children.

After her husband was crippled with infantile paralysis in 1921, she began to make political speeches, overcoming her own shyness and developing a public presence while keeping his name before voters in New York State. Coached in journalistic skills by Louis Howe, a newspaperman who was Franklin Roosevelt's chief advisor, she edited the *Women's Democratic News* and started to write for mass periodicals, mainly women's magazines. She also began speaking on New York radio stations. In addition, she taught history, literature and current events at Todhunter School in New York City, a private girls' school.

Following Franklin Roosevelt's election as governor of New York in 1928, she wrote more than twenty magazine articles, gaining an independent income from them. According to one son, Elliott Roosevelt, it was important to his mother's self-esteem to earn money in her own right. Topics, drawn from her own experiences, included women and politics, modern marriage, housekeeping, education, and her own philosophy of life, which called for overcoming personal adversity by drawing on inner resources and thinking of others.

Following her husband's election as President in 1932, her journalistic activity increased. She wrote newspaper columns, gave sponsored radio broadcasts, and became a staple of women's magazines. Offering an unsophisticated view of such subjects as daily life in the White House, her comments, allegedly nonpartisan, reinforced Franklin Roosevelt's New Deal political philosophy of offering government aid to the poverty-stricken as the nation battled the Great Depression of the 1930s.

From 1933 to 1935, for example, she wrote "Mrs. Franklin D. Roosevelt's Page" in the *Women's Home Companion*, then the nation's top-selling women's periodical, which urged readers to send her letters in care of the magazine. In columns based on these letters, Roosevelt, who received $1000 a month from the *Companion*, addressed controversial issues such as improving sweatshop conditions and outlawing child labor as well as less contentious subjects like national holidays and gardening. When critics complained that she traded on her husband's name for both print and broadcast work, she justified commercial contracts as first lady on grounds that she donated most of her earnings to charity. In later years she used the income for living expenses as well as charity.

In the 1940s she was paid $2500 a month for a question-and-answer column, "If You Ask Me," that gave her views on personal relationships as well as political topics. It was published in the *Ladies' Home Journal*, which had serialized the first portion of her autobiography, *This Is My Story*, in 1937, for $75,000. When the *Journal* balked at serializing the second volume of her autobiography, *This I Remember*, rights to both it and her column were purchased in 1949 by *McCall's* magazine, a move that helped *McCall's* overtake the *Journal* in circulation.

Her most famous journalistic venture, a daily syndicated diary of her activities, called "My Day," began on December 30, 1935, and continued until shortly before her death in 1962. Billed as a personal chat with her readers, the column introduced them to the people she met and the places she went, humanizing the Roosevelt administration and showcasing the accomplishments of women. By 1938 it appeared in sixty-two newspapers with a total circulation of more than four million.

Appointed a United Nations delegate after Franklin D. Roosevelt's death in 1945, she served until 1952, continuing to write and broadcast. She was one of the first women to participate in public affairs programming on television. "My Day" emerged as a platform for her political views, allowing her to oppose McCarthyism, speak up for civil rights and the establishment of Israel, and back presidential candidates. After leaving the United Nations, she worked as a volunteer on behalf of the organization, referring to it in her magazine articles and columns.

Eleanor Roosevelt died in New York City on November 7, 1962, leaving behind a legacy of activism on behalf of liberal causes along with more than a dozen books, many based on her personal experiences and hopes for social betterment. Her journalism was an unique undertaking that personified interest in presidents' wives as public figures. It also claimed their right to their own careers.

Further Reading

Beasley, Maurine H., Holly C. Shulman, and Henry R. Beasley. *The Eleanor Roosevelt Encyclopedia*. Westport, CT: Greenwood Press, 2001.

Beasley, Maurine H. *Eleanor Roosevelt and the Media*. Urbana: University of Illinois Press, 1987.

Black, Allida M. *What I Hope to Leave Behind*. Brooklyn: Carlson, 1995.

———. *Casting Her Own Shadow*. New York: Columbia University Press, 1996.

Chadakoff, Rochelle, ed. *Eleanor Roosevelt's 'My Day,'* vol. 1. New York: Pharos, 1989.

Cook, Blanche Wiesen. *Eleanor Roosevelt*, vols. 1, 2. New York: Viking, 1992, 1999.

Eleanor Roosevelt Papers, "Anna Eleanor Roosevelt," http://www.gwu.edu/~erpapers/abouteleanor/erbiograpy.html.

Emblidge, David, ed. *Eleanor Roosevelt's 'My Day'*, vols. 2, 3. New York: Pharos, 1990, 1991.

Lash, Joseph P. *Eleanor and Franklin*. New York: Norton, 1971.

Roosevelt, Eleanor. *The Autobiography of Eleanor Roosevelt*. New York: Harper & Brothers, 1961.

Seeber, Frances. "'I Want You to Write Me': The Papers of Anna Eleanor Roosevelt." In, eds. *Modern First Ladies: Their Documentary Legacy*, edited by Nancy Kegan Smith, and Mary C Ryan. Washington, D.C.: National Archives and Records Administration, 1989.

MAURINE H. BEASLEY

RUSSELL, CHARLES EDWARD

Charles Edward Russell (1860–1941) was born to a career in journalism and social activism. He was the son of Davenport, Iowa, newspaper editor Edward Russell and his wife, Lydia Rutledge. His fraternal grandfather, William Russell, quit a distillery job to become a temperance activist. His maternal grandfather, William Rutledge, was a clergyman leader in Iowa's Underground Railroad. Charles began work at his father's *Davenport Gazette* when he was twelve, wrapping newspapers in the mailroom. He advanced to typesetter as a teenager and became managing editor at twenty-one, embracing his father's admonition to "terrify evil doers" by "arousing the conscience" of his readers (Russell 1933, 4).

Russell's antipathy toward corporate interests was heightened when financial troubles forced his father to sell the *Gazette* to a railroad company. For twenty years Russell championed progressive causes, first as night editor of the *Minneapolis Tribune* in 1883, then as managing editor of the *Minneapolis Journal* in 1884, and the *Detroit Tribune* in 1886. He vaulted to national attention as Chicago correspondent for Joseph Pulitzer's *New York World* with his sympathetic reporting on strike leaders who were hanged on November 11, 1887, for the Haymarket Square bombing. He became a crime reporter for the *New York Herald* in 1889 and was promoted to assistant managing editor in 1892. It was reporting the "misery, want, and destitution" of the immigrant community on New York's Lower East Side that pushed Russell into socialism (Russell 1914, 69–70).

Russell's newspaper career reached a peak during his three years as city editor of the *New York World*, the nation's widest circulating newspaper. With the help of Sunday editor Arthur Brisbane, Russell pushed the *World's* Sunday circulation to six hundred thousand. William Randolph Hearst, publisher of the *New York Journal*, attempted to break Pulitzer's position with New York readers by making Russell his managing editor in 1897. Three years later Hearst promoted him to publisher of the *Chicago American*. The death of Russell's wife in 1902 and his subsequent physical collapse cut short his populist appeals.

Russell re-emerged in 1904 with a series of articles on the beef trust for *Everybody's* magazine. Over the next decade his investigate reports on railroad fraud, election graft, slum landlords, and race relations appeared in *Everybody's*, *Cosmopolitan*, *Pearson's* and *Hampton's*. Russell believed the work of the muckraker was the gathering of information, "the discovery of innumerable and indispensable details" that proved one's case and mobilized the public to action (Russell 1908, 285–287). His advised other muckrakers "never give credence to any claim without complete investigation" (Russell 1907, 346–347). Russell's pitiless description of the Georgia prison system in *Everybody's* magazine in June, 1908, led to a special session of the state legislature. His attacks on Trinity Church that same year helped to force America's wealthiest church to clean up its tenements. Concern for racial justice led him to become a founding member of the National Association for the Advancement of Colored People.

Russell joined the Socialist Party in 1908 and ran unsuccessfully for governor of New York in 1910 and 1912, for mayor of New York City in 1913 and for United States senator in 1914. He declined the Socialist nomination for president in 1916 and would later be expelled from the party for his support of United States entry in World War I.

Russell received the Pulitzer Prize for biography in 1927 for *The American Orchestra and Theodore Thomas*. His autobiographical *Bare Hands and Stone Walls*, published in 1933, completed a career of public service that trusted readers to do the right thing when journalistic detective work revealed the hidden situation and gave them news they needed to know.

Further Reading

"Charles Edward Russell." *Contemporary Authors*, vol.. Detroit: Gale Group, 2002.

Miraldi, Robert. "Charles Edward Russell: 'Chief of the Muckrakers'." *Journalism and Mass Communication Monographs*. Columbia, SC: Association for Education in Journalism and Mass Communication, 1995.

Miraldi, Robert. *The Pen Is Mightier: The Muckraking Life of Charles Edward Russell*. New York: Palgrave Macmillan, 2003.

New York Times, April 24, 1941.

Papers of Charles Edward Russell, Manuscript Reading Room, Library of Congress, Washington, D.C.

Russell, Charles Edward. *Bare Hands and Stone Walls: Some Recollections of a Side-line Reformer*. New York: Charles Scribner's Sons, 1933.

——. *Doing Us Good and Plenty*. Chicago: C.H. Kerr, 1914.

——. *The Greatest Trust in the World*. New York: Ridgway-Thayer, 1905.

——. *Lawless Wealth: The Origin of Some Great American Fortunes*. New York: B.W. Dodge, 1908.

——. *A Pioneer Editor in Early Iowa: A Sketch of the Life of Edward Russell*. Washington, D.C.: Ransdell, 1941.

——. *These Shifting Scenes*. New York: Hodder & Stoughton, 1914.

——. *The Uprising of the Many*. New York: Doubleday, Page, 1907.

——. *Why I Am a Socialist*. New York: Hodder & Stoughton, 1910.

Bruce J. Evensen

S

SAID, EDWARD

Edward Said (November 1, 1935–September 24, 2003) is perhaps best known in the journalism and mass communication field for two books that discuss how the West produces knowledge about the "non-west" in three important sites of knowledge production—universities, the military and foreign offices of the government, and mass media. The books are *Orientalism* and *Covering Islam*.

Said's most important impact on the study of journalism as an institution and as a practice, is perhaps his elaboration of Michel Foucault's theories of the relationship between power and knowledge. In *Orientalism,* Said used Foucault as a fulcrum to lift the veil masking the linkages between Western imperialism and the production of knowledge about the "Orient"—which for Said meant the Near and Middle East (though his ideas have been fruitfully applied more broadly). For Said, Orientalism is the "systematic discipline by which European culture was able to manage—and even produce—the Orient politically, sociologically, militarily, ideologically, scientifically, and imaginatively during the post-Enlightenment period." Said calls this process of knowledge production of the Orient a discourse, a term that refers, in the Foucauldian sense, to the historical interconnection between institutions, the powerful people who define the terms of debate and research, and the subsequent texts that emerge from this web of relationships. This "discursive formation" directs, guides, and massages Western "knowledge" about the Orient so that it takes on certain shape and form, contains certain themes and emphases that not only identify the Orient as backward and uninspired but also establish the West as fundamentally superior.

The title of the second book, *Covering Islam*, is meant to convey the double meaning of simultaneously *reporting on* and *covering up* Islam. The subtitle of the book is "How the Media and Experts Determine How We See the Rest of The World." Said's central criticism of American journalism is that many reporters use the label "Islam" to create unfounded generalizations, often relying on academic experts (typically American or European), U. S. government officials, and pro-Israel lobbyists who claim to know the "Arab mind." The discursive formation of Orientalism, says Said, explains the prevalence of these unflattering, negative images and the relative absence from media coverage of the well-researched, more complex views of Islam that are plentiful in the public realm and available for consultation by reporters.

Despite the structuring power of Orientalism, Said acknowledges the existence of alternative points of view written and distributed by a relatively small number of intellectuals and journalists. For Said, these writers represent an apex of scholarly and journalistic practice because they reveal that "knowledge" and "news" about Islam is fundamentally tied to Western domination and conquest of the Middle East.

The author of more than fifteen books on literary theory, Middle East politics, and classical music, among other topics, Said earned his BA in 1957 from Princeton. He earned his MA in 1960 and PhD in 1964, both from Harvard. He taught Comparative Literature at Columbia from 1989 until his death in 2003. Said was also a renowned opera critic and an activist for Palestinian rights.

Further Reading

Ashcroft, Bill, and Pal Ahluwalia. *Edward Said: The Paradox of Identity.* London and New York: Routledge, 1999.

Said, Edward. *Orientalism.* New York: Vintage, 1978.

——. *Covering Islam: How the Media and the Experts Determine How We See the Rest of the World.* New York: Vintage, 1981.

——. *Culture & Imperialism.* London: Chatto and Windus Ltd., 1993.

——. *Representations of the Intellectual.* London: Vintage, 1994.

——. *Out of Place: A Memoir.* New York: Random House, 1999.

Sprinker, Michael, ed. *Edward Said: A Critical Reader.* Oxford: Blackwell, 1992.

HEMANT SHAH

SALISBURY, HARRISON E.

One of the twentieth century's most distinguished foreign correspondents, the Pulitzer Prize-winning Harrison Evans Salisbury (November 14, 1908–July 5, 1993) wrote numerous articles and books about world events, especially those in the former Soviet Union, China, and other communist countries. He was born in Minneapolis, Minnesota, and after enrolling in the University of Minnesota there to study chemistry, he quickly became a cub reporter and then editor in 1929 for the campus newspaper, the *Minnesota Daily*. He also wrote for the *Minneapolis Journal*. In 1930 he joined United Press in St. Paul and went on to report from Chicago, Washington, D.C., and New York City.

By 1943 he was United Press's London bureau manager.

Salisbury covered World War II in England, North Africa, the Middle East, and eventually, Russia. His series of articles on the war for *Collier's Weekly* formed the basis for his first book, *Russia on the Way* (1946).

Salibury's interest in the Soviet Union continued to develop, and in 1949 he became a Moscow correspondent for the *New York Times*. This was a challenging assignment, given the anti-communist atmosphere in the United States during the 1950s. His reports were often censored by Soviet authorities. In 1955 he returned to New York City as a general staff member and published in the *Times* a series of articles about political and social life in Russia under communist rule. Some editors at the *Times* and conservative critics outside the paper, considered him a "Communist dupe." His series, however, won the Pulitzer Prize for international reporting, solidifying his reputation as a leading foreign correspondent of the postwar era.

Salisbury covered both the civil rights movement and the Vietnam War. He covered civil rights issues in the American South starting in the late 1950s. His reports should be remembered when one considers the context for the multi-million dollar libel suit against the *Times,* which was resolved in favor of the newspaper in 1964 in the *New York Times vs. Sullivan* case. As assistant managing editor for the *Times* starting in September 1964, Salisbury now spent more time in the United States. But he continued to travel and report from abroad sometimes, including in December 1966 when he visited Hanoi, as the first Western reporter allowed in wartime North Vietnam. His historic, eyewitness reporting from the enemy capital revealed that American bombs had hit civilian neighborhoods and other nonmilitary areas and directly disputed U.S. government claims that the bombing was going well. He became the first mainstream, well-respected journalist to oppose the Vietnam War. The resulting angry attacks on Salisbury and the *Times* may have cost him a Pulitzer Prize that year, for what was arguably the most compelling news story of the year.

Salisbury became the *New York Times'* first Op-ed page editor in 1970. He retired from the *Times* in 1973 as associate editor and continued to write books about international politics, including those in China. His many books include the bestseller *The 900 Days* (1969), a powerful account of the siege by the German army of Leningrad; *Black Night, White Snow: Russia's Revolutions 1905–1917* (1978); *Without Fear or Favor: The "New York Times" and Its Times* (1980); *The Long March: The Untold Story* (1985); *Tianamen Diary: Thirteen Days in June* (1989); and two autobiographical works, *Journey for Our Times* (1983) and *A Time of Change* (1988). His papers are located at Columbia University in New York City.

Further Reading

Obituary. *New York Times*, July 7, 1993, D19.
Salisbury, Harrison E. *The 900 Days: The Siege of Leningrad.* New York: Harper and Row, 1969
——. *American in Russia.* New York: Harper, 1955.

——. *Black Night, White Snow: Russia's Revolutions 1905–1917.* Garden City, NY: Doubleday, 1978.
——. *A Journey for Our Times: A Memoir.* New York: Harper & Row, 1983.
——. *The Long March: The Untold Story.* New York: Harper & Row, 1985.
——. *Tianamen Diary: Thirteen Days in June.* Boston: Little, Brown, 1989.
——. *A Time of Change: A Reporter's Tale of Our Time.* New York: Harper & Row, 1988.
——. *Without Fear or Favor: The* New York Times *and Its* Times. New York: New York Times, 1980. Also published as *Without Fear or Favor: An Uncompromising Look at the* New York Times. New York: Ballantine, 1981.

NANCY L. ROBERTS

SALON.COM

One of the first and best-known Internet-only publications, Salon launched its Web-based magazine in 1995 under the leadership of David Talbot of the *San Francisco Examiner* and a handful of his friends from the newspaper, including publisher David Zwieg, writers Gary Kamiya, Laura Miller, Joyce Millman, Scott Rosenberg, and Andrew Ross, and art-director Mignon Khargie. Based in San Francisco, Salon.com's full and part-time staff as well as a cadre of freelancers produced original content. At first a bi-weekly, Salon became a daily in February 1997. The original URLs for Salon were www.salon1999.com; www.salonmag.com, so the magazine did not become Salon.com until 1999 when it purchased the domain name, www.salon.com.

As an icon of the late 1990s and early millennium digiterati, Salon.com is known for its insightful articles and essays that often center on the American political system. It is also perceived to skew toward a more liberal viewpoint. One of its best known former bureau chiefs was Sidney Blumenthal, who was a high-ranking aide in the Bill Clinton White House. Formerly conservative columnist and talk show host Arianna Huffington was a regularly contributing columnist. The content sites, updated daily or more frequently, include News and Politics, Opinion, Technology & Business, Arts & Entertainment, Books, Life, and Comics.

In descriptions and reviews, Salon was called "intriguing and intelligent" (by the *Washington Post*), "truly compelling" (*Time*) and "smart and provocative" (*Forbes*). Its readers in the early twenty-first century were primarily older (97 percent were above twenty-one years old) with an average household income of $78,342, and 74 percent had earned a college or graduate level degree.

Salon.com also was known for its online community, and in particular, purchasing The Well, a well-known virtual community made up of intellectuals and early Internet users chronicled by Howard Rheingold in his best-selling non-fiction book, *Virtual Community: Homesteading on the Electronic Frontier* (1993). Salon.com used the software that powered The Well to run its own online forums (called "Table Talk") but housed the original online community as well.

Salon.com used advertising on its site to keep the publication free for readers, but in 2003 it moved to a model of charging subscribers $35 a year to read stories without also having to view advertising. In 2005, Salon.com had 80,000 subscribers, but another 730,000 per month choose to view the stories for free in exchange for first viewing full-page advertisements that lead into them. Before this time, the magazine was known in the dot com community for its financial troubles. In the summer of 1999, Salon.com offered an Initial Public Offering on the NASDAQ stock exchange and its offering was mediocre. In the several years following the IPO, Salon.com's stock has been delisted from the NASDAQ exchange and currently trades as an over-the-counter penny stock at less than 50 cents per share, and it announced ever-mounting losses and debt. The magazine's subscribers essentially saved it after a financial crisis in 2000 when founding editor Talbot appealed to them for donations. Salon.com had sixty full-time employees during the dot com boom of the middle to late 1990s, and that number was down to twenty-three full-time employees ten years after its founding.

In October of 2003, Chief Executive and President of Salon Media Group, Michael O'Donnel, announced he was leaving the company. Talbot, still the company chairman and editor-and-chief of the magazine took his place, and Betsy Hambrecht, Salon's CFO, became the new president. Joan Walsh took over as editor in February 2005. As of early spring 2005, Salon.com had made a quarterly profit for the first time in its existence, benefiting from a resurgent online ad market and an established subscription business.

Although Salon Media Group was still headquartered in San Francisco in 2006, most of its editorial operation was based in New York and it also had a smaller bureau in Washington, D.C.

Further Reading

Rheingold, Howard. *The Virtual Community: Homesteading on the Electronic Frontier.* Reading, MA: Addison-Wesley Publishing Company, 1993.
http://www.salon.com.

SHAYLA THIEL

SANGER, MARGARET

Margaret Sanger (September 14, 1879–Septembr 6, 1966) almost single-handedly launched the American birth control movement at a time when American society was just emerging from the morally constrained Victorian era. With only a few years of formal education, she educated herself about women's health and reproduction issues and sought to disseminate this information through lectures and publications. Governmental and Catholic Church officials repeatedly attempted to prevent her from doing this by censoring and prosecuting her under the nation's "Comstock" or obscenity laws, but Sanger always succeeded in turning official prosecution into publicity for herself and the movement.

Margaret Sanger was born in Corning, New York, the sixth of eleven children. Her father, Michael Higgins, an Irish immigrant, was a Socialist who worked as a stonemason. Her mother, Anne Purcell, became pregnant eighteen times and bore eleven children before she died at the age of forty-eight of tuberculosis. Margaret escaped the grinding poverty of the family by attending a private Methodist boarding school on the Hudson River, Claverack College, which she was able to pay for by working in the kitchen and dining room. After just three years, however, she had to leave the school to nurse her dying mother, run the household, and supervise her younger siblings.

While she was nursing her mother, Margaret began to read medical texts and dreamed of becoming a medical doctor. Entry into the medical profession was limited for women, however, and in 1900 she took one of the few routes open to them when she took a job as a probationary nurse at White Plains Hospital. Here, at a dance, she met socialist William Sanger, an up-and-coming architect, whom she married in 1902. They had three children and Margaret continued to work sporadically as a visiting nurse.

Margaret attended Socialist meetings with William and in the next decade became acquainted with some of the leading socialist and radical thinkers of the period. She joined the Socialist Party and was soon giving lectures to married women on sex and reproduction. These were so enthusiastically received that in 1912, the Socialist newspaper, *The Call*, invited her to write a column based on her lectures. This column, *What Every Mother Knows*, was so popular that a second series, *What Every Girl Should Know*, was announced soon after. Here, Margaret Sanger and *The Call* were treading on dangerous ground when they chose to publish anything about sex and reproduction, for this was a forbidden subject under the "Comstock Law." Passed by Congress in 1873 and named after anti-vice reformer Anthony Comstock, the law defined any information about contraception, sex, and reproduction as obscene and forbade the sending of such obscene material through the U.S. mail. Thus, the first column in the second series, which was to deal with venereal disease, was forbidden publication by the U. S. Post Office, which also forbade *The Call* to run any more sex-related articles by Sanger.

The Post Office's actions only spurred Sanger on. Frustrated in her attempt to learn more about these subjects, Sanger in 1913 went to France, where both contraceptive devices and abortion were legal. Upon returning to the States some months later, she and a group of like-minded feminists coined the term "birth control" and founded the National Birth Control League. In March 1914, Sanger began to publish a feminist journal, *The Woman Rebel*, whose primary purpose was to provide women with scientific information about reproduction and contraception. More than this, *The Woman Rebel* was a deliberate challenge to authority. Its motto, which appeared below the title on the front page, was "No Gods, No Masters." Its first issue featured articles denouncing established religion, capitalism, marriage, property laws favoring men, and the Comstock Law. The U. S. Post Office responded immediately by banning the issue from the mail, though Sanger and her friends succeeded in mailing out dozens of copies, a few at a time. In the April issue, Sanger challenged the U.S. Post Office, declaring this was a free speech matter and she would publish in spite of its action. The April issue was also banned. In the May issue, Sanger published an article warning readers of the dangers of abortion brought on by the failure to use birth control. The U.S. Post Office denounced the paper as "indecent, lewd, lascivious and obscene," seized all copies, and arrested Sanger. Though she was indicted on nine counts of sending obscene material through the mail, she continued to publish and distribute *The Woman Rebel* through the fall while awaiting trial. At the same time, she published a pamphlet, *Family Limitation*, in which she gave specific birth control advice, complete with formulas and drawings. This, too, was banned from the mail and its distribution prohibited.

Sanger fled to Europe before her trial took place. She returned to the States to face trial in October 1915, but after her young daughter Peggy died, public sympathy for Sanger mounted and the U. S. Attorney's office, fearing the trial might make her a martyr, dropped charges in February, 1916. Sanger launched a national speaking tour to promote birth control clinics, and eventually opened the first in Brooklyn. She especially wanted to awaken working women. There was "nothing new and radical about birth control," she told a New York audience in early 1916. "Aristotle and Plato advocated it. Practically all great modern thinkers have advanced it, for it is an idea that must appeal to all mature minds" (*New York Times*, Jan.18, 1916, 7).

Sanger was arrested again in 1916, along with her sister, Ethel Byrne, following a raid on her Brooklyn clinic. Both were found guilty of disseminating information about birth control and sentenced to thirty days, but the government's actions backfired and aroused sensational newspaper coverage and public outrage. While she awaited trial, Sanger had founded the Birth Control League of New York and while she served her sentence, the first issue of its monthly journal, *Birth Control Review*, appeared. In 1920, she published her first book, *Woman and the New Race*, in which she urged labor unions to oppose any laws suppressing birth control information. In that same year, Margaret and William were divorced. She married Noah H. Slee, a South African millionaire, in 1922, although she kept the name Sanger for the rest of her life.

Sanger grew in stature and influence. In 1921, she founded the American Birth Control League and organized the first national birth control conference in New York (where she was arrested once again). In the same year, she spoke in Japan, China, and Korea and in 1927 organized the first World Population Conference in Geneva. Then, in 1929, police raided her Clinical Research Bureau in New York and she was arrested under the Comstock Law. Her trial became a showcase for birth control and civil liberties advocates and a guilty verdict was overruled on appeal. Such raids and arrests continued in a number of states, however, well into the 1960s.

Sanger remained a leader in the birth control movement well into her seventies and enjoyed the eventual defeat of the federal Comstock Law and the official endorsement of a host of organizations from the U.S. Federal Council of Churches to the American Medical Association.

Further Reading

Archer, Jules. "Margaret Sanger." In *Breaking Barriers: The Feminist Revolution from Susan B. Anthony to Margaret Sanger to Betty Friedan*. New York: Viking Press, 1991.

Chesler, Ellen. *Woman of Valor: Margaret Sanger and the Birth Control Movement in America*. New York: Anchor Books, 1993.

Cronin, Mary. "The Woman Rebel." In *Women's Periodicals of the United States: Social and Political Issues*, edited by Kathleen Endres and Therese L. Lueck, 446–453, Westport, CT: Greenwood, 1996.

Cullen-Dupont, Kathryn. *American Women Activists' Writings" An Anthology, 1637–2002*. New York: Cooper Square Press, 2002.

Gray, Madeline. *Margaret Sanger*. New York: Vanguard Press, 1930.

Hunt, John Gabriel, ed. *The Dissenters: America's Voices of Opposition*. New York: Gramercy, 1993.

Katz, Esther, ed. *The Selected Papers of Margaret Sanger*. Urbana: University of Illinois Press, 2003; see also http://adh.sc.edu (accessed April 9, 2007).

Sanger, Margaret. *My Fight for Birth Control*. New York: Farrar and Rinehart, 1931.

——. An *Autobiography* New York: W.W. Norton and Co., 1938.

——. *Woman and the New Race*. New York: Truth Publishing Co., 1920.

ELIZABETH V. BURT

SATELLITE TECHNOLOGY

The introduction of communication satellites by the United States during the early 1960s led to major changes in both the domestic and international flow of news. Communication satellites are capable of transmitting different kinds of news products—including pictures, text, sound, and data. Their introduction has been especially important for dramatically increasing the volume of news exchanged internationally. Satellite developments since the 1970s have also resulted in a significant decrease in the cost of international news gathering and exchange. Thanks largely to the introduction of this new technological innovation, more news is flowing around the world more cheaply. Although communication satellites are used for all forms of news products, the most important innovation made possible by satellites was the global transmission of live television news pictures. For the first time, viewers around the world could simultaneously experience actual news events live via satellite. The use of communication satellites for global news gathering and transmission has thus played a crucial role in the process of globalization allowing the world to become more interconnected and interdependent.

The immediate incentive for the development of communication satellites was the cold-war inspired space race between the United States and the Soviet Union following the successful launch by the Soviets of the first earth orbiting satellite, Sputnik I, in October 1957 and the first human in space, Yury Gagarin, in April 1961. Communication satellites were particularly important to the United States because their development could demonstrate to the world not only the superiority of U. S. political and economic institutions but also the potential benefits to all countries of space exploration. Instead of allowing private companies to launch privately owned communication satellites that would mainly serve wealthy individuals and businesses in developed countries, government officials in the United States decided to organize a single global system. President John F. Kennedy signed new legislation, the Communications Satellite Act of 1962, to create a new company, Comsat, which played a key role in establishing the first international system for satellite communications, Intelsat. The system achieved world-wide coverage in 1969 when geosynchronous satellites were placed into orbit over the Atlantic, Pacific, and Indian Oceans. A geosynchronous satellite appears to an observer on the earth to remain at the same point overhead at all times because it orbits at an altitude where it moves at the same rate as the earth's rotation. By the beginning of the 1970s, over sixty countries belonged to Intelsat, including twenty-eight members operating fifty ground stations.

The first experiments with the transmission of news events by communication satellites were conducted by the United States during the early and mid-1960s. One of the first geosynchronous satellites, *Syncom 3*, provided continuous coverage of the 1964 Summer Olympics from Tokyo to the United States. The first major global television news event broadcast live via satellite by the Intelsat system to millions of people around the world was the Apollo moon landing in 1969. Major events in 1972—notably President Richard Nixon's visit to China and the attack by Palestinian terrorists at the Olympic Games in Munich, Germany—were even more important for convincing news executives in the United States and the American public of the importance of communication satellites for instantaneous news coverage of major news events. Communication satellites played an important role in bringing the realities of the Vietnam War to Americans during the late 1960s and early 1970s. Satellite transmissions from ground stations in Japan or Thailand of filmed events in Vietnam gave the war a strong sense of immediacy.

Satellite transmissions of television news by the Intelsat system was limited until the early 1980s. Intelsat was mainly established to facilitate international telephone traffic. Intelsat's membership primarily represented government telecommunication administrations. The rate structure and global regulatory patterns favored telephone usage. Intelsat charged for short-term usage (per minute). Television broadcasters could only afford to use the Intelsat system for special events with guaranteed large audiences.

While the use of communication satellites for international broadcasting remained limited until the 1980s, the domestic use of communication satellites for broadcasting in the United States opened up more quickly. A decision by the Federal Communications Commission in June 1972, known as the "open-skies policy," authorized competition among domestic communication satellite carriers. Unlike the international system during the 1970s, which was controlled by Intelsat, the domestic system was open to competition between private companies. Western Union, RCA, and AT&T launched nine communication satellites during the mid and late 1970s. Although these satellites were mainly used to relay domestic telephone traffic, cable television companies also became important users beginning in the mid-1970s. Networks were slower to adopt the use of communication satellites for domestic service; however, they did begin to take advantage of satellite capabilities, especially for program syndication. The first U. S. network to make a major commitment was the Public Broadcasting System (PBS). It contracted with Western Union for satellite service and initiated a transition from terrestrial relays in 1978. The success of this transition led other broadcasters to follow PBS's lead. By the end of 1979, fifty U. S. television stations were equipped with earth stations able to receive and make copies of television broadcasts from satellites. By 1981, this number had increased to 250.

The Intelsat system began to adapt to the needs of the broadcast industry beginning in the early 1980s. Part of the pressure came Ted Turner when he made plans for his twenty-four-hour news channel, Cable News Network (CNN). During 1980, executives at CNN convinced the Intelsat board of governors to adopt a new rate structure allowing for the full-time use of satellite channels. Changes to the cost structure also resulted from pressure from news agencies such as Visnews, based in the United Kingdom. Camera crews working for Visnews and other organizations produced television film packages that were then shipped to broadcasters around the world using air freight services. Executives at Visnews recognized the advantage of using communication satellites to transmit television broadcast packages to multiple locations from a single satellite uplink. Intelsat costs again were the major barrier. Lobbying during the early 1980s convinced Intelsat and national telecommunication administrations to introduce a new rate structure allowing for regular ten- to fifteen-minute satellite transmissions of international TV news packages at a regular time every day.

A process of liberalization accelerated beginning in the late 1980s, which has led to a further lowering of rates for international satellite transmissions. This process has facilitated the expansion of CNN and other twenty-four-hour news channels serving global markets. Organizations specializing in the global flow of news footage have also expanded through the use of communication satellites. By 2000, two agencies, Reuters Television (formerly Visnews) and Associated Press Television News (APTN), controlled most of the global video products used by broadcasters around the world. Although the broadcast networks in the United States—CBS, ABC, and NBC—as well as U. S. cable news stations such as CNN used satellite new feeds from their own foreign correspondents, they also relied on the services of Reuters Television and APTN.

An additional incentive for the expanded use of communication satellites for television news beginning in the 1980s was the development of new forms of electronic news-gathering (ENG). Broadcasters converted from the use of film cameras to portable battery-operated electronic cameras using new videotape technology. The electronic format meant that pictures could be edited in the field using portable editing equipment. All the equipment used by mobile news crews could fit into a small truck. News crews in the field could then send the footage directly to the station using small microwave transmitters or by way of a satellite uplink using portable transmission antennae. The combination of ENG with satellite news gathering (SNG) became more common by the late 1980s for television stations in the United States covering regional or national news events. This development tended to lessen control by networks of local television stations. Instead of having to rely on news feeds from networks, local stations could use their own video news footage collected in the field.

New developments in the miniaturization of SNG during the 1990s also expanded access in the United States to live international news. The broadcast networks and cable news channels began to use portable "flyaway" satellite dishes, which could be disassembled and flown as baggage accompanying news crews to distant locations. The major international news event that introduced the potential of these new innovations to American television viewers was the 1990–1991 Gulf War. Live broadcasts from Iraq, Israel, and Saudi Arabia created a sense of immediacy for U. S. audiences, including over one hundred million viewers during the first night of the war. Correspondents reporting on the war while under fire, using portable satellite uplinks, also created a sense of drama unique to live programming broadcast from highly mobile new crews.

Although the most important news development facilitated by communication satellites has been the global transmission of live television news pictures, the new technology has also been important for other innovations in news coverage, including most importantly instantaneous access to all forms of news coverage using the Internet. For both global television news and news over the Internet, communication satellites play the crucial role providing instantaneous global coverage. The new capability for immediate access does have potential negative implications. For example, governments often feel pressured to formulate policy decisions immediately based on television-influenced public opinion without carefully evaluating different positions. Also, the fast pace and high volume of instantaneous news coverage made possible by communication satellites has interfered with traditional processes of fact-checking. Instantaneous news has challenged journalistic conventions, especially with the expansion of news over the Internet. Finally, communication satellites have played an important role in the formation of global media conglomerates, mainly based in the United States, which increasingly control the global flow of media products.

Further Reading

Butrica, Andrew J, ed. *Beyond the Ionosphere: Fifty Years of Satellite Communications.* Washington, D.C.: NASA, 1997.

Hachten, William A., and James F. Scotton. *The World News Prism*, 6th ed. Ames: Iowa State University Press, 2002.

Higgins, Jonathan. *Satellite Newsgathering.* Woburn, MA: Focal Press, 2000.

Inglis, Andrew F. *Behind the Tube: A History of Broadcasting Technology and Business.* Boston, MA: Focal Press, 1990.

McNair, Brian. *Cultural Chaos: Journalism, News and Power in a Globalised World.* New York: Routledge, 2006.

Pelton, Joseph N., Robert J. Oslund, and Peter Marshall, eds. *Communications Satellites: Global Change Agents.* Mahwah, NJ: Lawrence Erlbaum Associates, 2004.

Slotten, Hugh R. "Satellite Communications, Globalization, and the Cold War." *Technology and Culture* 43, no. 2 (April 2002): 315–350.

Sterling, Christopher H., and John Michael Kittross. *Stay Tuned: A History of American Broadcasting.* 3rd edition. Mahway, NJ: Lawrence Erlbaum Associates, 2002.

Thussu, Daya Kishan. *International Communication: Continuity and Change.* London: Arnold, 2000.

Whalen, David. *The Origins of Satellite Communications, 1945–1965.* Washington, D.C.: Smithsonian Institution Press, 2002.

HUGH R. SLOTTEN

SATURDAY EVENING POST

The *Saturday Evening Post* (1821–1969; 1970–) is a national mainstream American magazine that claims descent from Benjamin Franklin's *Pennsylvania Gazette*. It rose to prominence in the early to mid-twentieth century, becoming a significant resource for American political and business news on a weekly basis. It also published a variety of short fiction from writers who later became famous, and its habit of publishing paintings, rather than photographs, on its cover stimulated the careers of noted American artists. At its peak in 1960, the *Post* boasted more than six million subscribers from across the country, but a change in editorial policy that included the weeding out of "undesirable" subscribers, together with changing industry conditions for magazines in the late 1960s, led to the magazine's initial downfall. As a weekly source for mainstream news and information, the magazine ceased publication in 1969. New owners took over the magazine and reinstated its publication in 1970, changing its focus to nostalgia. In this format, the *Post* continued circulation into the twenty-first century, maintaining both a printed magazine, published bimonthly, and a World Wide Web presence.

A number of editors stewarded the magazine, but arguably the most influential of them was George Horace Lorimer, who served as the *Post*'s editor from 1899 to 1936. Hired by Cyrus H. Curtis, whose Curtis Publishing Company purchased the *Post* in 1897, Lorimer guided the *Post* in its ascent from a marginal publication to a high-circulation must-read mainstream American weekly. Lorimer also gave the *Post* a voice that he claimed was particularly middle-class, particularly American, and decidedly conservative. Throughout his editorials, Lorimer wrote consistently about what he viewed as uniquely American ideals of hard work, initiative, free enterprise, and fair play. Articles under Lorimer's control demonstrated a strong bias toward a rags-to-riches myth; he printed a high number of stories about how men succeeded in business despite starting with little to no capital. His practice of hiring young people to sell magazine subscriptions had its roots in this philosophy. Lorimer relied on youth to sell his magazines and emphasized the development of manly traits in youth-oriented stories printed in the magazine. As historian Jan Cohn suggests, the content of the magazine under Lorimer's hands set up an image and construction of American life as a paradigm for readers to follow. It was the *Post*'s mission to promote and refine an American ideology.

Lorimer fostered publication of business and political news that supported his idealized American values, often writing business stories himself under pseudonyms. He also faithfully read all letters directed to the *Post* and responded to them through the editorial pages. A fiscal conservative, Lorimer encouraged debate and hired new writers, such as radical reporter David Graham Phillips, to bring other voices to the publication. However, the publication was known by some in its time to be a big business booster, an anti-labor union force, and a capitalist organ. Stories, articles, and editorials consistently touted the benefits of self-reliance and freedom from government interference in business and in the daily lives of American citizens. During the Great Depression of the 1930s, this editorial position made New Deal efforts seem un-American in that they took away American citizens' rights to work for themselves and, in the *Post*'s view, hampered the rights of individuals to be free from daily governmental interference in their lives, a position that remained a source of occasional debate in *Post* editorials through its final publication in 1969.

Lorimer's consistent support of new writing and artistic talent, a support continued by subsequent *Post* editors, made the magazine an outlet for some of the most influential writers of their time. Short fiction and nonfiction written by Willa Cather, Jack London, Sinclair Lewis, H. G. Wells, Rudyard Kipling, Theodore Dreiser, and Stephen Crane, as well as many others, offered a varied look at the many roads and cultures of American life. Louis L'Amour, Rose Wilder Lane, Zane Grey, and others continued the tradition of American short story fiction and literary nonfiction published in the *Post* well into the 1960s, making the magazine an important resource for scholars of the American short story, literary journalism, and American studies.

In 1916, Lorimer hired a young Norman Rockwell to create cover art for the *Post*. Rockwell's association with the magazine lasted for more than forty-five years, and yielded some of the artist's most famous and influential work. Pieces such as *Four Essential Human Freedoms*, taken from President Franklin D. Roosevelt's 1941 address to Congress, finished and published in 1943, established Rockwell as a premier American artist. Rockwell finished 317 cover pieces for the *Post* before his final publication in December, 1963, when an editorial decision was made to stop publishing paintings on the magazine's front cover. Other illustrators associated with the magazine in the 1950s included Joseph Leyendecker, who Rockwell mentored and who was known for his Deco style, Charles Marion Russell, and Walter Everett.

When Lorimer retired as editor in 1936, circulation had soared to nearly three million subscribers. Under subsequent editorial leadership, the magazine continued to draw subscribers until 1960, when circulation peaked at six million readers. The introduction of television into American homes during the 1950s and 1960s led to a downward spiral in circulation for many magazines of the period, and the *Post* was not immune to the economic crisis that swept the publishing industry at that time. A disastrous effort to cut subscriber lists and, in doing so, make the magazine an exclusive publication, ignored long-time middle-class mainstream readers who had supported the magazine through economic ups and downs for more than sixty years. The magazine that had brought a wave of new writers and artists to the forefront of American culture and had given an unparalleled voice to middle America ceased to be relevant to the very people to which it was trying to appeal. The *Post* as a mainstream middle-American icon ceased publication in 1969.

In 1970, entrepreneurs Beurt and Cory SerVaas revitalized the magazine, turning it into a niche magazine focused on American nostalgia. In the early twenty-first century, it was published bimonthly and maintains a presence on the World Wide Web.

Further Reading

Cohn, Jan. *Creating America: George Horace Lorimer and* The Saturday Evening Post. Pittsburgh: University of Pittsburgh Press, 1989.

Harvey, Anne-Marie. "Sons of the Sun: Making White, Middle-Class Manhood in Jack London's David Grief Stories and *The Saturday Evening Post*." *American Studies* 39, no. 3 (1998): 37–68.

Holder, Stephen C. "The Family Magazine and the American People." *Journal of Popular Culture* 1973 7, no. 2 (1973): 264–279.

"Norman Rockwell and The Saturday Evening Post," http://www.curtispublishing.com/sep.htm, (accessed Sept. 22, 2006).

Ryant, Carl G. "From Isolation to Intervention: 'The Saturday Evening Post,' 1939–42." *Journalism Quarterly* 48, no. 4 (1971): 679–687.

Wilcox, Gary B., and Moriarty, Sandra E. "Humorous Advertising in the Post, 1920–1930." *Journalism Quarterly* 61, no. 2 (1984): 436–439.

AMY MATTSON LAUTERS

SCHENCK V. U.S. (1919)

In March 1919, four months after the Armistice brought the First World War to a close, the United States Supreme Court handed down its first major interpretation of the First Amendment guarantee of freedom of expression. *Schenck v. United States* (1919) considered the appeal of Charles Schenck and Elizabeth Baer, both socialists, who had been convicted of circulating a pamphlet the Justice Department said was intended to obstruct the recruiting and enlistment service. Congress eschewed federal legislation limiting the freedoms of speech and the press for more than one hundred years after the 1801 expiration of the 1798 Sedition Act. Not until World War I did the federal government again enter the free speech arena. This time Congress enacted the Espionage Act of 1917, which made it a crime to "convey false reports or false statements" that would interfere with the war effort, to "cause or attempt to cause" insubordination or disloyalty in the military, or to "willfully obstruct the recruitment of soldiers." Close on its heels, the Sedition Act of 1918 made it a crime to "willfully utter, print, write, or publish" language disloyal to the United States, or to bring the government, the military, or the flag into disrepute, or to encourage others to "support or favor the cause of any country with which the United States is at war."

The defendants published a two-sided leaflet. One side was titled, "Long Live the Constitution of the United States. Wake Up America. Your Rights are in Danger." The other side was headlined, "Assert Your Rights." The leaflet quoted the Thirteenth Amendment ban on slavery and compared the draft to indentured servitude. The document called on people to petition for a repeal of the draft. The leaflet mailing list included some men who had been called up for military service. No evidence was ever introduced that the leaflet had any effect on draftees or on anyone else. The government argued that the intent of the leaflets was to disrupt the draft.

The defendants argued that the First Amendment barred Congress from enacting any law abridging the freedoms of speech and press. Justice Oliver Wendell Holmes Jr. wrote the unanimous opinion for the Supreme Court rejecting their interpretation of the First Amendment. He relied on what came to be known as the "clear and present danger" doctrine.

"The most stringent protection of free speech would not protect a man in falsely shouting fire in a theatre and causing a panic," Holmes wrote. The legal question, he said, "is whether the words used are used in such circumstances and are of such a nature as to create a clear and present danger that they will bring about the substantive evils that Congress has a right to prevent." To Holmes, the fact that the country was at war was the key. "When a nation is at war many things that might be said in time of peace are such a hindrance to its effort that their utterance will not be endured so long as men fight."

Critics at the time, including Harvard law professor Zechariah Chafee and federal judge Learned Hand, pointed out that Holmes' clear and present danger test provided inadequate protection for the kinds of political speech necessary to foster democratic governance. Historians since have noted that President Woodrow Wilson and Congress equated public opposition to Wilson's foreign policies with disloyalty to the nation, rather than viewing public discussion as necessary to democratic decision-making. The Supreme Court's deference to legislative authority and lack of familiarity in 1919 with viewing the First Amendment as a means of fostering public sovereignty contributed to what today is viewed as an overly narrow reading of the Constitution. During the World War I era, there were more than two thousand lower court convictions based on the Espionage and Sedition Act statutes. Holmes' view of what constituted clear and present danger in the Schenck case did not provide sufficient protection in any of them. In the *Abrams* case (1919) that soon followed, though, Holmes thinking about the clear and present danger test did begin to take on a broader meaning.

Further Reading

Alschuler, Albert W. *Law Without Values: The Life, Work and Legacy of Justice Holmes.* Chicago: University of Chicago Press, 2000.

Burns, James MacGregor, and Stewart Burns. *A People's Charter: The Pursuit of Rights in America.* New York: Knopf, 1991.

Cohen, Jeremy. *Congress Shall Make No Law: Oliver Wendell Holmes, The First Amendment and Judicial Decision Making.* Iowa City: Iowa State University Press, 1989.

Schenck v. United States. 249 U.S. 47 (1919).

Stone, Geoffrey R. *Perilous Times: Free Speech in Wartime.* New York: W.W. Norton & Co., 2004.

White, Edward G. *Justice Oliver Wendell Holmes: Law and the Inner Self.* New York: Oxford University Press, 1993.

JEREMY COHEN

SCHORR, DANIEL

Daniel Schorr's career in journalism spans five continents and more than six decades. He served CBS as a reporter for Edward R. Murrow in postwar Europe, then in the United States with Walter Cronkite during Watergate. In 2007, he was a senior news analyst for National Public Radio.

Daniel Schorr was born August 31, 1916, in New York City to parents fleeing pre-World War I persecution in Telechan, a village in what is now Belarus. His father, Louis, died when he was six—leaving a deathbed request that the $2,000 life insurance policy be used to send Schorr and his only sibling, polio-striken younger brother Alvin, to college.

A top student at the Bronx Jewish Center and fluent in Hebrew, Schorr became president of the Hebrew Society during high school, and wrote for the DeWitt Clinton High School newspaper. His exemplary grades earned him a tuition-free scholarship to the College of the City of New York, where he reported for CCNY's *The Campus*. He earned a B.S. degree in 1939. An accomplished tenor in the synagogue choir, he contributed music articles to the *New York Times*, the paper for which he aspired to work. During World War II, he was drafted and served in Army Intelligence.

Schorr reported for the short-lived *Jewish Daily Bulletin*, then its parent company, the Jewish Telegraphic Agency. He moved to the Hague to work for ANETA, the news agency of the Netherlands East Indies (now Indonesia). There, he freelanced stories for *Time, Newsweek,* the *New York Times,* the *Christian Science Monitor,* ABC, CBS and the *London Daily Mail*. In 1950 Schorr was the inaugural winner of the Netherlands' journalism award named for the nation's founder: William the Orange.

Schorr's first network radio broadcast was a live two-minute broadcast over crackling shortwave for ABC's World News Roundup covering the May 1948 Congress of Europe where Winston Churchill called for a new United States of Europe to counter Soviet aggression. Schorr also covered Indonesia's independence from Holland, the abdication of Dutch Queen Wilhelmina (noted for her heroic radio broadcasts from her exile in London during World War II), and the launch of the North American Treaty Organization (with inaugural NATO Supreme Commander Dwight D. Eisenhower).

As a stringer for CBS, Schorr's coverage of the dramatic Holland flood that broke the dikes and killed more than two thousand led to an offer from Edward R. Murrow. Still desiring a post with the *Times*, Schorr contacted them about the CBS offer but was rejected. In his autobiography, *Staying Tuned: A Life in Journalism* (2001), Schorr wrote that years later he was told that *Times* Managing Editor Turner Catledge "ordered a freeze on the hiring of Jews as correspondents...concerned that the disproportionate representation of Jews on the staff might hamper *Times* coverage of some future Middle East war." Schorr covered the U.S. State Department and related international events for CBS as part of Murrow's fabled team, which included Eric Sevareid, Howard K. Smith, and David Schoenbrun. When the Soviet Union admitted a handful of journalists in 1955, he was sent to Moscow—along with the tools of the new television news age: a Bell & Howell 16mm handheld camera and a wind-up Magnemite tape recorder. The Soviets tapped his phone lines, limited his sources, and required a KGB review before airing. Schorr and NBC's Irving R. Levine kept lists of visiting friends from the West who smuggled out some film and audiotape. His stories included a 1957 interview of Nikita Khrushchev on CBS' *Face the Nation* (filmed in Moscow), the first-ever press tour of Siberia, the launch of Sputniks I & II, and Khrushchev's visits to Poland, the United States and Paris. Because Schorr refused to cooperate with Soviet censors, he was banned from returning to the USSR.

In 1959, connections in the Netherlands allowed Schorr access to the famous Frank family hideaway at No. 263 Princes Canal, Amsterdam, as part of the CBS' Nazi war crime documentary *Who Killed Anne Frank?* For Murrow's *CBS Reports* he produced an hour-long documentary, *Poland--Country on a Tightrope,* that included stark footage of Nazi concentration camp Auschwitz. "I was not prepared for what I would see," Schorr said in his 2001 autobiography. "I had to read parts of my script several times, trying to control a catch in my throat."

Schorr also orchestrated exclusive interviews with estranged Spanish cellist Pablo Casals and an 8-minute interview with Fidel Castro regarding Cuba's relations with the U.S.S.R. that aired in its entirety on the *CBS Evening News.* He also covered the hour-by-hour erection of a fence, then a wall, between East and West Berlin beginning in the fall of 1961. The harrowing reports included stories of East German guards shooting would-be escapees, U.S. and Soviet tanks facing off at Checkpoint Charlie, East Berliners escaping through tunnels, and President John F. Kennedy's visit to West Berlin.

In 1966 Schorr covered President Lyndon B. Johnson's domestic programs, civil rights and the environment, including the Peabody Award-winning documentary *The Poisoned Air.* The FBI questioned friends and associates of Schorr's—and created a file—in the early 1970s when the Richard M. Nixon White House was angered by his reporting. His coverage of the Senate Watergate hearings earned him his three Emmys. During one live broadcast, Schorr inadvertently read his name over the air as part of the infamous Nixon enemies list when handed a just-obtained copy right before air time. Schorr was threatened with jail time in 1976 by the House Ethics Committee after leaking an exclusive copy of the U.S. House of Representatives' secret report on the CIA and FBI to the *Village Voice.* For failure to reveal his source, he faced contempt of Congress charges, which later were dropped. However, the episode created serious problems for Schorr at CBS. Chairman William S. Paley wanted him dismissed and after Schorr was interviewed by Mike Wallace on *60 Minutes*, he resigned from CBS News in September, 1976. Schorr later wrote about these events in *Clearing the Air* (1977).

On May 21, 1979, Schorr became the first employee of Ted Turner's fledgling Cable News Network as reporter and senior news analyst. He covered the release hostages from Iran and the elections of 1980 and 1984, but left CNN in 1985 in a dispute with Turner over limits to his editorial freedom. Schorr narrated the 1994 miniseries *Watergate* and made brief appearances as a newscaster in three motion pictures: *The Game, The Net,* and *The Siege.*

Schorr is author of two memoirs. His honors include a lifetime Peabody Award, the Society of Professional Journalists Hall of Fame, a Polk Radio Commentary Award, and a duPont-Columbia Golden Baton. He and wife, Lisbeth, live in Washington. They have two children.

Further Reading

Boyer, Peter J. *Who Killed CBS? The Undoing of America's Number One News Network.* New York: Random House. 1988.

Carter, Bill. "Daniel Schorr Wins Top duPont-Columbia Journalism Award." *New York Times*, January 26, 1996, B17.

Schorr, Daniel. *Clearing the Air.* Boston: Houghton Mifflin, 1977.

——. *Don't Get Sick in America.* Nashville, Aurora Publishers, 1970.

——. Introduction to *Taking the Stand: The Testimony of Lieutenant Colonel Oliver L. North.* New York: Pocket Books, 1987.

——. *Staying Tuned: A Life in Journalism.* New York: Pocket Books, 2001.

KEVIN C. LEE

SCIENCE AND TECHNOLOGY REPORTING

The earliest examples of American science reporting are found within the first colonial newspapers. Knowledge of disease, farming, and weather were paramount to the survival of settlers from Europe, and the news reflected this.

Benjamin Harris' *Publick Occurences*—America's first newspaper, although it was published only once (on September 25, 1690)—reported fevers and smallpox outbreaks in the colonies. While Harris stressed abatement of disease in Boston, he also warned that the smallpox "unhappily spreads in several other places, among which our Garrisons in the East are to be reckoned some of the Sufferers." This brief report from a significant but extremely short-lived publication foreshadowed the content and tone of science reporting to come. Historians have noted four similarities to modern science reporting: An emphasis on public health and medicine, attention to the local angle, emphasis on "progress," and a connection to military concerns. Harris also incorporated God and prayers into his reporting of disease, another common theme in science journalism during the colonial period and one that remained prominent through the mid-nineteenth century.

As for longer-lived early American newspapers, the structure and nature of science news remained constant through the eighteenth century. Scientific phenomena directly affecting daily existence were a constant theme in newspapers, and that news was typically written by one person—the publisher—who, although unbound by the later journalistic norms of objectivity and facticity, often provided vital information to readers. Disease continued to be a central theme in colonial papers, with publishers debating fiercely the new practice of inoculations through the 1720s. James Franklin's *Hartford Courant* argued against the smallpox inoculation. Benjamin Franklin, James' younger brother, took the scientific themes of the colonial press even further. As both a scientist and printer, he frequently reported on scientific themes in his *Pennsylvania Gazette*, including his own experiments with electricity in the 1750s.

The nineteenth century brought dramatic changes to journalism practices, and reporting of science and technology reflected those changes. At first, science news was slow to spread throughout the growing country. It took months for reports from Lewis and Clark's expedition through the American West to travel back to the public. News of inventions—Fulton's steamboat, the steam train, and Morse's telegraph, were reported in newspapers, but not extensively. During the Penny Press era, however, technological, social, and economic shifts began to increase the demand for, and dissemination of, science and technology news in the popular press.

The economic shift from subscriber-based revenue to advertising revenue spurred the practice of "objective" reporting as newspapers and magazines looked for larger, more diverse, audiences to make their publications attractive to advertisers. At the same time, both the natural and social sciences were relying more than ever on empirical evidence and scientific method. Journalism followed with its shift from emphasizing partisan political commentary to increasing reliance on "facts." The late 1800s saw the rise of professionalism in many fields, including journalism and medicine. And, the technological revolution both fed the need for technology news, and provided the means for distribution with advancements in printing technology, photography, and the invention of the telegraph.

Science reporting during this time came from a variety of sources: The scientists themselves, writing for scientific journals or the burgeoning new field of popular science magazines; magazine reporters with some specialized knowledge of their fields; newspaper reporters covering breaking stories of developments and, at times, disasters; and pseudo journalists borrowing from scientific method and journalistic reporting techniques to produce wild stories of space aliens or scientific miracles.

The Journals

Even before 1800, the need for detailed and accurate information about disease and epidemics, and advancements in education, medical science, and printing technology, led to the first scientific journals in the United States. In 1797, the quarterly *Medical Repository*, the first medical journal in America, was introduced in New York. With articles titled "Plague of Athens," "Remarks on Manures," "On the Cholera of Infants," as well as foreign and domestic medical news and notes in its inaugural issue, the new journal offered a much-needed resource for American physicians. Yet the groundbreaking publication did not enjoy its journalistic monopoly for long. Each successive decade from the founding of *Medical Repository* until the Civil War saw more journals published.

By the mid-1800s, hundreds of scientific journals—ranging from standard medicine to homeopathic and botanic content—were published, although many did not survive. Historian James Cassedy writes that in this "golden age of medical wrangling" most surviving journals depended on a partisan stance to build and maintain an audience. "Their columns alternated from condescension to sarcasm, from enthusiastic advocacy to better invective, all with the aim of discomfiting or defeating medical foes" (1983, 144).

Two of the most enduring scientific journals were *Nature* and *Science*—both peer reviewed journals that survive and thrive today. *Nature*, originally published in Britain (but now an international publication), was founded in 1869 by English astronomer Sir Joseph Norman Lockyer. Vowing in its original mission statement to "place before the general public the grand results of Scientific Work and Scientific Discovery," *Nature* set the stage for the American journal *Science*, founded eleven years later by journalist John Michaels and funded in part by Thomas Edison. Like other scientific journals of the time, *Science* struggled in its early years, briefly shutting down in 1882 before being restarted in 1883 by entomologist Samuel Scudder. Scudder sold the publication to psychologist James McKeen Cattell in 1894, and the journal gained a stronger foothold in 1900 when it became the journal of the American Association for the Advancement of Science (AAAS).

Daily and Popular Press

In the daily press, the journalistic beat system began to develop in the late 1800s, and reporters began to specialize in particular areas. With medical science quickly advancing with the development of germ theory and other break-through discoveries, and the technological revolution in full swing, science and technology reporters had no shortage of information to work with. Yet science information in the mainstream daily press was often inaccurate, and sometimes intentionally fabricated to increase readership. Most reporters were still generalists and had no specialized knowledge of science, medicine, and technology.

The Penny Press and Yellow Journalism eras produced their share of sensationalistic, and outright false, "science" stories. Perhaps best remembered was the 1835 story of the discovery of bat-like moon creatures. Benjamin Day's *New York Sun* reported the fictitious "astronomical discoveries," credited to British Astronomer Sir John Hershal, with convincing scientific observations: "We could perceive that their wings possessed great expansion and were similar in structure of those of the bat, being a semitransparent membrane expanded in curvilinear divisions by means of straight radii, united at the back by dorsal integuments" (August 25, 1835). In the years that followed came more sensationalized and often questionable reports or cures, inventions, and amazing scientific achievements. Among the most famous scientific journalism stunts was the *New York Herald's* effort to find missing explorer David Livingstone. Editor James Gordon Bennett, Jr., sent foreign correspondent Henry M. Stanley on the assignment in 1869. After a long, arduous, expensive expedition to Africa, Stanley found Livingston on Nov. 19, 1871, in Ujiji, Central Africa. Bennett had his headlines. Working for Joseph Pulitzer's *New York World* in 1888, journalist Elizabeth Cochrane, writing as Nellie Bly, combined investigative reporting with stunt journalism, faking insanity to gain access to an asylum and reporting first hand on the abysmal conditions.

Despite trends of sensationalism spawned by fierce economic competition, nineteenth-century newspapers did play a crucial role in reporting and debating scientific breakthroughs and theories. In March 1860, the *New York Times* astutely observed that Charles Darwin's *Origin of the Species*—published a few months earlier—was "revolutionary" and could potentially "necessitate a radical reconstruction of the fundamental doctrines of natural history" (*New York Times*, March 28, 1860). The *New York Herald* lauded "Edison's Light … The Great Inventor's triumph in Electric Illumination" on December 21, 1878. Edison was astute in using the press, frequently giving interviews that appeared in the Sunday Supplements, all in an effort to publicize and market his new inventions.

Popular magazines with scientific themes offered, as they still do, an important option for general readers—usually accurate and detailed information about science and technology aimed at non-scientists. With the publishing of *Scientific American* in 1845, which now claims the distinction of being the longest continuously published publication in the United States, popular magazines made science accessible to average people. *National Geographic* was launched by the National Geographic Society in 1888 to "the increase and diffusion of geographic knowledge." In its early days, the magazine offered scientific news not through photography, but through often technical accounts of anthropological, archeological, geographic, and astronomical advancements and expeditions. By 1900, though, editor Gilbert H. Grosvenor, hired by Society President Alexander Graham Bell, began to publish general interest articles aimed at a wider audience. In 1905 Grosevenor made his now-famous decision to fill the magazine with photography.

At the turn of the twentieth century, the culture of science, facticity and objectivity had permeated American thought and discourse. Journalists, during the last years of the nineteenth century, had begun to see themselves, as historian Michael Schudson put it, "as scientists uncovering the economic and political facts of industrial life more boldly, more clearly, and more 'realistically' than anyone had done before" (Schudson, *Discovering the News*, 71). Still ahead were a deadly pandemic, two world wars, and technological revolutions in travel and communication—events that further shaped and dramatically altered the nature of American science reporting.

War and Pandemic

The technological and scientific advancements of the early twentieth century were exciting and frightening, and inventions and world events whetted the public's appetite for scientific news. The simultaneous and interwoven occurrences of World War I and the 1918 influenza pandemic further challenged science writers to accurately report vital technological and health information. Meanwhile, trends within journalism—particularly the rise of the muckracking journalist, the rise of the newspaper columnist, and the founding of specialized news services—provided new forms of reporting science.

In addition to the medical professionals working as columnists, a few noted editors helped to expand coverage of science in major American newspapers. Carr Van Anda, hired as managing editor of the *New York Times* in 1904, had studied astronomy and physics before becoming a reporter. His knowledge and interest in scientific subjects led to more in-depth coverage by the *Times*. Meanwhile, E.W. Scripps of Scripps-Howard was also exploring ways to better cover science. In 1921, Scripps launched The Science Service—a project he had been working on for about a decade. Scripps intended the service to be used as a link between scientists and journalists, with the ultimate goal of delivering accurate and understandable scientific information to the public. Chemist and writer Edwin E. Slosson was selected as the first editor of the Science Service. His track record was impressive—he had contributed hundreds of articles to popular magazines, had served as editor of *The Independent*, and had written eighteen books. Under the leadership of Slosson, the Science Service covered scientific discoveries with an even hand, avoiding the earlier style of overt sensationalism, as well as producing human interest stories connecting the practicalities of science to everyday life. The Science Service sold its news articles and packages to newspapers nationwide.

Scientific topics in the popular press in the first years of the new century ranged from inventions in transportation and communication to archeology and medicine. Polar exploration was a popular topic in major newspapers and magazines. During the 1908–1909 race to the South Pole, publications fought hard, and paid well, to gain story rights. The race between Frederick Cook and Robert Peary, played out in ongoing and dramatic coverage of major publications, including the New York dailies.

By the beginning of the twentieth century, science reporting in the daily press had moved away from the lurid imaginings of the Yellow Journalism era to more realistic and truly fact-based information. Magazine reporters increased their attention to science. Some muckraking journalists, for instance, turned their attention to scientific and medical frauds and their stories led to important reforms. In *Collier's Weekly*, journalist and author Samuel Hopkins Adams exposed patent medicine fraud in a 1905–1906 series of investigative articles. The series, titled "The Great American Fraud," analyzed the content of popular medications, and the harm they did to users. Adams' series has been credited with leading to passage of the 1906 Pure Food and Drug Act.

Meanwhile, popular magazine reporters, including those working for women's magazines, focused attention on cleanliness and sanitization, with an emphasis on fighting germs. Germ theory had influenced not only science and health discourse, but prompted new ideas regarding housewifery and child care. Articles in a myriad of magazines, from *Good Housekeeping* to *Scientific American*, warned of disease dissemination through common household activities, and gave advice on sanitation and disinfectants.

This new stress on health and disease prevention was ineffective though in preventing the two most deadly events of the new century—World War I, the first war to see air combat and chemical weapons, and the 1918 influenza pandemic. War correspondents were challenged to make sense of the new technological and chemical weapons. Journalists covering combat and those at home had to make sense out of an unprecedented health threat to America and abroad. When the German army introduced poison gas in 1915, American newspapers described the effects of the new weapon, but had few details scientific details. Will Irwin of the *New York Tribune* wrote "The nature of the gasses carried by the German asphyxiating shells remain a mystery. Whatever gas it is, it spreads rapidly and remains close to the ground. It is believed not to be specially deadly" (*Tribune*, April 25, 1915). Within weeks, journalistic reports described more dire effects. "Death Is Slow Torture by Suffocation" one *New York Times* headline read (May 7, 1915). Partly in response to the use of chemical weapons in the war, and the obvious need for public information about chemistry, the American Chemical Society launched a news service a few years later.

In the spring of 1918, as World War I still dominated international news, a first wave of the influenza pandemic hit the United States. A second, more deadly wave, hit

that fall, challenging both scientists and journalists to find effective ways to relay possibly life-saving information to the public. Daily newspapers focused on local casualty numbers and information from public health officials. Magazines and journals tended to present stories exploring possible causes of the pandemic, and man's struggle to control it through the power of science. By 1918, scientific method and an emphasis on empirical information prevailed in science reporting, as did a tendency to use military metaphors in reporting disease. Scientists and medical professionals, according to the press, were at war with a poorly understood enemy.

After World War I ended and the pandemic abated, print media continued to feed the public's interest in science and technology news. *Time* magazine was launched in 1923, with *Life* and *Look* following in the 1930s. Though all three were general interest publications, each regularly included science information written for a mass audience, as well as photographs. The major daily papers, led by the *New York Times*, began to report on experiments with radiology and atomic energy. In 1934, William L. Laurence of the *New York Times*, one of the first full-time science reporters in the United States, and David Dietz of Scripps-Howard newspapers launched the National Association of Science Writers. Its initial membership of twelve grew to more than two thousand over the next seventy years. Laurence was also credited with leading the journalistic coverage of atomic energy, and ultimately, the A-bomb.

Late Twentieth to Early Twentieth Century

The post-World War II space race, combined with television's rapidly growing popularity, sparked a new wave of interest in technology and science. The competition between the Soviet Union and the United States to launch a manned space craft was covered extensively in daily news, popular magazines, and the scientific press. Television began to air live broadcasts of missile launches. In 1969, the public's desire for understandable scientific information peaked with plans for the first manned moon landing. By July 20, 1969, when Apollo 11 landed, NASA had accredited thousands of print and broadcast journalists to cover the mission. The print and broadcast coverage continued though the remainder of the Apollo program, and later chronicled the development of the Space Shuttle. The live television broadcast of the Challenger Space Shuttle disaster on January 28, 1986, once again created a need for accurate, and almost instantaneous, scientific information to be disseminated to the public.

In final decades of the twentieth century, journalists covered health and environmental issues extensively. Growing concerns about dwindling environmental resources, and the publication of Rachel Carson's *Silent Spring*, contributed to the environmental movement, and a media-fueled public debate about consumption of natural resources. The AIDS epidemic created a new urgent need for accurate public health information. The *San Francisco Chronicle* led coverage by appointing the first full-time AIDS beat reporter in 1982, mirroring a general trend toward more specialized science and technology reporters on the staff of general population publications.

Into the twenty-first century, political and social discourse over events and issues such as weapons technology, genetic engineering, space exploration, devastating natural disasters, famine and disease, has further expanded the need for specialized and knowledgeable science reporters. The major U.S. newsweeklies, as well as most major American newspapers, had full-time science reporters on their staffs by the 1990s. Since 1978, the *New York Times* carried a special science section on Tuesdays, and other news publications followed with expanded, and packaged, science and technology coverage. Television news also added science reporters or medical practioners to their staffs to both report and analyze science and health news. A rapid expansion in media technologies, combined with a trend toward media integration, affected the dissemination of science news in the last years of the century by creating a complex network of science news outlets. The National Geographic Society began producing television specials as early as 1965, and launched "Horizon," a ninety-second daily radio spot, in 1980. Science societies and publications more than a century old began to expand into cyberspace, adding web sites, blogs, and podcasts. NationalGeographic.com, ScientificAmerican.com, Smithsonian.com, and Science.com each, for instance, offer news sites, interactive features, and online stores for related products.

Since the mid-eighteenth century, reporters covering science and technology have gathered news the same way as other general assignment and beat reporters: They have covered scientific meetings and conferences, relied on sources within the scientific community, used written records and transcripts of scientific proceedings, and have followed tips from press releases, and more recently, video and electronic news releases. Popular newspapers and magazines also often rely on news from scientific journals, rewriting and repackaging scientific research into information for the layman. Scientific news values also mirror those of the general interest press. Scientists, from Thomas Edison, Marie Curie, Sigmund Freud, and Albert Einstein to Carl Sagan and Steven Hawking, have attracted media coverage. Disease and disaster have also warranted extensive news coverage throughout the history of American journalism. Controversy over scientific theory, health treatments, or research ethics also attracts journalistic attention. In-depth scientific information, and issues as opposed to event coverage, has been rarer in the mainstream press. While scientific and technological knowledge increases, ethical and policy debates rage, and communications technology expands, journalists continue to look for ways to relay complex scientific concepts so necessary to navigate the modern world.

Further Reading

Cassedy, James H. "Muckraking and Medicine: Samuel Hopkins Adams." *American Quarterly*, Spring 1964.

——. "The Flourishing and Character of Early American Medical Journalism, 1797–1860." *The Journal of the History of Medicine and Allied Sciences*, vol. 28, 1983.

Copeland, David A. "'A Receipt Against the Plague': Medical Reporting in Colonial America." *American Journalism*, Summer 1994.

Foust, J.C. "E.W. Scripps and the Science Service." *Journalism History*, Summer 1995.

McClary, Andrew. "Germs are Everywhere: The Germ Threat as Seen in Magazine Articles, 1890–1920." *Journal of American Culture*, vol. 3, 1980.

Nelkin, Dorothy. *Selling Science: How the Press Covers Science and Technology*. New York: W.H. Freeman and Company, 1995.

MEG SPRATT

SCIENTIFIC AMERICAN

Scientific American first published on August 28, 1845, as a weekly single-paged newsletter promising to deliver "the most interesting news of passing events, general notices of progress of Mechanical and other Scientific Improvements; American and Foreign." The publication's masthead went on to become even more specific, outlining an impressive menu of essays on mechanics, chemistry, architecture, arts and trades, and even "curious philosophical experiments." Founded by Rufus Porter, an energetic and prolific inventor, the primary purpose of the early *Scientific American* was to promote inventions and inventors. The first issues presented an eclectic mix of science and technology information, poetry, humorous or philosophical anecdotes, and catalogues of recent patents. The publication's emphasis on patents, and its illustrations (at first in the form of woodcuts) from the first issue on, made it unique among other American magazines at the time.

Porter sold the magazine in 1846 to Orson Desaix Munn and inventor Alfred Ely Beach, whose father had founded the *New York Sun*. Under the management of Munn and Company, *Scientific American* expanded to eight pages, dropped the non-scientific content, and placed an even greater emphasis on inventions and patents, opening the first branch of the U.S. patent office in 1850. On January 1, 1945, *Time* magazine honored the one hundredth anniversary of *Scientific American*, writing: "A crusader from birth, the magazine has been in the thick of the hurly-burly of U.S. invention. Through its Manhattan editorial office trooped Morse, Gatling, the Maxim brothers, Edison, many another great inventors."

The magazine continued to grow with quickly expanding disciplines of science. In the early years of the twentieth century, it continued aggressively tracking advancements in transportation, offering stories about the automobile and airplane. *Scientific American* printed dozens of descriptive articles of technical experiments and successes in transportation, including a short article on December 26, 1903, noting the "successful experiments at Kitty Hawk, N.C. with an aeroplane." The magazine had already printed an illustration of the Wright brothers' airplane almost two years earlier. In 1921, *Scientific American* began publishing monthly. During that decade, the magazine continued its success in reporting on scientific and technological developments long before other media. Reports on television and the potential of space travel appeared in *Scientific American* before 1930. The magazine printed a detailed navigational description of Charles Lindbergh's historic transatlantic flight in 1927, covered the splitting of the atom in 1932, and looked ahead to postwar technology in a 1943 feature.

After more than a century of ownership, Munn & Company sold *Scientific American* in 1948 to *Life* magazine writer Gerard Piel, *Life* science editor Dennis Flanagan, and Donald H. Miller. Piel and Miller took over as publisher and general manager, respectively, with Flanagan editing the magazine. The three established Scientific American Inc. and shifted the authorship of *Scientific American* from exclusively staff to contributors from a variety of scientific backgrounds. From then on, the magazine's list of contributors expanded to impressive, and often well-known, men and women of scientific backgrounds. Guest writers included Albert Einstein, describing his general theory of gravitation in 1950, Jonas Salk reporting in 1955 on his development of a polio vaccine, Robert K. Jarvik writing of his Jarvik-7 artificial heart in 1981, and Francis Crick, writing about brain science in 1979.

By the end of the twentieth century, new technologies, global communication, and the still growing need for scientific information accessible to the general public combined to change *Scientific American's* geographic and technological reach. Flanagan retired as editor in 1984, leaving the magazine with a healthy circulation of more than six hundred thousand—up from forty thousand when he, Piel and Miller purchased it. Scientific American, Inc. was sold to a German publishing group in 1985, though the magazine continued to publish out of New York. In 1996, the magazine launched its web site, www.sciam.com. In 2001, the print version of the magazine unveiled its first extensive redesign since 1948. By the first few years of the twenty-first century, the magazine was publishing more than a dozen international editions in Europe, the Middle East, Asia, and South America. By 2006, the web site had grown to include interactive features, including a science blog and an "Ask the Experts" column, as well as a Science Talk podcast.

Further Reading

"50, 100 and 150 Years Ago." *Scientific American*, September 1995.
"A Century of Progress." *Time*, January 1, 1945.
"Transfusion." *Time*, October 6, 1947.
Triumph of Discovery: A Chronicle of Great Adventures in Science (150 Years of Scientific American). Edited by Scientific American. NY: Henry Holt and Co. 1995.

MEG SPRATT

SCOPES TRIAL

In the spring of 1925, the Butler Bill, which prohibited the teaching of evolution in public schools, became law in Tennessee. The law's constitutionality was questionable and the American Civil Liberties Union sought to challenge a piece of legislation it viewed as a threat to the separation of church and state.

When John Thomas Scopes was arrested for teaching evolution, the great "Monkey Trial" (July 10–21, 1925) soon commenced in Dayton, Tennessee. The case was essentially a religious rather than a constitutional battle, as well as a personal battle between fundamentalist leader and three-time candidate for president, William Jennings Bryan, and the famous jurist, Clarence Darrow. What ensued was called by many at the time the trial of the century, and was covered by more than two hundred journalists and such media notables as H.L. Mencken. In addition, the Scopes trial was broadcast by Chicago radio station WGN, whose coverage made the Dayton trial the first remote-control national radio hook-up in history.

The trial began Friday, July 10, and as it progressed, Mencken wrote, Bryan "grew more bitter. What the Christian Scientists call malicious animal magnetism seemed to radiate from him like heat from a stove" (*Baltimore Sun*, July 27, 1925).

Not until Monday, July 20, did the climatic battle between Bryan and Darrow take place when Bryan was called as a witness. What followed was an intense cross-examination witnessed outdoors by two thousand spectators as Darrow left Bryan literally slurring his words in defense of the fundamentalists' position on evolution. One journalist covering the trial, Paul Anderson, reported it in the simplest of terms: "Bryan was broken, if ever a man was broken. Darrow never spared him. It was masterly, but it was pitiful."

The next day the jury was given its charge. Nine minutes later it returned with a guilty verdict. The jury, significantly, fixed no fine but Judge John Raulston fined Scopes $100.

Five days later, on July 26, William Jennings Bryan died in his sleep.

Eleven months later the Tennessee Supreme Court ruled in *Tennessee vs. Scopes* that under the state constitution any fine of more than $50 must be levied by the jury. The judgment, therefore, was reversed, not on the constitutional issues the defense hoped for but on a technicality. Of course, the case could still be appealed to a federal court except for one minor point: Upon the suggestion of the Tennessee Supreme Court, the attorney general entered a *nolle prosequi*, which meant the original indictment was dropped. Now there was nothing to appeal. The case, indeed, had finally ended.

Given its rather inauspicious ending, one is left to wonder about the legacy of the Scopes. It probably marked a high point of the fundamentalist movement for that time. As scientists, writers, and intellectuals mounted attacks against the opponents of evolution, favorable press coverage of fundamentalism faded. Within two years of the trial, anti-evolution laws had been repealed in ten states that had them. Following the trial, John Scopes quietly entered graduate school at the University of Chicago where he earned a masters' degree in geology.

Further Reading

de Camp L. Sprague. *The Great Monkey Trial*. Garden City, NY: Doubleday & Company, 1968), 408.

Glock, Charles Y. and Rodney Stark. *Religion and Society in Tension*. Chicago: Rand McNally and Company, 1965, 242.

Ginger, Ray. *Six Days or Forever*. Boston: Beacon Press, 1958, 191.

Scopes, John Thomas and James Presley. *Center of the Storm*. New York: Holt, Rinehart and Winston, 95–96.

Sheldon Norman Grebstein, ed. *Monkey Trial*. Boston: Houghton Mifflin Company, 1960, ix.

The World's Most Famous Court Trial: State of Tennessee v. John Thomas Scopes [Complete Stenographic Report of the Court Test of the Tennessee Anti-Evolution Act at Dayton, July 19, 1925, Including Speeches and Arguments by Attorneys]. New York: Da Capo Press, 1971, 47.

Zetterberg, Peter ed. *Evolution versus Creationism: The Public Education Controversy*. Phoenix, AZ: Oryx Press, 1983.

LLOYD CHIASSON JR.

SCRIPPS, E. W.

E. W. (Edward Willis) Scripps (1854–1926) built one of the nation's first successful media empires, which included a chain of newspapers, a features syndicate, and a wire service. The Scripps chain served small and medium-sized cities mostly in the Midwest and West. Scripps papers were known for their political independence, reforming zeal and working class orientation, as well as their hostility to the influence of advertisers in the news columns. During his life, Scripps started or purchased more than forty newspapers. Through a combination of shrewd management and fact-based journalism, Scripps attracted readers and earned substantial profits.

Scripps was born in Illinois in 1854, the youngest of thirteen children. His career in journalism began at age eighteen when he took a position as minority stockholder and circulation solicitor for the *Detroit Evening News*, a cheap, working-class paper managed by several of his older siblings. His ambition for greater control over newspaper affairs propelled him to the city editor's desk, where he showed great skill at putting together a popular paper. That ambition soon moved Scripps to demand his own paper and, after pressuring his older brothers, he was able to start the *Cleveland Press* in 1878. By the end of the decade, Scripps controlled all of the family newspaper properties, and had purchased or founded many more, often in conjunction with business partner Milton McRae.

Scripps' political leanings tended toward reform, civic improvement, and sympathy with the "common man." He believed that newspapers performed a vital function in the democratic process by spreading the information necessary for self-government, but only when they were free of partisan or commercial influence. The Scripps papers supported labor unions and workers' rights. They also joined Progressive era crusades against government corruption, political bosses, unfair business practices, and dangerous consumer goods. To minimize pressure from advertisers, Scripps prohibited full-page ads and sought patronage from family-owned neighborhood businesses and refused advertising from any business or organization that attempted to shape news content. Chicago's *Day Book* (1911–1917) was an unsuccessful attempt to publish a newspaper entirely without advertising.

Several common tactics formed the base of the Scripps business plan. This was an era of intense local newspaper competition and several other entrepreneurs, most notably William Randolph Hearst, aggressively developed national chains. First, Scripps sought markets in which he could successfully compete on a limited budget. He generally avoided the big cities on the East Coast and instead operated in places like Kansas City, Dallas, and San Diego where there were fewer rivals. Scripps positioned his paper as a morning edition if there was a successful afternoon publication, and vice versa. He worked hard to avoid direct competition with Hearst and other powerful publishers. Scripps was also aware of market segmentation. Most newspapers of the era were either partisan or written for the business class. Scripps hunted markets where there was no "penny paper" so he could capitalize on what was in most cases an untapped reader base. His papers included many cartoons, jokes, and columns written in a very simple, direct style that was interesting as well as informative. Excited to have a paper that spoke for them, working class readers responded by buying Scripps papers.

Other aspects of Scripps' newspaper management involved cost-cutting tactics. He looked to buy newspapers at below-market values or to set up a new paper in a part of town where expenses would be minimal. Scripps papers often operated with used presses and heavily worn type. Reporters in this era were notoriously underpaid, and Scripps tended to pay less than anyone, even if it meant losing talented staff. According to one scholar, reporters sometimes had to furnish their own stationary, pencils, and even toilet paper, in addition to sweeping out the office at the end of the day. Many employees, however, were given the opportunity to own stock in the company to augment their meager earnings. To save newsgathering and production costs, Scripps papers were usually limited to four to eight pages and printed with narrow margins on the cheapest available newsprint. This also limited the space for advertising, which ensured that advertiser pressure would be minimized.

The cost of newsgathering also factors in Scripps' establishment of a features syndicate and other mechanisms for sharing content among his papers. Each newspaper was required to provide its local news to the members of the chain at no cost, thus giving each paper access to news from around the nation. Many rival newspapers made use of the Associated Press wire service, but obtaining an AP franchise was difficult and expensive. Scripps initiated his own wire service, which eventually became the United Press International after mergers and acquisitions, to provide copy to the chain newspapers. The wire service later became a significant source of income for the company as a competitor to the AP, but it initially served as a low-cost alternative for the chain. The syndicate that eventually became the Newspaper Enterprise Association, in 1902, had the same premise. Illustrations, cartoons, and feature columns created at one Scripps newspaper made the rounds to the rest of the papers. One content analysis has demonstrated that Scripps papers tended to carry less local news than the average newspaper of the time. Scripps required his papers to carry the wire service and syndicate material because gathering local news required an active staff of reporters and increased operational costs.

Scripps' personal life was somewhat eccentric. He married Nackie Benson Holtsinger in 1885 and together they had six children. However, Scripps had affairs and was fairly open about having mistresses in different cities that he visited on business. He also was a heavy drinker and, at times, reclusive. One of his life-long interests was a large ranch, called Miromar, outside of San Diego. Scripps spent a great deal of time there while maintaining close control over his newspaper empire from a distance. He also loved the sea and spent much of the last decade of his life traveling on his yacht, the *Ohio*. He died on the ship on March 12, 1926.

Further Reading

Baldasty Gerald. *E.W. Scripps and the Business of Newspapers.* Urbana: University of Illinois Press, 1999.

Gardner, Gilson. *Lusty Scripps.* New York: Vanguard, 1932.

Knight, Oliver H., ed. *I Protest: Selected Disquisitions of E.W. Scripps.* Madison: University of Wisconsin Press, 1966.

McGabe, Charles R. *Damned Old Crank.* New York: Harper, 1951.

Trimble, Vance H. *The Astonishing Mr. Scripps: The Turbulent Life of America's Penny Press Lord.* Ames: Iowa State University Press, 1992.

ROBERT A. RABE

SCRIPPS-HOWARD

In a long and tumultuous career, E. W. Scripps burned through many partnerships. When Scripps plucked Roy W. Howard from the editorial desk of his flagship Cincinnati *Post* to manage the newly created United Press in 1908, however, he not only found an amicable partner but a steward who would guide Scripps' newspaper empire until his heirs were ready to assume leadership. In 1999, Scripps and Howard were named by *Editor and Publisher* magazine as two of the top twenty-five most influential newspaper figures of the 20th century.

In 1895, E. W. Scripps took on a partner, Milton A. McRae, to help direct his newspaper enterprises, which he referred to collectively as "The Concern." McRae retired in 1905, but his heirs would remain involved in the Scripps-McRae League until the 1920s.

As he continued to expand his newspaper chain, Scripps was frustrated by the monopolistic practices of the Associated Press—which would not sell its wire services to upstart papers in markets where it had established customers. After the turn of the century, Scripps began to lay the groundwork for a rival service to supply his own papers with wire news—and to profit by selling that news to other papers.

Characteristically avoiding a grand and risky strategy, Scripps did not found and market the United Press (UP) overnight. Instead, he quietly acquired the means to form a rival national wire service in small portions. Between 1900 and 1906, he and his partner organized the Scripps and McRae Press Association, a small wire service, in the Midwest and the Scripps News service on the West Coast. The final piece of the puzzle was a small wire service called the Publishers Press, which Scripps and McRae acquired in 1906.

Scripps launched the United Press in 1907 and chose John Vandercook to serve as general news manager. Within a year, however, Vandercook died and Scripps tapped Roy Howard to take his place.

Enter Roy Howard

Roy Wilson Howard was born in Ohio in 1883. After high school, he worked at the *Indianapolis News* for $8 per week. After stints at the *Indianapolis Star* and the *St. Louis Post-Dispatch*, Howard took a position as assistant managing editor of Scripps' *Cincinnati Post*. After four years as general news manager of the UP, he was appointed president in 1912.

E. W. Scripps had a brilliant business mind but he also possessed an abrasive personality (even the company's Web site describes the founder as "a tough customer"). As his news empire and personal wealth grew, he increasingly lived like a hermit at Minimar, his San Diego estate, and on his yachts. Beginning in 1918, he suffered a series of strokes, which some family members said led him to make irrational personal and professional decisions thereafter.

Howard, in contrast to his mentor and benefactor, was a dynamic raconteur who traveled widely and loved to practice the newsman's trade. In his memoir *Damned Old Crank,* Scripps described Howard as "a striking individual, very small of stature, with a large head and speaking countenance, and eyes that appeared to be windows for a rather unusual intellect. His manner was forceful, and the reverse from modest. Gall was written all over his face. It was in every tone and every word he voiced. There was ambition, self-respect and forcefulness oozing out of every pore of his body."

At United Press, Howard interviewed world leaders and personally took charge of the wire service's coverage of World War I. The UP scored many scoops over the Associated Press during the war, but Howard was responsible for its most infamous story: In 1918, he erroneously reported, based on a forged diplomatic dispatch, that an armistice had been signed four days before the actual end of the war. His flash ignited celebrations across America. Rival Associated Press took great pleasure in reporting a few hours later that the UP bulletin was in error; the gaffe tarnished the reputation of the United Press for years to come.

Despite his momentous error, Howard made the United Press a great success. When he became president of UP at age 29 in 1912, it was strictly an evening service of from 10,000-12,000 words per day. Howard encouraged livelier writing and feature stories. In 1919, he inaugurated morning service. UP had 392 clients in 1909 and 745 in 1919.

E. W. Scripps, meanwhile, had begun an extended retirement in 1908. He chose his son James to run the family business in his stead, but the two feuded constantly. James also feuded with his brother Robert and tried to thwart the younger man's rise in the company. In 1920, dissatisfied with James' leadership and tired of arguing with him, E. W. chose Robert and Roy Howard to run the Scripps-McRae League, which was renamed Scripps-Howard in 1922. James left the company, taking seven newspapers with him to start his own chain, but he died suddenly in 1921. E.W. Scripps died on his yacht, Ohio, off the coast of Liberia in 1926.

Now fully in charge of the company, Roy Howard and Robert Paine Scripps worked well together, according to a statement by Howard that appears in Sidney Kobre's *Foundations of American Journalism*: "Bob Scripps and I are as different as it is possible for two men to be. Ours is a most fortunate combination. Our faults seem to checkmate each other and our abilities to supplement each other."

While Robert shared his father's pro-worker, liberal political views, Howard dominated the company's newspapers and took their editorial direction in a more conservative direction. He was chilly towards organized labor, opposed President Franklin D. Roosevelt's court reorganization scheme and endorsed Republican Wendell Wilkie in his bid to unseat Roosevelt in 1940; Scripps newspapers would not endorse a Democrat again until 1960.

Robert P. Scripps died in 1938— on a yacht, as his father had—and Howard and two other Scripps executives ran the company as trustees until the next generation of Scrippses came of age. The company branched into radio in the 1930s and into television in the 1940s.

The Next Generation

In 1953 Charles E. Scripps, grandson of E. W. Scripps, was named Chairman of the Board of the E. W. Scripps Co. and Roy Howard's son, Jack, was named president. Roy Howard became president and editor of the firm's *New York World Telegram and Sun*. He died in 1964.

In 1960, after a decade of mergers and acquisitions, Scripps-Howard was the nation's largest newspaper chain, with twenty dailies and eight Sunday papers. Its newspapers were in head-to-head competition in only half of their markets.

The corporate organization of E.W. Scripps' many enterprises has a tangled and complicated history. As "The Concern" branched into ancillary enterprises, Scripps-Howard became a distinct division largely responsible for newspapers and broadcast stations.

Headquartered in Cincinnati, in 2006 the enterprise operated as the E.W. Scripps Company and the Scripps-Howard News Service was just one of its many media properties. The E. W. Scripps Company went public in 1988 but

family members maintain majority ownership and administer the company through a trust.

The E. W. Scripps Company owned twenty-one newspapers in 2006 and was the ninth largest newspaper publisher in the country. It also controlled or owned a stake in broadcast television stations, cable channels such as the Food Network and the Shop at Home Network, online media ventures, and the United Media syndicate. In a July 2005 interview with the author, Director of Communication and Investor Relations Mark Kroeger explained that a major re-branding in 1982 diminished the use of the Howard name in corporate enterprises, but the legacy of the partnership between the Scripps and Howard families lives on in the company's news service and the philanthropic Scripps-Howard foundation.

The E. W. Scripps Co. had approximately 7,355 full-time employees and 1,568 part-time employees and in 2004 reported revenues of nearly $2.2 billon; signaling the company's shift in new media directions, news and newspapers accounted for less than a third of that revenue. The company continued to use the motto Roy W. Howard adopted in 1922: "Give light and the people will find their own way."

Further Reading

Anon. "Our Pioneers," http://scripps.com/heritage/history.html (accessed April 10, 2007).

Baldasty, Gerald J. *E.W. Scripps and the Business of Newspapers.* Urbana and Chicago: University of Illinois Press, 1999.

Casserly, Jack. *Scripps: The Divided Dynasty.* New York: Donald I. Fine, Inc., 1993.

Gordon, Gregory. *Down to the Wire: UPI's Fight for Survival.* New York: McGraw Hill, 1990.

Stewart, Kenneth and John Tebbel. "Scripps-Howard" in *Highlights in the History of the American Press,* edited by Edwin Hopkins Ford and Edwin Emery. Minneapolis: University of Minnesota Press, 1954.

MIKE DILLON

SENGSTACKE, JOHN H.

John Sengstacke (November 25, 1912–May 28, 1997) emerged as a leading black newspaper publisher in World War II, when he was a strong advocate for more press rights as well as more racial equality despite intense government pressure for he and other black publishers to desist. After the war, despite a rapid decline in both circulation and influence on black newspapers, he continued as an outspoken advocate for black rights and published the *Chicago Defender* for fifty-seven years until his death in 1997, by which time he had established sixteen other black papers.

He was born on November 25, 1912, in Savannah, Georgia, and went to grade school in Woodville in the central part of the state. After graduating from Brick Junior College in North Carolina in 1929, he earned a business administration degree from Hampton Institute in Virginia in 1934. He later studied not only at Chicago's Mergenthaler Linotype School and the School of Printing but took business administration courses at Northwestern University and journalism classes at Ohio State University.

Sengstacke's first newspaper experience was on a paper owned by his father, the *Woodville Times*, where his jobs included advertising, editing, and printing. After his graduation from Hampton, his uncle, Robert Abbott, named him vice president and treasurer of the Robert S. Abbott Publishing Company, which published the *Defender* where Sengstacke had worked on summer vacations, and a year later he was named general manager. Abbott started the weekly newspaper in 1905 and had made it the country's largest and most influential black paper by the 1910s, when it developed a sensationalistic style that played up black inequalities and was one of the major factors causing an increase in the black migration from the South into the North. At one point in the 1920s, it had about 250,000 paid circulation and even more readership as it was estimated that for every paid subscription another two and five people looked at each copy.

As Abbott's health declined sharply in the late 1930s, Sengstacke virtually ran the *Defender* and then became president upon his uncle's death in 1940. Although the paper had severe financial setbacks during the Depression, he quickly turned it around and reestablished it as one of the country's top two black newspapers along with the *Pittsburgh Courier*, which had overtaken the Chicago paper in circulation and influence in the 1930s.

In 1940, Sentstacke quickly established himself as a leader in the black newspaper industry by holding a three-day meeting of black publishers in Chicago for the purpose of "harmonizing our energies in a common purpose for the benefit of Negro journalism." Nineteen newspapers sent representatives and out of the meeting came the Negro Newspaper Publishers Association (NNPA), which later was renamed the National Newspaper Publishers Association. While there had been various national organizations of black publishers and editors for all but five years since 1875, the NNPA would become the longest lasting of them, and Sengstacke would be its president six times.

During World War II, the NNPA, whose member papers had a circulation of about five million, had several notable accomplishments. On February 5, 1944, following a request by Sengstacke, President Franklin D. Roosevelt met with thirteen editors and publishers of the NNPA for thirty-five minutes. Then, three days later, Harry McAlpin of the *Atlanta Daily World* became the first black White House correspondent. This followed NNPA negotiations with the White House with Sengstacke playing a major role.

Sengstacke's biggest accomplishment during the war may have been a concession that Sengstacke got from U.S. Attorney General Francis Biddle during a meeting in June 1942. After Biddle said black newspapers were hurting the war effort by continually playing up racial injustices and criticizing the government, he threatened to take some of the publishers to court. Sengstacke retorted that black newspapers had always written this type of material and were not about to stop. At the end of their meeting, Biddle agreed to not indict any of the black publishers if they did

not become more critical, but he hoped they would tone down their criticism. Sengstacke happily passed this on to the other publishers.

Following the war, despite battling a downturn in circulation and influence on his paper, Sengstacke became the country's most prominent black publisher. In 1956, he turned the *Defender* into one of the country's few daily black newspapers; he helped found a major firm selling advertising space in black papers; and he was appointed to various positions by four U.S. presidents. But nothing showed his prestige more than in 1970 when he became the first black elected to the board of directors of the American Society of Newspaper Editors. As the *New York Times* wrote after his death, "Citizen Sengstacke ...was not just a publisher; he was a national power center" who "embodied the Negro press" (January 4, 1998).

Further Reading

Ottley, Roi. *The Lonely Warrior: The Life and Times of Robert S. Abbott*. Chicago: Henry Regnery, 1955.

Pride, Armistead S., and Clint C. Wilson II. *A History of the Black Press*. Washington, D.C.: Howard University Press, 1997.

Staples, Brent. "Citizen Sengstacke." *New York Times*, Jan. 4, 1998.

Thomas, Robert McG. Jr. "John Sengstacke, Black Publisher, Dies at 84." *New York Times*, May 30, 1997.

Washburn, Patrick S. *A Question of Sedition: The Federal Government's Investigation of the Black Press During World War II*. New York: Oxford University Press, 1986.

Wolseley, Roland E. *The Black Press, U.S.A.: A Detailed and Understanding Report of What the Black Press Is and How It Came to Be*. Ames: Iowa State University Press, 1971.

PATRICK S. WASHBURN

SEVAREID, ERIC

Growing up in the 1960s and 1970s necessarily meant waiting for the *CBS Evening News* where Eric Sevareid (1912–1992) offered perspective and analysis on two of America's most tumultuous decades. It had been a generation before on CBS Radio in 1940, as Sevareid reported the fall of France and the Battle of Britain, that Americans first became familiar with the voice that long-time colleague Dan Rather described as "deeply calming and extraordinarily authoritative." Andy Rooney considered Sevareid "the best thinker and writer that broadcast journalism has ever had." Winner of three Peabody awards and two Emmys, Sevareid helped invent broadcast journalism, observing he had spent a lifetime "trying to look at America, but in the end find myself looking with America" ("Eric Sevareid Remembered").

Arnold Eric Sevareid was born in Velva, North Dakota, on the southern bank of the Mouse River, as it swirls past the geographical center of North America, above a bluff where the Indian maiden Sakakawea introduced Lewis and Clark to the New World. Veteran CBS News broadcaster Charles Kuralt thought Sevareid "had Jefferson's rural ideal of what America could be." ("Eric Sevareid") Sevareid long remembered the "huddled community of painted boards" in his youth where "wheat made all men essentially equal" (Sevareid 1976, 6). His father, Alfred Eric Sevareid, a second generation Norwegian pioneer, was the town banker and hired man. His mother, Clare Pauline Elizabeth Hougen, was the daughter of an itinerant Lutheran minister. It was in the town's library, next door to his father's bank, that young Sevareid spent his weekends reading, the books taking him places that seemed "more beautiful and more real" than his actual surroundings (Sevareid 1976, 5).

Drought and bankruptcy forced the family to move to Minot in 1925 and Minneapolis a year later, where Sevareid edited the high school newspaper. After graduating in 1930, he and a friend took a twenty-two hundred mile canoe trip up to Hudson Bay. The adventure became the basis of his first book, *Canoeing with the Cree*, published five years later. By that time, Sevareid was a newspaper veteran, having graduated the University of Minnesota, where he majored in political science and economics and reported the Depression as a short-lived socialist for the *Minnesota Daily*, before moving on to the *Minneapolis Journal*, where he received death threats after going undercover to report on the Silver Shirts, a local fascist group. On May 18, 1935, Sevareid married Lois Finger, student leader and law school graduate.

The Sevareids sailed for Europe in the fall of 1937, where he edited the Paris edition of the *New York Herald-Tribune* and reported preparations for war as night editor of United Press. Edward R. Murrow was impressed by the quality of Sevareid's writing and hired him as a radio reporter for CBS News in August 1939. A month later Sevareid reported to American listeners the outbreak of World War II. After the birth of twin boys in April 1940, Sevareid sent his family home and became on June 16 the first journalist to report the surrender of France. As German storm troopers high stepped past the Place de la Concorde down the Champs Elysees before a beaming Adolph Hitler at the Arc de Triomphe, Sevareid famously reported "Paris lay inert, her breathing scarcely audible, her limbs relaxed and her blood flowing remorselessly through her manifold veins. Paris was dying like a beautiful woman in coma, not knowing or asking why" ("Eric Sevareid").

Sevareid joined Murrow in London to report "an endless summer" of mass bombing raids that marked the Battle of Britain. Sevareid noted that civilian response to "the frightful terror" gave the war "a positive meaning" in which class differences dissolved, creating a democracy of communal courage. Murrow's relentless reporting which captured the essence of the lived moment also inspired him as "the first great literary artist of a new medium of communication." Sevareid had also developed an international following. He concluded his final London broadcast in October 1940 by reporting, "When all this is over, in the days to come, men will speak of this war, and they will say: I was a soldier, or I was a sailor, or I was a pilot; and others will say with equal pride: I was a citizen of London"(Sevareid 1976, 166–179).

In the fall of 1940, Sevareid began a lecture tour across America, urging the country to be ready for war. Based in Washington, he reported on the Roosevelt administration's preparations for war, occasionally clashing with CBS chief William Paley, who wanted the network to maintain a strict neutrality. In August of 1943, Sevareid had to parachute into Burma, when a transport plane developed engine trouble. He walked out of the Assam jungle a month later and went on to report war news in Chungking, during the Allied advance in Italy and among guerilla fighters in Yugoslavia. He accompanied American troops to southern France and crossed the Rhine on their final assault into Germany. Near the end of the war he reported, "Only the soldier really lives the war. The journalist does not. War happens inside a man. It can never be communicated. A million martyred lives leave an empty place at only one family table. That is why, at bottom, people can let wars happen" ("Eric Sevareid").

After the war Sevareid reported on the founding of the United Nations and became the network's chief Washington correspondent, leading their election coverage as CBS News transitioned to television. Kuralt considered Sevareid's "a giant of a broadcaster," whose "fine large head set on broad shoulders" made him "look the part." But Sevareid was "never really very comfortable with television." The lights and cameras distracted him. Sevareid had been told "to see in my mind's eye a small group of friends before me. What really happened is that I began to feel a different presence in the studio, the presence of America" ("Eric Sevareid").

Beginning in the fall of 1963 and for the following fourteen years, Sevareid delivered four hundred-word, two-and-one-half minute long news analysis three and four times weekly on the *CBS Evening News*. At the height of the Vietnam War and Watergate crises in 1973 and 1974, twenty million Americans in 16 percent of all U.S. households, tuned in. Many shared the sentiment of veteran CBS news producer Don Hewitt who said, "Eric Sevareid has a better fix on America" than anyone in public life" ("Eric Sevareid"). Sevareid was guided by the principle that "democracy is not a free ride. It demands more of its citizens than any other arrangement. There can be no rights or privileges without responsibility" ("Eric Sevareid"). He was an early critic of the Viet Nam War, stating on June 21, 1966, that the Johnson administration was transforming a civil war into an international crisis. He had little sympathy for violent student protesters, charging on December 5, 1966, that they were the most privileged generation in American history. He had contempt for Richard Nixon whose administration labored "not to destroy opponents arguments, but in destroying opponents personally" and in the end "destroyed itself" (Schroth 1975, 390).

CBS News President Bill Leonard believed Sevareid was more responsible than any individual for "creating broadcast journalism that inspired millions." It had been Sevareid's view that the deadly realities of the twentieth century made the period "the age of the journalist, more than the age of the artist, the teacher or the pastor." That was why "there has never been a generation where it's been such a privilege to be a journalist." Washington had been "the greatest news center since ancient Rome." But the real story had been "the American people and their tough, undiminished instinct for what is fair" ("Eric Sevareid").

Sevareid's final work was the fifty-year remembrance of Pearl Harbor. He reported "We can never forget what we have seen of human stamina and resilience, and we know that the special vitality of the American people remains within them" ("Eric Sevareid"). That gave Sevareid reason to hope that the nation's greatest days might still be before it. After his death, Andy Rooney of *60 Minutes* spoke for many when he said, "If you had to pick the single greatest broadcast journalist there ever was, you'd pick Eric Sevareid. I feel sorry for all the people too young to know how great he was" ("Eric Sevareid").

Further Reading

Bliss, Jr., Edward J. *Now the News: The History of Broadcast Journalism.* New York: Columbia University Press, 1991.

Cloud, Stanley, and Lynne Olson. *The Murrow Boys: Pioneers on the Front Lines of Broadcast Journalism.* Boston: Houghton Mifflin, 1996.

"Eric Sevareid Remembered." *CBS News Special Report*, July 9, 1992.

Halberstam, David. *The Powers That Be.* New York: Alfred A. Knopf, 1979.

Leonard, Bill. *In the Eye of the Storm: A Lifetime with CBS.* New York: G.P. Putnam's Sons, 1987.

Matusow, Barbara. *The Evening Stars.* Boston: Houghton Mifflin, 1983.

Papers of Eric Sevareid, 1930–1992. Library of Congress. Washington, D.C.

Schroth, Raymond A. *The American Journey of Eric Sevareid.* South Royalton, VT: Steerforth Press, 1995.

Sevareid, Eric, ed. *Candidates 1960: Behind the Headlines in the Presidential Race.* New York: Basic Books, 1959.

——. *Canoeing with the Cree.* New York: Macmillan, 1935.

——, ed. *Conversations with Eric Sevareid: Interviews with Notable Americans.* Washington: Public Affairs Press, 1976.

——. *In One Ear.* New York: Alfred A. Knopf, 1952.

——. *Not So Wild a Dream.* New York: Atheneum, 1976, originally 1946.

——. *Small Sounds in the Night.* New York: Alfred A. Knopf, 1956.

——. *This Is Eric Sevareid.* New York: McGraw-Hill, 1967.

Smith, Sally Bedell. *In All His Glory: The Life of William Paley, the Legendary Tycoon and His Brilliant Circle.* New York: Simon and Schuster, 1990.

BRUCE J. EVENSEN

SINCLAIR, UPTON

Upton Beall Sinclair Jr. (September 20, 1878–November 25, 1968) has been called the "king of the muckrakers," a cadre of Progressive Era journalists who exposed corruption in politics and corporate America during the decade and a half before the United States's involvement in World War I. Although journalists best remember Sinclair for the *Brass Check* (1920), an exposé of how reliance on advertising corrupts the press, it was *The Jungle* (1906), a fictional account based on research in the Chicago stockyards that exposed barbaric working conditions and unsanitary processes, that brought him national attention. *The Jungle* often is credited with mobilizing the necessary public outrage to force meat

and drug inspection laws through Congress, where corporate interests had stalled the legislation. Some also claim *The Jungle* pioneered such techniques as coupling first-hand research with fictional devices, used by so-called New Journalism practitioners during the 1960s and 1970s.

Sinclair, however, differed from other muckrakers in ways that added to his historical significance and eventual prominence. He was ten years younger than the median age for the muckrakers as a group and continued writing what contemporaries called "the literature of exposure" well beyond muckraking's high-water mark in the first decade of the 1900s. He was able to do this by self-publishing many of his important works while his colleagues generally worked for and published in magazines geared to middle-class audiences. A prolific writer, Sinclair's works have been translated into more than forty languages. One of his bibliographers credits Sinclair with eighty-six major books and countless magazine articles, pamphlets, speeches, plays, and works in other than print media. Sinclair was a committed ideologue who espoused Socialism in his writings as the solution for the excesses of capitalism. A tireless self-promoter, he repeatedly fell from public attention during his ninety-year life only to reinvent himself—first as an unsuccessful writer of fiction, then as a muckraker and critic of American institutions, next as a politician, and finally as the author of a series of popular historical novels.

Sinclair was born in Baltimore to an alcoholic traveling salesman and the daughter of a well-to-do family. Both parents had their roots in the old South aristocracy, and many relatives had suffered financial reverses because of the Civil War. Sinclair grew to early adulthood during the Gilded Age, when obsession with success through hard work, ingenuity, and perseverance was almost universal in American society. His family's failures and his own early reverses quickly taught him that hard work did not guarantee success and undoubtedly led to his own preoccupation with obtaining social justice for the working class.

He did not attend public schools until age ten. A few months before his fourteenth birthday, he began classes in the City College of New York. After completing his bachelor's, Columbia University admitted him as a special student. He spent the next four years studying literature and philosophy. Sinclair supported his college studies by writing freelance pieces, especially "half-dime novels" for a publisher of juvenile fiction. After Columbia, Sinclair moved to the Canadian woods to try writing serious fiction, generally with poor results, and married the first of three wives. He divorced the first and outlived the others.

A patron introduced him to socialism and he joined the Socialist Party in 1904 and became a contributor to *Appeal to Reason*, a Socialist weekly that serialized *The Jungle* in 1905. Although Sinclair had a working-class audience in mind as he did the first-hand observations in the Chicago meat packinghouses upon which the book is based, his completed manuscript resonated with middle-class readers and politicians, who worked quickly to pass reform legislation. Sinclair later wrote other fictionalized muckraking accounts such as *King Coal* (1917) and *Oil!* (1927) but he is better known for the "Dead Hand" series and the "Lanny Budd" historical novels. Published between 1918 and 1927, the six books in the "Dead Hand" series offer a systematic critique of organized religion, the press, public and higher education, artists, and writers. Sinclair began writing the eleven volumes in the "Lanny Budd" series after his nearly successful race for the governorship of California on the Democratic ticket in 1934. The third book in the series, *Dragon's Teeth* (1942), won a Pulitzer Prize in 1943. The books chronicle the international adventures of a single protagonist between 1911 and 1950. Besides the 1934 gubernatorial race, Sinclair ran unsuccessfully on the Socialist ticket for the U. S. House, U. S. Senate, and the California governorship. He was one of the founders of the American Civil Liberties Union and its Southern California affiliate. An active commentator on public affairs to the end of his life, his last book-length work, an autobiography, was published in 1962.

Further Reading

Harris, Leon. *Upton Sinclair: American Rebel.* New York: Thomas Y. Crowell, 1975.

Mattson, Kevin. *Upton Sinclair and the Other American Century.* Hoboken, NJ: John Wiley & Sons, 2006.

Mitchell, Greg. *The Campaign of the Century: Upton Sinclair's Race for Governor of California and the Birth of Media Politics.* New York; Random House, 1992.

Reaves, Shiela. "How Radical Were the Muckrakers? Socialist Press Views, 1902–1906." *Journalism Quarterly* 61, no. 4 (1984): 763–770.

Sinclair, Upton B. *Autobiography.* New York: Harcourt, Brace & World, 1962.

Stein, Harry H. "American Muckrakers and Muckraking: The 50-Year Scholarship." *Journalism Quarterly* 56, no. 1 (1979): 9–17.

RANDALL S. SUMPTER

SMITH, HOWARD K.

"Truth is not equidistant between right and wrong," Howard K. Smith (May 12, 1914–February 15, 2002) wrote in his eighty-second year, looking back on a forty-year career covering Adolf Hitler, Joseph McCarthy, the Ku Klux Klan, and the collapse of the Berlin Wall. "All that is necessary for the triumph of evil is for good men to do nothing," he had wanted to say quoting Edmund Burke at the end of a 1961 television documentary. But CBS Chairman William S. Paley objected, so Smith, one of "Murrow's boys," switched to ABC, and helped establish the network's credibility as co-anchor and commentator on the *ABC Evening News.*

Howard K. Smith, a night watchman for the Missouri Pacific Railroad, married Minnie Gates, daughter of a Cajun riverboat captain, and lived in Ferriday, Louisiana, a small river town one big bend above Natchez. Howard Kingsbury Smith, the youngest of their three small children, would witness the fall of the Third Reich, the coming of the Cold War, the rise of American racism, and would one day write the political obituary of Richard Nixon. From an early age, Smith saw himself as "an observer of events." Feeling "rootless" and "alienated from my region" he decided to embark on a journalist's life of "skepticism and discovery."

Smith lettered in track and was elected class president at Tulane University. His mother's death just before graduation in 1936 made it "the most miserable time of my life." He spent a tuition-free summer studying at Heidelberg University and found Germans "enthusiastic" over Hitler's militarization of the Rhineland. Smith made $15 a week as a beginning reporter on the *New Orleans Item*, where "I did a lot of phoning and honing" general assignment stories. As a young reporter, he interviewed Franklin Roosevelt during a visit to New Orleans and thought the president "somewhere between God and Abraham Lincoln." In September, 1937, as a Rhodes Scholar in Europe, Smith saw Hitler at Munich's opera house and wondered how such "an ordinary, mild-looking man" could have "Germans cheering and saluting," while "the world trembled before him." At Oxford, Smith learned "to relax and drink" as Neville Chamberlain's "policy of appeasement" failed to satisfy Hitler's "raging paranoia." By early 1939 "the world seemed to come apart." Hitler dismembered Czechoslovakia. His opponents seemed paralyzed in fear. Smith's "only relief from despair" was writing for a Labour periodical, where he castigated those "afraid to confront the Antichrist." Hitler invaded Poland on September 1. Two days later, Britain declared war on Germany. On that day, Smith went to London's Fleet Street and on the strength of his German-language skills got a job with United Press. Immediately joining him there was Charles Collingwood, a close colleague through their years as broadcast journalists.

Smith filed stories in Copenhagen on Russia's attack in Finland. He arrived at the United Press office in Berlin on January 1, 1940, where he was teamed with Richard Hottelet, another man who would make his mark in network news. At Foreign Office briefings Smith was given with other reporters "the Leader's line." Despite exhaustive efforts, "interviews with members of the political power structure were way off limits." When he approached "torture-master" Heinrich Himmler, who appeared to "a pale-looking office drudge" with a question, SS men pushed Smith away. Smith wrote "night leads" for evening newspapers in the United States, detailing fighting along German's Western Front beginning on May 10, 1940. He flew to the Rhine and reported from casemates and pillboxes along France's ruined Maginot Line. Smith thought "Britain's situation now seemed hopeless." In late August, however, he was able to report that Britain's first bombers had reached Berlin. Smith reported the firebombing throughout September, despite efforts by the Germany's Propaganda Ministry to limit access to bomb sites and unscheduled Gestapo raids on UP's Wehrmacht office, beginning in early 1941.

In the spring of 1941, Smith began filing stories for the *New York Times* and reporting for CBS News. Collingwood and Hottelet soon joined him. He was struck by Edward R. Murrow's reports from London and his "talent for finding the essence of things" while "describing it in thrifty, fine prose." Smith's one minute, fifteen second broadcasts to America were heard twice daily as the Battle of Britain raged. On June 22, 1941, he reported the foreign ministry announcement that Germany had launched an attack against the Red Army along its Russian front. Eight hundred thousand Russian prisoners and twelve thousand tanks were taken in the first month of fighting. Smith reported the Fuhrer's October 3 declaration at Berlin's Sportsplast that 2.5 million Russians were prisoners. As war in the East bogged down, however, Foreign Office censors ordered Smith to read their account of the fighting. He refused. In November, he was banned from broadcasting in Germany. He filed stories for the *Times* under an alias. On November 30, Smith became engaged to a Danish journalist Benedicte Traberg after a four-day courtship. They would be married for sixty years and have two children. Six days later, on December 6, 1941, Smith became the last American reporter to leave Berlin. The next day Japan attacked Pearl Harbor and the United States was drawn into the war.

From Switzerland, Smith wrote *Last Train from Berlin*, a bestseller widely circulated in Occupied Europe and throughout the United States. From Bern, Smith reported on fighting in the Balkans for CBS radio and *Time*. In 1944 he reported on the French resistance at Plateau de Glieres. By late summer he was reporting for CBS from Allied Headquarters in Versailles. In Paris he met William S. Paley, CBS network founder, and Murrow, who had become the network's chief European Correspondent. Along with Hottelet, Collingwood, Eric Severaid, Larry LeSeuer, Winston Burdett, and Bill Downs, Smith became one of "Murrow's boys," groomed for leadership roles in the fast-emerging world of broadcast journalism. Smith followed the fighting through the Low Countries and Germany until the end of the war, including the decisive Battle of the Bulge that produced nearly two hundred thousand casualties. He was the American pool correspondent who reported the surrender of German forces to Russian Marshal Georgi Zhukov in a Berlin suburb.

Between 1946 and 1957 Smith was the chief European correspondent for CBS News, which had grown to include an expanding television operation. This included his coverage of the trial of Nazi war criminals at Nuremberg. Smith was a regular contributor to Murrow's news show *See It Now*. Along with Orson Welles, Aaron Copland, and Leonard Bernstein, Smith's name was one of 151 listed in *Red Channels* a publication that claimed to report on "Communist influence in radio and television." Smith was charged with being "a premature anti-Nazi." Paley initiated a loyalty oath that Smith, Murrow, and other network employees reluctantly signed swearing that they "had never been a member of any Communist organization." In 1957, Smith, based in Washington, became a correspondent on the network's fifteen-minute nightly *Douglas Edwards and the News*. In September he reported violent opposition to the court-ordered desegregation of a Little Rock, Arkansas, high school. Daily television coverage greatly stimulated the civil rights movement in America. With Walter Cronkite, Smith narrated a CBS special on American mili-

tary preparedness in the aftermath of Sputnik. *Behind the News with Howard K. Smith* premiered on CBS in 1959. Smith was picked to moderate the famous first televised debate between Richard Nixon and John Kennedy in 1960.

In 1961 Smith went to Birmingham, Alabama, where he witnessed clansmen beating up civil rights workers. He clashed with Paley over his *CBS Reports* special called "Who Speaks for Birmingham?" Paley criticized Smith for "editorializing." Smith resigned, as his mentor Murrow had done months before. "Paley said it was against CBS rules to take sides on a controversial issue. I said, I wish you had told me that when I took sides against Hitler." Network news, Smith and Murrow were painfully finding out, "wasn't mainly a medium for informing the public." Instead, it was "an entertainment business, operated primarily to make and expand a profit. In a crunch, it needed bigoted and fair-minded viewers alike."

Howard K. Smith: News and Comment was a weekly news show that premiered on ABC in 1961. It focused on disarmament, a "do-nothing" Congress, and ran a controversial "political obituary" of Richard Nixon after he lost the 1962 California governor's race. Smith also hosted ABC's Sunday public affairs program *Issues and Answers* and reported regularly on its nightly news show. In 1966, Smith launched *Scope*, a weekly documentary focusing on the Vietnam War. Smith became a hawk on winning the war. After the TET offensive of January 1968 he urged "escalation on an overwhelming scale." Attacked in the liberal press, he criticized network newsmen for "conformist thinking" that often had "the depth of a saucer."

In March 1969, Smith became co-anchor of the *ABC Evening News* with Frank Reynolds. In 1971, Harry Reasoner replaced Reynolds and Smith's role was expanded to include commentaries. His 1971 prime time, hour-long interview with President Nixon received a large rating. As evidence mounted in the Watergate scandal, Smith was the first major television analyst to call for Nixon's resignation. In 1975, Smith relinquished his co-anchor role to concentrate on commentaries. By 1977, he thought Roone Arledge had made the evening news a "Punch and Judy Show" by rotating four co-hosts. Two years later he retired.

Smith became a heroic figure for many journalists who followed him such as Peter Jennings, Bill Moyers, and Sam Donaldson. Smith's hero had always been Murrow who "excelled in the art of communicating" while giving citizens the news they needed to know. That had always been his aim, too.

Further Reading

Cloud, Stanley, and Lynne Olson. *The Murrow Boys*. Boston: Houghton Mifflin, 1996.

Gunther, Marc. *The House That Roone Built: The Inside Story of ABC News*. Boston: Little, Brown, 1994.

"The Life and Career of Howard K. Smith," a one hour interview, originally broadcast on C-Span on June 29, 1989, and rebroadcast on December 20, 2003.

New York Times, February 19, 2002, C9.

Smith, Howard K. *Events Leading Up to My Death: The Life of a Twentieth-Century Reporter.* New York: St. Martin's Press, 1996.

———, *Last Train from Berlin: An Eye-Witness Account of Germany at War.* London: Phoenix Press, 2000, originally 1942.

BRUCE J. EVENSEN

SMITH, WALTER WELLESLEY ("RED")

Walter Wellesley "Red" Smith (September 25, 1905–January 15, 1982) was among the greatest sports columnist in American history, his 1976 Pulitzer Prize for commentary attesting to his literary brilliance and his dexterity with a firm grasp of the power of metaphor. "Writing a column is like opening a vein and letting the words bleed out, drip by drip," he observed.

Red Smith was born in Green Bay, Wisconsin, where his father ran a grocery business. While attending Notre Dame University, Smith pursued a career in journalism. After graduation in 1927, he started as a reporter for the *Green Bay Press-Gazette.* The following year, he took a job as a copy editor at the *St. Louis Star* for a raise of $15 per week. When the managing editor fired most of the sports department in November 1928, he assigned Smith to write sports. Smith's first story demonstrated his aptitude for viewing events from unusual points of view: reporting on a local university's evening football practice, he wrote it from the ground-level perspective of a glowworm.

Eager to move east, Smith jumped to the *Philadelphia Record* in 1936 and then the *New York Herald-Tribune* in 1945. He remained there for twenty-two years, writing a daily sports column that catapulted him to prominence. Smith's "Views of Sport" became the most widely syndicated column in the nation. Smith's lean prose demonstrated his gift for wry humor. Detailing the ineptitude of a New York Giants baseball team, Smith wrote, "They couldn't hit the ball or catch it, pick it up, or hold it, and [manager] Rigney kept calling the bullpen for another bull."

Smith was also a master storyteller with a razor-sharp memory. Noticing an obituary for the Rev. Harold J. Martin, Smith recalled him as an ambidexterous pitcher for Fordham University and several minor league clubs before he took holy orders. Smith wrote:

> When he was pastor of a church in Ogdensburg, New York, the parish needed money for a playground. Under the name of Doc O'Reilly, the priest went to work pitching for a semi-pro team and achieved a local renown that eventually brought him to the attention of Bishop Joseph H. Conroy, who put on a storm.
>
> The idea of a priest giving scandal, putting off collar and cassock for a ball player's flannels! A man of God appearing in public as a professional athlete! And for what?
>
> "Seventy-five dollars a game," Father Martin said.
>
> "Seventy-five dollars!" His Excellency said. "Do you think they could use a third baseman?"

Smith's newspaper, eventually renamed the *World Journal Tribune,* failed in 1967. Bereft of a newspaper home, the dean of American sports columnists found an unlikely harbor at *Women's Wear Daily* for four years, until the *New York Times* signed him in 1971.

While with the *Times* in 1976, Smith became only the second sportswriter to win a Pulitzer Prize. The judges chose Smith for his "unique erudition, the literary quality, the vitality and the freshness of viewpoint." Smith's clever turns of phrase enabled him to be sardonic without scalding. He described beefy Columbia University football coach Lou Little as "a formidable trencherman who could hold his own at table with world-class feeders." Recalling the merits of a good-hit, no-field baseball player, Smith wrote, "during his thirteen seasons of big league baseball, Rudy York was an outfielder, a third baseman, and a catcher as well as a first baseman. If this suggests the adjective 'versatile,' it is misleading. No matter where he was stationed in the field, Rudy York always played the same position. He played bat."

Smith could also be somber and evocative when the story required. "When the iceman cometh, it doesn't make a great deal of difference which route he takes, for the ultimate result is the same in any case," Smith wrote when a former Yankee great died suddenly at age forty-two. "Nevertheless, there was something especially tragic in the way death came to Tony Lazzeri, finding him and leaving him all alone in a dark and silent house—a house which must, in that last moment, have seemed frighteningly silent to a man whose ears remembered the roar of the crowd as Tony's did."

Smith remained with the *Times* until his death in 1982. In his last years, he phoned in his column to a tape recorder from his house in Connecticut. Smith told friends he never wanted to retire from writing, plying his trade until the end. "I just want to fall into my typewriter," he said. He nearly achieved that goal, dying of heart failure four days after what proved to be his final column was published.

Further Reading

Anderson, Dave, ed. *The Red Smith Reader.* New York: Random House, 1982.

Berkow, Ira. *Red: A Biography of Red Smith.* New York: Times Books, 1986.

Smith, Red. *Red Smith on Baseball: The Game's Greatest Writer on the Game's Greatest Years.* Chicago: I.R. Dee, 2000.

———. *Red Smith on Fishing Around the World.* Garden City, New York: Doubleday, 1963.

———. *Strawberries in the Wintertime: The Sporting World of Red Smith.* (New York: Quadrangle, 1974.

———. *To Absent Friends from Red Smith.* New York: Atheneum, 1982.

RALPH FRASCA

SOCIALIST PRESS

The socialist movement sustained hundreds of newspapers and magazines at its height between the 1880s and 1930s, including several daily newspapers published in most of the languages spoken by the United States' predominantly immigrant working class. Cities such as Chicago, Detroit and New York were home to publications representing every socialist tendency, from anarchist to social democratic. Most of these papers were ensconced in vibrant working class communities, owned or sponsored by ethnically based mutual aid societies, political organizations, singing societies and other cultural groups, and union locals. (Indeed, the distinction between socialist and labor newspapers is somewhat arbitrary—many papers simultaneously served as the official organ of one or more unions, a mutual aid society and a political party, and several union-published newspapers gave strong backing to radical causes.) Others were ideological organs, published to promote a particular tendency or to explore theoretical debates within the socialist movement. Together, they formed a rich mosaic of humor and literary journals, magazines and newspapers published in dozens of languages in every state.

The country's largest socialist organization, the Socialist Party, refused as a matter of policy to own its own press, and as a result was served by an array of loosely aligned publications each free to pursue its own editorial vision. In 1912, party supporters issued more than three hundred English- and foreign-language daily, weekly and monthly publications. While many of these papers were owned by party-affiliated foreign language sections or local publishing associations, others were issued by sympathetic craftsmen who hoped to make a modest living while supporting the cause. The best known of these, the Kansas-based *Appeal to Reason,* built up a circulation of more than six hundred thousand subscribers (distributing hundreds of thousands of additional copies of special issues) for the eclectic weekly in which orthodox socialists shared the columns with radical populists and reformers, and advertisements for patent medicines and get rich quick schemes. The paper's blend of hard-hitting investigative journalism, folksy columns, poetry, and jokes, and news of farmer, labor, and socialist organizations reached an audience that extended far beyond the socialists' core supporters. Key to its success was the Appeal Army, a network of volunteer supporters who sold subscriptions, distributed newspapers in their communities, and formed the basis for Socialist Party organizations in many Southwestern rural communities. But the *Appeal to Reason* drifted away from the party after founder J.A. Wayland committed suicide in 1912, and broke with the socialists altogether under the pressure of World War I.

The Socialist Party was hardly alone in the field. The pre-existing Socialist Labor Party published newspapers in several languages, and what was probably the first English-language socialist daily in the world, the *Daily People* (1900–1914). Following a bitter split with a faction supported by the party's German-language daily, the Socialist Labor Party insisted on strict party control of the press. The *People* (which as of 2006 continued publication, if on a much-reduced schedule) served largely as a commentator on the day's events and a popularizer of socialist doctrine that assumed most readers got their news elsewhere. As other socialist organizations formed, they quickly launched their own periodicals to hold together their supporters and reach out to prospective sympathizers. Immigrant-based mutual aid associations published newspapers that often espoused socialist ideals while maintaining independence of any particular party. And many unaligned socialists issued periodicals, whether as independent forums for discussion and reflection, as with *Monthly Review,* or to provide an alternative view of events unencumbered by party control.

The Socialist Party press was especially influential in the years leading up to the Russian Revolution. In addition to local newspapers and more ideological journals such as Charles H. Kerr's flagship *International Socialist Review,* the party was served by several daily newspapers, including English-language dailies in Chicago, Milwaukee, New York, Oklahoma City, and Seattle. Many of these papers offered not only news of the labor and socialist movements and political commentary, but also attempted to provide a comprehensive news report. The *Milwaukee Leader,* longest-lived of these papers (1911–1942), aided the city's powerful Socialist Party (which held the mayor's office and several city council seats for much of this period), helping the party win support outside of its traditional German immigrant base, and also served as the official organ of the city's Federated Trades Council. The *Leader* emulated its commercial rivals, including business, sports and women's pages and extensive advertising. But it had difficulty adapting to the consolidation that swept the industry in the postwar years, narrowing the space for niche publications of all sorts.

Foreign-language papers proved more resilient, firmly rooted in community institutions and less subject to mainstream competition. In 1910, Chicago socialists were issuing five daily newspapers (in Czech, English, German, Slovene and Yiddish—later adding dailies in Lithuanian and Polish) and several weeklies. One of those dailies, the *Chicagoer Arbeiter-Zeitung* (1877–1924), demonstrates that these papers were as much community organs as party ones. The *Arbeiter-Zeitung* began life as the organ of the Socialist Labor Party; by 1884 the majority of the German-speaking movement had aligned themselves with the anarchist International Working People's Association, and August Spies (later executed in 1887 as one of the Haymarket Martyrs) was elected as editor; in 1910, the shareholders voted to affiliate with the Socialist Party.

The Socialists Party's foreign-language sections sometimes relied on sympathetic publishers but more typically organized cooperative societies that simultaneously served to buffer editors from stultifying day-to-day oversight while maintaining broad oversight for the movement. Such societies typically issued stock—owned by union locals, mutual aid societies, workers' choirs, party sections, and the like—and held regular meetings where the editor reported on his conduct of the paper, editorial and business policies could be debated, and the editor could at least in theory be removed if the community he served was dissatisfied. Even if it was relatively rare for an editor to lose his position, such elections served to reinforce an ethos of community control and to transform the nature of the relationship between readers (who often contributed reports of events they were involved with) and the journalists who served them. Stockholders in the *Arbeiter-Zeitung* exercised their right to replace editors whose politics or performance they found unsatisfactory fairly often; there were heated contests in many of these societies particularly as the socialist movement divided in the aftermath of the Russian revolution. That conflict was particularly heated in the Finnish community, where socialists had already lost control of the Duluth-based daily *Socialisti/Industrialisti* to Industrial Workers of the World supporters in 1913. The Communists ultimately won control of two of the party's three Finnish-language dailies, integrating them into a network of cooperatives, ethnic halls and other institutions that lent strong support to the party's Finnish- and English-language activities for decades to come.

Readers wrote for their newspapers, elected their editors, and donated funds to cover their deficits. Editors spoke at union rallies, opened their papers' columns to announcements and other news from community organizations, and mobilized readers behind labor campaigns. When police arrested the entire editorial staff of the daily *Chicagoer Arbeiter-Zeitung* in 1886 in the aftermath of the Haymarket explosion, blacklisted McCormick Reaper worker Gus Belz and other readers stepped forward to take their places. When Belz died (at age thirty-one) two years later of tuberculosis, his obituary noted that he had worked such long hours at the paper that he practically lived in its offices for several months.

Such a close relationship between readers and newspapers was more typical of immigrant papers than of their English-language counterparts. Although papers such as the *Chicago Daily Socialist* (1906–1912) boasted that every reader was also a reporter and established institutional mechanisms to ensure accountability, and all working-class papers published articles written by union officials and other community members, in practice the English-language Socialist press tended to rely more heavily on paid staff to produce newspapers that straddled the divide between emulating the mainstream press and following a more community-oriented model that blurred the distinction between readers and communicators.

Many of these papers survived the movements that gave them birth and sustained them for many years, adapting as their communities changed. The Finnish-language Socialist daily *Raivaaja*, for example, continues publication as a nonprofit ethnic weekly. The Lithuanian-language Chicago daily *Naujienos* followed its social democratic leanings into the Democratic Party, and survived into the 21st century as a semiweekly. The New York-based *Forward* continued to publish weekly editions in Yiddish, Russian and English, emphasizing its roots as a defender of unionism and "moderate, democratic socialism." As of 2006, the revived Socialist Party USA now publishes its own magazine, *The Socialist,* and a few local newsletters, as do several other socialist organizations. Magazines such as *In These Times* and the *Progressive Populist* hearken back to the tradi-

tion of the *Appeal to Reason.* But these publications in the early twenty-first century could no longer claim the influence once wielded by a socialist press that counted some two million readers, with local newspapers in nearly every state.

Further Reading

Bekken, Jon. "'No Weapon So Powerful': Working-Class Newspapers in the United States." *Journal of Communication Inquiry* 12(2), 1988.

Bekken, Jon. "The First Anarchist Daily Newspaper: The Chicagoer Arbeiter-Zeitung." *Anarchist Studies* 3(3), 1995.

Green, James R. *Grass-Roots Socialism*. Baton Rouge: Louisiana University Press, 1978.

Hoerder, Dirk, ed. *Essays on the Scandinavian-North American Radical Press, 1880s–1930s.* Bremen, Germany: Labor Newspaper Preservation Project, 1984.

Hummasti, Paul G. "'The Workingman's Daily Bread,' Finnish-American Working Class Newspapers, 1900–1921." In *For the Common Good,* edited by Michael Karni, and Douglas Ollila. Superior, WI: Tyomies Society.

Shore, Elliott. *Talkin' Socialism: J.A. Wayland and the Role of the Press in American Radicalism, 1890–1912.* Lawrence: University Press of Kansas, 1988.

Streitmatter, Roger. *Voices of Revolution: The Dissident Press in America.* New York: Columbia University Press, 2000.

JON BEKKEN

SOCIETY OF PROFESSIONAL JOURNALISTS

The Society of Professional Journalists began on April 17, 1909, when students at DePauw University organized Sigma Delta Chi (Talent, Truth, and Energy), an honorary fraternity for aspiring newspapermen. The Society's early growth paralleled the establishment of college journalism curricula throughout the United States, but despite its campus origins, within two decades it came to be dominated by professional chapters made up of "alumni" and other newsmen working in cities around the country. By 1960, seeing the need for a broad-based professional association for journalists, delegates at the annual convention voted to abandon the fraternity structure and reorganize as a national professional society. In 1973 the delegates followed up by changing the organization's name to "Society of Professional Journalists, Sigma Delta Chi." The fraternity name was dropped in 1988. As a national organization of rank-and-file journalists, it has played an influential role in the movements to raise professional standards, defend journalistic freedom, and increase access to government information.

In 1956, the organization drafted model open records and open meetings laws and initiated a long campaign that helped lead to the enactment of the federal Freedom of Information Act in 1966 as well as to passage of open records and open meeting laws in every state by 1983. It began a similar effort in 1971 to pass state "shield" laws to prevent reporters from being forced to reveal their sources and in 2005 started a campaign to pass a federal shield law.

In 1973, the Society adopted a code of ethics at its national convention that called on journalists to "seek truth" and defend First Amendment freedoms while taking a hard line against sensationalism, conflicts of interest and the acceptance of even small gifts. Posted in hundreds of newsrooms and included in many journalism textbooks, its inspirational tone and applicability to all media soon made it the best known code of journalistic ethics in and out of the profession.

One of the most important developments in expanding the organization's membership was the decision in 1969 to admit women. Total membership rose from twelve thousand in 1959, to a peak of just over twenty-four thousand in 1984. The Society lost numbers during the 1980s and 1990s as potential members joined the many special interest journalism organizations then emerging. But membership had stabilized by the late 1990s at about nine thousand and the SPJ remained the nation's largest general interest journalism organization. In 2005, it had some 10,000 members, 68 professional chapters, and 175 campus chapters. The majority of members were working journalists from all media with journalism students and faculty members making up most of the rest.

With a paid staff of less than a dozen at its headquarters in Indianapolis, much of the SPJ's work is done by volunteers, especially at the chapter level. Many professional chapters have long histories in their localities, presenting professional development programs, running local journalism contests and campaigning for increased press freedom.

SPJ is also known for *Quill*, its magazine on journalism issues published continuously since 1912; the national Sigma Delta Chi Awards, originally called the Distinguished Service Awards, awarded annually since 1939; the Mark of Excellence Awards for college journalists, awarded annually since 1972; and its Legal Defense Fund, created in 1972 to aid journalists in free press cases.

Further Reading

Bostrom, Bert N. *Truth, Talent and Energy: 75 Years of Service to Journalism*. Chicago, IL: Society of Professional Journalists, Sigma Delta Chi, 1984.

Clayton, Charles C. *Fifty Years for Freedom: The Story of Sigma Delta Chi's Service to American Journalism: 1909–1959*. Carbondale: Southern Illinois University Press, 1959.

Glenn, William M. *The Sigma Delta Chi Story*. Coral Gables, FL: Glade House, 1949.

The Society of Professional Journalists' web site at http://www.spj.org.

GUY T. BAEHR

SOCIETY REPORTING

To quote Lady Bracknell in Oscar Wilde's *The Importance of Being Earnest*, "Never speak disrespectfully of Society…Only people who can't get into it do that." The play, written in 1899, poked fun at the dictates of society at the very time that the Society Page was a popular and important fixture in most newspapers. From the onset of society reporting in 1840, stories about the comings and goings of men and women of high social status have been a favorite among readers—including those who were being written about and those who only aspired to achieve such stature.

An early example of society reporting can be traced to James Gordon Bennett, publisher of the *New York Herald*, who sent a reporter to cover a costume ball given at the home of Mr. and Mrs. Henry Brevoort on February 25, 1840. William H. Attree, who had been a sports reporter, donned a suit of armor to attend the event. He alienated most of the guests at the ball, but his slightly tongue-in-cheek report delighted *Herald* readers. Thus, the Society Page was born.

Society reporting first emerged at a time when proper women shunned being in the news. A woman's name was to appear in public only when a woman married and when she died. Bennett, long remembered for his willingness to mock Victorian morals, flaunted this taboo. When Bennett's techniques resulted in selling more newspapers, other journals followed suit.

Bennett's attention to society was perhaps rooted in the fact that he himself was scorned by the very people his paper was writing about in a slightly sarcastic tone. Bennett cared not at all if he alienated the social elite with his columns, but his wife and son suffered because of this devil-may-care attitude. As a result of his snide coverage of New York's high society, Bennett's wife moved with her young son to Europe.

Although Bennett never allowed a woman to write his society news, society reporting in other newspapers became the purview of women reporters. At many papers, the social news was penned under a standard pseudonym no matter who the writer actually was. Reports from New York and Washington also were syndicated.

Newspapers usually hired at least one person to write about social issues, and to accurately and intricately describe the clothes and costumes women wore to the best parties. Not only was it important to report who attended the parties, but readers delighted in extensive descriptions of how the women were dressed. In the era before newspapers and magazines were capable of publishing photographs, this was especially crucial and helped women keep abreast of fashion trends in the urban centers of the United States.

William Randolph Hearst, in the 1890s, introduced the society columnist in his *New York Journal*. Using the already established Hearst pseudonym *Cholly Knickerbocker*, Ivy Ross wrote for the newspaper chain for thirty-two years. The column transformed society reporting from a formal style in which the writer seemed awestruck by her subjects into a chatty, gossipy item in which the pillars of New York society were referred to by their first names or at times their nicknames.

While society reporting more likely flourished in urban centers than rural outposts by its very nature, it approached an art form in both New York City and Washington, D.C., where politics was also a part of the game. Ruth E. Jones served as society editor on all of the Washington dailies, the *Herald*, the *Times* and the *Post*, and reigned as queen of the social writers during the 1930s. That mantle was then assumed by Hope Ridings Miller, who wrote for a decade for the *Washington Post*. A friend of Eleanor Roosevelt, Miller startled her loyal readers in the early days of World War II when she stopped coverage of parties and society in favor of reports of volunteer efforts and military life. After she left the *Post* in 1944, she wrote a syndicated column on Washington society.

At the *Chicago Tribune*, society reporting appeared under the name *Nancy Randolph*. Inez Callaway was the woman behind the name. She memorized the city's *Social Register* and made it her business to stand outside while guests arrived at parties so that she could report their attendance at the event and their wardrobe (a forerunner, if you will, of later television reporting from the Red Carpet).

Another notable society writer was May Birkhead, who launched her long career with the sinking of the Titanic in 1912. Birkhead was aboard the cruise ship *Carpathia* when it picked up passengers from the sunken ship. She interviewed survivors, photographed them and provided copy to the *New York Herald*.

Society reporting gradually expanded to include engagement and wedding announcements for people living within the circulation area. In the 1950s and 1960s those announcements included the photograph of the bride only, but by the 1970s the groom was often included in the picture. Early in the new millennium, the respectable *New York Times* announced in 2002 its new policy of publishing announcements of same-sex commitment ceremonies in its Styles of the Times section each Sunday. Other newspapers followed this example.

Society reporting metamorphisized in late twentieth century. While news reports of America's ruling families—the Trumps, the Kennedys, the Hiltons, and the Rockefellers, to name a few—were still fodder for newspapers and magazines, the edges of society reporting blurred with entertainment reporting. Detailed reports of the gowns women were wearing at a New York matron's party for her debutante daughter have given way to live reports on cable television stations like *E!*, the *TV Guide* station, and *Style*, of the Red Carpet events before the Oscars, Emmys, Golden Globes, People's Choice, and other award shows. Hosts such as comedian Joan Rivers chatted with each star as they pass by and then commented on their clothing and their lapses into bad taste. Weekly publications such as *People* and *Us* magazines created icons of Hollywood celebrities, and newspapers often responded to this trend by transforming their Society Pages into columns that track the stars rather than the social climbers. At the same time, the term "Socialite" degenerated from a description of someone with philanthropic aspirations in the 1950s and 1960s into a stereotypical portrayal of someone who pursues a hedonistic life.

Further Reading

Mead, Rebecca. "State of the Unions." *Commonweal*, September 27, 2002, vol. 129, no. 16, 5.

Ross, Ishbel. *Ladies of the Press*. New York: Harper & Brothers, 1936.

Schudel, Matt. "Washington Society Chronicler Hope Ridings Miller Dies at 99." *Washington Post*, 5 May 2005, B06.

AGNES HOOPER GOTTLIEB

SOCIOLOGY

Since sociology emerged in the United States in the last decades of the nineteenth century, it has shared certain things with the news. Sociologists have written articles for newspapers, produced research that attracted journalistic interest, and brought experience as journalists to the social scientific study of society. Both sociology and the news have been officially guided by commitments to investigating and publishing truth about the human world. Both grew to be dominated by standards of objectivity. Both have housed aspirations to reform along with practices that maintain the status quo. One might address any of these topics in discussing the historical relation between sociology and the news, but the focus of this entry is more specific: the evolution of the sociological study of news and its production, content, readership, social roles, and impacts.

The Early Years

American sociology grew out of the social science movement of the post-Civil War era, which blended faith in science with efforts at liberal reform. Sociology was the last developed of the core social sciences. Sociological writings were published in the United States by the 1870s, but it was not until 1892 that the newly opened University of Chicago appointed the nation's first chair of sociology. In 1894, Columbia University established a similar chair, the same year the first course in sociology was offered at the University of Michigan. Over the next twenty years, news was a subject of sociological inquiry at these universities.

At Chicago, reformist and practical impulses blended with the analytic. "The power of the press has never been so great, so decisive, so irresistible as it is now," V.S. Yarros wrote; sociologists needed to find ways to direct it toward "the interest of righteousness and moral progress" (1899, 382). Yarros' colleague and former journalist George Vincent picked up the challenge in 1903 by offering a course entitled the History and Organization of the American Press. Borrowing an idea from John Dewey's laboratory school, Vincent called the course "a laboratory experiment in journalism," which gave students a historical overview of the development of the American press, visits to Chicago newspapers, and a hands-on effort creating a paper of their own—this a year before Joseph Pulitzer offered to fund a journalism school at Columbia, and nine years before it opened. Vincent (1904) advocated that sociology departments hire journalists who could "combine practical experience with academic tastes" as a way to instruct students about the news.

In 1913, Chicago did just that by hiring Robert Park, whose doctoral study in Berlin was sandwiched between early experience as a newspaper reporter and later work as publicist for Booker T. Washington's Tuskegee Institute. His press experience arguably shaped "the reportage of urban culture" by Chicago sociologists in the 1920s (Linde, 1996). During Park's tenure at Chicago, newspaper study was a staple research area of the department, classically focused upon the immigrant and urban press as a socializing and community-building agency (e.g., Thomas & Znaniecki 1918; Park 1922). Park (1923) added theoretical dimensions to Vincent's early emphasis on news' historical development, charting what he called "the natural history" of newspapers as tied up with the needs and social currents of the historical eras in which they evolved.

Elsewhere, sociologists analyzed the news in different ways. At Michigan, Charles Horton Cooley (1909) offered one of the earliest important theoretical accounts of the news and its social functions. He called news "organized gossip" and suggested that it played similar roles as face-to-face gossip of earlier eras—solidifying ties among those who exchanged it, enforcing moral standards by drawing attention to transgressions of them, and giving a sense of vicarious participation in the activities of others. His *Social Organization* is the start of the interpretive sociology of news in the United States, but it lacked the empirical base of the Chicago studies. At Columbia, meanwhile, Alvan Tenney and his students developed a more rigorous "scientific analysis of the press" based on counting column inches dedicated to particular subjects. It was an early version of content analysis, which Tenney (1911) hoped could be used to observe and predict "the 'social weather'" with the sort of accuracy meteorologists enjoyed with the climatic weather.

In these earliest studies, we see projects and research styles that persist into the present. Historical, interpretive, critical-reformist, and scientific-positivist impulses were all part of the original mix, and they have remained so ever since. Haltingly, relations were charted between news and public opinion, socialization, community identification, politics, moral codes, and the circulation of feelings and ideas. The mood was more hopeful than it was at other times in the century, with cautious optimism that news and sociology could both be agents of positive change and public engagement. That optimism did not last past World War I, though pre-war research trajectories in the sociology of news continued under Park at Chicago and via the dissemination of Columbia-style content analysis in studies of the Connecticut country newspapers (Willey 1926) and of the portrayal of African Americans in Philadelphia's white dailies (Simpson 1937).

The three most noteworthy contributions in the interwar period, however, came from figures marginal to academic sociology: Walter Lippmann, Robert and Helen Lynd, and Helen McGill Hughes. Lippmann, a working journalist and public intellectual, provided a realist's take on the routines of news gathering and the limits of readership that were more sophisticated than anything that preceded and much that followed. He described a world governed by "stereotypes" held by readers and perpetuated by the press, and he rejected much of the reformers' more idealized democratic conceptions of what news might do. This was a view picked up in a different way by the Lynds, who were not trained as sociologists. Their widely read *Middletown* (1929), a social anthropology of a "typical" American community (Muncie, Indiana), examined among other topics the way Middletowners got their information. In good scientific style, the Lynd's marshaled statistics and counted column inches to characterize the newspapers of the mid-1920s, to which they added characterizations of readers not unlike Lippmann's conclusions. Readers were poorly informed and often not up to the tasks of democratic citizenship. Their analysis fell to the left of Lippmann's politically, however, and they added a brief analysis of how the news buttressed "the interests of the business class who buy advertising." Also to the left of Lippmann was Helen McGill Hughes, who was trained as a sociologist at the University of Chicago, but like other women of her era did not enjoy a full-time academic position and worked from the margins of her field. Her *News and the Human Interest Story* (1940) is perhaps the single best book-length sociological study of news before the 1970s, though it has rarely been recognized as such. Extending Park's natural history approach, she perceptively analyzed the stereotypical narratives of the human interest story and discussed its cultural and economic functions from its origins in the penny press of the 1830s to her own day.

The Sociology of News since the 1940s

Sociologists continued to analyze newspapers in the early 1940s (see *Annals,* 1942), but increasingly they turned their attention to "mass communication," a new covering term for radio, motion pictures, newspapers, popular magazines, and soon television as well. The rise of mass communication research coincided with a growing research presence in journalism schools, which supplemented professional training with historical and social scientific study of news as well. Communications broke off from sociology in the late 1940s, led by Wilbur Schramm and his new Institute for Communication Research at the University of Illinois (and a later one at Stanford). Sociologists continued to do most of the heavy theoretical and empirical lifting in the 1940s and 1950s, however, with New York and Chicago again the key intellectual sites. At Columbia, Paul Lazarsfeld and Robert K. Merton headed up the Bureau for Applied Social Research, whose election studies and audience research established "the two-step flow" model of mass communication whereby news and other media information were seen as traveling first to "opinion leaders" and then via conversation to others in their social networks (see Katz and Lazarsfeld, 1955). From Merton came the idea that the news did not perform only social functions but had dysfunctional consequences as well, including an ability to "narcotize" those who regularly read it (Lazarsfeld and Merton 1948). Bernard Berelson (1949) picked up another line of Columbia audience research and showed how the news offered readers a number of "gratifications," only a few of which had much to do with staying informed or being a good citizen, while Warren Breed's (1955) study of newsroom routines put empirical meat on the bones of Lazarsfeld and Merton's (1948) insight that news generally upheld the status quo. News production was also the focus of an important study by David Manning White (1950), a student of Schramm's from Illinois, whose analysis of news selection or "gatekeeping" by a newspaper wire editor was a minor classic. Irving Janowitz (1952) meanwhile extended Chicago-style community-based newspaper studies to the neighborhood weeklies of the city and its expanding post-war suburbs, while two graduate students at Chicago, Gladys and Kurt Lang, pioneered the sociological analysis of television news events and their public images (collected with others in Lang and Lang, 1968).

After having been subsumed for a time within mass communication research, the sociology of news returned with a vengeance in the late 1970s, led by Gaye Tuchman, Michael Schudson, Herbert Gans, and Todd Gitlin. If early sociologists talked about the newspaper's natural history, this generation mapped its historical contingencies. News footage from the war in Vietnam had resonated powerfully with many Americans, including Tuchman, whose research was precipitated by images she viewed in 1966. Watergate was a second backdrop for the revival, putting the press center stage in the national consciousness and establishing one agenda item for a round of work that was more skeptical, analytical, and critical than straightforwardly supportive of contemporary journalistic work. Tuchman (1978) and Gitlin (1980) looked at how the news portrayed women and the New Left respectively, blending careful empirical work with sophisticated theories of ideology and society; Schudson (1978) re-invigorated the historical sociology of news in his account of the rise and partial fall of objectivity as a journalistic value; and Gans (1979) observed newsroom practices and offered reformist calls for a new "multi-perspectival news." The field remains vibrant today, with more recent work focusing on subjects like news and collective memory (Zelizer 1998), televised news-oriented media events (Dayan and Katz 1992), and the critical political economy of the news (Hallin 1994).

Further Reading

Annals of the American Academy of Political and Social Science, vol. 219 (January, 1942). A special issue devoted to discussing the news from sociological perspectives, with articles by Helen McGill Hughes, Malcolm Willey, Paul Lazarsfeld, and Alfred McLung Lee.

Berelson, Bernard. 1949. "What 'Missing the Newspaper' Means." In *Communications Research, 1948–49,* edited by Paul F. Lazarsfeld and Frank N. Stanton, 111–129. New York: Harper and Brothers; rpt. in Peters and Simonson, 254–262.

Breed, Warren. 1955. "Social Control in the Newsroom." *Social Forces* 33, 326–355; rpt in Wilbur Schramm, ed., *Mass Communications.* Urbana: University of Illinois Press, 1960, 178–194.

Cooley, Charles Horton. 1909. *Social Organization: A Study of the Larger Mind.* New York: Charles Scribner's.

Dayan, Daniel, and Katz, Elihu. 1992. *Media Events: The Live Broadcasting of History.* Cambridge, MA: Harvard University Press.

Gans, Herbert J. 1979. *Deciding What's News: A Study of CBS Evening News, NBC Nightly News, Newsweek, and Time.* New York: Vintage.

Gitlin, Todd. 1980. *The Whole World Is Watching: Mass Media in the Making and Unmaking of the New Left.* Berkeley: University of California Press.

Hallin, Daniel. 1994. *We Keep America On Top of the World: Television Journalism and the Public Sphere.* New York: Routledge.

Hughes, Helen McGill. 1940. *News and the Human Interest Story.* Chicago: University of Chicago Press.

Janowitz, Morris. 1952. *The Community Press in an Urban Setting.* Glencoe, IL: Free Press.

Lang, Kurt, and Lang, Gladys Engel. 1968. *Politics and Television.* Chicago: Quadrangle.

Lazarsfeld, Paul & Merton, Robert K. 1948. Mass Communication, Popular Taste, and Organized Social Action. In, *The Communication of Ideas,* edited by Lyman Bryson, 95–118. New York: Harper; rpt. in Peters and Simonson, 230–241.

Linder, Rolf. 1996. *The Reportage of Urban Culture: Robert Park and the Chicago School.* Cambridge: Cambridge University Press.

Lippmann, Walter. 1922. *Public Opinion.* New York: Harcourt Brace.

Lynd, Robert S., and Lynd, Helen. 1929. *Middletown: A Study in American Culture.* New York: Harcourt Brace.

Park, Robert E. 1922. *The Immigrant Press and Its Control.* New York: Harper and Brothers.

Park, Robert E. 1923. "Natural History of the Newspaper." *American Journal of Sociology* 29 (3): 80–98. Reprinted with other Park articles on the sociology of news in Everett Hughes, ed., *The Collected Papers of Robert Ezra Park,* vol. 3. Glencoe, IL: Free Press, 1955.

Peters, John Durham, and Peter Simonson, eds. 2004. *Mass Communication and American Social Thought: Key Texts, 1919–1968.* Lanham, MD: Rowman and Littlefield.

Schudson, Michael. 1978. *Discovering the News: A Social History of American Newspapers.* New York: Basic Books.

——. 2005. "The Sociology of News Production Revisited (Again). In *Mass Media and Society,"* 4th ed., edited by James Curran and Michael Gurevitch,. London: Arnold.

Simpson, George E. 1936. *The Negro in the Philadelphia Press.*

Tenney, Alvan, A. 1912. "The Scientific Analysis of the Press." *The Independent* LXXIII. October 17.

Thomas, William I., and Znaniecki, Florian. 1918. *The Polish Peasant in Europe and America: Monograph of an Immigrant Group,* 5 vols. Chicago: University of Chicago Press.

Tuchman, Gaye. 1978. *Making News: A Study in the Construction of Reality.* New York: Free Press.

Vincent, George E. 1905. "A Laboratory Experiment in Journalism." *American Journal of Sociology* 11(3): 297–311.

White, David Manning. 1950. "The Gatekeeper: A Case Study in the Selection of News." *Journalism Quarterly* 27: 77–128.

Willey, Malcolm. 1926. *The Country Newspaper: A Study of Socialization and Newspaper Content.* Chapel Hill: University of North Carolina Press.

Yarros, V.S. 1899. "The Press and Public Opinion." *American Journal of Sociology,* 5(3): 372–382.

Zelizer, Barbie. 1998 *Remembering to Forget: Holocaust Memory through the Camera's Eye.* Chicago: University of Chicago Press.

PETER SIMONSON

SOURCES OF INFORMATION FOR JOURNALISTS

Why and how journalists use the information sources they do to create their stories is a matter of deep interest and broad scholarly attention. Sociologist Michael Schudson has discussed "political economy" approaches to the study of news, which take news organization ownership patterns as the primary determinant of content; "sociological" approaches, which take the competitive interactions between sources and news professionals and among news professionals themselves to be the primary determinant; and "cultural" approaches that see the ideas and beliefs of journalists to be the primary determinant. This entry places the discussion of sources of information for journalists in the sociological context as a way to understand how journalistic information practices have developed, evolved and continue to influence why news looks the way it does.

Information Sources for Early Newspapers

Some of the earliest colonial newspapers were established by postmaster/printers who had easy access to official royal and colonial government information because they also had the printing contracts for governmental bodies. As postmasters, these early publishers also had access to incoming and outgoing mail and to the newspapers arriving from overseas. Postmasters had authority to open many official documents that came to the colonial governor. Merchants and ship captains relied on the postmaster to alert townspeople to the availability of goods or space on cargo ships.

Sources of information for these early publishers were primarily weeks- or months-old clippings of stories from foreign newspapers, official government notices, ship arrivals and other commercial intelligence, texts of sermons delivered, and information about activities in other colonies gathered from the letters exchanged by colonists. Occasionally, the newspaper would include an essay by the publisher, poetry, literary or creative writing and other miscellaneous content. By far, however, most information was simply reprinted from "official" sources.

A regular postal carriage rate for newspapers in 1758 greatly expanded the policy of exchange of newspapers between editors, free of any postal charge. This provided editors with access to news from all over the colonies, which they clipped and reprinted in their own publications. Newspaper editors began incorporating accounts of arrests, trials, deaths, fires, epidemics and the weather from many local communities, thus shifting the focus of what was newsworthy beyond simply "official" activities.

Newspaper publishers aligned themselves with the colonial or British side of events leading up to the Revolutionary War and content inevitably became more political. By the end of the war, political commentary was a typical feature of most newspapers. New political parties and local political leaders founded newspapers to espouse their emerging views. Party press editors reprinted important news items, columns, commentaries and information from the national party newspaper with which they were aligned and from like-minded local dailies and weeklies from around the country. Newspapers disseminated party ideologies and political candidates' views.

The Interview as a Method for Gathering Information

The development of the postal system, railroad route expansions, pony and pigeon posts and other transportation technologies in the nineteenth century allowed newspapers to gather information more quickly and from a wider geographical range than previously. Journalism historian Donald Shaw found that between 1820 and 1860, newspapers more actively undertook original news gathering, accompanied by a decline in the use of news clipped from other papers. The role of the reporter, separate from the publisher/editor, also emerged during this time. Shaw found that reporters accounted for one newspaper story out of ten in the early part of the 1820–1860 period, but for one story in five by the end of that time period.

As newspaper readership increased along with advances in literacy and the new affordability of the "penny press," the traditional function of the newspaper to provide a *record* of important actions of government was joined by a new function, that of storytelling or *reporting* on the feats and foibles of the average working-class audience member. Stories written to entertain joined those that recorded official information.

One of the new information gathering techniques to emerge was the interview. Prior to the 1850s, it was unknown for a reporter to speak to a politician or other news source to gather comments on the record. Scholars credit penny press editors and reporters with the introduction of the interview as they began including verbatim accounts of their conversations with individuals they encountered while gathering information for their stories. However, this form of information gathering remained unfamiliar enough so that when Horace Greeley interviewed Mormon leader Brigham Young for a story in the *New York Tribune* in 1859, Greeley felt he needed to explain to his audience what he was doing with the "question and answer" format.

The outbreak of the Civil War in 1860 greatly accelerated the adoption of the interview as a method of information gathering. Newspaper readers demanded the most recent accounts of battles, generals' decisions, military strategies and troop life. Newspapers hired many more reporters to cover the far-flung battle arenas across the country. These reporters relied on their own eyewitness accounts and interviews with both high-ranking officials and the rank-and-file soldiers to write their stories. The use of multiple sources became an established practice.

Of course, the interview is now one of the most important methods of information gathering for journalists in every medium. Sources and journalists have become experts at the give-and-take of the interview format. Many institutions send their top officials to executive training sessions to learn how to parry with a journalist to fend off unwanted questions and scrutiny during an interview. Given how entrenched the interview method is in modern journalism, it is hard to imagine a time when it was a novelty.

The Influence of the Telegraph and Wire Services

The invention of the telegraph in 1844 provided yet another new information gathering technique for journalists. The first wire service, the Associated Press, was founded in 1849 and quickly incorporated news by telegraph among its methods. And once again, the demands for news during the Civil War accelerated the adoption of reporting "by telegraph." As telegraph lines extended into the countryside, small daily and weekly newspapers began to get the same news as their big-city rivals. When the Atlantic Ocean telegraph cable was laid in 1866, news transmissions from Europe became much more timely and accessible.

News Beats and Routines of Information Gathering

During the latter part of the nineteenth century, as the great editors of the penny press died, a generation of well-trained journalists arose. These professionals were accustomed to reporting facts and conveying drama in their stories; they largely rejected the expression of editorial opinion that had been the hallmark of American journalism until that time. By the 1890s, the structural organization of corporate journalism had taken its modern form. Special sections of the newspaper and topic "beats" were the norm. Sports coverage, financial news, literary content, fashion pages, society announcements, and comics claimed space in the newspaper alongside the traditional records of government and institutional activity.

News beats developed around those institutions and community locations where journalists could rely on regular access to newsworthy activities. The beat names are self-evident: cops and courts; local government; education; sports; agriculture; business; the national desk. Each of these beats provided at least one major institutional location (a courthouse, a mayor's office, a school board meeting, a sports stadium, a farming cooperative, a company headquarters, Congress or the White House) and officials who could reliably provide journalists with current, newsworthy information. Publicity agents, widely adopted by big business during the late nineteenth and early twentieth centuries, helped disseminate information about their corporate clients to media professionals strapped for time.

The invention of broadcasting introduced a new imperative into the journalistic routines of information gathering. In addition to gathering accurate accounts for the written medium, journalists working in the radio and television media had to gather appropriate sound and moving pictures to accompany their stories. The need for a reliable process for gathering content in time to craft and edit a story to meet a broadcast deadline further narrowed the range of locations where journalists might seek for news.

The Associated Press wire service began providing information for broadcasters in 1941 and as television technology moved from film to tape to live electronic transmission, the deadline pressures mounted. The cost of assigning camera crews and the small number of reporters and producers in most television newsrooms means assignment editors rely heavily on pre-scheduled, pre-announced and pre-packaged events to generate coverage. Local broadcasters also monitor police scanners and emergency responder radio frequencies throughout the day to decide where to send their "live" crews. This obviously affects the types of stories television viewers see in their newscasts.

Critiques of Sourcing Practices

Research over several decades has documented that modern news organizations rely on routine channels of information for a large proportion of their stories. These include speeches, news releases, news conferences, trials and legislative hearings and other non-spontaneous events. Public relations professionals have established strong connections with media organizations and have found great success with newsrooms that are willing to reprint or rebroadcast the PR professionals' items, sometimes verbatim and unedited.

Journalists also still rely heavily on official sources—especially those affiliated with national, regional or local government, whose authority and legitimacy is generally assumed. In the age of subject specialization, journalists also rely heavily on political, scientific, business and military experts, especially as news organizations attempt to cover more complex problems and issues. The vast proliferation of interest groups and advocacy organizations has led to another major source of information for journalists, who turn to such partisans for much of their "on the one hand, on the other hand" reporting.

The crusading investigative journalist who attempts to break out of the reliance on official sources and routine information channels occasionally has some success. Starting in the 1970s, some journalists began using what was called "computer-assisted reporting" or CAR. By gathering records from institutions and independently analyzing them using newly-accessible computer systems, journalists were able to free themselves from their dependence on institutional spokespersons to interpret official information. Advances in desktop computers and powerful data analysis software made such CAR techniques widely available in even the smallest newsrooms by the end of the twentieth century. But investigative journalism is the exception for most corporate news organizations that need to meet shareholders' profit expectations, advertisers' demand for noncontroversial content environments for their ads, and readers' skepticism of the overreaching of what they see as the elite media class.

Modern Sources

Media organizations have legitimately been criticized for their failure to incorporate voices outside the mainstream, safe, "official" view of society. Journalists Bill Kovach and Tom Rosenstiel have argued that news organizations need to provide a forum for the voiceless to be heard. At the same time, they criticize journalists' reliance on the most extreme voices when a controversial issue is the subject of news coverage. They argue that an appropriate role for modern journalists is to report, verify, and synthesize information from as wide a spectrum of sources, views and perspectives as possible, while adhering to the tenets of sound journalistic practice. Journalists should identify a common set of issues for public attention and provide the relevant information for an informed discussion.

Journalism educators Kathleen Hansen and Nora Paul have outlined a model for information gathering that provides journalists with a means of conceptualizing their information tasks and helps them to identify information from a wide spectrum of sources. They note that journalists gather information through monitoring, searching and interviewing. Monitoring methods include personal observations, tracking information through electronic means and regularly "checking in" with sources. Searching methods include the techniques of identifying and retrieving information in print and electronic form and identifying expert sources. Interviewing includes both face-to-face and all of the other means of communicating with sources (telephone, e-mail, text-messaging, etc.).

Journalists use these methods to gather information from informal, institutional, scholarly and journalistic sources. Informal sources include those "person-on-the-street" sources that rarely see their perspectives or views represented in the media. Public opinion polls conducted by news organizations attempt to capture the attitudes and intended behaviors of informal sources by interviewing "average" community members for the poll. The new communications channels of weblogs, Internet chats, forums and newsgroups provide many avenues of access to informal information sources, making the journalists' job of diversifying their sources much easier.

Institutional sources are those that produce official records of activity (governmental bodies, businesses, churches, political organizations, trade unions, etc.) and the individuals who hold leadership roles in those organizations. These do not have to be limited to the narrow range of institutions usually tapped by journalists. The wide accessibility of institutional information in electronic form has greatly expanded the opportunity for journalists to conduct independent analyses and write stories outside the "spin" of official institutional spokespersons.

Scholarly sources provide expert perspective on the wide and complex range of issues on which modern media focus. The print and electronic literature produced by scholars and the individual scholars themselves can provide journalists with a means for understanding what institutional sources may be proposing or what informal sources may be doing.

Journalists have relied on experts since the adoption of the interview, but journalists are now able to independently identify appropriate scholarly information that helps them interpret information for their audiences.

Journalistic sources comprise the vast array of content produced by news organizations in all media. Journalists have always relied on their colleagues and competitors for cues about what it news. Broadcast journalists scan the morning newspapers as they prepare their newsgathering plan for the day. Online journalists compile news reports from a wide variety of sources to generate the links and value-added content they include in their online stories. Newspaper journalists monitor the all-news broadcast channels in the newsroom all day to make sure they are on top of breaking stories. The elite national media (the *New York Times*, the *Wall Street Journal*, the *Washington Post*, the network news programs, the wire services) have always set the news agenda for local and regional media outlets.

These information sources can be used by journalists to widen the news net they cast as they define what is newsworthy in their communities and for their audiences. Journalistic information practices will no doubt continue to evolve as news delivery mechanisms, audience preferences and media ownership trends change. At the core of such journalistic practices, however, there will always be the imperative to record what is important and report what is interesting.

Further Reading

Dicken-Garcia, Hazel. *Journalistic Standards in Nineteenth-Century America*. Madison: The University of Wisconsin Press, 1989.

Hansen, Kathleen A., and Nora Paul. *Behind the Message: Information Strategies for Communicators*. Boston, MA: Allyn & Bacon, 2004.

Kovach, Bill, and Tom Rosenstiel. *The Elements of Journalism: What Newspeople Should Know and the Public Should Expect*. NY: Crown Publishers, 2001.

Schudson, Michael. *The Power of News*. Cambridge, MA: Harvard University Press, 1995.

Shaw, Donald Lewis. "At the Crossroads: Change and Continuity in American Press News 1820–1860." *Journalism History* 8(2) (Summer 1981): 41.

KATHLEEN A. HANSEN

SPACE COVERAGE

When American astronaut Steve Robinson walked in space in July 2005 to repair the Space Shuttle Discovery, people around the world watched on international cable networks via a National Aeronautics and Space Administration (NASA) satellite feed. The vast, supportive prime-time news coverage, which came two years after a second shuttle disaster with the explosion of the Space Shuttle Columbia, was embraced and encouraged by NASA, who opened its operations to media representatives from around the world.

In 1958, at the height of the Cold War when the United States was in major competition with the Soviet Union

(U.S.S.R.), the newly founded NASA treated media coverage differently. Back then, a cloud of secrecy and security shielded NASA operations and buffered journalists trying to cover the early space program.

If a single event can be pinpointed as the starting point of the space race, it was the Soviet launch of Sputnik I on October 4, 1957. The world's first artificial satellite was the size of a basketball, weighed 183 pounds, and took some ninety-eight minutes to orbit the earth. It ushered in a new era of political, military, technological, and scientific developments.

The signing of the Space Act of 1958 helped to forge the framework for NASA's public affairs office. Section 203 (a) (3) of the act stated that NASA shall "provide for the widest practicable and appropriate dissemination of information concerning its activities and the results thereof." NASA public relations chief, Walter Bonney, wrote that NASA must maintain a positive information program designed to provide the people of the United States with maximum information about the agency's accomplishment.

Everything accelerated on April 2, 1959, when NASA introduced the first seven Mercury astronauts. Only a few feet away, more than two hundred newspaper, magazine, radio, and television reporters clambered for the ten-page press packet being handed out by public affairs specialists. The relationship between the agency and the press was not altogether harmonious. NASA, using strict Air Force public affairs protocols drafted during World War II, kept tight reins on information, allowing journalists restricted but uniform access to the astronauts as they performed their official duties. The astronauts' personal stories and off-duty lives were off limits, as NASA sold those rights to *Life* magazine.

Early space reporters had their work cut out for them at Cape Canaveral. By the time the astronauts arrived at Cocoa Beach in May 1959, the first reporters were already firmly entrenched there. The Associated Press assigned Howard S. Benedict to the Cape, while United Press International sent Al Webb. Fairchild Publications, publishers of *Aviation Week*, assigned Mary Bubb, while Doug Dederer was there from the *Cocoa Tribune*. Jay Barbree represented NBC News. These individuals were staples in the full-time Canaveral Press corps. Soon—and especially on launch dates—they would be joined by hundreds more, including Walter Cronkite of CBS News, Jules Bergman of ABC News, and Roy Neal with NBC, who created and staffed NASA's first broadcast press pool. John Noble Wilford was the *New York Times'* full-time science and space reporter, and *Life* reporters Don Schanche, Sr. and Ralph Morse wrote regular, contracted articles about the astronauts' daily lives.

Benedict said the first few months were a "fireworks display" as NASA tested rocket after rocket—and many exploded. "Since no trust had been formed between the two groups, we'd gather on a beach south of the Cape on high sandy knoll which we named 'Bird Watch Hill,' with cameras aimed at the launch site. When they (the Air Force) were launching a new missile, they didn't like us taking pictures; a lot of time they'd come in with a helicopter and swoop down on us and we'd scatter for the bushes. By the time we'd collected our senses, the missile was out of sight or had blown up," Benedict said.

Perhaps no journalist epitomizes the history of space coverage more than veteran CBS anchor Walter Cronkite. Cronkite had a keen interest in the early space program, keeping large notebooks on each of the Mercury Flights. He said in an interview with National Public Radio in 2002 that he owed astronaut John Herschel Glenn a part of his career, because Cronkite covered his launch extensively in early 1962. Cronkite was one of the foremost boosters of America's technological prowess and when the United States launched the first manned space flight to the moon in July, 1969, he provided, the Museum of Broadcast Communications noted, "Walter to Walter coverage" for twenty-seven of the thirty hours that Apollo XI took to complete its mission.

Through Gemini and Apollo, NASA loosened access to the astronauts, so reporters had more chance to work with them on official and off-duty stories. But as access improved, the actual volume of news coverage of space was reduced incrementally. After the round-the-clock Apollo XI moon landing in 1969 and the Apollo XIII accident in space in 1970, coverage became limited to the briefest launch and landing coverage. Only the largest newspapers and wire services continued thorough coverage, and most newspapers and television stations depended on those resources. The "space race" was no longer as exciting as it had once been.

Even the voyages of the Space Shuttle vehicles did not receive the coverage of the early days. Except for historic firsts like the launch of Columbia April 12, 1981, or for disasters, the missions received only cursory reporting from the networks. In fact, on January 28, 1986, all networks except CNN had cut away from the Challenger lift-off—only CNN and the Associated Press (led by Howard Benedict) were still reporting when the shuttle exploded.

Larry Klaes noted in a 2003 column in *Space Daily*, "The Space Shuttle *Columbia* Mission STS-107" was a case in point. Outside of the fact that the first Israeli astronaut was on this flight, the general public probably knew or cared little of what the mission objectives were. Most media coverage was brief and often buried amidst unrelated news." The *Columbia* disintegrated on re-entry over Texas on February 1, 2003, killing all seven crew members. The incident demonstrated the danger of space travel and its aftermath did reveal that a profound and continuing public interest did remain for reporting on space.

Further Reading

Carter, J.R. "View From the Birdwatch: Media, Memory, and America's Mercury Astronauts," Doctoral Dissertation, University of Southern Mississippi, 1996.

Klaes, Larry. "Living In The Space Age." *Space Daily: Your Portal to Space*. Los Angeles, February 6, 2003

"NASA History Office online," http://history.nasa.gov/tindex.html (accessed April 10, 2007).

"Walter Cronkite Biography," http://www.museum.tv/archives/
etv/C/htmlC/cronkitewal/cronkitewal.htm (accessed April
10, 2007).

GINGER CARTER MILLER

SPANISH-AMERICAN WAR AND THE PRESS

One of the most enduring questions in American journalism concerns the role of the press in the U.S. government's decision to declare war against Spain in 1898. In short, did the press—specifically New York's sensationalistic "yellow" newspapers, the *World* and *Journal*—whip the public into such a frenzy that war with Spain was inevitable? Although recent scholarship suggests that the yellow press had no direct role in the decision to wage war, scholars have posited different views on this for a century and the definitive answer may never be known.

Exit Spain, Enter America

Spain's vast empire in the New World had been depleted early in the nineteenth century, when most of its colonies took advantage of Spain's struggle against Napoleonic rule and gained their independence. By the 1890s, Cuba was one of Spain's only remaining colonies, and its citizens seemed increasingly determined to break free as well. In 1895—the same year that publisher William Randolph Hearst arrived in New York to "out-Pulitzer" Pulitzer with his *Evening Journal*—the Cubans officially began their war of independence.

Initially, the United States took little notice of what appeared to be a band of guerillas fighting the Spaniards in Cuba. But certainly by 1898, that had changed. And in 1898 several events, most dramatically the explosion of a U.S. battleship in Havana's harbor, galvanized public opinion against Spain. In June 1898, the United States invaded Cuba. By August, the war was over and the United States was ready to begin its path as a world power.

"The *Journal*'s War"

In the decades following the Spanish-American War, both contemporaneous and historical accounts pointed to the era's spectacularly sensationalistic and crusading "yellow journalism" and its jingoistic war cries as the impetus for America's decision to force Spain out of Cuba, which had been under Spanish rule for nearly four hundred years.

William Randolph Hearst in particular garnered much of this scrutiny. He had devoted significant column space and reporting resources in his *New York Journal* to the Cuban revolution well before American intervention. Hearst was keenly interested in the drama taking place just miles off America's shoreline. As a story, the Cuban resistance to Spain certainly lent itself to sensational treatment, with cruel villains, shocking injustices and the romantic quest of a nearby colony striving for independence from the merciless European power.

In perhaps the most famous scene from the yellow journalism era, Hearst exchanged telegrams with an employee he had sent to Cuba in anticipation of military action. The employee, artist Frederic S. Remington, had reportedly sent a telegram complaining that all was quiet, war seemed unlikely and he wanted to return. Hearst's reply was confident: "Please remain. You furnish the pictures and I'll furnish the war." This story, recounted by only one person, journalist James Creelman in his memoirs, gained an even greater hold in the popular conception of Hearst and the Spanish-American War when it was echoed in a scene from the film *Citizen Kane*, a thinly veiled fictionalized biography of Hearst. However, serious historians have dismissed the telegram story as unlikely over the years, and there is evidence that Creelman would have been in Europe at the time and could not have witnessed it.

The hubris contained in this supposed telegram, however, does reflect the spirit of unabashed self-promotion that was a hallmark of the yellow press and of Hearst in particular. And this trait, in turn, muddied later interpretations of a famous epigram that the *Journal* ran on its front page for three days, once the war was underway, asking: "How Do You Like the *Journal*'s War?" As historian Joseph Campbell points out, however, that epigram was intended to be an ironic retort to the *Evening Post*, which had accused the yellow press of "fomenting" the war.

What had Hearst's *New York Journal* done to earn this accusation? The paper had been aggressively calling for American intervention in Cuba and placing stories of Spanish atrocities on its front page prior to the war. In fact, Spain *was* guilty of numerous forms of oppression and abuse. In 1896, Spain had sent General Vaeriano Weyler to command its forces in Cuba, and Weyler had immediately implemented the policy of *reconcentrado*, rounding up people in the countryside into concentration camps, where they could be prevented from joining or supplying the rebels. In the following years, hundreds of thousands of Cuban citizens had died—many from starvation and abuse in the concentration camps. It did not take long for Hearst's *Journal* to nickname Weyler "Butcher."

But not all accounts of Spanish misdeeds were true. Indeed, the *Journal,* true to its yellow form, tapped into the Victorian fixation with female chastity and vulnerability by exploiting and often exaggerating stories of this nature. An 1897 headline about Weyler is illustrative: "Weyler throws nuns into prison. Butcher wages brutal warfare on helpless women." And that same year, Frederic Remington illustrated an article about American women being searched by Spaniards aboard a passenger ship. Remington's picture suggested the women had been stripped naked in front of several male Spaniards, when in fact they had been taken to private quarters and searched respectfully by females. The *Journal* undertook its boldest crusade ever soon thereafter—successfully breaking a Cuban political prisoner named Evangelina Cisneros out of a Havana jail. Playing up a questionable detail—that the beautiful nineteen-year-old was facing harsher punishment for resisting the advances of a Spanish officer—the *Journal*'s account by reporter Karl

Decker described how he valiantly rescued Cisneros and smuggled her onto a ship bound for New York.

The Role of Other Newspapers

Notably, most of the colorful anecdotes about press coverage a year before the Spanish-American War star Hearst and his *Journal*. Although both Hearst and Pulitzer are often accused of pounding the drums of war in concert, they treated Cuba quite differently before 1898. This changed near the end of February of that year, but the timing suggests that Pulitzer's *World* was following public sentiment by then, not leading it.

On February 15, 1898, when the *U.S.S. Maine* mysteriously blew up and sunk into the Havana harbor, casting suspicion on Spain despite the lack of any motive or evidence, the *World* merely followed the dictates of yellow journalism, filling its front pages with headlines and illustrations of the dramatic event that took nearly 266 American lives. The *Journal*, on the other hand, also carried a banner headline that screamed: "War sure! Maine Destroyed by Spanish; this proved absolutely by the torpedo hole." Just two weeks later, however, Pulitzer's *World* also began calling for war. And, frustrated by the slowness of the investigation into the explosion's cause, Pulitzer also claimed that the *World* had sent its own team of divers to the wreck and found fifty "proofs" that the Maine was blown up by a mine or torpedo.

And yet, despite these accounts, and despite the fact that other newspapers were pointing a finger at the yellow journals, scholars have found little evidence that the New York *World* or *Journal*—or even the yellow journals throughout the urban centers of America—had any direct impact on the foreign policy of President William McKinley, or even upon public opinion itself. Instead, W. Joseph Campbell's 2001 book, which analyzes an enormous collection of primary and secondary sources, makes the most complete case yet that the Remington-Hearst telegram exchange never happened, and that the yellow press, with such low credibility, could have had any significant influence concerning the Spanish-American War.

Moreover, a 2006 study of ten newspapers from that era—including both yellow and conservative papers—cast doubt on the claim that the yellow press stood out dramatically from other papers in coverage of Cuba leading up to the war. Although 39 percent of stories from the yellow press had a pro-Cuba bias, compared to 15 percent in conservative papers, *neither* type of newspaper showed much sympathy for Spain. And perhaps more significantly, given the understanding that scholars have of the media's ability to set the public agenda, that study also found that conservative papers carried three times as many stories about the conflict on their front pages than the yellow papers.

In that study, John Maxwell Hamilton and colleagues concluded that both conservative and yellow newspapers "put the Cuban question on the agenda of the public —and its leaders—and did so in a way that arguments for the war could take root and grow." When Congress declared war after several months of debate, President McKinley knew that the action was in line with public sentiment.

In any event, once the Spanish-American War began, it garnered an enormous amount of press coverage, with newspapers sending reporters to Cuba to bring home stories of what U.S. Ambassador to England John Hay famously called the "splendid little war" being waged by the increasingly prosperous and influential United States against a fading imperial power.

Further Reading

Campbell, W. Joseph. *Yellow Journalism: Puncturing the Myths, Defining the Legacies.* Westport, CT: Praeger, 2001.

Creelman, James. *On the Great Highway: The Wanderings and Adventures of a Special Correspondent.* Boston: Lothrop Publishing, 1901.

Hamilton, John Maxwell, Renita Coleman, Bettye Grable, and Jaci Cole. "An Enabling Environment: A Reconsideration of the Press and the Spanish-American War." *Journalism Studies* 7, no. 1 (2006): 87–103.

Nasaw, David. *The Chief: The Life of William Randolph Hearst.* Boston: Houghton Mifflin, 2000.

Swanberg, W. A. *Citizen Hearst: A Biography of William Randolph Hearst.* New York: Charles Scribner's Sons, 1961.

Wisan, Joseph E. *The Cuban Crisis as Reflected in the New York Press (1895–1898).* New York: Octagon Books, reprint edition, 1965.

EMILY ERICKSON

SPORTING NEWS

Often referred to as the "Bible of Baseball," the *Sporting News* was founded in 1886 in St. Louis, Missouri, by Alfred H. Spink, whose family would run it for ninety-one years. The publication was quickly successful, allowing Spink to pursue a variety of interests, including taking a musical show on the road. He persuaded his brother, Charles Spink, to return home from Montana to manage the magazine during his absences. The arrangement soon became permanent, as Charles Spink won a power struggle to gain control and Alfred Spink moved to Chicago. Charles was succeeded by his son, J.G. Taylor Spink in 1914.

The *Sporting News* was associated with the rise of the St. Louis Browns professional baseball team, which won a World Series in 1886. Although initially covering a variety of sports, the magazine had become devoted entirely to baseball by 1906 and was styled at the time as a "Weekly Journal Devoted to the Advancement of the Interests of Organized Baseball."

Taylor Spink always looked for ways to tie the publication in with major league baseball. He cultivated a friendship with American League President Ban Johnson, who purchased copies at a reduced rate and sent them to members of the American Expeditionary Force during World War I. The nickname "Bible of Baseball," embraced heartily by Spink, caught on during the 1940s, especially after a 1942 *Saturday Evening Post* story carrying that title also labeled

Spink as "Mr. Baseball." Indicative of the publication's status in the game, as one of his numerous publicity stunts Bill Veeck conducted a funeral service for the pennant hopes of the Cleveland Indians in 1949, and last rites were read from the *Sporting News*. Baseball, indeed, was covered in minute detail by the magazine, which added minor league box scores in 1922.

The minutiae were often leavened by a spirited editorial voice full of invective, under Charles and Taylor Spink. In the early days, women might be referred to as "harpies," and the proprietors of another publication, *Printer's Journal* were described as "four dirty, drunken, lousy printers." Taylor Spink's cozy relationship with major league baseball did not prevent Spink from saying of Commissioner Kenesaw Mountain Landis: "...Mr. Landis shows that he is possessed of vanity and weakness inherent in most autocrats."

Landis exercised his autocratic powers to take away the *Sporting News'* status as publisher of the *Official Baseball Guide* between 1942 and 1947. It was restored, however, by Landis' successor, Albert Chandler.

By 1942, the *Sporting News* had begun some coverage of football, and other sports followed. Taylor Spink died in 1962, and was succeeded by his son, C.C. Johnson Spink, who did not institute any dramatic changes. In 1969, the magazine moved to a suburban location. Finding himself childless at sixty and without a natural successor, Johnson Spink sold it to the Times Mirror Corporation in 1977.

No doubt, baseball in some part owes its status through much of the twentieth century as "the national pastime" to the fact that it had become so closely joined with a nationally prominent publication, a relationship that no other sport enjoyed. Baseball fans' unique enthusiasm for statistics can perhaps be attributed in some measure to the *Sporting News'* efforts to assemble such data in the weekly magazine and its annual publications.

Further Reading

Reidenbaugh, Lowell. *The Sporting News: The First 100 Years, 1886–1986*. St. Louis: Sporting News Publishing Company, 1985.

GORDON JACKSON

SPORTS BROADCASTING

Sports broadcasting in the United States can be traced back to 1899 when Guglielmo Marconi was brought to this country under the auspices of the *New York Herald* to report the America's Cup races via wireless telegraphy. Marconi saw it as an opportunity to demonstrate his new invention. For the *Herald* it was an opportunity to scoop the competition and have the news in print even before the boats reached shore. The minute-by-minute account of the race that Marconi provided proved to be a great success. It was with this event that the link between sports and broadcasting technology became one of the defining aspects of the relationship from then on. The technological aspect of the relationship between sports and broadcasting is, however,

only one dimension of this dynamic partnership. There are historical, political, economic, psychological, and social aspects of this relationship that entwine with the technological in complex ways to shape one of the great forms of American entertainment.

The relationship between sports and the media is one of mutual dependence with both positive and negative effects. This symbiotic combination has helped each survive and has changed the form and content of both. The broadcast media have, for example, elevated several sports events to spectacle status. They have the capacity to confer status and build an audience for a sport. Likewise, sporting events have the capacity to deliver an audience to the media and supply them with programming content. In addition, the sports industry has been very useful as a marketing tool for consumer media. The latest example is that of the satellite television industry where the desire to see and hear sports aids the penetration of technology into various markets through the sale of satellite dish services. Historically, sports have shown they have the capacity as marketing vehicles for the sale of broadcast hardware to consumers. Boxing and baseball, for example, were integral in the sale of radio receivers when radio was a new technology and television sets, when it was new. The combination of popularity and immediacy, then, feeds the symbiotic relationship between sports and broadcast media that together form a fruitful and dynamic interaction.

Enormous economic consequences emerge from this interface. Entrepreneurs market sports equipment and clothing and purchase television advertisements that can cost millions of dollars for a thirty-second spot. Multi-year contracts for television rights to broadcast various sports have cost commercial networks billions of dollars and the continuing popularity of televised sports ensures that the networks will keep on budgeting vast sums of money for the rights to cover them and that commercial sponsors will continue to underwrite these costs. Socially and psychologically, mediated sports can motivate people to get involved in healthy physical activities. There is also, however, the potential for less physical activity associated with the over use of the media. Additionally, much has been written about the exposure to sports through the mass media and the distortion of body image leading to negative attitudes about oneself and others. Scandals associated with athlete exploitation, gambling, and the use of performance enhancing drugs have also been related to sports broadcasting.

With the evolution of the broadcast media there has been an enhanced commitment of air time to sport. Indeed, sports have become a fundamental part of our television diet and can be found in many forms and formats. Local television news shows often have a sports segment embedded in the show to bring national, state, and local sports highlights to the audience. Reality TV programs often involve some sort of athletic skills. Game shows quiz contestants on their sports knowledge or engage them in competitive sport-like events. With the advent of cable and satellite technology, the television and radio audience can now tune in to a practically endless stream of live sports, sports talk shows, sports specials, highlights, and reruns of entire broadcasts from events that just recently happened or replay those that happened years ago in a "classic sports" format.

Television

A number of studies have illustrated the importance of media to sports. While radio and other media have played vital roles in the development of this relationship, the dominant medium since the late 1950s has been television. More than anything, television has helped to globalize sports, bringing events like the Super Bowl to a worldwide audience numbering in the hundreds of millions.

Arguably, television has transformed sports more than any medium—broadcast or otherwise. The time of day that baseball games are played has been altered to accommodate television scheduling needs. The increase of night baseball, for example, allowed networks to attract viewers during the prime time viewing hours. Football changed in many ways because of television. From the size of the letters and numbers on the players' jerseys to make them more visible to commercial timeouts, football has gone through many innovations to satisfy the visual, auditory, economic, and time-oriented needs of television. Football telecasts employed such technologies as slow-motion instant replay, improved cameras and zoom lenses, parabolic microphones, an electronic chalkboard called a telestrator. During Super Bowl XXXV, Columbia Broadcasting System (CBS) introduced Eyevision: a computerized form of instant replay that allowed the viewer to see the action in three dimensional space from a variety of angles. Many of these technologies were created, or improved, exclusively for use during football broadcasts.

Golf also underwent a major transformation because of television. The requirements of TV production literally changed the way the game was played. Once a private exercise traditionally played in an atmosphere of austere silence where the number of strokes required to complete a round of eighteen holes mattered little, golf was transformed into a public entertainment where the number of strokes under par a player takes during a multiple-round tournament matters greatly. Before television, the most interesting tournaments were played under the rules of match play where two men competed one against the other. What mattered under the rules of match play was the number of individual holes each player won. Two of the four championships Bobby Jones won when making his grand slam in 1930 were played under these rules. For television, match play had two basic weaknesses: it was impossible to predict how long a match would last, and it could be decided on a hole where no television cameras were stationed. If, for example, a player won the first ten holes, the match was essentially decided (his or her rival could not make up the difference over the final eight holes). Match play rules had to be abandoned for television. This resulted in the score keeping known today in which each player's number of strokes are compared to par at any given point in the tournament. Of course, television changed golf in other ways too, not least of which was the size of the crowds, or gallery, that attended major golfing events.

Indeed, sports and television have evolved much since the early days of the medium. In 1946, the National Broadcasting Company (NBC) introduced television by showing a Joe Louis—Billy Conn heavyweight prize-fight. Soon after, taverns rushed to install television sets to attract crowds during boxing and wrestling events. Over the years both sports have changed and the way people view them has changed. Now relegated to pay-per-view status, free, live viewing of boxing's major events is a thing of the past. And when we think of professional wrestling today we think of the ultra-hyped spectacle of the World Wrestling Entertainment (WWE) franchise whose promoter, Vince K. McMahon helped shape this popular made-for-television sport which includes heroes and champions with names such as Blackjack Mulligan, Sergeant Slaughter, Big Show, and Booker T. The scantily clad women wrestlers are also a far cry from early television fare. The evolution of sexualized and ultra-violent sports is one of the byproducts of the relationship between sport and television. Taking the best (or worst) of boxing and wrestling, Ultimate Fighting is an example of the extreme form of violent sport that has found a popular place on television.

A broadcast sport that rose in popularity thanks to television was car racing, especially the National Association for Stock Car Auto Racing (NASCAR) circuit, which in 2007 was the second most popular spectator sport behind football. NASCAR has been particularly good at enhancing the visual experience of the races by placing cameras in places such as on the driver's helmet in a heads-up display configuration and in various places in and around the cars to provide the television audience with spectacular and unique views of the race. For example, in one race a camera was placed in the wheel well of a car so that the television audience could watch the sparks and heat that were generated when the brakes were applied to the fast-moving vehicle. NASCAR has also been ahead of many other major sports in the use of new media technologies (see below).

Programming

Several programs were important in the development of sports television. The *Gillette Cavalcade of Sports*, one of the earliest television shows, broadcast some of the biggest boxing names from 1946 until 1960 on NBC. The American Broadcasting Company's (ABC) *Wide World of Sports* hit the television airwaves on April 29, 1961. From track and field to gymnastics, and from cliff diving to wrist wrestling, this weekly series would bring a variety of sporting events to the American public. Originally conceived as a summer replacement program, it first broadcast the Penn and Drake Relays live from Philadelphia, Pennsylvania, and Des Moines, Iowa, respectively. Broadcasting the twenty-four-hour grand prix auto race from Le Mans in 1965, it became the first sports program to telecast via satellite.

Known for their innovative sports programming, ABC inaugurated *Monday Night Football* (*MNF*) on September

21, 1970, with a game between the New York Jets and the Cleveland Browns from Cleveland, Ohio. The original commentators for the show were Howard Cosell, Keith Jackson, and Don Meredith. Jackson was soon replaced by former New York Giant football star Frank Gifford and through the years the *MNF* announcing team would go through many personnel changes. Through the 2005 season, Al Michaels and John Madden announced the games for what became the second longest running prime time television show after *60 Minutes*. Over the years, *MNF* pioneered several technological innovations including enhanced slow motion replays and computerized graphics such as the first down marker superimposed onto the field during play.

ESPN

On September 7, 1979, Scott Rasmussen and his father Bill Rasmussen along with Donny Stanley and his son Cardell launched ESPN, an abbreviation for *Entertainment and Sports Programming Network*. This American cable television network was dedicated to broadcasting sports-related programming twenty-four-hours a day. Its signature telecast, *SportsCenter*, was the network's debut show.

ESPN started as an alternative to the short sports segments found in most local television newscasts. In the beginning it was a small operation that often had to broadcast unorthodox sporting events such as tractor pulls, fairly unknown international sports such as Australian Rules Football, and the short-lived United States football League games to attract viewers. In landing the contract to show National Football League (NFL) games on Sunday nights in 1987, ESPN marked a turning point in its development from a small cable network to a marketing giant. In 2006 ESPN took over the Monday Night Football franchise. ESPN's influence today reaches into more than just the television medium. The ESPN radio network was launched on January 1, 1992, *ESPN The Magazine* in 1998, and its restaurant franchise, ESPN Zone in 1998.

Made-for-TV Sports

Sports existed long before television was invented and unlike other forms of television programming, exist independent of the medium. There are, however, some sports and sports events that are made for television. As already mentioned, ultra-violent sports are one byproduct of the sports-broadcasting relationship. "Extreme sports" such as the X Games and SlamBall are two other examples. The X Games, short for Extreme Games, are an extreme-sports version of the Olympics with summer and winter games. ESPN's Director of Programming, Ron Semiao, came up with the idea for the X Games in 1993. After two years in development, the first X Games were held from June 24 to July 1, 1995 in Middletown, Rhode Island, and Mount Snow, Vermont, with athletes competing in twenty-seven events in nine sports categories: bungy jumping, eco-challenge, in-line skating, skateboarding, skysurfing, sport climbing,

street luge, biking, and water sports. In 1997 the inaugural Winter X Games was televised from Big Bear Lake, California, from January 30 to February 2. The winter games consist of sports such as snowboarding, ice climbing, snow mountain bike racing, super-modified shovel racing and a cross-over multi-sport event. SlamBall, the brainchild of twenty-eight-year-old Mason Gordon is, simply put, basketball played on a court of trampolines. Slam Ball made its television debut on August 3, 2002, as a six-episode summer series on The Nashville Network (TNN; in 2003 TNN became Spike TV). With its violent mid-air collisions and spectacular dunks, SlamBall attracts a large, young and diverse audience for television.

Not all made-for-TV sports are extreme or violent in nature. The World Professional Figure Skating Championships created by former Olympic figure skating gold medalist Dick Button, The Superstars (also created by Button), and the World's Strongest Man competition are a few examples. One of the more famous television publicity stunts was a tennis match between Bobby Riggs and Billy Jean King. Riggs, a tennis champion in his youth, was fifty-five and a well-known tennis hustler in 1973 when he challenged King who was the women's tennis champion at the time. Billed as the "Battle of the Sexes," the match was shown on television during prime time and an estimated fifty million viewers watched. King defeated Riggs in three sets 6–4, 6–3, 6–3.

Radio

It is with the first electronic mass medium, radio, that the roots of sports broadcasting are found. The first sports game to be broadcast on radio was a major league baseball contest between the Pittsburgh Pirates and the Philadelphia Phillies from Forbes Field on August 5, 1921. Later that year the World Series was broadcast. Prizefights were another sport that was, early on, part of radio fare. Around this time KDKA, arguably the first full service commercial radio station, was broadcasting boxing via live remote pick-ups. In October 1922, American Telephone & Telegraph (AT&T) broadcast a football game between Princeton and the University of Chicago via long-distance telephone lines from Stagg Field in Chicago to WEAF in New York. In November a Harvard-Yale game was broadcast in a similar manner. The first professional football (NFL) game to be broadcast on radio was between the Detroit Lions and the Chicago Bears on Thanksgiving Day, November 29, 1934. Graham McNamee was the sportscaster for the game.

Sportscasters

MacNamee and the rest of radio's first generation of sports announcers, including Harold Arlin, Tommy Cowan, Ford Frick, Ted Husing, and Grantland Rice were most responsible for making their craft an art form. In those early days there was an emphasis on excitement and enthusiasm at the expense of accuracy. For an announcer who might be broadcasting from a studio that was miles away from the game site, recreating the event from wire service reports meant that sound effects and colorful language were needed to manufacture the illusion that they were reporting the play-by-play live from the event. Among the early sportscasters, working his first job at WOC in Davenport, Iowa, as a football announcer was Ronald W. Reagan who, forty-eight years later would become the fortieth president of the United States.

The second generation of radio sportscasters—Mel Allen, Red Barber, Jack Brickhouse, Lindsay Nelson, and Bill Stern—would make the transition to television and pave the way for a later generation of television announcers including Bob Costas, John Madden, Jim McKay, Al Michaels, Ray Scott, Pat Summerall, Dick Vitale, and Jack Whitaker, to name a few. Phyllis George is generally given credit for breaking sportcasting's gender barrier in 1975 when she joined *The NFL Today*, although for a brief time Myrtle Power did color commentating for CBS in the 1950s. The color barrier was broken by Jocko Maxwell in 1935 when he went to work as a sportscaster for WHOM in Jersey City, New Jersey. More recently, several African Americans have distinguished themselves as sports announcers and commentators including Irv Cross, brothers Greg and Bryant Gumbel, Jayne Kennedy, Joe Morgan, Ahmad Rashad, O.J. Simpson, and James Brown.

Radio has recently played a lesser role in live sports broadcasting. However, with the advent of XM satellite radio, a technology that eliminates static, some say that radio's romance with live baseball will be rekindled. Sports enthusiasts can find many sports talk programs on XM and Sirius satellite radio as well.

New Media

The term, "new media" is sometimes synonymous with digital media and computer-based media formats, especially the Internet. The Internet provides a vast store of information for the sports enthusiast that is easy to search with more current information than traditional print media. The quality and credibility of the information is, however, dubious at times. New media include, however, more than just the Internet: the latest forms of television, CD, DVD, cell phones, video games, converged technologies, multimedia, satellite radio, and other emerging forms of media.

There is much yet to be determined regarding the ways in which the relationship between sports and new media will develop. What is certain is that they will continue to evolve and influence each other in ways similar, and perhaps dissimilar, to the older media of television and radio with sports. In fact, emerging patterns of sports content usage in conjunction with new media are evident. On the Internet, for example, there are web sites for practically all major and minor league teams, league web sites, sports news, fan web sites and discussion boards for fans, as well as sports-related gambling and opportunities for sales and marketing of sports products. Some recent figures show that in one month as many as twelve million people visited sports Web sites such as espn.com, sportsline.com, CNNSI.com, and Foxsports.com. The Internet is also, at least in part, to be credited with fueling the growing popularity of fantasy sports leagues.

New media services are becoming increasingly important for the transmission of highlights from top sporting events. Mobile phones have led the way in this area by offering services that allow sports fans to play video clips of spectacular plays or receive text messages with the latest results. Moreover, the medium allows for a more truly interactive experience than traditional broadcast media with services such as chat rooms, discussion forums, and surveys. Greater fan participation and interactivity are, incidentally, hallmarks of the new media. In addition, sports content can be customized to suit user needs. Indeed, the relationship between new media and sports offers the consumer more choices in media content and information than ever before. Some satellite television services offer fans content "on-demand" to be viewed anytime at the viewer's leisure. And some services allow viewers to put several games on their screen at the same time, select what replays and camera angles they want, and other services that the viewer controls.

The use of new media technologies generally allows more flexible, individualized management of sports content, facilitating the circulation of information. But questions remain. Will new media services deepen fan interest or whittle away at sports viewership? Will fan interest in fantasy leagues erode loyalty to real teams? One thing is evident, however, new media have the potential to transform the way fans consumer sports content.

Further Reading

Baker, Aaron and Todd Boyd, eds. *Out of Bounds: Sports, Media, and the Politics of Identity.* Bloomington: University of Indiana Press, 1997.

Boyle, Raymond, Peter Flood, and Deirdre Kevin, eds. *Sports and Media: Recent Economic, Legal, and Technological Developments.* Mahwah, NJ: Lawrence Erlbaum, 2004.

O'Neil, Terry. *The Game Behind the Game: High Stakes, High Pressure in Television Sports.* New York: St. Martin's, 1989.

Patton, Phil. *Razzle-Dazzle: The Curious Marriage of Television and Professional Football.* Garden City, NY: The Dial Press, 1984.

Powers, Ron. *Supertube: The Rise of Television Sports.* New York: Coward-McCann, 1984.

Rader, Benjamin G. *American Sports: From the Age of Folk Games to the Age of Televised Sports.* Upper Saddle River, NJ: Prentice Hall, 2004.

Schultz, Bradley. *Sports Media: Reporting, Producing, and Planning.* New York: Focal Press, 2005.

Smith, Ronald A. *Play-by-Play: Radio, Television, and Big-Time College Sport.* Baltimore: The Johns Hopkins University Press, 2001.

Wenner, Lawrence A., ed. *Mediasport.* London: Routledge, 1998.

Wiggins, David K., ed. *Sports in America: From Wicked Amusement to National Obsession.* Champaign, IL.: Human Kinetics, 1995.

LAWRENCE J. MULLEN

SPORTS ILLUSTRATED

Perhaps the best known and most influential American sports publication, *Sports Illustrated*, began as part of the Henry Luce publishing empire, and remains today a property of Time-Warner. It was launched in 1954 after a polling effort centered in Columbus, Ohio sought to determine the directions in which post-war America's interests might turn. The concept was that the magazine would contextualize sports, and give fans a deeper perspective on the games they watched on television. Luce himself was not much of a sports fan, but eventually became strongly committed to the project.

The times were propitious for a national sports magazine. By 1954, millions of Americans already owned television sets—by the end of the decade more than 90 percent of homes had TVs—which made sports all the more popular to the fans who were not always prepared to go to a game in person. The Boeing 707, the first modern jet airliner, made transcontinental travel easier and allowed professional sports at the highest level to expand to the West coast. The American middle class grew significantly during the 1950s, making luxuries such as a sports magazine more widely affordable.

Many think that the magazine found its signature style in 1960 when Luce named Andre Laguerre managing editor. Laguerre was a worldly and highly literate foreign correspondent. Given enormous latitude by Luce, he made *Sports Illustrated* into a writer's magazine that encouraged high style and a broad, sophisticated perspective. As James Michener wrote of it in his 1976 book *Sports in America*: "Only the *New Yorker*, among contemporary magazines, has been as effective in sponsoring good writing with a certain wry touch."

The stable of exceptional writers was notable for a Texas contingent, such as Tex Maule and Dan Jenkins, and East Coast Ivy Leaguers such as George Plimpton and Frank Deford. Out of the contrasting approaches emerged what might be thought of as the *Sports Illustrated* style—thoughtful and literate, but with a sharp, witty edge and plenty of one-liners. A couple of generations of sports writers have grown up weaned on this style, including Rick Reilly, a featured columnist through the 1990s and into the twenty-first century.

The content of the magazine has always been sports in general, with the main focus on professional and college football and basketball, major league baseball and hockey, but the emphasis has varied depending on the managing editor at the time. The degree to which it has been thought of as a writer's magazine has varied as well, with the high point generally acknowledged as the Laguerre tenure from 1960 to 1974.

Sports Illustrated has also been renowned for its visual imagery. Its often stunning color photography has made celebrities out of photographers too, most prominently Walter Ioos. Its most widely discussed visual imagery, however, has been the annual swimsuit issue, heralding the arrival of spring since 1964. The issue has become almost a separate franchise unto itself.

More than any other publication, *Sports Illustrated* made sports a prominent part of post-war American life, and much less perceived as an enthusiasm of the uneducated. If sports metaphors have become a principal lens through which Americans understand their lives, *Sports Illustrated* was one of those publications that can take much of the credit for that development.

Further Reading

The Anniversary Book: 1954–2004. New York: Sports Illustrated Books, 2004.

MacCambridge, Michael. *Franchise: A History of Sports Illustrated Magazine.* New York: Hyperion, 1997.

GORDON JACKSON

ST. LOUIS GLOBE-DEMOCRAT

One of two remaining "major metro" daily newspapers in St. Louis in the mid- and late-twentieth century, the *St. Louis Globe-Democrat* was put to rest in 1986 after 134 years in operation, leaving St. Louis a one-paper city.

The paper began as the *Missouri Democrat* in 1852 in a bustling, prospering river city with a population of nearly eighty thousand, which would more than double by 1860. The original editor and one of the owners was William McKee, who would stay at the helm until 1872, when he and one of the other two editors broke away to form the *St. Louis Globe*. Undercutting the *Democrat's* prices and providing a superior product, the *Globe* forced the remaining owner of the *Democrat* to sell and the two papers merged in 1874. At the time there were eight other dailies in St. Louis competing for circulation. The chief competition then was the *Republican*, as Joseph Pulitzer had not yet begun to put out the *Post-Dispatch*, which would be the *Globe-Democrat's* main competitor through the twentieth century. Mckee's tenure ended with his death in 1877, one year before Pulitzer merged the *Post* and *Dispatch*.

Founded in part to give voice to the Free-Soil point of view, the *Missouri Globe-Democrat* became a most prominent Abolition paper in a border state. Abraham Lincoln, who benefited from the paper's support, said that it was worth more to the North in the Civil War than ten regiments of soldiers. The *Globe-Democrat* served as an early proving ground for such writers as Theodore Dreiser, James Redpath, and Henry Morton Stanley. The paper followed many of the trends of American journalism, becoming decidedly yellow during the period when Pulitzer and William Randolph Hearst were inaugurating yellow journalism in New York. It had a brief flirtation with radicalism during the Populist-Progressive era. Always involved with promoting the welfare of St. Louis, the paper became a friend and backer of young Charles Lindbergh, who rode to glory in the *Spirit of St. Louis.*

The *Globe-Democrat* was noteworthy for being owned by the same family for one hundred years. In 1955, upon the death of E. Lansing Ray, it was sold to S.I. Newhouse, owner of a chain of papers. Newhouse perhaps ensured its eventual demise by selling the main building and printing presses to the *Post-Dispatch* in 1959, consequent to a work stoppage over pension issues. After a ninety-nine-day shutdown, the paper reopened for business, being printed on a contract basis by the *Post-Dispatch*, as it would be for the remainder of its existence.

Despite its Free-Soil and Abolitionist roots, and the brief radical period, by the middle of the twentieth century the *Globe-Democrat* was well known for a conservative editorial viewpoint. Among those penning its editorials was Patrick J. Buchanan, later to become a syndicated columnist and wordsmith for the Richard Nixon and Ronald Reagan administrations. The *Globe-Democrat* editorial page was Buchanan's first job in journalism.

By late 1983 the Newhouse chain was ready to put the paper into bankruptcy. It was rescued from this fate briefly by two different ownership groups, neither of which was able to keep the paper in operation for longer than a period of several months. Its archives can be found in the Mercantile Library of St. Louis, located in the Thomas Jefferson Library at the University of Missouri-St. Louis.

Further Reading

Bauman, Duncan G. *Behind the Headlines: Stories About People and Events Which Shaped St. Louis.* Tucson, AZ: Patrice Press, 1999.

Hart, Jim Allee. *A History of the St. Louis Globe-Democrat.* Columbia: University of Missouri Press, 1961.

See also: Abolitionist Press; Columnists; Hearst Press; Newhouse Publishing; Samuel I. Newhouse; Joseph Pulitzer; *St. Louis Post Dispatch*; Sensationalism; Yellow Journalism

GORDON JACKSON

ST. LOUIS POST-DISPATCH

John A. Cockerill, Joseph Pulitzer's "perfect" editor, was in his second floor office at the *St. Louis Post-Dispatch* (1878–) at five in the afternoon on October 13, 1882, meeting with business manager John McGuffin and composing room foreman Victor Cole when two men burst into the room. One of them, local lawyer Alonzo Slayback, had been called a "coward" in print by Cockerill after Slayback had called the paper "blackmailers" at a political meeting.

> "Is that for me?" McGuffin remembered Slayback saying, when he saw a gun on a table beside Cockerill.
>
> "No," Cockerill replied. "Only for self-defense."

Slayback pulled a gun from his pocket and, according to testimony, aimed it at Cockerill. McGuffin rushed for the gun. Cockerill grabbed his pistol and fired. Slayback was killed almost instantly.

The rival *Missouri Republican* charged the killing was the "fruit" of the "*Post-Dispatch* aggressive and sensational school of journalism." *Harper's Weekly* concurred. The killing came "as a direct result of personal journalism." Had Cockerill been killed "there would have been a poetic justice in the transaction." The *Post-Dispatch*, however, had its defenders. The *St. Louis Criterion* admired "the progressive and fearless spirit of the *Post-Dispatch*" that "has accomplished much for morality in this city." William Rockhill Nelson, publisher of the *Kansas City Star*, editorially observed "the personal journalism of the *Post-Dispatch* is the hope and protection of the country." The paper had "antagonized all the evil elements in St. Louis, and has not hesitated to attack wrong, however securely entrenched in power."

The *St. Louis Post-Dispatch* was only in its fourth year when its editor was acquitted in the killing of a local political operative. The paper's publisher, thirty-six-year-old Joseph Pulitzer, a Hungarian immigrant, had come to St. Louis at the close of the Civil War looking for work. He tended mules, loaded cargo, and waited on tables before a chess-playing partner, Carl Schurz, got him a reporting job on the *Westliche Post*, the city's leading German-language daily. By 1871, the hard-working Pulitzer was part-owner of the paper. Pulitzer's burning opposition to what he saw as "the corruption, the lawlessness, and the profligacy of the Grant administration" led him to support Liberal Republican Horace Greeley in 1872 and, breaking with Schurz, Democrat Samuel Tilden in 1876. Convinced that the closely fought election had been stolen by Republicans, Pulitzer was eager to publish a paper of his own. In 1878 he bought the *St. Louis Evening Dispatch* at a sheriff's sale for $2,500, merged it with the *Evening Post* and on December 12, 1878, created the *St. Louis Post-Dispatch*.

"The *Post and Dispatch* will serve no party but the people," the paper editorially argued in 4,020 copies of its first four-page edition. It pledged to be an enemy of "all frauds and shams" and a proponent "of the principles upon which our government was originally founded." During the 127 years in which the *Post-Dispatch* remained in the Pulitzer family, the paper was generally a supporter of liberal causes and the Democratic Party. In a January 10, 1879, editorial, Pulitzer explained "democracy means opposition to all special interests." The Republican Party, he was certain, was "the party of corporations, the favored classes, and money." The "issue of all issues," according to the paper, "is whether corporations shall rule this country or whether the country shall again rule the corporations." In February 1879, the paper demanded the Missouri legislature force the affluent to pay their "fair share" of the tax burden. Over the threats of advertisers, the paper published tax returns of public men it charged with "tax dodging." Later that month the paper exclusively reported secret state senate hearings into a gambling ring connected to Missouri's governor.

By March 1879, circulation for the *Post-Dispatch* had soared five-fold. In two months, St. Louis's only competing paper for evening readers folded. During the next three years the *Post-Dispatch* solidified its widening reputation for reform-minded journalism by its investigation of corrupt insurance companies, bankers, brothel owners, and gas company and streetcar monopolists. The paper ran a series of stories on police corruption and "a servile press" that remained silent in the face of public malfeasance. In addition to social responsibility, the *Post-Dispatch* also relied on sensation to stimulate and sustain circulation. The paper gave front-page attention to a love triangle that ended in murder. The "wife of a well known investor," the paper reported on April 23, 1879, had had "her throat slashed" as a bloody demonstration of "the wages of sin." December 1880 page one stories took on gambling dens that "ruined boys from the best families." The paper's January 1881 "raids" on the city's seedy theaters exposed "man-traps baited with harlots and rot-gut whiskey." The paper was regularly sued for libel and routinely won its court cases. Pulitzer publicized the fact that he carried a gun for his own protection.

After the Cockerill-Slayback scandal the *Post-Dispatch* saw a circulation slump and the flight of some advertisers. Cockerill was reassigned and Pulitzer concentrated on publishing his new acquisition, the *New York World*. Pulitzer's business partner John Dillon became editor of the *Post-Dispatch* with Charles Jones succeeding him in February 1895. In January 1903, seventeen-year-old Joseph Pulitzer II went to work on the *Post-Dispatch* at $20 a week and was told by his father to "study, watch and learn what workers and managers are doing." He kept a daily journal that early recognized that "the life and blood of a newspaper" was "its circulation which springs from its news." In 1906, after studies at Harvard, young Pulitzer returned to work on the paper. He got his aging father's permission to ban patent medicine ads from the paper. At his father's death in 1911, Pulitzer became publisher of the *Post-Dispatch*, a position he maintained for forty-four years.

The *Post-Dispatch* won nine Pulitzer Prizes for journalistic excellence during Joe Pulitzer's tenure at the paper. Its 1927 investigation led to the impeachment of an Illinois judge. Paul Y. Anderson received the award in 1929 for reporting a naval oil lease scam. The paper's chief Washington correspondent Charles Ross won a Pulitzer for his 1931 reporting on the Depression. The *Post-Dispatch* went to court in 1937 to have forty thousand ballots invalidated in a voter registration fraud that won the paper another Pulitzer Prize. Other award-winning investigations included a campaign against German militarism in 1940, an end to the city's smoke pollution in 1941, and a campaign for stricter mine safety in 1948. In 1949, it exposed a payoff scheme between the Republican Party and Illinois editors and three years later revealed widespread corruption within the Internal Revenue Service. The paper's veteran cartoonist, Daniel Fitzpatrick, won his Pulitzer Prize in 1955. Bob Broeg, veteran sports writer and editor on the *Post-Dispatch*, won the J.G. Taylor Spink Award in 1979 for a lifetime of excellent work. Prize-winning cartoonist Bill Mauldin was given a star on the St. Louis Walk of Fame in 1991.

For thirty-one years Joseph Pulitzer III managed the *Post-Dispatch*, starting in 1955. He was followed by Joseph Pulitzer IV and Michael Pulitzer. By this time the paper had become a St. Louis cultural institution and a national opinion leader. Its editorial page editor, Robert Lasch, won a Pulitzer Prize in 1966 for his denunciation of U.S. policy in Vietnam. Subsequently, the paper was known for its advocacy of a woman's right to an abortion and the abolition of capital punishment. Its daily readership of 727,000 in 2000 made it the twenty-sxith most widely read newspaper in the nation. On January 31, 2005, the *Post-Dispatch* along with fourteen other daily and seventy-five weekly and bi-weekly newspapers owned by the Pulitzer Company were sold to Lee Enterprises, a multi-media company, for $1.46 billion. The agreement stipulated that the new management "for at least five years" would have to operate the *Post-Dispatch* under a covenant written by Joseph Pulitzer in 1911 that pledged "to always fight for progress and reform, to never tolerate injustice or corruption, to never lack sympathy with the poor, and to always remain devoted to the public welfare."

Further Reading

Brain, Denis. *Pulitzer: A Life*. New York: John Wiley & Sons, 2001.

Broeg, Bob, ed. *Front Page: A Century of News and Sports/St. Louis Post-Dispatch*, St. Louis: River City Publishers, 1982.

McWilliams, Jim. *Mark Twain in the St. Louis Post-Dispatch, 1874–1891*. Troy, NY: Whitston Publishing, 1997.

Pfaff, Daniel W. *Joseph Pulitzer II and the Post-Dispatch: A Newspaperman's Life*. University Park: Pennsylvania State University Press, 1991.

——. *No Ordinary Joe: A Life of Joseph Pulitzer III*. Columbia, MO: University of Missouri Press, 2005.

Rammelkamp, Julian S. *Pulitzer's Post-Dispatch, 1878–1883*. Princeton, NJ: Princeton University Press, 1967.

BRUCE J. EVENSEN

STANLEY, HENRY M.

Originally named John Rowlands, after a man who claimed to be his father, the person whom history knows as Henry Morton Stanley (January 28, 1841–May 10, 1904) was born in Denbigh, Wales, the illegitimate son of Elizabeth Parry. With meager circumstances, his only formal education was at the nearby St. Asaph Workhouse. In 1858 he shipped out of Liverpool as a cabin boy on a packet boat bound for New Orleans. There he met Henry Hope Stanley, who became his benefactor and namesake. In 1861, he sent Rowlands to Cypress Bend, Arkansas, to train as a storekeeper.

Finding that vocation unappealing, young Henry Stanley, as Rowlands now called himself (he added his middle name later) joined the Dixie Greys in 1861 and began a checkered Civil War career. Captured at the Battle of Shiloh, he was sent to Camp Douglas near Chicago, but several weeks later he was released, having agreed to join the Union army. Becoming ill and unable to serve in the ranks, he was discharged. Later he enlisted briefly in the U. S. Navy. With the war winding down, he deserted and headed west.

There he began working as a journalist. The *Missouri Democrat* employed him first as a freelance roving reporter and later as a special correspondent to cover the campaign against the Plains Indians in 1867. His reporting for this paper established him as a correspondent, and East Coast newspapers reprinted his colorful and vivid dispatches about the Indian wars. Independently, he also sent them to newspapers in Chicago and Cincinnati. Accordingly, in December 1867, he went to New York City to capitalize on his experience and reputation. There he met James Gordon Bennett Jr.

The younger Bennett had assumed control of his father's *New York Herald*. Stanley knew that the *Herald* led all American newspapers in reporting international news, and he offered to cover, at his own expense, a punitive expedition the British were launching to rescue a group of British hostages that Theodore, the Emperor of Abyssinia, held, if Bennett would pay for his dispatches. Bennett agreed and told Stanley that, if his reports were up to standard, he could expect a permanent position with the *Herald* upon his return. Stanley left little to chance. En route to join the expedition, he met the chief telegraphist at Suez and bribed him to assure that his dispatches from the campaign would be cabled first. Consequently, his reports of the fall of Magdala, the release of the hostages, and the death of Theodore beat those of all the other correspondents, and because of a subsequent break in the cable, they even arrived in London before the official military dispatches. Bennett, good to his word, gave Stanley a permanent position as a roving foreign correspondent for the *Herald*. In 1869 Bennett had a grander assignment to offer Stanley, and summoned him from Spain to meet him in Paris. That meeting marked the beginning of Stanley's great work—finding Dr. David Livingstone, the famous Scottish missionary-explorer.

Livingstone was somewhere in Central Africa, and, aside from rumors, had not been seen in over three years. However, Bennett was in no hurry to find Livingstone. He had Stanley pursue assignments in the Middle East and India before going to Zanzibar to begin the search. Stanley departed Zanzibar March 21, 1871, with a well-equipped expedition, heading for Ujiji, a trading center on the eastern shore of Lake Tanganyika. Driving his men relentlessly and overcoming perilous conditions, he reached Ujiji on November 10. There he found the missionary-explorer, greeting him with the later oft-repeated statement, "Dr. Livingstone, I presume." He stayed with Livingstone four months, and together they explored the northern end of Lake Tanganyika. Meanwhile, his dispatches to the *Herald* were a national and journalistic sensation. Some critics and rival newspapers tried to question their authenticity. But when Stanley arrived in England in 1872 bearing Livingstone's journals and letters to friends, the expedition was verified and the criticism silenced. The enterprising American journalist was now famous.

Africa remained the focus of his activity. Bennett sent him to cover the British campaign against the Ashanti Kingdom in West Africa in 1873. The following year he led an Anglo-American expedition sponsored by the *London Daily Telegraph* and the *New York Herald* back to Africa to complete Livingstone's explorations. Veteran African explorers called this four-year expedition the greatest exploration of the century. Afterwards, Stanley returned to Africa for five more years (1879–1884), commissioned by King Leopold II of Belgium to establish stations and sign treaties that would lead to the formation of the Congo Free State. From 1887 to 1889, he led his final expedition to Africa to rescue the governor of the southern province of the Sudan. Following the successful rescue, he guided the expedition out of Africa by reaching its eastern coast, becoming the first known man to traverse the width of Africa in both directions.

Stanley spent the remainder of his life lecturing and writing about Africa. In 1890 he married Dorothy Tennant; he served as a member of Parliament from 1895–1900, and he was knighted in 1899. He made a final trip to Africa in 1897 for the opening of the railway from the Cape to Bulawayo. Suffering a stroke in 1903, he died on May 10, 1904, in England, at Furze Hill, his country home near Pirbright, Surrey.

Stanley's achievements earned him the reputation as the greatest of the explorers of Africa and as an extraordinary journalist. His expeditions were crucial to the opening of Central Africa and to the subsequent missionaries' attraction to the region. His work also encouraged the later nineteenth-century "scramble for Africa." His finding Livingstone was one of the greatest exclusive stories in nineteenth-century journalism, and his newspaper-sponsored expeditions brought great credit to the *New York Herald* and the *London Daily Telegraph*. Stanley's African dispatches and later books contributed to the growth of the human-interest factor in journalism. Most important of all, he expanded the scope and content of foreign correspondence.

Further Reading

Casada, James A. "Henry Morton Stanley: The Explorer as Journalist." *Southern Quarterly* 15 (1997): 357–369.

Farwell, Byron. *The Man Who Presumed: A Biography of Henry M. Stanley.* New York: Henry Holt and Company, 1957.

Hall, Richard. *Stanley: An Adventurer Explored.* London: Collins, 1974.

McLynn, Frank. *Stanley: The Making of an African Explorer.* London: Constable, 1989.

Stanley, Dorothy, ed. *The Autobiography of Sir Henry Morton Stanley.* London: Sampson Low, Marston and Co., 1909.

Stanley, Henry Morton. *How I Found Livingstone.* New York: Scribner's, 1872.

JAMES D. STARTT

STANTON, ELIZABETH CADY

Elizabeth Cady Stanton (November 12, 1815–October 26, 1902) was an intellectual of the nineteenth-century woman's rights movement who became an outspoken and radical spokeswoman for woman suffrage. She attacked the historic and contemporary male dominance of social, political, and economic institutions both in lectures and in writing. In these she argued that women should demand equal status in the church, in marriage, in the economy, and in politics. In 1868 she and Susan B. Anthony established the *Revolution,* a radical woman suffrage publication, which she edited until 1870. With Anthony and others she founded the National Woman Suffrage Association in 1868, and when it merged in 1890 with the American Woman Suffrage Association to become the National American Woman Suffrage Association, served as the new organization's first president. Stanton was always more radical than the mainstream of the suffrage movement and continued to shock and alienate many of its participants even in her final years.

Elizabeth Cady was born in Johnstown, New York, not far from Albany. She was the daughter of Daniel Cady, an attorney who served in Congress and later became a New York State Supreme Court Judge, and Margaret Livingston Cady, who came from a prominent political family. Elizabeth was the fourth of six children; her only brother died at the age of eighteen when she was eleven. As a child, Elizabeth began to spend time in her father's law office, listening to his meetings with townspeople and debating legal resolutions with him. She received encouragement from her father's clerk, her oldest sister's husband, Edward Bayard, who introduced her to history, politics, and many of the subjects girls were not encouraged to study at that time. An eager pupil, she attended Johnstown Academy and then Emma Willard's Troy Female Seminary, from which she graduated at the age of seventeen.

Once her official schooling was completed, Elizabeth found an intellectual outlet in the spirited debates that occurred at the home of her cousin, reformer Gerrit Smith, where discussions focused on anti-slavery, temperance, and woman's rights. There she met Henry Brewster Stanton, a thirty-four-year-old orator for the New York abolitionist movement. When Henry and Elizabeth married in 1840, she succeeded in omitting the word "obey" from the marriage ceremony, one early declaration of her resolution to maintain her independence even within marriage. Shortly after the wedding, they departed to London to attend the World Anti-Slavery Convention.

Elizabeth Cady Stanton had hoped to participate in the anti-slavery convention, only to discover that women were excluded as delegates and speakers. Thus she found herself in the company of feminist Lucretia Mott and the two spent days walking around London, discussing the role of women. They continued their friendship through correspondence and occasional meetings as Henry and Elizabeth moved from Johnstown to Boston and then to Seneca Falls, New York. When Mott came to the area for an annual Quaker meeting in 1848, they met for an impassioned discussion of the condition of women and decided to call a convention to make their points public. Stanton modeled a statement of principles on the Declaration of Independence to present to the convention, which was attended by two hundred people. Her Declaration of Sentiments made the bold statement that "all men and women are created equal," and then went on to describe man's historical tyranny over women. It made twelve resolutions, including the need for women to overthrow the male monopoly in the church, to secure equal participation with men in the trades, commerce, and education, and to obtain the right to vote.

The reaction by the press and the church was venomous. Perhaps because of such a violent response, Stanton became all that more adamant, writing letters of protest to newspapers that had described her and her ideas inaccurately and speaking in a variety of venues to argue woman's rights. She also wrote for reform papers, such as Amelia Bloomer's the *Lily* and Paulina Wright Davis's *Una.* In 1854 she spoke before the New York State legislature on the disabilities of women before the law, the first woman ever invited to address a committee of the legislature. She then delivered the same speech to the New York Woman's Rights Convention, after which fifty thousand copies were distributed to the press, women's groups, and reform organizations all over the country. Soon after, Horace Greeley asked to publish her columns in the *New York Herald.*

Stanton developed a public career as the spokeswoman for the woman's movement, despite opposition from family and friends. In 1866, she ran (unsuccessfully) as an independent for Congress on a platform including free speech, free press, and universal suffrage. She and Susan B. Anthony campaigned in Kansas for a woman suffrage referendum (which was defeated) and in the process picked up the financial backing of the wealthy eccentric, George Train, to publish a reform newspaper to be called the *Revolution.* The first issue appeared in 1868 and for the next two years, Stanton wrote about a range of subjects, many of them controversial topics such as prostitution, birth control, the exploitation of servant girls, and the need for employment equity. At the same time, she, Anthony, and a number of like-minded women founded the National Woman Suffrage Association. More moderate members of the suffrage movement shortly after established the American Woman Suffrage Association and a second publication, the *Woman's Journal.* The woman's movement could not sustain both publications and in 1870 Stanton and her associates relinquished editorial control of the *Revolution.* The paper declined and eventually succumbed in 1872.

Although she no longer had a publication at her disposal as she had had with the *Revolution,* Stanton continued to publish her writings in the general-circulation press and, eventually, the various publications of the suffrage movement, including the *Woman's Journal.* As woman suffrage became a familiar idea in the last decades of the nineteenth century, Stanton was recognized as the intellectual leader of the woman's movement. She was often invited to contribute to national magazines such as *Arena* and *Forum* and her arguments often appeared when newspapers published "for and against" packages during local suffrage campaigns. She was a co-author of the first three volumes of the mammoth *History of Woman Suffrage* (completed in 1885) and in 1895 was the lead author of the highly controversial *Woman's Bible.* In that year, her eightieth, a tribute was held for Stanton at the Metropolitan Opera House in New York. More than three thousand people attended and the *New York Sun* reported, "This is Stanton Day in New York. The brave and estimable woman will be honored today as no other American woman ever was honored in her lifetime."

Further Reading

Baker, Jean. *Sisters: The Lives of American Suffragists*. New York: Hill and Wang, 2005.

Cullen-Dupont, Kathryn. *American Women Activists' Writings: An Anthology, 1637–2002*. New York: Cooper Square Press, 2002.

Griffith, Elisabeth. *In her Own Right: The Life of Elizabeth Cady Stanton*. New York: Oxford University Press, 1984.

Siegerman, Harriet. *Elizabeth Cady Stanton: The Right Is Ours*. New York: Oxford University Press, 2001.

Stanton, Elizabeth Cady, Susan B. Anthony, and Ann D. Gordon. *The Selected Papers of Elizabeth Cady Stanton and Susan B. Anthony, vol 3, National Protection for National Citizens, 1873 to 1880*. New Brunswick, NJ: Rutgers University Press, 2003.

Ward, Geoffrey C., Martha Saxton, Ann D. Gordon, and Ellen Carol DuBois. *Not for Ourselves Alone: The Story of Elizabeth Cady Stanton and Susan B. Anthony: An Illustrated History*. New York: Alfred A. Knopf, 1999.

ELIZABETH V. BURT

STARS AND STRIPES

Stars and Stripes is a daily newspaper distributed to American military personnel overseas. It is authorized by the Department of Defense Directive 5122.11 that states it is "editorially independent of interference from outside its editorial chain-of-command." Both General John J. Pershing, commander of American troops in France during World War I, and General Dwight D. Eisenhower, supreme commander of Allied Forces in Europe in World War II, defended that freedom.

Many think that *Stars and Stripes* began in World War I, perhaps because of the recognition it was to receive, but actually it started during the Civil War; Union soldiers, using the facilities of a captured newspaper plant in Bloomfield, Missouri produced four one-page papers.

The World War I edition of *Stars and Stripes* began publishing February 8, 1918, by order of General Pershing and continued publishing until June 13, 1919. Some of the recognition it got was after the fact as *Stars and Stripes* alumni became noted journalists. Best known of these were Harold Ross, co-founder of the *New Yorker;* Grantland Rice, the renowned sportswriter; and Alexander Wolcott, drama citric of the *New York Times*. There were also others less well-known journalists who held major positions in U.S. newspapers.

When *Stars and Stripes* began publishing in 1918, there were U.S. troops scattered among British, French and Italian troops. It was the newspaper's mission to promote unity and troop morale. General Pershing commended publication's success in this regard. The circulation peaked at 526,000.

Stars and Stripes resumed publication in England in 1942 and followed U.S. forces into France and Italy. It was to be a newspaper first and foremost for the combat soldiers.

Bob Moora, co-editor of the paper when it was in London, was quoted in *The Story of the Stars and Stripes* as saying:

> This is the paper for Joe; after that it's a newspaper; after that it's a trade journal whose special readers are soldiers; and after that it isn't anything else no matter what the brass says.

Moora emphasized that *Stars and Stripes* was not a public relations organ and was not an arm of the military public relations offices. Members of *Stars and Stripes* were enlisted men, and every public information office was headed by an officer, but Public Information Officers found their rank did not matter when they dealt with *Stars and Stripes*. Bill Mauldin, the cartoonist and perhaps the most famous staff member, drew cartoons that symbolized the perspective of *Stars and Stripes*. They featured Willie and Joe, a pair of unkempt infantry soldiers. One of Mauldin's most memorable cartoons had Willie and Joe with a neatly dressed, beribboned solider somewhere behind the lines. The soldier was pointing to one of his ribbons and saying "this pretty one is for being in this theater of operations." Willie and Joe, of course, had no such ribbon.

Mauldin won the Pulitzer Prize for editorial cartooning in 1945 and would win one years later as an editorial cartoonist for the *Chicago Sun Times*.

Staff members did not sit in the office. They went on missions with the fighting men. They flew with bombers on attacks against Germany. They were there at D-Day. They jumped with paratroopers in France. Some were killed in combat situations. As U.S. forces advanced in France and in Italy, *Stars and Stripes* followed. There were as many as thirty-two separate editions and twenty-five publishing locations in Europe, North Africa, the Middle East, and finally the Pacific. The latter edition did not begin until a week after the end of the war in Europe in April 1945.

The end of World War II did not mean the end of *Stars and Stripes*. In 2006, it was a newspaper with an average daily readership of 365,000. The European edition had offices in Griesheim, Germany, and the Pacific edition has offices in Tokyo. Layout and composition was done at the central office in Washington, D.C., and transmitted by satellite to printing facilities in Germany, Italy, Japan, Kuwait, South Korea, Iraq, Afghanistan, Qatar, and Bahrain. Copies were provided to service personnel in forty-eight countries, and the paper was also available online.

The staff was no longer the enlisted personnel of the World War II era. With the end of that war, the paper moved to a civilian staff. However, the civilian staffers continued the emphasis on covering the troops. *Stars and Stripes* reporters joined U.S. troops in the field in Korea and Vietnam and embedded with military units in Kuwait and Iraq and Navy ships in the Middle East.

Further Reading

Hutton, Bud and Andy Rooney. *The Story of The Stars and Stripes*. New York: Farrar & Rinehart, 1946.

Serial & Government Publications Division, Library of Congress. *The Stars and Stripes, 1918–1919: A Talented Editorial Staff,* http://memory.loc.gov/ammem/sgphtml/sashtml/staff.html (accessed April 10, 2007).

Stars & Stripes, http://www.estripes.com/ (accessed Sept. 24, 2006). The Library of Congress. *Stars and Stripes: The American Soldiers' Newspaper of World War I, 1918-1919.* http://memory.loc.gov/ammem/sgphtml/sashtml/sashome.html.

GUIDO H. STEMPEL III

STEFFENS, JOSEPH LINCOLN

The day before he died, Lincoln Steffens (April 6, 1866–August 9, 1936), writing a preface to a collection of his life's work, said he saw journalism as a great "teacher." As one of the Progressive period's foremost investigative reporters he had "breathed the news," hoping to give his readers life-saving instruction. His "systematic search" for remedies to the problems of city management would lead him from socialism and communism to Christianity and the single tax, while leaving behind a journalism of exposure that chronicled the urban corruption of his day.

Steffens passion for reform seems to have stemmed from his grandfather, the Rev. Joseph Steffens, a "bold defender of the faith, once delivered to the saints." He was born to Joseph Steffens and Elizabeth Louisa Symes Steffens in the Mission District of San Francisco, and raised in Sacramento, where his father was a prosperous banker. Steffens was drawn to police reporting at the *New York Evening Post* in 1892 after extensive studies in ethics, philosophy and psychology at universities in California, Berlin, Heidelberg, Leipzig, and Paris. He teamed with Police Commissioner Theodore Roosevelt and Jacob Riis of the *Evening Sun* to expose the corruption of Tammany Hall. As city editor of the *New York Commercial-Advertiser*, beginning in 1897, he hired Hutchins and Norman Hapgood and Abraham Cahan, to explore the problems of ghetto life in a news magazine format.

Steffens became managing editor of *McClure's Magazine* in September, 1901, where he set a standard for investigative reporting by exposing patterns of bribes, privilege and condoned criminality then flourishing in Chicago, St. Louis, Minneapolis, New York, Philadelphia, and Pittsburgh. The "Shame of the Cities" series, later published as a book in 1904, argued that political corruption triumphed over hard-working Americans who had "little time or interest in public business." Steffens noted that "the law-abiding backbones of our society, in city after city, start out for moral reform," but lost courage and "turn back." Steffens sought to tell the stories of individuals who took on the interests. He became convinced that "whenever anything extraordinary is done in American municipal politics, whether for good or for evil, you can trace it almost invariably to one man." The series solidified Steffens growing reputation as one of the leading muckrakers of the Progressive period and made him a national celebrity. Steffens detective work on municipal avarice appeared as a book, *The Struggle of Self-Government*, published in 1906.

Along with friends Ray Stannard Baker and Ida Tarbell, Steffens bought a controlling interest in *American Chronicle* in 1906, where he continued to write articles championing municipal reform. As a free lancer, Steffens hoped to mobilize public opinion by creating a nationwide movement for reform. *The Upbuilders* was a collection of these pieces, focusing on the competition between public and private interests. It was published in 1909. Three decades of unparalleled immigration had brought to America a vast urban population of seventeen million men and women largely untutored in the obligations of self-government. They found in Steffens the sworn enemy of big city machines that preyed upon them. Steffens ceaseless crusade against civic corruption hoped readers would recognize that "the misgovernment of the American people is misgovernment by the American people."

For the remainder of his life, Steffens worked for political and economic reforms that would prevent government from favoring the privileged. His celebrity status led him to personally negotiate guilty pleas of two anarchists who bombed the *Los Angeles Times* building in 1911, killing twenty-one. He would promote the early careers of Walter Lippmann and John Reed. He interviewed Vladimir Lenin in 1919 and reported admiringly, "I have seen the future, and it works." Married twice, he became a father at sixty. At his death, the *New York Times* report (August 10, 1936), he was widely regarded as "one of the best reporters and one of the most relentless searchers after truth in his generation."

Further Reading

Evensen, Bruce J. "The Evangelical Origins of the Muckrakers." *American Journalism* 6, 1989.

——. "The Media and Reform, 1900–1917." In *The Age of Mass Communication*, edited by Wm. David Sloan. Northport: Vision Press, 1998.

——. "Progressivism, Muckraking and Objectivity." In *Fair & Balanced: A History of Journalistic Objectivity*, edited by Steven R. Knowlton, and Karen L. Freeman. Northport: Vision Press, 2005.

Fitzpatrick, Ellen F., ed., *Muckraking: Three Landmark Articles.* Boston: Bedford Books, 1994.

Horton, Russell. *Lincoln Steffens.* New York: Twayne Publishers, 1974.

Kaplan, Justin. *Lincoln Steffens: A Biography.* New York: Simon and Schuster, 1974.

McClure, S.S. *My Autobiography.* New York: Frederick Ungar, 1963.

Palermo, Patrick F. *Lincoln Steffens.* Boston: Twayne Publishers, 1978.

Papers of Lincoln Steffens. Lincoln Steffens Collection, Columbia University. New York, NY, and Special Collections, Bancroft Library, University of California at Berkeley.

Steffens, Joseph Lincoln. *Lincoln Steffens Speaking.* New York: Harcourt, Brace, 1936.

Steffens, Lincoln. *The Autobiography of Lincoln Steffens.* New York: Harcourt, Brace, 1931.

——. *The Shame of the Cities.* New York: Sangamore Press, 1957, originally 1904.

——. *The Struggle for Self-Government.* New York: McClure, Phillips, 1906.

Stein, Harry. "Lincoln Steffens: Interviewer." *Journalism Quarterly* 46, 1969.

Winter, Ella, and Granville Hicks, eds. *The Letters of Lincoln Steffens*. New York: Harcourt, Brace, 1938.

BRUCE J. EVENSEN

STONE, LUCY

Lucy Stone (August 13, 1818–October 18, 1893) was a pioneering feminist who promoted her ideas through public speaking and the press. In 1870, she established the *Woman's Journal*, which became the nation's leading woman suffrage publication. Stone was the eighth of nine children born to Francis and Hannah Matthews Stone in West Brookfield, Massachusetts. At sixteen, she entered one of the few professions open to unmarried middle-class women—teaching. She continued her education, attending Mount Holyoake Female Seminary and Oberlin College in Ohio, from which she graduated in 1843 with honors, the first Massachusetts woman to receive a college degree.

Stone joined the abolition movement and accepted a job as lecturer for the American Anti-Slavery Society. Here she met other independent-minded women like herself who were frustrated by the social and legal restraints placed upon them. In 1850 she called the first national woman's rights convention in Worcester, Massachusetts.

It was through her work as a lecturer that Stone met abolitionist and woman's rights advocate Henry Blackwell. When they married in 1855 Lucy retained her maiden name while Henry renounced all legal rights to his wife's services and property and granted her complete freedom to pursue a public career. This she did, and in 1866, was one of the principal founders of the American Equal Rights Association, whose goal was to promote suffrage for blacks and women.

During the next two years, the woman's rights movement split over the wording of the Fourteenth and Fifteenth Amendments, which eventually guaranteed the right to vote to all male citizens regardless of "race, color, or previous condition of servitude." The more radical faction, led by Elizabeth Cady Stanton and Susan B. Anthony, not only opposed the amendments but also espoused far-reaching social changes, including equal employment and pay, divorce, and property rights. The more moderate faction, to which Stone and Blackwell belonged, instead, focused on promoting women's right to vote and avoided issues that would alienate influential members of the community. In early 1869 Stanton and Anthony established the National Woman Suffrage Association and began to publish a short-lived journal, *Revolution*. Six months later, Stone was among the group that founded the rival American Woman Suffrage Association and under its auspices, she and Blackwell published the first issue of the *Woman's Journal* in January 1870.

The *Woman's Journal* spoke for and to the growing number of women in the public sphere—professionals, writers, and clubwomen—but largely ignored the needs and interests of poor and working-class women. Assisted by Blackwell and later their daughter, Alice, Stone held most of the editorial responsibilities at the *Journal*, wrote copy, recruited writers, and solicited financial support and advertising from their offices in Boston. In 1883, she expanded her editorial reach when she launched a syndicated column about women, which was eventually published in one thousand American newspapers. In 1888, "The Woman's Column" became a four-page, subscription-based weekly edited by Alice Stone Blackwell.

When the two factions of the suffrage movement reconciled their differences and merged to become the National American Woman Suffrage Association in 1890, the *Woman's Journal* became its official organ with Lucy Stone at its helm. Through the pages of the *Women's Journal* and "The Woman's Column," Stone created a community of sisterhood for women across the nation and imprinted upon generations her vision of woman's proper role in American society.

Further Reading

Blackwell, Alice Stone. *Lucy Stone: Pioneer of Women's Rights*. Boston: Little, Brown and Company, 1930.

Endres, Kathleen L., "The Woman's Column." In *Women's Periodicals of the United States: Social and Political Issues,* edited by Kathleen Endres and Therese L. Lueck. Westport, CT: Greenwood, 1996, 459–463.

Masel-Waters, Lynne. "A Burning Cloud by Day: The History and Content of the 'Woman's Journal.'" *Journalism History 3:4* (Winter 1976–77): 103–110.

Million, Joelle. *Woman's Voice, Woman's Place: Lucy Stone and the Birth of the Woman's Rights Movement*. Westport, CT: Praeger, 2003.

Rodier, Katherine. "Lucy Stone and the Woman's Journal." In *Blue Pencils and Hidden Hands: Women Editing Periodicals, 1830–1910*, edited by Sharon M. Harris, and Ellen Gruber Garvey. Boston: Northeastern University Press, 2004.

Spencer, David R. "The Woman's Journal" In *Women's Periodicals of the United States: Social and Political Issues,* edited by Kathleen Endres, and Therese L. Lueck. Westport, CT: Greenwood, 1996, 468–478.

ELIZABETH V. BURT

STONE, MELVILLE ELIJAH

Few nineteenth-century journalists had a better business sense for the future of the profession than Melville E. Stone (August 22, 1848–February 15, 1929), co-founder of the *Chicago Daily News* and long-time general manager of the Associated Press, nor a greater understanding of journalism's social responsibility. Stone saw that the speed and growing complexity of modern living required news that was concise, accurate and impartial. This guided his creation of a newspaper and a news-gathering association that served as templates in the economic and philosophic development of twentieth-century journalism.

Melville was the second of six sons born to the Rev. Elijah Stone and Sophia Louisa Creighton Stone, when the couple led a Methodist congregation in Hudson, Illinois, a small community in the center of the state. The two had met at Knox College in nearby Galesburg, and shared the school's evangelical animosity toward slavery. The couple was active in the Underground Railroad and transmitted to their children the importance of individual initiative in the moral universe. In 1860, Stone's father became pastor of the Des Plaines Street Methodist Church, just west of Chicago's business district. It was here in 1864 that Stone began his career in journalism as an idealistic Lincoln Republican. His enthusiasm, however, eroded during five years of reporting and editing for papers—the *Chicago Tribune*, the *Chicago Republican*, and the *Chicago Post and Mail*—he considered more dedicated to partisan politics, personalities, and profit than their sense of civic responsibility.

In 1869 Stone got out of the newspaper game and married Martha Jameson McFarland. The Great Chicago Fire of 1871 destroyed his iron foundry and led to Stone's leadership in civic organizations dedicated to rebuilding the city. Late in 1875 Stone became convinced that Chicago needed a newspaper that had a communitarian regard for the city's future. With two partners he launched the one-penny *Chicago Daily News* on December 23, 1875, promising the paper would "give the greatest amount of news in the smallest possible space" with "dignity and decency." As editor, Stone claimed the paper was "more than a mere business enterprise." Instead, it offered "a true perspective of the world's developing history" that "a woman could read aloud in mixed company" (*Chicago Daily News*, December 23, 1875, 1; and December 20, 1876, 2).

In July of 1876 Stone persuaded a former schoolmate, Victor Lawson, publisher of Chicago's *Skandinaven*, to strengthen the paper's financial footing. The paper's emphasis on public works and social welfare was a hit with the city's working class and newly professional readers. By the end of the year the *Daily News* at fourteen thousand was Chicago's widest circulating afternoon daily. The paper's business principles were rigidly Sabbatarian. It closed Sunday, refused liquor ads, and established a fixed ad rate. Schoolboys became *Daily News* carriers and stores were encouraged to hold ninety-nine cents sales so that customers would have a penny to spend on the *Daily News*. The paper's editorial staff was among the best in the nation. Stone recruited Eugene Field to write columns and George Ade and Finley Peter Dunne became the paper's star reporters.

Stone and Lawson initiated the *Morning News* in 1881, which soon became the *Chicago Record*. The *Daily News*, however, was Stone's surpassing municipal achievement, its communitarian concerns gaining it by 1885 the city's widest circulation at one hundred thousand. By 1888 the circulation of the *Daily News* surged to two hundred thousand, second largest in the nation behind Joseph Pulitzer's *New York World*. Stone sold his interest in the paper to Lawson for $350,000 and traveled with his wife and three children to Europe. He returned to Chicago in 1890, leading the drive for civil service reform, while becoming president of the Globe National Bank. In 1893 he became general manager of the Associated Press, immediately contracting with

Reuters in Great Britain and affiliated agencies throughout Europe for the exclusive right to use their news in the United States. Under Stone's guidance the Associated Press became a cooperative, non-profit venture, owned by member newspapers who voluntarily shared the news. Stone saw public service as good business and insisted that Associated Press stories be accurate and balanced. He urged members to produce fair and impartial reporting because "for a self-governing people an honest news service is of the highest value" (*New York Times*, February 16, 1929, 7).

When a competing news agency, United Press, went into receivership in 1897, Associated Press became the dominant news organization in the United States, eventually growing into a network of twelve hundred newspapers during twenty-eight years of Stone's leadership. Stone was relentlessly resourceful in getting and making news. He chartered a fleet of tugboats to report the Spanish-American War, when the Spanish government cut cables to prevent war reporting. In July 1903, Associated Press scooped the world in reporting the death of Pope Leo XIII, ending his twenty-five-year papacy. A year later Stone traveled to St. Petersburg on the eve of the Russo-Japanese War and won a pledge from Czar Nicholas II to keep transmission lines open during the conflict. In August of 1905 he became personally involved in a Portsmouth, New Hampshire, peace parley that led to a settlement of the crisis.

Stone worked tirelessly to open Associated Press bureaus across Europe and around the world and to standardize the content of that coverage. During World War I, Associated Press supplied an average of seventy thousand words daily to newspapers in New York City alone. In 1918, the United States Supreme Court agreed with Stone's legal claim that news is a commodity and because it had commercial value a news story was the property of the paper that had obtained it.

When Stone died, *New York Times* publisher Adolph S. Ochs spoke for many when he observed that few men had done more to serve the public good. The development of a highly professional, non-partisan news service "owned and controlled by the papers it served" had helped lift journalism from the private pleasure and profit of publishers to a national resource with public responsibilities. This re-direction greatly encouraged "the freedom and independence of the press," Ochs claimed. "No warrior or crusader ever fought for a better principle" (*New York Times*, February 16, 1929, 7).

Further Reading

Abbot, Willis J. "Melville E. Stone's Own Story." *Collier's* 65, February 7, 1920, 51.

Cooper, Kent. *Kent Cooper and the Associated Press*. New York: Random House, 1959.

Dennis, Charles H. *Victor Lawson: His Time and His Work*. Chicago: University of Chicago Press, 1935.

Gramling, Oliver. *AP: The Story of News*. New York: Farrar and Rinehart, 1940.

"M.E.S." His Book. New York: Harper & Brothers, 1918.

Nord, David Paul. "The Business Values of American Newspapers: The Nineteenth-Century Watershed in Chicago." *Journalism Quarterly* 61, 1984, 265–273.

Nord, David Paul "The Urbanization of Journalism in Chicago." *Journal of Urban History* 11, August 1985, 411–441.

Papers of Melville E. Stone. Midwest Collection. The Newberry Library. Chicago, IL.

Rosewater, Victor, *History of Cooperative News-Gathering in the United States.* New York: D. Appleton, 1930.

Schwarzlose, Richard Allen. *American Wire Services: A Study of Their Development as a Social Institution.* New York: Arno Press, 1979.

Smythe, Ted Curtis. *The Gilded Age Press, 1865–1900.* Westport, CT: Praeger, 2003.

Stone, Melville E. *Fifty Years a Journalist.* New York: Greenwood, 1968, originally 1921.

BRUCE J. EVENSEN

STRYKER, ROY EMERSON

Roy Emerson Stryker (November 5, 1893–September 27, 1975) was best known for his work as the director of the Farm Security Administration photography project. Between 1935 and 1943 he employed well-known photojournalists and amassed a collection of photographs that documented the Great Depression and American culture. The pictures, which were widely used by the print media, provided some of the most powerful images of that era in American history.

Stryker was born on November 5, 1893, in Great Bend, Kansas, but spent his youth on a ranch in Montrose, Colorado. After serving in the military during World War I, he studied economics at Columbia University with Rexford Guy Tugwell. In 1924 Stryker served as Tugwell's teaching assistant and illustrated an economics textbook that Tugwell co-authored with Thomas Munro titled *American Economic Life and the Means of Its Improvement.* While compiling images for the book, Stryker realized that photographs could be used to convey complex information to a mass audience, and became captivated by the idea of using photography as a tool for visual communication.

In 1935 President Roosevelt created the Resettlement Administration to combat rural poverty, and appointed Tugwell director of the agency. Tugwell immediately formed the Historical Section—Photographic as part of the Resettlement Administration's Information Division, and hired Stryker to supervise the project. Although Stryker was not a photographer, he knew that photography would be a useful instrument to present evidence of the rural poverty that was worsened by the Depression. He employed a group of photographers including Arthur Rothstein, Walker Evans, and Dorothea Lange to create images that documented the widespread suffering and publicized New Deal agricultural relief efforts. The photography project generated over 160,000 images of American life, which circulated in books, newspapers, and popular magazines such as *Look, Survey Graphic, Time,* and *Fortune.*

After the Resettlement Administration was absorbed into the Department of Agriculture in 1937 and renamed the Farm Security Administration, Stryker instructed his photographers to portray a positive image of rural America and to focus on the success of the New Deal programs. By 1941, however, Stryker and his photographers began turning away from documenting the Depression and toward portraying a nation mobilizing for war. In 1942 the photography unit was transferred into the Bureau of Publications and Graphics of the Office of War Information's Domestic Operations Branch. Congress eliminated the Domestic Operations Branch in 1943, and Stryker resigned from the agency.

Later that year, Stryker accepted a job with Standard Oil directing a photography project for the company's public relations division. The images circulated in Standard Oil's publication *Photo Memo,* as well as in other print media. When the company reduced the size of the project due to budgetary constraints, Stryker resigned in 1950, and accepted a position with the Pittsburgh Photographic Library supervising a photographic study of the people of Pittsburgh. From 1952 to 1958 Stryker directed his final documentary study for the Jones and Laughlin Steel Corporation Public Relations Department, where the photographs appeared in the company publication *Steel Pix* and in *Fortune* magazine. After 1958 Stryker acted as a visual consultant for several news magazines and taught seminars on photojournalism at the University of Missouri. Stryker returned to Montrose, Colorado in 1962, and died in Grand Junction on September 27, 1975.

Further Reading

Curtis, James. *Mind's Eye, Mind's Truth: FSA Photography Reconsidered.* Philadelphia: Temple University Press, 1989.

Finnegan, Cara A. *Picturing Poverty: Print Culture and FSA Photographs.* Washington and London: Smithsonian Books, 2003.

Hurley, F. Jack. *Portrait of a Decade: Roy Stryker and the Development of Documentary Photography in the Thirties.* Baton Rouge: Louisiana State University Press, 1972.

Kidd, Stuart S. *Farm Security Administration Photography, the Rural South, and the Dynamics of Image Making, 1935–1943.* Lewiston, NY: Edwin Mellen Press, 2004.

Natanson, Nicholas. *The Black Image in the New Deal: The Politics of FSA Photography.* Knoxville: The University of Tennessee Press, 1992.

Stryker, Roy Emerson, and Nancy Wood. *In This Proud Land: America 1935–1943 As Seen in the FSA Photographs.* Greenwich, CT: New York Graphic Society, Ltd., 1973.

MICHELE KROLL

STUDENT JOURNALISM

Students in American schools and colleges have published newspapers, magazines and yearbooks as part of their educational experience. This practice of journalism is distinct from the training of journalism students, who are pursuing a degree qualifying them for employment as professional journalists. Student journalists have not yet chosen journalism as a career and they usually work after classroom hours, although some of their work may be directed and completed during formal classes taught by faculty.

Students at the William Penn Charter School in Philadelphia, Pennsylvania, published the earliest known student newspaper during the American Revolution while the city was under British military occupation. Twenty-five hand-written issues were published during 1777–1778, after which it ceased publishing. The earliest continuing student publication at a secondary school was the *Literary Journal* of the Boston Latin School, founded in 1829. By 1900, 276 student newspapers, magazines or yearbooks had started publishing in secondary schools located in thirty-seven states with increasing numbers in public high schools. While begun primarily as extracurricular activities by students, school publications were often paired up with journalism classes to help improve the students' work. The first high school journalism class was offered in Salina, Kansas, in 1912.

In 1998, the student press existed in nearly 97 percent of United States high schools if one counted the following activities: a journalism course for credit, a yearbook, a newspaper, a news magazine or a television or radio station, according to a national study by Jack Dvorak of Indiana University at Bloomington. He estimated more than seventeen thousand high schools offered one or more of these student journalism opportunities. In a 2002 study, Dvorak found 31 percent of high schools offered students an electronic journalism experience including radio, television or online media study or participation.

Among colleges, *The Dartmouth* of Dartmouth College in New Hampshire, first published in 1799, claims to be the oldest college newspaper, although *The Yale Daily News* asserts it is the oldest daily newspaper, independent since its founding in 1878. By the early twenty-first century, the modern college student press included 3,163 print publications at colleges and universities with at least 1,000 student-run radio and television stations.

To learn what other staffs were doing elsewhere, student editors began meeting together after World War I, often at local college campuses. Such meetings gave birth to national organizations such as the National Scholastic Press Association (1921), the Journalism Education Association (1924), the Columbia Scholastic Press Association (1925), and the Quill and Scroll Society (1926) along with many state and regional groups. They offered conferences for editors and faculty advisers to teach one another about best practices. These groups also provided contests, gave awards, completed evaluations and published books and other teaching aids for self-improvement by student journalists. The NSPA launched a college division, the Associated Collegiate Press (1933) to provide these services to the college student press. Advisers working with that group eventually formed what became College Media Advisers, Inc. in 1954.

Throughout its history, at both high school and college levels, the student press covered campus news and features of interest to students, written by students, and concerning student activities. But there were exceptions to this local orientation. During World War II, sixty student publications sold more than half a million dollars in War Stamps and Bonds to help fund the American war effort. Post-war growth took place as new schools were added rapidly with the surging enrollments caused by the baby boom. As schools and colleges opened new buildings and campuses, student publications and broadcast media were added as well.

The Civil Rights era, the Vietnam War protests and the emerging growth of student activism greatly affected student journalists. Coverage expanded to include more issues traditionally considered to be of "off-campus" interest. Conflicts arose between student editors and either administrators or those students who were more interested in traditional coverage. Some of these conflicts resulted in censorship attempts that escalated to court battles. A 1969 decision by the U. S. Supreme Court in the case of *Tinker v. Des Moines School District* recognized that students in public schools did not "shed their constitutional rights. . . ." A separate line of court cases established the right of college student journalists to a free press in public colleges.

The Student Press Law Center (SPLC), founded in 1974, took up the work of protecting the rights of student editors in much the same way that the Reporters Committee for a Free Press aided professional journalists facing legal challenges to their work. The SPLC's work on behalf of student journalists was seriously hampered by a 1988 Supreme Court decision sharply limiting the rights of the high school student press.

In *Hazelwood School District v. Kuhlmeier*, the Court held that the First Amendment did not require schools to affirmatively promote particular types of student speech as long as the refusal was "reasonably related to legitimate pedagogical concerns." In its opinion, the Court tried to distinguish *Hazelwood's* limitation of, from *Tinker's* securing of, student rights to free speech and expression. Ultimately, the impact of *Hazelwood* was to encourage renewed efforts to censor student journalists, usually aimed at improving the public relations image of schools in the local community. The Court seemed more intent on allowing schools to tighten controls over student behavior, and less concerned about educating students as young citizens in their constitutional rights.

One consequence of this enhanced effort to control student expression was reflected in a major national study of First Amendment attitudes among more than one hundred thousand high school students, teachers, administrators and student journalists. Titled "The Future of the First Amendment" and released in 2005, the report suggested that most high school students had "little appreciation for the First Amendment." However, student journalists were "more likely to believe that students should be allowed to report controversial issues without approval of school authorities" than other students. From its beginning in 1777, student journalism has always struggled to make its voice heard.

Further Reading

Dvorak, Jack. Journalism Student Performance in Language Arts [computer file]. ERIC Clearinghouse on Reading English and Communication. Bloomington, IN, 1999.

EDMUND J. SULLIVAN

SUBURBAN NEWSPAPERS

Often considered a stepchild to big-city daily newspapers, suburban newspapers' forte is intensive coverage of their communities, which is proving to be an ever-more valuable commodity. The suburban press shines at giving readers what they want by focusing coverage on such close-to-home topics as families, schools, commuting, crime, high school sports, and local government. While most suburban newspapers have substantially smaller circulations than their big-city counterparts, some newspapers domiciled in the suburbs have circulations that rival the papers downtown.

Newsday, based in Melville, New York, circulates more than four hundred thousand papers a day in the Long Island suburbs as well as in the New York City borough of Queens. In Southern California, *The Orange County Register*, based in Santa Ana, sells more than three hundred thousand copies a day. These suburban-based publications not only have strong circulations, but impressive editorial products as well. *Newsday*, considered by many to be the exemplar of suburban journalism, has won 17 Pulitzer Prizes, and the *Register* has won three of the coveted awards.

Suburban newspapers can often boast of substantial circulations thanks to multiple publications operating under a parent organization's banner. Liberty Group Publishing, based in suburban Chicago, has readership of more than two million thanks to its three hundred publications, including sixty-four dailies, in sixteen states. Many suburban newspapers are members of a chain of papers serving communities surrounding a large city. Gannett, the nation's largest newspaper group in terms of circulation, operates many newspapers that could be considered suburban.

Circulations of many suburban newspapers continue to rise, sometimes at the expense of the metropolitan dailies, as readers continue their migration to the suburbs. Not to be confused with small-town weeklies or dailies in rural locations, suburban newspapers typically operate on the fringe of a metropolitan area. The term "suburban newspaper" surfaced as early as 1877 when the *West Roxbury* (Massachusetts) *Gazette* renamed itself the *Boston Suburban News*. It was about that time that newspapers on the outskirts of metropolitan areas in Boston and Chicago began printing multiple suburban publications from a central printing plant.

The growth of the suburban press rapidly accelerated after World War II as city dwellers began heading to nearby towns seeking more room, less crime, better schools, and less congestion. Unfortunately for the big-city dailies, the middle class and the affluent were leaving the cities. Their departure did not go unnoticed by the metropolitan dailies

which began paying closer attention to the burgeoning communities on their doorsteps.

For example, the *Los Angeles Times* began publishing regional weekly editions in 1952. By 1957, the *Times* was publishing seventy- to eighty-page special sections for such communities as the San Fernando Valley, Orange County, the San Gabriel Valley, and the town of Glendale. However, it was not until the 1970s that many of the other metropolitan dailies began taking life in the suburbs seriously by beefing up coverage from the main office or by staking a physical presence in suburban communities with small newsroom and advertising offices often in storefront locations.

The suburban editions of the metropolitan dailies took such forms as weekly inserts or daily zoned editions. For example, the *Chicago Tribune* launched in 1972 a thrice-weekly tabloid called *The (Little) Trib* in an effort to duplicate the work of the already established suburban newspapers. The *Washington Post* successfully expanded into the Maryland and Virginia suburbs in the 1960s—slightly ahead of most metros. As of 2006, it retained a high circulation penetration throughout its metropolitan region. The metros that got to the suburbs early in the game tended to flourish.

Suburban publishers did not appreciate the incursion of the big-city newspapers on their turf. In 1967, Paddock Publications, a well-regarded, editorially respected suburban chain, opted to boost the frequency of its sixteen papers from weekly to thrice weekly in response to the launch of daily suburban newspaper on its turf by Field Enterprises, which was publishing the *Chicago Sun-Times* and the *Chicago Daily News*. That short-lived publication is long gone, but a Paddock publication, now known as the *Daily Herald*, has become the third-largest daily newspaper in Illinois with a circulation of more than 140,000. It has long been considered a must-read publication for residents of Chicago's northwest and western suburbs.

In Milwaukee, in 1972, Community Newspapers Inc. filed an anti-trust suit against the *Milwaukee Journal*. The suburban newspaper chain was attempting to stop the big-city daily from invading its territory after the *Journal* began producing special suburban sections. Both parties later agreed to dismiss the suit.

But the dailies could hardly be blamed for invading the suburbs. A report in trade publication *Editor and Publisher* on March 13, 1965, indicated that suburban dailies in the metropolitan areas surrounding the nation's ten largest cities boosted circulation by 80.5 percent between 1945 and 1964. By contrast, according to that report, circulations of the metro dailies in the nation's ten largest markets increased by only 1.9 percent.

The grim circulation numbers did not get much better through the rest of the century. A report published by the Newspaper Association of America found that daily newspaper circulation continued to stagnate from 1965 to 1998. Paralleling the plateau of daily circulation was a threefold increase in circulation of weekly newspapers to 74.3

million. Most of this increase occurred in the suburbs and satellite cities near the metropolitan areas.

The trend appears to be continuing, if not getting worse for the metropolitan dailies. In the San Francisco Bay region, for example, the area's two largest dailies—the *San Francisco Chronicle* and the *San Jose Mercury News*—reported daily circulation losses in the spring of 2005 of 6.5 percent and 3.4 percent, respectively. Meanwhile, two suburban operations reported slightly higher daily circulation. The *Contra Costa Times* reported a gain of .0.4 percent and the Alameda Newspaper Group saw its circulation increase by 0.3 percent.

Particularly problematic for the metropolitan dailies was their traditional strength in providing national and international coverage. But media analysts noted that readers—especially younger ones—were increasingly inclined to access that kind of information via the Internet. That still left local news, but the suburban press has long been savvy at delivering that element for its local readers. For many of the metro dailies, they still must overcome the perception that they are interlopers on the hotly contested suburban turf.

The departure of the middle class and affluent not only contributed to the diminution of circulation but to the erosion of the advertising base, the lifeblood of any successful newspaper. The suburban refugees embody the demographics that national and local advertisers particularly covet. Advertisers quickly recognized that the newly relocated residents of the suburbs were attracted to the more intimate coverage of their communities provided by the suburban weeklies and dailies.

Some metropolitan dailies have adopted a "if you can't beat 'em, buy 'em" mentality with regard to suburban dailies or suburban weeklies. The *Philadelphia Inquirer* in the 1990s, for example, bought ProMedia Management, a chain of suburban weeklies and shoppers serving suburban and Montgomery and Bucks counties.

During that same period Hollinger International, publisher of the *Chicago Sun-Times*, began buying up its suburban competitors with the purchase of more than one hundred Chicago-area dailies, weeklies, and Internet sites. In 2005, Hollinger began reorganizing the properties into three divisions in an effort to make it more competitive with the *Chicago Tribune*, the dominant daily in that region.

Despite the fact that the big-city metros have been taking the suburbs much more seriously, many maintain that the suburban weeklies and dailies are much more attuned to what's going on in their communities. The news staffs of the suburban weeklies and dailies, in many cases, genuinely want to cover the communities.

Covering the suburbs is a much less desirable beat for reporters at the metro dailies, who tend to dismiss the suburbs as overly homogenous and uninteresting. They would prefer the meatier, more high-profile coverage of the downtown institutions such as police, the courts and city hall or more specialized beats such as the environment, medicine or technology. Editors tend to assign their lower-paid, least-experienced reporters to suburban beats or suburban bureaus. The typically well-educated, highly mobile, sophisticated, and often single reporters themselves tend to be much different from the well-entrenched, family-focused readers they are writing for in the suburbs.

By the early twenty-first century, the suburban press had consistently shown that it could deliver the kind of information that people in the suburbs truly cared about and were willing to buy. The suburban press had outgrown its reputation for simply presenting just the good news or focusing on insignificant events. The suburban press continued to present such bread-and-butter fare as the school lunch menu or the weekly recreation schedule, but it was increasingly exploring complex political and social issues affecting its readership.

Further Reading

Davis, Nancy M. "Ring Around the Metros." *Presstime*. August 1, 2001.

Lister, Hal. *The Suburban Press: A Separate Journalism*. Columbia, Missouri: Lucas Brothers Publishers, 1975.

Morton, John. "Suburban Sprawl." *American Journalism Review*. November 2000: 64.

Moses, Lucia. "Here no evil SUB no evil: But if Journalists Continue to Look Down on the Suburbs, Newspapers May Alienate Their Markets." *Editor and Publisher*, January 21, 2002: 20.

Rosenthal, Phil. "Hollinger to Teorganize Sun-Times, Sister Papers." *Chicago Tribune*. August 21, 2005, section 3,1.

Sim, John Cameron. "19th Century Applications of Suburban Newspaper Concepts." *Journalism Quarterly*, Fall 1975: 627–631.

EDMUND LAWLER

SUNDAY SUPPLEMENTS

The widespread appearance of the urban Sunday newspaper in the wake of the Civil War greatly expanded the role of the newspaper as a source of entertainment. The daily penny papers that appeared in the 1830s were, of course, entertaining, but they had limited space. That meant that human interest stories were, by necessity, brief and appeared among a welter of hard news, editorials, stock reports, and police briefs. Daily newspapers also had another deficiency: because of their modest size and massive daily press runs they could not supply the existing demand for advertising lineage or the extended features that readers craved.

The Sunday newspaper was expansive, designed to be read at leisure; it focused on human interest, entertainment, and explanatory journalism, rather than breaking news. Special supplements, preproduced with extra care given to both content and appearance, allowed newspapers to either broaden or narrow their appeal to particular readers.

Supplements could be broad-based and focus on social events of wide public interest or could specifically target male sports fans or female homemakers. In fact, they more resembled magazines than newspapers and, like magazines, served as a conduit for nascent national firms who sought the widest possible distribution for their advertisements.

Clerics saw supplements, and the Sunday papers themselves, as competition and a symbol of creeping secularism on the Sabbath and opposed them. But despite local ordinances that forbid Sunday publication in some cities, religious protests were in vain. Working people, especially, eagerly turned to the supplements as a form of leisure on what was often their only day off from work.

To succeed, Sunday papers could not simply be bigger versions of the daily paper; their heft, and price, had to be justified, and the novel content of the supplements was well-suited to do just that. "It was the creation of the Sunday paper, stuffed with full-page ads, that truly opened the door to a multitude of entertainment features," according to the historian George H. Douglas.

The Sunday supplement, as a weekly publication, had more time and care to devote to the presentation of its articles, which brought readers short stories, inspirational essays, practical advice and celebrity profiles. In the early 1900s, the development of rotogravure, a specialized photoengraving process, allowed newspapers to reproduce artwork and photographs with relatively high quality. The first American newspaper to use the rotogravure process was the *New York Times*, which produced a special Christmas pictorial in 1912. In 1914, the *Times* became one of a half-dozen newspapers to regularly offer rotogravure sections in a separate section of the paper. In 1942, the *Times'* rotogravure feature became a part of its Sunday magazine.

While big urban papers created separate staffs just to gather and write Sunday feature material, newspapers big and small also depended on feature syndicates. Sunday papers were especially interested in reaching women readers because, while they typically were not breadwinners, they made many household purchasing decisions. William Randolph Hearst was a pioneer in the creation of "women's pages" and he also introduced "Annie Laurie," one of the first "sob sisters."

Comics, or funnies, which made their debut in 1893, were the most popular supplements of all. While Hearst did not invent the comic strip, in 1896 he did snatch a successful one, the Yellow Kid, from his rival, Joseph Pulitzer. Inspired by its popularity and success, Hearst papers began to develop other strips. In 1915, he introduced the King Features Syndicate to serve newspapers nationally. Today, King remains a force in the Sunday supplement business and distributes such popular comic strips as "Blondie," "Hagar the Horrible" and "The Family Circus," along with editorials, columns, puzzles, and games. The Universal Press Syndicate is another major supplier of comics, features and opinion columnists. Eventually, advertisers would produce their own supplements, multi-page mini-catalogues that described in detail the wares a particular firm had to offer. Newspapers profit by both charging to insert the ads and, in many cases, by printing them.

Sunday magazines are also widely circulated. *Parade Magazine*, which was founded by department store magnate Marshall Field III in 1941, and *USA Weekend* are among the most successful. Most of the bigger urban papers produce their own Sunday magazines—the *New York Times* Sunday magazine is among the biggest and most sophisticated and rivals high-toned journals such as *Harpers* and the *Atlantic Monthly* for depth, prestige and the quality of the writing.

Further Reading

Anon. King Features Syndicate History, http://www.kingfeatures.com/history/historyeFam.htm, (accessed April 11, 2007).

Douglas, George H. *The Golden Age of the Newspaper*. Westport, CT: Greenwood Press, 1999.

Hynds, Ernest C. *American Newspapers in the 1980s*. New York: Hastings House Publishers, 1980.

Moyes, Norman B., and David Manning White. *Journalism in the Mass Media*. New York: Ginn and Co., 1970.

MIKE DILLON

SWING, RAYMOND GRAM

Fred Friendly, veteran producer for Edward R. Murrow at CBS, thought Raymond Gram Swing (1887–1968) was "the closest thing that broadcasting ever had to a Walter Lippmann" (*The New York Times*, December 24, 1968). An estimated thirty-seven million nightly listeners on both sides of the Atlantic apparently agreed, making the soft-spoken minister's son one of the most respected of radio commentators before and during World War II.

Swing came from a distinguished, educated family that would shape his political views and encourage his sense of social responsibility. He was born in Cortland, New York, to Albert Temple Swing, a Congregational minister, and Alice Edwards Mead, the daughter of Elizabeth Storrs Mead, first president of Mount Holyoke College. His uncle, George Herbert Mead, became the nation's preeminent pragmatist and taught philosophy and social psychology at the University of Chicago. In 1893, Albert Swing became a professor in church history at Oberlin, the nation's first coeducational college. His son would say he was deeply influenced by Oberlin's progressive ideals, although only taking a year of classes there.

Albert Swing hoped his son would teach or enter the ministry. Raymond Swing saw reporting as his calling and he rose swiftly through the ranks. Starting with the *Cleveland Press*, while still in his teens, Swing graduated to the *Richmond* (Indiana) *Evening News*, the *Indianapolis Star*, the *Cincinnati Times Star*, and finally became managing editor of the *Indianapolis Sun* when he was twenty-three. Swing thought of himself as a reform-minded muckraker on the lookout for political corruption and corporate misbehavior.

When Swing married Suzanne Morin on July 9, 1912, his uncle gave them a wedding gift of a year in Europe, but the couple would soon divorce. While in Europe, however, Swing got caught up in the rush to war and became foreign correspondent for the *Chicago Daily News*. With Swing was based in Berlin, Paul Scott Mower in Paris, and Edward Price Bell in London, the paper became respected for reporting on World War I. Swing moved freely behind German and Turkish lines, reported on fighting in the Balkans, at Gallipoli and the Dardanelles. He scored an exclusive when he reported the introduction of the Germans' secret weapon, a 43-ton mobile howitzer known as the "Big Bertha" that proved critical in the August 1914 German advance on Liege. When the United States entered the war, Swing went to Washington to work for the War Labor Board.

After the war, Swing briefly edited the *Nation* before returning to Berlin as bureau chief of the *New York Herald*. He became one of the first Western reporters to visit Russia after the Bolshevik Revolution. On January 10, 1920, while based in London, where he worked for the *Wall Street Journal*, Swing married Betty Gram, a feminist, and agreed to take her name until their divorce in 1942. As Raymond Gram Swing he joined the foreign news service of the *Philadelphia Public Ledger* and the *New York Post* in 1924, and returned to Washington in the mid-1930s to write for the *Nation*, the *London News-Chronicle* and the *Economist*. His broadcasts began in 1935 for the British Broadcasting Company and grew to include nightly commentaries, starting in 1936, on America's Mutual Broadcasting System. His wide and growing following in the United States and Europe included Franklin Roosevelt and Winston Churchill. Swing's carefully-crafted two thousand-word, thirteen-minute summary and analysis of world events later won him lucrative contracts with the National Broadcasting Company and the American Broadcasting Company. His tireless reporting and scholarly prescience on a 120-station nationwide network on the eve of World War II made him one of America's most widely admired men.

"News," he told listeners on March 9, 1939, "is a combination of facts and a report of trends, and foreign news gets to be so much a report of trends, that facts when they reach the public do not always loom as they should." On May 30 he warned, "Whatever your newspapers report or fail to report, the nature of life for almost everybody, next year and for years to come, is perhaps being decided these days." On June 16 he reported, "The world crisis is at the boiling point." It waited for "what Hitler will next decide to do." He reported, "To get to the meaning of foreign news these days, the items have to be added up, not pulled apart." Two weeks before actual fighting broke out, he observed "the most obvious fact about the news from Europe is that things are going on which are not being reported" (August 16, 1939). On the eve of fighting he had vainly hoped the German people would not stand behind Hitler when the British and French stood beside Poland (August 28, 1939). He saw the war arising from Hitler's fundamental miscalculation. "The ordinary Englishman and the ordinary Frenchman" would fight "to check a single man in his ambition to dominate the world" (September 3, 1939). Eventually, Swing predicted, Americans would fight for the same thing.

After the war, Swing's popularity waned. His advocacy of peaceful coexistence with the Soviet Union led to his investigation by the House Committee on Un-American Activities. Eventually exonerated, he became a political commentator on the Voice of America from 1951 to 1953 and from 1959 to 1964. During the 1950s and 1960s, Swing was active in the World Federalist movement, arguing that nuclear weaponry created the necessity for stronger global government. To the end, he saw journalism as a critical instrument in giving citizens the information they needed to know to make democracy possible.

Further Reading

Fang, Irving E. *Those Radio Commentators!*. Ames: Iowa State University, 1977.
"Raymond Gram Swing," *Current Biography: Who's News and Why*, New York: H.W. Wilson, 1940.
Raymond Gram Swing Papers, Library of Congress, Manuscript Division, including his radio commentaries from 1938–1953, found in the library's Recorded Sound Reference Center.
Swing, Raymond. *Forerunners of American Fascism*. New York: J. Messner, 1935.
——.*"Good Evening!" A Professional Memoir*. New York: Harcourt, Brace & World, 1964.
——. *In the Name of Sanity*. New York: Harper & Bros., 1946.
——. *How War Came*. New York: W.W. Norton, 1939.
——. *Preview of History*. Garden City: Doubleday, 1943.
Van Pelt, Mark H. "The Cold War on the Air." *Journal of Popular Culture* 18 (Fall 1984).

BRUCE J. EVENSEN

SWISSHELM, JANE GREY

Jane Grey Swisshelm (December 6, 1815–July 22, 1884) was a journalist who was an unflinching advocate of the abolition of slavery, the integration of African Americans into schools and other institutions, women's property rights, and of women's right to work in the same jobs as men.

She was born Jane Cannon on December 6, 1815, in Pittsburgh. When she was eight years old, her father died and she helped support the family by making lace. Brought up as a Christian, she had a strong interest in religion. In 1836, she married James Swisshelm and the couple moved briefly to Louisville, Kentucky, where she began fighting slavery. Her newspaper stories sometimes appeared under the name Jennie Dean. The couple returned to Pittsburgh, and on December 20, 1847, Swisshelm issued the first copy of the *Pittsburgh Saturday Visiter* with its unique spelling to promote her antislavery passion. To appeal to a wider audience, she also published literary and general interest articles and market reports.

Because she worked in the office of the *Pittsburgh Commercial Journal* where her paper was printed, she demonstrated that a man and woman could work together respectably without arousing gossip. Swisshelm opened the shades and lighted the normally dark print shop so people could observe and she could avoid a scandal. Swisshelm wrote advice for women who worked in jobs then reserved for men, and she demonstrated her commitment by hiring female printers.

In 1850, she wrote Washington news for Horace Greeley's *New York Tribune* and became the first woman allowed into the press gallery of the U.S. Senate. For her own newspaper, she wrote fiery, probably false, reports against Whig leaders, especially after the Compromise of 1850, that so angered Greeley that he fired her.

After the failure of her marriage, she lost a fight for women's property rights in Pennsylvania and fled with her six-year-old daughter to St. Cloud, Minnesota, where her sister lived. There she again established a newspaper in which she fought for better treatment of African Americans and harsher treatment of Native Americans.

She angered St. Cloud's most influential business and political leaders and, after a bitter public exchange, a mob broke into the office of Swisshelm's newspaper, the *St. Cloud Visiter*, destroyed the press, and scattered type in the street and into the nearby Mississippi River. A note warned her not to repeat her offenses.

Swisshelm rebuilt her newspaper with financial help from St. Cloud and across the nation. She got so much mileage out of the incident that embarrassed St. Cloud leaders sued for a truce, but instead of suing her, they took on her male financial backers. In a settlement, the backers agreed not to mention the incident again, but Swisshelm said she had not agreed and reopened her newspaper as the *St. Cloud Democrat*.

This decidedly Republican *Democrat* displayed only lukewarm support for President Abraham Lincoln, and Swisshelm attacked him as lacking sufficient vengeance toward the Dakota Indians who attacked Minnesota settlers in 1862. Swisshelm referred to the Dakota as "those red-jawed tigers whose fangs are dripping with the blood of the innocents."

During the Civil War, Swisshelm obtained an appointment in the War Department. She founded the *Reconstructionist* in 1865 and her fierce criticism of President Andrew Johnson provoked him into firing her from her government appointment. With the loss of her job, she lost her income, and her paper failed. In retirement, Swisshelm wrote her autobiography, *Half a Century* (1880). She died four years later.

Further Reading

Endres, Kathleen. "Jane Grey Swisshelm: 19th Century Journalist and Feminist." *Journalism History* 2:4 (Winter 1975–76): 128–132.

Hoffert, Sylvia D. *Jane Grey Swisshelm: An Unconventional Life, 1815–1884*. Chapel Hill: The University of North Carolina Press, 2004.

Larsen, Arthur J. *Crusader and Feminist: Letters of Jane Grey Swisshelm 1858–1865*. St. Paul: Minnesota Historical Society, 1934.

Pierson, Michael D. "Between Antislavery and Abolition: The Politics and Rhetoric of Jane Grey Swisshelm." *Pennsylvania History* 60:3 (July 1993): 305–321.

Swisshelm, Jane Grey. *Half a Century*. Chicago: Jansen, McClurg & Company, 1880.

———. *Letters to Country Girls*. New York: J.C. Riker, 1853.

WILLIAM E. HUNTZICKER

SWOPE, HERBERT BAYARD

Considered by many to be one of the greatest reporters and editors—not to mention one of the most charismatic—of the twentieth century, Herbert Bayard Swope (January 5, 1882–June 20, 1958) was the personification of the Jazz Age, the period of his heyday as executive editor of the *New York World*. So great an impact did he have on the journalism of his era that at the time of his death, three decades after he left the paper, he was still known as "Swope of the World."

Born in St. Louis to German immigrants, Swope was encouraged to make writing his career after winning a local department store's essay contest. He took a reporting job on Joseph Pulitzer's *St. Louis Post-Dispatch*, soon moving to the *Chicago Tribune* before making his way to New York in 1909 and joining the staff of Pulitzer's flagship, the *World*.

The story that catapulted him to instant fame was the July 16, 1912, shooting of Herman Rosenthal, a local gambling-den operator, just hours after his secret grand jury testimony naming New York Police Lt. Charles Becker as his silent partner. As John Hohenberg, longtime administrator of the Pulitzer Prizes, put it, Swope went "storming into the bedroom of District Attorney Charles Whitman in the middle of the night … [and] showered both pleas and abuse on the prosecutor until he decided to begin an immediate investigation" and headed straight for Becker's precinct, balking a cover-up already in progress. Swope, wrote Hohenberg, was the only reporter who *could* have done that. The case concluded three years later with Becker's execution for the murder.

When World War I broke out, Swope insisted on being sent abroad, where he always seemed to be in the right place at the right time. His series of articles, "Inside the German Empire," was awarded the first-ever Pulitzer Prize for reporting in 1917. When the United States entered the war, Swope was named an assistant to Bernard Baruch on the War Industries Board.

In 1920, Ralph Pulitzer named Swope executive editor of the *World*, a position created just for him, which paid the then-astounding sum of $54,000 a year, plus two percent of the profits. But Swope earned his salary, leading the paper on a series of crusading exposés, the most important of which was an exposé in 1921 of the newly revived Ku Klux Klan and its growing influence outside the South. The paper also exposed Florida's peonage system, in which convicts were farmed out as cheap labor. In nine years, Swope's *World* won ten Pulitzer Prizes, including his own. He also left a lasting imprint on the newspaper world by originating the op-ed page, which featured a roster of brilliant columnists, including Heywood Broun and Franklin P. Adams. Stanley Walker, legendary city editor of the *New York Herald Tribune*, wrote of Swope: "He is as easy to ignore as a cyclone."

Swope's secret, wrote Hohenberg, was that he "deeply believed that the quality of moral indignation was what separated a good newspaper man from the competent technician. But he left the *World* in 1929—two years before the paper's demise—and became a private "policy consultant" to wealthy and powerful men. Over the next three decades, he became an influential figure in the worlds of politics and horse racing, "riding through life with a flourish of zest, known to everybody, knowing everybody," wrote the *New York Times*.

Further Reading

Harold Hutchings. "Swope, Famed Editor, Dies at 76 in New York." *Chicago Tribune,* June 21, 1958.

[Herbert Bayard Swope]. *New York Times,* June 21, 1958.

John Hohenberg. "Herbert Swope's Career," letter to the editor, *New York Times,* June 28, 1958.

E.J. Kahn. *The World of Swope.* New York: Doubleday, 1965.

Alfred Allan Lewis. *Man of the World: Herbert Bayard Swope.* Indianapolis, IN: Bobbs-Merrill, 1978.

Richard O'Connor. *Heywood Broun: The Life and Career of the Most Controversial Journalist of His Time.* New York: G.P. Putnam's Sons, 1975.

ERIC FETTMANN

T

TAPPAN, ARTHUR

Arthur Tappan (May 22, 1786–July 23, 1865), Christian reformer and abolitionist, was the leading supporter of American evangelical publishing and reform organizations in the 1820s and 1830s. Though not a publisher himself, his financial contributions to organizational publishing were unparalleled.

Tappan was born in Northampton, Massachusetts, on May 22, 1786, the son of Benjamin Tappan and Sarah Homes Tappan. He was the middle son in a trio of famous brothers that included Benjamin Tappan and Lewis Tappan. He married Frances Antill in 1810; they had six daughters and two sons. He died on July 23, 1865, in New Haven, Connecticut.

While holding fast to his native New England piety, Arthur Tappan made a fortune in New York in the silk importing business. He lived a simple life—"a cracker and tumbler of water sufficed for a luncheon," his brother Lewis recalled—so that he could pour his money into evangelical causes, including the American Bible Society and American Tract Society. In 1829 Tappan helped bankroll a project by the Bible Society to place a Bible into every home in America, one of the first efforts to produce truly mass media.

Tappan also believed that religious values could be instilled into regular daily journalism. In 1827 he founded the New York *Journal of Commerce*, which refused to accept liquor and theater advertising or to work its staff on Sunday. The paper became a leading daily under the subsequent ownership of David Hale and Gerard Hallock, and it was still in business in 2006.

In the 1830s Tappan, with his brother Lewis, took up the cause of antislavery. Arthur met the firebrand William Lloyd Garrison in 1830 and helped finance Garrison's radical abolition newspaper the *Liberator*. In 1833 the Tappans helped to found the American Anti-Slavery Society (AASS), which was organized like an evangelical missionary/publishing society. By 1835, with Arthur its chief financial supporter, the society was publishing four monthly periodicals, including a four-page newspaper, *Human Rights*, and a small-format tract series for children, the *Slave's Friend*. Most of these periodicals were distributed in bulk for free circulation. By 1835 the presses were churning out tens of thousands of copies each week. During the year ending May 1835 the society published more than one million periodicals, reports, and circulars. The society's main newspaper, the *Emancipator*, became a weekly in 1836, funded by Arthur Tappan.

The Panic of 1837 ruined Tappan's import firm, and the evangelical reform movement lost its financial angel. Tappan stayed with the AASS until 1840, when he and Lewis split with the Garrisonians over philosophy and tactics. Though Lewis soldiered on with the abolitionist cause, Arthur largely abandoned reform and abolition after 1841, as he struggled unsuccessfully to recoup his fortune.

When Arthur died, Lewis recalled that in the 1830s he had donated some $50,000 a year to evangelical and abolitionist organizations. This figure was surely inflated by fond memory, but the gist of it was true: Arthur Tappan was by far the leading benefactor of evangelical reform efforts, including publishing, in this Age of Reform.

Further Reading

Havas, John M. "Commerce and Calvinism: The *Journal of Commerce*, 1827–1865." *Journalism Quarterly*, 38 (Winter 1961): 84–86.

Friedman, Lawrence J. *Gregarious Saints: Self and Community in American Abolitionism, 1830–1870*. New York: Cambridge University Press, 1982.

David Paul Nord. *Faith in Reading: Religious Publishing and the Birth of Mass Media in America*. New York: Oxford University Press, 2004.

Tappan, Lewis. *The Life of Arthur Tappan*. New York: Hurd and Houghton, 1871. Reprinted by Negro Universities Press, Westport, Connecticut, 1970.

Wyatt-Brown, Bertram, "Arthur Tappan and Lewis Tappan." In *American National Biography*, vol. 21. New York: Oxford University Press, 1999.

——. *Lewis Tappan and the Evangelical War Against Slavery*. Cleveland: Case Western Reserve University, 1969. Reprinted by Louisiana State University Press, Baton Rouge, 1997.

DAVID PAUL NORD

TAPPAN, LEWIS

Best known as an evangelical Christian reformer and antislavery activist, Lewis Tappan (May 23, 1788–June 21, 1873) was involved in the creation of two lasting institutions in the field of business communication: the New York *Journal of Commerce* and Dun & Bradstreet, the business information company. Both were still operating in 2006.

Tappan was born on May 23, 1788, in Northampton, Massachusetts, the son of Benjamin Tappan and Sarah Homes Tappan, and the younger brother of Arthur and

Benjamin Tappan. In 1813 Lewis married Susan Aspinwall, with whom he had two sons and five daughters. After Susan's death in 1853, he married Sarah Jackson Davis. He died in Brooklyn, New York, on June 21, 1873.

Lewis Tappan's career as a reformer and businessman took off in 1827 when he joined his brother Arthur in New York City in the silk importing business and in an array of religious organizations and projects. One of these was the *Journal of Commerce*, founded by Arthur in 1827 to demonstrate that a regular commercial newspaper could also support religious values such as temperance and strict observance of the Sabbath. Lewis took over full management of the paper in 1828, put it on a sound financial footing, and arranged its sale to David Hale and Gerard Hallock in 1829. Hale and Hallock maintained the religious character of the paper, while quickly making it a leader in news gathering. Tappan's interest in religious journalism ran far beyond the *Journal of Commerce*. He was a founder of the New York *Evangelist* in 1830 and was a contributor to religious newspapers throughout his life. Like his brother Arthur, Lewis was also an avid supporter of the evangelical publishing societies, especially the American Bible Society and the American Tract Society.

In the 1830s Tappan turned his religious enthusiasm and managerial skill to the cause of antislavery. He was a founder of the American Anti-Slavery Society in 1833 and an important contributor to its early organizational and publishing success, including fund-raising and management of the society's weekly newspaper, the *Emancipator*. In 1835 he was the leading organizer of one of the most impressive publishing events of antebellum America—the Great Postal Campaign—which flooded the South with antislavery tracts, pamphlets, and newspapers. Lewis and Arthur Tappan broke with William Lloyd Garrison's wing of the antislavery movement in 1840, but Lewis remained an active abolitionist and antislavery publicist. He helped organize the antislavery American Missionary Association in the 1840s and was a driving force behind the association's newspaper, the *American Missionary*.

In 1841, to support his antislavery work and his family, Tappan launched the Mercantile Agency, the first American company to systematically gather and report information on business firms in order to evaluate their credit risk. The Mercantile Agency developed reporting methods similar to those of a national newspaper or wire service, employing both local correspondents around the country and professional traveling reporters. The Mercantile Agency evolved into the credit reporting and business information firm known today as Dun & Bradstreet.

Further Reading

Friedman, Lawrence, J. "Confidence and Pertinacity in Evangelical Abolitionism: Lewis Tappan's Circle." *American Quarterly*, 31 (Spring 1979): 81–106.
Wyatt-Brown, Bertram. "Arthur Tappan and Lewis Tappan." In *American National Biography*, vol. 21. New York: Oxford University Press, 1999.
Wyatt-Brown, Bertram. "God and Dun & Bradstreet, 1841–1851." *Business History Review*, 40 (Winter 1966): 432–450.
———. *Lewis Tappan and the Evangelical War Against Slavery*. Cleveland: Case Western Reserve University, 1969. Reprinted by Louisiana State University Press, Baton Rouge, 1997.

DAVID PAUL NORD

TARBELL, IDA MINERVA

Ida Tarbell (November 5, 1857–January 6, 1944) was born in a log cabin in Erie County, Pennsylvania, on November 5, 1857, into a politically active family. She was influenced by what she saw. She decided in high school not to marry so that she would have her freedom. Her father was an independent oil producer in western Pennsylvania. When his business failed, he claimed it was due to the practices of John D. Rockefeller's Standard Oil Company. She used these connections later in her career to expose corruption.

Tarbell was the only woman in class at Allegheny College when she enrolled in 1876. After graduation, she relocated to Ohio to teach science but resigned after two years. She then took an editorial job at the small magazine *The Chautauquan*, published in Meadville, Pennsylvania. She eventually started writing articles for the publication. After a few years, Tarbell left for Paris where she wrote various freelance stories for American syndicates; in this role, she interviewed Louis Pasteur and Emile Zola. These experiences helped to transform her into a more confident writer.

She returned to the United States for a position at *McClure's* magazine in 1894. There she wrote multipart biographies of Napoleon and Abraham Lincoln. She was promoted to associate editor in 1900 and began her research on Standard Oil and John D. Rockefeller. It was this muckraking series that would make her a famous investigative author, along with such other writers as Ray Stannard Baker and Lincoln Steffens.

Muckrakers were Progressive-era crusaders who strove to uncover injustices. The term was initiated by President Theodore Roosevelt in reference to these journalists' ability to expose corporate and political "dirt." Their work led to federal regulations such as the Pure Food and Drug Act and Hepburn Act of 1906, which regulated the railroads.

After Tarbell's series ran, the parts were collected and published as a best-selling book, *The History of the Standard Oil Company*, in 1904. Her series fueled public attacks on Standard Oil and on trusts in general, and the book is credited with the leading to the breakup of Standard Oil in 1911.

After a disagreement with publisher S.S. McClure in 1906, Tarbell, along with Baker, Steffens, and editor John Sanborn Phillips left McClure's and bought *American Magazine* from Frederick Colver. The magazine did well for a few years but World War I and a decline in interest in muckraking led to the selling of the magazine in 1915.

Tarbell then became active on the lecture circuit, at one point she gave forty-nine lectures in seven weeks. She also served on several federal committees on war, peace, and women's issues. She did not support most women's rights issues and did not fully support a woman's right to vote.

She died of pneumonia in 1944, at the age of eighty-six. Her work is often found in investigative reporting textbooks. In 2002, a postage stamp was issued with her picture. Tarbell's autobiography, *All in the Day's Work*, was reissued in 2003.

Further Reading

Tarbell, Ida. *All in the Day's Work: An Autobiography*. Urbana: University of Illinois Press, 1939, 2003.

——. *History of the Standard Oil Company*. New York: Harper Torchbooks, 1904, 1966.

Wilson, Harold. *McClure's Magazine and the Muckrakers*. Princeton, NJ: Princeton University Press, 1970.

KIMBERLY WILMOT VOSS

TECHNOLOGY, NEW

From weblogs, or blogs, to Podcasts, new technology is exerting a strong influence on journalism. This article offers a systematic look at four ways in which new or emerging technology is reshaping journalism, both for better or worse. First, technology affects the content of journalism, the news itself. Second, technology influences the ways that journalists do their work. Third, technology reshapes the structure, culture, and management of the newsroom and news organizations in general. Finally, technology alters the relationships between or among news organizations, journalists and their many publics, especially audiences, regulators, funders, and competitors.

News Content

Perhaps the most visible way that technology redefines journalism is through news content. Since at least the invention of photography and telegraphy in the early nineteenth century, emerging technologies have presented profound implications for news content. During the 1840s, the exhibition of photographs offered citizens new ways of learning about events. Although photographs did not commonly appear in newspapers until several decades later, the use of other types of images helped to redefine news as more than just words. Also during the 1840s, the Associated Press emerged as an economical means to utilize the telegraph in news delivery. The cost and unreliable nature of the telegraph (the longer the message the greater the likelihood the end of a message might be lost) led to the development of a specialized form of news writing called the inverted pyramid. Reporters who used the inverted pyramid style put the most important words in the first sentence, or lead, because that might be all they could rely on to get through via the telegraph. Less important facts came later. Editors could drop words, sentences or paragraphs from the end of the story first, knowing that the most important facts would remain. This was often important when laying out the pages of a newspaper, especially when on deadline.

Over the years, emerging technologies reshaped news content in other ways. The rise of radio, and then television, introduced first audio to news reporting and later moving pictures (first through film or newsreels shown in motion picture theaters and later on the small screen in the home). Radio and television news are so familiar today that we take them for granted, but only a few generations ago they were unheard of in journalism or the world at large.

During the 1960s and 1970s, the advent of videotape led to other important changes in news content. Television news had relied on film, but it was slow and made it difficult to report on daily events in anything close to real time. Videotape made it possible to shoot, record, transmit (often via satellite), edit and show to the audience moving pictures of current news events the same day. Research has shown that videotape changed the way news was reported. News stories shot on film as late as the early 1970s tended to run longer and feature fewer and longer cuts than similar stories shot and edited on videotape just a few years later. The late CBS News executive Bud Benjamin lamented influence of videotape. It gave entertainment undue influence in reporting, he thought, which resulted in the loss of serious reflection in television news.

Since the advent of the Internet and the World Wide Web, a variety of new technologies have continued to reshape the content of news, particularly the ways stories are told and by whom. Early on, gossip columnist Matt Drudge and his "Drudge Report" ushered in a new "unfiltered" form of news, using the term "news" somewhat loosely. Drudge rarely did any fact checking (i.e., checking out his leads with additional sources to confirm their authenticity) and typically ran the most salacious tidbits on his Internet web page (http://www.drudgereport.com) having now morphed or evolved into a blog, or weblog. Yet for all the criticism of the Drudge Report, it did break perhaps the biggest news story of the Bill Clinton administration—the president's affair with intern Monica Lewinski.

Weblogs, or blogs, emerged in the early years of the twenty-first century as a new way for anyone anywhere on the planet to post their own thoughts on any subject. Many blogs are produced by journalists, but many more are produced by laypersons with an interest in sharing their thoughts. Blogs, or online diaries, can take many forms, from text-based streams of consciousness to video reports on flood damage during or after natural disasters.

Similarly, Podcasts, or digital audio reports in MP3 (a compressed audio format typically used for music) downloadable off the Internet for playback on portable MP3 players (such as the Apple iPod, thus the name) or computers, have emerged as yet another way for news content to be reinvented. Many news organizations now routinely create audio content dubbed Podcasts for listeners to download and listen to while on the go. In some cases, newspapers, which otherwise might not venture into the world of audio-formatted news, are regularly creating Podcasts as a way to repackage their news for audiences that sometimes show little appetite for the printed word.

On another front, computers are becoming effective editors of news stories. Witness a project from the Natural Language Processing group at Columbia University's

Department of Computer Science, where scientists have a system to automatically track the day's news. "There are no human editors involved," the system's developers explain, "everything you see on the main page is generated automatically, drawing on the sources listed on the left side of the screen. Every night, the system crawls a series of web sites, downloads articles, groups them together into 'clusters' about the same topic, and summarizes each cluster. The end result is a web page that gives you a sense of what the major stories of the day are, so you don't have to visit the pages of dozens of publications" (http://newsblaster. cs.columbia.edu/). The researchers expect future enhancements to include "international perspectives, multilingual capability, and tracking events across days."

Some even more experimental forms of emerging technology also pose opportunities—or threats, depending on one's point of view—to reshape the news. Research using a technology known as mobile augmented reality, a cousin of virtual reality, is the basis for a new type of documentary experienced in three-dimensional form via a wearable computer with a see-through head-worn display, global positioning satellite system (GPS) and high-speed wireless Internet access (for an online example, see http://www1. cs.columbia.edu/graphics/projects/mars/mjwSd.html).

How Journalists Do Their Work

Although many of the most dramatic changes in journalism due to technology have been in the arena of news content, some of the most significant are in how reporters, writers and editors do their work. In the early days of modern journalism, reporters relied exclusively on their eyes and ears, a pen or pencil and paper to report the news. The advent of photographic, electronic and now digital technologies have all transformed the ways that journalists capture the news. Today's journalist is as likely to head out into the field equipped with a digital camera (possibly a cell-phone camera), audio recorder and mobile email device or laptop or hand-held computer as a pencil and notepad. Local television reporters who conducted interviews for a story would not only shoot video using a digital camera but also use a personal digital appliance, or PDA, to write a version of the story and file it wirelessly via email to the editor back at the station. This practice was common by the early twenty-first century. Reporters around the world relied increasingly on advanced technologies, including satellite phones and other high-tech devices, to capture, edit and deliver the news. Some posted their reports directly to the web via their blogs. Editing frequently took a back seat to speed, sometimes with dire consequences for accuracy and completeness.

Not always was technology so advanced. In some cases, reporters sat all day long in a central newsroom, only leaving their desk to make a bathroom run. Otherwise, they stared at their computer screen, interviewed sources via phone, kept an eye on television monitors for breaking news, and abandoned the traditional notion of good-old-shoe-leather reporting. It used to be said that nothing beats getting out into the field and talking face-to-face with sources and seeing things for oneself. Unfortunately, in the twenty-first century's super-competitive, highly consolidated, ultra-technological news world, this was less and less the case.

News Organization Structure

Largely behind the scenes, news organization structure, culture, and management were gradually being transformed by emerging technology. Among the most important influences of technology has been impact of telecommunications, computers and the Internet on how newsrooms are managed and organized. On a basic level, telecommunications, particularly the phone, has made it possible for reporters in the field to stay in constant or frequent communication with their editors back in a central newsroom. This distributed newsroom makes it possible for news organizations to cover effectively breaking stories and geographically large communities, especially in times of crisis, such as terrorist attacks or natural disasters. The oft-heard reporters cry, "get me re-write" emerged because of the telephone. The emergence of mobile or cellular phones has only expanded the role of telecommunications in the modern newsroom.

Computers and the Internet have made further fundamental changes in newsroom structure and management possible. Prior to the introduction of computer networks, newsrooms were organized as required by limitations of analog, or pre-computer, technologies. Information often moved slowly from reporter to editor, from copy desk to pagination and layout, or from audio or video editing booth to control room. With the rise of digital computer networks, particularly the Internet and broadband or high-speed networks, it suddenly became possible to completely reconceptualize and reorganize the modern newsroom. Newsrooms could be organized for maximum efficiency. Converged newsrooms became a logical development. Newsrooms could feature content of various types and modalities, whether text, audio or video, all shared among editors producing news for a continuous news cycle.

Relationships between and among Journalists, News Organizations, and the Public

It is often said that the most important role of journalism in a democratic society is to provide the information or knowledge that the public needs to make informed decisions. If that statement is even partially true, then it is essential that journalists and news organizations maintain a healthy relationship with its key public, including audiences, sources and those who provide the funding necessary to operate an independent news media system.

Technology plays a critical role in maintaining these relationships. Prior to the development of the so-called Penny Press in the mid-nineteenth century, newspapers reached only society's elite. They were too expensive for most people to afford and most of them tended to be highly partisan or commercial in content. New printing technology made low-cost, large-scale printing possible, and consequently, a new model, that of a cheap, mass-appeal daily newspaper emerged. What became known as the Penny Press marked the beginning of mass media. This news model endured largely unchanged for more than a century, through the emergence of other forms of media including radio and television. The rise of the Internet signaled a fundamental change. Audiences after World War II had begun to decline for most daily newspapers. Television audiences grew, but with the proliferation of channels via first analog and later digital cable, even television news audiences fragmented. The news audiences of the twenty-first century access many media alternatives; rarely does any one medium, channel, or print vehicle capture a significant portion of the audience.

Moreover, audiences during the twentieth century had become largely passive in their relationship to the news media and media in general. Media content, including the news, was made by centralized organizations that produced that widely appealing content in order to deliver audiences to paying sponsors. The rise of the Internet, World Wide Web, weblogs, or blogs, Podcasting and other new media, have turned the traditional centralized media model increasingly on its head. No longer are audiences limited to largely a passive role. Instead, they are increasingly active as people create their own web pages, blogs (online diaries), Podcasts and other digital media content for distribution online, sometimes to very small audiences and sometimes to millions.

At the same time, the role of the traditional news media as gatekeeper or filter of news is changing, even reducing, as alternative, less filtered voices emerge. Further, audiences are able to access customized news that fits their interests, eroding the role of the traditional news media in creating a common experience or public sphere.

Ethical Implications

All these changes present enormous challenges to the news media, journalists and the public from an ethical standpoint. There are more questions than answers. In a digital age, how free should the press be? Should the same freedoms that apply to "professional" journalists apply to bloggers? How should digitally altered photos or video be labeled? How can plagiarism be prevented or detected? Computerized systems for detecting plagiarism are being developed but it is unclear whether they will be adequate to prevent public trust in the media and media credibility or believability from further eroding.

Conclusions

Technology has exerted and continues to exert profound influences on the news media. Some of these effects are readily apparent, as blogs and Podcasts reach millions every day. Others are more subtle and behind the scenes, as news organizations create converged newsrooms to produce multimedia news coverage in a digital, networked age of globally competitive news media. Emerging technological trends suggest the changes are far from over. Stay tuned.

Further Reading

http://www.drudgereport.com (accessed April 11, 2007).

http://www1.cs.columbia.edu/graphics/projects/mars/mjwSd.html.

http://newsblaster.cs.columbia.edu.

Jenkins, Henry, and David Thorburn, eds. *Democracy and New Media*. Cambridge, MA: MIT Press, 2003.

New Media Bibliography. Poyntcronline (http://poynteronline.org).

Pavlik, John V., and Everette E. Dennis, eds. *Demystifying Media Technology: Readings from the Freedom Forum Center*. Mountain View, CA: Mayfield, 1993.

Vaughn, Stephen. comp. *New Communication Technologies: Their History and Social Influence*. Madison: University of Wisconsin Libraries, 2006 (http://newcomm.library.wisc.edu).

JOHN V. PAVLIK

TELECOMMUNICATIONS ACT OF 1996

The Telecommunications Act of 1996, (Pub. L. No. 104-104, 47 U.S.C. 151 et, seq. [1996]) became the first successful attempt by Congress to overhaul the Communications Act of 1934. The legislation rolled back decades of Federal Communications Commission (FCC) policy that structurally separated various segments of the telecommunications industry, by calling for a "pro-competitive, deregulatory national policy framework designed to accelerate rapidly private sector development of advanced telecommunications and information technologies and services to all Americans by opening all telecommunications markets to competition."

The 1996 Act represented a complex reform of American communication policy making by attempting to provide a level playing field in virtually all sectors of the communications industries. The Telecommunications Act's provisions fall into five general areas: radio and television broadcasting regulation, cable regulation, telephone services, Internet and online computer services, and telecommunications equipment manufacturing. The act abolished many of the cross-market barriers that prohibited dominant players from one sector of the communications industry from entering other sectors.

Radio and Television Broadcasting

The act significantly amended broadcast ownership rules removing limits on the number of television stations a media group could own, and raised the cap on the national penetration of group TV stations to 35 percent of the U.S. population. Limits on the number of radio stations that could be owned by one entity were abolished. Terms of license for both radio and television stations were extended to eight years and previous rules allowing competing applications for license renewals were dramatically altered in favor of incumbent licensees. During this act's first decade, public interest groups claimed that the new rules accelerated the trend toward increased control of most media outlets by a few media conglomerates.

Since its passage large broadcast networks have been able to acquire cable television systems, but television licenses are still prohibited from owning newspapers in the same market. The act affirmed the continuation of local marketing agreements (LMAs) and waived some restrictions on common control of radio and television stations in the top fifty markets, the one-to-a-market rule. In 2003, the FCC proposed sweeping changes in ownership rules under the biennial revision requirement of the act, but changes in the rules were then stayed as a result of a Court of Appeals ruling in *Prometheus Radio Project v. FCC* (case no. 03-3388).

While broadcasters won new freedoms in licensing and ownership in 1996, the act mandated that the industry develop a ratings system to identify violent, sexual and indecent or otherwise objectionable programming. Although development of a ratings system is required under the act, application of the system is voluntary. In conjunction with the establishment of a ratings system, the Telecommunications Act required television set manufacturers to install a blocking device, called the V-chip, in television receivers by 1998. Today most broadcast and cable networks provide program ratings for television show at the beginning of the program, although studies indicate few people use the V-chip option built into televisions.

The biggest concession to the broadcast industry centered around a provision that allowed the FCC to allocate extra spectrum for the creation of advanced television services, including high definition television (HDTV). Today many television stations in the United States are broadcasting in both digital and analog formats. Currently Congress has set an April 2009 deadline for the give back of analog channels, but that legislation had not been passed by both houses as of 2005. Broadcasters vehemently opposed the notion of paying for spectrum, but the act included provisions that would allow the commission to impose spectrum fees for any ancillary (non-broadcast) services that broadcasters may provide with these new allocations.

Cable Television

Dramatic changes in rate structures and oversight contained within the Telecommunications Act were meant to provide new opportunities and flexibility as well as new competition for cable service providers. Under the provisions of the act, uniform rate structure requirements were eliminated for cable operators where there was no effective competition from other service providers including the telephone company, multichannel video, direct broadcast satellites, and wireless cable systems. For smaller cable companies, programming tier rates and basic tier rates were deregulated in franchise areas where there are fewer than fifty thousand subscribers. Additionally, states and local franchise authorities were barred from setting technical standards, or placing specific requirements on customer premise equipment and transmission equipment.

Common carriers and other operators that utilize radio communications to provide video programming were dereg-

ulated under cable rules if the services were provided under a common carriage scheme. Joint ventures and partnerships between local exchange carriers and cable operators were barred unless the services qualified under provisions for rural exemptions. To date few common carriers have developed video services under these rules, but widespread deployment of optical fiber may allow for these services in the future.

In an attempt to spur competition between cable operators and local exchange carriers, Congress provided incentives for cable operators to compete with local telecommunications companies. Under the act, cable systems operators were not required to obtain additional franchise approval for offering telecommunications services. As a result, telephone services known as Voice Over Internet Protocol (VoIP) have grown rapidly among broadband users in the United States.

Telephone Services

The Telecommunications Act of 1996 contains sweeping provisions that led to wide-scale restructuring of the telephone industry in the United States. The act allowed the regional Bell operating companies to offer long-distance telephone service for the first time since the 1984 breakup of AT&T. At the same time, long distance companies and cable operators were allowed to provide local exchange service in direct competition with the regional Bell operating companies. Since the passage of the act, consolidation in the telephone section of the communication industry has led to the creation of several large conglomerates and the general decline of large long-distance companies.

Internet and Online Computer Services

The Telecommunications Act of 1996 generated substantial praise as a pro-competitive bill designed to allow anyone to enter any communications business and to let any communications business to compete in any market against other competitors. Supporters of the bill predicted job creation and lower telecommunications costs as two benefits likely to accrue as a result of its passage. Experts now disagree over whether the telecommunications sector has benefited economically since the passage of the act, but manufacturers of cable modems and network connectivity devices have benefited from rapid advances in the broadband sector as millions of Americans have switched from dial-up to cable and Digital Subscriber Line (DSL) services.

When passed, the act included several highly controversial provisions that various interests groups claim restricted speech or violated constitutional protections. Title five of the Communications Decency Act (CDA), called for the prohibition of transmission of indecent and obscene material via the Internet when the material was likely to be seen or read by a minor, and another provision required broadcasters to formulate a ratings scheme for programs. Within hours of the bill's passage, a number of civil liberties groups led by the ACLU sought an injunction against provisions of the act. Ultimately the Supreme Court ruled the CDA unconstitutional in *Reno v. ACLU* (521 US 844 (1997)).

Summary

Ten years after the passage of the Telecommunications Act of 1996, reaction to the legislation has been mixed. While some segments of the industry saw increases in competition, other sections of the act did not create the desired level of competition. Cable and direct broadcast television could be seen as competitors, and broadband services expanded but the transition to digital television was very slow. Critics of the act pointed to the reduced diversity in the broadcast marketplace as consolidation occurred. Others saw the expansion of the Internet and broadband services as an indicator of increased diversity of voices in public debate. Overall, the Telecommunications Act of 1996 during this period did not live up to expectations that it would spur competition in all sectors, provide protections for children against unfriendly programs and services, and bring advanced telecommunications services to all geographical areas of the United States.

Further Reading

Andrews, E.L. "Congress Votes to Reshape Communications Industry Ending a 4-Year Struggle." *The New York Times,* February 2, 1996,. A1, D6.

——. "What the Bill Already Did." *The New York Times,* February 2, 1996, A1, D6.

——. "President Signs Telecommunications Bill." *Cyber Times Extra, The New York Times,* February 9, 1996.

Bento Foundation, "Public Interest Issues in the Telecommunications Act of 1996," http://www.Benton/Goinon/telecompost.html (version February, 1996).

Carte, B. "The Networks See Potential For Growth." *New York Times,* February 2, 1996,. D6.

Clinton, W. "Statement By The President," Office of the Press Secretary, The White House (press release), February 1, 1996.

Clinton, W. "Remarks By The President In Signing Ceremony for the Telecommunications Act Conference Report." Library of Congress (press release), February 8, 1996.

Congressional Record: February 1, 1996 (House), http://wais.access.gpo.gov, H1145-H1179.

Corazzini, R.F., and Barr, H.J. Telecommunications Act of 1996 Impact on Cable. Internet http://www. com/pepper.Memos/Cable/telcabl.html (current version March 20, 1996).

Federal Communications Commission. (FCC 96-99, Implementation of Section 302 of CS Docket No. 96-46 the Telecommunications Act of 1996, Open Video Systems), http://www.fcc.gov/Bureaus/Cable/Notices/fcc96099.txt (version current March 20, 1996).

Gutmann, P. "Telecommunications Act of 1996 Impact on Broadcast." http://www. commlaw.com/pepper.Memos/Broadcast/telbcst.html (version current March 22, 1996).

Hinde, S. "The Greatest Telecommunications Show in Years: The 1996 Legislation Leaves Fund Managers Wondering: Which Company's Act is a Winner?" *The Washington Post,* wire services, March 24, 1996, HO3.

Hundt, R. "It's the End of the World as We Know It." http://www.fcc.gov/chairman.html (current version March 20, 1996).

Jones, K. "Net Access Providers Worried As FCC Rethinks On-Line Regulation." *Cyber Times Extra, New York Times,* February 29, 1996

Landler, M. "For Telephone Companies, Excitement Over New Markets." *New York Times,* February 2, 1996, D6.

Lewis, P. H. "Internet Courtroom Battle Gets Cyberspace." *Cyber Times Extra, New York Times,* March 20, 1996.

"The United States Telecommunications Act of 1996." http://www.ntia.doc.gov/opadhome/overview.htm, (accessed April 11, 2007).

Raysman, R., and Brown, P. (1996, March 12). "Liability of Internet Access Provider Under Decency Act." *New York Law Journal,* wire services, March 12, 1996, 3.

United States Congress, House of Representatives, 104 - H.R. 1555 , The Telecommunications Act of 1995, One Hundred Fourth Congress 1st. session, introduced 5/3/95.

United States Congress, Senate. *S.652 - The Telecommunications Act of 1996,* One Hundred Fourth Congress 2nd. Session, January 3, 1996.

United States Congress, *Joint Explanatory Statement of the Committee of Conference on S.652 - The Telecommunications Act of 1996,* One Hundred Fourth Congress 2nd. Session, January 3, 1996.

Walsh, M. (1996, February 27). "New Front Opens In Fight Against Indecency Law." *American Lawyer Media L.P. The Recorder,* wire services, February 27, 1996, 1.

FRITZ MESSERE

TELEGRAPH

With the advent of the telegraph, the contours of modern communication became visible. The telegraph—the first commercially practical application of electricity—separated communication from transportation and transformed nearly all aspects of American journalism.

From Invention to the Civil War (1840s–1860s)

Samuel F. B. Morse publicly inaugurated his invention by transmitting a Biblical passage — "What hath God wrought!"—from Washington to Baltimore on May 24, 1844. Over the next few days, Morse quietly inaugurated a new era in American journalism by repeatedly exchanging another message— "What's the news?"—with his assistant forty miles away. As telegraphy matured as an industry during the next twenty years, it fostered new routines and institutions, as well as a new ethos, in the gathering and distribution of news.

Before the telegraph, newspapers obtained out-of-town news through the mails. From 1792 to 1873, postal law allowed editors to exchange newspapers with one another postage free. Editors scanned exchanges from around the country for stories of interest to their local readers and simply reprinted them. For vital commercial and political news, editors looked to special expresses—relays of horseback riders—sporadically arranged by the Post Office in the 1820s and 1830s and sometimes organized by the newspapers themselves in the 1830s and 1840s. Correspondents also submitted stories by mail. In short, pre-telegraphic news moved at the speed of one or more transports—horses, stagecoaches, railroads, and boats.

The telegraph promised much faster news delivery, if the wires worked and editors were willing to bear the cost. Early telegraph lines, able to handle only one message at a time, were notoriously unreliable and expensive, especially compared to the nearly free news gathering by mail. In 1849, most customers paid about fifty cents to telegraph ten words from New York to Washington, though newspapers typically lowered their costs by using the wires during off-peak evening hours and by negotiating volume discounts. The costly and complex task of arranging telegraphic news gathering prompted newspapers to cooperate in the effort, organizing early versions of the Associated Press in upstate New York and New York City between 1846 and 1848.

After a slow start, the nation's telegraph network grew rapidly. The principal cities of the Ohio and Mississippi River valleys were tied into the national grid before 1850 and the transcontinental telegraph reached San Francisco in 1861. Newspaper readers who had once found the most up-to-date intelligence under columns headed "Latest Mail" or "By Express" now looked for it under "By Telegraph." Telegraphy also revolutionized foreign reporting. The 1866 completion of the Atlantic cable, an undersea telegraph, enabled American newspapers to publish European news less than a day old.

Western Union, a regional firm in the 1850s, emerged from the Civil War poised to absorb competitors. It became the first American company to dominate an economic sector—telecommunication—from coast to coast. As the technical and cost constraints of early telegraphy eased in the last quarter of the nineteenth century, the press dramatically increased its routine use of the wires to the point where the heading "By Telegraph" faded as a meaningless distinction.

The Telegraph and the Modern Newspaper (1860s–1920s)

At the end of the Civil War, news was delivered over eighty-four thousand miles of telegraph lines in the United States. Telegraph companies continued to add new lines and discovered in the 1870s how to multiplex—operate multiple circuits—on a single wire. Newspapers could now afford to have their own reporters supplement the dry, nationally standardized wire service stories with accounts that included interpretation or opinion tailored for their readers. In 1880, Western Union transmitted 611-million words of wire service copy and special dispatches; one paper that year paid more than $70,000 for its telegraph news.

The telegraph altered the dynamics of publishing daily newspapers in several ways. Urban newspapers issued multiple daily editions to accommodate the constant flow of dispatches. In their competition to attract subscribers, editors boasted about the volume of telegraph news they carried and about their spending to obtain special dispatches and expensive overseas cable reports. Newspapers also showcased their telegraph news by posting it on bulletin boards outside their buildings and, by the early 1900s, displaying it on electric screens. Telegraph news became one of the chief expenses in publishing a daily newspaper and one reason for consolidation in the industry.

Telegraph news became such a pervasive presence that it transformed journalism beyond the big cities. Many small-town papers increased their frequency to daily publication once they received a steady diet of telegraphic news. The distribution of news by telegraph also gave rural newspapers an edge in competing with city publications; they obtained news by wire and published it for local readers before city papers with similar reports could circulate in the countryside. Small newspapers without direct wire service managed to feature a few columns of telegraph news, albeit dated, in materials provided by newspaper syndicates.

The constraints of sending stories by wire contributed to the emergence of the modern news report—short accounts with brief factual sentences stripped of unnecessary verbiage and free of the reporter's opinions. To minimize costs and transmission time (operators could send about thirty words a minute in Morse code), reporters condensed their accounts by pruning articles, prepositions, and modifiers, plus they summarized sources' remarks rather than simply transcribing them. Many also devised codes for commonly used phrases and sentences. Cost-conscious editors admonished reporters that the telegraph was for facts while interpretation and analysis could be sent by the much slower but cheaper mails. Historians have long considered these telegraph-induced changes in news reports as steps toward the rise of journalistic objectivity and the inverted-pyramid story form (information arrayed in descending order of importance). Recent scholarship, however, suggests that the telegraph's effects were mainly indirect; instead, the business dynamics of the wire services, the press's growing reliance on institutional news sources, and cultural changes arguably played a larger role than technological constraints.

Reporters distinguished themselves through their ingenious use of the telegraph. In covering breaking news, reporters sometimes "held the wires" by paying the telegraph operator to send a long text, customarily the Bible, until the story was ready for transmission. This stratagem kept rival reporters from sending their accounts. Also, reporters who knew Morse code could eavesdrop as operators transmitted competitors' messages. Foreign correspondents who outsmarted censors in overseas telegraph offices by sneaking sensitive information into cable dispatches especially won plaudits from their editors and peers.

The telegraph partly divorced news reporting from news writing. Reporters who wired their skeletonized observations to the home offices relied on telegraph editors to flesh out the story. Skilled telegraph editors became remarkably adept at producing a well-rounded story from a bare-bones dispatch, but they always risked introducing serious errors in the process of reconstituting a story.

Separating telegraph reporting from writing also enabled newspapers to synthesize coverage of complex breaking stories from multiple wire reports and locations. When news of the 1906 San Francisco earthquake and the ensuing fires reached the *New York Sun,* for instance, the paper supplemented fragmentary reports from the city with news from telegraph offices surrounding the city, from individuals who contacted the *Sun,* and from government reports issued in Washington, D.C. Sitting in the *Sun's* office on the other side of the continent, a reporter familiar with San Francisco constructed stories from the bits and pieces of news that came over the wires.

Unlike earthquakes, however, most telegraph news was predictable, and gathering it became institutionalized in the decades after the Civil War. News-savvy government officials and institutions synchronized their practices and rhythms to accord with electrified journalism. Most such efforts involved subtle controls, such as giving telegraph reporters preferred access to news sources. More dramatically, as in times of national crisis such as the Civil War and the Spanish-American War, the authorities recognized that the telegraph provided a convenient choke point to censor news as it flowed to the public.

Arranging telegraphic coverage for the biggest events required elaborate planning. Four months before the 1888 Republican convention in Chicago, the party's press committee began working with Western Union and the press to install circuits that would allow special correspondents to send dispatches directly to newspapers in thirty cities. Convention planners even allowed the Associated Press to place a telegrapher directly in front of the speaker's stand. News of the nomination reached London, via the Atlantic cable, two minutes after the votes were tallied—and before delegates in the convention hall heard the official announcement. By one estimate, telegraph companies transmitted about 14.5 million words in connection with the convention.

The timeliness of telegraph news had pronounced consequences for readers and society by allowing people to respond to situations fast enough to affect their outcome. News of the great Chicago fire of 1871 and the Johnstown flood of 1889, just two of many disasters flashed to the nation over the wires, prompted outpourings of aid that eased the victims' plight. In the realm of politics, citizens far from Washington followed the daily or hourly news reports of congressional deliberations and pressured lawmakers by phone or telegram in time to influence legislation.

The rush of telegraph news, combined with its staccato nature—impulses of constantly revised intelligence—created emotionally charged public spectacles around the nation. In 1910, for example, former heavyweight champion Jim Jeffries came out of retirement as the "Great White Hope" in a bid to reclaim the title from an African American boxer, Jack Johnson. Telegraph companies upgraded the circuits from Reno, Nevada, to accommodate the voluminous dispatches filed by wire service reporters and dozens of special correspondents. For days before the July 4 fight, newspapers around the nation featured reports, many unabashedly racist, from the boxers' training camps. While twenty thousand boxing fans witnessed the match live, hundreds of thousands more gathered outside newspaper offices around the country to share the round-by-round telegraph bulletins posted by the papers. News of Johnson's decisive victory over the "Great White Hope" unleashed violence throughout the country in which mobs burned buildings, assaulted individuals, and killed many African Americans.

Eclipse of the Telegraph (1920s–1980s)

The telegraph continued to distribute news for the wire services well into the age of the telephone, radio, and television even as its role as a tool for individual reporters faded. For most stories, reporters found it simpler to telephone their newspapers rather than work through a telegraph operator. Reporters, however, still depended on the telegraph's transmission capacity to relay the huge volume of dispatches filed for political conventions and other major news events. As late as the 1960s, correspondents used submarine telegraph lines—and contended with foreign cable censors—to transmit stories from Vietnam to offices in the United States.

The value of the telegraph in distributing the wire services' output was enhanced by developing simpler equipment and new applications. The teletype, which substituted simple typewriter-like equipment for the sending and receiving apparatus that used Morse code, spread quickly through newsrooms after 1920. Radio and television stations also received much of their news by teletype, and some even incorporated its clattering sound into the background of their broadcasts to create a journalistic soundscape. In 1935 the Associated Press launched its Wirephoto service, which transmitted pictures to newspapers around the world over telegraph and telephone lines. This innovation capped more than fifty years of experimentation, much of it inspired by newspapers, in phototelegraphy. Another 1930s innovation, the teletypesetter, used the telegraph's electrical impulses to code tapes that operated automatic typesetters, saving considerable labor in preparing stock market tables and similar text.

In the 1980s, computers linked by sophisticated telecommunication networks finally replaced the telegraph as the basis for transmitting news. Even though telegraphy has passed from the journalistic scene, its imprint can be found in reporters' idiom (e.g., news "flashes" and "bulletins"), in television's rediscovery of news tickers (news briefs crawling across the bottom of the screen), and in the frenzied scramble to beat rivals in delivering news to the public.

Further Reading

Blondheim, Menahem. *News over the Wires: The Telegraph and the Flow of Public Information in America, 1844–1897.* Cambridge, MA: Harvard University Press, 1994.

Coe, Lewis. *The Telegraph: A History of Morse's Invention and Its Predecessors in the United States.* Jefferson, NC: McFarland, 1993.

Harnett, Richard M. *Wirespeak: Codes and Jargon of the News Business.* San Mateo, CA: Shorebird Press, 1997.

Kielbowicz, Richard, B. "The Telegraph, Censorship, and Politics at the Outset of the Civil War." *Civil War History* 40 (June 1994): 95–118.

Schwarzlose, Richard A. *The Nation's Newsbrokers,* 2 vols. Evanston, IL: Northwestern University Press, 1989 and 1990.

Thompson, Robert L. *Wiring a Continent: The History of the Telegraph Industry in the United States, 1832–1866.* Princeton, NJ: Princeton University Press, 1947.

RICHARD B. KIELBOWICZ

TEMPERANCE PRESS

The American temperance movement began in the early 1800s in a spirit of optimism, with the belief that heavy drinkers could be persuaded to voluntarily reduce their consumption of alcohol or abstain entirely. Temperance advocates initially relied on moral suasion and the rhetorical powers of the pulpit and the press to reform the individual, but as this seemed to have little affect on society as a whole, by the turn of the century they had begun to advocate the prohibition of alcohol and focus their efforts on federal, state, and local laws that would entirely ban its manufacture, transportation, sale, and consumption. Many temperance advocates felt strongly about this reform because they had seen wives beaten and families broken and left destitute as a result of problem drinking. Many advocates believe that excessive drinking cost society dearly in terms of crime and violence.

Hundreds of local, regional, and national temperance and prohibition societies were created between the 1810s and 1919, when the Eighteenth Amendment to the U.S. Constitution (the Prohibition Amendment) was ratified. The earliest of these included the Massachusetts Society for the Suppression of Intemperance (founded in 1813), the American Society for the Promotion of Temperance (established in 1826, it changed its name to the American Temperance Society in 1831 and reorganized as the American Temperance Union in 1836), the New York State Temperance Society (1829), the Order of the Sons of Temperance and its auxiliary, the Daughters of Temperance (1842), the Independent Order of Good Templars (1851), and the Woman's New York State Temperance Society (1852).

In the decades following the Civil War, three national organizations were established that survived into the twenty-first century. The Prohibition Party (1869), which never commanded more than 2.2 percent of the national vote, nevertheless kept the prohibition debate alive during political campaigns and elections, and eventually came to endorse other reforms such as woman suffrage and equal pay for equal work. The Woman's Christian Temperance Union (WCTU), founded in 1874, was the first national woman's organization devoted solely to temperance. It eventually expanded its platform to include a broad range of social reforms, including woman suffrage and labor laws and grew to become the largest women's organization in the United States, with more than 245,000 members by 1911. The Anti-Saloon League (ASL), until the 1940s a largely male organization, was founded in 1895. It united a broad-based coalition of church groups and temperance organizations, hired a professional staff, and became a national clearinghouse for prohibition activity, lobbying, legislation, and propaganda. It changed its name several times in the twentieth century—to the Temperance League (1948–1950), the National Temperance League (1950–1964), and the American Council on Alcohol Problems (1964–present). Along with the Prohibition Party and the WCTU, it was still active in 2006, by which time all three organizations had expanded their focus to include anti-drug campaigns.

Leaders of these organizations heartily believed in the power of the press, but because they frequently found general circulation newspapers either indifferent or opposed to temperance, they almost always established their own publications (1826–). (Many mainstream publications benefited from advertising from liquor interests.) While many of these temperance papers lasted only a few years and rarely had a circulation of more than a few thousand, others survived for decades and claimed national readerships of more than a million. These publications provided a vital communication network that allowed temperance advocates to create a sense of community, despite the great distances that sometimes separated them.

Temperance advocates published tracts and pamphlets as early as the 1780s, but did not establish regular temperance periodicals until the 1820s. In the century that followed, the numbers of these publications increased, so that by 1888, more than 180 were being published by temperance organizations, religious groups, and individual reformers. Prominent temperance periodicals published by national organizations included *The Journal of Humanity and Herald of the American Temperance Society* (1829–1833), the *Official Organ of the Independent Order of Good Templars* (published in New York state), the *Union Signal* (the voice of the WCTU from 1883 until the present), and the *American Issue* (founded in 1896 by the ASL).

Regional and local chapters of national temperance organizations also published their own organs. In 1888, for example, the Templars were publishing at least six regional or local periodicals, including the *Eastern Good Templar* (Boston), the *Western Good Templar* (Mauston, Wis.), the *Central Good Templar* (Findlay, OH), the *Good Templar at Work* (Selman, FL), the *West Virginia Good Templar* (Gerrardstown, WV), and the Swedish-language *Templarn* (Brooklyn, NY). In the same year, local branches of the WCTU were publishing local organs, including *Woman's Temperance Work* (New York City), the *Anchor* (Greensboro, NC), the *Temperance Banner* (Greensburg, PA), the *Woman's Journal* (Dallas, Texas), and the *Rock County Banner* (Clinton, WI). By 1910, the ASL, was publishing regional as well as thirty state editions of the *American Issue*, which by 1917 claimed a weekly circulation of 250,000.

Temperance papers were also published by local organizations and individual reformers. The *New York Olive Plant* (established 1842) was the first temperance newspaper edited by women. Amelia Bloomer, one of the organizers of the Woman's New York State Temperance Society, established *The Lily* (1849–1856), another woman's temperance newspaper. Siblings Emma and Thurlow Weed Brown established the *Cayuga Chief* in upstate New York in 1849 and renamed it the *Wisconsin Chief* when they moved it to that state in 1856. Brown became an organizer for the Order of Good Templars and eventually received funding from that organization to run the paper, though it remained independent. His sister ran the paper in his absence and took over its publication from his death in 1866 until her own in 1889.

While devoted primarily to temperance and then prohibition, these publications frequently promoted other reforms. Bloomer's *Lily*, for example, was one of the first American publications to promote woman's rights and is best known today for its campaign for women's dress reform, most notably the adoption of pantaloons, or "bloomers" as they came to be known. The WCTU's Union Signal eventually supported a number of causes, including woman suffrage, labor reform, pacifism, and child welfare. The ASL's *American Issue* was initially a "single-issue" publication, but after 1910, expanded its interests to include anything that might affect its push for prohibition. Thus it supported woman suffrage (in the belief that when women could vote, they would vote for prohibition). With the outbreak of war in Europe in 1914, the *American Issue* attacked German and Irish immigrants (who typically opposed prohibition), corrupt politicians (who it claimed were bribed by the liquor industry to block prohibition legislation), and the brewers (many of whom were of German origin).

Temperance publications reached their heyday in the decade preceding the passage of the Prohibition Amendment. After 1920, most discontinued publication or shifted their focus to other reforms. Two noteworthy exceptions were the *American Issue*, which continued publication until 1942, and the *Union Signal*, which was still being published as a quarterly journal of "Social Welfare and Change" in 2007.

Further Reading

Blocker, Jr., Jack S. *"Give to the Winds Thy Fears:" The Women's Temperance Crusade, 1873–1874*. Westport, CT: Greenwood Press, 1985.

Blocker, Jr., Jack S. *American Temperance Movements: Cycles of Reform*. Boston: Twayne Publishers, 1989.

Bordin, Ruth. *Women and Temperance: The Quest for Power and Liberty, 1873–1900*. Philadelphia: Temple University Press, 1981.

Gusfield, Joseph. *Symbolic Crusade: Status Politics and the American Temperance Movement*. Urbana: University of Illinois Press, 1966.

Odegard, Peter H. *Pressure Politics: The Story of the Anti-Saloon League*. New York: Columbia University Press, 1928.

Pegram, Thomas R. *Battling Demon Rum: The Struggle for a Dry America, 1800–1933*. Chicago: Ivan R. Dee Publisher, 1998.

ELIZABETH V. BURT

TERRORISM

From its early days, terror has entailed an aspect of mass psychology. Specifically, the word "terror" comes from the Latin word "terrere" which means "to frighten" or "to scare." The first use of large-scale terrorism was during the "popular" phase of the French Revolution. For example, in September 1793 the "Reign of Terror" was officially declared and activated, causing the execution of seventeen thousand people. Executions were conducted before large audiences and were accompanied by sensational publicity thus spreading the intended fear. Contemporary terrorists have become exposed to new opportunities for exerting mass psychological impacts as a result of technological advances in communications and transportation. Paralleling the growth in technology-driven opportunities for terrorist action were efforts by terrorists themselves to hone their communications skills.

The emergence of media-oriented terrorism led several communication and terrorism scholars to re-conceptualize modern terrorism within the framework of symbolic communication theory. During the 1970s, academic observers remarked increasingly on the theatrical proficiency with which terrorists conducted their operations. As Brian Jenkins concluded in his analysis of international terrorism: "Terrorist attacks are often carefully choreographed to attract the attention of the electronic media and the international press. Taking and holding hostages increases the drama. The hostages themselves often mean nothing to the terrorists. Terrorism is aimed at the people watching, not at the actual victims. Terrorism is a theater."

Modern terrorism can be understood in terms of the production requirements of theatrical engagements. Terrorists pay attention to script preparation, cast selection, sets, props, role playing, and minute-by-minute stage management. Just like compelling stage plays or ballet performances, the media orientation in terrorism requires full attention to detail in order to be effective. The growing importance attributed to publicity and mass media by terrorist organizations was revealed both in the diffusion of media-oriented terrorism as well as in the tactics of modern terrorists who have become more media-minded. One of the most influential theorists of modern terrorism was the Brazilian Carlos Marighella, whose *Mini-manual of the Urban Guerrilla* (1971) became a sourcebook for many terrorist movements all over the world. In his publications, Marighella outlined the various uses that can be made of the media: "To kidnap figures known for their artistic, sporting, or other activities who have not expressed any political views may possibly provide a form of propaganda favorable to the revolutionaries.... Modern mass media, simply by announcing what the revolutionaries are doing, are important instruments of the propaganda. The war of nerves, or the psychological war, is a fighting technique based on the direct or indirect use of the mass media...."

The terrorist campaign usually has four target audiences for its messages: the supporters; the population that it purports to serve; the enemy, or those attacked by the terrorist; and international public opinion. The messages vary from one target audience to another. To the terrorist organization's supporters, purported community, and potential recruits, the message is of pride, success, commitment, and vision. To the "enemy" population, the terrorists' message is of threat and fear, with the intention that this fear translates into moral breakdown, collapse of confidence in the government, and pressure on decision makers to accept the terrorists' demands. The success of this strategy depends on the degree to which fear or panic can be overblown out of all proportion to the actual threat. Finally, to the rest of the world, the terrorists' message is usually based on the determination to achieve noble political goals such as freedom, equal rights, self-expression, a free state, liberation of prisoners, and so on. The use of violence is justified as the only way to get world attention. One of the terrorists who orchestrated the attack on the Israeli athletes during the 1972 Munich Olympic Games testified:

> We recognized that sport is the modern religion of the Western world. We knew that the people in England and America would switch their television sets from any program about the plight of the Palestinians if there was a sporting event on another channel. So we decided to use their Olympics, the most sacred ceremony of this religion, to make the world pay attention to us. We offered up human sacrifices to your gods of sport and television. And they answered our prayers. From Munich onwards, nobody could ignore the Palestinians or their cause.

The "theater of terror" is a useful metaphor to examine modern terrorism as an attempt to communicate messages through the use of orchestrated violence. This metaphor materialized in dramatic form in October 2002, when forty-one Chechen terrorists took more than eight hundred people hostage in a Moscow theater, demanding an end to Russia's war against the Chechen homeland. Playing at the Moscow Theater that evening was a Russian musical about the Red Army during World War II. Thus, when heavily armed masked gunmen appeared onstage, the audience thought that it was a part of the production. A member of the audience in the Moscow Theater recalled thinking to herself, "Great acting!" However, it was acting in a very different sense, and that Moscow Theater was about to become the world's stage for yet another monstrous terrorist drama. When the terrorists exposed their explosive belts and declared that if the Russian army did not leave Chechnya they would blow up the entire theater, the hostages realized that they had just become actors in a horrifying and very realistic drama. Videotapes of the event as well as dramatic first-person interviews with the hijackers, the hostages, and the survivors, gives a vivid illustration of the "theater of terror" being actualized.

The most powerful and violent performance of modern terrorism to date, however, was the September 11, 2001, attack on U.S. targets. "The greatest irony," argued Brigitte Nacos in 2003, "was that the very terrorists who loathed America's pop culture as decadent and poisonous to their own beliefs and ways of life turned Hollywood-like horror fantasies into real life hell." In November 2001, shortly after the assault, Osama bin Laden discussed the attacks, describing the suicide terrorists as "vanguards of Islam" and arguing that "those young men said in deeds, in New York and Washington, speeches that overshadowed other speeches made everywhere else in the world. The speeches are understood by both Arabs and non-Arabs, even Chinese." From the "theater of terror" perspective, the September 11 attack on the United States introduced a new level of mass-mediated terrorism, a perfectly choreographed production aimed at international, Muslim, and U.S. audiences.

The targets chosen for September 11, for example, were symbols of American wealth, power, and national heritage. In the attacks on New York and Washington, "the architects of terror were successful in realizing some of their objectives," according to Nacos. "With their deadly assault Bin Laden and his followers managed to set America's public agenda for many months, perhaps even years." Several studies revealed that literally all Americans followed the news of the terrorist attacks by television, radio, and the Internet. All over the world there was a wave of shock and fear and a general tuning in to the mass media. The terrorists were spectacularly successful in the agenda-setting goal for which all terrorists strive. During the 1972 Olympic Games at Munich, the Black September terrorists' attack was watched live by an estimated audience of eight hundred million viewers all over the world. The advances in communication technology in the ensuing three decades, and the staggering visual images of the events on September 11 combined to make the al Qaeda attacks on America the most watched terrorist spectacle ever.

Moreover, by striking hard at America, the terrorists led the world media to present and discuss their claims and grievances in ways that far transcended the amount and prominence of the coverage before the attacks. Media coverage of Islam-related issues changed in a rather dramatic fashion after al Qaeda's attacks on September 11. Much of the coverage focused on attempts to answer President Bush's question: "Why do they hate us?" Such coverage served the terrorists by publicizing their causes, grievances, and demands. But bin Laden's most important target audience was not the American public but rather the populations of Muslim countries. In the eyes of many Muslims, Osama bin Laden was a greatt hero: the Arab media and especially several Arab news networks presented him as a world leader, a rising icon, and America's public enemy number one, thus promoting his status, popularity, and legitimacy among millions of Muslims. In the international media, from CNN to *Time* magazine and from al Jazeera to al Arabiya, bin Laden appeared frequently and prominently, sometimes even more frequently and prominently than the world's most important leaders. The "status conferral" function of the mass media elevated him to the level of a leading global figure.

The emergence of media-oriented terrorism and its growing sophistication in manipulating the media have led governments and media organizations to react by limiting terrorists' access to the conventional mass media, reducing and censoring news coverage of terrorist acts and their perpetrators and minimizing the terrorists' capacity for manipulating the media. However, the new media technologies, and especially computer-mediated communication and the Internet, allow terrorist organizations to send messages more freely and easily than through other means of communication. Al Qaeda, for example, used multimedia propaganda and advanced communication technologies in a most sophisticated way. One assessment of al Qaeda in 2003, noted this "long-established sophistication of bin Laden and al Qaeda's propaganda efforts—employing multimedia vehicles, including prerecorded video and audiotapes, CD-ROMs, DVDs, and the Internet; dramatically choreographed and staged dissemination opportunities; and other mass outreach techniques (e.g., via al Qaeda's phantom Alneda website and those of sympathetic, aboveground radical Islamic sites and organizations)."

The same advantages the Internet and advanced communication technology bring to the general public and to business (i.e., speed, easy access, and global linkage) help international terrorist groups organize their deadly and disruptive activities. Paradoxically, the very decentralized structure that the American security services created out of fear of a Soviet nuclear attack now serves the interests of the greatest foe to the West's security services since the end of the Cold War, namely international terror. The nature of the network, its international character and chaotic structure, the simple access, and the anonymity all furnish terrorist organizations with an ideal arena for action. The story of cyberspace presence of terrorist groups has barely begun to be told. In 1998, nearly half of the thirty organizations designated as Foreign Terrorist Organizations under the US maintained websites; by the end of 1999, nearly all terrorist groups had established their presence on the net. Whereas in the late 1990s there were perhaps a dozen web sites operated by terrorist organizations, by 2001, the number had burgeoned to more than 1,600 web sites associated with terrorist groups, and by 2005, 4,640 sites. The face of modern terrorism is decidedly different than the face of terror in the past: Postmodern terrorism is less centralized, less structured, less organized, and far more dangerous than the terrorism of the late twentieth century. The postmodern terrorist emerged—savvy with the latest technology, easily familiar with laptop and desktop computers, CD burners, e-mail accounts and the World Wide Web. The Internet expanded the terrorists' theater of operation, allowing full control over their own communications through the use of the developed world's own infrastructure in cyberspace.

Terrorism functions by delivering threats and promises, intended to create fear and helplessness among some target audiences and hope and sympathy among others. Whether it is the public arenas of France's Reign of Terror or the global coverage of the September 11, 2001, attacks, terrorists have been dependent on whatever means were available to let their actions and messages be known. With the advent cable and satellite television and then the Internet, the means of communication became internalized and controlled by the terrorists themselves. Media-oriented terrorism presented a tough challenge to democratic societies and their values. The threat was not limited to media manipulation and psychological warfare launched by terrorists; it also included the danger of restrictions imposed on the

freedom of the press and freedom of expression by those who try to fight terrorism. These developments could wind up having profound implications for democracies and their values, adding heavy prices in terms of civil liberties to the destructive effects of terrorism.

Further Reading

Bell, J. Bowyer. "Terrorist Script and Live-Action Spectaculars." *Columbia Journalism Review* 17 (1978): 47–50.

Brosius, Hans-Bernd, & Gabriel Weimann. "The Contagiousness of Mass-Mediated Terrorism." *European Journal of Communication* 6 (1991): 63–75.

Dobson, Christopher, and Ronald Paine. *The Carlos Complex: A Pattern of Violence.* London: Hodder and Stoughton, 1977.

Dowling, Ralph. "Terrorism and the Media: A Rhetorical Genre." *Journal of Communication* 56 (1986): 12–24.

Hoffman, Bruce. "Al Qaeda, Trends in Terrorism, and Future Potentialities: An Assessment." *Studies in Conflict and Terrorism* 26 (2003): 427–440.

Jenkins, Brian. *International Terrorism.* Los Angeles: Crescent Publication, 1975.

Karber, Philip. "Urban Terrorism: Baseline Data and a Conceptual Framework." *Social Science Quarterly* 52 (1971): 527–533.

Marighella, Carlos. "Mini-manual of the Urban Guerrilla." http://www.latinamericanstudies.org/marighella.htm (accessed April 11, 2007).

Nacos, Brigitte. "The Terrorist Calculus behind 9-11: A Model for Future Terrorism?" *Studies in Conflict and Terrorism* 26 (2003): 1–16.

Schmid, Alex., and de Graaf, J. *Violence as Communication.* Beverly Hills: Sage, 1982.

Tsfati, Yariv, and Gabriel Weimann. "www.terrorism.com: Terror on the Internet." *Studies in Conflict and Terrorism* 25 (2002): 317–332.

Weimann, Gabriel. "The Theater of Terror: Effects of Press Coverage." *Journal of Communication,* 33 (1983): 38–45.

——. "Media Events: The Case of International Terrorism." *Journal of Broadcasting and Electronic Media* 31 (1987): 21–39.

——. *WWW.Terror.Net: How Modern Terrorism Uses the Internet.* Special report, Washington, D.C.: United States Institute of Peace, 2004.

——. *Terror in the Internet: The New Arena, The new Challenges.* Washington, D.C.: United States Institute of Peace, 2006.

Weimann, Gabriel, and Hans-Bernd Brosius. "The Newsworthiness of International Terrorism." *Communication Research* 18 (1989): 491–502.

——. "The Predictability of International Terrorism: A Time-Series Analysis." *Terrorism,* 11 (1991): 333–354.

Weimann, Gabriel, and Conrad Winn. *The Theater of Terror: Mass Media and International Terrorism.* New York: Longman, 1994.

GABRIEL WEIMANN

THE NEWS HOUR

Broadcast television's first and only hour-long nightly news program, *The News Hour with Jim Lerher* from the Public Broadcasting Service (PBS), consistently tops surveys as "the most credible, most objective, and most influential" news program on television. It epitomizes the public service approach to news broadcasting, treating important issues in depth with scrupulous fairness and balance. *The News*

Hour (formerly *MacNeil-Lehrer Report*) has been prepared to bore viewers from time to time if that was the price of serious journalism. Nonetheless, in 2006, it attracted about three million viewers each evening, a "failure" by commercial television standards, but far above the daily circulation of serious newspapers such as the *New York Times* or the *Wall Street Journal*.

The program that became *The News Hour* grew out of the ashes of public television's first venture into journalism, the National Public Affairs Center for Television (NPACT), funded primarily by the Corporation for Public Broadcasting (CPB) and the Ford Foundation and fronted by former NBC journalists Robert MacNeil and Sander Vanocur. The Richard Nixon administration labeled as "liberal" NPACT in general, and the two lead reporters in particular. A Canadian, MacNeil drew ire for his work at the Canadian Broadcasting Corporation (CBC) and the British Broadcasting Corporation (BBC), where his reporting questioned America's role in Vietnam. When NPACT closed, MacNeil found refuge at WNET, the public television station in New York City, which subsequently launched the half hour nightly news program that evolved into *The News Hour*.

A former Marine officer, Jim Lehrer wrote and published fiction as a young man in Dallas, while working for newspapers in that city. The success of his fiction allowed Lehrer to leave his "day job" at the newspaper in favor of a part-time position as public affairs director of KERA, the Dallas public television station. There he obtained a Ford Foundation grant for a daily program in which reporters talked with one another and with an editor about the stories they covered that day, a "newsroom" format instituted at other public television stations at the time. Lehrer's television leadership in Dallas caught the eye of PBS, which brought him to Washington to head its public affairs programming in the wake of the Nixon attacks. Whatever his personal politics, his demeanor said "heartland" rather than liberal eastern elite, the persona of MacNeil and Vanocur. In his PBS executive role, he teamed with WNET's MacNeil to cover the Watergate hearings that led to Nixon's resignation and cleared the way for public television to revitalize public affairs programming.

WNET took the first step in 1975 with *The Robert MacNeil Report*, a nightly half-hour treatment of a single topic in the news. A "talking heads" program, MacNeil's "report" discussed the news more than reported it. At the same time that commercial television news began to exploit satellite technology and computerized graphics to bring more pizzazz to their broadcasts, MacNeil gave viewers a sober discussion of current issues and ideas. Lehrer served as Washington reporter for the MacNeil program. Their contrasting styles and personal chemistry quickly led to restructuring of MacNeil's program into the *The MacNeil-Lehrer Report* co-produced by WNET, where MacNeil remained based, and WETA in Washington, Lehrer's television home. They continued to cover one story each evening for a half hour.

While conservative leaders often condemned public tele-

vision in general for its "liberal bias," they nearly always exempted MacNeil-Lehrer from that charge, not surprising, perhaps, because the program invited so many Washington officials of all persuasions to appear on the program. The program prided itself on talking in depth with key decision makers, which caused some critics on the left to label the program the voice of the Washington establishment.

The team took a bold and controversial gamble in 1983. Over the objections of many public television stations protective of their air-time and concerned about costs for which they were partially responsible, the half-hour *Report* exploded into *The MacNeil/Lehrer News Hour*. Philosophically, the expanded format changed the purpose of the broadcast from a "supplement" to network television news to a competitor. The "hour" started with a news summary that covered the substance of the nightly network newscasts before launching into in-depth treatment of three or four of the stories reported in the summary. The three or four topics each evening, still featured the talking heads format, but included some original reporting and taped reports from the field. By 2005, the program had established relationships with about a dozen correspondents in different parts of the country, specialists in topics such as health, media, the arts, foreign affairs, politics, Congress, urban issues, education and technology. Most correspondents were based in the West and the Midwest, providing geographic diversity to reporting as well as topical diversity. The health correspondent led a unit devoted to that topic and separately funded by a foundation.

A major "underwriting" commitment from AT&T paid much of the increased cost of the hour-long format, setting a pattern of corporate funding, also somewhat controversial among those concerned about influence on content. Funding in 2005 came from Archer Daniels Midland, Smith Barney, CIT, Pacific Life, and the William and Flora Hewlett Foundation, in addition to PBS and its viewers, and the CPB.

About the same time, the duo took over ownership and responsibility for the broadcast from WNET and WETA, forming MacNeil/Lehrer Productions and hiring a former NBC News president, Les Crystal, as company president and executive producer for *The News Hour*. The Gannett newspaper publishing chain invested in the new production company, a further cause for concern among those fearful about the independence of news on public television.

MacNeil's retirement in 1995 led to another series of changes. The New York operation, where MacNeil had been based, closed down and MacNeil/Lehrer Productions consolidated at WETA in the Washington suburbs. Lehrer became sole host of *The News Hour with Jim Lehrer*. *The News Hour* spread MacNeil's duties among several senior correspondents, who shared interviewing responsibilities with Lehrer and anchored the program during his absences. In 2005, four persons served as senior correspondents: Gwen Ifell, formerly of NBC, and moderator of *Washington Week in Review*; Margaret Warner, from *Newsweek;*, Ray Suarez from National Public Radio; and Jeffrey Brown from the staff of Columbia University.

Further Readings

Engleman, Ralph. *Public Radio and Television in America: A Political History*. Thousand Oaks CA: Sage Publications, 1996.

Lehrer, Jim. *A Bus of My Own*. New York: GP Putnam's Sons, 1992; Hawk Publishing Group, 2000.

McNeil, Robert. *Looking for my Country: Finding Myself in America*. New York: Nan A. Talese/Doubleday, 2003.

Stewart, David, *The PBS Companion: A History of Public Television*. New York: TV Books, 1999.

JACK W. MITCHELL

THEATRE AND PERFORMANCE CRITICISM

Before 1800 Americans did not hold theatre in high regard; indeed, many thought it to be a dangerous institution. Critics, therefore, looked upon themselves more as censors than critics, delivering reviews that commented on a play's moral import rather than its aesthetic or dramatic qualities or cultural significance. In his 1832 history of the American theatre, William Dunlap identified an anonymous review in the *Maryland Gazette* of 1762 as the first review of a play.

The last decade of the eighteenth century and the first half of the nineteenth saw some change. A group of men calling themselves "scalpers and mountebanks" formed in the 1790s in New York to write anonymous reviews of New York productions. One calling himself "Philo Theatricus"—possibly of this group—authored a review, which appeared in the Boston *Columbian Centinnel* in 1794, of "Gustavas Vasa." A 1796 article on acting by a person with the same pseudonym appeared in the *Gazette of the United States*. A new Park Street Theatre opened in New York in January 1798 that some acclaimed for its qualities as a venue for dramatic performances. "The essential requisites for hearing and seeing have been happily attained," commented the *Daily Advertiser* and the *Commercial Advertiser*, but Washington Irving suggested that audiences needed improvement. With regard to gallery patrons, he wrote: "The noise in this part of the house is somewhat similar to that which appeared in Noah's ark; for we have an imitation of the whistles and yells of every kind of animal." Critics also remained wanting, at least in the opinion of Edgar Allan Poe, who, in 1836, characterized those who practiced theatre criticism as "illiterate mountebanks."

Few daily newspapers published regular reviews. Irving, who came to be regarded as the first drama critic of importance in the United States, wrote criticism for such publications as *The Salamagundi, Select Reviews,* and the *Analytic Magazine*. When newspapers did choose to cover a play, they usually sent untrained people to review an opening performance and only on condition that the producer be one who had purchased advertising in the paper. That practice led Walt Whitman to add to Poe's indictment of the state of theatre criticism. Reviews, he charged in 1847, often got written according to the "paid puff" system—an affliction that others complained about with regard to the music criticism of the day.

Romanticism and the Theatre

The growth of cities, improved transportation, and more leisure time provided conditions more favorable for theatre before the Civil War. A romantic theatre tradition, emphasizing melodrama and star actors who mastered a highly artificial rhetorical style, became popular. Whitman commented on the popularity of one of these, Edwin Forrest. He reported in a *Brooklyn Eagle* review of 1846 that "packed crowds of people" filled the Park Theatre "from footlights to lobby doors to see Mr. Forrest" in "The Gladiator," a role especially created for him. In describing Forrest's performance, he warned lesser talents about the dangers of this highly stylized romantic melodramatic acting. In the late 1850s, a leader of a moral and conservative school of criticism, William Winter of the *New York Tribune*, attributed the triumph of Edwin Booth in New York in the late 1850s to his "great personality" and his "imagination, insight, grace, intense emotion and melancholy refinement."

Moralists and puffers continued to dominate the profession through the Civil War. Henry Clapp Jr. emerged, however, just before the war to challenge these people and their criticism. He led a group of critics that met regularly in Pfaff's Restaurant in New York to discuss and critique current theatrical practice. In articles published in the *Saturday Review* and other weekly publications Clapp argued that aesthetic rather than moral criteria should be used to evaluate plays and their performance. He and his group found some support in the popular press that demanded bright and clever reviews rather than moralistic essays.

Realism and a Professional Criticism

The moralistic and conservative school reasserted itself after the war. But by the late 1870s, a number of critics—among them Harrison Grey Fiske, Epes W. Sargeant, and Edward Rothman—revived the cause of a more professional and better theatre and a criticism befitting it. William Dean Howells, in his capacity as editor of the *Atlantic Monthly*, added his voice to urge a more realistic native drama to take the place of the melodramatic works so popular in the 1830s, 1840s, and 1850s. A theatre weekly, the *New York Dramatic Mirror*, founded in 1879, joined Howells, Rothman, and others in the cause. They found a powerful ally and model in the dominant critical voice of the period, James Gibbons Huneker, who wrote for the *New York Recorder*, the *New York Advertiser*, and the *Sun*. These people and their publications began to gain some support from academicians, who, although they practiced a different kind of criticism from that of journalistic criticism, began to educate the public.

Developments in Europe and increased travel by Americans to that continent aided these people and publications to bring about change in America. Henrik Ibsen, George Bernard Shaw, and other European dramatists produced a realistic and naturalistic theatre that Americans such as Howells admired and urged be emulated in the United States. Shaw wrote theatre criticism that American critics found to be a model; he was "the great master of the art of criticism," according to twentieth-century critic Julius Novick. All contributed to the emergence of a more professional and vital theatre culture in the United States by the turn of the twentieth century. Described as closest in spirit to Huneker, George Jean Nathan championed a new American drama exemplified by the work of Eugene O'Neill in his writings for *Smart Set* (1909–1923). Critics found their power over the success of new plays growing. A notable example occurred when Alexander Woolcott, a reviewer for the *New York Herald*, the *Sun*, and the *New York World*, challenged the city's leading producers, the Schuberts.

Nathan and Woolcott dominated the New York critical world down to the advent in 1926 of Brooks Atkinson as a reviewer for the *New York Times*. Remaining in that position until 1960, Atkinson sustained Huneker's and other's advocacy of new and experimental work. He encouraged off-Broadway work in the 1950s. A New York Critics Circle was established in 1933 with Atkinson as its first head. Walter Kerr emerged as successor to Atkinson among New York newspaper critics. He wielded even more influence over the success of new plays and productions as the number of newspapers began to decline in New York. Kerr wrote extensively on criticism and urged colleagues to see a distinction between a newspaper critic, who often does no more than provide information as to what might be good this week, month or season, and a drama critic who looks at where a play stands in relation to the very best work that has preceded it and to its age in general.

Twentieth-Century Changes and Issues— Emergence of a National Theatre and Criticism

New forms of popular theatrical entertainment appeared, often to challenge those who preferred more serious theatre. Vaudeville, musical theatre, radio, movies, and television provided alternatives to live theatre and for some did not merit serious critical discussion. In New York, the musical theatre came to be associated with Broadway, and it seemed to require only the kind of notice Kerr saw as the typical product of a newspaper critic. Serious theatre and dramatic criticism tended to be associated more with off-Broadway productions. Hence, some critics preferred to work away from Broadway; others, like Henry Hewes, endeavored to take account of all theatrical productions.

Although New York continued to be regarded as the theatre and arts capital of the country, regional theatre flourished and by the 1960s had transformed theatre and the criticism associated with it into a national force. Chicago, Los Angeles, San Francisco, Minneapolis, and even smaller communities such as Montgomery, Alabama, with its Blount Theatre and Alabama Shakespeare Festival emerged as theatrical centers of note. The career of the Nashville, Tennessee, critic, Clara Hieronymus, exemplifies the growth of regional theatre and a new critical tradition to support it. In reminiscing about the past, she noted that in the old days theatre events were included in the society or "darling"

section of the newspaper, and "people who reviewed plays were supposed to praise." Anybody who challenged that unwritten rule, as she did, violated "a longstanding Southern tradition of being just nice to everybody."

Major critics from various parts of the country recognized the transformation of the theatre into a national institution. In 1974, they met at the Eugene O'Neill Theatre Center in Waterford, Connecticut, to establish an American Theatre Critics Association to "promote public awareness of the theatre as a national resource." In sponsoring the financially significant ATCA-Steinberg prize, it expanded an important role of critics already played (what with the Tony and the Pulitzer prizes) to shape theatrical awards. In 2004, the Association celebrated its founding by publishing interviews with a number of critics associated with its creation and early life. These included, in addition to Hewes, Hieronymus, and Novick, Eliot Norton, described as "the dean of American theatre critics"; Ann Holmes, who covered the birth of the resident theatre movement in the Alley Theatre in 1947; and Otis L. Guernsey Jr., viewed as perhaps the most prolific editor of theatre criticism in American history. For thirty-six years he edited the *Best Plays* annual, characterized by Rick Pender, arts and entertainment editor of the Cincinnati-based *City Beat,* as "a true compendium of American theatre and criticism." Four other lengthy interviews make up the collection *Under the Copper Beach: Conversations With American Theatre Critics.*

More serious theatre may have found itself challenged by the growth of an entertainment industry, but in the end it continued to find ways to grow and prosper. Commercial playhouses tended to dominate theatrical life in large cities by the end of the nineteenth century, but in 1916 independent theatre came into existence with the establishment of the Provincetown Players, which encouraged American playwrights and the development of an American theatre. Four years later the Theatre Guild was established by members of the Washington Square Players. It dedicated itself to the presentation of cultural plays by both Americans and Europeans and undertook a series for both radio and television. By the end of the century, some critics such as Novick had concluded that quality theatre could be made only under noncommercial auspices.

Another challenge came with a decline the number of newspapers after World War II. In New York, that meant that more power accrued to the *New York Times* to make or break shows in that city. Its many critics discussed theatrical events not only in New York but in other parts of the country and world as well. As the newspaper's chief drama critic from 1980 to 1993, Frank Rich was especially influential. Magazines and eventually electronic means of communication assumed greater importance in the 1960s, 1970s, and 1980s. Among the magazines, the *Nation*, the *New Republic*, the *New Yorker, Theatre Arts Magazine* published articles by such highly regarded and influential critics as Joseph Wood Krutch, Harold Cluer, Eric Bentley, Robert Brustein, Stanley Kauffman, and others. *Time* and *Newsweek* reached large audiences and included reviews by

Louis Kronenberg, T. E. Kalem, and Jack Kroll. Experimental, avant-garde, and alternative off-Broadway, and off-off Broadway theatre spawned its own critical culture that found expression in the writings of such people as Hewes and Novick and such publications as the *Village Voice*.

Then in the 1990s the Internet brought another way to comment and communicate about theatre. By the first decade of the twenty-first century the weblog and web journals made available unlimited space for exchange of ideas about plays and their performances. *The ArtsJournal.com* became one of these with access through it to newspaper and magazine articles published mainly in the United States, Canada, and the United Kingdom and to a number of weblog sites.

Further Reading

Banham, Martin, ed. *The Cambridge Guide to Theatre*. New York and Cambridge: Cambridge University Press, 1995.

Bladel, Roderick. *Walter Kerr: An Analysis of His Criticism*. Metuchen, N J: Scarecrow Press, Inc., 1976.

Comtois, M. E., and Lynn F. Miller, compilers. *Contemporary American Theatre Critics: A Directory and Anthology of Their Works*. Metuchen, N J. and London: Scarecrow Press, Inc., 1977.

Jenkins, Jeffrey Eric, ed. *Under the Copper Beach: Conversations with American Theatre Critics*. Millvale, PA: Foundation of the American Theatre Critics Association, 2004.

Londré, Felicia Hardison, and Daniel J. Waterman. *The History of Theatre in North America From Pre-Columbian Times to the Present*. New York: Continuum, 1998.

Wilmerth, Don B., and Christopher Bigsby. *The Cambridge History of the American Theatre*, 3 vols. New York: Cambridge University Press, 1998–2000.

Wilmerth, Don B., Christopher Bigsby, and Tice L. Miller, eds. *Cambridge Guide to American Theatre*. New York and Cambridge: Cambridge University Press, 1996.

CHARLES A. WEEKS

THOMAS, HELEN

Helen Thomas (August 4, 1920–) was a Hearst Newspaper columnist and a White House Bureau Chief for newspaper syndicate United Press International. She worked for United Press International (UPI) for fifty-seven years from 1943 to 2000. Thomas began covering the White House in 1960; she covered every president from John F. Kennedy through George W. Bush.

Thomas was born August 4, 1920, in Winchester, Kentucky to Lebanese immigrants. She was the seventh of nine children in the Thomas family. Although born in Kentucky, she was raised in Detroit, Michigan, and attended public schools there. Thomas graduated from Wayne State University (then Wayne University) with a degree in English.

After graduating from college, Thomas went to work for the *Washington Daily News* as a "copy girl." She left the that paper in 1943 and accepted a reporting position at United Press Radio where she was responsible for covering the Federal Bureau of Investigations, the Department of Justice, the Department of Health, Education, and Welfare (now Health and Human Services), and Capitol Hill.

In 1960, United Press International transitioned her from primarily radio to print, and assigned her to report on President-elect Kennedy. Thomas followed the president-elect into the White House and served as a White House Correspondent for approximately forty years for UPI. At the conclusion of each presidential news conference, Thomas was heard to say, "Thank you, Mr. President." Her concluding statement became an accepted practice among reporters.

In 1971, First Lady Pat Nixon announced that Thomas would marry Douglas B. Cornell, a reporter who was then retiring as the Associated Press's White House correspondent.

In 1972, Helen Thomas was the only print reporter to accompany President Richard Nixon on his historic trip to China. Subsequently, she accompanied presidents Gerald Ford, Ronald Reagan, George H.W. Bush, Bill Clinton, and George W. Bush on numerous trips abroad. During that period, she covered every economic summit.

In 2000, she resigned from UPI and accepted a reporting position at Hearst Newspapers. Thomas resigned from UPI when it was purchased by News World Communications which was associated with Sun Myung Moon's Unification Church. Allegedly she did not want to be affiliated with Moon.

President George W. Bush refused to call upon Thomas during his press conferences. When, after approximately three years, President Bush reluctantly did call upon her, she quickly warned him, "You're going to be sorry." Thomas asked the President Bush why he wanted to go to war with Iraq since every reason he had given to justify the war was inaccurate.

Thomas crusaded against sexism. She gave numerous speeches that encouraged young women to fight gender discrimination. "I've been a feminist since the day I was born," she explained.

Thomas was the first female officer of the National Press Club, the first female member and president of the White House Correspondents Association, and first female member of the Gridiron Club. She received numerous awards including the International Women's Media Foundation Lifetime Achievement Award and the National Press Club's 4th Estate Award.

President Bill Clinton presented her the first "Helen Thomas Lifetime Achievement Award" and she was inducted into the Society of Professional Journalists Hall of Fame.

Thomas was often referred to as "The First Lady of the Press." She wrote four books: *Dateline: White House* (1975); *Front Row at the White House* (2000); *Thanks for the Memories, Mr. President* (2002); and *Watchdogs of Democracy?* (2006). Her seat in the White House press briefing room was in the center of the front row just beneath the podium where the White House spokesperson stands, a seat reserved with a small brass plaque.

Further Reading

"Helen Thomas." *Mother Jones Radio.* http://www.motherjones.com/radio/2005/09/thomas_bio.html. (accessed April 12, 2007).

"Helen Thomas." http://www.goddesscafe.com/FEMJOUR/thomas.html (accessed April 12, 2007).

Thomas, Helen. *Dateline: White House.* New York: Macmillan Pub Co., 1975.

——. *Front Row at the White House: My Life and Times.* New York: Simon & Schuster, 2000.

——. *Thanks for the Memories, Mr. President.* New York: Simon & Schuster,. 2002.

——. *Watchdogs of Democracy?: The Waning Washington Press Corps and How It Has Failed the Public.* New York: Scribner, 2006.

JOHN ALLEN HENDRICKS

THOMAS, ISAIAH

Isaiah Thomas (January 19, 1749–April 4, 1831) wrote the first eyewitness account of an American battle, describing for newspaper readers that British soldiers during the 1775 Battle of Lexington "wantonly, and in a most inhuman manner fired upon and killed a number of our countrymen, then robbed them of their provisions, ransacked, plundered and burnt their houses!"

Thomas enjoyed a distinguished career publishing newspapers, almanacs, and magazines in Massachusetts for nearly forty years during the American Revolution and the early years of the Republic. However, Thomas made his greatest contributions to journalism as an organizer and historian. He created one of the largest early American printing networks, wrote the first American history of printing, and founded a scholarly archive to document the growth of both the printing trade and the early United States.

Thomas was born in Boston January 19, 1749, the fifth of Moses and Fidelity Thomas' five children. Moses left the family two years later, prompting Fidelity to seek other arrangements for her children. In 1756, she apprenticed the seven-year-old Isaiah to Boston printer Zechariah Fowle. Thomas remained until 1765, when a feud with his master prompted Thomas to depart. After working for other printers in Halifax, Nova Scotia, Portsmouth, New Hampshire, and Charleston, South Carolina, Thomas returned to Boston in 1770 and commenced the weekly *Massachusetts Spy*, a radical patriot newspaper. Thomas also began an almanac in 1771 and a magazine in 1774. Like his newspaper, these publications supported the Revolutionary cause.

When the war began in April 1775, Thomas moved his newspaper to Worcester, forty miles west of Boston. Thomas briefly joined the American militia and witnessed the battles of Lexington and Concord, which he described in an inflammatory and inaccurate manner in the *Spy*'s May 3 issue. According to Thomas, the British soldiers launched their attack despite being "unmolested and unprovoked." Their "thirst for blood" and "DESIGN of MURDER and ROBBERY" could not be stopped even by "the tears of defenceless women, some of whom were in the pains of childbirth, the cries of helpless babes, nor the prayers of old age, confined to beds of sickness."

Thomas remained in Worcester for the remainder of his life, but extended his printing activities throughout the northeast by creating a printing network. Following Benjamin Franklin's practice of offering partnerships to his workers, Thomas formed a partnership with his former apprentice Henry Tinges and sent him to the Massachusetts seaport village of Newburyport in 1773 to print a newspaper. Other apprentices-turned-partners Thomas dispatched to extend his printing network included David Carlisle in Walpole, New Hampshire; Elisha Waldo in Brookfield, Massachusetts; and Ebenezer Andrews in Boston and Springfield, Massachusetts and Albany, New York. Referring to himself and his partners, Thomas wrote, "They printed three newspapers in the country, and a magazine in Boston; and they had five bookstores in Massachusetts, one in New Hampshire, one at Albany, and one at Baltimore."

By the 1790s, Thomas decided to amass a documentary history of the new nation, featuring the journalistic products that played a central role in its creation. Concerned by the absence of a written history of the American press, Thomas yielded management of the *Massachusetts Spy* to his son Isaiah Jr. and began soliciting reminiscences from other printers. Responding to one of his inquiry letters in 1792, *Connecticut Gazette* printer Timothy Green recalled his family's printing dynasty as far back as his great-grandfather Samuel, who operated a printing press in Cambridge, Massachusetts, as early as 1649. Samuel "had a numerous Family—his sons Samuel, Bartholemew, and Timothy set up the same business in Boston; but my Grandfather who was his youngest Son, removed to New London, in the Year 1714, if I mistake not," Green wrote. Thomas also asked printers throughout the nation "to forward one or two of their papers" to him in Worcester.

Thomas collected these memories and samples of the early American press, augmented by his own extensive knowledge, into a two-volume work, *The History of Printing in America*, in 1810. The book has been reprinted many times. Although it contains numerous factual errors, his history remains a valuable source of anecdotal information about the early-American press. Thomas also used the correspondence of printers and his own vast library to establish the American Antiquarian Society in 1812. Its purpose was to collect and document the early history of the American press. As Thomas wrote, the Society would preserve documents and newspapers "to assist the researches of the future historians of our Country." The Society remains in existence today, its research library located in Thomas' adopted hometown of Worcester.

Further Reading

Frasca, Ralph. "Printers' Networks." In *History of the Mass Media in the United States*, ed. Margaret A. Blanchard. Chicago: Fitzroy Dearborn, 1998.

Hill, Benjamin Thomas, ed. *The Diary of Isaiah Thomas, 1805–1828*, 2 vols. Worcester, MA: American Antiquarian Society, 1909.

Marble, Annie Russell. *From 'Prentice to Patron: The Life of Isaiah Thomas*. New York: D. Appleton-Century, 1935.

Shipton, Clifford K. *Isaiah Thomas: Printer, Patriot and Philanthropist*. Rochester, NY: Leo Hart, 1948.

Thomas, Isaiah. *The History of Printing in America*. Worcester, MA: Isaiah Thomas Jun., 1810. Reprint edition ed. Marcus A. McCorison. New York: Weathervane, 1970.

RALPH FRASCA

THOMPSON, HUNTER S.

Hunter S. Thompson (July 18, 1937–February 20, 2005) was one of the most parodied American journalists of the twentieth century. His self-created literary image as a drugged-out, slightly out-of-control angry man drowning in a sea of personal irony while railing against a creeping American fascism has been well reproduced. It exists in most of his works, two major Hollywood movies (*Where The Buffalo Roam* [1980] and *Fear And Loathing In Las Vegas* [1998]), the character "Uncle Duke" in the nationally syndicated comic strip *Doonesbury* and the character "Spider Jerusalem" in the sixty-issue DC/Vertigo comic book series *Transmetropolitan*. Behind this self-mocking mask, however, was a hard-working prose stylist whose decades worth of carefully crafted newspaper and magazine articles, personal correspondence, online essays, and book narratives made Thompson a star among the "new" journalists of the 1960s and 1970s. A senior statesman of American letters, he was still producing work to some acclaim when he fatally shot himself in the head at age sixty-seven on February 20, 2005.

Hunter Stockton Thompson was born on July 18, 1937 (although some Thompson biographies incorrectly list the date as 1939) in Louisville, Kentucky. He entered the U.S. Air Force in 1956. He began his journalistic career as the sports editor of the *Command Courier,* his base newspaper. He left the Air Force a year later after angering top brass with his investigative reporting and by his moonlighting for a local newspaper. He moved to New York City for a brief time, attending night classes at Columbia University while working as a *Time* magazine copyboy. Personally inspired by the work of, characters in the novels of, and lives of writers like Jack Kerouac, F. Scott Fitzgerald, Ernest Hemingway, and Tom Wolfe, Thompson was determined to blaze an independent trail.

After a brief Caribbean stint for the *New York Herald-Tribune*, Thompson became first a South American correspondent, and later a national correspondent, for the *National Observer*. All the while he freelanced for publications like *Scanlan's Monthly*. An assignment for *The Nation* magazine on the Hell's Angels motorcycle gang led to a book contract and some fame.

But it was in *Scanlan's* that Thompson began experimenting with composing half-fictional, fragmented, and purposely-seeming stream-of-consciousness, first-person accounts of events. In these articles, he presented himself as an anti-hero often defeated by his own absurdity. This subset of "new" journalism he created was dubbed "gonzo journalism." A counter-culture magazine out of San Francisco named *Rolling Stone* first published his "gonzo" magnum opus, *Fear And Loathing In Las Vegas*. Thompson, having settled in Colorado, became one of *Rolling Stone*'s star journalists in the 1970s. In these articles, he was also an anti-hero often defeated by absurdity.

Scores of magazine articles, and book collections of articles past and current, would follow from the 1970s to shortly before his death. In 1997 and in 2000, Thompson published volumes of select letters in his approximately twenty-thousand-item collection of personal correspondence. By early 2001, Thompson was writing a semi-regular sports column for *ESPN.com*. His memoir, *Kingdom Of Fear*, was published in 2003.

Thompson's image often overshadowed his work. But Thompson's so-called "non-fiction" writing documents a turbulent era inf American history, and does so with all the satirical wit and precise detail of the then-young writer's literary heroes.

Further Reading

Anson, Robert Sam. *Gone Crazy and Back Again: The Rise and Fall of the Rolling Stone Generation*. New York: Doubleday, 1981.

Carroll, E. Jean. *Hunter: The Strange and Savage Life of Hunter S. Thompson*. New York: Plume, 1993.

Draper, Robert. *Rolling Stone Magazine: The Uncensored History*. New York: Doubleday, 1990.

Love, Robert, ed. *The Best of Rolling Stone: 25 Years of Journalism on the Edge*. New York: Doubleday, 1993.

McKeen, William. *Hunter S. Thompson*. Boston: Twayne Publishers, 1991.

Perry, Paul. *Fear And Loathing: The Strange and Terrible Saga of Hunter S. Thompson*. New York: Thunder's Mouth Press, 1992.

Thompson, Hunter S. *Hell's Angels: A Strange and Terrible Saga*. New York: Ballantine Books, 1996, originally published 1967.

——. *Fear and Loathing in Las Vegas: A Savage Journey to the Heart of the American Dream*. New York: Vintage, 1998, originally published in 1971.

——. *Fear and Loathing: On The Campaign Trail '72*. New York: Warner Books, 1983, originally published in 1973.

——. *Kingdom of Fear: Loathsome Secrets of a Star-Crossed Child in the Final Days of the American Century*. Foreword by Timothy Ferris. New York: Simon And Schuster, 2003.

——. *The Proud Highway: Saga of a Desperate Southern Gentleman, 1955–1967*. Edited by Douglas Brinkley. Foreword by William J. Kennedy. New York: Villard, 1997.

——. *Fear and Loathing in America: The Brutal Odyssey of an Outlaw Journalist, 1968–1976*. Edited by Douglas Brinkley. Foreword by David Halberstam. New York: Simon And Schuster, 2000.

Whitmer, Peter O. *When the Going Gets Weird: The Twisted Life and Times of Hunter S. Thompson*. New York: Hyperion, 1993.

TODD STEVEN BURROUGHS

THURBER, JAMES GROVER

James Thurber (December 8, 1894–November 2, 1961), humorist and cartoonist for the *New Yorker* magazine for over three decades, published some forty works, including collections of essays, cartoons, children's stories, and plays. He is best known for his depictions of the mild-mannered man turned hero, the domineering woman, and amusing cartoon caricatures.

James Grover Thurber was born in Columbus, Ohio, to Charles L. and Mary Thurber. His father was an adept clerk who worked for a number of politicians, including two Ohio governors. His mother, known as Mame, was a natural comedienne and true comic talent, according to Thurber. She once attended a faith healer's meeting disguised as a cripple, jumping up abruptly and claiming to be healed. On another occasion, she stunned waiting dinner guests by proclaiming that she had been delayed because of her dalliance in the attic with the postman.

Thurber lost sight in his left eye at age six when it was struck by a homemade arrow shot by his older brother while the pair were playing William Tell. Inflammation of the undamaged eye caused it to deteriorate for the next forty years, eventually resulting in blindness. Unable to participate in sports, he honed his writing. Thurber's story produced for the eighth-grade class was a fanciful tale in which he serves as unlikely hero by rescuing the group's "seairoplane" from near disaster. At East High School he wrote for the *X-Rays* school magazine, was elected class president and graduated with honors.

Thurber's initial experiences at nearby Ohio State University, which he attended from 1913 to 1917, were not so fortunate. The tall, awkward freshman received no invitations to join a fraternity and faltered badly in mandatory gym and military drill classes, hurdles that also prevented him from earning an OSU degree. However these early misadventures served as uproarious anecdotes in his later story "University Days." Thurber was befriended by Elliot Nugent, who became a lifelong confidant. The son of a noted playwright, Nugent admired Thurber's literary and creative skills and helped usher him into the Phi Kappa Psi fraternity, the Strollers drama club, the *Ohio State Lantern* newspaper and the *Sundial* magazine—which first published his drawings and essays, then elevated him to editor-in-chief.

Rejected for World War I military service, Thurber worked as a code clerk in Washington, D.C., Thurber's life was routinely punctuated by a series of mishaps that provided rich material for the humorist. His entrée to a U.S. office in Paris was a prime example. The American Peace delegation reportedly requested twelve or so code *clerks*, when in actuality they only required a dozen copies of the code *book*. En route to his ill-fated appointment abroad, Thurber succumbed to seasickness and discovered, upon docking, that an armistice ending the war had been signed two days earlier. His luggage was lost and Thurber could only afford an ill-fitting suit, which he described as something that could have been manufactured by the American Can Company. Recovering his suitcase later, the young

writer discovered that his mother, thoughtful of the privations of wartime, had judiciously packed Hershey bars into every nook; in storage they had melted all over his clothes.

Returning to Columbus in 1920, Thurber wrote and directed comedies for local theatre troupes and reported for the *Columbus Dispatch*. He also freelanced for the *Christian Science Monitor*, which mistakenly attributed his work to "Miss Jane Thurber." Although taunted by the *Dispatch's* gruff city editor with the nicknames "Phi Beta Kappa" and "Author," the skillful Thurber advanced to the city hall beat in Columbus. In wry happenstance, the first City Council meeting Thurber covered was interrupted by a fire that burned City Hall to the ground—leading to an extra edition of the paper in which his writing was prominently featured.

In early 1922, Thurber spotted Althea Adams' striking photo in the OSU yearbook and determined to meet and marry her. To the chagrin of his family, particularly his mother, Thurber did just that. However, Thurber's wife was domineering and fought often with his mother, later inspiring a composite character, the Thurber Woman, which figured prominently in his work. Thurber conceded that his stories written in the late 1920s featuring the sharp-tongued dialogue between Mr. and Mrs. John Monroe were near transcripts of his and Althea's colorful quarrels.

At his wife's behest, the couple moved first to Paris, where Thurber contributed to the Paris and Nice bureaus of the *Chicago Tribune*, then to New York, where the writer took a job with the *Evening Post* and contributed freelance pieces to *Harper's* magazine. After a series of rejections from the *New Yorker*, Thurber successfully submitted a story of a modest man who wins a world record for going round and round in a department store revolving door and humbly concludes that he did it all for his wife and kids. The humorist also developed a friendship with *New Yorker* editor E.B. "Andy" White, who helped him secure a job with the magazine, and the office next door to White's.

Thurber blossomed at the *New Yorker* under the tutelage of White, whom he credited for teaching him how to write well and for encouraging his first drawings for publication—spare line drawings of droll adults and clever animals, particularly dogs. In 1929, Thurber and White collaborated on a highly successful first book, *Is Sex Necessary?*, that poked fun at contemporary psychoanalysis. The humorist then published a collection of Monroe stories, pet humor and drawings: *The Owl in the Attic* (1931). A collection of memorable Thurber *New Yorker* cartoons was published in 1932: *The Seal in the Bedroom*.

Thurber's most celebrated work is his 1933 collection of embellished memoirs and accompanying drawings, *My Life and Hard Times*, which introduces the fabled characters of Walter Mitty, his demanding wife, and their perceptive pets. The book includes "The Night the Bed Fell," a chaotic 2 a.m. race for the attic to rescue father, who the family supposes has been crushed by a collapsing old bed, and "The Night the Dam Broke," where flood-fleeing citizens mistake soldiers' shouts of "the dam has *not* broken!" as "the dam has *now* broken!" Thurber and OSU friend Nugent collaborated on *The Male Animal* (1940), a play about university life and academic freedom that ran for 243 performances on Broadway in 1939 to 1940.

The humorist lost sight in his right eye in the early 1940s and suffered from alcoholism and recurring bouts of depression. He continued to contribute to the *New Yorker* after his move to Connecticut with second wife, magazine editor Helen Wismer. In 1958 he became the first U.S. humorist since Mark Twain to be "invited to the table" by Britain's legendary *Punch* humor magazine.

Thurber created several children's books in his later years: *Many Moons* (a Caldecott winner), *The Great Quillow*, *The 13 Clocks*, and *The Wonderful O*. He received honorary degrees from three universities and starred as himself 88 times in his Tony Award-winning Broadway play, *The Thurber Carnival* (1945). A 1969–70 TV show titled *My World and Welcome to It* was based on his life. OSU named a theatre for him in 1972 and in 1984 his family's 77 Jefferson Avenue residence in Columbus, Ohio, became the Thurber House, a museum of his life and work. Thurber died November 2, 1961, at age sixty-six of a blood clot in the brain while hospitalized for pneumonia. He had one daughter.

Further Reading

Bernstein, Burton. *Thurber: A Biography*. New York: Dodd, Mead, 1975 .

Grauer, Neil A. *Remember Laughter: A Life of James Thurbe.* Lincoln: University of Nebraska Press, 1994.

James Thurber Family Collection, Thurber House, Columbus, OH, http://thurberhouse@thurberhouse.org.

Kinney, Harrison. *James Thurber: His Life and Times*. New York: Henry Holt & Co., 1995.

Kinney, Harrison, with Rosemary A. Thurber, eds. *The Thurber Letters: The Wit, Wisdom, and Surprising Life of James Thurber*. New York: Simon & Schuster, 2002.

Thurber, Helen, and Edward Weeks, ed. *Selected Letters of James Thurber*. Boston: Little, Brown, 1981.

KEVIN C. LEE

TIME MAGAZINE

Debuting in 1923, *Time* was America's first successful "news magazine," a guided synthesis of the previous week's events. By the mid-twentieth century, *Time* was the nation's most influential periodical. "I do not always agree with Time," President John F. Kennedy wrote in 1963, "but I nearly always read it."

The magazine was the creation of Henry R. Luce and Briton Hadden, two young graduates of Yale University. Although the two men had decidedly modest journalistic credentials, consisting of brief stints at several big-city dailies, they possessed enormous self-confidence. They were convinced that they could create a new type of magazine. *Time* would summarize concisely (no entry at first was to run more than four hundred words) and "explain" the week's news—and not just news of politics and government. They intended to cover the arts and religion. Hadden and Luce

in a sense imagined themselves—busy, young, would-be upper-middle-class professionals—as the target market for *Time*. They needed a publication like *Time* to master an increasingly complex world. This conclusion was shared by other monitors of the news media in the early 1920s, notably Walter Lippmann, whom both men admired. Newspapers in effect offered too much news, too little context.

Time's fate, like those for all successful magazine startups, would depend on the periodical's distinctiveness. Unlike the popular weekly *Literary Digest*, which reprinted newspaper accounts, *Time* offered one omniscient voice (said to be "that of the Man in the Moon at the end of the current century"). To that end, stories were heavily edited and normally lacked bylines. The magazine gave great weight to newsmakers in explaining events. Individuals usually adorned *Time*'s cover. The magazine also developed a unique style. Sentences were often inverted ("Not yet ready was the President"), words invented ("cinemactress"), or rescued from obscurity ("tycoon"). At first, *Time*'s unique packaging of news disguised a great weakness. Until the 1930s, *Time* writers did little reporting; their entries were, in effect, smart summaries of newspaper clips. This was often cloaked by stories' inclusion of "knowing" details, like the color of someone's dress, which gave them an eyewitness quality absent in most daily papers. Finally, *Time* eschewed objectivity. Entries in the magazine would have a point-of-view, admiring or disdaining. Politically, the magazine honored more centrist Republicans, and mocked (often cruelly) the nation's more reactionary or revolutionary voices. Culturally, *Time* took few chances, tending to favor the safe and middle-brow. Of the magazine's founding partners, Hadden played the greater role in setting the magazine's content and tone. But the magazine continued to flourish after his death in 1929.

By then, *Time* was making money and finding an audience. Younger, college-educated Americans found the magazine engaging. *Time* also affected to a completeness that made reading it an obligation for many. Demand for the publication rose sharply in the 1930s, when the Great Depression and expansion of the federal government further complicated the world. The need for a guided synthesis never appeared more critical and only grew with the start of World War II. By late 1946, *Time* had a circulation of 1.6 million.

The typical readers were comfortably middle-class, residing in smaller cities or towns. Businesspeople, a 1946 survey indicated, constituted just under 60 percent of *Time*'s readership. *Time* subscribers were, by definition, more interested in national and international events, and frustrated by most newspapers' heavy emphasis on local occurrences. The arrival of *Time* in the mid-twentieth century was a signal event, affording readers their best and most clever rendering of the world, the arts, and sciences.

Time's growing popularity affected all of American journalism. Younger reporters imitated the magazine's peculiar style. And *Time*'s more interpretive news presentation prompted many larger dailies, beginning in the mid-1930s, to introduce Sunday sections that analyzed the week's news. More slowly, newspapers' daily reportage became more analytical.

Time's impact on journalism hardly satiated Luce's ambitions. He launched two other successful magazines, *Fortune* (1930) and *Life* (1936). And he began to concern himself with public affairs. Although he had disdained the more reactionary wing of the Republican Party, Luce became increasingly frustrated during Franklin D. Roosevelt's second term. The Democratic Roosevelt was too hostile to business, Luce concluded, forestalling full economic recovery. The outbreak of war in Europe made Luce all the more anxious. Fearful that Germany would emerge victorious, he joined forces with others urging Roosevelt to move the nation away from its traditional isolationism. Luce's magazines helped the largely unknown but internationalist Wendell L. Willkie win the 1940 Republican presidential nomination. To Luce's exasperation, voters proved less partial to Willkie in the general election campaign against Roosevelt.

Over the next quarter century, *Time* proved more editorially consistent, more closely reflecting Luce's views on politics and foreign relations. Its stories tended to favor the moderate wing of the Republican Party, while disparaging more conservative Republicans (including Joseph R. McCarthy Jr.) and most Democratic leaders. In foreign relations, *Time* proved an early proponent of containing the Soviet Union. Then, too, *Time* reflected Luce's dismay over the Communist takeover of China in 1949 (Luce was the son of China missionaries). When the United States intervened in South Vietnam in the 1960s, *Time* reassured readers as to correctness of America's involvement. "The Vietnamese conflict," *Time* declared in May 1965, "is the right war in the right place at the right time." Luce died in 1967 convinced that the United States would prevail.

To his detractors, Luce helped to create a mentality that encouraged a costly war in Vietnam and delayed the normalization of diplomatic relations with China. Yet critics were too quick to blame Luce alone and not acknowledge the extent to which his magazine was one of many editorial voices favoring the Cold War and hostility to Communist China. At the same time, it is worth recalling that *Time*'s readership tended to be limited to a segment of the middle-class, much of which was already inclined to be anti-Communist. (If anything, *Time* may have caused some small-town, middle western Americans to abandon their traditional isolationism.) More influential Americans, notably those living in New York and Washington, were much less dependent on *Time* for their view of the world. Overseas, however, many leaders considered *Time* a mirror of American opinion. Decrying "the evil influence of *Time* magazine in the [Far] East," one reader wrote Luce, "you are the dominant instrument for informing the East about American attitudes."

Nevertheless, *Time*'s increasing rigidity in the 1950s and 1960s left it vulnerable. The magazine's biases exasperated more liberal readers. "Mr. Luce is like a man that owns a shoe store and buys all the shoes to fit himself. Then he expects other people to buy them," complained Louisiana

Governor Earl Long. *Newsweek*, long an inconsequential competitor, seized upon this dissatisfaction in the 1960s with more aggressive reporting and a more liberal point of view.

Partly in response to *Newsweek*'s gains, *Time* underwent an editorial shift in the 1970s. Under editor Henry Grunwald, the magazine gradually shed its omniscient voice. *Time* moved to the political center; in November 1973 the magazine ran its first editorial, recommending that Republican President Richard Nixon resign. Beyond the momentous, more cover stories concerned trends as opposed to individuals. "It was no longer easy," Grunwald concluded, "to find individuals to personify what was significant in American society."

A more lasting threat to *Time*'s importance came from television. Network TV newscasts became an increasingly important informational option for the middle-class in the 1960s. Newspapers carried more of the interpretive journalism that *Time* had helped to invent. The advent of cable news networks, starting in 1980, marked still another challenge to *Time*'s position. Simply put, the information-seeking classes had a growing number of options in the late twentieth century. Fewer needed *Time* to comprehend the world.

Time abandoned its once daunting effort to summarize "all the news." Its news agenda became less comprehensive—and more indulgent. The number of overseas stories fell sharply between 1970 and 2000 while those involving fads and popular culture rose. All told, *Time* ran fewer but longer entries. This transformation reflected two editorial assumptions, that readers already knew the week's events. "Basically, we no longer feel that it is adequate to review last week's news," commented one bureau chief in 1990. Then, too, many younger Americans took information less seriously. So *Time* devoted new space to health or the sensational. On May 4, 1998, *Time* ran a long cover story on male impotency and included a five-page article on a school teacher who had a child by a thirteen-year-old male student.

Corporate pressures also affected the magazine. For more than sixty years, *Time* had been the centerpiece of a corporation whose primary business was magazine publishing. Journalists led Time Inc. But in the late 1970s and 1980s the parent company began deriving more revenue from cable television and other holdings. Time Inc. management showed decreasing indulgence toward Luce's first-born. In 1990, Time Inc. merged with Warner Communication, a film and music conglomerate. This and subsequent marriages further diminished the position of all Time Inc. magazines (which accounted for 13 percent of revenues in 2006). When Time-Warner failed to meet investor expectations, *Time* was subject to cost-cutting unimaginable a half-century earlier.

In the early 2000s, *Time* had become a "mature" magazine, one whose best days were two generations distant. After decades of steady growth, *Time*'s circulation failed to increase beyond four million between 1970 and 2006. No longer was *Time* a central factor in American journalism and politics. "In truth, *Time* has become all but irrelevant in the years since Luce died," wrote one former staff member in 1992, "a dentist's office magazine more often bought than read."

Further Reading

Baughman, James L. *Henry R. Luce and the Rise of the American News Media*, rev. ed. Baltimore: Johns Hopkins University Press, 2001.

Elson, Robert T. *Time Inc.: The Intimate History of a Publishing Enterprise 1923–1941*. New York: Atheneum, 1968.

——. *The World of Time Inc.: The Intimate History of a Publishing Enterprise 1941–1960*. New York: Atheneum, 1973.

Herzstein, Robert E. *Henry R. Luce, Time, and the American Crusade in Asia*. New York: Cambridge University Press, 2005.

Prendergast, Curtis. *The World of Time Inc.: The Intimate History of A Changing Enterprise: 1960–1980*. New York: Atheneum, 1986.

Wilner, Isaiah. *The Man Time Forgot: A Tale of Genius, Betrayal, and the Creation of Time Magazine*. New York : HarperCollins, 2006.

JAMES L. BAUGHMAN

TIMOTHY, ELIZABETH

Elizabeth Timothy (c. 1700–1757) was the first woman newspaper publisher and editor in colonial America. Like many other women printers who followed her, she entered the business out of necessity, following the accidental death of her husband. She published the *South-Carolina Gazette* from 1739 until 1746, when she turned it and the print shop over to her son, Peter. During those years, the newspaper grew and prospered with the growing community of Charleston and reflected many of the issues of the day.

Elizabeth Timothy was born in Holland and immigrated to America in 1731 with her husband, Louis, and four small children, settling in Philadelphia. After striking up a fortuitous acquaintance with Benjamin Franklin, Louis briefly held a post editing the short-lived German-language newspaper, *Philadelphia Zeitung*. In 1734, after that paper had failed, Franklin recruited Louis to publish the *South-Carolina Gazette*, which he had started up with a partner the year before. Franklin would get Louis started financially and would receive one-third the profits for six years, while Louis would put in the labor and time. After that, the paper would be his, or his oldest son's in the case of his death. His duties included publication of the Charleston newspaper, the state printing contract, and distribution, all of which Louis fulfilled successfully until his accidental death at the end of 1738.

The fate of the family fell to Elizabeth. Though she was well-educated for the period, she had never received formal training either as a printer or newspaper publisher. Left with six children to feed and clothe as well as one year to go on Louis's business contract, she took up her husband's burden and began publishing the paper, though in the name of her oldest son, Peter, who at thirteen, had started apprenticing in the print shop.

The newspaper faltered in the first year as Elizabeth Timothy learned the trade. Eventually, she changed its day of publication from Saturday to Thursday, increased the number of woodcuts in the layout to give the newspaper a lively appearance, increased the number of advertisements, and won Franklin's praise for her meticulous record-keeping. Under her management, the four-page newspaper published reprints from other newspapers, reports and commentaries on life in Charleston, reprints of addresses by colonial officials, poems and literary essays, and at least one-and-a-half pages of advertisements. In addition, the print shop published colonial documents and publications, sermons, and occasional historical treatises. Elizabeth also sold a variety of commodities, including Franklin's *Almanac*, beer, and flour.

Like most colonial newspapers of the day that were published under the censorious eye of colonial, church, and royal authorities, the *South-Carolina Gazette* under Elizabeth Timothy generally avoided controversy. In 1739 and 1740, for example, it did not publish any news about the numerous slave revolts that were breaking out in South Carolina, whose economy by this time was heavily dependent on slave labor and where whites were outnumbered two to one by slaves. It did, however, print the news when, in response to the Stono Rebellion of 1740, the colony passed strict laws banning slaves from congregating for any purpose. Elizabeth, who owned eight slaves at the time of her death, also frequently ran advertisements for the sale of slaves or concerning escaped slaves.

Religion was also a topic of some controversy and here Elizabeth was not so careful, publishing letters and sermons from a variety of opposing preachers that made the pages of the *Gazette* lively and occasionally rancorous. Between 1740 and 1742, for example, the *Gazette* published a series of pro and con essays over the controversial Reverend George Whitefield and his fundamentalist interpretation of Anglican doctrine. These essays sometimes skirted official censorship and in 1741, Elizabeth's fifteen-year-old son, Peter, was brought to court on a charge of seditious libel for publishing a letter in which the writer compared the local clergy unfavorably to the fiery evangelist Whitefield.

When Peter Timothy turned twenty-one in 1846, Elizabeth turned over full control of the newspaper to him. She briefly operated a book and stationary shop next to the printing office for at least the next year, and then apparently retired from public life. She continued as a woman of property, however, and colonial records show that in the last decade of her life she owned property in Charleston, slaves, and some valuables in addition to the *Gazette*.

Elizabeth Timothy not only kept the *Gazette* running at a time when the growing Charleston community depended on it, she turned it and the print shop over to her son as a healthy, thriving establishment. She also set an example for her son and other women, showing them a woman could accomplish anything when she put her shoulder to the wheel. When Peter died in 1781, his wife Anne Donovan Timothy took over the publication of the *Gazette* until her own death in 1791.

Further Reading

Copeland, David. *Colonial American Newspapers: Character and Content.* Newark: Delaware University Press, 1997.

Dexter, Elizabeth. *Colonial Women in America: Women in Business and the Professions in America.* Boston: Houghton Mifflin, 1934.

Marzolf, Marion. "Widow Printer to Big City Reporter." In *Up From the Footnote: A History of Women Journalists.* New York: Hastings House Publishers, 1977, 1–31.

Oldham, Ellen M. "Early Women Printers in America." *Boston Public Library Quarterly 10* (1958): 6–26, 78–92, and 141–153.

Schlipp, Madelon Golden, and Sharon M. Murphy. "Elizabeth Timothy: First Woman Publisher" In *Great Women of the Press*, 1–11, 203–204. Carbondale: Southern Illinois University Press, 1983.

Thomas, Isaiah. *The History of Printing in America with a Biography of Printers.* 1874, reprint New York: Burt Franklin, 1964.

ELIZABETH V. BURT

TODAY SHOW

The *Today Show* became the longest-running daily program on television and a major showcase for news on broadcasting's first network, NBC. It was continuously seen in NBC's 7 a.m. to 9 a.m. weekday time period from its first broadcast on January 14, 1952. The program was conceived by NBC television's first president, Sylvester "Pat" Weaver, when network TV was in only its fourth year. Most early television was limited to nighttime hours. Stations did not "sign on" until the afternoon. *Today* opened the morning period. Starting at 7 a.m., news, interviews, and light entertainment were cycled every thirty minutes. Viewers became accustomed to watching a segment of *Today* before leaving for work or school. As *Today* progressed through numerous producers, hosts, and contributors, its format has not changed.

Today helped to inspire many non-entertainment daytime television program, from cooking instruction to talk shows. Yet unlike other daytime programs, *Today* was defined as a news broadcast, although entertainment and news about entertainment were featured prominently during the show's two hours. The program was produced by the NBC news division. Most of NBC's best-known correspondents and news anchors, including John Chancellor, Frank McGee, Jessica Savitch, and Tom Brokaw, served as "Today Show" hosts. In 1976, Barbara Walters left the *Today Show* to become co-anchor of *ABC Evening News*, with Harry Reasoner. In 2006, *Today Show* host Katie Couric moved to CBS to anchor its evening news program.

Today also was significant for bringing women into television. In 1953, female guest hosts were added to the program's all-male on-air team. Some of the first women seen on TV in a public affairs setting were author Joyce Brothers, consumer expert Betty Furness, and numerous entertainers including Estelle Parsons, Helen O'Connell, and Betsy Palmer. This rotating arrangement continued until 1964 when Barbara Walters was given a permanent *Today Show* role.

The program contributed as a news source as a day's first account of national and world events. Newscasts began and ended each half-hour segment. Benefiting *Today* were NBC correspondents and facilities all over the world. News on *Today* was most prominent during developing major national and international stories such as the Cuban Missile Crisis in 1962 and the Iran Hostage Crisis in 1980. Viewers who had been asleep had tuned to *Today* for overnight developments. Many people watched the terrorist attacks of September 11, 2001, unfold live on the *Today Show.*

Today was launched in 1952 with Chicago TV personality Dave Garroway as host. Sports announcer Jack Lescoulie also appeared. A chimpanzee named J. Fred Muggs brought comic relief. Each half-hour cycle opened with a live camera view of crowds on the street at NBC headquarters in New York's Rockefeller Center. Helped by the chimp, Garroway and Lescoulie gave *Today* its relaxed yet serious style. John Chancellor succeeded Garroway in 1961. When Chancellor became an NBC foreign correspondent in 1962, announcer Hugh Downs advanced.

Today reached its largest audiences in the 1960s and early 1970s with Downs and Walters as co-hosts. In 1967, sport wit Joe Garagiola became a third member of the team. Audiences savored Walters's revealing interviews with entertainers and world leaders. It was on *Today* that most Americans saw the first scenes of overnight violence that in the 1960s had rocked major cities. Because night had reached Asia, viewers awoke to each day's news from the Vietnam War. In addition, *Today* joined with NBC News in televising the feats of John Glenn and other early astronauts. The first space missions were morning events. *Today* won Emmy Awards in 1966, 1968, and 1970.

The program's continued to flourish in 1971 after Downs was hired by ABC News. Joining Walters and Garagiola was Frank McGee, one of NBC's most popular news figures. In 1972, *Today* provided some of the first scenes inside the People's Republic of China. A *Today* crew was selected to accompany President Richard Nixon during Nixon's historic visits with Mao Tse-tung and Chou En-lai.

Fortunes changed in 1976. As noted, Walters followed Downs to ABC. On ABC's *20/20*, Downs and Walters would team for twenty more years. More ominous for *Today* was ABC's 1976 launch of a rival program called *Good Morning America*. A new *Today* team of Brokaw and Jane Pauley could not stop a loss of viewers to ABC. *Good Morning America* was produced by ABC's entertainment division and hosted by Hollywood actor David Hartman.

In 1977, NBC briefly experimented with an all-female team of Pauley and Jessica Savitch. During the 1980s and 1990s, as ratings still tumbled, *Today* assignments passed from Brokaw and Pauley to Chris Wallace, Linda Ellerbee, Bryant Gumbel, and Deborah Norville. As hosts were replaced, the most popular *Today* figures became weather-caster Willard Scott and movie critic Gene Shalit. A cloud hung over the program when the public learned that Gumbel had tried to have Scott and Shalit removed.

Further challenge came in 1986 when Fox television began. In 1994 Fox acquired powerful TV stations in most cities. Rather than a national morning program, Fox had each station develop its own version of *Today*. These local programs multiplied and claimed the highest ratings. For the first time, viewers in all regions saw live morning programming. In the West, *Today* viewers had not seen live TV but a recording of telecast made three hours earlier in New York. The local programs concentrated on weather, traffic, and school closure information that *Today* could not provide.

Despite increased competition, *Today* again became the main source of national and world news in the morning period. In 1996, the program reclaimed first place in the national audience ratings when Couric and Matt Lauer were paired. Couric and Lauer became prominent TV celebrities. The weekday program expanded to three hours (7a.m.–10 a.m.). Weekend *Today* broadcasts began. In 2000, *Today* reprised its 1952 innovation of showing crowds in Rockefeller Center. Upstairs studios were abandoned. The entire program was televised from a streetside location.

Today was honored as a landmark when broadcasters observed its fiftieth anniversary in 2002. Of television's hundreds of thousands of programs, only one other, NBC's *Meet the Press* started in 1947, had been seen for a longer period.

Further Reading

Davis, Gerry. *The Today Show: An Anecdotal History*. New York: Morrow, 1987.

Kessler, Judy. *Inside Today: The Battle for the Morning*. New York: Villard Books, 1992.

Metz, Robert. *The Today Show: An Inside Look at 25 Tumultuous Years ... and the Colorful and Controverial People Behind the Scenes*. Chicago: Playboy Press, 1977.

CRAIG ALLEN

TRAVEL JOURNALISM

Travel and travel accounts began with the first Americans. Native Americans recorded their many trips in oral and pictographic ways, a way of communication revived and expanded in the late nineteenth and twentieth centuries by means of photography, radio, and television. Travel narratives often framed oral legends that sought to explain origins, as in the case of a trip down the Colorado River by a young Hopi Indian to find a bride and through that marriage introduce to his people the Snake clan. Europeans brought with them written language. Through it they produced narratives of exploring expeditions. Later, Europeans often submitted reports in the form of diaries or travel accounts in an effort to describe the land and its inhabitants to prospective settlers or investors or to summarize diplomatic missions to Native American groups.

The Nineteenth Century: Reading, Writing, and Travel

A major culture of reading, writing, and travel emerged in the nineteenth century. The writer and critic H.T. Tuckerman observed in 1868 that "if the social history of the world is ever written, the era in which we live will be called the nomadic period." He cited the advent of ocean steam navigation, the railway, electricity, and the telegraph as innovations that encouraged writing and reading about travel and travel itself. He also included as encouragements leisure and money. "When we analyze the motives of our American nomadic tribe, we find, first of all, that many of the individuals thereof have made money, and naturally wish to enjoy it."

Newspapers and periodical publications formed part of this culture and endeavored to help people decide the great question, as Tuckerman put it: "To go or not to go." Monthly publications included articles and essays on foreign travel and places, and they published copious excerpts from travel books, almost two thousand of which were published, according to William Stone, before 1900. The first issue of *North American Review* (1815) contained an article on Paris and the French, and *Scribner's Monthly* ran a series of articles on a number of European cities later in the century. *New England Magazine* and *American Monthly Magazine* offered their readers travel sketches written by Nathaniel Hawthorne. Editor for fifteen years at the *Atlantic Monthly*, novelist William Dean Howells, traveled to Europe and wrote about his time there in *Venetian Life* (1866) and *Italian Journeys* (1867). Beginning in 1870, the *Nation* and *Atlantic Monthly* published some of the first travel sketches of Henry James. He followed these with book-length travel accounts and in 1907 published what some regard as his most remarkable travel book, *An American Scene*, composed after a long absence from the United States.

Newspapers employed writers to travel and to publish. The *New York Tribune*, a paper founded by Horace Greeley, joined the *Saturday Evening Post* to encourage Bayard Taylor to go to Europe. Greeley asked Taylor to send back sketches of German life and society. Editor of the transcendentalist journal *Dial*, Margaret Fuller, traveled in Europe and published letters and pieces in the *Tribune*, many of them recounting events associated with the 1848 revolutions. In the early 1850s, the California newspaper *Alta California* told Samuel Clemens (Mark Twain) to go to Europe and compose travel letters "'on such subjects and from such places as will best suit him.'" He set sail on board *The Quaker City* with other "pilgrims," as he called them, and produced accounts of the trip that enabled him to hone his skills as an entertaining, satiric but insightful observer of people and their ways. Ultimately these pieces became part of *The Innocents Abroad*, the first of five travel books he wrote. Greeley himself went to Europe and wrote a series of letters addressed to the "reading class." He published them as a book, *Glances at Europe* (1851). He also went west and recounted his experiences in articles and eventually a book, *Overland Journey from New York to San Francisco* (1860).

The Twentieth Century and Beyond: Mass Travel and Travel Journalism

Rapid demographic and economic growth continued throughout the nineteenth century and into the twentieth and with it the transformation of travel into mass tourism. Many more people had wealth and leisure to spend on travel. New ways of getting about—the automobile and the airplane—became available. To serve and shape this group, a tourist industry took form. In the 1840s, the Englishman Thomas Cook set an example to be followed elsewhere. He saw potential in the new railroads and began to organize large group tours. He ran an excursion train from Leicester to Loughborough in England on July 5, 1841, a distance of twelve miles. Five hundred seventy people took part. Cook then went on to make a business of travel as a travel agent and author of guidebooks.

Less sophisticated magazines and newspapers than some of those mentioned above played a major role in the creation of a national mass culture for travel and leisure activity in the United States. Beginning in the 1880s, magazines such as *Ladies Home Journal, Cosmopolitan, McClure's,* and *Collier's* joined the *Saturday Evening Post*, which had been in existence since 1821, to play an important role in shaping this culture. Innovative publishing technologies and aggressive marketing strategies undertaken by such people as the publishers William Randolph Hearst and Joseph Pulitzer made the newspaper the journalistic counterpart of F. W. Woolworth's "Five and Ten Cent Store." These publications made travel an important part of their content.

Magazines devoted exclusively to travel began to appear. Of these, the *National Geographic* became the best known and most successful. Beginning in 1888 as a scientific journal with limited appeal, it quickly abandoned that format to become a glossy publication with a reputation for being impartial and genteel, occupying, "a space between science and entertainment" (Lutz and Collins 1993) and appealing to Americans increased interest in the larger world after the Spanish-American War and the acquisition of new territorial possessions. It took advantage of new photoengraving technology to make vivid photos its principal appeal to a mass audience. Its first photos appeared in 1896, and in 1905 it published photographs of the forbidden city of Lhasa, Tibet. Its first nature photographs appeared in 1926, introducing a dimension to the magazine that became a more important focus in the last quarter of the century as people became more aware of threats to the health of the planet. In 1984, it launched a new magazine, the *National Geographic Traveler*, designed to encourage readers, in the words of the editor of *National Geographic*, Gilbert Grovesner, "to go and experience first hand" what before they might only have read about in the pages of the *Geographic*. *National Geographic* found the moving pictorial images of television congenial as a way to augment its reach through a series of programs for that medium.

Mass media complemented mass tourism. Newspapers began to include travel sections, and the larger ones made use of many people to provide articles. The advent of the automobile brought about organizations such as the American Automobile Association and such publications as *Westways*, which began describing itineraries and advocating better roads in the first decade of the twentieth century. Before 1945, magazines ran advertisements for popular car models that stressed the delights of a weekend or Sunday motor excursion into the country at a time before the car culture transformed—in the words of James Kunstler—much of the American landscape into "a geography of nowhere." A plethora of travel magazines entered the market with such names as *Holiday, Travel & Leisure, Trailer Travel* to appeal to this culture and even suggest other types of journeys. Magazines such as *Arizona Highways* and *Nevada Magazine* appeared to promote travel in particular states. As travel and tourism expanded, especially after World War II, some newspapers—particularly in the West—and regional publications such as *High Country News* and *Northern Lights* began to discuss issues related to tourism: its potential as an alternative to environmentally damaging extractive industries, as a threat to the environment itself if not carefully managed, or as a kind of "devil's bargain," a selling of place, history, and cultural identity in exchange for seasonal low-wage employment.

Beginning in the 1920s, radio and television offered themselves as new means for people to access information and diversion. Both produced notable travel personalities and journalists. Perhaps the most successful of these was the radio personality, Lowell Thomas, Jr. Before his long radio career, Thomas had established a reputation as both a world traveler and an effective speaker. While in the Middle East he had met Thomas Edward Lawrence and won his confidence. His talks about those experiences in such places as the Royal Albert Hall in London attracted large audiences. William Paley of the Columbia Broadcasting System took note and in 1931 asked Thomas to talk extemporaneously for fifteen minutes in front of a microphone. Thomas proceeded to talk about his experiences in India, about pygmies in Malaya, and mysterious ceremonies in Afghanistan. His performance impressed Paley, who offered him a job. Thus began "the longest continual daily broadcast in the history of radio," according to Norman Bowen. Thomas's programs mixed news and travel and were transmitted from mountain tops, the depths of salt mines, from ships at sea, and from airplanes. A highlight of his radio career came in the 1950s when he traveled to what had been the forbidden land of Tibet in response to an invitation from its government then feeling threatened by China. On the occasion of a dinner in his honor in 1965, Walter Cronkite, the event's chair, read a letter from former President Harry Truman in which Truman dubbed Thomas "the Methuselah of radio broadcasts."

Few, if any, television personalities could match Thomas' range and influence. One person who came close was Charles Kuralt, whose "On the Road" program had a lengthy career and represents some of the best that television came to offer in the way of informational travel journalism. Kuralt developed in-depth television essays on people and places he found interesting and representative of a certain diversity in America at a time of growing homogenization of both landscape and culture. Pictures and the spoken word made up these essays, but Kuralt decided to write a book about these travels, for as he put it "television journalism is no field to enter if you have intimations of immortality; one's best work vanishes at the speed of light, literally."

Television expanded to include cable, with channels numbering in the hundreds and including some devoted exclusively to travel. The 1990s saw the addition of the computer as a standard household fixture and with it access to the Internet which increasingly became one of if not the principal ways people accessed information and ideas. With expanding numbers of cable channels and the spread of the Internet, a form of niche journalism devoted to travel also grew. While some commentators concluded that the rapid developments communication and transportation had made the world one neighborhood, other writers such as the historian Paul Fussel concluded that not all these changes were for the good and that by the late twentieth century, travel in the old sense of the word had become impossible.

After World War II, at least two organizations came into existence to further the professional development of travel journalists and engage issues related to their work and their subject. In the 1956, a Society of American Travel Journalists formed and now numbers over thirteen hundred. It sponsors annual "Lowell Thomas Awards" for distinguished travel writing and coverage. In 1991, two New Jersey travel writers, Bob Nesoff and Dan Schossberg, established the North American Travel Journalists Association. It aimed to promote the professional development of members, which within ten years numbered about five hundred, and to meet the demands of the travel industry. It held annual meetings, sponsored an annual travel journalist's competition, and published, with MSNBC Travel, *Travelworld Magazine*.

Further Reading

Barnes, Trevor J., and James S. Duncan, eds. *Writing Worlds: Discourse, Text, and Metaphor in the Representation of Landscape*. London and New York: Routledge, 1992.

Bowen, Norman R., ed. *Lowell Thomas: The Stranger Everyone Knows*. Garden City, NY: Doubleday & Company, Inc., 1968.

Cole, Garold L. *Travels in America From the Voyages of Discovery to the Present: An Annotated Bibliography of Travel Articles in Periodicals, 1955—1980*. Norman: University of Oklahoma Press, 1984.

Dorson, Richard M. *America Begins: Early American Writing*. New York: Pantheon, 1950.

Dulles, Foster Rea. *Americans Abroad: Two Centuries of European Travel*. Ann Arbor: University of Michigan Press, 1964.

Edmonds, Margot, and Ella E. Clark. *Voices of the Winds: Native American Legends*. New York: Facts on File, Inc., 1989.

Fussell, Paul, ed. *The Norton Book of Travel*. New York: Norton, 1987.

Hulme, Peter, and Tim Youngs, eds. *The Cambridge Companion to Travel Writing*. New York: Cambridge University Press, 2002.

Kunstler, James Howard. *The Geography of Nowhere: The Rise and Fall of America's Man-Made Landscape*. New York: Touchstone, 1993.

Kuralt, Charles. *On the Road with Charles Kuralt*. New York: Putnam's, 1985.

Lutz, Catherine A., and Jane L. Collins. *Reading National Geographic*. Chicago: University of Chicago Press, 1993.

Norris, Scott, ed. *Discovered Country: Tourism and Survival in the West*. Albuquerque: Stone Ladder Press, 1997.

Ohmann, Richard. *Selling Culture: Magazines, Markets, and the Class at the Turn of the Century*. New York: Verso, 1996.

Rothman, Hal K. *Devil's Bargains: Tourism in the Twentieth-Century American West*. Lawrence: University Press of Kansas, 1998.

Tuckerman, H. T. *America and her Commentators. With a Critical Sketch of Travel in the United States*. New York: Charles Scribner. 1864.

——. "Going Abroad." *Putnam's Magazine* (Jan.–June 1869), 530–538.

Warhus, Mark. *Another America: Native American Maps and the History of Our Land*. New York: St. Martin's Press, 1997.

Ziff, Larzer. *Return Passages: Great American Travel Writing, 1780–1910*. New Haven, CT: Yale University Press, 2000.

CHARLES A. WEEKS

TRUTH IN ADVERTISING

Established members of the advertising community sought to protect consumers, force disreputable competitors out of business, and embellish their own image through a truth-in-advertising campaign in the early twentieth century.

Many advertisements in the late nineteenth century were "outright lies," historian Daniel Pope has noted. Hawking miracle-working patent medicines or elaborate get-rich-quick schemes to unsuspecting consumers, these types of advertisements sullied the reputations of legitimate advertisers. Reading notices, disguised advertisements appearing as news in newspapers and magazines, also came under attack for being fraudulent, misleading, deceitful, and dishonest.

Recognizing the validity of these accusations and their deleterious effect on the industry, established advertisers formed the Associated Advertising Clubs of America (AACA) in 1906 to improve the industry's ethical standards and to promote professionalism. Driven by the Progressive Era belief that publicity could solve problems, this national organization pushed for truth in advertising at its 1911 convention.

By this time, the industry was ready to confront the problem through government regulation. *Printers' Ink*, the leading advertising journal founded by George P. Rowell in 1888, became the chief advocate for the truth-in-advertising movement soon after the convention. The journal promoted truth in advertising using the "rotten apple" theory. One wrong statement in an advertisement undermined consumers' confidence in all ads, and one discredited advertiser harmed all advertisers.

Printers' Ink editor John Romer asked attorney Harry Nims, author of *Nims on Unfair Competition*, to write a model statute outlawing dishonest advertising. Recommending state, not federal, legislation to take advantage of the local advertising clubs, Nims drafted a 153-word sentence making it a misdemeanor for any one selling a product whose "advertisement contains any assertion, representation or statement of fact which is untrue, deceptive or misleading." The local clubs could monitor advertisements and investigate complaints, Nims reasoned. Following up on his idea, AACA leaders formed a national vigilance committee in 1912 to encourage local clubs to begin their own "vigilance" work. By mid-1914, about one hundred local committees were active around the country.

At the same time, *Printers' Ink* lobbied state legislatures to enact the truth-in-advertising statute. Ohio was the first state to enact the law in 1913, followed by Minnesota, after a particularly active local advertising club fought for it. By 1921, twenty-three states had adopted the statute outlawing fraudulent advertising, though some diluted its provisions.

Critics complained that the laws did not go far enough in regulating the advertising industry because they did not prohibit exaggerated advertising claims nor did they address the subtly persuasive techniques becoming more popular such as appealing to body image or status symbols. Some critics also thought national legislation would have been more effective at cleansing the marketplace of fraudulent advertisers. The Federal Trade Commission, created by Congress in 1914, eventually filled this role, though initially it focused on protecting businesses—not consumers—from unfair competition.

By World War I, the advertising industry had moved beyond the truth-in-advertising movement to emphasize service during the national crisis. Soon after, the local advertising clubs evolved into the Better Business Bureau.

Although the truth-in-advertising campaign and subsequent *Printers' Ink* statutes did not dramatically alter the nature of American advertising, they did help to purge the industry of the most blatant abuses. Language from the model statute also contributed key elements to the modern definition of what constitutes deceptive advertising.

Further Reading

Presbrey, Frank. *The History and Development of Advertising.* Garden City, NY: Doubleday, Doran & Company, Inc., 1929.

Fox, Stephen. *The Mirror Makers: A History of American Advertising and Its Creators.* New York; William Morrow and Company, Inc., 1984.

Pope, Daniel. *Making of Modern Advertising.* New York: Basic Books, Inc., 1983.

Printers' Ink: A Journal for Advertisers; 50 Years, 1888–1938. New York: Printers' Ink Publishing Company, 1938.

Schultze, Quentin J. "'An Honorable Place': The Quest for Professional Advertising Education, 1900–1917." *Business History Review* 56 no. 1 (Spring 1982): 16–32.

LINDA LAWSON

TURNER, GEORGE KIBBE

The daughters of the poor "flood east through narrow streets in a winter's twilight," George Kibbe Turner (1869–1952) wrote, "returning to their homes in the East Side tenements. The exploitation of young women as money-making machines has reached a development on the East Side of New York probably equaled not anywhere in the world" (Weinberg and Weinberg 1961, 420). Turner's investigation of Tammany Hall's determination to "wholesale the bodies" of the daughters of the poor "at good profit" and to push their plan nationwide (Weinberg and Weinberg 1961, 429) would contribute to passage of the Mann Act making it a federal crime to transport women across state lines for purposes of prostitution.

One of the Progressive Era's most effective muckrakers, Turner was born in Quincy, Illinois, the son of Rhodolphus K. Turner, a real estate broker, and Sarah Ella Kibbe Turner. Turner's lifelong interest in Progressive causes was stirred at Williams College, where he graduated in 1890, and during a fifteen-year apprenticeship as a reporter at the *Springfield* (Massachusetts) *Republican* under taskmaster Samuel Bowles. Turner became a contributor to *McClure's Magazine* in 1899 and a staff writer seven years later, specializing in urban problems.

In 1906, Turner traveled to Galveston, Texas, to report on the aftermath of the September, 1900, hurricane that killed six thousand of the town's thirty-seven thousand residents, and destroyed half the homes and businesses. Later that year, Turner wrote in *McClure's* about a "revolution in local government," established when local commissioners successfully oversaw the city's rebuilding (*McClure's Magazine*, October 1906, 611). The construction of a seawall, the raising of the city's grade, and the building of a causeway connecting the island to the mainland converted Turner to the cause of commission government. Twelve million copies of his article were reprinted and in the decade-long debate that followed more than three hundred cities experimented in non-partisan commission forms of government.

Turner reported on Chicago's "dealers in dissipation" in 1907, and observed that "the basic guarantees of civilization" had broken down (Kibbe 1907, 576–577). He uncovered a citywide conspiracy involving ward politicians, police, and the courts, that netted liquor, prostitution, and gambling interests $135 million annually. Turner's reporting prompted civic reformers to demand action. Chicago's vice commission, launched in 1910, became the model for Progressive-minded reforms in cities across America.

Public reaction to Turner's muckraking was even more immediate in 1909 after *McClure's* published his article "Tammany's Control of New York by Professional Criminals" that alleged the complicity of city officials in New York's growing prostitution problem. "Daughters of the Poor," published in *McClure's* five months later, detailed the "closely organized machine" of slum politicians that preyed upon New York's tenement population while exporting procurement to other large cities (Weinberg and Weinberg

1961, 412–413). In January 1910, Turner was subpoenaed for two days of testimony before a grand jury investigating organized crime in the city. The publicity led to Congressional passage of the Mann Act on June 25, 1910, and vice commission initiatives in Minneapolis, Portland, Hartford, and other American cities.

Turner muckraked corporate capitalism for *McClure's* in a seven-part series co-written with John Moody between 1910 and 1911. Thereafter, he turned to fiction and film scripts. Turner married Julia Hawks Parker in 1892. Some historians see Turner as the author who contributed to the moral panics stemming from America's uncertain encounter with modernity. Others see him as one of the most effective muckraking reformers of the Progressive Era.

Further Reading

Bridges, Lamar W. "George Kibbe Turner of *McClure's Magazine*." *Journalism Quarterly* 61, 1984.

Filler, Louis *Crusaders for American Liberalism*. New York: Harcourt, Brace, 1939.

New York Times, February 16, 1952.

Turner, George Kibbe. "The City of Chicago: A Study of the Great Immoralities." *McClure's Magazine*, April 1907.

——. "The Daughters of the Poor." *McClure's Magazine*, November 1909.

——. "Galveston: A Business Corporation." *McClure's Magazine*, October 1906.

——. "The Men Who Learned to Fly." *McClure's Magazine*, February 1908.

Weinberg, Arthur, and Lila Weinberg, eds. *The Muckrakers: The Era in Journalism That Moved America to Reform*. New York: Simon and Schuster, 1961.

Wilson, Harold S. *McClure's Magazine and the Muckrakers*. Princeton, NJ: Princeton University, 1970.

BRUCE J. EVENSEN

TURNER, TED

Born Robert Edward Turner III on November 19, 1938, in Cincinnati, Ted Turner began in the media by selling space on his father's billboards. When Turner was twenty-four, he became president of Turner Advertising when his hard-driving father committed suicide in 1963. The young Turner built his father's ailing billboard business into a multibillion-dollar media empire, which included the first twenty-four-hour television news channel. In 1995, he merged his Turner Broadcasting Company with Time Warner in exchange for a reported $7.5 billion and corporate vice presidency in charge of cable operations.

In the early 1970s, Turner purchased WTCG (Channel 17), a struggling Atlanta UHF television station losing more than $600,000 a year when people were not used to turning to the high channels. If that were not enough, he purchased a failing Charlotte station with a higher UHF channel number. He then negotiated with the Atlanta Braves to offer them regional coverage through cooperation with other stations, including Charlotte. Both Turner and the Braves gained from the exposure; Turner eventually bought the team and the Atlanta Hawks of the NBA.

Turner changed his Atlanta station to WTBS (for Turner Broadcasting System) and transmitted it to local cable companies via satellite. Turner paid only for use of the programs in one market, even though a satellite beamed his superstation's signal worldwide. Local stations complained that Turner's use of the same programs that they bought in syndication was unfair competition. Always identifying with the underdogs, Turner said he represented people in rural areas and small towns who had no local stations. They argued that Turner ought to pay more for retransmission covering so many markets at one time. Turner won the first round with congressional inaction.

Turner often criticized the major networks for corrupting American morals, but his alternative provided baseball, professional wrestling, recycled network shows and old movies, some showing more violence than network television. With his own station, he seemed indifferent, even hostile, to news, until he hit on the idea that the world needed access to news for twenty-four hours a day.

While the major networks were cutting their worldwide presence, Turner began building the Cable News Network (CNN), which went on the air June 1, 1980, with an emphasis on live reporting. Turner knew nothing about the techniques or ethics of news, but he hired experienced and committed journalists at a time the major networks were cutting them.

Reese Schonfeld, who had worked for UPI Television and UPI Movietone news, taught Turner the news business and some basic news concepts, such as preventing advertisers from having veto power over anchor selection and persuading Turner from using his news channel to further his own personal agenda. CNN's executives believed they could succeed in Atlanta (away from New York) because they had a dedicated, non-union staff. The low-budget operation made many mistakes at first, allowing critics to say CNN meant Chaos News Network and Chicken Noodle Network. Clearly, the critics underestimated the appeal of live remotes from hot spots around the world. On December 31, 1981, he opened a second channel, CNN Headline News that provided news summaries and updates every half hour.

When the Gulf War began in early 1991, CNN's crew, including reporters Peter Arnett, Bernard Shaw, and John Holliman were the only ones allowed to remain broadcasting from Baghdad, even while American planes bombed the city. As the world watched the war live on television, some network affiliates took CNN feeds along with those from their own networks. At the same time, however, American military leaders severely restricted reporters' access to the troops. The war, followed by other dramatic events covered live, like the murder trial of sports celebrity O.J. Simpson and the siege of the Branch Davidian compound near Waco, Texas, established CNN's reputation and made it profitable. Live television gave international terrorists an immediate audience for bizarre hostage taking and other dramas. CNN also gave extensive coverage to other, perhaps less significant stories such as the trial involving Lorena and John Wayne Bobbitt in 1993–1994 and to the Nancy Kerrigan-Tonya Harding scandal in 1994.

Before his merger with Time Warner, Turner threatened to buy CBS to return it to traditional values and, at the same time, Rupert Murdoch in 1995 promised to create an alternative Fox News channel that would be more conservative than Turner's. In the same year, Turner and Murdoch got into a legal battle over which all-news channel would get access to New York City's cable system operated by Time Warner. The feud got messy, as the *New York Times* wrote: "Ted Turner was likening Rupert Murdoch to Hitler, Mr. Murdoch was running cartoons in *The New York Post* portraying Mr. Turner as a straitjacketed nutcase, and Mr. Turner's wife, Jane Fonda, was dissing Rudolph Giuliani's wife, Donna Hanover. And that's when everyone was still on the high road."

As a sailor, Turner often won and hated to lose. Turner took up sailing as a teenager and won the America's Cup in 1977. He won Britain's Fastnet race in 1979 in a storm that smashed other yachts and killed other participants. With CNN in the planning stage, executives thought their plan may be scuttled when they heard news reports that Turner himself was missing during that storm.

Hoping to get into movies, Turner purchased the financially troubled MGM studios in 1986. Although he did not realize how troubled, he acquired an incredible archive that provided the content for several cable networks, including WTBS, Turner Network Televison (TNT), Turner Classic Movies, and, after the purchase of Hanna-Barbera, the Cartoon Network. Under pressure to meet payments on his MGM purchase, Turner ceded some control over Turner Broadcasting Sytem to a group of cable operators and began investing in land. He tried unsuccessfully to buy CBS Television. In 1995, Turner merged with Time Warner, owner of cable companies, providing a distribution method for Turner's movies.

Turner's private life was often stormy. His first marriage in 1960 was to Judy Nye, whom he met during a sailing regatta in which he defeated her; she was one of the few female skippers competing in 1959. They had two children, Laura Lee and Robert Edward Turner IV. Ted and Judy divorced soon after his father's death. Ted married Jane Smith from Birmingham, Alabama, on June 2, 1964. They had three children. After the failure of his second marriage and some very public affairs, Turner married the actress Jane Fonda December 21, 1991, and they increased their land and livestock holdings. By early 1997, they owned 1.3 million acres in ranches in Montana, New Mexico, and Nebraska, placing them among the nation's top landowners. They began stocking their Flying D ranch near Bozeman, Montana, with bison. They ran 12,000 bison on their 107,000-acre ranch and charged hunters $9,500 per animal they took. Turner and Fonda divorced in 2001 and, in 2002, he opened the first Montana Grill, a restaurant promoting bison meat.

In 2003, Turner announced that he would step down as vice chairman of AOL Time Warner. Although he initially supported the merger of AOL with Time Warner Communications, Turner lost billions when the stock of the merged company dropped in value.

Further Reading

Auletta, Ken. *Media Man: Ted Turner's Improbable Empire.* New York: W. W. Norton & Company, 2004.

Bibb, Porter. *It Ain't as Easy as It Looks: Ted Turner's Amazing Story* New York: Crown Publishers, Inc., 1993.

Goldberg, Robert, and Gerald Jay Goldberg. *Citizen Turner: The Wild Rise of an American Tycoon.* New York: Harcourt Brace and Company, 1995.

Schonfeld, Reese. *Me and Ted Against the World: The Unauthorized Story of the Founding of CNN.* New York: Collins, 2001.

Smith, Perry M. *How CNN Fought the War: A View from the Inside* New York: Birch Lane Press, 1991.

Whittemore, Hank. *CNN: The Inside Story: How a Band of Mavericks Changed the Face of Television News.* Boston: Little, Brown and Company, 1990.

Williams, Christian. *Lead, Follow or Get Out of the Way: The Story of Ted Turner* New York: Times Books, 1981.

WILLIAM E. HUNTZICKER

TV GUIDE

Once the "bible" for television's most faithful audience, *TV Guide* is a national weekly entertainment magazine that combines local program listings for network, cable, and paid television with celebrity interviews and articles on popular television shows. Currently owned by News Corp. and available for delivery in only the United States, the magazine was an outlet for highly opinionated political commentary in the past, but, in keeping with the larger trend in media over the last decade, today's *TV Guide* comfortably accommodates to the contemporary obsession with entertainment celebrities.

The magazine was founded in the early 1950s by publishing entrepreneur Walter Annenberg (also owner of the *Philadelphia Inquirer* and the *Daily Racing Form*, a former U.S. ambassador to Great Britain, and a noted philanthropist). In 1952, after purchasing three local television guidebooks (Chicago's *Television Forecast,* Philadelphia's *Local Televiser,* and New York's *Television Guide*) that had been introduced in 1948, Annenberg combined them into a national publication that used identical feature content for all editions and customized local channel listings for each city.

The first national issue of *TV Guide* hit the newsstands on April 3, 1953, with Lucille Ball and her son, Desi Arnaz, on the cover. Approximately 1,560,000 copies were distributed in 10 cities, an initial circulation that only reached a fraction of the 25 million television households in the United States at the time.

In concert with the enormous popularity of television, *TV Guide* was a major publishing success. One interesting aspect of its early success was the fact that in the 1950s many newspapers, reluctant to promote what they perceived to be a new media competitor, refused to include TV listings. As a result, *TV Guide* was for a while the only available source for what was on TV. And television itself was changing the values for American homes, with popular shows such as *Leave it to Beaver* and *American Bandstand* portraying the perfect on-screen families that viewers hoped to emulate. Television became increasingly popular in 1954, when color sets came into being, and by the 1960s millions of viewers began tuning in to the hit programs featured within the pages of *TV Guide*, including the popular Sunday evening variety show *The Ed Sullivan Show* and the renowned sitcom *I Love Lucy*.

In the decades following its birth, as the number of households owning a television set reached 97 percent by the mid-1970s, the interest in *TV Guide* was also experiencing a steady increase in numbers throughout the country. By the time the publication achieved its peak circulation of twenty million in 1977, it could claim to be the largest-selling magazine in the world, and observers speculated that Annenberg was making one million dollars a week from the publication.

In its early years, *TV Guide* saw itself as a guardian of the public taste, harshly judging television shows that its editors considered to be beneath the American public's intelligence. For example, it often criticized the game shows and the high number of westerns that dominated the network schedules. Moreover, the magazine promoted the concept of what was called "dialsmanship," encouraging its readers to make informed viewing choices. In keeping with a belief in the television's potential for information as well as entertainment, in the late 1950s and early 1960s, *TV Guide* employed such celebrated critics as Cleveland Amory and Judith Crist, and published "think pieces" by such authors as sociologist Margaret Mead, novelist John Updike, and even John F. Kennedy. In the 1970s, to remain consistent with Annenberg's loyalty to the Republican Party, the magazine published columns by Pat Buchanan and an essay by then-Vice President Spiro Agnew.

A few years later in 1982, *TV Guide* experienced one of its finest hours when it published an article that indicted CBS News for airing a poorly reported and biased documentary, *The Uncounted Enemy: A Vietnam Deception*, accusing General William Westmoreland of lying to Americans concerning the strength of the Viet Cong troops in the months before the 1968 Tet offensive. Afterwards, CBS News admitted that it had violated its own in-house guidelines for investigative pieces, and Westmoreland eventually filed a $120 million libel suit against CBS. After an eighteen-week jury trial in New York City, however, Westmoreland and CBS mutually agreed to an undisclosed private settlement.

In 1989, Annenberg sold *TV Guide* magazine, along with his other properties, to fellow media mogul Rupert Murdoch for $3 billion. By the time of the sale, however, the publication was no longer known for its more enterprising forms of journalism. Celebrity pieces had in large part replaced *TV Guide*'s critical essays and investigative reporting, and soon the magazine's editorial department was moved from Radnor, Pennsylvania, to New York City.

In the mid-1990s, a new editor, Steven Reddicliffe, was hired to improve newsstand sales. With a background at *Entertainment Weekly* and *Parenting* magazines, Reddicliffe stressed what was termed the "collectible factor." Individual issues of the magazine began to focus on specific personalities and events (e.g., NASCAR racers, boy bands, etc.) and the line between television and movies was blurred. As a result of these editorial changes, the magazine's balance sheet showed some improvement, and in the late 1990s, the magazine was merged with United Video Satellite Group to form a broadcast television version of its programming grids. In 2000, Gemstar purchased the magazine, a move that allowed the new *TV Guide* to list VCR codes for programming along with broadcast dates, times, and synopses.

In the midst of these content and ownership shifts at the magazine, television itself was clearly undergoing a major transformation. The three major networks lost their dominance, cable and satellite options proliferated, and viewership became divided into increasingly smaller segments. In addition, listings competition from Internet sites forced the magazine to publish 126 different weekly editions to encompass every one of its regional variations in programming.

Despite its best efforts, the magazine's prospects at the opening of the twenty-first century were somewhat clouded. Circulation problems included a drop of 30 percent to nine million subscribers. Even more troubling given all the changes in the television landscape of the last decade, there was, according to some observers, some uncertainty as to who was the publication's primary readership. This in turn depressed advertising rates; by way of illustration, the cost per thousand for an advertisement in the magazine (the standard measure of value in the media industry) was approximately $12, compared to $40 for the average consumer magazine in America.

Looking to the future, it is hard to predict what might lie ahead for the publication. Its stock price has over time declined considerably, from a high of $80 a share to somewhere below $15. Founded just over fifty years ago at the dawn of the then-new medium of television, *TV Guide*'s program listings have always been the magazine's raison d'etre. What's on TV tonight? The nation wanted to know, and, for more that five decades, *TV Guide* told them. But given both the variety of informational sources available today and the fractionalization of television programming itself, the role of a single integrated national print product is far from certain.

Further Reading

Altschuler, Glenn C., and David I. Grossvogel. *Changing Channels: America in TV Guide*. Champaign, IL: University of Illinois Press, 1992.

Baker, Russ. "Murdoch's Mean Machine." *Columbia Journalism Review* 37, no. 1 (1998): 51–56.

Editors of TV Guide and Adam West. *TV Guide Guide to TV: The Most Definitive Encyclopedia of Television*. New York: Barnes & Noble Books, 2004.

Harris, Jay S., ed. *TV Guide: The First 25 Years*. New York: Simon & Schuster, 1978.

Lasswell, Mark and TV Guide. *TV Guide: Fifty Years of Television*. New York: Crown Publishing Group, 2002.

DAVID ABRAHAMSON
HAIWEN LU

U.S. INFORMATION AGENCY

As the United States government's primary overt propaganda agency throughout the Cold War, the U.S. Information Agency (USIA) (1953–1999) has had a subtle, yet sustained influence on U.S. and international journalism since the late 1940s.

The U.S. Information and Education Exchange Act (Public Law 402), better known as the Smith-Mundt Act of 1948, established the program mandate for American information and cultural programs abroad. Under this act, President Dwight D. Eisenhower created the USIA on August 3, 1953, as an independent government agency for conduct of most officially sponsored publicity and information programs overseas. The new agency brought together the USIA's administrative staff, an overseas arm known as the U.S. Information Service (USIS), and the government's single largest news and information project, the Voice of America (VOA), to coordinate publicly acknowledged "information activities" designed to promote U.S. national security interests during the emerging Cold War.

The USIA did not control well-known propaganda and information programs such as Radio Free Europe and Radio Liberty, however. For most of their existence, those projects were secretly operated by the Central Intelligence Agency as ostensibly private, civilian organizations. The U.S. Department of Defense also conducted both publicly acknowledged and covert information operations independent of the USIA, particularly in war zones and areas under military occupation.

In 1999, most of USIA was reorganized as a branch of the U.S. Department of State for conduct of what are now known as "public diplomacy" activities overseas. Those operations are now led by the under secretary of state for Public Diplomacy and Public Affairs. A newly created U.S. Broadcasting Board of Governors took control of most government-funded broadcasting, including the Voice of America radio network and its television and film distribution arm, Worldnet.

The USIA employed about 6,350 people at the time it was absorbed into the State Department. Some 40 percent of these were citizens of foreign countries engaged in U.S.-sponsored information operations abroad.

The USIA and more recently the State Department have resisted calling their work "propaganda," preferring instead to use that term to describe information operations that are hostile to the United States. Some retired USIA executives tend to be more frank, however. Alvin Snyder, director of the USIA's television and film service during the Ronald Reagan administration, referred to the agency's work during those years as "American propaganda [versus] Soviet lies." The former USIA director during the George H. W. Bush administration, Bruce Gelb, may have captured the USIA's self image best when he described the USIA as "never propagandists but rather dedicated 'sales' representatives for the greatest global product of them all: America, our Constitution … [and] our unquenchable belief in the benefits to all people of a market-based economy."

The USIA played a substantial role in American and international journalism throughout its life, as do its successor organizations in the State Department today. There is no simple way to measure this impact, but examples include the USIA's service as the primary source of official information and quotations about U.S. international actions, policies and aspirations for both American and international journalists; training programs for as many as five thousand international journalists per year, particularly those from global hot spots; exchange and travel programs for journalists and journalism educators; provision of substantial logistic support, background information and local contacts for selected American journalists traveling abroad; placement in non- U.S. media of tens of thousands of news and commentary articles, newsreels, video, audio, and Internet feeds regarded as favorable to U.S. national security interests; and significant engineering and financial support for building communication systems in poor countries, especially in Southeast Asia and parts of Africa. The USIA also established well-known Foreign Press Centers for international journalists in Washington D.C., New York, and Los Angeles, which are now managed by the U.S. Department of State.

Throughout its life, the USIA was the principal source of information on overseas public opinion for the U.S. government, including for the intelligence community. It conducted or contracted for polls in some seventy-seven nations and has trained native pollsters throughout the former USSR, Central Asia, Bosnia, Haiti, Nepal, and the Palestinian Authority. The agency also established a large publishing plant in the Philippines that printed tens of millions of magazines, pamphlets, posters, handbills, and books in scores of languages.

The USIA's Voice of America radio, Worldnet television and film service, and affiliated radio, television, and Internet operations remain major news media today, claiming to reach more than one hundred million users per week. The VOA's network of journalists and stringers stretches from "Hong Kong to Los Angeles, London to Capetown, Beijing to Rio de Janiero," wrote Alan Heil, the VOA's long-time deputy director, and includes remote hot spots such as Chad, eastern Congo, the Horn of Africa and southern Lebanon. Many VOA stringers work simultaneously for private media organizations or for news services such as the Associated Press. VOA shortwave and AM frequency broadcasts reach almost the entire earth, although at this writing they are being jammed in the Peoples Republic of China. The VOA and Worldnet distribute radio, television and news-oriented films to at least eleven hundred radio and television stations worldwide.

Other broadcasting projects now affiliated with VOA include Alhurra (Arabic satellite TV service), Radio Sawa (twenty-four-hour Arabic news and entertainment radio in the Middle East), Radio Farda (news and entertainment in Persian aimed at Iran), Radio Free Europe/Radio Liberty (news and other programming for Eastern Europe and nations of the former USSR), Radio Free Asia (news in nine East Asian languages), and Radio and Television Marti (news and programming aimed at Cuba).

Further Reading

Current State Department and Broadcasting Board of Governors reports on continuing news media and public diplomacy projects, http://www.state.gov/press and http://www.bbg.gov (accessed April 13, 2007).

Snow, Nancy. *Information Warfare*. New York: Seven Stories Press, 2004.

Snyder, Alvin A. *Warriors of Disinformation: American Propaganda, Soviet Lies and the Winning of the Cold War, An Insider's Account*. New York: Arcade Publishing, 1997.

USIA. "United States Information Agency: A Commemoration," http://dosfan.lib.uic.edu/usia (accessed April 13, 2007).

CHRISTOPHER SIMPSON

U.S. NEWS & WORLD REPORT

U.S. News & World Report began weekly publication with a somewhat different name and format in May 1933. Its arrival and that of *Newsweek* a few months earlier presented *Time* with two competitors after a decade of monopoly as a weekly newsmagazine.

United States News derived from the *United States Daily*, a national newspaper edited and published by David Lawrence since 1926. Seven years of financial losses persuaded Lawrence and his investors, who had provided more than a million dollars for the daily, to switch to a weekly schedule. However, *United States News* retained its newspaper format until January 1940; upon transforming itself from a broadsheet page size to a standard magazine page size, the publication thereafter referred to itself as a newsmagazine.

Having spent some of his career with the Associated Press and most of his time covering the White House and Congress, Lawrence had enough experience by 1920 to establish an independent news syndicate based in Washing-

ton, D.C. This provided him the requisite insider's knowledge to produce informative articles on national politics and policy, and supplied a substantial stream of revenue to create ancillary news syndicates on commerce and financial information.

Lawrence decided to focus *United States News* on the inner workings of government and government's effects on the private sector. One of the publication's earliest regular features was "Washington Whispers," a compendium of behind-the-scenes tidbits.

Lawrence, a journalist in his mid-forties whose reputation had attracted wealthy investors, committed *United States News* solely to national events and issues, while the other newsmagazines included international news. Also unlike the other newsmagazines, *United States News* based its operations in the nation's capital, not New York City. During his forty-year tenure as editor, Lawrence set a production deadline of Friday, one day ahead of the competition, to ensure that his publication would arrive by mail first.

United States News did not thrive during the Depression era, but it survived. By the start of World War II, the weekly had a circulation of about ninety thousand subscribers and newsstand readers, giving *United States News* approximately one-fifth the circulation of *Newsweek* and one-twelfth that of *Time*.

Lawrence then created a second newsmagazine for international news in 1946, *World Report*. This weekly relied on a handful of correspondents to report dramatic news in the postwar world, with particular attention paid to the threat of Communism. Many loyal readers of *United States News* also subscribed to *World Report*, an indication of Lawrence's popular esteem.

United States News combined with *World Report* in early 1948, a recognition by Lawrence that whatever rationale he once had for separate national and international publications no longer was logical in the postwar world. With a shortened title and ampersand, the new combination of *U.S. News & World Report* quickly gained more readers, attaining paid circulation of a half-million copies by the early 1950s.

U.S. News & World Report maintained a writing style and format quite different from its competitors. Lawrence, a former newspaper reporter, preferred to hire newspaper editors and reporters. Their writing was more straightforward, less descriptive than the prose in either *Time* or *Newsweek*. Correspondents tended to work alone on articles, rather than the group effort at the larger newsmagazines. Correspondents at *U.S. News & World Report* stayed on their beats longer, and acquired expertise and a network of sources that allowed them to compete effectively against the much larger competitors.

Lawrence also favored shorter articles, and would present two or three related stories on the same subject rather than a single lengthy piece. However, the newsmagazine occasionally suffered from a seemingly disorganized approach to the news by publishing related articles in different sections of an edition rather than placing them together.

U.S. News & World Report emphasized text more than

illustrations. The cover was strikingly different, usually simply headlines for a few major articles and only rarely a full-page photograph or illustration. The idea was to highlight a variety of topics.

The question-and-answer interview article also was a distinctive feature of *U.S. News & World Report*. The newsmagazine regularly presented three- to four-page articles consisting of apparently verbatim responses by a newsmaker to questions posed by a correspondent or editor. Presidents, international leaders, and a variety of noteworthy individuals explained their decisions and policies without journalistic interpretation.

Lawrence and his editors rarely paid attention to popular culture, arts, or entertainment either. *U.S. News & World Report* devoted its pages to hard news about legislation, politics, policy, social issues, and developments in commerce, finance, and industry. The newsmagazine ignored celebrities, fashion, and other trendy items.

The no-nonsense editorial approach provided readers with more articles on politics and policy than the other newsmagazines. Correspondents supplied extensive coverage of federal regulatory agencies and tax laws. Much space was allocated every week for coverage of highly specific news of interest to businesses and affluent citizens. It was a nuts-and-bolts type of journalism not seen in the other newsmagazines.

Graphics on inside pages played a major role. Charts and graphs displayed statistical information, monetary data, and other numerical amounts to accompany text. The newsmagazine used photographs, but until the 1970s did not let them dominate a page. Text mattered most.

In its viewpoint, and in Lawrence's back-page opinion columns, *U.S. News & World Report* favored business over labor, state government authority rather than federal government power, and militant anti-Communism. During the postwar decades of dramatic changes in the nation and world, *U.S. News & World Report* often attributed such events to the influence of Communists and their sympathizers.

The public liked the editorial identity. By the mid-1960s, the newsmagazine distributed 1.4 million copies a week to subscribers and newsstand buyers. Although still solidly in third place, *U.S. News & World Report* had significantly closed the gap to slightly less than half *Time*'s circulation and one-third less than *Newsweek*'s.

The Vietnam War set *U.S. News & World Report* further apart from its competitors. The newsmagazine favored comments from policymakers and politicians who wanted to expand military operations into Laos and Cambodia, and to confront China with military force for its support of the Vietnamese Communists. Articles also relied on anonymous remarks from military commanders who criticized the Johnson administration's restraints on bombardment of northern Vietnam. The newsmagazine was the first to warn its readers that American military operations probably would not succeed. Congressional opponents of war policy received scant coverage, except when vilified by congressional supporters of the war. And, for most of the war *U.S. News & World Report* suggested that antiwar organizations were directed or influenced directly or indirectly by Communists.

Its hard-line stand attracted a loyal readership of two million subscribers and newsstand buyers by the mid-1970s. *U.S. News & World Report* remained third among the newsmagazines, maintaining approximately the same proportion of circulation.

The Lawrence era ended with his death in February 1973. He had sold the magazine company to its employees a decade earlier.

The 1970s and 1980s were years of transition for *U.S. News & World Report*. Its cover design changed to emphasize the major article in each edition and it ran cover blurbs—brief headlines—to refer to secondary articles. Business news expanded, and the newsmagazine emphasized coverage of technology. It also published its first annual ratings of colleges and universities in 1983, a feature that has become a trademark.

Despite a new look and more varied editorial strategy, *U.S. News & World Report* endured years of stagnant circulation, a condition that afflicted its competitors, too. In 1984, the newsmagazine's employee owners sold the publication to Mortimer Zuckerman, a publisher and real estate developer.

Several editors-in-chief came and went by the early 1990s, along with the replacement of most long-time correspondents and editors. Gradually, the newsmagazine concentrated on single-topic editions rather than breaking news and focused on service-oriented articles rather than politics and policy. Circulation briefly increased to nearly 2.5 million copies by the late 1990s.

The transformation generated interest among advertisers. *U.S. News & World Report* gained advertising pages through most of the 1990s while its competitors lost pages.

Long an early adapter of technology, *U.S. News & World Report* converted to electronic production during the 1970s. Its newsroom had video-display terminals, pagination, and digital photography before the larger newsmagazines did. *U.S. News & World Report* had an online site in 1995 when the Web was in its infancy; the newsmagazine formed a separate online staff several years later.

Although it has changed much during its lifetime, *U.S. News & World Report* continued to have a distinct editorial identity in the early twenty-first century.

Further Reading

Landers, James. *The Weekly War : Newsmagazines and Vietnam*. Columbia: University of Missouri Press, 2004.

Lawrence, David. *U.S. News & World Report: A Two-Way System of Communication*. New York, Newcomen Society in North America, 1969.

JAMES LANDERS

UNDERGROUND PRESS

Attempts to define and write the history of the underground press in the United States began almost as soon as the term itself was applied to a class of alternative news periodicals rising to prominence in the mid-1960s. They appeared to have distinct characteristics, yet proved very difficult to define as a category separate from alternative newspapers. The term itself emerged during the 1960s.

A 1994 gathering at DePaul University in Chicago drew some boundaries between underground newspapers and the alternative press. Following the first of what would become the Annual Underground Press Conference, managing editor of *Serials Review*, Ken Wachsberger, characterized the term "underground press" as generally referring "to the dissident press of the Vietnam Era." Its heyday spanned from 1965 until around 1973, but underground newspapers still existed well into the twenty-first century. Most continued to express views outside the mainstream of thought. During the late 1960s, if not later, many of these publications faced regular government harassment.

Perhaps 1,500 underground newspapers existed in the United States by 1969, with at least 227 aimed at or written by U.S. soldiers. However, the voice soldiers who opposed the Vietnam War did not achieve prominence in the media history literature until independent scholar James Lewes documented, in a 2001 *Media History* article entitled "Envisioning Resistance: The GI Underground Press During the Vietnam War," the work of U.S. GIs who started such underground newspapers as *Attitude Check*, *A Four Year Bummer*, *A'bout Face!* and *All Ready on the Left*. Until Lewes' offering, the history of the Vietnam War generally was constructed from military, government, and political voices, with some critics in the mix.

Generally speaking, underground newspapers aimed to provide investigative reporting uncovering perceived moral and ethical wrongdoing by "the establishment." Such controversial topics as the civil rights movement, the Vietnam War, the emergence of the gay rights movement, and, in the last phases of the era, the struggles for justice for Vietnam veterans, the environmental movement, and the proto-animal right rights movement dominated the periodicals. This countercultural orientation came along with generally left-leaning politics.

Typically, underground newspapers formed to cover topics and perspectives that their editors and publishers contended were neglected by the mainstream press. Usually, they lost their most talented writers and much of their audience to mainstream media, then imploded. That result sometimes occurred because of infiltration and disruption by political foes, or the FBI's COINTELPRO program, which existed to spy upon and dismantle opponents of U.S. foreign policy. Occasionally, key personnel were lost to arrests for possession of marijuana or other involvement with illegal drugs.

If those arrests can be counted as attempts to silence the press, then the most notorious police repression of the underground press occurred in Cleveland, Ohio, where the newspapers were perhaps less political but more clearly countercultural than anywhere else in the United States. In Cleveland, the underground press was under the influence of the charismatic street poet and publisher known as d.a.

levy (few people knew his name was Darrell Allen).

While others were publishing political exposés, levy was publishing translations of the Tibetan Book of the Dead. After repeated arrests and police beatings, and at least one conviction for allegedly uttering public obscenities, levy shot himself in 1968. Publishers he inspired include rjs (Robert Jay Sigmund), Al Horvath, and tl kryss (Tom Kryss). They largely focused on producing poetry and silk screened prints. Exactly why and how they attracted the intensity of official mistrust and overt repression remains a mystery.

One line of thought about the underground press was that it originated with a tabloid called *The Oracle*. However, two underground publications shared that name: one based in San Francisco, and the other in New York City's Greenwich Village. And they were not related. Which holds status as the original remains a question. Those who held out *The Oracle* as the original underground newspaper cited its countercultural orientation, generally left-leaning politics, and its base of advertising support from personals, entertainment (especially associated with music), and the commercial sex trade. The latter ads were increasingly explicit over time.

This definition recognized underground newspapers of the 1960s as distinctly different in economic support from the heavily politically subsidized "left" press preceding the underground era. In that respect, they were also viewed as separate and apart in values and tone from the rather prudish and stodgy Marxist Party newspapers, which had proliferated and thrived in the United States between the 1920s on into the 1960s. Competition for audience share from the underground press largely drove the Marxist papers into economic collapse and journalistic irrelevance in the 1960s.

Despite this distinction, there were evident bridges from the "left" press to the underground press. One was the influential role of veteran "left" press freelance reporter Henry Gitano, better known later as Henry Spira. Gitano was especially noted as the first U.S. journalist to travel to Cuba and interview Fidel Castro after Castro ousted dictator Fulgencio Batista. He also is noted for traveling in Mississippi in the early 1960s with the Freedom Riders, who were registering black voters.

Gitano became Spira while transforming himself into a New York City high school teacher later in the 1960s. In 1976 he founded Animal Rights International, which is remembered as the original U.S. animal rights activist group. Spira returned to journalism briefly as a contributing editor to the short-lived newspaper, the *Humane Family*. Toward the end of his life he was an occasional guest columnist for the monthly newspaper, *Animal People*. As a reporter, Spira/Gitano set a standard for investigative reporting, independent of political propagandizing. As such, his work exemplified the best of underground newspaper reportage on controversial subjects of the day.

Another line of thought about the origins of the underground press framed them as existing throughout U.S. history. San Jose State University journalism department founder, Dwight Bentel, defined them as publications flourishing in many different places and times almost since the advent of mass circulation itself. In an article appearing in a 1976 issue of the Berkeley, California-based underground newspaper, *Samisdat*, Merritt Clifton traced the origins of underground newspaper publishing back to Isaiah Thomas, whose defiance of the Stamp Act after 1765 helped to incite the American Revolution. Thomas' engraver, Paul Revere, he argued, was the first underground newspaper cartoonist for his famous engraving of the Boston Massacre. In this respect, Paul Revere can be viewed as ancestral to the career of wildly popular underground cartoonist-turned-countercultural-icon, R. (Robert) Crumb, who, among his other accomplishments, influenced animated filmmaking with his movie, *Fritz the Cat*.

Political reporting by Robert Scheer in his independent news magazine, *Ramparts,* was generally recognized as outstanding even by the right-leaning mainstream news periodicals of the day. Some of his more memorable writings centered on the Vietnam War and CIA activity in Latin America.

Claiming no relation to Robert Scheer, Max Scheer, founded the *Berkeley Barb*. At its peak, it was the most widely distributed underground newspaper in the United States. The *Barb* originated as one of several attempts by liberal and radical Berkeley intellectuals to undermine area readership dominated by the distinctly conservative *Berkeley Daily Gazette*, *Kensington Hilltop Mirror*, and *Oakland Tribune*.

Another Berkeley intellectual, Len Fulton, founded the nationally distributed *Small Press Review*, which is still published monthly. He also created the Dustbooks publishing empire. While Fulton and others generally foundered economically, the *Barb* caught lightening in a bottle by employing underground poet John Thompson, who signed his articles "j poet." Thompson is noted for igniting the Free Speech Movement that appeared to detonate the epoch of campus activism.

From that point forward, Max Scheer seemed to have a knack for finding the young writers who were most closely associated with whatever phase of activism or countercultural activity was just about to explode in the limelight. As a result, he managed to position the *Barb* as the newspaper of record when it came to covering the peace movement, the emergence of the Black Panther Party (which had its own underground newspaper), and just about anything else going on in Berkeley that was controversial.

However, the *Barb* paid notoriously poorly. Eventually, disgruntled staffers broke with Sheer. Some formed the *Berkeley Tribe*, a look-alike publication that cut deeply enough into the *Barb*'s support base to encourage Scheer to downgrade the quality of the newspaper's content. He began focusing on publishing sexually oriented material that supported sex trade advertising.

Although the *Barb* produced several journalists who went on to mainstream distinction, by the mid-1970s the *Barb* no longer enjoyed any sort of journalistic standing. Among the reporters becoming prominent are Steve Wasserman, who became editorial page editor for the *Los Angeles Times*, and Dave Haldane, an award-winning *Los Angeles Times* investigative reporter.

While the *Berkeley Tribe* was a substantial rival to the *Barb*, its major journalistic rival in the San Francisco Bay area was the *Bay Guardian*, edited by Hunter S. Thompson. Dozens of others came and went, including the *San Jose Redeye*.

Berkeley was the largest center of underground press activity in the United States. Other major centers were Los Angeles, Detroit, and Madison, Wisconsin, where the scene seemed to evolve out of labor newspapers, which had a local tradition.

Underground newspapers seemed to endure in communities where there was a clear need for an alternative voice. Consequently, they thrived in New Orleans, where Robert and Darlene Head for a decade produced the *NOLA Express,* and in Austin, Texas, where Hal and Caroline Wylie produced *The Gar*.

The Detroit scene produced the beginning of the end of the era, in one sense, when increasing reliance on music industry advertising eventually led the publishers of *Cream* to realize that their audience might be more interested in rock-and-roll than in politics. As the era of campus activism waned, with the end of the Vietnam War-era draft, underground newspapers tended to evolve into the "alternative press" of today, consisting of ad-heavy weekly entertainment periodicals, distributed free, with often relatively little serious news content.

Further Reading

Armstrong, David. *A Trumpet to Arms: Alternative Media in America*. Los Angeles: J. P. Tarcher, Inc., 1981.

Glessing, Robert J. *The Underground Press in America*. Bloomington: Indiana University Press, 1970.

Johnson, Michael L. *The New Journalism: The Underground Press, the Artists of Nonfiction, and Changes in the Established Media*. Lawrence: University Press of Kansas, 1971.

Peck, Abe. *Uncovering the Sixties: The Life and Times of the Underground Press*. New York : Pantheon Books, 1985.

Romm, Ethel Grodzin. *The Open Conspiracy: What America's Angry Generation Is Saying*. New York: A Giniger Book, published in association with Stackpole Books, 1970.

MERRITT CLIFTON
DEBRA A. SCHWARTZ

UNITED PRESS INTERNATIONAL (UPI)

For decades United Press (and its successor United Press International) was known as the innovative, aggressive wire service. UPI emphasized crisp, sharp writing and it pioneered a separate news wire for broadcast and an audio service for radio stations. Its correspondents were young and hard driving.

News agencies like United Press International and the Associated Press provide news and features for newspapers, broadcast stations and groups that cannot have their own correspondents at the scene of every news event. To accomplish this, AP and UPI have bureaus and correspondents scattered through the United States and the world. UPI was the smaller by most any measurement.

For decades UP/UPI and the AP fought for supremacy. On a corporate level, it was a battle to see which could contract with the most and/or biggest newspapers and broadcast stations.

Often, it was a personal duel between the UPI and the AP correspondents covering the same event to see whose story won the most "play," that is, whose version appeared in the most newspapers that subscribed to both news services.

UPI staffers, whose wages generally were lower and who were often outnumbered, made up for it in enthusiasm and *esprit de corps*. They were told to write "so it can be understood by the Omaha Milkman" (Packard 1951, 7. He changed the city to Kansas City for purposes of his book), a phrase familiar to all Unipressers. The UPI alumni, known as "downholders" because of management's frequent orders to "downhold" expenses, are spread throughout the journalism profession.

In the days before the dominance of television news, UPI and the AP shaped the agenda of coverage for the rest of the news media. UPI's Louis Cassels, the most prominent religion columnist of the day, remarked that two of the most powerful persons in Washington at any one moment were the two persons sitting in the "slot" at UPI and AP. This was true, Cassels said, because the "slot" determined what stories were going to move on the wire and when—and because most high officials in Washington monitored the wires carefully and acted accordingly.

At its peak in the 1970s, UPI had about 170 bureaus. In the United States, the general practice was to put bureaus in a state's largest city and the capital city.

Other bureaus were scattered throughout the world.

At the turn of the millennium, UPI had declined to the point that it had few bureaus abroad or in the United States and the AP had a virtual monopoly as the American news agency. AP's competition abroad was by then mainly the British news agency Reuters or Agence France Presse (AFP).

The list of famous Unipressers was impressive. Overseas, Westbrook Pegler, later a nationally syndicated columnist, covered World War I. Webb Miller, a famed foreign correspondent, covered eleven wars during the period between and including the two world wars (he hated war as is suggested by the title of his autobiography, *I Found No Peace*). Walter Cronkite, the CBS anchor, was UP's chief correspondent in Europe during World War II. Russell Jones won a Pulitzer Prize for his coverage of the 1956 Hungary uprising. Henry Shapiro covered the Soviet Union during most of the Cold War, along with Harrison Salisbury, who went on to the *New York Times*. Joe Galloway, barely in his twenties at the time, was the correspondent in Vietnam who later wrote the best-selling *We Were Soldiers Once ... And Young*. Thomas L. Friedman of *the New York Times* and winner of three Pulitzer prizes got his start with UPI.

At home, UPI's stable of famous bylines was vast. Allen Drury, who wrote *Advice and Consent* (1959), covered the

U.S. Senate. David Brinkley later was an NBC anchor. Merriman Smith, Helen Thomas, and Al Spivak were perhaps the most famous—and talented—team ever of White House correspondents. Few sports writers could turn a phrase as well as Oscar Fraley, who also wrote TV's *The Untouchables*.

These reporters were backed up by relatively unknown editors and writers whose by-lines rarely appeared on a dispatch. Lucien Carr, a UPI news editor in New York and Washington, was the "intellectual" in Jack Kerouac's "beat" generation coterie. UPI emphasized sharp, concise writing—and among the best at this were David Smothers, the ex-Quiz Kid, in Chicago, Robert M. Andrews in London and Washington, and Jack Warner in Atlanta.

One of the best leads ever to move on the UP/UPI wire was written by Merriman Smith, then in his mid-twenties:

> TUTTNALL, Ga. (UP) — Six Negro men in the death house atop Georgia's Tuttnall Prison started singing early this morning but by lunchtime their song was ended. "Oh you sinners, better get ready, God is comin'," they chorused loudly, hour after hour, until the electric chair had claimed every one of them in the largest mass execution in state history (quoted by Robert J. Donovan in his Foreword to *Merriman Smith's Book of Presidents: A White House Memoir*, ed. Tim Smith. New York: W.W. Norton, 1972, 21).

Though probably not by design, UPI played a part in the women's and civil rights movements. Among the top-flight UPI correspondents who dominated coverage in state capitals were Hortense Meyers in Indiana, Barbara Frye in Florida, Bessie Ford in Mississippi, Roberta Ulrich in Salem. Charlotte Moulton was the dean of Supreme Court reporters.

Other leading state house correspondents included Seymour Hersh (later one of the country's top investigative reporters in Pierre), Dick Charnock in Boise, John Herbers (later with the *New York Times*), in Jackson, and Bill Cotterell in Atlanta.

UPI lagged far behind in putting African Americans on its staff. Yet its influence on the civil rights movement may have been significant. Often the local journalists in a city had been there so long they had become part of the community's social and power structure. UPI correspondents, often young and with few more possessions than what they could toss in the back seat of a car, were transferred frequently. This was true in the South in the 1960s.

So, a young UPI staffer would transfer to a city that was experiencing racial unrest and civil rights demonstrations. Sometimes the local media ignored those demonstrations. The young UPI staffer, not knowing any better, would cover the story in detail, thus forcing competitors to do the same. The result was that for the first time, these demonstrations began to get covered and the nation began to pay attention.

Its photographers excelled too. UPI (and AP) photographers never achieved the celebrity status their magazine counterparts enjoyed only because, until the 1970s, their names were not published with their work. But the photo credits in today's coffee-table books reveal that most are by UPI or AP photographers.

Stanley Tretick took the famous picture of young John F. Kennedy Jr. peeking from under his father's desk and the poignant photo of John-John saluting as his father's bier passed. David Hume Kennerly, who became official White House photographer for President Gerald R. Ford, won a Pulitzer for his coverage of the Vietnam War. Tom Schaefer while with Acme earlier snapped one of the photos of General Douglas Macarthur wading ashore in the Philippines during World War II. Frank Cancellare took the picture of a beaming President Harry S Truman carrying a copy of the *Chicago Tribune* saying "Dewey Wins" the 1948 election.

The agency also established UPI Audio, a service for client radio stations and UPITN, a newsfilm service for television stations and networks. It had its own staff of correspondents, including such "golden throats" as Bill Reilly, Pye Chamberlayne, Gene Gibbons, Denis Gulino, and Tom Foty.

But by the end of the twentieth century, much of UPI's glory, its staff and bureaus, was gone. What had happened? The forerunner of the modern AP was established in 1848 by a group of New York City area newspapers, which eventually sold news to other newspapers. From the beginning it was a "co-operative," as contrasted to UP, which was a private corporation. The first United Press had a meteoric rise and fall in the 1890s. One of its clients was E.W. Scripps, and when it tumbled, he organized the Scripps-McRae Press Association which distributed news files from its own correspondents as well as other newspapers. He bought the competing Publishers' Press Association and Laffan News Agency.

In 1907, Scripps combined several of these services into a single agency—United Press Associations. And Roy Howard, at twenty-four barely half Scripps' age, became general manager of the new agency. His assignment, as Morris put it, was to "buck the Associated Press on a shoestring" with a young staff that was "usually underpaid and grossly overworked" (Morris 1957, 23, 24, 42).

The International News Service was formed by William Randolph Hearst in 1909. It always struggled in third place in a three-way race, and in 1958, it merged with United Press to form UPI.

For all of Howard's considerable drive, he also perpetrated UP's perhaps most infamous error. In Europe as World War I was drawing to an end, Howard, acting on a tip from an American intelligence officer with confirmation from an American admiral, filed an urgent story saying the Allies and Germany had signed an armistice. But it was November 7, 1917—four days before the armistice actually was signed.

UP's Raymond Clapper, reporting on the 1920 Republican convention, wrote that Warren G. Harding had been chosen as the GOP presidential nominee in a "smoke-filled room," a phrase that made it into the lexicon. About the same time, another term emerged that survived for all future Unipressers— "downhold." It followed the wire service practice of using cables.

By 1919 UP was highly profitable with 745 newspaper clients. During Karl Bickel's presidency, from 1923 to 1935, the number of client newspapers increased from 867 to 1,300 in 49 countries, and the number of bureaus from 50 to 81 (Morris 1957, 197). In 1937 the American Newspaper Guild (CIO) organized the UP staff. By 1941, as World War II started, UP served 462 papers in 38 other countries (Harnett-Ferguson 2003, 64). It had become dominant in South America.

UP President Hugh Baillie endorsed a plan in 1935 to make UP the premiere news service for radio stations, and soon a separate broadcast wire was established. This style of writing emphasized short, simple words and sentences ... with lots of ellipses and pronunciations inserted ... to make for easy reading by the newscaster and easy listening. The wire, known as UPR, became one of the company's best sources of revenue.

Unlike the dismal days at the end of the century, UP's leadership changed infrequently. Howard served until 1920; Karl Bickel from 1923 to 1935. The pugnacious Baillie (bayh-lee) led UP for twenty years, never forgetting he was a correspondent and often seeming to spend more time abroad chasing stories than running the news agency. Then the urbane Frank H. Bartholomew served from 1955 to 1962.

Bickel—and UP—were directly involved in several big stories involving Charles Lindbergh. An enterprising UP correspondent arranged to keep a telephone open at the side of the field as Lindbergh's 1927 transatlantic flight neared Paris, and within five minutes after *The Spirit of St. Louis* landed, all UP clients knew it. At home, five years later, Bickel fielded a telephone call in his apartment from Charles Lindbergh that the famed flier's son had been kidnapped... and a few days later, another call that Lindbergh was ready to pay a ransom. Later, when AP flashed the wrong verdict in Hauptmann's trial on the death of the Lindbergh child, UP got it correct.

In 1935 when Huey Long was shot in Louisiana, UP reporter I.I. Femrite at the hospital overhead a doctor say "he's dead." Femrite quickly phoned a flash to the news desk. At the state capital Femrite's colleague, J. Alan Coogan, in a diversionary ploy, strolled casually through the press room, even bumming a match from the AP correspondent to light a cigarette. The AP reportedly asked, "Do you think Huey's going to die tonight?"

Bickel had persuaded Benito Mussolini, a journalist, to write stories for United Features. Webb Miller, who had been a journalist colleague of the man now known as Il Duce, noted the Italian armed buildup in Ethiopia in 1935 and so prepared, Miller was ready with his flash: ITALIAN ADVANCE INTO ETHIOPIA STARTED AT FIVE A.M. (Morris 1957, 207). Baillie called it "one of the great beats of news-service history" (Baillie 1959, 93). Later, in a one-on-one interview, Mussolini asked Baillie if UP was on Italy's side. "We are favorable to you to the extent that we are not favorable to you. It balances," Baillie replied (Baillie 1959, 96).

When the Japanese attacked Pearl Harbor in 1941, Frank

Tremaine in Honolulu was awakened by the sound of the antiaircraft guns. In moments he was making calls and then his wife joined in phoning to the UP bureaus in San Francesco and Manila what they were seeing and hearing.

"United Press grew and gained prestige under Baillie, but weakness in the 'financials' started in the 1950s..." and Ferguson noted (2003, 104). By 1957, UP had 4,833 newspaper and broadcast clients and 4,000 employees worldwide. In 1951, Argentine dictator Juan Peron closed *La Prensa*, one of UP's major clients in South America, costing UP about a half million dollars a year in revenue. In 1958, UP merged with the Hearst-owned, money-losing International News Service (INS) to form UPI—and the AP filed the story first to score an embarrassing scoop. Most INS employees and some UP personnel were laid off. Al Spivak and Hortense Meyers were among the INS employees who joined the new UPI.

The 1960s were days of tumult in the United States—the civil rights demonstrations, the feminist movement, 1963 John F. Kennedy and 1968 Martin Luther King and Robert Kennedy assassinations, the Vietnam war. Lucinda Franks and Tom Powers combined to write a Pulitzer-winning story on the background of Diana Oughton, a young woman from a wealthy, small-town Illinois family who was killed in a New York townhouse where bombs were made. Ironically, it was one of those ordeals that have provided the single incident most identified with UPI.

Merriman Smith was in the "pool" car as President Kennedy rode from the airport into Dallas. (A "pool" is the handful of reporters, always including the major news services, assigned to accompany the president when the entire White House press corps is unable to.) There was a shot, then a pause, and two more shots. Smith, a gun fancier, was probably the one who said, "Those were shots!" Smith, sitting in the front seat, picked up the phone in the car, called the Dallas bureau, and dictated: "BULLETIN—THREE SHOTS WERE FIRED AT PRESIDENT KENNEDY'S MOTORCADE IN DOWNTOWN DALLAS." Smitty, as he was widely known, refused to give up the phone despite the AP's Jack Bell's attempts to wrestle it away so he could file too. Later, as Air Force One carried the slain president and the new president, Lyndon B. Johnson, back to Washington, Smith composed the story of how the day had unfolded—and it won a Pulitzer Prize.

In the 1970s, UPI was on the cutting edge in the use of computers, and this led to the eventual elimination of the "operators," who had been organized by the Commercial Telegraphers Union and put the stories into tape to move on the Teletype machines. This meant that a reporter now could write a dispatch at a computer, file it, have it read out by an editor also at a computer, which filed it directly to the newspapers that in turn, could print it from direct from the computer. Quite literally, the reporter on the scene had typed the very print appearing in the newspaper.

What lay ahead were wholesale, non-stop changes for next decades, in owners, management and editors, in wave after wave of staff lay-offs, and in pay cuts. Perhaps worse, the UPI began to lose its innovative edge. The financial drain continued. By 1972 UPI was losing $2 million a year and the loss was mounting. UPI pulled out of several states, such as the two Dakotas, giving up an attempt to file a state-wide news file. UPI was struck by the Wire Service Guild for three weeks in 1974. UPI froze wages in 1979. UPI President Rod Beaton failed in an attempt to sell limited partnerships in UPI to other newspaper publishers.

Scripps-Howard made known in 1979 that it no longer could keep subsidizing UPI. It became common knowledge that UPI was up for sale. Reuters and the new cable network, CNN, logical buyers, took a look the UPI books and decided against buying. It was even suggested that UPI be given to National Public Radio. Media giant Rupert Murdoch and years later evangelist-broadcaster Pat Robertson expressed an interest.

Finally, in 1982, Scripps sold UPI debt-free to two thirty-ish entrepreneurs, Doug Ruhe and Bill Geissler, for $1 and secretly gave them $5 million to keep it afloat. Within hours UPI was back in debt. They hired expensive consultants and entertained "grand dreams" (Gordon and Cohen 1990, 147), but the drain continued. The next year the *New York Times* cancelled its contract although it later extended until 1986.

The next few years were chaotic. Wave after wave of clientele shrinkage, staff layoffs, and cuts in pay swept the company. Morale suffered. The personnel exodus continued at every level. In a seven-year period, there were seven UPI presidents.

Ruhe and Geissler began selling off parts of UPI: its remaining stake in UPITN, the electronic data base, photo library, which contained priceless pictures, the foreign photo staff and overseas picture contracts. UPI faced bankruptcy, and obtained Chapter 11 protection in 1985. (Chapter 11 allows a company to keep operating while keeping the creditors at bay and preventing them from closing it down.) The two owners feuded with Chairman and Chief Executive Officer Luis Nogales.

Although Beaton and Editor-in-Chief H.L. Stevenson departed or were replaced, Unipressers continued putting out a comprehensive news report, continuing to match and often to beat the AP. Under the direction of Managing Editor Ronald E. Cohen and Chief Investigative Reporter Greg Gordon, UPI ran detailed, candid dispatches each day about the company's mounting problems, for which they eventually paid with their jobs. UPI was the first news service to call the close 1976 election for Jimmy Carter over President Gerald R. Ford.

The next buyer, in 1985, after a bankruptcy court battle, was Mario Vazquez-Rana, who owned a large group of newspapers in Mexico. In weeks, the top three UPI editors were gone. The rest of the staff was shaved as well, including the charismatic Nogales.

In 1987 Vazquez-Rana turned over control of UPI to Dr. Earl Brian, who had been a member of Ronald Reagan's California Cabinet. There were more layoffs and pay cuts and closing of bureaus. Worldwide News Inc., with connections to the Saudi royal family, bought the agency in 1992.

Finally, its client base almost depleted and only a shell of a staff remaining, it was sold in 2000 to the News World

Communications, established by the Rev. Sun Myung Moon, founder of the Unification Church, and owner of the arch-conservative *Washington Times*. UPI's icon, Helen Thomas, quit in protest.

What had led to the comatose state of UPI? The AP was a co-operative that did not need to show a profit. The AP thus could sell its service for less. UPI was a private organization that was increasingly subsidized by the increasingly disenchanted, proliferating Scripps-Howard Trust family. So, the Scripps family finally stopped subsidizing UPI.

Stephen Vincent Benet, in a study of UP in *Fortune* in May 1933, had stated: "…every UP executive has come from the ranks" (Harnett-Ferguson 2003, 123). (This was not true, of course, during recent years when many if not most of the top echelon had no previous wire-service experience.) In the outlying bureaus, often outstanding correspondents were "promoted" to regional executives, the fancy UP term for salesman. But the traits that made a person a good correspondent were not the traits that would create a successful salesman. Many of these regional executives quit, and UPI had lost both good reporters and salesmen.

Afternoon newspapers had become a dinosaur because of ever-earlier deadlines and the required distribution of the evening papers through rush hour traffic. Thus, UPI suffered a shrinking newspaper market.

As one Unipresser put it: "Both Beaton and Charles Scripps, however, ignored entreaties from Bernard Townsend, a Scripps financial vice president, to explore the growing world market for business and financial information."

Television eroded newspapers as the primary source of news for the general public. Newspapers and newspaper groups started their own syndicates that distributed their own stories. Many newspapers felt that it made more sense to take one basic service—generally preferring the AP—and a supplemental service, rather than both AP and UPI.

By 2005, the combined New York headquarters and once powerful Washington bureau had shrunk to sixteen persons, who "were genuinely concerned not only about their livelihoods, but also about the longevity of an organization that they had taken a great amount of pride being involved with" (Preciphs 2005, 41).

Further Reading

Baillie, Hugh. *High Tension*. New York: Harper & Brothers, 1959.

Gordon, Gregory, and Ronald E. Cohen. *Down to the Wire: UPI's Fight for Survival*. New York: McGraw-Hill, 1990.

Harnett, Richard M., and Billy G. Ferguson. *Unipress: Covering the 20th Century*. Golden: Fulcrum, 2003.

Herbers, John. "The Reporter in the Deep South." *Nieman Reports*, double issue, Winter 1999 and Spring 2000.

Miller, Webb. *I Found No Peace*. New York: Simon and Schuster, 1936.

Moore, Harold G., and Joseph. Galloway. *We Were Soldiers Once … And Young: Ia Dang—The Battle That Changed the War in Vietnam*. New York: Random House, 1992.

Morris, Joe Alex. *Deadline Every Minute*. New York: Doubleday & Co., 1957.

Packard, Reynolds. *Lowdown* (originally published under the title *The Kansas City Milkman*). New York: Bantam, 1951.

Preciphs, Joi L. "Participant Observation of Editorial Functions and Workplace Culture at United Press International." Unpublished master's research paper, University of Missouri School of Journalism, 2005.

WES PIPPERT

USA TODAY

"If *USA Today* (1982–) is a good paper," grumbled *Washington Post* executive editor Ben Bradlee, "then I'm in the wrong business."

"Bradlee and I finally agree on something," quipped *USA Today*'s founder Al Neuharth. "He is in the wrong business."

Many in the mainstream media charged the paper's large charts, pie graphs and downsized stories amounted to "junk-food journalism." A *Newsweek* headline in January 1983 labeled *USA Today* "The Big Mac of Newspapers." Jonathan Yardley, a *Washington Post* columnist, claimed "McPaper" gave "readers only what they want. No spinach. No bran. No liver." CBS News veteran Charles Kuralt, however, did not agree with "the heavy hitters of big-time journalism" who sneered at *USA Today*. The paper was "a reliable way for many to find out what's going on in the world" and that "is not only good for journalism; it's good for the country," he said.

USA Today began life on September 15, 1982, at the foot of Capitol Hill when President Ronald Reagan, Senate Majority Leader Howard Baker, and Speaker of the House of Representatives Thomas "Tip" O'Neill stood beside Gannett Publishing president Allen H. Neuharth to receive their complimentary copies of the paper's first press run. All 155,000 copies of that first edition were sold in the Washington-Baltimore corridor that day. Twenty-five years later, the nation's most-widely read newspaper had a circulation of 2.3 million. It would be years, however, before the paper turned a profit. Early opponents observed the country already had a national newspaper, some mentioning the *Wall Street Journal* while others added the *New York Times*, but the flamboyant Neuharth, who had helped build Gannett into the country's largest newspaper chain, was convinced the company could deliver a general-interest daily that would appeal to nationwide readers.

"The Nation's Newspaper" began life in Rosslyn, Virginia, a Washington, D.C., suburb, with two-thirds of its 218 reporters, average age thirty-three, on loan from Gannett's other eighty-eight papers, under a leadership team of Neuharth, Editor John J. Curley, Executive Editor Ron Martin, and Chief News Executive John C. Quinn. For staffers, these were the "Gang of Four." A staff guide told reporters and editors, "our readers are upscale, well informed and looking for a supplement to their regular newspaper. So our stories may contain less background on events, more emphasis on what's new." Quinn's view was that "exploding media have increased hunger for news/info, but none has met market needs for news/info-in-a-hurry that is more portable than TV news." Quinn wanted the paper's focus to be on the future. He urged reporters and editors "to look ahead, to look at solutions." Curley thought the chances were only "40/60" that the paper would succeed. *USA Today* would be based on a "space age" newspaper design Neuharth had successfully launched in Cape Canaveral, Florida. The management team was a constant and terrorizing presence in the newsroom. The pressure was intense. "I was terrified," said Money section managing editor J. Taylor Buckley. "We feared the feedback from the chiefs. Always negative." Sheryl Bills, Life section managing editor, was equally anxious. "It's hard to believe we could endure mentally, physically." A characteristic note of caustic criticism from Neuharth to Curley and Quinn in December 1982 read, "Do I have to do everything myself? Page one is a disaster. Dull stories. Dumb editing. No stories that help the reader. No good pix of women or minorities—just the usual white males. The blue sky came out purple. At this rate *USA Today* will never see the New Year."

The paper's four sections—news, money, sports, and life—became a heavily illustrated "mix," according to managing editor Peter Prichard, of "hard news and features of wide interest" that "had to say, 'read me.'" That meant de-emphasizing foreign news, the assassination of Lebanese leader Bashir Gemayel was buried on an inside page of the paper's first edition, while summarizing the news of all fifty states in an "Across the USA Roundup." *USA Today*'s full-page of national weather included a color map that became the most imitated part of the paper. As circulation expanded westward, the map was tilted to take the focus off the East Coast. The newspaper was marketed through vending machines that looked like television sets and was heavily marketed to the business traveler through giveaways on airlines and at airports and hotels. The paper was sent via satellite to regional distribution hubs, allowing it to push back deadlines and capture the latest news and sports scores. The paper does not print on Saturday and Sunday. Its starting price of 25 increased to 35 cents in August 1984, 50 cents in August 1985 and 75 cents in September 2004.

For its first few years, *USA Today* struggled to survive. Losses ran in the millions. Neuharth had planned the paper as a "second read," designed to complement a local newspaper. Joe Welty, the paper's vice president for advertising, had a hard time finding buyers. Madison Avenue wanted to know, "What niche does *USA Today* have? Where is the hook? Why do we need to be in this newspaper?" Gannett's business plan estimated the paper might sustain losses of $40 to $50 million in its first year of operation. Fourteen million of it was to assure full color production quality printed on deadline. Neuharth suggested the "losses" were "investments" in the company's future. Critics were condescending and unremitting. *USA Today* was "a multimillion dollar attempt to create a national newspaper," the Associated Press reported, "on rented presses." *The New Republic* reported, "Gannett is known for expert marketing and mediocre journalism and its latest endeavor is the product of both." Ben Bagdikian sized it up in the *Columbia Journalism Review* as "a serious blow to American journalism" with "no serious sense of priorities."

Circulation was approaching one million when *USA Today* debuted in Chicago on March 9, 1983. Its lead story quoted "a source" saying police had "in sight" a suspect in the killing of seven Chicago area residents who had been killed after taking Tylenol capsules laced with cyanide. No one was ever charged in the case, and Neuharth barred "sources said" from appearing in the paper. As circulation spread to Atlanta, Detroit, Philadelphia, Pittsburgh, Boston, Cleveland, Houston, Denver, Seattle, Los Angeles, Cincinnati, Nashville, Phoenix, New Orleans, Dallas/Ft. Worth, and San Francisco problems persisted. The paper's business office was understaffed and poorly trained. Home delivery plans were a shambles. The paper's Minneapolis office processed subscription orders on three by five index cards. It would be April 1983 before the paper was able to launch in New York City. As late as July 1984 it was losing $10 million a month. The tide turned by the start of 1985, when *USA Today* was able to reach 80 percent of the U.S. population. Six months later, the paper's research showed two-thirds of its readers had attended college and nearly half were making more than $35,000 annually, better demographics than competing magazines. Circulation stood at 1.3 million. This helped boost paid advertising to twelve and a half pages and within a year translated to a three-quarters gain in ad revenue. By April 1987, circulation had climbed to 1.75 million. On May 6, 1986, an International Edition of *USA Today* began appearing in Switzerland. A July 1986 survey showed the paper's daily readership averaged 4,792,000. As the 1980s ended, the paper was beginning to show a profit and gain respect. Initial misgivings by minorities and religious groups had faded. It had surpassed the *New York Daily News* in circulation and would soon breeze by the *Wall Street Journal* for the number one spot.

In the 1990s, critics continued to carp, "*USA Today* doesn't rub off on your hands or mind." Some of the criticism was justified. In March 2004, the paper admitted that veteran reporter Jack Kelley had fabricated eight major stories during his ten years at *USA Today*. Those who decried the rise of "corporate newspapering" and the "Wal-marting of America" made the ninety-nine-newspaper Gannett Publishing empire and *USA Today* a poster child of what was wrong with America's $60 billion newspaper industry.

But the Kelley episode was not typical of the paper. Neuharth argued that the paper "informs, entertains, and debates. But it doesn't dictate. We don't force unwanted objects down unwilling throats." The paper's political and public opinion polling received wide distribution. Neuharth, who turned the daily operation of the paper over to Curley, began writing columns highly critical of America's pre-emptive war in Iraq, characterizing George W. Bush as "an unwise commander in chief" with an obligation "to bring our troops home sooner rather than later." During this period it became a strong advocate of campaign finance reform and limiting the role of lobbyists. On May 11, 2006, a major page-one story claimed the National Security Agency had been "secretly collecting the phone call records of tens of millions of Americans" in the aftermath of terrorist attacks on the nation. The charges would lead to a Congressional investigation and court suits.

Since 2001, *USA Today* has been headquartered in a thirty-acre complex in McLean, Virginia. Once reviled, it had become widely imitated by mainstream newspapers needing to modernize in the age of the Internet. The paper won grudging admiration from previous critics by luring top flight talent to strengthen its writing and reporting. Those who saw *USA Today* as an innovator on the eve of the digital age praised its adaptation to new market forces.

Further Reading

"Allen Harold Neuharth." In Charles Moritz, ed., *Current Biography 1986*, New York: H.W. Wilson, 1987, 409–413.

"Gannett: A Brief Company History" and "Gannett: Company Profile," http://www.gannett.com, (accessed November 6, 2006).

Neuharth, Al. *Confessions of an S.O.B*. New York: Doubleday, 1989.

Prichard, Peter S. *The Making of McPaper: The Inside Story of USA Today*. Kansas City: Andrews, McMeel & Parker, 1987.

Roberts, Gene, ed. *Leaving Readers Behind: The Age of Corporate Newspapering*, Fayetteville: University of Arkansas Press, 2001.

Ritzer, George. *The McDonaldization of Society: An Investigation into the Changing Character of Contemporary Social Life*. Thousand Oaks, CA: Pine Forge, 1996.

BRUCE J. EVENSEN

V

VANDERBILT TELEVISION NEWS ARCHIVE

The Television News Archive collection at Vanderbilt University in Nashville, Tennessee, was created by Nashville insurance executive and Vanderbilt alumnus Paul C. Simpson in 1968. Simpson was inspired to create the archive after a visit to television newsrooms during a business trip to New York revealed that the networks at the time did not preserve their news broadcasts because of the expense of videotapes and the immense storage space that would have been required. Most of the first twenty years of television history in the United States has disappeared because of this early attitude.

The Television News Archive collection consists of videotapes of more than thirty thousand network evening news broadcasts produced by ABC, CBS, and NBC from August 5, 1968, to the present and various CNN daily news programs from October 2, 1995, to the present. The archive also includes more than nine thousand hours of news-related programming such as special reports, coverage of presidential press conferences and political campaigns, and national and international events such as the wars in Afghanistan and Iraq and the terrorist attacks on the United States on September 11, 2001. The archive is a non-profit organization maintained by grants and contributions from individuals, foundations and scholarly institutions.

The editorial staff of the archive creates the listings, summaries and descriptions of the broadcasts in the collection. Archive staff members summarize each evening news segment with the names of anchors and reporters, names of persons involved in the event reported, and a summary of the event. Each news item in a broadcast is separately described with a beginning and end time noted. Staff members also summarize and describe special news broadcasts such as political conventions, presidential press conferences and breaking news events, although not to the level of detail as the evening news broadcasts.

Prior to 1994, the summaries were published in a monthly printed reference tool titled *Television News Index and Abstracts*. Now, all of the descriptive information is entered into the TV-NewsSearch database, which includes more than 705,000 records describing individual items of content. The database, which has been available since 1994, can be searched by keywords of titles and descriptions, by dates, by broadcast type, by reporter and even by the advertisements that ran during the broadcast. Access to the collection's TV-NewsSearch database is through subscrip-

tion; additionally, users pay fees for videotape loans from the collection if they wish to have access to the actual tapes of broadcasts.

Description of the Collection

Regular evening news programs in the collection include:

ABC Evening News: August 5, 1968–present
CBS Evening News: August 5, 1968–present
NBC Evening News: August 5, 1968–present
CNN WorldView: October 2, 1995–November 3, 2000
CNN Wolf Blitzer Reports: February 1, 2001–December 21, 2001
CNN NewsNight: November 5, 2001–present

Some of the major special reports included in the collection include:

Each Republican and Democratic political convention since 1968 and corresponding election coverage
Each televised presidential State of the Union Address since 1968
Most major speeches delivered by U.S. presidents since 1968
Presidential news conferences
Coverage of international crises, wars and world events involving the United States

The late-night news program *Nightline* from ABC is also included:

ABC *Nightline*: March 24, 1980–September 12, 1988, occasional coverage
ABC *Nightline*: September 12, 1988–present, comprehensive coverage

The collection does not include local news coverage from any broadcast market. Also, the collection does not include news segments from broadcast magazine programs such as *60 Minutes*, *20/20*, *Dateline NBC* and similar shows unless the segment is on a topic directly related to the U.S. presidency or major world events.

Copyright Issues

Historically, early television producers did not seek to voluntarily register their programs with the Library of Congress for copyright deposit purposes. Prior to the 1976 Copyright Act, broadcasting a program did not per se constitute publication, nor were network television programs sold or leased in copies. Therefore, there were serious questions about what constituted "publication" for a broadcast program within the meaning of copyright law. The passage of the revised law and advances in affordable home videocassette recording technology led television networks to become more aggressive about registering their materials for copyright protection. ABC and CBS began depositing copies of their evening news programs with the Library of Congress starting in the late 1970s, as did PBS for the *MacNeil-Lehrer NewsHour.*

The television networks have periodically challenged the archive's right to duplicate and loan copies of broadcasts for which the networks claim copyright ownership. CBS filed a copyright infringement lawsuit against Vanderbilt University in 1976, but dropped the suit in 1978 after the revised Copyright Act included a fair-use clause which allowed for noncommercial duplication of news broadcasts. When the archive moved their descriptions online in 1994, the networks again complained because they feared that wider Internet access would greatly increase public use of copyrighted material that the networks wanted to control and for which they wanted to receive revenues.

The networks objected to the archive's production of compilation tapes. If an archive user requests the staff to produce a tape with relevant news segments edited together from a series of broadcasts (a common request from researchers who are studying news coverage of an event over time), the staff will comply with the request. Users sign an agreement that they will not duplicate, rebroadcast or publicly show the compilation tapes. Once a researcher makes a request for such a compilation, the tape becomes part of the archive collection when it is returned and becomes available to others with a similar interest. The networks object because they consider compilation tapes to be new content which competes with network productions.

The achive home page on the Internet (tvnews.vanderbilt.edu) includes a statement that indicates "all material of the Television News Archive must be used within the restrictions of the United States copyright legislation. Specifically, Copyright Public Law 94-553 includes provisions regarding copyright of audiovisual works and archiving of television news broadcasts." The archive relies on the agreements signed by individual users to ensure compliance with the law.

The Motion Picture, Broadcasting & Recorded Sound Division of the Library of Congress began acquiring master copies of evening news broadcasts from the archive in the early 1990s when ABC and CBS stopped depositing their broadcasts (NBC had never deposited their *Evening News* broadcasts with the Library of Congress). However, master videos acquired from the archive are not available for viewing at the Library of Congress due to copyright concerns.

Scholarly Use of the Archive

With the exception of the networks' own archives, the Vanderbilt collection is the most comprehensive record of television news in the United States. Scholars and students in many academic disciplines use the archive to locate stories, track coverage of specific topics and evaluate the tone of news. The archive's own web site includes citations and summaries for more than eighty scholarly articles that make reference to the archive as a source for the researchers' study. Scholars from such disciplines as communications, political science, sociology, history, public health, economics, international relations and criminology have relied on the archive to provide information for content analysis of television coverage.

Researchers Scott Althaus, Jill Edy, and Patricia Phalen found that the abstracts prepared by archive staff members reflect important elements of news when compared to the verbatim transcripts of the programs, but may be unreliable as substitutes for the actual news stories themselves. Staff at the archive do not intend for the abstracts to serve as a surrogate for the verbatim transcripts of the content. Hence, serious researchers may be best served by identifying the appropriate broadcast segments through the TV-NewsSearch database and then ordering full transcripts or seeking videotape loans to be confident that their content analyses reflect the actual content that was broadcast.

Technology Changes and the Future of the Archive

Several Internet search engine firms have developed a computerized system for transcribing and abstracting television broadcasts and assigning keywords that can be searched electronically. The television broadcasts need to be converted into digital format, but once they are, they can be easily stored and made accessible via the Internet. This has the potential to provide much more accurate search results than the systems based on human-generated abstracts. These search engine companies are working with the television networks to develop a fee-based system that could offer users access to an unlimited, fully searchable digital video library of network content.

This has implications for the Vanderbilt Archives, obviously, but it is not clear how such systems might affect the future. Even if the television networks strike a deal with the Internet search firms to make their content available digitally for a fee, it would not preclude the archive staff from continuing to tape the news broadcasts and abstracting them for use by researchers. But users might find it much more efficient, convenient, and accurate—and therefore be willing to pay—to use the Internet-based systems that might become available. It remains to be seen how these technological developments will influence the Vanderbilt Television News Archive.

Further Reading

Althaus, Scott L., Jill A. Edy, and Patricia F. Phalen. "Using the Vanderbilt Television Abstracts to Track Broadcast News Content: Possibilities and Pitfalls." *Journal of Broadcasting & Electronic Media*, 46(3) (September 2002): 473–492.

Dillon, John F. *The Vanderbilt Television News Archive: Its History, Operations, and an Outline for its Use.* Murray, KY: Murray State University, 1987.

Rawley-Saldich, Anne. "Access to Television's Past." *Columbia Journalism Review,* (November/December 1976): 46–48.

Simpson, Paul C., with Patricia G. Lane, and F. Lynne Bachleda. *Network Television News: Conviction, Controversy, and a Point of View.* [A history of the Vanderbilt Television News Archive] Franklin, TN: Legacy Communications, 1995.

KATHLEEN A. HANSEN

VANITY FAIR

Few magazines have as interesting a history as *Vanity Fair* (1868–1936, 1983–). Since its founding almost a century and a half ago, the publication has gone through a number of different iterations, and in each instance it proved to be one of the intriguing periodicals of its time.

Debuting in 1868 as a weekly magazine in Great Britain, *Vanity Fair*'s coverage focused on politics, society, and literature. It was best known for its caricatures of prominent figures by such artists as Thomas Nast, James Jacques Tissot, and Carlo Pellegrini. All told, more than two thousand of these caricatures appeared in the publication, with a variety of subjects that included artists, athletes, royalty, actors, soldiers, and scholars.

Thomas Nast bought the publication in 1913, renaming it *Dress and Vanity Fair*, but after only four issues the magazine was transformed and relaunched in 1914 with the original name under the editorial direction of Frank Crowninshield. Crowninshield was one of the major cultural arbiters of his time and an ideal choice for editor. He had, for example, organized the Armory Show in New York City which introduced Cubism to the United States, and his connections in the art world and Manhattan society were legendary.

Under Crowninshield, *Vanity Fair* covered all the topics he presumed to be part of an urbane and sophisticated conversation—art, sports, drama, humor—and he recruited the most celebrated *literati* of the age as contributors, including e.e. cummings, Aldous Huxley, T. S. Eliot, Theodore Dreiser, F. Scott Fitzgerald, H. L. Mencken, Edgar Allen Poe, Carl Sandburg, Ezra Pound, George Bernard Shaw, and photographer Man Ray.

A victim of the Great Depression, *Vanity Fair* was folded into *Vogue* in 1936, disappearing until the name was revived in 1983 by Condé Nast Publishing as a somewhat pretentious upscale society monthly. A year later, however, Christina (Tina) Hambley Brown, formerly at Britain's gossipy *Tattler* magazine, became the editor, and the publication quickly repositioned itself to respond to the American obsession with celebrity, wealth, and scandal. Circulation increased significantly under Brown's editorship, as did the stable of prominent writers she attracted from other magazines with notably generous contributors' fees.

Brown departed to edit the *New Yorker* in 1992, and Edward Graydon Carter, one of the original founders of *Spy* magazine, became *Vanity Fair*'s editor. Carter continued Brown's efforts by enlisting well-known writers such as Gail Sheehy, Christopher Hitchens, David Halberstam, and Marie Brenner, and by pursuing an eclectic editorial mix of articles on high and low culture, celebrities, politics, travel, and entertainment.

Harkening back to a strategy perfected by Crowninshield, who in the 1920s created society events for the magazine to cover, Carter's *Vanity Fair* has kept the tradition alive with its lavish annual post-Academy Awards party in Hollywood. To its readers' evident delight, no effort is spared on either the party or the magazine's coverage of it.

Further Reading

"Christina Hambley Brown." *Wikipedia,* http://en.wikipedia.org/wiki/Tina_Brown.

Collins, Amy Fine, "The Early Years, 1914–1936." *Vintage V.F.,* http://www.vanityfair.com/magazine/vintage/earlyyears/

Friend, David. "The One-Click History," *Vintage V.F.,* http://www.vanityfair.com/magazine/vintage/oneclickhistory.

Mott, Frank Luther. *A History of American Magazines: 1885–1905.* Cambridge, MA: Harvard University Press, 1957.

Peterson, Theodore. *Magazines in the Twentieth Century.* Urbana: University of Illinois Press, 1964.

Tebbel, John, and Mary Ellen Zuckerman. *The Magazine in America: 1741–1990.* New York: Oxford University Press, 1991.

"Vanity Fair magazine," *Wikipedia,* http://en.wikipedia.org/wiki/Vanity_Fair_magazine (accessed April 16, 2007).

DAVID ABRAHAMSON
NICOLE PRICE FASIG

VIDEOTAPE

Videotape changed news reporting. It gave coverage greater immediacy and eventually it allowed more people to participate in newsgathering. But at the outset the technology was so cumbersome and expensive that it seemed impractical. In 1956, CBS-TV affiliates watched in Chicago as Ampex exhibited the first commercially viable quadruplex Video Tape Recorder (VTR). The machine weighed almost half a ton, cost about $90,000, and recorded images only in black-and-white. Over the next four years, as prices declined, Ampex sold six hundred VTRs, most to the major television networks, ABC, CBS, and NBC, which used them to cover such news events as President Dwight D. Eisenhower's inauguration in 1957. The technology continued to improve as machines became lighter and recorded in color, and by 1959, it was being used more frequently in news reporting. In Moscow at the American National Exhibition, an Ampex VTR recorded in color Vice President Richard Nixon's so-called "kitchen debate" with Soviet Premiere Nikita Khrushchev. In November, 1963, videotape did not capture John F. Kennedy's assassination—that was shot on an 8mm home movie camera by Abraham Zapruder—but it did record the murder of Lee Harvey Oswald by Jack Ruby. And it also played an important role in the television coverage of the Kennedy funeral that helped bind the nation together in a shared experience. NBC, for example, used more than twenty VTRs in its reporting of events in the terrible hours following the president's death.

The advantages of videotape became clear to newsmen. It could record sound synchronously with images, and they could be played back at once, and if necessary, edited, all without the usual prolonged chemical processing involved with film. Television stations could erase videotape and reused it over and over again. Videotape also added spontaneity and timeliness to TV news coverage. Certainly 8mm and 16mm film had earlier speeded news reporting, but videotape provided even greater immediacy. "Video is … instantaneous, electronic, and replayable" on many different screens simultaneously, said an early proponent of the medium (Price 1972, 4). The Oswald shooting, which was carried live on TV, was then rebroadcast by television stations around the country only seconds after it happened.

Videotaped changed other types of reporting and broadcasting. With its ability to offer instant replay, it transformed sports coverage during the 1960s. CBS, for example, used instant replay in covering the Army-Navy football game in December, 1963, a game called by the well-known announcer Lindsay Nelson. Instant replay greatly increased the popularity of football on television. In 1964, CBS bought the rights to televise National Football League games and recouped its investment quickly when Ford Motor Company and Philip Morris agreed to sponsor the broadcasts. Advertisers liked videotape, too, and it soon replaced film in most television commercials. By 1965, about one in three TV shows were videotaped. During the 1960s, the number of TV stations that used VTRs increased about six fold. In the decade that followed, the stations with this technology more than doubled again.

Despite the advantages and increasing popularity of videotape, many reporters during the 1960s and 1970s had reservations about the medium. A number of people who worked in television still preferred film over videotape because they found it easier to play and it could store more content than magnetic tape. During the 1967 Arab-Israeli War, newsmen found film cheaper and easier edit than videotape. During the 1970s, many local television reporters continued to weigh the pros and cons of using videotape versus film. The technology "was big and bulky," recalled one reporter who first saw videotape in 1976 while working in Rockford, Illinois. "The camera operator and audio guy were tethered together. A hand held 16mm film camera was actually more flexible but not as instantaneous."

Social and political activists tended to be enthusiastic about videotape during the 1960s. Some of them believed that videotape would bring "an image-making revolution equal to" the ones produced in still photography by Kodak and Polaroid, and they thought that videotape (and other portable media such as 8mm and 16mm cameras) could augment the underground press. Filmmaker Jonas Mekas wrote about the revolutionary potential of these media for *The Village Voice* and proposed using them to develop an alternative journalism that would reveal the true nature of the Vietnam War, expose racism, and publicize the deplorable conditions in prisons and asylums. Still other activists foresaw a day when the technology would become more affordable and the VTR would become a powerful instru-

ment to "create a video democracy" (Armstrong 1981, 72). Some expected that it would make "censorship nearly powerless" (Youngblood 19970, 114).

During the 1960s, the technology was still too costly for most people to own—indeed, *Time* magazine reported in 1965 that "few Americans" had ever seen a recorder. That would soon change, however. In 1965, Sony introduced the Portapak, a portable video recorder and camera that was less expensive and lighter than TV video cameras. It cost from $1,000 to $3,000 compared to the $10,000 to $20,000 needed for the TV camera. Some compared the Portapak's empowerment of independent cameramen and individual citizens to the portable Bolex 16mm film camera used during the early 1940s, or to offset printing that changed newspaper publishing during the 1960s.

Videotape became more and more accessible to both professionals and ordinary citizens during the latter third of the twentieth century and early twenty-first century. Professional cameramen liked it better than film because they felt it allowed them to report on real people in a more authentic manner. With the appearance of ever more mobile and inexpensive technology, such as video surveillance cameras and camcorders, there was a veritable explosion in citizen-produced images used in news reports. One of the major news stories of 1991, for example, was made possible by the amateur videotape made of Los Angeles police officers beating Rodney King. In 2004, home video shot during the Christmas Day tsunami following the Sumatran earthquake provided some of the most powerful images of this catastrophe. By the early twenty-first century, the technology had developed to the point where literally millions of people were capable of recording events. The technology posed serious challenges for journalists and the public as they attempted to assess which of the events they watched were truly newsworthy and which ones were not.

Further Reading

Armstrong, David. *A Trumpet to Arms: Alternative Media in America*. Los Angeles: J. P. Tarcher, Inc., 1981.

Barnouw, Erik. *Image Empire: A History of Broadcasting in the United States: Volume III — from 1953*. New York: Oxford University Press, 1970.

Block, Jerry. "How NBC-TV Newsreel Crews Filmed the Israeli-Arab War." *American Cinematograher*, 48 (December 1967), 868.

Bluth, Joseph E. "More Facts About Vidtronics," *American Cinematographer*, 48 (November 1967), 803.

Daniel, Eric D., C. Denis Mee, and Mark H. Clark, eds. *Magnetic Recording: The First 100 Years*. New York: IEEE Press, 1999.

Fischel, Robert. "Color Film Preferred." *American Cinematographer*, 46 (January 1965): 46.

Hearst, Jr., William Randolph, Frank Conniff, and Bob Considine. *Khrushchev and the Russian Challenge*. New York: Avon Book Division, 1960, 1961, 167–72 (original title *Ask Me Anything — Our Adventures with Khrushchev*, McGraw-Hill Book Company).

Junker, Howard. "Underground Channels." *New Republic*, 157 (September 9, 1967), 33–34.

Marlow, Eugene, and Eugene Secunda. *Shifting Time and Space: The Story of Videotape*. Westport, CT: Praeger, 1991.

Mekas, Jonas. *Movie Journal : The Rise of the New American Cinema, 1959–1971*. New York: Macmillan Company, 1972, 132–136, 186–188, 235–236.

Pierce, Bill. "Videotape: Tomorrow's 35-mm?: A Still Photographer Makes the Transition from 35-mm to Electronic Filming in a Week End." *Popular Photography*, 57 (August 1965), 90–91.

Price, Jonathan. *Video-Visions: A Medium Discovers Itself*. New York: New American Library, 1972, 1977.

Rush, Michael. *Video Art*. London: Thames & Hudson, 2003.

Stockert, Hank. "Is Filming Technology Losing Ground?" *American Cinematographer*, 46 (April, 1965), 228.

"Taping Untapped Markets," *Time*, 85 (February 19, 1965), 90–92.

Youngblood, Gene. *Underground Cinema*. New York: E. P. Dutton Co., Inc., 1970.

STEPHEN VAUGHN

VIETNAM WAR

The Vietnam War, which ended in 1975, was America's longest, most contentious foreign war. Four U.S. presidents deployed more than two million combat personnel to South Vietnam, Cambodia, and Laos, at a peak force in 1969 of 543,054 combatants, resulting in 58,152 U.S. combat deaths and 153,303 seriously wounded, not including civilian casualties. Indochinese casualties on both sides were in the millions. Yet, Vietnam received scant press attention until the United States took over the war in 1965. Americans' ignorance of the growing U.S. commitment could be viewed as a major failure of American journalism.

Despite many challenges, Vietnam War correspondents continued a tradition of outstanding American war reporting and were honored by many Pulitzer Prizes, the foremost American award for journalistic excellence. Press casualties in Vietnam, especially among risk-taking photographers, outpaced those of any other American war.

Following withdrawal of French colonial rulers from Vietnam in 1954, U.S. President Dwight D. Eisenhower saw Southeast Asia as the place to contain the spread of global Communism. His administration financed the anticommunist regime in South Vietnam of nationalist leader Ngo Dinh Diem. Colonel Edward G. Lansdale helped Diem to take control of the southern capital of Saigon. However, Diem's government was handicapped by political corruption and lack of popular support. Despite more American weapons, advisors, and aircraft (U.S. pilots secretly flew combat missions) over the next several years, Diem's army failed to stop Communist rebels, who viewed Diem as a puppet of U.S. imperialism.

In 1960 the rebel guerrillas, nicknamed the Vietcong, pledged to overthrow Diem and to reunify Vietnam. Communist North Vietnam sent weapons and political organizers into the south over a network of footpaths known as the Ho Chi Minh Trail. President John F. Kennedy responded by increasing the contingent of U.S. military advisors to 16,300 and by sending new helicopters and armored personnel carriers.

A military coup in late 1963 left Saigon in chaos. The Vietcong took control of most of the countryside. Bolstered by the North Vietnamese Army (NVA), the Vietcong threatened South Vietnamese cities, so President Lyndon Johnson authorized sustained bombing of North Vietnam (Operation Rolling Thunder) and sent U.S. combat troops to South Vietnam in 1965. A large contingent of Western correspondents, photographers, and television crews accompanied the troops, and Vietnam became front-page news.

The U.S. military commander, General William C. Westmoreland, believed that mobile force deployment by helicopters and overwhelming firepower eventually would deplete the enemy, so he disregarded the political struggle. The Vietcong viewed its struggle as primarily political and exploited the propaganda value of civilian casualties to win support of the Vietnamese peasants. Three years of bloody, indecisive combat caused the United States to realize its attrition strategy would not work, but it took another five years to withdraw from the conflict, leaving the Saigon government to defend itself in 1973. Saigon capitulated in 1975. Political relations between reunified Vietnam and the United States were normalized in 1995, but the war's legacy of doubt and regret remains.

The Diem Regime

From 1960 to 1965 only a handful of American wire service and newspaper correspondents regularly covered events in Saigon.

On January 2–3, 1963, the biggest setback of the war to date for Diem's Army of the Republic of Vietnam (ARVN) at the village of Ap Bai in the Mekong Delta showed that the Vietcong were improving their tactics and weapons. The U.S. Army advisor at Ap Bai, Lieutenant Colonel John Paul Vann, leaked his criticism of ARVN leadership to Neil Sheehan of United Press International (UPI). As ARVN setbacks and political resistance to Diem mounted, Military Assistance Command Vietnam (MACV) in Saigon hardened its stance toward the Saigon press corps. In July 1964, Barry Zorthian, MACV's chief public affairs officer, tried to regain journalists' confidence with his new "Maximum Candor" press policy. Free travel and tours of Vietnam were provided for several dozen newspaper editors. But candor slowly gave way to obfuscation, and a credibility gap emerged between the official MACV line and eyewitness accounts. The correspondents came to regard the daily MACV briefings in the Rex Hotel in Saigon as little more than public relations exercises, which by 1966 acquired the irreverent nickname "five o'clock follies."

Diem was a Roman Catholic who suspected Buddhists of collaborating with the Vietcong to overthrow his government. He used the Mat Vu secret police of his brother, Ngo Dinh Nhu, to persecute Buddhist pagodas. Malcolm Browne's Associated Press (AP) wire photo of the ceremonial self-immolation of Buddhist monk Quang Duc in Saigon on June 7, 1963, stunned newspaper readers around the world and won a Pulitzer Prize for Browne in 1964. Unmoved, Diem continued his repression, and more monks committed ritual suicide for the cameras. The Mat Vu targeted the western media for reprisal. The Diem regime's most strident critic, David Halberstam of the *New York Times*, feared for his life and went into hiding. Halberstam's reporting was honored with a Pulitzer Prize in 1964.

U.S. Escalation

By December 1965, Johnson increased U.S. forces in Vietnam to 184,300, which were followed by hundreds of American journalists, all hunting for a story. On March 20, 1965, AP reporter Peter Arnett and photographer Horst Faas saw ARVN troops carrying gas canisters into combat. The gas turned out to be non-lethal tear gas used to control civilian crowds. MACV refused comment. The AP released the story two days later. Media sensationalism about illegal "poison gas" could have been averted if MACV had disclosed use of the gas. Both Arnett and Faas accompanied troops often into the field for their pictures and stories. In 1965, Faas won a Pulitzer Prize for his combat photography in South Vietnam. The following year, Arnett won a Pulitzer Prize for International Reporting.

Westmoreland believed that superior U.S. technology eventually would win a war of attrition, so he sent "search and destroy" missions to wipe out enemy units. On August 3, 1965, a Columbia Broadcasting System (CBS) television news crew accompanied one such mission. Millions of American viewers were shocked by correspondent Morley Safer's so-called "Zippo lighter" filmed report showing Marines nonchalantly burning the village of Cam Ne near Danang. Military leaders felt the report made U.S. soldiers, not the Vietcong, look like immoral aggressors. MACV accused Safer of manipulating the situation, but Safer actually had deleted some violent scenes from his report. Westmoreland wanted to clamp down on the media, but the Pentagon feared a hostile response and continued with voluntary news guidelines and pandered to journalists who made the military look good.

Beginning in January 1966, a national television audience watched the war policy debate of the U.S. Senate Foreign Relations Committee, chaired by Democratic Senator J. William Fulbright of Arkansas. Fulbright had brokered the president's war powers in the Congress, but now he had second thoughts. The proceedings had little effect on public opinion, and Congress waited another three years to limit war appropriations.

Late in 1966, detailed dispatches and photographs filed from North Vietnam's capital city of Hanoi by Harrison Salisbury, assistant managing editor of the *New York Times*, showed devastated civilian areas and untouched defense works, which contradicted Defense Secretary Robert McNamara's claims about "surgical" bombing strikes. The administration counterattacked by accusing Salisbury of near-treason. A board of publishers caved in to this pressure and in 1967 revoked Salisbury's Pulitzer Prize for his Hanoi reporting. Months later the architect of Rolling Thunder, McNamara, repudiated the bombing campaign to

a Senate subcommittee, to the disbelief of hawkish senators. The admission cost McNamara his job.

Turning Point: The Tet Offensive

Despite Westmoreland's confident declarations about a vanquished foe, the Vietcong proved strong enough in January and February 1968 to attack simultaneously in dozens of cities and military outposts throughout South Vietnam. A Vietcong suicide squad held the U.S. Embassy in Saigon for more than six hours. On February 1 in Saigon, AP photographer Eddie Adams and National Broadcasting Company cameraman Vo Suu photographed General Nguyen Ngo Loan, chief of South Vietnam's national police, executing a Vietcong officer. Adams' photograph dominated newspapers the next day and won a Pulitzer Prize in 1969. In Hué, Communists held a fortress known as the Citadel for twenty-five days of the most savage fighting of the war. Later were revealed the mass graves of nearly three thousand Hué citizens murdered by the Vietcong during its political purge in the city. Despite admitting it had been caught off guard by the enemy offensive, MACV claimed tactical victory during Tet. For a time, Americans patriotically rallied around their flag, but disillusionment soon set in.

Westmoreland believed the attacks on cities masked the enemy's real intention to capture the remote U.S. mountain base at Khesanh near the demilitarized zone separating North and South Vietnam. He reinforced the Khesanh garrison and prepared emergency replacements. When the NVA attacked in strength, Westmoreland ordered saturation bombing of the perimeter—the most intensive strategic bombing campaign to that date in the history of warfare. When the enemy withdrew after a nine-week inconclusive siege, the base was abandoned, triggering charges that Westmoreland had wasted the lives of U.S. servicemen to defend a meaningless outpost. Westmoreland was replaced by General Creighton W. Abrams in June 1968.

Westmoreland never forgave the media, particularly television, for doubting his assessment of the Tet Offensive. In 1982, he filed a $120 million lawsuit against CBS News for libeling him in a documentary, *The Uncounted Enemy: A Vietnam Deception*. CBS based its report on claims of former Central Intelligence Agency analyst Sam Adams, who said the general had intentionally underestimated enemy strength prior to the Tet Offensive in order to justify his optimism. After eighteen weeks of testimony in a New York courtroom, CBS settled out of court. However, a pall on Westmoreland's reputation lingered.

CBS television news anchor Walter Cronkite personally inspected the Tet action and returned to New York convinced of the war's futility. On February 27, 1968, Cronkite broke with journalistic objectivity by broadcasting his opinion that the United States was mired in a stalemate in Vietnam. Losing Cronkite's support stunned Johnson, who was facing a reelection campaign. On March 31, 1968, Johnson addressed the nation on television and announced that he would not seek another term. On November 5, 1968, Richard M. Nixon won the presidency by promising Americans an honorable end of the war.

Vietnam War Controversies

The most controversial battle of the Vietnam War was fought in May 1969 on a mountain named Dong Ap Bia near the Laotian border. Repeated heavy bombardment and twelve frontal assaults over nine days were needed to overcome the enemy's mountaintop position. News reports repeated the Marines' mocking nickname for the mountain, "Hamburger Hill." The battle became a public relations nightmare for the Nixon administration when Senator Ted Kennedy of Massachusetts decried the battle's senseless waste of American youth. Some of the battle's veterans sent letters of support to Kennedy.

A sensationalized incident captured headlines for months and increased disillusionment over the war. On June 20, 1969, Colonel Robert B. Rheault and seven of his "Green Berets" in the Fifth Special Forces Group executed a suspected North Vietnamese spy named Thai Khac Chuyen at the request of a station chief of the Central Intelligence Agency. Because Rheault lied to MACV about the affair, Abrams had the soldiers arrested for murder. The story broke in the *New York Times* in August. After MACV refused comment, civilian attorneys of the accused suggested to the press that Abrams was motivated by a personal vendetta. Congress received protest letters from families of the accused. The Green Berets case soon swelled into a general debate on the war. After several months, President Nixon intervened, and the soldiers were released for lack of evidence.

The June 27, 1969, "Faces of the Dead" issue of *Life* magazine is believed by many to have influenced the American public as much as any other media event of the Vietnam War and is remembered as the zenith of *Life's* journalism. The magazine featured the photographs of most of the 242 U.S. troops killed during the previous weeks of fighting. The dead soldiers' innocence was captured in pictures from high school yearbooks and personal memorabilia. No editorial copy was needed to communicate a compelling anti-war message. Because the military draft deferred college students, the faces of the dead were disproportionately working class.

The worst war atrocity in U.S. history was uncovered by Seymour Hersh on November 16, 1969. Hersh's syndicated story told of the murder of more than five hundred Vietnamese peasants during a search and destroy mission on March 10, 1968, in My Lai, a hamlet in the northern part of South Vietnam. In a news release in September, 1969, the Army announced the arrest and pending court martial of U. S. troops and Hersh followed up this lead. He confirmed that a massacre had occurred when he interviewed an officer accused of personally executing 109 of the villagers, First Lieutenant William Calley. Follow-up stories revealed photographs of the massacre by an Army photographer and accusations of a cover-up by the Army. Calley's case became a referendum on the war. A military court convicted Calley, who was paroled in 1975. Hersh won the 1970 Pulitzer Prize for international reporting.

Vietnamization and U.S. Withdrawal

In July of 1969, Nixon announced his war plan: the ARVN would take over the fighting, while U.S. troops assumed garrison duties and eventually withdrew. Although a French attempt at "Vietnamization" in the early 1950s had failed, Nixon maintained that superior U.S. firepower would make it work this time. Even the South Vietnamese doubted their chances against the NVA.

The change of mission for U.S. troops, plus a greater reliance on conscripts, hurt morale and discipline. With announcement of troop withdrawals, an American soldier's personal mission was reduced to surviving his yearlong tour of duty. The Saigon government profited from trade in narcotics, so many GIs used drugs to relieve the tensions of combat duty, which further reduced combat readiness. On November 13, 1970, a broadcast by CBS reporter Gary Shepard about widespread pot smoking at Firebase Ares caused a national scandal back home.

Low morale was blamed for outbreaks of GI insubordination. The first reported incident in August 1969 concerned the Twenty-third Infantry Division stationed in Song Chang Valley south of Danang. An AP story by Peter Arnett and Horst Faas stated that Alpha Company had refused to renew its attack after five attempts to recover a downed helicopter had been turned away by ferocious enemy fire. Military spokesmen claimed the mutiny was limited to a few men, but the soldiers told reporters the entire company balked. Nine days later a second unit refused its orders. Several newspaper columnists dismissed the incidents and blamed Arnett and Faas for harming GI morale.

The anti-war movement was losing patience with apparent lack of progress to end the war. On October 15, 1969, massive war protest "moratoriums" were staged in Washington, D.C., and other major cities. Attention from the national media served to legitimate anti-war sentiments. Nixon addressed a national television audience on November 3 and asked the "silent majority" of Americans to trust him to win an honorable peace in Vietnam. The speech restored his standing and deflated the protestors, who staged another moratorium on November 15.

Another televised Nixon address six months later shocked the nation and sparked protests on college campuses across America. On April 30, 1970, Nixon announced a combined U.S.-ARVN ground invasion of Cambodia to suppress NVA sanctuaries. Although intended to bring the war to swifter conclusion, the operation's long-term effects were to cause civil strife in America and to destabilize the neutralist regime of Cambodia's leader, Prince Norodom Sihanouk. On May 4, 1970, a violent clash between students and national guard troops at Kent State University in Ohio left four students dead and seven wounded. Undergraduate John Filo won a Pulitzer Prize for his photo of Mary Vecchio decrying the death of fellow student Jeffrey Miller.

The image was transmitted by the AP and became a bitter icon of the Vietnam War.

Nixon wanted to show that his "Vietnamization" policy was working. He proposed an ARVN incursion into Laos with U.S. air support to interdict enemy strongholds. Launched on January 29, 1971, Operation Lam Son 719 targeted the Laotian town of Tchepone fifty kilometers northwest of the old U.S. base at Khesanh. Hoping to surprise the enemy, Abrams embargoed all news coverage of the operation. Reporters protested that the huge ARVN convoy hardly could have escaped the enemy's attention. The reporters were right. The North Vietnamese were prepared to repel the attack and inflicted heavy losses, especially of U.S. helicopters. Eventually Nixon ordered Abrams to loosen his press restrictions. Pilots were authorized to transport journalists to the battle zone. On February 10, a helicopter with the first load of photographers was shot down with all lives lost, including *Life* magazine's Larry Burrows, AP's Henri Huet, UPI's Ken Potter and ARVN Sergeant Vu Tu. An NVA counterattack on February 19 routed ARVN troops and transformed Lam Son into a public relations fiasco for the White House. Nixon later told Kissinger that their worst enemy seemed to be the press.

In June 1971, the *New York Times* began publishing installments of the *Pentagon Papers,* a forty-seven volume classified internal analysis of Vietnam War miscalculations, which were turned over to *Times* reporter Neil Sheehan by their author, former Defense Department official Daniel Ellsberg. A federal injunction stopped publication on grounds of national security and theft of government property. The *Times* got around the injunction by giving the documents to a rival paper, the *Washington Post.* Two weeks later the U.S. Supreme Court ruled 6–3 to dismiss the injunction because the papers, though embarrassing to the government, did not threaten national security.

Due to thawing of relations with Red China and the Soviet Union and a preliminary breakthrough in Paris peace talks with the North Vietnamese, Nixon won a landslide reelection victory in 1972. On January 23, 1973, Nixon and Kissinger proclaimed "peace with honor" in formal agreements to be signed on January 27 in Paris by all warring parties. The United States agreed to withdraw, leaving the ARVN to defend its own country. Nixon guaranteed continued air and logistical support. The release of U.S. prisoners of war commanded the news agenda for months. The search for U.S. soldiers missing in action was concluded in 1995.

Despite these foreign relations victories, Nixon was forced to resign in disgrace on August 9, 1974, after the press uncovered White House malfeasance in the so-called Watergate scandal. As soon as Vice President Gerald R. Ford was sworn in as the new chief executive, he reassured South Vietnam of continued U.S. support, but Congress already had begun cutting war funding. Eight months later, Saigon collapsed before an NVA assault on April 30, 1975. News film of frantic refugees, rooftop evacuations, and helicopters jettisoned from aircraft carrier decks symbolized for the American people a quarter century of failed government policies and the end of innocence.

Press Impact during the Vietnam War

Democracies cannot fight long wars without public support. As messengers of bad news about the Vietnam War, the media inevitably were caught up in the war's controversy and marked by it. The war spawned several mistaken ideas about the wartime role of the American press, which persist despite having been thoroughly debunked by scholars.

The incorrect notion that the American television networks brought home the horrors of war to the American viewing public, thereby handicapping a military solution, was born in 1966, when Michael J. Arlen's *New Yorker* column referred to Vietnam as America's first "living-room war." In fact, the networks were skittish about violating viewers' sensibilities. Subsequent analyses of newscasts showed that most news programs avoided graphic violence.

Another persistent misunderstanding casts Vietnam War correspondents as belligerent, anti-establishment critics who broke rules to make the government look bad. Research shows the vast majority of journalists cooperated fully with MACV's guidelines. Only six journalists of the thousands certified by MACV were stripped of their credentials.

Perhaps the greatest myth about news coverage of the Vietnam War, one that nevertheless has guided U.S. military planners since, was promulgated by Spiro T. Agnew, Nixon's vice president. Agnew accused the American press of serving the enemy cause by influencing U.S. public opinion against the war. Opinion polls conducted throughout the conflict showed that the news media actually trailed behind the public in its growing disapproval of the U.S. war effort. Critical news commentaries late in the war merely served to confirm already held anti-war attitudes.

Vietnam was the only uncensored U.S. war in the post-telegraph era. Government press handlers' efforts to be open with correspondents eventually were confounded by Washington's desire to cast the war effort and its South Vietnamese ally in the best possible light. A credibility gap resulted. Many correspondents found their questioning dispatches toned down or disregarded altogether by stateside editors, who were persuaded by the more optimistic "big picture" painted by MACV and the Pentagon.

The Pentagon decided free press access prevented an otherwise certain military victory in Vietnam. The Joint Chiefs of Staff appointed a former MACV press officer to lead a panel on the issue. In 1984 the Sidle Commission's recommendations for limited press pools in conflict zones were sold to the American public as reasonable safety measures and were key to the military's mastery of press access during the Persian Gulf War of 1990–1991.

Further Reading

Cook, Russell J. *The Vietnam War (The Greenwood Library of American War Reporting, Volume 7).* Westport, CT: Greenwood Press, 2005.

Fawcett, Denby, et al. *War Torn: Stories of War from the Women Reporters Who Covered Vietnam.* New York: Random House, 2002.

Hallin, Daniel. *The "Uncensored War": The Media and Vietnam.* New York: Oxford University Press, 1986.

Hammond, William M. *Reporting Vietnam: Media and Military at War.* Lawrence: University Press of Kansas, 1998.

Just, Ward S. *To What End: Report from Vietnam.* Boston: Houghton Mifflin Company, 1968.

Karnow, Stanley. *Vietnam: A History,* 2nd. rev. ed. New York: Penguin Books, 1997.

Landers, James. *The Weekly War: Newsmagazines and Vietnam.* Columbia: University of Missouri Press, 2004.

Prochnau, William. *Once Upon a Distant War: David Halberstam, Neil Sheehan, Peter Arnett — Young War Correspondents and Their Early Vietnam Battles.* New York: Vintage Books, 1996.

Reporting Vietnam (Part One: American Journalism 1959–1969, Part Two: American Journalism 1969–1975). New York: Literary Classics of the United States, Inc., 1998.

Sheehan, Neil. *A Bright Shining Lie: John Paul Vann and America in Vietnam.* New York: Vintage, 1989.

Wyatt, Clarence R. *Paper Soldiers: The American Press and the Vietnam War,* rev. ed. Chicago: University of Chicago Press, 1995.

RUSSELL J. COOK

VOICE OF AMERICA

Soon after becoming Director of the Voice of America (VOA) (1942–2006) in 1965, broadcast journalist John Chancellor defined VOA as functioning "at the crossroads of journalism and diplomacy." That phrase captures both the nature and mission of the first (and still largest) official international broadcast service of the United States. Its primary function is to inform listeners in other nations about life in the United States. However, its Charter (P.L. 94-350) requires that it also "present the policies of the United States clearly and effectively and will also present responsible discussion and opinion on these policies." Any journalist would recognize the wide range of possible interpretations for "effectively" and "responsible." Since VOA is government-funded, those interpretations are likely to reflect the political agendas of the Executive and Legislative Branches, including the Departments of State and Defense. In such a situation, journalism and diplomacy may operate at cross-purposes, and VOA's history offers many illustrative examples. However, its history also displays a commitment to broad, balanced coverage that, if inconsistent, nevertheless has earned it a worldwide reputation for reliability second only to that of the BBC World Service.

World War II

The Voice of America was created in 1942 by amalgamating several private international broadcasting services and placing the new service under the jurisdiction of the Office of War Information. Its first transmission in February 1942 began with the statement "Daily, at this time, we shall speak to you about America and the war. The news may be good or bad. We shall tell you the truth." Wartime censorship did not make it easy to tell "the whole truth," but VOA often noted American battlefield losses. However, it rarely featured negative news on the home front, such as the River Rouge, Michigan "race riots" in 1943.

Occasionally, it contradicted U. S. government policy. For example, a 1943 broadcast referred to the "moronic little king" of Italy (Victor Emmanuel II) even as U. S. diplomatic efforts were underway to persuade the king to withdraw his support for Italian dictator Benito Mussolini. The problem stemmed from distance (official guidance from Washington often was slow to reach VOA headquarters in New York City), but also a measure of policy-maker contempt for broadcasting as an instrument of diplomacy.

The U. S. Congress generally accepted the need for an international broadcast service during the war, although some Republican members criticized VOA (and OWI in general) for its overwhelmingly favorable coverage of President Franklin D. Roosevelt, even though VOA did not broadcast to the United States. Some also were concerned that the service would continue following the war, fearing that a peacetime government-run Voice of America would be manipulated by the administration.

The Cold War

After the war, VOA operated on a sharply reduced budget, with Congressional appropriations providing only temporary support. In December 1945 it came under the control of the State Department. Soon, Associated Press and United Press withdrew their services, not wishing to be linked with a "propaganda operation." The Smith-Mundt Act made United States government international informational and educational services permanent in 1948, mainly because of concern over increasingly virulent anti-Western propaganda coming from the Soviet Union and its allies. The resulting war of words between the West and the East lasted until the early 1990s, and VOA played a prominent role in it, but a role soon shared with other U. S. government (largely CIA) supported services such as Radio Free Europe, Radio Liberty, and numerous clandestine radio stations.

VOA journalism early in the Cold War was reminiscent of its work during World War II, with strong attacks on the enemy (Communist governments), support for their long-suffering people, positive treatment of democratic institutions, and emphasis on U.S. military and economic strength. The attacks moderated by the end of the 1950s, as it became evident that the United States would not intervene militarily to challenge Soviet control in Eastern Europe.

The Rise of the Third World

As a substantial portion of the world moved from colonial rule to independence after the World War II, and these newly emerging Third World nations became increasingly important targets for international broadcasting. Both the West and the Communist-bloc nations attempted to develop political and economic alliances with them, and invested heavily in establishing language services to reach them. VOA broadcasts emphasized U. S. financial and technological aid to the emerging nations, along with generally positive treatment of the U. S. Civil Rights movement. They criticized dictatorial practices of Communist governments, while highlighting U. S. economic and military strength.

VOA also covered events taking place within the new nations—an indication of American respect but also recognition that access to information about Third World nations in general, even immediate neighbors, was so limited. Gathering such information was difficult, since VOA had few correspondents or stringers in those nations. Supervision of program content emanating from VOA foreign language services also became more challenging: few U. S. citizens were capable of monitoring the accuracy of translations from English into Hausa or determining whether commentary from a Hindi service staff member was in accordance with official U. S. policy.

One newly independent nation—Vietnam—eventually posed a major challenge for VOA journalists. By the mid-1960s the United States was deeply involved in supporting the southern portion of the divided nation. White House and State Department pressure on VOA to support American policy intensified, despite rising public discontent in the United States over the Vietnam War (what the VOA referred to as a "conflict"). When the American embassy in Saigon was evacuated in 1975, the State Department forbade VOA to cover it, even though every other major international broadcast service was doing so.

A Bid for Independence

After the United States Information Agency (USIA) became VOA's parent in 1953, the State Department continued to influence VOA by issuing guidelines, involving itself in personnel decisions (especially through U. S. embassy control over VOA foreign correspondents), and sometimes restricting VOA's coverage of such sensitive issues. The restrictions on covering the evacuation of Saigon strengthened the determination of VOA journalists to seek independent status for the service. In 1975, two private bodies—the Murphy Commission and the Stanton Panel—filed reports with the United States Congress recommending independent status for VOA, with provision for State Department-supervised broadcasts setting forth official U. S. policy.

In 1978, Congress approved the restructuring of USIA, keeping VOA within it. While some members favored independence, far more wanted it to remain within USIA, where Congress could exercise oversight of an operation some regarded with suspicion, particularly when it portrayed (as in its evenhanded coverage of Watergate) a less than unified United States. In 1979, VOA implemented a self-commissioned report recommending that its foreign correspondents be separated as much as possible from U.S. embassies—no diplomatic passports, commissary privileges, or embassy housing—in return for greater freedom to report from the field. It seemed to have immediate utility, since a VOA correspondent could interview officials from both sides in the Nicaraguan civil war during 1979–1980 even though

the U. S. embassy had no official contact with the rebel Sandinistas.

The Collapse of Communism

During the 1970s, the U. S. and Communist governments were less critical of one another, which reduced pressure on VOA to attack Communism. In the 1980s, however, the Republican administration revived some of the 1950s Cold War when President Ronald Reagan denounced the Soviet Union as the "evil empire." Pressure mounted on VOA to support the administration by featuring outspoken anti-Soviet figures such as Alexander Solzhenitzyn and devoting more attention to the USSR's problems. Although the VOA complied to some extent, administration supporters often criticized it for not doing enough. That again caused newsroom staff to regard themselves as "second class" journalists, although they took pride in their reporting on the injustices of the *apartheid* policies of the South African government despite some Congressional criticism.

By the early 1990s, Eastern Europe and the Soviet Union itself discarded Communism. VOA, Radio Free Europe, and Radio Liberty claimed some credit in bringing that about, but government officials questioned the need to continue such services, now that the Cold War was over. In 1998, Congress approved a unified structure for them, headed by a presidentially appointed Broadcasting Board of Governors (BBG). The budget was cut, and VOA came under the same overall administrative roof with the CIA-originated Radio Free Europe and Radio Liberty, causing its journalists to wonder whether listeners might lose trust in VOA newscasts.

The BBG also developed "tactical" services aimed at specific nations or regions, such as Radio Sawa to the Middle East, and Radio Farda to Iran. Radio Sawa replaced VOA's Arabic service, aimed chiefly at opinion leaders, with a heavily youth-oriented program schedule featuring more emphasis on music than on news and current affairs, raising fears of a diminished role for VOA journalists. Just after the September 11, 2001, suicide attacks, VOA prepared a program containing several views on that event, including excerpts from an interview conducted by the head of its Pashto Service with Afghanistan's Taliban leader Mullah Muhammad Omar, who regarded the attacks as justifiable. The State Department strongly opposed using Omar's observations. BBG members were divided on whether to include them. VOA Acting Director Myrna Whitworth decided to go ahead with the broadcast. Within months, the Pashto Service head and Whitworth were reassigned to other positions within VOA.

Many VOA journalists regarded the changes in program services and reassignments of personnel as diminishing the importance of objective journalism. Days after the reassignment of their News Director in July 2004, 450 staff members submitted petitions to Congress, calling for an investigation of the BBG on the grounds that it was exercising undue political influence over VOA and endangering its credibility. Congress did not respond. In February, 2006, the BBG proposed restructuring VOA's schedule by eliminating several language services and substantially reducing the English service, including much of the journalistic programming. The BBG stated that this would provide additional funding for broadcasts to Muslim nations, but critics saw it as one more diminution in the importance of journalism. The crossroads of journalistic freedom and politically-influenced diplomatic necessity remain an unresolved bone of contention between VOA's journalists and Washington's various political forces (including administrative appointees within VOA). That situation seems destined to continue so long as VOA remains a government-funded service.

Further Reading

Alexandre, Laurien. *The Voice of America: From Détente to the Reagan Doctrine*. Norwood: Ablex, 1988.

Browne, Donald R. "The Voice of America: Policies and Problems." *Journalism Monographs*, no. 43, 1976.

Heil, Alan.*The Voice of America: A History*. New York: Columbia University Press, 2003.

Krugler, David. *The Voice of America and the Domestic Propaganda Battles, 1945–1953*. Columbia: University of Missouri Press, 2000.

Pirsein, Robert W. *The Voice of America: a History of the International Broadcasting Activities of the United States Government, 1940–1962*. New York: Arno Press, 1979.

Rawnsley, Gary D. *Radio Diplomacy and Propaganda*. New York: St. Martin's Press, 1996.

Schulman, Holly C. *The Voice of America: Propaganda and Democracy, 1942–1945*. Madison: University of Wisconsin Press, 1990.

Snyder, Alvin A. *Warriors of Disinformation: American Propaganda, Soviet Lies, and the Winning of the Cold War — An Insider's Account*. New York: Arcade, 1995.

DONALD R. BROWNE

WALL STREET JOURNAL

The *Wall Street Journal*, based in New York City and owned by Dow Jones & Company, is the United States' only true national business daily, and the first American newspaper to aspire and achieve national circulation. In addition to an American edition, the paper—unique among American newspapers—also publishes Asian and European editions, operates one of the few successful subscription-only news web sites, and provides content to the financial news cable channel, CNBC. As of 2005 the *Journal's* American print circulation was second only to *USA Today* (1,750,000). In late 2005 the newspaper, long a weekday paper, was planning to add a weekend edition published on Saturday with a higher proportion of softer life-style oriented coverage, in part, as a reaction to declining circulation, an affliction it shares with many other American newspapers. Since World War II the paper has gradually expanded its coverage of non-business matters although at heart it remains a business paper.

The paper, the key profit center of Dow Jones, has been controlled since the late 1920s by the Bancroft family which in a manner reminiscent of the role the Sulzberger family plays for the *New York Times* shields it from some of the commercial and political pressures involved in being one of a handful of influential and high-circulation print media outlets in the U.S. In contrast to the Sulzbergers, the Bancrofts are less involved in the day-to-day management of the newspaper.

The newspaper boasts a very affluent and politically influential readership. According to 2003 estimates, the average annual income of a *Journal* reader stood at over $200,000. In the United States, its chief competitors among dailies are the *New York Times* and the *Financial Times,* although it now also contends with a plethora of television and Internet-based purveyors of business news.

The *Journal* was founded in 1889 as an outgrowth of a financial newsletter published by Dow Jones & Company, a firm established by Charles H. Dow, Edward D. Jones, and Charles M. Bergstresser who identified the growing need for accurate information as New York City became a national and then global financial center. In its early years many reporters exploited their positions as disseminators of financial news to collaborate with speculators and companies. This problem characterized many other publications as well. Although almost totally eradicated at the *Journal*, it reappeared with the trial of one of its reporters, R. Foster Winans, in the 1980s, who was found guilty of insider trading after he traded in stocks he later wrote about in a daily stock market column.

For many years the paper was considered of secondary importance to the Dow Jones' main revenue producer, its news wire. During the early years of the twentieth century, it remained supportive of big business and relatively critical of anti-trust policies. The *Journal* was a staunch booster of the stock market in the years preceding the 1929 crash. During the Great Depression, the paper teetered on the brink of extinction.

From World War II onwards the paper under the direction of Bernard (Barney) Kilgore broadened its coverage to include, aside from strictly financial news, in-depth coverage of economics as well as American politics and society, and foreign affairs while avoiding technical economic or financial terminology. This editorial move was made in an effort to broaden the newspaper's appeal beyond the financial community and make it into a national publication. This effort was successful as Kilgore's reign coincided with a rapid advance in circulation figures and the appearance of a nationwide subscription base. The expansion was helped by the war's transformation of the American economy from a quilt of regional and local economies into an integrated national economy.

One of Kilgore's most notable innovations was the partial rejection of the traditional "inverted pyramid" style of writing which demanded the inclusion of the key facts of any issue or event in the first few paragraphs of a story (the 5 Ws). Instead, Kilgore instituted a more narrative style that stressed detailed description and polished writing, the exposition of an argument and a counter-argument—an early example of interpretive journalism. The "What's News" feature, a page-one digest of news stories introduced in 1934, was expanded into two columns, a business and finance column and a worldwide column. Considerable effort was put in the paper's front page with the assumption that as a second paper for many American business people it did not have to feature every piece of breaking news but instead should provide the most exhaustive and accurate analyses of key business and political trends to supplement the reader's hometown newspaper. In addition, the *Journal's* front page is noted for the "A-head" story, first instituted in 1941 under Kilgore, which features frequently quirky topics such as a 1981 story on a Scottish dentist who developed braces for sheep.

The *Journal's* editorial pages under the editorship of

Robert Bartley between 1972 and 2003 became renowned for their staunch free market positions continuing the paper's long standing support for Republican policies and administrations. The pages have been held by many as paragons of engaging and influential editorial writing while others have criticized them for sometimes circumventing the truth and ignoring facts already reported in the news columns to buttress ideological beliefs.

The *Journal* had to continuously fight against its image as a boring, narrow-interest newspaper. Some of this image no doubt came from its long-time reluctance to use color and a heavy reliance on text. In 1979 the paper began including small half-column portrait heads of newsmakers using a dot laying technique to illustrate stories—a feature now closely identified with the paper. Color was introduced on its front page only in 2002 at the same time that a section featuring personal finance and life-style issues was added.

Until late into the twentieth century, the newspaper's editorial staff was predominantly male with the exception of the World War II years when the *Journal* recruited women to replace men who had gone to war.

Further Reading

Auletta, K. "Family Business; Annals of Communications." *New Yorker* 79(33): (November 3, 2003), 54–67.

Rosenberg, J.M. *Inside the Wall Street Journal.* New York: Mac-Millan, 1982.

Royster, V. *My Own, My Country's Time.* Chapel Hill: Algon-quin, 1983.

Scharff, E. E. *Worldly Power: The Making of The Wall Street Journal.* New York, Plume, 1988.

ROEI DAVIDSON

WALLACES FARMER

For more than a century, *Wallaces Farmer* has been one of the most prominent farm journals in the United States. Founded in 1895 by three members of one family, it began as *Wallace's Farm and Dairy* and then *Wallaces' Farmer and Dairyman*. The shift in the apostrophe's location proclaimed that it was a family publication. The first editor was the patriarch, Henry Wallace (1836–1916). A Presbyterian minister, he had entered agricultural journalism in 1880, soon became editor of the *Iowa Homestead*, but, after clashing over editorial policy with the business manager, James Pierce, lost his position. He quickly joined forces with two of his sons, Henry C. and John, in the new venture. By the beginning of the twentieth century, it had become profitable, dropped *and Dairyman* from the name, and adopted a slogan: Good Farming — Clear Thinking — Right Living.

Based in Des Moines and focused on corn-belt farmers, *Wallaces' Farmer* had a broad range, including politics and religion as well as farming. The Wallaces used the magazine as an instrument of reform. They sought to persuade farmers to discard their disdain for "book farming" and treat farming as an intellectual as well as a physical enter-prise. Such changes, they assumed, would make farming more productive, more rewarding, and more satisfying and persuade bright boys and girls to stay on the land. Thus, the nation would get the large and talented farm population it required for success. Hoping to build what they called a "distinctly rural civilization" outside the cities, the reformers were determined to prevent the United States from becoming totally urban in population and culture.

For four decades, the Wallaces edited their magazine, and it enabled them to become wealthy and prominent. President Theodore Roosevelt appointed Henry to a Country Life Commission in 1908 (created to improve the quality of agricultural and rural life). After his death in 1916, Henry C. (1866–1924) succeeded him as editor and served until Warren Harding called upon him in 1921 to become secretary of agriculture. His son, Henry A. (1888–1965), then took over and remained editor until 1933 when Franklin Roosevelt chose him to represent agriculture in the president's cabinet.

Shortly before Henry A. moved to Washington, the family lost ownership of the magazine. They had purchased their rival, the *Iowa Homestead*, in 1929, but the Great Depression seriously damaged their business, enabling Dante Pierce, James's son, to take control of *Wallaces' Farmer and Iowa Homestead*.

The magazine remained in business well into the twenty-first century. Along the way, it removed the apostrophe and became simply *Wallaces Farmer*. It maintained its focus on Iowa farmers, trying to help them become profitable. They became the scientific and productive farmers the Wallaces had encouraged them to be. In fact, they participated in an agricultural revolution. Contrary to the hopes of the Wallaces, however, the revolution did not hold farmers on the land. Instead, it substituted technologies for people, sharply reducing the size of the farm population.

By the twenty-first century, *Wallaces Farmer* had become significantly different from what it had been when the Wallaces were in command. It was no longer family-owned. Instead, it was part of a large nation-wide combine, the Farm Progress Companies. Its circulation was only about a quarter of what it had been at its peak following the merger of 1929 when circulation included about 250,000 paying subscribers. The magazine, like Iowa farmers, had felt the force of the agricultural revolution.

Further Reading

Culver, John C., and John Hyde. *American Dreamer: A Life of Henry A. Wallace.* New York: W.W. Norton & Company, 2000.

Kirkendall, Richard S. *Uncle Henry: A Documentary Profile of the First Henry Wallace.* Ames: Iowa State University Press, 1993.

Wallaces Farmer, http://www.wallacesfarmer.com.

Winters, Donald L. Winters. *Henry Cantwell Wallace as Secretary of Agriculture, 1921–1924.* Urbana: University of Illinois Press, 1970.

RICHARD S. KIRKENDALL

WAR OF 1812

Officially, the War of 1812 began when the United States Congress declared war on Great Britain on June 18, 1812. The tensions that produced the war dated back to the 1790s and had grown during the early 1800s as Britain found herself at war once more with France. The major issues revolved around trade restrictions as Britain sought to strike at her enemy by cutting off trade with the United States. Throughout the conflict with Great Britain, the American press discussed and debated the various issues involved while providing their readers with details of the war.

War almost broke out in 1807 when the British ship *HMS Leopard* fired on the *USS Chesapeake* when her captain refused to allow a search for deserters. American casualties included three dead and eighteen wounded. Many Americans pushed for war, but President Thomas Jefferson was able to avoid it at the time. Pressure built over the next five years until war seemed unavoidable.

The American press played an important role in the years of growing tension. Newspapers provided information about the arguments with Great Britain prior to the war and details of the military conflict once war was declared. But the role of the press in the War of 1812 was complicated because of how it functioned prior to the war. Political partisanship had dominated the American media since the American Revolution, and those divisions influenced the press coverage of the arguments with Great Britain. The Republican press generally supported the administrations of Thomas Jefferson and James Madison as they responded to British actions, while the Federalist newspapers initially urged caution and came out strongly against the war once it had begun. Thus, the coverage of the War of 1812 got caught up in the political partisan battles of the early Republic.

Perhaps the most important newspaper during the Republican administration of James Madison was the *National Intelligencer*, edited by Joseph Gales Jr. and William Winston Seaton. Throughout the war, Gales and Seaton provided as much information as they could acquire on military activities and the actions of Congress. Their battle reports appeared in newspapers throughout the nation because editors knew that Gales and Seaton, as the semiofficial government paper, had good access to government reports.

The *National Intelligencer* also led the debate over whether the war with Britain was a good idea. Even before war was declared, Gales and Seaton urged Americans to stand firm in face of British oppression. In the April 14, 1812, issue, they declared that "our wrongs have been great; our cause is just; and, if we are decided and firm, success is inevitable." Once war was declared, they said that the time for debate had ended. On June 27, 1812, Gales and Seaton stated that "This is not the time for debating the propriety of war. WAR IS DECLARED, and every patriot heart must unite in its support."

For Gales and Seaton, the time for discussion about the war had ended. But for many other newspaper editors, particularly those who supported the Federalist Party, the war against Great Britain never made much sense. These disagreements about the validity of the conflict continued until war's end. Some editors perceived the war as unavoidable, but the Federalists saw it as a big mistake. Throughout the war, Federalists argued that the war was being fought over meaningless issues and that it was a waste of lives and money. Several leading Federalist newspapers came out openly against the war with Britain. Included in this group were the *Federal Republican* in Baltimore (Maryland), the *United States Gazette* in Philadelphia, the *Alexandria* (Virginia) *Gazette* and *New York Evening Post*. As these papers became more vocal in their opposition to the war, the issue arose of how much press criticism could be allowed during times of crisis. Madison, as author of the First Amendment and a supporter of a free press, could not sanction government action against such critics, even when they seemed to undermine the success of the government's war effort. Many people, however, did not agree with the president, and in some parts of the country, opposition became increasingly dangerous. Mobs drove both the *American Patriot* (Savannah, Georgia) and the *Norristown Herald* (Pennsylvania) out of business in 1812. Crowds threatened other Federalist editors with bodily harm if they did not end their opposition. The worst example of mob violence against a Federalist editor occurred in Baltimore in June 1812 when a mob destroyed the office and equipment of the *Federal Republican*. Attacks on British sympathizers and anyone suspected of secretly trading with the British continued in Baltimore for two more months.

Once Congress actually declared war and Americans braced for armed conflict, the press tried to keep readers informed about battles and other related events. News reports about victories and defeats appeared on a regular basis. During most of the war, the news was not good because the American military lost more than it won. By and large, the Federalist press used losses to criticize the war, while the Republican newspapers sought to put as good a face as possible on the efforts of the U. S. military forces. The U.S. Navy received great praise from all the newspapers throughout the war because it succeeded very well. During the fighting in 1812, it was the only branch of the military that won anything. When covering land engagements, many of which the United States lost, Republican newspaper editors sought to emphasize success and downplay defeat. They reported every victory, no matter how small. Blame for defeats, such as the loss of Detroit in 1812, fell on the generals in command. Such news stories served as propaganda, and Republican editors continually used them to urge Americans to fight until the United States achieved victory.

The War of 1812 also spurred journalistic developments. Since newspapers constituted the primary source of news about the war, readers wanted current information. Editors increasingly tried to get news in a timely manner. Larger newspapers hired express riders to move news fairly rapidly around the country. Stories started appearing only days after events, a great improvement over the several weeks time lag that existed during the American Revolution. Newspaper editors also encouraged better delivery of newspapers to their readers. The postal service delivered newspapers on an ever-increasing system of post roads. By the end of the War of 1812, nearly forty-four miles of roads crossed the country and stagecoaches were hired to improve mail delivery. The growth of post roads made acquiring a newspaper fairly simple for Americans who lived near them.

Another development that slowly began at this time was a desire for if not objectivity, at least political neutrality in the press. Most newspapers during this era were far from objective, and few editors even considered it necessary. However, there were some who thought the press should be less partisan. One of the first editors who tried to accomplish this goal was Hezekiah Niles. He founded *Nile's Weekly Register* in Baltimore, in September 1811. He promised to be politically neutral and sought to provide an unbiased printed record of the actions of the national government. In his prospectus, Niles promised that the *Register* would be open to people of all political outlooks. During the more than twenty years that he edited the *Register*, the journal never endorsed or opposed any political candidate and Niles sought to present a balanced view of the various political issues of the day. Niles became one of the most respected journalists of the era and set a standard that would become the goal of more journalists by the end of the nineteenth century.

Newspapers continued to experience growth during the War of 1812, but the rapid expansion of paper that had characterized the years since the end of the American Revolution ceased. As had been true earlier during the Revolution, the war with Great Britain interfered with the press and discouraged its growth. When James Madison entered office in 1809, 329 newspapers appeared throughout the country. When peace finally came in 1815, the number had grown by fewer than a hundred, to 413.

News of the war's end and the signing of the Treaty of Ghent elicited much comment in the newspapers. Many Americans rejoiced over the news and public celebrations took place throughout the country. People stopped working and joined together to rejoice over the heroic efforts of soldiers and diplomats. For many Americans who believe that the conflict, despite it setbacks, had been success, the War of 1812 only confirmed the rightness of the republican experiment that had begun in 1776. The majority of the American newspaper publishers in the United States agreed with these sentiments. Even if they disagreed over whether the war had been a good idea or not, both Republican and Federalist newspaper editors rejoiced that the war had ended.

Further Reading

Humphrey, Carol Sue. *The Press of the Young Republic, 1783–1833.* Westport, CT: Greenwood Press, 1996.

CAROL SUE HUMPHREY

WASHINGTON POST

The *Washington Post* (1877–) was the dominant daily newspaper in Washington, D.C., during the late twentieth and easrly twenty-first centuries, and is perhaps best remembered for its dogged reporting during the Watergate scandal of the Richard M. Nixon administration (1969– 1974). But the *Post* was an influential paper well before the 1970s. *Post* cartoonists coined the phrases "Remember the Maine" in 1899 and "McCarthyism" in 1950. The paper was a leading voice against President Franklin D. Roosevelt's "court packing" effort in 1937. It was the first major newspaper to hire an ombudsman to oversee editorial practices.

The *Post* won numerous national awards including at least thirty-seven Pulitzer Prizes—two of which marked the respective high and low points of *Washington Post* journalism. In 1973, the Watergate series won a Pulitzer Prize for public service reporting. Then in 1981, the paper won the Pulitzer for feature writing, but the prize was revoked after *Post* editors discovered that the winning story was a fabrication. In 2007, the newspaper maintained strong readership and influence, and its corporate parent, the Washington Post Company, controlled a wide array of media properties including magazines, broadcasting stations, cable systems, and online news outlets.

Early Years

The *Washington Post* was founded at the end of post-Civil War Reconstruction by politically-minded journalist Stilson Hutchins, who wanted his "Democratic daily" to be an influential voice in Washington. The paper's first edition on December 6, 1877, was a four-page issue printed on rag paper and sold for three cents a copy. Within a decade the *Post* gained circulation and credibility by upgrading equipment, buying out rival papers, and becoming the first city paper to publish seven days a week. By the turn of the century, the *Post* had changed hands three times and performed steadily, but by the 1930s it was in steep decline. The paper was poorly managed, scarcely competitive, and on the brink of bankruptcy—an especially vulnerable position in a city with plenty of newspapers to fill any vacuum. By 1930, the *Post* had the lowest readership of Washington's five daily papers, lagging far behind the *Evening Star* which was the circulation leader in Washington and the city's most influential paper.

By 1933 the ailing *Post* was in receivership, and a judge ordered it sold at auction to satisfy creditors. At the June 1933 auction, two serious buyers—media giant William Randolph Hearst, and the estranged wife of Edward B. (Ned) McLean, the *Post*'s departing publisher—were outbid substantially by an agent for wealthy Republican financier Eugene Isaac Meyer. Like the paper's original founder, Meyer wanted a chance to exercise influence in the nation's capitol, and upon purchasing the *Post* (for $825,000) he vowed to reshape it into an independent newspaper. Many in Washington presumed Meyer would use the paper to advance his own business-oriented views, but he managed largely to uphold his promise of independence for the *Post*.

Under Meyer's leadership the *Post* gained ground as its popularity and readership grew. It won its first Pulitzer Prize in 1936 for editorial writing, and over time the paper emerged as a serious competitor to the dominant *Evening Star*—a paper that by World War II had more total advertising lineage than any newspaper in the country. Up to the 1950s the *Evening Star* was considered the "establishment newspaper" and the strongest daily in Washington, and some felt it had great political influence on Capitol Hill. The *Post* was running third in a field of four daily papers, but it was improving, adding talent like the much-admired cartoonist Herbert L. Block ("Herblock") who joined the *Post* in 1946 and became a fixture on the editorial page. In 1954 Meyer bought out his rival morning paper, the *Times-Herald*, thereby securing a monopoly on the morning news market and knocking the *Star* out of first place for good.

In the space of twenty years, Eugene Meyer had transformed the *Post* into a robust enterprise and the city's dominant news source. He shifted the emphasis from news stories to the editorial pages, hoping to capture the attention of politicians and power brokers. He made a series of smart business decisions that turned the *Post's* fortunes around and brought both prestige and revenue to the organization. In 1946 Meyer's brilliant son-in-law, Philip K. Graham, took over as publisher, with plans to turn the *Post* into a "miniature *New York Times*." When Meyer died in 1959, Philip Graham took the helm of the *Washington Post*.

Graham, Bradlee, Pentagon, and Watergate

By the 1960s the Washington Post Company had grown significantly and acquired a string of media properties. Philip Graham purchased *Newsweek* magazine in 1961, and launched a joint news service with the *Los Angeles Times* in 1962. The *Post* was gaining influence even as publisher Philip Graham began to exhibit the mental instability that would end with his suicide in August, 1963. Following Graham's death his widow, Eugene Meyer's daughter Katharine (Kay) Meyer Graham, took over the organization. After a halting start she began to reshape the *Post*, changing the editorial guard and redistributing financial resources. In 1965, Kay Graham hired *Newsweek's* D.C. bureau chief, Benjamin Bradlee, as a deputy managing editor of the *Post*. The ambitious Bradlee took over as managing editor within the year, and the newspaper entered a vigorous phase of growth and innovation that would lead to its now-legendary role in the Watergate affair.

Ben Bradlee brought energy and savvy to the *Post* and soon gained the full trust of Katharine Graham. One of Bradlee's innovations was the "Style" section, launched in 1969 and instantly provocative. He wanted to replace the *Post's* predictable women's section with something that would chronicle a changing American culture for both genders. "Style" gave the *Post* an outlet for non-traditional news, for lifestyle stories, and for a kind of subjective writing traditionally unacceptable on hard-news pages. Readers and competitors were skeptical at first, but eventually "Style" became a much-imitated success for the *Washington Post*.

Graham and Bradlee saw their paper as fully able to compete with the *New York Times*. Bradlee had reshaped the newsroom and recruited journalists from papers and magazines around the country, forging a top-flight news staff. He rewarded gutsy journalism and encouraged competition among reporters—strategies that made for a vibrant but often cut-throat newsroom atmosphere. Then in 1971, in the thick of public protest about the war in Vietnam, Bradlee's *Post* was utterly scooped when the *New York Times* published the "Pentagon Papers"—a series of stories based on a highly classified government report chronicling decades of U.S. strategy and folly in Indochina.

The Pentagon Papers saga was a turning point for American journalism, and for the *Washington Post*. In 1971, former defense analyst Daniel Ellsberg leaked a classified Pentagon report to the *New York Times*. The seven thousand-page report made it clear that the U.S. had been involved in Vietnam far longer than most Americans realized, and that many administrations had erred and stumbled in their handling of the burgeoning conflict. The report was explosive, and the *Times* had the exclusive story but kept it wraps until June 13, 1971, when it ran a series of articles based on the secret report. Nixon's Justice Department got a court order forbidding the *Times'* to publish more Pentagon stories, which the *Times* appealed in federal court. Meanwhile, the *Post* got hold of its own copy of the Pentagon report, raising the competitive ire of the *Times*.

With a court order in force against the *Times*, the *Post* had either to hold its own stories, or publish them and risk a federal contempt citation. *Post* management had recently decided to take the company public, and any criminal liability would jeopardize the stock offering and hence the company's financial future. After much tense discussion and argument, Bradlee decided to publish the Pentagon stories and Kay Graham gave the go-ahead. After the *Post's* stories were published, a federal court issued another injunction against the paper. In 1971 the U.S. Supreme Court ruled that the injunctions against the *Times* and *Post* had violated the First Amendment. For the *Post*, its decision to publish was a triumph of journalistic responsibility and courage.

One year later that courage set a course for the *Post* after two of its junior reporters got wind of a burglary at the Watergate Hotel. What began as a minor local story (the burglary got barely a mention in the *Times*) eventually grew into the biggest news story of the era, as reporters Bob Woodward and Carl Bernstein followed the trail of thieving, spying, wiretapping, and deceit all the way to the Nixon White House. Watergate cost Richard Nixon his presidency and catapulted the *Post* to national and international prominence, and the paper rode the wave of Watergate fame for many years.

Then in 1981 the *Post* had something of a course-correction. A talented young reporter, Janet Cooke, wrote a riveting feature story about an eight-year-old inner city heroin addict. Despite some uncertainty inside the newsroom about the story's veracity, Bob Woodward nominated "Jimmy's World" for a Pulitzer, and it won the 1981 prize for feature writing. But eventually Cooke's tale unraveled and the *Post* had to accept that the story was fabricated—as was much of Cooke's resumé. The affair launched an investigation of *Post* editorial practices by the National News Council, and a somber self-assessment by the *Post* itself.

Modern Times

In the early twenty-first century, the *Washington Post* was part of a mature news organization. Katharine Graham and Ben Bradlee both retired in 1991, the same year Kay Graham passed the publisher's torch to Donald E. Graham who had spent years working in the ranks of the *Post* organization. In 1993, Donald Graham became chairman of the board for the Washington Post Company. Katharine Graham's memoir, *Personal History,* won the Pulitzer Prize for biography in 1998. Under Donald Graham's leadership the Post Company moved into new territory—Spanish language papers, youth publications, and Internet news, acquiring the popular online zine Slate.com in 2004. The company's flagship newspaper, the *Washington Post,* remained an influential and respected publication, and still informed a significant part of the mainstream American news content.

Further Reading

Bradlee, Ben. *A Good Life: Newspapering and Other Adventures.* New York: Simon & Schuster, 1995.

Bray, Howard. *The Pillars of the Post: The Making of a News Empire in Washington.* New York: W.W. Norton & Company, 1980.

Broder, David. *Behind the Front Page.* New York: Simon and Schuster, 1987.

Graham, Katharine. *Personal History.* New York: Vintage Books/Random House, 1998.

Kelly, Tom. *The Imperial Post.* New York: William Morrow & Company, 1983.

Roberts, Chalmers. *In the Shadow of Power: The Story of the Washington Post.* Cabin John, MD: The Seven Locks Press, 1989.

WENDY E. SWANBERG

WASHINGTON, BOOKER T.

Booker T. Washington (April 5, 1856–November 15, 1915) emerged as a black leader in the 1890s when he advocated controversially that blacks should accept an accommodationist role in society. For the remainder of his life, this provoked a national, heated discussion. He played up his stance by working closely with the black press, including owning several newspapers, and dealt almost ruthlessly with those who did not support him.

He was born a slave on April 5, 1856, in Franklin County, Virginia, and graduated in 1875 from Hampton Normal and Agricultural Institute, where he worked as a janitor to pay his room and board. After teaching in Virginia and attending a seminary in Washington, he returned to Hampton in 1879 as a teacher and then two years later became the principal and organizer of a new black school at Tuskegee, Alabama. By the time he died in 1915, Tuskegee Institute, which he started from scratch without buildings, students, or faculty, had an endowment of $2 million.

Washington embraced vocational education because he felt it made it possible for blacks to earn a good living by being proficient at a skill or trade. In a speech at the Cotton States and International Exposition in Atlanta in 1895, he firmly established himself as the country's major black leader, at least according to whites, when he encouraged blacks to become good friends with white southerners, take jobs they could get, and work hard to succeed. "The wisest among my race understand that the agitation of questions of social equality is the extremist folly and that progress in the enjoyment of all the privileges that will come to us must be the result of severe constant struggle rather than of artificial folly," he continued.

He played up this accommodationist master plan for blacks, which quickly brought opposition from those who wanted to continue fighting vigorously for equality, with what became known as the "Tuskegee Machine." Operating somewhat secretly, it went about trying to prevail over those who opposed Washington's views. It did this by sending out a torrent of public relations releases and editorials to the press; paying a black syndicated columnist to play up Washington's views; and placing or withholding advertising to black editors, depending on whether they supported Washington's compromise program. It also surreptitiously purchased several newspapers and controlled them firmly while secretly giving subsidies to others.

One of Washington's main supporters was Thomas Fortune, who founded the *New York Age* in 1883 and made it into the country's leading black newspaper by the end of the century with its protests against lynchings, discrimination, mob violence, and disenfranchisement. It regularly ran material supplied by Washington until 1907 when Fortune, faced with financial difficulties, sold the paper, not realizing the buyer was one of Washington's agents, which made the black leader a main stockholder. Washington sold the paper several years later in order to avoid disclosing his ownership. Washington and his "Tuskegee Machine" continued vigorously fighting his enemies, both in and out of the press, until he died of arteriosclerosis in 1915.

Further Reading

Harlan, Louis R. *Booker T. Washington: The Making of a Black Leader, 1856–1901.* New York: Oxford University Press, 1972.

Harlan, Louis R. *Booker T. Washington: The Wizard of Tuskegee, 1901–1915.* New York: Oxford University Press, 1983.

Logan, Rayford W. *The Betrayal of the Negro from Rutherford B. Hayes to Woodrow Wilson*, 5th ed. New York: Collier Books, 1970.

Pride, Armistead S., and Clint C. Wilson II. *A History of the Black Press*. Washington: D.C.: Howard University Press, 1997.

Smock, Raymond W., ed. *Booker T. Washington in Perspective*. Jackson: University Press of Mississippi, 1988.

Spencer, Samuel R. Jr. *Booker T. Washington and the Negro's Place in American Life*. Boston: Little, Brown and Co., 1955.

PATRICK S. WASHBURN

WATERGATE

The Watergate scandal (1972–1974) was the biggest American political scandal since Teapot Dome during President Warren G. Harding's administration. Unlike the earlier crimes for profit, Watergate was about political dirty tricks. Like Teapot Dome, Watergate had a special prosecutor who obtained criminal convictions of White House officials. Unlike the earlier scandal that did not impact the president or his political party, Watergate became a constitutional crisis that forced President Richard M. Nixon's resignation and contributed to the Republican Party losing the White House in the 1976 presidential election.

Watergate was the name of a Washington, D.C., hotel and office complex. In the early 1970s, its sixth floor housed the Democratic National Committee (DNC) headquarters. A surveillance squad hired by the Republican Party broke into the DNC offices to plant bugging devices and wiretaps. The wiretaps were monitored from the seventh floor of the Howard Johnson Motor Lodge across the street. Three weeks later, on June 17, 1972, they broke in again to fix phone taps and to photograph documents. This time they were caught, when Watergate night watchman Frank Wills noticed a taped-over door lock. The police arrested five men: Bernard Barker, Virgilio González, Eugenio Martínez, James W. McCord Jr., and Frank Sturgis.

Though White House Press Secretary Ron Ziegler dismissed the break-in as a "third-rate burglary," the perpetrators had embarrassing ties to President Nixon, who was running for reelection. McCord was officially employed as Chief of Security at the Committee to Re-elect the President (CRP, also known pejoratively as CREEP), and McCord's notebook confiscated by the police had the telephone number of E. Howard Hunt, who had previously worked for Nixon's White House. These White House connections generally were disregarded, however, because the Nixon campaign had a comfortable lead in opinion polls and did not need to resort to political espionage.

Yet, like the tip of a political iceberg, the Watergate incident eventually emerged as a massive conspiracy to abuse executive power. The conspiracy's crimes included bribery, destruction of evidence, eavesdropping, extortion, illegal campaign contributions, illegal use of the Central Intelligence Agency (CIA) and the Federal Bureau of Investigation (FBI), phone tapping, political burglary, political sabotage, obstruction of justice, using taxpayers' money for private purposes, and tax fraud. The press's revelation of these crimes depended on luck, perseverance, and assistance from a secret source within the government.

Nixon and the Press

During his long and distinguished career in politics, Nixon had a love-hate relationship with the press. The antipathy between Nixon and the press undoubtedly traced back to his days as a member of the U. S. House Committee on Un-American Activities (HUAC) in the late 1940s, his senatorial campaign against Helen Gahagan Douglas in 1950, outspoken criticism of liberals in politics and the press during the Cold War, and his failed 1962 gubernatorial race in California. When Nixon as president could control the news agenda, he excelled, but when journalistic enterprise took over, he felt vulnerable.

Nixon had early success in the news spotlight. As a young U.S. Congressman from California, he gained nationwide fame on HUAC investigating Alger Hiss, a U.S. State Department official accused of passing secret documents to a Soviet spy ring. Hiss was convicted of perjury. In 1950 Nixon cashed in on his image as a tough-minded anti-Communist and won his race for U.S. Senator by a wide margin, although critics charged that he had smeared his opponent, Douglas.

When the Republican Party nominated World War II hero Dwight D. Eisenhower as its candidate for the U.S. Presidency in 1952, Eisenhower asked an elated Nixon to be his vice-presidential running mate. However, Nixon's ascendancy seemed to falter just as it got started, when the press accused Nixon of having accepted improper campaign contributions. Eisenhower was reticent to intervene, so Nixon defended himself on national television. The public accepted Nixon's emotional protests of innocence, and Eisenhower's confidence in his running mate was restored. The speech became known by the name of Nixon's dog, "Checkers," and in it he announced that the pet was the only gift he had accepted and he was not going to give it back.

After eight years as an exceptionally active and newsworthy vice president, Nixon became the Republican Party's presidential nominee in 1960 against a young Democratic senator from Massachusetts, John F. Kennedy. Nixon lost by two-tenths of one percent of the popular vote in one of the closest national elections in U.S. history. The margin of victory later was pegged to Kennedy's superior showing in four televised debates, in which Nixon was the better debater but appeared weak and indecisive to the television audience.

Nixon returned to California to practice law in Los Angeles. He won the Republican nomination for governor of California in 1962, but after losing the election by a wide margin, he blamed his defeat on unfair press coverage. Bitterly, he announced to reporters, "You won't have Dick Nixon to kick around anymore." His political retirement was apocryphal, however, as Nixon continued to keep a close eye on Republican politics. When conservative Republican Barry Goldwater lost a landslide election to incumbent President Lyndon B. Johnson in 1964, Nixon was able to reestablish himself as his party's leader. In 1966 he successfully campaigned on behalf of Republican congressional candidates. Then, after a series of primary victories in 1968, Republican Party leaders concluded that he had the best chance to win the White House and nominated him to be their candidate.

As in 1960, the 1968 popular vote was exceedingly close, but this time Nixon came out on top. Nixon defeated Democratic Vice President Hubert H. Humphrey, who ran after President Lyndon B. Johnson bowed out in March because of discouraging developments in the Vietnam War. Nixon ran on a "peace with honor" platform, though he was vague about specifics. A key to Nixon's victory was a split of Democratic Party strength in the South. Some votes went to racial segregationist Governor George C. Wallace of Alabama, who won forty-six electoral votes for the American Independent Party. Nixon's television commercials cast their candidate as a moderate conciliator who was firm on the rule of law. Once again, Nixon succeeded politically when he, and not the press, was in control of his own image. Even before moving into the White House in 1969, one of Nixon's top priorities was assure his reelection in 1972.

Watergate Investigation Led by the *Washington Post*

Washington Post metro editor Barry Sussman assigned Bob Woodward and borrowed Carl Bernstein from the paper's Virginia bureau to report the Watergate break-in story. Their first dispatch was on the burglars' arraignment on the day of the burglary. Cued by the Associated Press wire, their second story noted that burglar James McCord served currently as the Chief of Security at CRP, the DNC's rival. Their third story on June 20, 1972, followed the clue that police found two burglars had contacts to White House employee E. Howard Hunt. When Woodward tried to call Hunt, he got the office of Charles W. Colson, a special counsel to the President. The White House identified Hunt as a consultant to Colson. Slowly other puzzle pieces dropped into place to suggest a well-organized effort by the White House to spy on the DNC.

During a news conference on June 22, President Nixon denied White House involvement in the burglary. The *New York Times,* the *Boston Globe,* and CBS News looked more deeply into the burglary story but did not find much. However, the *Washington Post* stuck with the story. Woodward and Bernstein reported that the White House had assigned Hunt to look into the private life of Senator Edward Kennedy. To help confirm story facts and keep the two reporters on track, Woodward consulted a secret source inside the government, which turned out to be the number two official at the FBI, W. Mark Felt. Code named "Deep Throat," Felt's identity was kept from the public until May 31, 2005, when his family announced Felt's role in the Watergate affair—a claim later confirmed by Woodward.

The Watergate Cover-Up

On June 23, 1972, President Nixon and White House Chief of Staff H. R. "Bob" Haldeman discussed using the CIA to obstruct the FBI's investigation of the Watergate break-ins (a tape recording of their conversation later was made public). The CIA was restricted by law from spying within the United States, but agreed to help the White House by claiming to the FBI that an active investigation would compromise the CIA's agents, thereby jeopardizing national security. Nixon and Haldeman's real fear was that the FBI would discover what former Attorney General John Mitchell called "White House horrors"—criminal and unethical maneuvers undertaken by Hunt and his subordinate, G. Gordon Liddy, in a special investigations unit, nicknamed the "Plumbers." The Plumbers investigated leaks of information to the press and ran various sabotage operations against the Democrats, Vietnam War protestors, and other political enemies.

Among notorious Plumbers' operations was the break-in at the office of the psychiatrist of Daniel Ellsberg, a former Pentagon and State Department employee who had leaked a secret government study, the "Pentagon Papers," to the *New York Times.* Though not critical of the Nixon White House directly, the Pentagon Papers embarrassed the government in general and threatened to undermine support for Nixon's war policies. Hunt and Liddy found nothing useful when they broke into the psychiatrist's office, and their role was not revealed until 1973. However, the judge in Ellsberg's trial for espionage, theft, and conspiracy dismissed the case because of evident government misconduct.

CRP Director John Mitchell, along with campaign managers Jeb Stuart Magruder and Fred LaRue, approved Hunt and Liddy's espionage plans, including the break-ins. Whether Nixon was directly involved is unclear. The evidence shows that Nixon knew about the Watergate break-in later and directed its cover-up, including dispensing hundreds of thousands of dollars of hush money to the burglars to plead guilty and to keep quiet about their White House connections.

The *Washington Post,* the *New York Times,* the *Los Angeles Times, Time* magazine, and *Newsweek* magazine continued to report misappropriated campaign funds and break-in links to the White House, but the charges had little effect on Nixon's reelection bid. Thwarted by perjury of White House officials and the cover-up payoffs, the FBI's investigation of the break-in had stopped with seven men—the burglars, McCord and Liddy—while the candidacy of Democratic challenger, Senator George McGovern of South Dakota, was self-destructing. McGovern won the Democratic nomination by opposing Nixon's Vietnam War policies, but his appeal to moderates for support made him appear to waffle on his anti-war stance. His indecisiveness and incompetence became a campaign issue when the press uncovered mental illness in the personal history of his nominee for vice president, Senator Thomas Eagleton of Missouri. In November, Nixon won the landslide election he had been seeking all his life.

On January 8, 1973, a U.S. District Court convicted the original Watergate burglars, plus Liddy and Hunt, of conspiracy, burglary and wiretapping. All except McCord and Liddy pleaded guilty. Trial judge John Sirica, known as "Maximum John" because of his harsh sentencing, gave sentences of thirty-years' imprisonment, but indicated he would reconsider if the defendants would cooperate with his effort to learn the true Watergate story. During the trial, the *New York Times* had published Seymour Hersh's report that the Watergate conspirators had been promised $1,000 a month to keep silent. Sirica wanted to know who made the payments. A short time later, John McCord complied with Sirica's offer, implicated the CRP in the burglary and the payoffs, and admitted to perjury. The federal prosecutor, Earl Silbert, convened a new Watergate grand jury, and the cover-up began to unravel. On April 19, the *Washington Post* reported that Mitchell and presidential counsel John Dean had approved and helped to plan the Watergate burglary. The Watergate story had new life on newspaper front pages.

The Senate Watergate Investigation

McCord's revelations dramatically recharged interest in Watergate. On April 30, 1973, Nixon attempted to blame a rogue element in his administration. He coerced the resignations of Haldeman and John Ehrlichman, two of his most powerful aides, and fired counsel John Dean, whom Nixon blamed for failing to keep him informed. Nixon also gave authority to new Attorney General Elliot Richardson to appoint an independent Watergate prosecutor and promised a clean sweep in the White House. On May 18, Richardson named Archibald Cox as prosecutor. Cox was inexperienced in criminal law but was staunchly independent.

Meanwhile, a special U.S. Senate committee, chaired by Sam Ervin of North Carolina, subpoenaed White House staff members. The committee's star witness was disaffected White House counsel Dean, who felt he was been set up by Nixon to take the blame for Watergate. Dean's detailed testimony implicated nearly every White House staff member, including Nixon, of obstruction of justice to cover up the Watergate burglary, but Dean stopped short of accusing the president of planning the break-in itself. The hearings were broadcast to a rapt television audience throughout the summer of 1973 and devastated Nixon's political support. The Senate committee probe began to focus on the president himself, as famously stated by Republican Senator Howard Baker of Tennessee: "What did the president know and when did he know it?"

On July 13, 1973, Alexander Butterfield, deputy assistant to the President, told the Senate Watergate committee about a secret audio taping system that automatically recorded everything in the Oval Office. Both the committee and Special Prosecutor Cox soon subpoenaed the tapes as essential to their investigations. Nixon refused, citing the principle of executive privilege. When Cox refused to drop his subpoena, Nixon ordered Attorney General Richardson to fire Cox as special prosecutor. When Richardson and his deputy William Ruckelshaus refused in turn to fire Cox, Nixon compelled their resignations on October 20—the so-called "Saturday Night Massacre." The new acting head of the Justice Department, Solicitor General Robert Bork, dismissed Cox. Widespread condemnation caused Nixon to declare to a gathering of Associated Press managing editors, "I am not a crook."

For a year, Nixon and new special prosecutor Leon Jaworski struggled over control of the tapes, until July 24, 1974, when the U.S. Supreme Court ruled unanimously (Justice William Rehnquist recused himself) that Nixon's claim of executive privilege over the tapes was void. Nixon and Haldeman's taped conversation of June 23, 1972, provided the "smoking gun" that prosecutors were looking for against Nixon. On July 27, the House of Representatives Judiciary Committee started official impeachment proceedings against Nixon for obstruction of justice, abuse of power, and contempt of Congress. With political support crumbling and many of his aides indicted or convicted, Nixon addressed a national television audience on August 8, 1974, and announced he would resign effective noon the next day. Nixon was succeeded in the presidency by Gerald R. Ford, who on September 8 issued a broad pardon that immunized Nixon from punishment for any crimes he might have committed as president.

Aftermath

President Nixon's resignation and the imprisonment of some of his aides did not end the effects of Watergate. The scandal led to more transparent government, such as revision of campaign financing laws, the amendment in November, 1974 of the Freedom of Information Act (1966), and new requirements for financial disclosures by government officials. The public came to expect other unofficial types of personal disclosure, such as releasing recent income tax forms. Because the taping of Oval Office conversations had been Nixon's downfall, the practice ended, at least to public knowledge.

Watergate also led to far more aggressive news reporting on politicians' public and private lives. Shortly after Nixon's resignation, for example, Wilbur Mills was forced to resign his powerful post in Congress because of a drunken driving accident, the type of an infraction that previously the press usually overlooked. Inspired by Woodward and Bernstein's heroics, a new generation of journalists enthusiastically embraced investigative reporting, and journalism school enrollments ballooned across the country. Woodward and Bernstein went on to successful careers as authors. Riding high from its lead role uncovering Watergate, the *Washington Post* lay claim to national newspaper status.

Because Nixon and many other Watergate conspirators were lawyers, the scandal also sullied the public image of the legal profession. To improve its standing and to head off government regulation, the American Bar Association launched a major reform in 1983 — the Model Rules of Professional Conduct — which law school students are required to study and which remain in effect.

Popular culture adopted the "gate" suffix for later political scandals, such as "Koreagate" during 1976, "Contragate" during President Ronald Reagan in the 1980s, and "Whitewatergate" during President Bill Clinton administration in the 1990s.

Meanwhile, in the wake of Nixon's resignation, the former president and others attempted to rehabilitate his image. The efforts were partly successful. Upon his death in 1994, he was honored as a senior statesman with little mention of the devastating scandal that forced the first resignation of a U.S. president.

Further Reading

Bernstein, Carl, and Bob Woodward. *All the President's Men*. New York: Simon and Schuster, 1974.

Buchwald, Art. *I Am Not a Crook*. New York: Putnam, 1974.

Dash, Samuel. *Chief Counsel: Inside the Ervin Committee — The Untold Story of Watergate*. New York: Random House, 1976.

Jaworski, Leon. *The Right and the Power: The Prosecution of Watergate*. New York: Reader's Digest Press, 1976.

Kutler, Stanley I. *The Wars of Watergate: The Last Crisis of Richard Nixon*. New York: Knopf : Distributed by Random House, 1990.

Lang, Gladys Eden, and Kurt Lang. *The Battle for Public Opinion: The President, the Press, and the Polls during Watergate*. New York : Columbia University Press, 1983.

Nixon, Richard M. *The White House Transcripts: "Submission of Recorded Presidential Conversations to the Committee on the Judiciary of the House of Representatives by President Richard Nixon"* (introduction by R.W. Apple, chronology by Linda Amster). New York: Viking Press, 1974.

Schudson, Michael. *Watergate in American Memory: How We Remember, Forget, and Reconstruct the Past*. New York: Basic Books, 1992.

Sirica, John J. *To Set the Record Straight: The Break-in, the Tapes, the Conspirators, the Pardon*. New York: Norton, 1979.

Staff of the New York Times. *The End of a Presidency*. New York: Holt, Rinehart and Winston, 1974.

Sussman, Barry. *The Great Coverup: Nixon and the Scandal of Watergate*. New York: Crowell, 1974.

White, Theodore H. *Breach of Faith: The Fall of Richard Nixon*. New York: Atheneum Publishers, 1975.

RUSSELL J. COOK

WATTERSON, HENRY

Widely described as the last survivor of the era of personal journalism, Henry Watterson (February 16, 1840–December 22, 1921) reigned over the editorial page of the *Louisville Courier-Journal* for more than fifty years, attracting national attention far beyond his paper's immediate influence with his brilliant, original phrasemaking and unwavering principles. As the *Boston Globe* wrote of him, "Marse Henry," as he was known, made "a pedestal by the sheer force of [his] personality and then [occupied] it through storm and sunshine for more than half a century."

Born in Washington, D.C., to a member of Congress, Watterson hoped to become a pianist, but those dreams were shattered when he irreparably injured his hand. So, at an early age, he worked in Washington and in New York as a musical critic for several papers before returning south when the Civil War broke out.

Though opposed to secession, he joined the Confederate army, serving as an aide first to Gen. Nathan Bedford Forrest and then to Gen. Leonidas Polk, becoming the chief of Confederate scouts. But his active military service was cut short because of poor eyesight, so Watterson became editor of several newspapers, most notably the *Chattanooga Rebel*. It was an auspicious choice; as the *New York Times* wrote of him: "He was something of a rebel always, impatient of authority, fond of jabbing august ribs. His journalism was a perpetual cavalry charge."

After the war, he revived a newspaper in Nashville, then was hired to edit the *Louisville Journal*; when he quadrupled circulation within six months, he initiated a merger with the *Courier*, giving him an ownership share, as well. Watterson, like most editors of the era, concerned himself solely with politics and the editorial column; with his spirited defense of Abraham Lincoln's memory during Reconstruction, and advocacy of education for newly freed ex-slaves, he quickly achieved prominence as the voice of the new South. And his paper employed twice as many editorial writers as it did news reporters.

In 1872, he was one of four prominent editors who formed the liberal Democratic movement that nominated Horace Greeley for what became a disastrous run for president. Four years later, he was one of Democrat Samuel Tilden's strongest backers—and, in the wake of the disputed election, publicly called for one hundred thousand supporters to march on Washington to prevent Rutherford Hayes' swearing-in. At the same time, Watterson was elected to Congress, but only served a few months.

That was the end of Watterson's unquestioned allegiance to the Democrats, though he served as a delegate to its national conventions until 1892. He broke with President Grover Cleveland, refused to support nominee William Jennings Bryan in 1896 and opposed Woodrow Wilson's candidacy in 1912. Yet when World War I broke out in 1914, Watterson advocated for United States involvement, arguing: "To hell with the Hohenzollerns and the Hapsburgs."

Throughout, Watterson epitomized the nineteenth-century standard of the writing editor; as the *Los Angeles Times* noted, to Watterson a newspaper was an editor's "consecrated sword of combat and chivalry. In those days, an editor who did not write was a rifle without trigger. It was unthinkable and impossible."

In 1902, Watterson sold the *Courier-Journal* to Robert Bingham, but remained on as an editorial writer until 1919, when he was asked to retire because of his opposition to the League of Nations. On his death two years later, the *Boston Globe* wrote: "Mr. Watterson was not always right. No man who passed so rapidly from one side to another could be right much more than half of the time. But Mr. Watterson was always genuine. He wrote and printed exactly what he happened to believe at the time of writing, which is a good deal."

Further Reading

Wall, Joseph Frazier. *Henry Watterson: Reconstructed Rebel*. New York: Oxford University Press, 1956.

ERIC FETTMANN

WEEKLY READER

The *Weekly Reader* (1902–) has changed its name over the years but not its mission to teach children American values while informing them. Editors today explain that the magazine's purpose has always been to teach children how to think, not what to think. Nevertheless, many stories then and now celebrate the power of optimism, the inevitability of overcoming poverty through hard work, as well as the cost of patriotism and the healing efficacy of serving others.

Until recently, the newspaper often avoided harsh subjects unless extensive media coverage made such efforts futile. One topic that was impossible to steer clear of, though, was the Cold War. The *Weekly Reader* introduced many boys and girls to the U.S.-Soviet conflict in the 1950s and 1960s. Maps prominently displayed the Iron Curtain countries of the Soviet bloc. And when other types of grim stories appeared, they offered hope often in the form of a child empowered by quick thinking, integrity, and persistence to make a difference.

Charles Palmer Davis created the forerunner of *Weekly Reader*, *Current Events*, in 1902 because only two of his daughter's twenty-four classmates in the one-room schoolhouse in Agawam, Massachusetts, could name the U. S. president, William McKinley. The former newsman decided to devote his life to helping young people learn what was going on in the world. *Current Events* was published twenty five times during the school year for middle and high school students.

On May 20, 1902, the first headline, "AWFUL VOLCANO ERUPTION Thirty Thousand People Lost Lives in One Minute. St. Pierre, Martinique, in Ruins. It is the Worst Volcanic Eruption Since the Destruction of Pompeii," may have been shocking for middle school and high school students, but one of the three survivors of the disaster, a little girl, Havivra Da Ifrile, peered into the smoking crater just minutes before it exploded. Her quick thinking and perseverance enabled her to escape to a cave along the coast where she had often played pirates with the other kids. She saw the rivers of lava engulf her friends and neighbors as she fled but, nevertheless, remained hopeful even during the showers of flaming embers that burned her and charred her little boat. The French cruiser, *Suchet*, rescued the unconscious girl, who had drifted two miles out to sea in the seared and battered dingy. Of course, this story reflected American belief in the power of positive thinking as well as respect for underdogs who beat incredible odds.

Children as newsmakers, not victims or individuals too inexperienced to matter, appear repeatedly in the pages of *Current Events* and later *My Weekly Reader*. Perhaps, this sensitivity to his readers' need to feel important inspired Davis to choose stories, like the crowning of the boy Spanish King, which also ran in the first edition. Over time, these messages reminded students that everyone—no matter how young or powerless—can contribute to society as well as overcome formidable obstacles.

Demand for news of current events skyrocketed. In 1917,

Davis incorporated his company, American Education Press, and relocated to Columbus, Ohio. Prosperity generated new publications, including *Current Science* in 1927, a paper published sixteen times a year for middle-school students. A year later, *Current Events* became *My Weekly Reader*.

A teacher and reading expert who was director of elementary schools in York, Pennsylvania, Eleanor Johnson, was the founder and editor-in-chief of the *Weekly Reader*. She took over on September 21, 1928, and extended the reach of the publication to elementary school students. She mixed morals freely with news, translating complex issues into terms children could understand. For example, the first headline in *My Weekly Reader*, "TWO POOR BOYS WHO MADE GOOD ARE NOW RUNNING FOR THE HIGHEST OFFICE IN THE WORLD!" converted the presidential race into a Horatio Alger plot. Diligence, a bit of luck, and lots of determination enabled the heroes, Herbert Hoover and Al Smith, to prevail.

Interspersed amid the news items were poems, cartoons, and adages (reminiscent of the didactic *McGuffey Eclectic Readers*) that instructed children in health and social mores. For example, this item ran in the first issue: "Our little Buddy is robust and ruddy/Disease germs he knows how to foil/For just like a man, he takes all he can/From a bottle of cod-liver oil."

Occasionally, appeals for cultural unity took a grim turn. In fact, in 1935, a sketch depicted a skull labeled "Death" eating an endless stream of humans while Mars, the grinning god of "War" waved his sword. It accompanied an article, "The League Acts for Peace." This time, no miracle child saved the day. After a frank essay about humanity's penchant for killing to expand territory, the piece ended with this question, "Will the League of Nations be able to bring peace and order to a troubled world?"

In 1940, *My Weekly Reader* added the tag line "The Junior Newspaper" to its masthead. Of course, the stories shifted with the times from isolation in the late 1930s to support of World War II after Pearl Harbor. Articles applauded technology increasingly from the 1950s to the present. In the 1980s, the *Weekly Reader* began reporting on controversial subjects without giving them a happy ending. For instance, in 1982, the *Weekly Reader* ran a banner headline: "Unemployment: Over 11 Million U. S. Workers Are Unemployed." The story ended bleakly: "'Its like death, but you go on breathing,' says one unemployed worker."

Since 1902, an estimated eighteen billion copies of the *Weekly Reader* have circulated in classrooms teaching children to draw conclusions about the consequences of events. The *Weekly Reader* celebrated its century mark in 2002. In 2006, the Weekly Reader Corporation published sixteen newspapers for students in kindergarten through grade twelve, including READ® (1951), Know Your World®Extra (1967), Teen NewsweekTM (1999).

One theme has remained constant in *Weekly Reader* throughout its evolution—motivating children to take action to help others, especially after devastation. In October, 2005, the *Weekly Reader* web page for kids featured a story taken from its printed pages: "Earthquake Shakes Pakistan." The first paragraph starts with the children in Kashmir going to school on the morning of October 8, just as they always had. Then, "their world collapsed." The writer relates the gruesome details—thirty thousand dead and more fatalities expected. But, the site also offered advice for raising money for victims of disasters, like the tsunami, the hurricane along the Gulf Coast, or the earthquake in Pakistan.

Further Reading

Carpenter, Walter Duane. "Values, Leaders and My Weekly Reader: An Historical Study." PhD disseration, The University of Nebraska—Lincoln, 2006.

Mott, Frank Luther. *A History of American Magazines, 1885–1905.* Cambridge, MA: Harvard University Press, 1957.

Richards, Marc. "The Cold War According to My Weekly Reader," *Monthly Review: An Independent Socialist Magazine* (October 1, 1998) 50:5,3 3–47.

Weekly Reader: 60 Years of News for Kids, intro. Hugh Downs. New York: World Almanac, 1988.

PAULETTE KILMER

WHITE, SALLIE JOY

Sallie Joy White (1847–1909) became the first woman staff reporter on a Boston newspaper in 1870 and during the next thirty-nine years served as a role model for women aspiring to enter the field of journalism. Like other newspaperwomen of the time, she wrote mostly about society, fashion, and the home and toward the end of her career published a popular advice column under the pen name "Penelope Penfeather." She helped found the New England Woman's Press Association in 1885 and was thereafter repeatedly elected to office in both women's and mixed-sex press organizations. In 1894, a contemporary described White as "first as well as foremost of 'all-round' women journalists in New England... known not only throughout New England but throughout the United States."

Sallie Joy White was born Sarah Elizabeth Joy in Brattleboro, Vermont, in 1847. The only child of Rhoda and Samuel Sargent Joy, she lived a privileged middle-class existence and was able to attend school through her teenage years, during which she published freelance articles in Vermont papers. After her graduation and the death of her father in 1865, she moved to Charlestown, Massachusetts, where she found work first as a teacher, then as a librarian, continuing at the same time to publish numerous pieces in New England newspapers and magazines. At the same time, she became a member of the suffrage movement.

In 1870, Sarah Elizabeth was hired by the *Boston Post* to cover the Vermont suffrage convention. Her success in this assignment secured her a permanent position at the *Post* and she was soon publishing articles on prominent women, women's clubs, suffrage meetings, public lectures, society events, and housing conditions in the Boston slums. She withdrew briefly from her newspaper career in 1874 when she married musician Henry K. White, Jr., with whom she had two daughters, though she continued writing as a freelancer during the marriage. When Henry abandoned the family after the birth of their second daughter in 1879, she increased the volume of her work and in 1885, under the name Sallie Joy White, succeeded in landing a permanent position at the *Boston Herald*, where she was to remain for the next twenty-one years.

In that same year, White and five other Boston newspaperwomen established the New England Woman's Press Association (NEWPA), and White was elected its first president. After completing her five-year presidency at NEWPA in 1891, White established and became the first president of the Boston Woman's Press Club. She also became active and held office in a number of other press organizations, including the International League of Press Clubs.

White published several books on women's work, including *Housekeepers and Homemakers* (1888) and *Business Openings for Girls* (1899). The latter included a chapter on "Newspaper Workers" in which she advised young women to get as much education and training as possible. Because it was difficult for young women to get education and training in news reporting through the conventional methods open to men, White established educational and mentoring programs in the women's press organizations she helped found. Upon her death in 1909, White was remembered by her contemporaries for three accomplishments: her success as a newspaperwoman; her role in providing support and guidance for women following in her path, and her unswerving dedication to the field she had chosen while still a teenager.

Further Reading

Beasley, Maurine H., and Sheila J. Gibbons. *Taking Their Place: A Documentary History of Women and Journalism*, 2nd ed. State College, PA: Strata Publishing, Inc., 2003.

Blair, Karen J. *The Clubwoman as Feminist: True Womanhood Redefined, 1869–1914.* New York: Holmes and Meier, 1980.

Burt, Elizabeth V. "A Bid for Legitimacy: The Woman's Press Club Movement, 1880–1900." *Journalism History* 23, 2 (Summer 1997), 72–84.

——. "New England Woman's Press Association." In *Women's Press Organizations, 1881–1999*, edited by Elizabeth V. Burt. Westport, CT: Greenwood Press, 2000.

——. "Pioneering for Women Journalists: Boston's Sallie Joy White," *American Journalism*, 18 (Spring 2001): 39–63.

Lord, Myra B. *History of the New England Woman's Press Association.* Newton, MA: Graphic Press, 1932.

Marzolf, Marion. *Up From the Footnote: A History of Women Journalists.* New York: Hastings House, 1977.

Ross, Ishbel. *Ladies of the Press.* New York: Harper and Bros., 1936.

White, Sallie Joy. *Housekeepers and Homemakers.* Boston: Jordan Marsh and Co., 1888.

——. *Business Openings for Girls.* New York: The Werner Company, 1899.

Willard, Frances E., assisted by Helen M. Winslow and Sallie Joy White. *Occupations for Women: A Book of Practical Suggestions for the Material Advancement, the Mental and Physical Development, and the Moral and Spiritual Uplift of Women.* New York: Success Company, 1897.

ELIZABETH V. BURT

WILL, GEORGE F.

George F. Will (May 4, 1941–) is a syndicated newspaper columnist, book author, and television commentator. Known for his erudition and lofty prose style, he staked out for himself the high Tory position in postwar American conservatism.

Born in 1941, Will grew up in Champaign-Urbana, Illinois, the son of a philosophy professor at the University of Illinois. After graduating from Trinity University in Connecticut, he studied at Oxford University in England. He has said that his steady support for a strong American military posture stems from a visit to the Berlin Wall during that period in the early 1960s when it had just been built. Following Oxford, he earned a PhD in political philosophy from Princeton University.

His academic career was short-lived, and included stints at Michigan State and the University of Toronto. He then took a position with Senator Gordon Allott of Colorado in 1970. Once in Washington, he set up shop as an opinion journalist, serving as Washington correspondent first for the *American Spectator* and then *National Review,* for which he was Washington editor from 1973 to 1976. In 1974 he began writing a syndicated column for the Washington Post Writers Group, an effort that reaped a Pulitzer Prize for commentary in 1977. In 1976 be began writing a bi-weekly column for *Newsweek* magazine. His television commentary began with Agronsky & Company in the mid-1970s, and continued on to the ABC show *This Week with David Brinkley,* launched in 1981.

Will has published several collections of his columns, along with works of political philosophy and two books on baseball. His high-brow enthusiasm for the sport, and for the hapless Chicago Cubs became part of popular lore, prompting a skit on the popular television comedy, *Saturday Night Live.*

Always a self-proclaimed conservative, Will encountered controversy during the 1980 election when he helped Republican candidate Ronald Reagan prepare for a debate, and afterwards commented on television that Reagan had done splendidly. There was, however, often tension between Will and "movement conservatives," some of whom believed that he had ingratiated himself with the Washington establishment by trampling on the carcass of Richard Nixon. Will occasionally exacerbated these tensions by attempting to distinguish himself from "soi dissant" conservatives, generally of the libertarian variety, whom he deemed insufficiently attuned to the proper purposes of government.

Will counts himself a part of the Tory tradition, which seeks to cultivate a virtuous citizenry, and is willing to use the good offices of government toward that end. As a practical matter, however, the shortcomings of Americans rather than their virtues are what elicited his keenest thought. He was perhaps strongest as a cultural critic, in which capacity he capably defended Victorian traditions of literacy and high culture from the barbarian incursions of modern times. His erudition—some have commented that the baton was handed from Walter Lippmann—gave him an air of intellectual authority on such matters unique in mainstream American commentary.

The principal use he found for American government, however, was national defense pursued aggressively. Ultimately, his legacy may be joined to that of the neoconservatives: both came to prominence as social critics defending tradition, but found their true passion in the encouragement of American military adventures abroad.

Further Reading

Will, George F. *Men at Work: The Craft of Baseball.* New York: Macmillan, 1990.
——. *The Pursuit of Happiness, and Other Sobering Thoughts.* New York: Harper & Row, 1978.
——. *The Pursuit of Virtue and Other Tory Notions.* New York: Simon and Schuster, 1982.
——. *Suddenly: The American Idea Abroad and at Home, 1986–1990.* New York: Free Press, 1990.

GORDON JACKSON

WINCHELL, WALTER

From the Jazz Age to the beginning of the Cold War, Walter Winchell (April 7, 1897–February 20, 1972) was "the country's best-known and most widely read journalist as well as among its most influential" (*New York Times*, February 21, 1972). At his peak, one of every three Americans read Winchell's nationally syndicated gossip column and listened to his weekly radio program that brought celebrity, crime, and war news and views to sixty million Americans.

Walter Winchell was the first of two sons born in Harlem's Jewish ghetto to Jacob Winchel, a womanizer who occasionally sold silk for women's underpants, and Jennie Bakst Winchel, the daughter in a family recently arrived from Russia. Jennie sewed, but the ends never met. The Winchels were stalked by rent collectors from tenement to tenement, forcing six moves in nine years. Walter often lodged with relatives and sometimes strangers. He found it humiliating.

By nine, Walter was an experienced hustler. He peddled papers along 116th Street and earned extra nickels on rainy days by holding an umbrella over unsuspecting passengers outside the Lenox Avenue subway station. At ten, he got his name in the *Evening Sun* when he was hit by a trolley bus. He liked the attention. At twelve he ushered and plugged songs at Harlem's Imperial Theater. It gave him "an exciting, breathless feeling" (Gabler 1994, 13). He dropped out of sixth grade and began touring Vaudeville with other child performers. Along with Georgie Jessel, the Newsboy Sextette sang and danced and battled one another with rolled up newspapers across Tin Pan Alley. Walter added an "l" to his last name because he liked its look on the marquee. He played Loew's vaudeville circuit with Rita Greene, starting in 1917. It was small-time stuff.

From July of 1918 until the Armistice five months later, Winchell served in the Naval Reserve. Ever after, he liked wearing the uniform. Winchell married Greene on August 11, 1919, and the couple played the Pantages circuit from

Rockford, Illinois, to Bay City, Michigan. For amusement, Winchell began writing a backstage gossip sheet for fellow vaudevillians called "The Newsense" and tacked it on the call board. *Billboard*, a Vaudeville trade paper, began publishing Winchell's "Stage Whispers" in February 1920. In April they were signed with the initials "W.W." In June, Winchell's "Pantages Paragraphs" and "Merciless Truths" began appearing in the *Vaudeville News*, a trade paper distributed free of charge to theater goers. In five months, Winchell gave up hoofing for a Corona portable typewriter when he was promoted to assistant editor at the *News*. His salary doubled to $50 weekly and his cut on every ad he solicited was raised to 20 percent.

Winchell loved having a byline and the money and growing reputation that came with it. He roamed Times Square and Broadway at all hours searching for items that appeared in his "Broadway Hearsay." He realized "the later it grew, the more interesting the conversation became" (Gabler 1994, 50). Veteran newspaperman Stanley Walker remembered the young Winchell as "astonishingly alert," an "electrically nervous little man" who was "possessed with an almost maniacal curiosity" (Thomas 1971, 29). Winchell said he kept a "killer" schedule out of a persistent fear of going hungry again. His marriage became an early casualty. Winchell and Greene separated in March 1922. The divorce became final in September 1928. By then, Winchell had established himself as America's wise guy, the columnist who let readers in on everything during the Roaring Twenties.

Jazz journalism became the antidote to the monotony of industrial living for millions of readers, and few were better at feeding their appetite for celebrity and scandal than Walter Winchell. The mainstream press decried the excesses of tabloid journalism, but when it saw the circulation that could be stimulated by reporting sex, crime, sport, sentiment and sensation, got in on the act. Leisure culture's growing fascination with the distinctive and dramatic, the rude and the romantic was furthered by columnists preoccupied with personalities, the self and showmanship. Winchell's big break came in September 1924 when he was hired by Bernarr Macfadden's to do a daily column "Your Broadway and Mine" for the fledgling *New York Graphic*, called by critics "The Pornographic." Columnists were not new. Ring Lardner, Heywood Broun, Alexander Woollcott, Christopher Morley, Franklin P. Adams, and Mark Sullivan were New York-based writers enjoying a wide readership. Regular reporting on the Broadway scene, however, in a language that reached the masses was new. Winchell's capacious energy and ear for vernacular raised Broadway chatter to a widely reviled, but often-imitated art.

Winchell gave gossip a new grammar, furthering a trend started by Sime Silverman in the pages of *Variety*. Winchell wrote a couple in love were "uh-huh," "that way," "making whoopee," "on the verge," or "Adam and Eveing it." It was a clever way to report repetitive kinds of stories and to slide around libel laws. To get married was to be "welded," "sealed," "merged," or "middle-aisled." Expectant parents were "infanticipating," "baby-bound," "getting storked," or

awaiting a "blessed event" with "blessed expense." Those planning divorce had gone "phfft," were "wilted," "soured," "curdled," "straining at the handcuffs," and were going to "tell it to a judge." Legs were "shafts" and passion "push" along Broadway, the "Hardened Artery."

In June 1929, Winchell was lured by William Randolph Hearst to the *New York Mirror* for $500 a week plus half of all revenue earned in nationally syndicating his column. "Walter Winchell on Broadway" ran thirty-three years with the paper. By 1923, Winchell had taken a common law wife, June Magee. Their first daughter died of a heart ailment soon afterwards. As an adult, their son committed suicide. The family lived in suburban Westchester, while Winchell slept in Manhattan's San Moritz Hotel. Throughout the 1930s, it became his custom to hold court at Table 50 in the Cub Room of the Stork Club, the center of New York's café society. Press agents were his legmen, hoping to get their clients names in Winchell's column. Doormen, head waiters, cab drivers, and cigarette girls at New York's major nightclubs—El Morocco, the Copacabana, Lindy's, the Onyx Club, the Blue Angel and Leon and Eddie's—fed Winchell material and feared his "drop dead" list, when the information was wrong.

Winchell's life as a wise-cracking columnist became the basis of Warner Brothers highly successful film *Blessed Event* in 1932. That was the year Winchell began his Sunday night broadcasts on NBC's Blue Network, sponsored by Jurgens Lotion. His million dollar voice, enhanced by his incessant tap of a telegrapher key, created a sense of urgency and was good theater. "Good evening, Mr. and Mrs. America and all the ships at sea—let's go to press" became instantly familiar to a generation of listeners. By the time Winchell played himself in Twentieth Century Fox's 1937 film *Wake Up and Live,* he was a millionaire. His militant anti-fascism won him private audiences with Franklin D. Roosevelt at the White House. His work as a crime reporter won him exclusives from J. Edgar Hoover.

Winchell's strong anti-Communism made him an early supporter of Joseph McCarthy. A tiff with Josephine Baker in 1951 led to charges he was a racist. He was attacked as a journalistic fraud by the *New York Post* and attacked back. In 1952 Winchell took his radio show to television but it was dropped by ABC in 1954. A TV drama "The Walter Winchell File" was cancelled after five months in 1956. Winchell's narrative voice gave authenticity to *The Untouchables,* ABC's crime series that premiered in 1958. His Las Vegas act, where he simulated his radio show and soft-shoed with a chorus girl, was not well received. In 1962 he lost his column when a strike at the *Mirror* closed the paper.

In his later years, Winchell still rushed off to crime scenes even though no paper would hire him. He handed out mimeographed copies of his column to many patrons of El Morocco who did not know who he was. He lived long enough to become a caricature of himself. His lasting legacy, however, became journalism's unalterable course of making the private public through the creation of a culture of celebrity that has become both folklore and a mainstay for the masses.

Further Reading

Bessie, Simon Michael. *Jazz Journalism: The Story of Tabloid Newspapers.* New York: E.P. Dutton, 1938.

Cohen, Lester. *NY Graphic: The World's Zaniest Newspaper.* Philadelphia: Chilton Books, 1964.

Gabler, Neal. *Winchell: Gossip, Power and the Culture of Celebrity.* New York: Alfred A. Knopf, 1994.

Herr, Michael. *Walter Winchell: A Novel.* New York: Vintage Books, 1991.

Kamp, John Peter. *With Lotions of Love.* New Haven, CT: Constitutional Educational League, 1944.

Klurfeld, Herman. *Winchell: His Life and Times.* New York: Praeger, 1976.

McKelway, St. Clair. *Gossip: The Life and Times of Walter Winchell.* New York: Viking Press, 1940.

Mosedale, John. *The Men Who Invented Broadway: Damon Runyon, Walter Winchell and Their World.* New York: Richard C. Marek, 1981.

Page, Francis. *Confucius Comes to Broadway.* New York: Windom House, 1940.

Papers of Walter Winchell. Billy Rose Theatre Collection. New York Public Library.

Stuart, Lyle. *The Secret Life of Walter Winchell.* New York: Boar's Head Books, 1953.

Thomas, Bob. *Winchell.* New York: Doubleday, 1971.

Weiner, Edward Horace. *Let's Go to Press: A Biography of Walter Winchell.* New York: Putnam, 1955.

Winchell, Walter. *Winchell Exclusive: Things That Happened to Me and Me to Them.* Englewood Cliffs, NJ: Prentice-Hall, 1975.

BRUCE J. EVENSEN

WOLFE, TOM

Thomas Kennerly Wolfe (March 2, 1931–) was one of America's leading literary journalists and popular novelists in the second half of the twentieth century. A flamboyant stylist and satirical chronicler of American mores and manners, he often focused on the pursuit of status, clashing social stratums and what he perceived as the intellectual poverty of liberal pieties. Along with Gay Talese, Truman Capote, Norman Mailer, Joan Didion, and Hunter S. Thompson, Wolfe was one of the better-known members of a loose-knit and influential school of American literature known as the New Journalism, a genre of non-fiction writing that employed fiction devices, such as interior monologue, long passages of dialogue, and shifting points-of-view, with the traditional fact-gathering techniques of a newspaper reporter. Writing in Harold Hayes' *Esquire* and Clay Felker's *New York* magazines, Wolfe gained particular attention as for his sharp-eyed coverage of the 1960s and 1970s' colorful cultural landscape. Later, as a novelist, he garnered fame—and a considerable fortune—limning the excesses of Wall Street in the 1980s.

Wolfe, who is of no relation to the novelist Thomas Wolfe, was born in Richmond, Virginia; his father was an agronomist and agriculture magazine editor; his mother quit medical school to stay at home and raise a family. Wolfe was graduated from the prestigious St. Christopher's School in Richmond and, in 1951, from Washington and Lee University in Lexington, Vorginia. He earned a PhD in American studies at Yale University in 1957; his dissertation: "The League of American Writers: Communist Organizational Activity among American Writers, 1929–1942."

While in graduate school, Wolfe took a position as a general assignment reporter with the *Springfield Union* in Springfield, Massachusetts. In 1959, he joined the *Washington Post*, where he was a general assignment reporter, feature writer, illustrator and forcign correspondent. In 1960, he won the Newspaper Guild's award for foreign reporting for his coverage of the Cuban revolution. In 1962, he moved to New York, where he worked for the *New York Herald-Tribune* as a general assignment reporter and a writer for the newspaper's Sunday magazine, *New York*. During his first year in New York, he also began freelancing for *Esquire* magazine. His first story for the magazine, on the custom car culture of Southern California, was stymied by writer's block. But Wolfe, at an editor's behest, typed up his rough notes, which the editor decided to publish, largely unedited. The article's exclamatory, overly punctuated, onomatopoetic style soon became Wolfe's trademark as a journalist and helped spawn the "New Journalism." Later, Wolfe often cited the Serapion Brothers, a group of experimental writers in the Soviet Union in the 1920s, as an additional influence on his writing.

Wolfe's articles from the early 1960s were collected in the *Kandy-Kolored Tangerine Flake Streamline Baby* in 1965. He published several other collections: *The Pump House Gang* (1968); *Mauve Gloves & Madmen, Clutter & Vine* (1976) and *The Purple Decades* (1982). His first book-length work of journalism was *The Electric Kool-Acid Test* (1968), a innovative account of novelist Ken Kesey, his friends, known as the Merry Pranksters, and their role in the early days of the psychedelic movement. Later, in *Radical Chic and Mau-Mauing the Flak-Catchers* (1970), Wolfe displayed his conservative leanings by skewering a fundraiser for the Black Panthers hosted by Leonard Bernstein. Wolfe also co-edited, with E.W. Johnson, an anthology of magazine articles and book excerpts by numerous journalists called *The New Journalism* (1973). Besides journalism, Wolfe published two books of criticism: *The Painted Word* (1975), a critique of modern art, and *From Bauhaus to Our House* (1981), an attack on modern architecture. He also published his illustrations, which often ran in *Harper's* magazine, in a book called *In Our Time* (1980). Throughout much of the 1970s, Wolfe worked on a book about the astronauts, *The Right Stuff* (1979), which became a popular motion picture. During the early and mid-1980s, as the interest in the New Journalism faded, Wolfe began a serialized novel in *Rolling Stone* magazine, and a substantially revised version of that work became *The Bonfire of the Vanities* (1987), a Trollope-like saga of the downfall of a wealthy philandering bond salesman, Sherman McCoy; it also became a motion picture. Wolfe's bestselling fiction did not impress more serious literary minds, however. Novelists John Updike, John Irving, and Norman Mailer, described Wolfe's fiction as more entertainment than literature. Wolfe responded by calling the three novelists "the Three Stooges." Wolfe further damaged his reputation with the literary establishment when, in 1989, he published an essay in *Harper's* called "Stalking the Billion-footed Beast." In the article, he argued that American novelists were mired in their own minds and needed to return to the social realism and naturalism of writers such as Emile Zola, as Wolfe himself had done in *The Bonfire of the Vanities* and would do again in his second novel, *A Man in Full* (1998), which concerned the growth of Atlanta, Georgia, and the modern South. Later, Wolfe published a collection of essays and short fiction, *Hooking Up* (2000), which included the novella *Ambush at Fort Bragg*, previously serialized in *Rolling Stone,* and *Tiny Mummies*, a famous 1965 article in *New York* magazine that mocked *The New Yorker* magazine. The article, when it was originally published, ignited fierce debates among journalists about the accuracy and ethics of Wolfe and the New Journalism, which critics at the time derided as "parajournalism."

Like several of the New Journalists, Wolfe became a celebrity often profiled in the media; he cultivated the role by making frequent speeches and public appearances, as well as by wearing only tailor-made white suits, often with a matching homburg. He also coined or made popular such phrases as "good ol' boy," the right stuff," "pushing the envelope," "the Me Decade" and "masters of the universe." Wolfe's novel, *I Am Charlotte Simmons* (2004) concerned college life at the end of the twentieth century. By mid-2006, Wolfe, in his mid-seventies, said in interviews that he was researching a novel on immigration in the United States.

Further Reading

Bloom, Harold. *Tom Wolfe*. Philadelphia: Chelsea House Publishers, 2000.
McKeen, William, *Tom Wolfe*. New York: Twayne's, 1995.
Ragen, Brian Abel. *Tom Wolfe, A Critical Companion*. Westport, CT: Greenwood Press, 2002.
Shomette, Doug. *The Critical Response to Tom Wolfe*. Westport, CT: Greenwood Press, 1992.
Weingarten, Mark. *The Gang That Wouldn't Write Straight*. New York, Crown, 2005.

NICK RAVO

WOMAN SUFFRAGE PRESS

More than thirty woman suffrage journals were published during the seven decades of the woman suffrage movement (1849–1921). These journals, which were published by individuals as well as state and national organizations, expressed the beliefs and goals of the suffrage movement at a time when this information was largely excluded from and ridiculed by the general circulation press. Suffrage publications aided in recruiting, mobilizing, and sustaining support and membership in the movement and established a sense of community among suffragists who were often separated by great distances and unable to meet.

In addition to women's right to vote, suffrage publications discussed a wide range of issues affecting women, including labor laws, employment, education, and marriage and divorce laws. When woman suffrage was guaranteed in all elections with the passage of the Nineteenth Amendment to the U.S. Constitution in 1919, several of these journals continued publication to address issues of citizenship and womanhood.

First Suffrage Journals—Pre-Civil War

Women's right to vote first became a political issue in 1848, when a gathering of men and women met in Seneca Falls, New York, to discuss the "social, civil and religious rights of women." At the end of the convention, sixty-eight women and thirty-two men signed a "Declaration of Principles" in which, among other things, they called on women to secure for themselves the "sacred right to the elective franchise." Shortly after this, Amelia Jenks Bloomer, one of the women who had attended the convention, established *The Lily* (1849–1858). The eight-page monthly started as a temperance journal, but within the year was emphasizing suffrage. Bloomer also promoted a variety of reforms, including the introduction of "bloomers" (pantaloons to be worn under a knee-length skirt). Bloomer sold the *Lily* in 1854 when her husband relocated his business to a frontier town where it would have been impractical to continue publication. The journal lost impetus under the new owner, Mary Birdsall of Richmond, Indiana, and ceased publication in 1858.

A second publication to result from the Seneca Falls Convention was the *Una* (1853–1855), launched by Paulina Wright Davis, a wealthy Providence, Rhode Island, socialite. Davis edited the paper on her own until 1855, when she was joined by Caroline Healy Dall, and moved the publication to Boston. Davis sought to attract working-class and immigrant women readers, and addressed issues that affected them such as poverty and child labor in addition to broader women's issues such as suffrage, temperance, and women's rights. Unfortunately, the *Una's* target audience could not afford the one-dollar subscription rate. Plagued by a shortage of funds and the responsibility of running the paper on their own, Davis and Dall discontinued publication in October 1855.

The next year, Lydia Sayer Hasbrouck, a homeopathic physician, established *The Sibyl: A Review of the Tastes, Errors and Fashion of Society* (1856–1864) in Middletown, New York. The bi-weekly journal supported a range of reforms in addition to women's rights, including abolition, temperance, and dress reform. Like other feminist papers, it published subscribers' letters and served as an important place for women from different regions of the country to express and share their views. Hasbrouck continued publication during most of the Civil War, but suspended the journal in 1863, unable to continue in the face of rising publication costs and increasing family and professional demands.

Post-Civil War Suffrage Journals

Following the Civil War, the woman suffrage movement split over the passage of the Fourteenth and Fifteenth

Amendments to the Constitution, which eventually guaranteed the right to vote to all *male* citizens regardless of "race, color, or previous condition of servitude" but made no mention of women. The more radical faction, led by Elizabeth Cady Stanton and Susan B. Anthony, established the National Woman Suffrage Association (NWSA) and in early 1868, began to publish the *Revolution* with Anthony as proprietor, Stanton and Parker Pillsbury as editors, and the wealthy Francis Train as their financial backer. From the beginning, the *Revolution* was controversial and adopted a belligerent tone, alienating potential advocates and angering many supporters. Stanton called for women's political enfranchisement as the first, basic right, then went on to call for additional reforms, including liberalized divorce laws, equal pay, equal employment opportunities, and unionization. The paper also advocated many causes espoused by Train, including the Irish rebellion and open immigration. It soon ran into financial difficulties when Train was jailed by the British government for his pro-Irish sentiments and his support was cut off. By 1869, he and Pillsbury were no longer involved in the paper and Stanton recruited Paulina Wright Davis, former editor of the *Una,* as corresponding editor. Deprived of Train's financial support and unable to raise sufficient funds through subscriptions, Anthony sold the *Revolution* in 1870 to Laura J. Bullard, who was more moderate in her support of woman's rights. Under Bullard's hand, the publication became more of a literary and socially oriented publication, and was merged into the New York *Christian Enquirer* in 1872.

In response to Stanton and Anthony's actions, the more conservative suffragists established the American Woman Suffrage Association (AWSA) and in 1870 began to publish the *Woman's Journal*, which continued publication until 1917. Edited and published by Lucy Stone and her husband Henry Blackwell, and after their deaths by their daughter, Alice Stone Blackwell, the *Journal* appealed to moderates who supported woman suffrage but not all of the social and political reforms espoused by Stanton and Anthony. Financed by various suffrage organizations as well as wealthy benefactors, the weekly *Journal* prospered until, in 1917, it was merged with several other suffrage publications to become *The Woman Citizen.*

The Woman's Tribune (1883–1909) was the second-longest surviving suffrage journal. Clara Bewick Colby established the *Tribune* as the weekly organ of the Nebraska Woman Suffrage Association, but was soon filling its pages with news of a variety of women's organizations as well as topics such as "Household Hints" in an attempt to expand the readership base. Perhaps because of these digressions, Colby lost the association's support in 1884 and thereafter published the paper with her own money in Beatrice, Nebraska, Washington, D.C., and, finally, Portland, Oregon. Free of editorial control, Colby expanded the paper's topics to include regular columns on hygiene, literature, law, fashion, art, and finance, hoping to make it an important paper in suffrage circles. Though the *Tribune* reached 9,200 subscribers in 1890, she was never able to turn a profit. Attempts to win sponsorship from the National American

Woman Suffrage Association (NAWSA) (formed in 1890 as a result of the merger of the AWSA and the NWSA) failed, probably because of the *Tribune's* broad-based editorial content. Colby's financial problems became more severe at the end of the century, when she and her husband separated. In 1904, in anticipation of the upcoming campaign in Oregon, she moved to Portland. The Oregon suffrage amendment failed, however, and the *Tribune's* financial situation continued to slip. Colby discontinued publication in 1909, citing financial problems.

Regional Publications

Other suffrage journals were published by regional groups and often expressed local concerns. The *Woman's Exponent* (1872–1914) was published by and for Mormon women in Salt Lake City. Edited by Lulu Greene Richards (1872–1877) and Emmeline B. Wells (1877–1914), the *Exponent* created a place in which its readers' needs could be expressed and at the same time sought to present a favorable picture of Mormon women to the often hostile outside world. When Utah women won the right to vote in 1896, the *Exponent* continued covering suffrage campaigns in other parts of the nation. In 1914, the rising cost of publication and the failure to entice new subscribers led the eighty-six-year-old Wells to discontinue publication.

Another regional publication was the *Ballot Box* (1876–1878), which became the official voice of the NWSA in 1878, when its name was changed to the *National Citizen and Ballot Box* (1878–1881). The journal was established by the Toledo Woman Suffrage Association to support state suffrage and under Sarah Langdon Williams the monthly publication enjoyed spirited debate, sufficient subscribers, and financial stability. In 1878 family issues forced Williams to sell the *Ballot Box* to Matilda Gage of the NWSA, who moved it to Syracuse, New York. Gage recruited Stanton and Anthony as corresponding editors and changed the journal's mission to secure federal, rather than state, suffrage. Despite her ambitious plans, financial difficulties and the lack of resources forced Gage to suspend publication of the *National Citizen and Ballot Box* in late 1881.

The *Wisconsin Citizen* (1887–1917) was published almost single-handedly for its first twenty-five years by the Rev. Olympia Brown, the president of the Wisconsin Woman Suffrage Association (WWSA) from 1884 to 1913. Brown used the journal to publicize her legal battle against the state, which refused to allow her to vote in 1887, to keep the movement alive despite repeated defeats, and, in later years, to blast the state's powerful brewing and liquor industries for defeating suffrage campaigns. A younger faction within the WWSA forced Brown out of office in 1913, partly because of those failed campaigns. They elected journalist Theodora Youmans to replace her and the new president took over the *Citizen* within the year. Youmans used the *Citizen* to publicize her goals as president and, in the last years, to promote the national campaign for a federal amendment at the expense of legislation within the state. Overextended and overworked, Youmans discontinued publication of the

Citizen in 1917, replacing it with a typewritten monthly bulletin sent to newspaper editors.

Other suffrage journals include the *Pioneer* (1869–1873), published in San Francisco by Emily A. Pitts; *The New Northwest* (1881–1887), published in Portland, Oregon, by Abigail Scott Duniway; the *Woman Voter* (1910–1917), published by the New York City Woman Suffrage Party; the *Western Woman Voter* (1911–1913), published in Seattle; the *Suffragist* (1913–1921), published by the militant National Woman's Party; and *The Woman Citizen* (1917–1927), published by the NAWSA as the result of the merger of the *Woman's Journal*, *Woman Voter*, and *National Suffrage News*.

Despite the disadvantages these women journalists faced during the late nineteenth and early twentieth centuries, their work taken as a whole helped to raise the public's consciousness of women's rights and contributed to changes in the American political and social climate in ways that eventually led to the ratification of the Nineteenth Amendment in 1920.

Further Reading

Buechler, Steven. *Women's Movements in the United States*. New Brunswick, NJ: Rutgers University Press, 1990.

Burt, Elizabeth V. "Dissent and Control in a Woman Suffrage Periodical: 30 Years of the *Wisconsin Citizen*." *American Journalism* 16, 2 (Spring 1999): 39–62.

Endres, Kathleen L., and Therese L. Lueck, eds. *Women's Periodicals in the United States: Social and Political Issues*. Westport, CT: Greenwood Press, 1996.

Flexner, Eleanor. *Century of Struggle: The Woman's Rights Movement in the United States*, rev. ed. Cambridge, MA.: Belknap Press, 1975.

Lumsden, Linda. "'Excellent Ammunition' Suffrage Newspaper Strategies During World War I." *Journalism History* 25, 2 (Summer 1999): 53–63.

Steiner, Linda. "Finding Community in Nineteenth Century Suffrage Periodicals." *American Journalism* 1, 1 (Summer 1983): 1–15.

Solomon, Martha Solomon, ed. *A Voice of Their Own: The Woman Suffrage Press, 1840–1910*. Tuscaloosa: The University of Alabama Press, 1991.

ELIZABETH V. BURT

WOMEN JOURNALISTS

Women have played a vital role in American journalism since the colonial period, though their numbers and influence were limited by a combination of economic, legal, and social factors until the mid-twentieth century. After the late 1960s, increased educational opportunities, social and cultural changes brought about by the women's movement, and the advent of equal opportunity legislation led to greater participation of women in the journalistic workforce. Their numbers increased, some won highly visible assignments covering political and international news or as television anchors and correspondents, and others finally broke through the "glass ceiling" to hold positions as editors, publishers, and board members at a handful of media

companies. These gains slowed in the 1990s, however, and by 2007, women journalists were still a minority in the newsroom and boardroom and their salaries continued to lag behind those of their male counterparts. This disparity and women's under representation in the news workforce continue to be points of concern today for educational groups, media corporations, feminists, and critics, who view women's equal participation in the news industry as a democratic imperative as well as an assurance for the future of the industry itself.

The Colonial and Revolutionary Periods

The first newspaper publishers in America were printers who produced a variety of materials, including pamphlets, religious tracts, official documents, and public notices in addition to weekly four-page newspapers. These printers, almost always male, were sanctioned by the colonial government and often held official printing contracts. They were assisted by male journeymen and apprentices and, informally, their wives and daughters. When a printer died or became incapacitated, it was often his wife or widow who carried on the business until her male children were old enough to take legal possession. Women were rarely recognized for their contributions during this time, however; their official role was to serve as wife and mother. They had no legal rights, little formal education, and no formalized training in the trades. Their role as printer was often obscured by the fact that their name rarely appeared on the newspaper or in official records as publisher.

Despite this, historians have identified at least sixteen women who published newspapers, tracts, and pamphlets during the colonial and revolutionary periods. The first of these was Catherine Anna Zenger, who, for nine months in 1734, published the *New York Weekly Journal* for her husband, Peter, who was imprisoned and awaiting trial for seditious libel. When he died in 1746, she continued publishing the paper and running the print shop until she turned it over to her oldest son and the legal heir in 1749. Elizabeth Timothy published the *South-Carolina Gazette* from 1739 until 1746, following the death of her husband, Louis. During these years, the *Gazette* served as an important source of information for the growing Charleston community. The mother of six children, Elizabeth Timothy kept the business going until her oldest son and the official heir, Peter, turned twenty-one.

During the revolutionary period, Mary Katherine Goddard and her mother, Sarah Updike Goddard, ran the *Maryland Journal* for Mary's brother, William, from 1773 to 1784 while he traveled around the colonies seeking business opportunities. Mary Goddard made the Baltimore paper one of the most vigorous voices of the growing rebellion against colonial rule and in 1777 was selected by the Continental Congress to issue the first official publication of the Declaration of Independence. She made the *Journal* one of the best newspapers in the colonies, but was removed as publisher by William when he resumed control of the paper in 1784. There were also other women involved in journalism during this period. Mary Crouch, who was strongly opposed to the Stamp Act of 1765, published *The Charleston Gazette* in South Carolina until about 1780, and then moved the paper to Salem, Massachusetts, where it continued for several years.

In the years following the Revolution, women continued to take up the business of printing and newspaper publishing upon the death or absence of husbands, fathers, and brothers. While most of them ran the business for fewer than two years, a few did so for nearly a decade. Ann Barber of the *Newport Mercury* published her paper from 1800–1809; Sarah Hillhouse published the *Monitor* in Washington, Georgia, from 1803 to 1811; and Catherine Bose Dobbin published the *Baltimore American* from 1811–1820. In sum, thirty-two women acted as newspaper publishers from the colonial period until 1820.

The Early Nineteenth Century

After the 1830s, when city newspapers began to print daily editions and hire regular correspondents and reporters, a few women made their name as staff writers or regular correspondents. Others established themselves as editors of women's magazines or even established their own publications. These were the exceptions, however, for most women publishing in newspapers and magazines did so on an ad hoc basis. They contributed letters, poems, stories, and observations, were paid by the published word, and rarely set foot in a publishing office.

One of the earliest women to make a name for herself in nineteenth-century journalism was Anne Royall, who became known for her eccentricity, political acumen, and devotion to democratic government. Widowed and destitute, she moved to Washington in 1831 at the age of 61, and began to publish *Paul Pry,* the first of two political newspapers. She published this until 1836, then launched a second newspaper, *The Huntress,* which continued until shortly before her death in 1854. Critical and outspoken, she exposed graft and corruption, campaigned for internal improvements, free schools, and free thought and speech. Another original was the feminist Margaret Fuller, who had established herself as the editor of the *Dial,* a transcendentalist journal. In 1844 she was hired by Horace Greeley to be the literary critic for his *New York Tribune*, but she also wrote exposés on public institutions and women's rights. Because it was not socially acceptable for a middle-class woman to work in the public eye, Fuller worked from a room in Greeley's home and sent her material to the *Tribune* by messenger.

Some women journalists used their positions to critique social conventions while at the same time paying lip service to those that required them to conform to the prevailing ideal of "the lady." Sarah Josepha Hale edited the popular *Godey's Lady's Book* from 1837 until 1877, publishing the expected articles on home, family, food, and fashion. But at the same time, she critiqued the very fashions she featured, promoted women's education, and advocated that widowed or unmarried women be able to support themselves. Sarah

Willis Parton, who wrote under the pen name "Fanny Fern" for the weekly *New York Ledger* from 1853 until 1872, was appreciated by both male and female readers for her wry wit as well as her direct language, despite the fact that she dealt with many potentially sensitive topics such as woman suffrage, dress reform, prostitution, and poverty. Jane Cunningham Croly ("Jennie June"), who began her forty-year newspaper career at the *New York Herald* in 1855, used her fashion, society, and women's columns to promote the expansion of woman's sphere to include civic activism and improvement.

Post-Civil War Years

Following the Civil War, women slowly made gains in the public sphere, partly because of their earlier involvement in the abolition movement, partly because of the growing woman's movement. This was reflected in journalism, where the numbers of women increased and the roles they played widened, despite rules and restrictions that favored male journalists. A small number of women ventured into the world of political journalism, including Mary Clemmer Ames, who covered Congress from 1866 to 1884 for the *New York Independent* and the *Brooklyn Daily Union,* and Sarah Lippincott ("Grace Greenwood"), who published columns in the *New York Times* from 1873 to 1878 that attacked corruption in Washington, supported women government workers, and condemned the return of white supremacy in the South. By 1879, twenty women were covering Congress as weekly columnists, but in that year, a Capitol rules change barred them from the press galleries on the grounds that only the main representatives of daily papers (all of whom were male) were to be allowed.

As advertisers, whose influence in journalism increased substantially during the late nineteenth century, began to value the importance of women consumers, newspapers established women's columns, pages, and sections in an effort to attract these readers. These pages required women writers and editors, and by the early 1880s, many of the larger city newspapers had at least one woman on staff. In that year, the U.S. Census counted 288 women—less than 3 percent of all working journalists—as full-time journalists, while perhaps three times that number were part-time correspondents and contributors While the majority of these wrote about affairs of the domestic sphere (family, food, and children) or society (weddings, births, and gossip), some used these pages to comment on social ills and promote civic reform. Some who became leaders in the growing woman's movement served as catalysts for change. Sallie Joy White, who became the first woman staff reporter on a Boston newspaper in 1870, eventually wrote a popular column under the pen name "Penelope Penfeather," and continued writing for Boston papers until her death in 1909. She was a suffragist, promoted women's education and their place in the professions, and in 1885 helped found the New England Woman's Press Association (NEWPA). Helen M. Winslow was a staff writer at the *Boston Advertiser* from 1883 to 1890 and the *Boston Herald* in 1891, the fashion editor at *Delineator* for seventeen years, and the founder and editor of *Clubwoman*, the publication of the General Federation of Women's Clubs. She was an officer in NEWPA as well as several others women's organizations and regularly used her columns to promote women's interests, especially suffrage.

Other women entered the field of journalism through their advocacy for a particular reform. The woman suffrage movement, for example, published more than thirty journals between 1849 and 1920. Though most of these were short-lived, each provided an opportunity for women to edit and write for their own publication which was dedicated to their own needs and interests. In 1870, for example, Victoria (Claflin) and Tennessee Claflin ran *Woodhull and Claflin's Weekly*, a paper that supported woman suffrage and free love, and in 1872, published an English translation of the *Communist Manifesto*. The paper also helped to cause a national scandal when it carried rumors an affair between the wife of journalist Theodore Tilton and Rev. Henry Ward Beecher. Another example was the feminist Lucy Stone who became the founding editor of the longest-lived suffrage publication, the *Woman's Journal* (1870–1917). Upon her death in 1893, she was succeeded by her daughter, Elizabeth Stone Blackwell, who had grown up in the *Journal* offices and the suffrage movement.

The temperance movement also provided women an opportunity to enter journalism. In 1883, the Women's Christian Temperance Union established the *Union Signal*. This national weekly, which focused primarily on temperance and prohibition, came to follow the dictum of WCTU leader Frances Willard to "do everything" and eventually promoted a slew of reforms, including woman suffrage, welfare reform, women's labor issues, health reform, and pacifism. By 1911, the WCTU claimed nearly a quarter-million members and the *Union Signal*, filled with articles by staff writers, contributors, and movement leaders, likely had triple that number of readers.

A third reform movement of the period was launched almost single-handedly by one woman journalist, Ida B. Wells, the African American editor of the Memphis *Free Speech*. She gained notoriety in 1892 when she began writing editorials against lynching, her life was threatened, and her newspaper office was burned. Wells moved to the North where she continued her anti-lynching campaign on the staff of the black publication, *New York Age*. She founded anti-lynching societies, lectured throughout the United States and England, published several books, and continued to write for several newspapers until her death in 1931.

Front-Page Women

By the last decades of the nineteenth century, newspapers had adopted modern-day news values that identify "news" as events of significance, usually involving change and conflict, and affecting significant portions of the population. At the same time, there was a growing taste for "human-interest" stories that emphasized the triumphs and tragedies of the human condition. While women at this time were typically deemed physically and psychologically unfit to enter into the helter-skelter world of breaking news (politics, war, crime, and disaster), they were considered ideal for some of the human-interest stories that required a sympathetic approach and a compassionate tone. These stories allowed women to break out of the women's pages and a few even made it onto the front page where the most important stories appeared. Because it was still considered a novelty for women to work for newspapers, the editors often publicized the fact by attaching the woman's byline to the story, something that was newsworthy in itself at that time.

The most famous of these front-page women was Elizabeth Cochrane ("Nellie Bly"), who won a reputation as a stunt reporter in 1887 after she got herself committed to a insane asylum and then reported her story in lurid detail for the *New York World*. Her most renowned stunt was her 1889 trip around the world in seventy-two days, but she also wrote about social issues, including labor strikes, the living conditions of workers, gambling, and prostitution. Wisconsin reporter Zona Gale also enjoyed front-page exposure with her stories in the *Milwaukee Journal* in 1900 and eventually worked her way to New York, where she landed a job with the *Evening World*. Here she used her considerable personal charms to win the confidence of witnesses in murder trials, striking mill workers, and champion boxers before launching a highly successful career as a playwright and novelist. During World War I, though women journalists were banned by the military authorities from the front lines, a few managed to circumvent regulations to cover the war effort. Rheta Childe Dorr, for example, followed the women's "Battalion of Death" in Russia and later gained access to training camps in France by joining the staff of the YMCA.

The success of the woman suffrage amendment in 1919, the end of World War I, and the ensuing optimism of the Jazz Age encouraged women to enter the work force and the number of women reporters doubled between 1920 and 1930. Some entered the emerging fields of radio, advertising, and public relations, but most of those in print journalism continued to work for the women's pages and women's magazines. Despite their recently won political equality, they were still restricted by quotas in both the newsroom and the journalism schools that had opened during the first decades of the twentieth century, and most male press clubs remained closed to them. Those who succeeded in establishing and maintaining a career were single-minded and determined. One particularly successful woman was Dorothy Thompson, a newspaper columnist who achieved celebrity status for her coverage of the European political scene during the 1930s and 1940s. She was an early critic of Adolph Hitler and was expelled from Germany in 1934 because of her unflattering portrait of the dictator. Back in the United States, she toured the country to lecture on the dangers posed by Hitler and his Nazi party. From 1936 to 1958 she published a political column three times a week, "On the Record," first for the *New York Herald-Tribune* and later for other papers.

With the beginning of World War II, as male reporters and editors were drafted into the military, news organizations were forced to fill their places with women. More than one hundred received accreditation from the War Department, though they still faced antagonism from military authorities and male reporters and were generally restricted from the front lines. A few, including Marguerite Higgins of the *New York Herald-Tribune* and *Life* photographer Margaret Bourke-White, won recognition for their extraordinary work and continued in high-profile careers. Once the war ended and men returned from the military to claim their old positions, however, most of the women who had filled editorial and news assignments were moved back to the women's pages or fired.

They eventually found new opportunities during the post-war economic boom, when many newspapers took advantage of the developing consumer-driven economy by transforming their traditional women's pages into expanded "home" and "lifestyle" sections. Here, women journalists wrote about the latest domestic technology and trends in homemaking and child rearing. Just as they had in the 1890s, some used the women's pages to talk about serious social issues and, eventually the rising women's liberation movement. Others found work with the growing number of women's magazines, which also took advantage of the economic boom. Women seeking jobs in the news department, the wire services, radio, and the emerging television news industry, however, were turned down by managers who explained they needed someone they could send anywhere, who were more likely to have accessibility to male sources, who would not have family and childcare issues interfering with her work, who would be tough and reliable, and who would fit into the (male) newsroom.

The Women's Movement and Later

Women finally received a weapon to use against job discrimination with the passage of Title VII of the Civil Rights Act of 1964 and the establishment of the federal Equal Economic Opportunities Commission (EEOC). They began to organize across the country and in the next decade filed successful complaints with the EEOC against news organizations, including the Associated Press, the *New York Times*, the *Washington Post*, and NBC. At the same time, feminist groups organized public demonstrations, boycotts, and sit-ins to protest the media's failure to adequately represent women and their interests as well as their sexist representation and misrepresentaton of women in news and advertising. Women journalists wrote about these events in radical new feminist publications such as *Ms.* as well as in some of the traditional women's magazines, including *Redbook* and *Cosmopolitan*.

The lawsuits, court rulings, and publicity drove news organizations to improve their hiring and promotion of women journalists and to expand their news sections to include what had been traditionally relegated to the women's pages as merely "women's issues." Opportunities increased dramatically for women in the next two decades. Quotas were dropped by journalism schools and by 1985 female students had begun to outnumber male students (though male professors continue even today to outnumber and outrank female professors). The number of women in the journalism workforce grew steadily to 30 percent in 1970, 40 percent in 1980 and 48 percent in 2001. They were hired to cover the entire gamut of news, including sports, crime, politics, and war, although "hard news" continued to be dominated by male reporters. Some women journalists were promoted to editorial positions, but here growth was slow and by 1985, fewer than 12 percent of editors were women. Women even made it into the publisher's office and the boardroom. Companies such as Gannett and Lee Enterprises were the most receptive in this regard. The television news industry also gradually opened its doors to women journalists and increasingly hired them as reporters, although usually not on the political beat. By the late 1980s, most local television stations had a man-woman anchor team. Some women enjoyed stints as anchorwomen on national television news including Barbara Walters, Diane Sawyer, Leslie Stahl, and Elizabeth Vargas. In 2006, Katie Couric, a former co-host for NBC's *Today Show*, became the evening anchor of CBS Evening News, a position formerly occupied by such male newscasters as Douglas Edwards, Walter Cronkite, Dan Rather, and Bob Schieffer.

Despite such gains, the trend toward hiring more women journalists slowed during the mid-1990s, and by 2001, had come to a halt. The percentage of women in the journalistic workforce began to drop for the first time in 150 years and they remained significantly underrepresented in management positions where news decisions are made and corporate policy was formed. As in all professions, they continued to be paid less than their male counterparts, just eighty-one cents to the dollar, according to a study published in 2003. Surveys showed that they shared the same professional values as their male counterparts, but were less likely to seek management positions. They were less likely to plan on staying in the field for the rest of their professional lives, perhaps because of the difficulties they faced in advancing, perhaps because of the eventual demands of motherhood and family. By 2005, women held just 27 percent of management positions and their numbers had decreased to 43 percent of the journalistic workforce. These statistics were troubling for those who believed women must take an equal part in the news industry to represent a realistic and balanced view of the world and to ensure the very future of the news industry.

Further Reading

Beasley, Maurine H., and Sheila J. Gibbons. *Taking Their Place: A Documentary History of Women and Journalism,* 2nd ed. State College, PA: Strata Publishing, Inc., 2003.

Belford, Barbara. *Brilliant Bylines: A Biographical Anthology of Notable Newspaperwomen in America.* New York: Columbia University Press, 1986.

Burt, Elizabeth V., ed. *Women's Press Organizations: 1881–1999.* Westport, CT: Greenwood Press, 2000.

Creedon, Pamela J., ed. *Women in Mass Communication*, 3rd ed. Newbury Park, CA: Sage Publications, 2006.

Edwards, Julia. *Women of the World: The Great Foreign Correspondents.* Boston: Houghton Mifflin, 1988.

Endres, Kathleen L., and Therese L. Lueck, eds. *Women's Periodicals in the United States: Social and Political Issues.* Westport, CT: Greenwood Press, 1996.

Henry, Susan. "Exception to the Female Model: Colonial Printer Mary Crouch." *Journalism Quarterly*, 62 (1985):725–733, 749.

Marzolf, Marion. *Up From the Footnote: A History of Women Journalists.* New York: Hastings House, 1977.

Schlipp, Madelon Golden, and Sharon M. Murphy. *Great Women of the Press.* Carbondale: Southern Illinois University Press, 1983.

Signorielli, Nancy, ed. *Women in Communication: A Biographical Sourcebook.* Westport, CT: Greenwood Press, 1996.

ELIZABETH V. BURT

WOMEN JOURNALISTS, AFRICAN AMERICAN

The contributions of African American women journalists are a legacy of service to their ethnic heritage, gender, and communities. Battling the double bind of racism and sexism, their history weaves through the black and mainstream press, and the American women's movement, fashioning an indelible component of the American press.

By the early 1800s, America had established twenty-five years of a free press and two hundred years of slavery. For American citizens and freed African Americans, an industrialized newspaper industry became a family enterprise. The first newspaper published by African Americans, *Freedom's Journal* appeared in New York City in 1827. Founding fathers Samuel Eli Cornish and John Brown Russwurm sought to address the social and economic concerns of free blacks living in New York State, which abolished slavery the same year. Published slave poet Phyllis Wheatley was profiled along with other successful entrepreneurs, teachers, preachers, and writers. Antebellum African American women journalists were most likely of privilege, and the more visible educators, orators and writers. Their writing concentrated on ending slavery and "uplifting the race" through civic and moral education. They rallied the cause of women's rights

Mary Ann Shadd Cary (1823–1893) was born free in Wilmington, Delaware. She was an educator and editor with the *North Star,* published by former slave Frederick Douglass. After passage of the Fugitive Slave Act in 1850, Cary moved to Canada and urged resettlement there in her weekly *Provincial Freeman.* Cary belonged to the National Woman Suffrage Association (NWSA), founded in 1869.

White female journalists, known as "literary ladies," mostly wrote at home, in a decided moral voice on social, church, and education issues. Some female writer-activists debated abolition and women's rights. Of note were Jane Grey Swisshelm (1815–1884), owner of *The St. Cloud Visitor*; and Elizabeth Cady Stanton (1815–1902) a friend of Douglass.

Frances Ellen Watkins Harper (1825–1911) worked as a sewing instructor and, in 1854, began writing and lecturing for the abolitionist press in Philadelphia. Harper joined the American Women Suffrage Association (AWSA), founded

the same year as the more radical NWSA, which protested the 1870 passage of the Fifteenth Amendment to the Constitution, granting African American men voting rights.

Gertrude Bustill Mossel (1855–1948) approached journalism with an evangelical spirit. During the 1880s, she contributed to among others the *Philadelphia Times,* the *Philadelphia Echo,* and the *Independent.* She was an editor for the women's columns of the *New York Age,* the *Indianapolis World* and the *New York Freeman.* In her book, *The Work of the Afro-American Woman* (1894), Mossel noted journalism was a viable career for educated women of color traditionally employed as seamstresses and teachers.

Civil War, Emancipation, and Reconstruction—events from 1861 to 1877—increased opportunities for women in nursing, teaching, and journalism. Nearly two dozen white women abolitionists were Congressional reporters, although they were denied seats in the press gallery.

Women formed their own professional clubs: Sorosis, the first, in 1868; the Women's National Press Association in 1882; the Women's Press Club of New York in 1889; and in Boston, the Federation of Women's Press Clubs in 1891. These clubs excluded African American women journalists well into the 1960s. The National Colored Press Association (NCPA) began in 1880.

In 1886, *Journalist,* the precursor to *Editor & Publisher* magazine, estimated that five hundred women worked as journalists in American newspapers. On January 26, 1889, the trade publication devoted an entire issue to women journalists. Lucy Wilmot Smith (1861–1888), who belonged to the NCPA, wrote the article "Some Female Writers of the Negro Race," which featured ten journalists and cited sixteen other contributors. As recorded in *The Black Press in the Middle West, 1865–1985* (1996), Smith's article appeared in the Indianapolis black weekly *Freeman* one month later.

Three years later, I. Garland Penn's *The Afro-American Press and Its Editors* (1891), listed about twenty black female journalists in this benchmark tome. The "Princess of the Press," Ida B. Wells-Barnett (1862–1931), figured prominently in both Smith's and Penn's publications. Born in Mississippi six months prior to the Emancipation Proclamation, Wells-Barnett's byline stamped newspapers from the Midwest to the East Coast: First, at *The Evening Star,* a journal for public school teachers; and others such as the *Kansas City Gate City Press,* the *Chattanooga Justice,* the *Little Rock Sun,* the *Detroit Plaindealer,* the *Washington Bee,* and the *New York Age.* Wells-Barnett wrote for and later purchased the *Free Speech and Headlight,* renaming it the *Memphis Free Speech.* Here, she published a scathing series of anti-lynching editorials. After her offices were destroyed by a mob, she fled to New York City and the paper folded in 1892.

Wells-Barnett was a co-founder of the National Association for the Advancement of Colored People (NAACP) and instrumental in starting its magazine, *Crisis.* In 1895, Wells-Barnett became publisher and succeeded her now husband, Ferdinand Barnett, as editor of Chicago's first black newspaper, the *Conservator.* The Barnetts's civic activism and stewardship during the Great Migration of blacks moving from the south to the north, World War I, and the sanctioned separatism of the Jim Crow years helped to shift the capital of the black press from New York to Chicago.

Penn described Victoria Mathews (1861–1907) as the most well-liked-writer of her time. Self-educated, Matthews was raised in New York by her mother, a fugitive slave from Georgia. Matthews was a "sub reporter" for several New York papers including the *New York Times* and the *Herald* in the late 1800s. An active clubwoman, Matthews's work appeared in black newspapers such as the *Boston Advocate, Washington Bee, Richmond Planet, New York Globe,* and *New York Enterprise.*

Battling the Barriers of Race and Sex

Origins of the black women's club movement date to an 1892 New York fundraiser coordinated by Matthews for Wells-Barnett. Journalists from Boston, New York, and Philadelphia attended, including activist Mary Church Terrell (1863–1954), the daughter of two former slaves from Memphis who became wealthy realtors. In 1896, Terrell founded the National Association of Colored Women (NACW) and served as its president until 1901. For seven decades, Terrell used the press for civil rights activism. She wrote for the NACW organ, *The Woman's Era;* the *AME Church Review*; the *New York Age;* and had a current events column in the *Norfolk Journal and Guide.* Terrell's articles on the "race problem" were often refused, but during the 1930s and 1940s, the *Boston Globe* and the *Washington Post* printed her letters to the editor. She advocated for black soldiers, and in 1949 asked the *Post* to stop using the word "Negro." She authored in 1940 *A Colored Woman in A White World.*

Josephine St. Pierre Ruffin (1842–1924) and Josephine Silone Yates (1859–1912) were regular contributors to the *Woman's Era* newspaper, which Ruffin founded. Yates initiated the first black woman's club in Kansas City, and served as the second president of the NACW. Both were proponents of an integrated women's club movement.

In 1900, more than one thousand women convened for the predominantly white General Federation of Women's Clubs meeting. Ruffin who was of mixed ancestry and a member of several prestigious women's clubs in New England was turned away. The black *Wisconsin Weekly Advocate,* a Booker T. Washington supporter, buried coverage of this incident.

The Twentieth-Century Legacy

By the turn of the century, close to 2,200 women, black and white, were journalists. Their beats still considered women's work; the majority of them staffed the women's pages and reported on the church, domestic concerns and society life. A handful of white women such as Elizabeth "Nellie Bly" Cochrane (1864–1922) and Ida Tarbell (1857–1944) gained fame as investigative reporters examining social ills

and the business practices of the leading industries.

African American newspapers developed editorial policies reflecting the social philosophy of W.E.B. DuBois or Booker T. Washington. Some African American women journalists balanced career and personal life by marrying men of like persistence.

Geraldine Pindell-Trotter (1872–1918) was the wife of William Monroe Trotter (1872–1934), a Harvard graduate and principle with W.E.B. Dubois in the Niagara Movement. Pindell-Trotter was associate editor for her husband's newspaper, the *Boston Guardian* (1901). She advocated for women and children, and World War I African American troops.

Alice Dunbar Nelson (1875–1935) was the widow of poet Paul Laurence Dunbar (1872–1906). She edited the women's page of the *Journal of the Lodge* and *AME Church Review.* Her column "From a Woman's Point of View" began in 1926 in the *Pittsburgh Courier;* and "Little Excursions Week by Week" was a staple of the black syndicated press.

Amy Jacques Garvey (1895–1973) was the wife of Marcus Garvey (1887–1940), a Pan-African leader and president of the Universal Negro Improvement Association (UNIA). Jacques Garvey was a managing editor of UNIA's the *Negro World,* and the one-page column "Our Women and What They Think." Jacques Garvey chronicled a three-volume history of the UNIA in the 1960s.

The West, Wars, Depression, and Expansion

Post-bellum America was a flurry of industrialization and immigration to the nation's urban centers. African Americans seeking escape from the virulent conditions of Jim Crow, migrated north and west. Although women's suffrage passed in 1920, race and gender discrimination did not ease for African American women; the journalists intensified their focus on racial, social and economic equality. Until the mid-twentieth century, an ethnically diverse America on the cusp of global involvement saw opportunity in California.

Delilah Beasley (1871–1934) began writing at age twelve for the *Cleveland Gazette* and contributed regularly to the *Cincinnati Gazette.* She moved to California in 1910; held various occupations in the health field; and documented the lives of African Americans in the West. Beasley argued fervently against stereotypical images and descriptions of African Americans. She collaborated with the NAACP, protesting the film, *The Birth of A Nation* (1915). She wrote an *Oakland Tribune* column, "Activities Among Negroes," and the book, *The Negro Trailblazers of California* (1919).

Editor and publisher of the oldest black paper in the West, the *California Eagle,* Charlotta Bass (1874–1969) confronted racial injustice in local and national government, and in her community during the Depression and World War II. In 1925, she proved victorious in a libel suit filed by the Ku Klux Klan; and in 1943 was the first African American to serve on a Los Angeles grand jury. In her column, "On the Sidewalk," Bass celebrated the accomplishments of African American women, and vehemently recommended that African Americans boycott businesses that discriminated.

Lucile Bluford (1911–2003), the second black student to study journalism at the University of Kansas, served the *Kansas City Call* for seventy years. She became editor in 1955, and was part owner of the paper founded in 1919. It grew to be one of the nation's largest black weeklies. She sued the University of Missouri in 1939 when denied admission to the graduate program. Her loss in the suit resulted in the start of a program at Lincoln University in Jefferson City.

Another nonagenarian, Marvel Cooke (1903–2000) entered journalism during the Harlem Renaissance as a society editor for the *Amsterdam News*. There, in the 1930s, she organized a strike of the employees for membership in the Newspaper Guild. She later joined the staff of the liberal, all-white, daily *Compass* as the only woman and African American. Here, Cooke wrote a series on domestics by going undercover as a day laborer.

Alice Allison Dunnigan (1906–1983) was the first African American woman to cover Congress, the White House, and travel with a U.S. president. She was a Washington correspondent for the *Chicago Defender*, which was a member of the Associated Negro Press (ANP). Dunnigan served as ANP Washington chief for fourteen years, and broke the color line of the Women's National Press Club in 1955.

Era Bell Thompson (1905–1986) moved from North Dakota to Chicago during the Great Depression. She worked for *Ebony* magazine for three decades. Publisher John Johnson sent her South and throughout the African people's diaspora.

Often called the "first lady of the black press," Chicago native Ethel Payne (1911–1991) was the first African American female journalist to move from print to network broadcasting. Known for her stealth reporting during the civil rights movement, Payne worked as a librarian, and then, the U.S. Army. The *Chicago Defender* published her award-winning appeal for the adoption of World War II African American and Japanese babies. Payne was the only African American woman to witness signings of the Civil Rights and Voting Rights acts of the mid 1960s. She was a commentator for CBS radio and television; and covered the Vietnam War and apartheid in South Africa.

Healing the Divide—A Second Wave

In 1968, the Kerner Commission, formed to investigate the race riots of preceding years, identified economic disparity a key factor in African Americans' frustration. The report noted that African Americans comprised less than 5 percent of editorial positions in mainstream media; and most managers, numbering less than 1 percent, worked for the black press. The report mandated that mainstream media—the nation's mirror—integrate the industry through increased employment; access to academic training; and editorial inclusion to address the concerns and needs of African Americans.

Dorothy Gilliam (1936–), former city columnist for the *Washington Post* entered mainstream media from the black press during the civil rights movement. Gilliam covered the integration of Little Rock's Central High and was one of two African Americans in the 1961 class of Columbia University Graduate School of Journalism.

Nancy Hicks Maynard (1946–) became a reporter for the *New York Times* in 1968 after leaving the *New York Post*. She co-founded the *Institute for Journalism Education* with her husband Robert Maynard, former owner of the *Oakland Tribune*.

A contemporary in television, Belva Davis (1933–), won five Emmys and was the first African American female news anchor on the West Coast in 1967.

Pamela Johnson (1945–), in 1981, became the first female African American publisher of a white-owned newspaper, the *Ithaca Journal*, in New York State. A decade earlier, Johnson was the first African American woman appointed to the faculty of the University of Wisconsin, where she earned her doctorate.

According to *Media Report to Women* (December 2005), 37.5 percent of women work in daily newsrooms and 17.2 percent are minority women, which is not exclusive to African American women. Men still hold the majority of managerial positions, while women (of all backgrounds) remain the majority of college journalism students since 1977.

Increased opportunity in employment, diversity in education, and a passing of the baton has had its rewards. Ten years after being banned from the San Diego Padres locker room, Claire Smith (1953–) became in 1994, the first woman to head the New York chapter of the Baseball Writers Association of America. Gwen Ifill (1955–), who wrote for the *Boston Herald American*, the *Baltimore Evening Sun*, the *Washington Post,* and the *New York Times*, succeeded pioneer African American journalist Charlayne Hunter-Gualt (1942–) as a correspondent for the PBS program *The News Hour with Jim Lehrer*. Ifill, in 2004, was the first African American woman to moderate a vice-presidential debate.

African American women awarded an individual Pulitzer Prize in the 1990s included Isabel Wilkerson (1960–) in 1994 and Margo Jefferson in 1995, both of the *New York Times*; and E.R. Shipp (1955–) of the *New York Daily News*, in 1996. In 2006, Robin Givhan (1964–) of the *Washington Post* won for criticism of fashion. She was the first fashion writer to be nominated, and win.

Further Reading

Beasley, H. Maurine, and Sheila J. Gibbons. *Taking their Place: A Documentary History of Women and Journalism*. Washington, D.C.: American University Press, 1993.

Broussard, Jinx Coleman. *Giving a Voice to the Voiceless: Four Pioneering Black Women Journalists*. New York & London: Routledge, 2004.

Cairns, Kathleen A. *Front-Page Women Journalists, 1920–1950*. Lincoln: University of Nebraska Press, 2003.

Mills, Kay. *A Place in the News: From the Women's Pages to the Front Page*. New York, Columbia University Press, 1990.

Pride, S. Armistead, and Clint C. Wilson II. *A History of the Black Press*. Washington, D.C.: Howard University Press, 1997.

Gibbons, Sheila, ed. *Media Report to Women*, http://www.mediareporttowomen.com/statistics.htm (accessed April 16, 2007).

Salem, Dorothy C., ed. *African American Women: A Biographical Dictionary*. New York: Garland, 1993.

KISSETTE BUNDY

WOMEN'S MAGAZINES

Magazines have historically reflected and responded to women's unique and changing roles in American society. Remnants of the earliest women's magazines may be glimpsed in contemporary publications that attempt to mobilize constituencies and effect positive change in the lives of women. Yet, even more enduring are profit-driven magazines that address women as consumers. The influence of advertising is a historical constant in women's magazines, even as they struggle to remain viable in the digital age.

Eighteenth Century

Previously excluded from political affairs, women emerged from the American Revolution with a significant political role, albeit exercised within the home. The notion of "Republican Motherhood," as described by Linda Kerber, fused private female virtues with civic obligations. As wife and mother, a woman needed to be educated in the ideals of republicanism so that she could instill them in her children and encourage them in her husband. As a result, women were afforded greater educational opportunities and increasingly, their rights and responsibilities became a source of public interest. As printers looked for new audiences and women began to cultivate the reading habit, magazines emerged to address that group exclusively.

The first American women's magazine, *The Lady's Magazine and Repository of Entertaining Knowledge*, was begun by William Gibbons in Philadelphia in 1792. Another magazine, *Ladies Museum*, was launched at the turn of the century by Philadelphia bookseller and editor, Isaac Ralston. Both magazines followed in part the model set by English periodicals such as *The Lady's Magazine, or Polite Companion for the Fair Sex*, published in 1759. British women's magazines had a small but loyal audience among wealthy Americans, and that fact did not escape the attention of enterprising publishers in this country.

A wide variety of information was already being printed during the period, but technologies were still relatively crude. Thus, magazine pages were composed primarily of text, punctuated with an occasional design element. A one-year subscription cost about $2, a figure equivalent to three days' salary for a skilled laborer. The early women's magazines carried little to no advertising.

These early periodicals were intended for elite readers, evidenced by their content and cost. American women's magazines emphasized literature, fashion, and etiquette. But in keeping with women's new political ken, contribu-

tions also addressed women's education and suffrage. In fact, the first issue of *The Lady's Magazine and Repository of Entertaining Knowledge* included an excerpt from Mary Wollstonecraft's *A Vindication of the Rights of Woman* (1792).

Scholars such as Amy Beth Aronson have argued that women readers of this period were not a passive audience suggestible to male editors' paternalistic advice, but rather were actively engaged in the critical selection and understanding of magazine content. One reason was the slapdash fashion in which information was arranged. For example, an item that began as an observation might end as a poem. Stories were not always presented in their entirety, and material was occasionally misclassified in tables of contents. Negotiating the magazines' haphazard content was "an exercise in versatility," as Aronson wrote.

Importantly, early women's magazines relied on reader contributions and as such, provided opportunities for amateur writers to question authority, debate issues of concern to women, and build consensus. This is noteworthy since women of the period were allowed few chances to express themselves in public forums. Still, it remains open to interpretation whether these early magazines promoted women's political independence or cemented their traditional domestic, maternal role.

Nineteenth Century

The nineteenth century is considered by some historians to be the "golden age of magazines." As leisure time and literacy increased among Americans, so too, did the number of periodicals offering information and entertainment. Improved printing technologies and favorable postage rates further encouraged general-interest magazines, which proliferated throughout the 1800s. By the 1830s, nearly fifty women's magazines had appeared, many short-lived and nearly all of them unprofitable. By 1860, some six hundred magazines were being published and more than one hundred women's magazines had come and gone. By the end of the century, more than four thousand mass market publications were in circulation and magazine reading was part of most Americans' routines.

Whereas women readers of the previous century were addressed as individuals with limited political prerogative, the most popular magazines of the nineteenth century courted women as consumers of household goods. Publishers became more reliant on advertising revenues to sustain their periodicals, particularly as the mass production of branded goods increased and manufacturers and distributors clamored for promotional opportunities. Singer sewing machines, cosmetics, and "safety" bicycles were among the products advertised to women. By the 1880s, the amount of paid advertising a publisher procured for a magazine was a good indicator of its life expectancy.

Perhaps the most well-known women's magazine from this period was *Godey's Lady's Book*, published in Philadelphia from 1830 to 1898. The magazine was founded by Louis Godey and a partner who soon bowed out of the venture. Godey then hired as his editor Sarah Josepha Hale, whose foundering publication, *Ladies' Magazine*, he bought and merged with his own. Hale, an accomplished writer and an advocate for women's education and property rights, served as *Godey's* editor for forty years. *Godey's* soon earned a reputation for its literary quality. Hale published the work of established writers, such as Ralph Waldo Emerson and Harriet Beecher Stowe, as well as poetry and essays by promising new writers. However, provocative subjects were avoided. Hale was a reformer, but she believed women's province was the home and opposed suffrage. Further, the magazine did not devote any content to slavery or the Civil War, at Louis Godey's insistence. Rather, *Godey's* published articles on history, travel, care of home and family, and sheet music and book reviews. Some historians have argued whether the magazine owed its success to its hand-colored fashion illustrations, which showed readers the latest European styles and also provided work for women artists. Even if it had no claim to intellectual heft, *Godey's* had a winning formula, and was a model for many other women's magazines that were launched in the nineteenth century, such as *Woman's Home Companion*, *Good Housekeeping*, and *Ladies' Home Journal*.

Female editors of women's magazines were rare during this period, although Louisa Knapp Curtis enjoyed a highly successful tenure as editor of *Ladies' Home Journal* from 1883 to 1889. Her husband, Cyrus H. K. Curtis, published the magazine and boosted its circulation with creative strategies such as discounted subscription rates, rewards for subscribers, advertising campaigns to promote the magazine, and solicitation of national advertisers. *Ladies' Home Journal* was the first magazine to garner one million subscribers and, until the 1950s, had the largest circulation of any women's magazine.

Whereas many titles concentrated on the home, other women's magazines derived from pattern companies and emphasized fashion, such as *McCall's*, *Delineator*, and *Pictorial Review*. Other magazines that targeted upper- and middle-class women and focused on fashion and culture were *Vogue* and *Harper's Bazar* (later *Harper's Bazaar*).

Although some women's magazines took a stance on suffrage alongside other editorial material, their content was characterized by a philosophical inconsistency. As Mary Ellen Zuckerman has shown, articles addressed political issues and described women who were pursuing careers and interests independent of men, but fiction and editorials were conservative, affirming women's place in the home. Overwhelmingly, content directed women's attention to homemaking. These editorial contradictions were the result of a society in flux, a mixed bag of reader contributions, and in some cases, reflected the personal beliefs of a magazine's editor or publisher.

At the same time, several journals were created for the explicit purpose of promoting women's rights. They resembled newspapers in format, but are often categorized as magazines since many of them were published on a monthly basis. One of the earliest such publications was *The Lily*, in which founder Amelia Bloomer promoted suffrage, temperance, and women's dress reform. *The Una* was founded in 1853 by suffragist and abolitionist Paulina Wright Davis; it was owned, edited and written solely by women. *Woman's Journal* was launched in 1870 by Lucy Stone, a co-founder of the American Woman Suffrage Association. One of Stone's partners in forming the AWSA, Josephine St. Pierre Ruffin, began a periodical in 1890 to promote black women's rights, the *Woman's Era*. Most prominently, Susan B. Anthony and Elizabeth Cady Stanton, co-founders of the National Woman's Suffrage Association, began a weekly in 1868 called *The Revolution* in which they argued for suffrage, equal pay for equal work, and an eight-hour work day. Although these publications enjoyed loyal readership, their circulations remained small and so too, did their coffers. Despite their relatively short runs, these periodicals demonstrated the increasing prominence of women, and the need for forums in which to discuss issues that specifically affected women's lives.

Twentieth Century

The popularity of magazines continued to intensify during the twentieth century, and gave rise to the "Seven Sisters," the name given to the top-selling women's magazines: *Ladies' Home Journal*, *McCall's*, *Good Housekeeping*, *Family Circle*, *Woman's Day*, *Redbook*, and *Better Homes and Gardens*.

Ownership of magazines tended toward concentration. Publishers who produced multiple titles could charge advertisers higher rates to reach the readers of all their magazines. Bigger profits allowed publishers to further improve the production values of their magazines, and hire established writers to generate content. The Hearst Corporation, for example, published *Good Housekeeping*, *Harper's Bazaar*, *Cosmopolitan*, *Pictorial Review*, *Delineator*, and many other popular titles. Of course, this meant that the fate of an individual magazine was directly affected by the success or failure of its parent company. When Hearst's finances were strained to the point of bankruptcy in 1937, unprofitable magazines were sold or folded.

Magazine content was affected by the dramatic social and political changes of this century. In the early 1900s, women's magazines encouraged readers to take up community service, manifesting the preoccupations of the Progressive movement. Also characteristic of the era was an interest in investigative reporting that uncovered corruption and waste in the public and private sectors; magazines proved the ideal site for that kind of long-form journalism. When William Randolph Hearst bought *Cosmopolitan* in 1905, he began to publish the work of muckraking journalists such as Ida Tarbell and Upton Sinclair.

With the outbreak of World War I, the content of women's magazines took on an international character, describing the social and political history of Europe, and how war was affecting Europeans. When the United States entered the conflict in 1917, articles and editorials instructed women on ways they could contribute to the war effort, such as food conservation and relief work. Magazines that had taken up the issue of suffrage now minimized such content and even criticized concerns for women's rights as selfish in wartime. As with other mass media in wartime, magazines were subjected to government pressure, such as Woodrow Wilson's "advice" to *Ladies' Home Journal* editor Edward Bok that he should emphasize home front preparedness over straightforward news of the war.

Content in women's magazines during World War II was similarly affected by censorship and propaganda, as magazines and advertisers worked with government to boost morale and build support for the war effort. When large numbers of men vacated jobs as they were called into service, the magazines encouraged women to step in, although they were careful to emphasize that employment was "for the duration." Most magazines counseled women to maintain an attractive appearance no matter how filthy the work might be, and to remain focused on the home and family to which they would return full-time at war's end. Equal pay and the continued employment of women were two postwar issues that magazines covered, but few took a decisive editorial stand, arguably squandering any gains women made with their wartime contributions.

As the women's movement gained momentum in the 1960s, magazines increasingly came under fire for encouraging women's domesticity rather than their political autonomy. Betty Friedan argued in *The Feminine Mystique* that magazines represented women as "gaily content in a world of bedroom, kitchen, sex, babies, and home," contradicting the average American woman's experience. Unhappy housewives were instructed to overcome their frustrations with energetic cleaning. "Beat the daylights out of your rugs or super-polish every table in your house," a 1950 *McCall's* article told readers. They should do so with the magazine's advertised products, of course.

The idealized domesticity espoused in so many women's magazines was an indication of the close relationship between editorial content and advertising. Magazines had to compete with newspapers, television, and radio for advertisers, and so the editorial side was more beholden than ever to provide "complimentary copy," as Gloria Steinem, a founding editor of *Ms.* magazine, called it. Competition in the media marketplace was heightened by the fact that publishing costs increased after World War II and profit margins decreased. Newsstand purchases diminished as more people moved to the suburbs, and magazines became more reliant on subscriptions, which were expensive to post and to service. Thus, while readership continued to grow, a healthy circulation did not always ensure a magazine's long life. Advertising revenue now accounted for more than half of a magazine's profit.

This century also gave way to specialization, a way to court readers with specific interests and in turn, attract more advertisers. Among the broad category of women's magazines emerged several subgenres that appealed to working-class women: pulp magazines such as *Love Book* that emphasized romantic fiction, confession journals including *True Story*, and fan magazines. At mid-century, *Vice Versa*, the first lesbian magazine was published in Los Angeles.

Though none of these titles was very successful at attracting advertisers, they offered an alternative perspective among publications aimed at middle-class women. Perhaps more successful were efforts to capture the teenage market. *Seventeen*, aimed at girls ages twelve to twenty-four, emphasized fashion and first appeared in 1944. It eventually achieved a circulation of more than two million. Many other similar publications with such titles as *Cosmo Girl*, *Teen*, and *Girl's Life Magazine* targeted the teen market.

The upheaval of the 1960s and 1970s made way for niche magazines that further narrowed audiences. One of the most dramatic transformations was that of *Cosmopolitan*, which was recast in 1965 by Helen Gurley Brown as a journal for single working women preoccupied with sex and popular culture. As a contrast, Gloria Steinem's *Ms.*, launched in 1972, became a leading feminist publication and in 1989, became one of the few magazines to publish an ad-free format. Other magazines dedicated to professional women, such as *Working Woman* and *Working Mother*, provided career advice, tips on financial planning, and strategies to cope with workplace issues. *Essence*, a magazine targeted to middle-class black women, was founded in 1970.

In the 1980s and 1990s, magazines targeted to "older" women appeared on newsstands. Three magazines aimed at readers aged thirty to fifty were launched with varied success, *Mirabella, Lear's,* and *More*. Although magazines continued to be popular reading material, they faced stiff competition from other mass media, such as cable television and the Internet.

Twenty-First Century

Faced with competition for consumers and more importantly, for advertisers, from the Internet and other emerging technologies, magazine publishers struggle to remain viable in a digital age when the number of online niche publication grew substantially. Interestingly, many of their strategies are souped-up versions of traditional ones, such as cooperative advertising and subscriber discounts. Ownership is more concentrated than ever.

By now, all major periodicals have an online presence. Some publishers, such as Hachette Filipacchi, moved to web-only versions of their titles when print advertising flagged. Online efforts range from digitized versions of the printed page to sites that feature video, message boards, and podcasts. An effort to cultivate the magazine habit among young readers is apparent now in a cornucopia of titles targeted to teenage girls and young adults. Condé Nast combined material from its three bridal magazines on a single interactive web site that allows users to "try on" wedding gowns, create a wedding scrapbook, and customize content by their location. Perhaps harkening to the earliest women's magazines, some online magazines call for user-generated content and allow that to dominate their web sites, no matter how hodgepodge.

Magazines remain profit-driven and thus, intent on wooing advertisers. In 2006, revenue spent on Internet advertising exceeded the amount spent on magazines, although the products being advertised have changed little. Magazines may cooperate with technology companies to retain advertisers. Google, for example, bought ad space in magazines and then resold it via online auction. One result was the appearance of new advertisers in magazines whose rates they could not previously afford.

In the early twenty-first century, women often edited the top women's magazines, although they moved rapid-fire from one title to another. This was particularly true as magazine ownership became concentrated among fewer companies. A successful editor at one title was easily trans-ferred to revive a troubled magazine owned by the same parent corporation.

Publishers continue to generate new magazines every year. As women's lives become more complex, magazines targeted to their niche interests may always be relevant, even if they are used as a springboard to web-based resources.

Further Reading

Aronson, Amy Beth. *Taking Liberties: Early American Wom-en's Magazines and Their Readers*. Westport, CT: Praeger, 2002.

Harris, Sharon M., and Ellen Gruber Garvey, eds. *Blue Pencils and Hidden Hands: Women Editing Periodicals, 1830–1910*. Boston: Northeastern University Press, 2004.

Tebbel, John, and Mary Ellen Zuckerman. *The Magazine in America, 1741–1990*. New York: Oxford University Press, 1991.

Walker, Nancy A. *Shaping Our Mothers' World: American Wom-en's Magazines*. Jackson: University Press of Mississippi, 2000.

Zuckerman, Mary Ellen. *A History of Popular Women's Maga-zines in the United States, 1792-1995*. Westport, CT: Green-wood Press, 1998.

BARBARA G. FRIEDMAN

WOMEN'S NATIONAL PRESS CLUB

The Women's National Press Club (WNPC) (1919–1970) was founded at a time when women journalists were excluded from the Washington-based National Press Club (NPC), where male journalists, publicists, and lobbyists met with national and world leaders. The WNPC provided women journalists working in the nation's capital their own access to important news sources. It also provided them a place to network and publicized their achievements. In 1970, the WNPC admitted its first male members and reor-ganized as the Washington Press Club (WPC) (1970–1985). The next month, after bitter debate, the male NPC voted to accept applications from women. By 1985, equal opportu-nity legislation had brought about a surge of women in the news industry, and it became clear that the coexistence of the two organizations had become redundant. In 1985, the WPC merged with the NPC and thereafter women and men journalists were granted equal membership opportunities in the organization.

The WNPC was founded by three publicists who had worked for the National Woman's Party, the militant arm of

the suffrage movement, and three Washington journalists. Over the years, some members continued to concern them-selves with women's issues, but in keeping with the jour-nalistic ideals of neutrality and impartiality, the club did not officially endorse feminist positions. The first president was Lily Lykes Rowe (later Shepard), a correspondent for the *New York Times*. Other early presidents included Cora Rigby (1920–1926), the Washington bureau chief for the *Chris-tian Science Monitor*; Genevieve Forbes Herrick (1933), a correspondent for the *Chicago Tribune*; and Winifred Mal-lon (1935), the first woman political writer in the *New York Times's* Washington bureau.

By the 1970s, the WNPC had about five hundred mem-bers, primarily fulltime women journalists. It also accepted women whose work in public relations brought them in regular contact with the press and by the 1960s, women in broadcast journalism were also admitted. The WNPC's most illustrious member was Eleanor Roosevelt, who for two years wrote a daily syndicated newspaper column, "My Day." Dur-ing her years in the White House, Eleanor Roosevelt gave women journalists a boost when she held "women only" press conferences so that news organizations would have to hire newspaperwomen to cover them. The organization was noted for its luncheons featuring influential speakers from the political, literary, and journalistic worlds. These were "news making" events that lent prestige to the women jour-nalists who attended them and assured their bylines in their newspapers.

The gender barrier imposed by the male NPC broke down gradually over the years as the result of pressure, lob-bying, and changing times. In 1946 the WNPC began to allow men to cover its annual dinners. In the 1950s, the NPC permitted women journalists to observe its luncheons from the balcony overlooking its dining hall. In 1964, Presi-dent Lyndon B. Johnson directed the State Department to inform the NPC that it would schedule visiting dignitaries there only if the men's club allowed women journalists to cover speakers on the same basis as men. When the NPC reluctantly agreed, this eliminated the need for the separate women's organization.

The WNPC (and its later version, the WPC) played an important role in the acceptance of women journalists in Washington. Its merger with the NPC in 1985 symbolized the success of that goal, but was a loss for many women who failed to find the same camaraderie in the less exclu-sive NPC.

Further Reading

Beasley, Maurine H. "The Women's National Press Club: Case Study of Professional Aspirations." *Journalism History* 15:4 (Winter 1988): 112–121.

——. "The Women's National Press Club" In *Women's Press Organizations: 1889–1999*, edited by Elizabeth V. Burt, 283–229, Westport, CT: Greenwood Press, 2000.

Black, Ruby. *Eleanor Roosevelt: A Biography*. New York: Duell, Sloan and Pearce, 1940.

Furman, Bess. *Washington By-Line*. New York: Alfred A. Knopf, 1949.

Winfield, Betty Houchin. "Mrs. Roosevelt's Press Conference Association: The First Lady Shines a Light." *Journalism History* 8:2 (Summer 1981): 54–55, 63–70.
WNPC Papers. Archives of the National Press Club. 529 14th St., N.W., Washington, D.C.

ELIZABETH V. BURT

WOMEN'S PAGES

The women's pages in American newspapers can be counted as a victim of the women's movement of the 1960s. Their regular presence in virtually all daily newspapers is long gone. But in their heyday, the women's pages of a newspaper provided advice, recipes, fashion, society news, and gossip to women readers throughout the United States for nearly a century. Today, the women's pages of almost all daily newspapers have been carefully subsumed into gender-neutral feature sections headlined with terms like "Accent," "Today," "Style," or "Living."

The Women's Pages trace their lineage back to eager nineteenth century publishers who recognized, as part of a tide of rising consumerism, that women were economic forces to be reckoned with in their own homes. These publishers, anxious for increased advertising revenues, believed that if women could be enticed to be newspaper readers, advertisers would send more dollars their way. The development and growth of Women's Pages also closely parallels the evolution of department stores in the United States.

The earliest attempts to attract women readers can be found in the Penny Press era. Horace Greeley, for example, hired Margaret Fuller to write for his *New York Tribune* in 1844. He never explained his reasoning behind bringing Fuller to his newspaper but, in an era prior to journalist bylines, when most writing was anonymous, Fuller's articles were marked with an asterisk. Thus, women were able to know which articles were written by Fuller. After Fuller, other women used alliterative, flowery pen names to identify their work to circumvent the social taboo that a woman's name should never appear in print.

After the *Tribune*, other newspapers followed suit, bringing a woman on staff or accepting freelance articles from women and then publishing them with bylines. This served a two-fold purpose of informing women readers of articles that were written by women, but also allowing editors to distance themselves from the writing of women and flagging the articles so that the male readers would know.

Women like Jane Cunningham Croly, whose penname was "Jenny June," Sara Payson Willis Parton, who wrote under the "Fanny Fern" pen name, and Sara Clarke Lippincott, journalism's "Grace Greenwood," provided the nation's newspapers with a woman perspective while at the same time opening a new career path to literate women who needed to earn their keep.

In the second half of the nineteenth century, as urban culture grew and journalism flourished, newspapers opened their doors to a quota of one woman in the news room, a regrettable necessity (from the male editor's position) born from the recognized growing audience of woman readers.

From early columns like "Gossip With and For Ladies," which Jenny June wrote in a weekly New York newspaper beginning in 1853, the concept of an entire section of articles aimed solely at women grew. Newspaper magnate Joseph Pulitzer is generally credited with institutionalizing the Women's Page section in his newspaper, the *New York World*.

In 1891, his *Sunday World* began featuring an entire page devoted to women and by 1894, his daily newspaper had a regular "For and About Women" page. An anchor to this section in the *World* and other newspapers always was advertising aimed specifically at women readers.

The Women's Pages were basically ignored by the newspaper executives. There was an unstated and unwritten rule that the sections would offend no one, ruffle no feathers and cause no controversy. Beyond that, the women who wrote and edited the pages were left to their own devices.

By the turn of the century, photography in newspapers extended to the women's pages so that fashion and styles could be featured, along with extensive advice about food, beauty, love, etiquette, good health and housekeeping.

Popularity of Women's Pages escalated. Many of them took on a boilerplate look due to the increasing popularity of syndication, which allowed for the growth of advice columnists like Dorothy Dix. Her lovelorn column began in the *New Orleans Daily Picayune* in 1896 reached about sixty million readers during the height of its popularity through her death in 1951. Other advice columns, like Dear Abby (which is still published in 2006 by the daughter of the original Abby) and Ann Landers (which ceased publication with the death of the author in 2002) became cornerstones of the women's pages.

The women's pages changed little throughout the first half of the twentieth century. During World War II, when women were hired in newsrooms to fill positions left vacated by men who were drafted into the Army, the Women's Pages assumed an air of patriotism that recognized women were working in the war effort and provided information to help them juggle work and home. After the war, however, a wave of renewed domestic fervor was evidenced in the women's pages. The era of *Leave it to Beaver* and *Father Knows Best* on television was reflected in the celebration of domesticity in the women's pages. That complicity with the status quo was blown to bits in the late 1960s as the women's movement, seeking equality in the workplace, at home and in the political and social arenas, took aim at the women's pages and questioned why women and their issues were segregated into a section that by its very title isolated it from the power makers of society.

The *Washington Post* was among the first of the nation's elite newspapers to bow to criticism of the Women's Pages. In January 1969, under the section editorship of a man, the "Style" section debuted. Its goal was to appeal to the entire newspaper readership with emphasis on books, the arts, entertainment and leisure time. Half a decade later, most newspapers in the United States had made the shift to the new format.

The pendulum swung back again. In 1991, the *Chicago Tribune* created a weekly "WomaNews" section as part of its "Tempo" lifestyle section. This was in reaction to concern that women were turning away from newspapers as a source of information. The goal of the new section was to provide women with relevant news that connected with their lives as both professionals and parents. Health and business news were well represented. Critics of the newfangled section complained that it could become a ghetto where news about women was dumped and then ignored by the country's power brokers. They expressed concern that this new section was actually a retrograde maneuver because it was taking women's news out of the news sections; proponents of the new section countered that it was actually providing a forum for news and information that would have gone unreported before.

While the WomaNews section never achieved the regularity of the daily women's pages of the bygone era, it was syndicated to sixty other newspapers by 1993. The movement never resurged, however, to regain the position as a daily section aimed specifically at women.

Further Reading

Beasley, Maurine H., and Sheila J. Gibbons. *Taking Their Place: A Documentary History of Women and Journalism.* Washington, D.C.: American University Press, 1993.

Dubey, Anita. "A Woman's Place in the News," *Ryerson Review of Journalism* (Spring 1993), http://www.rrj.ca/issue/1993/spring/160/ (accessed April 17, 2007).

Gottlieb, Agnes Hooper. *Women Journalists and the Municipal Housekeeping Movement, 1868–1914.* Lewiston, NY: Edwin Mellen Press, 2001.

Guenin, Zena Beth. "Women's Pages in American Newspapers: Missing Out on Contemporary Content." *Journalism Quarterly* (Spring 1975): 66–69, 75.

Tuchman, Gaye, Arlene Kaplan Daniels, and James Benet, eds., *Hearth and Home: Images of Women in the Mass Media.* New York: Oxford University Press, 1978.

Van Gelder, Lindsy, "Women's Pages: You can't Make News Out of a Silk Purse." *Ms.* magazine (November 1974).

AGNES HOOPER GOTTLIEB

WOMEN'S PRESS ORGANIZATIONS

Since the first women's press organizations were founded in the United States in the 1880s, they have played an active role in the preparation, recognition, and assimilation of women in journalism. In that time, the number of women in the journalistic work force has increased from less than 3 percent to more than 48 percent.

The roles women routinely occupy in the news industry have expanded from a limited number of positions as correspondent, society writer, and woman's page editor to include positions as print and broadcast reporter, managing editor, and publisher. In the expanding communications industry of the twentieth and twenty-first centuries, women writers found their place in related fields as well, including public relations and advertising. As women's place in the profession changed, so too did the interests, goals, and strengths of women's press organizations. These changes contributed to an evolving vision of the role of women journalists, assisting them in defining themselves and contributing to their acceptance by the profession as well as the public. In addition, women's press organizations, often closely related to major women's movements of the nineteenth and twentieth centuries, have helped to put women's issues on the public agenda.

Women's Press Organizations in the Nineteenth Century

During the second half of the nineteenth and the first part of the twentieth century, press clubs existed in many cities and states, but were organized by men and were typically closed to female membership. There were rare exceptions. The Missouri Press Association, founded in 1867, permitted a few women members in the early years, usually because they were married to an editor and assisted him in the publication of his newspaper. Other women who worked at newspapers, either as full-time society writers and editors or part-time contributors, were excluded from such clubs.

It was not until the 1880s that women journalists banded together to create their own press clubs and associations. The first of these was a group of correspondents in Washington, D.C., who formed the Ladies' Press Club in 1881 with Emily Edson Briggs ("Olivia" of the *Philadelphia Press*) as their first president. (By 1883, the club had renamed itself the Woman's National Press Association.) Their purpose was to provide a source of "mutual help and encouragement" for the female correspondents working in the nation's capital, especially for the "coming generation" of women journalist. Next to organize was a group of women attending the North, South, and Central American Exposition in New Orleans in 1885. The women, who worked for newspapers in Boston, St. Louis, and Indianapolis, established the National Woman's Press Association as an umbrella organization that would spark the creation of women's press organizations in cities and states throughout the country.

By the early 1900s, some two dozen women's press organizations had been established in more than seventeen states. Several national and international groups had also been established, including the National Federation of Women's Press Clubs in 1891 and the Woman's International Press Union in 1898. The principle goal of these groups during these years was to provide a venue where women journalists could talk about their work, discuss professional issues, and mingle with their professional sisters, a luxury often denied them in the workplace where they might be the only woman employed at a newspaper. Another important function of women's press organizations was to legitimize their members in the eyes of the public. To this end, they sought publicity in the press by submitting material to the society columns of the general circulation press, the columns of women's publications such as the *Woman's Journal,* and the "club notes" of trade journals such as *The Journalist* and *The Fourth Estate.* By 1900, the society columns in local papers regularly ran reports of the doings of the individual clubs, including their weekly meetings, their fund raisers, their annual balls. Other events attracted coverage in the news pages when the speakers were prominent social or political figures.

Many of the founders of women's press organizations were active in the woman's club movement, which created synergy and networking opportunities. Jane Cunningham Croly, "Jennie June," who established the Woman's Press Club of New York City (1889–1980), is credited with launching the woman's club movement in 1868 when she founded Sorosis and was instrumental in establishing the General Federation of Women's Clubs in 1890. Julia Ames and Frances E. Willard, founding members of the Illinois Woman's Press Association (1885–present), were both officers of the Woman's Christian Temperance Union. Their influence led many of the early women's press organizations to share the benevolent and reformist characteristics and interests of the woman's club movement. The New England Woman's Press Association (1885–1982), for example, formed a benefit society called Samaritana in 1893 that distributed funds among a number of local charitable institutions and established a journalists' fund that it maintained for the next eighty years to aid distressed journalists who needed assistance. One of the early projects of the Illinois Woman's Press Association was to provide an inexpensive lodging house for working women and in 1886 the association announced a campaign to raise $1,500 to fund the project.

Many of the women involved in press associations were also active in the woman suffrage movement and several of their organizations eventually took a formal position on the reform. In 1911, for example, both the Kansas Woman's Press Association (1891–1913) and the Southern California Women's Press Club (1893–1939) endorsed suffrage. In 1914, the New England Woman's Press Association sent a delegation to march in the May 2 suffrage parade in Boston, and on October 1915 and October 1917, the Woman's Press Club of New York City turned out in force in the woman suffrage parades on New York's Fifth Avenue.

Toward the end of the nineteenth century, some press organizations, such as the National Editorial Association (founded in 1885), began to enroll both men and women as members. By 1900, woman's press groups were also affiliated with a dozen state, regional, and city male press organizations. Some of these typically male-only organizations also began to admit female members, as in the case of the Pennsylvania State Editorial Association, and the St. Paul Press Club. In a handful of other cases, press associations were established by men and women working together. One of these, the International League of Press Clubs was organized in 1891 and within two years a woman, Sallie Joy White of the New England Woman's Press Association, was elected a first vice president.

Women's Press Organizations in the Twentieth Century

By 1900 the U.S. census reported 2,193 women journalists, who made up 7 percent of the journalistic workforce; women's press organizations were established in at least seventeen states and claimed more than seven hundred members. Yet many of the organizations founded in the nineteenth century, which had been closely affiliated with the woman's club and suffrage movements, lost vitality or died out as their members aged, retired, and passed away and once the federal suffrage amendment became law in 1919. The Michigan Woman's Press Club (1892–1914) and the Missouri Woman's Press Association (1896–1915) suspended meetings during the early years of World War I. The Woman's National Press Association became inactive during the mid-1920s, and other organizations, such as the Woman's Press Club of Kentucky (founded in 1890), vanished quietly.

At the same time, a new generation of women journalists rose up and began to establish their own organizations, seemingly oblivious to those that already existed. Washington women journalists organized the Women's National Press Club in 1919, despite the existence of the still active but fading Woman's National Press Association. Likewise, women in New York established the New York Newspaper Women's Club (1922–present, with a change of name to the Newswomen's Club of New York in 1972), though the Woman's Press Club of New York City was still active. In this case, the new organization became more exclusive than the old, admitting only women working for newspapers, while its predecessor continued to admit all women writers. The general trend, however, was to become more inclusive. The New England Woman's Press Association, which had originally limited membership to newspaperwomen, revised requirements to embrace women professionals in the emerging communication fields, such as public relations and radio, as well as in the broader fields of literature and magazine writing. These organizations also sponsored scholarships and youth auxiliaries in the hope of attracting women to the profession and securing their allegiance to the organization. By the 1960s, this became a common practice.

There was also a surge of interest in reestablishing a national umbrella organization, and in 1936, four state organizations—the Illinois Women's Press Association, Ohio Newspaper Women's Association (1920–2004), Presswomen of Portland (Oregon), and the Woman's Press Club of Indiana (1913–present)—federated to form the National Federation of Press Women (NFPW). An early requirement that affiliated clubs restrict their membership to women working for newspapers was eventually changed so that the NFPW and its affiliates came to embrace a wide variety of women in communications, including those in advertising, public relations, and broadcast. During the 1940s, responding to these developments as well as the recruiting efforts of the NFPW, several new organizations were created, including Minnesota Press Women (1940–1982), and Colorado Press Women (1941–present).

The Removal of Gender Barriers

Until the 1970s, many of the women who founded and joined women's press organizations did so largely because they were excluded from male press organizations and isolated within the journalism profession, which for most of its existence has been male-dominated. They soon learned, however, that the women's press organizations provided a sense of power, solidarity, and identity women could rarely experience in mixed-sex organizations. Nevertheless, as women gained legitimacy in journalism, the barriers excluding them from male-only press clubs began to slowly come down so that by the early 1960s women in some localities had the option of choosing whether to belong to a women's organization, a mixed-sex organization, or both.

As the twentieth century women's movement brought pressure through public opinion and legal action, the most recalcitrant of male press organizations—the National Press Club and Sigma Delta Chi—removed their exclusionary policies and admitted their first women members in 1971 and 1972, respectively. Following these developments, many women's press organizations abandoned membership descriptions that defined members in term of gender, although they usually retained the word "women" or "woman's" in their name and maintained their purpose of supporting the efforts of women within the profession. Other women's press organizations went even further and, in addition to admitting men, dropped the word "women" from their title in an effort to attract new members. In 1995, the name of Texas Press Women (founded in 1893 as Texas Woman's Press Association) was changed to Texas Professional Communicators. By the end of the century, twelve of the NFPW's forty-four affiliates were using a name without the designation "women."

Even as women's press organizations merged with men's and gender distinctions were dropped after the 1970s, participation in the established press organizations declined across the board. Changing lifestyles and a decrease of available time for voluntary and professional activities led to the demise of some of these organizations, including the Woman's Press Club of New York City, Minnesota Press Women, and the Woman's Press Club of Cincinnati. Others simply became inactive without taking formal action: the New England Woman's Press Association ceased activity after 1982; and during the 1990s, at least four NFPW affiliates became inactive. Others survived by capping costs, reducing the frequency of meetings, redefining their mission, and stepping up recruiting efforts.

At the same time, new women's press organizations were established in response to emerging issues and needs. In 1985, a group of women journalists and journalism educators established JAWS: Journalism and Women Symposium to support the personal growth and empowerment of women in the newsroom. In 1987, women sports journalists created the Association for Women in Sports Media to address the difficulties they faced in covering male athletes, the poor coverage of women's sports, the lack of legitimacy accorded both women athletes and women sports reporters, and inequities of pay. And in 1988, a group of Dallas, Texas, journalists established the Association for Women Journalists (AWJ) to protest a demeaning promotional campaign in a local newspaper. In its mission it stated it was "dedicated to supporting women in journalism and promoting respectful treatment of women by the media." By 2005, the three organizations were still active and the AWJ had grown to seven chapters.

Since the 1880s, women's press organizations have provided women journalists with the professional and emotional support they have needed to function in the workplace, to survive gracefully during times of little progress, and to eventually overcome some of the barriers preventing them from gaining full access to their profession. Even in the first decade of the twenty-first century, however, women journalists still had not attained full access. In 2005, they still earned less than their male counterparts, lagged behind in receiving promotions and plum assignments, and remained in the minority in managerial positions. The women's press organizations of the twenty-first century still had much to accomplish.

Further Reading

Beasley, Maurine H. "The Women's National Press Club: Case Study of Professional Aspirations." *Journalism History* 15, 4 (Winter 1988): 112–121.

Blair, Karen J. *The Clubwoman as Feminist: True Womanhood Redefined, 1868–1914.* New York: Holmes and Meier, 1980.

Bradshaw, James Stanford. "Mrs. Rayne's School of Journalism." *Journalism Quarterly* 60 (1983): 513–517.

Burt, Elizabeth V., ed. *Women's Press Organizations: 1881–1999.* Westport, CT: Greenwood Press, 2000.

Croly, Jane Cunningham. *The History of the Woman's Club Movement in America.* New York: Henry G. Allen & Company, 1898.

De La Torriente, Donna Duesel. *So We All Can Be Heard: A History of The Illinois Woman's Press Association, 1885–1987.* Streamwood, IL: Illinois Woman's Press Association, 1987.

Deverell, William, and Tom Sitton, eds. *California Progressivism Revisited.* Berkeley: University of California Press, 1994.

Gottlieb, Agnes Hooper. "Networking in the Nineteenth Century: Founding of the Woman's Press Club of New York City." *Journalism History* 21:4 (Winter 1995): 156–163.

Kulczycky, Larissa C. et al. *The First 85 Years: The History of Women in Communications, Inc.* Arlington, Virginia: Women in Communications, Inc., 1994.

Lord, Myra B. *History of the New England Woman's Press Association.* Newton, MA: Graphic Press, 1932.

Scott, Anne Firor. *Natural Allies: Women's Associations in American History.* Urbana: University of Illinois Press, 1993.

Women's Institute for Freedom of the Press. "Women's Media Organizations." *Directory of Women's Media,* http://www.wifp.org (accessed April 17, 2007).

ELIZABETH V. BURT

WOODWARD, BOB

Bob Woodward (March 26, 1943–), considered a premier investigative journalist, first won fame for his role in reporting the Watergate scandal that led to the resignation of President Richard M. Nixon in 1974. As half of the youthful *Washington Post* reporting team known as "Woodstein," Woodward and his colleague, Carl Bernstein, relentlessly pursued a tale of corrupt campaign activities that led to Nixon himself following a 1972 burglary of the Democratic National Committee offices at the Watergate, a Washington office complex. Their reporting, carried on in the face of indifference by other news media, involved Woodward's use of a confidential source referred to as "Deep Throat," whose identity was kept concealed until 2005.

In his book, *The Secret Man*, published after "Deep Throat" was revealed to be W. Mark Felt, the number two official in the Federal Bureau of Investigation, Woodward wrote that keeping his source's name secret proved that he could be trusted. As a result, he was able to get interviews for subsequent best-selling books.

Following Watergate, for which the *Washington Post* won the 1972 Pulitzer Prize for public service, Woodward continued his career at the *Post*, where he was named an assistant managing editor in 1981. Writing books pertaining mainly to power and politics, portions of which were excerpted in the *Post* and *Newsweek*, which the *Post* owns, Woodward demonstrated he was a quintessential Washington "insider." His books revealed infighting, socializing, and political strategizing at the highest levels.

Born in Geneva, Illinois, to Alfred E. Woodward, a circuit judge, and his wife, Jane Upshur, Woodward was the oldest of six children. He attended Yale University on a ROTC scholarship, majoring in history and English literature. After five years of service with the U.S. Navy following graduation, he decided in 1970 to try journalism and talked his way into a two-week tryout at the *Post*. He failed the tryout but was sent to get experience on a weekly newspaper, the *Montgomery County Sentinel*, in the Maryland suburbs. After uncovering misconduct in county government, Woodward was hired back at the *Post* in 1971, where he cultivated police and governmental sources while investigating consumer abuses and health code infractions.

To investigate the Watergate burglary, *Post* editors paired him with Bernstein, another young reporter but one with more journalistic experience and stronger writing skills. Since the personalities of the two differed, Woodward was meticulous while Bernstein was impetuous, the two had to learn to work together as described in their acclaimed 1974 book, *All the President's Men*. Made into a movie with Robert Redford playing Woodward, it drew attention to Woodward's surreptitious meetings with "Deep Throat" at night in an underground parking garage. Many people believe that the movie attracted an influx of students to journalism schools in the 1970s hoping to emulate the achievements of "Woodstein."

"Woodstein" collaborated on another best-selling book, *The Final Days* (1976). Based on voluminous reporting, it reconstructed life in the White House prior to Nixon's resignation to avoid impeachment stemming from Watergate-linked improprieties. It received some criticism for use of anonymous sources and inclusion of intimate details about the Nixon family. Bernstein left the *Washington Post* in 1976.

Prolific Author

Woodward's next book, *The Brethren* (1979), written with Scott Armstrong, offered the first exposé of the internal workings of the U.S. Supreme Court. Although some reviewers complained of poor taste, it also sold well. Woodward then turned aside briefly from Washington subjects to write *Wired: The Short Life and Fast Times of John Belushi* (1982), a biography of the actor who died of a drug overdose. Upset by the portrayal of her husband's addiction, Belushi's widow tried unsuccessfully to block distribution of the book.

Meanwhile, at the *Washington Post,* Woodward, who became editor for local news in 1979, supported the hiring of Janet Cook, who claimed to be a Vassar graduate. When Cook won a 1980 Pulitzer Prize for a story on "Jimmy," an eight-year-old heroin addict, it came to light that she had lied about her educational background and fabricated the "Jimmy" story. The *Post* returned the Pulitzer and Cook resigned. The debacle led the publisher of the newspaper, Donald Graham, to tell Woodward, who had approved the story, that he would never be editor of the *Post*, the position he had hoped to attain.

Subsequently concentrating on books, Woodward, known for his tireless work habits, published behind-the-scenes accounts of the Washington power structure. Over a two-decade period he wrote books on the CIA (Central Intelligence Agency), presidential election campaigns, leadership of the Gulf War, the Clinton White House, the legacy of Watergate as it affected the presidency, Alan Greenspan and the Federal Reserve system, and the Bush administration's response to the terrorist attacks of September 11, 2001. Most of his books, which drew heavily on key sources, some anonymous, and paper trails of internal documents, received mixed reviews. Some critics contended Woodward offered too much detail instead of analysis, but he was lauded with having access to top officials and ferreting out information. *Plan of Attack* (2004), a study of the decision-making leading up to the war in Iraq, won praise on the grounds Woodward still possessed the ability to open the White House to public scrutiny thirty years after Watergate.

Ironically Woodward himself was scooped on the release of the identity of "Deep Throat." In 2005 the family of Mark Felt, who was in ill health, revealed his name in an article published in *Vanity Fair* magazine. Woodward himself had said he would not identify his source during the source's lifetime, instead using the nickname, "Deep Throat," taken from a pornographic movie of the 1970s.

In 1970 Woodward divorced from Kathleen Middlekauff whom he had married in 1966. A 1974 marriage to Francie Barnard resulted in one child, Mary Taliesin. It ended in divorce in 1979. Woodward lives in Georgetown with his wife, Elsie Walsh, a writer for the *New Yorker,* whom he married in 1989. They have a daughter, Diana.

Further Reading

Bernstein, Carl, and Bob Woodward. *All the President's Men.* New York: Simon and Schuster, 1974.

Havill, Adrian. *Deep Truth: The Lives of Bob Woodward and Carl Bernstein.* New York: Carol Publishing Group, 1993.

Kelly, Tom. *The Imperial Post: The Meyers, the Grahams and the Paper That Rules Washington.* New York: Morrow, 1983.

O'Connor, John D. "'I'm the Guy They Called Deep Throat.'" *Vanity Fair,* May 2005, 86–89, 129–33.

Woodward, Bob. *The Agenda: Inside the Clinton White House.* New York: Simon and Schuster, 1994.

——. *Bush at War.* New York: Simon and Schuster, 2002.

——. *The Choice.* New York: Simon and Schuster, 1996.

——. *The Commanders.* New York: Simon and Schuster, 1991.

——. *Maestro: Greenspan's Fed and the American Boom.* New York: Simon and Schuster, 2000.

——. *Plan of Attack.* New York: Simon and Schuster, 2004.

——. *The Secret Man: The Story of Watergate's Deep Throat.* New York: Simon and Schuster, 2005.

——. *Shadow: Five Presidents and the Legacy of Watergate.* New York: Simon and Schuster, 1999.

——. *Veil: The Secret Wars of the CIA, 1981–1987.* New York: Simon and Schuster, 1987.

——. *Wired: The Short Life and Fast Times of John Belushi.* New York: Simon and Schuster, 1984.

Woodward, Bob, and Carl Bernstein. *The Final Days.* New York: Simon and Schuster, 1976.

Woodward, Bob, and Scott Armstrong. *The Brethren: Inside the Supreme Court.* New York: Simon and Schuster, 1979.

MAURINE H. BEASLEY

606

YELLOW JOURNALISM

Yellow journalism is the term attached to the sensationalistic, graphically flamboyant journalism emerging in New York at the end of the nineteenth century. It was coined by the *New York Press,* which used it derisively in 1897 to label the news coming from two of its fellow New York papers, the *World* and the *Journal.* The term alluded to a comic-strip character dubbed "The Yellow Kid," who symbolized the frenzied competition between the two papers that pushed them to such journalistic extremes. Although the *World* and the *Journal* were the original "yellow journals," their profitable approach to news was picked up by other newspapers in New York and across the country in the 1890s.

The Father of New Journalism

Although older accounts of yellow journalism have placed its genesis with the competition between publishers Joseph Pulitzer and William Randolph Hearst, more recent treatments see it as simply the amplification of the "new journalism" that Pulitzer brought to New York City in 1883.

By the time he arrived, the ideals of an aggressive, independent journalism for the working class were mellowing with the commercial success they had achieved in previous decades. New York publishers like Charles Dana and Whitelaw Reid had wrested their pages away from the influence of politicians and drawn a broad working-class readership with frank, well-written news, and biting political commentary. By the early 1880s, however, the energetic independence of that era was foundering.

Pulitzer hastened the end of that era by bringing his model of journalism to the scene—one that had made his *St. Louis Post-Dispatch* an enormous success. Like the *Post-Dispatch,* Pulitzer's *World* shunned the style of traditional newspapers. Instead, the Hungarian-born Pulitzer vowed to carry more *interesting* news, targeted at the growing population of urban working- and middle-class Americans. Appealing to this growing market by charging only two cents for the *World,* Pulitzer was also able to deliver more readers to his advertisers. Although this commercial business model had emerged decades earlier, Pulitzer took it to a new level by building a newspaper that saw its readers as consumers of entertainment, leisure, and retail goods.

A key to this approach was the creation of a dramatically different *looking* newspaper. Visually, the *World*'s pages exploded with huge, alliterative headlines and illustrations—a marked departure from its counterparts, which topped tidy columns of text with modestly sized titles. Pulitzer even brought color to the newsprint with the yellow-skirted urchin in the comic strip "Hogan's Alley" (later retitled "The Yellow Kid").

But the content of its pages also set the *World* apart from the rest of New York's newspapers. The *World* carried bright, gossipy features, including fashion and leisure pieces to reach women, as well as ample coverage of scandal, vice and corruption. Pulitzer maintained that the *World,* like the *Post-Dispatch,* was published for the underdog, which meant the paper would not hesitate to uncover abuses of power. Indeed, it would seek out these stories and promote them as crusades on behalf of the *World*'s readership.

These crusades, reported in sensationalistic terms, comprised a mix of idealism and unabashed self-promotion. They have remained some of the most colorful anecdotes from this era. In 1887, for example, journalist Nellie Bly (Elizabeth Cochran) feigned insanity in order to report on the conditions at the infamous asylum on Blackwell Island. Her piece, which detailed systemic abuses of the women there, led to an investigation of the institution and a significant boost in funding for the state's department of charities and corrections. The *World* drew more readers through participatory crusades as well, such as its fundraising campaign to purchase a base for the Statue of Liberty, which France had recently given the United States. This created a sense of pride and efficacy among the *World*'s immigrant readers, many of whom found their names on the paper's front page for contributing hard-earned pennies to the cause.

Despite New York's saturated newspaper market—the city already had twenty-six English-language dailies when Pulitzer first arrived—the *World* ultimately demonstrated to the city's other papers that they would have to incorporate at least some facets of Pulitzer's new journalism into their pages to achieve similar circulation success. Pulitzer's tactics ultimately earned him credit as the father of "new journalism"—a less political, more sensationalistic, commercial, and entertaining form of journalism for the masses. And, although the form did not earn its "yellow" label until Pulitzer's nemesis entered the picture, the latter was merely an extension of Pulitzer's original model.

"Out-Pulitzering" Pulitzer

The success of the New York *World* inspired William Randolph Hearst, son of U.S. Senator George Hearst, to replicate

Pulitzer's model with the *San Francisco Examiner*, turning that newspaper around just as Pulitzer had done with the *Post-Dispatch* and the *World*. Hearst had convinced his father to let him run the *Examiner* after he was expelled from Harvard. The paper had been neglected for years, having served its purpose as a vehicle for promoting the elder Hearst's political career. Now, using Pulitzer's techniques, Hearst revived it and quickly had it turning a profit. Then he announced his next challenge: to "out-Pulitzer" Pulitzer in the great New York City newspaper market.

Hearst got his foot in that market when he managed to buy the struggling *New York Morning Journal* in 1895. He then set up shop in Pulitzer's own building and began pumping his formidable inheritance into the operation. But the *Journal*'s circulation was so small that Pulitzer did not take notice of his new rival until Hearst began using his war chest to put together a new editorial staff in a startlingly efficient manner—by stealing the staff away from Pulitzer.

One of the early raids began with Hearst's attempt to hire the *World*'s Sunday editor, Morrill Goddard. When Goddard said he needed the rest of his staff, Hearst quickly agreed and hired them all—including R.F. Outcault, the illustrator of "The Yellow Kid" comic strip. Pulitzer persuaded them to come back for nearly twenty-four hours, but ultimately lost the battle. The entire Sunday editorial team joined the *Journal* for good. Hearst then began running "The Yellow Kid" in his paper, only to find that Pulitzer had hired another illustrator to continue the strip in the *World*.

It was this famous episode of one-upmanship that epitomized the driving force behind yellow journalism and, by traditional accounts, earned the practice its label. But it was the content and style of Hearst's and Pulitzer's papers that earned yellow journalism its derision. Hearst's plan to "out-Pulitzer" Pulitzer resulted in a circulation war that amplified the characteristics of new journalism and inspired condemnation from the city's conservative press.

Hearst did ultimately make good on his plan to outdo Pulitzer. Headlines grew larger and more sensational, and the *Journal* was criticized for covering trivial news too often and covering important news irresponsibly with sloppy reporting and brazen writing. Hearst's crusades, while flavored with some of the same reformist impulses as Pulitzer's, were also so self-congratulatory that this alone may have been sufficient to raise the ire of other journalists and publishers. But Hearst also spent enormous amounts of money to *get* the news—to pay generous salaries to talented writers and editors, and to get news coverage from overseas. He also popularized the use of bylines and made reporters like Stephen Crane and Richard Harding Davis into journalistic celebrities. And he did all this while the *World*, led by an increasingly blind and fraught Pulitzer, battled vociferously to keep pace, engaging in the same practices while simultaneously castigating the other for its foibles.

Yellow journalism's heyday, and the roots of its decline, traditionally corresponds with the Spanish-American War of 1898. Earlier historians even credited, or blamed, the war on the sensationalistic jingoism of the two yellow jour-

nals. Hearst's *Journal* had been calling for U.S. support for Cuban resistance to Spain's colonialist rule long before the United States declared war on Spain. Indeed, Hearst's telegraph to *Journal* artist Frederic Remington, replying to the artist's request to leave Havana because there was no military action, is easily one of the most famous anecdotes in the history of U.S. journalism. "You supply the pictures," Hearst told the young man, "and I'll supply the war." However, apart from the biographical account of this scene by a journalist who was almost certainly not there to witness it, there is no indication that the exchange took place. And most historians—particularly after Joseph Campbell's meticulous 2001 book debunking the myths of yellow journalism—do not credit the sensationalistic journals with that kind of policy power.

In any case, by the war's end that same year, the excesses of yellow journalism had reached a frenzied peak and the public was beginning to weary of the screaming scare headlines, scandal news and contradictory, unsubstantiated reporting that marked the yellow journals' war coverage. By the beginning of the twentieth century, the very brief yellow journalism era was over. However, many of its characteristics stayed behind in more subtle variations as the press became a modern professional institution.

Further Reading

Campbell, W. Joseph. *Yellow Journalism: Puncturing the Myths, Defining the Legacies*. Westport, CT: Praeger, 2001.

Juergens, George. *Joseph Pulitzer and the New York World*. Princeton, NJ: Princeton University Press, 1966.

Kobre, Sidney. *The Yellow Press and Gilded Age Journalism*. Tallahassee: Florida State University Press, 1964.

Lubow, Arthur. *The Reporter Who Would Be King: A Biography of Richard Harding Davis*. New York: Scribner, 1992.

Milton, Joyce. *The Yellow Kids: Foreign Correspondents in the Heyday of Yellow Journalism*. New York: Harper & Row, 1989.

Smythe, Ted Curtis. *The Gilded Age Press, 1865–1900*. Westport, CT: Praeger, 2003.

Stevens, John D. *Sensationalism and the New York Press*. New York: Columbia University Press, 1991.

EMILY ERICKSON

YOUTH TELEVISION NEWS

The evolution and practices of youth television news in American journalism is a phenomenon driven by new media technology and generations of viewers who primarily receive their news information visually. After the first regular news broadcast, *Tele-topics*, on NBC in 1939, the "television babies" of the four succeeding decades, and their children, still rely on television news to learn about their communities and the world. The monumental difference is how television audiences access news because of the digital media revolution.

Most Americans born mid-twentieth century witnessed the nation's most volatile and iconic events—the assassination of John F. Kennedy, the Vietnam War, the civil rights and women's movements—through the abbreviated, visual narrative known as broadcast television news. And, whereas the music of a generation often defines it, the stylized production values of MTV (Music Television) created by Robert Pittman provided the blueprint for youth television news of the 1980s and beyond.

Premiering in 1981, MTV, celebrated and excoriated for its exportation of Western pop culture through the music video, used the narrowcasting technology of cable to target the youth audience, opening the portal for global distribution of a visual, youth culture.

As its audience matured, so did MTV Networks, Inc. In the 1990s, more news content began to appear along with dramatic, reality, and entertainment shows. Topics for news coverage included youth crime, teen violence, and drug use. The network promoted voter registration and reported on presidential elections from 1992 and 2004. The MTV Generation partied with aging Baby Boomers at a MTV-sponsored inaugural ball for saxophonist and president-elect Bill Clinton, who, during a 1992 "Rock the Vote" forum, was queried by a young audience member on his choice of style in undergarments.

Following the events of September 11, 2001, MTV began offering more global news programming. In 2001, the network collaborated with CNN (Cable News Network) on reports from Afghanistan by CNN correspondent Jason Bellini to foster cultural exchange between American and Afghani youth. The half-hour program "Confronting Iraq" in 2003 examined the possibility of another Gulf War, complete with non-traditional editing techniques and rock music.

Taking full advantage of new media technology, MTV. com, the Internet web site, included video streaming and pod casts of interviews with music artists and public figures. The network had satellite channels worldwide.

The success of MTV to attract and hold the youth market did not escape traditional broadcasters for long. In 1989, WSVN in Miami, Florida, then recently affiliated with the fledging Fox Network after being dropped by NBC, began airing nightly, local newscast designed to hold the "short attention spans" of eighteen to twenty-four year-olds. The station led in the ratings for this age group, and placed second for all audiences in the city. Sunbeam TV Corp., which created the format, duplicated it after purchasing the CBS affiliate, WHDH in Boston, in 1994. The program thrived in both markets despite the culture differences of the cities and the parent networks.

Young viewers wanted brief stories, creatively shot and tightly edited. They also required that the content be relevant to their lifestyles, and reported by anchors and reporters who looked and spoke like them. Producers had to balance all of these factors without communicating news that was too graphic in image, tabloid in content or commercial in presentation.

Growing an audience and talent bank was also crucial to the evolution of the genre. *Nick News* on Nickelodeon, part of the MTV network, first aired in 1991. Hosted by former network correspondent Linda Ellerbee, *Nick News* was for pre-teens and had a traditional news show format of four to five information segments. Ellerbee often appeared on-

camera in casual pants, and sneakers. Her company, Lucky Duck Productions, also produced *Nick News* specials. Titles included "Kids, Terrorism and the American Spirit; Faces of Hope: The Kids of Afghanistan"; and the controversial 2002 "My Family is Different," which featured children of same-sexed parents. A program on the scandal surrounding White House intern Monica Lewinsky and former President Clinton won a Peabody award. Its young viewers often debated on the Nickelodeon web site, that the stories were about adult issues, not what "kids" really cared about.

Channel One News, an in-classroom news program for public schools, was criticized for its news content and its inclusion of commercials in the twelve-minute newscasts. Introduced in 1990 by Chris Whittle, the network contracted with over ten thousand schools in the United States to air its broadcasts in exchange for television equipment and access to its archive of educational programming. Critics claimed many of the ads were for consumer items that were tied to soft news programming. Channel One was sold to Primedia in 1994, and changed its broadcast headquarters from Los Angeles to Washington, D.C., in 2006. The network boasted a daily teen audience of over eight million, a Peabody award, and a 2005 Webby People's Voice Award for the Best Youth Site on the web.

Another school-based news program modeled after Channel One, *Youth News Network,* was initiated in Canada. Similar public and political opposition caused it to fold.

Channel One, which collaborated with MTV and CNN often relied on news footage from networks such as ABC, proved a training ground for young journalists who moved to more traditional, mainstream television news. Past Channel One correspondents included Lisa Ling, formerly of ABC, and later with National Geographic Channel; Tracy Smith, national correspondent for the *CBS Early Show*; and Anderson Cooper, anchor of CNN's *Anderson Cooper 360*.

Syndicated morning news program, *The Daily Buzz* began in 2002 and rapidly became one of the most popular three-hour, weekday news programs for American youth. Its format was relaxed with quirky segment titles such as "Dot Com Dish," "Mr. Moviephone," "Rumor Control," and "News by the Numbers." A correspondent who often danced to a clip of pop music reported news on the quarter-hour during the "Plugged into the News" segment. Owned by ACME and Emmis Communications the program's flagship station was WBDT in Dayton, Ohio. Syndicated in more than 139 markets affiliated with the former WB, now the CW network, it reached 39 percent of American viewers from the 6:00 a.m. to 9:00 a.m. time slot. The show was produced in 2006 in Orlando, Florida, and the program's web site was a panoply of Internet connectivity including a link to the program store.

The television news journalists of the twenty-first century will come from today's new media users. The technology—satellite, viral video (video clips shared over the Internet), podcasting—evolved at a rapid pace, and innovation was usually a young person's game. Web stars were made...and faded daily. Amanda Congdon (1981–), dubbed "The Web's Anchorwoman," co-created the video podcast

Rocketboom in 2004. The daily news show has a comedic edge and had a strong Internet following. TiVO, the leading brand of digital video recorders, offered Congdon and co-producer Andrew Michael Baron a distribution deal in the millions. Congdon left the show in 2006.

Further Reading

Denisoff, Serge R., *Inside MT*. New Brunswick: Transaction Publishers, 1988.

Hendershat, Heather, ed. *Nickelodeon Nation: The History, Politics, and Economics of America's Only TV Channel for Kids.* New York: New York University Press, 2004.

Manning, Steven. "The Television News Show Kids Most Watch." *Columbia Journalism Review,* March/April (2000).

Schofield, John. "Ads Come to Class; Cash-strapped Schools Take a Closer Look at YNN." *Maclean's,* April 5, 1999.

Sherr, Susan, and Meredith Staples. "News for a New Generation Report 1: Content Analysis, Interviews, and Focus Groups." *CIRCLE Working Paper 16,* July 2004.

Yalof, David, and Kenneth Datrich. *Future of the First Amendment: What America's High School Students Think About Their Freedoms.* Miami: John S. and James L. Knight Foundation, 2005.

KISSETTE BUNDY

YOUTH'S COMPANION

Nathaniel Willis launched the *Youth's Companion* (1827–1929) on April 16, 1827 with Asa Rand in Boston to provide righteous stories that could not find space in Willis' publication, the *Boston Recorder*. In the era of keeping the Sabbath, Christians were expected to spend Sunday contemplating the Lord, and the *Youth's Companion* staff hoped to save souls. The staff changed the title on August 9, 1834, to *Youth's Companion and Sabbath School Recorder* and on May 20, 1836, to the *Youth's Companion*.

Although Willis tried to entertain while edifying, his newspaper resembled Bible tracts. The *Youth's Companion* shifted from Puritanism to Victorian sentimentalism after Daniel Ford became editor in 1857. For five years, Ford kept Willis' name on the masthead and ran didactic stories. But after 1860, he featured adventure and humorous stories—sometimes without a moral but never containing crime or sex. He borrowed short items from other periodicals including French, German, and English magazines.

Ford, a devout Christian and astute businessman, sought lively fiction and articles that upheld Victorian standards. Ford and his partner, John Olmstead, parted ways when Ford offered coupons to subscribers. Olmstead considered such tactics bribery.

In 1872, Ford merged Merry's Museum with the *Youth's Companion*. Theodore Roosevelt, Grover Cleveland, William James, Willa Cather, O. Henry, Mark Twain, Bret Harte, William Dean Howells, Winston Churchill, Lincoln Steffens, William Cullen Bryant, Thomas Huxley, Jack London, John Quincy Adams, Francis Scott Key, and Emily Dickinson contributed poetry, short stories, and think pieces. By this time, while the original purpose of the magazine continued to be apparent, its goal had also come to include providing "wholesome entertainment for the children of democracy" (Kelley 1974, 4). The circulation of the monthly magazine also increased dramatically from about 4,800 when Ford and Olmstead took control to about 480,000 by the mid-1890s. By then, many of the magazine's first young readers had introduced the *Youth's Companion* to their own children.

To protect his privacy, Ford published the paper as the Perry Mason Company, which became Perry Mason and Company, in 1900. Most modern readers recognize "Perry Mason" as Earl Stanley Gardner's flamboyant detective. As a boy, Gardner enjoyed reading the *Youth's Companion*.

Ford claimed that the *Youth's Companion* staff, not Francis Bellamy alone, had written the Pledge of Allegiance and felt the magazine deserved credit for originating the loyalty oath. In fact, the *Companion's* new home, not far from Boston's Public Library, was a five-story, brownstone that became known as the "Pledge of Allegiance" Building.

The World's Fair edition of *Youth Companion* on May 4, 1893, made history twice—first for amassing 650,000 subscriptions and second in selling a single ad for more than anyone had ever paid before; the lithograph of the winning Paris Salon Painting of 1891, "The Awakening of Cupid," cost Mellin's Foods $14,000.

After the Columbian Exposition, subscriptions returned to normal levels. Circulation figures rose steadily from 1892 until 1907. Like the rest of his staff, Ford's name never appeared in the magazine until after he died in 1899. The next two editors had worked as staff members for many years. The first, Edward Stanwood, served until 1911 when Charles M. Thompson took over. When Ellery Sedgwick, who owned the Atlantic Monthly Company, bought *Youth's Companion* in 1925, it had 305,445 subscribers. He merged it with the *American Boy* in 1929.

Further Reading

Baer, John W. *The Pledge Of Allegiance: A Centennial History, 1892–1992.* Annapolis, MD: Free State Press, Inc., 1992.

Gillian, Avery. *Behold the Child: America's Children and Their Books 1621–1922.* Baltimore: Johns Hopkins University Press, 1994.

Kelly, R. Gordon. *Children's Periodicals of the United States.* Westport, CT: Greenwood Press, 1984.

——. *Mother Was a Lady: Self and Society in Selected American Children's Periodicals, 1865–1890.* Westport, CT: Greenwood Press, 1974.

Meigs, Cornelia et al. *A Critical History of Children's Literature.* London: Macmillan Company, 1969.

Mott, Frank Luther, *A History of American Magazines: 1850–1865.* Cambridge, MA: Harvard University Press, 1938.

——. *A History of American Magazines: 1885–1905.* Cambridge, MA: Harvard University Press, 1957.

Peterson, Theodore, *Magazines in the Twentieth Century.* Urbana: University of Illinois Press, 1964.

Tebbel, John, and Mary Ellen Zuckerman. *The Magazine in America: 1741–1990.* New York: Oxford University Press, 1991.

PAULETTE D. KILMER

Z

ZENGER, JOHN PETER

John Peter Zenger (October 26, 1697–July 28, 1746) was the defendant in a landmark 1735 case that Gouvernor Morris, one of the drafters of the Constitution, later called—perhaps with some overstatement—"the germ of American freedom, the morning star of that liberty which subsequently revolutionized America."

Zenger immigrated to America from Germany and in 1710 became an apprentice to William Bradford, New York's only printer at that time. In 1733, Zenger became the printer of the *New York Weekly Journal*, an independent political newspaper highly critical of New York colonial governor William Cosby for his misconduct and abuses of office.

After unsuccessful attempts by the governor to prosecute the pseudonymous authors of critical editorials in the *Journal*, Cosby had a bench warrant issued for Zenger's arrest in November 1734, accusing him of seditious libel for publishing writings that "raise[d] factions and tumults among the people of this Province, inflaming their minds with contempt of His Majesty's government, and greatly disturbing the peace thereof." Under English law, any criticism of the government could be prosecuted as seditious libel, even if it was true. The duty of the jury in a seditious libel trial at that time was only to determine whether the defendant had indeed printed the material; whether it constituted seditious libel was a matter of law for the judge to decide.

Zenger was initially represented by two defense attorneys, one of whom was James Alexander, a founder and financial supporter of the *Journal* who may also have been the author of the critical editorials. After those lawyers were disbarred for objecting to the fairness of a trial presided over by judges hand-picked by Crosby, famed Philadelphia lawyer Andrew Hamilton stepped in to serve as defense counsel.

With Alexander's advice, Hamilton devised a novel defense strategy. He admitted that Zenger had printed the allegedly libelous material and that the law was not on his side. But he urged the jury to acquit his client anyway, based on the right of colonists to speak the truth against abuses of power such as Cosby's. Hamilton argued that the law of England need not be applied the same in America and that a "not guilty" verdict would send a message of support for truth and freedom against tyranny that would be heard across the colonies.

Hamilton's plea for jury nullification worked and the jury quickly found Zenger not guilty. The verdict demonstrated the growth of public opposition to seditious libel prosecutions. Zenger's wife, Anna, continued publication of the *Journal* during the months Zenger was imprisoned. While the case set no legal precedent, it helped establish the defense of truth in libel cases, and generally marked the beginning of greater press freedoms in America. Alexander's 1736 account of the trial helped spread the cause of freedom of speech and press in England and America and established the reputations of both Zenger and Hamilton. Zenger later became public printer for the colonies of New York and New Jersey.

Further Reading

Alexander, James. *A Brief Narrative of the Case and Trial of John Peter Zenger, Printer of the New York Weekly Journal*, edited by Stanley N. Katz. Cambridge, MA: Belknap Press, 1963.

Covert, Catherine L. "'Passion Is Ye Prevailing Motive': The Feud behind the Zenger Case." *Journalism Quarterly* 50, 1 (Spring, 1973): 3–10.

Putnam, William L. *John Peter Zenger and the Fundamental Freedom*. Jefferson, NC: McFarland & Co., 1997.

KATHLEEN K. OLSON

Index

Index